ENCYCLOPEDIA OF
AMERICAN
CULTURAL &
INTELLECTUAL
HISTORY

ADVISORY BOARD

ENCYCLOPEDIA OF
AMERICAN
CULTURAL &
INTELLECTUAL
HISTORY

VOLUME II

MARY KUPIEC CAYTON • PETER W. WILLIAMS
EDITORS

Charles Scribner's Sons
an imprint of the Gale Group
New York • Detroit • San Francisco • London • Boston • Woodbridge, CT

Charles Scribner's Sons
1633 Broadway
New York, New York 10019

1 3 5 7 9 11 13 15 17 19 20 18 16 14 12 10 8 6 4 2

Printed in the United States of America

The paper used in this publication meets the requirements of ANSI/NISO Z39.48–1992 (Permanence of Paper).

Library of Congress Cataloging-in-Publication Data

Encyclopedia of American cultural and intellectual history / Mary Kupiec Cayton, Peter W. Williams, editors.
     p. cm.
    Includes bibliographical references and index.
    ISBN 0-684-80561-8 (set : alk. paper) — ISBN 0-684-80558-8 (v. 1 : alk. paper) —
ISBN 0-684-80559-6 (v. 2 : alk. paper) — ISBN 0-684-80560-X (v. 3 : alk. paper)
    1. United States—Civilization—Encyclopedias.   2. United States—Intellectual life—Encyclopedias.   I. Cayton, Mary Kupiec.   II. Williams, Peter W.

E169.1 .E624 2001
973'.03—dc21

2001020005

CONTENTS OF THIS VOLUME

Part 10 Geography and Cultural Centers

Broad Geographical Constructs

Major Cultural Regions

Urban Clusters and Other Cultural Units

Part 11 Nature, Human Nature, and the Supernatural

Part 12 The Political Order

CONTENTS OF THIS VOLUME

CONTENTS OF OTHER VOLUMES

ALPHABETICAL TABLE OF CONTENTS

Essay titles have been simplified to make a useful overview.
See index in volume 3 for a full analytical breakdown.

ENCYCLOPEDIA OF
AMERICAN
CULTURAL &
INTELLECTUAL
HISTORY

Part 6

WORLD WAR II AND THE 1950s

OVERVIEW: WORLD WAR II AND THE 1950s

George Cotkin

WORLD WAR II

American intellectuals and the popular culture worked hand in hand to assure American success once the United States entered the Second World War in December 1941. Although a handful of intellectuals opposed the war effort for pacifist reasons or Trotskyist politics, most intellectuals, as well as the population at large, viewed the war as a necessary fight. Patriotic unity was the keyword in the war effort, and through motion pictures, radio, and other visual images, popular culture would help to support and define the war. War films attempted to finesse ethnic and racial divisions at home by presenting military units of Americans from diverse backgrounds who managed to work heroically together toward a common goal. Even the classic American loner could become involved in the war effort. In *Casablanca* (1942), hard-bitten Rick Blaine, played by Humphrey Bogart, attempts to remain neutral but finds that his past idealism and submerged romanticism make it impossible for him to ignore the atrocities of the Nazis. In the end, Rick does the right thing, killing an evil Nazi, forgoing the love of his life for a greater good, and deciding to join with his French friend to fight "the good war."

Music also played a role in the war effort. Swing music, especially in the hands of the orchestra leader Glenn Miller, who served as a captain in the Army Air Force, became a unifying force, bringing together ethnic and geographical regions through a common musical idiom. Miller's swing music was a war weapon, transforming the musical repertoire of traditional American military bands and, in the process, increasing the morale of American troops. American culture worked full time to promote patriotism at home, through bond drives, civil defense, and recycling programs. Defense work in large urban areas resulted in a major migration of African Americans, and many women, presented in the media through the image of "Rosie the Riveter"

took advantage of new opportunities in wartime industries.

World War II was also a boom time for American intellectual and scientific life. Nazi repression led to a wide-scale exodus of European thinkers (mostly Jewish) to America. They brought with them much of their European intellectual baggage, but many exuberantly entered into American life and the war effort. Billy Wilder quickly adapted to the American environment as a filmmaker, and he used his skills and German cultural background in his work with the U.S. Army's Psychological Warfare Division. During the war and immediately after, European émigrés transformed and enriched American intellectual life. In architecture, members of the Bauhaus school brought an aesthetic of high modernism; surrealist and expressionist artists challenged the reigning styles of American painting; Arnold Schoenberg revolutionized avant-garde musical composition, and members of the Frankfurt school helped to deepen American sociology both empirically and theoretically. And, of course, the arrival of European scientists such as Albert Einstein, Leo Szilard, Edward Teller, and a host of other refugee physicists made the production of the atomic bomb, and later the hydrogen bomb, into grim but perhaps necessary realities.

The United States emerged from World War II as the world's preeminent political, military, and economic power. This was to be, as Henry Luce of *Time* had predicted in 1941, the "American Century." That vision was soon realized, as America became a dominant intellectual and cultural power as well. Not surprisingly, the postwar years were marked by optimism, confidence, and "grand expectations." But heightened desires, especially in a world of change, often elicit opposite feelings of anxiety and confusion. The unity that had been sustained during World War II would soon begin to crack under the weight of its own internal contradictions and the tensions of a new set of problems. Once American global hegemony had been established, it was challenged, first by the Soviet Union's takeover of eastern Europe and then by the Soviet atomic bomb blast in 1949. In that same year, China became Communist. The world was resisting American expectations. In such a climate, confidence and anxiety, containment and exploration, consensus and conflict all co-existed and helped to define American intellectual and cultural life in the postwar years.

CONTAINMENT

The doctrine of containment, as developed by U. S. State Department intellectual George F. Kennan and in the Truman Doctrine of 1947, was designed as a military and economic policy to counter the threat of Communism's expansion in Europe and Asia. Each move by the Soviet Union, or by its presumed revolutionary proxies in nations such as Greece or Turkey, would be met with American resistance. Acceptance of the logic of containment led to problems, as it committed the United States to a permanent cold war, blurred distinctions between nationalist and communist revolutions abroad, and produced an insane weapons race and a foreign policy that was often as simplistic as it was self-righteous.

The containment of Communism abroad also defined life at home in postwar America. If American policy abroad failed to stem the red tide, then the cause must be found at home. Well-known spy cases involving State Department official Alger Hiss and Julius and Ethel Rosenberg convinced many that internal subversion was sapping American resolve against the Communist threat. Thus, beginning with President Truman's Federal Employee Loyalty program, continuing with the zealous witch-hunting of the FBI led by J. Edgar Hoover, and culminating with the fanaticism of Senator Joseph McCarthy's tirades against Communist subversion, the attempt to contain Communism abroad transformed itself into a home-front assault against any ideas deemed antagonistic to a unified anti-Communist front.

Containment had metaphorical possibilities that reached beyond the borders of the narrowly political. As large numbers of women entered the work force, social critics such as Marynia Farnham and Ferdinand Lundberg, in *Modern Women: The Lost Sex* (1947), worried that the family was under siege, that it was necessary to contain the aspirations of women. Moreover, from the perspective of containment, cultural protests, from the development of

rock-and-roll music to the emergent civil rights movement, were viewed as threats to be suppressed. In such an atmosphere, it often appeared that the postwar world demanded intellectual consensus, vapid theorizing, and a conformist culture.

BOUNDARIES

Despite attempts to impose rigidity and to contain challenges, the postwar years were intellectually rich. Rather than the era being defined solely by the notion of containment, perhaps an allied metaphor of boundaries is equally appropriate. Containment is about the fixing of borders, the imposition of limits. Boundaries depend on borders, but they are fluid entities, expanding as much as containing. As the influential theologian Paul Tillich and others in the period used the term, boundary situations brought forth anxiety in the face of death and conformity. But such anxiety also opened the individual up to courage and creativity. Boundaries became opportunities for growth. In certain paintings of the immediate postwar years, a concern with boundaries gave energy to the work of art. In the paintings of Barnett Newman, such as *Onement 1* (1948), and Mark Rothko, *Number 7* (c. 1951), the line between fields of color acts less to contain each of the fields than to figure as a place where the action is, where meaning is to be discerned, where the boundaries are to be transgressed in a heroic search for transcendence. In this fashion the culture of the postwar era may be read as a narrative of courage and creativity as much as of cowardice, conformity, and containment.

ANTI-COMMUNISM

Courage and creativity, however, often absented themselves in the mania to discover Communist subversion at home and abroad. The postwar years witnessed a "red scare," which largely crushed a left culture in the United States, contained political protest, and promoted conformity. In entertainment, the blacklist effectively kept actors, directors, and screenwriters with left-wing allegiances from practicing their trades. Publishers hesitated to issue books critical of the anti-Communist paranoia, and editorial voices of dissent were often silenced. Former Communists such as the journalist Whittaker Chambers and others confessed to congressional investigating committees their "sin" of having been members of the party and willingly named the names of others who had been with them in the movement. Many former Communists literally created for themselves a new profession, that of anti-Communist intellectuals devoted to using their knowledge of Communist byways to ferret out dangerous influences in American life.

Many intellectuals, however, were deeply divided about how best to respond to the hysteria of anti-Communism, even when they were unanimous in supporting the containment of Communism abroad. Some intellectuals rejected McCarthyism as counterproductive, seeing the senator as an ineffective and dangerous buffoon. Others jumped on the McCarthy bandwagon claiming that the means of the senator were justified by the ends of obliterating Communist subversion. Liberal anti-Communists such as the historian Arthur M. Schlesinger Jr. and the theologian Reinhold Niebuhr, the founders of Americans for Democratic Action, sought to devise a third way, a "vital center" in Schlesinger's phrasing, that would uphold the economic and social programs of the New Deal, vigorously pursue the cold war abroad, and vigilantly oppose Communism at home, with a minimum of disruption to civil liberties. Yet the lines of civil liberties were clouded and often obliterated. The philosopher Sidney Hook, who in his earlier years had done much to wed Marxism with American pragmatism, argued that professors at the nation's colleges should be fired from their jobs if they were members of the Communist Party. Since the party was, in Hook's analysis, inherently antagonistic to civil liberty and democracy, a Communist would only use democratic liberty to pursue totalitarian ends. In contrast, heresy, or criticism of American policy, was valuable and protected by the First Amendment and academic freedom. But such discriminations were rarely respected, as federal agencies and conservative administrators banished many professors with left-wing inclinations from the academy. The ultimate chilling aspect of this red scare was not simply the removal of hundreds of faculty or the nonhiring of certain professors, but the consensus and conformity that it promoted.

Consensus about the dead-end of totalitarianism (both Communist and fascist) was a staple of the postwar intellectual. Totalitarian thinking was an "escape from freedom," in the phrase of the social philosopher Erich Fromm, while the political philosopher Hannah Arendt understood totalitarianism as a deadly response to the dislocations caused by modernity. While the Soviet Union presented a real threat because of its messianic idealism, most intellectuals were convinced that historical development was in the direction of the liberal

state. Yet this widely shared perspective was often a source of concern as much as it was of satisfaction. Although the sociologist Daniel Bell titled his 1962 book *The End of Ideology,* he revealingly subtitled it *On the Exhaustion of Political Ideas in the Fifties.* Conformity at home had diminished political debate and possibility.

A similar consensus about the dangers of totalitarianism was apparent in American popular culture. Many second-rate films, such as *The Red Menace* (1949) and *The Steel Fist* (1952) were predictable vehicles for anti-Communist sentiments. *My Son John* (1952) presented the public with the danger of communism as an ideology eating into the heart of American family life. The ideal of unity in wartime, necessitated anew by the hostilities of the Korean War, remained a staple in Hollywood films of the 1950s. The desire for unity and the recognition of common enemies also informed science fiction and horror films in this period. Here the alien presence (as a blob, vicious plants, or monsters created by radioactivity) often patently implied the threat of the Soviet Union and the People's Republic of China. Only by the joining of advanced science and concerted community action could the American way of life be protected.

Yet it would be mistaken to imply that films in this period were mere propaganda pieces. Even when the film had a particular political message, in the hands of talented directors and actors, it could rise to the level of the highest art, as in two films from this period, *High Noon* (1952) and *On the Waterfront* (1954). In *High Noon,* the town marshal Will Kane, played by Gary Cooper, stands up against the forces of complacency and evil without help from the community. In essence, the film may be read as a critique of the red scare and an encomium on the heroism of defying the status quo. In a similar vein, although with a highly different subtext, *On the Waterfront,* was an attempt by talented artists such as Elia Kazan, Budd Schulberg, and Lee J. Cobb to rationalize or explain the heroism of standing up for truth, for turning against false friends, for naming names—something all of them had done when called before the House Committee on Un-American Activities in 1951 and 1952.

While overt political protest in film was rare, especially in an era when any taint of political leftism would result in the blacklisting of a screenwriter, director, or artist, in other realms of American culture voices of political protest were heard, often in original form. Dwight Macdonald founded *politics* magazine in 1944 as a humanistic, almost anarchistic, response to the "root that is man." The literary-social critic Irving Howe and the sociologist Lewis Coser launched *Dissent* in 1954 as a journal dedicated to democratic socialism. Powerful critiques of McCarthyism and the logic of corporate capitalism were found in the work of the sociologist C. Wright Mills and the journalist I. F. Stone. But they remained distinctly minor voices in the era.

CONFORMITY AND CORPORATE CULTURE

Conformity was deeply embedded in the postwar years, promoted in part by the demands of the policy of containment and the red scare. In troubled times, conformity helped to ease anxiety by limiting the range of options and by supporting consensus around options deemed reasonable and valuable. The corporate liberal economy that boomed in the 1950s was fed by the cold war; American economic power abroad and rising productivity and increasing wages at home also aided conformity and complacency. Modern advertising promoted consumer goods which, in turn, standardized tastes and values. In industrial relations, the earlier model of industrial strife was replaced by the reassertion of managerial authority (helped in part by the anti-labor provisions of the Taft-Hartley Act), but balanced by worker satisfaction with increased wages and shorter hours in many key industries. Even the American university system enrolled as a full-fledged member of the corporate liberal establishment. In the cold war era, and with the influx of new students taking advantage of the GI Bill, the university system expanded tremendously in the 1940s. By 1956 half of all servicemen had taken advantage of the act. While small liberal arts schools continued to survive, the new model of university life was the research university, closely connected to government, science, and industry, with applied research and generous grants working to implicate professors and students in the cold war militarization of American society.

In the university and business worlds a new ideal of success came into being. Success accrued from competent work rather than from flashes of brilliance, from getting along rather than from rocking the boat. A corporate culture of conformity had, as analyzed in the work of the social analyst David Riesman and others, created a new character type—the "other-directed" individual. According to Riesman's famous thesis, the dominant character type of the nineteenth century had been "inner directed"—rigid, driven to succeed by hard work, a moralistic individualist. With the shift from a pro-

THE LONELINESS OF THE OTHER-DIRECTED TYPE

If the other-directed people should discover how much needless work they do, discover that their own thoughts and their own lives are quite as interesting as other people's, that, indeed, they no more assuage their loneliness in a crowd of peers than one can assuage one's thirst by drinking sea water, then we might expect them to become more attentive to their own feelings and aspirations.

Source: Riesman, *The Lonely Crowd* (1950), pp. 571–572.

ducer to a consumer economy, from factory to white-collar production, the emerging character type required qualities of efficiency and compromise to function as an efficient and satisfied cog in the corporation.

In some cases, the corporation became more than the employer, it became the ideal society for the other-directed personality. Lines or boundaries between work and family, society and the individual diminished; IBM executives worked, lived, and played together. Their needs were anticipated and dictated by the corporation. Wearing the same type of suit and shirt, IBM executives were viewed as interchangeable parts. When an executive was relocated to a new community, he and his family had little need to worry about social disruption—the corporation knew precisely what type of suburban house and community would be proper for the executive. The increasing availability of air-conditioning, moreover, promised to erase the vagaries of climate, thus allowing for one of the most important internal migrations in American history, from the unionized eastern and Midwestern states to the southwestern and western United States. Conformity also colored the trip west, as the mobile family might now stay at a chain of hotels, eat in a chain of restaurants—all marked by familiar (if unexciting) accommodations and food.

The power of conformity in postwar culture was confronted and often challenged, as in the protests of the Beat writers such as Jack Kerouac and Allen Ginsberg. In "Howl" (1955–1956) Ginsberg ranted against "Robot apartments! invisible suburbs! skeleton treasuries! blind capitals! demonic industries!

spectral nations! invincible houses! granite cocks! monstrous bombs!" (p. 132).

Although David Riesman and fellow social analyst William H. Whyte criticized the conformity of the corporation, they demurred from a full frontal assault. Whyte praised the cooperative spirit of the modern corporation and even maintained that the rules of corporate life, while often stifling, could create space for the individual to flourish. He worried mainly that the rush to a rule-driven corporate culture had gone too far. Similarly, while Riesman sympathized more with the inner-directed character than the other-directed character type, he recognized that an irreversible shift had occurred, and that the new character type had a greater capacity for social interaction and happiness. Riesman himself, in the view of *Time* magazine, figured as the new other-directed character, as he was presented in 1954 as a family man, a connoisseur of fine wine and food, and a team player. The lines that had once been seen to separate the elitist and threatening "egghead" intellectual from the middle-class consumer had been obliterated. Intellectuals, *Time* assured its readers, were helping now to build rather than to destroy American society.

RELIGION

Many Americans considered it a salient fact that religion was a strong presence in the postwar world. More Americans than ever professed to religious beliefs; *Time* magazine celebrated the prominence of theologians such as Paul Tillich and Reinhold Niebuhr with cover stories. Membership in churches and synagogues skyrocketed. Even intellectuals got in on the act. In a symposium in *Partisan Review* some intellectuals professed to a personal faith in a manner that would have been unimaginable twenty years earlier. However, many of these same intellectuals also bemoaned what they viewed as the new-born conformity of American religion. Will Herberg's influential *Protestant, Catholic, Jew* (1955) found that America had become a tripartite nation of religious sentiments but that worshipers seemed without doctrinal enthusiasms. Faith in the value of faith appeared to be the new religious ideal. Churches, in this view, had grown silent on sin, and salvation seemed assured. Churches now functioned as social centers, places where congregants found a sense of community and a vague feeling of satisfaction. Even the religious revivals of the period led by the Reverend Billy Graham appeared as earnest and optimistic, hardly challenging to the pro-

prieties of middle-class life. Graham's message, in addition to a strong dose of anticommunism, was that God was love. The heavy weight of sin that appealed to followers of theologians such as Reinhold Niebuhr was absent. God, as the movie star Jane Russell exclaimed famously, was a "livin' doll" (Miller and Nowak, *The Fifties,* p. 100).

CRITICS AND ARTISTS

The postwar years were heady ones for American critics and artists. In an era when popular culture seemed to threaten the monuments of modernist art, American critics deemed themselves essential to the task of protecting high art and to defining the canon. In literature, critics such as Lionel Trilling, Leslie Fiedler, Dwight Macdonald, Alfred Kazin, and Edmund Wilson gained a status as exalted as that of the novelists they reviewed. The New Criticism, as practiced by Cleanth Brooks, Robert Penn Warren, and Allen Tate, promoted reading and criticism as rigorous method; texts assumed importance by dint of their internal logic and the strength of their symbolic structure. Understanding a text required the powerful guidance of the critic.

A heady feeling also ran through the currents of American fiction in this period. A new breed of Jewish American writer—Saul Bellow, Bernard Malamud, Norman Mailer—captured in different ways the experiences of assimilation and alienation. Themes of alienation were also central to the work of many southern-born writers publishing in this period—Walker Percy, Carson McCullers, Flannery O'Connor, and William Styron. This literature of alienation served as a counterpoise to the conformity that dominated American culture, and it suggested that the absurdity and alienation of the postwar world must be confronted and that, perhaps, through creativity it might be overcome.

In the world of painting, American artists achieved remarkable breakthroughs in technique, intent, and reputation. Abstract expressionism came to be the style favored by American painters. Although the range of abstract expressionism was large—from the drip canvases of Jackson Pollock to the color-field work of Newman and Rothko to the dancing strokes of Franz Kline—all forms of expression were linked by a deep concern with the logic of their medium, with a rejection of traditional forms of representation, with a desire to transcend the rational creative mind in favor of the unconscious or spontaneous gesture. Through the act of working out their inner needs on the canvas, these artists were, in effect, engaged in acts of heroic creativity, acts that challenged the borders of the conformist world. In their work, dissociated as it seemed from the social criticism that motored the work of artists in the 1930s, abstract expressionism could, some argued, be appropriated for the ends of the cold war. Their works signaled a shift from Paris to New York as the center of culture, and were part and parcel of the rejection of politics, new symbols of American power, weapons in the cultural cold war that could be contained, consumed, and exported.

In reality, abstract expressionist art resists such containment. While some critics recognized its value as a cultural export, others, such as the Republican congressman George Dondero, railed against it as incomprehensible and hence subversive. The refusal of the artists to discipline their instincts and to dampen their spontaneity also suggests that the work of abstract expressionism may have been critical of conformist, rationalistic culture. And while abstract expressionism did triumph and displace French art, American intellectuals and producers of culture rarely declared independence for the American mind from Europe. American critics worshiped the adopted Anglican tones of T. S. Eliot and they celebrated the European monuments of high culture—the Danish philosopher Søren Kierkegaard, the Russian novelist Fyodor Dostoevsky, and the Czech writer Franz Kafka were popular in this era.

WOMEN AND THE FAMILY

The postwar years attempted to contain women to the sphere of the family. In a very real sense, the 1950s were a dark age for women. Postwar reconversion was directed toward placing returning GIs back in gainful employment; the propaganda machine stressed women's responsibility to return to the home and to raise a family. Women in the postwar years did marry younger and did have families—these were, after all, the years of the baby boom. But while women were giving birth and raising families, they also remained employed in greater numbers than ever before—albeit in less well-paying jobs than earlier. Women, as Betty Friedan declared in *The Feminine Mystique* (1963), were chafing in their assigned roles as suburban housewives, consigned to the family circle and to occasional jobs without prospects. Women intellectuals, though present, were an endangered species in this era, despite the important work represented by

women such as Hannah Arendt, Mary McCarthy, and Elizabeth Hardwick. In the discipline of philosophy, talented women such as Hazel E. Barnes and Marjorie Grene were pushed to do translations or popularizations in continental philosophy, a branch of study that was perceived to be less exacting and rigorous than "male" analytic philosophy.

While the boundaries that contained women in this period were real and rigid, they were hardly absolute. Images of women as social leaders and strong personalities competed with the stereotype of women as contented homemakers. Even in television, the presumed bastion of the ideal family, divergent possibilities emerged. To be sure, 1950s television celebrated the nuclear, suburban family; in shows such as *Leave It to Beaver, The Donna Reed Show,* and *Ozzie and Harriet* the male had a career outside of the home, while the female sphere was contained within the role of looking pretty and taking care of home and children. The *I Love Lucy* show managed to challenge, however feebly, the racial and ethnic boundaries of postwar culture by having a white woman married to a Cuban bandleader. While the show posed little overt challenge to either the ideal of the housewife or the dichotomy between the rational male and the ditzy female, in every episode Lucy Ricardo did attempt to break out of the boundaries set for women. This should not be surprising, since the actress Lucille Ball brought to the show well-honed acting skills, a perfect sense of timing, and a strong perfectionist streak. Her marriage to Desi Arnaz was rocky, and those tensions were often reflected in the "war of the sexes" that occurred on the screen. Ball's character is consumed with dreams of being in show business, despite slim talents. Yet the desire for some financial independence and control define Lucy's on-screen existence as she takes on a host of jobs—working on a candy assembly line or pitching juiced-up vitamin supplements on television ads. Although comedic failure follows her every attempt at liberation from the home, Lucy nonetheless is clearly in rebellion from the expectations and boundaries—a fact that even comedy could not conceal. Moreover, when Lucille Ball became pregnant, she and Desi managed to push the network and the show's sponsor, Philip Morris, to work into the show the theme of Lucy's pregnancy—a first for television.

THE CRISIS OF MASCULINITY

Boundaries of masculinity in the postwar years were both contained and challenged. During World

8

War II, homosocial service stressed male camaraderie and bonding as essential to personal survival and winning the war. Once the war had concluded, American males were expected to reassume the old patriarchal order. On television, most male authority figures were bland, responsible, middle-class family men, whose sexual identification and power were rarely questioned. Only when cast as working class, as with William Bendix in *The Life of Riley* or Jackie Gleason in *The Honeymooners,* did television males gain personality, but at the expense of respectability.

However, in much of popular culture and intellectual life in the postwar years the boundaries of maleness were challenged and expanded, mainly because the traditional patriarchal model of the inner-directed character was shifting to the other-directed individual. Traditional male autonomy and power appeared to be in question. In the film *Rebel without a Cause* (1955), James Dean's character does have an apparent cause for rebellion; he is particularly irked by his father, portrayed by Jim Backus, who is unable to exercise patriarchal authority. Most tellingly, in one scene, Backus is shown wearing an apron.

In postwar culture, the new male was increasingly pictured as a rebel, pushing the boundaries of sexual propriety and responsibility. One form of rebellion was captured in the swinger image developed by Frank Sinatra and Hugh Hefner, which did little to question patriarchal power, although it did seek to change its expression. Here the male was no longer self-denying or family oriented so much as a machine for pleasure; women were objects for his sexual gratification; the world of consumer items became a phantasmagoria of pleasure possibilities, as exemplified in Hefner's *Playboy* magazine founded in 1953. Less amenable to the world of consumption and corporate ideals were the screen portrayals of young rebels. In *The Wild One* (1954), Marlon Brando's character, a motorcycle gang leader, when asked what he is rebelling against, responds, "Waddya got?" James Dean, while often inarticulate on screen, clearly rejected the corporate mentality and challenged heterosexuality with his admitted bisexuality and emphasis on emotional acting. The rebelliousness of the Beat writers—Kerouac, Ginsberg, William Burroughs—was more than a function of their spontaneous prose and an appreciation for the open road. They dismissed the traditional masculine ideal of the male as breadwinner, opting instead for the vagabond life. After a period of sexual uncertainty, Ginsberg embraced his homosexuality, as did Burroughs. The bonds of ho-

moerotic friendship between Kerouac and Ginsberg, as well as with the Beat writer Neal Cassady, were powerful. Despite the Beat push against the bonds of patriarchal, heterosexual lifestyles, they remained wedded, especially in the case of Kerouac, to a world of male solidarity; women in the Beat movement were shunted to the side, expected to play supportive roles to the flowering artistic genius and energy of the males.

MAILER'S REBELLION

Revolt against the conformity of the white patriarchal world reached its apogee, and most problematic expression, in the work of Norman Mailer. By 1956, Mailer was a celebrated literary lion, with three novels under his belt. In these novels, Mailer deeply identified with the outsider and the attitude of alienation. How, he asked, in a bureaucratic, constrained, conformist world could one find resources for rebellion that touched the soul of liberation? Mailer's solution, in his widely read essay "The White Negro" (1957), captures much of the essential critique of conformity and the blurring of boundaries that challenged containment culture in the 1950s. At the same time, Mailer attempted to link his fate to that of African American culture as he perceived it.

Mailer depicted dominant white culture as bereft of feeling, hurtling toward nuclear annihilation, dismissive of spontaneity, and boringly conformist. Whereas some artists in the immediate postwar years had turned to Native American culture for spiritual and artistic inspiration, Mailer (along with the Beats) identified with the creativity and freedom other artists discovered in African American culture. Mailer, in the process, managed to strip black life of its context and to transform black suffering into the stuff of redemption. According to Mailer, precisely because blacks were marginalized and discriminated against, on the cusp of violence, their lives were granted meaning and access to creativity in ways closed to whites. Mailer's vision of African American life was, to put it mildly, myopic. Ignoring the centrality of church, community, and family in the black experience, he reduced African American life to its criminal or rebellious elements—the dope dealer, pimp, and criminal. He came to praise these individuals in an eerie reversal of racist representations. Mailer waxed rhapsodic about liberation through murder and found in the style of the hipster a model that would allow white males to gain freedom through transcendental rebellion.

Mailer was hardly alone in his rebellion. According to many, teenagers, too, were pushing the boundaries of respectability. Suddenly juvenile delinquency was threatening the nuclear family. Youth gangs threatened the social order. Comic books, with their graphic depictions of violence and sexuality, became the subject matter of congressional hearings. Soon thereafter, the comic book industry "voluntarily" adopted codes of decency to censor offending materials from the impressionable eyes of young people. Pushed out of the comic book niche, *Mad* magazine dedicated itself to taking swipes at cultural conformity and good taste. J. D. Salinger's novel *The Catcher in the Rye* (1951) similarly, skewered adults of the 1950s from the perspective of teenager Holden Caulfield, who views every adult as a phony.

AFRICAN AMERICANS

However problematic and imperialist Norman Mailer and other white artists were in their appropriation of black culture for their own psychic needs, they did presage a more general and significant shift in American culture. Not since the 1920s had white American cultural boundaries expanded so much to include African American culture. With expansion and exploration of the boundaries, of course, came attempts at containment.

Ralph Ellison's novel *Invisible Man* (1952) was quickly recognized as a brilliant work of fiction. But Ellison's self-conscious irony, wordplay, and symbolism did not readily fit the genre of race writing. Thus, the liberal critic Irving Howe questioned the value of the novel on political grounds. In response, Ellison declared that he would never compromise or reduce his art to that of sociological or protest literature. While Ellison's work is a powerful critique of racial realities in America, it is also a work of the imagination, a work that seeks to transcend racial categories by exploring the boundaries of identity. In a similar fashion, Richard Wright moved away from the type of sociological literature of racism that had gained him a following in the 1930s and 1940s. In *The Outsider* (1953), Wright began with the premise of racism, but he attempted to universalize the conditions of alienation that afflicted African Americans as much as whites to explore the possibility of freedom and the weight of responsibility to others.

Not all African American artists in the postwar years shared the cultural expansiveness of Ellison and Wright. Dismayed by the white appropriation

JOINING THE STRUGGLE

In going underground, I whipped it all except the mind, the *mind*. And the mind that has conceived a plan of living must never lose sight of the chaos against which that pattern was conceived. That goes for societies as well as for individuals. Thus, having tried to give pattern to the chaos which lives within the pattern of your certainties, I must come out, I must emerge. . . . I'm shaking off the old skin and I'll leave it here in the hole. I'm coming out, no less invisible without it, but coming out nevertheless. And I suppose it's damn well time. Even hibernations can be overdone, come to think of it. Perhaps that's my greatest social crime, I've overstayed my hibernation, since there's a possibility that even an invisible man has a socially responsible role to play.

Source: Ellison, *Invisible Man* (1952), pp. 571–572.

of black jazz, African American musicians such as Charlie Parker and Dizzy Gillespie attempted with bebop music to create a musical idiom so drenched in the rhythms and syncopations of the black experience that it could not be appropriated by whites. Indeed, the essential culture of hip, in its argot of young blacks addressing one another by "hey, man," was a protest against the racist reduction of black men to boys in white culture. Although successful musically and largely confined to black musicians and composers, bebop culture's boundary quickly became blurred, as many whites came to champion it, even if they were not able to appropriate it musically.

ROCK AND ROLL

In the 1950s a new form of music developed which would further thrust the African American into the center of American cultural life. Rock and roll was largely beholden to the rhythm and blues tradition of African Americans. It was an expansive musical idiom, capable of including New Orleans–style jazz and even the cadences of country music. But in its purest form and initial energy, rock and roll pushed racial barriers as singers such as Little Richard, Chuck Berry, and Fats Domino became heroes for a new generation of young people, both black and white. Yet the cultural terrain of early rock and roll was racially charged and contested. For every boundary of race that was destroyed, a new one was erected. Fundamentalist religious groups burned piles of rock and roll records on moral and racist grounds. They believed, not without reason, that rock often challenged social and sexual proprieties. Record companies, never hesitant to exploit the profits associated with an emerging youth culture, but also worried about racial divisions undermining sales of records, attempted to develop alternatives to black music. Thus record companies manufactured clean-cut white singers such as Pat Boone to sing "cover" versions, without innuendo or sexual energy, of songs by Little Richard. While African American music remained central, and African American performers appeared regularly on such popular television shows as Dick Clark's *American Bandstand,* interracial dancing on the program was strictly forbidden.

In an era when African Americans were, through direct action in Montgomery, Alabama, and Greensboro, North Carolina, directly challenging the racism and segregation of America, rock and roll helped to make the boundaries between the races a bit less exacting, opening up many young whites to the protests of African Americans for equality.

Although containment and consensus were deeply etched into the culture and ideas of postwar America, the very boundaries that it erected were open to question, to new sets of possibilities. Rather than being an intellectual and cultural dark age between the social protest of the 1930s and the renewed protests of the 1960s, the postwar era had its own energy and protest. In those border areas formed by the tension between containment and courage, creative activity and social criticism flowered, making the transition to the counterculture era of the 1960s less a leap than a logical continuation.

BIBLIOGRAPHY

Overviews

Chafe, William H. *The Unfinished Journey: America Since World War II.* New York, 1986.

Diggins, John Patrick. *The Proud Decades: America in War and Peace, 1941–1960.* New York, 1988.

Graebner, William S. *The Age of Doubt: American Thought and Culture in the 1940s.* Boston, 1991.

Halberstam, David. *The Fifties.* New York, 1993.

Lhamon, W. T., Jr. *Deliberate Speed: The Origins of a Cultural Style in the American 1950s.* Washington, D.C., 1990.

May, Lary, ed. *Recasting America: Culture and Politics in the Age of Cold War.* Chicago, 1989.

McClay, Wilfred M. *The Masterless: Self and Society in Modern America.* Chapel Hill, N.C., 1994.

Miller, Douglas T., and Nowak, Marion. *The Fifties: The Way We Really Were.* Garden City, N.Y., 1977.

Patterson, James T. *Grand Expectations: The United States, 1945–1971.* New York, 1996.

Pells, Richard H. *The Liberal Mind in a Conservative Age: American Intellectuals in the 1940s and 1950s.* New York, 1985.

Whitfield, Stephen J. *The Culture of the Cold War.* 2d ed. Baltimore, 1996.

Specialized Studies of the Period

Boyer, Paul. *By the Bomb's Early Light: American Thought and Culture at the Dawn of the Atomic Age.* New York, 1985.

Belgrad, Daniel. *The Culture of Spontaneity: Improvisation and the Arts in Postwar America.* Chicago, 1998.

Brick, Howard. *Daniel Bell and the Decline of American Radicalism: Social Theory and Political Reconciliation in the 1940s.* Madison, Wisc., 1986.

Ehrenhalt, Alan. *The Lost City: Discovering the Forgotten Virtues of Community in the Chicago of the 1950s.* New York, 1995.

Erenberg, Lewis A., and Hirsch, Susan E., eds. *The War in American Culture: Society and Consciousness during World War II.* Chicago, 1996.

Heilbut, Anthony. *Exiled in Paradise: German Refugee Artists and Intellectuals in America from the 1930s to the Present.* New York, 1983.

Jumonville, Neil. *Critical Crossings: The New York Intellectuals in Postwar America.* Berkeley, Calif., 1991.

Leja, Michael. *Reframing Abstract Expressionism: Subjectivity and Painting in the 1940s.* New Haven, Conn., 1993.

Lipsitz, George. *Rainbow at Midnight: Labor and Culture in the 1940s.* Urbana, Ill., and Chicago, 1994.

Marty, Martin E. *Modern American Religion: Under God, Indivisible, 1941–1960.* Vol. 3. Chicago, 1996.

May, Elaine Tyler. *Homeward Bound: American Families in the Cold War Era.* New York, 1988.

McCann, Graham. *Rebel Males: Clift, Brando, and Dean.* New Brunswick, N.J., 1993.

Meyerowitz, Joanne, ed. *Not June Cleaver: Women and Gender in Postwar America, 1949–1960.* Philadelphia, 1994.

Powers, Richard Gid. *Not without Honor: The History of American Anticommunism.* New York, 1995.

Ross, Andrew. *No Respect: Intellectuals and Popular Culture.* New York, 1989.

Savran, David. *Taking It like a Man: White Masculinity, Masochism, and Contemporary American Culture.* Princeton, N.J., 1998.

Schrecker, Ellen W. *No Ivory Tower: McCarthyism and the Universities.* New York, 1986.

Sumner, Gregory D. *Dwight Macdonald and the "Politics" Circle.* Ithaca, N.Y., 1996.

Primary Sources

Bell, Daniel. *The End of Ideology: On the Exhaustion of Political Ideas in the Fifties.* New York, 1962.

Ellison, Ralph. *Invisible Man.* 1952. Reprint, New York, 1992.

Friedan, Betty. *The Feminine Mystique.* 1963. Reprint, New York, 1997.

Fromm, Erich. *Escape from Freedom.* New York and Toronto, 1941.

Ginsberg, Allen. *Collected Poems, 1947–1980.* New York, 1984.

Herberg, Will. *Protestant, Catholic, Jew: An Essay in American Religious Sociology.* Garden City, N.Y., 1955.

Kerouac, Jack. *On the Road.* 1957. Reprint, New York, n.d.

Mailer, Norman. *Advertisements for Myself.* 1959. Reprint, Cambridge and London, 1992.

Mills, C. Wright. *The Power Elite.* New York, 1956.

Riesman, David. *The Lonely Crowd: A Study of the Changing American Character.* New Haven, Conn., 1950.

Salinger, J. D. *The Catcher in the Rye.* 1951. Reprint, Boston, 1991.

Schlesinger, Arthur M., Jr. *The Vital Center: The Politics of Freedom.* 1949. Reprint, New York, 1988.

Whyte, William H. *The Organization Man.* New York, 1956.

Wright, Richard. *The Outsider.* 1953. Reprint, New York, 1993.

WORLD WAR AND COLD WAR

Paul Boyer

As in all historical time periods, American cultural and intellectual life in the 1940s and 1950s was decisively shaped by the era's larger social and political realities. Especially important in influencing this period's thought and culture were World War II and the cold war, vast global crises that profoundly engaged the American people, including intellectuals, opinion molders, cultural creators, and cultural critics.

From 1941 to 1945 the United States waged a war against foes who seemed the antithesis of all that Americans held dear. After 1945 a new conflict loomed: a confrontation with the Soviet Union conducted on the ideological and cultural plane no less than the military and strategic. Deepening the anxieties of the early cold war era was a superpower nuclear arms race.

These vast developments profoundly shaped America's intellectual and cultural life. In contrast to the contentious 1930s, World War II brought an ideological consensus as citizens rallied behind the Allied cause. Grassroots support for the war, while authentic, was powerfully reinforced by government propagandists, opinion molders, and mass-culture creators. At the same time, government leaders and the shapers of opinion offered scenarios of the postwar order and America's role in it.

In the early postwar years, the administrations of Harry S. Truman (1945–1953) and Dwight D. Eisenhower (1953–1961) sought to sustain the wartime ideological consensus, turning it now against a new global foe, Communist Russia. After a short, sharp debate a new ideological consensus on cold war issues did take shape, a consensus that involved the silencing of dissent and a coarsening of the discussion of international issues.

The domestic ideological and cultural fallout from World War II and the cold war extended well beyond the immediate issues raised by these international conflicts. Attitudes toward racial and ethnic relations, the themes of movies and television shows, even the nation's religious life—all were in-

fluenced by the larger realities of America's global role in these years. The specter of thermonuclear war—the legacy of America's wartime development and use of the atomic bomb—also found frequent cultural expression in the early cold war.

WORLD WAR II: FIGHTING FASCISM, DEBATING THE FUTURE

In the early 1930s, reacting to the Wall Street crash and the onset of the Great Depression, many American intellectuals and writers took a bleakly pessimistic view of capitalist America. President Franklin Delano Roosevelt's New Deal proved a rallying point for millions, but even as the New Deal unfolded, Roosevelt's critics, from conservative businessmen and reactionary demagogues on the right to communists and socialists on the left, continued to make this a decade of bitter ideological contention.

By the later 1930s, however, as European Fascist dictatorships and Japanese militarists menaced the Western democracies, including the United States, intellectuals and cultural producers of all kinds presented a more positive view of American democracy and the strength of ordinary Americans, even in times of crisis. John Steinbeck's *The Grapes of Wrath* (1939), Thornton Wilder's play *Our Town* (1938), and Carl Sandburg's biographical portrayal of Abraham Lincoln as the quintessential product of the midwestern heartland all date from this cultural moment.

Understandably, this upbeat view of America grew even more pervasive and emotionally compelling during World War II. The war against Nazi Germany, Fascist Italy, and Japan's imperialistic warlords rallied the United States to unprecedented levels of national unity. "Remember Pearl Harbor," the slogan recalling the Japanese surprise attack of 7 December 1941, became a national rallying cry.

Mobilizing Public Opinion for War Government propaganda, coordinated by the Office of War

Information, reinforced this spontaneous support for the war. Journalistic reports from the front and even war photos and newsreels were censored to build support for the war and avoid anything that might undermine morale. Not until late in the conflict did carefully selected photographs of American dead appear in the press.

Corporate America cooperated in the propaganda effort. Business executives volunteered as "dollar-a-year men" in wartime agencies. Corporate advertisers ran ads promoting patriotic themes. Tobacco companies gave free cigarettes to military hospitals (thereby creating a new generation of smokers). American business, its reputation tarnished by the stock market crash and the Depression, trumpeted its patriotic contribution. In *America Unlimited* (1944), a U.S. Chamber of Commerce official proclaimed, "Credit for the most astounding production job in all human history must go primarily to American capitalism."

The mass media joined in. Radio soap operas featured wives and sweethearts bravely carrying on while their menfolk went off to war. Singer Kate Smith provided a wartime anthem with her soaring renditions of "God Bless America." Bing Crosby lifted spirits with the sentimental ballad "White Christmas." Juvenile fans of the *Dick Tracy* radio show who collected scrap metal for the war effort had their names inscribed on the program's "Victory Honor Roll." Even comic strip characters, such as the hero of "Terry and the Pirates," donned uniforms.

Hollywood went to war as well. Movie stars like John Wayne and Ronald Reagan appeared in patriotic films; movie celebrities such as Bette Davis and Bob Hope promoted war bond drives or entertained the troops. Director Frank Capra's "Why We Fight" series explained the war's meaning to the troops. Humphrey Bogart gave up Ingrid Bergman to Paul Henreid, a courageous Czech anti-Nazi resistance leader, in the film *Casablanca* (1942). Government officials reviewed movie scripts to make certain they struck the proper themes.

The message of this propaganda was simple: America was fighting to overthrow dictatorships and to preserve democracy and freedom in the world.

This wartime propaganda and cultural mobilization, undertaken to build national unity in a time of crisis, helped shape the post-1945 cultural and ideological climate. Both the idealized representations of American life and the portrayal of America's foes as the embodiment of evil carried over into the early postwar era.

WARTIME PROPAGANDA: COMMUNITY AND FAMILY VS. FASCIST ANIMALS

Anticipating a 1950s cultural theme, the propagandists of 1941–1945 often defined American war aims in terms of community life and family togetherness. One war bond poster featured a winsome little girl with a message written in a childish scrawl: "Please help bring my daddy home." The illustrator Norman Rockwell offered a heartwarming view of grassroots Americans—speaking in town meetings, tucking their children into bed, enjoying Thanksgiving dinner—built around the "Four Freedoms" (freedom of speech, freedom of worship, freedom from want, freedom from fear) proclaimed by President Roosevelt in 1941.

The representations of the enemy were equally stark. While anti-German propaganda focused on Adolf Hitler and the Nazis, the anti-Japanese propaganda took on distinctly racist overtones, portraying Japanese in grotesque stereotypes and even as monkeys or vermin. A Walt Disney propaganda cartoon represented the Japanese as rats to be exterminated.

Defining America's Postwar World Role Political leaders and media opinion molders took advantage of the wartime unity to prepare Americans for global leadership in a postwar era when democratic values, international cooperation, and a liberal capitalist system as regulated in the public interest by Progressive-era and New Deal reforms—it was hoped—would spread worldwide. President Roosevelt, determined to preempt the isolationist forces that had defeated Woodrow Wilson's League of Nations after World War I, promoted a liberal vision of a postwar order led by a new international organization. Aiding Roosevelt in this effort was the fact that a key isolationist voice in the 1930s, the America First movement, had been discredited by Pearl Harbor and by America's subsequent declaration of war.

Roosevelt persuaded Wendell Willkie, the defeated 1940 Republican presidential candidate, to join in the effort to prepare Americans for their postwar world role. After a grueling global tour of the Allied nations, Willkie published an internationalist-minded account called, appropriately, *One World* (1943).

Even before Pearl Harbor, an expansive vision of America's future role had been offered by the media tycoon Henry Luce in a *Life* magazine editorial, "The American Century," published in February 1941. Updating Wilson's vision of America's global destiny, Luce insisted that the aim of the approaching war must be not only to defeat freedom's enemies, but to establish U.S. dominance worldwide—a dominance that would promote peace, justice, democracy, and the free enterprise system. "We must . . . be the Good Samaritan of the entire world," Luce insisted. But even after America's immediate enemies were defeated, Luce predicted, a protracted postwar struggle would ensue against the forces of "Tyranny"—his euphemism for Communism and the Soviet Union. Elaborating his vision of America as "the most powerful and vital nation in the world," Luce proclaimed: "Let us not be staggered by it. Let us rise to its tremendous possibilities."

These two visions—of a cooperative international order and of a world dominated by the United States—contained obvious internal contradictions. But the contradictions were glossed over in the effort to articulate America's postwar aims. The United Nations Charter, adopted at a fifty-nation conference in San Francisco in June 1945, seemed to embody the idealistic vision of a new and finer international order emerging from the carnage of war. In fact, World War II had unleashed forces that would overwhelm the United Nations; shattering the Grand Alliance of the United States, Great Britain, and the Soviet Union; and mocking both Roosevelt's dream of global amity and Henry Luce's scenario of a benign Pax Americana.

The Atomic Bomb Enters the Cultural Arena

On 6 August 1945 President Harry Truman announced that a new secret weapon, the atomic bomb, had been dropped on the Japanese "military base" of Hiroshima. As the utter destruction of Hiroshima and Nagasaki (bombed three days later) became known, the reaction was sharp and instantaneous. On one hand, Americans welcomed the new weapon, especially when Japan surrendered a few days later, ending the war. On the other, the bomb unleashed an intense ethical debate over the morality of the mass killing of civilians, even in a just war, and anxious speculation about the future. Visions of atomic destruction pervaded the culture. On 19 November 1945 *Life* magazine ran a feature imagining World War III as "The Thirty-Six Hour

Mushroom Cloud over Nagasaki, 9 August 1945. The chilling end of World War II became a symbol that would drive the cold war. © Bettmann/corbis

War," with illustrations of New York City devastated by missiles. Public figures, editorial writers, and radio news commentators spoke of the future in the gravest terms. Even country music songs, such as Fred Kirby's "Atomic Power," written on 7 August 1945, the day after the Hiroshima bombing, offered nightmarish visions of atomic annihilation.

Other cultural voices, however, echoing the hopeful theme President Truman had incorporated in his atomic bomb announcement, offered bright visions of a technological utopia ahead—a world transformed by atomic energy. "Electricity too cheap to meter," some predicted. Both the frightening and the hopeful themes would continue to shape American thought and culture through the cold war era and beyond.

For the idealists who were calling for a new world order to replace the rivalries and conflicts of the past, the atomic bomb seemed the clinching argument. Norman Cousins, editor of the *Saturday Review of Literature,* published an impassioned editorial, "Modern Man Is Obsolete," on 18 August 1945, proposing a world government. Published in book form, Cousins's appeal found an answering echo across the nation.

The internationalist response to the bomb also inspired the Acheson-Lilienthal Report of 1946, calling for the international control of atomic energy under the United Nations. Americans rallied to the cause, including scientists who had worked on the atomic bomb. *One World or None* (1946), a collection of essays by atomic scientists and others, posed the alternatives starkly: either global cooperation or global destruction. In the 1951 movie *The Day the Earth Stood Still,* the same message is preached by extraterrestrial beings who arrive in a spaceship. But the space visitor who delivers this warning is attacked by fearful citizens—a parable of the rapidly changing cultural climate as the 1950s dawned.

INTO THE COLD WAR

During World War II, the United States and the Soviet Union forged an alliance of convenience against a common foe, Nazi Germany. With the war's end, however, long-standing sources of tension, both strategic and ideological, quickly resurfaced. The most intense and dangerous phase of the resulting conflict, dubbed the cold war, began in the late 1940s and extended through the early 1960s. This all-encompassing struggle affected all facets of American life, including the intellectual and cultural spheres. The most obvious initial effects came in the ideological realm as Americans debated the nature of the Soviet threat and how best to counter it.

Redefining America's Mission in a Cold War World Some prominent Americans continued to espouse the Rooseveltian vision of a cooperative world order under the leadership of the United Nations. FDR's widow, Eleanor Roosevelt, firmly supported the United Nations. So did Henry A. Wallace, vice president in Roosevelt's third term and secretary of commerce in the Truman administration. In a summer 1946 memo to Truman, Wallace lamented "the irrational fear of Russia . . . being built up in the American people by certain individuals and publications." In a New York speech that September, Wallace urged renewed effort to find accommodation with the Soviet Union.

But the ideological climate was changing rapidly, and when Secretary of State James F. Byrnes bitterly protested Wallace's speech, Truman dismissed Wallace. The deepening hostility between the United States and the Soviet Union reflected both the bold confidence of an atomic-armed America and alarming evidences of Moscow's belligerence and intransigence. The Soviet dictator Joseph Stalin was imposing his will ever more ruthlessly, not only in Russia but also in Eastern Europe, from 1945 to his death in 1953.

Among the statesmen and intellectuals who played important roles in shaping America's cold war ideology were the diplomat George F. Kennan, the theologian Reinhold Niebuhr, and the historian Arthur M. Schlesinger Jr. Early in 1946, Kennan, a foreign-service officer in Moscow, sent to Washington a "Long Telegram" setting forth his views of Soviet aims and how the United States should respond to them. In expanded form, Kennan's essay appeared as "The Sources of Soviet Conduct" in the July 1947 issue of the influential journal *Foreign Affairs.* Although the article was simply signed "X," Kennan's authorship soon became known.

Kennan portrayed the Soviet Union, motivated both by Communist ideology and by Russia's long-standing strategic aims, as constantly probing for weak spots on its periphery, into which Soviet power might flow. The appropriate response to Russia's "patient but deadly struggle" to expand its influence and crush all foes real and imagined, argued Kennan, was a policy of *containment:* unremitting vigilance and resistance to Soviet power probes wherever they occurred. Warmly endorsed by Secretary of Defense James Forrestal, a fiercely militant early cold war warrior, and popularized by the Luce publications and other media outlets—often in more belligerent terms than Kennan himself had employed—Kennan's containment doctrine and the assumptions underlying it became a cornerstone of U.S. policy in the early cold war era.

Although couched in the cool language of strategic analysis, Kennan's essay embraced a vision of America's mission first formulated by the New England Puritans and elaborated by the advocates of the nation's policy of "Manifest Destiny" in the late nineteenth century. Americans should be grateful, Kennan insisted, to "a Providence which, by providing [them] with this implacable challenge, has made their entire security as a nation dependent on their pulling themselves together and accepting the responsibilities of moral and political leadership that history plainly intended them to bear."

Reinhold Niebuhr, of German immigrant stock, attended Yale Divinity School, briefly led a parish in Detroit, and after 1928 taught at Union Theological Seminary in New York City. Like other intellectuals, he moved leftward in the 1930s, rejecting both capitalist ideology and progressive reformism in favor of Marxism. But disillusionment soon set in, and in numerous books and essays he exhorted Americans to abandon their idealistic naïveté and sentimental optimism and recognize the power calculations that underlie the behavior of nations and social groups.

By the late 1940s Niebuhr emerged as an articulate shaper of cold war ideology, preaching full-scale resistance to the Soviet Union on the military and ideological fronts. To avoid war, he advised, do not be too afraid of it. He welcomed the apocalyptic terms of global confrontation with which President Truman in March 1947 called for U.S. aid to help Greece and Turkey resist Communist insurgencies. Communists were especially fearsome, Niebuhr warned in *Irony of American History* (1952), because in their absolutist zeal they tried to impose by force the social ideals that Western liberals only fitfully pursued. Although critical of America's tendency toward moral smugness, Niebuhr insisted that the United States, with its freedom of expression and relatively open politics, offered far greater promise of a reasonably just social order than did Moscow. Niebuhr exerted enormous influence in the early cold war era, providing an ideological framework for U.S. cold war policy. One journalist called him "the official establishment theologian." Popularized versions of his message appeared in such magazines as *Time, Life,* and *Reader's Digest.*

Arthur Schlesinger Jr., a New Deal liberal and biographer of such Democratic icons as Andrew Jackson and Franklin D. Roosevelt, sought to articulate a cold war liberalism that would be progressive on domestic issues but firmly anti-Soviet and free of any hint of collaborating with Communists. In the late 1930s, in response to the Nazi threat, Stalin had proposed an anti-Fascist "Popular Front" uniting the Communist and non-Communist left. Many American leftists had embraced the Popular Front; but in the altered ideological climate of the early cold war, the idea that one might make common cause with Communists on any issue became anathema.

In *The Vital Center* (1949), Schlesinger elaborated his version of cold war liberalism, vigorously anti-Communist but committed to extending the New Deal's liberal agenda domestically. The Soviet Union could never be negotiated with, only defeated, Schlesinger implied, if not in war then through the West's "technological dynamism." He spent little time identifying legitimate Soviet security interests or exploring international realities that did not fit his starkly bipolar worldview.

Indeed, few of these early cold war intellectuals paid much heed to the poverty-stricken regions of Latin America, Africa, and Asia that lay outside the arena of direct U.S.-Soviet confrontation. The United States would pay a price for this neglect, but in the early cold war era, these issues seemed peripheral to the urgent business of mobilizing against the perceived Soviet threat.

As Kennan, Niebuhr, and Schlesinger articulated a cold war ideology for liberals, conservative intellectuals were shaping an anti-Communist position congenial to their worldview. Key figures in this effort included Friedrich Hayek, William F. Buckley Jr., and Whittaker Chambers.

Hayek, an Austrian economist who immigrated to England before settling at the University of Chicago, is best remembered for *The Road to Serfdom* (1944), a powerful polemic that denounced not only Communism but also socialism and welfare-state liberalism as stepping-stones to totalitarianism. Only a libertarian state permitting the maximum individual freedom and a largely unregulated economic order, suggested Hayek, would provide immunity to the Communist virus. Although Hayek's critique of New Deal–style policies offended liberals, his analysis appealed to conservatives in the postwar anti-Communist climate. Named a Book-of-the-Month Club selection and excerpted in *Reader's Digest,* Hayek's work helped undergird a resurgent conservative ideology that would influence American politics for decades.

William F. Buckley Jr., son of a wealthy Catholic family, attended Yale, whose liberalism and apostasy from its Christian roots he lamented in *God and Man at Yale* (1951). A fervent anti-Communist, Buckley played a central role in rallying conservatives to the cold war banner through the *National Review,* founded in 1955. Buckley's magazine provided a forum for an array of cold war ideologues, including James Burnham, author of such polemics as *The Coming Defeat of Communism* (1950); *Containment or Liberation?* (1954), a critique of Kennan's containment doctrine as insufficiently militant; and *The Web of Subversion* (1954), on the dangers of homegrown Communists.

Whittaker Chambers, a *Time* editor and former Communist, rocketed to fame in 1948 with his charges that Alger Hiss, a State Department official in the 1930s, was a Communist who had passed secret documents to Chambers. In dramatic hearings before the House Committee on Un-American Activities, Hiss vehemently denied Chambers's charges. However, dogged investigation by a young California congressman, Richard Nixon, eroded

C. WRIGHT MILLS

C. Wright Mills stands out among the social thinkers of the 1950s for his radical engagement with contemporary issues, from the nuclear arms race to the psychological effects of modern capitalism. Born in Waco, Texas, in 1916, Mills graduated from the University of Texas and earned a Ph.D. from the University of Wisconsin in 1941. Appointed professor of sociology at Columbia in 1948, he ruffled feathers not only for his radical politics but for his unconventional lifestyle, including his fondness for riding a motorcycle.

Influenced equally by Karl Marx and Max Weber, Mills called for the close study of social structures but criticized the "objective" and "value-free" sociological research then dominant in the profession. Sociologists—and indeed all academics—he insisted, should be actively engaged with the issues of their day. His own increasingly polemical work breathed indignation with social injustice and exploitation and what he saw as the destructive psychological effects of the modern corporate order. In *The Sociological Imagination* (1959) he wrote:

> Nowadays men often feel that their private lives are a series of traps. They sense that within their everyday worlds, they cannot overcome their troubles, and in this feeling, they are often quite correct: What ordinary men are directly aware of and what they try to do are bounded by the private orbits in which they live; their visions and their powers are limited to the close-up scenes of job, family, neighborhood; in other milieux, they move vicariously and remain spectators. And the more aware they become, however vaguely, of ambitions and threats which transcend their immediate locales, the more trapped they seem to feel.

For Mills, the cold war and the nuclear arms race ranked high among causes of this feeling of entrapment. He saw corporate profit-making as a major force propelling the cold war. (Indeed, President Dwight Eisenhower would point to a similar link in his 1961 Farewell Address with its warnings about the power of the nation's "military-industrial complex.") In *The Causes of World War III* (1958), Mills observed:

> The . . . combat readiness on both sides is already devastating. The development of this equipment is cumulative: One "ultimate weapon" follows another in geometric progression, and the case for the acceleration in both war camps is quite adequate for the end in view. Never before has there been an arms race of this sort—a scientific arms race, with a series of ultimate weapons, dominated by the strategy of obliteration. At every turn of this "competition," each side becomes more edgy and the chances become greater that . . . the U.S. radar man in Canada or his Russian counterpart in Siberia will trigger the sudden ending.

Mills's combative radicalism stood out starkly in the cautious intellectual climate of the 1950s, making him seem more a man of the 1930s or the 1960s. He reacted warmly to evidences of renewed social activism, publishing a prescient "Letter to the New Left" in 1960. But he did not live to see the full flowering of youthful radicalism. Mills died of a heart attack in 1962, at the age of forty-five.

Hiss's story and led to his conviction and imprisonment on perjury charges (the statute of limitations on treason having expired).

Chambers, a gifted writer, capitalized on his fame by writing *Witness* (1952), a spiritual autobiography that reinforced the view of the cold war as not merely a strategic rivalry between two superpowers, but a religious crusade against a demonic and cunning foe—a crusade to which the West must commit all of its material and ideological resources if it had any hope of winning. In the same confessional vein, *The God That Failed* (1950) offered a collection of essays by former Communists, including the novelist Richard Wright.

Cold War Culture on the Homefront   As the cold war ideological consensus took shape, it influenced American culture in complex and subtle ways. Secret government funds flowed to cultural organizations and publications deemed helpful to the anti-Communist cause. The State Department sponsored European tours by jazz musicians such as Dizzy Gillespie, recruiting them for the cultural cold war. *Life* magazine celebrated abstract expressionism, particularly the work of Jackson Pollock, as evidence of America's cultural freedom in contrast to Russia's rigid control of artists and writers.

The cold war's cultural fallout also included widespread fears of subversion, pressures for intellectual conformity, and suspicion of deviant opinions. This repressive climate peaked in the early 1950s during the heyday of Senator Joseph R. McCarthy and his headline-grabbing search for Communists in government and in other realms of American life.

The House Committee on Un-American Activities, meanwhile, pursued its own campaign to expose domestic disloyalty, grilling citizens who belonged (or had once belonged) to a long list of "subversive" organizations compiled by the attorney general. Scholars, writers, and artists were summoned to testify or named as a danger to the republic. Careers were shattered and reputations ruined. Hollywood screenwriters were blacklisted. Teachers and professors were required to sign "loyalty oaths."

Some writers and moviemakers addressed the issue directly. Arthur Miller's play *The Crucible* (1953) used the Salem witchcraft episode of 1692 as a metaphor for contemporary anti-Communist paranoia. The makers of the 1952 film *High Noon,* starring Gary Cooper as a western sheriff who is cravenly abandoned by the townsfolk as he prepares to meet a gang of desperadoes out to kill him, explicitly intended it as a warning against surrendering to ideological bullies.

Other cultural commentaries on the contemporary political climate were more allusive. In the film *Invasion of the Body Snatchers* (1956), set in a picturesque California town, sinister space aliens take over the bodies of townspeople, who remain outwardly unchanged. The movie both criticized and contributed to the prevailing paranoia about internal subversion.

Director Elia Kazan made his 1954 movie *On the Waterfront,* in which Marlon Brando reports waterfront corruption to the authorities, to justify his decision to appear as a friendly witness before the House Committee on Un-American Activities. Movies such as *I Married a Communist* (1950), *My Son John* (1952), John Wayne's *Big Jim McLain* (1952), and the television series *I Led Three Lives* (1953–1956), based on the memoirs of an FBI agent who had infiltrated the U.S. Communist Party, sought to reinforce public concerns about domestic Communist subversion.

The obsession with domestic Communism faded after a 1954 television broadcast by newsman Edward R. Murrow exposing Senator McCarthy's tactics, and McCarthy's censure by the Senate later that year. But suspicions of domestic subversion remained a cultural force through the 1950s.

The cold war's domestic impact took other forms as well. Popular television series such as *Leave It to Beaver* and *Father Knows Best* that celebrated suburban domesticity and a stable, patriarchal social order have been interpreted as culturally conservative productions designed to contain the forces of change at home as the nation girded up for ideological struggles abroad, and to underscore the centrality of the American family in contrast to the all-powerful state in the Soviet system.

The cold war contest with the Soviet Union also encouraged scrutiny of racial prejudice and discrimination in American life. As early as 1944, in *An American Dilemma: The Negro Problem and American Democracy,* the Swedish economist Gunnar Myrdal had noted the paradox that while America waged war against racist foes abroad, racial segregation prevailed at home. America would confront this issue even more directly, Myrdal predicted, in the postwar era. Indeed, as America hosted the United Nations and courted darker-skinned peoples in the cold war competition with the Russians, the embarrassment of continued racism at home attracted increasing notice. These considerations, plus growing African American political activism, pushed the Truman administration to embrace a far-reaching civil rights agenda, set forth in *To Secure These Rights* (1947), the report of a presidential commission.

Anti-Semitism also came to the fore in the early postwar era as the full horror of the Nazi Holocaust emerged. During the war, Washington had scarcely reacted as evidence of the Nazis' extermination program filtered out, and U.S. public opinion had earlier opposed admitting large numbers of Jewish refugees from Nazism. (U.S. immigration officials did, however, admit a substantial number of refugee scientists, writers, composers, musicians, and scholars who were fleeing Nazism, most of them Jewish. This cadre of emigré intellectuals would profoundly influence many realms of American thought and culture in the postwar era.) After the war, as shocking accounts of the death camps documented with horrifying photographs were published, anti-Semitism at home faced increasing censure. Laura Z. Hobson's *Gentleman's Agreement* (1946), made into a successful movie (1947) starring Gregory Peck, documented patterns of anti-Semitic discrimination in American life.

The ideological constraints of the cold war consensus—combined with a booming consumer economy—affected 1950s social thought in many ways. Former radicals like the critic Dwight Macdonald, the sociologist Daniel Bell, and the historian Daniel Boorstin espoused more conservative positions in the postwar era, directing their critical energies to capitalism's cultural effects, rather than its political and economic dimensions.

Macdonald, in a series of essays collected in *Against the American Grain* (1963), defended high culture not only against America's mass culture but also against a watered-down version of high culture he called "midcult." Daniel Bell, in the title essay of *The End of Ideology* (1960), argued that the Marxist critique of capitalism—a critique that he and many other intellectuals had embraced in the 1930s—had been discredited by events and was irrelevant to the conditions of postwar American society. Boorstin in *The Image* (1962) offered an incisive critique of media "pseudo-events" and the many other ways modern American culture substituted the shallow and the ersatz for authentic experience. But Boorstin did not extend his analysis to the consumer-capitalist system that underlay the cultural phenomena he criticized. Indeed, few social critics of the 1950s discussed modern capitalism, issues of social class or gender, the lives of the poor and disadvantaged, discrimination against minorities, or indeed any social realities that lay beyond the suburban, middle-class culture that was the target of their criticism.

A notable exception to this conservative cultural criticism was the maverick Columbia University sociologist C. Wright Mills. In *White Collar* (1951) and *The Power Elite* (1956), Mills explored the class structure and power relationships in contemporary America, as he understood them, in radical ways that were rare in the cautious intellectual climate of the early cold war era.

As the first wave of the wartime and early-postwar baby-boom generation reached adolescence in the mid- and later 1950s, attention focused on this demographic bulge in the population. With suburban teenagers enjoying ample disposable income thanks to postwar prosperity, Hollywood filmmakers, record-company executives, drive-in restaurant owners, and the marketers of clothing, soft drinks, portable radios, and record players all sought to tap this lucrative market. But in this conservative cold war era that so insistently celebrated family values and parental authority, fears of adolescent rebelliousness and worse—both in inner cities and in suburbia—eddied through the culture. In *Seduction of the Innocent* (1954), the psychiatrist Frederic Wertham warned of the dangerous effects of sex and violence in comic books. A kind of national hysteria about "juvenile delinquency" led to congressional investigations and dire cultural commentary, and spawned such cautionary movies as *Blackboard Jungle* (1955), *Rebel without a Cause* (1955), and *The Wild One* (1953), featuring Marlon Brando as leader of a motorcycle gang that invades a peaceful California town. Leonard Bernstein's hit musical *West Side Story* (1957) retold the story of Romeo and Juliet in a context of New York City street gangs. The rise of rock 'n' roll in the mid-1950s, with its high-decibel songs of adolescent anger, angst, and sexual urgency, typified by a young Elvis Presley not yet tamed by Hollywood, intensified conservative handwringing about the younger generation.

As an anodyne to these fears, many cultural voices emphasized the importance of religion as both a source of social and familial stability and a point of contrast between the United States and the officially atheistic Soviet Union. Church attendance soared; the Advertising Council promoted the slogan "The Family That Prays Together, Stays Together"; Congress in 1954 added the phrases "In God We Trust" to the nation's coinage and the phrase "under God" to the pledge of allegiance; and television programs featuring the Protestant evangelist Billy Graham and the Catholic bishop Fulton J. Sheen attracted millions.

The Cultural Expression of Nuclear Fear The impact of nuclear weapons on American thought and culture, so noticeable in the earliest months of the Atomic Age, continued even after the initial shock of the bombing wore off. Cultural attention to nuclear issues peaked in 1954–1963 amid widespread attention to the hazards of radioactive fallout from atmospheric hydrogen-bomb tests in the Pacific. Novels such as Nevil Shute's *On the Beach* (1957)—made into a successful film by Stanley Kramer—and scores of science fiction stories, including Walter Miller Jr.'s *A Canticle for Leibowitz* and Pat Frank's *Alas, Babylon* (both 1959), offered imagined scenarios of a postnuclear future. The satirical songwriter Tom Lehrer addressed nuclear dangers in many of his songs, which enjoyed great popularity on college campuses. Television programs such as *The Outer Limits* and Rod Serling's *The Twilight Zone* frequently explored the social effects of nuclear fear, the consequences of genetic mutation, or life after a nuclear war.

The film industry, ever sensitive to shifts in the public mood, offered a series of mutant movies in the middle and later 1950s, including *Them!* (1954), *The Incredible Shrinking Man* (1957), the Japanese import *Godzilla: King of the Monsters* (1956), and many others. In nearly all of these films, the grotesque mutations are triggered by atomic radiation. In *Them!*, terrifying giant ants emerge from the atomic test site in New Mexico. In *The Incredible Shrinking Man*, the hapless hero begins to shrink after his sailboat passes through a radioactive cloud—the fate that actually befell a Japanese fishing boat in 1954, causing death and illness to the crew.

In 1955, Ralph Edwards's popular television program *This Is Your Life* featured "the Hiroshima Maidens," a group of young Japanese women brought to America by Norman Cousins for reconstructive surgery. In a staged moment of reconciliation, a crew member of the *Enola Gay*, the plane that dropped the Hiroshima bomb, presented a check to the representative of the Hiroshima Maidens. In an outpouring of sentiment, twenty thousand viewers sent in contributions.

Nuclear fear shaped American religion in these years as well. The evangelist Billy Graham first burst into public attention with a Los Angeles tent revival in September 1949, just as the Russians exploded their first atomic bomb. Cried Graham, "An arms race unprecedented in the history of the world is driving us madly toward destruction! . . . Time is desperately short. . . . Prepare to meet thy God" (Boyer, 1994, p. 239).

Other religious leaders sought to soothe nuclear anxieties. In *A Guide to Confident Living* (1948) and other books, the Reverend Norman Vincent Peale advised fearful Americans to "say confidently to yourself 'Through God's help and the application of simple techniques, I will be free from fear. Believe that—practice it, and it will be so'" (pp. 133, 146).

The nuclear theme faded with the signing of the Limited Nuclear Test Ban Treaty in 1963, but for nearly twenty years it had been a shaping influence in American thought and culture—and it would become so again in the early 1980s.

CONCLUSION

By the early 1960s, the conservative political climate, cautious cultural criticism, and rigid cold war ideological consensus that had prevailed for more than a decade were changing rapidly. With the election of John F. Kennedy as president in 1960, the Democrats regained the White House after Republican Dwight D. Eisenhower's eight-year incumbency. In the aftermath of the 1962 Cuban Missile Crisis and the test ban treaty, the cold war entered a marginally less dangerous stage, while a series of arms control treaties held promise that the ultimate nuclear confrontation might be avoided. A cycle of American thought and culture that had begun with the outbreak of war in 1941 was drawing to a close as new cultural currents and new ideological configurations emerged.

See also **Intellectuals and Ideology in Government; International Relations and Connections** *(in this volume);* **Technological Enclaves** *(volume 3).*

BIBLIOGRAPHY

General

Boyer, Paul S. *Promises to Keep: The United States since World War II.* 2d ed. Lexington, Mass., 1995.

Graebner, William S. *The Age of Doubt: American Thought and Culture in the 1940s.* Boston, 1991.

Pells, Richard. *The Liberal Mind in a Conservative Age: American Intellectuals in the 1940s and 1950s.* New York, 1985.

World War II

MOBILIZING PUBLIC OPINION FOR WAR

Blum, John M. *V Was for Victory: Politics and American Culture during World War II*. New York, 1976.

Dower, John W. *War without Mercy: Race and Power in the Pacific War*. New York, 1986.

Koppes, Clayton, and Black, Gregory D. *Hollywood Goes to War: How Politics, Profits, and Propaganda Shaped World War II Movies*. New York, 1987.

Laurie, Clayton D. *The Propaganda Warriors: America's Crusade against Nazi Germany*. Lawrence, Kans., 1996.

Roeder, George H., Jr. *The Censored War: American Visual Experience during World War Two*. New Haven, Conn., 1993.

Westbrook, Robert B. "Private Interests and Political Obligation in World War II." In *The Power of Culture: Critical Essays in American History*, edited by Richard Wightman Fox and T. J. Jackson Lears. Chicago, 1993.

Winkler, Allan M. *The Politics of Propaganda: The Office of War Information, 1942–1945*. New Haven, Conn., 1978.

Wyman, David S. *The Abandonment of the Jews: America and the Holocaust, 1941–1945*. New York, 1984.

DEFINING AMERICA'S POSTWAR ROLE

Baughman, James L. *Henry R. Luce and the Rise of the American News Media*. Boston, 1987.

Dallek, Robert. *Franklin D. Roosevelt and American Foreign Policy, 1932–1945*. New York, 1979.

Gaddis, John Lewis. *The United States and the Origins of the Cold War, 1941–1947*. New York, 1972.

The Cold War Era

REDEFINING AMERICA'S MISSION IN A COLD WAR WORLD

Ehrman, John. *The Rise of Neoconservatism: Intellectuals and Foreign Affairs, 1945–1994*. New Haven, Conn., 1995.

Fowler, Robert Booth. *Believing Skeptics: American Political Intellectuals, 1945–1964*. Westport, Conn., 1978.

Fox, Richard. *Reinhold Niebuhr: A Biography*. New York, 1985.

Gardner, Lloyd C. *Architects of Illusion: Men and Ideas in American Foreign Policy, 1941–1949*. Chicago, 1970.

O'Neill, William L. *A Better World: The Great Schism: Stalinism and the American Intellectuals*. New York, 1982.

Walker, J. Samuel. *Henry A. Wallace and American Foreign Policy*. Westport, Conn., 1976.

COLD WAR CULTURE

Biskind, Peter. *Seeing Is Believing: How Hollywood Taught Us to Stop Worrying and Love the Fifties*. New York, 1983.

Brands, H. W. *The Devil We Knew: Americans and the Cold War*. New York, 1993.

Jackson, Walter A. *Gunnar Myrdal and America's Conscience: Social Engineering and Racial Liberalism, 1938–1987.* Chapel Hill, N.C., 1990.

Lawson, Steven F. *Running for Freedom: Civil Rights and Black Politics in America since 1941.* 2d ed. New York, 1997.

Lipsitz, George. *Class and Culture in Cold War America: A Rainbow at Midnight.* New York, 1981.

May, Lary, ed. *Recasting America: Culture and Politics in the Age of Cold War.* Chicago, 1989.

Powers, Richard Gid. *Not without Honor: The History of American Anticommunism.* New York, 1995.

Schrecker, Ellen W. *No Ivory Tower: McCarthyism and the Universities.* New York, 1986.

Whitfield, Stephen J. *The Culture of the Cold War.* Baltimore, 1991.

CULTURAL CRITICS OF THE 1950S

Horowitz, Irving Louis. *C. Wright Mills: An American Utopian.* New York and London, 1983.

Jumonville, Neil. *Critical Crossings: The New York Intellectuals in Postwar America.* Berkeley, Calif., 1991.

Liebowitz, Nathan. *Daniel Bell and the Agony of Modern Liberalism.* Westport, Conn., 1985.

Schaub, Thomas Hill. *American Fiction in the Cold War.* Madison, Wisc., 1991.

Nuclear Weapons in American Thought and Culture

Boyer, Paul S. *By the Bomb's Early Light: American Thought and Culture at the Dawn of the Atomic Age.* New edition with a new preface by the author. Chapel Hill, N.C., 1994.

George, Carol. *God's Salesman: Norman Vincent Peale and the Power of Positive Thinking.* New York, 1993.

Martin, William C. *A Prophet with Honor: The Billy Graham Story.* New York, 1991.

Oakes, Guy. *The Imaginary War: Civil Defense and American Cold War Culture.* New York, 1994.

Shaheen, Jack G., ed. *Nuclear War Films.* Carbondale, Ill., 1978.

Winkler, Allan M. *Life under a Cloud: American Anxiety about the Atom.* New York, 1993.

THE CULTURE AND CRITICS OF THE SUBURB AND THE CORPORATION

James Hudnut-Beumler

The United States underwent substantial social change in the twenty years following the end of World War II. The postwar period witnessed the emergence of a United States transformed by its new status as a world superpower, by unparalleled affluence, by social and geographical mobility, by the rise of television, and by changes in long-standing patterns of race relations. Accompanying these social transformations was a body of social criticism that was likewise unprecedented in American social and intellectual history. The postwar era proved in many ways to be the golden age of the American social critic. The critics' leading concerns emerged directly out of the social changes taking place and often focused on two leading social realities: the corporation and suburbanization.

Corporate and suburban life figured prominently in the concerns of social observers precisely because the corporations and suburbia grew so rapidly in the postwar years that they appeared in some way responsible for the striking changes observed in the postwar culture. Indeed, white-collar employees were far more likely to work for a publicly held corporation after the war than before. New college graduates and returning GIs were especially likely to work for large-scale institutions and to live in new housing created on farmland at the fringe of established cities, in what became known as suburbia. Some leading corporations in major urban areas such as New York City, Boston, and Chicago intensified the dual trend by relocating their headquarters to suburban locations. The meaning of suburbia and the corporation thus became preoccupations of social critics, and these institutions came to represent more than themselves in discourse about postwar social developments.

World War II marked a decisive break with prewar American culture and with the moral and social concerns of the prewar generation. The social critics of the 1930s had focused largely on the question of whether some form of socialism would better serve the needs of the have-nots and the common man.

The postwar American critics, however, worked in a society without breadlines, and they had the example of Joseph Stalin as an argument against the viability of some forms of socialism, especially Soviet-style Communism. Indeed, after Americans had been gathered into the largest armed force in the nation's history, many social critics worked from the premise that America too had become collectivized and that one of its most pressing problems was how to preserve the autonomy of the individual.

By making Americans affluent and America powerful, the war and its aftermath gave social critics two new questions to ponder: Toward what end was American global power to be used? And, in the formulation of John Kenneth Galbraith, "affluence for what?" The war, by uprooting people from their homes and delaying home-building starts for an additional period of years beyond the depression, helped guarantee that residential mobility, suburbanization, and even cultural homogenization would occur soon after its conclusion. These trends would also come to disturb critics. They asked questions about life in these new settlements, which seemed curiously like army base life, and about the people living in them, who seemed more like one another than ever before and less like the more ethnically diverse populations of the prewar cities. Consideration of the nature and meaning of this assimilation became a major preoccupation of social critics in the 1950s.

The ominous ending of World War II, with the deployment of the atomic bomb, also affected the substance of criticism, as the postwar international settlement resolved itself into a cold war conflict between the Western powers and the Eastern European Communist bloc, with both sides armed with weapons of mass destruction. The atomic cloud hanging over the peace of the late 1940s and 1950s changed the context for domestic criticism insofar as the American dilemma was how to differentiate the nation morally from its rival and from the former great powers brought low by the war.

American anticolonialism was an expression of this impulse overseas. At home, the desire to be worthy of global might fostered a growing concern for the contradiction of segregation, which denied at home what soldiers had fought to protect and defend abroad.

Critical social thought in the postwar period can be distinguished most by its willingness to be critical of the very culture of its authors. A comparison of social criticism to the etiquette, church, and business literature of the period shows just how radical the critics were in relation to the how-to-succeed nature of these other genres, which were positively Victorian in their assumptions about how people could get ahead by means of firm handshakes, correct manners, and a positive, can-do attitude. Unlike critical journalism and social thought from 1890 through the Great Depression, postwar criticism tended to take as its object not the rich, the poor, or the benighted other, but instead the critics' own social class or the homogenized American society in general in which the critics themselves held a stake.

One of the more effective forms of social criticism employed in the postwar period was the non-fiction travelogue. Such documentary studies allowed people to see unpleasant realities as viewed by an innocent traveler. The critic was hidden behind the choice of what to reveal, but the results could often be devastating. Thus, Gunnar Myrdal's *An American Dilemma* (1944), an account of what a Swedish observer saw concerning race relations in the United States, was doubly potent since the author did not seem to have an ax to grind. The portrait of America was unflattering, but its author was no more to blame than a photographer for a subject's real appearance. "Harvest of Shame," a 1960 television documentary on CBS, hosted by Edward R. Murrow, proved the viability of the genre in a new medium. Here the tragedy of migrant worker life was allowed to unfold before the eyes of middle-class television viewers who had mentally consigned such realities to prewar John Steinbeck novels and their own dimming memories of dust-bowl days during the depression.

While the travelogue and documentary showed average Americans who others were, it was the literary form of the jeremiad that told them who they were. The jeremiad, or social sermon modeled on the rhetoric of the prophet Jeremiah, had been used throughout American history to communicate the twin message that something terrible was happening in contemporary life but that there was still a glimmer of hope if people would attend to the error of their ways and repent. More than a scolding it is the critical form best employed by those who wish to correct their own people and offer an alternative vision to existing social norms. The form proved irresistible to the postwar critics of the corporation and the suburbs.

DAVID RIESMAN

One of the earliest and most influential of the jeremiads was David Riesman's *The Lonely Crowd.* First published in 1950, the book stayed in print and sold well for two decades. Riesman and his collaborators, Reuel Denney and Nathan Glazer, sought to point out the defects of a then-emerging postwar character type different from both "tradition-directed" people living in premodern circumstances and "inner-directed" people whose morality grew out of a sense of duty during a time of transitional growth such as the United States experienced through World War II. The new type that Riesman observed lived in a time of incipient decline, a time when industrialization and social development had freed people from a need to strive for survival and from received moral absolutes. In this new era, people were far less likely to be influenced by received norms or religious and cultural traditions; rather, they paid greatest attention to the behavior of their peers. Riesman called this emergent character type "other-directed." The problem with a culture of other-referencing, sheeplike individuals was that far from being truly free, the culture's members were subject to the tyranny of the group. None or few could be said to exercise autonomy, that is, to do things for their own reasons.

An other-directed society was subject to easy manipulation and to cultural stagnation, Riesman thought. In politics, it was harder for advocates of valid social objectives and aspirations to succeed than it was for naysayers to veto change. Politics also became a spectator sport where "inside dopesters" cared more about the dirt on politicians than about the results of the process. Child rearing was geared to producing children who excelled at not "sticking out." The mass media seemed especially crafted to help people learn what they ought to want as consumers. And consumers they were, for in a time when production aims were exceeded, people were to be valued more for their role as acquirers of things and entertainment than for any other role or personal quality.

In the economic arena, Riesman depicted a transition from a time when men worked with hard materials and sought self-approval in craft and hard work to one in which the manipulation of others with a "glad hand" determined one's economic success more than the invisible hand of Adam Smith's economics. Riesman expressed the academic's characteristic outrage that the spoils of money, sex, and expense accounts were so freely given to those who produced so little of social or intellectual value. In contrast to other academic critics, however, he showed considerable skill at explaining why this phenomenon was the natural outcome of prevailing social forces and how this kind of success was apt to leave its possessors both lonely and feeling stifled by others.

Part of Riesman's success as a social critic lay in his ability to present power and class analysis in the 1950s without sounding like a Marxist. Another part lay in his talent for holding a mirror to American society and explaining to college students their parents while portraying what they, the students, would likely become in corporate and suburban life. Finally, Riesman made for popular reading insofar as he suggested there might yet be a way to escape conformity by achieving "autonomy." This possibility fed into an acute desire to be individually significant in a society whose institutions kept reinforcing the sense that one was simply a part of a mass culture.

JOHN KENNETH GALBRAITH AND C. WRIGHT MILLS

The central criticism of the corporation in the postwar period was that, by virtue of its growth in size and dynamism, it was a mass, impersonal social force that overwhelmed individual autonomy. In part the criticism simply affirmed the common wisdom of the day, voiced effectively by the theologian Reinhold Niebuhr in *Moral Man and Immoral Society* (1932), that human beings tended toward greater evil when gathered into collectivities. What Niebuhr argued before the war seemed doubly true to Americans after their confrontations with fascism and Communism, and even their own experiences of being cogs in the war effort machine.

By the 1950s corporations seemed ready to perpetuate organization on a mass scale with only a change in uniforms and products. Vance Packard's *Hidden Persuaders* (1957) dissected advertising to expose its tricks and cynicism, including its manufacture of wants—aspects of capitalism later categorized as "consumerism," a term lacking Packard's moral edge. John Kenneth Galbraith's *American*

Capitalism (1952) and *The Affluent Society* (1958) went further, arguing that the problem was not just that the salesman and flacks for the American corporation were corrupt but rather that the whole enterprise of American capitalism was flawed. As an economist, but also as an observer who seemed to rise above his peers in the academy, Galbraith knew that far from being the free-market expression of a totally free democratic people, corporate capitalism in America was the stuff of oligopolies, cartels, manufacturer's associations, "fair market" pricing, and deals with the government that set the rules of the game. Nevertheless, Galbraith's enduring popularity owes not merely to his gift for lucid criticism, but also for his almost prophetic vision. Repeatedly throughout the postwar period his analysis proved prescient, and he inspired the public and its leaders—not the least being another Harvard man, President John F. Kennedy—to use America's vast wealth to produce public goods such as better health, more education, and less poverty.

If Galbraith was one of the last great patrician liberal democrats, then C. Wright Mills, a sociologist based at Columbia University, was one of the first tenured radicals. In a series of books produced through the 1950s, Mills delighted in biting the hand that fed him in the cool tones of the sociological study. In *White Collar: The American Middle Classes* (1951) and *The Power Elite* (1956), his method was to characterize whole classes of people and to describe the interaction of these classes with one another in a vast social system. Rarely in Mills's sociology did a real, named person appear. Mills used this narrative strategy, which usually makes for dull reading, to critical advantage as he depicted with flair the problems of elected politicians, government bureaucrats, white-collar workers, and corporate CEOs, leaving the reader with the impression that it did not matter which person occupied the post because in any case, the job experience, challenges, and frustrations would be exactly the same. Social roles in the economy were archetypes to which holders of those roles necessarily had to conform. For Mills, the supposedly powerful were caught in a contradiction. They could exercise power only while they retained power, and they could retain power only by acting predictably. Unlike the nobles and aristocrats of a former age, and unlike the robber barons of the nineteenth century, the American power elite consisted of almost anonymous men whose power and low-level recognition lasted only until they were replaced. Autobiographies of politicians, generals, and business leaders might make it seem as though men made their own

C. Wright Mills. Mills analyzed conformity fostered by bureaucratic power stuctures, including those of academia. ARCHIVE PHOTOS

destinies. But the truth was that the elite leaders were caught up in a permanent war complex consisting of the military, the corporations, and the government, which set the terms of their leadership. Still, Mills placed responsibility for the decisions of the elite on the elite itself and insisted that its members be accountable to all Americans and not only to their own interests. When Dwight D. Eisenhower left office in 1961 he would echo these themes, warning Americans against the power of what he called "the military-industrial complex" and the ways that its interests ran counter to their own.

When Mills compared the plight of the contemporary middle classes to the condition of earlier generations, he saw even bleaker prospects for the contemporary generation. The old middle classes of the nineteenth century had been shopkeepers,

farmers, and small manufacturers who typically owned the means by which their livings were made. The functions they performed were indispensable to society and were conducted on such a localized scale that competition from large-scale enterprise was not a threat. By contrast, the white-collar workers of the mid-twentieth century were wage workers in suits. Worse yet, they entertained the illusion that the system was working for them. White-collar people, believing themselves better served by the political economy than were laboring men and women, opposed the interests of organized labor and endorsed business values that undermined their own position in society by strengthening the hold of large-scale enterprise and bureaucracy over them. When they became frustrated by their wages, housing, entertainments, opportunities, and quality of life they were apt—when politically conscious at all—to cede more power to the sphere of business, which would in time only compound their frustration and their powerlessness. More common among white-collar people were those who were politically indifferent, only minimally sacrificing their time and selves to meaningless work in exchange for the cheap thrills of entertainment and instant gratification. Therefore, by donning suits and going to work for large corporations, the middle classes, despite the huge numbers they represented, were the most politically impotent group in American society.

WILLIAM H. WHYTE

Unlike the Marxist Mills, the assistant managing editor of *Fortune* magazine, William H. Whyte, presented his critique of the corporation with minimal theory but to even greater effect in a 1956 bestseller, *The Organization Man.* For Whyte, American life was characterized by the pursuit of personal security through conformity. The corporation was both an institution and a metaphor for other large-scale bureaucratic institutions like the academy, the church, and the military that provided safety to the men and women who were willing to pledge their organizational loyalty to these institutions, which Whyte lumped together as constituting "the organization." In taking up the plight of the organization man, Whyte expanded on a theme introduced by David Riesman in the *The Lonely Crowd,* that of the personally debilitating effects of conformity. Many people, Whyte wrote, were troubled by the effects of belonging to corporations, suburbs, churches, and neighborhood groups: "And they sense that by their immersion in the group they are frustrating other urges, yet they feel that responding to the group is a moral duty—and so they continue, hesitant and unsure, imprisoned in brotherhood" (p. 365).

The conflict between the individual and the organization was, for Whyte, inevitable. Its denial was, moreover, bad for both the individual and for the organization, which—freed from criticism—was nearly deified. Living the organization's way spilled over into the suburbs, where the wives of organization men worked hard to conform to the expectations of their neighbors and thus to minimize their own individuality. The wives also oriented domestic life in a "filarchy," Whyte's term for a child-centered existence where even one's friends were chosen not out of common interests among adults but on the basis of who had children the same age as one's own offspring. Whyte was no utopian, but he counseled, much like Riesman before him, that persons situated within organizations ought to resist the lure of conformity and seek to remain authentically individuated from their corporate jobs and suburban neighbors.

THE CHURCH OF SUBURBIA

Mills, Whyte, and another popular writer of the era, Will Herberg, reserved special criticism for the religious institutions of their day. Mills, writing in the *Nation* what he called "a pagan sermon to the Christian clergy" (March 1958, pp. 199–202), argued that the churches and their clergy were failing to do what their own profession of faith and traditions committed them to do, namely to resist the power of the military-industrial complex and the statecraft that relied upon threats of nuclear war to accomplish national objectives. For Whyte, the church of suburbia was especially beholden to the "social ethic" of the organizational way. Wherever young organization people gathered in a community, Whyte noticed, "the urge for a more socially useful church manifests itself" (p. 417). This was only logical, he thought, since they needed what others had historically taken for granted: "For those who stay put in one place, the church has always been socially useful, and the by-products of church affiliation they take as a matter of course. But the transients cannot. Stability, kinship with others—they want these demonstrated, and in the here and now." The result of this need was that the churches and synagogues were faced with an "irresistible temptation" to make the facilitation of friendship their chief appeal. The quest for friendship was the quest of the suburban transient population of organization people. This quest defined their expectation of religious fellowship, an expectation that the churches were only too happy to adopt as their own.

Will Herberg The content of friendship-oriented religiosity also concerned Will Herberg. His *Protestant, Catholic, Jew* (1955) is a distillation of historical fact, sociological theory, and community studies into a coherent, popularly accessible essay that critiqued contemporary religion as the religion of the "American Way of Life." A union organizer who had come to maturity through his experiences in various Communist organizations before World War II, Herberg was trained by his past disillusionments to recognize an ideology masquerading as genuine truth. His work turned on a paradox. Americans in the postwar years were becoming both more religious and more secular. He resolved the paradox by asserting that their dominant religion was a secular faith in the American Way of Life, a belief in abundance, fairness, having some (unspecified) faith, education, the benign corporation, the good government, the family, and a home in the suburbs. The residual post–melting pot faith communities of Protestantism, Catholicism, and Judaism had for the most part, he believed, become outlets for this one, common underlying faith in the way things were in America and in faith itself. For Herberg, this kind of faith simply was not worth having because it was rootless and without any referent outside the world of contemporary America. His recommendation that Americans seek out a biblical faith rooted in the God of Abraham, Isaac, and Jacob was a different solution on its surface from those offered in the other jeremiads, yet at its root was strikingly similar in its assertion that meaning in life was not to be found in either corporate devotion or a suburban paradise.

Gibson Winter   The best single jeremiad on suburban life came from another religious writer, Gibson Winter. Winter issued an attack on suburban Christianity in an article in the *Christian Century* (28 September 1955) and in his book *The Suburban Captivity of the Churches* (1961). Unlike many of the other postwar social critics, Winter knew suburbia well from personal experience. Yet as a Christian and a person trained to think sociologically, he did not like what he saw.

Suburbia was, for Winter, the ultimate extension of two hundred years of industrialization, and a dominant social reality, by which Winter meant to indicate the swing of power of all types from the cities to suburbia within the generation just past. While recognizing that suburban locations varied considerably from one another in some respects, he argued that they formed a single group "by reason of their state of mind rather than by their geographical similarity" (p. 1112). He allowed that suburban settlements ranged from modest to high income and that houses in them ranged from ranch to colonial. Nevertheless, Winter wrote, the suburban mind had three common elements regardless of those differences. The first and most important was the principle of advancement in life. For the suburbanite, success was not defined in terms of skill or service; rather, success equaled "advancement with a pay raise," this being "the real meaning of work" (p. 1112). The second element in this mindset was the permeation of the management point of view. Even lower-income suburbanites saw work "in terms of production needs, cost problems, and profit drives" (p. 1112). It did not matter that most suburbanites lacked the prestige and checkbooks of top management; one of the first steps on their way to advancement was to think like top management. The third element was the attitude that came with a high degree of mobility. Suburbanites never saw themselves as "rooted, anchored, placed." Therefore, although they might live in the same place for a dozen years, they would still regard their friendships and organizational commitment as temporary. All of this added up to a pattern that promoted an overextension of activities. Suburbanites, because of a desire for advancement and the insecurity generated by mobility, found themselves "unable to refuse organizational obligations . . . one of these being the church" (p. 1112).

As much as Winter disliked the mentality of suburbia, he despised how it disordered his church. Suburbia had introduced its conception of success into every aspect of the church's being. In spite of infusing the church and its programs with energy and enthusiasm and filling the offering plates, pews, and educational facilities to overflowing, suburbia had brought the churches into captivity. Suburban and corporate criteria—advancement in financial terms and in numerical growth—had crowded out more traditional measures of Christian success, such as salvation, redemption, care of the poor, and witness to the power of the cross. The location of the church in suburbia had also insulated it from the world of work, community, urban housing, and the cities. In suburbia, secularization had found its fullest and final expression, since a society in which the church was confined to a private, suburban sphere was a society without any real religious influence. Winter, much like Mills, believed this acute secularization constituted a national tragedy because it was happening at a time when America's world leadership necessitated a "prophetic church at home." The suburban church was anything but prophetic. "Suburban domination may well be God's word of judgment upon us as his church," Winter wrote. "For our trespasses and complacency we have been delivered to Babylon" (p. 1114). When Winter's article appeared in the *Christian Century*, the reaction was immediate, so much so that *Time* magazine carried news of the article to its readership, together with extracts from it under the title "Last Train to Babylon" (10 October 1955, p. 73).

The very mass culture that the critics decried helped to spread their ideas on a tide of mass market paperbacks, themselves a postwar innovation. Discussing American intellectual history more generally, Louis Hartz argued that Americans had slogans rather than ideas. To some degree the charge applied to the social critics themselves, for though they championed ideas over mindless obedience to the mass, their ideas rather easily dissolved into slogans that conveyed the message of 100,000-word books. By simply using the era's leading titles, one can summarize the central thrust of the criticism: Americans were a *People of Plenty* (1954, David Potter), living in an *Affluent Society* (Galbraith), a *Mass Culture* (Dwight Macdonald), dominated by a *Power Elite* (Mills), members of a *Lonely Crowd* (Riesman). Each player was an *Organization Man* (Whyte), a *Man in the Gray Flannel Suit* (1955, Sloan Wilson). Whether they be *Protestant, Catholic, Jew* (Herberg) or something else did not matter much, for their churches were in *Suburban Captivity* (Winter), their homes had a *Crack in the Picture Window* (1957, John Keats), and their children were *Growing up Absurd* (1960, Paul Goodman).

The line between literature and social criticism was a very narrow one in the 1950s. Some of the most trenchant social critiques offered during the postwar period were embedded in novels. More than the nonfiction works of criticism, many of these novels were so successful in capturing the spirit of the times and what was wrong with American life in such an abiding way as still to be widely read at the beginning of the twenty-first century. Among these books are Sylvia Plath's *The Bell Jar* (1962), which captured the dilemma of being young, bright, and female in the 1950s; Ralph Ellison's *Invisible Man* (1947); and Richard Wright's *Black Boy* (1945) and *Native Son* (1940), which conveyed with tremendous power the feeling of being black in white racist America. J. D. Salinger's *Catcher in the Rye* (1951) evoked other feelings, feelings about being young, male, and aimless. Kurt Vonnegut's *Slaughterhouse-Five* (1968) and Joseph Heller's *Catch 22* (1961) effectively broke the image of World War II as a well-executed effort of selfless Americans.

MIDCENTURY CRITICS AND LATE-CENTURY ISSUES

The early post–World War II period was a fertile time for social criticism. Over a brief span of years the critics neatly anticipated most of the concerns of the next half century. Indeed, books of the 1990s such as Alan Wolfe's *One Nation After All* (1998), Stephen Carter's *The Culture of Disbelief* (1993), and Francis Fukuyama's *The End of History and the Last Man* (1992) reveal that authors of that decade were still working from social-critical agenda from midcentury. Some issues that were—in retrospect—clearly latent in the 1950s, however, were barely noticed then. Themes like the role and status of women and the issue of race, beyond the obvious fact of the color line, asserted themselves in the 1960s only through the intellectual leadership of popular critics like Betty Friedan and Martin Luther King Jr. The postwar critics were overwhelmingly white, male, and privileged and their social concerns, though presented as general in nature, inevitably reflected their social locations. Yet no critics of the 1950s could have anticipated the ways in which mid-1960s legislation that vastly increased immigration would bring back issues that those critics had counted as finally settled: the issues of language, assimilation, and acceptable diversity.

In light of American cultural diversity at the dawn of the twenty-first century, it is tempting to see the concerns of postwar critics as parochial in scope and irrelevant to later developments. However, it is fairer to credit them with establishing the mode of critical social introspection that has enabled American society to assimilate dramatic changes in gender roles and in the ethnic composition of common institutions such as schools, and also to accept the presence of openly gay and lesbian people in the workplace and the media. It is perhaps a result of the thinking of postwar social critics that Americans in the late twentieth century tolerated otherness to a much greater degree than a century before.

See also **Industrialism and Its Critics** *(volume 1);* **Technology; Political Economy; Twentieth-Century Economic Thought** *(volume 3); and other articles in this section.*

BIBLIOGRAPHY

Primary Works

Galbraith, John Kenneth. *American Capitalism.* Boston, 1952.

———. *The Affluent Society.* Boston, 1958.

Herberg, William. *Protestant, Catholic, Jew: An Essay in American Religious Sociology.* Garden City, N.Y., 1955.

Macdonald, Dwight. "A Theory of Mass Culture." *Diogenes* 3 (summer 1953): 1–17. Reprinted in Rosenberg and White, pp. 59–73.

Mills, C. Wright. *White Collar: The American Middle Classes.* New York, 1951.

———. *The Power Elite.* New York, 1956.

Myrdal, Gunnar. *An American Dilemma: The Negro Problem and American Democracy.* New York, 1944.

Riesman, David. *The Lonely Crowd: A Study of the Changing American Character.* New Haven, Conn., 1950.

Rosenberg, Bernard, and David Manning White, eds. *Mass Culture: The Popular Arts in America.* Glencoe, Ill., 1957.

Whyte, William H. *The Organization Man.* New York, 1956.

Winter, Gibson. "The Church in Suburban Captivity." *Christian Century* (28 September 1955).

———. *The Suburban Captivity of the Churches: An Analysis of Protestant Responsibility in the Expanding Metropolis.* Garden City, N.Y., 1961.

Secondary Works

Hudnut-Beumler, James. *Looking for God in the Suburbs: The Religion of the American Dream.* New Brunswick, N.J., 1994.

Pells, Richard. *The Liberal Mind in a Conservative Age: American Intellectuals in the 1940s and 1950s.* New York, 1985.

WOMEN AND FAMILY IN THE SUBURBAN AGE

Anita L. Larson

The development and growth of suburbs in the post–World War II era accompanied a modern resurgence of family and domesticity associated with the end of the war. Family offered stability in an insecure postwar world, but the security and satisfaction of traditional gender roles experienced by many women and men also limited women who yearned for personal fulfillment beyond domestic roles that revolved around family and home.

SUBURBAN GROWTH

The first modern suburb of the post–World War II era covered what had once been thousands of acres of farmland on Long Island in New York State. Using modern assembly-line techniques, the developer William Levitt quickly built small, inexpensive houses to sell to returning veterans and their spouses. Anxious to own their own homes, young, white, married couples flocked to the suburban community called Levittown. The homes were not only small, initially consisting of a living room, kitchen, bathroom, and two bedrooms, but uniform in floor plan and exterior design as well. Schools, churches, and shopping centers soon followed in the development of this first "bedroom" community. Despite criticisms that the homogeneity of Levittown was bland and boring, the affordable home ownership that it offered became part of the modern American dream for those who were white and middle class. The pattern of suburban growth that was initiated in Levittown was repeated throughout the 1950s, as the white-collar and blue-collar middle class flocked to housing developments in suburbs located as far as twenty miles from the city.

After years of economic depression followed by a world war, women and men appeared to be eager to return to the traditional roles of domesticity for women and wage earning for men. Life in the sub-

urbs, with its affordable and modern housing, seemed to offer such a promise, as men could commute by train or car to work in the city while women remained at home to tend to their children. An essential part of the eagerness to return to traditional roles included starting families as quickly as possible. The soaring birth rates of the baby boom associated with the 1950s began with the end of the war and continued for approximately ten years before the birth rates dropped slightly, followed by an appreciable drop in the late 1950s. While birth rates increased, marriage age declined, as did the divorce rate. Family, it would seem, had taken on a new importance in the United States and, in some ways, it had.

DOMESTIC IDEOLOGY AND GENDER ROLES

Critics of the late-twentieth-century family often point to the family of the 1950s as the standard-bearer of what families should be. Reruns of popular 1950s television shows such as *The Adventures of Ozzie and Harriet* and *Leave It to Beaver* are singled out as reminders of what has been lost with the reconfiguration of families that took place in the late twentieth century. Single-parent households, working mothers, and blended families apparently replaced the two-parent, one-wage family, giving rise to the belief that the long-revered traditional family was no more. But social historians of the family and the 1950s have come to understand that the traditional family of the post–World War II era was not the last of its kind, as previously believed, but a new development, unique in the history of the family. The postwar family was in some ways a throwback to the Victorian era, but with a modern twist: the belief in the nuclear family as the source of all personal fulfillment and attainment in life.

The nuclear family took center stage in American life in the 1950s. Extended family ties, frequently offered up as one of the hallmarks of the traditional family, were disrupted and even looked upon with suspicion as young couples were encouraged to strike out on their own, often at some distance from relatives and the older generation. As corporate growth and increasing bureaucratization rendered work impersonal and meaningless, a man's identity came not from his work but from his roles as husband and father. For women, ambitions and aspirations outside the home were strongly discouraged. A woman's work was her home, her identity to be found in her domestic roles. Even home design of the 1950s underscored this new emphasis on the nuclear family. The suburban ranch house, with the "family room" as the center for recreation and family activity, replaced the older arrangement of gender-specific rooms that embodied the ideology of Victorian separate spheres. Family had indeed taken on a new importance, unlike anything that had come before.

The belief in the family as a stabilizing force in society did not originate with the postwar era (family was a cornerstone of Puritan society, for example) but was raised to new heights as Americans struggled with the instability that followed World War II. The fear of communism permeated the postwar era, and the family was perceived to be one of the best weapons in the civilian arsenal to fight it. Good citizens, raised in the ideals of civic responsibility, democracy, and individualism, came from solid families with devoted mothers and fathers, thereby rendering one immune to subversive elements that weakened the social fabric. Good citizenship also came to include ownership of a single-family home, preferably in one of the newly growing suburbs, because owning a home, the developer Levitt claimed, made one impervious to communism. As the family became the place in which all one's emotional and sexual needs were to be met, the home also came to symbolize the political rhetoric of communist containment on the domestic cold war front. Personal security in an age of political insecurity came from harnessing potentially dangerous social forces such as premarital sex and homosexuality within the nuclear family, in much the same way dangerous forces such as the atom bomb and communism were to be harnessed and contained in the world at large.

Popular culture often reflected this new emphasis on the nuclear family of the 1950s. Television situation comedies of the era, such as *Father Knows Best, The Adventures of Ozzie and Harriet,* and *Leave It to Beaver,* featured the ups and downs of family life. Homemaking moms and wage-earning dads

worked out family misunderstandings with patience and kindness. When David wanted a bedroom separate from younger brother Ricky, for example, Ozzie and Harriet talked about the advantages and disadvantages of sharing a room, which led to a misunderstanding about Ozzie needing a room of his own. By the end of the episode, the misunderstandings had been straightened out: David and Ricky continued to share a bedroom and Harriet realized that her fears that Ozzie needed a room of his own were unfounded. Several cups of hot chocolate and family discussions helped the Nelson family successfully smooth out their "conflict."

Home was supposed to be a fun place, and family life was portrayed as satisfying and fulfilling in the popular television comedies. When sons Ricky and David entertain friends at home, Harriet and Ozzie often join in the fun. Ozzie demonstrates football plays for the guys, dances with the young girls, and sings along with Ricky, who plays songs on the guitar. Harriet shares cooking, beauty, and fashion tips with the teen girls, and cheerfully feeds the crowd that has gathered at the Nelson home. In one specific episode, Ozzie and Harriet join in a teen outing that includes a hayride and barbecue at a riding stable where Ricky has been taking lessons. Television sitcoms such as *The Adventures of Ozzie and Harriet* presented family togetherness as the ideal way to spend time.

The belief in family as the center of one's life dictated that women accept their domestic role as the true expression of their womanhood. Wife and motherhood were the primary roles to which women should aspire. For example, the physician Leo Kanner of Johns Hopkins Hospital, speaking before a meeting of the American Medical Association in Washington, D.C., claimed that problems between mothers and children were due to "the fact that young women are no longer reared for the main purpose of becoming wives and mothers" (as reported by Jane Stafford in a syndicated column that appeared in the *Columbus Citizen Journal,* 7 December 1949). Professionals in psychology and psychiatry argued that to be feminine was to be passive and dependent. A woman's happiness, they stated, came not from competition or achievement, but in her subordination to men and acceptance of her domestic role in life.

And for many women, primarily those of the white middle class, domestic life in the suburbs was good. They enjoyed being homemakers and eagerly read the popular magazines of the day such as *Ladies Home Journal, Good Housekeeping,* and *Women's Home Companion,* which provided suggestions for home decorating on a budget, recipes for cooking elegant but easy family meals, child-rearing tips from leading experts such as Dr. Benjamin Spock, and marital advice on how to keep a husband happy and fulfilled. These modern homemakers reveled in the new technology of washing machines, garbage disposals, and dishwashers in the continuing quest to keep their families and homes clean. They formed mothers' clubs to establish community rules to ensure the safety of their children, while bridge clubs, coffee klatches, and neighborhood get-togethers served as venues for socializing for women in the suburbs. Many women truly enjoyed homemaking and raising a family. For these women, domestic life was fulfilling.

CONTRADICTIONS IN IDEOLOGY

For many other women, however, the ideal of full-time domesticity in a new suburban ranch house was not reality. Women of color had been employed outside the home for years, balancing the competing demands of home, family, and wage earning. Crushing poverty still existed for many Americans, regardless of race or ethnicity, forcing many women into the paid workforce in order to support their families. Moreover, many African Americans and newly arrived Hispanic immigrants from Mexico and Puerto Rico flocked to and remained in the cities, while white Americans moved to the suburbs and the new housing developments, which often barred racial and ethnic minorities. Despite the transformation of the rural countryside into suburban communities in the postwar years, farm life still existed for some Americans, and the physical labor women and men performed was no less arduous, despite modern appliances and mechanized farm equipment.

White middle-class women increasingly entered the workforce during the postwar era as well. Many of these women had career ambitions that threatened to take them outside the home and away from their domestic roles. Others sought paid employment to supplement the family income. Some looked to employment outside the home when their children reached school age or beyond as a way of filling the time they now had on their hands. Whatever the reason for entering the paid work force, the number of working women, often mothers in their mid-thirties and older, increased during the decade, albeit in low-paying, menial jobs deemed suitable for women.

While the roles of wife and mother were fulfilling for many women, popular magazines, such as *Redbook* and *McCall's,* featured articles that addressed the problems of the modern housewife. In response to women's complaints of restlessness, fatigue, or general despair, doctors diagnosed these women as maladjusted and not accepting of their domestic and therefore feminine role. The writer and homemaker Betty Friedan said it was something else. In her 1963 book *The Feminine Mystique,* Friedan identified the general malaise experienced by white, middle-class, suburban housewives in the 1950s who had embraced domesticity as the "problem that has no name." Marriage and children were simply not enough for women, she claimed. Friedan's book resonated for the hundreds of thousands of white, middle-class, college-educated women who traded careers and further education for marriage and family, only to find domestic suburban life wanting.

Containment of these women's desires and aspirations, far from promoting personal happiness and national security, often resulted in desperately unhappy women, for not every woman found the role of homemaker as emotionally satisfying as she was told it would be. For these women, life in the suburbs was filled with meaningless activities and endless days of suffocating boredom. Isolated in housing developments located miles from the cities, women were cut off from extended family, virtually trapped in their homes and neighborhoods during the day. Car ownership, which became a necessity in the sprawling suburbs, did little to alleviate women's feelings of confinement, as few families owned more than one car, especially at the beginning of the decade. And despite the increase in modern, labor-saving appliances, housewives in the 1950s spent more time on housework than in the past. Cleanliness standards and food preparation became more demanding as more houses contained washing machines, vacuum cleaners, and modern ranges. Often the housewife of the mid-twentieth century took care of her home and family without domestic help, in contrast to the middle-class, white Victorian woman, who routinely employed and supervised servants to perform household chores and assist in child rearing.

The ambivalence many women experienced as they contemplated their domestic roles and public aspirations was often reflected in the mass media. Nonfiction stories, in popular magazines as diverse as *Harper's, Atlantic Monthly, Reader's Digest,* and *Coronet,* often reported on women whose nondomestic activities included careers, civic organizations, and

Betty Friedan. Friedan was a founding member and first president (1966–1970) of the National Organization of Women. © BETTMANN/CORBIS

political participation. White middle-class women in the suburbs participated in parent-teacher associations and church organizations, while African American women actively worked in the civil rights movement in the South, for example, but these additional activities rarely challenged womens' domestic role. Such activities were more likely to be presented as the extension of a woman's natural domesticity into a more public realm, as women were rarely in positions of authority or policy making.

Newspapers of the postwar era often reflected the same ambivalence and contradictions. For example, when Dr. Millicent Carey McIntosh, dean of Barnard College and mother of five, spoke before the Women's City Club of New York City in 1947, she told her audience that having careers could actually make women better mothers by constructively directing their energy and training away from their children. The Women's National News Service picked up the event and an Ohio newspaper (*Dayton Daily News,* 26 April 1947) reprinted the story. Two years later, another Ohio newspaper (*Columbus Citizen Journal,* 7 December 1949) reported on Dr. Kanner's address before the American Medical Association. Dr. Kanner asserted that single women should not become "secretaries, nurses, salesgirls, the factory-piece worker, the laboratory technician, the librarian or the nurse." The child becomes a "substitute for the typewriters, the cash registers, the machine, the test tube, the book shelf or the medicine cabinet," Dr. Kanner claimed, because the punctuality, meticulousness, and perfectionism demanded in such jobs would be transferred to the home.

The debate over working women centered not so much on women who were compelled to work outside the home for financial reasons, but on women who chose to work at careers outside the home rather than make motherhood their career. Doubts that domesticity could truly be as fulfilling as it was claimed to be lurked just below the surface as newspaper columnists, such as Mrs. Walter Ferguson of the *Columbus Citizen Journal,* and Ida Jean Main, feature writer for the *Dayton Journal Herald,* debated the value of the housewife versus the career woman, underscoring that the belief in domestic fulfillment was based on predominately white middle-class values and aspirations.

Contradictions also extended beyond the homemaker versus career woman debate. As homemakers, women were encouraged to be active consumers but were held responsible for the economic burdens their spending placed on their husbands. At the same time, they were discouraged from taking jobs outside the home to earn the needed extra income. Young women quickly learned the tricks necessary to attract a man, but were held in contempt for having trapped the unsuspecting man into marriage. Married women were told to expect their marriages to be sexually fulfilling, provided they maintained a passive sexual role, while being reminded that sexy and sexual wives held on to husbands.

Motherhood contained the most contradictions. While women clearly benefited from the advances in medical science that reduced the life-threatening complications once associated with giving birth, the use of anesthetics and other medications left many women feeling disconnected and alienated from the birth experience. Medical professionals replaced what was once a female ritual of support and assistance: male obstetricians replaced midwives, nurses replaced female relatives and friends. Mothers were instructed to nurture and guide their children, but were cautioned that too much mothering resulted in immature, unstable adults unable to cope in a complex world.

Men were not immune from the contradictions of the era either. While the family ideology of the time prescribed the role of homemaker for women, men were supposed to find their needs met in the comfort of their home and the security of family life after a hard day at the factory or office. Messages to men were often confused, mixing a tough competitive masculinity with a tender concern for hearth and home that threatened to undermine the very nature of that masculinity. Feature articles in Ohio newspapers (*Columbus Citizen Journal,* 20 October 1955 and 5 July 1956), for example, encouraged men to be handy in the kitchen and skilled at the backyard barbecue. *Better Homes and Gardens* regularly devoted several articles to men under the category "Building, Remodeling, and Maintenance." Cooking sections also featured articles such as "Men's Recipe Winners" or "When a Man Takes Hold of the Spoon" (*Better Homes and Gardens,* February 1950).

Television situation comedies presented the same mixed message regarding men's domestic roles. In one particular episode of *The Adventures of Ozzie and Harriet,* for example, Ozzie and his poker-playing buddies valiantly try to prepare a meal for soon-to-arrive dinner guests. Due to a mix-up, Harriet is enjoying an afternoon at the movies, so it is up to the men to save the evening. Wearing aprons and stirring pots of food do not necessarily undermine the masculinity of Ozzie and his pals. But when one of the men suggests cutting the spaghetti with a pair of scissors and another explains that he learned his cake-frosting technique the summer he worked as a bricklayer, the message is unmistakably clear: men are not all that compe-

tent in the kitchen, despite their good-faith effort. The last-minute appearance of Harriet with a tray of appetizers, and Ozzie's attempt to organize an after-dinner poker game, reinforce notions of appropriate masculine and feminine behavior.

According to one unidentified male writer for the *Columbus Citizen Journal* (20 October 1955), it was bossy women who no longer knew how to love a man that undermined masculinity, and his proof came in the form of independent women who often used trickery to get and keep their men. To avoid becoming "she-men," the American male was exhorted to exert his natural masculinity, to "growl" at women now and then (*Dayton Journal Herald,* 12 July 1948). Fathers were especially suspect, as they no longer commanded respect in their own home, claimed Associated Press feature writer Hal Boyle in a feature reprinted in the *Columbus Dispatch* (14 June 1956). Boyle waxed nostalgically and humorously on the old-fashioned father who commanded both love and respect from his children.

Phyllis Battelle, author of a six-part series entitled "What's Wrong with American Men?" (*Dayton Journal Herald,* 22–27 June 1959), argued that fathers were no longer "he-men" but "mild-mannered fellows" who diapered babies, took out the trash, and mixed drinks for the cocktail hour. The sociologist Helen Hacker called these types of fathers "mother-substitutes," Battelle reported. And the confusion that resulted from changing gender roles directly contributed to the rise of male homosexuality, said psychiatrist Dr. Cornelius Beukenkamp Jr., who was featured in Battelle's series. On a similar note, writer Andre Fontaine asked the question, "Are we staking our future on a crop of sissies?" in an article of the same name, which appeared in *Better Homes and Gardens* (December 1950). Adding to the mixed messages and confusion surrounding male gender roles, Fontaine encouraged fathers to become more involved in child care, including diapering and bottle feeding baby sons, as well as doing handyman projects with their sons, to avoid raising "pantywaist" boys who think and act like their mothers.

The source of man's problem, according to Battelle's series, was American women. Battelle cited such experts as psychiatrist Dr. Karl Menninger, novelist Pearl Buck, and anthropologist Margaret Mead, who argued that as women entered the paid workforce and gained positions of power, they disrupted the natural gender order, creating unhappy, neurotic women as well as effeminate men. The physician Marynia F. Farnham and Ferdinand Lundberg (described as a newspaper reporter, economist, historian, and biographer) authored the 1947 best-selling and controversial book *Modern Woman: The Lost Sex.* Farnham and Lundberg also pointed to women as the source of men's inadequacies, claiming that men were being so dominated by their wives that they were becoming submissive alcoholics and homosexuals. Dr. George T. Harding, professor of psychiatry at Ohio State University, echoed similar sentiments in an address before the Institute of Scientific Studies for the Prevention of Alcoholism in Loma Linda, California, in 1958 (*Columbus Dispatch*, 11 June 1958). Thelma Whalen, a social worker and executive director of the Family Service Agency in Dallas, Texas, identified four types of women who were responsible for causing their husband's alcoholism. Whalen's descriptions, which appeared in the 1954 issue of the *Quarterly Journal of Studies on Alcohol,* published by Yale University, was picked up by the Associated Press and reported in an Ohio newspaper (*Columbus Dispatch*, 3 January 1954).

Even more frightening, perhaps, than a "social structure made up of he-women and she-men," according to psychiatrist Irene Josselyn, was the belief that women had become the stronger sex—financially, emotionally, and physically. In Battelle's series, writer Diana Trilling, marriage expert Abraham Stone, anthropologist Margaret Mead, and psychiatrists Cornelius Beukenkamp Jr. and Theodore Reik all argued that the change from what had been regarded as the traditional, time-honored, and natural order of things created a dangerous loss of male identity and masculinity. But whereas Harrison Smith, editor of the *Saturday Review of Literature,* and historian Arthur Schlesinger Jr. argued that the relentless drive for success and conformity of the middle class contributed to the loss of male identity, other experts such as Stone, Mead, Beukenkamp, Reik, Josselyn, Farnham, Lundberg, and anthropologist Geoffrey Gorer were just as quick to blame women for pushing men too hard to succeed at all costs. The result, they claimed, was that men were no longer "real men," but emasculated weaklings who could no longer assert their masculinity.

DOMESTIC VIOLENCE

In a culture that looked to traditional gender roles to provide security in an unstable world, changing notions of masculinity and femininity could be especially frightening. Maintaining a modern version of traditional roles that revolved around home and family for both men and women was essential to

the preservation of the American way of life. It was not much of a reach, therefore, for a society that longed for male aggressiveness and encouraged female passivity to cast domestic violence as normal, perhaps even natural, behavior. Moreover, the increasing privatization of family that was part of the domestic ideology of the time served to keep family secrets, such as alcoholism, drug addiction, incest, and rape, quietly hidden. So it was with domestic violence, which was "contained" within the home as an individual and mostly private matter.

It is not surprising that domestic violence has been largely bypassed in the histories of the postwar era, as it was not regarded as a contemporary social problem in the 1950s. Historians are only now beginning to document the darker side of family life in that era. And while it may be difficult to determine the extent of domestic violence, it is a mistake to assume that there was little awareness of it, or, that wife beating was not viewed as a problem simply because domestic violence was not defined as a *social* problem. In the very public discussions that appeared in advice columns in local newspapers, domestic violence was recognized as a serious matter. But it was also clearly considered a personal problem and a private concern.

Even though women were encouraged to accept their domestic roles without complaint, it is clear that some women did not passively accept the abuse and violence that often came with that role, nor were they always encouraged to do so. Women advice columnists such as Dorothy Dean and Betty Fairfax, who dispensed marital advice in daily newspaper columns, understood the danger behind issuing threats to a potentially violent husband but often praised women who stood up to brutish husbands nonetheless. Dorothy Dean told one woman who signed her letter "Blue" to "show some spunk" when Blue's violent husband became overly controlling and physically abusive. Encouraging women to fight back served to keep much violence from being regarded as problematic by perpetuating the notion that some violence in a marriage was normal. Responses that did not encourage the use of mutual violence offered women unrealistic suggestions instead. Miss Fairfax advised "Worried" to ask her husband if she might take classes to improve her life and to insist that her husband, who had beaten her every Friday night during their six-year marriage, be cordial to her friends.

Dean and Fairfax were products of the time, and in some ways their responses come as no surprise. Placing the responsibility on the wife to change her husband's behavior was a typical response. But columnists did not shy away from the issue or disguise the violence with euphemisms. The letters they published in their columns have the ring of authenticity. The isolation that many women described, their lack of personal financial resources, and the threats their husbands shouted at them are now recognized and labeled as classic behaviors of systematic domestic abuse. But the naive and simplistic answers, mixed with confusing messages that encouraged women to accept some violence as normal by meeting violence with violence, served to privatize the very problem that was being publicly discussed.

Confusion over changing gender roles in the postwar era also added to the contradictions surrounding domestic violence. The slogan "Husbands Beat Wives" promoted a Betty Crocker brand cake mix in a newspaper advertisement, while the ad copy continued "in cake baking contests from coast to coast." The ad reassured men that they, too, could bake cakes that were as tasty and light as the cakes their wives baked from scratch. Despite concerns that men were quickly losing their masculinity, this ad drew on the understanding that men who baked cakes were no less virile than men who were physically aggressive. Men who took up baking simply found a different outlet for "besting" their wives, and on their wives' turf no less. The advertisement was really aimed at women, however, as the copy went on to describe the special ingredients that saved time in the kitchen and distinguished cake mixes from scratch cakes. By having some fun with gender-role reversal, the advertisers reinforced the traditional female gender role of domesticity and drew upon people's awareness of abuse at the same time.

Post–World War II America was a much more complex world than public memory has acknowledged, and the modern 1950s family was part of that complexity. The traditional gender roles placed family at the center of American life, which provided a sense of security in an age of political and social insecurity. At the same time, gender roles were so narrowed for women (and men) that women such as the white, middle-class, college-educated women surveyed by Betty Friedan in the early 1960s, or the white, middle-class women surveyed by University of Michigan psychologist E. Lowell Kelly in 1955, and later analyzed by historian Elaine Tyler May, chafed under the restrictions that denied women an identity independent of their roles as wife and mother. Doctors, psychiatrists, and marriage counselors labeled women who were unable or unwilling to subordinate their aspirations and ambitions as failures as women. But to think that all suburban housewives were unhappy with their lot distorts the history as much as the "happy days" myth has clouded our understanding of this era. The traditional gender roles and the domesticity that some women and men found so comforting eventually became untenable to women who had contained ambitions and desires that went beyond the domestic realm. The result was the resurgence of the feminist movement in the 1960s that sought to redefine womanhood beyond the roles of wife and mother.

See also **Women** (in this volume); **Consumerism; Family** (volume 3); and other articles in this section.

BIBLIOGRAPHY

Coontz, Stephanie. *The Way We Never Were: American Families and the Nostalgia Trap.* New York, 1992.

Cowan, Ruth Schwartz. *More Work for Mother: The Ironies of Household Technology from the Open Hearth to the Microwave.* New York, 1983.

Evans, Sarah M. *Born for Liberty: A History of Women in America.* New York, 1989.

Friedan, Betty. *The Feminine Mystique.* New York, 1963.

Halberstam, David. *The Fifties.* New York, 1993.

Harvey, Brett. *The Fifties: A Woman's Oral History.* New York, 1993.

Kaledin, Eugenia. *Mothers and More: American Women in the 1950s.* Boston, 1984.

Lundberg, Ferdinand, and Marynia F. Farnham. *Modern Woman: The Lost Sex.* New York, 1947.

May, Elaine Tyler. *Homeward Bound: American Families in the Cold War Era.* New York, 1988.

Meyerowitz, Joanne, ed. *Not June Cleaver: Women and Gender in Postwar American, 1945–1960.* Philadelphia, 1994.

Winkler, Allan M. *Life under a Cloud: American Anxiety about the Atom.* New York, 1993.

Woloch, Nancy. *Women and the American Experience.* New York, 1994.

THE DESIGN OF THE FAMILIAR

Catherine Gudis

The pop artist Andy Warhol was fond of making pronouncements. One such legendary assertion was, "I like boring things." Another was, "I want to be a machine." These were odd statements for an artist to make in the early 1960s. After all, an artist was supposed to create anew, to explore individual acts of genius, not to enjoy the sameness and repetition that leads to boredom. Nevertheless, Warhol emerged as a cultural marker of 1950s commercial excess, an era punctuated by the scarcity of the Great Depression on the one side and by the unrest of civil rights activities and the Vietnam War on the other.

Warhol's statements—like his art—extolled machine made and mass-produced goods, the banal and repetitive elements of everyday life in the affluent society of 1950s America. He called attention to the elements that comprised the jumble of material life as it was lived through the mass media and mass-marketed consumer products. His subjects were the familiar goods and the daily barrage of images that had become so widely distributed in American society, so ever present, that they were hardly noticed. But Warhol noticed the otherwise ephemeral elements of visual culture, such as the ad, the fashion magazine, and the tabloid newspaper. He also took as the source of his work the standardized brand names and packaging in which daily life was wrapped—the seemingly ubiquitous Brillo soap pads, Campbell's soups, Heinz tomato ketchup, Del Monte peach halves, and Coca-Cola. In so doing, he drew attention to the design of the familiar.

Pop artists such as Warhol weren't the only public figures to highlight the design of mass media forces such as advertising, television, and billboards and the standardized goods they promoted. Roy Lichtenstein, one of the founding figures of pop art, borrowed characters, dialogue, and illustration techniques from popular post–World War II comic books, such as *Secret Hearts* and *G.I. Combat*. His paintings even featured benday patterns—the large, regularly spaced dots used for shading in comics and commercial art. Like Lichtenstein, pop painter James Rosenquist, who supported himself by painting commercial billboards in New York's Times Square in the late 1950s, similarly used commercial techniques in his fine arts work. His paintings combined dramatically enlarged fragments from ads—the moist Duncan Hines cake mix, the front headlights of a Ford V-8, and the whitewall tires of a Chevrolet—that remain familiar despite being shorn from their context and original scale. Pop artists helped focus attention on elements of daily life that were otherwise difficult to discern. Pop architects Robert Venturi, Denise Scott Brown, and Steven Izenour (also called VSBA, or Venturi, Scott Brown, and Associates) did the same for the auto-oriented highway "strip" when they explored the vibrant complexity and contradictions of the unplanned and commercially driven built environment in their 1968 book *Learning from Las Vegas*. Like Warhol, they found fascination in the blaring billboards along the strip, where the speed and mobility of the motorist had influenced the designs of buildings and signs. Again, the ephemeral qualities of life in the fast lane were stressed, where the quick glance was all that could be expected from motorist passersby.

The members of VSBA embraced what their contemporary, the journalist Tom Wolfe, boisterously described as the booming expressions of American wealth seen through material excesses ranging from the family car, "a 425-horsepower, twenty-two-foot-long Buick Electra with tail fins in back and two black rubber breasts on the bumper in front," to the ranch-style suburban house, "with wall-to-wall carpet you could lose a shoe in." Wolfe similarly extolled the raucously flamboyant signs that VSBA also saw on the Vegas strip. He described the meeting of architecture and advertising at road's edge as soaring, oscillating, towering signs in shapes Wolfe coined as "Boomerang Modern, Palette Curvilinear, McDonald's hamburger parabola, Mint Casino Elliptical, Miami Beach Kidney."

The Venturi group quoted from Wolfe, in part because he created a language that descriptively captured the characteristics of the vernacular commercial landscape, an arena designed not by planners or the big-name architects one could read about in museum catalogs, but by businesspeople whose aims were market driven. The designs were specific to the needs of the companies to communicate their commercial function to an automotive audience. The term "vernacular" historically suggests indigenous building traditions, regionally determined and employed. For pop artists and architects like Warhol and VSBA, the vernacular was driven by the needs of commerce to communicate to undefined masses of consumers. In this commercial vernacular, clear representational imagery—quickly seen and understood—was employed so that there was no room to guess the meaning or purpose of the sign or building (as in a hot dog stand in the shape of a hot dog); recognizability might also be ensured by the use of traditional elements of design and architecture of the past, such as a pitched roof to signify "house," a broken pediment for furniture that would read as status-seeking "Chippendale," curving tree-lined streets to signal upper-crust "garden suburb."

In taking note of these signs and symbols of the ordinary landscape of 1950s and 1960s America, Venturi, Scott Brown, and Izenour were also offering an antidote of acceptance to what they saw in the popular and professional press as a dismissal of the familiar, in all its jumble of design forms. In particular, they were responding to the derision of the urban critic Peter Blake, who, in a book only a few years before, had described the increasingly automobile-oriented landscape as "God's Own Junkyard." For Blake, billboards, cars, and roadside businesses blighted the natural landscape that had so recently been opened to the view of the masses of Americans through the construction of the federal interstate highway system. Many contemporary critics saw the throwaway culture of American material life as the sign of domination by corporate forces. The journalist Vance Packard, for instance, described those forces under the names "The Hidden Persuaders," "The Waste Makers," and "The Status Seekers" (all titles of his popular books). Packard, along with the communications critic Marshall McLuhan, called for a careful eye to the effects of mass media images upon the public mind.

For Blake, Packard, and McLuhan, the barrage of goods and images that marked industrial life in the postwar era was phantasmagoric but numbingly so.

Each of these figures pointed out conflicts that relate to the idea of design and the idea of the familiar. They grappled with the notion that design in the mechanical age meant the effacing of the individual in favor of a corporate mentality of conformity; the despoliation of nature by technology and the machine; and the loss of the real through the domination of the mass-reproduced image. Foremost among their goals was to awaken what seemed a disengaged and detached public to recognize that they were being bamboozled by the persuasive and seductive forces of mass media and mass consumerism according to which there could never be too much or too many of anything. Underlying their projects, however, was a focus on design—how and why the world looked the way it did and who was responsible. For them, individual designers were rarely named or nameable, as the forces behind the age of mass materialism were far larger than any one artistic genius might lay claim to.

In each of these cases, from Warhol to McLuhan, the critic or celebrant pointedly sought out the order undergirding the seeming jumble of material life. Each sought to stir their audience, to provide an opening or a fissure in what was otherwise an evenly stuccoed wall of ordinariness, of the commonplace, of that which is so apparent as to be impossible to see, much less to get some critical distance from. All called attention to the ordinary landscape, that which was rarely recognized as designed and whose manufacture, distribution, and consumption had exponentially increased in the postwar period without much attendance to the means and effects of such large-scale change.

Mass-produced and nationally distributed goods are at the root of the familiar and are key elements in the design of dominant middle-class material culture and the larger built landscape of 1950s America. Mass production and national distribution are also factors that point out the intrinsic contradictions of the phrase "the design of the familiar," the same contradictions that Warhol took delight in highlighting through his art and life. For while the word "design" suggests the hand of the individual strategizing the form and function of two- and three-dimensional objects, the "familiar" suggests something that is easy to recognize because it has been experienced before, it isn't wholly novel or new. Whereas "design" suggests individualism and originality, the "familiar" is about repetition and the reproducible. In the age of mass production and national distribution both of these definitions become exaggerated by sheer quantity, more and more difficult to discern or to gain critical distance from as the authorial intentions of the designed and the ancestry of the familiar become more difficult to trace. Their common roots, however, are intertwined in the cultural events of an earlier period, when design emerged as part of an economic program in which private industry allied itself with public agencies and sought scientifically rational means by which to balance mass production with mass consumption.

HISTORICAL BACKGROUND: FORGING A NEW CONSUMER CONSCIOUSNESS

In the 1940s and 1950s the American economy was boosted first by defense spending then by a rise in real income as veterans returned to work and industry pumped out the products that people had been denied in the long years of depression and wartime conservation. Many of the factors that influenced the outpouring of consumer items in this period—mass production, increased automation, national distribution, over-the-top advertising, and promotional campaigns—weren't new to mid-twentieth-century America. Indeed, Henry Ford had been mass producing his "tin lizzies" or Model Ts since the 1910s; General Electric had been distributing domestic appliances nationally from around the same date. Ford's techniques for developing scientifically rationalized means of efficient mass production to a large number of other industries had been designed but were interrupted by World War I, only to be re-engaged in the 1920s. Throughout, cries of concern reverberated in the popular press and business journals: How on earth could Americans ever consume the vast quantities of goods they were now capable of producing? How would growing capacities for production ever be matched by consumption? These same questions littered the business journals and professional journals of the 1940s and 1950s.

From the turn of the twentieth century through the post–World War II period, American industrialists, politicians, and businessmen were preoccupied by these fears that "natural" laws of supply and demand were not enough to disperse and distribute the mass of goods being produced. They determined that more aggressive intervention was necessary, that businessmen needed to manipulate prices and output, and that they needed to forge alliances with one another and with the state in order to do so effectively. Moreover, they needed to mold a new consumer consciousness or to preach, as one industrial manager put it in 1927, "a new economic gospel of consumption." This was a social program, whereby industry and government would strengthen the social and political power of private corporations as the purported providers of economic stability through enhanced consumption.

This was the climate in which advertisers and industrialists could paternalistically proclaim their educational role and responsibility for diffusing desire and higher standards of living to all classes of people. As one billboard designer wrote in 1922, "Advertising is a factor in modern merchandising" because it brings "potential wants out of the depths of subconscious minds and establishes them among the group of active and immediate motives which control action." The idea was that if Americans were properly trained in consumption, they would want better and more commodities and go to greater efforts to gratify their desires; as luxuries became defined as necessities, efforts to maintain and improve standards of living would breed economic stability. After all, workers would have to return to work and what they produced would, in turn, have a continued consumer market.

By the 1900s professional advertising agencies were handling most national campaigns, particularly for products that were new, such as Kodak cameras; automobiles by Pope, Ford, and Oldsmobile; and rubber tires by Fisk, Kelly-Springfield, and Firestone. Ads for domestic goods that promised convenience and new dimensions in healthful living also multiplied, including those for the Gillette disposable razor; bar soap by Ivory; and breakfast cereals by Quaker Oats, Cream of Wheat, and Kellogg's. By the 1920s the advertising art director and the industrial designer also emerged as important proselytizers in the new economic gospel of consumption. Their jobs were not merely to convey the practical functions of the products to be packaged and promoted, but to amplify the subjective associations or psychic by-products of their consumption. Themes of individualism, progress, and modernity dominated advertisements for products as varied as Palmolive soap, General Motors cars, and Arrow shirts. Part of the task at hand was to suggest that modernity was about consumption and that goods, even standardized and mass-produced goods, would grant freedom and autonomy, not to mention class ascension.

Advertisers employed this approach in different ways. For instance, the manufacturers of Listerine managed to create a new market for their old product by making up a scientific-sounding description for bad breath, "halitosis," and then offering the means of curing it with their medicinal mouthwash. They innovated the use of halftone photographs montaged with dramatic "life stories" to make their points. For image makers, incorporating such new design and marketing techniques meant a simple retooling of the concepts that had informed print media in prior decades; they did not need to change the hardware by which the products were manufactured or the ads were printed, they simply had to alter the superfice—the image.

The same lessons were not so simple for other industries to learn, however, as the case of the automotive industry suggests. By the mid-1920s the market for cars neared saturation and the industry was faced with the problem of how to stimulate consumption without entirely retooling their large-scale and expensive factory production line. Henry Ford had built his reputation on the production of one unchanging, mass-produced motor car for the masses: the Model T, available in "any color as long as it's black." But what would happen when the nearly indestructible tin lizzie had made its way through the ranks of the masses? As the story goes, at that point, the masses went to General Motors. Alfred Sloan was the president of GM in the 1920s and his vision was quite clear: the "purpose of GM was to make money, not just to make motor cars." He realized that technical improvements to the body and engine of the car interfered with this goal, and left that to Ford. Instead, he kept the assembly line going but gave the cars that came off the line a change of clothing once a year. He hired Harley Earl in 1927 as his fervent preacher of this new gospel of consumption, which went under the name "styling." With Earl, he got a master illusionist who understood the ways of Hollywood and took them to the road, molding fantasies of chrome and color on wheels. Earl and Sloan institutionalized the automotive industry's program of increased obsolescence through the initiation of the yearly model change. With it, they created the illusion of technological change or progress, when in fact they had only superficially modified the same basic mechanical features. But what embellishments they were! Earl created an expressive vocabulary of automotive forms that grew more exaggerated as years went by: radiator grilles, taillights, trim, bumpers, fenders, and—in a move that would be prophetic for all cars of the 1950s—the tail fin, inspired by a Lockheed fighter plane and first seen on the 1948 Cadillac.

DESIGN IN THE SERVICE INDUSTRY

Styling, as GM practiced it, was the domain of numerous other manufacturers as well, particularly those who designed domestic appliances and other durable goods. Most frequently, their designs were not left entirely to the industrial engineers but were bolstered by marketing and promotional programs that extended into a variety of media and that contributed to the overall identity of the corporation. For designers of both print media and products, however, the problem was how to create an identity that would be recognizable across different media and that would connect different products to the same company. Even more significant was how to make mass-produced designs seem individualized and varied, yet not too far outside accepted standards of style. After all, consumers wanted a sense of individuality but they did not want to be too different from those they aspired to be like. These concerns became particularly important as the same products were sold increasingly on a national and international basis. The ease with which a consumer might recognize the package and distinguish the product from others serving exactly the same function emerged as a key project for the nascent field of graphic and industrial designers.

Many business leaders began to look toward the fine and applied arts for means by which to make their goods seem different from the rest, to seem individualized and appealing no matter how many of the same products were churned out annually. To give products and companies an identity is a difficult task under any conditions. This is especially true for products that are either new or have no easily reproducible image to present, as was the case for electrical and gas companies, pharmaceutical companies, and firms that were involved in packaging and distribution.

The first American company to develop a fully integrated design program, managing the appearance of all elements of the corporation, from its stationery to its architectural exteriors and interiors, was the Container Corporation of America (CCA), run by Walter Paepke. The CCA manufactured cardboard boxes and packed other people's products for national distribution. As the railroad and motor truck began to mass distribute the goods of assembly-line production across the country, the need for packaging grew exponentially too, and

Paepke was determined to maintain his stronghold on the business. In 1935 he hired Egbert Jacobson to direct a newly formed design department. They set out to construct a unified image of CCA that was communicated through the consistent and co-ordinated use of a logo and sans serif typeface on the company's products and printed materials, a series of distinctive advertisements utilizing modernist design and avant-garde art, and a functionalist corporate architectural style that sought to forge links to the abstract forms of the print and package designs.

Paepke's sponsorship of modern European designers as well as modern artists made him a leading force in design and packaging in Chicago and the United States. This sponsorship of art and design on behalf of the corporation was widely extolled in business journals and the popular press. For Paepke, this publicity was part of his corporate design. He sought the appearance of modernity, the quality of the new, and the potential for a universal means of expression that many European artists, designers, and industrialists had been exploring through governmentally sponsored workshops beginning in the 1910s with the German Werkbund and continuing with the Bauhaus in the 1920s and 1930s.

Paepke established the precedent of hiring designers to direct both the graphic production of advertisements and the overall public face of the company in all its guises, from internal memos to product design. This integrated design scheme helped to identify the company through the establishment of a "look" that did not directly reflect the products or services of the company, but instead communicated the essence of the organization's activity by allusion, minimal text (oftentimes a one-word headline), and dynamic compositions using generous amounts of white space and contrasting tones. While "institutional" advertising—selling the company rather than any one product itself—was not an uncommon practice and actually exceeded individual product advertising in the late 1930s through the wartime years, Paepke's association with cutting-edge art from around the world—an affiliation that would extend far beyond the pages of print advertisements as the years wore on—brought a groundbreaking new dimension. It would prove exemplary to many corporations, advertising agencies, artists, and designers in the years through the 1950s.

Paepke's project was not just the orchestration of all elements of the company's appearance but the construction of an image that, by virtue of its association with new and modern art, spoke of the company's higher aspirations. These aspirations were in part paternalistic, put forth to edify the public and to elevate their tastes and faculties for art. These lofty goals allowed companies to justify their hiring of designers and their investment of money and research into design. However, the problem of how to explain and adopt an identity was a vexing one. How could a designer and a company leader lend an identity to a corporation and its mass-produced goods and services? How could they determine the "personality" of an inanimate object—a bureaucratic organization? In answer, some companies merely sought to appear forward thinking, new and modern, poised to move ahead. This was a popular approach during the depression years of the 1930s, as designers were employed to galvanize public recognition—if not for the immediate need of promoting business, at least to guarantee a future for the firm.

The job of industrial and graphic designers—those who designed products as well as the printed materials promoting and wrapping them—was publicized most grandly of all by the depression-era world's fairs that took place in Chicago in 1933 and in New York in 1939. These were publicity stunts on behalf of big corporations that wanted to compete with one another and to bring to the public eye their distinctive corporate presence.

Fairs in this period were blatantly commercial corporate events. They were aimed to bolster public faith in the corporation and in the promise of future economic well-being provided by the corporation. For instance, the 1939 New York World's Fair looked both backward to an agricultural age of abundance and forward to a technological utopia of abundance. It was the product of a New Deal partnership of private corporations and the federal government, funded by President Franklin Roosevelt and major companies such as Ford Motor Company, General Motors, Westinghouse, and others. Though a visionary world of tomorrow was imagined at the fair, a real world of tomorrow was being built: a corporation-driven, consumption-oriented welfare state led by private companies supported by federally sponsored policies.

Corporate-sponsored design played a big role in communicating and advertising this bright rosy future. Like no fair before or since, the New York World's Fair was the province of a new breed of industrial designers, many of whom came from the fields of advertising, illustration, engineering, architecture, and theater design. (Vocational programs in industrial design were just beginning.) Walter Dorwin Teague, Norman Bel Geddes, Raymond

Loewy, and Albert Kahn were a few of the designers commissioned by the major corporate sponsors of the fair. With its focus on science, transportation, and communications, the fair was an important arena in which companies could familiarize audiences with the newest developments in radio, television (the first shows began broadcasting on opening day), plastics, domestic electrical use, and styled automobiles. Audiences could glimpse into the future City of Lights in the Consolidated Edison Building, where Teague helped portray twenty-four hours in the life of New York City in a time-elapsed light show of twelve minutes. At the Westinghouse Pavilion, visitors could root for Mrs. Drudge or Mrs. Modern as they watched the Battle of the Centuries between the housewives' handwashing versus the 1940 Westinghouse dishwasher; in the same pavilion one could also see the seven-foot-high robot Elektro and his robotic dog, Sparko.

Some of the most popular displays at the fair were those on the Transportation Zone, oriented toward the future of automobile travel. The design of the Ford Pavilion, by Kahn, and the General Motors Pavilion, by Bel Geddes, reflected an American translation of European modernist design. Incorporating poured and reinforced concrete into its contemporary simplicity of forms, Kahn constructed a spiral ramped Road of Tomorrow as a dramatic runway on which the year's new model in a variety of colors was paraded before throngs of spectators. Audience members who entered the exposition hall then became part of the show, climbing into a new Ford to ride themselves down the ramp into the colorful future. (By this point, Ford was scurrying to catch up with GM by offering styled model changes.)

For GM, Bel Geddes also glamourized the future possible through advanced automobility in his elaborate designs for "frictionless" travel, which he envisioned for the year 1960. According to his plan, high-speed limited-access expressways would connect city and country by 1960, and traffic congestion as well as overcrowded city centers would be things of the past. Highways, like the cars and buildings presented at the fair, would be streamlined—designed for speed without unnecessary parts hindering the flow of traffic. Bel Geddes's car designs were also part of this Futurama display, incorporating the teardrop shape that engineers had determined to be the most wind-resistant form for machine-aged travel.

Many other products on display at the fair were designed to embody speed and movement, particularly those that traveled across space and time, such

as the Kodak camera, the radio, the telephone, and the record player. Many were presented in the new plastics and acrylics being developed. They incorporated thin horizontal streamlining stripes and rounded corners to suggest their modernity, as speed and the idea of mobility became the driving force of functionalist design. Buildings, too, bore the influence of the machine. Designers drew upon America's agricultural past, by incorporating shapes reminiscent of grain silos, as well as on its mechanical future, with variations on factory-sash glass windows and futuristic-looking finned pylons. Throughout the fairground, the settings for these objects were controlled spectacles, dramatic tableaux in which the facts of labor and industry were aestheticized and the future projected as a corporation-constructed technological utopia disconnected from the facticity of depression life. Critical to the fabrication of this dreamworld were the powers of the stylists, whose jobs had grown from molding the appearance of goods and images to molding new technologies of production and psychologies of consumption.

WARTIME STYLING/POSTWAR MODERN LIFE

Many of the new materials and the uses for them that were presented at the New York World's Fair did not have a commercial outlet until wartime years, and, even then, this was by default, as limitations were imposed on manufacturers by the Federal Reserve Board and the War Production Board, whose goals were to control the use of natural resources for defense needs and to reduce nonessential production of consumer goods. Such limitations on materials needed for defense meant that research into substitutes gained favor. For instance, when aluminum was no longer available for ice trays, plastic ice trays were produced; when cast iron and enameled steel for pots and pans were not available, Pyrex, a tempered glass that could withstand high and low temperatures, gained popularity.

Defense uses for new materials also had an eventual effect on the designs and demand for consumer goods. Acrylics such as Lucite and Plexiglas, developed in 1935, had never really garnered a market, in part because they were seen as poor substitutes for glass. Defense uses of these materials in military aircraft as clear window bubbles helped expand their market and brought them to the attention of consumers. What would eventually be called Tupperware had a similar start, when the durable yet flexible polyethylene found use as an insulating material. In the late 1940s, its chemist-developer Earl Tupper began producing storage containers out of this material and innovated a national marketing program through a system of home parties.

Many of the new materials and production techniques honed for the defense industry, especially for the aviation industry and home construction (to erect shelters quickly for defense workers) promised to revolutionize postwar life too. For instance, airplane manufacturers such as Vultee and Douglas Aircraft had discovered that new fixatives could be used to attach aluminum sheeting to plywood panels, which were light, easy to refabricate, and ideal for fulfilling President's Roosevelt's challenge to the aviation industry to build enough planes to help England win the war. Easy-to-produce prefabricated parts like these could similarly be used for mass housing construction, a need which was already pressing in the United States since the depression had halted home construction and defense needs had continued the building moratorium. Standardized components that could be easily and quickly assembled on site by unskilled workers were one such wartime practice used for defense housing in California and New York and applied later by companies such as Levitt & Sons to suburban tract housing developments.

Systems of modular and prefabricated construction found easy adaptation from wartime uses to postwar furniture production. Charles Eames, for instance, developed a molded and laminated plywood form for use as leg splints for wounded soldiers. After the war he used laminated plywood for a great number of furniture designs, most notable being the Eames chair, mass manufactured by the Herman Miller Company.

Many of the new materials and techniques of production inspired forms that were biological or organic in origin, a complete contrast to the synthetic nature of the materials employed. The exotic repertoire of sculptural items included bubble-shaped lamps by George Nelson, tulip-shaped molded plastic chairs by Eero Saarinen, and biomorphic abstractions in bent wire sculptures, jewelry, and furniture by Harry Bertoia. The Herman Miller Company and Knoll Associates were two of the biggest mass producers and distributors of these simple postwar designs for the modern home and office, many of which are still in production in the twenty-first century. Their use of simple industrial materials, free-formed sculptural shapes, and a low-slung casual approach embodied ideas for postwar modern living as it was envisioned in mass magazines and architectural journals alike.

Many postwar designs employed organic forms that were more figurative, too, such as wispy outlines of birds, butterflies, spiders, bows, and starbursts populating all manner of interior and graphic design, from fiberglass draperies to plastic laminate Formica tables to vinyl adhesive Con-Tac paper. Both the abstract biomorphic forms of Eames and Saarinen and these representational images joined to fashion a forward-looking new look for American design. The atom bomb and then space travel pushed the look forward in time, too, as a vocabulary of forms for domestic and commercial graphics, buildings, and consumer goods incorporated sci-fi imagery of boomerangs, rocket ships, flying saucers, and parabolic arches. The roots of this design style were in wartime and postwar defense research, funded by the government, engineered by the corporation, and styled by the troops of designers who were finding employment in a rapidly growing professional arena at the crossroads of art and industry.

POSTWAR CORPORATE IDENTITY

By the post–World War II years, designers had established their importance to industry and were in huge demand as the rate of production and consumption increased exponentially due to increases in real income, spending, automation, population, and mass-media communication. All of these factors contributed to the shape and appearance of daily material life in the postwar period and to the role of the designer and the corporation in its shaping. Automation changed the kinds of jobs that people got—they supervised machines rather than doing the labor of machines—and also shifted jobs to areas of administration, research, and distribution. The stylist's job became firmly entrenched in research and development, which now integrated production, marketing, consumer studies, and distribution. Modern market analysis, attempting to identify just who comprised the mass at the receiving end of the magazines, newspapers, and radio and television signals, emerged as the next step in scientifically engineering consumption.

Raymond Loewy, who was among those first-generation industrial designers of the 1930s to publicize the important role the designer played in industry, was one among many figures fascinated with how modern technology applied to product styling and modern market analysis. He was also a proponent of styling as a means of continuously reworking packaging and design, and did redesign for Coca-Cola, Lucky Strike, Westinghouse Electric Company, Greyhound Bus, Shell, and Standard Oil (Esso). In fact his motto, and the title of his 1951 book, was Never Leave Well Enough Alone, and his mantra was that "good design" is "an upward sales curve." Loewy and numerous designers, including Henry Dreyfuss, Donald Deskey, J. Gordon Lippincott, and H. Creston Doner, were hired by big companies such as Libbey-Owens-Ford glass company, Revere Copper and Brass, Dow Chemical Company, Monsanto, and others, to develop new design ideas and products for the postwar world. Many of the designers ran big firms, with large numbers of designers and other specialists employed, and worked in all media and all aspects of design to manufacture not just the look but the overall identity of their corporate clients.

The colorful commercial effusion that marked the post–World War II years was dramatically enhanced by the domestic application of synthetic and mineral materials from plastics to asbestos as well as technological improvements in color printing, broadcasting, and Technicolor films. Speed and mobility were key words for this commercial expansion and for designs aimed toward these goals. As Americans bought more cars than ever before and became a suburban nation, their lifestyles became characterized by social, physical, and economic mobility. As the Cadillac's tail fin grew in length during the 1950s, becoming more like rocket fuselages by 1959, the chief stylist for Chrysler, Virgil Exner, gave its products a "forward look" too, first with uplifted tail fins and then with a dynamic new logo of two superimposed boomerangs. The same winged, or parabolic, form was used in the design of Knoll's butterfly chairs, Isamu Noguchi's coffee tables, RCA's portable televisions, and Herman Miller's trademark. Meanwhile, abstract shapes aimed at capturing the modernity of the atomic age and the speed of space travel were employed in products and ads ranging from wallpaper and clocks to laundry detergent. All were material enticement for mobility and consumption.

Graphic designers such as Paul Rand, Saul Bass, and Lester Beall all took a pragmatic approach to design, incorporating lessons learned both from European modern art and, ironically, from market researchers who suggested that the masses did not like or understand abstract art. They understood that the speed of modern life and the limited attention people were willing to pay to any one image or object had an effect on how designers should work on behalf of business. Rand, for instance, employed elements of modern art such as collage and montage. Often he included whimsical line drawings and singular words that he used in striking contrast and toward expressive ends. Fundamentally, he believed that a synthesis of words, type, and image was required to keep communication simple and direct; ultimately, he believed that basic shapes and typefaces could communicate universally and timelessly. Increasingly in the 1950s and 1960s, Rand took his ideas into the realm of corporate identification, where he created trademarks for companies such as IBM, ABC, and Westinghouse. For all of these logos, he used simple distinct forms, which in subsequent years he continued to redesign.

Working in Los Angeles, Saul Bass employed a similar tradition of graphic design reduced to a single dominant image often centered in the space of the composition. In particular, Bass reduced the essence of an ad to a glyph, with one image telling a whole story or with simple pictographs expressing a complex message. In his film title sequence and advertising campaign for The Man with the Golden Arm (1955), for instance, he constructed the image with a reduced vocabulary of chunky horizontal and vertical forms that combined first to represent a silhouetted man and then recombined to spell out the name of the film.

Artists whose works could be rendered easily for recognizability and appropriateness to the product were increasingly hired by enlightened corporate heads and advertising agencies in the 1950s. Commercial art schools and funding to attend them through the GI Bill helped expand the professional pool of designers available for commercial work. Commercial art programs had begun in the interwar period, with the first major in industrial design offered at Carnegie Institute of Technology (now Carnegie Mellon University) in Pittsburgh, starting in 1935 as part of a program initiated by Donald R. Dohner, who had worked as a designer for Westinghouse Electric Company. Dohner was then asked to set up a similar program at Pratt Institute in New York. Meanwhile, in Chicago, Walter Paepke was busily orchestrating support for the establishment of the New Bauhaus (eventually called the Institute of Design), under the German émigré László Moholy-Nagy. Along with other graduates of the German Bauhaus, Moholy-Nagy offered classes in the tradition of the European modernist tradition. However, despite Paepke's efforts, the school was never able to gain the full support of Chicago industrialists, perhaps due to the lofty philosophical approach of some of the faculty, and eventually became part of the Illinois Institute of Technology. Paepke's support for design in industry was undiminished, and in 1951 he inaugurated what would soon become a yearly design conference at the Aspen Institute of Humanist Studies in Colorado, which brought together international leaders in industry, government, and design. These conferences, as well as museum and department store exhibits featuring "good design," were means by which the application of art to industry was promoted as an industry unto itself. Many of these programs, including industrial design exhibitions presented at the Museum of Modern Art (MOMA) in New York starting in the 1930s, such as "Machine Art" (1934) and "Bauhaus" (1938), predicated the idea of good design on European and Scandinavian modernist examples, especially of furniture. With MOMA's series of exhibitions called "Good Design," which ran from 1950 to 1955, European modernism was further institutionalized as the canon of industrial design.

Despite what was going on in the museum, city and suburban streets told a different story of American design. There, a variety of commercial artists, including those who later gained fame for their pop art, such as James Rosenquist, Robert Rauschenberg, and Andy Warhol, made their living as illustrators, billboard sign painters, window display designers, and advertising photographers. Not everyone who worked in the commercial arts in the 1950s ended up in museum exhibitions, however. Most made work that stayed on the street and in the shop and home.

In fact, a different kind of design museum could be experienced on the streets and highways of postwar America. There, the commercial landscape seen from a moving automobile offered another lesson in the "economic gospel of consumption" initiated by advertisers in the decades before. During the period from 1930 to 1958, automobile production and ownership increased five times as fast as the population. By 1953 plans were laid for federal funding of over 40,000 miles of interstate express highways. Nevertheless, the number of cars produced in the twelve years between 1946 and 1958, if placed bumper to bumper, would require more than the 55,000 miles of highway lanes that had been built in that same period. Cars and highways had become the dominant feature of American life.

Along the roadside, both regional and multinational companies made their presence felt, some incorporating the same lessons that designers in other arenas had learned. The logo and the simplified image had a natural home on the billboards and signage all along the roadside, where speed and mobility were the guiding design forces. Aimed to be seen at high speeds and to communicate quickly and easily, many nationally spreading franchises, from Howard Johnson's to McDonald's, incorporated the same simplified design aesthetic of bold colors, simple forms, and an expressive array of energized lines meant to be read quickly and themselves embody the speed and mobility of their audience passersby. Why else did the franchises take on such bold colors and soaring shapes or geometric contrasts—the steeply pitched orange roofs of HoJo's, the golden arches and forward tilting cantilevered roof of McDonald's, and the blinking arrows of Sonic gas stations and drive throughs too numerous to mention? Not only were Americans driving more, in more cars, but they were moving more, too, changing houses, towns, and suburbs at a rapid rate, unmatched by any previous generation. Their mobility was enabled by and then contributed to the growth of the suburban tract developments springing up across the country, another example of the rapid rise in standardized mass production that fostered the appearance of individualism by means of the availability of numerous models or varieties of the same type.

Integral to this highway landscape of mobility were the larger-than-life pictures and structures of outdoor advertisements or billboards. It was to this landscape that architects such as Robert Venturi, Denise Scott Brown, and Steven Izenour and artists such as Andy Warhol called attention. For these pop artists, the ordinary and the banal elements of contemporary daily life in the postwar period were a rich source material. Their project was nothing short of an aesthetic cultural anthropology, a mining of the people and places around them for evidence of life lived. In their cases, however, the people and places were not to be found in an exotic otherworldly environment but right in their own backyard, through the picture windows of the split-level ranch house and across the manufactured lawn of the suburban development.

See also **Industrialism and Its Critics; The Popular Arts** *(volume 1);* **Popular Culture in the Public Arena; Postmodernism and the Arts** *(volume 2);* **Technology; Consumerism; Architecture; Advertising; Myth and Symbol** *(volume 3); and other articles in this section.*

BIBLIOGRAPHY

Primary Sources

Blake, Peter. *God's Own Junkyard: The Planned Deterioration of America's Landscape*. New York, 1964.

Galbraith, John Kenneth. *The Affluent Society*. Boston, 1958.

Giedion, Sigfried. *Mechanization Takes Command: A Contribution to Anonymous History*. New York and Oxford, 1948.

Kaufmann, Edgar, Jr. *What Is Modern Design?* New York, 1959.

Lippincott, J. Gordon. *Design for Business*. Chicago, 1954.

Loewy, Raymond. *Never Leave Well Enough Alone*. New York, 1941.

McLuhan, Marshall. *The Mechanical Bride: The Folklore of Industrial Man*. Boston, 1951.

Nelson, George, and Henry Wright. *Tomorrow's House*. New York, 1946.

Packard, Vance. *The Hidden Persuaders*. New York, 1957.

Venturi, Robert, Denise Scott Brown, and Steven Izenour. *Learning from Las Vegas*. New Haven, Conn., 1968; Cambridge, Mass., 1972.

Wolfe, Tom. *The Kandy-Kolored Tangerine-Flake Streamline Baby*. New York, 1966.

Wright, Russel, and Mary Einstein Wright. *Guide to Easier Living*. New York, 1954.

Secondary Sources

Albrecht, Donald, ed. *World War II and the American Dream*. Washington, D.C., 1965.

Banham, Reyner. *Design by Choice*. New York, 1981.

Blaszczyk, Regina Lee. *Imagining Consumers: Design and Innovation from Wedgwood to Corning*. Baltimore and London, 2000.

Forty, Adrian. *Objects of Desire: Design and Society 1750–1980*. London, 1986.

Friedman, Mildred, ed. *Graphic Design in America: A Visual Language History*. New York, 1989.

Gartman, David. *Auto Opium: A Social History of American Automobile Design*. New York and London, 1994.

Hine, Thomas. *Populuxe*. New York, 1990.

Liebs, Chester H. *Main Street to Miracle Mile: American Roadside Architecture*. Baltimore and London, 1995.

Mamiya, Christin J. *Pop Art and Consumer Culture: American Super Market*. Austin, Tex., 1992.

Marchand, Roland. *Advertising the American Dream: Making Way for Modernity, 1920–1940*. Berkeley, Calif., 1985.

———. *Creating the Corporate Soul: The Rise of Public Relations and Corporate Imagery in American Big Business*. Berkeley, Calif., 1998.

Margolin, Victor, ed. *Design Discourses: History, Theory, Criticism*. Chicago and London, 1989.

Marling, Karal Ann. *As Seen on TV: The Visual Culture of Everyday America in the 1950s*. Cambridge, Mass., 1994.

Meikle, Jeffrey. *American Plastic: A Cultural History*. New Brunswick, N.J., 1995.

——. *Twentieth Century Limited: Industrial Design in America.* Philadelphia, 1979.

Miller, Daniel. *Material Culture and Mass Consumption.* Cambridge, Mass., 1987.

Olins, Wally. *Corporate Personality: An Enquiry into the Nature of Corporate Identity.* New York, 1978.

Pulos, Arthur J. *The American Design Adventure, 1940–1975.* Cambridge, Mass., 1988.

Sloan, James Allen. *The Romance of Commerce and Culture: Capitalism, Modernism, and the Chicago-Aspen Crusade for Cultural Reform.* Chicago and London, 1983.

Smith, Terry. *Making the Modern: Industry, Art, and Design in America.* Chicago and London, 1993.

Tedlow, Richard. *New and Improved: The Story of Mass Marketing in America.* New York, 1990.

Woodham, Jonathan M. *Twentieth Century Design.* Oxford and New York, 1997.

THE PROFESSIONAL IDEAL

Bruce A. Kimball

The ideal of the professional reached its apogee during the 1950s, having ascended in influence and popularity since the late nineteenth century, when it was first announced in such statements as "The True Professional Ideal," an address by John F. Dillon, the president of the American Bar Association (ABA), in 1894. This idealization of—and idealism about—professions was increasingly voiced in popular and professional discourse during the first half of the twentieth century, while scholars, led by the sociologist Talcott Parsons, developed a theory explaining and legitimating the high status and authority of professions. The 1950s marked a turning point, however. In subsequent decades the approbation gradually receded and was displaced by criticism and cynicism about professions, which predominated during the closing decades of the twentieth century and was accompanied by a competing theoretical framework.

Over the course of this ascendance up to the 1950s and subsequent decline, the fundamental charactcristics of the professional ideal—expertise, association, service—remained intact, having been formulated through a long historical process. In order to understand the professional ideal and its peaking in the 1950s, it is therefore necessary to begin with an account of this historical process through which the meaning of "profession," and its cognates, was informed by cultural, economic, and political influences, as well as by the nature of the groups to which the term referred.

HISTORICAL BACKGROUND OF THE PROFESSIONAL IDEAL

The Profession of the Clergy and the Ethic of Service Prominent historical interpretations have attributed the genesis of professions in America to the mid-eighteenth century (Samuel Haber) or the late nineteenth century (Burton J. Bledstein). While these periods witnessed significant developments in the professions, the origins of the professional ideal lie in the understanding of "profession" in the early seventeenth century and, particularly, in the seminal influence of the clergy, who have been neglected by most historical interpretations written during the twentieth century. Yet, a careful examination of the meaning of "profession" and the nature of the clergy, beginning in the 1600s, reveals significant developments that contributed to the emergence of the professional ideal centuries later.

In the religious culture of the English colonies of the future United States, the word "profession" early in the seventeenth century was employed most prominently in the sense of one's religious vow or affirmation. This denotation was gradually extended to the act of joining, or belonging to, a religious sect and finally to the sect itself. One's "profession" meant, most commonly, one's religion. During the seventeenth century, the special weight and dignity of "profession" in this religious sense was extended to the group whose work was uniquely entwined with advancing religion, namely, the clergy. Three factors contributed to this development. First, "profession" had long had a second, minor denotation of the vow or affirmation of competence in some art or craft. Thus, in 1611 the King James Bible clarified the phrase "to maintain good works" with the gloss "professe honest trades" (Titus 3:14). Second, the Protestant clergy were the preeminent vocation in the English colonies by almost any standard: they earned greater income, enjoyed higher social status, and exercised greater cultural authority than any other vocational group. Third, the heavily Calvinist influence upon the religious culture in the colonies led to emphasizing and dignifying secular vocations as the fulfillment of a Christian's spiritual calling.

By the early 1700s, these three factors, particularly the preeminence of the Protestant colonial clergy, resulted in the special weight and dignity of "profession" in its religious sense being extended to the occupational sense. The facts that "profession" came to refer to a corporate group of persons, that it began to denote the work of those persons, and that it began to signify the most dignified kind of work undertaken in society are developments explained by the religious culture and by the dominance of the Protestant colonial clergy.

While the vocational sense of "profession" thus grew more dignified, it also became narrower, as manifested by the appearance of two new terms. "Liberal professions" and "learned professions" were coined early in the eighteenth century and denoted the preeminent occupation of theology and the three fields with which it had been closely associated since the founding of universities in the early 1200s: law, medicine, and learning. Those medieval universities comprised four faculties: one devoted to each of the four fields, whose close association and higher status were recognized by the introduction of these two new, interchangeable terms, "liberal professions" and "learned professions."

Interwoven in these events was one further semantic development of great import. The Protestant colonial clergy informed the meaning of "profession" with an ethic of selfless service. This ethic, being a central tenet of Christian theology, was shaped by the dialectical character of that doctrine. Selfless service implied that the servant would gain in status through the act of selflessness. In their treatises and sermons addressing their occupational role and standing, the colonial ministers therefore often invoked such biblical texts as "So the last shall be first, and the first last" (Matthew 20:16); "For whosoever will save his life shall lose it; and whosoever will lose his life for my sake shall find it" (Matthew 16:25); and "Whosoever will be great among you, shall be your minister: And whosoever will be your chiefest, shall be servant of all" (Mark 10:43–44).

By the mid-eighteenth century, the conventional meaning of "profession" had thus been transformed from "vow" to "vocation," while acquiring greater dignity and becoming narrowed to four fields, as well as being informed with a dialectical sense of selfless service to others.

Professional Lawyers and Association
As the new United States emerged from the throes of the American Revolution, religion, theology, and the clergy were gradually eclipsed by politics, jurisprudence, and attorneys. Lawyers rose to juridical, political, social, and economic preeminence among vocations, notwithstanding eruptions of the longstanding antilawyer animus immediately after the Revolutionary War and during the Jacksonian period

of the 1820s and 1830s. This shift in the attractiveness of the professions was reflected in the assessment of vocational choice made in 1779 by the future jurist Hugh Henry Brackenridge: "The next fair young lady for whom I conceived an affection was *Miss Theology* . . . yet we both saw the necessity of ceasing to indulge my fond thought of a union. . . . The present object of my soft attentions is a *Miss Law,* a grave and comely young lady, a little pitted with the small pox. . . . This young lady is of a prudent industrious turn, and though she does not possess at present any very great fortune, yet what she has in expectancy is considerable" (pp. 312–313).

During the period of lawyers' ascendance, extending from the second quarter of the eighteenth century through the third quarter of the nineteenth century, they necessarily adopted in their discourse the vocational dignity and service ethic that the colonial clergy had infused in the rhetoric of profession. Conversely, lawyers informed the meaning of "profession" and its cognates with their own characteristic influence.

First, there was a shift in the meaning of the adjective "professional," which, prior to the nineteenth century, was employed rarely and most often in the sense of "religious." One's professional interests generally denoted one's religious interests in the colonial period. In the first half of the nineteenth century, lawyers adopted and popularized the term "professional," whose meaning was transmuted from its religious usage to the customary modern meaning of "vocational." Second, attorneys adumbrated the theological service ethic implying selflessness with a new meaning of "professional service." This new denotation was the contractual and feeable use or benefit to a client; consequently, the term "professional service" henceforth became profoundly ambiguous, signifying selfless but billable activity on behalf of another.

Finally, the nature of the legal vocation informed the subsequent understanding of "profession" and "professional" by defining and emphasizing the professional association as a characteristic of "profession." The devotion of lawyers to politics and polity led them by nature to associate. Lawyers "naturally constitute *a body;* . . . the analogy of their studies and the uniformity of their methods connect their minds as a common interest might unite their endeavors," wrote Alexis de Tocqueville in 1835 in *Democracy in America* (vol. 1, pp. 283–284). Like the new meanings of "professional" and of "service," the importance of professional association derived from the preeminence of attorneys, as well as their devotion to association and polity.

Professors, Professionals, and Functional Expertise Between the 1860s and the 1910s another transformation occurred in the professions, culminating in the emergence of the professional ideal. This transformation involved a shift in status both within the echelon of liberal or learned professions and for that echelon as a whole. Law declined to the position that it has held for most of American history and to which it seems especially well suited: the second-best profession. Whether due to the seeming amoralism of the advocacy system, to the fact that lawyers must lose half of their cases, or to the long-standing Anglo-American animus toward lawyers, the legal profession seems to attract an extraordinary amount of criticism, particularly when it is put forth as the foremost profession. Attorneys fare much better when counseling in the shadow of another preeminent profession, which then attracts the bulk of egalitarian criticism directed against elites.

As the status of law declined, so did the entire echelon of liberal and learned professions, while the educational professions ascended dramatically within that echelon and became for a brief period the most attractive among the learned professions. This happened, in part, because a gender boundary in education substituted for the sectarian, institutional, and occupational boundaries in the other professions, resulting in relative mobility for male educators and restrictions upon women in the field. In the late nineteenth century, men crossed the institutional and occupational boundaries within the field of education far more often and easily than happened subsequently in the field or contemporaneously in other learned professions. Male schoolteachers became university professors who became school superintendents who became college or university presidents and vice versa. Meanwhile, gender prejudice confined women, who made up about 65 percent of educators in 1900, largely to schoolteaching within the field of education; and schoolteaching became the most attractive profession available to women. Consequently, education became the most attractive profession for men and for women, within their respective spheres.

These developments were accompanied by several changes in the meaning of "profession" and its cognates. A practitioner of a profession had previously been called most often by the noun "professor," whose secondary denotation was "teacher." A "professor of law" most commonly referred to a lawyer prior to the 1860s. During the final third of the nineteenth century, the term "professor" came to signify no longer the practitioners but their teachers, who were becoming the elite of each profession. A "professor of law" meant most commonly a member of a law school faculty by the 1890s. The exemplar in this regard was Harvard Law School's appointment in 1873 of James Barr Ames as the first full-time faculty member, someone who had never practiced law and who thus pioneered the profession of professional school professor, distinct from the practitioner of a profession. Meanwhile, the recently popularized adjective "professional" was adopted as a noun to refer to practitioners in general, thereby supplanting the previous usage of the term "professor."

Another change occurred as these new professors informed the meaning of "profession" with a characteristic of their vocation: learning. This semantic development appeared through two changes in usage. First, the term "liberal professions" became outmoded and disappeared. Then, ironically enough, "learned" was sloughed away from "learned professions" as the adjective became redundant when learning became cardinal for all professions. The noun "professions" alone began to refer to the expanding group of vocations that were seeking the legitimacy of learning, as manifested in the phenomenal development of professional education. This development appeared not so much in the absolute number of professional schools as in the elevation of academic standards, which was championed by Harvard Law School during the deanship of Christopher Columbus Langdell between 1870 and 1895 and then James Barr Ames from 1895 to 1910.

Notwithstanding this early influence of law schools, it is important to recognize that learning was understood by the end of the nineteenth century as functional expertise modeled upon the natural sciences. That new understanding was codified through a series of decisions by the U.S. Supreme Court concerning occupational licensing. In the 1880s states began enacting laws requiring that more and more occupations be licensed and then raising the educational requirements for those licenses. Those laws were challenged by current and prospective practitioners on the grounds that they abridged contractual obligations and property rights of citizens. But the U.S. Supreme Court, beginning in *Dent v. West Virginia,* 129 U.S. 114 (1889), upheld the state's licensing statutes insofar as the occupation's expertise was difficult and valid and exercised a function related to the public good.

By the end of the nineteenth century, this long historical process of successively preeminent ministers, lawyers, and professors had prepared the ground for the idealization of "profession." The term denoted a dignified vocation practiced by "professionals" who offered selfless and contractual service, membership in a strong association, and education in functional expertise modeled on the natural sciences. This conception then became hypostasized as leading professionals, such as ABA president Dillon, announced the "true professional ideal." Professionals, such as the lawyer James C. Carter Jr., advocated making "a nearer approach to the ideal" (1890). The editor and educator Albert E. Winship maintained that workers "cannot vote themselves a profession. . . . It must come from an indefinable sentiment generally recognized, born of idealizing an occupation" (1892). Successive presidents of the Carnegie Foundation for the Advancement of Teaching, which sponsored the 1910 report by the educational reformer Abraham Flexner on medical education, as well as notable studies of other professions, commended "the dominant ideal . . . of regard for the honor of the profession."

ASCENDANCE OF MEDICINE AND THE PROFESSIONAL IDEAL

It was telling that the expertise at issue in *Dent v. West Virginia*—and that came to serve as the courts' standard in subsequent cases—was medicine, which thereby established the constitutional standard for occupational licensing between 1890 and 1930. The characteristics of the professional ideal fit medicine remarkably well; and the ascendance of the announced ideal during the first half of the twentieth century cannot be understood apart from the contemporaneous elevation of medicine to "queen of the professions" (Hughes, 1963, p. 1), just as the clergy had reigned three centuries earlier.

The ascent of medicine was surprising in light of its history. Given doctors' attendance on unmentionable bodily functions and their long-standing disagreements about therapies, which, in any case, were ineffective, medicine had long lagged behind the other liberal professions—scarcely preferable to teaching and far less attractive than law or theology. Once medical licensing and education were aligned with the standard of functional science, medicine fit remarkably well into the professional ideal, whose characteristics derived from the vocations of theology, law, and education in American culture. This fit tightened further after the appearance in 1910 of Flexner's *Medical Education in the United States and Canada*. The Flexner Report provided the stimulus,

the blueprint, the confirmation, or the legitimization (depending on the scholarly interpretation) for raising admission standards to medical schools and the further elevation of the profession. The raising of standards in medical science, medical education, the medical profession, and medical ethics and their intimate association is conveyed in the introduction to the Flexner Report, written by Henry S. Pritchett, the first president of the Carnegie Foundation for the Advancement of Teaching (1905–1930).

In 1925 the first public opinion survey of vocational status indicated that physicians had passed lawyers and clergy, although not professors, in public esteem. Within a decade, another survey of "representative citizens" of small towns and cities reported that physicians ranked first "in the *order of your admiration*" for twenty-five occupations (Hartmann, "The Prestige of Occupations," 1934), and this status was confirmed in surveys during the 1940s and 1950s. As with other preeminent professions in the past, the personal income and public expenditures in the field rose dramatically, eclipsing that of other professions.

Thousands of articles and books appeared on the topic of professions in the course of the twentieth century. In 1970 Wilbur E. Moore and Gerald W. Rosenbloom published *The Professions*, a fifty-six-page bibliography of sources "selected" from "a truly tremendous literature" on the topic. While the literature mounted, many scholars tried unsuccessfully to systematize these writings and arrive at a definition of a profession, an effort that has been periodically declared both fruitless and wrongheaded. Yet even those who announced in one decade that there was no agreed-upon criteria of a profession could be found in the following decade seeking such criteria. Overall, it is difficult to generalize about this contradictory mass of twentieth-century writings beyond the assessment of Eliot Freidson, a leading scholar, "that scholarship concerned with the professions is in an intellectual shambles" ("Are Professions Necessary?" 1984, p. 5).

Nevertheless, some basic distinctions may be made. Most of the literature written during or before the 1950s praised professionals and encouraged their commitment to professionalism. To be sure, cynicism and caustic criticism about professions were expressed, as had happened during the Jacksonian Period. In 1906 George Bernard Shaw penned the line "All professions are conspiracies against the laity" in his play *The Doctor's Dilemma*. But the dominant viewpoint was laudatory, even among acerbic social critics, such as Thorstein Veblen. In 1915 Flexner maintained in "Is Social Work

INTRODUCTION TO THE FLEXNER REPORT

In 1910 the educational reformer Abraham Flexner prepared a report for the Carnegie Foundation for the Advancement of Teaching, titled *Medical Education in the United States and Canada.* Henry S. Pritchett, an astronomer, former president of the Massachusetts Institute of Technology, and president of the foundation, wrote the following in his introduction to the Flexner report:

The significant facts revealed by this study are these:

(1) For twenty-five years past there has been an enormous over-production of uneducated and ill trained medical practitioners. This has been in absolute disregard of the public welfare and without any serious thought of the interests of the public. . . .

(2) Over-production of ill trained men is due in the main to the existence of a very large number of commercial schools, sustained in many cases by advertising methods through which a mass of unprepared youth is drawn out of industrial occupations into the study of medicine.

(3) Until recently the conduct of a medical school was a profitable business, for the methods of instruction were mainly didactic. As the need for laboratories has become more keenly felt, the expenses of an efficient medical school have been greatly increased. . . . Colleges and universities have in large measure failed in the past twenty-five years to appreciate the great advance in medical education and the increased cost of teaching it along modern lines. Many universities desirous of apparent educational completeness have annexed medical schools without making themselves responsible either for the standards of the professional schools or for their support.

(4) The existence of many of these unnecessary and inadequate medical schools has been defended by the argument that a poor medical school is justified in the interest of the poor boy . . . ; but the facts set forth in this report make it evident that this argument is insincere, and that the excuse which has hitherto been put forward in the name of the poor boy is in reality an argument on behalf of the poor medical school.

(5) A hospital under complete educational control is as necessary to a medical school as is a laboratory of chemistry or pathology. . . .

In view of these facts, progress for the future would seem to require a very much smaller number of medical schools, better equipped and better conducted than our schools now as a rule are; and the needs of the public would equally require that we have fewer physicians graduated each year, but that these should be better educated and better trained. . . .

The development which is here suggested for medical education is conditioned largely upon . . . an educational patriotism on the part of the institutions of learning and a medical patriotism on the part of physicians.

By educational patriotism, I mean this: a university has a mission greater than formation of a large student body or the attainment of institutional completeness, namely, the duty of loyalty to the standards of common honesty, of intellectual sincerity, of scientific accuracy. A university with educational patriotism will not take up the work of medical education unless it can discharge its duty by it; or if, in the days of ignorance once winked at, a university became entangled in a medical school alliance, it will frankly and courageously deal with a situation which is no longer tenable. It will either demand of its medical school university ideals and give it university support, or else it will drop the effort to do what it can only do badly.

By professional patriotism amongst medical men I mean that sort of regard for the honor of the profession and that sense of responsibility for its efficiency which enable a member of that profession to rise above the consideration of personal or of

CONTINUED NEXT PAGE

professional gain. . . . Perhaps in no other of the great professions does one find greater discrepancies between the ideals of those who represent it. No members of the social order are more self-sacrificing than the true physicians and surgeons, and of this fine group none deserve so much of society as those who have taken upon their shoulders the burden of medical education. On the other hand, the profession has been diluted by the presence of a great number of men who have come from weak schools with low ideals both of education and of professional honor. If the medical education of our country is in the immediate future to go upon a plane of efficiency and of credit, those who represent the higher ideals of the medical profession must make a stand for that form of medical education which is calculated to advance the true interests of the whole people and to better the ideals of medicine itself.

a Profession?" that "what matters most is professional spirit" (1915, p. 903–904). In 1931 the first Minnesota Occupational Scale ranked "professional" at the top of seven groups of occupations. In 1935 the political scientist Harold J. Laski observed in the essay "The Decline of the Professions" that "it is impossible to draw up an indictment against a profession." In 1954 Henry T. Heald, chancellor of New York University, affirmed that "prosperity and . . . happiness can both be attributed—insofar as we attain them—to the professions: to their growth, to their ever-increasing assumption of responsibility in providing for the needs and wants of the people" (pp. 1–2).

This idealization of—and idealism about—the professions was accompanied by a theoretical framework explaining and legitimating the professions based upon their functional expertise. The full complexity and many variations of the theory cannot adequately be stated here. In a word, this functionalist analysis held that specialized scientific knowledge that serves a social function and is usually produced in a university constitutes the legitimating foundation of a profession. Many scholars contributed to articulating this functionalism, but the leading proponent was the sociologist Talcott Parsons.

In 1939 Parsons published an important essay, "The Professions and Social Structure," which, after several reprintings and revisions, led to his authoritative article on professions in 1968, by which point the functionalist view was on the wane. Parsons took for granted that "cognitive rationality" was invested in "the intellectual disciplines—the humanities, and the sciences natural and social." These disciplines were institutionalized in "the university-academy complex" that provided the basis, first and foremost, for "the profession of learning itself," second, for "the 'applied' branch of the professions

. . . its historic focuses . . . represented by the two fields of law and medicine." In fact, "professionalization" was "a process which in one aspect is almost synonymous with that of rationalization" (pp. 536–537, 544).

The functionalist analysis was generally accompanied by the affirmation that professions were relatively high-minded and selfless. The attribution of the long-standing service ethic to professions thus persevered through the first half of the twentieth century. In 1933 the supreme court of Washington State gave legal standing to the ethic of selfless service by upholding the exemption of "professions" from an excise tax on business activities on the grounds that: "A profession is not a money getting business. It has no element of commercialism in it. True, the professional man seeks to live by what he earns, but his main purpose and desire is to be of service to those who seek his aid and to the community of which he is a necessary part" (*State ex rel. Stiner v. Yelle* 174 Washington 402, 411).

The declaration and advance of the professional ideal between the late nineteenth century and mid–twentieth century were thus accompanied by the ascendance of medicine. Commensurately, there was a remarkable proliferation of vocations seeking to emulate the major professions, especially physicians, and thereby to acquire the dignified title. This endeavor was also pursued by women, who were virtually excluded from the major professions and entered primarily the four so-called "minor professions" of schoolteaching, social work, nursing, and journalism.

POST-1950 SHIFT

Even as Talcott Parsons was refining his analysis, scholars and outside observers began to voice criticism of professions and professionals, whose numbers were nevertheless growing dramatically. In the frequently cited article "Toward a Definition of Profession" (1953), Morris L. Cogan noted that a minor, but vocal chorus of complaint could be heard, and Myron Lieberman echoed that point in his popular textbook *Education as a Profession* (1956). Typical of this transitional period was the approach of Milton Friedman and Simon Kuznets in *Income from Independent Professional Practice* (1945) and Howard Becker in "The Nature of a Profession" (1962), each of whom noted the possibility of a cynical interpretation of professions but who, respectively, doubted "that the symbol of the profession is used simply as a device by which the self-interest of the work group can be furthered" (p. 137) and wished to avoid being "accused of cynicism or muckraking" (pp. 39–40). Scholars and observers became less deferential as time passed, and by the 1980s the professions, individually and collectively, were under vehement attack by scholars, a development that attracted the widespread attention of the popular press by the 1990s.

Commensurately, medicine became the target of widespread criticism in the decades after the 1950s. By 1980 the increasing number of malpractice suits and third-party payers undermined the cultural authority and financial standing of the profession, which became "proletarianized" as more physicians entered large health companies than private practice. The number of medical school applicants began to fall while the number of medical schools continued to rise, leading to a decline, some said, in the quality of medical graduates. By the 1990s the popular press from the *Boston Globe* (18 March 1990) to the *San Francisco Chronicle* (31 December 1987) was asking, "What's ailing doctors?"

As the normative judgment of the professional ideal, and the leading profession of medicine, shifted more and more after the 1950s and Parsons's benign judgment was supplanted by skepticism and disfavor, a different theoretical framework was introduced to explain and evaluate the professions. This new analysis was inaugurated by Everett C. Hughes, who began offering courses and seminars on the sociology of professions at the University of Chicago in the late 1940s. As Hughes later described it in *The Professions in America* (1965), these courses "invariably attract many people from outside sociology. As often as not, they want to write a paper to prove that some occupation—their own—has become or is on the verge of becoming a true profession. The course gives them a set of criteria for their demonstration. Librarians, insurance sales-

men, nurses, public relations people, YMCA secretaries, probation officers, personnel men, guidance directors, city managers, hospital administrators, and even public health physicians have been among them" (p. 4).

In response to this adulatory enthusiasm, Hughes founded a study group at Chicago during the 1950s that developed a critical view of professions, particularly medicine, to the point of expressing resentment at its prestige and authority and suspicion of its knowledge. This critical, sociological analysis of professions unfolded during the 1960s and was given prominent expression in 1970 in the award-winning book *Profession of Medicine* by Eliot Freidson, who wrote:

> I assume that the analytical variables of social organization are more useful discriminants than those of norms, attitudes, or ethics and that, in fact, the former has a closer relationship to behavior than the latter.... Medicine, then, in this sociological usage, is an organized consulting occupation which may serve as the discoverer, carrier, and practitioner of certain kinds of knowledge, but which is not a body of knowledge as such. (pp. 4–5)

In contrast to the functionalist thesis that cognitive rationality naturally and necessarily legitimates professional authority over a social function, Freidson averred, "Obviously, an occupation does not 'naturally' come by so unusual a condition as professional autonomy.... A profession attains and maintains its position by virtue of the protection and patronage of some elite segment of society.... Its position is thus secured by the political and economic influence of the elite which sponsors it" (pp. 72–73).

As the critical, post-1950s analysis was developed in prominent works by Magali Sarfatti Larson (1977) and Andrew D. Abbott (1988), among others, it became no less complex and even more variegated than its predecessor, and has been called "a radically sociological view," a "power analysis," a "dominance model," "the alternative 'capitalist' model," "a constructivist view," and a "structuralist theory." The central emphasis of the new analysis is on the organizational structure of professional associations and the socioeconomic structures that sustain the associations.

In its extreme versions, this analysis challenges the claims of professionals that they possess objective expertise and regards professions as self-conscious monopolies seeking to establish control of a market in order to maximize their authority, income, and prestige. The challenge to functional expertise and, hence, to the legitimacy of professional authority is intimately linked with charges that the ethic of service was invented to disguise the self-interest of professionals and thereby deflect criticism of their authority and prestige. For example, Sydney A. Halpern's *American Pediatrics* (1988) adopts this analysis of medical pediatrics and is said to conclude that the specialty "developed deliberately and consciously as the best way to enhance the careers, social status, and income of doctors. . . . The suggestion that specialization has been caused in part by the tremendous increase in scientific knowledge is given very little attention" (John P. Hubbell, *New England Journal of Medicine* 320 [1989]: 1358).

Overall, twentieth-century scholarship about the professions and the professional ideal reveals two marked shifts that began in the 1950s: a normative shift from approbation to criticism and a theoretical shift from a functionalist to a structuralist analysis. These simple sketches of functionalism and structuralism do not do justice to the subtleties of scholars' individual analyses. But it is important to gain a sense of the large picture. The conceptual distinction between the pre-1950s and post-1950s views turns on whether functional expertise or organizational and social structure are regarded as the taproot of professional authority, status, and remuneration.

This conceptual distinction is not the only way to explain the normative and theoretical shifts, however. Bruce A. Kimball's analysis, *The "True Professional Ideal" in America* (1992), has attributed both shifts to a third shift: the change in social status of the professoriate over the course of the twentieth century. Studies of the social status of occupations before World War II indicate that college and university professors were highly regarded. By 1950 it was evident that professors had begun to decline as a cultural elite. As C. Wright Mills observes in his book *White Collar*:

> The increase in enrollment and the consequent mass production methods of instruction have made the position of college professor less distinctive than it once was. . . . The type of man who is recruited for college teaching and shaped for this end by graduate school training is very likely to have a strong plebeian strain. . . . The Arts and Sciences graduate schools, as the president of Harvard has indicated, do not receive "their fair share of the best brains and well-developed, forceful personalities." Law and medical schools have done much better. (pp. 129–130)

The boom in higher education between about 1955 and 1970 stemmed the decline in prosperity and esteem of professors, but subsequent decades witnessed increasing disenchantment with and criticism of the professoriat. The relative status of the academic profession thus changed markedly and concurrently with the normative and theoretical shifts in scholarship analyzing the professions. In fact, these changes were not only correlated but may be profoundly related. The functionalist view legitimating the professions during the first half of the twentieth century was, in effect, crediting the academy—the source of functional expertise—with professionals' achievements. During and after the 1950s, as M.D.s and J.D.s more and more outstripped Ph.D.s in social and economic status and cultural authority, scholarly resentment toward professions arose, and the structuralist analysis was developed to justify that new attitude.

This, at least, is a plausible explanation for why the theoretical shift is correlated both with the normative shift and with professors' decline in social and economic status in the decades after 1950. To be sure, this correlation does not prove that the change in status caused the other two shifts. But it does offer a plausible explanation, just as both functionalism and structuralism plausibly explain the idealization of—and idealism about—the professional.

Whatever interpretation ultimately prevails, it will have to explain the ascendance of the professional ideal early in the twentieth century, its peaking during the 1950s, and its subsequent decline in the United States. Such an interpretation will also have to account for the gradual appearance of the fundamental characteristics of the professional ideal—expertise, association, service—as they emerged from the beginning of the seventeenth century through the long historical succession of ministers, lawyers, professors, and physicians.

See also **Education; Law and the American Mind; Medicine; The Role of the Intellectual; Elite vs. Popular Cultures; The American University; Learned Societies and Professional Associations** (*volume 3*).

BIBLIOGRAPHY

Abbott, Andrew D. *The System of Professions: An Essay on the Division of Expert Labor.* Chicago, 1988.

Becker, Howard S. "The Nature of a Profession." In *Education for the Professions.* Edited by Nelson B. Henry. Chicago, 1962.

Bledstein, Burton J. *The Culture of Professionalism: The Middle Class and the Development of Higher Education in America.* New York, 1976.

Brackenridge, Hugh Henry, ed. *The United States Magazine: A Repository of History, Politics, and Literature* 1 (1779): 312–313.

Carter, James C., Jr. "The Ideal and the Actual in the Law." *Reports and Transactions of the American Bar Association* (1890): 1–10.

Cogan, Morris L. "Toward a Definition of Profession." *Harvard Educational Review* 23 (1953): 33–50.

Counts, George S. "The Social Status of Occupations: A Problem in Vocational Guidance." *School Review* 33 (1925): 16–27.

Dillon, John F. "The True Professional Ideal." *Reports and Transactions of the American Bar Association* (1894): 409–422.

Flexner, Abraham. *Medical Education in the United States and Canada.* New York, 1910.

———. "Is Social Work a Profession?" *School and Society* 1 (1915): 900–912.

Freidson, Eliot. *Profession of Medicine: A Study of the Sociology of Applied Knowledge.* New York, 1970.

———. "Are Professions Necessary?" In *The Authority of Experts: Studies in History and Theory.* Edited by Thomas L. Haskell. Bloomington, Ind., 1984.

Friedman, Milton, and Simon Kuznets. *Income from Independent Professional Practice.* New York, 1945.

Gusfield, Joseph. "American Professors: The Decline of a Cultural Elite." *School Review* 83 (1975): 595–616.

Haber, Samuel. *The Quest for Honor and Authority in the American Professions, 1750–1900.* Chicago, 1991.

Halpern, Sydney A. *American Pediatrics: The Social Dynamics of Professionalism, 1880–1980.* Berkeley, Calif., 1988.

Hartmann, George W. "The Prestige of Occupations: A Comparison of Educational Occupations and Others." *Personnel Journal* 13 (1934): 144–152.

Heald, Henry T. *The Responsibility of the Professions to Future Society.* New York, 1954.

Hughes, Everett C. "Professions." In *The Professions in America.* Edited by Kenneth S. Lynn and the editors of *Daedalus.* Boston, 1965. Pp. 1–14.

Kimball, Bruce A. *The "True Professional Ideal" in America: A History.* Cambridge, Mass., 1992.

Larson, Magali Sarfatti. *The Rise of Professionalism: A Sociological Analysis.* Berkeley, Calif., 1977.

Laski, Harold J. "The Decline of the Professions." *Harper's* 171 (November 1935): 676–685.

Lieberman, Myron. *Education as a Profession.* Englewood Cliffs, N.J., 1956.

Metzger, Walter P. "A Spectre Is Haunting American Scholars: The Spectre of 'Professionism.'" *Educational Researcher* (August–September 1987): 10–19.

Mills, C. Wright. *White Collar: The American Middle Classes.* New York, 1951.

Moore, Wilbert E. *The Professions: Roles and Rules.* New York, 1970.

Parsons, Talcott. "The Professions and Social Structure." *Social Forces* 17 (1939): 457–467.

———. "Professions." In *International Encyclopedia of the Social Sciences.* Vol. 12. New York, 1968.

Starr, Paul. *The Social Transformation of American Medicine.* New York, 1982.

Suzzallo, Henry. "The Reorganization of the Teaching Profession." *Addresses and Journal of Proceedings of the National Education Association* (1913): 362–379.

Veblen, Thorstein. *The Higher Learning in America: A Memorandum on the Conduct of Universities by Business Men.* New York, 1918.

Winship, Albert E. *Is There a Science of Pedagogy?* Boston, 1892.

THE IDEAL OF SPONTANEITY

Daniel Belgrad

The spontaneous gesture, understood as an act of freedom originating in the unconscious, defined an important countercultural impulse in the 1940s and 1950s in art, music, and literature. The ideal of spontaneity was expressed in abstract expressionist gesture painting and collage, in Projective verse and Beat poetry, in bebop jazz, Gestalt therapy, and happenings. Fusing ideas from surrealism, Jungian and Gestalt psychology, Taoism and Zen Buddhism, existentialism, and Alfred North Whitehead's "process philosophy," the postwar aesthetic of spontaneity emphasized two principles that otherwise had little currency in wartime and cold war American society: the principles of intersubjectivity and body-mind holism. (Intersubjectivity is the metaphysical proposition that reality is not already there, outside of us, but emerges through our interactions. Body-mind holism rejects the notion that the intellect is of different stuff—higher, better, or more spiritual—than the body.) These two principles challenged the traditional humanistic paradigm that defined the human being as a thinking mind in an objective universe; instead, the human body-mind was conceived of as one with nature, constituted through a ceaseless, unconscious interplay between self and environment. The social implications of these principles were far-reaching, suggesting a cultural revolution dedicated to recovering emotional "authenticity" and environmental awareness. In this way, the postwar culture of spontaneity became the intellectual heritage of the 1960s counterculture.

DISAFFECTION WITH CORPORATE LIBERALISM

The ideal of spontaneous improvisation, which had been valorized previously in the Romantic movement of the nineteenth century and in early-twentieth-century modernism, was revitalized in the United States by the outbreak of World War II,

due to psychological and social pressures experienced by American artists and intellectuals in relation to the war. These included a horror of Nazism, a disillusionment with Stalinist Communism, and disgust with a corporate-bureaucratic-advertising culture in the United States itself.

Nazism's war machine, its psychological manipulation of the masses through new media technologies, and its welding of forward-looking social engineering to racist myth raised doubts among thinking people the world over about the vaunted "progress" of Western civilization. The Great War, now renamed the First World War, began to appear not as a singular rite of passage into modernity but as the first of a series of violent convulsions endemic to the modern order. Doubts about the psychological balance of "modern man" triggered artists' efforts to recover, through spontaneity, unconscious possibilities that might offer an alternative to the apparent cultural cul-de-sac of scientific progressivism.

In America in the 1930s many idealistic and socially minded artists and writers had embraced Karl Marx's "scientific socialism" in response to the Great Depression. Yet, as Stalinism triumphed in the Soviet Union, the artistic freedom of these leftists was compromised by directives from the Communist International defining socialist propaganda as the only legitimate form of art. Restive under this tightening regimen and disillusioned by the Hitler-Stalin pact, several abstract painters abandoned the influential, leftist American Artists Congress in 1940, and turned to experiments with surrealist automatism in search of a new mode of socially relevant art.

The ideal of spontaneity connoted a rejection not only of Nazism and communism but also of the corporate liberal ideology that had come to occupy the American political center. When World War II began, the power balance within President Franklin Roosevelt's New Deal administration shifted away from democratic leftism and social experiment toward the hierarchical authority structures and "information management" strategies of corporate capitalism. The corporate liberal culture fostered by the war emphasized managerial bureaucracies, conformity to standards and regulations, and the "psychological warfare" of advertising campaigns. American artists and writers who rejected this cultural package found recourse in an ideal of spontaneity that espoused the values of democratic small-group dynamics, unpremeditated action, and "authentic" interpersonal communication.

SURREALISM AND JUNGIAN PSYCHOLOGY

As poets and painters who were disaffected with communism and corporate liberalism turned from topical political commitments to deep questions about the limitations of Western metaphysics, they turned to surrealism and Jungian psychology for the basis of a new aesthetic rooted in spontaneity. Painters like Adolph Gottlieb, Robert Motherwell, Jackson Pollock, William Baziotes, Willem de Kooning, Gerome Kamrowski, Mark Rothko, Arshile Gorky, and Peter Busa, and poets like Charles Olson and Robert Creeley, turned to "psychic automatism" as a technique for transcribing the contents of their unconscious minds, in hopes of creating new cultural forms that would articulate the "collective unconscious" of their society.

The surrealist movement, which had developed in Europe in the early 1920s under the leadership of the French poet André Breton, espoused automatism (akin to the "free association" invoked by Freudian psychoanalysis) as the key to cultural revolution through art. Influential surrealists in New York City and Mexico City encouraged automatist experiments among American artists; most important among them were John Graham, Matta Echaurren, and Wolfgang Paalen. The resulting art aimed to challenge the viewer's awareness by offering not a depiction of accepted reality but what Paalen called a "prefigurative image": a cryptic artifact of the artist's psychological quest, alluding to an alternative construction of reality (Dyn, 1, p. 9).

The analytical psychology of Carl Jung, influential in American art circles from the mid-1930s through the 1940s, also championed an art based on symbols emerging spontaneously from the unconscious. Jung, departing from orthodox Freudianism, defined such symbols as representations of a social "collective unconscious," revealing the antidote to modernity's spiritual malaise. The abstract expressionist style of painting originated in the

automatic painting of such "archetypal," "mythic" images in an "anti-illusionist" cubist plane, exemplified by works such as Adolph Gottlieb's *Eyes of Oedipus* (1941), Mark Rothko's *The Omen of the Eagle* (1942), and Jackson Pollock's *The She-Wolf* (1943).

AMERICAN INDIAN ART

Prompted by Jungian psychology, early abstract expressionist painters as well as poets like Charles Olson looked to the symbols and myths of "archaic" cultures for an alternative system of values. They believed that these cultures preserved important practices and attitudes that the West had lost, particularly in their ways of integrating the life of the unconscious into public decision-making processes, and in their sense of the moral relations of humans toward the natural environment. Self-consciously American in their sense of the need for a break with European tradition, the emerging avant-garde took particular interest in the possibility of adapting cultural materials from Native American sources.

Avant-garde interest in American Indian cultures was guided by the Jungian concept of "participation mystique," which Jung had adopted from the French anthropologist Lucien Lévy-Bruhl. Participation mystique referred to a mental attitude that did not place humanity outside and above nature, but within it, and therefore always engaging it intersubjectively. In *Dyn* magazine, which Robert Motherwell helped him to publish in Mexico City, Wolfgang Paalen praised the totem poles of the Haida tribe of America's northwest coast as representative of a worldview different from the rational ideal of Western science, with its "pretended Zero-point of observation . . . like a chaste sword tip inserted between perception and interpretation." American Indian art in general, he felt, embodied participation mystique as a usable principle for modern culture: "not distinguishing clearly between the subjective and the objective, [it] identifies itself emotionally with its environing world" (1, p. 48, and 4, p. 18).

Among American painters who worked within this nexus of automatism, Jungian psychology, and American Indian art during the war years were Richard Pousette-Dart, Adolph Gottlieb, and Jackson Pollock. Gottlieb's "Pictograph" series and Pollock's celebrated practice of laying his canvas on the floor while painting both derived from Native American arts showcased at the Museum of Modern Art's "Indian Art of the United States" exhibit of 1941. The "Indian Space" painters, associated with Kenneth Beaudoin's *Iconograph* magazine in 1946, also worked in this vein. Charles Olson explored the same terrain through poetry with his "The Kingfishers" of 1949, a meditation on the possibility of reviving the values of Amerindian cultures long since destroyed by European conquest.

PROJECTIVE VERSE

Olson's "The Kingfishers" is an early example of the "open" or dialogical poetry form that he would theorize in his seminal "Projective Verse" essay of 1950. In 1951 Olson became rector of Black Mountain College in North Carolina, a place that was in the late 1940s and early 1950s a focal point for spontaneous experiments across the arts. Olson's essay became the basis of a spontaneous poetics embraced by the "Black Mountain" poets, including Robert Creeley, Denise Levertov, and Ed Dorn, and endorsed by William Carlos Williams and the Beats.

The practice of projective verse relied on the twin notions of "syllabism" and "kinesis." The first, derived from Ernest Fenollosa and Ezra Pound, suggested that the poet's mind was unconsciously attuned to a complex of meanings historically accruing in each syllable. The second conceived of the poem as an object thrown by the poet, like a ball or a rock, in a transfer of energy to the reader-listener. It emphasized the oral quality of poetry as a breath from the poet's body. Olson's spontaneous "composition by field" charged the poet with integrating mind and body to trace the flux of energy across the unconscious mind and transmit it, so as to transform the culture at large.

IDEOGRAMS

In the mid-1940s the avant-garde's project to recover participation mystique gravitated toward experiments with the communicative potential of the glyph or ideogram, a kind of "scripture-writing" that hovers between figurative and abstract representation. Picture-symbols define a stage of abstract expressionist painting that includes such works as Jackson Pollock's *Guardians of the Secret* (1943), Willem de Kooning's *Orestes* (1947), Lee Krasner's *Composition* (1949), and even Ben Shahn's *A Glyph for Charles* [Olson] (1951). The editors of *Tiger's Eye* magazine reproduced some of these works in juxtaposition with images of textiles and petroglyphs from the Andean Indians of Peru.

Ideograms were meant to articulate ideas emerging from the artist's unconscious physical and emotional perceptions and inexpressible in either words or conventional imagery. In 1947 the abstract expressionist painter Barnett Newman coordinated an exhibition of "The Ideographic Picture" at the Betty Parsons Gallery in New York and wrote that the participating artists "evoke their world of emotion . . . without the props of any known shape. This is a metaphysical act" (Johnson, *American Artists on Art*, p. 19). Charles Olson believed that the sensory appeal of such picture-writing, epitomized for him in the glyphs of the Maya Indians of Central America, preserved the ideal psychological balance between the concrete and the abstract (*Selected Writings*, p. 113). In *Dyn* magazine, Robert Motherwell modified the surrealists' call for an art of "pure psychic automatism" to call for "plastic automatism": a spontaneous method that recognized the sensory medium of painting as an indispensable tool of thought (*Dyn* 6, p. 13).

EXISTENTIALISM AND EINSTEIN

The avant-garde's ideographic experiments shared much with existentialist philosophy's celebration of subjective experience over fixed concepts. ("Existence precedes essence," asserts an existentialist slogan.) When French existentialism reached New York soon after the Allied liberation of Paris, it quickly gained influence in the artistic and intellectual community. Willem de Kooning's paintings from the late 1940s onward, as well as the words he used to describe them, notably make use of an existentialist approach or vocabulary. This vocabulary also defined the writer-philosopher Harold Rosenberg's influential description of abstract expressionist gesture painting as "action painting." Yet, in important ways, the American ideal of spontaneity diverged from existentialism and was aligned instead with the pragmatism of John Dewey and the "process philosophy" of Alfred North Whitehead.

The existentialism of Jean-Paul Sartre and Hannah Arendt, who described its precepts in the influential *Partisan Review,* emphasized the angst of each mind's "I," trapped in an intrinsically absurd social and physical world and compelled to make something meaningful of this. In this context, dramatic unconventional action was valorized as an assertion of freedom and authenticity. However, Charles Olson's projective verse, Robert Motherwell's plastic automatism, and Jackson Pollock's gesture-field painting emphasized not the plight of the alienated consciousness, but the continuity of conscious and unconscious thought processes and the unity of the physical, emotional, and intellectual worlds.

Gesture-field painting, first developed by Jackson Pollock in the winter of 1946–1947, took plastic automatism beyond the symbolism of ideographic painting into the purely gestural brushstroke. The skeins of "drips" or gestural strokes that define Pollock's mature style present the interaction of body, unconscious, and conscious mind, and paint in a "physiological automatism" incorporating a new awareness of the body. Dewey and Whitehead had asserted that the body, as the site of cognition, links the individual to the outside world at once physically and psychologically. Thus Motherwell, who studied philosophy at Harvard, wrote that art must express the "feeling" of the unified body-mind in engagement with a plastic environment ("Beyond the Aesthetic," in O'Hara, *Robert Motherwell*, p. 37). This principle is embodied in the gesture-field paintings of, among many, Pollock, Jack Tworkov, James Brooks, and Helen Frankenthaler; in the collages of Motherwell and Lee Krasner; and in the poetic collage of Olson's magnum opus, *The Maximus Poems* (published between 1953 and 1956).

Alfred North Whitehead's "process philosophy," summarized in his book *Adventures of Ideas* (1933), explored the metaphysical implications of Einsteinian physics. Whereas Newtonian physics, relying on Euclidean geometry, had posited a universe of discrete particles interacting only occasionally, Whitehead suggested a geometry based on overlapping volumes in constant flux. From this perspective, every point is a palimpsest, showing traces of prior events, and every piece of matter is a patterned "event" in a field of energy. Every human, Whitehead wrote, is a "society" of "occasions," a stable yet malleable (that is, "plastic") pattern of energy. Breaking down the distinctions between objects and actions and between identity and society, this vision placed emphasis on the plastic dialogue through which every body-mind defines itself and develops in relation to its surroundings. The palimpsests of postwar gesture-field painting and collage were artistic expressions of this plastic dialogue, exemplified by Pollock's *Sounds in the Grass: Shimmering Substance* (1946) and Motherwell's *Yellow Envelope* (1956). Olson's "The Ridge," written on Pearl Harbor Day 1954, describes American society itself as a plastic medium with which the socially conscious artist grappled (*Maximus Poems*, pp. 184–185).

GESTALT THERAPY

The Gestalt therapy of Paul Goodman and Fritz Perls developed this "field" theory into a psychological model that became the basis of "encounter group" therapy and the human potential movement. Goodman, who taught for a summer at Black Mountain College, was a conscientious objector during World War II. He described corporate-liberal America as founded on the "introjection" of authority: a neurotic mandate to "swallow things whole" rather than engage one's reality with a healthy level of aggression. As a result, he believed, the aggression was turned inward, and the mind's "I" became an internalized deputy of the social authority, bullying and manipulating the hapless organism; "self-control" was pitted against the organic needs of the individual, leaving one's identity self-consciously split against itself. The solution, he wrote, in a Gestalt revision of the Viennese psychologist Wilhelm Reich's earlier call for "sexual revolution," was spontaneity, defined as a flexible, emotional engagement with one's immediate surroundings or "social-animal-physical field."

According to Goodman, conscious "concentration" and spontaneous awareness were distinguished by the quality of attention associated with each. In the first, attention was deliberate: a kind of fixed determination that dissipated one's energy through the effort of self-mastery. Such discipline, he wrote, was trained so deeply into the minds and bodies of contemporary Americans that to relinquish it would be difficult; their psychological lives were composed of "thousands and thousands of struggling motions so minute . . . but we see them in the delicate tendons taut and in the pitiful eyes. . . . It is hard to do the easy thing . . . as an artist draws the easiest line" (*Possibilities* 1, p. 7). The more a person learned to rely on spontaneous awareness, however, the more of this energy would be released for active engagement with one's surroundings. The result would be a synergy indicating personal and social health, rooted in feelings and inspiring actions that the introjected intellect would otherwise disallow. Spontaneity could thus be both personally therapeutic and, in the context of corporate liberalism, socially revolutionary.

ZEN BUDDHISM

An important source for Goodman's Gestalt therapy was Chinese Taoism, which was also a crucial ingredient of Japanese Zen Buddhism. In the 1950s Zen grew in popularity on both the East and West coasts, largely due to the lectures and writings of Alan Watts, Aldous Huxley, and D. T. Suzuki. Like field theory, Zen insisted on the illusory nature

AN INTERVIEW WITH TOSHIKO TAKAEZU CONDUCTED BY DANIEL BELGRAD ON 10 AUGUST 1993 AT THE ARTIST'S HOME IN QUAKERTOWN, NEW JERSEY

For many authors, artists, and musicians, spontaneity was a means to challenge the cultural power of privileged Anglo-American "insiders." The aesthetic of spontaneity questioned the course of "Western civilization" and emphasized "honesty," "awareness," and "authenticity" over the mastery of traditional forms. It therefore provided a path to cultural authority outside the established institutions of high culture and more accessible to aspirants from immigrant, working-class, and minority backgrounds. Bebop jazz was, for instance, the music of a generation of urban blacks who refused to concede the superiority of the Anglo-American symphonic tradition. The poets William Carlos Williams, Charles Olson, Allen Ginsberg, Jack Kerouac, and LeRoi Jones were all intensely aware of their ethnic identities. (Kerouac was raised speaking Québecois French, and that oral culture permeates his later novels.) Among abstract expressionist artists, the pattern is equally clear: many, like Jackson Pollock, boasted working-class origins; several grew up in ethnic enclaves, including Peter Voulkos, Theodoros Stamos, Adolph Gottlieb, Jack Tworkov, and Lee Krasner.

The abstract expressionist potter Toshiko Takaezu was born in 1922 to Japanese parents who worked in the Hawaiian sugar plantations. Japanese was her first language. She studied pottery in 1951 at the University of Hawaii, and then at the Cranbrook Academy of Art in Michigan, under the tutelage of Finnish potter Maija Grotell. There she met Bernard Leach, Shoji Hamada, and Soetsu Yanagi, and eventually developed a pottery style rooted in the Japanese Zen aesthetic.

In 1955, Takaezu traveled to Japan, both to study the art of making ceremonial tea bowls and to strengthen her sense of identity with her parents' culture of origin. With her sister, she lived for a month at a Zen temple at the Daitokuji complex in Kyoto. As she recalls, "I decided at that time that there were a few things that I really wanted to know about my heritage . . . and going to Japan was one way—not only of learning how to do pottery, [but]—being with potters you can talk to them. And all communication would be something that was part of our medium. Communication, other things would happen. That's what I was interested in."

As the decade progressed, she began to increase the scale of her pieces until they were human-sized, and to alter her thrown forms by slapping or gouging them, to emphasize the clay's plasticity. Like many others, Takaezu compares this plastic dialogue to dancing. Explaining her reasons for creating works of human scale, she observes: "You become part of it . . . when you make bigger things. . . . You can move along the piece, around it . . . and there is a kind of feeling that you dance with the piece, there's a feeling that you're in tune with the piece, with the motion of the dance, with the glaze and the brushstroke."

She has directed much attention to applying the glaze, a process that she likens to painting on the surface of the pot. In the course of her career, she gradually achieved greater looseness and spontaneity in her brushstroke, as self-conscious design was supplanted by a reliance on bodily gesture. As she explains: "I just want to flow. . . . You need that kind of freedom, of a certain type. Your whole body gets to be part of everything, and you become free." It is this interrelation

CONTINUED NEXT PAGE

that she credits for the quality of *shibui* in her work, a Zen term that she understands as "understated aliveness." As she says, "You can't force [the clay] completely . . . so you're in tune. You play. It's interrelation, interplay with the clay. But the clay has much to say on its own. You can't really control that. . . . And when you finish a piece, . . . the piece is alive."

In 1966, Takaezu returned to Hawaii with a solo exhibition at the Contemporary Art Center in Honolulu. In 1968, she began teaching at Princeton University, a bastion of American high culture; she held this post until her retirement in 1992. In 1995, she was honored with a traveling exhibition in Japan, confirming the integration of cultures that her art has achieved.

---

of fixed subject-object relations. "Buddha taught that there is no ego, either in man or in dharma [nature]," wrote the Zen master Sokei-An in his magazine, *Cat's Yawn;* "In accordance with the movement of the water, the reflection of the moon on the water assumes many shapes." Zen taught the boon of unself-conscious awareness and the primacy of action and experience over words and concepts.

Zen aesthetics valorized spontaneity, sincerity, and imperfection; works that bore witness to the process of their creation (like a ceramic bowl with glaze cracked and bubbly from the kiln) were particularly valued. In the 1950s, the confluence of Zen aesthetics and the abstract expressionist discourse revitalized the craft of pottery in America and endowed it with fine-art status. Bernard Leach, Shoji Hamada, and Soetsu Yanagi toured the United States in 1952, demonstrating the Japanese pottery aesthetic. The Americans they influenced included Peter Voulkos, Toshiko Takaezu, Warren Mackenzie, and Mary Caroline Richards. Their work emphasized the plastic dialogue between artist and clay.

The composer John Cage espoused Zen as the basis of a method that relinquished his agency as a creator. Cage's chance composition methods and the complete silence of his *4'33"* (*Four Minutes and Thirty-three Seconds,* 1952) used the cachet of art as a mere framing device to entice audiences into an aesthetic awareness of their own everyday reality. Summarizing his position for Julian Beck and Judith Malina of the Living Theatre in 1952, he wrote:

> instantaneous   and unpredictable
> nothing is accomplished by writing a piece of music
> nothing is accomplished by hearing a piece of music
> nothing is accomplished by playing a piece of music
>   our ears are now in excellent condition
>   (Cage, *Silence,* p. xii)

PERFORMANCE ART

In the 1950s the ideal of improvisational interaction led artists to explore new media that involved the whole body-mind and rewarded instantaneous responsiveness. Some painters, including Robert Rauschenberg, Allan Kaprow, and Jim Dine, expanded on the bodily motions used in gesture-field painting and collage, until their "environments" and "happenings" elided the boundary between painting and performance arts. The Beats accomplished a similar transformation of literature, with oral poetry readings that sometimes included jazz musicians.

In modern dance, Katherine Litz, José Limón, and Merce Cunningham (who developed a lifelong partnership with John Cage) broke with the storytelling technique of Martha Graham to make the body's kinetics and the dancers' interactions themselves the subjects of the dance. Cunningham used chance composition to isolate body parts and their motions, breaking down the rote combinations of movement conditioned by modern life. In this sense, his artistic project had much in common with the Gestalt therapy of Paul Goodman, who also wanted to replace physical habit with spontaneous awareness. After 1953 Cunningham's choreography relied on improvised interactions among the dancers; each expressed individuality and yet participated in the overall dance, creating an interdependence that Cage described as "polyattentiveness" (Copeland, *What Is Dance?,* p. 321).

BEBOP JAZZ

Bebop was another postwar performance art in which intersubjective improvisation played a key role. Bebop jazz musicians like Charlie Parker, Max Roach, and Miles Davis turned away from the "big band" jazz of the 1930s in order to develop a new style rooted in conversational prosody. Prosody in this sense refers to what a spoken statement contains in addition to word-symbols: its tempo and tone quality, for instance, which contribute much to the meaning of utterances in a face-to-face dialogue.

Before bebop, big band swing music had assimilated jazz to the European orchestral form. It emphasized working in unison to create a pleasing blend of sound, and band leaders ran their organizations like small corporations, fining their sidemen for lateness or for infractions of dress or deportment. Bebop was by contrast an improvisational music, in which authority was passed from soloist to soloist in turn. As the improvisational musician Ann Farber explained, "Our aim is to play together with the greatest possible freedom— which, far from meaning without constraint, actually means to play together with sufficient skill and communication to be able to select proper constraints in the course of the piece. . . . No single instrumentalist or structure establishes absolute dominance. Instead, voices and structures keep weaving in and out, modifying and reshaping one another" (Rohn, p. 118).

In turning away from the Western orchestral tradition and the bureaucratic discipline associated with swing, bebop musicians reasserted what LeRoi Jones in *Blues People* called the "Africanisms" of jazz: call-and-response improvisations, polyrhythms, and prosodic tone. These elements asserted the countercultural values of intersubjectivity and body-mind holism. The improvisational interaction required each musician to be attuned to what the others were playing. Polyrhythm inscribed the intersubjective nature of time: time not as an abstract unit but as a relation between two or more internal, subjective realities. Prosodic tone, which was emphasized in the "dirty" timbre of buzzing trumpets, squeaking saxophones, and nonsense "scat" syllables, explored the border between mental ideas and physical feelings where music meets utterance, and words become pure sound.

THE BEATS

The Beats exported the ideas of the postwar avant-garde to the youth counterculture of the 1960s. The writers Jack Kerouac and Allen Ginsberg were at the core of a "beat generation" that brought together projective verse, bebop jazz prosody, gesture fields and happenings, Gestalt therapy and Buddhism, marijuana and mescaline. The term "beat" was coined to refer to their preference for the margins of American society, and for the dispossessed whose survival strategies they admired more than affluence and sophistication. Spontaneous Beat writing pursued the integration of conscious and unconscious thought, in order to bring to awareness the ideological contradictions underpinning corporate-liberal culture and normally hidden from the conscious mind. "You manifest the process of thoughts—make a model of consciousness," Ginsberg explained to Ezra Pound; "anyone with sense can always see the crazy part" (Ginsberg, *Composed on the Tongue*, p. 9).

Kerouac's novel *On the Road* (1957) was a best-selling travelogue of the Beats' bohemian lifestyle, but his *The Subterraneans* (1958) and posthumously published *Visions of Cody* (1972) are better examples of his vision of a literature founded on "spontaneous bop prosody." These works underline Kerouac's commitment to a dialogical or conversational form modeled on the structure of bebop. *Visions of Cody* is not so much a novel as a palimpsest of conversations, remembered or transcribed exactly as they transpired. "Not 'selectivity' of expression but following free deviation (association) of mind into limitless blow-on-subject seas of thought," wrote Kerouac in his manifesto, "Essentials of Spontaneous Prose" (1957) comparing his spontaneous "sketching" technique to a bebop horn solo; "Satisfy yourself first, then reader cannot fail to receive telepathic shock and meaning-excitement by same laws operating in his own human mind" (Charters, *The Portable Beat Reader,* p. 57).

Believing, like Olson, Motherwell, and Goodman, in the truth of an "energy field," the Beats used the feeling of excitement as an index of authenticity, defined as communicating close to the bone of physical-psychological need. They therefore tried, often aided by drugs, to write on the edge of consciousness, where inarticulate emotions threatened to take over and reduce their writing to the "howl" of pure prosody, as in the final line of Ginsberg's poem "Kaddish": "Lord Lord Lord caw caw caw Lord Lord Lord caw caw caw Lord" (Charters, *The Portable Beat Reader,* p. 98).

The Beats also participated in the revival of oral poetry readings sparked by the "San Francisco poetry renaissance." Like performance art, poetry readings emphasized the immediate physical presence of artists and auditors; like bebop sessions, they transformed prosody from a literary abstraction into an aural experience. Oral readings also maximized spontaneity, since moments could not be erased or revised; as events taking place in real space and time, readings shared with life itself an element of contingency that written texts lacked. The Beat lifestyle, defined by confessional conversation, sexual experiment, modern jazz, drugs, and oral poetry, extended the principles of intersubjectivity and body-mind holism from late modernist precepts into a countercultural way of life.

THE STRUGGLE FOR CULTURAL AUTHORITY

By the late 1950s the ideal of spontaneity had led to the creation of new forms across the spectrum of American arts and letters. Furthermore, it had generated a countercultural sensibility that actively challenged the values of the corporate-liberal center. Academic intellectuals and the mass media joined in deriding spontaneous artists as paradoxically alienated and conformist; impotent and mindless; juvenile delinquents and pretentious charlatans; the critic Frank Butler in "On the Beat, Nature of Beat" called them "an anti-intellectual and anti-artistic gang of sentimental dabblers and semi-criminal nihilists, devoted to destruction, motivated by pettiness, and equipped with mediocrity" (*American Scholar* 30, no. 1, 1960, p. 91); the journalist Paul O'Neil in *Life* called them "loafers, talkers, passive little con men, lonely eccentrics, mom-haters, cophaters, exhibitionists with abused smiles and second mortgages on a bongo drum—writers who cannot write, painters who cannot paint" (30 November 1959, p. 119). Such shrill invectives did not impede the growth of a youth counterculture; but the regi-

men of spontaneity often exacted its own toll in the currency of poverty, drug addiction, and psychological disintegration. In the early 1960s, notwithstanding, the ideal of spontaneity grew to political significance. The principles of intersubjectivity and body-mind holism informed diverse countercultural beliefs and practices including tribalism, nudism, environmentalism, pacifism, psychedelia, and open sexuality.

The culture of spontaneity was a common heritage of the New Left and the hippies. The 1962 "Port Huron Statement" of the Students for a Democratic Society paraphrased Paul Goodman in its call for American universities to cultivate a spontaneous quality of mind. Bob Dylan's 1965 underground classic, "Subterranean Homesick Blues," was spontaneous poetry set to rock music; the California "acid tests" were drug-induced happenings emphasizing group improvisation. At the Gathering of Tribes for the First Human Be-In in 1967, twenty thousand hippies gathered in San Francisco's Golden Gate Park to smoke marijuana, ingest LSD, protest the Vietnam War, and listen to the poets Allen Ginsberg, Michael McClure, Gary Snyder, the political activist Jerry Rubin, and the music of Jefferson Airplane, the Grateful Dead, and Janis Joplin. In his 1968 *Armies of the Night*, the American novelist Norman Mailer described the New Left's march on the Pentagon as an improvisational theater event; in the same year, the improvisational Living Theatre brought public nudity to the level of social protest with its audience-participation performance, *Paradise Now*. Thirty years earlier, artists and writers had turned away from political subjects to questions of psychology and metaphysics; in the 1960s, their heirs felt the pull of politics again, as events held forth the promise of a spontaneous cultural revolution.

See also **Anti-modern Discontent between the Wars; Radical Alternatives** *(volume 1);* **Countercultural Visions; Native Americans; Psychology, the Mind, and Personality** *(in this volume);* **The Scientific Ideal; Painting; Fiction; Poetry; Music; Dance; Myth and Symbol** *(volume 3).*

BIBLIOGRAPHY

Magazines

Black Mountain Review (1954–1957)

Dyn (1942–1944)

Iconograph (1946–1947)

It Is (1958–1960)

Possibilities (1947–1948)

Tiger's Eye (1947–1949)

Books

Allen, Donald, and Warren Tallman, eds. *Poetics of the New American Poetry.* New York, 1973.

Ashton, Dore. *The New York School: A Cultural Reckoning.* New York, 1972.

Belgrad, Daniel. *The Culture of Spontaneity: Improvisation and the Arts in Postwar America.* Chicago, 1998.

Berliner, Paul F. *Thinking in Jazz: The Infinite Art of Improvisation.* Chicago, 1994.

Cage, John. *Silence: Lectures and Writings.* Middletown, Conn., 1961.

Charters, Ann. *The Portable Beat Reader.* New York, 1992.

Cohen, Selma Jeanne, ed. *Dance as a Theatre Art: Source Readings in Dance History.* New York, 1974.

Copeland, Roger, and Marshall Cohen, eds. *What Is Dance? Readings in Theory and Criticism.* New York, 1983. Pages 307–324 are of particular relevance.

Davis, Miles. *Miles: The Autobiography.* New York, 1989.

Duberman, Martin. *Black Mountain: An Exploration in Community.* New York, 1972.

Fields, Rick. *How the Swans Came to the Lake: A Narrative History of Buddhism in America.* 3d ed. Boston, 1992.

Gibson, Ann Eden. *Issues in Abstract Expressionism: The Artist-Run Periodicals.* Ann Arbor, Mich., 1990.

Ginsberg, Allen. *Composed on the Tongue.* Bolinas, Calif., 1980.

Gitler, Ira. *Swing to Bop: An Oral History of the Transition in Jazz in the 1940s.* New York, 1985.

Guilbaut, Serge. *How New York Stole the Idea of Modern Art: Abstract Expressionism, Freedom, and the Cold War.* Translated by Arthur Goldhammer. Chicago, 1983.

Hartman, Charles O. *Jazz Text: Voice and Improvisation in Poetry, Jazz, and Song.* Princeton, N.J., 1991.

Hoover, Thomas. *Zen Culture.* London, 1988.

Johnson, Ellen H., ed. *American Artists on Art, from 1940 to 1980.* New York, 1982.

Jones, LeRoi. *Blues People: Negro Music in White America.* New York, 1963.

King, Richard. *The Party of Eros: Radical Social Thought and the Realm of Freedom.* Chapel Hill, N.C., 1972.

Kirby, Michael, ed. *Happenings: An Illustrated Anthology.* New York, 1965.

McClure, Michael. *Scratching the Beat Surface.* San Francisco, 1982.

Motherwell, Robert. *The Collected Writings of Robert Motherwell.* Edited by Stephanie Terenzio. New York, 1992.

O'Hara, Frank. *Robert Motherwell.* New York, 1965.

Olson, Charles. *Maximus Poems.* Edited by George F. Butterick. Berkley, Calif., 1983.

———. *Selected Writings.* Edited by Robert Creeley. New York, 1965.

Ong, Walter. *Orality and Literacy: The Technologizing of the Word.* New York, 1982.

Perls, Frederick, Ralph F. Hefferline, and Paul Goodman. *Gestalt Therapy: Excitement and Growth in the Human Personality.* New York, 1951.

Richards, Mary Caroline. *Centering in Pottery, Poetry, and the Person.* Middletown, Conn., 1964.

Rohn, Matthew L. *Visual Dynamics in Jackson Pollock's Abstractions.* Ann Arbor, Mich., 1987.

Ross, Clifford, ed. *Abstract Expressionism: Creators and Critics.* New York, 1990.

Roszak, Theodore. *The Making of a Counter Culture: Reflections on the Technocratic Society and Its Youthful Opposition.* Garden City, N.Y., 1969.

Sandler, Irving. *The Triumph of American Painting: A History of Abstract Expressionism.* New York, 1970.

Slivka, Rose. *Peter Voulkos: A Dialogue with Clay.* Boston, 1978.

Zumthor, Paul. *Oral Poetry: An Introduction.* Translated by Kathryn Murphy-Judy. Minneapolis, Minn., 1990.

THE CULTURE OF SELF-IMPROVEMENT

Joseph F. Kett

Like the boat so often reconstructed that ancient philosophers debated whether indeed it was still the same vessel, the connotations of self-improvement have changed since the eighteenth century from a stress on self-discipline to an emphasis on personal adjustment and, in the last few decades, to a preoccupation with self-release. Despite the ever-changing objectives of promoters of self-improvement, however, its practitioners have long been attracted by its promise of intellectual, spiritual, and psychological self-betterment.

In the eighteenth century the confluence of several intellectual and social developments gave rise to the idea that the individual could improve his inner essence by self-consciously cultivating his faculties of reason and will. Self-improvement was compatible with the Christian's duty to shepherd time, but its advocates rejected Calvinist determinism for free will and extolled the disciplined cultivation of the faculties both as a prerequisite for acquiring knowledge and truth, and as an end in itself. In *The Improvement of the Mind* (part I, 1741; part II, 1751), the English Dissenting clergyman Isaac Watts equated self-improvement with the application of logic to the reading of books, to the conduct of conversation and debate, and to the practice of teaching and writing. Watts's guide to self-improvement circulated widely in America, especially in the nineteenth century, when it was reissued as a vademecum for students.

By then, self-improvement had acquired a wider range of associations, most of which were traceable to Benjamin Franklin's writings and career. Franklin's founding of the Junto in 1727 introduced Philadelphians (and, after the 1790 publication of his immensely popular *Autobiography,* introduced everyone) to mutual improvement, self-improvement in a collegial group. The *Autobiography* also laid out his pursuit of "moral perfection" and printed excerpts from the "little book" in which he daily recorded his progress and regress in his conquest of vice and his serial mastery of the thirteen virtues

that he had identified. Franklin's career hinted at the subversive conclusion that individuals could reinvent themselves to their advantage. No one could mistake the fact that Franklin had reinvented himself in many forms: the ingratiating printer's apprentice who made sure that his social superiors knew about his bookish ways; the successful retired printer who engaged in projects of public utility; the American who so affected the simple manners of his country that he dazzled the sophisticated French court and persuaded an absolute monarch to finance a republican revolution.

DEMOCRATIZING SELF-IMPROVEMENT

Watts and Franklin remained the best-known writers on self-improvement for generations, but nineteenth-century advocates of self-improvement added new wrinkles. In the second quarter of the nineteenth century, Unitarian clergymen advanced self-improvement not merely as an alternative to the vicious amusements afforded by frivolity and the tavern, but also as an alternative to the revival's insistence on religious-conversion experiences. Inclined to conflate religion and ethics, as well as the disinterested pursuit of knowledge and spiritual grace, Unitarians portrayed life as a steady elevation of behavior and wisdom rather than as a jagged fluctuation between spiritual gloom and spiritual euphoria. In the course of the nineteenth century, this conception of the life course as a steady improvement of the self gradually gained currency among conservative Protestants, who increasingly shared the Unitarian concern with building character, habitual rectitude.

Faculty psychology exerted a strong influence on nineteenth-century self-improvement. Reading books with attention would exercise the faculty of reason, which then would enable the individual to control his baser passions. But self-improvement was more than self-discipline. Self-improvement guides advocated plain living and high thinking. They assumed that exposure to masterpieces of literature and art would impart to each person a more humane and liberal outlook on life and an elevation above sectarianism and partisanship. Within the confines of faculty psychology, some writers, especially those influenced by Emersonian Transcendentalism, directed self-improvement toward the cultivation of the higher affections, the "social powers," our "intuitional nature," moral "courage" (Emersonian self-reliance), and the experience of natural beauty.

The usual nineteenth-century synonyms for self-improvement were "self-education" and "self-culture." "Culture," which originally signified the cultivation of plants, came to be applied to the cultivation of the faculties through disciplined study. The Unitarian clergyman William Ellery Channing entitled his widely reprinted lecture on self-improvement "Self-Culture." He first delivered it in 1838 at Boston's Franklin Institute, an institution of mutual improvement intended primarily for mechanics. During the course of the nineteenth century, mutual improvement took the form of an extraordinary variety of organizations: Franklin societies, young men's societies, belles-lettres societies, mercantile and apprentice library societies, debating and literary societies (mostly for whites but some for "free people of color"), societies to sponsor libraries and lectures, and the ubiquitous lyceum, which a contemporary accurately defined as a "literary club of almost any description" ("Seventh Annual Report," p. 629). After the Civil War women played an increasingly prominent role in mutual-improvement societies. They did this both in the women's clubs, which until the end of the century were devoted primarily to "culture-study," and in the Chautauqua movement, which started in 1874 as a summer school for Sunday School teachers and quickly evolved into a far-reaching adult education enterprise.

In the course of the nineteenth century, the increasing diversity of the audience for self-improvement did not alter the stated goals of most of its advocates: personal ethical elevation through disciplining and harrowing of the faculties, and exposure to the finer intellectual and aesthetic products of Western culture. In 1869 Matthew Arnold defined culture in terms that would make him an icon among late-nineteenth-century self-improvers: the effort to make "the best that has been thought and known current everywhere, to make all men live in an atmosphere of sweetness and light" (Arnold, p. 70).

Despite the ever-expanding boundaries of nineteenth-century self-improvement, which developed a considerable following among apprentices, artisans, and clerks, self-improvement guides usually avoided the crude pitch embodied in the title of P. T. Barnum's most popular lecture: "The Art of Money-Getting." Channing told his Franklin Institute audience that self-culture is "not struggling for another rank" ("On the Elevation," p. 42). But self-improvement in the form of acquiring facility in writing and public speaking was useful in an oratorical age marked by widespread aspirations to public life. In addition, the prevailing equation of moral with material progress, embodied in Walt Whitman's declaration that Americans' "almost maniacal appetite for wealth" was part of "amelioration and progress" (Whitman, p. 261), helped to establish a link, more often implied than overtly stated by self-improvement tracts, between self-culture and getting on in the world.

Nineteenth-century self-improvement guides struck a modern note by vastly multiplying the number of improvable faculties beyond the old standbys—reason, memory, and will. With its cross listing of thirty-seven distinct faculties, each embodied in a different region of the brain, the "Self-Improvement Directory Table" compiled by the popular phrenologist Orson Fowler resembled Franklin's "little book" more than Channing's earnest exhortation that mechanics practice self-improvement as a kind of Unitarian duty. In 1880 James Freeman Clarke, a prominent Unitarian clergyman with Emersonian leanings, blessed phrenology as an indispensable tool for achieving "self-knowledge" and lauded it for its revelation of the luxuriant multiplicity of human powers. Contemporaries had little trouble recognizing the revolutionary implications of phrenology: that mental powers did not depend on rank, station, or previous education; that someone weak in one quality might be strong in another; and that all powers could be improved. It is not surprising that a collection of Fowler's writings was posthumously published as *Education and Self-Improvement.*

CHANGES SINCE 1945

The rich and variegated tradition of self-improvement in America contains more continuity than may be realized. Since 1945 and especially since 1960, however, the language expressing the desire for self-improvement has experienced considerable change. We now read less about self-discipline and "character," and more about "self-actualization," "self-directed behavior modification," and "self-realization." The numerous shelves headed Self-Improvement in trade bookstores now groan under the weight of such titles as *Awaken the Giant Within, The Self-Hypnosis Kit, The Power Is Within, Care of the Soul, Napoleon Hill's Keys to Success: The Seventeen Principles of Personal Achievement,* and *The Complete Idiot's Guide to Beating the Blues.*

Both the titles and content of some of these manuals are traceable to the tradition variously labeled Mind Cure, New Thought, or Positive Thinking. This tradition gradually developed from the teachings of Mary Baker Eddy and William James in the late nineteenth century, through Orison Swett Marsden and Ralph Waldo Trine's works in the early 1900s, to Norman Vincent Peale's books of the 1950s. Advocates of positive thinking told their readers that happiness and unhappiness were states of mind and that life could be turned around by some mixture of autosuggestion and religious faith. What most strikes the bookstore browser, however, is the extent to which recent self-improvement manuals are permeated by the language of psychotherapy rather than religious faith, by their preoccupation with formulae and methodical "steps" (the "kit") to improvement, and by their orientation toward the release rather than soothing of the inner self.

These newer associations of self-improvement coalesced in the Human Potential Movement, the outgrowth of informal discussions between professional and amateur psychologists and psychiatrists, including Frederick Perls, Abraham Maslow, Aldous Huxley, Alan Watts, Richard Price, and Michael Murphy. In 1962 these men and others gathered at Big Sur Hot Springs in California, on property owned by Murphy's family. Human Potential substituted self-fulfillment for mainstream psychology's emphasis on personal adjustment. Whereas adjustment implied the legitimacy of established social norms and roles, Human Potential enthroned the sovereignty of inner experience, which it then sought to enhance by a variety of techniques. These included various Chinese exercise systems and "sensory awareness," which took the form of massage-like mutual touching and exercises to relax or control bodily functions. Another technique was Gestalt therapy, an idea popularized by Perls but owing more to Jacob Levy Moreno. Moreno was an Austrian psychiatrist who in the 1920s had agreed with Martin Buber's dictum that industrialization and urbanization had destroyed meaningful social relationships but who then advanced a therapy,

which he called psychodrama, to revitalize interpersonal relationships. In psychodrama, the therapist becomes the director of a kind of play in which the members of the group act out real or imagined life scenes, sometimes playing themselves, sometimes others. Perls drew on this method for Gestalt therapy, while giving it a twist toward reestablishing contact with a lost or deadened self.

Psychodrama replaced the therapist, patient, and couch with the "encounter group." Since Charles Horton Cooley's formulation of the concept of the "social self" in the early 1900s, educators, government officials, and students of industrial management had been exploring the effects of the group on individual behavior. In the 1930s the human relations movement had blessed the idea of organizing workers into groups to discuss job-related problems. In the 1940s Kurt Lewin, a Gestalt psychologist who conducted the Research Center for Group Dynamics at M.I.T., pioneered the concept of group dynamics. Lewin redirected attention from the problem being solved to the group itself, which became a laboratory for working out failures in interpersonal communication. Lewin had studied industrial management and his methods were widely employed by business training programs in the 1950s, usually under the rubric of "sensitivity training" or the "T-group." Late in his life, however, he became preoccupied with exploring the subtle differences in the ways individual members of a group perceived both the group objective and the relationships among group members. It was more a step than a leap from group dynamics to encounter sessions, in which the group as such had no external objective to attain.

The Big Sur Hot Springs seekers owed something to Jack Kerouac and Allen Ginsberg's attacks on the work ethic and "fitting in." They also absorbed their interest in Zen and other forms of Eastern mysticism, and by the early 1960s they were developing ties, mainly through the efforts of Alan Watts and Aldous Huxley, to the research on psychedelic drugs being conducted at Harvard by Timothy Leary and Richard Alpert. On balance, there was nothing especially American about the Human Potential, or "awareness," movement. Perls and Lewin were refugees from Nazism. Elsa Gindler, the founder of sensory awareness and a familiar figure at Big Sur Hot Springs after 1963, had developed her ideas as a young calisthenics teacher in Wilhelmine Berlin. The Big Sur group was also influenced by the writings of a renegade Freudian, the Austrian Wilhelm Reich, who had argued for the acting out rather than the necessary repression of inner drives,

NORMAN VINCENT PEALE

Born in rural Ohio in 1898, the son of a Methodist clergyman, Norman Vincent Peale trained at Boston University Seminary and then held pastorates in Brooklyn and Syracuse before being summoned in 1932 to the pulpit of the then-dwindling Marble Collegiate Church in Manhattan. Peale's first success was to boost the church's membership, which he accomplished with a mixture of friendliness (the church "where you are a stranger but once") and counseling sessions that aimed more to cure than save the souls of parishioners troubled by fear of failure, alcoholism, and marital difficulties. Peale stayed at Marble Collegiate for over fifty years, and by 1940 he had started a radio show and written two inspirational books, *The Art of Living* (1937) and *You Can Win* (1938). By his death in 1993 he had authored or co-authored over forty books, including the best-seller *The Power of Positive Thinking* (1952), which made him a celebrity ("God's Salesman") and whose popularity greatly increased the circulation of his inspirational magazine, *Guideposts*.

Peale's writings drew on New Thought, an early twentieth-century form of applied Christian psychotherapy that told people to get "in tune with the infinite." New Thought writers usually had described God as the All Supply, Higher Consciousness, Mind, or Omnipresent Spirit, man as an individuation of this divine spirit, and Jesus as a channel of the divine power. Peale mingled elements of New Thought with Protestant evangelicalism and the American Dream. Dressing his message in folksier terms than All Supply, Peale moved New Thought from the periphery to the center stage of American religion. His message itself was uncomplicated: self-empowerment through recognition and acceptance of the divine power within is the road to peace of mind; "you do not need to be defeated by anything." Critics dismissed him as a rich man's Billy Graham (Peale had conservative political views and many ties to corporate America) and as a pantheist in a gray flannel suit. But his books remained popular even as his visibility declined; by the late 1980s the *The Power of Positive Thinking* had sold some fifteen million copies. Peale rode the crest of the religious revival of the 1950s, but his continuing appeal rests on another wave that shows no sign of breaking: the quest of Americans for a better quality of life and their higher expectations for personal happiness.

and by the Australian F. Matthias Alexander, who had developed a technique for enhancing self-awareness by self-conscious attention to bodily movements. Nor can it be said that there was much public interest in the activities of the Big Sur Hot Springs group, whose occasional attempts to offer extension courses in Human Potential foundered for want of takers.

In 1964 Michael Murphy and Richard Price changed the name of the Big Sur group to the Esalen Institute, which soon became a scheduled stop for dissident intellectuals affiliated with unconventional psychotherapies, the antiwar movement, and the burgeoning counterculture, such as Norman O. Brown, Joan Baez, and Ken Kesey. Esalen grew as a well watered plant in the garden of the counterculture; the mélange of ideas and methods behind Human Potential began to acquire a wider following. "Growth" centers sprang up elsewhere on the West Coast and in Chicago and New York, and in 1967 Murphy inaugurated a San Francisco branch of Esalen, housed, thanks to Episcopal bishop James A. Pike (a frequenter of Esalen), in the diocesan headquarters on Nob Hill.

By the early 1970s Esalen was facing a challenge from EST, an acronym for Erhard Seminars Train-

Norman Vincent Peale (1898–1993). Among Peale's early influences were William James and Ralph Waldo Emerson. © OSCAR WHITE/CORBIS

ing. A former salesman of automobiles, correspondence courses, and Great Books, Werner Erhard acknowledged his debt to such inspirational tracts as Napoleon Hill's *Think and Grow Rich*. Erhard's methods contained elements of Gestalt, Zen, Scientology, martial arts, and sensory awareness, but Erhard oriented these less toward self-awareness as an end than toward self-help as a means of success. Popularized in Britain and America after the publication in 1860 of Samuel Smiles's *Self-Help*, the ideal of self-help emphasized the building of self-esteem more than the cultivation of talents, a component of self-improvement that Smiles deprecated. Self-help could lead to material success but, as depicted in the turn-of-the-century writings of Orison Swett Marsden and in Norman Vincent Peale's *The Power of Positive Thinking* (1952), it smacked more of Mind Cure's substitution of inner peace for outward disappointment. In contrast, Erhard aimed to mobilize the psyche for success which EST defined as "getting your act together" rather than "letting it all hang out." In the 1970s as many as half a million persons, mostly white and affluent, paid Erhard and other EST trainers handsome fees, $300 to $500, for

a weekend that promised to transform them from underachievers to take-chargers.

In the 1970s self-enhancement began to loom larger in the cultural associations of self-improvement than in 1960s-style self-discovery. In 1741 Isaac Watts had warned against "the pride of your own reason" and a "vain conceit of your intellectual powers," and counseled prayer to God that "He would bless all your attempts and labors in reading, study and conversation" (Watts, pp. 14–15). The culture of self-enhancement also exhorted self-improvers to recognize the inadequacy of their capacities, but it replaced prayer with a variety of techniques to increase the personal powers of the self-improver. For example, in 1979 ten members of the New York Yankees were put through a regimen of visual enhancement designed to increase their visual concentration, visual acuity, and spatial awareness. The objective in this case was a kind of elevation, specifically of their batting averages, and the context was a training program, not an encounter session or "self-directed learning activity." But aids to functional enhancement—greater physical vitality, faster reading comprehension, sexual amplitude, and more satisfactory interpersonal relationships—increasingly filled the shelves of trade bookstores, which not infrequently classified them under self-improvement.

So numerous and widely diffused did techniques for self-enhancement become that in 1984 the Army Research Institute asked the prestigious National Academy of Sciences to investigate the effectiveness of literally scores of enhancement techniques. Some of these, such as the Hawthorne effect (the effect on one's performance that results merely from being selected for an experiment), dated to the 1930s, specifically to Elton Mayo's famous investigations of the correlatives of worker performance at General Electric's Hawthorne plant in Chicago. But most were of recent vintage: biofeedback (techniques to inform subjects about their heart rate, brain frequencies, finger temperature, and other internal events as a prelude to mastering control of internal events in order to enhance performance); hemispheric laterality (techniques to relax either or both right and left brain hemispheres); and stress-management methods (biofeedback, drugs, meditation).

SELF-IMPROVEMENT AS PATHOLOGY

The therapies that sprouted in the 1960s and 1970s were sufficiently numerous, diverse, and conflicting to defy easy classification, but their critics increasingly identified disquieting resemblances among them. Linguistically, they all amounted to "psychobabble." Politically, they were attacked for substituting self-absorption for activism. (In a different form this charge had been leveled at nineteenth-century self-improvement for its preoccupation with the "mountainous Me.") In 1966 Philip Rieff identified a disturbing "triumph of the therapeutic." Rieff targeted the Freudians Carl Jung and Wilhelm Reich for abandoning the master's "mature" recognition that therapy could do no more than return the individual to "an environment in which the ego could fight more capably for itself in the subtle and universal war of all against all," and for substituting an empty promise of salvation by ersatz ontologies (Jung's "archetypes") or sacralized impulses (Reich's sanctification of sex). In 1973 Peter Marin described Esalen as runaway "narcissism," a term popularized by Christopher Lasch's *The Culture of Narcissism* (1978).

Lasch demurred from the contention of many psychiatrists that human personality structures were relatively unchanging. Therapists, he noted, were reporting fewer cases of classical Freudian disorders in the form of obsessional phobias and fixations and more cases of clients who complained of an inability to experience close relationships, of vague but pervasive feelings of emptiness and depression, and of violent oscillations of self-esteem—all symptoms of narcissism. He then contended that narcissism represented the psychological effect of a social and cultural change that had rendered the individual increasingly dependent on corporate and bureaucratic structures. The modern individual was not the isolated, self-sufficient master of his destiny, the icon of the nineteenth century, but an increasingly vulnerable being. The nineteenth-century tradition of self-improvement had reminded Americans of their divinely ordained duty to cultivate their talents and to measure their progress by their advance in virtue and social usefulness. In contrast, the modern success myth told them that success could only be gauged by money-getting and surpassing others, by the will to win. In the increasingly dominant corporate and bureaucratic worlds, the will to win, now stripped of its quondam associations with virtue, primarily took the form of pleasing others, and in the post–Dale Carnegie age, manipulating others. Even more than money, Lasch argued, what had come to matter was gaining the esteem of others; publicity had become the ratification of success. Lasch targeted not just the positive-thinking phase of success ideology but the twentieth-century reform tradition that had progressively stripped the family of its socializing functions and invested these in schools and experts. Child-rearing manuals called upon parents to be perfect nurturers, yet assumed their incapacity to so act and thereby left mothers fluctuating between feelings of omnipotence and failure, the seeds of narcissism.

ALTERNATIVE EXPLANATIONS

To make his case, Lasch had to assume that pathology "represents a heightened version of normality" (p. 38), that patients who reported symptoms labeled narcissistic by therapists were just the tip of an iceberg formed by modern social and cultural forces. But there are other ways to interpret the vogue of awareness therapy. At its simplest, resort to psychotherapy rests on an individual's decision to consume a specialized service. This decision can be viewed as a sign of underlying pathology and pathetic dependency, but it may merely signify more respect for professionalism, more options, and new freedoms.

The period since 1945 has witnessed an intensification and extension of the consumer culture that first flowered in the 1920s. One aspect of this culture has been its encouragement of the purchase of specialized products and services as anodynes for customary behaviors and qualities that are newly labeled as problematic. For example, buy Listerine and cure "halitosis." Another has been its penchant for questioning and then classifying Americans into ever more specialized categories. Public-opinion polling grew out of market research, which itself was a handmaiden of advertising. On a parallel track, the rise of intelligence testing created new categories of mental deficiency and, ultimately, new services such as special education.

People accustomed to being polled, tested, and classified began to think of themselves, and others, in terms of their classifications. The first mass administration of intelligence tests—the army alpha and beta tests during World War I—almost immediately led to the first wave of national anxiety over Americans' stupidity, the menace of the "feebleminded." During the interwar period, literally hundreds of new intelligence tests, usually more skill-specific than the alpha tests, came on the market each year, and new tests purporting to measure "personality" and occupational proclivities, such as the Minnesota Multi-Phasic Personality Inventory and the Coudert Preference Test, were devised. During World War II, the armed forces' General Classification Tests were routinely administered to nearly 15 percent of the entire male population of the United States.

World War II gave an enormous boost to psychology as a profession. Membership in the American Psychological Association grew by more than 1,100 percent between 1940 and 1970, and that of the American Psychiatric Association rose 760 percent. (Since 1970 each organization has more than doubled its membership.) During the war, "sykewarriors" advised the government on propaganda, morale, the screening of recruits, and even the selection and training of spies and saboteurs. The war did more than stimulate demand for psychologists and psychiatrists. It also nudged psychology and psychiatry from their traditional preoccupation with neurophysiological disorders toward recognition of the social and cultural determinants of what was coming to be known as mental health. The apparent fanaticism of the Germans and Japanese suggested that otherwise normal people could be induced to act abnormally by their environments. Wartime investigations of "war neuroses" led to the same conclusion, especially after psychologists established that breakdowns occurred more often in combat units than among noncombatant soldiers, and that the symptoms of neuroses in the air forces differed from those in ground units. By signing the National Mental Health Act (the bill had originally been entitled the National Neuropsychiatric Institute Act) into law in 1946, President Truman gave official support to clinical psychology's newly acquired commitment to maintaining the mental equilibrium of normal people.

The war experience also encouraged soldiers to engage in psychological self-help. Recruits were lectured on ways to control fears and resentments. Innumerable GIs read *Psychology for the Fighting Man.* Written by psychologists and then neatly packaged by a professional journalist into readily comprehensible prose, the book warned soldiers of "danger signals" and advised them how to cope with sexual deprivation and how to own up to fear. By the 1950s ex-soldiers were taking the sort of corporate personality tests derided by William H. Whyte in *The Organization Man* (1956), and reading Whyte's appended advice on "How to Cheat on Personality Tests." To propose that personality testing had gone too far was to acknowledge that it had gone very far. The employment of personality tests by businesses was part of a larger cultural tapestry marked by popular acceptance of expert definitions of private selves. Psychological self-help and corporate se-

lection/training programs based on personality profiles were different sides of the same coin.

Popular and psychological forms of self-help predated the Human Potential movement, which blasted the emphasis of adjustment that had marked psychology in the 1940s and 1950s. Awareness therapy hinged on the assumption that clients would be happier if they understood the repressive nature of the institutions to which they had been told to adjust. Human Potential was attracting something close to a mass following by the 1970s. This development would never have occurred without the broader acceptance by the public of psychological self-definitions and self-help, but the popularization of Human Potential also reflected a cultural reorientation, one marked by changed attitudes toward marriage, gender, and work.

Congress's decision in 1957 to establish a Joint Commission on Mental Illness and Health—another sign of rising interest in the mental adjustment of normal people—ultimately led to the compilation of data that affords insight into the changing values of Americans between the 1950s and the 1970s. The congressional staff asked the Survey Research Center at the University of Michigan to conduct an intensive survey of average Americans in order to answer such questions as whether the respondents felt "adequate," whether they solved problems by themselves, and where they turned for help. Thus, the focus was on subjective mental health and individual strategies for coping with problems. In 1976 the Survey Research Center conducted a similar interview survey, employing many of the same questions as the 1957 survey, and in 1981 Joseph Veroff, Elizabeth Douvan, and Richard A. Kulka compared results of the two surveys in *The Inner American.*

The Inner American documented significant changes between 1957 and 1976. By the 1970s Americans had become less inclined than in the 1940s and 1950s to expect fulfillment through participation in established social institutions, and more inclined to judge all affiliations by the extent to which they yielded personal emotional satisfaction. Expressed more abstractly, there had taken place a diminution of role standards as the basis for defining adjustment. Fewer Americans in the 1970s than in the 1950s accepted the proposition that marriage and parenthood were indispensable to happiness, and more of them rated their jobs by the degree of personal satisfaction they imparted, especially in their relationship with other workers, than by such formal features as salary and working conditions.

The Inner American also underscored changes in attitudes toward family relationships. Parents in

1976 stressed the "relational, interpersonal" aspects of parenthood more than their 1957 counterparts. This was especially true for fathers, who by 1976 had grown more likely than in the 1950s to evaluate their relations with their children by the degree of emotional intimacy achieved rather than by more traditional measures, such as financial support and physical care. Fathers who sought more intimacy with their children disclosed another prominent feature of the culture of self-improvement that had emerged since the 1960s: its tendency to elevate the importance of personal contacts with others as a solution to difficulties. Between the 1950s and the 1970s the proportion of Americans who sought to assuage personal difficulties by prayer declined, while the proportion of those who sought to address their problems by reaching out to others rose.

Identifying these changes is easier than explaining them. The youth rebellion and cultural upheaval of the late 1960s and early 1970s occurred amid affluence. Those who by traditional measures should have been contented obviously were not. Affluence itself opened a wider range of options to individuals, who enjoyed unprecedented freedom to choose among alternative "life styles" (a revealing neologism). In addition, the rebellions of the mid- to late 1960s targeted types of authority in families, schools, and workplaces—the stress on specialized gender roles, life adjustment, and conformity—that have often been described as traditional but that had been severely disrupted by the Great Depression and World War II, only to become more secure and more brittle during the 1950s. Combined with the rising prestige of psychotherapy, a trend evident before 1960, this configuration of value changes between the 1950s and 1970s created clients for types of psychotherapy that were oriented more to release than to adjustment.

THE PERSISTENCE OF EDUCATION

The shelves devoted to self-improvement in trade bookstores now only whisper the once resonant exhortation that individuals impose on themselves a regimen of study to acquire a liberal education, the keystone of President Charles W. Eliot's five-foot shelf of "Harvard Classics" in the 1920s. Yet self-improvement continues to take the old-fashioned form of education. As a Massachusetts prison inmate in the 1940s, Malcolm Little (the future Malcolm X) devoured books by Will Durant, Arnold Toynbee, H. G. Wells, and Gregor Mendel. When asked by a journalist to identify his alma mater,

Malcolm bluntly replied: "Books." In 1967 Eric Sevareid introduced Eric Hoffer, the sometime migrant worker and longshoreman turned philosopher, author, and Berkeley lecturer, to a national television audience. In addition, since 1970 vast numbers of adults, especially women from their mid-twenties to mid-thirties, have made the decision to start, or return to, college. Like the rising utilization of therapeutic services, the surge of college re-entrants reflected supply-side factors. As the baby boomers moved through the educational system, colleges started to worry about declining future enrollments and began to offer more programs tailored to adult students. On the demand side, as calls for gender equality in occupational opportunity mounted in the 1970s, women, who as late as 1967 were significantly less likely than males to attend or to persist in college, now elected to secure the baccalaureate. By 1984 the percentage of women aged 24–29 attending and graduating from college was virtually the same as that for men.

Inasmuch as many of these late commencers or re-commencers have sought academic credentials and "job improvement" by enrolling in degree programs, it can be argued that college reentry has lacked the voluntarism and spontaneity of true self-improvement. But the meaning of self-improvement has always been protean and culturally contextualized; it has never excluded participation in educational institutions, and it has not necessarily been incompatible with job improvement. Chautauquans in the late nineteenth century reported benefits from joining study groups that we would unhesitatingly label psycho-social and that resembled the avowed motives of the adult women who, their horizons extended by the women's movement, have poured into institutions of higher education in recent decades: to break out of an isolating domestic situation, to boost self-esteem by responding to a new challenge, and to learn something. In the early twentieth century, the astoundingly numerous clients of correspondence schools, which soaked their advertisements in images of Benjamin Franklin and other icons of self-improvement, were motivated by an explicit desire for social mobility that would not have embarrassed Franklin, the self-taught printer turned gentleman.

The surge of college enrollments by adults in the late 1900s underscores an aspect of self-improvement that has rarely been detected by those culture critics who reflexively conflate self-improvement with therapy for sick souls: its strong correlation with educational attainment. No less striking than the growth of psychotherapy and the phenomenon of college reentry has been the increase in the median number of years of schooling completed by Americans aged twenty-five and over. As late as 1940 more than 60 percent of all persons aged 25–29 had not completed high school, a figure that by 1986 had fallen to 16 percent. In addition to the obvious point that increases in college entry and reentry ultimately depend on higher rates of high school graduation, abundant survey evidence points to the strong correlation between higher levels of education attainment and increased resort to self-improvement in virtually any form, from taking an adult-education class to embarking on a self-directed learning project.

Today, we hear few of the exhortations to self-improvement that resounded through the nineteenth century. Like Sherlock Holmes's dog that did not bark, this is a revealing clue to the direction of change. In a consumer culture marked by a penchant for popular psychology and high levels of educational attainment, the market for self-improvement guides and activities seems sufficiently well established as to require little encouragement from moralists. More often, moralists and social critics blast the popular penchant for self-improvement as evidence of an underlying social pathology. But if the popularity of self-improvement is a sign of disease, the disease is unlikely to be cured any time soon.

See also **Working Class; Humanitarianism** (in this volume); **Success; Twentieth-Century Economic Thought; Individualism and the Self; Lyceums, Chautauquas, and Institutes for Useful Knowledge** (volume 3); and other articles in this section.

BIBLIOGRAPHY

Primary Sources

Clarke, James Freeman. *Self-Culture: Physical, Intellectual, Moral and Spiritual.* Boston, 1880.

Peale, Norman Vincent. *The Power of Positive Thinking.* Englewood Cliffs, N.J., 1952.

Trine, Ralph Waldo. *In Tune with the Infinite.* New York, 1897.

Watts, Isaac. *The Improvement of the Mind.* With Corrections, Questions, and Supplement by Joseph Emerson. Boston, 1858.

———. *The Improvement of the Mind; or, A Supplement to the Art of Logic. In Two Parts.* Exeter, N.H., 1793.

Secondary Sources

Anderson, Walter Truett. *The Upstart Spring: Esalen and the American Awakening.* Reading, Mass., 1983.

Arnold, Matthew. *Culture and Anarchy.* Cambridge, U.K., 1950.

Cawelti, John. *Apostles of the Self-Made Man.* Chicago, 1965.

Channing, William Ellery. "On the Elevation of the Laboring Classes." In *Works of William Ellery Channing, D.D.* Boston, 1880.

Clecak, Peter. *America's Quest for the Ideal Self: Dissent and Fulfillment in the 60s and 70s.* New York, 1983.

Cooter, Roger. *The Cultural Meaning of Popular Science: Phrenology and the Organization of Consent in Nineteenth-Century Britain.* Cambridge, U.K., 1984.

Fowler, Orson. *Memory and Intellectual Improvement Applied to Self-Education and Juvenile Instruction.* New York, 1893.

George, Carol V. R. *God's Salesman: Norman Vincent Peale and the Power of Positive Thinking.* New York, 1993.

Herman, Ellen. *The Romance of American Psychology: Political Culture in the Age of Experts.* Berkeley, Calif., 1995.

Howe, Daniel Walker. *Making the American Self: Jonathan Edwards to Abraham Lincoln.* Cambridge, Mass., 1997.

Kett, Joseph F. *The Pursuit of Knowledge under Difficulties: From Self-Improvement to Adult Education in America, 1750–1990.* Stanford, Calif., 1994.

Lasch, Christopher. *The Culture of Narcissism: American Life in an Age of Diminishing Expectations.* New York, 1978.

Latner, Joel. *The Gestalt Therapy Book.* New York, 1973.

Marchand, Roland. *Advertising the American Dream: Making Way for Modernity, 1920–1940.* Berkeley, Calif., 1985.

Marrow, Alfred J. *The Practical Theorist: The Life and Work of Kurt Lewin.* New York, 1969.

Meyer, Donald B. *The Positive Thinkers: A Study of the American Quest for Health, Wealth, and Personal Power from Mary Baker Eddy to Norman Vincent Peale.* Garden City, N.Y., 1965.

Rieff, Philip. *The Triumph of the Therapeutic: Uses of Faith after Freud.* New York, 1966.

"Seventh Annual Report of the American Lyceum." *American Monthly Magazine* 9 (1837): 629.

Susman, Warren. *Culture and History: The Transformation of American Society in the Twentieth Century.* New York, 1984.

Veroff, Joseph, Elizabeth Douvan, and Richard A. Kulka. *The Inner American: A Self-Portrait from 1957 to 1976.* New York, 1981.

Whitman, Walt. "Democratic Vistas." *The Works of Walt Whitman.* New York, 1968.

FRANCO-AMERICAN CULTURAL ENCOUNTERS AND EXCHANGES

Randolph Paul Runyon

When national cultures interact, they tend to remake each other in their own image. Such is the conclusion one might draw from the intersection of French and American culture, high and low, in the 1940s and 1950s. Each misread the other, which is not to say that misreadings cannot produce genuine insights.

In literature, cinema, music, and other cultural arenas, American influence on France during World War II and the postwar years was preponderant. Americans were the heroic liberators of 1944, and gratitude mixed with enthusiasm, for all things American persisted throughout the postwar years among the masses, although some intellectuals and members of the Communist Party tried to stir up anti-American sentiments. Once the war was over, the French did have reason to complain about the U.S. government's conscious policy of overwhelming their country with products of American culture. The Blum-Byrnes Agreement of 1946 required the French to remove their limit on the importation of American movies and set aside only four weeks in any three-month period for the showing of French films; as a result, French film production dropped 50 percent by 1947 and did not fully recover until the 1960s.

The presence of American army bases on French soil, which persisted until 1967, and the gum-chewing GIs and their radio stations and PXs—veritable paradises to the French, who were under food rationing until 1949—offered a tantalizing window on American popular culture. Army jazz bands toured the countryside, while jazz clubs offered musical apprenticeship to a generation of French musicians.

To an increasingly urbanized France in some danger of losing touch with its past, America looked like the future, both a dream and a nightmare: a consumer society where old values might well be lost.

AMERICAN INFLUENCES ON FRENCH WRITERS

In the 1940s the French writer and philosopher Jean-Paul Sartre covered three American novelists with high praise: William Faulkner, Ernest Hemingway, and John Dos Passos, calling Dos Passos "the greatest writer of our time" (quoted in Lehan, *A Dangerous Crossing,* p. 39). One might say that while Sartre chose well in the first two instances, the third was somewhat questionable. Apart from Dos Passos's intrinsic literary value, it is difficult to see how Faulkner's dense prose and Hemingway's directness and clarity could have attracted allegiance from the same critics as they did from Sartre. How could things turn out so differently on the other side of the Atlantic?

In part, it was because Sartre, himself a novelist, was behaving like every other writer who stakes out his identity at the price of rejecting his immediate forbears. In Sartre's case, it was Marcel Proust, whose *In Search of Lost Time* has many qualities that render it a masterpiece, but among them are its analytic approach to human experience and its place as the culmination of a literary tradition of psychological exploration. Sartre also had little regard for Henry James because he was too much like Proust, and he rejected James Joyce as a model for future novelists for the same reason.

Wishing to free himself from what he felt was an oppressive literary inheritance, Sartre was delighted to find that American novels of the 1930s and 1940s were just what he was looking for—spontaneous, natural, and even brutal works, the products of an unlearned talent unencumbered by the traditions of much depth or philosophical content. Their heroes "never explain themselves. . . . They live because they spurt suddenly as from a deep well. To analyze them would be to kill them" (quoted in Mathy, *Extrême-Occidents,* p. 130). American writers, in other words, would do well to leave the deep thoughts to the Europeans and "stick to . . . novels with fast-paced plots and monosyllabic dialogue featuring characters who were not introspective and spent little time contemplating the meaning of their lives" (Pells, *Not Like Us*, p. 252). It is an old story dressed up in new guise: innocent America discovered by decadent Europe. "Once again, Old World effete aristocrats of the mind are left to admire and envy the muscular body of the Whitmanesque woodsman" (Mathy, p. 131). It could also be expressed as pragmatic America versus ideology-obsessed Europe—terms that would continue to define the difference between the two cultures for decades.

The content and settings of these novels, including Dos Passos's delineation of the excesses of American capitalism and Faulkner's depiction of rural poverty and racial injustice, held some interest for French writers. Furthermore, they found in these novels' characters fellow victims of the absurdity of a godforsaken modern world. Above all, it was the writers' narrative techniques that caught the eye, and, despite their innocent naïveté, made them for Sartre the last word in literary modernism. "On the whole," the French writer Simone de Beauvoir recalled, "we found that the technique of French novelists was quite rudimentary, compared to that of the great Americans" (quoted in Bosquetti, "Sartre in the Age of the American Novel," p. 87, note 14). Despite the tone of condescension one might see in the refusal to grant philosophical or psychological depth to these writers (which seems particularly unjust in Faulkner's case), this interest in technique is more important than might be realized by those who do not appreciate just how deeply the French believe in the poet Stéphane Mallarmé's dictum that one makes poetry with words, not with ideas. French critics found in Faulkner, Hemingway, and Dos Passos "narrative discontinuity, an objective or impersonal style, simultaneity of action, and dialogue (or monologue) that did not so much express thought or sentiment as reveal the uncertainties of all forms of human communication" (Atherton, "Americans in Paris," p. 909). This disjointed way of telling a story spoke well to Sartre's concern for human alienation. It was both modernist and subversive protest literature, he thought, against the capitalist system responsible for that alienation. Also, by incorporating aspects of popular culture—the detective story, the style of gangster films, street speech—it could tear down old hierarchies and undermine the classical tradition.

The admiration of French critics extended to hard-boiled detective writers like Raymond Chandler, James M. Cain, and Dashiell Hammett. Albert Camus's landmark novel *L'étranger* (The stranger, 1942) may even have borrowed some elements from Cain's *The Postman Always Rings Twice* (1934). Both end in a murderer's cell with the protagonist communicating with a priest and about to be executed for a crime. There is in each work a strikingly parallel beach scene with a woman. Both are narrated with "the same detached, objective, narrative eye, describing surface reality, speaking in clipped sentences, each sentence recording a physical impression, and each impression a distinct and separate thing" (Lehan, p. 65).

But Hemingway is the more generally acknowledged source. The crime Camus's character commits, mechanically pulling the trigger of his revolver but without the intent to kill, may find its analogue in Hemingway's *A Farewell to Arms* (1929), when Lieutenant Henry mechanically pulls the trigger and shoots a sergeant. Sartre noticed a stylistic influence, once quipping that he had heard that Camus's novel "was Kafka written by Hemingway" but on closer inspection could find no Kafka (Lehan, p. 56). To produce the effect of estrangement that his protagonist experiences at his trial, where he senses himself an intruder in his own life, seeing in the prosecutor's account of his actions an unconnected jumble of events, Camus "applies a Hemingway technique: narration is reduced to instant-long notations as if the frames of a movie film had been run through slowly enough for the cuts between frames to appear" (Atherton, p. 913).

In his observations on American novels in *L'homme révolté* (The rebel, 1951), Camus writes of their "innocent" protagonists, in touch with the physicality of the world but little else, seeing them as figures locked in an absurd universe. The protagonist of *The Stranger* is similarly innocent, but unlike the American characters, he undergoes growth and enlightenment.

Sartre went beyond merely preaching the gospel of the American school in his lectures and essays; he also practiced it, in the series of novels entitled *Les chemins de la liberté* (The paths of liberty, 1945). This is especially true of *Le sursis* (The reprieve, 1945), the second volume, in which he appropriated Dos Passos's technique in *U.S.A.* of jumping from one narrative line to another.

An American influence of a different sort is evident in the work of Boris Vian, who was enamored of American detective and science fiction novels as well as American popular music. A tireless propagandist for jazz in his reviews and articles and a musician himself, he wrote novels in which he "sought to transcribe the atmosphere, the sonorities, and the rhythm" of this popular art form (Tournès, "L'americanisation de la culture française," pp. 70–71).

The influence of Hemingway, Faulkner, and company on French literature reached a final flowering in the 1950s with the *nouveau roman,* the French new novel, whose exponents included such writers as Alain Robbe-Grillet, Michel Butor, and Claude Simon (winner of the 1985 Nobel Prize for literature). Butor, who won the prestigious Prix Renaudot for *La modification* (U.S. title, *A Change of Heart*) in 1957, thereby winning a wider audience for a genre that until then had received only critical success, attended a lecture by Sartre in 1944 in which he first heard of Dos Passos and Faulkner. "It is absolutely certain," he later recalled, "that a good part of the problematic of my own novels developed from the reflections which came to me during that lecture" (quoted in Bosquetti, p. 84).

Sartre's synthesis of the phenomenology of Edmund Husserl and Martin Heidegger and his observations on the American neorealist novel emerged in the French new novelists' tendency to focus on the surface of things, to let them remain unexplained and to stress their "being there." Examples might include the orange seeds that keep changing their position on the heating grate in the railway compartment in *La modification* or the intense scrutiny of tomato segments in a Robbe-Grillet novel. So much did these novelists let their narrator's gaze linger on visual phenomena normally overlooked by more traditional writers that the movement was at first called "l'école du regard," the school of looking. The description of such phenomena took the place of psychological analysis and, to some extent, of the interior life of their characters. "The New Novelists, in their way of considering description, recalled Sartre's considerations on Hemingway and his art of rendering the resistance of things and the time flow by pausing on the objects" (Bosquetti, p. 84).

But the new novelists were by no means alike in all respects. The "zero degree of writing" that French critics noted in certain neorealist American novels is most evident in the spare prose of Robbe-Grillet's novels, including *Les gommes* (The erasers, 1953), *Le voyeur* (The voyeur, 1955), and *La jalousie* (Jealousy, 1957). It is less evident in Butor's work, including *Passage de Milan* (Passage from Milan, 1954), *L'emploi du temps* (Passing time, 1956), and *La modification,* especially in the latter, which is rich

Jean-Paul Sartre in 1964. Sartre's thought influenced a great number of American writers, among them John Barth and Richard Wright. © Hulton-Deutsch Collection/Corbis

in references to mythology, Vergil, and Dante. It is least evident in the luxuriant prose of Claude Simon, author of *Le vent* (The wind, 1957), *L'herbe* (The grass, 1958), and *La route des Flandres* (The Flanders road, 1960). Simon's closest American analogue is Faulkner. The Mississippian's influence is evident on every page, in the lengthy and syntax-stretching sentences, the passion for family sagas, the insistently repeated recollections of moments from a distant past shrouded in mystery, and the tendency to tell events backward and to make a riddle out of the story he is telling through a certain reticence to explain.

FRENCH INFLUENCES ON AMERICAN WRITERS

While existentialism was certainly talked about among American writers and intellectuals in the 1950s, and a certain "pop existentialism" gained popularity on college campuses, much of what existentialism denotes antedates Sartre, finding its roots in Søren Kierkegaard, Friedrich Nietzsche, and Fyodor Dostoevsky. It was similar to the "absurd," a concept developed by Camus but not original with him, as it could be considered an appropriate response to any of the great catastrophes that periodically afflict the human race, especially when Christianity or whatever the reigning religion is has lost its power to persuade.

Nevertheless, certain American novelists of the 1950s did enter into conversation with the French on these topics. In John Barth's *The End of the Road* (1958), a doctor offers Sartrean advice to Jacob Horner, who is overcome with an inability to act: "Choosing is existence: to the extent that you don't choose, you don't exist" (quoted in Lehan, p. 176)—and then recommends that he read the French philosopher. Richard Wright, who lived in Paris in the postwar years, found that Sartre and Camus were "writing of things that I have been thinking, writing, and feeling all of my life" (cited in Lehan, p. xvi); his novel *The Outsider* (1953) is explicitly existentialist in the French manner. Norman Mailer, who called himself the first American existentialist, wrote in *Advertisements for Myself* (1959) of the "hipster," a native American variety of existentialist, neither cerebral nor indebted to Sartre but "based on a mysticism of the flesh." Joseph Heller's *Catch-22* (1961) is an exploration of the absurd, more Kafkaesque than Camusian, and a treatment of a world run like a perfect bureaucracy, not disordered but all too structured. Saul Bellow and Walker Percy also treated existentialist themes but not in a way specifically indebted to Sartre or Camus.

The *nouveau roman* was another possible French influence on American writers, but it is difficult to make an absolute case because of the abundance of other models. Barth, whose later novels are "metafictional" in the way that many French new novelists' are, which is to say self-referential and tending to immensely complicate the relationship between reader and text, denied any French influence on his work, and rightly so. If he had a model, it was the Argentinean writer Jorge Luis Borges, whose stories swallow their own tail, like a Barth narrative. Barth argues, too, that literature has always been metafictional, just not always obviously so. At the 1982 conference where Barth made these remarks, Robert Coover, another novelist whose work might be likened to the *nouveau roman,* declared that if he had to name the French writer who had influenced him the most, it would be the Irish author Samuel Beckett—not one of the *nouveaux romanciers.* The novelist Jonathan Baumbach, however, suggested

that the French connection was very real and that its very denial made it all the more evident.

AMERICAN FILMS THROUGH FRENCH EYES

As American novels of the 1930s and 1940s found a receptive audience among certain French critics and later influenced writers as diverse as Camus and Simon, American films of the same era enjoyed a similar second life. In both cases, the French found qualities and value that Americans either ignored or denied were there. Among the novelists, Hammett, Cain, and Chandler were prized along with Hemingway and Faulkner. Although Hollywood movies of the 1930s and 1940s were dismissed by American critics as mass-produced big studio products, in France in the early 1950s they began to receive critical analysis and praise. But as Sartre used the American novelists to counterbalance a native inheritance, in opposition to which he sought to establish his own identity, the young critics of *Cahiers du Cinéma,* a periodical started in 1951, called attention to American directors of the studio era to point the way to a new way of making films, in rebellion against their immediate predecessors, the 1940s "cinema of quality," which produced lavish but stodgy re-creations of French literary classics.

But, Americans may wonder, were the French seeing qualities that weren't really there? The question itself suggests a fundamental cultural difference, the one between an American tendency to value content over style and a French one to do just the opposite. The young writers for *Cahiers du Cinéma*—François Truffaut, Eric Rohmer, and Jean-Luc Godard, who would go on to make films themselves later in the decade—argued that despite the Hollywood studio moguls' dictating plot, characters, and setting, the directors were the real *auteurs* of the films. Through camera angles, cutting, pacing, lighting, and the relation of one scene to another, such directors as Nicholas Ray, William Wyler, John Ford, Preston Sturges, Howard Hawks, and Alfred Hitchcock were able to write with the cameras as with a pen, and a personal vision emerged, despite the restrictions placed on them by studio bosses (and the capitalist conglomerates behind them). Besides, wrote the *Cahiers* critics, plot, characters, and dialogue are not specific to, and are therefore irrelevant to, cinema. It is the *mise-en-scène* that counts. It has been charged that because these critics were not fluent in English, they did not realize just how hackneyed the scripts of some of these films were and that their attention was caught by what they could understand: majestic, brooding landscapes in a John Ford Western or an exchange of glances on a darkened street—purely visual aspects. Yet their reevaluations of these directors have in many instances stood the test of time and have brought deepened enjoyment to American film buffs who now see their native directors in a fresh light.

It remains to be seen whether the French enthusiasm for the American comic actor Jerry Lewis, evident as early as 1956, will lead to a similar change of heart among American critics and viewers. As with the author Edgar Allan Poe and the entertainer Josephine Baker, Lewis's critical reputation is significantly higher, to the bewilderment of some, in France than at home. Some things gain in translation, but it should be noted that the French discovered what a master comic Buster Keaton was long before Americans did, and they could do so because they take comedy seriously. The French comic tradition includes Fernandel, Louis de Funès, and the remarkable director Jacques Tati. In Jerry Lewis, they could see a descendant of Tati's Monsieur Hulot, an innocent klutz who spreads disaster wherever he goes. As Lewis's biographer Shawn Levy remarks, "A country capable of producing and appreciating a Tati was obviously a place where the comic film was respected as a style of movie making with a heritage and a grammar all its own" (Levy, p. 331). Frank Tashlin, the director of the Jerry Lewis and Dean Martin film *Artists and Models* (1955), —a considerable success in France, was considered a competent hack at home but was relished in Paris as a wickedly funny satirist of the American way of life. American critics, perhaps too caught up in the American dream themselves, just did not get it, but the French did. It should be pointed out that, among the *Cahiers* critics (and New Wave directors), Truffaut did not like Lewis but Godard did; this may have had something to do with their politics. In his seminal 1954 article in *Cahiers du Cinéma*, "A Certain Tendency of the French Cinema," Truffaut complains of the "cinema of quality" that it is anticlerical, antimilitary, and antibourgeois; he could evidently be offended by the kind of social critique Lewis would later be perceived as making. Godard, on the other end of the political spectrum, would later flirt with Maoism.

Putting their theories into practice, by 1959, the year Truffaut's *Les 400 coups* (The four hundred blows) was released, these critics were creating the *nouvelle vague* (New Wave) school of movie making that brought global prestige to French cinema from 1959 to 1964. Although Godard dedicates his 1960 film *A bout de souffle* (Breathless) to Monogram Pictures, a Hollywood B-movie studio, and has his hero imitate Humphrey Bogart and quote William Faulkner, the influence of the American films that the *Cahiers* articles praised is readily apparent neither here nor in the films of Truffaut, Rohmer, or other New Wave directors. What is evident is a freshness of approach and a genuine ability to turn the camera into a writing instrument as they maintained their favorite Hollywood directors had done.

New Wave films played well in U.S. art houses, but the breakthrough French film was *And God Created Woman* (1956), starring Brigitte Bardot. Within two years, it earned $4 million in the United States. Although definitely not a New Wave film, it awakened American audiences to the new frankness in sexuality that French films could offer.

THE NEW WAVE AND THE NEW HOLLYWOOD

The typical French New Wave film, as David Bordwell and Kristin Thompson define it in *Film Art: An Introduction* (pp. 465–467), had a casual look, was filmed on location in available light with a hand-held camera that was often in motion, and contained humorous if esoteric references to other films. Protagonists drifted through life; plots drifted, too, surprising the viewer with shifts in tone and confounding expectations. Endings were ambiguous, like the freeze-frame at the conclusion of *Les 400 Coups,* which does not let us know what will become of the protagonist.

We do know what will happen to Butch Cassidy and the Sundance Kid at the end of George Roy Hill's 1969 film, but the freeze-frame there puts us in mind of Truffaut's film and is emblematic of the influence of the French New Wave on what became known as the "new" Hollywood, as studios strove to meet the demands of a new and younger audience. Other films that showed a New Wave influence include Richard Lester's *Petulia* (1968), Brian De Palma's *Greetings* (1968) and *Hi, Mom!* (1970), Melvin Van Peebles's *Sweet Sweetback's Baad Asssss Song* (1971), and the work of Dennis Hopper and Martin Scorsese. Cinema in Britain, Italy, and Sweden was undergoing a renaissance at the same time as in France, and the resulting various styles reappeared in a rich assemblage of Hollywood creations. Perhaps the most lasting French contribution was the auteur theory itself. Adopted by American film critics, and having filtered through to the general public, it gave the new Hollywood director star billing. One went out to see—and occasionally one still does—a Francis Ford Coppola, a Woody Allen, or a Robert Altman film, as opposed to one with a particular cast.

The French film industry helped Hollywood renew itself, but at the cost of being overshadowed by the new vitality coming from American directors. By 1970 the U.S. film industry would again dominate the world scene, and more powerfully than before.

PAINTING, POPULAR MUSIC, COMIC BOOKS

American culture of the 1950s, however, did not penetrate all areas of French life. Although by the beginning of the decade the world art market had shifted from Paris to New York, French art critics refused to recognize this fact or to acknowledge the importance of American abstract expressionism. In the immediate postwar years, they "continued to think of pictorial art as an elitist, refined, and intellectual product, characteristics that did not apply to the radical newness of a violent American painting that exploded the notions of balance and good taste so dear to the criticism of that time" (Tournès, p. 70). French Marxists, who dominated critical discourse until 1953, persisted in defending socialist realism from the decadence of abstraction. An abstract painter like Pierre Soulages had to go to the United States to gain recognition. The Museum of Modern Art in New York City bought his first paintings in 1948, and in 1950 he had a successful gallery exhibition in New York, yet he was totally unknown in his homeland.

In parallel fashion, Sidney Bechet, born of Creole ancestry in New Orleans, Louisiana, and now recognized as one of the greatest jazz clarinetists and saxophonists, never enjoyed the success in America that he found in France. After his triumph at the Paris Jazz Festival of 1949, he became to the French the very incarnation of jazz and took up permanent residence in that country, where his biggest hit, "Les Oignons" (Onions), sold more than a million copies by 1958. Beyond introducing American jazz tunes, Bechet also made jazz arrangements of French songs, thus opening an even larger public to African American music. Music hall singers like Yves Montand and Charles Aznavour went out of their way to hire jazz musicians to accompany them on stage and in the recording studio.

American rock and roll, however, ran into a roadblock with the French language, which just was not conducive to its harsh, driving beat. Its initial appearance in France in 1956 met with failure. But in 1960 a native French version of rock emerged, a softer "yé-yé" style that brought sudden success to young singers like Johnny Halliday and Sylvie Vartan. In the 1980s and 1990s, rap music translated more readily, its rhythms remarkably well suited to the run-on patter of Parisian street talk. Occasionally, French popular songs would succeed on the other side of the Atlantic: "La vie en rose" (music by R. S. Louiguy, lyrics by Edith Piaf) reigned as number one for fourteen weeks on the Lucky Strike Hit Parade in 1950; likewise, "Autumn Leaves" (music by Joseph Kosma, original lyrics by the French poet Jacques Prévert) held the top spot for sixteen weeks in 1955.

Although popular in France in the 1930s, American comic books were not available after the war because of a 1949 French law that forbade the importation of "publications destined for the young" judged immoral or vulgar. This cleared the way, however, for the development of a specifically francophone school, beginning with Hergé, a Belgian who drew the critically acclaimed *Tintin* books. In the 1990s, "la bande dessinée" became an enormously successful literary and artistic genre that French cartoonist-authors developed in different directions from their American counterparts.

PRO- AND ANTI-AMERICANISM IN FRANCE

Despite Sartre's having glimpsed in certain American novelists an opening to existential freedom, soon after World War II he began to see the culture that produced them as alienating, a smothering threat to freedom and to revolutionary change. There were other anti-American voices: The Communist Party and the Catholic Church both saw American popular culture as a threat to morals. It was only after a prolonged struggle with both of these cultural forces that the Coca-Cola Company was able to introduce their product into France in 1953; by then, "Coca-colonization" had become a synonym for American cultural imperialism. The same year saw the founding of *L'Express,* modeled after *Time* magazine, which soon became the adopted magazine of "les cadres," the new managerial class founded on largely American principles. Its founder and editor, Jean Jacques Servan-

Schreiber, told his readers that the French had much to learn from the American way of doing business.

The French philosopher Raymond Aron countered Sartre's complaints about the American menace by pointing out that despite his alleged sympathies for the masses, he was just an elitist at heart:

> Why do the intellectuals not admit to themselves that they are less interested in the standard of living of the working class than in the refinements of art and life? Why do they cling to democratic jargon when in fact they are trying to defend authentically aristocratic values against the invasion of mass-produced human beings and mass-produced commodities? (quoted in Mathy, pp. 161–162)

Sartre's elitism is a French phenomenon, historically conditioned by the peculiar isolation of French intellectuals from the real world, according to Mathy:

> The prestige and authority of the humanist tradition, reinforced throughout the school curriculum, the permanence of aristocratic models of cultural taste and judgment, and the centralization of intellectual activities in Paris, helped the literati to insulate themselves from the scientific and economic trends at work in the society at large. More so than in Germany, Britain, or the United States, French writers and philosophers continued to adhere to precapitalist, antiscientific values and categories of understanding and felt empowered to resist the growing materialism, positivism, and hedonism of the modern world. (*Extrême-Occident*, pp. 252–253)

Not so elitist, however, is the anti-Americanism expressed in the 1990s by Michel Houellebecq, a young novelist representative of the children of the generation of May 1968, when student riots in Paris brought down the de Gaulle government, considered a watershed in twentieth-century French history. These children, the French Generation Xers, rejected the revolutionary ideals of their parents. Like Houellebecq, the narrator in his *Les particules élémentaires* (1998) lacks Sartre's educational background (at the École Normale, producer of the best and brightest). In the midst of detailing his inability and that of his friends to achieve the normal human fulfillment of love and marriage as their grandparents had, he gives a capsule history of French attitudes toward love and marriage during the 1950s and 1960s, a time of wrenching change, with particular stress on the disastrous influence of American hedonist culture. Initially, he explains, modernization itself was at fault, for as the salaried sector (les cadres) increased and agriculture was abandoned, the "mariage de convenance" gave way to the "mariage d'amour."

> It was thus with a unanimous impatience that young people in the 1950s waited *to fall in love,* all the more so for the fact that the decline of agriculture and the accompanying disappearance of village communities allowed almost unlimited range to the search for a marriage partner. . . . It is no exaggeration to say that the 1950s and early 1960s were a veritable *golden age of romantic sentiment.* . . . However, at the same time libidinal mass consumption from North America (Elvis Presley songs, Marilyn Monroe films) was spreading throughout western Europe. Along with refrigerators and washing machines, the material accompaniment to a couple's happiness, came the transistor and the record player, which were to bring to the fore the behavioral model of *adolescent flirtation.* The ideological conflict, latent throughout the 1960s, burst to the surface at the beginning of the 1970s in [French teen magazines], crystallizing around the question, How far can one go before marriage? During the same years, the libidinal-hedonist option of North American origin received a powerful boost from the libertarian press. . . . Though ostensibly attacking capitalism, these periodicals agreed with the entertainment industry on one essential thing: the destruction of Judeo-Christian moral values, the celebration of youth and individual liberty. (*Les particules élémentaires,* pp. 69–71)

Thus, here is a twist on the old idea of innocent America and decadent Europe, although it had already been present in the early 1950s, as Catholics and communists alike denounced the corrupting power of American mass culture. In the perennial misunderstandings (or all too vivid understandings) floating between American and French culture, one can have it both ways: America the innocent, free of the weight of European learning; America the decadent, corrupting the youth of the world.

See also **American Expatriates Abroad; Artistic, Intellectual, and Political Refugees; International Relations and Connections** (*in this volume*).

BIBLIOGRAPHY

Atherton, John. "Americans in Paris." In *A New History of French Literature,* edited by Denis Hollier, pp. 908–914 Cambridge, Mass., 1989.

Barth, John, with Jonathan Baumbach, Robert Coover, and John Hawkes. "American Parallels: An Afterword." In *Three Decades of the French New Novel*, edited by Lois Oppenheim, pp. 195–209 Urbana, Ill., 1986.

Bordwell, David, and Kristin Thompson. *Film Art: An Introduction*. 5th ed. New York, 1997.

——. *Film History: An Introduction*. New York, 1994.

Bosquetti, Anna. "Sartre in the Age of the American Novel." In *Situating Sartre in Twentieth-Century Thought and Culture*, edited by Jean-François Fourny and Charles D. Minahen, pp. 71–92 New York, 1997.

Hillier, Jim, ed. *Cahiers du Cinéma: The 1950s*. Cambridge, Mass., 1985.

——. *Cahiers du Cinéma: The 1960s*. Cambridge, Mass., 1986.

Houellebecq, Michel. *Les particules élémentaires: Roman*. Paris, 1998.

Lehan, Richard. *A Dangerous Crossing: French Literary Existentialism and the Modern American Novel*. Carbondale, Ill., 1973.

Levy, Shawn. *King of Comedy: The Life and Art of Jerry Lewis*. New York, 1996.

Mathy, Jean-Philippe. *Extrême-Occident: French Intellectuals and America*. Chicago, 1993.

Pells, Richard. *Not Like Us: How Europeans Have Loved, Hated, and Transformed American Culture since World War II*. New York, 1997.

Tournès, Ludovic. "L'américanisation de la culture française." *Historiens et Géographes* 358 (July–August 1997): 65–79.

Truffaut, François. "A Certain Tendency of the French Cinema" *Cahiers du Cinéma* no. 31 (January 1954). Also in *Movies and Methods: An Anthology*, edited by Bill Nichols, pp. 224–237 Berkeley, Calif., 1976.

THE WORLD ACCORDING TO HOLLYWOOD

Christopher Ames

HOLLYWOOD AND WORLD WAR II

World War II had a transforming effect on Hollywood, and Hollywood significantly shaped how Americans perceived and experienced the war. In the years of American involvement in the war, 1942 to 1945, over eight hundred of the fifteen hundred films released by Hollywood made references to the war. While actual combat was featured in some of these films, many Hollywood films dealt with other aspects of the war experience: the draft, wartime shortages and rationing, foreign resistance movements, military training, the enemy, international cooperation, espionage, and life on the home front. Nearly all of Hollywood's great directors made films that involved the war: Alfred Hitchcock, Charlie Chaplin, Howard Hawks, George Cukor, Billy Wilder, Otto Preminger, William Wyler, Fritz Lang, George Stevens, Cecil B. DeMille, Preston Sturges, John Ford, William Wellman, James Whale, Mitchell Leisen, Douglas Sirk, Spencer Williams, Sam Wood, Victor Fleming, Jean Renoir—even Busby Berkeley in *The Gang's All Here* (1943). Workman-like studio directors Edward Dymytryk and Raoul Walsh filmed five or six war movies each. Michael Curtiz, whose *Casablanca* (1942) remains the most famous movie of the war, made six other films with war themes, including the documentary *This Is the Army* (1943).

Hollywood mobilized for the war and turned its considerable resources to patriotic support of the Allied cause. Hollywood stars promoted the sale of war bonds and entertained GIs abroad and in the Hollywood Canteen. Studios conserved paper and limited the construction of sets, costumes, and wigs. Directors Frank Capra, John Huston, Darryl Zanuck, George Stevens, William Wyler, and John Ford all worked for the military, filming training movies and documentary footage in battle, much of which later found its way into fiction films. Ford's raw color footage of D-Day is said to have inspired Steven Spielberg's vivid treatment of the invasion in his film *Saving Private Ryan* (1998).

Since only 10 percent of Americans actually saw military action in the war, while 85 million Americans attended movies weekly, Hollywood had a powerful role in shaping popular images and attitudes regarding the war. Moviegoing was more popular during the 1940s than it has ever been—before or since. So World War II movies make particularly good objects for studying how social anxieties and desires are figured in popular culture. The unabashed propaganda aspects of war films make obvious what popular entertainment often conceals: that social and political beliefs are advocated and interrogated through the narratives of popular culture. In reading the cultural messages of a film genre or cycle, the World War II film is a good place to start.

Hollywood's treatment of the war began before President Roosevelt used federal muscle to encourage it; in fact, the interventionist implications of a variety of films released between 1937 and 1941 led to a Senate investigation headed by the isolationist Gerald P. Nye. He charged that Hollywood was abusing its access to the hearts and minds of America by pushing a particular political agenda. The investigation was quickly thwarted by Nye's immoderate and sometimes anti-Semitic remarks, by Wendell Wilkie's spirited defense of the Hollywood producers who hired him, by the overwhelming popular support for Roosevelt's stated position of "all aid short of war," and, ultimately, by the bombing of Pearl Harbor, which ended U.S. isolationism and rendered the investigation moot.

The sensitivity in Hollywood to the rise of European fascism had several sources, among them the strong Jewish presence in studio front offices and practical concerns that Nazi-occupied territories would not import American films. Given the outright propaganda of the American war years, it is hard to realize that films like Charlie Chaplin's *The Great Dictator* (1940), *Personal History* (based on Vincent Sheean's best-seller), and the British-made indictment of Nazi government, *Pastor Hall* (1940),

CASABLANCA

Casablanca (1942) is the most popular film to emerge from Hollywood's treatment of World War II. But during production, Warner Bros. thought of it as a run-of-the-mill topical melodrama. Once it was finished, however, the studio knew it had created something special, a feeling confirmed at the box office and at the Academy Awards. Rushed out in November 1942 to capitalize on the Allied capture of Casablanca, the film was extraordinarily popular, grossing three times its production cost and winning Oscars for best screenplay, best director, and best picture. The movie has grown in stature since its release, becoming one of the most shown films on television, and cited among the best films ever made by the British Film Institute in 1983.

What gave *Casablanca* this lasting appeal? Some of the credit must go to what has been called "the genius of the system," as *Casablanca* exemplifies the assembly line artistry of the studios. Both producer Hal Wallis and director Michael Curtiz were very successful at churning out high-quality pictures, and the fortuitous mix of several different writers, the renewed popularity of the song "As Time Goes By," and career-defining performances by Humphrey Bogart, Ingrid Bergman, and a host of character actors gave *Casablanca* an appealing mixture of sentimentality and sting.

Part of the movie's appeal is owed to good timing. *Casablanca* is clearly an interventionist film, as was the play on which it was based, *Everybody Comes to Rick's,* written by Murray Burnett and Joan Allison in 1940. But the movie was made after Pearl Harbor, and thus the interventionist message was no longer controversial propaganda but rather a reinforcement of the wisdom of American commitment.

The interventionist message is hard to miss. When Rick initially asserts, "I stick my neck out for nobody," the local police chief, Louis, responds, "A very wise foreign policy"—in case the parallel is unclear. Rick speaks to Americans everywhere when he muses to the piano player, Sam: "It's December 1941 in Casablanca. What time is it in New York? I'll bet they're asleep in New York. I'll bet they're asleep all over America." Rick's conversion from selfish neutrality to passionate commitment is made all the more convincing by Bogart's tough-guy outsider style. His committed sacrifice represents America's as a whole in a way that makes the American audience feel good about itself.

Hollywood casting created a great deal of authenticity in evoking a Casablanca filled with refugees of Nazi terror. At least two dozen of the seventy-five cast members were actual refugees. Ironically, most Nazi roles in Hollywood were played by refugee Jews. The OWI classified *Casablanca,* approvingly, as a United Nations film, a film that emphasized the multinational character of the Allied effort; it includes a sympathetic Russian bartender, as well as a good German one, and a member of the Norwegian resistance.

Curtiz's use of Rick's bar as a global microcosm emerges in the brilliantly manipulative scene of the singing of "The Marseillaise." A group of German soldiers begins singing "Watch on the Rhine." Curtiz pans through disapproving reaction shots, then Victor orders the orchestra to play the French national anthem. Rick gives a curt nod of approval. Eventually the whole barroom crowd is on its feet, drowning out the German soldiers. As the song reaches its climax, Curtiz moves

CONTINUED NEXT PAGE

94

through a series of emotional close-ups: an émigré singing through tears, Victor beaming forcefully, Ilsa admiring him with moist eyes. The war of national songs reflects the larger war and demonstrates the heroism and populist strength of the resistance; the insular community of Casablanca symbolizes a world trapped in mortal conflict.

The film's sentimental theme of ennobling sacrifice probably explains why it has continued to charm audiences. It takes a tough guy like Bogart to deliver the weepy moral with conviction: "Ilsa, I'm no good at being noble. But it doesn't take much to see that the problems of three little people don't amount to a hill of beans in this crazy world. Someday, you'll understand that. Here's looking at you, kid." The speech mingles romance with stoicism, condescension with sentimentality, American independence with allegiance to a greater cause. The OWI noted that the movie demonstrated "that personal desires must be subordinated to the task of defeating fascism." It is a moral told in dozens of wartime films; in this one it is captured with such enduring grace and wit that it defined a kind of American hero.

were controversial for fear that they might offend Nazi Germany. Indeed, the Production Code Administration quashed *Personal History* (it later became, in a greatly depoliticized form, Hitchcock's *Foreign Correspondent* [1940]). In the postwar years, the makers of these films would come to be known by the revealing term, "premature antifascists," and such premature antifascism would, during McCarthyism, leave these same filmmakers prey to charges of communism and anti-Americanism.

The breakthrough interventionist film was *Confessions of a Nazi Spy* (1939), produced by the relatively liberal Warner Bros. Based on an actual incident in which Nazi spies were tried in a U.S. federal court, *Confessions* was filmed in a pseudo-documentary style. By focusing on Nazi infiltration of America, the movie emphasized the danger the Nazis posed to this country. The peroration of the district attorney to the jury reads like an exhortation to American intervention in Europe. Though *Confessions* exaggerated the Nazi presence in America, that plot device allowed the movie to argue forcefully against isolationism.

The bombing of Pearl Harbor put an end to debates over isolationism. With America engaged in a total war, Hollywood turned its production lines to making wartime products, just as automobile factories were converted to munitions plants. President Roosevelt, in typical fashion, assigned the dissemination of war-related information to a complex variety of federal commissions, most notably the Bureau of Motion Pictures (BMP) and the Office of War Information (OWI).

Neither commission had actual censorship power over the industry. The BMP and the OWI worked in an advisory capacity, producing guidelines and manuals, reviewing scripts and completed films, and communicating their opinions to the studios. The organizations hoped to persuade Hollywood to promote patriotic values and convey truthful information about the war. An OWI manual asked filmmakers to apply seven questions to all their wartime products, the first of which was "Will this picture help win the war?" Such a question was fundamentally different from Hollywood's usual question, "Will this film make money and entertain people?"

Though Hollywood was wary of censorship, the studios threw themselves enthusiastically into producing war propaganda, both subtle and obvious. Oddly, the OWI often found itself in the position of asking studios to tone down their wartime rhetoric, to be less obviously propagandistic or less racist and simplistic in depicting the enemy, particularly the Japanese. Composed of Roosevelt liberals, the OWI often advocated political messages (especially with regard to cooperation with the Russians and the Chinese) that the largely conservative studios were reluctant to promulgate. Still, the OWI did influence film content, often through their manual, which was occasionally quoted verbatim by preachy characters in films. And by reinforcing certain propagandistic themes, the OWI intensified the generic uniformity characteristic of Hollywood; many films of wartime Hollywood seem ideologically interchangeable.

The combat film, for example, typically introduced the audience to a democratically diverse platoon, possibly containing an Irishman, an Italian, a baseball fan from Brooklyn, a young greenhorn, an experienced vet, and even a black man (as in *Bataan* [1943]), in spite of the fact that actual American military units were not integrated. The combat plot centers on a well-defined but elusive objective, and it presents a bloody and costly battle that causes the soldiers to reflect on the value of their sacrifices. American soldiers are depicted as fighting for the American way of life, for home and democracy, and for the end of foreign dictatorships—not for acquisition or conquest. Inevitably the home front appears in many more movies than the actual depiction of combat, because it reinforced what Americans felt they were fighting for. As Koppes and Black analyze it, "By making the war pervasive in the depiction of ordinary lives, the movies would show that the country was united, with everyone participating equally."

Wartime patriotism even influenced historical movies set before World War II. Critical historicism asks us to analyze the context in which a film is made in addition to the historical period in which it is set. This double focus is most obvious in the World War I films that offered World War II implications. *All Quiet on the Western Front* (1930) was rereleased in 1940 in response to the new war; *Sergeant York* (1941), in which Gary Cooper portrays a pacifist who becomes a military hero in the First World War, effectively responded to qualms about newly instituted conscription preceding American involvement in World War II. More intriguing as an example is the 1944 comedy *Meet Me in St. Louis,* which, set at the turn of the century, contains no literal topical references at all. The film's relevance to 1944 comes across most vividly in the powerful and sentimental rendition Judy Garland gives of the song "Have Yourself a Merry Little Christmas." The lyrics, slightly altered for the film, promise that "next year all our troubles will be out of sight," echoing the propaganda line popular in 1944—"home next year"—as the end of the war became foreseeable. To a 1944 audience, the implications of the tearjerker would have been obvious: families separated by the war prayed that fate would reunite them, while those on the home front bravely "muddled through," to use another propaganda phrase. The nostalgia of *Meet Me in St. Louis* reinforces the wartime verities of American home and family—what we fight for.

FILM GENRES IN THE 1950s

The most critically successful film of the 1940s was a war film that signaled the end of war films: William Wyler's *The Best Years of Our Lives* (1946). Wyler's film follows three serviceman—from different branches of the service and different social classes—returning to home life in the fictional Boone City. The film deglamorizes the war and speaks frankly about the difficult adjustments returning veterans faced: marital problems, underemployment, postcombat trauma, alcoholism, and mixed popular support. Harold Russell, an actual wounded veteran with metal hooks replacing hands lost in an explosion, gives a riveting performance in a role that symbolizes the physical and psychic wounds that veterans had to overcome. The film depicts returning servicemen as people who have become so used to the company of men that they feel awkward with women and in domestic situations. Women are shown to have become more independent and self-sufficient on the home front, and all three men have difficulty accepting those changes.

The film struck a chord; it was fabulously successful at the box office and won all the Academy Awards it was nominated for, including best director, best actor, and best picture. In the film, the veterans are reluctant to talk about their wartime heroics, and this reluctance reflected a change in the home audience appetite as well. "By the summer of 1946," Thomas Schatz reports, "not a single war film was in release or in production" (*Boom and Bust*, p. 368). When war films returned in the 1950s, many would have the critical, antiromantic edge of *The Best Years of Our Lives. Stalag 17* (1953) showed prison and privation bringing out the worst in people, not the best; *From Here to Eternity* (1953) included a character whose refusal to box in an army league symbolized a kind of conscientious objection; *The Caine Mutiny* (1954), in another context, revealed the harshness of strict military rule; *The Bridge on the River Kwai* (1957) was replete with ironies, as prisoners struggled to survive by aiding the enemy and finally sabotaging their own work; *Paths of Glory* (1957) showed the corruption of military leadership in World War I; and William Wyler's *Friendly Persuasion* (1956) focused on Quakers committed to nonviolence. The appetite for military propaganda had ended with the war.

While Hollywood returned to telling familiar stories in the forms of Westerns, crime pictures, melodramas, and romances, the postwar period and the 1950s saw the rise of three distinctive and in-

The Best Years of Our Lives (1946). Returning veterans Harold Russsell and Dana Andrews *(left and center)* confront an intransigent system in William Wyler's optimistic treatment of postwar America. © BETTMANN/CORBIS

teresting film genres: the social-problem film, film noir, and the science fiction movie.

The Best Years of Our Lives anticipates the social-problem film in tone and content. This genre arose out of the decline of the studio system in the 1950s. While American prosperity led to a sharp rise in single-family homes and in persons attending college, Hollywood endured a steadily declining box office. The studio system was assailed by antitrust actions that led to divorcement, the forced sale of theater chains held by production studios. Above all, film began to lose out to other forms of entertainment—from night baseball to the big competition, television. Hollywood reacted to television by trying to differentiate its product. Greater emphasis on color photography, on extreme widescreen projection (CinemaScope), and on novelties like 3-D accompanied a turn to controversial topics too volatile for television, as the censorship of the produc-

tion code weakened (it was eventually overturned in 1960).

Successful films dealt with such topics as alcoholism (*The Lost Weekend* [1945]), drug addiction (*The Man with the Golden Arm* [1955], *A Hatful of Rain* [1952]), mental illness (*The Snake Pit* [1948]), violent crime and its psychological causes (*Anatomy of a Murder* [1959], *Rope* [1948], *Compulsion* [1959], *Vertigo* [1958]), interracial relationships (*Island in the Sun* [1957], *Pinky* [1949]), anti-Semitism and racial prejudice (*Gentleman's Agreement* [1947], *Intruder in the Dust* [1949], *The Defiant Ones* [1958]), and youth rebellion (*Rebel without a Cause* [1955], *Blackboard Jungle* [1955], *The Wild One* [1954]).

A fascinating Hollywood example of the social-problem film genre is *On the Waterfront* (1954), which deals with the issue of union corruption. In typical Hollywood fashion, the film focuses on the heroic efforts of one uncorrupted individual opposing a mob. But this powerful film also has a political subtext; both the writer, Budd Schulberg, and the director, Elia Kazan, had cooperated with the HUAC investigation of communism in the motion picture industry that led to the painful and needlessly divisive blacklist. That they contrived to produce an emotional film in which the hero does the right thing by informing on others was read by many as cleverly disguised self-justification.

The suspiciousness that characterized a decade in which the government pressured workers in the film industry to inform on their colleagues emerged in many forms. This threatening milieu provided a context for the most interesting genre to arise out of postwar Hollywood, film noir. The term "film noir" was coined by French critics in response to a flood of literally and figuratively dark movies that entered France after the wartime embargo. It refers to movies from the 1940s and 1950s, generally inexpensively produced, that were characterized by violence, adultery, corruption, and ambiguous or unhappy endings. But the term also refers to a visual style that emphasized nighttime location shooting, rain-slicked streets, oblique framing, and lighting that, unlike traditional Hollywood three-point lighting, cast long shadows. As R. Barton Palmer puts it, "Film noir, in brief, offers the obverse of the American dream" (*Perspectives in Film Noir*, p. 6). Film noir presents a message that runs contrary to the usual Hollywood themes, in a style equally contrary to the classic Hollywood style.

Of the four influences the contemporary director Paul Schrader identifies as leading to film noir—postwar disillusionment, international postwar realism, the influx of German expatriates into Hollywood, and the rise of the hard-boiled tradition in detective novels—three reflect the cataclysm of World War II. To postwar audiences, noir films possessed an existential edge and a toughness that seemed particularly authentic; noir films depicted ordinary individuals as lonely and threatened by ambiguous forces, the dark roads of the films representing the unilluminated stretches on a metaphorical road of life.

As the genre developed in the 1950s, it naturally reflected the distrust and cynicism of blacklisting and the cold war. The late film noir *Kiss Me Deadly* (1955) inserts cold war themes into the hard-boiled detective context. Private investigator Mike Hammer spends the movie in a violent and mysterious search for an object dubbed "the great whatzit." Like the precious statuette of the earliest famous noir film, *The Maltese Falcon* (1941), the "great whatzit" functions as an empty signifier that motivates a plot of ruthless competitive searching. But in *Kiss Me Deadly*, the mysterious sought after object is revealed to be some sort of deadly, glowing, radioactive substance connected with "Trinity, Los Alamos, the Manhattan Project." The firestorm that ends the film embodies the fears of nuclear annihilation that colored the late 1950s.

Similar fears spurred a flowering of the science fiction genre in the 1950s. Futuristic films about space travel and scientific innovation had been around as long as the technological medium of film itself, and they continue to the present day. But in the 1950s, critics agree, this relatively minor genre assumed much greater importance: "it was only after 1950 that [science fiction] film emerged as a critically recognized genre" (Sobchak, *Screening Space*, p. 12). Technological innovations that made space travel increasingly plausible were doubtless influential in stimulating the American collective imagination in this direction, as represented in the highly regarded *Destination Moon* (1950). But many of those innovations—such as the V-2 rocket—grew out of World War II, and space exploration as a theme became inescapably linked to the cold war and the concepts of an arms race and a space race.

It should come as little surprise that one of the most popular 1950s subgenres of science fiction was the alien invasion film. Fears of actual foreign invasion were addressed and assuaged imaginatively through science fiction. Transforming the human enemy into inhuman monsters was a predictable by-product of this form of cultural expression. These films present alien invaders not susceptible to our normal means of defense: they may replicate like plants or viruses, as in *The Thing* (1951); resist all weaponry, as in *The War of the Worlds* (1953); or insidiously mask themselves in the guise of our neighbors, as in *Invasion of the Body Snatchers* (1956). That these films played out an anxiety about the perceived communist menace seems plausible; indeed some films, such as *The Flying Saucer* (1950) and *Project M-7* (1953), explicitly mingle communists and space invaders. As with wartime films, alien invasion films emphasize how human cooperation—particularly between scientists and the military—and social orderliness are necessary to defeat the invaders. The imperative force of the final command in *The Thing*—"Keep watching the skies"—echoes the literal messages of wartime posters and movies.

The red scare and the arms race were inextricably conflated with the anxieties of the nuclear age, the new consciousness of the human ability to destroy the planet. Many of the monster films of the science fiction genre feature atomic mutants: the giant ants of *Them!* (1954), the monster of *It Came from beneath the Sea* (1955), the villains of *Attack of the Crab Monsters* (1957), even the radioactive lava of *X—the Unknown* (1956). As in *Kiss Me Deadly*, the name for fear and grotesque monstrosity is the atom bomb; these monsters are, in the words of one critic, "instruments of punishment for nuclear misuse" (Kane, *Take One* 2, p. 10).

In *The Day the Earth Stood Still* (1951), a sympathetic extraterrestrial being comes to Earth to warn against nuclear proliferation. This film struck such a powerful chord that it was echoed in many accounts given by persons claiming to have been abducted by UFOs in the 1950s. The extraterrestrial visitor in the film gains our attention by, significantly, stopping all power—electrical and otherwise—so that society comes to a halt. Science fiction films both celebrated and warned against the influence of science; their popularity expressed widespread anxieties stimulated by the cold war and the nuclear age. But these films were also entertainingly fantastic and escapist, they worked to exorcise and assuage the fears they embodied.

WALT DISNEY AND THE AMERICAN IMAGINATION

The Hollywood combination of the fantastic, the escapist, and the socially conservative emerges powerfully in the 1950s in the films of Walt Disney. Indeed, Disney has probably attracted more attention from historians of American culture than any other filmmaker. Because Disney defined himself as prototypically American, and because he deliberately and successfully created a mythology for American children, his works reveal powerfully the latent ideologies of twentieth-century American culture.

Pioneering the animated short film and developing the first animated feature (*Snow White and the Seven Dwarfs* [1937]), Disney Studios became one of the most powerful forces in Hollywood. With the advent of World War II, the Disney studios turned their efforts to supporting the Allied cause, to an even greater extent than the rest of Hollywood. For eight months following Pearl Harbor, army troops were actually housed at Disney Studios, and throughout the war, over 90 percent of the studio was dedicated to government projects, including training and health films. A remarkably successful cartoon, "The New Spirit" (1942), used Donald Duck to urge Americans to pay their income tax promptly to aid the war effort. In 1943,

Disney won an Oscar for an anti-Nazi animated short called *Der Führer's Face.*

Disney's most enduring work of the war years is the animated feature *Bambi* (1942). The product of years of animation and careful research on animal movement, *Bambi* is a triumph of realistic animation that remains visually effective to this day. Though *Bambi* features the familiarly charming Disney animal characters and provides one of the cutest Disney heroes in the little deer of the title, it is a remarkably disturbing children's film. The influence of the war is evidenced in young Bambi's traumatic encounter with humankind, the deadly power of guns, the brutal death of his mother, and a destructive forest fire. Admirably, the film teaches children about death in a natural context, but the urgency of such lessons is related to the violent death and destruction wrought by humankind. The film critic Roger Ebert hyperbolically calls the movie "a parable of sexism, nihilism and despair, portraying absentee fathers and passive mothers in a world of death and violence."

The sexism Ebert refers to lies in the way *Bambi* uses the traditional sex roles of deer—the father uninvolved with the raising of the child—as an apparent model of human behavior. This reinforcement of traditional gender roles—in the face of the changes spurred by the war—also characterizes two of Disney's other most successful full-length cartoons that framed the 1950s, *Cinderella* (1950) and *Sleeping Beauty* (1959).

Disney turns *Cinderella* from a story about a teenager freeing herself from a limiting life into a meditation on motherhood. Both Cinderella and the Prince have lost mothers, yet substitute mothers abound—most memorably in the form of the wicked stepmother who enslaves her late husband's child. Cinderella is rescued by a fairy godmother, a surrogate good mother who enables Cinderella's venture into the world. But the movie reduces the role of this figure from the folk tale, rendering the fairy godmother comically absent-minded. The real good mother of the Disney version is Cinderella herself, who tends to a debilitating array of chores with unbroken good cheer, and mothers a host of mice and family pets invented by Disney. She works tirelessly and cheerfully for her charges in contrast to the selfish stepmother. Ironically, Cinderella's obedient performance of myriad chores gives her the inner beauty requisite to attract the Prince, whose marriage proposal makes it no longer necessary for Cinderella to slave away.

The family tensions that grip young viewers— wicked stepmother, jealous step siblings—exist within the class structure of the film as well. Cinderella is treated as a servant, and the movie offers the democratic message that she deserves to share her sisters' privileges. Yet Cinderella has her own servants of a sort. The comical mice usurp the role of the original fairy godmother: not only are they transformed into carriage horses, but they sew her a ball gown and rescue her from her locked room. Watching the splendid animation, one cannot help but think of all the "mice" working as animators in the Disney factory, a cadre of mostly female workers engaging in the repetitive labor necessary for such filmic accomplishments. The division of labor implicitly lauded in *Cinderella* was replicated at the Disney studios, where the most mechanical, repetitive labor in animation was performed by female workers.

The happy ending is achieved through the amorous intervention of the virtually mute Prince. It is in such conclusions that Disney cartoons most famously reinforce traditional views of women's roles. In *Sleeping Beauty* the Prince must again rescue the damsel in distress. The main character's animated beauty, a trait so important it becomes her name, interestingly resembles the feminine ideal embodied in Barbie, the popular doll introduced the year before. But this beauty is somnolent, and it requires the Prince's kiss to undo the wicked spell of Maleficent, the harpy of this fairy tale.

The dark Disney antimothers—the wicked stepmother of *Cinderella*, Maleficent of *Sleeping Beauty*—parallel the femmes fatales of film noir. In film noir, women combine seductiveness, evil, and power. Their fatal quality arises from their ability to entice the male hero away from his mission. While film noir women are corrupt wives, Disney female villains are corrupt mothers, and they typically possess the only sexuality in the films. Perhaps these destructive women reflect social anxiety about the changing and expanding role of women during and following the war. The change in the status of women is surely one of the biggest transformations of the 1900s. At the century's midpoint, we see those changes reflected in nightmarish caricatures, both in the dark black-and-white of noir films and the vivid color of Disney's animation.

The political implications of Disney's productions have both attracted and resisted explication. A recent collection of essays promises "to develop vocabularies for the political in the seemingly apolitical world of Disney" (Bell et al., *From Mouse to Mermaid*, p. 2). In the most sustained examination of Disney's politics, Watts argues that Disney began as a liberal, sentimental populist. Mickey Mouse

was a common man figure, a feisty and irrepressible opponent of the dark forces of the depression. "The Three Little Pigs," the most popular animated short ever, was widely viewed as a parable about ordinary folk (the pigs) using their wits and industry to rally against the Big Bad Wolf at the door. Critics have similarly read the dwarfs in *Snow White* as a model for collective labor. But in the early 1940s three events shifted Disney to the political Right: a bitter strike at Disney Studios, the spread of World War II, and the anticommunist investigations in Hollywood. Walt Disney became an outspoken anticommunist, and his genial populism darkened into a jingoistic Americanism. These changes were reflected throughout the Disney ouevre, including an increased emphasis on preserving the traditional family as a bulwark against social chaos—what Watts calls the "Disney doctrine"—and an increased fascination with patriotic heroes from American history—in live-action features and television. The most famous of these was Davy Crockett, whose television show sparked a 1950s coonskin-cap craze as widespread as the 1930s' response to "The Three Little Pigs." Davy Crockett's heroism "symbolized the American character in the death struggle with the Communist foe" (Watts, *The Magic Kingdom*, p. 317).

In the 1950s Disney solidified its vast reach into American culture. While other film studios floundered in the face of divorcement and television, Disney expanded. Disney added to the interrelated network of cartoons, comic books, children's books and toys, regular forays into live-action films, the creation of a variety of television programs, and the development of a revolutionary new amusement park. Walt Disney envisioned the amusement park as a created utopian township, a village devoted to pleasure. And he populated the town with versions of his animated characters (played by actors in costumes, built into rides, and displayed iconically on signs and souvenirs). Thus, the transient world of motion pictures could be reified in a form inviting audience participation. From a business point of view, theme park and feature film promoted one another, as when one of Disney's earliest and biggest live-action features, *20,000 Leagues under the Sea* (1954), quickly metamorphosed into a submarine ride at the new Disneyland, which opened in 1955. The vertical integration of studio and theater was replaced by the horizontal integration of different forms of entertainment, an industry trend pioneered by Disney and dominant today when studios are owned by conglomerates involved in book and magazine publishing, sports franchises, cable networks, recording labels, and theme parks.

Disney continues to have an extraordinary influence on children; its stores dot shopping malls across the country, Florida's Disney World has become the most popular tourist destination on Earth, and Disney animated features remain the most popular children's movies. The fantasy expert Jack Zipes notes that when Americans recall classic fairy tales, they generally remember the Disney version, a version he identifies as "capitaliz[ing] on American innocence and utopianism to reinforce the social and political status quo" (Bell, pp. 21–22). Disney's enduring role in American family life has its roots squarely in the 1950s, at the midpoint of the century and the midpoint of Walt Disney's career (1923–1966).

It is wise, however, to be cautious in interpreting the social messages of the movies in the 1940s and 1950s. Walt Disney always scoffed at what "the professors" said about his work, yet the form of the fable invites moral interpretation and analysis. Our understanding of eras past is necessarily textual, and Hollywood's products should be read in the context of other artifacts and historical explorations of culture. In so doing, one sees not a mere reflection of the times, but many intriguing resonances between popular culture and social changes.

See also **Film** *(volume 3)*.

BIBLIOGRAPHY

Hollywood and World War II

Basinger, Jeanine. *The World War II Combat Film: Anatomy of a Genre.* New York, 1986.

Dick, Bernard F. *The Star-Spangled Screen: The American World War II Film.* Lexington, Ky., 1985.

Harmetz, Aljean. *Round Up the Usual Suspects: The Making of "Casablanca"— Bogart, Bergman, and World War II.* New York, 1992.

Koppes, Clayton R., and Gregory D. Black. *Hollywood Goes to War: How Politics, Profits, and Propaganda Shaped World War II Movies.* New York, 1987.

Lebo, Harlan. *Casablanca: Behind the Scenes.* New York, 1992.

Myers, James M. *The Bureau of Motion Pictures and Its Influence on Film Content during World War II: The Reasons for Its Failure.* Lewiston, Ky., and New York, 1998.

Shull, Michael S., and David Edward Wilt. *Hollywood War Films, 1937–1945: An Exhaustive Filmography of American Feature-Length Motion Pictures Relating to World War II.* Jefferson, N.C., 1996.

Siegel, Jeff. *The Casablanca Companion: The Movie and More.* Dallas, Tex., 1992.

Film Genres of the 1940s and 1950s

Cameron, Ian, ed. *The Book of Film Noir.* New York, 1993.

Gow, Gordon. *Hollywood in the Fifties.* New York, 1971.

Johnson, William, ed. *Focus on the Science Fiction Film.* Englewood Cliffs, N.J., 1972.

Kane, Joe. "Nuclear Films." *Take One* 2 (July–August 1969): 9–11.

Maxfield, James F. *The Fatal Woman: Sources of Male Anxiety in American Film Noir, 1941–1991.* Madison, Wis., 1996.

Menville, Douglas. *A Historical and Critical Survey of the Science-Fiction Film.* New York, 1975.

Palmer, R. Barton. *Hollywood's Dark Cinema: The American Film Noir.* New York, 1994.

Palmer, R. Barton, ed. *Perspectives on Film Noir.* New York, 1996.

Polan, Dana. *Power and Paranoia: History, Narrative, and the American Cinema, 1940–1950. New York, 1986.*

Roffman, Peter. *The Hollywood Social Problem Film: Madness, Despair, and Politics from the Depression to the Fifties.* Bloomington, Ind., 1981.

Schatz, Thomas. *Boom and Bust: The American Cinema in the 1940s.* History of the American Cinema, Vol. 6. New York, 1997.

Schrader, Paul. "Notes on Film Noir." In *Film Genre Reader II,* edited by Barry Keith Grant. Austin, Tex., 1995.

Silver, Alain, and James Ursini, eds. *Film Noir Reader.* New York, 1996.

Sobchack, Vivian. *Screening Space: The American Science Fiction Film.* 2d ed. New York, 1987.

Telotte, J. P. *Voices in the Dark: The Narrative Patterns of Film Noir.* Urbana, Ill., 1989.

Walt Disney and American Culture

Bell, Elizabeth, Lynda Haas, and Laura Sells, eds. *From Mouse to Mermaid: The Politics of Film, Gender, and Culture.* Bloomington, Ind., 1995.

Giroux, Henry A. *The Mouse That Roared: Disney and the End of Innocence.* New York, 1999.

Jackson, Kathy Merlock. *Walt Disney: A Bio-Bibliography.* Westport, Conn., 1993.

Maltin, Leonard. *The Disney Films.* New York, 1995.

Schickel, Richard. *The Disney Version: The Life, Times, Art, and Commerce of Walt Disney.* New York, 1968.

Shale, Richard. *Donald Duck Joins Up: The Walt Disney Studio during World War II.* Ann Arbor, Mich., 1982.

Smoodin, Eric, ed. *Disney Discourse: Producing the Magic Kingdom.* New York, 1994.

Watts, Steven. *The Magic Kingdom: Walt Disney and the American Way of Life.* New York, 1997.

ANALYTIC PHILOSOPHY

Michael Goldman

Analytic philosophy was the dominant school of philosophy in American universities during the second half of the twentieth century. While it is easy to assert this with confidence, it is by no means easy to say exactly what analytic philosophy is. Most philosophers know it when they see it, but attempts to capture it by means of a simple definition—an approach characteristic of analytic philosophy itself—inevitably are defeated by numerous counterexamples—which is likewise a technique common in analytic philosophy.

There are a variety of characterizations of analytic philosophy. Some describe what analytic philosophy is, others illuminate it by means of contrasts with other approaches. For any characterization, however, it is possible to point to one or more analytic philosophers or analytic philosophic approaches that do not fit the description. Since there is no seminal or founding figure, and no body of canonical literature in analytic philosophy, the absence of agreement among scholars is not surprising.

ANALYTIC PHILOSOPHY AS ANALYSIS

Although analytic philosophy became known for its desire to rid philosophy of nonempirical metaphysics, its initial manifestation nevertheless harbored an extreme metaphysical commitment of its own. Early analytic philosophy, represented by the logical atomism of Bertrand Russell and Ludwig Wittgenstein, was committed to the assumption that the proper way to understand the world is to understand the parts out of which it is constituted. In terms of philosophical practice this frequently amounted to an attempt to provide definitions of problematic concepts. Russell's *Analysis of Mind* (1921) and *Analysis of Matter* (1927) are paradigmatic. The goal was to substitute for these concepts—always in a propositional context, never standing alone—equivalent statements about the elements that constituted the reality to which the proposition referred. Ultimate definitions were called "atomic sentences" and were descriptions of the fundamental units of reality. Philosophers' definitions were not intended to be scientific findings; instead, philosophers focused on the meaning of propositions that referred to ontologically basic units of reality, such as mind, matter, universals, particulars, numbers, time, causality, and the like, and the general principles that characterize the behavior and interaction of these different kinds of reality. While some holistic philosophical systems assert the reality of an undivided One, logical atomism, the first version of analytic philosophy, takes the position that the fundamental elements of reality are particular, distinct items, and that reality, rather than being a single whole, is constituted by these items in their relationship to each other. Whatever laws these items obey are laws peculiar to these items. Reality is the interaction of particular elements, each obeying the physical laws appropriate to them. Thus, to understand reality requires a person to understand the parts out of which it is constituted, the laws that govern those parts, and the relationships those parts enter into with each other.

Such a metaphysical bias is clearly congenial to the physics (and politics) that prevailed in Western thinking for most of the twentieth century. As physicists sought and discovered new truths about what they took to be the fundamental elements of the physical universe, and as Western individualism became more and more the dominant political ideology in the world, it is not surprising that the metaphysical assumptions underlying this physics and this politics should be taken by philosophers to reflect the necessary structure of reality.

One feature of this approach that may serve to explain both its metaphysical significance and the way it reflects prevailing social assumptions concerns the nature of relations. Philosophers traditionally distinguish between internal relations and external relations. An external relation is one that a fully defined and self-sufficient element enters into with another fully defined and self-sufficient element. A molecule of gas is a fully defined and self-sufficient element, and it can attract, repel, or collide with another fully defined and self-sufficient molecule of gas. Neither molecule is redefined by this interaction, though each may have its behavior altered by it. A self-interested actor in the marketplace is a fully defined and self-sufficient economic unit that can interact with others, guided only by its own self-interested motivations. It is not redefined by its interaction with others, though it may change its behavior in response to them. An internal relation, by contrast, is constitutive of an element and partially determines the laws that govern its behavior. Thus, if some item is what it is only because of its relation to some other items, such that in the absence of those other items it would be a different thing, then its relation to those other items is an internal relation. Certain analytic philosophers deny there are any internal relations. Atoms are what they are independent of other atoms, and people are what they are independent of other people. Even if human beings are significantly influenced by others, they are not constituted by them.

This same kind of atomism was brought to bear on another major branch of philosophy, epistemology. According to this view, knowledge is built out of elements, each one of which is a "simple" perceptual "given." A person's knowledge of a table, for instance, can be analyzed into his or her direct perceptual acquaintance with a brown, rectangular "sense-datum" (an immediate unanalyzable private object of sensation), perhaps linked with a hard tactile sense-datum or a sharp auditory sense-datum. What the person knows is a complex sum of individual perceptions and logical inferences that he or she draws from them. Again, the whole is constituted by its parts. By contrast, a Gestalt theory of knowledge suggests that human knowledge of particular parts may be based on inferences from more primary knowledge of a whole.

While logical atomism was the first movement in analytic philosophy, and while most analytic philosophers still deny internal relations, the specific tenets of logical atomism no longer attract many adherents.

ANALYTIC PHILOSOPHY AND THE SYNTHETIC A PRIORI

Another dimension of analytic philosophy concerns its relationship to so-called synthetic *a priori* knowl-edge. There is some knowledge that can be had only by means of sense experience. Ordinary beliefs about the world around us, for instance, as well as sophisticated beliefs found in the sciences, require observational evidence. Such knowledge is said to be *a posteriori*, or empirical. Other knowledge does not depend on empirical investigation; rather it is knowable simply by reflection; that two plus two are four, that a brother is a male sibling, that it is either raining or not raining, etc. Such knowledge is said to be *a priori*. Propositions can be divided in yet another way: some are about what the Scottish philosopher David Hume called the relations of ideas or concepts. That a bachelor is unmarried or that a triangle has three sides are examples. The German philosopher Immanuel Kant called such propositions "analytic." Other propositions intend more and are not about ideas or concepts but are about the external world, such as that tigers are found in India; these propositions are referred to as "synthetic."

It might be supposed that these divisions map directly onto each other: that analytic propositions and a priori propositions are one and the same, and that synthetic propositions and a priori propositions are one and the same. This was the position of Hume. Kant argued, however, that this is not so, that there are propositions that express more than the relationship of ideas but that, nevertheless, the mind is capable of knowing independent of any empirical observations. This is the so-called synthetic *a priori* and is the realm into which (according to Kant) fall mathematics, metaphysics, and possibly morality and aesthetics.

It is characteristic of analytic philosophy that it denies the existence of the synthetic a priori. In his *Enquiry Concerning Human Understanding* (1758) David Hume wrote:

> If we take in our hand any volume . . . let us ask, *Does it contain any abstract reasoning concerning quantity or number?* [that is, relations of concepts] No. *Does it contain any experimental reasoning concerning matter of fact or existence?* No. Commit it then to the flames, for it can contain nothing but sophistry and illusion.

Analytic philosophy insists that any claims about matters beyond mere tautologies, such as logical truths or truths by definition, are solely the province of science to investigate. It is characteristic of analytic philosophy to defer to the natural and social sciences whenever these disciplines issue findings about the world. Logical positivism, the second major movement in analytic philosophy, did not burn books, but instead declared meaningless any asser-

104

tion that was neither empirically verifiable nor simply conceptual.

Such a position requires that philosophy abandon its traditional claim to reveal profound truths about "man and his place in nature." But once the sciences are granted dominion over all synthetic propositions, what is there left for philosophy to do? The answers to this question help to illuminate the research program for much analytic philosophy in the twentieth century.

Mathematics   As examples of synthetic a priori propositions Kant pointed to the truths of mathematics. That seven plus five are twelve is not something found in the very concepts of seven, five, plus, and twelve, but is nevertheless known entirely without empirical investigation. Analytic philosophy must deny this, but (inasmuch as mathematics does not require empirical investigation) to do so it must show that the propositions of mathematics are conceptual truths, following logically from the definition of the key terms. This project was not new to the twentieth century. The German mathematician-philosophers Gottfried Wilhelm Leibniz and Gottlob Frege tried to do this in the seventeenth and nineteenth centuries, respectively. However, it was the work of the mathematician-philosophers Bertrand Russell and Alfred North Whitehead in *Principia Mathematica* (1910–1913) that almost succeeded in showing that arithmetic can be derived from definitions of numbers and arithmetical operations. Their near success allowed philosophers to continue to deny the synthetic a priori, and also gave them confidence that the powerful new tools of modern symbolic logic could be used to clear away that tangle of metaphysical baggage that the history of philosophy had bequeathed.

Metaphysics   Much of that baggage was inherited from post-Kantian philosophers in the German idealist tradition, and Georg Wilhelm Friedrich Hegel was a chief target for analytic philosophers. Hegel insisted upon the inevitable progress of history, in which a dialectical process would assure that the Absolute, or Reason, would come to know itself in a grand synthesis in which Freedom would come to be realized. This kind of confusing jargon was objectionable to analytic philosophers, since it used terms that had no clear empirical meaning and purported to tell us synthetic truths about "man and his place in nature" without the slightest bit of empirical evidence. Although philosophers in the twenty-first century recognize there is a definite metaphysical orientation to analytic philosophy, in

the early twentieth century analytic philosophers insisted that metaphysics was a thing of the past, and that the "new" philosophy would finally eliminate all the confusions sown by its predecessors. It would do so by showing that so many of the alleged problems of metaphysics result from not understanding the meaning of the key concepts and from treading where science alone ought to tread.

Morality   In his 1903 *Principia Ethica,* the influential English realist philosopher and professor G. E. Moore succeeded in persuading many philosophers that morality is not an empirical science; that knowing that a course of action leads to happiness, pleasure, the greatest good for the greatest number, the survival of the species, and so on, is not the equivalent of knowing that it is good or right. Moore's own solution, the existence of a "moral sense," was not consistent with the empirical bias of analytic philosophy. Instead, an extremely ingenious solution emerged, primarily in A. J. Ayer's *Language, Truth, and Logic* (1935) and Charles Stevenson's *Ethics and Language* (1944). One must not assume that all uses of language are descriptive in nature. Moral language needs to be understood not as descriptive but as emotive and persuasive. In other words, to use moral language is to express an attitude toward something in a way designed to persuade others to share that attitude. Such an approach opens a whole new research program. What, precisely, are the uses of different forms of moral language? What is being done in the process of reasoning about morality? This approach to morality reinforced the growing interest in language as central to philosophy.

Similar treatment of other value areas, like aesthetics and religion, soon followed. However, since the mid-1960s, philosophers became willing to engage in debate about normative issues. Largely in response to student demand for "relevance" in the civil rights and Vietnam era, attention since the mid-1960s turned to issues of civil disobedience, war, violence, and, later, biomedical and professional ethics. It is difficult to reconcile such focus with the underlying analytic metaethics, but the concept of "reflective equilibrium" is an ingenious way to engage in such debate without forcing one to make any commitments to ontologoical or epistemological matters. The idea is to compare one's "intuitions" about particular cases with various moral theories that are proposed to deal with them, and to try to create a balance of harmony between the initial judgments and the theories, adjusting the judgment to the theory and the theory to the

105

judgment in the hope of creating a workable synthesis to which general consent can be attained.

Mind   The nature of the mind has been a traditional concern of analytic philosophers. However, given the great respect for natural science among analytic philosophers it is not surprising that philosophical thinking about the mind developed in conjunction with psychological theory. The dominance of behaviorism in early-twentieth-century psychology was mirrored in philosophical behaviorism, which held that terms that purport to refer to mental states (such as "anger," "jealousy," "fear") in fact refer to a wide variety of behavioral states. Thus the use of mentalistic language need not be taken to imply the existence of a nonempirical realm populated by unobservable entities like "minds" or their contents. (Gilbert Ryle's *The Concept of Mind* [1949] is central here.) As behaviorism waned in psychology, however, the task of analytic philosophers shifted. It became a research project of the 1980s to explain how cognitive psychology can use mentalistic terms without commitment to mental objects. Great imagination and ingenuity characterize this project, and the development of computers that mimic—to some degree—the functions of the mind has opened new avenues for exploration. In the 1980s and 1990s this led to emergence of functional analysis and related approaches in the intersecting fields of artificial intelligence, cognitive psychology, and philosophy of mind.

Epistemology   Analytic attempts of the 1920s and 1930s to analyze knowledge in terms of basic statements of immediate sense experience proved untenable. Consistent with the desire to deal with the clarification of concepts, epistemologists of the 1950s and 1960s tried to refine the traditional definition of knowledge as a justified true belief. These definitions ran into serious obstacles, but have not been entirely abandoned. But, like philosophy of mind, epistemology seeks to be a handmaiden to the sciences, and much epistemology since 1970 has been defined as "naturalized" epistemology—that is, a theory of knowledge that accepts a causal theory of perception and knowledge and it does not attempt (as the French mathematician-philosopher René Descartes did, for example) to find any sort of transcendent justification for the beliefs that are caused in the human mind by the normally reliable perceptual and cognitive processes.

Language   It is not surprising that language has been a central focus of study in analytic philosophy.

Since Wittgenstein's logical atomism suggested that an ideal language would be one that "pictured" reality, analytic philosophers turned their attention to the nature of language, and in particular to the distinction between meaning and reference. Since the logical positivist rejected as meaningless any sentence that was not either scientific or true "by definition," questions about "sameness of meaning," "synonymity," and "analyticity," all related concepts, were brought to the center of attention. The logical positivist position further inflamed debate about the relationship of language and its alleged referents. Additionally, the recognition of the nondescriptive language of value discourse opened a whole new field of inquiry into the various functions of language. Finally, the later work of Wittgenstein (*Philosophical Investigations,* 1953) radically shifted attention to the role of "language games," in which meaning is seen as being found in the use of words and expressions rather than in any external referent that might be thought to be their denotation. A surprising development from this was the emergence of "ordinary language" philosophy, a movement that sought to dissolve philosophical problems by showing that they do not arise when philosophers use language as the ordinary person uses it. Influenced by their studies with and of Wittgenstein, thinkers Norman Malcolm and Max Black brought this approach to Cornell University, where it flourished in the 1940s, 1950s, and 1960s.

Science   During much of analytic philosophy's dominance in the twentieth century, its most respected subfield was the philosophy of science. Since analytic philosophy is committed to empiricism, and since science is, perhaps by definition, the source of empirical knowledge, it became important for analytic philosophers to understand how science works. To some extent, this inquiry is epistemological. What is the scientific method? Why is it reliable? How does it overcome traditional skepticism about perception and induction? How does it explain phenomena? To some extent it is ontological. To what do the theoretical terms so essential to modern science refer? Since they do not seem to be empirical terms, how can the commitment to empiricism be reconciled to science? How can science be justified in making lawlike statements (infinite in their intention) when all empirical evidence is necessarily limited and finite? These questions led to research programs in the 1920s and 1930s that resulted in extraordinarily ingenious, if ultimately wrongheaded, solutions. Theoretical terms and lawlike statements, in one view, have no meaning at all:

they are merely devices scholars use to allow them to infer empirical propositions. When the radical empiricism that led to this view was abandoned, attention shifted to the defense of science's epistemological privilege not only in analytic philosophy but in the culture at large. The suggestions of Bacon and Mill—that an algorithm could establish the laws of nature—were rejected. There was an initial assumption of analytic philosophers (led by Rudolph Camp at the University of Chicago and Carl Hempel at Princeton University) that scientific laws could at least be confirmed by objective methods. This assumption, however, was severely challenged by Karl Popper and his falsification theory and then by Thomas Kuhn's (at the University of California at Berkeley and Princeton, respectively) historical investigations. The failure of various attempts to establish and defend that privilege has led to a serious retreat from some of the dogmas of analytic philosophy.

Logic More than any other school of philosophy, analytic philosophy has emphasized logic both as a tool and as an independent field of study. Since the domain of philosophy is circumscribed by the denial of the synthetic a priori and the allocation of synthetic truths to science, philosophers were constrained to operate in the realm of logically necessary truths. Consequently, the full power of logic needed to be explored and new techniques of inference established. Wittgenstein and Russell pioneered this work in connection with their logical atomism. Since every element of reality can (allegedly) be described in terms of a simple sentence, reality as a whole can be described as logical functions of simple sentences. Certain complex sentences turn out to be true regardless of the truth of their components. (For instance "A or not-A" is true or false whatever A may be.) In such cases the complex is a tautology. Others turn out to be false regardless of the truth of their components. (For instance "A and not-A.") These are contradictions. In the *Tractatus Logico-Philosophicus* (1922) Wittgenstein introduced the "truth table," a method of determining whether any such complex is a tautology or a contradiction. If so, it is a proper field of philosophical commentary or inquiry. If not, it belongs to science. Russell demonstrated the power of the new logic in his "theory of descriptions." Statements such as "The present king of France is bald" appeared to raise metaphysically and epistemologically difficult problems, inasmuch as there is no present king of France. Must one accept an ontol-

ogy populated by endless imaginary beings? And more problematically, how can one determine the truth of this claim? Russell argued that such sentences can be analyzed into two separate sentences: there exists something that is the present king of France, and that something has the property of baldness. Since the first sentence can be determined by empirical methods to be false, the conjunction is also false. Many saw in Russell's analysis the tremendous power of logic for the future of philosophy. In the United States, the logicians Alonzo Church (active from the 1940s to the 1950s) and W. V. O. Quine (active from the 1950s to the 1990s) continued this tradition of cutting-edge work in logic.

THE STYLE OF ANALYTIC PHILOSOPHY

While there are considerable differences among analytic philosophers with respect to the content of their theories, there is something about their style of doing philosophy that most clearly distinguishes them from other philosophers. Analytic philosophers are problem oriented. They are driven by the desire to solve a problem or answer a question rather than by the desire to understand a system or to articulate or develop the theories of some great philosophical figure. Characteristically, analytic philosophers refer to their philosophical forebears only to illuminate the position they themselves are trying to develop. There is no great concern to get the philosopher "just right." This sharply contrasts with other styles of philosophy that are very much concerned with getting at correct interpretations. It contrasts even more sharply with schools of philosophy that take a given system almost as gospel, seek to plumb its most obscure depths for insights into anything and everything, and consider inconsistency with the master to be refutation of the idea. Thomist philosophy, Marxist philosophy, and some followers of the philosophers Edmund Husserl and Martin Heidegger fall into this latter category.

The methods analytic philosophers use may appear quite strange, though many of them can be found in Socratic dialogues. The counterexample and thought experiment are central. Socrates was engaged in a typical analytic project in Plato's *Republic* when he sought to define the concept of justice. Cephalus suggested that justice is telling the truth and paying your debts. To this Socrates replied by inventing a scenario—a thought experiment: Imagine a friend has lent you a weapon but has since gone mad. He asks for the return of the weapon. Surely it would not be right to return it to a madman; nor would it be right always to tell the truth to a madman. Consequently this definition of justice must be mistaken—there is a counterexample to it.

It is instructive to understand why this method works. Since analytic philosophy is committed to discovering conceptual truths—truths that do not depend on the specific condition of the empirical world at any particular time—the claims analytic philosophers put forward must stand up against all possible worldly conditions. Here "possible" does not simply mean "likely" or "plausible," or even "consistent with the laws of nature"; rather, it should be taken to mean "non-contradictory." So, as long as there is nothing logically contradictory in a friend's going mad, the very possibility of its happening defeats the proposed definition. The logic of this approach is unassailable, but it leads to some extremely bizarre scenarios in the analytic literature: brains in vats, kidnapped women attached to critically ill violinists, fields filled with cardboard cutouts of barns, immobilized innocents forced to blast falling babies out of the sky with bazookas, and so on. The casual reader who encounters these examples will be forgiven for thinking that analytic philosophy is either irrelevant or downright insane. Unlike some styles of philosophy, analytic philosophy has not garnered much popular following or support, though it remains dominant in the academy.

WHY AMERICA?

There can be no dispute that the roots of analytic philosophy are found in the work of Russell, Moore, and Wittgenstein at Cambridge University, and philosphers like Moritz Schlick, Hans Reichenbach, and Rudolf Carnap in and around the Vienna Circle in Austria. So it is natural to wonder why it blossomed in the United States. In the mid-nineteenth century American philosophy was heterogeneous. There were New England Transcendentalists, scatterings of Scottish philosophy taught quite frequently by university presidents, and, surprisingly, a strong strain of Hegelianism, found in Ohio and St. Louis, Missouri. (It is alleged that John Roebling, the designer of the Brooklyn Bridge and, before that, the Suspension Bridge over the Ohio River at Cincinnati, was influenced in his engineering by Hegelian principles!) By the later part of the nineteenth century, however, the pragmatism of Charles Sanders Peirce and William James began to gain the ascendency. It abjured the romantic excesses of European speculative metaphysics and, in its hardheaded, no-nonsense style, seemed more compatible with the pragmatic spirit driving the expansion of America. Peirce's work in logic paved the way for Whitehead and Russell's *Principia Mathematica,* and his pragmatic theory of meaning presaged the logical positivists' verification theory. The work of John Dewey in the first quarter of the twentieth century cemented the ascendency of pragmatism. Dewey was a "reformed" Hegelian and spread his pragmatic message from the University of Chicago to Columbia University, drowning the Midwestern Hegelians in his wake. Analytic philosophy seemed consistent in spirit with this hardheaded pragmatism. Like pragmatism it rejected metaphysical speculation and asked of any philosophical theory or position what the practical (that is, empirical) implications of accepting it or rejecting it might be. It also insisted that there must be an answer.

The emergence of Nazism in Germany and Austria hastened the spread of analytic philosophy. A number of leading continental positivists, among them Carnap and the philosopher of science Reichenbach, fled to the United States, where they took up positions in leading graduate programs (the University of Chicago and the University of California at Los Angeles, respectively). A German student of theirs, Carl Hempel, found a place at Princeton in the 1950s. Curiously, another group of émigrés, those associated with phenomenology and with the Frankfurt school of critical theory, were less welcomed in these programs and remained at the New School for Social Research in New York City, which had established a "University of Exile" for such émigrés. The New School remains a leading institution for the study of nonanalytic philosophy, and especially continental philosophy. For several reasons, then, the American intellectual orientation was congenial to analytic philosophy in the first four decades of the twentieth century, and became even more so when the "end of ideology" spirit began to pervade the political and social landscape in the 1950s. The spirit of analytic philosophy was congenial to the rejection of "isms"—especially Marxism and fascism. Schools required by charter to adhere to nonanalytic principles, primarily Catholic (Thomistic) schools, have not become as dominated by analytic philosophy as have the major nonsectarian universities. But even at places like Notre Dame it is possible to find and study with analytic philosophers.

THE PRESENT AND FUTURE OF ANALYTIC PHILOSOPHY

Even at the height of its influence from the 1950s to the 1970s analytic philosophy was creating arguments that might undermine its very foundations. In his influential 1951 essay, "Two Dogmas of Empiricism," W. V. O. Quine challenged the distinction between analytic and synthetic propositions. He proposed instead a pragmatic distinction between propositions that are central to one's sphere of beliefs (and hence unlikely to be dislodged on the basis of ordinary empirical discoveries) and propositions more peripheral to one's belief system (and hence vulnerable to the usual sorts of empirical refutation). If this distinction replaces the analytic-synthetic distinction, the conceptual certainty that philosophical claims are supposed to harbor is replaced by a more tentative pragmatic certainty that can be undermined when changes in one's conceptual scheme demand it.

This challenge was reinforced by the rising influence of Wittgenstein's 1953 work, *Philosophical Investigations,* in which he suggested that socially grounded "language games" are the basis of meaning. This too undermines the conceit that philosophical claims have a certainty based in the socially transcendent meaning of terms or concepts, and instead finds more relativistic grounding for these claims.

In addition to challenges to the concepts of analyticity and necessity, there were important challenges to the empirical assumptions of analytic philosophy. The empirical reliability of science was initially based on assumptions about the indubitability and incorrigibility of basic observational reports. As early as 1933, however, Rudolf Carnap in a long untranslated piece "Über Protokollsätze" suggested that there is an inevitable element of arbitrariness, or at least pragmatics, in deciding what statements one is willing to call epistemologically certain. While Carnap's piece remained untranslated, other philosophers were raising similar challenges. In 1979 Richard Rorty's *Philosophy and the Mirror of Nature* emerged as the culmination of challenges not only to analytic epistemology, but to the very idea that what people call knowledge, even scientific knowledge, provides them with a representation of reality at all.

In addition to assumptions about the reliability of empirical observation, the epistemological respect reserved for science was based on assumptions about the rationality of its methods of testing, explanation, proof, and, ultimately, progress. These assumptions, which philosophers of science had long tried to justify through their rational reconstructions of scientific method, which culminated in Ernest Nagel's brilliant *Structure of Science* (1961), were dealt an extraordinary blow by Thomas Kuhn's historical and philosophical investigations in *The Structure of Scientific Revolutions* (1962). Kuhn argued that science is as much grounded in social power as it is in objective epistemology, that (as Norwood Russell Hansen had argued earlier in *Patterns of Discovery,* 1958) observation is necessarily determined by theory as much as theory is determined by observation, and that progress in science requires explanation at least as much in sociopolitical terms as it does in epistemological and empirical terms.

All of these tendencies, which emerge from analytic philosophy itself, undermine the initial analytic project of finding conceptual truths untainted by speculative metaphysics and irrefutable by empirical investigation. Instead, the significance of culture, whether it be understood in terms of Wittgenstein's "language games," Kuhn's "normal science," Rorty's "conversations," or other formulations, can no longer be ignored. Additionally, works by feminist theorists within the analytic tradition have revealed the extent to which philosophical theory has been colored by the patriarchal structures that are embedded in culture, and postcolonial theorists have made similar arguments concerning the Eurocentric bias of philosophical theory. As a consequence scholars are beginning to see some convergence between the Anglo-American analytic approaches and the continental postmodern approaches, to the extent that both recognize the role of culture in the formation of what used to be considered "necessary" truths. It remains the case, however, that the responses to this recognition are quite different: the continental approach is much more speculative and playful, the analytic approach tends toward the pragmatic and "naturalistic."

It is interesting to note that these developments have not undermined the methods of analytic philosophy. While counterexamples and thought experiments may not reveal the necessary truths they had originally been assumed to reveal, they remain powerful methods for testing and comparing "intuitions." Perhaps they function as another way of describing those beliefs that remain at the core of W. V. O. Quine's epistemological sphere. Additionally, in his very influential work *A Theory of Justice* (1971), John Rawls provided another conceptual justification in the articulation of what he called "reflective equilibrium," a method by which people try to bring their pre-philosophical intuitions in line with philosophical theory in such a way as to retain whatever they think is valuable about each while demanding consistency among the elements. Thought experiments and counterexamples are valuable in this enterprise.

See also **New Philosophical Directions** *(in this volume);* **Social Construction of Reality** *(volume 3).*

BIBLIOGRAPHY

Excellent introductions to the various fields of analytic philosophy can be found in the Foundations of Philosophy Series edited by Elizabeth Beardsley and Tom L. Beauchamp (Englewood, N.J., 1966).

An excellent bibliography of analytic philosophy up through the late 1950s can be found in A. J. Ayer, ed., *Logical Positivism.* (Glencoe, Ill., 1959). The remainder of this bibliography lists items mentioned in the text and important post-1958 works.

Armstrong, D. M. *Perception and the Physical World.* London, 1961.

Ayer, Alfred J. *Language, Truth, and Logic.* 2nd ed. London, 1946.

Austin, J. L. *Sense and Sensibilia.* Oxford, reconstructed from the manuscript notes by G. J. Warnock, 1962.

Carnap, Rudolf. "Über Protokollsätze." *Erkenntnis* 3 (1932).

Chisholm, Roderick M. *The Foundations of Knowing.* Minneapolis, Minn., 1982.

Hansen, Norwood Russell. *Patterns of Discovery: An Inquiry into the Conceptual Foundations of Science.* Cambridge, U.K., 1958.

Kripke, Saul A. *Naming and Necessity.* Cambridge, Mass., 1980.

Kuhn, Thomas S. *The Structure of Scientific Revolutions.* 2nd ed. Chicago, 1970.

Malcolm, Norman. *Knowledge and Certainty, Essays and Lectures.* Ithaca, N.Y., 1963.

Moore, G. E. *Principia Ethica.* Cambridge, U.K., 1903.

Nagel, Ernest. *The Structure of Science: Problems in the Logic of Scientific Explanation.* New York, 1961.

Quine, W. V. O. *From A Logical Point of View: Logico-Philosophical Essays.* Cambridge, Mass., 1953. Contains "Two Dogmas of Empiricism."

———. *Word and Object.* Cambridge, Mass., 1960.

Rawls, John. *A Theory of Justice.* Cambridge, Mass., 1971.

Rorty, Richard. *Philosophy and the Mirror of Nature.* Princeton, N.J., 1979.

Russell, Bertrand. *The Analysis of Matter.* London, 1927.

———. *The Analysis of Mind.* London, 1921.

———. *Problems of Philosophy.* Oxford, 1959.

Russell, Bertrand, and Alfred North Whitehead. *Principia Mathematica.* Cambridge, U.K., Vol. 1, 1910, Vol. 2, 1912, Vol. 3, 1913.

Ryle, Gilbert. *The Concept of Mind.* London, 1949.

Sellers, Wilfrid. *Science, Perception, and Reality.* London, 1963.

Stevenson, Charles L. *Ethics and Language.* New Haven, Conn., 1944.

Strawson, P. F. *Individuals: An Essay in Descriptive Metaphysics.* London, 1959.

Wittgenstein, Ludwig. *Tractatus Logico-Philosophicus.* London, 1961.

———. *Philosophical Investigations.* Oxford, 1953.

Part 7

THE 1960s AND 1970s

OVERVIEW: THE 1960s AND 1970s

Allan M. Winkler

The 1960s and 1970s were turbulent years in America. The United States began the era on a hopeful note, strong and secure in its mission at home and abroad. The nation enjoyed extraordinary prosperity within its own borders and stature as the dominant power on the world stage. The cultural consensus that had prevailed in the decade and a half after World War II led most Americans to assume that such conditions would continue indefinitely. By the end of the 1960s, however, that sense of stability was gone. Young Americans in colleges and universities began to question the values of their parents and to join in the struggle to redress inequities in American society. Reform efforts brought progress on a number of fronts but in the process unleashed forces that could not be contained. As society became more turbulent, many Americans joined in the campaign to end the disastrous war in Vietnam that was fast spiraling out of control. Their challenges to conventions brought about significant changes in the intellectual and cultural norms of the United States. Patterns of literature, music, and art all changed, so that by the time the 1970s came to an end, the mood and appearance of the nation was altogether different than it had been before.

POLITICAL IDEOLOGY

Most Americans in the early 1960s relished their prosperity and believed that abundance was here to stay. They agreed with historian David Potter's observation in *People of Plenty*, published in 1954, that "in every aspect of material plenty America possesses unprecedented riches" (p. 84), and accepted as a matter of course their continued enjoyment of the benefits of "The Affluent Society," in economist John Kenneth Galbraith's 1958 phrase (Galbraith, p. 1). Sociologist Daniel Bell spoke for many of them in *The End of Ideology* in 1960 when he noted that "there is today a rough consensus among in-

tellectuals on political issues: the acceptance of a Welfare State; the desirability of decentralized power; a system of mixed economy and of political pluralism" (pp. 402–403).

Electoral politics reflected these intellectual assumptions. Democrat John F. Kennedy ran for the presidency in 1960 with the stated intention of moving the country toward a "New Frontier." The nation was thriving, but it could do even better. Kennedy's first inaugural address stated the challenge in clarion terms: "And so, my fellow Americans: Ask not what your country can do for you—ask what you can do for your country" (*Public Papers*, 1962, p. 3).

Kennedy's administration embodied a sense of optimism. At the age of forty-three, he was the youngest man ever elected president, and he conveyed an image of youth and vitality. He surrounded himself with talented staff members, fifteen Rhodes Scholars among them, and entertained Nobel Prize winners in the White House. He tapped the talents of liberal intellectuals such as Harvard professor Arthur M. Schlesinger Jr. Drawing on the example of Franklin D. Roosevelt, he wanted to be an activist who plunged into the political world and performed in the thick of the fight.

Despite his popularity, Kennedy failed to achieve most of his goals. His domestic program never really got off the ground, and efforts to promote aid to education and to cut taxes failed to get through Congress. In foreign affairs, Kennedy sometimes seemed to move from one crisis to the next, as the confrontation over Russian missiles in Cuba followed the debacle at the Bay of Pigs. Struck down by an assassin in Dallas, Texas, in November 1963, Kennedy was succeeded by Lyndon B. Johnson, former majority leader of the Senate, who was determined to take over where Kennedy had left off. Addressing the nation in the aftermath of the assassination, the new president said, "Let us continue" (*Public Papers*, 1965, p. 9).

Johnson, though further removed from the intellectual world than Kennedy, was one of the most talented politicians of his age. He had an expansive sense of the possibilities of reform and hoped to create what he called a "Great Society," which would have something in it for everyone. When he was reelected president in his own right in 1964, he was ready to push for implementation of his plan. What followed in the next two years was the greatest wave of legislative activity since Franklin D. Roosevelt's New Deal in the 1930s. Johnson pushed through a tax cut and two civil rights bills, a system of Medicare for the elderly and Medicaid for the poor, a poverty program, measures creating national endowments for the arts and humanities, and much more.

But then the liberal consensus evaporated. Johnson ran afoul of public opinion with his ill-fated commitment to victory in the war in Vietnam, and the opposition undermined his political base. In the 1964 presidential election, he had defeated conservative Republican candidate Barry Goldwater in a landslide. Now conservative forces regrouped and created what commentator Kevin Phillips called an "emerging Republican majority" (p. 1). Richard Nixon, formerly vice president under Dwight D. Eisenhower in the 1950s, was elected president in 1968. His election marked the end of the era of liberal reform and a reorientation of American politics that continued for the next thirty years. Nixon understood that it was impossible to roll back the government's expanded role altogether, but he was determined to scale it back, rationalize it, and shift resources from the federal establishment to state and local governments where he believed they belonged. Nixon tumbled from grace—and power— as a result of the Watergate scandal in the early 1970s, in which Republicans wiretapped the Democratic National Headquarters and then attempted to subvert an investigation when the crime unraveled. Nixon and his party also lost out in 1976 when Democrat Jimmy Carter entered the White House in a political reaction to the revelation of the Republican abuses. Yet the reaction to the turbulence of the 1960s and 1970s continued; the country remained more conservative than before, and with the election of Ronald Reagan as president in 1980, the right wing in American politics demonstrated that it was now the dominant political force.

REFORM

The 1960s and 1970s were marked by concerted efforts at reform, and reform movements provide a framework for the period. First, the civil rights movement expanded the opportunities available to African Americans, who had faced serious discrimination in the past. Then a related movement sought to achieve equality for women, who had long been considered second-class citizens. Before this era ended, Latinos and Native Americans were likewise clamoring for equal rights. And both an environmental movement and a consumer movement used similar tactics to achieve their own goals.

The Civil Rights Movement Agitation for black equality predated the 1960s. The seeds of protest were sown in the World War II years, when African Americans demanded that discrimination come to an end. The legal efforts of the National Association for the Advancement of Colored People (NAACP) culminated in the *Brown v. Board of Education* decision of 1954, which stated that separate but equal schools were inherently unconstitutional and must be desegregated "with all deliberate speed." The Montgomery bus boycott the next year demonstrated the efficacy of nonviolent direct action and forced the desegregation of local transportation facilities.

In the next few years, a number of authors, James Baldwin among them, gave an intellectual grounding to the effort to gain equal rights. In a variety of different books, both fiction and nonfiction, he described what it was like growing up black in white America and articulated the desperate need for change. In *The Fire Next Time* (1962), for example, he concluded:

> If we . . . do not falter in our duty now, we may be able, handful that we are, to end the racial nightmare, and achieve our country, and change the history of the world. If we do not now dare everything, the fulfillment of that prophecy, recreated from the Bible in song by a slave, is upon us: *God gave Noah the rainbow sign, No more water, the fire next time!* (p. 141)

Meanwhile, a number of new civil rights organizations became important. The Reverend Martin Luther King Jr., a leader of the Montgomery boycott, established the Southern Christian Leadership Conference (SCLC) and became the most eloquent and visible black leader in the land. The Student Nonviolent Coordinating Committee (SNCC) recruited young Americans into the battle for equality.

Confrontations included sit-ins at lunch counters and freedom rides aimed at desegregating buses and bus terminals in the South. Though the protesters were nonviolent, often their opponents were not. Slowly, images of vicious confrontations, transmitted on television, created a constituency for further reform.

Lyndon Johnson made civil rights his first priority when he became president. "No memorial oration or eulogy could more eloquently honor President Kennedy's memory than the earliest possible passage of the civil rights bill for which he fought so long," he told Congress (*Public Papers*, p. 9). Using his extraordinary political skills, Johnson pushed through the Civil Rights Act of 1964, which banned racial discrimination in all public accommodations. The next year, he helped bring about passage of the Voting Rights Act of 1965, which authorized the U.S. attorney general to send federal examiners to register voters where local officials had arbitrarily obstructed the registration of blacks. In but a few years after passage, a million new African Americans had registered to vote, and their voice changed the nature of political and cultural debate.

Then the movement ran out of steam. A backlash set in, as some whites protested that gains for blacks came at their expense. In the *Bakke* decision of 1978, the Supreme Court ruled that rigid racial quotas were unconstitutional, though schools and other institutions could take race into account. As school systems in both the North and South resorted to busing, in an effort to achieve racial balance, critics protested what they felt were arbitrary and unacceptable methods that eroded local authority. Richard Nixon embraced a "Southern strategy" that involved seeking the support of whites who were bothered by the rapid rate of progress and ready to slow the process down.

The Women's Movement A women's movement developed out of the agitation for civil rights and likewise framed the period. Women involved in the struggle for black equality realized that they were being mistreated too. They disliked being expected to do most of the menial chores both in the workplace and at home, while their male counterparts made all the decisions and received more professional gains. They also felt sexually exploited, and resented comments like that of SNCC leader Stokely Carmichael who, when asked what the position of women in the movement should be, allegedly replied, "prone." They decided to use the same nonviolent techniques they had been practicing in the civil rights movement to bring about equality for themselves.

Betty Friedan provided the intellectual grounding for the movement. In her powerful 1963 book *The Feminine Mystique,* she articulated "a strange stirring, a sense of dissatisfaction, a yearning that women suffered in the middle of the twentieth century in the United States." Women, she argued, felt trapped by the assumption "that they could desire no greater destiny than to glory in their own femininity" (p. 11).

Legislation played an important part in the effort to end sexual discrimination. Title 7 of the Civil Rights Act of 1964 included a provision, added at the last minute, banning discrimination on the basis of gender as well as race. It gave women the legal tool they needed to attack exploitation. Later, Title 9 of the Education Amendments of 1972 prohibited gender bias in federally assisted educational activities and required equitable funding for women's athletics.

Active protest was equally important. In 1966, a group of twenty-eight women, including Friedan, established the National Organization for Women to bring women into the mainstream of American society. Two years later, women staged a highly visible protest demonstration at the Miss America pageant at Atlantic City, New Jersey, where they nominated a sheep as their candidate for beauty queen and set up a "freedom trash can" for bras, girdles, hair curlers, and other "instruments of torture." They also unfurled banners announcing "Women's Liberation" to the world.

New publications in the 1970s spread the principles of the women's movement. Activist Gloria Steinem and several other women founded *Ms.* magazine in 1972. *The New Women's Survival Catalogue* provided helpful advice to female readers ready to strike out on their own, while *Our Bodies, Ourselves* encouraged women to understand and control their own bodies.

Passage of the Equal Rights Amendment (ERA) in 1972 sparked a backlash. The constitutional amendment stated simply that "Equality of rights under the law shall not be denied or abridged by the United States or by any State on account of sex." Conservatives such as Phyllis Schlafly, who argued that the amendment would do nothing to help women and would only take away rights they already enjoyed, organized a nationwide campaign to prevent ratification. Schlafly and her allies succeeded in their quest. Ten years after passage, the unratified amendment was dead.

The Latino Struggle Latinos, like women, learned important lessons from the civil rights movement. While the roots of their struggle likewise dated back to the World War II years, their protest

115

movement came into its own in the 1960s and 1970s, as they too began to practice the politics of confrontation.

César Chávez, founder of the United Farm Workers, led the struggle. This labor organization represented the migrant farm workers of the West, who had long been exploited and overlooked. Chávez first took on the grape growers of California, demanding better pay and working conditions and recognition of the union. Eventually the large corporations came to terms, particularly after they were shown to have rigged union elections in their effort to defeat the farm workers' campaign. After victory in this strike, Chávez called for similar boycotts of lettuce and other products. These campaigns likewise ended in success. In 1975 Chávez succeeded in winning passage in California of a measure requiring growers to bargain collectively with elected representatives of the union. This victory gained national visibility for both Chávez and his movement.

Chicanos—Mexican Americans—were equally active on other fronts. Some formed organizations, such as Young Chicanos for Community Action, which served as a defensive patrol in the East Los Angeles area. Others became politically active. In Texas, José Angel Guttiérrez formed a citizens' organization that developed into the La Raza Unida political party, which gained strength in the 1970s in the West and Southwest. Despite occasional gains, however, Latinos faced continued discrimination and recognized that their struggle had just begun.

The Movement for Native American Rights

Indians, too, campaigned for equal rights. Long suffering from second-class status, they now began to assert themselves. A National Indian Youth Council sought to reestablish a sense of Indian pride. Native Americans promoted their own values and designs in art galleries, museums, and shops. Author N. Scott Momaday gained visibility when his novel *House Made of Dawn* won the Pulitzer Prize in 1968. In it, Momaday showed Indians struggling with contemporary life but finding a sense of harmony from their own cultural traditions. Author Vine Deloria Jr. gained even more attention in 1969 for *Custer Died for Your Sins,* a manifesto challenging the treatment of Indians in the past and urging them to take control of their own lives. The film *Little Big Man,* starring Dustin Hoffman, provided a sympathetic portrayal of an Indian reflecting on the changes he had seen over the course of a long life and was a major hit in 1970. All of these works provided readers and viewers—Indian and non-Indian alike—with a vivid sense of Indian history and culture.

Native Americans also adopted confrontational tactics. They protested the encroachment on their land in a pattern that dated back over several centuries. They demanded protection of long-abused water rights and reasserted traditional fishing rights. In 1972 George Mitchell and Dennis Banks, two Chippewa in Minneapolis, founded the American Indian Movement (AIM) to help neglected Indians in the city. In 1972 AIM organized the Broken Treaties Caravan to Washington, D.C., which occupied the Bureau of Indian Affairs. The next year, AIM took over the South Dakota village of Wounded Knee, where the American army massacred the Sioux in 1890. Pressure politics paid off. In 1975 Congress responded by passing Indian Self-Determination and Education Assistance Acts that provided a framework for federal policy in the decades ahead.

The Environmental and Consumer Movements

In these same years, several other movements also provided a focus for the period. The modern environmental movement began when naturalist Rachel Carson published *Silent Spring* in 1962. She attacked the use of chemical pesticides, particularly DDT, which increased crop yields but had harmful side effects. Chemicals infiltrated the food chain with lethal results. As Carson wrote, "This pollution is for the most part irrecoverable; the chain of evil it initiates not only in the world that must support life but in living tissues is for the most part irreversible" (p. 6).

As Americans became aware of the impact of pesticides, industrial waste, and automobile exhaust, they became more vocal in their demands for change. Earth Day in 1970 celebrated the world's natural resources and highlighted continuing threats. Activists warned of the environmental destruction that could occur from a nuclear accident, particularly after the mishap at Three Mile Island near Harrisburg, Pennsylvania, in 1979.

Environmental agitation brought about legislative results. Johnson's Great Society in the 1960s included the vision of an environment that was pleasing to live in, and he pushed through legislation halting the depletion of the nation's natural resources. In the 1970s, during Nixon's presidency, Congress passed the Clean Air Act, the Water Quality Improvement Act, and the Resource Recovery Act, and authorized a new Environmental Protection Agency (EPA) to help control pollution.

The consumer movement was related to the environmental movement. As affluent Americans indulged themselves in all kinds of new purchases, they began to worry about unscrupulous sellers who were dedicated to making a profit above all else. In the 1970s, the consumer movement sought to protect the interests of the purchasing public and to make business more attentive to customer demands.

Activist Ralph Nader led the movement. He first became interested in the issue of automobile safety and published *Unsafe at Any Speed: The Designed-in Dangers of the American Automobile* in 1965. Many cars, he argued, were simply coffins on wheels, for collisions, even at low speeds, could kill both drivers and passengers. His efforts led to passage of the National Traffic and Motor Vehicle Safety Act of 1966, which set minimum safety standards and made provision for compliance. Volunteers who joined Nader became known as "Nader's Raiders" and focused attention on consumer interests at all levels of government.

THE IMPACT OF THE VIETNAM WAR

The Vietnam War of the 1960s and 1970s likewise circumscribed the entire period and had a devastating impact on American life. Involvement in a struggle that had been going on for decades escalated in these years, until more than half a million American men were fighting in a conflict few of them were able to comprehend. As opposition to the war mounted, protesters challenged policies and priorities that had governed the nation since World War II, and helped redirect the course of intellectual and political life.

The roots of the conflict dated back to the colonial era, when France had been in control of Vietnam. An independence movement sought to rid the region of European masters, and then challenged the Japanese during World War II when they defeated the French. Ho Chi Minh, a Communist revolutionary, hoped to lead the country as the war ended in 1945, but the French were determined to return and so the struggle for Vietnamese independence continued. Because the United States wanted France's support for its cold war containment policy in Europe, it funded most of France's expenses in the Vietnam War.

The United States became even more involved following the French defeat at Dien Bien Phu in 1954. An international agreement in Geneva divided Vietnam at the seventeenth parallel, with Ho

Chi Minh in power in the north, and an anti-Communist government in control in the south. The Dwight D. Eisenhower administration supported Ngo Dinh Diem, the South Vietnamese leader, with financial aid and military advisers.

Kennedy increased the American commitment in the 1960s. The number of advisers rose from 675 when Eisenhower left office in 1961 to 16,000 at the time of Kennedy's death in 1963. But even that assistance failed to promote the stability in southern Vietnam that the United States sought. Diem proved unpopular in his own country, and guerrillas, known as the Viet Cong, challenged his regime, aided by Ho Chi Minh and the North Vietnamese. The government in the south began to disintegrate.

Following Kennedy's assassination, Johnson was determined not to lose in Vietnam, and that commitment shaped American policy for the next five years. In August 1964, in the Gulf of Tonkin Resolution, he received authorization from Congress to take whatever measures were necessary to prevent attacks on American forces, and that measure provided authorization for the war. After Johnson won reelection that November, escalation began in earnest, and the number of American soldiers serving in Vietnam rose from 25,000 at the start of 1965 to 543,000 in 1968.

As the war intensified, opposition in the United States began to mount. Scholars such as Hans Morgenthau of the University of Chicago began to mount an intellectual challenge to American involvement in the war. Students soon joined in the challenge to basic assumptions—first propounded by President Harry S. Truman in the immediate aftermath of World War II—about the need to battle communism around the globe. A teach-in at the University of Michigan in March 1965 examined both sides of the question of American involvement in Vietnam. It was followed by other sessions, which became more like one-sided antiwar rallies, on campuses around the country. Working through Students for a Democratic Society (SDS) and other radical organizations, activists campaigned against the military draft, attacked ROTC military training units on campuses, and sought to discredit companies that made napalm—a chemical jelly that sears off human flesh—and other tools of war.

The antiwar movement expanded. Women Strike for Peace, the strongest women's group fighting against the war, proclaimed "Stop! Don't drench the jungles of Vietnam with the blood of sons." Opposition intensified during the Tet offensive of 1968, when North Vietnam mounted a ferocious attack on provincial capitals and district towns in South

Vietnam, even striking the American embassy in the national capital of Saigon.

Literature helped highlight the absurdity of the war. In 1961, Joseph Heller published *Catch-22*, which was set in World War II but became a commentary on the war in Vietnam. Pilots flying missions in Heller's outrageous account could only be relieved on the grounds of insanity, but if they were able to articulate their fury and frustration at the futility of the war, they were deemed too sane to be sent home. The work of Kurt Vonnegut became equally popular. *Slaughterhouse-Five,* published in 1969, dealt with the firebombing of Dresden, in Germany during World War II, but came to reflect the furious bombing of Vietnam. *Welcome to the Monkey House,* which appeared in 1968, also highlighted the absurdity of American actions during these years.

Television helped mobilize resistance to the war. Over a period of years, Americans became troubled by the images of burning villages and wounded soldiers that appeared on the nightly news. During the Tet offensive, television networks broadcast scenes never screened before. One clip showed the chief of the South Vietnamese National Police look at a Viet Cong prisoner, lift his gun, and then blow out the brains of the captive. Viewers watched the corpse drop to the ground, blood spouting from his head. Horrified, many of them wondered what their own nation was doing fighting in such a war, and began to ask whether it could be won.

The war produced a fragmentation in American political culture and led to the election of Republican Richard Nixon in 1968. Nixon promised to bring the nation together with a plan that would extricate the United States from the fighting while still winning the war. But further opposition mounted as stories surfaced about a horrible massacre at the village of My Lai in South Vietnam, where an American infantry company slaughtered women, children, and old men in cold blood.

The national rift grew even deeper in mid-1970 when Nixon decided to invade neighboring Cambodia to clear out enclaves that he claimed were aiding the Communists in Vietnam. The United States, he said, would not stand by as a "pitiful, helpless giant" and let the Communists take over. (*Public Papers,* 1971, p. 409). Nixon's invasion caused a revival of the antiwar movement on college campuses. At Kent State University in Ohio, students faced members of the National Guard, called up by the governor of the state. As tension reached a fever pitch, the soldiers fired without provocation on the students, killing four and wounding nine.

Students around the country were outraged by the attack, and by a similar one at Jackson State University, a black institution in Mississippi. In response, many colleges closed early that spring.

At long last the struggle came to an end. Protracted negotiations brought a ceasefire early in 1973, and in the spring of 1975 the North Vietnamese finally consolidated their control over the entire country. American soldiers came home, but the legacy of the struggle during the 1960s and 1970s lingered on. In foreign policy, many Americans questioned their nation's stance in world affairs; they challenged the assumptions about America's role as world policeman that sustained the cold war. In human terms, the war caused the deaths of more than 58,000 American men, with even more dying from war-related ailments in later years. Financially, the nation spent over $150 billion in a losing struggle that disrupted the economy and prompted an inflationary spiral that plagued the country for years to come. Socially, the conflict sparked a cynicism about government that continues to this day.

SOCIAL AND CULTURAL CHALLENGES

The push for social reform and opposition to the war in Vietnam led to an upheaval in American intellectual and cultural life that likewise framed these two decades. Young people in particular rejected the patterns of their parents. Some became involved in radical political activity; many more expressed themselves by adopting new standards of sexual behavior, music, and dress.

Colleges proved to be a breeding ground for political activity. In the 1960s and 1970s, many more students were in college than ever before. The baby boom generation of the post–World War II years came of age, and most young people sought out some form of higher education. By the end of the 1960s, college enrollment was more than four times higher than it had been in the 1940s.

Some of these students joined the struggle for civil rights. Hopeful at first about the prospects for peaceful progress, they gradually became discouraged at the slow pace of reform. To try to promote more rapid social change, some students organized Students for a Democratic Society (SDS) in 1960. Two years later, SDS issued a manifesto, written largely by Tom Hayden, a student at the University of Michigan. The Port Huron Statement declared: "We are people of this generation, bred in at least modest comfort, housed now in universities, looking uncomfortably at the world we inherit" (p. 1).

It deplored the isolation and estrangement that were part of modern life and called for a "democracy of individual participation" instead. SDS leaders wanted to create a new political movement, a New Left. Folksinger Bob Dylan captured the sense of incipient change in his powerful song "The Times They Are A-Changin'."

The first blow of the student rebellion came on the West Coast, at the University of California in Berkeley. In September 1964, university officials refused to allow civil rights activists to distribute promotional material outside the main campus gate. In response, the students challenged the restriction and asserted their right to free speech. When police arrested one of the student leaders, students surrounded the police car and kept it from moving all night. University regents retaliated by bringing charges against the students, prompting a student occupation of the administration building and then a student strike. Mario Savio, one of the leaders, termed the university an impersonal, odious machine that had to be stopped.

The increasing anger at the escalation of the Vietnam War refocused the student movement. In the late 1960s, as more and more students joined protest activities, confrontation became a way of life. In the first six months of 1968, hundreds of thousands of students staged demonstrations at more than one hundred educational institutions in the United States. One of the most dramatic episodes occurred at Columbia University in New York City, where students challenged both university involvement in military research and a plan to build a new gymnasium for students on the fringes of the black Harlem community.

A year later, in October 1969, the Weathermen, a radical fringe group of SDS, launched a violent attack in Chicago to demonstrate that the revolution had really arrived. They took their name from a line about not needing a weatherman to know which way the wind blows in the Bob Dylan song "Subterranean Homesick Blues." The Weathermen rampaged through the streets with clubs, pipes, chains, and rocks, attacking police and anyone else who tried to stop them.

The New Left was a powerful force for a brief time. It helped stop the war in Vietnam and highlighted inequities in American society. But as it turned extreme, it offended more conventional Americans and lost its base of support.

Even more young people became caught up in the counterculture in the 1960s. Whether or not they were politically active, they were often troubled by the emptiness of old patterns and became intent on finding new ways of asserting their individuality and independence. The "hippies" of the era wore their hair long and grew beards. Both men and women donned jeans and other simple garments. Most young people stressed spontaneity above all else and rejected traditional marital customs in favor of a freer sexuality. The oral contraceptive pill allowed people to experiment sexually without the threat of pregnancy and had a revolutionary impact on social life.

At the same time, hallucinogenic drugs became part of the counterculture. Many students sampled LSD and subscribed to the advice of researcher Timothy Leary, who counseled them to "tune in, turn on, and drop out." Many more smoked marijuana regularly, as it became even more popular than alcohol on college campuses.

Law professor Charles Reich summed up the changes taking place in his book *The Greening of America* (1970). He applauded a new consciousness that he claimed was taking over from the tired patterns of the past.

Similarly, music reflected the changes that were occurring. By the mid-1960s, rock music had begun to push aside the folk music that had been popular throughout the decade. Though such singers as Joan Baez, Bob Dylan, and Peter, Paul, and Mary remained popular, even more people listened to the the Beatles and the Rolling Stones, and a host of new groups, all playing a hard-driving rock music that reflected the intensity of the period.

The art world changed as well, as artists reflected the mood of dissent. "Op" artists painted sharply defined geometric figures in clear colors, very different from images of the past, while "pop" artists such as Andy Warhol, Roy Lichtenstein, and Jasper Johns commented ironically on the materialism of American culture with bald representations of everyday objects like soup cans.

While the counterculture had an underside that was most visible in places like Haight-Ashbury in San Francisco, where the hippies gathered, it changed cultural norms around the country. Young people led the way, but soon some of the elders too were listening to different music, dressing differently, and experimenting with drugs.

In the 1970s both political activism and the more dramatic manifestations of the counterculture began to fade. More people followed their own bent in what was, according to social commentator Tom Wolfe, the "Me" Decade (p. 26). Millions of Americans looked inward rather than outward, in narcissistic quests for personal salvation. Some embraced transcendental meditation; others became

119

interested in Zen. Still others became involved in cults; the Hare Krishna movement, the Unification Church of the Reverend Sun Myung Moon, and the Children of God drew people, mostly young, into their midst.

THE 1960s AND 1970s IN PERSPECTIVE

The United States changed dramatically in the 1960s and 1970s. Old norms that reflected American values at the start of the period gave way to new ones that were dominant at the end. In political, cultural, and intellectual configurations, the nation was very different at the end of the 1970s than it had been when the 1960s began. The Vietnam War shattered America's confidence in its mission and its might, and led to a widespread debate about what role the United States should play in the larger world. Protest movements exposed inequities and inequalities in American life, and forced what for some Americans was an uncomfortable process of social and cultural change. But even as change occurred, a backlash developed that altered the contours of national life. The political world experienced tremendous upheaval. The Democratic Party coalition that had governed American politics for nearly fifty years gave way to a new conservative movement, spearheaded by Ronald Reagan, which dominated the decade ahead. Turbulence and upheaval were the hallmarks of the 1960s and 1970s. As the period drew to an end, the sense of confidence and security that had predominated in the past were gone; the world seemed far more chaotic than before.

BIBLIOGRAPHY

Primary Works

Baldwin, James. *The Fire Next Time.* New York, 1962.

Bell, Daniel. *The End of Ideology: On the Exhaustion of Political Ideas in the Fifties.* Glencoe, Ill., 1960.

Carson, Rachel. *Silent Spring.* Boston, 1962.

Friedan, Betty. *The Feminine Mystique.* New York, 1963.

Galbraith, John Kenneth. *The Affluent Society.* Boston, 1958.

Hayden, Tom, et al. *The Port Huron Statement of the Students for a Democratic Society.* New York, 1962. A copy of the third printing is available in the Labadie Collection, Hatcher Graduate Library, University of Michigan. The document is widely reprinted in anthologies on the 1960s and also appears in Allan M. Winkler, *The Recent Past: Readings on America since World War II.* New York, 1989.

Heller, Joseph. *Catch-22.* New York, 1961.

Nader, Ralph. *Unsafe at Any Speed: The Designed-In Dangers of the American Automobile.* New York, 1965.

Phillips, Kevin P. *The Emerging Republican Majority.* New Rochelle, N.Y., 1969.

Potter, David Morris. *People of Plenty: Economic Abundance and the American Character.* Chicago, 1954.

Public Papers of the Presidents of the United States: John F. Kennedy: 1961. Washington, D.C., 1962.

Public Papers of the Presidents of the United States: Lyndon B. Johnson: 1963–1964. Washington, D.C., 1965.

Public Papers of the Presidents of the United States: Richard Nixon: 1970. Washington, D.C., 1971.

Reich, Charles A. *The Greening of America: How the Youth Revolution Is Trying to Make America Livable.* New York, 1970.

Vonnegut, Kurt. *Slaughterhouse-Five; or, The Children's Crusade: A Duty-Dance with Death.* New York, 1969.

———. *Welcome to the Monkey House: A Collection of Short Works.* New York, 1968.

General Works

Farber, David. *The Age of Great Dreams: America in the 1960s.* New York, 1994.

Hodgson, Godfrey. *America in Our Time.* Garden City, N.Y., 1976.

Matusow, Allen J. *The Unraveling of America: A History of Liberalism in the 1960s.* New York, 1984.

Winkler, Allan M. *Modern America: The United States from World War II to the Present.* New York, 1985.

———. *The Recent Past: Readings on America since World War II.* New York, 1989.

Politics and Ideology

Dallek, Robert. *Flawed Giant: Lyndon B. Johnson, 1960–1973.* New York, 1998.

Kearns, Doris. *Lyndon Johnson and the American Dream.* New York, 1976.

Kutler, Stanley I. *The Wars of Watergate: The Last Crisis of Richard Nixon.* New York, 1990.

Parmet, Herbert S. *JFK: The Presidency of John F. Kennedy.* New York, 1983.

Reeves, Richard. *President Kennedy: Profile of Power.* New York, 1993.

Reform Movements

Acuña, Rodolfo. *Occupied America: A History of Chicanos.* 4th ed. New York, 2000.

Evans, Sara. *Personal Politics: The Roots of Women's Liberation in the Civil Rights Movement and the New Left.* New York, 1979.

Hoxie, Frederick E., and Iverson, Peter, eds. *Indians in American History: An Introduction.* 2d ed. Wheeling, Ill., 1998.

Sitkoff, Harvard. *The Struggle for Black Equality, 1954–1992.* Rev. ed. New York, 1993.

The Vietnam War

Appy, Christian G. *Working-Class War: American Combat Soldiers and Vietnam.* Chapel Hill, N.C., 1993.

Herring, George C. *America's Longest War: The United States and Vietnam, 1950–1975.* New York, 1979.

———. *LBJ and Vietnam: A Different Kind of War.* Austin, Tex., 1994.

Karnow, Stanley. *Vietnam: A History.* New York, 1983.

Social and Cultural Protest

Anderson, Terry H. *The Movement and the Sixties: Protest in America from Greensboro to Wounded Knee.* New York, 1995.

Gitlin, Todd. *The Sixties: Years of Hope, Days of Rage.* New York, 1987.

Roszak, Theodore. *The Making of a Counter Culture: Reflections on the Technocratic Society and Its Youthful Opposition.* Garden City, N.Y., 1969.

Wolfe, Tom. *The Electric Kool-Aid Acid Test.* New York, 1968.

RACE, RIGHTS, AND REFORM

Clayborne Carson

Interracial relations have become increasingly important concerns for nations that have experienced movements to protect or expand the rights of minority groups. In the United States, these issues gained salience during the 1960s and 1970s as a result of the growing militancy of African American advancement efforts, but many other nations also confronted demands from minorities within racially and culturally diverse populations, especially when such nations experienced rapid changes in racial-ethnic composition due to immigration. During the late twentieth century, while multiethnic confederations such as the Soviet Union and Yugoslavia were unable to survive intact, former slave societies such as Brazil and the United States, former colonial powers such as France and Great Britain, and European settler states such as Rhodesia (Zimbabwe) and South Africa each struggled in different ways and with different degrees of success to find solutions to problems associated with racial and cultural diversity. In the United States as well as South Africa, the advent of sustained and massive civil rights protests during the 1950s marked the beginning of a major transformation of racial advancement strategies in the two countries and of scholarly understandings of race and racial relations.

Before the 1960s most studies of interracial and interethnic relations reflected the widely held assumption among social scientists that the displacement of traditional racial-ethnic values and behavior patterns by those associated with urban-industrial society—that is, modernization and assimilation—were universal and inexorable social trends. This assumption led many social scientists to view as temporary, or at least tractable, the problems associated with intercultural contact in dynamic, democratic Western societies that were characterized by extensive social and geographic mobility, mass communications institutions, and free secular education systems. While recognizing that antiblack racism in the United States was especially resistant to change, most American students of American racial relations accepted the optimistic perspective of Gunnar Myrdal's *An American Dilemma* (1944), which saw white racial prejudice as the main obstacle to black advancement and racial discrimination as an anachronism that was contrary to the traditional political values of the American creed.

The black Marxist sociologist Oliver C. Cox and a few other scholars questioned Myrdal's emphasis on attitudinal factors, but the Swedish sociologist set the tone for subsequent research about African Americans when he asserted, "American Negro culture is not something independent of general American culture. It is a distorted development of general American culture" (p. 928). Myrdal's influence was evident in the Supreme Court's 1954 decision in *Brown v. Board of Education of Topeka, Kansas,* which declared unconstitutional racial segregation in public schools and gave encouragement to broader efforts to combat racial discrimination and segregation. During the decade after the *Brown* decision, issues of race and racial relations attracted the attention of a number of leading American scholars, including many who served as presidents of their disciplinary associations, who became involved in public discussions of race relations in general and black-white relations in particular. These included E. Franklin Frazier, Nathan Glazer, and Talcott Parsons in sociology; Gordon Allport, Kenneth Clark, Thomas Pettigrew, and Arnold Rose in social psychology; and John Hope Franklin, Oscar Handlin, Richard Hofstadter, and C. Vann Woodward in ethnic and social history.

The sustained African American protest movements of the 1950s and 1960s undermined prevailing assumptions about racial relations, however, for they revealed the potential intensity of black-white conflict in the United States, the strength of the emergent feelings of racial identity among mobilized African Americans, and the myriad possible consequences of interracial relations in modern societies. Major civil rights reforms protected and expanded the rights of African Americans and other victims of discrimination, but the mass movements that spurred these reforms also fostered new types of intercultural conflict and collective consciousness among African Americans as well as among women and other victims of discrimination.

THE AFRICAN AMERICAN STRUGGLE FOR CIVIL RIGHTS

The *Brown* decision marked the culmination of years of multifaceted efforts to alter the prevailing climate of opinion among Americans regarding racial matters, civil rights litigation spearheaded by the Legal Defense and Education Fund of the National Association for the Advancement of Colored People (NAACP), and many individual acts of defiance against the Jim Crow system of discrimination and segregation. When the Supreme Court announced in 1955 that its earlier *Brown* decision would be enforced "with all deliberate speed," southern white officials became more obstinate, hoping to postpone integration in the public schools. Given southern resistance to federal court decisions and the Dwight D. Eisenhower administration's lukewarm support for those decisions, African Americans soon realized that they would have to prod the federal government into action. The changing climate of black-white relations during the late 1950s was indicated by the success of the Montgomery, Alabama, bus boycott campaign in 1956; by President Eisenhower's 1957 decision to send federal troops to Arkansas to enforce a federal court order desegregating Little Rock's Central High School; and by the passage of the Civil Rights Act of 1957, the first such significant legislation since the era of Reconstruction.

While the Montgomery protest leader Martin Luther King Jr. emerged as the best-known American civil rights leader, the African American protest movements of the 1960s were not under any centralized leadership and eventually developed goals that extended beyond civil rights legislation. The lunch-counter sit-in protests that began on 1 February 1960, in Greensboro, North Carolina, ignited a wave of protests by black college students. King's Southern Christian Leadership Conference (SCLC) and the NAACP attempted to provide guidance for student protesters after the initial sit-in, but student activists insisted on forming their own local groups under student leadership. Representatives of these local groups came together at an Easter weekend

MARTIN LUTHER KING JR.'S GANDHIAN IDEAS

The recipient of the 1964 Nobel Prize for peace, King was a major contributor to the African American tradition of social gospel Christianity, combining spiritual leadership as a Baptist minister with civil rights activism. During his undergraduate years at Morehouse College and his graduate studies at Crozier Theological Seminary and Boston University, King became familiar with the thought of the Indian independence leader Mahatma Gandhi, but he adopted Gandhian concepts of nonviolent social change only after becoming a leader of the Montgomery bus boycott movement. He once explained that "the spirit of passive resistance came to me from the Bible, from the teachings of Jesus. The techniques came from Gandhi." Even as other black political activists questioned King's nonviolent strategy during the 1960s, King continued to insist that militant nonviolence was the only workable alternative to destructive violence. In *The Trumpet of Conscience* (1967), King noted that African Americans had "experimented with the meaning of nonviolence," but added that "the time has come for man to experiment with nonviolence in all areas of human conflict and that means nonviolence on an international scale."

gathering at Shaw University in North Carolina in April 1960 to form the Student Nonviolent Coordinating Committee (SNCC).

During the spring and summer of 1961, student activists unexpectedly forced federal action after the Congress of Racial Equality (CORE) sent a small group of "freedom riders" through the southern states. Although the interracial CORE contingent ended its campaign after it was attacked by white mobs in Alabama, the Nashville student activist Diane Nash quickly recruited other students to continue the Freedom Ride into Jackson, Mississippi, where police quickly arrested them and charged them with violating the state's segregation laws. The brash freedom riders placed the new administration of John F. Kennedy on the defensive. Despite imprisonment, a cadre of young freedom riders associated with SNCC and CORE resolved to leave college to become full-time organizers in Black Belt areas of the Deep South. Kennedy had to balance his desire to support civil rights against his fear of upsetting southern whites. Along with his brother, Attorney General Robert Kennedy, the president tried to stop the rides through behind-the-scenes efforts to steer students toward voter registration efforts instead of further desegregation protests. Although some student activists recognized the need for such efforts, their demands for "freedom now" made them unsympathetic to the Kennedy administration's cautious approach to civil rights reform.

In Deep South areas containing substantial black populations, racial control was at stake and white resistance to civil rights reforms was particularly intense. Mississippi was especially notorious because of its history of lynchings and other acts of racial violence. In 1962 the United States Commission on Civil Rights warned of the "danger of a complete breakdown of law and order," noting, "citizens of the United States have been shot, set upon by vicious dogs, beaten and otherwise terrorized because they sought to vote." During the fall of 1962 President Kennedy sent federal troops to Oxford, Mississippi, when a large mob of whites rioted in a violent protest against the admission to the University of Mississippi of a black student, James Meredith. In June 1963 a white supremacist shot and killed the NAACP leader Medgar Evers at his home in Jackson, Mississippi. Robert Moses, a SNCC worker who directed the voting rights effort of Mississippi's Council of Federal Organizations (COFO), implemented a strategy of developing leadership at the "grassroots" level rather than relying on top-down leadership. The sustained voting rights struggle in Mississippi, and similar efforts in southwest Georgia and central Alabama, strained relations between the Kennedy administration and civil rights workers seeking federal support and protection.

Mass Militancy and the Civil Rights Act of 1964

The southern black protest movement escalated in intensity during the spring and summer of 1963. At the beginning of the year, the Reverend Fred Shuttlesworth of Birmingham, one of the many grassroots civil rights leaders and a founder of the Alabama Christian Movement for Human Rights, invited SCLC to assist his campaign to overcome racial segregation. King and other SCLC leaders prepared a plan called "Project C" (for "confrontation") designed to provoke confrontations with local white officials. Televised confrontations between nonviolent protesters and brutal police with

clubs and police dogs attracted northern support and resulted in federal intervention to bring about a settlement that included civil rights concessions. King's April 1963 "Letter from Birmingham City Jail," written after a group of white ministers denounced his involvement in the protests, provided hints of the new militancy that had become evident in the African American freedom struggle. King argued that white resistance to black equality had forced blacks to move outside legal channels to express their discontent. He also warned that whites who refused to negotiate with nonviolent black leaders would soon have to deal with more militant leaders. Frustrated blacks, he argued, might turn to black nationalism, "a development that will lead inevitably to a frightening racial nightmare."

By the end of the Birmingham campaign, other mass protests had begun in other cities, including some in the North. During 1963 an estimated 930 public protest demonstrations took place in more than one hundred cities. Each of the national civil rights organizations tried to offer guidance for the mass marches and demonstrations that culminated in the Birmingham protests of spring 1963, but unlike the lunch-counter sit-ins, which generally were well organized and peaceful, the larger protests began taking on a life of their own. Some of the larger protests during the spring and summer of 1963 involved poor and working-class blacks who sought economic as well as civil rights gains. King and other nonviolent leaders feared that they might lose control of the black struggle to black nationalist leaders, such as Malcolm X of the Nation of Islam.

Faced with militant black demands for civil rights reforms, President Kennedy belatedly identified his presidency with the civil rights cause when he announced support for the legislation that would eventually become the Civil Rights Act of 1964. Yet, when the veteran civil rights leader A. Philip Randolph proposed a march on Washington to give blacks an opportunity to express their discontent in a nonviolent way, President Kennedy initially objected to the idea. Randolph warned the president that black citizens were bound to take to the streets and he asked, "Is it not better that they be led by organizations dedicated to civil rights and disciplined by struggle rather than to leave them to other leaders who care neither about civil rights nor about nonviolence?" The March on Washington for Jobs and Freedom, held on 28 August 1963, was the largest single demonstration of the black civil rights movement, attracting more than 200,000 people to the Lincoln Memorial for a program that included speeches by leaders of major civil rights groups. The

MALCOLM X'S CHALLENGE

As a minister of the Nation of Islam, Malcolm X's caustic criticisms of King's nonviolent strategy and integrationist goals attracted a considerable following among discontented African Americans, especially in New York and other large cities. Yet, while attacking national civil rights leaders, he also identified himself with the grassroots activists of the southern civil rights protest movement. His desire to move from rhetorical to political militancy led him to become increasingly dissatisfied with Elijah Muhammad's apolitical stance. As he later explained in the *Autobiography of Malcolm X*, "It could be heard increasingly in the Negro communities: 'Those Muslims *talk* tough, but they never *do* anything, unless somebody bothers Muslims.'" After a pilgrimage to Mecca in April 1964, Malcolm moved toward orthodox Islam, and, after returning to the United States, he left the Nation of Islam to form a new political group, the Organization of Afro-American Unity (OAAU), which was intended to unite the African-American freedom struggle. After his assassination in February 1965, Malcolm's views reached an even larger audience through the publication of the *Autobiography*, written with the assistance of Alex Haley, and of anthologies of his speeches, as well as the release of Spike Lee's film biography in 1992.

SNCC chairperson, John Lewis, used his speech as an opportunity to express the growing frustrations many activists felt toward "politicians who build their careers on immoral compromise and ally themselves with open forms of political, economic, and social exploitation." Lewis's speech was the most controversial one delivered at the march. But King's address called upon the nation to live up to its liberal political ideals: "I have a dream that one day this nation will rise up and live out the true meaning of its creed: 'We hold these truths to be self-evident, that all men are created equal.'"

The March on Washington was a major event in a decade of struggle, but the black-white coalition that supported civil rights reform came apart during the years afterward. Civil rights leaders recognized that they were caught in the middle between increasingly angry blacks, frustrated by the slow pace of change, and white political leaders who resisted rapid social change. Even moderate black leaders reacted with rage a few weeks after the march when a bomb planted in a Birmingham church killed four black children. Speaking on behalf of an angry group of black spokespersons who confronted President Kennedy at the White House, King warned that "the Negro community is about to reach a breaking point." King warned that "if something isn't done to give the Negro a new sense of hope and a sense of protection, there is a danger we will face the worst race riot we have ever seen in this country." Malcolm X of the Nation of Islam saw Kennedy's assassination a few months later as an outgrowth of a violent climate that white leaders condoned—a case of the "chickens coming home to roost."

The new president, Lyndon Baines Johnson, did not have a reputation as a strong advocate of civil rights. To the surprise of some activists, however, Johnson pushed through Congress the historic Civil Rights Act of 1964. Although the new legislation did not eliminate all barriers to racial equality, it was among the most important reforms of the period after World War II. The most dramatic result of the Civil Rights Act was the elimination of "whites only" public facilities. Other less-noticed provisions of the legislation also caused major changes in American life, not only in the South but also in the North. Title VII of the Civil Rights Act dealt mostly with racial discrimination aimed at African Americans, but the legislation also outlawed employment and educational discrimination against women and nonblack minorities.

Mississippi Voting Rights Movement Despite passage of the 1964 Civil Rights Act, substantial racial barriers remained in the South. This was particularly true in the rural areas of Mississippi and Alabama where blacks outnumbered whites. In such areas, widespread poverty among blacks made desegregation of public facilities a less important racial goal than political and economic gains. By the end of 1963, Robert Moses and other Mississippi civil rights organizers had concluded that blacks in the state were unlikely to make gains unless the federal government intervened to protect them. Hoping that the presence of whites would bring national attention and restrain racist violence, they developed a plan to recruit many white volunteers to work in Mississippi. In June 1964, just as the Mississippi Freedom Summer project began, three civil rights workers, James Chaney, Mickey Schwerner, and Andrew Goodman, failed to return from a trip to investigate the burning of a black church near Philadelphia, Mississippi. Their disappearance attracted national attention and led to a massive investigation by the Federal Bureau of Investigation (FBI), which had been reluctant to offer protection to civil rights workers. Following a massive search involving military personnel, the bodies of all three men were found in August, buried in an earthen dam.

Presenting the extensive evidence of widespread violence against voting rights advocates, the Mississippi Freedom Democratic Party (MFDP) challenged the seating of Mississippi's all-white "regular" Democratic delegation to the Democratic National Convention, which was held that August in Atlantic City, New Jersey. Despite vivid testimony from Fannie Lou Hamer, an SNCC worker, the MFDP delegation did not unseat the regular delegation. President Johnson feared that he would lose southern white support and refused to support the MFDP. The new party's support began to weaken as liberal leaders such as Hubert Humphrey, many black politicians, and even Martin Luther King himself felt pressures from Johnson. Many former supporters urged MFDP delegates to accept a compromise that would give them two "at-large" seats along with a promise to ban racial discrimination at the next convention in 1968. Most of the MFDP delegates opposed such a compromise, insisting that they had risked their lives and that politicians should therefore be willing to take political risks.

The MFDP challenge in 1964 marked the beginning of a major transformation of African American politics. Disappointment with the failure of Democratic leaders to back the MFDP challenge created a sense of disillusionment among civil rights activists. Many agreed with Fannie Lou Hamer's conclusion that "we learned the hard way that even though we had all the law and all the righteousness on our side, that white man is not going to give up his power to us." Black organizers involved in the Freedom Summer project were disturbed that the presence of college-educated white volunteers had undermined the confidence of less-educated black leaders. After the tumultuous summer, some civil rights workers even began to question whether the ideal of racial integration was achievable. Moreover, the African American freedom struggle had forced the Democratic Party to confront the challenge of maintaining the support of both southern whites and the expanding black electorate. Since the shift during the 1930s of the allegiance of black voters from the Republican Party of Abraham Lincoln to the Democratic Party of Franklin D. Roosevelt,

Democratic presidents had sought to respond to black demands for civil rights reform without alienating southern segregationist politicians whose support was vital to the party. President Lyndon B. Johnson, who succeeded Kennedy after the latter's assassination late in 1963, could not avoid confronting his party's racial dilemma, which now manifested itself as escalating black militancy and festering white resentment.

After the SCLC initiated a major voting rights campaign in central Alabama during 1965, the SCLC and SNCC jointly planned a march on Sunday, 7 March, from Selma to the state capitol in Montgomery. At the Pettus Bridge on the outskirts of Selma, police on horseback attacked the marchers using tear gas and clubs. Television and newspaper pictures of policemen attacking nonviolent protesters shocked the nation and angered black activists. The violence of this "Bloody Sunday" brought hundreds of civil rights sympathizers to Selma. White officials obtained a court order against further marches, but many blacks were determined to mobilize another march. Young SNCC activists challenged King to defy the court order, but King was reluctant to do anything that would diminish public support for the voting rights cause. After several postponements of the march, civil rights proponents finally gained court permission to proceed. The Selma-to-Montgomery march was the culmination of a distinct stage of the African American freedom struggle. It led to the passing of the Voting Rights Act of 1965 but it was also the last major racial protest action to receive substantial white support.

Although the enactment of major civil rights legislation dealt a decisive blow against the overt, legalized racial discrimination of the southern Jim Crow system, during the remainder of the century the overall advancement of African Americans continued to be shaped less by governmental initiatives to eliminate racial inequities in education, employment, and housing (which remained controversial and politically vulnerable) than by large-scale economic and social forces.

RESPONSES TO LIBERAL RACIAL REFORM

The civil rights legislation of the 1960s not only broadened the scope of federally protected civil rights but also provided a foundation for subsequent movements on behalf of women, resident aliens, poor people, homosexuals, people with disabilities, and many other groups that traditionally suffered discriminatory treatment. Moreover, the struggle to achieve African American advancement fostered increasingly intense feelings of group consciousness among many African Americans and comparable transformations of consciousness among members of other oppressed groups that mobilized to achieve collective goals. Constrained by the prevailing conservative trend away from governmental activism and toward greater dependence on market forces to shape patterns of social mobility, post-1960s changes in American patterns of ethnic and racial relations have been complex and sometimes contradictory—levels of overt racial discrimination and prejudice have declined, but economic stratification and isolation remained a fact of life in American race relations. When compared to the landmark civil rights legislation of the 1960s, subsequent racial and civil rights reform efforts of the rest of the century focused mainly on defensive efforts to protect previous gains rather than on expanding the scope of civil rights.

Although Lyndon Johnson succeeded in enacting the pending civil rights legislation, he also presided over the disintegration of the liberal coalition that made possible not only racial reform but also Johnson's own Great Society programs. A chasm that would last beyond the decade opened between Kennedy-Johnson liberals and civil rights activists after the MFDP was spurned at the Democratic Party convention in August 1964. MFDP backers such as Fannie Lou Hamer, Bob Moses, and Stokely Carmichael subsequently repudiated the conventional liberalism of Johnson, Hubert Humphrey, and Walter Mondale. Johnson's landslide win over Barry Goldwater in the 1964 election marked the last major victory for the national liberal coalition. It was the last presidential election of the century in which most white Americans voted for the candidate favored by the majority of black Americans. After the spring 1965 Selma-to-Montgomery voting rights march, Johnson proclaimed "we shall overcome" in mobilizing support for new voting rights legislation, but the Voting Rights Act of 1965 and the Economic Opportunity Act of 1964 were not enough to ameliorate the festering racial grievances that would explode in the Watts section of Los Angeles during August 1965 and in many other cities through the end of the 1960s. During the summer of 1967, for example, twenty-three people were killed in a rebellion in Newark, New Jersey, and forty-three were killed in Detroit. Such racial violence revealed that civil rights reform had not

changed material conditions of life for most African-Americans.

During the 1960s American society fractured in ways it never had before, not only along the color line but also along lines that were scarcely visible at the start of the decade. Social divisions stood out in stark relief as rapid cultural and political challenges tested the viability of nearly every institution. The African American struggle for equal treatment stimulated a series of other struggles to reshape the identity of Americans, both collectively and as members of distinctive groups. In the course of those multiple efforts, the conviction of some people that "we shall overcome" was overwhelmed by a wave of unresolvable arguments over who, exactly, "we" were. The disintegration of the black activist community once known as The Movement mirrored that of the surrounding American society. That fracturing may have been the inevitable result of the inclusion in American political life of groups that had previously been excluded, oppressed, or silenced. (Similar mass rebellions, often led by young people, were evident in many different countries, including France, Czechoslovakia, and Mexico, suggesting that the international mass culture and increasingly rapid social change encouraged political dissent as well as assimilation.)

African American militancy continued to increase during the last half of the 1960s. Mass struggles had produced expectations that were difficult to fulfill. Blacks could enter restaurants, but many lacked the money to pay for a meal. Blacks could vote, but they still had not gained the power to improve their lives through the political system. As civil rights activists began to question their own long-term goals, many began to respond to influences from outside their own movement. During the last year of his life, Malcolm X's ideas converged with those of many veterans of the civil rights struggle. His ideas remained popular among militant young activists in the civil rights movement after his assassination in February 1965.

SNCC workers were particularly attracted to Malcolm's ideas. In May 1966, Stokely Carmichael became SNCC's new chair, replacing John Lewis, a veteran of the sit-ins and Freedom Rides who was now considered insufficiently militant. Carmichael had helped black residents of Lowndes County, Alabama, establish the all-black Lowndes County Freedom Organization, which became the prototype for the Black Panther Party. Carmichael soon provided a slogan that seemed to symbolize SNCC's own disillusionment with white liberals as well as the resentments of black ghetto residents: "We want Black

Power." During a voting rights march through Mississippi, Carmichael and other advocates of black power criticized white allies who insisted that blacks remain nonviolent. "Let them preach nonviolence in the white community," Carmichael said.

Although black power was a political slogan, it also symbolized a broader cultural transformation. African Americans began to express their enhanced sense of pride through art and literature as well as through political action. The playwright and poet LeRoi Jones, who changed his name to Amiri Baraka, became a leader of the Black Arts movement, which sought to create positive images for blacks. Popular black singers such as James Brown and Aretha Franklin expressed the spirit of "soul." Sports figures such as Cassius Clay, who changed his name to Muhammad Ali, also identified with black power sentiments. During the playing of the national anthem at the 1968 Olympics, two African American athletes raised clenched fists in a "black power salute" on the victory stand after their event. At numerous colleges and universities, black students demanded black studies programs that would emphasize the contributions of African and African American people.

As the decade came to an end, racial divisions persisted. Few political leaders of the period were able to transcend the boundaries that divided Americans. Instead, the prominent leaders at the end of the decade often exploited fears and prejudices based on race, gender, ethnicity, or sexual orientation. When they crossed rhetorical swords during 1967, black power advocate H. Rap Brown and Maryland governor Spiro Agnew epitomized styles of political speech that would exacerbate social divisions. Brown gained a moment of fame when he proclaimed violence "as American as cherry pie," not as a complaint but as a prescription for black liberation. Agnew, for his part, capitalized on Brown's notoriety to catapult himself from obscurity to the vice presidency as a proponent of "law and order." Richard Nixon's "southern strategy" encouraged white voters to abandon the Democratic Party and resulted in a narrow victory over the Democratic presidential candidate, Hubert Humphrey.

Common themes of the new literature of racial relations were the notions that black-white relations should be understood as power relations and that the black freedom struggle inherently strengthened African American racial cohesion. The novelist James Baldwin suggested this new current in *The Fire Next Time* (1963), writing that the only thing whites had that black people need or should want

was power. By 1965, when the American Academy of Arts and Sciences brought together the writings of leading race scholars in *Daedalus,* the thesis that power rather than attitudinal change would bring about progress in race relations had become widely embraced but also served as a major point of contention. For many social scientists who previously had worked for civil rights reforms, greater attention to the role of power in intergroup relations did not involve an abandonment of the view that assimilation was the eventual goal of the black struggle.

Mainstream social scientists were slow to recognize the strength of the emergent militant African American consciousness that had become evident among black activists of the mid-1960s. Nevertheless, some mainstream scholars who noted the rise of black militancy and of the white backlash against that militancy realized that civil rights reforms would not satisfy the heightened expectations that mobilized African Americans. The prevailing social movement theories of the 1950s had encouraged the belief that a protest movement often fulfilled the psychological needs of participants rather than serving as effective political instruments. Nathan Glazer was among the white scholars who insisted that his commitment to equal rights remained strong but that militant blacks had become unrealistic in their demands. Still assuming that assimilation remained the main black objective, Glazer and his coauthor Daniel Patrick Moynihan, in their influential 1963 work *Beyond the Melting Pot,* questioned the feasibility of assimilation as a national goal. Glazer set the tone for a neoliberal (or neoconservative) departure in the racial literature by distinguishing between black goals that were consistent with liberal values and those that were not. He condemned black militants for demanding group advancement rather than expanded individual opportunities and for challenging the rights of Jews and other ethnic groups to maintain "an area restricted to their own kind" and passing on to their children "advantages in money and skills." Milton Gordon's *Assimilation in American Life* (1964) similarly insisted that assimilation had its limits and that, although minority groups had rapidly acquired the dominant culture, "structural separation on the basis of race and religion" would continue for the foreseeable future.

Glazer's suggestion that ethnicity remained an important force in American life became a central aspect of the American literature of racial relations. While Glazer questioned the limits of assimilation, a few social scientists and observers of American racial relations saw African American racial distinctiveness as a positive attribute that should be preserved and developed. These writings took seriously the notion of cultural relativism and saw distinctive black behavior patterns not as a problem to be solved or an expression of undeveloped or premodern racial consciousness but as a pattern of cultural adjustment to be understood on its own terms. This stream had its roots in the critiques of modern mass culture that were published with increasing frequency during the 1950s. The view of contemporary black culture as an alternative to the white middle-class way of life was present in the Beat literature of the 1950s and, as a minor theme, in the black literature of the period. During the mid-1960s this view gained popularity as a result of such works as Baldwin's *The Fire Next Time,* Ralph Ellison's *Shadow and Act* (1964), and LeRoi Jones's *Blues People* (1963). In 1966, Charles Keil published *Urban Blues,* which was soon followed by other firsthand accounts of black life emphasizing the distinctiveness of African American culture. This literature coincided with writings by young black intellectuals—such as those associated with the Black Arts movement—who formulated the concept of "soul" to describe the distinctive ways blacks created their own world within urban-industrial America.

Affirmative Action   Even before the Civil Rights Act of 1964 many civil rights proponents recognized that a legislative ban on overt racial discrimination might not address many of the economic problems facing African Americans. King, for example, argued for governmental policies that would compensate for the historical wrongs committed against African Americans. Although the term "affirmative action" was not widely used during King's lifetime, in his book *Why We Can't Wait* (1964), King compared the social reforms he favored to the GI Bill of Rights that gave World War II veterans special concessions, including home loans and special advantages in competition for civil-service jobs. King admitted that African Americans could never be adequately compensated "for the exploitation and humiliation" they had suffered in the past, but he proposed a "Negro Bill of Rights" as a partial remedy for these wrongs. He insisted that African Americans should be compensated through "a massive program by the government of special, compensatory measures which could be regarded as a settlement in accordance with the accepted practice of common law." He added that "such measures would certainly be less expensive than any computation based on two centuries of unpaid wages and accumulated interest."

Although the Civil Rights Act of 1964 banned only "intentional" employment discrimination, the federal offices established to enforce the law soon recognized that proof of intent in individual hiring decisions was more difficult to obtain than was evidence of previous hiring patterns. By 1968 the Office of Federal Compliance of the Labor Department issued "goals and timetables for the prompt achievement of full and equal employment opportunity." The first extensive use of affirmative action programs in the United States occurred during the administration of Richard Nixon. These programs, in part intended to serve as a safety valve for black discontent, resulted from the gradual shift from legislative and legal remedies for racial injustice to administrative-bureaucratic remedies by government agencies. Because affirmative action programs allocated benefits and preferential treatment to groups rather than simply eliminating discriminatory policies, they came under increasing attack during the 1970s from neoliberals and neoconservatives. Although the Supreme Court backed "temporary, voluntary, affirmative action" in *United Steelworkers of America v. Weber* (1979), Nathan Glazer's *Affirmative Discrimination: Ethnic Inequality and Public Policy* (1975) was among the numerous works that denounced "quotas" and viewed affirmative action programs as departures from the principles undergirding the civil rights legislation of the 1960s. The conservative black economist Thomas Sowell also joined the attack against affirmative action programs, insisting in *Markets and Minorities* (1981) that unregulated labor markets were a preferable means to combat employment discrimination.

Despite such criticism, affirmative action programs survived long after the African American protest movements had subsided because they served a variety of constituencies. First, such programs served the needs of African Americans who benefited from programs that offered jobs and other concrete benefits rather than abstract opportunities. Second, they allowed federal agencies charged with enforcing civil rights laws to achieve their mission mainly through the establishment of goals and guidelines rather than through protracted prosecution of institutions that may have violated civil rights laws. Third, they were usually established by public and private institutions that were willing to offer these benefits to minorities and women in return for the advantages of being in compliance with federal guidelines, which include a reduced likelihood of civil rights litigation and negative publicity.

RACE, RIGHTS, AND REFORM IN A CONSERVATIVE ERA

The insurgents of the late 1960s could not have imagined that the tumult of the decade would lead to an era of conservatism rather than to a revolution, but black insurgency gave way to defensive battles to protect hard-won civil rights gains. The protest movements and cultural rebellions of the 1960s produced expectations of change that were only partly fulfilled. By the end of the 1970s studies of African Americans increasingly focused on the economic hardships facing urban blacks rather than the political inequalities suffered by southern blacks. Many women and racial minorities benefited from civil rights reforms, but they advanced more as individuals than as members of mobilized groups. A decade of unprecedented political activism and participation among previously excluded groups ironically brought about a decline in the belief that political action could transform the world for the better.

One black political scientist and activist, Ronald Walters, noted with dismay that "there was very little internal intellectual Black ferment" and "no consensus and no debate over the structure and function of the Black social system." Nevertheless, during the late 1960s and the 1970s, several main lines of racial analysis emerged.

Neocolonial Analyses of Racial Relations

The most significant theoretical approach to emerge from the writings of militant black intellectuals of the 1960s was the use of the colonial analogy to describe the position of non-Europeans in European societies. Many of these writings were influenced by the work of Frantz Fanon, particularly his *Wretched of the Earth* (1963), but an early African American statement of the colonial thesis can be found in the work of Harold Cruse. Perhaps the most widely read of the colonial arguments was Stokely Carmichael and Charles V. Hamilton's *Black Power* (1967).

Afrocentrism

African American racial thought of the late 1960s and 1970s featured an increasing emphasis on black cultural distinctiveness and on the underlying similarities uniting the cultures of people of African descent. Influenced by pioneering African American writers such as W. E. B. Du Bois and Carter G. Woodson, by the Black Arts movement of the 1960s, and by African intellectuals such as the Senegalese Cheikh Anta Diop (especially in his 1974 *African Origin of Civilization*), African American writings initiated a concerted effort to shape popular understanding of Africa's cultural achievements. Pioneering works of the Afrocentric movement included Chancellor Williams's *The Destruction of Black Civilization* (1971), Ivan Van Sertima's *They Came before Columbus* (1976), and Molefi Kete Assante's *Afrocentricity* (1980).

Unlike proponents of neocolonial ideas, who did not gain much support outside academic and activist circles, advocates of Afrocentrism gained considerable popularity among African Americans by offering an analysis of race relations that emphasized the need for countering notions of European cultural superiority rather than mobilizing political struggles against political and economic oppression.

Neoliberalism

Although the range of racial thought expanded considerably during the 1960s and 1970s, the underlying themes of liberal racial thought of the 1950s were still evident at the end of the period. Indeed, many neoconservatives and Afrocentrics saw themselves as engaged in an ongoing debate with proponents of racial liberalism, who, for their part, conceded that African American culture was more distinctive and resilient than was once supposed, but still insisted that African Americans should move toward assimilation and modernization. The most thoughtful statement of neoliberalism's racial positions was the sociologist William Julius Wilson's *The Declining Significance of Race* (1978).

See also **African Americans; Social Reform** *(in this volume);* **Race** *(volume 3); and other articles in this section.*

BIBLIOGRAPHY

Asante, Molefi Kete. *Afrocentricity: The Theory of Social Change.* Buffalo, N.Y., 1980.

Baldwin, James. *The Fire Next Time.* New York, 1963.

Carmichael, Stokely, and Charles V. Hamilton. *Black Power: The Politics of Liberation in America*. New York, 1967.

Clark, Kenneth B. "Introduction: The Dilemma of Power." In *The Negro American*. Edited by Talcott Parsons and Kenneth B. Clark. Boston, 1966.

Cruse, Harold. "Negro Nationalism's New Wave." In his *Rebellion or Revolution?* New York, 1968.

Diop, Cheikh Anta. *The African Origin of Civilization: Myth or Reality*. Translated from the French by Mercer Cook. New York, 1974.

Ellison, Ralph. *Shadow and Act*. New York, 1964.

Fanon, Frantz. *The Wretched of the Earth*. New York, 1963.

Glazer, Nathan. *Affirmative Discrimination: Ethnic Inequality and Public Policy*. New York, 1975.

Glazer, Nathan, and Daniel Patrick Moynihan. *Beyond the Melting Pot: The Negroes, Puerto Ricans, Jews, Italians, and Irish of New York City*. Cambridge, Mass., 1963.

Gordon, Milton Myron. *Assimilation in American Life: The Role of Race, Religion, and National Origins*. New York, 1964.

Hannerz, Ulf. *Soulside: Inquiries into Ghetto Culture and Community*. New York, 1969.

Jones, LeRoi (Amiri Baraka). *Blues People: Negro Music in White America*. New York, 1963.

Keil, Charles. *Urban Blues*. Chicago, 1966.

King, Martin Luther, Jr. *Why We Can't Wait*. New York, 1964.

Myrdal, Gunnar. *An American Dilemma: The Negro Problem and Modern Democracy*. New York, 1944.

Sowell, Thomas. *Markets and Minorities*. New York, 1981.

Van Sertima, Ivan. *They Came before Columbus*. New York, 1976.

Walters, Ronald W. "Toward a Definition of Black Social Science." In *The Death of White Sociology*. Edited by Joyce Ladner. New York, 1973.

Williams, Chancellor. *The Destruction of Black Civilization: Great Issues of a Race from 4500 B.C. to 2000 A.D.* Dubuque, Iowa, 1971.

Wilson, William Julius. *The Declining Significance of Race: Blacks and Changing American Institutions*. Chicago, 1978.

COUNTERCULTURAL VISIONS

Fred Pfeil

"One must, once in a lifetime, when the time was right, have believed in the impossible": thus states the narrator of German feminist Christa Wolf's classic novel *The Quest for Christa T.* (1968; English translation, 1970, p. 52). The specific locus of the narrator's remark is East Germany in the late 1940s and early 1950s; the nearest specific referent for "the impossible" she has in mind, a genuinely democratic socialist state. Yet her rueful but intransigent comment applies with at least equal force to the United States of America in the 1960s and 1970s, where the time was also right for an extraordinary upwelling of "impossible" countercultural beliefs.

What were the primary forms and characteristics of those beliefs? How did they develop and mutate, among which groups did they circulate? What forms of social practice did they generate or legitimate; and what long-term effects have they had? No simple or unqualified answer to any of these questions will suffice; nor can this brief essay provide any more than a schematic map of a much more complicated force field, together with a few broad generalizations on that field's tangled circuitry.

Such mapping might as well begin with a crude sorting of the countercultural dreams and practices of the time into three categories: (1) those initially developed to counter the racism of the dominant culture; (2) those formed in opposition to its undemocratic character; and (3) those formed in reaction against mainstream white culture's inauthentic and psychologically unsatisfying "way of life." Though only the last of these three currents of resistance and revolt received the curse and blessing of the label "counterculture" at the time, the other two deserve the name just as surely. For the New Left and the various antiracist movements of African Americans and other "minority" peoples each had its own countercultural dreams of the impossible; moreover, in their endogenous developments and exogenous cross-fertilizations with both one another and the hippie "counterculture," they were

destined to generate new movements in their turn before their reserves of hope were spent.

CONTEXTS AND PREFERENCES

What then were the enabling conditions and discourses that made the time right for these dreams and revolts? Like any and all countercultural visions, they depended to a surprising extent on key features of the dominant to which they declared themselves opposed. Politically, both the civil rights movement and the New Left of the early 1960s took their initial cues from the cold war claim of the United States to be the foremost exponent and instance of democracy in the world. Economically, albeit in divergent ways, all three currents were also enabled and fueled by the long boom in American capitalism, thanks to which in real terms the income of the average worker doubled between 1946 and 1973; this context of affluence and high employment in effect reduced the risk of dissent for white counterculturalists of all stripes, while fueling the outrage of African Americans and other minorities stagnating at the bottom of the heap. And ideologically, the hippies and freaks of 1960s counterculture inherited large chunks of their critique from those mainstream cold war culture critics (from the sociologist David Riesman to the art critic Clement Greenberg and the humanistic psychologist Abraham Maslow) who throughout the 1950s decried the shallowness of mass-produced culture and the alienated, zombie-like conformity it supposedly spawned.

As in the founding moment of all such countercultures, moreover, in their initial moment each of these three currents of opposition may be said to have jump-started itself by cross wiring some elements of the dominant culture with other repressed or marginalized cultural elements and themes. Like the Southern Christian Leadership Conference that helped inspire it, the Student Nonviolent Coordinating Committee (SNCC) conducted its nonviolent voter registration campaigns and founded its Freedom Schools in the name of a vision in which the tepid and hypocritical clichés of American democracy were infused with a traditionally black Christian emphasis on deliverance, redemption, and the achievement of the "beloved community" of the just. As John Lewis prophetically declared in an address at the historical 1963 March on Washington, "We shall splinter the segregated South into a thousand pieces, and put them back together in the image of God and democracy" (quoted in Hampton and Fayer, eds., p. 167). Similarly, the founders of the New Left simultaneously drew on mainstream tropes of Jeffersonian democracy and invoked the radical vision of the Industrial Workers of the World, or "Wobblies," and their dream fifty years earlier of a directly democratic, fully participatory political and economic anarchy. And so, too, a horde of largely white, largely middle-class kids, who had imbibed from their most cultivated elders an existentialist contempt for the inauthenticity of plastic mass culture and premasticated middlebrow culture, followed up various invitations from aging Beat figures such as Allen Ginsberg and Gary Snyder to blow their minds, or go tribal, or both, at their first opportunity.

These countercultural visions and movements hardly showed up all together or all at once. The young activists of SNCC inherited the spiritually infused vision of "black and white together" from the civil rights struggles of the 1950s; the founding manifesto of the New Left, the Port Huron Statement, was adopted by the Students for a Democratic Society (SDS) in 1962; and the hippie counterculture did not appear on anyone's radar screen until 1965 or so. Many of the founding members of the New Left, moreover, were themselves veterans of the civil rights struggle, while a multitude of white baby boomers shifted unselfconsciously back and forth between political and cultural radicalism from the mid-1960s through to the mid- or late 1970s and beyond, constructing new identities from various permutations of communist "hippie," activist movement–oriented radicals, and drug-abusing "freak."

Thus, inevitably, our three counterculture visions and movements inspired and influenced one another in complex ways that have yet to be fully teased out. Certainly, their coexistence and fraught but real affiliations encouraged the sense among their adherents and opponents alike that most so-called baby boomers, born just after World War II and coming of age in the 1960s and after, were rad-

ically at odds with white mainstream society: so much so, indeed, that a long pamphlet (or short book) called *The Student as Nigger* made the round of the campuses in the late 1960s, urging white students not only to identify themselves as closely and literally as possible with black people, but also to imagine themselves as the new revolutionary class.

AUTHENTICITY, ALIENATION, EVANESCENCE

Black activists, who by this time had themselves moved from nonviolent egalitarianism to militant nationalism of one stripe or another, found such arguments appalling at best. Yet to some extent they too had come to confuse and conflate alienation in the psychological sense of the term as subjective estrangement, with its more objective senses such as economic subordination or political disenfranchisement. If many white radicals, hippies, and freaks looked on blacks as embodiments of a cultural and existential authenticity they themselves lacked by virtue of having been reared in a hypocritical and sterile mainstream, many Black Power advocates, in the Black Panthers and elsewhere, followed Frantz Fanon, the Martinican psychoanalytic theorist of the African decolonization movement, in arguing that to overcome the psychic, social, and cultural effects of centuries of enforced subordination, American blacks, like their African brothers and sisters, would have to construct and maintain an opposition to the norms and practices of white society that would be as forceful as it was absolute.

This turn from a nonviolent struggle for civil rights under the aegis of the vision described in Martin Luther King Jr.'s "I have a dream" speech to an at least potentially violent struggle for black "national liberation" under the slogan of "Black Power" was essentially the result of a stalemate that befell the strategy of civil disobedience in the face of entrenched racism outside the segregationist South: as, for example, in the housing projects and zoning laws of Mayor Richard Daley's Chicago; or in the rebuff the Democratic Party handed the duly constituted, SNCC-organized Mississippi Freedom Democratic Party, when it refused seats to the delegates at the Democratic National Convention of 1964. But in their concern with personal and psychological liberation from internalized inferiority—with militant resistance as, in effect, a form of collective psychotherapy—black nationalists from the Panthers to the US Organization, like most if not all subsequent visionary movements from second-wave feminists to gay liberationists, were in thrall to notions of psychospiritual self-development that were symptomatic of the entire countercultural field more or less throughout the period.

Perhaps it would be best to allow this historically distinctive politics of subjective authenticity to call out in its own voice. Here are three quotations: first, the most famous utterance of Mario Savio, leading spokesperson for the Free Speech Movement at the University of California at Berkeley, near the beginning of the 1960s; second, from Michael Rossman, a longtime Berkeley activist looking back in the late 1970s on more than fifteen years of struggles, from the Free Speech Movement's nonviolent campaign for free expression on the University of California, Berkeley campus, to the antiwar movement's demonstrations, to the anarchic street war to claim and redeem a vacant lot owned by the university as a communal "People's Park"; and third, from Sandra Cason (Casey Haydon) looking back from 1990 at the appeal of the civil rights struggle in the early 1960s to young whites like herself.

Savio: There is a time when the operation of the machine becomes so odious, makes you so sick at heart, that you can't take part, you can't even tacitly take part. And you've got to put your bodies upon the gears and upon the wheels, upon the levers, upon all the apparatus, and you've got to make it stop. And you've got to indicate to the people who run it, to the people who own it, that unless you're free, the machine will be prevented from working at all. (Quoted in Teodori, p. 156)

Rossman: Emboldened to risk and dare only by each other's presence, we were out there on the existential edge, where what we knew dropped off into the unknown, toward a vision of a different reality. Everything was torn loose for a time: our careers cast off, our lives at times in jeopardy, our very conceptions of who we were and how to be a person among persons were shaken and revised. . . . In this chaos and mystery, alone together and equal facing the unknown, no one led or followed. We were cast in a desperate spontaneous democracy, which was our ultimate and only magic. (Rossman, p. 46)

Cason: You've got to remember, this was the early sixties. Kids on college campuses were reading the existentialists. The black students [in SNCC] were like heroes. They were like existentialist heroes, and people wanted to get close to this. It was beautiful, it was happening. And it drew white intellectuals. It was more real, or more profound, than most anything else happening. They wanted to get close to it. (Quoted in Hampton and Fayer, p. 186)

Ultimately, this emphasis on subjective liberation, on the necessity and centrality of feeling empowered, authentic, and free, would find its most crystalline expression in the most enduring slogan of the time, second-wave feminism's injunction that "the personal *is* the political." But the assumption, as the 1962 Port Huron Statement put it, that the "goal of man and society should be . . . finding a meaning in life that is personally authentic" (in Miller, p. 332) was at the center of every countercultural movement and vision of the period, and had profound implications and effects for all those in its grip.

Some of those implications and effects can, indeed, be teased out from the quotations just given. Note, for example, the significance of Savio's characteristic distinction between his "you" and the "machine." The countercultural discourse of the period is everywhere informed by the assumption that subtends this distinction: that the dominant society and its conventions are both entirely distinct from and wholly inimical to the true self they degrade and repress; and, conversely, that the true self requires only to be loosed from the imprisoning grip of the dominant society in order to realize itself. For those who adhered to a nationalist, or, in the later years of the period, a feminist perspective, the repressed self to be liberated had, to be sure, a collective aspect, insofar as it naturally arose from and partook of some much larger, communal essence of Blackness, Africanicity, or Womanhood. For others, especially in the counterculture, the selfhood to be found and freed might be more amorphously "tribal" in its communality, especially when "tribal" was used by spokespersons such as Gary Snyder to suggest a preconscious "knowledge of connection and responsibility" that both preceded and went "beyond society" (Snyder, pp. 121, 122). In any case, in all these modalities and more, as the Vietnam War rolled on despite the rising tide of student protest, as Panther-style militance was countered more and more with government infiltration, subversion, and violence, and as Timothy Leary's injunction to "turn on, tune in, drop out" via the use of psychedelic drugs found more and more youthful adherents, the sense of existing society as a dysfunctional, alien, absurd yet potentially lethal machine, on the one hand, and of the self's links to others as deriving from some pool of communality lying beneath or beyond the social and seemingly outside of historical time, on the other hand, became an ever more fundamental axiom of countercultural common sense.

Accordingly, this same common sense also came to include an entrenched suspicion, or outright hostility, to any and all fixed institutions or organizational forms. For white counterculturalists—Free

Mario Savio at Berkeley, 1966. Savio (1942–1996) faced punishment for his fiery leadership, including suspension for a four-month jail sentence. © Bettmann/corbis

Speech advocates, antiwar activists, white feminists, and hippie freaks alike—such suspicion ran especially deep. That "desperate, spontaneous democracy" Rossman speaks of, beyond and outside all imprisoning social forms, was felt to be the only valid social engagement, one whose validity resided solely in its existential evanescence. Likewise, when one of Leonard Wolf's interviewees is asked to describe how "given the vast industrial complex of our society," the change she foresees from competition and hierarchy toward community and compassion is to take place, her answer, virtually on principle, is, "I don't really know, that's not what I'm into" (p. 33). At their best, the radically egalitarian and antihierarchical impulses behind such refusals fueled the construction or adoption of new forms of domestic and political organization, from communes, coparenting, and experiments in nonmonogamous sexual relationships to consensus decision-making and consciousness-raising groups. At worst, they led to a variety of ineffective or antithetical outcomes: communes in which at most only a few people, usually women, did the actual work; experiments in "free love" that left some or all of their participants either numb or writhing with pain; meetings and "actions" which, formed in chaos, occurred as chaos. Or, more ominously still, they opened power vacuums in every such arena into which any and all kinds of "power trippers" found the opportunity to "do their own thing"—as did the parodically rigid Marxist-Leninist ideologues who first strolled unimpeded into the ranks of SDS and ultimately drove a stake through its heart; as did the murderous Hell's Angels at the Altamont rock concert in 1969 (intended as the West Coast version of the giant countercultural extravaganza of Woodstock held the preceding year); as did the Reverend Jim Jones, leader of the antiracist, anticapitalist, communal People's Temple in Jonestown, Guyana, where in 1978, nearly ten years after Altamont, on his command more than nine hundred followers committed suicide by drinking poisoned Kool-Aid.

More commonly, however, this suspicion of form and hostility to organization, together with the accompanying emphasis on the liberation of the self, tended in turn to fuel the sense that the struggle to construct, via all those existential moments of subjective truth and personal-tribal authenticity, some new and better world had, within just the past month or minute, ultimately been lost. Of course such events as Martin Luther King's and Bobby Kennedy's assassinations in 1968, or the police riot at the 1968 Democratic Convention in Chicago, or the murders of black and white students at Jackson State and Kent State in 1970, poured gasoline on the fire of such catastrophism; but the counterculture's perpetual sense of imminent failure or collapse scarcely needed such events to sustain its jittery self. The necessary vertiginousness of any and every moment of achieved authenticity and freedom is, indeed, inscribed within the terms of Rossman's evocation of the revolutionary-utopian moment. Accordingly, it is hardly startling to find on the same Jefferson Airplane album— *Volunteers* (1969)—the uptempo "Look what's happenin' out on the street / Got a revolution, gotta revolution," almost side by side with the plaintive suggestion, in the apocalyptically elegiac "Wooden Ships," that the game is already lost, and the only valid choice left is to be "Very free / And gone." Two years before, as Jesse Kornbluth's 1968 anthology attests, contemporary accounts in the underground press of the notorious "Summer of Love" in San Francisco were already riddled with brooding grief over "the death of hippie." And by the summer of 1970, despite the widespread moratoria on classes called in the wake of the U.S. government's invasion of Cambodia, to bring the nation's campuses to a halt, the student antiwar movement was relentlessly rumored to be on its last legs. Such bleak prophecies, moreover, by and large proved self-fulfillingly correct. If, after all, as the era's troubadour Bob Dylan aptly sang it, "There's no success like failure / And failure's no success at all," the failures they predicted were by definition preordained.

MILITANT DISINTEGRATION

By the late 1960s, meanwhile, the militant nationalist rhetoric of black liberation, now often laced with a dash of Marxist anti-imperialism drawn from a usually hazy acquaintance with the works of Lenin or Mao, provided the inspiration and example for a host of other new nationalist or liberationist movements, from the American Indian Movement to the Chicano Brown Buffaloes, whose adherents tended to view nonviolent Gandhian campaigns (like that of Cesar Chavez and his United Farm Workers on behalf of Latino migrant workers) with something like the same contempt Black Panthers

reserved for what was left of the civil rights movement. Moreover, in both the positively enabling influence of their militant discourses and equally in the negative incitements of their often outrageously sexist practices, most antiracist organizations and movements and the New Left alike spurred the explosive emergence of a new feminist movement, whose liberatory discourse in its first years mixed all the countercultural voices and visions of the time—antiracist, radically democratic, and anti-"straight" culture—into an especially fervid and exciting "antipatriarchal" perspective. (The "Documents" section of Robin Morgan's *Sisterhood Is Powerful,* which appeared in 1970 and was the foremost feminist anthology of its time, provides a lively sample of this variety and intensity, which remain impressively tangible even today.)

To be sure, the countercultural vision animating these largely young, white, middle- and uppermiddle-class "second-wave" feminists was not altogether clear or consistent, especially around issues of sexuality and reproduction. Some feminists, viewing gender as the linchpin of all oppressive social relations, envisaged a revolution which, by liberating women and men alike from any and all naturalized definitions of "womanhood" and "manhood," might ultimately lead to the eradication of homophobia, racism, and even capitalism itself. Insofar as such feminists, unlike most or all the other visionary rebels of the 1960s and 1970s, critiqued and transcended the notion that somehow underneath or beyond their oppression women as a whole embodied some untrammeled wisdom and authentic being, their writings—Shulamith Firestone's *The Dialectic of Sex* (1970), for example, or Dorothy Dinnerstein's *The Mermaid and the Minotaur* (1976)—arguably forwarded the most advanced and intransigently radical critiques and countercultural visions of the period, and so remain inspiring and important today.

Yet by the same token, the social changes they called for were so fundamental and comprehensive—ranging as they did from the technological elimination of natural childbearing by women, to the extirpation of the roots of heterosexual desire, to the transcendence of the gendered division of the private-public sphere itself—they seemed all the more hopelessly (or even, to some women and many more men, frighteningly) utopian, and all the less capable of being realized in the lived relations of the present. Thus, in theory and practice alike, the moment of such critiques and visions, and of movements like Boston's left-feminist revolutionary action-collective, Redstockings, quickly passed.

137

Astute political analysts like Harold Cruse (quoted in Marable) noted even at the time that black nationalism was, contrary to the views of its adherents, less a revolutionary ideology than a reformist sheep in a revolutionary-anarchist wolf's clothing; so too what came to be known and practiced most often as "radical feminism" was for the most part radically essentialist in theory but reformist and "entryist" in practice, a celebration of women's putatively essential "difference" (for example, as nurturant mothers, or as sisters linked inextricably on what the feminist poet and essayist Adrienne Rich famously called "the lesbian continuum" or as beings ineradicably closer to nature than men) combined with an insistence on equal rights and participation in a social order that otherwise may remain untransformed.

Yet even so—or perhaps because this was so?—feminist critique and practice have proved far more vital and effective than any of the other visionary movements of the 1960s and 1970s. Their presence today is discernible, albeit incompletely and unevenly, in a host of once quite decisively counterhegemonic institutions and advances many Americans now take for granted: for instance, women's clinics and bookstores and rape hotlines, along with abortion rights and tougher legislation and enforcement against domestic abuse. In this respect, both the florescence of second-wave feminism in the early 1970s and its continued vitality stand in especially marked contrast to the equally swift dissolution of the hippie counterculture of the 1960s in the new decade.

To some extent, of course, what happened in the 1970s was simply that the insignia and accoutrements of that counterculture—long hair for men, for example—gradually lost their transgressive cachet in most parts of the country. But it is also the case that as the most radically antinomian of the period's countercultures, the world of the hippies and freaks was paradoxically most vulnerable to co-optation or assault from without, and, in its radical hostility to most or all forms of structured organization, to collapse from within. Already in the late 1960s, as many hippies moved the site of their alternative dreams from the city to the country, fueling a typically utterly disorganized and decentralized communal "movement," the streets they left behind were increasingly awash in speed and heroin, pushed by crime syndicates who easily shouldered aside the relatively benign traffickers of mescaline, acid, psylocibin, and marijuana. Yet by 1976, of the estimated two thousand rural communes that had existed in the United States in 1970, only a

handful were left; by the mid-1980s, most of these too were extinct, along with every Digger-style free clothing or free food store. Moreover, throughout the early 1970s, in a telling shift from their prior allegiance to an ethic of doing "whatever feels right," many former hippies and freaks in country and city alike had switched over virtually without a beat to some form or other of a fairly extreme submission to guru-centered spiritual authority and had reappeared as, for example, Jesus Freaks, Hare Krishnas, or followers of the Reverend Sun Yung Moon (known as Moonies).

Nor, in the early and mid-1970s, was this phenomenon limited to former hippies and freaks. Throughout the time, and often under the cover of an increasing tendency for the countercultures of authenticity to give way to countercultures based on one notion or another of identity, a general trend toward exclusivist and authoritarian structures was under way. At times it came accompanied by fantastic scenarios of guerrilla warfare that were as dangerous as they were absurd, as in the lethal adventurism of the Symbionese Liberation Army (its motto, "Death to the Fascist Insect That Preys upon the Life of the People") or the Weather Underground. More often, taking its warrant from the same assumption that fueled so much countercultural thought and action of the time—that revolutionary subjectivity lay somehow in a pure state within the oppressed subject—it followed as well from an insistence that "the master's tools will never dismantle the master's house," and therefore took the form of an endless series of harsh and disabling arguments over just who the true revolutionary subject was whose every instinct should be respected, and every word obeyed.

To be sure, the bitter internecine squabbles, internal coups d'état and separatist splitting that plagued feminist, leftist, and minority counterculturalist groups throughout the 1970s were at least in part justified by the tendency within all such groups to define both oppression and liberation solely in terms of the interests and perspectives of the dominant within each group: black men, for example, in black nationalist organizations; white middle-class heterosexual women in feminist camps; white men within leftist groups. But the tendency was politically disabling, if not downright depoliticizing, all the same—and especially ruinous, as Marable recounts, for those "black militants who defeated themselves" in the 1970s as "organizationally fractious, nationalist groups took turns in purging various tendencies out of their respective formations" (p. 136)—especially insofar as it became increasingly unclear exactly what sort of countercultural vision or strategy truly did preside over the potentially endless divisiveness of sorting out ideologically pure sheep from impure or upstart goats.

The question of whether and to what extent this 1970s turn toward what would come to be called "identity politics" was itself inevitably inscribed within the countercultural logic of authenticity and its accompanying projects of personal liberation can probably never be settled decisively. What is clear, however, is that by the mid-1970s the once wide-open territory in which large dreams of personal and cultural transformation could be both dreamed and, in part at least, acted out was being not only hived off, but closed down and commodified as well. Certainly the end of the long postwar economic boom around 1974, and the subsequent class struggle waged from above, which sent real average wages into a twenty-odd-year decline, played their own large parts in reducing the countercultural space in which to dream and act. Nor is it any secret that by the late 1970s a counter-countercultural ideological struggle was also under way, much of it backed by strong corporate funding, to demonize the impossible dreams of the 1960s as the source of all contemporary ills and to supplant them with the reactionary social, cultural, and political dreams of the New Right.

LEGACY AND PROSPECT

Under all these pressures, and in the hangover of their own overheated rhetoric and overblown expectations, it is small wonder that the countercultures of the 1960s and 1970s, now on the defensive, turned to downsizing themselves. For some, a shift from a way of life centered on the quest for a fully liberated individual and collective identity to a more or less vaguely alternative "lifestyle" was aided and abetted by a capitalist-consumerist market always willing to find and furnish new market niches with the appropriate "authentic" commodities: from "natural cosmetics" to Native American dreamcatchers, African drums to "peasant" clothing from around the world. For others, such downsizing involved forming a myriad of small communities and organizations as a step toward settling in for what was increasingly seen as a long hard struggle to keep hope and possibility alive in situ. Thus it is both notable and symptomatic that the single new countercultural vision to appear in the 1970s, that of Green or environmental consciousness, was, on the

one hand, seized upon with singular rapacity by the marketeers of advanced capitalism, even as, on the other hand, its most novel and arguably radical feature consisted of its insistence on "thinking globally, acting locally" and regarding "small" as "beautiful" (Schumacher).

More generally, though the fires may have banked down that fueled the countercultures of the 1960s and 1970s in their various, complexly intermingled and cross-fertilizing quests for an existential affirmation of previously negated subjectivities, the energies set loose by those quests are still with us today. Nor, despite the contradiction they never resolved, or even fully faced, between individual fulfillment and collective liberation, have they been wholly canalized into so many lifestyle choices and privatized pursuits. Even at the bitter moment of Reaganism ascendant, they could still be discerned in the pollster Daniel Yankelovich's finding that "a majority of Americans" believed "our civilization is unbalanced, with excessive emphasis on the instrumental, and insufficient concern with the values of community, expressiveness, caring, and with the domain of the sacred" (p. 229). And their half-life endures, especially though not exclusively within white and nonwhite middle-class culture, where lives are lived and gender, sex, and racial identities constructed within and through a structure of feeling that allows immeasurably more scope for expressivity, equality, and freedom than could have been imagined had the 1960s not taken place. Likewise, at the beginning of the twenty-first century a host of countercultural practices continued to work themselves out and through a wide variety of institutions, groups, and communities: from the former New Left radicals and hippies of the northern California bioregional community that Jentri Anders calls "Mateel" to a Sufi commune in upstate New York, from former SNCC leader Bob Moses's Algebra Project for inner-city black children to the campaign to save the black activist and journalist Mumia Abu-Jamal from execution and abolish the death penalty.

In all these forms and sites and a myriad of others, despite the long winter of Reaganite reaction and the false spring of Clintonian neoliberalism, the countercultural visions of the 1960s and 1970s continued their circulation through the capillaries of the body politic. Meanwhile, to revisit those visions in the time of their flowering, we must bypass those once-popular works, now quaintly dated at best, that bore the impress of the counterculture into the mainstream: the jingly vacuousness of the "rock musical" *Hair,* the glib prophecies of *The Greening of America,* and its silly view of human history as the passage from "Consciousness I" first to the individualist "II," and now, soon, to the neo-tribal "III," coming soon to a world near you. Rather, we should look back at the oracles and calls to arms it issued in its own time and to its own people: to Mitchell Goodman's raw anthology of dispatches from the various fronts at their most feverish pitch of activity in *The Movement toward a New America* (1970); or to those visions in their most crystalline and comprehensive synthesis near the end of the period, in Marge Piercy's urgent and beautiful utopian science-fiction novel, *Woman on the Edge of Time* (1976). And we must look back to look ahead, toward that moment no one of us can foretell, when some new version of belief in the impossible, starting in from where the 1960s counterculture left off, yet from somewhere new as well, will open the sky of our collective desire and expectation once again.

See also **The Ideal of Spontaneity; The Struggle for the Academy; American Expatriate Artists Abroad; Artistic, Intellectual, and Political Refugees** *(in this volume);* **The Visual Arts; Journals of Opinion; Film; Marxist Approaches** *(volume 3); and other articles in this section.*

BIBLIOGRAPHY

Anders, Jentri. *Beyond Counterculture: The Community of Mateel.* Pullman, Wash., 1990.

Callenbach, Ernest. *Ecotopia: The Notebooks and Reports of William Weston.* 1975. Reprint, New York, 1990.

Case, John, and Rosemary C. R. Taylor, eds. *Co-ops, Communes, and Collectives: Experiments in Social Change in the 1960s and 1970s.* New York, 1979.

Cluster, Dick, ed. *They Should Have Served That Cup of Coffee: Seven Radicals Remember the Sixties.* Boston, 1979.

Dinnerstein, Dorothy. *The Mermaid and the Minotaur: Sexual Arrangements and the Human Malaise.* New York, 1976.

Echols, Alice. *Daring to Be Bad: Radical Feminism in America, 1971–1975.* Minneapolis, 1989.

Evans, Sara. *Personal Politics: The Roots of Women's Liberation in the Civil Rights Movement and the New Left.* New York, 1979.

Farber, David. *Chicago '68.* Chicago, 1988.

Firestone, Shulamith. *The Dialectic of Sex: The Case for Feminist Revolution.* New York, 1970.

Gitlin, Todd. *The Sixties: Years of Hope, Days of Rage.* New York, 1987.

Goodman, Mitchell, ed. *The Movement toward a New America.* Philadelphia and New York, 1970.

Hampton, Henry, and Steve Fayer, eds. *Voices of Freedom: An Oral History of the Civil Rights Movement from the 1950s through the 1980s.* New York, 1990.

Jacobs, Ron. *The Way the Wind Blew: A History of the Weather Underground.* New York, 1997.

Kornbluth, Jesse, ed. *Notes from the New Underground: An Anthology.* New York, 1968.

McAdam, Douglas. *Freedom Summer.* New York, 1988.

Marable, Manning. *Race, Reform, and Rebellion: The Second Reconstruction in Black America, 1945–1990.* 2d ed. Jackson, Miss., 1991.

Matthiessen, Peter. Sal si puedes: *Cesar Chavez and the New American Revolution.* New York, 1969.

Miller, James. *"Democracy Is in the Streets": From Port Huron to the Siege of Chicago.* New York, 1987.

Morgan, Robin, ed. *Sisterhood Is Powerful: An Anthology of Writings from the Women's Liberation Movement.* New York, 1970.

Muñoz, Carlos. *Youth, Identity, Power: The Chicano Movement.* New York, 1989.

Omi, Michael, and Howard Winant. *Racial Formation in the U.S.: From the 1960s to the 1990s.* 2d ed. New York, 1994.

Payne, Charles. *I've Got the Light of Freedom: The Organizing Tradition and the Mississippi Freedom Struggle.* Berkeley, Calif., 1995.

Piercy, Marge. *Woman on the Edge of Time.* New York, 1976.

Reich, Charles. *The Greening of America.* New York, 1971.

Rossinow, Doug. *The Politics of Authenticity: Liberalism, Christianity, and the New Left in America.* New York, 1998.

Rossman, Michael. *New Age Blues: On the Politics of Consciousness.* New York, 1979.

Roszak, Theodore. *The Making of a Counter Culture: Reflections on the Technocratic Society and Its Youthful Opposition.* Garden City, N.Y., 1969.

Schumacher, E. F. *Small Is Beautiful: Economics as if People Mattered.* New York, 1973.

Snyder, Gary. *Earth House Hold: Technical Notes and Queries to Fellow Dharma Revolutionaries.* New York, 1969.

Teodori, Massimo, ed. *The New Left: A Documentary History.* Indianapolis, Ind., 1969.

Ture, Kwame (Stokely Carmichael), and Charles V. Hamilton. *Black Power: The Politics of Liberation in America.* Rev. ed. New York, 1992.

Wolf, Leonard, ed. *Voices from the Love Generation.* Boston, 1968.

Yankelovich, Daniel. *New Rules: Searching for Self-Fulfillment in a World Turned Upside Down.* New York, 1981.

POPULAR CULTURE IN THE PUBLIC ARENA

Steve Waksman

In the twenty-first century, the 1960s remained a crucial point of reference in the contemporary cultural landscape and an era of American history decidedly shrouded in certain myths about the national past. A decade of social and political unrest, the "years of rage" as the sociologist Todd Gitlin has memorialized them, the 1960s started with the hope of a new liberal establishment and ended with the rise of the "silent majority." Consequently, the transition from the 1960s to the 1970s is alternately told as a story of decline—from the collective euphoria of social action to the self-serving narcissism of the "me decade"—or as a story of the restoration of order (in which case the truly happy ending to the narrative does not come until 1980, when Ronald Reagan's presidency solidified the rise of conservatism to the forefront of American public life). Within this divided historical narrative, popular culture is also typically cast into two principal roles: (1) as the provocateur of transformation, carrying within it some of the more hopeful and, indeed, radical values of the burgeoning counterculture; or (2) as the space of a new hedonism within which any sense of collective engagement was overwhelmed by the array of pleasures offered by an expansive consumerism. In fact, popular culture in its manifold forms was both of these things and more, and the path that it followed was not so straightforwardly one of either decline or progress. Observing the interrelated spheres of media, film, and popular music, historians can begin to see how popular culture during both the 1960s and 1970s consolidated the power of certain social formations while at the same time opening the way for new styles of expression, new types of sensation, and a loosening of certain social constraints.

Historically, popular culture has been viewed as a "lower" form of culture by many of the critics and intellectuals whose task it is to propagate the terms of cultural evaluation. Such judgments, which have by no means vanished in the contemporary intellectual landscape, are most often aimed at the sup-

posed content of popular culture, which is seen to be aimed at a lowest common denominator of audience appeal and thus to leave its audiences unchallenged. Setting aside the assumption that "popularity" necessarily entails a diminution of aesthetic or intellectual content (and noting ironically that one of the most vigilant highbrow critiques of popular culture, Allan Bloom's *The Closing of the American Mind,* also became one of the best-selling books of the late 1980s), it is important to note that the arguments directed against the artistic value of popular culture largely miss the point. The popular culture of the 1960s and 1970s put forth some charged and at times quite challenging messages regarding the issues of the time. Yet the power of those messages rested not strictly in what the creators of that culture had to say but in how audiences responded to those messages, and how the content of the era's popular culture was framed by a new media environment that itself encouraged the partial dissolution of old-guard cultural values. By shifting the focus of critical scrutiny away from an understanding of culture as a collection of great works and toward an understanding of culture as representative of the environments that people inhabit and the ways that they experience cultural forms and messages, historians can best appreciate how popular culture shaped and reflected the struggles and values of one of the most turbulent periods in twentieth-century history.

At this level of critical analysis, the decades of the 1960s and 1970s were marked by considerable change in the levels of experience made available through popular culture. Such change might appear difficult to measure—"experience" may seem a nebulous category, hardly an objective criterion for research into social and cultural history. Nonetheless, when observing the discourses that surrounded popular culture during these years, it is striking how wide a range of commentators was beset by the notion that something significant was changing in the ways that audiences were interacting with popular

143

culture, and in the possibilities for different types of responses and experiences that were opened by the dominant cultural forms of the day. Specifically, television, film, music, and generally, the entire apparatus of mass cultural production were perceived to be expanding the range and the power of cultural representations in both form (the uninterrupted flow of televised representations, the radical juxtapositions of "underground" film, the sensory overload of high-volume rock and roll) and content (the representation of controversial or taboo subjects such as war, racial conflict, and explicit sexual activity). It was in this blend of impressions and meanings that popular culture exerted its greatest impact, as the rush of sensations transmitted by media channels and popular forms became cause for comment, critique, and celebration.

MEDIA SENSATIONS

Only during the 1960s, perhaps, could a theorist of media have become a media darling. Marshall McLuhan's dictum that "the medium is the message" (or alternately, "the medium is the massage," as the title of his 1967 collaboration with Quentin Fiore put it) has become almost commonsensical in the age of the Internet and the electronic information revolution, and McLuhan is viewed by many as the "prophet of the information age." But amid the late-twentieth-century wave of fascination with new media and new technologies, we should remember that McLuhan was not responding primarily to computers and their attendant technologies, although he was more aware of their presence and their implications than many. McLuhan's ideas about the importance of the medium, and the media, and the irony-tinged celebrity he achieved during the mid-1960s, were principally concerned with an earlier wave of electronic media: the telegraph, radio, film, and, above all, television. Television was the quintessential "cool medium" for McLuhan, meaning that it was the medium that invited the greatest amount of participation from its audience. Presenting viewers with a low-intensity experience, TV pointed toward the subversion of the overarching visual emphasis that had dominated Western societies since the time of the German inventor-printer Johannes Gutenberg and the rise of a print-based culture; with television, the individual viewer was opened up to a new sort of media experience, a "daily session of synesthesia" that foregrounded the aural and tactile dimensions of everyday perception (*Understanding Media*, p. 275).

McLuhan's optimistic reading of the "participatory" qualities of the television viewing experience might seem almost quaint to a contemporary reader, and yet his evaluation of television and its place within the broader media system highlights some key aspects of the changing role of media and, by extension, of popular culture during the decades of the 1960s and 1970s. Whether viewed positively or negatively, this era was marked by the recognition that media spectacle of various sorts increasingly dominated the patterns of everyday life in the United States and abroad (McLuhan, after all, was Canadian). From electoral politics to the struggle for civil rights to the growing conflict over the Vietnam War, American knowledge of national and international events was tied to the expanding reach of television and other visual media to represent the major events of the day. More was at issue than the content of media representations, however; as McLuhan himself routinely pointed out, the power of media lay not so much in *what* was shown as in *how* things were shown, and in how the media established new modes of sensory experience that framed human perceptions in (ostensibly) new ways. While McLuhan observed that the medium was not only the message but the massage, then, so did Susan Sontag assert in a different context that "in place of a hermeneutics we need an erotics of art" (*Against Interpretation,* p. 14). For both writers, the key issue was that media, art, and culture in the new environment conveyed information that was less factual or intellectual than it was bodily, sensual.

As such, the new media were perceived by two of the most influential critics of the day to be breaking down many of the long-cherished values and boundaries that had held "culture" together for its proponents. These included not only the separation of mind and body implied by the preceding insights, but also, and perhaps more notably, the boundary between "high" and "low" cultures that had been fundamental to the structure of American culture since at least the late nineteenth century and that had been reinforced by the "culture of containment" that emerged in the early phases of the cold war. Sontag's essay "One Culture and the New Sensibility," first published in 1965, became a veritable manifesto for this new perspective on media, culture, and the arts, albeit one that was shaped by a decidedly "high culture" perspective. Yet Sontag's essay was itself a response to certain trends in the art world that were already quite well established, revolving around the seemingly oxymoronic category of "pop art."

144

Campbell's Soup Can, **Andy Warhol (1965).** This work is among the most popular symbols of twentieth-century American art. © 2000 ANDY WARHOL FOUNDATION FOR THE VISUAL ARTS/ARS, NEW YORK [BURSTEIN COLLECTION/CORBIS]

Indeed, while Sontag and McLuhan were among the key intellectual voices to discuss the significance of the "new sensibility," it was Andy Warhol, the crown prince of pop art, who did the most to put those new ideas into some kind of practice. The commercial sheen of Warhol's soup cans, Brillo boxes, and Marilyn Monroe prints are, of course, the best known examples of Warhol's affinity for an aesthetic of mechanical reproduction so indebted to the imagery of popular culture. In his memoir of the 1960s, *Popism* (1980), Warhol offered a description of his work process that reveals how deeply rooted were his tendencies to reorganize the boundaries between fine and commercial art, "high" and "popular" materials. Warhol's story begins with a visit to his studio by the noted art dealer Ivan Karp:

When Ivan came by, I had all my commercial art drawings stashed away out of sight. As long as he didn't know anything about me, there was no sense bringing up my advertising background. I still had the two styles I was working in—the more lyrical painting with gestures and drips, and the hard style without the gestures. I liked to show both to people to goad them into commenting on the differences, because I still wasn't sure if you could completely remove all the hand gesture from art and become noncommittal, anonymous. I knew that I definitely wanted to take away the commentary of the gestures—that's why I had this routine of painting with rock and roll blasting the same song, a 45 rpm, over and over all day long—songs like the one that was playing the day Ivan came by for the first time, "I Saw Linda Yesterday" by Dickey Lee. The music blasting cleared my head out and left me working on instinct alone. In fact, it wasn't only rock and roll that I used that way—I'd also have the radio blasting opera, and the TV picture on (but not the sound)—and if all that didn't clear enough out of my mind, I'd open a magazine, put it beside me, and half read an article while I painted. (p. 7)

McLuhan's "daily session of synesthesia" here comes to life through Warhol's artistic practice, although the points of mediated reference have widened. Whereas McLuhan characterized television as in itself a multisensory conductor, Warhol emphasized the convergence of media experiences available at the level of everyday painterly activity. The televised image, the repetitive blare of rock and roll, the distraction of popular print media all fuse together in Warhol's account in a manner that suggests the recombinative possibilities made available by the new media, possibilities that were a key source of inspiration for Warhol in his own disruptive approach to the creation of culture.

There is another level of meaning at work in Warhol's comments worth noting: the various distractions provided through media channels enabled him to produce an art that was, by his account, devoid of gesture, "noncommittal, anonymous." Warhol celebrated these effects (or this apparent lack of affect) in his art; indeed, he concluded the above passage in *Popism* with the assertion that of the two different styles that occupied him at the time, his favorite was "the cold 'no comment' paintings," which comes as no surprise to those familiar with his art. Others were less sanguine in their judgments concerning the new pervasiveness of mediated culture. Across the ocean in France, the social theorist and filmmaker Guy Debord and other members of the Situationist Party viewed everyday life as the site of political struggle, and argued that the new media threatened to colonize everyday experience and to displace independent will or action with the uninterrupted flow of representations. Closer to home, the film critic Jonathan Rosenbaum reflected upon some of the changes that had beset

American life in the years between the 1950s—the period of his childhood—and the late 1970s, when he wrote his quasi-autobiographical account of moviegoing, *Moving Places* (1980). Considering the place of his critical writing amid the other activities and experiences that occupy an ordinary day, Rosenbaum noted the following:

> A garden stroll through a supermarket: this describes Hollywood's activity and my own with equal precision, whether it's scanning an aisle of breakfast cereals, waiting for a free bank teller, following a narrative, or pursuing a line of thought—all these activities preferably performed as though conducted by music. How could I have guessed in the early fifties that Muzak would answer my constant prayer for God's own chorus singing down to earth and swelling the air, fulfilling the dream so perfectly that I'm not even aware of its daily effects on me? Who would have guessed that making life into a musical would deaden the senses rather than exalt them? (p. 45)

Should only life become a musical. . . . What once seemed an almost utopian vision of a life surrounded by music had for Rosenbaum turned into something far less desirable at the end of the 1970s. Everyday spaces such as the supermarket were now organized according to the rhythms of mass-produced culture, much as Warhol's art was organized by such rhythms. Rosenbaum's judgment of this circumstance stands in marked contradiction to that of Warhol's; he heard not the proliferation of creative possibility but something more akin to what the French social theorist Jacques Attali described as "a silence in sound, the innocuous chatter of recuperable cries" (*Noics*, p. 124). But as social critics try to make sense of the contrast between Rosenbaum's tacit denouncement of the deadening powers of Muzak and Warhol's description of the ability of his "blasting" rock and roll to clear his head, as they try to understand how these two perspectives shed light upon the place of popular culture in the society of the 1960s and 1970s, they need to be mindful of the separation that exists not only in the judgments of these two notable figures, but in their points of reference. Rock and roll and Muzak, after all, may both be a part of the economy of repetitive desire that is contemporary consumer culture, but they offer different pleasures, different sensations. The assault upon the senses generated by the pervasiveness of media-driven sound and spectacle during the 1960s and 1970s, and continuing into the present day, offers a compelling drama of the interplay between power and its lack, silence and creativity, bodily stimulation and bodily restriction; and accordingly, while some have sought to escape or combat the onslaught, others have sought instead to submerge themselves within it.

UP FROM THE UNDERGROUND

> When people describe who I am, if they don't say, "Andy Warhol, the Pop artist," they say "Andy Warhol the underground filmmaker." . . . But I don't even know what the term *underground* means, unless it means that you don't want anyone to find out about you or bother you. . . . But if that's the case, I can't see how I was ever "underground," since I've always wanted people to notice me. . . . From the different types of movies people applied [the term "underground"] to, you couldn't figure out what it meant—aside, of course, from non-Hollywood and nonunion. But did it also mean "arty" or "dirty" or "freaky" or "plotless" or "nude" or "outrageously camp"? (Warhol, *Popism*, pp. 46–47)

Certainly part of the impetus behind the swell of "underground" film activity in the 1960s arose from the desire to work outside of, or underneath, the principal flow of mainstream film and media activity. Yet as Andy Warhol tellingly observed, the "underground" was by no means so strictly defined, nor were its boundaries so rigid as the term would seem to imply. There were, of course, artists and critics who wished to maintain the underground as a separate sphere of artistic activity dominated by the aesthetic impulses of the American and European avant-garde. Such was the position of Jonas Mekas, perhaps the principal champion of underground cinema (or the "new American cinema," as it came to be called in the early 1960s), who specifically argued against a "people's" definition of cinema in his dogged efforts to bring experimental works to the surface of public attention through his activities as filmmaker, distributor, and critic. Despite Mekas's insistent positioning of underground film as a phenomenon outside of mainstream cinematic activity, though, it is more fruitful to acknowledge that the cinematic underground can best be understood in constant dialogue with the mainstream. The 1960s and 1970s were a period when the interaction between these different levels of filmic activity was most pronounced. The underground was at its most public and visible during these years, and the censorship battles surrounding some of the key underground works of the era not only drew attention to what might otherwise have remained obscure pieces of work, but led the way toward the broader loosening of restraints surrounding the cinematic representation of taboo subjects, most notably those concerning sexuality, as indicated by Andy Warhol's previous comment on the indeterminate nature of underground film.

Sex and sexuality were indeed key elements of underground film during the 1960s, at the same time as sex was becoming more explicitly central to "above-ground" narrative cinema. For experimental filmmakers, however, the representation of sex and nudity was rarely an end in itself, the way it would become within the "sexploitation" films and the more explicit narrative pornographic films that emerged into the public spotlight in the late 1960s and early 1970s. Carolee Schneemann's *Fuses,* made during the years 1964 to 1967, was one of the most sexually explicit films of the underground movement, consisting almost entirely of shots of Schneemann and her lover James Tenney engaged in various acts of intercourse, interspersed with occasional images of Schneemann alone or of Schneemann's cat, Kitch, observing her human counterparts at play. Over the course of the film's twenty-one minutes, the copulating forms of Schneemann and Tenney come to stand for a combination of love and lust unchecked by social or psychological inhibition, especially notable in an era before feminism had turned female pleasures and desires into a central political concern.

Also significant is Schneemann's connection to what Jonas Mekas called the "Baudelairean cinema" and the 1960s film critic Gene Youngblood called "synaesthetic cinema": her effort to capture not just images of sexual intercourse but to somehow approximate the sensations stimulated by intercourse in a manner that returns us to Susan Sontag's call for an "erotics of art." Thus did Schneemann later discuss her desire in making *Fuses* to get "closer to tactility, to sensations in the body that are streaming and unconscious and fluid," the accomplishment of which required that she "make cameras and light meters and tripods all part of my body. I had to enjoy them in some way" (Haug, *Wide Angle,* p. 25; MacDonald, *A Critical Cinema,* p. 139). The bodies in *Fuses* are not represented in a straightforward, fully objectified manner, but are instead refracted through Schneemann's almost assaultive approach to editing and reassembling the footage she shot in cooperation with Tenney. During Schneemann's filmmaking process, she baked parts of the film in the oven, soaked other parts in acid, and rearranged the overall flow of images so that the end result "closely approximates the actual experience of sex in which the body of one's partner becomes fragmented into tactile zones and exaggerated mental images" (Youngblood, *Expanded Cinema,* p. 119).

What makes *Fuses* such a provocative and powerful piece of filmmaking—its visual and ideological fluidity—also kept it sequestered squarely within the province of film festivals and art museums. Whereas Schneemann envisioned sex as one aspect of a much broader movement toward some kind of personal and political liberation, the movement of explicit sexual content toward the mainstream of American popular culture involved a much more narrow approach to the representation of sexuality, one that too often strictly delimited the possible meanings that sex could assume. Much debate has ensued in the late twentieth century about the social effects of pornography, especially concerning the representation of women as objects, and as victims, of an aggressive male sexuality. Viewed historically, however, the public emergence of pornographic films as a significant aspect of commercial narrative cinema, marked most obviously by the considerable and surprising success of *Deep Throat* upon its release in 1972, reflected nothing so much as the ambivalence surrounding the public exhibition of explicit sexual content, especially where women's sexual pleasure was concerned.

Deep Throat is focused around the story of a woman, Linda, and her search for sexual gratification. As such, the film marks a clear response to the increased public acknowledgment of female pleasure and desire that was an outgrowth of the "sexual revolution," promoted both by the political claims of radical feminists and the medical views of sexologists like William Masters and Virginia Johnson. Yet a close examination of the plot of the film reveals that *Deep Throat* is just as clearly an effort to contain any threat posed by this new prominence of women's sexuality to existing hierarchies of sexual difference and sexual desire. When the film opens, Linda suffers from an inability to achieve a satisfying orgasm. After several efforts to remedy her problem, she consults Dr. Young, who correctly diagnoses her lack of sexual stimulation. Linda, as it turns out, has a clitoris in the back of her throat rather than in the usual location; and consequently, the only fully stimulating sexual experience she can have involves the practice of "deep throat," a form of fellatio that requires a man of unusually generous endowment. With this narrative conundrum, *Deep Throat* announces its true intentions: to construct a version of female pleasure necessarily tethered to the pleasures and desires of a more knowledgeable and experienced (and thus, more powerful) man. By placing her clitoris outside of her own reach, *Deep Throat* divests Linda of the control over her pleasure that both Masters and Johnson and feminists had sought to establish, and replaces the utopian mutuality between man and woman depicted by Carolee Schneemann in *Fuses* with a decidedly hierarchical relationship within which biology does indeed become destiny.

Over the course of the 1970s, the wave of "porno chic" ushered in by *Deep Throat* and its counterparts receded. Pornography remained a highly profitable endeavor, but the exhibition of pornographic films moved from its public position back into more privatized realms with the emergence of home video in the late 1970s and early 1980s. Even at the height of visibility, though, pornographic films retained an aura of "dirtiness" that made them an uneasy presence in the public sphere. The uneasiness surrounding the public exhibition of pornography, in turn, played a significant role in one of the most influential films of the 1970s, Martin Scorsese's *Taxi Driver* (1976). As discussed by Lesley Stern in *The Scorsese Connection*, Travis Bickle, the protagonist of *Taxi Driver*, is a character obsessed with dirt, filth, and pollution; and this obsession renders Bickle's interest in pornography ironic and, ultimately, deadly. When Travis takes the pure white object of his desire, Betsy, to a pornographic film for their first date, the male-dominated narratives of power and pleasure that drive so much film pornography are displaced by his humiliation when Betsy flees the scene in distaste. This humiliation sets the stage for Travis's reinvention of himself as a killing machine through a regime of physical and psychological activity that leads him back to the porn theater. As Travis imaginatively shoots the characters onscreen with the tip of his finger, Scorsese, actor Robert De Niro, and screenwriter Paul Schrader bring their protagonist to "that precarious terrain where sexuality and violence intermesh," where the spectacle of sexual pleasure gives way to an image of masculinity disfigured by the surrounding filth of the New York streets.

BRING THE NOISE

It's time for a new national anthem. America is divided into two definite divisions. . . . The easy thing to cop out with is sayin' black and white. That's the easiest thing. You can see a black person. But now to get down to the nitty-gritty, it's gettin' to be old and young—not the age, but the way of thinking. Old and new, actually . . . because there's so many even older people that took half their lives to reach a certain point that little kids understand now. (Hall and Clark, *Rock*, p. 25)

The scene: the Woodstock rock festival, summer 1969. Jimi Hendrix, the closing act of the festival, played in the morning to a thin representation of the weekend's audience; only thirty thousand of the festival's half-million participants remained to see the guitarist's set. Amid the remnants of one of the decade's most notable collective gatherings, Hendrix played a strong if uneven set, showcasing his new Electric Sky Church band that represented a renewed impulse by the black guitarist to align himself with other African American musicians. The highlight of the set, however—and some would say, the festival—was essentially a solo turn by Hendrix, who followed a group jam with a devastating rendition of "The Star-Spangled Banner" that gave musical form to his expressed desire to create a new national anthem. Sounding out the main melody of the song with the loud blasts of his distorted electric guitar, Hendrix moved his rendition of the anthem toward sheer electronic noise during the third verse; "And the rocket's red glare" descended into a series of atonal shrieks and growls the likes of which interrupted and punctured the remainder of his performance. As disruptive as these sounds were, Hendrix's blend of physical and electronic effects also seemed to flow from the melody of the anthem. By the time the guitarist converted the climactic note of "free" (in "O'er the land of the free") into a shrill bit of feedback that descended into a miasma of sound, one had the sense of having heard not just a rendition of the national anthem but a full-fledged reinvention of it, such that the original could never be heard in quite the same way again (Waksman, *Instruments of Desire*, pp. 171–172).

Charles Shaar Murray, the most astute of Hendrix's many critics and biographers, called the guitarist's performance of the "Star-Spangled Banner" at Woodstock "probably the most complex and powerful work of American art to deal with the Vietnam War and its corrupting, distorting effect on successive generations of the American psyche" (*Crosstown Traffic*, p. 24). Hendrix translated the fractiousness of the war at home and abroad and the damage it did to American patriotism into a war between music and noise that was at once a supreme act of defamiliarization and a stunning political critique. Also significant was that Hendrix's rendition of the national anthem demonstrated the power of the electric guitar to express and represent the most pressing conflicts of the era, to give voice to the shifts in cultural and political understanding for which the 1960s are most remembered. One could well argue that, amid the wave of significant performers who held the spotlight during the 1960s,

148

the electric guitar was the true "star" of the decade, as an instrument that emblematized new pleasures and possibilities for change. So it was that Bob Dylan's decision to use the electric guitar at the 1965 Newport Folk Festival became such a challenging and conflict-ridden occurrence, exposing the tension between old-guard notions of folk authenticity and a new generation yearning to blend folk idealism with rock excitement. So it was, too, that a rock band like Detroit's MC5 could view the electric guitar as an instrument designed to foment not just musical but political disorder, and could occupy a central place in their short-lived vision of cultural revolution through rock and roll. John Sinclair, the long-time manager of the MC5, wrote the following in accompaniment to the band's first album, the live *Kick Out the Jams:*

> There is no way to get at the music without taking in the whole context of the music too—*there is no separation.* We say the MC5 is the solution to the problem of separation, because they are *so together.* The MC5 is totally committed to the revolution, as the revolution is totally committed to driving people out of their separate shells and into each other's arms. . . .
>
> The MC5 will make you feel it, or leave the room. The MC5 will drive you crazy out of your head into your body. The MC5 is rock and roll. Rock and roll *is* the music of our bodies, of our whole lives—the "resensifier," [singer] Rob Tyner calls it. We have to *come together,* people, "build to a gathering," or else. Or else we are dead, and gone. (*Guitar Army,* p. 110)

If rock and roll was the "resensifier"—that which awakened the body to new heights of sensual enjoyment, which in turn made for an experience of connectedness that for Sinclair had significant political implications—then the electric guitar was the instrument that made such resensification possible. For the MC5, the heavily amplified sounds of the electric guitar opened the way toward the dissolution of social, sexual, and political boundaries through the radical deployment of noise. Noise, as defined by Jacques Attali, is a mode of music making that disturbs the existing social and musical order; it represents the boundary between acceptable and unacceptable musical practices, and indicates the power of sound to organize and shape social experience. The MC5, with their deliberate use of the electric guitar and amplification to generate a disorderly noise, sought to embody the utopian project of taking "pleasure in the instruments, the tools of communication" in a manner designed to demarcate a realm of autonomous desire in which the "separation" between worker and consumer, performer and audience, would be abolished (Attali, *Noise,* p. 135; Waksman, *Instruments of Desire,* p. 233).

Of course, such utopian visions were not to come to pass. If the electric guitar gave rise to a politics of sensation in line with the most radical possibilities of 1960s popular culture, it also played into the expansion of rock music's economic base in a way that mitigated against the realization of those possibilities. Even those hallowed, quasi-pastoral gatherings at events such as the 1967 Monterey Pop Festival and Woodstock were ultimately as significant for showing the full potential of rock as a mass medium as they were for consolidating the counterculture. Jacques Attali himself warned of the difficulties of enacting a program for aesthetic and political transformation; as much as he acknowledged the potential for noise to engender such changes, he also declared that "inducing people to compose using predefined instruments cannot lead to a mode of production different from that authorized by those instruments. That is the trap" (*Noise,* p. 141). With the rise of arena rock in the 1970s, emblematized in the music of hard rock and heavy metal stalwarts such as the ever-innovative Led Zeppelin and the more basic, pounding Grand Funk Railroad, the noise of the electric guitar was effectively normalized to fit the predefined contours of the commercial music industry. What the rock critic Robert Duncan called the "loud*est*ness" of hard rock made large, arena-size concerts the new standard for live presentation of the music, and arguably created conditions in which the technological trappings of rock substituted for any meaningful evocation of passion or commitment. Yet this foreclosure of musical and political possibilities was never complete. However adulterated, "the noise" remained notable in its power to disturb, its potential for provocation, or more basically in its ability to give meaning to those existing at "the lower reaches of the rock hierarchy . . . where a kid sits hunched over his amp, ready to enact again the mythic hustle that is rock 'n' roll" (Goldstein, *Harper's,* October 1971, p. 32).

See also **The Popular Arts; The Athlete as Cultural Icon** (*volume 1);* **The Design of the Familiar** (*volume 2);* **Elite vs. Popular Cultures; Culture for Mass Audiences; Periodicals; Film; Television; Radio; Advertising; Public Murals; Music; Dance; Fashion** (*volume 3).*

BIBLIOGRAPHY

Attali, Jacques. *Noise: The Political Economy of Music.* Translated by Brian Massumi. Minneapolis, Minn., 1985.

Biskind, Peter. *Easy Riders, Raging Bulls: How the Sex-Drugs-and-Rock-'n'-Roll Generation Saved Hollywood.* New York, 1998.

Debord, Guy. *Society of the Spectacle.* Detroit, Mich., 1983.

D'Emilio, John, and Estelle Freedman. *Intimate Matters: A History of Sexuality in America.* New York, 1988.

Duncan, Robert. *The Noise: Notes from a Rock 'n' Roll Era.* New York, 1984.

Goldstein, Richard. "Also Sprach Grand Funk Railroad." *Harper's* 1457 (October 1971): 32–44.

Hall, Douglas Kent, and Sue C. Clark. *Rock: A World Bold as Love.* New York, 1970.

Haug, Kate. "An Interview with Carolee Schneemann." *Wide Angle* 20, no. 1 (1988): 20–49.

James, David E. *Allegories of Cinema: American Film in the Sixties.* Princeton, N.J., 1989.

Levine, Lawrence. *Highbrow/Lowbrow: The Emergence of Cultural Hierarchy in America.* Cambridge, Mass., 1988.

MacDonald, Scott. *A Critical Cinema: Interviews with Independent Filmmakers.* Berkeley, Calif., 1988.

McLuhan, Marshall. *Understanding Media: The Extensions of Man.* Introduction by Lewis H. Lapham. New York, 1964.

McLuhan, Marshall, and Quentin Fiore. *The Medium Is the Massage: An Inventory of Effects.* New York, 1967.

Mekas, Jonas. *Movie Journal: The Rise of the New American Cinema.* New York, 1972.

Murray, Charles Shaar. *Crosstown Traffic: Jimi Hendrix and the Post-war Rock 'n' Roll Revolution.* New York, 1989.

Rosenbaum, Jonathan. *Moving Places: A Life at the Movies.* 1980. Reprint. Berkeley, Calif., 1995.

Ross, Andrew. *No Respect: Intellectuals and Popular Culture.* New York, 1989.

Sinclair, John. *Guitar Army: Street Writings/Prison Writings.* New York, 1972.

Sontag, Susan. *Against Interpretation, and Other Essays.* New York, 1966.

Stern, Lesley. *The Scorsese Connection.* Bloomington, Ind., 1995.

Waksman, Steve. *Instruments of Desire: The Electric Guitar and the Shaping of Musical Experience.* Cambridge, Mass., 1999.

Warhol, Andy, and Pat Hackett. *Popism: The Warhol Sixties.* San Diego, Calif., 1980.

Williams, Linda. *Hard Core: Power, Pleasure, and the "Frenzy of the Visible."* Berkeley, Calif., 1989.

Youngblood, Gene. *Expanded Cinema.* Introduction by R. Buckminster Fuller. New York, 1970.

INTELLECTUALS AND IDEOLOGY IN GOVERNMENT

David Steigerwald

Judging by the amount of writing on the subject, especially the widely noted books of Russell Jacoby and Edward Said, contemporary intellectuals at the end of the twentieth century were more anxious about their public roles than at any time in the previous hundred years. They feared political seduction, despised the bureaucratic career, and lamented the demise of the public intellectual, that heroic individual who, as Said defines the type, "speaks the truth to power."

But if the important question of the intellectuals' proper public role was particularly keen as we entered the twenty-first century, it was so because ideas themselves had come to figure prominently in the attainment and exercise of power. Public intellectuals might be rare, but intellectual products are in high demand. To meet that demand, a hybrid type of intellectual has emerged: the political intellectual, whose ambition is to turn abstract ideas into public policy and who is willing to join the politician toward that end. Like purists, political intellectuals disdain bureaucrats, but they claim expertise on the basis of knowledge that is bureaucratic in nature. They offer their boldest ideas for blatant political uses but believe that their ideas are too compelling to be compromised. They are not content with mere jeremiads, as the public intellectual may be; they want power. But they cloak ambition with the self-assurance that they alone know what is in the nation's best interests.

Three developments account for the emergence of this hybrid type: the state's demand for instrumental knowledge; the transformation of electoral politics from a party-based process to an image-based form of marketing; and the ongoing need of politicians for an "agenda."

In the first case, the needs of the cold war state for information of all sorts was so vast that the existing bureaucracies could never supply enough, and the state looked to outside sources, universities and think tanks that were often staffed by people who were specialists but who also routinely convinced themselves that the larger public good depended on their expertise. As a rule, these budding political intellectuals have regarded the federal bureaucracy with condescending scorn, even though they themselves hail from knowledge bureaucracies and are quite willing to accept government positions. There, they see themselves boring from within, countering the stodgy bureaucracy by subverting it. In contemporary America, the philosopher and the functionary have tended to be one and the same.

Meanwhile, the persistent decline in party loyalty has broken the hold of long-held party positions on candidates who, thus liberated from confining doctrine, market themselves. Political marketing depends on many things, including the candidate's "attractiveness," but the candidate's Big Idea—"the vision thing," a rather bewildered President George Bush called it—has become the centerpiece of marketing strategy. The essence of these strategies is to broach whatever idea has the most resonance in the public mind. It is far less important that the Big Idea is an accurate analysis of the state of the nation than that it tweaks the interest, panders to the biases, or plays to the anxieties of the largest number of constituencies. And there is no lack of intellectuals who are prepared to push their views for those purposes.

Yet contemporary politicians need ideas for more than just rhetorical purposes. Once elected, they must at least feign the attempt to fulfill campaign rhetoric. The philosopher's unruly abstractions have to be fashioned into instrumental knowledge, and it is the self-appointed duty of the political intellectual to turn the Big Idea into concrete policy.

THE RISE OF THE THINK TANK

The governmental appetite for useful knowledge, the exploitation of grand ideas, and the minor empowerment of the intellectuals have all run hand-in-hand, however distinct their origins. World War II brought expert knowledge into regular government service by demanding everything from theoretical physics to manufacturing engineering. The cold war defense establishment heightened the demand, so much so that neither the Defense Department nor its private contractors could keep up with research and development. The department turned to universities for many of its needs, but a new sort of institution, the think tank, also developed. Postwar think tanks, the prototype for which was the RAND Corporation, were mostly self-sustaining, research-and-development contractors of government services. They were extra-bureaucratic, formally independent from governmental agencies but dependent on them for contracts. Thus beholden to their clients, think-tank researchers had reason to be as pusillanimous as the proverbial functionary.

Yet there was an important difference. Where the mere functionary kept his job if he just got along, the think-tank researchers, as James Allen Smith ably points out in *The Idea Brokers* (1991), "had to 'market' their services. . . . Ideas were 'sold' and research 'products' were supplied. . . . For the individual researcher working in this environment, skills and methods had to be developed that were useful, that is to say, 'marketable'" (pp. 201–202). The need to market themselves made experts more eager to influence policy, because influence meant reputation and continued contracts.

THE STEVENSON PRECEDENT

If think tanks helped turn instrumental knowledge into marketable knowledge, the market was a peculiar one, driven as it was by a political system similarly bent on marketing ideas. As early as the mid-1950s, when Adlai Stevenson began to seek advice from a group of liberal intellectuals, including Arthur M. Schlesinger Jr. and John Kenneth Galbraith, political hopefuls have tried to use ideas for electoral ends. It is no surprise that Stevenson should have been among the first to approach intellectuals. He cultivated the image of a gadfly, an absentminded dreamer and lover of great books. Not that he was an intellectual in any meaningful sense. Galbraith called Stevenson's intellectual front "an amiable fraud." "There could be doubt as to whether . . . he ever read a serious book. . . . No one was so relentlessly admiring of mine," Galbraith

quipped. "He was always about to read them" (*A Life*, p. 288).

It must be said, in any event, that the intellectuals sought Stevenson more than he courted them. This was particularly true for Schlesinger and Galbraith, who up until then were public intellectuals in the best sense; their best works were accessible commentaries on important issues of the day. Schlesinger helped define cold war liberalism in *The Vital Center* (1949) and regularly wrote on current events. Galbraith produced two extremely important books on American public life: *American Capitalism* (1952) and *The Affluent Society* (1958). The two men defined the liberal critique of cold war society: Americans, they argued, had exchanged the nation's core values for the goodies of the affluent society. The challenge of the cold war was only secondarily the Soviet military threat or the ideological war for the hearts and minds of postcolonial peoples; the deepest threat, they believed, lay in the nation's spiritual doldrums, which an inspired leader like Stevenson might fruitfully dispel.

Stevenson's convenient marriage to the intellectuals contained two important hints of the future. First, it diminished ideas by turning them directly to the purpose of political image building and made ideologues out of serious intellectuals. Schlesinger and Galbraith were putting forward ideas that were entirely legitimate and not without real power of their own. But uniting them with Stevenson the candidate was in effect to put an important body of social criticism to the service of political image making, which could not help but to undermine the integrity of the liberal critique. Second, Stevenson was not deeply loved within the Democratic Party. Indeed he took pride in not being a partisan. By appealing to the intellectuals, Stevenson was building an agenda independent of the party base.

The disengagement of political principles from party constituencies had a peculiar consequence for the intellectuals who took part in it. Convinced that they were public intellectuals, Schlesinger, Galbraith, and those who followed them were in truth increasingly detached from the public for which they claimed to speak. The lonely intellectual "speaking truth to power" is one thing. The politically connected intellectual dishing out agendas to those seeking power while moving farther and farther away from contact with the daily lives of citizens is quite another. Given the recent history of such intellectuals, it is almost surely a recipe for political disaster, the corruption of ideas, and chronic disappointment for the intellectuals themselves.

KENNEDY AND THE "NEW POLITICS"

Instead of awakening to such dangers, Stevenson's intellectual companions left him when someone new emerged who had a better chance of political success and who was even more eager to include intellectuals in governing. That someone, of course, was John F. Kennedy, whose solicitation of intellectuals was a complicated blend of personal disposition, political style, electoral objectives, and governing intentions. In 1960, Kennedy made himself the first practitioner of the so-called new politics, in which image, particularly televised image, counts increasingly over party platforms, local loyalties, or definitive plans for the future. Kennedy made good use of his looks and persona, but he had no real direction, much less a blueprint for governing. His primary motivation was to get elected, and in this cause, the intellectuals were of real use. For he borrowed heavily from the liberal critique of cold war America, infusing it with positive spin when he beckoned America to "the New Frontier" and made his famous inaugural call for national self-sacrifice.

Once elected, Kennedy had to craft programs that somehow or other got America moving again. He depended on intellectuals who, like him, had strong ideals but were determined to put those ideals into play. Kennedy admired thinkers who directed themselves to problem solving rather than abstract theorizing; the think-tank researcher was more his type than the muddle-headed philosopher. He wanted, as the journalist Theodore White famously called them, "action intellectuals." There was no dearth of aspirants. After eight years of Dwight Eisenhower, America's intellectual class was eager to lend its expertise to the refreshingly new administration. To recruit them, the Kennedy transition team launched a "talent search" under his brother-in-law Sargent Shriver. Successful applicants were to be brash and self-confident, with a hearty scorn for bureaucracies. No conservative ever despised the federal bureaucracy more strongly than the Kennedy liberals, and few have so actively sought to subvert it. As James Allen Smith notes, the talent search sought not to fill the top positions in government so much as the lower echelon of the bureaucracy, because those were the places where real work was done.

Foreign Policy Once ensconced, the Kennedy intellectuals hammered ideas into policy, nowhere more fervidly than in the area Kennedy felt most deeply about, foreign affairs. While determined to stand tough against the Soviets, he also wanted a new approach to the third world that appealed to anticolonial movements. Kennedy called for a change in attitude but had no concrete idea about how to hone it into policy. For that, he looked to Walt Whitman Rostow, a Massachusetts Institute of Technology economic historian whose brief but influential treatise *The Stages of Economic Growth* (1960) propounded a general theory of social development that could be made to yield practical policy. Rostow argued that societies pass through regular patterns of modernization. They begin in a traditional stage of static technology, where the struggle for survival is keen and rigid family and clan hierarchies dominate. Then, for reasons he was never clear about, a combination of technological change, entrepreneurial behavior, and new ideas would nudge traditional societies into a trajectory of stages: the pre-"takeoff" stage; the takeoff stage; the "drive to maturity"; and the "high mass-consumption" stage. At each stage, new political and social elites rise to power and have an interest in defending the status quo, but at the final stage, where technological and material affluence are widely shared, something like a middle-class democracy emerges. U.S. policy, accordingly, should foster the modernization process. Aid should be directed toward raising agricultural productivity, and the levels of foreign economic aid should be increased.

Stages was not the only line on Rostow's résumé. He had been widely critical of the foreign policy bureaucracy. In "The Fallacy of Fertile Gondolas" (1957), he argued that America had "a bias towards practical, usable thought, embodied in living experience" that, when put to use in government, became the tool of "the operator," the bureaucrat devoted to solving small problems but numb to grand theory. In "a world of extremely rapid change, where the survival of our society hinges on prompt innovation," Rostow argued, the operator was too slow-footed. Policy makers needed to surrender "the illusion that our affairs can successfully be handled . . . in layer after layer of interdepartmental committees" in favor of unifying visions. For example, the National Security Council, which Kennedy later asked Rostow to help reorganize, "would be vastly improved if it had an independent staff of first-rate men, freed of ties to particular bureaucracies, paid to think in terms of the totality of our policy problem, empowered to lay proposals on the table." The bureaucracy would still exist, Rostow conceded, "but its processes must be made to grind on something other than departmental vested interests and the preconceived views of men anxious, above all, to avoid controversy or trouble" (*Essays on a Half-Century*, pp. 42–55).

Apparently Kennedy considered Rostow himself first-rate, and he placed him prominently in the policy-making bureaucracy as head of the State Department's Policy Planning Staff and asked him to work specifically on the mounting problems of Southeast Asia.

As a career move, Rostow's *Stages of Economic Growth* had its fair share of genius, but in the larger sense it also reveals the pitfall of trying to apply broad-ranging ideas to specific policies. His ideas were central to two initiatives: the Alliance for Progress, the administration's program of massive economic and military aid to Latin America, and the commitment to uphold the regime of Ngo Dinh Diem in South Vietnam. The Alliance for Progress was directly modeled on Rostow's framework; intended to fend off the spread of "Castroism," it funneled economic and military aid to Latin nations that in turn were expected to launch land reform and agricultural development. It was, at best, a qualified failure. Rostow assumed that the old oligarchies would yield power to rising middle classes, but the traditional elite refused to pass away gently. Meanwhile, the military aid enormously increased the power of decidedly undemocratic armies and contributed to the long struggle with military dictatorship that marked Brazil, Guatemala, Chile, and Paraguay.

The Alliance raises a fundamental question: What happens when the Big Idea turns out to be wrong? Had Rostow merely counseled Kennedy to exhort Latin American elites to live up to humane ideals, he might have been ineffective, but he would have done less damage. This is all the more the case in regard to the Vietnam War, the vigorous prosecution of which Rostow promoted through his entire tenure in Washington. The nation might well have been better served had policy been in the hands of bumbling and inefficient bureaucrats instead of "first-rate men."

Domestic Policy The Kennedy intellectuals did little better on the domestic front. In 1961, the administration set out to develop a program on juvenile delinquency, no pressing problem but one close to the heart of the president's sister, Eunice, "a world-class nagger" whom the Kennedy brothers wanted to placate. They naturally looked for the latest in academic theorizing and found Richard Cloward and Lloyd Ohlin, two Columbia University sociologists whose *Delinquency and Opportunity* (1960) argued that delinquency was a rational response to the social conditions many young urban males confronted. Faced with blank prospects, they reasonably turned to crime. As mundane as this proposition might sound, in 1961 it contrasted sharply with long-enduring assumptions that deviancy was a function of race, innate inferiority, or simple sinfulness.

The Cloward-Ohlin thesis made its way into the basic structure of the juvenile-delinquency (JD) program, which was set up under the auspices of Robert Kennedy's Justice Department. The JD group developed a $30 million pilot program for urban community centers in selected cities, all modeled on one that the Ford Foundation had set up in Harlem, which relied on community participation, volunteer workers, and grassroots activism.

JOHNSON'S "GREAT SOCIETY"

The program might have been little more than an odd historical footnote except that, after Kennedy's death in 1963, Lyndon Johnson was in a hurried search for programs that might justify his succession to the presidency. From the start, Johnson set out to prove himself more liberal than Kennedy, and so he expanded initiatives already in the works and launched a continuous search for Big Ideas. When Johnson decided to launch his War on Poverty, he questioned the Kennedy domestic advisers about what they had been working on. Besides the tax-cut program and a program for rural development, the juvenile-delinquency program was all there was. This was not enough for Johnson. Looking at the pilot program's $30 million budget, he told aides to "add another zero," and suddenly an experimental program designed to test an academic thesis ballooned into a massive nationwide initiative, formalized in the Economic Opportunity Act of 1964.

A deeply insecure man, Johnson was touchy about his lack of intellectual credentials, a deficiency he sought to alleviate by organizing experts into task forces for nearly every problem that seemed politically fruitful to fix. When he first committed to an ambitious domestic program in 1964, Johnson told his audience that the Great Society would be based on "the best thought" of the day. No one was ever more interested in Big Ideas than Johnson; no one was ever more determined to use them for strictly political purposes. Eric Goldman, Johnson's go-between with the intellectuals, later explained in *The Tragedy of Lyndon Johnson* (1969) that to LBJ "an idea was a suggestion, produced on the spot, of something for him to do tomorrow—a point to be made in a speech, an action . . . for him to take promptly, a formula to serve as a basis for legislation to be hurried to Congress" (pp. 131–132).

To Goldman, the heart of Johnson's "tragedy" lay in the slapdash deployment of programs built around theoretical claims. Johnson was in too big a hurry to understand the hesitant and qualified nature of ideas. By the time tentative ideas passed through the political calculations of the inner circle, any integrity they originally had was lost. But if Johnson's ambition mutilated ideas, his haste created any number of breaches into which political intellectuals could step with their pet projects, so long as they made those projects sound good.

The War on Poverty was one such project. Johnson had little understanding of the JD program, and the intellectuals involved in it, particularly Richard Boone, had objectives that were far different from Johnson's. They made local community action a central part of the overall poverty program by insisting that federal monies be awarded to those projects that ensured the "maximum feasible participation" of local citizens. They sold community action as a way of demonstrating local initiative; after all, the president wanted the Great Society to be a "hand up, not a hand out." But the community-action advocates inside the Office of Economic Opportunity had decided, in a twist on the Cloward-Ohlin thesis, that people were poor because they lacked power; community action was supposed to be practical instruction in grassroots political action, through which poor folk would learn to protect and extend their own interests.

It was a subversive idea, exactly what the subversives in the administration intended. They wanted to undercut both urban political machines, which they believed repressed poor folks, and the federal bureaucracy, which wanted cumbersome, conventional programs. They succeeded in both cases, with disastrous consequences.

As with Rostow, their ideas, exquisite in theory, were profoundly flawed in practice. Community action empowered not poor people but people who claimed to speak on their behalf—demagogues, long-time radicals, social workers. Because the urban machines were an essential Democratic constituency, community action became a program in which a Democratic administration funded opponents of local Democrats. It was political self-immolation, something to which the intellectuals had given no thought.

And why should they, since they thought of themselves as renegades even as they shaped policy? More interested in politicizing the poor than in dol-

ing out the same old programs, they executed end runs not only around the existing executive bureaucracies but around Congress as well. Weaned in the antibureaucratic ground wars of the juvenile delinquency program, where they had been led by David Hackett, a boyhood friend of Robert Kennedy, they had come to think of themselves as guerrilla fighters. One of their foremost critics, Daniel Patrick Moynihan, described them as "young, bright, energetic New Frontiersmen, with an important sprinkling of career professionals" who lived "off the administrative countryside, invisible to the bureaucratic enemy but known to one another, hitting and running and making off with the riches of the established departments" (*Maximum Feasible Misunderstanding*, p. 75).

The outrage of local political leaders wound its way back to Washington, where it came to reside in a Congress unwilling to pay for social disruption. More important, community action did nothing to solve the problem of urban poverty, in part because it was built on a fundamental flaw. The guerrillas had gotten it in their heads that to be poor was a result of powerlessness, when, as Moynihan pointed out, to be poor is not to have money. The program requisitioned hundreds of millions of dollars, precious little of which went into the pockets of poor people. Any antipoverty program administered through the existing bureaucracies with conventional public-works projects would surely have been more successful. In this form, the program could have been administered on the ground by local Democratic Party machines and would have been easier to explain to Congress. Not only was the Labor Department jockeying to do just this, but important elements in the civil rights movement advocated this route in the so-called Freedom Budget.

What had happened? Moynihan's explanation remains a good one. The intellectuals, more interested in social change than in the careful execution of social-science analysis, took a modest juvenile program and distorted it into an ill-conceived strategy for grassroots revolution. The disaster resulted, so Moynihan argued, from the emergence of a new character in American public life: intellectuals trained in social science who saw it as both their professional obligation and political duty to extend their expertise to practical problem solving. The professional reformer was neither a public intellectual in the strict sense nor a social scientist in the proper sense. These activists parlayed their expertise into influence only to ignore the need for careful study and cautious adjustments of solutions to practical results.

By ignoring the basic strictures of social science, the intellectuals called attention to a deeper problem, according to Moynihan. They would never have gotten near power were it not for "the increasing introduction into politics and government of ideas originating in the social sciences which promise to bring about social change through the manipulation of . . . the hidden processes of society" (p. xiii). Of course politicians want that manipulative magic to deliver for their constituents; of course the social scientists eagerly offer their services for that purpose. But manipulating murky social processes "remains an occult art. And a highly uncertain one" (p. xiii). In his haste, the politician could not wait for clarification; in his self-interest, the social scientist could not admit his uncertainty.

INTELLECTUALS IN RESIDENCE: THE NIXON YEARS AND AFTER

In his book, Moynihan put his finger on exactly what emerged after the Kennedy years: political intellectuals who not only have an expertise and a product to sell, but whose self-interest rests in persuading the politicians that their particular recommendations are politically valuable. Moynihan saw this development clearly, perhaps because he was one of most determined of the new type. His criticism of the War on Poverty, cogent as it was, was completely disingenuous. Having lost out in the struggle for influence in the liberal administrations of Kennedy and Johnson, he accepted an invitation to join the Nixon administration. Richard Nixon wanted a "true intellectual in residence," as he once wrote Moynihan, mostly because Kennedy had made it fashionable. Moynihan had the Ivy League credentials, and he had been in the Kennedy administration. "He's so stimulating," Nixon told an aide. The two men shared a deep-seated hatred of the activist Left. But Moynihan's only use was for distinctly narrow ideological purposes. Moynihan's own Big Idea was a guaranteed annual income to replace the welfare system, and he knew that he had to sell it for its political effect. Nixon reportedly was intrigued when Moynihan explained that the scheme would bring down the liberal welfare system and rid the government of pesky social workers, but even that promise was not enough to sustain Nixon's interest.

The increasing relationship between ideas and politics since the Kennedy years has produced nothing like the "serious assembling of facts" that Moynihan claimed was necessary to modern gover-

President-Elect Richard Nixon Introducing Daniel Patrick Moynihan, 1968. The Harvard intellectual Moynihan headed the newly created Council on Urban Affairs and later served as U.S. senator from New York. © Bettmann/Corbis

nance. Instead it has made the political intellectual a routine figure in public life and spawned a growth industry in the mass-production of polemical ideas.

Indeed, just as more and more political intellectuals turn up, the think tanks that were once given to the production of supposedly objective social science have increasingly become devoted either to the promulgation of a decided point of view on a particular issue or to a distinct ideological position. All of the forces congealing to increase the demand for the political intellectual—the decline of party loyalty and the rise of political marketing foremost among them—have encouraged the proliferation of ideological institutions. Moreover, argues the political scientist David Ricci, the decline in party loyalty has made voters increasingly reliant upon the experts or spokespersons who articulate positions that appeal to their biases. Think tanks, Ricci notes, have both grown in and contributed to the dissonant atmosphere of contemporary America, because where ideological competition increases, ideologically inspired organizations flourish. Whatever the various causes, hundreds of such organizations arose over the last three decades of the twentieth century; as of the early 1990s there were a hundred or so inside the Washington beltway alone.

With the mass production of polemical ideas, political intellectuals are no longer content to inhabit the lowest levels of the federal bureaucracy, as was the case with the antipoverty guerrillas. Now they can be independent of those bureaucracies and still have influence over the course of practical policy, sometimes even more so. As James Allen Smith points out, the entrepreneurial obligations of the think tank intellectual make it all the more necessary to have a direct impact on policy, because therein lies the key to holding the attention of politicians and of impressing potential contributors of the organization's effectiveness. The politicization of ideas serves not only as a marketing device for politicians but also more and more for intellectuals themselves, a phenomenon, Smith suggests, that has done more than anything else to change the think tank's definition of its role. "The metaphors of science and disinterested research that informed the creation and development of the first think tanks," he writes, "naive as they sometimes were, have now given way to the metaphor of the market and its corollaries of promotion, advocacy, and intellectual combat" (*The Idea Brokers*, p. 194).

THE FAILURE OF THE STOCKMAN REVOLUTION

The blurring of instrumental knowledge with partisanship has surely increased with the demand for compelling ideas in the political sphere. But for the intellectuals who broach the Big Ideas, compromise and disillusionment continue to be the order of the day. The cases of David Stockman in the Reagan administration and Robert Reich under President Bill Clinton show us as much.

Stockman was, as he put it, the point man for the "supply-side intellectuals" in the Reagan administration. Inspired to a political career by Senator Moynihan, he was elected to Congress from Michigan in 1977 and was quickly appalled by the waste of interest-group politics. In the House of Representatives he joined Jack Kemp's small group of renegades cobbling together a political doctrine around Arthur Laffer's theory that cutting taxes would encourage growth and actually increase governmental revenues. Stockman's own Big Idea, to which the others were not altogether congenial, was that long-term economic health required the dismantling of the welfare state, which, he believed, had been financed by the inflationary monetary policies of the

1970s. Stockman's so-called grand doctrine was intended as a revolutionary prescription for "risky and mortal combat with all the mass constituencies of Washington's largesse—Social Security recipients, veterans, farmers, educators, state and local officials, the housing industry, and many more" (*The Triumph of Politics*, p. 8).

The Kemp group convinced itself that the strength of its own convictions and the vigor of a vanguard was enough to pull off its revolution. "Like all revolutionaries," Stockman wrote, "we wanted to get our program out of the fringe group where it had been hatched and into the mainstream. The brave new world it promised was too good and urgent . . . to be left under a bushel of ideological scribblings" (p. 9). So they hitched their fortunes to Ronald Reagan, an affable fellow, who like many politicians had a general sense of direction but nothing in the way of concrete programs. Kemp converted the Reagan inner circle through the appeal of tax cuts, Stockman was put in place as the head of the Office of Management and Budget, and the vanguard had entered the palace.

The brief history of Stockman's failed revolution is easy to recount. The administration's agenda included four pillars: tax cuts, increases in defense spending, an aggressive assault on the federal bureaucracy, and a determination that all these would be carried out within a balanced budget. Supply-side theory said it was possible. The theory, however, took no account of inflation, and with inflation at 12 percent when Reagan took office, supply-side doctrine could work only if draconian budget cuts were adopted. Stockman was not averse to doing so. He freely admitted that "my blueprint for sweeping, wrenching change . . . would have hurt millions of people in the short run. . . . It required the ruthless dispensation of short-run pain in the name of long-run gain" (p. 11).

But inducing such pain was politically impossible. Politicians did not have the courage to pull it off. That included Reagan insiders, who permitted the revolution to devolve into fiscal irresponsibility by cutting taxes and increasing defense spending without taking the ax to the federal bureaucracy. Any schoolchild could do the math and understand that a huge budget deficit would result.

While he never relented in his criticism of the inner circle, Stockman did come to see that politicians were not primarily to blame for the failure of his revolution. The welfare state was not dismantled because Americans themselves—at least those organized in the countless constituencies, from industry groups to senior citizens—were unwilling to join the revolution.

YET ANOTHER BIG IDEA: ROBERT REICH AND LABOR POLICY

Politics frustrated Stockman's grand doctrine, a conclusion no different from how the liberal activists of the War on Poverty interpreted the failure of their revolution and no different from how Robert Reich, who served as labor secretary in the first Clinton administration, interpreted the failure of his Big Idea. Reich was an intellectual by occupation, a professor at Harvard's Kennedy School and author of a number of books before joining the Clinton administration. Two things recommended him for a role there. He was an old friend of Clinton's and he had just published his one noteworthy book, *The Work of Nations* (1991), a widely read effort to cut between free traders and protectionists in the debate over economic globalization. It was futile, indeed, positively harmful to try to preserve manufacturing industry when transnational corporations were free to seek out low-cost labor, he argued; at the same time, the government was responsible for helping its displaced citizens reorient themselves in the global economy. Reich's Big Idea called for a national industrial policy that acquiesced in globalization but maintained "positive investment" in people through job training and education spending. By reconciling the liberal spirit of activist government with a commitment to free trade, Reich's Big Idea sat well with Clinton's middle-of-the-road strategy.

Like Stockman, Reich found himself beset by two foes: interest groups and political marketing. As labor secretary, he expected to get hassled from both business and labor, since he intended to do neither's bidding. Still he was astonished at the institutionalization of interest-group claims. Reich was more dismayed that his ideas never won the day. He constantly lost arguments to the conservatives in the administration, especially the treasury secretaries Lloyd Bentsen and Robert Rubin, who were committed to placating Wall Street. Clinton, meanwhile, could juggle many things and make it all sound coherent, but in doing so he lost sight of the basic problems the administration was committed to addressing—the widening gulf between the rich and poor, stagnating or declining wages for many workers, and deepening economic insecurities. When the Republican sweep in the 1994 off-year election delivered a body blow to White House morale, Reich

strenuously argued that the "anxious class" was paying the Democrats back for ignoring those very issues.

It was a perfectly plausible interpretation, but whether or not is was correct was immaterial. Clinton responded by hiring the political consultant Dick Morris to guide him into the 1996 re-election campaign. Reich began to suspect Morris's hand when Clinton lurched to the right in 1995, but what most troubled him was how Morris went about his business. To Morris, principles were merely products to be tried out on audiences. He would make Clinton into whatever sold, regardless of ends. "The President likes your ideas," he told an aghast Reich. But Morris wanted to test those ideas—in opinion polls. "I can know within a day or two whether they *work*. Anything under forty percent doesn't work. Fifty percent is a possibility. Sixty or seventy, and the President may well use it." Morris later told Reich that he had to stop talking about "job insecurity or stagnant wages or the widening gap between the rich and the rest." There would be no talk about the things that mattered most. What's the point of an election, Reich asked, if not to stand for something? "To be *elected*," Morris responded (*Locked in the Cabinet*, pp. 271–277). Reich's serious recommendations, ideas that he hoped would have real effect in people's daily lives, were coopted as mere products for public consumption and reduced to nothing more meaningful than deodorant or blue jeans.

The marketing of ideas is only one side of the equation. Like the intellectuals who immediately preceded him, Reich entered public life because he was certain his Big Idea was the right idea, so right, in fact, that policy had to be shaped around it for the betterment of the nation. But there are always others who have similar ambitions and equally strong convictions and are willing to compete over influence. In such an atmosphere, the most likely result is that ideas will cancel each other out.

And that is not a bad thing. Even at their best, when they have committed themselves in all good faith to changes they believe fulfill the common good, political intellectuals only get burned, and their stories—these stories—serve mostly to reinforce the age-old Machiavellian truth that the prince and the philosopher should not get their roles confused. In those few cases during the 1960s where they actually wielded power, the intellectuals wreaked havoc, and we can take some comfort that Stockman, for one, was deprived of the opportunity to trifle with the lives of fellow citizens. Indeed Stockman is instructive here. In *The Triumph of*

Politics, he admits that his "grand doctrine" failed because it was just that, a theory of "elegant idealism" that inherently clashed with the "messy, expedient compromises of daily governance." Those compromises are, after all, the stuff of public life. Although "politicians can be a menace," Stockman writes, even worse is ideological hubris, "the assumption that the world can be made better by being remade overnight. . . . It can't be done. It shouldn't have been tried." The only thing worse than the typical politician, in the end, is the political intellectual.

See also **The Struggle for the Academy; Constitutional Thought; International Relations and Connections** *(volume 2);* **Political Economy; The Role of the Intellectual; Government** *(volume 3).*

BIBLIOGRAPHY

Cloward, Richard, and Lloyd Ohlin. *Delinquency and Opportunity: A Theory of Delinquent Gangs.* New York, 1960.

Cotkin, George. "The Tragic Predicament: Postwar American Intellectuals, Acceptance, and Mass Culture." In *Intellectuals in Politics: From the Dreyfus Affair to Salmon Rushdie,* edited by Jeremy Jennings and Anthony Kemp-Welch. London, 1997.

Elshtain, Jean Bethke. *Democracy on Trial.* New York, 1995.

Gaddis, John Lewis. *Strategies of Containment: A Critical Appraisal of Postwar American National Security Policy.* New York, 1982.

Gagnon, Alain G., ed. *Intellectuals in Liberal Democracies: Political Influence and Social Involvement.* Westport, Conn., 1987.

Galbraith, John Kenneth. *The Affluent Society.* Boston, 1958.

———. *American Capitalism: The Concept of Countervailing Power.* Boston, 1952.

———. *A Life in Our Times: Memoirs.* Boston, 1981.

Goldman, Eric. *The Tragedy of Lyndon Johnson.* New York, 1969.

Jacoby, Russell. *The Last Intellectuals: American Culture in the Age of Academe.* New York, 1987.

Lasch, Christopher. *The Revolt of the Elites and the Betrayal of Democracy.* New York, 1995.

Lemann, Nicholas. *The Promised Land: The Great Black Migration and How It Changed America.* New York, 1991.

Marris, Peter, and Martin Rein. *Dilemmas of Social Reform: Poverty and Community Action in the United States.* New York, 1967.

Matusow, Allen. *The Unraveling of America: A History of Liberalism in the 1960s.* New York, 1984.

McGann, James G. *The Competetion for Dollars, Scholars, and Influence in the Public Policy Research Industry.* Lanham, Md., 1995.

Moynihan, Daniel Patrick. *Maximum Feasible Misunderstanding: Community Action in the War on Poverty.* New York, 1969.

Paterson, Thomas G. "Bearing the Burden: A Critical Look at JFK's Foreign Policy." *Virginia Quarterly Review* 54 (spring 1978): 193–212.

Reich, Robert B. *Locked in the Cabinet.* New York, 1997.

———. *The Work of Nations: Preparing Ourselves for Twenty-First Century Capitalism.* New York, 1991.

Ricci, David. *The Transformation of American Politics: The New Washington and the Rise of Think Tanks.* New Haven, Conn., 1993.

Rostow, W. W. *Essays on a Half-Century: Ideas, Policies, and Action.* Boulder, Colo., 1988.

——. *The Stages of Economic Growth: A Noncommunist Manifesto.* Cambridge, U.K., 1960.

Said, Edward. "Intellectuals in the Postcolonial World." In *The New Salmagundi Reader,* edited by Robert and Peggy Boyers. Syracuse, N.Y., 1996.

——. *Representations of the Intellectual.* New York, 1994.

Schlesinger, Arthur M., Jr. *A Thousand Days: John F. Kennedy in the White House.* Boston, 1965.

——. *The Vital Center: The Politics of Freedom,* Boston, 1949.

Smith, James Allen. *The Idea Brokers: Think Tanks and the Rise of the New Policy Elite.* New York, 1991.

Stefanic, Jean, and Richard Delgado. *No Mercy: How Conservative Think Tanks and Foundations Changed America's Social Agenda.* Philadelphia, 1996.

Stockman, David. *The Triumph of Politics: How the Reagan Revolution Failed.* New York, 1986.

SECOND-WAVE FEMINISM

Sara M. Evans

The "second wave" is a term used to denote feminist activism in the United States from the mid-1960s to the end of the twentieth century and possibly beyond. The "first wave" consisted of the long struggle for women's suffrage that began with the Seneca Falls Convention in 1848 and concluded in 1920 with the passage of the Nineteenth Amendment to the Constitution, which granted women the right to vote. Some historians restrict the second wave to the years between 1966 (the founding of the National Organization for Women) and 1982, when the deadline for ratification of the Equal Rights Amendment arrived just three states short of the requisite majority of thirty-eight states. Certainly those dates can serve to demarcate a surge of activism. But like the first wave, the second will probably have many swells and crests before it fully wears itself out. The second wave has been declared "dead" more than once, yet feminism remains a powerful force in American life.

ORIGINS

Feminism erupted onto the American landscape during a time that was already turbulent with social movements: conflict over the Vietnam War, racial strife, and a national crisis over the meaning and inclusiveness of democracy. The 1960s challenged Americans to rethink the most fundamental aspects of personal as well as political life, indeed of human identity. As it did so, it mobilized a new kind of political power that could be felt in the bedroom as well as in the courtroom, the boardroom, or the halls of Congress.

The second wave was initiated by educated, middle-class women whose lives had been dramatically changed by their growing access to higher education and labor force participation. Their lives were at odds with traditional middle-class gender ideology (which the feminist author Betty Friedan later named the "feminine mystique") and they faced constant discrimination. Until 1963 it was legal to pay women and men different wages for exactly the same work. Newspaper job listings were separated into men's and women's jobs. Professional women were regularly accused of being improper mothers because of their devotion to their work.

In 1961, newly elected President John F. Kennedy, under pressure from the director of the Women's Bureau, Esther Peterson, appointed a presidential Commission on the Status of Women to reexamine women's place in the economy, the family, and the legal system. The founding of the first explicitly feminist organization of the second wave, the National Organization for Women, can be traced directly to the work of that commission, which was chaired by the former first lady Eleanor Roosevelt until her death in 1962.

The President's Commission on the Status of Women put women's issues back on the national political agenda by recruiting a network of powerful women. Commission members and their staff included lawyers, government officials, union organizers, academics, and white women and women of color. Their report, published in 1963, documented in great detail the ongoing realities of employment discrimination, unequal pay, legal inequities, and lack of child care and other social services. Soon governors in virtually every state appointed commissions to conduct similar state-level investigations. That year several milestones took place: the Equal Pay Act made different rates of pay for the same work illegal; a presidential order required the federal Civil Service Department not to discriminate on the basis of sex; and Betty Friedan published her book, *The Feminine Mystique,* which explored the causes of the frustrations of contemporary women in traditional homemaking roles.

The following year, Title VII of the 1964 Civil Rights Act included "sex" alongside race, creed, and national origin as prohibited grounds for employment discrimination. Women suddenly had a potentially powerful and far-reaching legal tool. The Equal Employment Opportunity Commission (EEOC), an agency established to enforce Title VII, received a flood of complaints from women. But the bureaucrats were slow to take them seriously, and women on the inside like Catherine East, the executive secretary of the president's Commission on the Status of Women, and Aileen Hernandez, an African American member of the EEOC, began to spread the word that women needed their own civil rights organization.

FOUNDING OF NOW, WEAL, AND NWPC

The National Organization for Women (NOW) was born over lunch at the 1966 Third National Conference of the Commission on the Status of Women. Its stated purpose was "to take action to bring women into full participation in the mainstream of American society now, exercising all the privileges and responsibilities thereof in truly equal partnership with men." Modeled on the National Association for the Advancement of Colored People (NAACP), NOW set out to use lobbying and legal and direct action tactics to pressure new laws and better enforcement into being.

Using the United Auto Workers (UAW) women's department as their headquarters, NOW sparked pickets and demonstrations across the country against sex-segregated want ads and "men only" clubs. They also pressured the government to enforce antidiscrimination laws, especially Title VII. By 1968, the membership insisted on an endorsement of the Equal Rights Amendment (ERA), which forced UAW women to withdraw from NOW until their union supported the ERA. The issue of abortion precipitated another split, as lawyers who wanted to focus on legal and economic issues left NOW to found the Women's Equity Action League (WEAL). While NOW remained the largest membership organization of the second wave, the proliferation of other groups, many with very specific concerns, turned out to be a source of strength for the movement as a whole.

A third key feminist organization, the National Women's Political Caucus (NWPC), was founded in 1971 with a specific focus on policy issues. Leaders of NOW and WEAL joined with civil rights activists like Fannie Lou Hamer, congresswoman and caucus co-founder Bella Abzug, and journalist Gloria Steinem to create a grassroots organization with chapters in every state. The purpose of the NWPC was to place women's issues (such as child care, the ERA, abortion, and affirmative action) on the agenda of national political parties, to encourage women to get involved in electoral politics, and to pressure the parties to nominate women for office. The NWPC quickly became a major force in both Democratic and Republican Parties. The strong leadership of women of color facilitated its ability to build broad coalitions on issues of civil rights and social justice.

WOMEN'S LIBERATION

While NOW laid the organizational and legal groundwork for a new push for women's rights, a younger generation of women launched a more radical feminist movement that named itself "women's liberation." The women's liberation movement emerged in the fall of 1967, when small groups of women active in civil rights, antiwar, and student movements began to meet spontaneously in several cities, including Chicago, New York, and Seattle. For these women, the civil rights movement offered an environment in which they could begin to challenge dominant ideas and learn the skills of building a movement in small group settings. The civil rights movement advanced a set of ideas that highlighted the radical egalitarianism of American tradition; similarly, the student New Left grew into a movement in which young women honed political skills and imbibed a deep belief in "participatory democracy." Feminism arose when these movements, which had provided a unique kind of free space for women, also replicated the restrictive stereotypes of the broader culture. Young women who shared the New Left conviction that it was essential to embed their ideals in their daily lives found that when it came to relationships between women and men, egalitarian ideals did not hold. In the student movement, however, women found a voice with which to name the problem of sexism and the skill to initiate a burst of female activism. Having broken the middle-class rules of female decorum and discovered themselves as political actors, they named the movement's sexism and immediately broadened their analysis to society as a whole.

The women's liberation groups engaged in "consciousness raising," a technique for using the prism of their own experience to rethink everything they had been told. In small groups women talked about everything from family roles, to sexuality and the body, to work, education, and ambition. Telling stories from their own lives about marriage, motherhood, menstruation, orgasm, work, and school, they challenged accepted ideas about women. Consciousness raising was a brilliant tool that released thousands of women from isolation through the discovery that others shared their experience and empowered them through the strength of sisterhood. An early articulation of consciousness raising was the "Redstockings Manifesto" from a group in New York City: "We cannot rely on existing ideologies as they are all products of male supremacist culture. We question every generalization and accept none that are not confirmed by our experience."

Women's liberation groups captured media attention with flamboyant guerilla theater tactics. A group that called itself WITCH (Women's International Terrorist Conspiracy from Hell) hexed a bridal fair and Wall Street. Soon "WITCH actions" appeared across the country. At the 1968 Miss America Pageant several women gained access to the balcony where they unfurled a huge "Women's Liberation" banner. Outside the building, their collaborators crowned a live sheep, tossed "objects of female torture"—girdles, bras, curlers, issues of *Ladies Home Journal*—into a "freedom trashcan," and auctioned off an effigy of Miss America ("Gentlemen, I offer you the 1969 model. She's better in every way. She walks. She talks. *And* she does housework"). From this demonstration came the epithet "bra burners," though no bras were actually burned at the event. In general, media coverage sensationalized and mocked women's liberation with nicknames like "women's lib" and "libbers." Yet in those first few years, publicity of any sort sufficed to bring women out in droves.

Through 1968 and 1969, the women's liberation movement grew at an accelerating rate. Unlike NOW chapters, small consciousness-raising groups had no structure and no officers. They sprang up in schools, neighborhoods, offices, and carpools. Some lasted for many years, others met a few times and disbanded, but by 1969 every major city (and many small towns) had one or more groups. Each group set out to discover the root cause of women's oppression and to design a strategy for action to challenge that cause. The energy of their ideas found expression in dozens of mimeographed articles, manifestos, newsletters, and, by 1969, journals that included *Notes from the First Year* (New York), *Up from Under* (New York), *No More Fun and Games* (Boston), and *Women: A Journal of Liberation* (Baltimore). In 1970, two members of New York Radical Women published books that offered pathbreaking analyses of sexism and patriarchy: Shulamith Firestone wrote *The Dialectic of Sex* and Kate

Millett wrote *Sexual Politics*. A third, Robin Morgan, edited one of the first collections of essays from the women's liberation movement, *Sisterhood Is Powerful*.

Consciousness-raising groups were seedbeds for what grew into diverse movements focused around issues ranging from women's health, child care, violence, and pornography to spirituality and music. The groups formed child care centers, bookstores, coffee houses, shelters for battered women, and rape crisis hotlines—new institutions they could wholly own. At the same time, other feminists built enclaves within mainstream institutions, including unions, churches, and synagogues, and professional associations.

MAKING THE PERSONAL POLITICAL

Feminism grew rapidly into a mass movement because it touched women at a deeply personal level, giving political voice to issues that had gone unchallenged and bringing new opportunities for action. Under the microscope of consciousness raising, politics encompassed virtually all of life. The immense creativity unleashed by the women's movement between 1967 and 1975 owed much to the practices that encouraged local initiatives and allowed issues and ideas to flow from grassroots experiences. NOW's structure encouraged the creation of "task forces" at the local and national levels on virtually every topic. The task forces, in turn, issued a string of reports—on sexism in education, legal discrimination, violence against women—with recommendations for action. Women's liberation, with its antistructure, antileadership, and "do your own thing" ethos, spawned thousands of projects and institutions, as consciousness-raising groups put their words into action.

When NOW called for a "women's strike for equality" on 26 August 1970, in commemoration of the fiftieth anniversary of the passage of the Nineteenth Amendment to the Constitution granting women the right to vote, the national scope of this new movement became visible to activists and observers alike. Its insistence on the politics of personal life was likewise on display as women took action under the slogan "Don't iron while the strike is hot." In New York City, between 20,000 and 50,000 women staged the largest women's rights rally since the suffrage movement, completely blocking Fifth Avenue during rush hour. Branches of a movement springing from different roots intertwined in theatrical and humorous actions in forty U.S. cities: women in Indianapolis performed a piece on the middle-class female life cycle, from "sugar and spice" to "Queen for a Day"; Boston women chained themselves to a huge typewriter; women in Berkeley marched with pots and pans on their backs; New Orleans reporters ran engagement announcements under photos of future grooms; stewardesses carried posters challenging discriminatory airlines rules: "Storks Fly—Why Can't Mothers?"

Consciousness raising called attention to language as a prism through which women's lives could be shaped, distorted, or diminished. Once women identified the politics and the power of language, they used it to press for change wherever they were—with dramatic results. A group of NOW activists in Chicago, who worked for several major publishing houses, formed Women in Publishing in 1971. They were the force behind "Guidelines for Equal Treatment of the Sexes in McGraw-Hill Book Company Publications," an eleven-page statement that had been distributed to all editorial employees and eight thousand authors of textbooks, reference works, trade journals, educational materials, and children's books. In October 1974, the *New York Times Magazine* published excerpts from the guidelines, which incorporated key feminist ideas about sex roles and individual choice in the mid-1970s, stating: "Men and women should be treated primarily as people, and not primarily as members of opposite sexes."

WOMEN'S STUDIES

Women's liberation found another institutionalized and mainstream outlet in the creation of women's studies programs on campuses across the country. Women's studies began with isolated courses, frequently at "free universities" or other informal, alternative settings. Soon professors and students also collaborated to teach a wide range of courses about women. In 1970, Sheila Tobias put together a collection of seventeen syllabi and bibliographies. Two years later, the Commission on the Status of Women of the Modern Language Association compiled sixty-six syllabi from about forty different schools for publication in *Female Studies II.*

As word of the courses spread through the movement as well as academic channels, students at many universities were the first to demand "women's studies" courses, and they frequently participated in teaching experimental and interdisciplinary offerings. Rapidly growing caucuses created a kind of synergy as student demands bolstered the professional aspirations and intellectual agendas of a rapidly growing cohort of academic women. Following on the heels—and in the mold—of newly formed Afro-American or black studies programs, women's studies programs appeared on hundreds of campuses by the mid-1970s.

POLITICS OF THE BODY

Consciousness raising also meant that feminist deliberation would center on the most intimate, personal aspects of womanhood. Groups analyzed childhood experiences for clues to the origins of women's oppression; they discussed relations with men, marriage, and motherhood; and they talked about sex. Frequently, discussion led to action. New York Radical Women, for example, held a public "speak-out" in which they told stories of personal experiences with abortion and challenged the authority of male "experts" who had been invited to speak at a legislative hearing on abortion reform. Thousands of women, hearing about such speakouts, experienced a release from lonely silence.

Soon women's liberation groups became the "shock troops" of abortion rights, joining an already active abortion law reform movement. For the most part, they sought to intervene directly, offering services and assistance to women and public education, rather than lobbying for reform. Numerous groups, for example, began to help women seeking illegal abortions find competent doctors. Word-of-mouth communication usually resulted in a flood of requests. In Chicago, members of the socialist-feminist Chicago Women's Liberation Union began doing counseling and referrals in 1969. Calling themselves Jane, they shifted, in 1971, from making the referrals to doing the abortions themselves. Between 1971 and 1973, the abortion collective performed 11,000 illegal abortions, with a safety record that matched that of doctor-performed legal abortions. At about the same time that Jane was formed, members of another consciousness-raising group—made up primarily of graduate students and writers for an underground newspaper in Austin, Texas—volunteered to research the legal risks involved in abortion referral. That research by Sarah Weddington revealed a line of judicial precedent that suggested the real possibility of challenging laws against abortion in court. Thus began the process that resulted in the landmark Supreme Court case, *Roe v. Wade,* in which Sarah Weddington argued her first case at the age of twenty-six.

The self-help, challenge-authority ethos of women's liberation also generated a diverse movement for women's health. The Boston Women's Health Collective grew from a project of Bread and Roses, a women's liberation group that saw itself as both socialist and feminist. They taught a course and published a pamphlet called *Our Bodies, Ourselves.* That pamphlet-turned-book, still in print after many editions, exemplified the widespread effort among women's groups to empower women in relation to their bodies. Several clinics on the West Coast pioneered techniques of gynecological self-examination. All of these projects demystified medical "expertise" by giving women direct information, conveyed through personal stories and narratives with an emphasis on the importance of sexual self-determination.

Efforts to increase women's sexual autonomy frequently sparked concerns about the problem of sexual violence, as well. One of the classic realizations in consciousness-raising groups had to do with the sexual objectification and vulnerability of women in public. The first rape crisis hotline, established in Washington, D.C., in 1972, was followed by the rapid emergence of rape crisis centers across the country. In addition to the initiatives of women's liberation groups, by the mid-1970s NOW chapters had formed more than three hundred local and state rape task forces. Rape crisis centers provided counsel and advice to rape victims, assisted victims in dealing with police and medical personnel, set up speakers bureaus, offered self-defense courses and training for professionals, and created support groups for victims.

The movement to create shelters for battered women grew from a similar impulse. The first such shelter, Women's Advocates in St. Paul, Minnesota, began as a consciousness-raising group in 1971. When the group members reached the stage of wanting to take action, they started by writing a handbook on divorce and setting up a telephone service to provide legal information. Soon they were flooded with requests for emergency housing. They collected pledges to support the rent on a small apartment and a telephone answering service in 1973, but the demand was so great that members took women into their own homes. By 1974, when Women's Advocates "officially" opened, the collective already had eighteen months' experience working with battered women. Other shelters grew out of rape crisis hotlines and coalitions of battered women and feminist activists.

Women's liberation also provided a unique space for the emergence of a public identity for lesbians. Discussions of sexual autonomy (at a time when the counterculture celebrated sexual freedom and expression, and when a gay liberation movement had just begun in 1969) inevitably challenged the norms of heterosexuality. Validated by the notion that the personal is political and by the separatist politics of black power, they began to articulate a specifically lesbian feminist point of view.

The energy unleashed by the emergence of lesbian feminism was another source of turbulence in the women's movement, but one that eventually brought about a broader change in society. For several years, serious tensions persisted between lesbian and heterosexual women. Within many NOW chapters and consciousness-raising groups, lesbians felt silenced and ostracized. Some separatist groups formed, most famously The Furies in Washington, D.C., from 1971 to 1973. Others brought women's liberation and consciousness raising into the newly forming gay liberation movement where they also struggled against male dominance. By 1977, even the well-established feminist leader Betty Friedan was willing to acknowledge publicly the crucial role of lesbian leadership in the movement as a whole, and to embrace the battle against homophobic prejudice and discrimination as part of the larger struggle for women's rights.

PROFESSIONS OPEN UP

By the early 1970s there were active women's caucuses in most professional associations in the humanities and social sciences. Some focused on obstacles to professional advancement. Others also challenged the intellectual premises of their professions.

Bernice Sandler initiated one of the most far-reaching challenges to discrimination in colleges and universities after she was denied tenure at the University of Maryland. Discovering that she was far from alone in this experience, Sandler approached WEAL about taking action. In January 1970, WEAL filed a complaint with the U.S. Department of Labor demanding a review of all colleges and universities holding federal contracts, to determine whether they complied with antidiscrimination regulations. Two hundred and fifty institutions were targets for more specific charges of sex discrimination. By the end of the year, more than 360 institutions of higher education were in court because of suits brought by women willing to make public charges against discriminatory employers—both for themselves and for women as a class.

In response to similar pressures, most professional schools began to pay new attention to their own employment patterns and to drop barriers and quotas designed to limit the enrollment of female students. The proportion of women in law schools and medical schools rose dramatically in the 1970s. By 1990, women earned 40 percent of all law degrees and one-third of all medical degrees. In turn, the increase in the numbers of women "in the pipeline" laid the basis for an ongoing dynamic of change within many professions. Among the first to make headlines were women who had been waiting, fully prepared, for ordination as members of the clergy. In 1970, two Lutheran denominations approved the ordination of women. In 1972, Sally Priesand became the first female rabbi. Most major denominations experienced turbulence, as "women's liberation" presentations appeared on the agendas of major national meetings. Episcopalians seated female deputies for the first time in 1970, but denied ordination on the grounds that women were not in the "image of Christ." In 1974, eleven women deacons participated in an "illegal" ordination ceremony, which their church initially declared "invalid." In 1976, after two more years of intense debate and politicking, the Episcopal Church reversed itself on the ordination of women and recognized the earlier ordinations of these rebellious pioneers.

RACE AND CLASS: FEMINISM DIVERSIFIES

While the second wave emerged most visibly among middle-class women for whom the experience of discrimination was not complicated by issues of race or class, very soon working-class and minority women asserted their issues by founding their own feminist organizations. Women Employed in Chicago and 9to5 in Boston used the techniques of community organizing to bring clerical workers into the women's movement. They challenged the demeaning sexism of jobs in which women were presumed to be the "office wife," expected to serve coffee and food regardless of their job description. They also built effective strategies around the enforcement of antidiscrimination laws to force several large corporations to institute affirmative action plans, to equalize pay scales of women and men, and to post jobs and open up career ladders for clerical workers. While Women Employed and 9to5 experimented with new forms of organizing, women in the labor movement founded the Coalition of Labor Union Women (CLUW). Though there were

strong advocates for women in several unions, traditional union divisions not only prevented concerted action, they kept female activists in different unions from knowing each other, even when they worked in the same city.

Several CLUW founders recalled the atmosphere of change in the early 1970s, when women were on the move and looking for labor unions to join. Those who were active in NOW, WEAL, or commissions on the status of women felt the pressure of expectations: "When are you people going to do your part?" When a founding meeting for CLUW was called in 1974, more than three thousand women showed up—twice the expected attendance. In subsequent years, despite the serious internal divisions that occurred between 1974 and 1977, CLUW became an important training ground in leadership skills as well as a support group for women. For many, active involvement in CLUW translated into leadership roles in local unions.

Women of color were involved in the second wave from the outset, notably Aileen Hernandez and the lawyer Pauli Murray. Yet their distinctive concerns remained relatively unarticulated until the formation of a series of new organizations in the mid-1970s, such as the National Black Feminist Organization (NBFO), MANA, a national Latina organization, National Conference of Puerto Rican Women, Asian Women United, and Women of All Red Nations. A chapter of the NBFO in Boston, the Combahee River Collective, articulated "A Black Feminist Statement," a radical, socialist feminist perspective that emphasized the centrality of race: "As black women we see black feminism as the logical political movement to combat the manifold and simultaneous oppressions that all women of color face" (in Moraga and Anzaldúa, *This Bridge Called My Back*, p. 362). Their statement of purpose became one of the most influential documents in the evolution of feminist theory in the 1980s.

THE GOLDEN YEARS: POLICY BREAKTHROUGHS

From late 1968 to about 1975, lawmakers rushed to appease a newly aroused constituency that potentially represented more than half of the voting public. Courts, prodded by feminist lawyers from WEAL and NOW-LDEF (NOW Legal Defense and Education Fund), began to rule that protective laws were discriminatory and thereby in violation of Title VII of the Civil Rights Act. In March 1969, the Supreme Court ruled in *Weeks v. Southern Bell* that it was no longer necessary to demonstrate that many, or even most, women could not perform a specific job requirement to justify a hiring restriction. Instead, employers (and states) would have to show that all or "substantially all" women could not perform the required task. The choice of whether to accept a particularly difficult job would rest with the woman, as it already did with men. The *Weeks* decision and similar cases, executive orders forbidding discrimination, and the many EEOC complaints under Title VII began to convince key union leaders and other former opponents of the Equal Rights Amendment that the protective laws unfairly prevented women from access to higher paying jobs. By 1970, the ranks of ERA supporters included the League of Women Voters, Business and Professional Women, the Young Women's Christian Association (YWCA), the American Association of University Women, Common Cause, and the United Auto Workers. Together they formed a coalition that succeeded in mounting a massive two-year campaign that allowed Representative Martha Griffiths to collect the 218 signatures needed to bring the ERA to the House floor. By 22 March 1972, both houses of Congress finally approved the ERA, and at the end of the year, twenty-two of the needed thirty-eight states had ratified it.

Landmark legislation in the early 1970s included Title IX of the Higher Education Act, which stated, "No person in the United States shall, on the basis of sex, be excluded from participation in, be denied the benefits of, or be subjected to discrimination under any education program or activity receiving federal financial assistance." This set the stage for a revolution in women's athletics. The 1974 Women's Educational Equity Act (WEEA) originated with a secretary on Capitol Hill in 1972 and drew on studies like the Princeton Chapter of NOW's "Dick and Jane as Victims." It provided several million dollars in seed money for demonstration projects to improve education for girls. The Equal Credit Opportunity Act (ECOA) guaranteed women, for the first time, independent access to credit in their own names.

LIBERAL/RADICAL/SOCIALIST/ CULTURAL FEMINISMS

A radically egalitarian outlook that challenged most any hierarchy characterized the second wave. All feminists believed themselves to be radicals, but the nature of their radicalism differed considerably. Over time, a number of distinct feminist perspectives evolved in different branches of the second wave.

Liberal feminism characterized many of the founders of NOW, WEAL, the NWPC, and other policy-oriented feminist groups. Their goals were to bring women "into full participation in the mainstream of American society." Believing that the most effective forms of change would be gained through legal and political channels, they set out to work "within the system." Radical feminism, born in the early days of women's liberation out of the New Left, placed a strong emphasis on eradicating sex roles as the root cause of all forms of oppression. They were strong advocates of separation from the male-dominated left wing. Deeply suspicious of any essential notions of "male" and "female," radical feminists set out to rework the cultural understandings of masculinity and femininity by raising a range of cultural issues regarding language, sexuality, motherhood, religion, and the family.

By 1975, two variants on radical feminism had become prominent: lesbian feminism and socialist feminism. Lesbian feminism emerged in the early 1970s. One of the early, classic essays, "Woman-Identified Woman," described lesbianism as central to feminism: "It is the primacy of women relating to women, of women creating a new consciousness of and with each other which is at the heart of women's liberation, and the basis for the cultural revolution" (Koedt et al., *Radical Feminism*, p. 176). The Furies and other groups built on this perception to analyze heterosexism—the implicit assumption that only heterosexual relationships are normal and valid—as an institution that functioned to oppress all women, both by restricting their choices and by threatening assertive women with the label of deviancy.

Socialist feminism flowered between 1972 and 1976, sparking a number of serious efforts to build a more coherent set of ideas and organizations than the first flush of radical feminism had been able to achieve. Socialist feminists were highly critical of the efforts of radical feminists to define sex as the primary source of all oppression and men as "the enemy." They also dissented from the more extreme visions of lesbian separatism. Although most socialist feminist organizations had disintegrated by the late 1970s, the influence of socialist feminism continued well into the 1980s, because it provided the intellectual foundation for a crucial cohort of emerging feminist scholars as well as a training ground for community and labor activists.

Cultural feminism, infused often with a lesbian sensibility but not necessarily a politicized separa-

167

tism, found expression in an enormous range of alternative service institutions, women's businesses, and cultural events from the mid-1970s forward. Sharp criticism of cultural feminists' emphasis on women's uniqueness (which slid easily into terms like "female nature") precipitated major debates, and yet these assumptions found their way into liberal feminist organizations and mainstream institutions far from the feminist counterculture. Because cultural feminist institutions and events gave space, voice, and a visible reality to an emerging lesbian subculture, they unleashed a new force, a new community in American society, generating energy that undergirded the persistence of feminism through the conservative backlashes of the 1980s.

FEMINISM IN THE POPULAR CULTURE

By 1975, at least two dozen feminist presses and nearly two hundred feminist periodicals existed. The most prominent bridge between the internal conversations generated by these publications (often within groups of women with specific professional or personal interests) and the broader public was *Ms.* magazine, whose preview edition, enclosed in an issue of *New York,* appeared in December 1971. *Ms.* set out to bring a feminist voice to the marketplace of women's magazines, to compete with them on the shelves of grocery stores for the attention of American women. Glossy, slick, professional, and run by professional journalists Gloria Steinem and Patricia Carbine, the first stand-alone issue of *Ms.* sold out its 300,000 copies within eight days, generating 36,000 subscriptions and 20,000 letters (Farrell, *Yours in Sisterhood,* p. 45). Through *Ms.,* a new form of address entered the popular culture. *Ms.* defined its title as a "form of address meaning whole person, female" as opposed to objectifying modes of address like "chick," "bitch," and "babe."

The dramatic growth of women's studies programs and the explosion in feminist scholarship continued for several decades. In addition, the second wave inspired the creation of research centers and "think tanks" to generate the professional expertise needed to advocate policy change. Among the earliest were the Center for the American Woman and Politics at Rutgers University, founded in 1971, and the Center for Women Policy Studies, a freestanding center in Washington, D.C., created in 1972 by two NOW members, economist Jane Roberts Chapman and attorney Margaret Gates. With the help of major funding from the Ford Foundation, at least fourteen more centers for research on women came into being by 1981.

Throughout the 1970s numerous second-wave programs and projects evolved into businesses and social service institutions. There were feminist credit unions and banks, bookstores, coffeehouses, health clinics, art galleries, media production companies, recording studios, publishing houses for fiction, nonfiction, and children's books, restaurants, and law firms. For the most part they strove to conduct their businesses according to feminist principles, though there were few guidelines. Those that survived by the early 1980s had adapted their earliest antihierarchical and antibureaucratic principles to incorporate some degree of specialization and professionalization as well as basic business principles required for bookkeeping and responsible budget management. Some remained as not-for-profit organizations; others evolved into profit-making enterprises.

Cultural feminism, catalyzed by lesbian feminism, took on an institutional reality with the emergence of feminist art galleries, "women's music" (with singers like Holly Near, Sweet Honey in the Rock, Meg Christian, and Cris Williamson), and proliferating women's music festivals. Works like Judy Chicago's *The Dinner Party* celebrated female form and women's history. The Michigan Womyn's Music Festival was the largest of many such events that drew thousands of participants. New Age spiritualism pervaded these countercultural events, which many experienced as utopian, if ephemeral, communities. Many of these events, while not always separatist in a highly politicized way, continue as spaces for solace, affirmation, and rejuvenation.

BACKLASH

The revival of feminism at first met little resistance beyond ridicule because it was so new, so surprising. A more organized opposition emerged, however, as the new movement demonstrated its clout. In 1972, Phyllis Schlafly, a right-wing activist, founded Stop ERA to lobby against the ratification of the Equal Rights Amendment with the message that most women did not want to be "liberated." Similarly, a movement to reinstitute laws against abortion—soon named the pro-life movement—emerged rapidly in the wake of *Roe v. Wade.* A new Right, with powerful roots in the Republican Party, took up the cultural issues raised by the women's movement, politicizing personal life even further. Where previous conservative movements had focused primarily on anticommunism and hostility to government involvement in the economy, the new Right emphasized "family values," opposition to abortion and the ERA, hostility to homosexuality, and antagonism to affirmative action for minorities and women. Faced with a spreading backlash focused on abortion, ERA, and women's athletics, and after 1975, a declining economy that made women easy scapegoats, the second wave shifted gradually from offensive to defensive, from ebullient optimism to tenacious persistence.

Both the breadth and the opposition to new feminism became visible in 1977 at the massive International Women's Year Convention in Houston, Texas, and the fifty state conferences that preceded it. State conferences, called to elect delegates for the Houston conference, became areas for battle between feminists and the right wing. While liberal feminists prevailed for the most part, they were unprepared for the strength of anti-abortion and anti-ERA forces in several states. The Houston conference, consisting of about 2,000 delegates and 18,000 additional observers, was highly diverse. Thirty-five percent of the delegates were nonwhite and nearly one in five was from a low-income household. Protestants represented 42 percent of the delegates, Catholics 26 percent, and Jews 8 percent (Rossi, *Feminists in Politics,* pp. 58–59, table 2.3). In an emotional move, the conference adopted, by significant majorities, a "Plan for Action," with the ERA as its centerpiece and major planks on reproductive freedom and minority and lesbian rights.

The ERA stalled after 1975. NOW led a massive lobbying effort in the late 1970s to extend the deadline for ratification until 1982, and under the leadership of Eleanor Smeal spearheaded a series of state campaigns reminiscent of the struggle for women's suffrage early in the twentieth century. Membership in NOW, the National Women's Political Caucus, and other active groups soared for a few years, and a new generation of women were schooled on the battlelines. Yet, it proved impossible to gain the required number of states for ERA ratification, and by the time the clock ran out in 1982, several states had even repealed their ratification.

SURVIVAL IN THE 1980S

The second wave, by many accounts, subsided after 1982. In the wake of the ERA's defeat, most national women's rights organizations—NOW, NWPC, NARAL (the National Abortion Rights Action League), and others—experienced a sharp contraction of membership. Cuts in government funding combined with membership losses destroyed many feminist groups. The conservative ethos of the Reagan administration abruptly reversed the political influence of the women's rights movement. Making effective use of cultural themes initially politicized by feminists—family, sexuality, and reproduction—the new conservatism reshaped the 1980 Republican Party platform, eliminating its longstanding endorsement of the ERA. Once elected, the new administration removed many feminists from positions on commissions and in federal departments, replacing them with employees hostile to affirmative action.

Despite shifts at the government level, thousands of institutions created in the 1970s continued into the 1980s. Hundreds of women's studies programs continued to grow, and feminist theory blossomed into a powerful intellectual force. Differences of race had become central issues for feminists by the late 1970s. Minority women had always held some leadership positions in organizations like NOW, and earlier articles had challenged the tendency to talk about "women" as a unified group from the perspectives of women who could not separate their femaleness from their racial, religious, and ethnic identities.

In the political arena, feminists regrouped on the margins, building new forms of political capacity with the creation of organizations like EMILY's List. EMILY is an acronym for "Early Money Is Like Yeast," and EMILY's List was created as a feminist political action committee to direct political contributions in a highly strategic effort to increase the success of feminist political candidates. Other mainstream institutions began to incorporate the perspectives of the second wave. Mainstream Protestant denominations rewrote hymnals and liturgies to make the language more inclusive (referring to humankind rather than brotherhood, for example, and offering images of God as mother as well as father). Girl Scouts promoted a wide variety of career-oriented badges. A flood of young women armed with degrees in business, medicine, and law began to transform the gender composition of many professions. Women "firsts" multiplied (astronaut, supreme court justice, vice presidential nominee of a major party) throughout the 1980s.

THE 1990S AND BEYOND

The second wave did not die in the 1990s, though it did subside, and popular stereotypes of feminists

169

as strident man-haters made feminism a label younger women often avoided. It enjoyed a resurgence following the *Webster* decision in which the Supreme Court approved state laws restricting access to abortion, and especially after the Senate hearings on the nomination of Clarence Thomas to the Supreme Court. The testimony of Anita Hill put sexual harassment back on the political agenda. The riveting view of a committee of white men roughly grilling a black, female law professor had much to do with the political mobilization in 1992, during which a record number of women were elected to state, local, and national office.

See also **Women in the Public Sphere: 1838–1877; Gender and Political Activism** *(volume 1);* **The Struggle for the Academy; Women** *(in this volume);* **Family; Gender** *(volume 3).*

BIBLIOGRAPHY

Baxandall, Rosalyn, and Linda Gordon, eds. *Dear Sisters: Dispatches from the Women's Liberation Movement.* New York, 2000.

Boston Women's Health Book Collective. *Our Bodies, Ourselves for the New Century: A Book by and for Women.* New York, 1998.

Brownmiller, Susan. *In Our Time: Memoir of a Revolution.* New York, 1999.

Collins, Patricia Hill. *Black Feminist Thought: Knowledge, Consciousness, and the Politics of Empowerment.* New York, 1990.

Davis, Flora. *Moving the Mountain: The Women's Movement in America since 1960.* New York, 1991.

Echols, Alice. *Daring to Be Bad: Radical Feminism in America, 1967–1975.* Minneapolis, 1989.

Evans, Sara. *Personal Politics: The Roots of Women's Liberation in the Civil Rights Movement and the New Left.* New York, 1980.

Farrell, Amy Erdman. *Yours in Sisterhood: Ms. Magazine and the Promise of Popular Feminism.* Chapel Hill, N.C., 1998.

Ferree, Myra Marx, and Beth B. Hess. *Controversy and Coalition: The New Feminist Movement.* Boston, 1985.

Ferree, Myra Marx, and Patricia Yancey Martin, eds. *Feminist Organizations: Harvest of the New Women's Movement.* Philadelphia, 1995.

Friedan, Betty. *The Feminine Mystique,* with new introduction and epilogue. New York, 1974.

——. *It Changed My Life: Writings on the Women's Movement,* with new introduction. New York, 1985.

Harrison, Cynthia. *On Account of Sex: The Politics of Women's Issues, 1945–1968.* Berkeley, 1988.

Hartmann, Susan M. *The Other Feminists: Activists in the Liberal Establishment.* New Haven, 1998.

Kaplan, Laura. *The Story of Jane: The Legendary Underground Feminist Abortion Service.* New York, 1995.

Koedt, Anne, Ellen Levine, and Anita Rapone, eds. *Radical Feminism.* New York, 1973.

Moraga, Cherríe, and Gloria Anzaldúa, eds. *This Bridge Called My Back: Writings by Radical Women of Color.* Watertown, 1981.

Rosen, Ruth. *The World Split Open: How the Modern Women's Movement Changed America.* New York, 2000.

Rossi, Alice S. *Feminists in Politics: A Panel Analysis of the First National Women's Conference.* New York, 1982.

Smith, Barbara, ed. *Home Girls: A Black Feminist Anthology.* New York, 1983.

Steinem, Gloria. *Outrageous Acts and Everyday Rebellions.* New York, 1983.

Thom, Mary. *Inside Ms.: Twenty-Five Years of the Magazine and the Feminist Movement.* New York, 1997.

Tobias, Sheila. *Faces of Feminism: An Activist's Reflections on the Women's Movement.* Boulder, 1997.

Walker, Rebecca, ed. *To Be Real: Telling the Truth and Changing the Face of Feminism.* New York, 1995.

THE DISCOVERY OF THE ENVIRONMENT

John Opie

THE ENVIRONMENT AND AMERICAN REFORM MOVEMENTS

In the early 1960s Americans were dismayed to learn that the natural world around them was far more damaged than they imagined. In the next two decades, this incredulity turned to anger and frustration over the default of industry to control waste and pollution, and of government to protect and secure the environment. Citizen groups mobilized a groundswell of public opinion that led to governmental intervention through law and regulation. Now, as never before in American history, environmental protection entered the American mainstream. This environmentalism built upon historic reform movements in America. For decades previously, Americans had crusaded over public health and urban blight. The modern environmental movement was also kin to antislavery, temperance, women's rights, and civil rights movements. The sociologist Robert Nisbet predicted that history would judge environmentalism as having been the single most important social movement of the twentieth century.

In some ways, modern concern for the environment was a surprising development, since Americans had long taken their air, land, water, and natural resources for granted as birthrights meant to produce perpetual wealth-making and a superior standard of living. Both the nation's agricultural bounty and industrial prowess depended upon notions of infinite resources. Nature was at the most an opponent to be beaten, and at worst obsolete and redundant. Most Americans had recognized that their landscape was being drastically altered, but, in general, changes were judged to be improvements. Eastern canal systems, a national railroad network, great water management projects in California, electric power generation in the Pacific Northwest, and a massive system of roads and highways, all treated the nation's geography as a challenge to be overcome. Industrial blight was accepted as a ra-

tional cost for "progress." Such material growth demanded consumption of millions of acres of soil, trillions of gallons of water, thousands of tons of coal, and millions of barrels of petroleum. Technological optimists like Herman Kahn and Julian Simon, both advocates of technological "fixes" for environmental problems, insisted that human inventiveness, not nature, was the world's "ultimate resource." Americans would continue to build a satisfying future through technological "fixes" just as they had done for the past 250 years. This enduring optimism contained a profound contradiction: humans had learned to control nature, but they believed they could not seriously harm nature. Manmade disasters were only small and temporary setbacks for an infinitely resourceful earth. The American landscape was a machine that could be tinkered with at our pleasure.

On the other hand, modern environmentalism built upon earlier traditions that defined the United States as "Nature's Nation." Thomas Jefferson, the father and son naturalists John and William Bartram, and others applied the eighteenth-century science of natural history to comprehend America's bounty. The nineteenth-century Transcendentalism of Ralph Waldo Emerson and Henry David Thoreau saw divinity in nature. John Muir, the founder of the Sierra Club, urged a similar devotion to wilderness preservation, which was played out in the national park movement. Nature was modernized into America's great resource by the late-nineteenth-century. Progressive concepts of efficient and multiple use were espoused by Gifford Pinchot, who turned conservationism into a nationwide movement, and by Theodore Roosevelt, whose policies as president supported that movement.

In the second half of the twentieth century it became painfully clear that technological improvement had not overcome the classic Four Horsemen of the Apocalypse: war, pestilence, famine, and death. Now a fifth threat grabbed Americans by the throat—industrial pollution. A small but influential number of writers had already been questioning un-limited industrial development and environmental degradation. The social critic Lewis Mumford lambasted the industrial city as an inhuman place. Bernard De Voto and the naturalist Joseph Wood Krutch decried a disappearing wilderness. The political critics William Vogt and Fairfield Osborn saw profound environmental threats in uncontrolled economic growth. A small number of scientists, led by René Dubos, Garrett Hardin, Paul R. Ehrlich, and Eugene Odum, were also convinced that humans were destroying the environment. The first multinational effort at environmental science, International Geophysical Year (actually mid-1957 to the end of 1959) was hailed as an attempt, admittedly short-lived, at scientific and environmental connectiveness.

By the 1960s, American hope for technology had shifted to a large-scale sense of technological letdown. One defining moment on the path to this letdown had taken place in 1945, when Americans began to agonize over a truly marvelous discovery—the near-infinite energy that humanity learned to release out of the core of the atom—which was first deployed as a military weapon to massacre 200,000 people in two Japanese cities. The threat of "nuclear winter" seemed to guarantee the global collapse of civilization, the likely extermination of humanity, and an end to most innocent plant and animal species. Americans put themselves in this difficult position because of their high expectations of technology, and disregard for its side effects as minor or easily corrected. At one time, nature, or wilderness, was viewed as the source of risk, to be tamed by technology. Now the tables were turned: once the source of safety, technology had become the source of risk. A seemingly endless series of acute industrial breakdowns were highlighted by deaths from a smog inversion in 1948 at Donora, Pennsylvania; a 1959 controversy over pesticide-contaminated cranberries in New England; and the recognition in 1961 that terrible infant deformities were the result of pregnant women having taken the tranquilizer thalidomide.

RACHEL CARSON'S *SILENT SPRING*

Threats to the natural world (and thus to its human inhabitants) became a national agenda with the publication of Rachel Carson's *Silent Spring* in September 1962. The book enjoyed thirty-one weeks on the *New York Times* best-seller list, with hardcover sales of more than a million copies, unusual

for a nonfiction book. The title *Silent Spring* refers to declining songbird populations as an unintended side effect of widespread use of synthetic pesticides, but that was only part of Carson's story. She sounded the alarm that chlorinated hydrocarbons, such as DDT, harmed not just insects and birds, but became pervasive in the world's environments. Introducing readers to the new science of ecology, with its emphasis on interconnections, she showed how hydrocarbons, as they moved along the food chain, became concentrated at increasingly dangerous levels in fatty tissues of plants, fish, animals, and humans, and threatened higher cancer risks and genetic disorders. She provided a credible analysis of the negative impact of DDT: it harmed the reproductive systems of fish and birds, remained in the food chain indefinitely, and did not easily degrade into nonpoisonous substances. Massive pesticide spraying had multiplied after World War II to become common in agricultural production and also in forest, roadway, and golf course maintenance, and in suburban developments. By the late 1950s, chemical pesticides had replaced all other pest-control methods. They were widely promoted, and accepted, as a kind of miracle product. Carson acknowledged that pesticides could be useful, but their indiscriminate spread disregarded the complex balances and interrelationships of nature. She wrote in dismay, "For the first time in the history of the world, every human being is now subjected to contact with dangerous chemicals, from the moment of conception until death" (*Silent Spring*, p. 15). In the words of Carson's biographer Linda Lear, Carson's book "made people stop in their tracks and see the world in a new way" (in Lear, 1993, p. 28).

THE SCIENCE OF ECOLOGY

One distinguishing feature of modern environmentalism was its foundation in rigorous science. In the early 1960s the word "ecology" was unknown to the public and to most scientists; by the early 1970s it was widely used and misused as a universal explanation of the environment. In fact, the word "ecology" had been coined a century earlier, in 1866, by the German biologist Ernst Haeckel, from the Greek word for the study of the home. Haeckel defined this new science as "the whole science of the relations of the organism to the environment including, in a broad sense, all the 'conditions of existence.' These are partly organic, partly inorganic." Over the next century, ecology gradually emerged as a viable science. In the decades after *Silent Spring*, ecology became attractive as the new "corrective" paradigm that contradicted the widespread opinion that science was primarily a servant to industrial capitalism as it gobbled up the world's natural resources. This newly defined environmental science began the arduous task of uncovering the nature and scale of worldwide pollution and ecological changes wrought by 250 years of industrialization.

Ecological science educated the public about how intimate and fragile the link was between an organism and its environment. Species could be wiped out by the destruction of their habitat, and no habitat was invulnerable from human contamination. When scientists discovered DDT in the fatty tissue of arctic fish and antarctic penguins, a thousand miles from any place where the pesticide was used, they realized that a local environmental problem quickly became global. Ecology's big-picture approach received more credibility as scientists in other fields began to explore and accept large-scale discoveries, notably the acknowledgment of plate tectonics in the earth sciences, global climate patterns (El Niño, the Antarctic ozone hole, global warming) in meteorology, and the modern synthesis of Darwinism and genetics. Still, most ecologists insisted that little yet was known about planetwide natural forces, much less man-made influences.

Ecology was also treated as a panacea. Laymen looked to ecologists to solve the world's environmental problems where other scientists and technologists had failed. Most professional ecologists were uncomfortable with claims put forth by nonecologists that solutions to environmental problems could also solve social problems. They worried about distortions that would weaken ecology's scientific credibility, particularly its co-opting by nonscientists as a tool for environmental advocacy and its trivialization into a notorious "pop" science. Nevertheless, by the 1970s, ecology appeared to provide a solid scientific base for environmental advocacy because it identified ways that human interference with nature had been clearly disruptive and dangerous. Ecosystem ecology provided an integrated way to view the environment and was quickly adopted by the public.

COMBINING SCIENCE, ADVOCACY, AND MORALITY

The publication of Silent Spring and its impact on public awareness of environmental issues has been compared to the impact that Harriet Beecher Stowe's Uncle Tom's Cabin (1852) had upon views about slavery in America. In an extraordinary synthesis that set a national agenda for the rest of the century, Silent Spring meticulously identified a technological risk, opened a rigorous scientific debate, reported on industrial indifference, created a high level of public concern, and demanded governmental responsibility. Like most American reformers, Rachel Carson insisted that the environmental debate was also a moral debate. Late in her life Carson spoke out: "Through our technology we are waging war against the natural world. It is a valid question whether any civilization can do this and retain the right to be called civilized. By acquiescing in needless destruction and suffering, our stature as human beings is diminished" (in Lear, 1993, p. 42). Scientific evidence of public danger seemed to compel a moral duty to warn about existing and potential harm. And if in a democratic society every person had an inalienable right to clean air and water and a fruitful land, it was the duty of government to protect this right.

ENVIRONMENTALISM GOES PUBLIC

The result of Silent Spring was, in the words of an editorial in the New York Times, the "noisy summer" of 1962. Rachel Carson's report caused a groundswell of public concern about environmental decline and threats to public health. The Kennedy administration was joined by high-level Democrats including Representative John Dingell of Michigan and Senator Abraham Ribicoff of Connecticut in a full-fledged government investigation of the abuse of pesticide use. Carson was attacked by the chemical industry, notably the Velsicol Corporation. Ezra Taft Benson, former agriculture secretary under President Dwight Eisenhower, said she was "probably a communist." Benson and other critics labeled her a "hysterical female." The petrochemical industry, while acknowledged as essential to modern life, was newly blamed for toxic dumps, air pollution, contaminated water supplies, and farm soils loaded with pesticides and herbicides. With Carson's ecological critique of chemical pesticides, Americans had their first rigorous understanding of an inherent defect in an important and useful technology. The public discovered technological "sin" at the very heart of its inventive prowess. Environmental protection became part of the national agenda after a CBS prime-time television special in April 1963 strongly restated Rachel Carson's evidence and conclusions. CBS went to great lengths for a balanced report, but what viewers saw was a calm and strong

Carson stating her deep concern in contrast to a blustering Dr. Robert White Stevens of American Cyanamid Corporation who represented the chemical industry.

After a decade of impassioned debate, DDT use was banned in the United States in 1972, and soon wildlife populations began to recover, represented by the bald eagle and the osprey. DDT was not an isolated case. In the early 1970s the useful synthetic PCBs (polychlorinated biphenyls), organic chemicals used for electric insulators, plastic food containers, epoxy resins, caulking compounds, wall and upholstery coverings, and contained in soap, paint, paper, waxes, and cosmetics, were found worldwide in cows' milk, fish meat, and human bodies. PCB production was banned in the United States in 1977, but already 1.2 billion pounds had been released into the environment, probably half in products still in use. Evidence revealed that its decomposition products were even more toxic than the original material.

RETHINKING THE AMERICAN EXPERIENCE: MODERN ENVIRONMENTALISM

The Biologists   Rachel Carson's agenda was taken up by a younger generation of environmental reformers and activists. They shaped public interest that lasted into the 1990s. Paul Ehrlich, also a biologist, in 1968 published *The Population Bomb,* which sold an astonishing three million copies. Not only did Ehrlich revisit the eighteenth-century thesis by Thomas Malthus that the world's population would inevitably outstrip food supply, but he also emphasized enormous global disparities—one American baby consumes the same resources as sixty Indian babies. Yet another biologist, Barry Commoner, authored *The Closing Circle: Nature, Man, and Technology* in 1971. Described as "the Paul Revere of ecology," Commoner emphasized the need for radical social, economic, and political changes to bring environmental justice in Western society. Commoner provided a set of environmental axioms that quickly entered the public debate: Everything Is Connected to Everything Else, Everything Must Go Somewhere, Nature Knows Best, and There Is No Such Thing as a Free Lunch. The biologist Garrett Hardin's influence came in two related ways, first in his 1968 *Science* article "The Tragedy of the Commons," which emphasized the unavoidable disaster if the world's growing population continued its uncontrolled competition for

limited natural resources. Hardin's 1974 *Bioscience* article "Living on a Lifeboat" saw tragedy in the battle between the rich (on the lifeboat) and poor (swimming in the water) for the world's limited resources.

The Economists   Economics entered the picture with the publication in 1972 of *The Limits to Growth,* by a team led by Jay Forester, Donnella Meadows, and Dennis Meadows. This was the first, albeit primitive, computer-modeled and international study of the long-term uncontrolled growth of population, resource consumption, and industrial output, and the resulting impacts upon food supplies and pollution. Using the new highly integrated approach, systems dynamics, the report projected global failure and human collapse early in the twenty-first century. In a pathbreaking 1973 essay, Herman E. Daly urged a global shift from uncontrolled growth ("maximization of GNP," the historic axiom of Western economics) to a "steady-state economy" that would sustain natural resources, address social issues, and yet protect desirable living standards. Daly's 1977 *Steady-State Economics* also emphasized that modern environmental (and human) problems had "no technical solution." Daly's work initiated the field of ecological economics and urged strategies for economic sustainability. Another economist, Kenneth Boulding, put forward the concept of "Spaceship Earth" (in opposition to "cowboy economics") as a way of conveying the absoluteness of global interdependency and the risk of global failure because of population growth and resource depletion.

History, Religion, Wilderness, and Gaia   The emerging environmental movement was also shaped by the historian Lynn White Jr.'s 1967 article "The Historical Roots of Our Ecologic Crisis," in the prestigious *Science* magazine. White argued that Christianity sharply separated humanity from the natural world and that it urged nature's use for human ends. White nevertheless saw in Christianity an alternative direction based on the teaching of St. Francis of Assisi that all creation was equal. In 1968 Edward Abbey wrote the nature classic *Desert Solitaire,* of which it was said, "Abbey almost single-handedly made it impossible for nature writing to lapse back into babbling brooks and heavenly birdsong" (Zakin, p. 136). David Brower, executive director of the Sierra Club in the 1950s and 1960s, captivated and energized Americans with exhibits, picture books, and newspaper advertisements that extolled America's remaining wilderness regions,

176

especially in the national parks, as "America's crown jewels." In the late 1970s, the British atmospheric scientist James Lovelock and the American microbiologist Lynn Margulis formulated the controversial but influential "Gaia hypothesis," suggesting that the Earth's climate and surface environments are influenced not only by material forces, but also by the very existence of life itself. Ahead of all of these writings by environmental philosophers, however, were the essays of the wildlife manager Aldo Leopold, whose 1949 *Sand County Almanac* became a classic. In it, Leopold summed up a land ethic in the dictum, "A thing is right when it tends to preserve the integrity, stability, and beauty of the biotic community. It is wrong when it tends otherwise" (*Sand County Almanac,* pp. 224–225).

ENVIRONMENTALISM ENTERS THE CULTURAL MAINSTREAM

Earth Day 1970 By 1970 we can justifiably speak of America's "environmental era," when the nation was galvanized into urgent action, and when environmental issues were absorbed into the public consciousness to become part of the mainstream.

The first Earth Day, observed on 21 March 1970, was peaceful, even festive, with major rallies in New York City and Washington, D.C., as well as on hundreds of college campuses. Earth Day was itself the product of the activism of the 1960s, a sense of crisis that had already produced an effective civil rights movement and the powerful anti–Vietnam War demonstrations. Most participants did not seek a social and economic revolution that would transform American industry and cities. This disappointed a radical faction. Earth Day was the brainchild of the Wisconsin senator Gaylord Nelson, who declared that environmental collapse was among the "most critical issues facing mankind," making "Vietnam, nuclear war, hunger, decaying cities, and all the other major problems one could name relatively insignificant by comparison" (in Gottlieb, p. 106). Nelson recruited twenty-five-year-old Harvard law student Denis Hayes as the national coordinator for Earth Day. Hayes took a more radical position: "Ecology is concerned with the total system—not just the way it disposes of its garbage." The Maine senator Edmund Muskie, a Democratic presidential challenger, connected Earth Day with the contemporary civil rights and antiwar issues: "Those who believe that we are talking about the Grand Canyon and the Catskills, but not Harlem and Watts, are wrong" (in Gottlieb, p. 112). Hayes

pointed out that the Vietnam War was "an ecological catastrophe." Earth Day activities elicited some corporate participation, from Monsanto Chemical, Dow Chemical, and the Ford Motor Company, along with two of the nation's most powerful utilities: Commonwealth Edison in Chicago and Consolidated Edison in New York City. A significant part of industry was suspicious of the entire idea and saw the marshaling of public opinion in Earth Day as a left-wing attack on capitalist society. The popular appeal of Earth Day indicated that Americans no longer accepted the disappearance of wilderness nor industrial pollution as inevitable costs of progress. Instead, environmental quality became an essential feature of the quality of life that they demanded as a national birthright. To the media, Earth Day was "Day One of the Fix-It."

NON-GOVERNMENTAL ORGANIZATIONS (NGOS)

Voluntary environmental organizations—nongovernmental organizations, or NGOs—came into their own in the 1960s and 1970s. Environmentalism appealed to a broad spectrum of Americans (though minorities were largely left out). Its organizations mostly enjoyed tax-free status, like the long-standing privileges of organized religion and philanthropy in American history.

Some NGOs had existed long before environmentalism caught the public imagination: the Sierra Club (1892), the National Audubon Society (1905), the National Parks and Conservation Association (1919), the Wilderness Society (1935), the National Wildlife Federation (1936), the Conservation Foundation (1948), and the Nature Conservancy (1951). They stayed in America's mainstream, willing to settle for reform in government policy without changes in society's basic culture. They expanded their original wilderness preservation mission into a wider environmental net to include population growth, energy efficiency, pollution control, global warming, and nuclear winter. They devised basic strategies: lobbying, lawsuits, scientific research, and electoral politics. Local grassroots efforts—often a combination of organizations labeled PIRGs (public interest research groups) and more-informal interest groups labeled NIMBYs (for "not in my back yard")—combated local environmental hazards by forcing public disclosure and government action against toxic dumps, pesticide spraying, air pollution, contaminated water supplies, radioactive wastes, and nuclear plants. They effectively compelled major corporations such as 3M, DuPont, and Dow to consider more closely the environmental consequences of their actions.

The 1970s saw a discernible shift in the practice of environmentalism from dedicated amateurs to highly skilled professionals. The old-line organizations added scientists, lawyers, and lobbyists to their staffs. Organizations such as Resources for the Future (1952), the Environmental Defense Fund (1967), and the National Resources Defense Council (1970) were dedicated to research, lobbying, and litigation. Early differences showed up among these groups. Some were politically pragmatic, looking to shape specific government policies, while others preached a total lifestyle change of voluntary simplicity to reduce consumption. Radical environmental activists turned to Greenpeace (1971) and Earth First! (1980). In one view, "lawyers from the Environmental Defense Fund may draft a bill, lobbyists from the Sierra Club may help push it past Capitol Hill, and a popularizer like Greenpeace may land the issue on the evening news," often without any coordinated planning. The radicals used tactics such as demonstrations, sit-ins, and occasional destructive violence toward logging and road-building equipment and power transmission lines. Advocates of "ecotage" found a model in the revolutionary characters of Edward Abbey's 1975 novel, *The Monkey Wrench Gang,* which gave advice on disabling a bulldozer or wrecking electric power pylons. The radicals believed environmental issues would not be resolved except through change in society's basic culture; within this view, a prevailing concept was that of "deep ecology," in which humanity is a participant, not the leader, in the natural world.

ENVIRONMENTAL LAW AND REGULATION: FEDERAL INTERVENTION

For decades, most environmental debates had focused on the natural environment. One climactic event was passage of the Wilderness Act in 1964, which led to the creation of dozens of protected, roadless areas. The act itself was the result of a public outcry that stopped a proposed federal dam in the isolated Echo Park of Dinosaur National Monument astride the northern Colorado–Utah border. A skilled media campaign against the dam was led by David Brower of the Sierra Club and Howard Zahniser of the Wilderness Society. Similarly, the public successfully opposed dams within each end of Grand Canyon National Park. However, the construction of a dam that created Arizona's Lake Powell and consumed the scenic Glen Canyon was a major loss for wilderness protection. Among so-called conservation agencies, the U.S. Forest Service remained predominantly a servant to the highly profitable forest industry. The Bureau of Land Management, lord over a quarter of the land of the lower forty-eight states, leased its western grazing and mining lands at minimal costs established in the 1870s and 1880s. Nevertheless, 90 percent of Americans believed that national parks and wilderness protection were essential to national well-being. Public pressure brought passage of the national Wild and Scenic Rivers Act of 1968, the Wild Free-Roaming Horse and Burro Act of 1971, and especially the Endangered Species Act of 1973. The latter act tested the nation's resolve as protection of the snail darter fish in Tennessee and the spotted owl in the Pacific Northwest was pitted against local economic interests.

By the mid-1960s, public interest also turned to the negative impacts of a mushrooming postwar industrial growth, symbolized by expansive highway construction, a riot of coal- and nuclear-fueled electric power plants, and the spread of manufacturing into suburban zones called, paradoxically, "industrial parks." Political lines began to be drawn in the late 1960s that would last into the 1990s. State legislatures and bureaucracies seemed uninterested in environmental cleanup and appeared to work hand-in-glove with local polluting industries. The general public, nongovernmental organizations, and the media increasingly looked to the federal government for intervention and cleanup. Americans had learned from the Depression of the 1930s, and from World War II in the 1940s, that the federal government could be the lead agent in achieving a better society.

Public doubts about technological progress and fears over pollution seemed to be confirmed as parts of the nation began to fall apart—the 1965 power blackout and garbage strikes in New York City, the burning of Cleveland's industrially polluted Cuyahoga River in 1969, the industrial eutrophication of Lake Erie, and the 1969 Santa Barbara oil spill on California beaches that killed sea life. This sense of public crisis and industrial denial was reinforced by the discovery of numerous "dead zones" created by toxic waste in Michigan, Virginia, New York's Hudson River and Love Canal, and the "Valley of Drums" near Louisville, Kentucky. Faith in environmental well-being was also shaken by the "energy crisis" during the winter of 1973–1974, when oil prices skyrocketed from $3 a barrel to more than $30 a barrel and Americans saw the end of a fifty-

Raking Oil-Soaked Hay at the Shoreline in Santa Barbara, California, 5 February 1969.
Several days earlier a Union Oil Company platform in the Santa Barbara Channel suffered
a blowout leading to a massive amount of oil being released from the ocean floor. The first
Earth Day happened the following spring. © BETTMAN/CORBIS

year era of low-cost abundant energy. Oil shortages and rising prices induced a public shift from energy consumption to energy conservation. An early director of the U.S. Environmental Protection Agency, William Ruckelshaus, identified a major shift in public opinion, which now had a "pervading sense that unless we acted immediately, something irreplaceable and indispensable would be lost forever."

The Environmental Protection Agency Environmental law was a means for Americans to put teeth into their overall environmental desires to clean up the air and water, to remove solid wastes and toxic chemicals, and to protect wilderness and endangered species. Public pressure led to passage of the landmark National Environmental Policy Act (NEPA) in 1969.

The first environmental law in American history was the 1899 Rivers and Harbors Act, which made dumping in America's waterways a criminal act leading to stiff fines and imprisonment. When it was rediscovered in the 1960s, the law was used effectively against companies and individuals who dumped liquid wastes, and it helped move the nation toward the 1972 Clean Water Act. But the sweeping rights granted by other old laws, such as the 1872 Mining Act, were still causing enormous environmental problems. Land containing potential

mineral wealth could still be purchased in 1998 at $2.50 an acre, and the private landowners enjoyed enormous freedom of action. For most of American history the demands for total autonomy by the private sector had been largely impossible to counteract, despite oversight by the Interstate Commerce Commission, the Food and Drug Administration, the Federal Trade Commission, and the Securities and Exchange Commission. In the twentieth century, only the U.S. Fish and Wildlife Service identified threats to wild species. Only one other agency, the U.S. Public Health Service, had a long history and mandate to raise doubts about the negative impacts of industrial development. By the 1990s, other agencies had joined to carry environmental regulation into business and private life, notably the Occupational Safety and Health Administration (OSHA), the National Institutes of Health (NIH), the Centers for Disease Control, and the National Oceanic and Atmospheric Administration (NOAA).

The NEPA did not create the Environmental Protection Agency (EPA), despite the similar initials. Rather, the NEPA created the president's Council on Environmental Quality (CEQ). The CEQ by the end of 1970 proposed a separate agency—the EPA—to consolidate the nation's environmental response, to treat "air pollution, water pollution, and solid wastes as different forms of a single problem." The EPA began operations on 12

December 1970, with a ready-made bureaucracy of six thousand government employees patched together from the air quality, pest control, solid waste, and drinking water units of other agencies. Most important, the EPA is the only regulatory agency whose administrator reports directly to the president. It was created as an independent agency, not part of a larger department, such as the Department of the Interior, where many said it belonged. The EPA opened its doors with extraordinary regulatory powers and has consistently enjoyed remarkable freedom of action. The EPA's tools included the universal requirement for environmental impact statements (EISs) in all public projects, the Clean Air Act and the Occupational Safety and Health Act, both passed in 1970, the Federal Water Pollution Control Act (Clean Water Act) of 1972, and the Endangered Species Act in 1973.

Harm-Based Policies Public demands for speedy and effective environmental cleanup urged action regardless of available technologies or economic costs. Air pollution began to emerge in the 1960s as a potent political issue that elicited the passage of federal legislation in 1963 and 1967. In Pittsburgh, the Group Against Smog and Pollution (GASP), became a vocal advocate of clean air, as did Chicago's Campaign Against Pollution (CAP). Lobbying by the Coalition for Clean Air moved the debate to Congress, where it was urged on by *Vanishing Air*, a persuasive report by John C. Esposito writing for Ralph Nader's "Raiders," and by presidential hopeful Edmund Muskie, who chaired the Senate Committee on Air and Water Pollution. When the new Clean Air Act was signed into law in December 1970, it dramatically enlarged the role of law and regulation in setting and fulfilling Americans' expectations for environmental cleanup. The federal presence became the dominant force for cleanup.

The Clean Air Act, reauthorized in 1977, allowed the EPA to press hard to prevent "significant deterioration" of high-quality air. By the 1970s, pollution began to cloud the pristine air (where sight lines had historically extended to sixty miles or more) at the Grand Canyon and the national parks, monuments, and wilderness areas of southern Utah. Some of the pollution was traced to the controversial coal-fired Four Corners power plant, which was subsequently required to limit power generation and retrofit smokestack cleaners. Pollution also came, environmentalists argued, from auto smog in Los Angeles. The goal of eliminating health problems from auto pollution was still far away. Between 1954 and 1982, the number of motor vehicles in the

United States had increased 320 percent. Industry and its allies complained about exceedingly expensive controls, about the need for some balance between marginal benefits and the cost of reduction, the threat of possible economic dislocations (job loss and factory closings), and the EPA's demand for "ample margin for safety" (setting thresholds above the minimum for health).

Technology-Forcing Policies Even more than bad air, water pollution has historically been closely related to human health. In the United States in particular, the ability of water to wash away, thin out, and distribute most substances made it the universal solvent for the removal of human and industrial wastes. Most of America's majestic rivers (and the Great Lakes) were casually used for waste dumping, regardless of impacts on local swimming, fishing, or health, and with astonishing indifference to people and towns downstream. Not until after World War II, with the great acceleration of industrial development, was public attention drawn to industrial chemical discharges as well as household pollution. Rivers that ran through cities like Pittsburgh, Cleveland, Chicago, Boston, and around New York City became cesspools of decay with little or no fish life and were disgustingly unattractive for public swimming or boating.

The 1972 Water Pollution Control Act Amendments, better known as the Clean Water Act, served as a major piece of "technology forcing" legislation in the way it revolutionized public responsibility for the nation's water supplies and waterways. Waste disposal was no longer a legitimate use of a river or lake. Some major corporations, such as 3M, DuPont, and Dow Chemical, switched to new technological strategies—pollution prevention, life cycle engineering, and industrial ecology—for upfront reduction of waste, extensive recovery, and continuous reuse.

The Clean Water Act, which was revised and strengthened in 1977, had positive results. Around the city of Cleveland, the water quality of Lake Erie and the Cuyahoga River improved dramatically. Fish returned to the lower Hudson River. Industrial pollution of the Ohio River system from above Pittsburgh to the Mississippi dropped significantly. Groundwater systems in eastern industrial states received protection in the nick of time. Despite the revolutionary steps mandated by the Clean Water Act of 1972, some polluters continued to insist that the issue of dumping waste into the nation's waters was overblown; they claimed that pollutants had a natural capacity to biodegrade.

Setting National Environmental Standards

Together with air and water, the first significant national law to deal with land-based hazardous and solid wastes was the Resource Conservation and Recovery Act (RCRA) of 1976. Before RCRA, most waste generators kept hazardous waste in slag piles, pits, ponds, and lagoons, or shipped it away to unknown sites where it was carelessly dumped. Public pressure followed the discovery of heavily toxic sites like Love Canal, under a public schoolyard near Niagara Falls in New York. As it became clear that children were poisoned and pregnant women were miscarrying due to exposure to the toxic environment, the school closed and neighboring houses were abandoned. Literally tens of thousands of other hazardous waste sites were uncovered nationally over the next two decades, with public attention drawn to the towns of Times Beach, Missouri, of Globe, Arizona, and of Centralia, Pennsylvania. The RCRA set a framework for regulating the cradle-to-grave system to control the generation, transportation, treatment, and disposal of hazardous wastes. Not all went well, however. The similar Superfund program was launched in 1980 by Congress as the biggest environmental effort in American history to identify and clean up tens of thousands of toxic waste dumps. By 1990 the Superfund was reviled for its interminable delays bordering on gridlock, its dense bureaucracy, its boondoggle for lawyers and consultants, and its trillion-dollar cost, of which only 12 cents of every dollar was used for actual cleanups.

By the 1980s and 1990s, environmental protection had become imbedded in the American mainstream. Yet, in 1994, a probusiness, antigovernment backlash led to the election of a conservative Republican Congress that challenged the government's commitment to environmentalism as part of an agenda that rejected so-called big-government programs in general. Nevertheless, a coalition of local communities, responsive industry, and government continued efforts to sustain the environmental progress of the 1960s and 1970s. It became clear that environmental protection was closely linked to shifts in the political process, economic well-being, and the moods of public opinion.

See also **The Natural World; God, Nature, and Human Nature** (in this volume).

BIBLIOGRAPHY

Primary Sources

Abbey, Edward. *Desert Solitaire.* New York, 1968.

———. *The Monkey Wrench Gang.* Philadelphia, 1975.

Carson, Rachel. *Silent Spring.* Boston, 1962.

Commoner, Barry A. *The Closing Circle: Nature, Man, and Technology.* New York, 1971.

Daly, Herman E. *Steady-State Economics.* New York, 1977.

———. "The Steady-State Economy: Toward a Political Economy of Biophysical Equilibrium and Moral Growth." In *Toward a Steady-State Economy,* edited by H. E. Daly (1973), 1–22.

Daly, Herman E., ed. *Toward a Steady-State Economy.* San Francisco, 1973.

Devall, Bill, and George Sessions. *Deep Ecology.* Salt Lake City, Utah, 1985.

Ehrlich, Paul R. *The Population Bomb.* New York, 1968.

Hardin, Garrett. "The Tragedy of the Commons." *Science* 162 (1968): 1243–1248.

———. "Living on a Lifeboat." *Bioscience* 24 (1974): 561–568.

Leopold, Aldo. *A Sand County Almanac.* 1949. Reprint, New York, 1989.

Lovelock, J. E. *Gaia: A New Look at Life on Earth.* New York, 1979.

Meadows, Donella H., Dennis L. Meadows, Jorgen Randers, and William W. Behrens III. *The Limits to Growth: A Report for the Club of Rome's Project on the Predicament of Mankind.* New York, 1972.

Simon, Julian, and Herman Kahn. *The Resourceful Earth: A Response to "Global 2000."* Oxford, U.K., 1984.

White, Lynn, Jr. "The Historical Roots of Our Ecological Crisis." *Science* 155 (1967): 1203–1207.

Secondary Sources

Bowler, Peter J. *The Norton History of the Environmental Sciences.* New York, 1993.

Callicott, J. Baird. *Companion to* A Sand County Almanac: *Interpretive and Critical Essays.* Madison, Wis., 1987.

Colten, Craig E., and Peter N. Skinner. *The Road to Love Canal: Managing Industrial Waste before EPA.* Austin, Tex., 1996.

Dunlap, Riley, and Angela Mertig, eds. *American Environmentalism: The U.S. Environmental Movement, 1970–1990.* Philadelphia, 1992.

Dunlap, Thomas R. *DDT: Scientists, Citizens, and Public Policy.* Princeton, N.J., 1981.

Gottlieb, Robert. *Forcing the Spring: The Transformation of the American Environmental Movement.* Washington, D.C., 1993.

Graham, Frank. *Since Silent Spring.* Boston, 1970.

Harvey, Mark W. T. *A Symbol of Wilderness: Echo Park and the American Conservation Movement.* Albuquerque, N. Mex., 1994.

Hays, Samuel P. *Beauty, Health and Permanence: Environmental Politics in the U.S., 1955–1985.* Cambridge, U.K., 1987.

Lear, Linda J. *Rachel Carson: Witness for Nature.* New York, 1997.

——. "Rachel Carson's *Silent Spring,*" *Environmental History Review* 17, no. 2 (summer 1993), 28.

McPhee, John. *Encounters with the Archdruid.* New York, 1971.

Meine, Curt. *Aldo Leopold: His Life and Work.* Madison, Wis., 1988.

Ophuls, William, and A. Stephen Boyan Jr. *Ecology and the Politics of Scarcity Revisited: The Unraveling of the American Dream.* New York, 1992.

Opie, John. *Nature's Nation: An Environmental History of the United States.* Fort Worth, Tex., 1998.

Sagoff, Mark. *The Economy of the Earth: Philosophy, Law and the Environment.* Cambridge, U.K., 1988.

Worster, Donald. *Nature's Economy: A History of Ecological Ideas.* 2d ed. Cambridge, U.K., 1994.

Zakin, Susan. *Coyotes and Town Dogs: Earth First! and the Environmental Movement.* New York, 1993.

VIETNAM AS A CULTURAL CRISIS

David Farber

Truong Nhu Tang, a high-ranking member of the National Liberation Front, was on the winning side of the Vietnam War. In 1967 he became a prisoner of the South Vietnamese National Police in Saigon. After prolonged torture he was allowed a visit from his father. "My son," his father had said to him, "I simply cannot understand you. You have abandoned everything . . . to follow the Communists. . . . They will betray you, and you will suffer your entire life." Truong had gently remonstrated with his father, "My dearest father, you have six sons. You should be content to sacrifice one of them for the sake of the country's independence and liberty." Eighteen years after that desperate meeting, Truong published *A Viet Cong Memoir* (1985, p. 260). The dedication page reads: "To my mother and father. And to my betrayed comrades, who believed they were sacrificing themselves for a humane liberation of their people."

As Truong's memoir shows, even many of the so-called winners of the decades-long Vietnam Wars believed that they had lost. Betrayal, heartbreak, horror, and loss tore at the souls of many who served their nations at such extravagant cost in the Vietnam Wars.

The Vietnam Wars, from 1945 to 1975, in which the Vietnamese fought first with the French, then with the Americans, and throughout with each other, destroyed much of the land of Vietnam. Millions of Vietnamese were killed or maimed. During the years the United States military fought in Vietnam, from roughly August 1964 to January 1973, some 58,000 Americans died and more than 135,000 were injured. Hundreds of thousands of combat veterans would bear the physical and emotional marks of their experiences in Vietnam for years after their time at war had ended. For the United States, these lives lost and damaged are a bitter monument to a war that achieved so little for either the United States or the people in Southeast Asia.

The Vietnam War did more than ravage those who fought in it—though their sacrifices stand at its heart of darkness. The Vietnam War forced Americans to rethink what they stood for in the world. The war forced Americans to ponder the honesty and integrity of their leaders. The war forced Americans to question the meaning of patriotism and the practice of loyalty. The war made some Americans hate and despise one another. The war made cynicism seem a reasoned response to the post–World War II faith in the essential nobility of the American experiment in democracy and global leadership. These cultural wounds—shattered beliefs, deepened divides, destroyed trust, discredited acts—caused by the Vietnam War debacle would haunt the body politic long after the last American soldiers had come home.

WHY WE FIGHT

In 1975, two years after President Richard M. Nixon declared that "peace with honor" had been achieved in Vietnam, Robert Stone won a National Book Award for the novel *Dog Soldiers* (1975). Stone tells a story of corrupt government officials, twisted counterculturalists, Hollywood scum, and lives lost in the backwash of the Vietnam War. The novel opens in Vietnam. John Converse, a second-rate journalist looking for kicks, is working out a drug deal with the book's hero, Ray Hicks, an ex-marine who lives by his own strict code of honor. In elliptical fashion, Converse tries to explain why he is asking Hicks to smuggle three kilos of heroin from Vietnam into the United States. To put it more crudely than Stone did, Converse tells Hicks that it is the war, a war in which everything Americans thought about themselves was turned around. Converse concludes: "You can't blame us too much. We didn't know who we were till we got here. We thought we were something else" (p. 57). *Dog Soldiers,* in brutal scenes of cynical violence, illuminated the fear that tore at American society by the last days of the Vietnam War: maybe the United States was not the "arsenal of democracy" and the "beacon of freedom" in the world. The war had torn apart some Americans' proud faith, earned during World War II and banked in the early cold war years, that God and truth and justice were always on their side.

The American people wanted to believe that the Vietnam War was a righteous struggle in a battle for freedom against repression. American presidents from Dwight D. Eisenhower to Richard M. Nixon instructed the American people that the United States fought in Vietnam for altruistic reasons. President Lyndon B. Johnson stated the matter most bluntly in a speech he gave at Johns Hopkins University on 7 April 1965. "We fight because we must fight if we are to live in a world where every country can shape its own destiny. . . . We want nothing for ourselves," he orated, "only that the people of South Vietnam be allowed to guide their own country in their own way" (Schulman, *Lyndon B. Johnson and American Liberalism,* p. 214). President Johnson told the assembled students and faculty that South Vietnam had been targeted for communist expansion by Communist China and that only the United States could prevent all of Asia from being "swallowed up . . . [by] a nation which is helping the forces of violence in almost every continent" (pp. 214, 215).

Focusing his audience's attention on the People's Republic of China, Johnson ignored the actual history of the Vietnamese struggle for nationhood. He spoke as if the Vietnamese had not been a colony of imperialist France for over a century. He did not mention that the Vietnamese had fought a war of independence (begun well before Communist China had come into existence) against the French for nearly ten years, finally defeating the French—despite American military aid to France—in 1954. He made no mention that this war of independence had been led by Ho Chi Minh, the Vietnamese nationalist communist. He omitted from his speech any mention that this same national hero was leading the effort to reunify Vietnam. He did not explain that the reunification process, guaranteed by the Geneva Accords that had ended the French-Vietnamese War, had been subverted by the Eisenhower administration in the mid-1950s because American officials had known at that time that Ho would have been the victor in any open national election. President Johnson, like presidents Eisenhower and John F. Kennedy before him and President Nixon after him, omitted much when he explained to Americans, "why we fight in Vietnam." Increasing numbers of Americans, as they watched the Vietnam War unfold and heard new voices speaking out against America's military intervention, began to doubt their presidents' honesty.

The Beginnings of Protest   In the first major protest against American policy in Vietnam, speakers raised the ugly possibility that the United States was not in Vietnam for any reason that could bring honor to the American people. That first rally took place on 17 April 1965 at the Washington Monument in Washington, D.C. The keynote speaker was Paul Potter, the young president of the Students for a Democratic Society (SDS), the organization that had called for the protest.

SDS had formed at elite universities in 1960. In 1962 core members of this group produced a manifesto, the Port Huron Statement, which declared: "We are people of this generation, bred in at least modest comfort, housed now in universities looking uncomfortably to the world we inherit. . . . Doubt has replaced hopefulness—and men act out a defeatism that is labeled realistic" (Miller, *"Democracy Is in the Streets,"* pp. 329, 331). This mordant view of the United States as a land awash in "defeatism" and spiritual disaffiliation was not a widely shared sentiment at the midpoint of John F. Kennedy's thousand days of "Camelot." But beginning in 1965, with the Vietnam War beginning to escalate, the SDS leaders' biting critique of the United States began to resonate with more and more Americans.

At the April 1965 anti-Vietnam protest, SDS president Paul Potter explained what he believed had gone wrong in the United States. "The incredible war in Vietnam," Potter said

has provided the razor, the terrifying sharp cutting edge that has finally severed the last vestige of illusion that morality and democracy are the guiding principles of American foreign policy. The further we explore the reality of what this country is doing and planning in Vietnam the more we are driven toward the conclusion of Senator [Wayne] Morse that the United States may well be the greatest threat to peace in the world today. That is a terrible and bitter insight for people who grew up as we did. . . . The pattern of repression and destruction that we have developed and justified in the war is so thorough that it can only be called cultural genocide. (Bloom and Breines, *Takin' It to the Streets,* pp. 214–215)

Potter did more than indict American policy in Vietnam. He fought to make sense of it, to link the Vietnam War to the core beliefs that he believed had made it possible. Rather than treat Vietnam policies

184

as an aberration, a mistake made by well-intentioned government officials, Potter connected the war to fundamental domestic policies as well. He asked the 15,000 or so antiwar protesters to ponder what had gone wrong in the United States:

> What kind of system is it that justifies the United States or any country seizing the destinies of the Vietnamese people and using them callously for its own purpose? What kind of system is it that disenfranchises people in the South, leaves millions upon millions of people throughout the country impoverished and excluded from the mainstream and promise of American society, that creates faceless and terrible bureaucracies and makes those the place where people spend their lives and do their work, that consistently puts material values before human values—and still persists in calling itself free and still persists in finding itself fit to police the world? (pp. 217–218)

By 1965 Potter and hundreds of thousands of other antiwar protesters had come to believe that the U.S. military intervention in Vietnam revealed the spiritual and cultural bankruptcy of a nation that was willing to put money and power ahead of morality. The United States, they insisted in rallies and protests throughout the nation, did not fight for altruistic reasons. The Vietnam War proved, instead, that the United States had become a power-hungry bully run by antidemocratic elites. The president and his advisers, antiwar protesters insisted, had deliberately lied to the American people about the causes and course of American involvement in Vietnam.

WHAT IS TO BE DONE?

For those Americans who believed that U.S. policy in Vietnam was unjust and who did not trust their government to develop a more honorable policy, hard questions followed. The most pressing one was how to challenge American policy in Vietnam. Americans from all walks of life would come to oppose government policy in Vietnam and work toward changing that policy. At the heart of the antiwar movement, however, were Americans whose social roles positioned them to ponder the propriety, wisdom, and morality of national policy: university-based intellectuals and scholars, religious figures, and students.

Intellectuals and Scholars By 1967 leading intellectuals had joined in the chorus of voices raised against American intervention in Vietnam. The most prominent intellectual journal in the United States in the last half of the 1960s, the *New York*

Review of Books (*NYRB*), became a focal point for antiwar analyses and polemics, publishing 262 critical articles on the Vietnam War between 1965 and 1975. Dozens of major scholars used the pages of *NYRB* to blast American policy and propose a new role for American academics.

The Massachusetts Institute of Technology linguistics professor Noam Chomsky issued the most well known of these intellectual calls-to-arms in a 23 February 1967 article, "The Responsibility of Intellectuals." Chomsky argued that during the 1950s and early 1960s, too many university-based scholars and intellectuals had become complicitous in the cold war's national security and military-industrial complex. Many of the most capable intellectuals had become servants to power, working as advisers to political and economic elites, helping to develop the secret policies that both subverted foreign governments and made a mockery of American democracy. Chomsky insisted: "It is the responsibility of intellectuals to speak the truth and to expose lies" (Schalk, *War and the Ivory Tower*, pp. 142–143). Intellectuals must use their intellectual training and expertise to rip away "the veil of distortion and misrepresentation" that hid "the will to power, cloaking itself in idealism," that drove American foreign policy.

For a great many American academics (mostly those in the humanities and social sciences, far fewer in the so-called hard sciences and professional-training fields), the Vietnam War marked a professional crisis in which they felt obliged to ponder the political responsibilities of their social roles. A vocal minority insisted that they had the right and obligation to extend their opposition to the war to their classrooms, scholarship, and professional activities. In several academic disciplines this issue came to an explosive head when self-described radical scholars asked their professional associations to pass resolutions against the Vietnam War. In the debates that ensued, academics divided not so much over the war itself but over the propriety of scholarly associations taking public stands on political issues. While scholars argued more vocally than most over the relationship between professional responsibility and civic duty, they were not alone in feeling that the Vietnam War raised hard questions about how and where, and even if, citizens should protest against wartime government policy.

Religious Figures and Churches Religious leaders, too, pondered their role in the debate over the Vietnam War. In the mid-1960s, during the first years of American military intervention, few church leaders spoke out against the war, preferring to issue bland statements of general support. The Presbyterian Church of the United States, for example, officially stated in 1967 its "loyalty to the government in this current conflict" (Hall, *Because of Their Faith*, p. 46). That same year, the Lutheran Church–Missouri Synod simply recommended that church members pray over the situation in Vietnam. At the local church, the Vietnam War as a political issue was rarely discussed. Most churchgoers seemed to prefer that the war be left outside their church's door.

This general avoidance of the Vietnam controversy by church leaders at both the national and local levels did not go unchallenged. In October 1965 the Reverend Richard Neuhaus, pastor of the prestigious Lutheran Church of St. John the Evangelist in New York City, spearheaded a petition drive that gathered the signatures of some one hundred New York City clergymen who supported the right of Americans to protest against the Vietnam War. Early in 1966 Neuhaus joined with Rabbi Abraham Heschel, Jesuit priest Daniel Berrigan and several others to form a National Emergency Committee of Clergy Concerned about Vietnam, later known as Clergy and Laymen Concerned about Vietnam (CALCV). The CALCV began a nationwide effort to mobilize religious leaders to speak out against the war both publicly and in their churches and synagogues. CALCV member and Stanford University theologian Robert McAfee Brown explained the group's position: "A time comes when silence is betrayal. That time has come for us in relation to Vietnam" (p. 34).

Between 1967 and 1969, a growing number of religious leaders openly opposed the war. Mainline Protestant denominations such as the United Church of Christ, the Lutheran Church in America, the United Presbyterian Church, and the United Methodist Church all declared themselves in favor of de-escalation of the war. Similarly, Jewish organizations such as the American Jewish Congress and the Union of American Hebrew Congregations took antiwar positions. CALCV membership increased to some 40,000 members. On 11 April 1967 the Reverend Martin Luther King Jr. quietly agreed to co-chair the organization. A week earlier, at a CALCV-sponsored event at Riverside Church in New York City, King had given his moral and spiritual weight to the antiwar cause in his first major address against the Vietnam War:

> We are at a moment when our lives must be placed on the line if our nation is to survive its own folly. Every man of humane convictions must decide on

the protest that best suits his convictions but we must all protest. . . . I oppose the war in Vietnam because I love America. I speak out against it not in anger but with anxiety and sorrow in my heart. . . . This war is a blasphemy against all that America stands for. (Farber, *The Age of Great Dreams*, p. 162)

King and like-minded clergyman insisted, on religious grounds, that it was the spiritual duty of Americans to oppose a war that was, in the words of the Roman Catholic magazine *U.S. Catholic*, "Wrong, unjust and immoral" (Hall, p. 65)

Outspoken activism against the war by religious leaders did not sit well with many churchgoing Americans. Self-described fundamentalist Christians overwhelmingly opposed such antiwar activism. A poll taken in mid-1968 showed that 91 percent of Protestant fundamentalists, most of them Southern Baptists, believed not in de-escalating American involvement in Vietnam but in increasing American military pressure against the communists. The most prominent evangelist in the United States, the Reverend Billy Graham, spoke for many conservative, religious Americans when he gently urged ministers just to stay away from the debate over government policy in Vietnam: "I fear that if the church, as the church, begins to try to dictate in politics, we're way off the main track" (Rorabaugh, *Berkeley at War, the 1960s*, p. 116). Both Presidents Johnson and Nixon worked hard at convincing religious leaders to maintain this position, at least in regard to the Vietnam War. Americans, by and large, were made uncomfortable by the politicization of the clergy. A Chicago policeman put this issue most directly to three ministers at an August 1968 antiwar protest at the Democratic National Convention: "You bastards. What are you doing here? You belong back at your church" (Farber, p. 182).

Throughout the war, polls showed that a majority of churchgoing Americans approved of their government's evolving policies in Vietnam. As a result, clergymen who did speak out against the war often found themselves facing angry congregations. As the religious monthly the *Lutheran* reported in May 1968, "Officially the churches may coo like a dove but the majority of their members are flying with the hawks" (Hall, p. 66). The war divided religious Americans. They angrily debated not just their government's Vietnam policy but, even more, the appropriateness of their church leaders using the pulpit to oppose or to support the Vietnam War. The politicization of the church, while not unique to the Vietnam era (mid-nineteenth-century abolitionists mobilized support through churches, as did anticommunists and civil rights activists in the mid–twentieth century), brought the Vietnam crisis out of the headlines and into the lives of millions of Americans.

Colleges The church-based debate over the Vietnam War gained little mass media attention during the 1960s. Far better known, then and now, were the fierce struggles over the Vietnam War that took place on college campuses across the United States. Students, faculty, administrators, politicians, and citizens angrily debated both the war itself and the role that institutions of higher education played in the war. A significant number of both faculty and students, as well as a sizable number of sympathetic administrators, believed that universities could and should have an important role in protesting against the American government's Vietnam policies. Others vehemently disagreed. As with the church, many simply felt that the university should not be a site of political protest. They insisted that college campuses should be oases of learning. The war forced Americans to consider just what their institutions of higher education were supposed to do and what limits should be placed on Americans' traditional freedoms of speech and assembly.

The first major campus-based response to the Vietnam War, the "teach-in" (the name derived from the civil rights sit-in movement of the early 1960s, which was in turn derived from the sit-down labor union tactic of the 1930s), were decidedly academic. The teach-in movement began at the University of Michigan in March 1965. By the end of that year it had spread to more than 120 colleges and universities. At these teach-ins, students and professors, often in all-night sessions attended by thousands of people, attempted to educate themselves on the situation in Vietnam. Rather than trust in the explanations offered by their government leaders or the information spread through the mass media, teach-in participants sought out alternative points of view on Vietnam, such as those offered by foreign commentators and radical Americans. They attempted to open up discussion based on their own research and inquiries. Many students and faculty came away from the teach-in experience with a growing skepticism about the veracity of mainstream perspectives on Vietnam and an increasing distrust of the men who were managing the war in Washington, D.C.

Campus activism against the Vietnam War radically escalated in the late 1960s. Teach-ins were replaced by campus-based protests, student strikes, and demands that neither faculty nor administrators assist the war effort in any fashion. Military recruitment and ROTC centers on campuses were picketed and even vandalized. Defense industry representatives who attempted to recruit on college campuses were often surrounded and harassed by hostile students. War-related faculty research, done at almost every major university in the nation, was condemned, and in some cases literally destroyed, by antiwar students and professors. By 1970 the most radical students were even participating in arson attacks, bombings, and the "trashing" of university campuses. This radical fringe of the antiwar movement, enraged by what had become America's longest war in history, had come to believe that the only way to stop the slaughter in Vietnam was, in their words, "to bring the war home" to the American people.

Such antiwar activism enraged a large majority of Americans. At the University of California at Berkeley, site of some of some of the most vehement antiwar protests, faculty, administrators, and students bitterly divided over the war and the right of antiwar protesters to demonstrate on campus. In 1967, for example, a high-ranking administrator publicly challenged the university chancellor, Roger Heyns, to stop all campus activism. "We are at war with the reds wherever they exist" (Rorabaugh, p. 116), he insisted, and demanded that the university security forces should "beat the living hell out of [campus protestors]." Chancellor Heyns, like most university presidents, rejected this advice, insisting that students had the right to protest against the war.

Most Americans disagreed with moderate university presidents like Chancellor Heyns. Opinion polls showed that upwards of 80 percent of all Americans believed that students should not protest against the war on their university campuses. Ronald Reagan successfully ran for governor of California in 1966 and then made a bid for the 1968 Republican presidential nomination by blasting student antiwar protesters (as well as other 1960s dissidents, such as civil rights demonstrators). To cheering audiences, he explained how you could spot a hippie protester: "[He] dresses like Tarzan, has hair like Jane, and smells like Cheetah" (Gitlin, *The Sixties,* p. 217). Far less humorously, Vice President Spiro Agnew spoke to many Americans' anger with student protesters in the tragic aftermath of the Kent State antiwar protests. During a chaotic May 1970 protest against President Nixon's expansion of the war into Cambodia, panicked National Guardsmen shot into a crowd of unarmed students,

187

Kent State University, May 1970. After a crowd of fifteen hundred protesters and spectators had seemingly dispersed, a group of a dozen National Guardsmen turned, aimed, and fired sixty-seven shots, killing four and wounding nine. © BETTMANN/CORBIS

killing four of them. In a logic that a majority of Americans found compelling, Agnew blamed the students for their own deaths, explaining that if they had not been protesting they would not have been shot. Though a majority of Americans by 1970 did want to see the United States escape from the Vietnam quagmire, an even larger majority was fed up with antiwar protesters who condemned the American war effort as a horrific, even immoral failure.

POLARIZATION

The Vietnam War and the protests it engendered polarized the nation. This fierce division did not simply reflect a difference in opinion over the American strategy in Vietnam. The war had opened up other fault lines in the United States. One of the ugliest was the gulf between those who fought and those who did not.

Unlike America's other twentieth-century wars, the Vietnam War was fought overwhelmingly by men whose hold on the American dream was weakest. About 80 percent of the men who served in Vietnam came from working-class and poor families. A disproportionate number of soldiers were African American and Latino. This sharp class and racial divide was, in large part, produced by delib-

erate government policies that through much of the war gave automatic draft deferments to college undergraduates, graduate students, and others in relatively privileged occupations. Government draft policy favoring young, white, middle-class men was, however, only part of the story. As William Strauss and Lawrence Baskir wrote: "The Vietnam draft cast the entire generation into a contest for individual survival ... the 'fittest'—those with the background, wit, or money—managed to escape" (Farber, p. 149). Americans were aware that young men from relatively elite backgrounds were using every means at their disposal to avoid serving in Vietnam. In America's undeclared and increasingly unpopular war, the unifying World War II ideals and practices of shared sacrifice and patriotic duty were shattered. In the wake of that breakdown, those Americans who did sacrifice, and those who struggled to maintain an unquestioning faith in their political leaders, felt betrayed by their fellow Americans. As the war went on and on, they also felt betrayed by their government, which refused, they believed, to do whatever was necessary to bring the war to a victorious conclusion.

For the men who fought and for their families, as well as for the many Americans who saw the Vietnam War as a just and necessary cause, blatant draft dodging and vocal antiwar protests were demoral-

188

izing and infuriating. Even as some of these veterans and prowar Americans lost their faith in the American war effort, most still despised the demonstrators and their mainly liberal political supporters. Throughout the United States, anti-antiwar demonstrators plastered their cars with bumper stickers that read, "Love It or Leave It" and "Support Our Boys in Vietnam" and proudly sported American flag lapel buttons. It was not so much that such people, most of them working-class Americans, approved of the war—in fact, more working-class people disapproved of their government's war policies than did higher-income Americans. It was more that they hated what they perceived to be the disloyalty of the protesters. Antiwar protest, many of them felt, was traitorous behavior at a time when Americans were dying in battle.

Antiwar Americans, on the other hand, could not fully comprehend what they perceived as blind, unreasoning faith in a failed, even immoral government policy. The broad mainstream of antiwar activists saw their protests as patriotic exercises in "real democracy." One middle-aged, middle-class antiwar stalwart, who first became involved through her church, stated that the protests "were self-critical but in a constructive way. . . . People listened to each other, the First Amendment was real. There was free speech" (Farber, p. 167). These Americans believed that, even at a time of war—especially a war they believed to be wrongly conceived—the American people had the right and the duty to defend the nation against egregiously mistaken policies taken by their government. They believed that American democracy, based on the sovereign right of the people to determine their collective fate, demanded such protest. This domestic battle over what it meant to be a good American during a difficult time tore the country apart.

LEGACIES

On 27 January 1973 the United States and North Vietnam signed a peace accord ending direct American involvement in the Vietnamese people's civil war. While the nation was relieved that no more Americans would die in the jungles and rice paddies of Vietnam, few accepted Nixon's cynical declaration that "peace with honor" had been achieved in America's longest war.

In 1961 President John Kennedy had inspired the nation with his ringing declaration that the United States would, "pay any price, bear any burden, meet any hardship, support any friend, oppose any foe, in order to assure the survival and the success of liberty" (Farber, p. 32). In the years that followed the Vietnam debacle, such cold war histrionics met with little public approval. President Gerald Ford spoke for the new conventional wisdom in 1975 when he told a national television audience: "I think . . . there are a number of lessons that we can learn from Vietnam. One, that we have to work with other governments that feel as we do—that freedom is vitally important. We cannot, however, fight their battles for them. Those countries who believe in freedom as we do must carry the burden" (McMahon, *Major Problems in the History of the Vietnam War*, p. 609). By the mid-1970s, pundits labeled as the "Vietnam syndrome" the unwillingness of Americans to send their young men and women to fight in foreign wars in the name of other nations' freedom. Some foreign policy experts, as well as President George Bush, have argued that this syndrome ended with America's swift victory in the 1991 Persian Gulf War. Even so, American political and military leaders, as well as the great majority of the American people, still carry with them the weight of the Vietnam debacle as they consider the limits of unilateral American military power in the world. In the decades following the Vietnam War, no American leader would speak of unbridled American force the way President Kennedy did in the pre–Vietnam War days of the early 1960s.

In 1976 the American people elected Georgia governor Jimmy Carter, a political outsider, to be their president. At the center of Carter's campaign had been a plain spoken declaration: "I'm not a lawyer, I'm not a member of Congress, and I've never served in Washington," along with a simple promise, "I'll never tell a lie." In a nation still traumatized by Vietnam (and the linked implosion of the Nixon presidency), such relatively humble characterizations matched the public's desire for a new kind of national leadership, one untainted by any connection to the Vietnam-era political establishment of either political party. Such "anti-Washington" election-time rhetoric would become a winning strategy in every post-Vietnam twentieth-century presidential election. The failure in Vietnam, compounded by many Americans' perception of failed federal antipoverty programs as well, had seared a deep, long-lasting distrust of government elites into American political culture.

Unlike the Vietnamese, who decades after the war still lived amid daily reminders of the conflict, most Americans—apart from those who had faced the enemy firsthand or who had lost a friend or loved one—slowly cut out the most painful malignancies that the war in Vietnam had metastasized through the body politic of the United States. In the last days of his presidency, even Ronald Reagan, the outspoken Vietnam "hawk" who had so vociferously lashed out against antiwar protesters as traitors, spoke of a national healing. On Veterans Day in 1988, the "Great Communicator" spoke gently of a time that knew little in the way of moderation: "Unlike the other wars of this century, of course, there were deep divisions about the wisdom and rightness of the Vietnam War. Both sides spoke with honesty and fervor. And what more can we ask in our democracy?" (McMahon, p. 614). And while Reagan did go on to claim that the American mission in Vietnam had been noble, his remarks were mainly aimed at creating a new national consensus about America's role in Vietnam. Regardless of the rancor and divisions back then, Reagan implored, the nation should join together now to pay homage to the veterans who fought, often at great personal sacrifice, for their country.

President Reagan's hope that all Americans could transcend the bitter divisions of the war by focusing on the sacrifices of those who fought it was a hopeful message. It was also a means of promoting a national amnesia about the murky, even deplorable causes and secret maneuvering that governed American policy in Vietnam. During the late 1960s and early 1970s, the Vietnam War tore apart the United States in ways almost unfathomable either to the generation that defeated the fascists during World War II or to the generation that came of age in the economic boom years of the late twentieth century. While the cultural crisis of the Vietnam War inflicted painful wounds—most especially political cynicism and a deep national divide—it was useful at the turn of the twenty-first century to also remember, as Reagan acknowledged, the meanings it had for American democracy. Americans' battle over their government's policy in Vietnam reinvigorated a great national debate about the role the United States should play in the world. More long lastingly, that great debate also restored a vigor to Americans' centuries-old struggle to find the means by which a free and democratic people can maintain the political sovereignty guaranteed them by their Constitution.

See also **World War and Cold War** *(in this volume); and other articles in this section.*

BIBLIOGRAPHY

Anderson, Terry H. *The Movement and the Sixties.* New York, 1995.

Appy, Christian G. *Working-Class War: American Combat Soldiers and Vietnam.* Chapel Hill, N.C., 1993.

Bao, Ninh. *The Sorrow of War: A Novel of North Vietnam.* New York, 1993.

Baskir, Lawrence M., and William A. Strauss. *Chance and Circumstance: The Draft, the War, and the Vietnam Generation.* New York, 1978.

Bloom, Alexander, and Wini Breines. *"Takin' It to the Streets": A Sixties Reader.* New York, 1995.

Dickstein, Morris. *Gates of Eden: American Culture in the Sixties.* Cambridge, Mass., 1997.

Engelhardt, Tom. *The End of Victory Culture: Cold War America and the Disillusioning of a Generation.* New York, 1995.

Farber, David. *The Age of Great Dreams: America in the 1960s.* New York, 1994.

———. *Chicago '68.* Chicago, 1988.

Farrell, James J. *The Spirit of the Sixties: Making Postwar Radicalism.* New York, 1997.

Gitlin, Todd. *The Sixties: Years of Hope, Days of Rage.* New York, 1987.

Hall, Mitchell K. *Because of Their Faith: CALCAV and Religious Opposition to the Vietnam War.* New York, 1990.

Levy, David W. *The Debate over Vietnam.* Baltimore, 1991.

Lyons, Paul. *New Left, New Right, and the Legacy of the Sixties.* Philadelphia, 1996.

McMahon, Robert J., ed. *Major Problems in the History of the Vietnam War: Documents and Essays.* Lexington, Mass., 1995.

Miller, James. *"Democracy Is in the Streets": From Port Huron to the Siege of Chicago.* New York, 1987.

Rorabaugh, W. J. *Berkeley at War, the 1960s.* New York, 1989.

Schalk, David L. *War and the Ivory Tower: Algeria and Vietnam.* New York, 1991.

Schulman, Bruce J. *Lyndon B. Johnson and American Liberalism: A Brief Biography with Documents.* Boston, 1995.

Small, Melvin. *Johnson, Nixon, and the Doves.* New Brunswick, N.J., 1988.

Stone, Robert. *Dog Soldiers: A Novel.* New York, 1987.

Truong, Nhu Tang. *A Viet Cong Memoir.* New York, 1985.

Young, Marilyn B. *The Vietnam Wars. 1945–1990.* New York, 1991.

Part 8

THE REAGAN ERA TO THE PRESENT

OVERVIEW:
FROM THE REAGAN ERA TO THE PRESENT

Eduard van de Bilt

Johanna C. Kardux

Two "revolutions," each developing out of the 1960s, had a major impact on American intellectual and cultural life in the 1980s and 1990s. One, named after the presidency of Ronald Reagan, the man best able to communicate its message to the nation, was political but reverberated in other areas of society as well; the other, variously called postmodernism or poststructuralism, was strictly academic at first but was eventually appropriated for political purposes. In many respects, the two revolutions clashed: representing a mass culture, the Reagan revolution idealized precisely the "American" values and beliefs that were critically interrogated by the intellectual elite that was influenced by "French" philosophy. As a result, the rise of political conservatism, epitomized by Reagan's election to the presidency in 1980, and the simultaneous ascendancy of poststructuralist theory put politics and the academy at odds. While proponents of the new critical theory became increasingly vocal critics of Reagan's efforts to restore traditional values, neoconservatives tried to regain control over the academic world by staging a public debate about the changes in the curriculum and in hiring and admission policies that, in the wake of the 1960s and 1970s, had transformed American higher education by the late 1980s. Far less visible, however, were the intersections between the two revolutions. Reagan's political agenda was as controversial as poststructuralist theory, and the opposition to each created unexpected alliances that do not easily fit into simple schemes. Moreover, both revolutions responded to, and were made possible by, processes of change that were well under way before Reagan won the presidency or poststructuralist theory entered academic discourse.

The combined impact of neoconservatism and poststructuralist ideas gave rise to public debates in which epistemological issues meshed with questions about the division of power and the status of minority groups in American society. Incorporating certain elements of poststructuralist discourse into their own political rhetoric, representatives of marginalized and oppressed groups and their supporters developed the notion of a multiethnic and multicultural society, demanding not only equal rights but also recognition of these groups' cultural identities and contributions to American history. Although these debates helped redefine race and gender relations in the United States, they were also divisive, frequently polarizing academic institutions and contributing to an atmosphere of political confrontation.

THE REAGAN REVOLUTION

Ronald Reagan's rise to power in 1980 was the result of a resurgence of political conservatism that, in hindsight, can be said to have begun in 1964, with the presidential election campaign of the Republican Barry M. Goldwater. The incumbent Lyndon B. Johnson easily defeated his Republican opponent in the race for the presidency. Yet, contrary to what many political analysts predicted at the time, Johnson's years in the White House did not mark the end of conservatism; instead, the liberal tradition of government regulations established during the Progressive and New Deal eras, which Johnson had hoped to expand with his own Great Society and War on Poverty programs, showed signs of strain that eventually led to its demise. The war in Vietnam split the coalition that had brought Johnson to power, turning students and advocates of alternative lifestyles against workers and liberal power brokers. This left-wing distrust of the federal administration fueled the doubts about the role of government prevalent among other groups in society, including those that had supported Goldwater. The rise of a counterculture and the revitalization of the feminist movement elicited strong and emotional reactions among Americans who regarded these movements' rebellion against traditional views of sexuality and other middle-class values and norms as evidence of the nation's moral disintegration.

At the same time, Johnson's efforts to secure equal rights for African Americans alienated the southern wing of his Democratic Party, as did the civil rights movement's policy shift from advocating equality of opportunity and "color blindness" to institutionalizing affirmative action programs. The Johnson administration's refusal to be frank about the extent of American involvement in the Vietnam War in the mid-1960s and the frustrations about the eventual loss of the war, combined with what many Americans considered to be unwarranted government support of minorities, fostered a distrust of government that survived Johnson's presidency and was reinforced under Richard Nixon's administration by the Watergate scandal. Any government that privileged particular groups within society was, in Reagan's view, part of the problem— a problem that he proposed to solve by eliminating programs aimed at supporting these groups, by downsizing government itself. Refurbishing nineteenth-century notions about the virtues of individualism and laissez-faire, the New Right replaced the Progressive Era and New Deal ideal of a benevolent government by the older (if narrowly conceived) Jeffersonian tradition characterized by suspicion of strong government.

The neoconservative movement of the 1980s offered its own economic, political, and cultural program as an alternative to a tradition it disdainfully and pejoratively labeled "liberal." In the realm of economics, Keynesian theory, which advocated government spending to create jobs and maintain purchasing power in times of depression or cyclical downturns, had to make way for a policy called supply-side economics, which consisted of lowering taxes and minimizing government interference in the private sector to stimulate economic growth. Politically, the neoconservative movement retained the anticommunist cold war rhetoric in foreign policy, trying to banish the humiliating memories of the Iran hostage crisis in 1976–1980 under President Jimmy Carter by demanding that the United States "stand tall" again; domestically, it called for a revival of the states' rights tradition. Culturally, it defined itself in opposition to what it considered the 1960s legacy of an excessively tolerant and relativist frame of mind, which was blamed for virtually all the ills that afflicted American society, from crime, drug abuse, and abortion to anything else that could be captured under the rubric of "un-American" behavior. Claiming for itself the title of "moral majority," the religious right made aggressive use of modern communication techniques to preach a mix of evangelical Christianity, patriotism, and "family values." Countering social trends from the 1960s on, which resulted in a majority of married women entering the labor force, conservative social thinkers and politicians tried to reintroduce a separate-sphere ideology, relegating mothers to the home, while ignoring that Reaganomics made it impossible for an increasing segment of the American population to support a family on one income.

Central to conservative thought was a renewed emphasis on the individual. Poverty was not a problem to be solved by the government, but by the individual who was believed to be at the root of the problem. Individual merit, rather than preferential treatment of disadvantaged groups, had to be restored as the basis of economic and social reward. Conservatives found support for these views in, for example, Charles Murray's *Losing Ground* (1984), which argued that the welfare system only exacerbated the plight of the minority groups whose condition it was supposed to ameliorate, because it prevented them from taking economic initiatives. Moreover, conservatives claimed that the emphasis on group interests that had crept into the debates about social issues not only conflicted with the constitutional rights and liberties of the individual but also threatened to divide society into competing ethnic and racial sections.

The fall of the Berlin Wall in 1989 and the collapse of the Soviet Union two years later indicated, in the neoconservatives' view, the success of their philosophy and, in a way, the end of ideology: lacking any alternatives, the American ethos centered around private initiative and the freedom of the individual to rule the world.

THE POSTSTRUCTURALIST REVOLUTION

In the academic world of the 1980s, another revolution of sorts occurred. Just as in the 1950s, when American intellectuals were profoundly influenced by existentialist philosophy, in the late 1970s another French school of thought began to have an impact, first in the language and literature departments of a few elite universities in the United States and by the mid-1980s at other universities and in other disciplines such as history and legal studies as well: poststructuralism. The publication of English translations of the French critic Jacques Derrida's *Of Grammatology* in 1976 and *Writing and Difference* in 1978 (both first published in France in 1967) introduced a new generation of American scholars and graduate students to deconstruction, a mode of reading texts that, together with the new feminist criticism that had started a few years earlier, became an important source of energy and innovation—as well as controversy—in American literary and cultural studies. As the complex ideas of Derrida, Foucault, and Lacan were introduced and made more accessible by American scholars such as Jonathan D. Culler in literary studies and Hayden V. White and Dominick LaCapra in history, the poststructuralist theories of the philosopher Derrida, the historian Michel Foucault, and the psychoanalyst Jacques Lacan caused a growing number of American scholars and students to rethink the presuppositions of their trade, raising questions about the presumed objectivity of scholarship—questions that, if not entirely new, nonetheless profoundly influenced their choice of methods and subjects of inquiry.

Although there were obviously differences among the three major French theorists (Derrida, Foucault, and Lacan), they shared a few key ideas. Drawing on the previous work of Friedrich Nietzsche, Sigmund Freud, and Martin Heidegger, all three called into question the concept of the rational, autonomous human subject that underlies modern Western thought and scholarship. Poststructuralist theory decentered the human subject, whose autonomy was radically undermined by forces outside his or her control, such as language (Derrida), discourse (Foucault), and the unconscious (Lacan). Two other common characteristics were antifoundationalism and antiessentialism. According to poststructural theory, there is no absolute truth, no ultimate foundation on which to ground meaning. All attempts to claim the truth or capture the totality of an object or historical experience are intellectually misguided and politically and socially repressive. Repudiating the concepts of essence or unity, poststructuralism celebrated difference and multiplicity.

Derrida, the most influential of the three in the 1980s, was influenced by but went beyond the linguistic theory of Ferdinand de Saussure, whose lectures were published posthumously in 1916, and French structuralists, who in the 1950s applied de Saussure's theory to anthropology and literary criticism (hence the coinage of the term "poststructuralism"). While de Saussure posited that the relation between language (signifier) and reality (signified) is arbitrary, Derrida argued that there is no "reality"—no transcendent "signified"—outside language. As Derrida put it, there is "no outside-the-text"; all is language. Meaning is, therefore, produced by (and not the source of) language.

While structuralists aimed to analyze the underlying structures, or signifying systems, of a culture or a text, Derrida dismantled (or deconstructed) these very structures, exposing them as constructs that were artificially imposed by the analysts themselves. Derrida pointed out, for instance, the Western habit of thinking in terms of binary oppositions, such as nature/culture, self/other, or white/black. Although these oppositions seem neutral, Derrida argued that they reflect the dominant value system, which privileges one term of the binary pair over the other—self over other, white over black—thus imposing a hierarchical order. A deconstruction of these binary oppositions revealed not only that they are ideologically motivated, but also that they are not truly opposites: for example, social practices that are traditionally defined as "natural" under scrutiny turn out to be "cultural," contingent upon place and time.

As a mode of analysis, deconstruction focused on those aspects of, or moments in, a text (or cultural discourse) that bring to light the breakdown of meaning. Each text, Derrida claimed, contains a contradiction or irreconcilable paradox (aporia), which subverts the overt meaning of the text and exposes the fact that there are no grounds, either inside the text or outside, for attributing a determinate meaning. As Derrida was well aware, his own texts were subject to the same deconstructive analysis.

Deconstruction and poststructuralist theory in general radically challenged two major traditions in the humanities and the social sciences in the United States—positivism and humanism. Rejecting the positivists' claim of objectivity, the French theorists maintain that thought, instead of an objective account, is always someone's storied version of events that cannot be known in themselves. In their view, all communication is an effort to establish control, and it is the critic's task to deconstruct or expose these efforts. At the same time, they undermined the humanist belief in the autonomy, centrality, and integrity of the human subject. Governed by external forces such as language and discourse, human individuals ultimately lack the initiative and agency attributed to them in the humanist tradition; since individuals are internally divided by conflicting impulses, human identity is neither unitary nor essential but rather a social construct.

Despite significant similarities, the three main French theorists and their disciples differed considerably from each other, some being more interested in showing how language or discourse and ideas are organized or structured, others intent on tracing the

197

contradictions in, or breakdown of, these efforts to construct reality. While some were more willing than others to acknowledge the political and ethical implications of their ideas, they all denied being the radical relativists or nihilists their opponents claimed them to be. Although their skepticism about human autonomy and rationality subverted traditional humanist claims about ethics and positivist claims of objectivity, some of their followers argued that the exposure of preconceptions and the displacement of hierarchical opposition, which was central to their work, potentially had ethical consequences and could easily be transformed into a political strategy, thus opening up the possibility of social and political change.

FEMINISM AND MULTICULTURALISM

French poststructuralist theory, frequently jargon-ridden and sometimes willfully obscure, might have been limited in impact to a coterie of Francophile theorists if, in popularized and politicized form, it had not fed into other contemporary social and intellectual movements, particularly feminism and multiculturalism.

The broad emancipatory crusades that emerged in the wake of the civil rights movement of the 1960s may have helped to provoke the conservative backlash of the Reagan revolution of the 1980s, but they nonetheless remained a force to be reckoned with in American society, because at least a number of the policies by which they aimed to bring about social change, such as affirmative action programs, had been institutionalized in the 1970s. Moreover, although liberals lost much of their political clout as a result of the New Right's rise to power, they continued to dominate the American academy in the 1980s. By the 1980s the new social history had transformed the discipline by rewriting history "from the bottom up," making "common" people and other groups that were previously neglected in historiography the focus of research and teaching. At the same time, as women's studies programs established in the 1970s flourished, the mid-1980s saw an enormous expansion of black studies, Native American studies, Chicano studies, and, by the 1990s, gay studies at American universities. Although many of these new programs remained rather isolated institutionally, they were crucial in bringing about a reform within the traditional disciplines, adding race, ethnicity, and sexual orientation to class and gender as crucial categories in historical, political, and cultural analysis. In fact, by the late 1980s they had largely replaced class as an analytical category, as the emphasis in the humanities shifted toward cultural studies.

The movement of "minority" issues from the margins to the center of academic life and discourse coincided with and was partly influenced by the demographic transformation of the United States in the 1980s and 1990s. An influx of millions of immigrants from Asia and Hispanic America rapidly changed the racial and ethnic composition of the nation. While the massive immigration caused resentment and fear among native white and older minority groups such as African Americans, exacerbating racial and ethnic divisions in the lower social strata, the increasing ethnic diversity of the American population gave moral incentive to the broad movement in academic, social, and political life called "multiculturalism."

Radicalizing the older, liberal vision of the United States as a pluralist society, multiculturalism aimed to make the college curriculum representative of the multiethnic and multicultural character of American society. After the breach (predominantly white) feminist historians and critics had made in the walls of patriarchy in the 1970s by exposing the gender politics that underlay the writing of history and the formation of the literary canon, the demand that the voices of nonwhite women and of other ignored and oppressed groups be heard as well was inevitable. As an intellectual and cultural movement, multiculturalism consisted of pressure groups within the academy, ranging from the moderate to the radical, rather than a formal organization. While the racial and ethnic diversity of the student and faculty body rapidly expanded as a result of affirmative action programs, at a number of major colleges and universities the core curriculum was revised. Texts by and about women and other excluded or marginal groups were substituted for some of the works of the "great authors," now debunked as "dead white males," that traditionally figured in required courses such as "Western Civilization." The more radical opponents of the Eurocentric tradition even called for the abolition of Western civilization courses, arguing that these only bolstered the existing power structures and their supremacist and racist ideologies.

Although few universities followed this radical route, by the end of the 1980s multiculturalism, feminism, and the new social history had a considerable influence on what was read and taught in undergraduate and graduate courses and, in the next few years, at American high schools. In most places, however, the changes took the form of an opening up of the literary and historical canon and the curriculum, making them more inclusive rather than displacing the old ones entirely, and creating space within them for the achievements of formerly excluded individuals and groups. The old metaphor of America as a melting pot made way for that of the mosaic or salad bowl, a new cliché that represented a multicultural, but not necessarily less nationalist, vision, celebrating the many colors and separate cultural identities that "made America great." Although the forces that brought the Democrat William Jefferson Clinton to the presidency in 1992 were complex, Clinton's outspoken allegiance to this moderate multicultural vision was an important factor, because his election was partly the result of his successful appeal to African American and women voters.

The career of the African American literary scholar Henry Louis Gates Jr. was emblematic of the furious pace with which multiculturalism gained institutional power and from there moved to the forefront of public debate. Gates's career took off in the mid-1980s, and he accepted increasingly influential teaching positions, successively at Yale, Cornell, Duke, and Harvard Universities, and even gained a place on *Time* magazine's list of the twenty-five most influential Americans in 1997 (together with the African Americans General Colin Powell and golfer Tiger Woods). Another example is the novelist Toni Morrison, who won the 1988 Pulitzer Prize for *Beloved,* a historical novel about the trauma of slavery, and who was called "the closest thing the country has to a national writer" in the *New York Times Book Review* in 1992. In 1993 she was the first African American writer to receive the Nobel Prize in literature, evidence that multiculturalism had become an international phenomenon. Needless to say, Gates and Morrison owed their achievements to their own talents and perseverance; nonetheless, it is difficult to imagine they would have been the public figures they became if it had not been for the rise of multiculturalism in the 1980s.

Within the academic realm, both feminism and multiculturalism interacted productively with poststructuralism. Making selective use of poststructuralist theory, feminism and multiculturalism promoted the circulation, and ultimately integration, of certain poststructuralist concepts in more mainstream thought. Derrida's deconstruction of binary logic, for instance, could easily be applied both to feminist critiques of patriarchal power structures and to multicultural critiques of cultural hegemony. Feminists used deconstruction, for example, to undo the

male-female binary, which they claimed to be the underlying paradigm in the patriarchal value system; similarly, multiculturalists focused on the self-other opposition, exposing the ways in which white males and Western cultures achieved and maintained dominance by defining nonmales and non-white or non-Western cultures as "other." While deconstruction contributed to the theoretical underpinnings of these more overtly political intellectual movements, feminist and multiculturalist applications of poststructuralist theory helped bring out its political implications.

As American cultural studies were politicized in the late 1980s, there was a shift in influence from Derrida to Foucault, whose work on power structures was more explicitly political and less textually oriented than Derrida's, while his concern with the outcast and the deviant spoke to the multiculturalists' interest in the oppressed. Foucault's contention that class conflict is only one source of social struggle and that power informs all social relationships through the discourses of gender, sickness, normality, and so on, was appropriated by American feminists and multiculturalists, who argued that gender and race were just as important factors as class in the process of constructing reality and exercising power. A politicized poststructuralist theory thus lent support to American (multi)cultural critics' foregrounding of the tradition of intolerance, oppression, and colonialism in the history of American and other Western democracies.

THE "CULTURE WARS"

Both poststructuralist theory and multiculturalism were heavily contested. Opposition against poststructuralism was particularly active in the discipline of history and the social sciences, where the older positivist and humanist modes of inquiry were strongest. Although by the late 1980s popularized poststructuralist ideas (and jargon) pervaded American academic discourse, the ascendancy of poststructuralism came to an end after the discovery in 1987 that one of the most influential scholars linked with this literary-philosophical movement, Paul de Man, had written for the collaborationist press in Belgium in 1941 and 1942, including at least one anti-Semitic article. De Man, a Belgian émigré and Yale professor who had died four years before the scandal erupted, was a close friend of Derrida's and his scholarly work contributed much to the transmission of poststructuralism in the United States. The affair made headlines in the *New*

York Times and led to a protracted controversy between deconstructionists and their detractors, who used de Man's secret past to discredit poststructuralism as a whole. While de Man's friends and supporters tried to explain his wartime writings as youthful aberrations, to others they served as proof of the dangerously nihilist nature of French theory. The fact that Derrida was strongly influenced by the German philosopher Martin Heidegger, whose Nazi sympathies in the 1930s are well documented, was adduced by critics as a case in point.

It has been argued by Alan B. Spitzer and others that what perhaps most damaged poststructuralism as a movement and deconstruction as an analytical method was not de Man's collaboration but the way the defense was conducted. Eager to establish the truth of the matter, de Man's defenders abandoned the radical skepticism characteristic of poststructuralist thought and practiced a kind of double-talk by applying conventional methods of fact-finding in order to exculpate de Man or at least point to extenuating circumstances. At the same time, Derrida's attempt to use a deconstructive reading of de Man's wartime articles to show how they subverted or even resisted their overt pro-German and anti-Semitic messages gave ammunition to accusations that deconstruction could be used to justify anything. While to antagonists on the Left, the de Man affair (or defense) signaled the politically conservative tendencies in poststructuralist thought, conservatives regarded it as proof that French theory eroded America's most cherished values.

Erosion of traditional values was also the charge leveled against feminism and multiculturalism in Allan Bloom's best-selling book *The Closing of the American Mind* (1987), which was published and widely reviewed at exactly the time the de Man affair made headlines. Young Americans today are morally confused, Bloom argued, because their education provides them with neither knowledge of the past nor a vision of the future. No longer committed to the traditional view of culture defined by the English poet and critic Matthew Arnold in the nineteenth century as "the best that is known and thought in the world" (by which Arnold meant the West), American universities had become "multiversities"; they substituted relativism disguised as tolerance for the universal truths and humane values that, in Bloom's view, were taught by the classics of the Western philosophical and literary tradition and the founding documents of American democracy.

Hardly a topic that would normally gain much public attention outside the academy, the debate about the curriculum suddenly became national news in the fall of 1990 and especially following the publication early in 1991 of Dinesh D'Souza's book *Illiberal Education.* While Bloom held the breakdown of authority in the 1960s accountable for America's "spiritual malaise," D'Souza asserted that multiculturalism had, in effect, established a new kind of authoritarianism that undermined American constitutional liberties and fostered a spirit of intolerance on American campuses. Gender, race, and ethnicity had replaced excellence as criteria for admission, hiring policies, and curriculum decisions; America's cherished tradition of merit-based individualism had made way for the politics of group identity. Two catchphrases, repeated in one headline after another to denote multiculturalism, helped whip the media into a moral panic: "thought police" and "political correctness" (conveniently abbreviated as PC). Both phrases, as the cultural critic and sociologist Todd Gitlin has pointed out, raised the specter of Stalinist orthodoxy. Multiculturalists were accused of turning the university campus—and, by extension, American society—into a totalitarian state by waving the banner of political correctness. To conservatives, multiculturalism became what communism had been before the fall of the Berlin Wall: the enemy, or, even more insidiously, a kind of fifth column, undermining from within the American Republic and the values for which it stood.

The "culture wars" were not fought only within the academic world. For example, multiculturalism also influenced museum exhibition policies, turning the museum into an increasingly politicized arena. The nature of the United States Holocaust Memorial Museum (founded in 1980 and opened in 1993) in Washington, D.C., was the subject of years of intense debate. In January 1995, plans for a Smithsonian Institution exhibit to commemorate the fiftieth anniversary of the dropping of the atomic bomb on Hiroshima had to be abandoned because veterans' groups and their supporters in Congress protested that the planned exhibit was "politically correct" and "unpatriotic" since it emphasized Japanese casualties. In 1989 a planned Corcoran Gallery exhibit of Robert Mapplethorpe's homoerotic photographs suffered a similar fate. Aiming to introduce diversity and create space for alternative points of view, organizers of museum exhibits entered a political minefield, often causing an uproar that alienated conservative visitors and sponsors and endangered the continuation of their programs.

The crusade against multiculturalism (and poststructuralism) obviously was part of the conservative backlash against the 1960s. Bloom and D'Souza, for example, were both closely affiliated with the New Right, receiving financial support from the conservative John M. Olin Foundation and moral support from President George Bush and other Republican politicians who joined the anti-PC bandwagon. The crusade created surprising bedfellows, however. The media campaign against multiculturalism actually started in the *Atlantic* and the *New York Times,* traditionally venues of liberal thought. Redefining multiculturalism as the "new orthodoxy" or even "new McCarthyism," New (and Old) Left intellectuals such as Eugene Genovese and Irving Howe ignored the movement's roots in the 1960s and joined conservatives in their defense of academic freedom and the canon. While clinging to the 1960s' ideal of the United States as a pluralist nation, liberal opponents of the multicultural movement were alarmed by what they saw as the fragmentation of academic disciplines and American society in general along ethnic and racial lines. Whereas conservatives worried about moral corruption, the liberals' chief concern was, in the words of Arthur M. Schlesinger Jr., "the disuniting of America." To a generation of liberal intellectuals like Schlesinger, whose lifetime's work derived its moral imperative from their allegiance to the struggle against racial segregation during the civil rights era, it was deeply disturbing to see how multiculturalism threatened to divide the United States, as Schlesinger put it, into "distinct and immutable ethnic and racial communities, each taught to cherish its own apartness from the rest."

To many of its opponents, multiculturalism came to serve as a convenient label for a mixed bag of perceived ills: affirmative action, curriculum reform, codes for speech and sexual conduct, and even poststructuralist theory. In their efforts to discredit these various policies and theories, the opponents tried to use the excesses and problematic aspects of one against the others. To D'Souza and others who criticized poststructuralism for blurring the lines between good and evil (the de Man affair being cited as a case in point) and for idolizing fragmentation, the link between French critical theory and affirmative action programs was obvious: both undermined clear-cut judgments based on established values and merit and endangered the bonds that held the nation together. Spanish language education for Mexican Americans, the privileges granted to African Americans and other ethnic minorities, and the widespread skepticism among intellectuals about the idea of national unity threatened to bring about the balkanization of the United States.

Conservatives gained important victories in the "culture wars." Affirmative action was abolished in California in 1997. Although even President Bill Clinton owed his reelection in 1996 to a shift toward the political right, implementing changes in the welfare system that had long been on the Republican agenda, the conservative victories were only partial. Because of its highly moralizing postures and stern policy proposals, the religious right that partly fueled the Reagan revolution and put George Bush in office also alienated many Americans. Efforts to redefine affirmative action to make it more acceptable to white men and the growing awareness of the inner-city problems that wreaked havoc in African American communities stalled the attempts to abolish the program completely.

THE CALL FOR A RE-UNITED STATES

Among intellectuals who have sought a way out of the culture wars, the American philosopher Richard Rorty deserves special mention. In the 1980s and 1990s, Rorty argued, in *Achieving Our Country* (1998), that American intellectuals on the Left betrayed the tradition of social reform and political activism represented by Rorty's own maternal grandfather, the social gospel theologian Walter Rauschenbusch, and the educational reformer John Dewey. Disillusioned by the Vietnam War, the Left abandoned its old alliance with the labor unions and withdrew itself into the ivory tower of the academy. The political Left made way for the cultural Left. While crediting the cultural Left with bringing about important changes in attitude in American society, Rorty argued that it failed to address underlying economic problems or offer political alternatives. By making cultural issues central in the public debate, the Left inadvertently collaborated with the Right, whose family-value rhetoric during the Reagan and Bush administrations successfully deflected attention away from economic exploitation and injustice.

To overcome the impasse in which the American Left was mired in the late 1990s, Rorty advocated a kind of synthesis between liberal humanism and poststructuralism on a philosophical level and between the activism of the older, reformist Left represented by Dewey and the insights of the (multi)cultural Left on a political level. Drawing on the tradition of American pragmatism, Rorty argued that a diagnosis of the ills of American society was pointless unless accompanied by an effort to remedy them. What the nation needs, according to Rorty, is a revitalized political Left that, in Emersonian terms, is the party of hope as well as the party of memory. While it is important to remember the failures of American democracy, Rorty suggests, it is even more important to formulate what Gitlin called "common dreams" of a better future.

The United States in the 1980s and 1990s was a nation deeply divided by culture wars, economic disparities, and political conflicts culminating in the impeachment procedures against President Clinton in 1998–1999. The greatest challenge confronting American intellectuals at the beginning of the twenty-first century was perhaps to help define an intermediate space between conflict and consensus, to find a balance between the recognition of diversity and the necessity of common values and ideals.

BIBLIOGRAPHY

The New Conservatism

Dionne, E. J., Jr. *Why Americans Hate Politics.* New York, 1991.

Johnson, Haynes. *Sleepwalking through History: America in the Reagan Years.* New York, 1991.

Murray, Charles. *Losing Ground: American Social Policy, 1950–1980.* New York, 1984.

Wills, Garry. *Reagan's America: Innocents at Home.* Garden City, N.Y., 1997.

Intellectual History and Poststructuralism

Appleby, Joyce, Lynn Hunt, and Margaret Jacob. *Telling the Truth about History.* New York, 1994.

Berkhofer, Robert F., Jr. *Beyond the Great Story: History as Text and Discourse.* Cambridge, Mass., 1995.

Cmiel, Kenneth. "Poststructural Theory." In *Encyclopedia of American Social History.* Vol. 1. Edited by Mary Kupiec Cayton et al. New York, 1993.

Culler, Jonathan D. *On Deconstruction: Theory and Criticism after Structuralism.* Ithaca, N.Y., 1982.

Norris, Christopher. *Deconstruction: Theory and Practice.* Rev. ed. New York, 1991.

Novick, Peter. *That Noble Dream: The "Objectivity Question" and the American Historical Profession.* Cambridge, Mass., 1988.

Spitzer, Alan B. *Historical Truth and Lies about the Past: Reflections on Dewey, Dreyfus, de Man, and Reagan.* Chapel Hill, N.C., 1996.

The Multiculturalism Debate

Bloom, Allan. *The Closing of the American Mind.* New York, 1987.

Boynton, Robert S. "The New Intellectuals." *Atlantic Monthly* (March 1995): 53–70.

D'Souza, Dinesh. *The End of Racism: Principles for a Multiracial Society.* New York, 1995.

——. *Illiberal Education: The Politics of Race and Sex on Campus.* New York, 1991.

Gitlin, Todd. *The Twilight of Common Dreams: Why America Is Wracked by Culture Wars.* New York, 1995.

Gutmann, Amy, ed. *Multiculturalism: Examining the Politics of Recognition.* Princeton, N.J., 1994.

Higham, John. "Multiculturalism and Universalism: A History and Critique." *American Quarterly* 45 (1993): 195–219.

Hollinger, David. *Postethnic America: Beyond Multiculturalism.* New York, 1995.

Hughes, Robert. *The Culture of Complaint: The Fraying of America.* New York, 1993.

Levine, Lawrence. *The Opening of the American Mind: Canons, Culture, and History.* Boston, 1996.

Rorty, Richard. *Achieving Our Country: Leftist Thought in Twentieth-Century America.* Cambridge, Mass., 1998.

Schlesinger, Arthur M., Jr. *The Disuniting of America: Reflections on a Multicultural Society.* New York, 1992.

Thernstrom, Stephan, and Abigail Thernstrom. *America in Black and White: One Nation, Indivisible.* New York, 1997.

RESURGENT CONSERVATISM

John A. Andrew III

The election of Ronald Reagan to the presidency in November 1980 brought conservatives to power in the United States for the first time in decades. Although Democrats still controlled the House, the Republicans held the Senate from 1980 to 1986 as a conservative tide seemingly swept the country. The 1994 congressional elections firmly deposed the postwar liberal hegemony and offered vistas of a conservative future. Reagan conservatives argued that this represented the first conservative mandate since the New Deal. This resurgent conservatism, however, also exposed long-standing fissures in conservative ranks. These fissures ranged from conflicts over definitions of conservatism to conflicting ideological, cultural, and political agendas within a segment of the political spectrum that had rarely exercised power in modern America.

The origins of this conservative resurgence, and its cultural and intellectual foundations as well as its ideological fragmentation, are to be found in the thirty-five-year period between the end of World War II and Reagan's election. Between 1945 and 1960 conservative intellectuals struggled to define a conservative ideology. Then, following the formation of Young Americans for Freedom in 1960, a new group of energetic conservative activists appeared on the American political scene. Reacting against the unwillingness of President Dwight D. Eisenhower and the Republican Party to dismantle the New Deal, these activists determined to provide voters a clear alternative to the reigning liberalism and to elect conservative candidates to public office. The theme of Arizona senator Barry M. Goldwater's 1964 campaign captured their goal: a choice, not an echo. By 1980 these activists, along with more recent recruits to the conservative cause, had embraced Ronald Reagan as a mechanism to advance their cause.

THE ROOTS OF REVIVAL

To understand what drove these individuals, as well as the conservative philosophy they articulated, a review of these earlier decades is critical. During that time several definitions of conservatism emerged. Throughout the 1950s most Americans believed that Eisenhower Republicanism represented conservatism. Conservative intellectuals, however, believed otherwise. Consigned to the fringes of American intellectual and cultural life, they labored to define and articulate their message. By the end of the 1950s, efforts had emerged to fuse these differing definitions into a holistic conservative philosophy. In these struggles lay the bedrock of what later became known as Reagan conservatism and the New Right.

The development of a coherent set of conservative principles faced an uphill struggle. Conservatism lacked any intellectual relevance to the concerns of most Americans, while the Great Depression and the New Deal had discredited conservative philosophies of the 1920s. In addition, following the struggles against totalitarianism and fascism, and in the face of new challenges from communism, Americans remained suspicious of any movements that were not centrist. As the historian Arthur Schlesinger Jr. warned in 1949, the real core of American ideals were to be found at "the vital center," not on the extremes.

Three Strains of Conservatism Nonetheless, conservative intellectuals developed two models of the ideal society, models that often proved fundamentally irreconcilable. One group drew on the work of Richard Weaver, whose 1948 book, *Ideas Have Consequences,* argued that certain transcendent values defined Western culture. Weaver complained that an orgy of relativism had led Americans to forget the fundamental concepts of original sin and the value of private property. Americans needed to embrace God, to buttress the moral and religious foundations of society upon which their great traditions rested. Joining Weaver were classical political philosophers like Leo Strauss, who emphasized the importance of natural law, and philosopher-historian Russell Kirk, whose book *The Conservative Mind* (1953) proved essential reading for an emerging generation of conservative youth. Together, these traditionalists stressed tradition, order, religion, community, and an organic model of society modeled on the ideas of the British political philosopher Edmund Burke. In such a society all individuals not only shared a common tradition; they were bound to each other by moral and institutional bonds. Traditionalists believed that moral permissiveness and narrow self-interest were the legacy of the modern world, a legacy they emphatically rejected.

The second model was a libertarian one. Led by men like the Austrian economist Friedrich von Hayek (whose 1944 book, *The Road to Serfdom,* excoriated the New Deal and national economic planning) and Frank Chodorov (who founded the Intercollegiate Society of Individualists in 1953), libertarians emphasized the free market and the importance of individualism. Freedom rather than order was their first priority. In economics, this group resolutely opposed the ideas of the British economist John Maynard Keynes and feared a rampant statism that, in the name of the common good, stripped individuals of their economic and intellectual freedom. The New Deal, with its emphasis on planning, labor rights, and progressive taxation, epitomized to them the dangers of state power. They insisted that such statist coercion eroded individualism, and in the process curtailed freedom, especially economic freedom. For libertarians, society was a collection of individuals rather than an interconnected, organic whole. Individuals, they believed, had the capacity for self-control and did not need coercive ordering mechanisms. Operating as free persons, their individual actions would collectively advance the good of society. Although not narrowly economic in emphasis, libertarianism nonetheless insisted that entrepreneurial capitalism and individual freedom were the bedrock of society. This focus highlighted the fundamental difference (and conflict) between libertarians and traditionalists, since the latter worried about an uncontrolled individualism exerting centrifugal forces on society that would destroy its organic whole.

A third strain of conservatism also emerged in the postwar years: anticommunism. What distinguished anticommunism from traditionalism and libertarianism was not so much its ideological underpinnings but its focus and priorities. Although liberals as well as conservatives embraced anticommunism, conservatives made it a crusade central to the operation of intellectual as well as public life. This postwar conservative anticommunism attracted men like James Burnham, Frank Meyer, and Whittaker Chambers. As former communists, these individuals became true witnesses, men who had seen the light and publicly recanted their previous ideological convictions. Because they had seen the lion in its den, they believed they understood better than most the dangers posed by communism to democratic societies. After 1955 many of these individuals joined William F. Buckley Jr. on *National Review,* a journal that was the voice of conservatism during its years in the political wilderness. Chambers's memoir, *Witness* (1952), became an ideological Bible to Buckley and his followers.

All types of conservatives shared at least one common bond: their opposition to liberalism. Buckley's strident attack on liberalism in his 1959 book, *Up from Liberalism,* typified their concern. Buckley argued that the United States had sacrificed its principles for flexibility, rendering the country vulnerable to opportunistic ideas. Liberals, he lamented, believed in human perfectability and relied on reason as the mechanism for social progress. That led them to embrace state power to promote equality and eradicate social and individual differences. Despite cold war liberalism's embrace of anticommunism, conservatives feared that this innate optimism left liberals unable to fully appreciate the dangers of communism. They were too willing to promote compromise and coexistence.

Fusionism   By the early 1960s, some conservatives, led by Frank Meyer, attempted to unite traditionalists, libertarians, and anticommunists under one banner. Best known as fusionism, it sought to synthesize conservative principles around individual freedom and anticommunism. Meyer's 1964 anthology *What Is Conservatism?* included both traditionalists and libertarians between its covers. Meyer insisted that what they held in common—belief in an objective moral order, an emphasis on human freedom, an opposition to state power—was far more important than their differences. This effort at synthesis was important, and ultimately successful. Although leading conservative thinkers like Richard Weaver, Willmoore Kendall, Russell Kirk, and L. Brent Bozell held firm to their fears of too much individual freedom, William F. Buckley Jr. and William Rusher used *National Review* to keep the camps together, in part through their common bond of anticommunism.

In addition, fusionists agreed that the decay of free market capitalism and individual freedom stemmed in large part from the decline of a religious belief in the centrality of God and a conviction that absolute truths existed. Grounded as it was in religious truths, fusionism excluded some conservatives, like Ayn Rand. Rand's best-selling novels *Atlas Shrugged* (1957) and *The Fountainhead* (1943) trumpeted the virtues of capitalism but substituted the almighty dollar for God as the object of worship. For this reason, Meyer, Buckley, and other conservative intellectuals despised Rand and her group of "objectivists." There had to be, Meyer insisted, an "immutable moral order" that fostered common values. This combination of antistatism and a belief in human freedom led conservatives in the late 1950s to defend southern resistance to integration. In the short term, that position put conservatives on the "wrong side" of history and perpetuated their marginalization.

Fusionism also revealed something else important about this new postwar conservatism: its underlying activist impulse. As Paul Gottfried and Thomas Fleming observed in *The Conservative Movement* (1988), Meyer and the fusionists defined that conservatism as a political force of "economic libertarianism, cultural traditionalism, local government, and militant anticommunism." This inevitably led to activism, and conservatives sought to effect a revolution in public policy and to reorient politics along a liberal-conservative rather than a Democratic-Republican axis. Meyer became vice chair of the New York Conservative Party, Buckley ran for mayor of New York City in 1961, and most of the writers at *National Review* became involved in political campaigns. The journal brought to bear on the issues of the day the overriding tenets of this new conservative philosophy and called for active participation in politics. The future mattered, they insisted, and only by abandoning pure philosophizing and injecting themselves into the political fray could conservatives hope to shape that future. By 1960 this seemed at best a long shot. But in the next four years a major change occurred, a change that served as a transition from the philosophizing of the 1950s to the political success of the 1980s.

FROM PHILOSOPHY TO POLITICAL PROGRAM

During the 1960s three developments emerged to transform conservatism from a philosophical framework to a political program, from a philosophy of conservatism into a philosophy of government. The first two followed the failure of conservatives to nominate one of their own as a running mate for Richard Nixon at the 1960 Republican National Convention in Chicago. Determined to take back the Republican Party from Eisenhower's "modern Republicanism" (which they considered far too accepting of the New Deal), men like Buckley, Rusher, and Marvin Liebman threw in their lot with a boisterous group of young conservatives to nominate the Arizona senator Barry Goldwater for vice president. They failed, but postconvention caucusing led to a conservative summit that September at Great Elm, the Buckley family estate in Sharon, Connecticut. More than one hundred men and women met at Sharon, drawn together by an apocalyptic vision that the United States stood at a crossroads between liberalism-socialism and conservatism. They formed Young Americans for Freedom, a conservative activist organization, and fashioned the Sharon Statement, a brief but forceful synthesis of essential conservative beliefs. Seeking power, they intended the Sharon Statement as a vehicle for electing conservatives to public office. It was a credo that spoke to fundamental principles rather than specific issues, and would guide the conservative political cause into the 1980s and beyond.

The second development stemmed directly from the efforts at Sharon. Soon after, activists began a campaign to make Barry Goldwater the 1964 Republican nominee. Richard Nixon's defeat at the hands of John F. Kennedy in the November 1960 elections cleared the way for a conservative capture of the Republican Party. Although Goldwater was often an unwilling vehicle for their cause and despite his crushing defeat by Lyndon Johnson in the 1964 elections, the campaign proved a significant turning point for conservatives. As the historian Charles Kesler has argued: "Convictions about the nature of man and the unchanging content of justice . . . deserve to be embodied in the aims and structure of a political party, which functions not only to win elections but to form citizens by educating their opinions" (Buckley and Kesler, *Keeping the Tablets*, p. 17).

Using the national stage to promote their credo, conservative activists raised millions of dollars in an

Young Americans for Freedom Picketing. St. Louis, February 1968. The group protested IBM's trade with Communist countries in Eastern Europe. © BETTMANN/CORBIS

unprecedented grassroots campaign that attracted more than 27 million voters to the 1964 Goldwater campaign. That fund-raising experience provided the groundwork for the future growth of conservativism. Led by Richard Viguerie, the Right developed lengthy mailing lists of true believers ready to contribute to conservative causes. When combined with a new cadre of political activists, these lists provided a mechanism to communicate conservative ideologies. Their revolutionary potential undergirded a forthcoming conservative resurgence. This was the first real stirring of political power on the Right. Perhaps even more significant in the long run, as several historians have noted, the Goldwater campaign shifted the focus of conservatism from a dedication to underlying truths to a concern for winning elections. In the short term, however, Goldwater's defeat appeared to confirm that conservatism was a cause primarily restricted to cranks and extremists.

The third development—the political, social, and cultural movements of the 1960s—changed all that. The Great Society, Black Power, affirmative action, anti–Vietnam War protests, and urban riots, together with other social, political, and cultural challenges, changed the nature of American liberalism and reshaped the ideological and political landscape. Many moderates, and some liberals, found themselves not only opposed to many of

these changes but also under attack from proponents of change. As the consensus frayed, many of them found refuge in conservative ranks. Although they did not really embrace the entire credo outlined in the Sharon Statement, they did share a dedication to traditional values once shared by liberals and conservatives, and a commitment to anti-communism. Their alienation from the course of late-1960s liberalism led these individuals into what became known as neoconservatism.

NEOCONSERVATISM

Although not all that numerous, neoconservatives proved important to the conservative resurgence for several reasons. Many were lifelong intellectuals and able to articulate ideas with great clarity. In addition, because most of them had been liberals throughout the postwar years, they brought a sense of credibility to the conservative cause that groups like the John Birch Society had not. They were not extremists; indeed, they abhorred extremism. They emphasized what was good about the United States, reasserting a sense of nationalism and exceptionalism that 1960s critics had ruthlessly attacked. While admitting that American society had its flaws, they insisted that it was basically good and certainly superior to that of most other countries. In short, they

THE SHARON STATEMENT

Adopted by the Young Americans for Freedom in conference at Sharon, Conn., 9–11 September 1960

In this time of moral and political crisis, it is the responsibility of the youth of America to affirm certain eternal truths.

We, as young conservatives, believe:

That foremost among the transcendent values is the individual's use of his God-given free will, whence derives his right to be free from the restrictions of arbitrary force;

That liberty is indivisible, and that political freedom cannot long exist without economic freedom;

That the purposes of government are to protect these freedoms through the preservation of internal order, the provision of national defense, and the administration of justice;

That when government ventures beyond these rightful functions, it accumulates power which tends to diminish order and liberty;

That the Constitution of the United States is the best arrangement yet devised for empowering government to fulfill its proper role, while restraining it from the concentration and abuse of power;

That the genius of the Constitution—the division of powers—is summed up in the clause which reserves primacy to the several states, or to the people, in those spheres not specifically delegated to the Federal Government;

That the market economy, allocating resources by the free play of supply and demand, is the single economic system compatible with the requirements of personal freedom and constitutional government, and that it is at the same time the most productive supplier of human needs;

That when government interferes with the work of the market economy, it tends to reduce the moral and physical strength of the nation; that when it takes from one man to bestow on another, it diminishes the incentive of the first, the integrity of the second, and the moral autonomy of both;

That we will be free only so long as the national sovereignty of the United States is secure: that history shows periods of freedom are rare, and can exist only when free citizens concertedly defend their rights against all enemies;

That the forces of international Communism are, at present, the greatest single threat to these liberties;

That the United States should stress victory over, rather than coexistence with, this menace; and

That American foreign policy must be judged by this criterion: does it serve the just interests of the United States?

Source: Andrew, pp. 221–222.

---

attacked the notion of "Amerika" propagated by the radical critique of American history and society.

The advent of neoconservatives made conservatism appear more moderate than in the past. They combined a cultural traditionalism with political moderation. What set them apart from traditionalists, libertarians, and even fusionists was their belief that the essential efforts of the New Deal were not only good but worth saving. They were, in short, modernists. They studied economics, law,

Milton Friedman. Widely regarded as one of the most significant libertarians of the last century, Friedman was awarded the Nobel Prize for economics in 1976. His writings advocate the extension of individual freedom. © ROGER RESSMEYER/CORBIS

During the 1970s neoconservatives became agitated about the nation's political course. To men and women like Jeane Kirkpatrick, Richard Perle, William Bennett, William Kristol, Norman Podhoretz, and Gertrude Himmelfarb, President Jimmy Carter epitomized what was wrong with the United States. He was, they believed, weak, vacillating, pessimistic about the country's future, and unwilling to use American power abroad. The Iranian hostage crisis, the oil crisis, and a persistent Vietnam syndrome of defeatism and retreat in foreign policy, together with the cultural changes initiated in the 1960s, led neoconservatives and paleoconservatives to make common cause. They opposed what they labeled a "culture of appeasement" and formed organizations such as the Committee for the Free World and the Committee on the Present Danger to challenge the human rights policies of the Carter administration. As the historian Gary Dorrien noted, their conservatism was "activist, interventionist, and stridently ideological," asserting that the United States had a "proprietary right" to "pursue its interests unilaterally in the world" (*The Neoconservative Mind*, p. 122).

THE NEW RIGHT

By the late 1970s, the neoconservatives were part of an emerging New Right. The New Right was an umbrella term rather than a specific philosophical strain of conservatism. It emphasized social, cultural, and moral questions as much as it did economic issues and big government. The New Right rested on an essentially traditionalist base and courted social and cultural conservatives among Democrats as well as Republicans. In many respects the New Right was as much a movement of political opportunism as one of political philosophy. While it opposed what it considered the oppressive interference of government in individuals' lives such as civil rights legislation and affirmative action, for example, it endorsed government support for school prayer and legislation against pornography. Perhaps its most significant characteristic was its search for power. This found clear expression in former treasury secretary William E. Simon's *A Time for Truth* (1978), which urged the formation of a new set of conservative institutions. An array of divergent groups now coalesced under the banner of the New Right. These included Paul Weyrich's Committee for the Survival of a Free Congress, former YAFer Howard Phillips's Conservative Caucus, and John Dolan's National Conservative Political Action Committee. As the

and political science and did not always share the religious and humanistic ideals of Richard Weaver or William F. Buckley Jr. Their defection from 1960s liberalism changed the conservative movement and contributed to its resurgence. The Old Right now became known as paleoconservatives, indicating a rejection of modernity and the existing social order. Despite the broadening of the conservative cause to embrace neoconservatives as well as paleoconservatives, the two groups rarely saw eye to eye and had little in common aside from their anticommunism and distaste for "new class" liberals (although many of them were new class professionals themselves). New class liberals, as seen by conservatives, were college-educated professionals interested in law, education, and the media and often disdainful of business careers and material values. Concerned with quality of life and personal freedom, they embraced social and cultural change and looked to the government to advance both.

historian Jerome Himmelstein has observed, what they held in common was a conceptualization of "freedom and individualism largely in terms of the right to pursue one's interests in a market context unhampered by external interferences" (Liebman and Wuthnow, *The New Christian Right*, p. 16).

Among the most important additions to the New Right cause was the mobilization of a New Christian Right. Led by televangelists such as Jerry Falwell and Pat Robertson, the New Christian Right attacked secular humanism and liberal Christianity. In their eyes, both fostered the evils of moral relativism and excessive permissiveness. Falwell and Robertson, together with groups like the Moral Majority and the Religious Roundtable, focused on the need for a more public profession of religion and religious values and traditional family life, while attacking pornography, abortion, homosexuality, and "welfare socialism." This concern with ethical and religious issues mobilized conservative evangelical Protestants and led them into the political arena. They were joined by new groups like Gary Bauer's Family Research Council and Robertson's Christian Coalition, directed by Ralph Reed.

In 1980 these groups united to back Ronald Reagan for the presidency. Through the issues they raised in that campaign, and throughout the 1980s and 1990s, they were attempting to join conservative philosophies to political issues. Ever since the formation of Young Americans for Freedom in 1960, conservatives had sought power. Now they had achieved it, and they meant to use it. Their list of issues and goals was lengthy and often was focused on reversing changes wrought by 1960s activists: opposition to abortion and support for prayer in the public schools in order to reverse earlier U.S. Supreme Court decisions; promotion of family values to reverse perceived social dislocation; opposition to affirmative action and what they considered other "special rights" legislation of the Great Society; support for an end to welfare dependency and virtually all forms of state intervention that helped the weak and powerless; opposition to an Equal Rights Amendment; and, most important throughout the 1980s, backing for a revival of a strong anticommunism in an effort to win the cold war.

DIVISIONS

While the 1980 election brought conservatives to power, the Reagan administration did not satisfy all conservatives. Reagan often paid lip service to conservatives' cultural, moral, and religious issues, but he appointed mostly neoconservatives to administrative positions. Determined to revive American prestige in the world and to attack economic problems and curb inflation, neoconservatives supported many aspects of the welfare state and most were not terribly interested in moral or religious issues. These emphases diverged significantly from the agendas of paleoconservatives and the Christian Right. The problem for conservatives in the 1980s and 1990s was how to keep their coalition together. Neoconservatives (predominantly Jewish), Catholics of the Old Right (from Buckley to Patrick Buchanan), various conservative intellectuals (including libertarians), blue-collar social conservatives (often Democrats), and religious conservatives had found common cause in their opposition to Great Society liberalism. They reached out to moderates in both parties and blue-collar Democrats (the so-called Reagan Democrats) who disapproved of affirmative action and opposition to the war in Vietnam, and were fed up with criticism of the United States. Their problem was not only to articulate a coherent philosophy, but to transform their often conflicting ideologies into a philosophy of government. During the 1980s, moreover, intellectual debate gave way to policy arguments among conservatives. As paleoconservatives of the Old Right like Buchanan and fundamentalist Christian conservatives gained ascendancy in the Republican Party, neoconservatives found themselves on the fringes of the movement. In the 1990s, as the Democratic Party moved firmly to the right, many neoconservatives returned to their original home within its ranks.

During the 1980s and 1990s these groups often focused on separate issues and went in different directions. Paramount in the 1980s was a revitalized anticommunism, marked by unprecedented defense spending and a commitment to win the cold war, together with the emergence of new economic theories to attack Keynesianism. Supply-side economics, with an emphasis on individual rather than governmental decision making, was popularized through the writings of George Gilder (*Wealth and Poverty*, 1981) and Jude Wanninski of the *Wall Street Journal* (*The Way the World Works*, 1978). They argued that a massive reduction in taxation would free up individual initiative and promote economic growth. This idea fit well with both traditionalist and libertarian philosophies, and reflected their intent to liberate Americans from bureaucracies and regulations.

CULTURAL CONSERVATISM

By the 1990s, as the cold war ended and inflation cooled, moral and cultural issues came to the fore. Grateful that Ronald Reagan had helped them achieve power, but enormously disappointed with George Bush's failure to endorse their efforts to legislate morality, conservatives sought to capture (or recapture) the Republican Party. They complained that conservatism lacked direction. Long in opposition both to liberalism and liberals in power, conservatives found the transition from an opposition philosophy to a governing philosophy difficult. While Paul Weyrich of the New Right insisted that "value-related" issues appealed to ordinary Americans who sought to take charge of their lives and preserve local control, a new phalanx of tax-exempt conservative think tanks, such as the Heritage Foundation, the Pew Trust, and the John M. Olin Foundation, and wealthy conservatives like Richard Scaife (of the Mellon family) and brewing magnate Joseph Coors, gave cultural conservatives intellectual and financial resources to promote their ideological and philosophical convictions.

Among the most public and outspoken of the cultural conservatives was William Bennett. Bennett insisted that cultural and moral decay threatened basic American values. Arguing that "American conservatism now sets the terms of our national debate" (*Our Children and Our Country*, p. 227), he spearheaded an effort to translate conservative philosophy into cultural change. A former secretary of education, he decried the "assault on intellectual and moral standards" as well as the "dumbing-down" of curricula. Education, he insisted, should impart "ethical standards and moral principles." Bennett penned a series of morality tales, *The Book of Virtues* (1993), that sought to unite moral principles and social policy. Allan Bloom's best-seller, *The Closing of the American Mind* (1987), agreed that a society's moral and spiritual core lay in its traditions. Those traditions, Bloom argued, had withered under a series of attacks, beginning in the 1960s, that had seriously damaged American cultural and intellectual life. Like Leo Strauss, Bloom blamed modernism for eroding traditional values.

Despite the popularity of Bloom's book, Bennett's contribution to the conservative cause was larger: it pulled together disparate developments to fashion a coherent interpretation of recent American history. Between 1960 and 1990, he observed, there was a 500 percent increase in violent crime, a more than 400 percent increase in illegitimate births, and a tripling of the percentage of children living in single-parent homes and of the teenage suicide rate. The divorce rate doubled, and SAT scores fell precipitously. These were not isolated events, he concluded, but a collection of "modern-day social pathologies" that heavy government spending had failed to alleviate. This "substantial social regression" had led to "social decomposition," and the human costs were high. He warned of an apocalypse: unless those "social pathologies are reversed, they will lead to the decline and perhaps even to the fall of the American republic" (*The Index of Leading Cultural Indicators*, p. 8). Because Bennett held several administrative positions during the 1980s, and because he was outspoken in his views, he perhaps best articulated the two core conservative beliefs: in an objective moral order and an unchanging human nature.

NEW TRIUMPH, NEW DIVISIONS

Conservatives' fortunes seemingly peaked in 1994 when they swept the off-year elections and captured control of Congress. Conservative author David Brooks insisted that the "vote reminded us that elections are not just political turning points; they are also cultural events. In November 1994 the conservative movement left the Sinai and completed its exodus into Jerusalem. . . . But the more important transformation is psychological. . . . Liberalism is no longer the mother planet" (*Backward and Upward*, p. vx). Wielding power was much different from seeking power, however, and conservatives continued to struggle over priorities. Divisions among cultural, political, and religious conservatives often proved more powerful than their commonalities. In the 1990s conservative divisions persisted, this time between libertarians and moralists. The philosophical truths of the Sharon Statement remained a framework for agreement on broad principles, but conflicting specific agendas reminded conservatives that the devil was in the details.

See also **Conservatism** (*in this volume*); **Political Economy; Government** (*volume 3*); *and other articles in this section.*

BIBLIOGRAPHY

Andrew, John A., III. *The Other Side of the Sixties: Young Americans for Freedom and the Rise of Conservative Politics.* New Brunswick, N.J., 1997.

Bennett, William. *The Book of Virtues.* New York, 1993.

——. *The Index of Leading Cultural Indicators.* New York, 1994.

——. *Our Children and Our Country: Improving America's Schools and Affirming the Common Culture.* New York, 1988.

Berman, William. *America's Right Turn: From Nixon to Bush.* Baltimore, 1994.

Blumenthal, Sidney. *The Rise of the Counter-Establishment: From Conservative Ideology to Political Power.* New York, 1986.

Brinkley, Alan. "The Problem of American Conservatism." *American Historical Review* 99, no. 2 (1994): 409–429.

Brooks, David, ed. *Backward and Upward: The New Conservative Writing.* New York, 1996.

Buckley, William F., and Charles R. Kesler, eds. *Keeping the Tablets: Modern American Conservative Thought.* New York, 1988.

Dorrien, Gary. *The Neoconservative Mind: Politics, Culture, and the War of Ideology.* Philadelphia, 1993.

Gottfried, Paul, and Thomas Fleming. *The Conservative Movement.* Boston, 1988.

Himmelstein, Jerome L. *To the Right: The Transformation of American Conservatism.* Berkeley, 1990.

Hixson, William B., Jr. *Search for the American Right Wing: The Analysis of the Social Science Record, 1955–1987.* Princeton, N.J., 1992.

Hodgson, Godfrey. *The World Turned Right Side Up: A History of the Conservative Ascendancy in America.* Boston, 1996.

Hoeveler, J. David, Jr. *Watch on the Right: Conservative Intellectuals in the Reagan Era.* Madison, Wisc., 1991.

Liebman, Robert C., and Robert Wuthnow, eds. *The New Christian Right: Mobilization and Legitimation.* New York, 1983.

Murray, Charles. *Losing Ground: American Social Policy, 1950–1980.* New York, 1984.

Nash, George H. *The Conservative Intellectual Movement in America since 1945.* New York, 1976.

Peele, Gillian. *Revival and Reaction: The Right in Contemporary America.* Oxford, 1984.

Rusher, William. *The Rise of the Right.* New York, 1984.

Stefancic, Jean, and Richard Delgado. *No Mercy: How Conservative Think Tanks and Foundations Changed America's Social Agenda.* Philadelphia, 1996.

Steinfels, Peter. *The Neoconservatives: The Men Who Are Changing America's Politics.* New York, 1979.

POSTSTRUCTURALISM AND POSTMODERNISM

William Pencak

The year 1968 was a significant year. It marked a turning point in history and consciousness that is recognized by both scholars and laypeople alike. The emergent New Left was defeated in the streets of Paris and New York; conservatism triumphed at the polls with the elections of the French president Charles de Gaulle and the American president Richard M. Nixon. The Soviet Union's suppression of the liberalizing regime of Alexander Dubček in Czechoslovakia finished off Communism for the Left as a viable alternative to a tarnished American capitalism that was fighting the Vietnam War and about to plunge into recession. Neither of the two competing world systems could plausibly justify its existence except through sheer power or by providing the good life for limited numbers of people. Many intellectuals believed that the world prophesied by the Irish poet William Butler Yeats in his "The Second Coming" (1921) had come to pass: "Things fall apart; the centre cannot hold. . . . the best lack all conviction, while the worst are filled with passionate intensity."

Yeats's rough beast slouching "towards Bethlehem to be born" was poststructuralism/postmodernism. Modernity had mirrored a confident Western world that insisted the world made by the great white men and nations—whether destined to terminate in the communist, capitalist, or mixed economy dream of heaven—the world of technical progress, material comfort, and popular enlightenment, applied to humanity as a whole rather than a segment thereof.

Postmodernism and poststructuralism are so closely linked that it is futile to try and separate them. Until the 1960s, structuralism, the dominant school of anthropology, reflected the claims of modernity. It maintained that societies were coherent entities whose institutions and symbols served functional purposes and provided stability. The most prominent structuralist, the French anthropologist Claude Lévi-Strauss, could thereby rationalize the customs of South American Indians, and the American cultural anthropologist Clifford Geertz memorably analyzed the role of the cockfight in Bali. But for modern societies, structuralism's ideological upshot was to minimize flaws and deviance, showing that these too were necessary to the stability of the system. Such ideas rang hollow in the late 1960s. For example, two major historical works—published by Seymour Mandelbaum in 1965 and Alexander Callow in 1966—justified the urban achievement of New York's notorious nineteenth-century "Boss" Tweed while America's cities raged out of control. Mario Puzo's novel *The Godfather* (1969) became a popular icon and an Academy Award–winning film. Meanwhile, politically protected organized crime increasingly impoverished minorities and the young while poisoning them with illegal drugs.

Isolated geniuses such as William Butler Yeats, Friedrich Nietzsche, Herman Melville, and Charles Sanders Peirce had long since pointed out that people could only pay homage to the emperor of modernity if they ignored the fact that he was clothed in bogus ideologies. However, the "post" alternative only came into its own after the climactic spring of 1968. It has flourished ever since in a never-ending series of variations on a theme articulated by Jean-François Lyotard in *The Postmodern Condition* (1984) as "incredulity toward metanarratives."

Intellectually speaking, postmodernism is the equivalent of the transglobal movement of economic capital. It makes no sense to differentiate between "American" or "European" postmodernism when the Italian literary critic Umberto Eco is as likely to be seen in Berkeley or Toronto as in Bologna; when the non-American philosophers Michel Foucault, Michel de Certeau, Vyacheslav Ivanov, and Jacques Derrida have all taught at the University of California; when the international journal *Semiotica* is also published at Indiana University and edited by the Hungarian-born Thomas A. Sebeok; and when the Bulgarian-born French psychoanalyst Julia Kristeva and the Indian literary

Charles Sanders Peirce (1839–1914). The young Peirce was a well-to-do gentleman who had career prospects before him as a scientist and philosopher. © BETTMANN/ CORBIS

theorist Gayatri Chakravorty Spivak teach at Columbia University. For all his or her skepticism toward the established order, the postmodern thinker is usually linked to a corporation (a university or institute), flies from one conference to another to consult with other scholarly entrepreneurs, and relies upon an international community to buy his or her products. David Lodge's novel *Small World* (1984) is a delightful commentary on postmodern academic life, a postmodern classic of its own. The novel exposes the ironies and pretensions of postmodern entrepreneurial scholarship.

Postmodern thinkers are aware of their ironic place in the new world order. In 1964, the German political philosopher Herbert Marcuse was the first to call attention to the way "radical" speech, protected and rewarded in universities, enabled "free" societies to render dissent inconsequential by separating intellectuals from the working-class constituencies likely to be receptive to their ideas. As privileged thinkers who majored in criticism and at best minored in protest, postmodernists reinforced the very structures their theory claimed to subvert. They would not have considered this an inconsis-

tency, but rather a symptom of the paradoxical structure of existence that must be sustained by inquiry to reflect accurately the world they purported to describe. Thus, this essay selectively examines some leading figures of postmodernism and poststructuralism and presents how their much-derided vocabulary—"deconstruction," "semiotics," "hyperreality," "simulacra," and "discourses," to list a few words—is useful for understanding the twentieth century's strange new world and the "texts" (artifacts, computer information, institutional structures, as well as books) it generated.

ROLAND BARTHES AND THE DEATH OF THE AUTHOR

Roland Barthes, the French essayist and social literary critic, wrote widely on semiotics, the formal study of symbols and signs. He began as a structuralist, helping to establish structuralism as an intellectual movement. Of his many works in the genre, his analysis of professional wrestling in his *Mythologies* (English translation, 1972) is perhaps the most famous. However, in 1967 he proclaimed "the death of the author," which means that any text cannot be interpreted according to the "intentionality" of the person who wrote it. Instead, its meaning changes according to the different interpretations individuals choose to give it, although for practical purposes "audiences" may be "constructed" which regard a text in a similar manner. Barthes went on to explore the "zero sign," or "writing degree zero," the empty space that lies at the heart of any text. But instead of mourning this lack of certainty, Barthes professed, readers should celebrate the fecundity and mystery at the core of a text, or of existence itself. Human freedom arises because people are privileged to interpret and then interpret their interpretations themselves in a never-ending dance of thought.

One of Barthes's most insightful and yet neglected writings, "Of African Grammar" (included in *S/Z*, 1974), argues cogently that writers ought not to be too clear in their writing, depriving their readers of the need to wrestle with the ambiguity and agony inherent in writing and in the world. Official rhetoric, like the words Richard Nixon used, attempts to make everything "perfectly clear" and to lay down the law. Such is the "fascist" language that would foreclose interpretation, according to Barthes. As such, it becomes necessary to steal or regenerate language—to seduce, cruise, stagger, torment, and enchant—to overcome the coercive

CHARLES SANDERS PEIRCE: PIONEER OF SEMIOTICS, FORERUNNER OF POSTMODERNISM

When they read postmodernists, students of the American philosopher Charles Sanders Peirce find themselves, like the professional baseball player and coach Yogi Berra, experiencing "déjà vu all over again." Now regarded by most scholars as the most original thinker of his time, Peirce spent the last twenty-seven years of his life in poverty and neglect in Milford, Pennsylvania, as leading universities eagerly hired philosophers who oversimplified his idea of "pragmatism" (William James, John Dewey, Josiah Royce) and never explored what he meant by "semiotics." A contemporary of the German philosopher Friedrich Nietzsche, Peirce worked out systematically what the German had expressed in brilliant aphorisms: that no intellectual certainty is possible and, therefore, that the philosophers, rulers, and scientists of the nineteenth-century West who claimed to direct the best of all possible worlds had built upon quicksand. Peirce argued that since thinking is parallel with the human adventure, certainty can only be achieved provisionally by communities of inquirers who agree to follow agreed-upon methods of inquiry. Anticipating Thomas S. Kuhn's theory of paradigms in *The Structure of Scientific Revolutions* (1962) and Michel Foucault's *epistémès,* or discourses, Peirce argued that, far from being continuous, ideas and society did not so much evolve as change radically from time to time through gigantic reactions against paradigms of thought that had ceased to describe experience.

According to Peirce, human freedom is possible since people are faced with overlapping worldviews (in times of crisis more than most). Human beings construct reality "semiotically": they select, partly by choice and partly out of necessity, signs to which they will attend from the universe to create a world for themselves that "pragmatically" works. Dying three months before the First World War broke out, Peirce prophesied the coming end of modernism: "The twentieth century in its latter half shall surely see the deluge tempest burst upon the social order—to clean up a world as deep in ruin as that greed-philosophy has long plunged it into guilt" (*Collected Papers of Charles Peirce,* vol. 6, p. 144–196).

Peircean-based semiotics is one of the two leading schools of semiotic thought in the late twentieth century, the other being derived from the French structuralists A. J. Greimas and Ferdinand de Saussure, who emphasized regular patterns of sign structure rather than the constant alterability Peirce stressed.

power of official discourse. As examples of language that ought to be subverted, Barthes stressed that words such as "tribes" or "terrorism" are used to stigmatize people without power, while words like "nations" and "police actions" signify comparable actions by the powerful.

MICHEL FOUCAULT AND THE GREAT CONFINEMENT

Likewise, Michel Foucault has sometimes been called a structuralist, for he stressed the omnipres-

ence and near omnipotence of the overlapping institutions that confine humankind in the modern world. Foucault began studying psychology in French insane asylums in the 1940s and was deeply disturbed by the way normality was equated with passive conforming. In his works, Foucault professed that the institutions that modernists historically considered beneficial—schools, prisons that reform rather than merely punish, mental institutions, and democratic government—are better understood as more insidious forms of controlling people. What historians usually called the Enlightenment is better understood as "the Great Confinement" according to Foucault. In the premodern world, physical coercion kept the masses in line: now, with the false belief that they rule themselves and live in a benign society, the tyranny that controls them is internalized. It is no longer necessary to torture criminals; people can be educated to assent psychologically to the institutional order that shapes their lives while providing the illusion of freedom. Whereas once power ruled overtly with the iron fist, now "capillaries" and "microtyrannies" insinuate themselves with the velvet glove of miseducation.

But Foucault argued that people are not necessarily trapped, which is why historians cannot really label him a structuralist. There are gaps, "spaces," between institutions where power does not reach. Here, Foucault argued, lies the possibility for freedom in the form of "heterotopia"—alternative ways of life that are mutually tolerant—which he distinguished from "utopia," which would only inflict new and more all-encompassing laws. Some scholars profess that the homosexual Foucault, unable to express himself in the rigid French academy, found such a heterotopia in the gay community of San Francisco, which led to his death from AIDS. His key contention is that freedom and creativity emerge through resistance against, rather than by means of, what he called "the great historico-transcendental destiny of the Occident" (*The Archaeology of Knowledge*, p. 209). He praised the "life of unreason" that "no longer manifests itself except in the lightning-flash of words such as those of Hölderlin, of Nerval, of Nietzsche, or of Artaud . . . resisting by their own strength that gigantic moral imprisonment which we are in the habit of calling . . . the liberation of the insane" (*Madness and Civilization*, p. 278).

Foucault is the postmodernist thinker most virulently attacked or defended by historians. Besides denying the peculiar virtue of Western civilization, he insisted traditional historians were embarked on an impossible quest in their desire to show causes and consequences. That historians will never definitively decide what caused World War I, or whether Napoleon's domestic policy was good for France, for instance, only reveals personal or "political" judgments as to how events are explained. Historians can only legitimately map the *epistémès*, or "discourses," of different eras and show how they either legitimate or provide resistance to the powers that be. The great American historian Carl Becker, who in many ways wrote postmodern history fifty years before its time, explained:

Michel Foucault (1926–1984). One of the most familiar of postmodern and gay icons. Many younger intellectuals have imitated his bald head and (usually) black wardrobe. © BETTMANN/CORBIS

If we would discover the little backstairs door that for any age serves as the secret entranceway to knowledge, we will do well to look for certain unobtrusive words with uncertain meanings that are permitted to slip off the tongue without fear and without research; words which, having from constant repetition lost their metaphorical significance, are unconsciously mistaken for objective realities. In the thirteenth century the key words would no doubt be God, sin, grace, salvation, heaven, and the like; in the nineteenth century, matter, fact, matter-of-fact, evolution, progress; in the twentieth century, relativity, process, adjustment, function, complex. In the eighteenth century the words without which no enlightened person could reach a restful conclusion were nature, natural law, first causes, reason, sentiment, humanity, perfectibility. (*The Heavenly City of the Eighteenth-Century Philosophers*, p. 47)

By not only believing in causes and effects and spending excessive energy in trying to demonstrate them, but even more tellingly by having refused to accept Foucault's method as historically valid at all, modernist historians revealed their innate conservatism. As Foucault perceptively remarked, "The cry goes up that one is murdering history whenever, in a historical analysis . . . one is seen to be using in too obvious a way the categories of discontinuity and difference, the notions of threshold, rupture, and transformation" (*The Archaeology of Knowledge,* p. 14).

PIERRE BOURDIEU, MICHEL DE CERTEAU, AND JACQUES LACAN: THE CRITIQUE OF SOCIAL AND PERSONAL IDENTITY

Three French thinkers—the sociologist Pierre Bourdieu, the Jesuit philosopher turned historical theorist Michel de Certeau, and the psychiatrist Jacques Lacan—questioned Foucault's notion that a coherent "power" defined any given community. Bourdieu's point is that different realms of society and thought—theory, fine art, literature, philosophy—develop their own distinctive "habitus": "systems of durable, transposable . . . principles which generate and organize practices and representations" (*The Logic of Practice,* p. 53). Texts, broadly conceived, must thus be understood as products and producers of both a specific historical context (this sort of inquiry is known as the new historicism) and of a specific disciplinary discourse. Bourdieu astutely argued that silence speaks volumes here: the theoretical articulation of the rights of lords, kings, and churches only multiplies when the traditional habitus of rituals such as feudal justice, court pageants, and celebrations of saints' days are under attack. Bourdieu fruitfully compared such symbolic exchanges of deference and noblesse oblige to resembling, and yet historically more persistent and powerful than, the marketplace exchange of goods. He also focused on the modern academic establishment and revealed it as a social system possessing its own habitus, rather than as the truth-seeking community of scholars standing apart from the structures of power in an exalted quest for objectivity.

De Certeau took the ideas of Bourdieu one step further. He professed that heterogeneity not only appears in habitus but also manifests itself in the decision-making abilities of apparently powerless and even victimized individuals. De Certeau focused on the "margins, limits, [and] silences," the "zones" science and rationality have left as their "unintelligible underside," the "object[s] lost by history" (*The Writing of History,* pp. 39–40). Rather than regarding a given social order as a monolith that is almost impossible to escape, he argued that societies are pluralistic. Historians studying sorcery, miracles, the lives of the oppressed, women, or alternative sexualities show that every society, even the most apparently rigid, is continuously being both recreated and resisted, through the "tactics" of its members. His *The Practice of Everyday Life* (1984) focuses on consumerism, a feature of modern life frequently despised by intellectuals, and shows how people "produce" a popular culture by choosing from a myriad of possibilities to define themselves. A consumer may thus be compared to a reader who "insinuates into another person's text [or array of products] the ruses of pleasure and appropriation; he poaches on it, is transported into it, pluralizes himself in it" (p. xxi).

In his internationally famous lectures in Paris, the psychoanalyst Lacan denied the coherence of the human person. He was expelled from the International Psychoanalytical Association for his radical theory that the Freudian unconscious of id, ego, and superego is itself the product of a particular culture. Thus, for example, people do not fear the father figure in their lives; rather, they are held in thrall by "the name of the father." Whereas Freudian analysis is protracted, emphasizing the control and understanding of desire, and is based on the psychiatrist's structuring of a personal narrative history to fit a general theory, Lacanian analysis is marked by rupture of the patient's narrative, sudden endings to sessions, and the effort to release suppressed *jouissance*—the human capacity for experiencing an undefinable "more than joy." By deconstructing human personality as possessing a coherent identity, Lacan extended postmodernist thought from the social to the personal.

LUCE IRIGARAY, JULIA KRISTEVA, AND THE FEMINIST CRITIQUE OF LACAN

Despite their radical denial of the Western social order, the male postmodernists, according to their feminist critics, could not shed their own patriarchal prejudices. The French feminist psychoanalyst and philosopher Luce Irigaray began as a student of Jacques Lacan but was expelled from his movement for insisting that his theories disregarded women. For Irigaray, Lacan's ideas mirrored the Western patriarchal order, where women were not recognized as full persons (that is, denied the right to hold office and undertake certain professions) but could only exist as men used and imagined them: as sexual or emotional beings valued for their appearance, as mothers and housekeepers, as icons of justice and freedom. In many works of Western art and literature, women achieve greatness by sacrificing themselves for men. Julia Kristeva argued that the female body is built around the womb, or chora. Thus, women experience an emptiness and absence innately while "phallic" men do not. Accordingly to Kristeva, women are historically silent as the female represents the prelinguistic, impossible-to-be-articulated existence that Lacan denied by "privileging" male discourse. Therefore, women should not be victimized, but their insights, which need to be expressed in poetic rather than argumentative language, must be granted a privileged "semiotic" place if humankind is to interpret and destabilize the patriarchal, "symbolic" world largely constructed by men. Representing the philosophical expression of the feminist movement, Kristeva and Irigaray urge women to recreate themselves and enrich society with their distinctive contributions.

JACQUES DERRIDA
AND DECONSTRUCTION

The French linguist Jacques Derrida is the trickster par excellence of the postmodernist movement. His playful analyses are deliberately provocative, building on other theorists to deny that humankind can never definitively know anything at all. Derrida takes the fragmentation of the postmodern scene to its logical extent and denies that humankind can definitively know anything. He rechristened reason as "logocentrism"—the belief that words can describe things accurately, or that "the signifier" can be identified with "the signified"—to deflate the claims of those who argued that the Western philosophical tradition provides accurate knowledge of the world. According to Derrida, there is always *différance* between any interpretation (or meaning) and the text (or object) one hopes to understand. Each effort to pin down meaning only begets complications. Derrida's method, called deconstruction, was summarized by the scholar Madan Sarup as "reading a text so closely that the author's conceptual distinctions on which the text relies are shown to fail on account of the inconsistent and paradoxical use made of these very concepts within the text as a whole" (*An Introductory Guide to Poststructuralism and Postmodernism,* p. 34). For instance, when Derrida "deconstructs" the Declaration of Independence, he asks, How can one "people" claim independence from another when only the document itself claims to constitute such a people?

Derrida also put terms that claim to describe reality under "erasure" in his own quirky, ironic style of writing, which he called "grammatology"—the deconstruction of the logocentric. For instance, he would write natural thusly and point out that the

Roman Catholic Church regards clerical celibacy as natural, and birth control and homosexuality as unnatural. For Derrida, a good way for scholars to deflate the pretensions of orthodox texts is to "privilege" the "marginal" or critical texts produced by outsiders, the despised, the undervalued—in other words, "others." Critics have uncharitably charged that Derrida denied the real world of joy and suffering when he claimed, "There is no reality outside the text." What he meant was that people cannot arrive at a final, definitive interpretation of any text by appealing to any set of supposedly true principles.

EDWARD SAID, ORIENTALISM,
AND ITS EXTENSIONS

One major criticism of postmodernism that falls flat is that it only exists as a parasite of the modernist condition its practitioners condemned. Critics argued that there would be no university, no serious listening to deconstructionists, were not the Western modernist tradition of free thought and critical inquiry that it attacks in place. This scholarly criticism brings up the vital importance of the work of the literary scholar Edward Said, who teaches English at Columbia University and is an internationally known leader of the Palestinian liberation movement. He exemplifies "postcolonial" theory, which integrates postmodern insights into a critique of imperialism. He showed that the Western world itself is a construct, wherein Russia, ancient Egypt, and the biblical Hebrews may belong. "The West" both incorporates the achievements of groups constructed as "the other" and at the same time disparages these peoples. (Similar arguments can also be made for aristocracy and capitalism vis-à-vis peasants and workers, men vis-à-vis women, and heterosexuals vis-à-vis homosexuals.) Ironically, the West in fact defines others in terms of a stereotype that projects its own desires and fears onto a scapegoated group.

Said's major work, *Orientalism,* shows that Western images of the Orient focused on the luxury, laziness, and sexual indulgences Europeans used to enjoy. Working independently, historians of American slavery had come to the same conclusion about racial prejudice. Scholars such as Winthrop Jordan noted that affluent whites who did no physical labor claimed African Americans were lazy and that black men lusted after white women—while masters' relations with slave women, such as the statesman

220

Thomas Jefferson's relations with Sally Hemings, were both tolerated and denied.

Said's orientalism may also be extended to the stereotyping of women and homosexuals. Similarly, twentieth-century men failed to educate women and then condemned them for lack of reason; they refused housework and child rearing the status of "work" to dub women "the weaker sex." The heterosexual stigmatized the homosexual as effeminate and decadent while laying claim to a civilization produced largely by same-sex communities (the Greek agora, the medieval monastery, the Renaissance stage). Postmodern and postcolonial history, along with feminism and queer theory, the preferred term for intellectual work dealing with homosexual identity and history, thus unearths the stories of the "subaltern," in the words of Gayatri Chakravorty Spivak, and enables him or her to speak, to present counternarratives, to subvert a "master narrative" still confused by conservatives with "history" per se.

JEAN BAUDRILLARD, SIMULACRA, AND HYPERREALITY

For many scholars, the postmodern world of the twentieth century had become the "artificial wilderness" of which the poet e. e. cummings warned, where information and texts exploded in cyberspace (as people meet, shop, and do research on the Internet) and in hyperreality (people vacation at Disneyland rather than go to Africa; conversely, they experience the third world on television). Even the natural survived as artificial constructs (national parks, tourism). In order to make sense of this, the philosopher Jean Baudrillard, whose work explores the effects of the profusion of late-twentieth-century consumer goods on society and human personality, coined the term "simulacrum" to describe an artificial object or experience that the public accepts as real through consumerism and advertising. People's thoughts and deeds are guided by what they see on television and shaped by reporters who provide canned interpretations. For instance, the sometimes-confused president Ronald Reagan became "the great communicator," while John Wayne, who never served in the armed forces and lived in the Los Angeles area for most of his life, became the archetypal American military and frontier hero. Through advertising people learned that athletic shoes, blue jeans, and toothpaste come in significantly different varieties—a reality that continues into the twenty-first century.

Such "simulacra" are not unreal, but hyperreal, they merge with American lives to become people's reality. Sometimes this takes the form of life imitating art: Ronald Reagan used his film experience to conduct foreign affairs; the rap artists Tupac Shakur and the Notorious B.I.G. who sang about violence were killed in shoot-outs. Desire to imitate the cinematic heroism of the actor John Wayne (who was not a war veteran) was frequently mentioned as a reason soldiers enlisted to fight in Vietnam. Production, advertisement, and consumption even of apparently threatening images, uniting whites and conservative blacks against simulated rebels, often becomes the basis of social stability. Baudrillard made headlines in intellectual circles when he proclaimed at the conclusion of the Gulf War of 1991 that it could not have happened: war could only be imagined and simulated through the media. Rather than denying reality, Baudrillard was trying to shock the public into no longer accepting media distortions as the basis for understanding it. He reasoned that even if people disagree about the slant placed on different events by television or newspaperes, they still accept such distortions as the starting point for their inquiries instead of, say, realizing that the events are presented at the hand of a manipulative media.

PERILS, PARADOXES, AND POTENTIALITIES OF POSTMODERNISM

In 1992, the author Francis Fukuyama presented posthistoricism as the antidote to postmodernism in his book *The End of History and the Last Man.* The modern welfare state/bourgeois democracy had to be the final stage of history, he argued, because any nation hoping to be of political or economic consequence had to adopt this form to keep abreast of the required intellectual developments (an educated class that can program computers, for instance). What other scholars saw as objections to his theory—third-world poverty, first-world crime and ignorance, and ethnic warfare all over the globe—Fukuyama viewed as residues that have yet to be adjusted into an essentially benign system. The real long-range problem is boredom: deprived of the need to accomplish great deeds that much of history has already accomplished, human beings are apt to become violent out of the human need to find meaning in life.

Fukuyama's book, of course, came hard on the heels of the end of communism and the defeat of the Iraqi leader Saddam Hussein in the Gulf War during a period of general prosperity among the leading capitalist nations. Like so many works of forecasting, he confused the trend of the hour with the course of human history. His gigantic assumption was that liberal capitalism would be able to compensate technologically for whatever environmental and military destructive power it could develop. However, Fukuyama's work and the status quo it philosophically defends should be an inspiration to twenty-first-century postmodernists. To be sure, they too are the product of their age: of a society that has lost confidence in traditional family, community, and moral values—values believed by those without a knowledge of history to have been much more powerful in the past. Hence political conservatives hysterically harp on moral values while defending a capitalist system that destroys them all over the world as it relocates industry to cheaper labor pools. Those who denounce postmodernism need to realize that the alternative may be Fukuyama and the deliberate abandonment of what the German sociologist Max Weber stressed in his 1919 essay "Science as a Vocation" is the main duty of the intellectual: to point out the inconvenient fact.

See also **Analytic Philosophy; Intelligence and Human Difference; Psychology, the Mind, and Personality; Anthropology and Cultural Relativism** *(in this volume);* **Individualism and the Self; Family; Ethnicity and Race; Race; Class; The Humanities; The Social Sciences; The Visual Arts; Architecture; Painting; Sculpture; Memory; Music; Dance; Social Construction of Reality** *(volume 3); and other articles in this section.*

BIBLIOGRAPHY

General Introductions

Appignanesi, Richard, and Chris Garratt. *Introducing Postmodernism.* New York, 1995. Although written and illustrated in a sophisticated comic book style, a very good place for beginning students to start. The series also includes *Introducing* (each of the following) *Semiotics, Barthes, Derrida, Foucault, Lacan, Baudrillard,* and *Feminism.*

Appleby, Joyce Oldham, Lynn Hunt, and Margaret Jacob. *Telling the Truth about History.* New York, 1994. Critical yet appreciative commentary on postmodernism and history.

Deely, John N. *Basics of Semiotics.* Bloomington, Ind., 1990. Short, basic introduction for beginners.

Docherty, Thomas, ed. *Postmodernism: A Reader.* New York, 1993. Good, short excerpts from many of the major figures.

Hughes, H. Stuart. *Sophisticated Rebels: The Political Culture of European Dissent, 1968–1987.* Cambridge, Mass., 1988. Includes other trends and locates postmodernism relative to them.

Jameson, Fredric. *Postmodernism; or, The Cultural Logic of Late Capitalism.* Durham, N.C., 1991.

Jenkins, Keith, ed. *The Postmodern History Reader.* New York, 1997. Includes short works by advocates and critics, and exchanges between them.

Kevelson, Roberta, ed. *Hi-Fives: A Trip to Semiotics.* New York, 1998. Shows application of postmodern ideas to various disciplines.

Nöth, Winfried. *Handbook of Semiotics.* Bloomington, Ind., 1990. Encyclopedic coverage with excellent bibliographies.

Sarup, Madan. *An Introductory Guide to Post-Structuralism and Postmodernism.* 2d ed. Athens, Ga., 1993. Perhaps the best starting point for studying the field.

Works by or about Specific Authors
The extensive writings of many of these authors prevents listing more than a few of the most important besides those cited in the text.

Barthes, Roland. *A Barthes Reader.* Edited by Susan Sontag. New York, 1982.

———. *Mythologies.* Translated by Annette Lavers. New York, 1972.

———. *S/Z.* Translated by Richard Miller. New York, 1974.

———. *Writing Degree Zero.* Translated by Annette Lavers and Colin Smith. New York, 1968.

Baudrillard, Jean. *The Gulf War Did Not Take Place.* Translated by Paul Paton. Bloomington, Ind., 1995.

———. *The Mirror of Production.* Translated by Mark Poster. St. Louis, Mo., 1975.

———. *Simulacra and Simulation.* Translated by Sheila Faria Glaser. Ann Arbor, Mich., 1994.

———. *Spectres of Marx.* Translated by Peggy Kamuf. London, 1994. Includes a critique of Fukuyama.

Becker, Carl Lotus. *Everyman His Own Historian.* 1935. Reprint, Chicago, 1966. Introduction by Jack L. Cross. Brilliant anticipation of the postmodern approach to history.

———. *The Heavenly City of the Eighteenth-Century Philosophers.* New Haven, Conn., 1932.

Bourdieu, Pierre. *Homo Academicus.* Translated by Peter Collier. Stanford, Calif., 1988.

———. *The Logic of Practice.* Translated by Richard Nice. Cambridge, U.K., 1990.

Bourdieu, Pierre, with Jean-Claude Passeron. *Reproduction in Society and Culture.* Translated by Richard Nice. Foreword by Tom Bottomore. London, 1977.

Callow, Alexander B. *The Tweed Ring.* New York, 1966.

De Certeau, Michel. *Heterologies: Discourses on the Other.* Translated by Brian Massumi. Minneapolis, Minn., 1986.

———. *The Practice of Everyday Life.* Translated by Steven Randall. Berkeley, Calif., 1984.

———. *The Writing of History.* Translated by Tom Conley. New York, 1988.

De Lauretis, Teresa. *Technologies of Gender: Essays on Theory, Film, and Fiction.* Bloomington, Ind., 1987. The first articulation of queer theory, the preferred term for intellectual work dealing with homosexual identity and history.

Derrida, Jacques. *A Derrida Reader: Between the Blinds.* Edited by Peggy Kamuf. Introduction and notes by Peggy Kamuf. New York, 1991.

———. *Of Grammatology.* Translated by Gayatry Chakravorty Spivak. Baltimore, 1976.

———. *Writing and Différence.* Translated by Alan Bass. Chicago, 1978.

Eco, Umberto. *Serendipities: Language and Lunacy.* Translated by William Weaver. New York, 1998.

———. *Travels in Hyperreality.* Translated by William Weaver. San Diego, Calif., 1986.

Eco, Umberto, with Richard Rorty, Jonathan Culler, and Christine Brooke-Rose. *Interpretation and Overinterpretation.* Edited by Stefan Collini. New York, 1992.

Foucault, Michel. *The Archaeology of Knowledge.* Translated by A. M. Sheridan-Smith. New York, 1972.

———. *Essential Works of Foucault.* Edited by Paul Rabinow. 3 vols. New York, 1997–1999.

———. *Madness and Civilization: A History of Insanity in the Age of Reason.* Translated by Richard Howard. New York, 1967.

Fukuyama, Francis. *The End of History and the Last Man.* New York, 1992.

Geertz, Clifford. *The Interpretation of Cultures: Selected Essays.* New York, 1973.

Irigaray, Luce. *The Irigaray Reader.* Edited and with introduction by Margaret Whitford. Cambridge, Mass., 1991.

Jordan, Winthrop D. *White over Black: American Attitudes toward the Negro, 1550–1812.* Chapel Hill, N.C., 1968. Foreshadows postmodern studies of how dominant cultures project their own shortcomings and hidden desires onto "others."

Kristeva, Julia. *The Kristeva Reader.* Edited by Toril Moi. New York, 1986.

Kuhn, Thomas S. *The Structure of Scientific Revolutions.* Chicago, 1962.

Lacan, Jacques. *Écrits: A Selection.* Translated by Alan Sheridan. New York, 1977.

Lévi-Strauss, Claude. *The Savage Mind.* Chicago, 1966.

Lodge, David. *Small World: An Academic Romance.* New York, 1984.

Lyotard, Jean François. *The Postmodern Condition: A Report on Knowledge.* Translated by Geoff Bennington and Brian Massumi. Minneapolis, Minn., 1984.

———. *Postmodern Fables.* Translated by Georges van den Abbeele. Minneapolis, Minn., 1997.

MacCannell, Dean. *Empty Meeting Grounds: The Tourist Papers.* London, 1992.

Mandelbaum, Seymour. *Boss Tweed's New York.* New York, 1965.

Marcuse, Herbert. *One-Dimensional Man: Studies in the Ideology of Advanced Industrial Society.* Boston, 1964.

Peirce, Charles Sanders. *Collected Papers of Charles Sanders Peirce.* Edited by Charles Hartshorne, Paul Weiss, and Arthur Burks. 8 vols. Cambridge, Mass., 1931–1958.

———. *The Essential Peirce: Selected Philosophical Writings.* Edited by Nathan Houser and Christian Kloessel. 2 vols. Bloomington, Ind., 1992–1998.

Pencak, William. "Foucault Stoned: Insanity Reconsidered, and History." *Rethinking History* 1 (1997): 34–55.

Said, Edward W. *Culture and Imperialism.* New York, 1993.

———. *Orientalism.* New York, 1978.

Spivak, Gayatri Chakravorty. *A Spivak Reader: Selected Works of Gayatri Chakravorty Spivak.* Edited by Donna Landry and Gerald MacLean. New York, 1996.

Stacewicz, Richard. *Winter Soldiers: An Oral History of the Vietnam Veterans against the War.* New York, 1997.

Tierney, William G. *Academic Outlaws: Queer Theory and Cultural Studies in the Academy.* Thousand Oaks, Calif., 1997.

Weber, Max. *From Max Weber, Essays in Sociology.* Translated by Hans H. Gerth and C. Wright Mills. London, 1991. Includes essays "Science as a Vocation" and "Politics as a Vocation," which anticipate the postmodern predicament of how to inquire and live morally in a world without certainty.

POSTMODERNISM AND THE ARTS

Amelia Jones

In the 1984 English-language edition of his book *The Postmodern Condition,* the French philosopher Jean-François Lyotard included an essay titled "Answering the Question: What Is Postmodernism?" In 1984 this was a heated and pressing question as hundreds of texts probed the uneasy boundaries of this contested phenomenon. The question of postmodernism was at the forefront of discussions in philosophy, the arts, architecture, and cultural studies in general. The term and the concept came, through these discussions, to define a broad social phenomenon as well as a cluster of cultural attributes. Postmodern discourse served to codify both postmodernism and—largely by opposition and resistance—the way in which modernism itself came to be understood.

Up until the development of the concept of postmodernism in the post–World War II period, modernism had largely been seen as a more or less direct cultural counterpart to modernization, the industrialization of the modern West. Its most radical arm was the avant-garde, comprised of artistic movements that, especially in the early twentieth century, sought to critique or destabilize the effects of the increasing bureaucratization of everyday life. Thus, members of what the scholar Peter Bürger has called the "historic avant-garde" in the visual arts from around 1910 into the 1920s—such as cubism, futurism, dadaism, and constructivism—produced works and performances that foregrounded or questioned the various European nationalisms and the massive growth of commodity culture and industrial capitalism during this period. Avant-garde architects linked to these movements proposed to overthrow outmoded revivalist styles and to produce buildings made with simplified forms to reflect a streamlined machine aesthetic and promote the possibility of lifestyles more in tune with the innovations of the industrial era.

Perhaps most infamously, in the 1910s the French artist Marcel Duchamp produced a number of "readymades," industrially produced objects that he signed and thus legitimated as works of art. The quintessential avant-garde gesture, the readymades subvert the separation of high and low culture so necessary to the functioning of the burgeoning art market and to a more conservative modernist conception of high art as autonomous from the social realm. As many have argued, the readymades sowed the seeds of a kind of cultural critique that came to the fore after World War II and came to define postmodernism.

With postmodernism, modernism itself began to be cast in a negative light as clinging to conservative conceptions of individuality and cultural value. In this way, modernism today is often conflated with the arguments of its least progressive representatives, such as Roger Frye and Clement Greenberg, writers who defined a rarefied, formalist notion of modernist artistic practice as linked to the creative expression of "pure" form, untouched by the concerns and pressures of economic and social systems.

The term "postmodernism" is applied to the arts developed in the immediate post–World War II period first in relation to contemporary poetry in the United States. By the mid-1960s Leslie Fiedler was using the term as a label for "pop" writers such as Kurt Vonnegut, and the art historian Leo Steinberg had deployed it to describe a development of an art that turned away from modernism's emphasis on the visual experience of nature, shifting the subject matter of art "from nature to culture" (Steinberg, *Other Criteria,* p. 84). By the early 1970s, writers such as Ihab Hassan broadened these definitions of postmodernism, proposing that it might represent a wholesale "mutation in Western humanism" (*The Postmodern Turn,* p. 89). But it was in the 1980s that debates surrounding the term and concept of postmodernism exploded into a full-scale industry in literary theory, philosophy, art discourse (that is, art criticism, art theory, and art history), architectural history, and urban theory. By the mid-1990s, however, debates about postmodernism had fizzled out—perhaps more by general acceptance of its parameters than because of its irrelevance.

MEANINGS OF POSTMODERNISM

Postmodernism in a general sense has thus been theorized as the "cultural logic" of the late capitalist economic and social structures, an epistemic shift in the belief systems of the West. Significantly, postmodernism is a phenomenon that has been coextensive with a series of social upheavals. These began in the 1950s with the revolutionary rise of the civil rights movement and the nascent resistance to authority on the part of the Beat writers and their assemblage artist colleagues, from Wallace Berman in California to Robert Rauschenberg in New York. They continued with the Black Power, Chicano, feminist, gay-lesbian, student, and New Left movements of the 1960s and 1970s. Along with these upheavals, the dissolution of national borders and nationalisms in the face of the end of the imperial era of Western expansion, the global permutation of technologies of communication and exchange, and the corporatization of public and private life around the world have encouraged a broad reevaluation of what it means to live and to produce and experience culture in a rapidly changing world. In particular, the previous notion of a "subject" or "individual" as fully self-knowing and in potential mastery of his environment, already challenged by the historic avant-garde, was increasingly seen as untenable in the face of the new demographic and economic global situation.

More specifically in relation to culture, postmodernism has been theorized as a loss either of the "real" itself or of a belief in the "real" (a deflation of modernist truth value). Postmodern culture is a "society of the spectacle," in which the referent, the thing in the world to which a sign or symbol refers, disappears beneath a "precession of simulacra" or an endless flow of disattached signifiers, symbols or sounds, that signify or have meaning, which refer only to other signs rather than to a pre-existing real (Baudrillard, "Precession of Simulacra," in Wallis, ed.). In this regime, as meaning itself comes to be posed as an open question rather than put forth as fact, the coherent, centered subject of Descartes's famous dictum "I think therefore I am" dissolves into a skein of contradictions. This post- or anti-Cartesian subject is the "decentered" subject of postmodernism: one whose gender, sex, race, ethnicity, nationality, and class are no longer taken for granted.

In literature in particular, in the postwar period the idea of meaning shifted away from fixity to undecidability; for example, antinarrative strategies took the place of the narrative closure of the nineteenth-century novel as the secure, truthful narrator (the third-person voice) was replaced by a first-person, explicitly subjective point of view. However, the distinction between modernism (for example, in the works of James Joyce and Gertrude Stein) and postmodernism (say, Don DeLillo's 1985 *White Noise*) is not clear-cut in this regard, since the shattering of narrative and dislocation of narratorial voice had occurred early in the twentieth century before being refined and extended in the postmodern period. What makes postmodern literature distinct, in degree if not in kind, is its relentless focus on the structures of representation itself, with an emphasis on paradoxes of appearance, the duplicity of perception, and the continual slippage of meaning. While modernist literature is characterized by an attitude of seriousness marked by an alienation from bourgeois culture, postmodern literature might be said to be playful, ironic, and fully engaged in contemporary media culture.

In the visual arts, postmodernism was, in the 1980s, increasingly codified by the dominant visual arts discourse based in New York City (the heart of the contemporary art market). This systemization was made in terms of a Marxian schema of value that bore closer resemblance to modernist value systems than its proponents tended to admit. In this schema "radical" postmodernism was identified with strategies relating to modernist avant-garde modes of production, in particular, photographic montage and collage: appropriation, pastiche, bricolage, allegory, and the undermining of originality through photographic reproduction. This kind of appropriation was evaluated positively as "good" postmodernism, in that it followed the example set by the historic avant-garde and took a critical stance toward capitalism and the art market in particular. In contrast, the resurgence of expressionistic painting and revivalist architectural styles during this period, which ostensibly benefited from, and even pandered to rather than critiquing, the over-inflated economy of the Reagan era, were labeled by dominant New York–based critics as "bad" modes of postmodern practice. The notion of "critique" thus became central to visual arts postmodernism through these debates, with feminist art and criticism making dramatic inroads in cultural visibility because of their obvious critical stance vis-à-vis traditional modernism.

Tucker House (1975), Venturi, Scott Brown and Associates, Inc. Venturi's solo and group projects are quintessential examples of the kind of populist postmodern architecture promoted by Charles Jencks. Vernacular forms are playfully quoted in a mannered pastiche of earlier architectural motifs and structures, producing hybrid and decorative buildings of the type now common in cheaply constructed shopping malls. COURTESY VENTURI, SCOTT BROWN AND ASSOCIATES, INC. PHOTO BY TOM CRANE

In architecture, Charles Jencks became the primary promoter of a celebratory conception of architectural postmodernism, one characterized by the rejection of the perceived elitism of modernist architecture, that is, its utopian aspirations and insistence on purity and monumentality over the eye- and body-pleasing effects of exterior decoration and intricate spatial forms provided by revivalist styles. Jencks drew on the earlier terms laid forth in the 1950s and 1960s by architects and theorists who had embraced popular culture, from members of the British Independent Group to Robert Venturi. In his classic of architectural theory, *Complexity and Contradiction in Architecture* (1966), Venturi called for hybrid elements and an inclusive rather than exclusive architectural logic. (Venturi's pithy claim against Ludwig Mies van der Rohe's modernist dictum "less is more" was a provocative "less is a bore.") Sparked by the perceived failure of modern architecture to achieve its ascetic, utopian goals,

postmodern architecture, Jencks argued, aims to speak directly to the public and is typified by a populism and pluralism shaped by revived historical and especially vernacular forms brought together in an eclectic mix. According to Jencks, postmodern architecture has a playful rather than critical relationship to modernist forms and styles and to social issues in general.

In sum, postmodern culture arose in multiple cultural sites during the post–World War II period in reaction to the perceived failures of modernism. However, as a number of philosophers and cultural theorists have argued, postmodernism did not suddenly appear in 1960 or in the 1980s. Rather, as viewed in alignment with the modernist radical (or "historic") avant-garde of the first quarter of the twentieth century, postmodernism was always present in modernism. But the modernist impulse to critique the "master narratives" that shore up the ideology of Western superiority became dominant only in the 1960s and after, when it began to be articulated—perhaps paradoxically—precisely as a critique of modernism itself (see Lyotard, *The Postmodern Condition*). Postmodernism is thus "new" not in the sense that it invents entirely innovative modes of cultural expression and analysis but to the extent that it brings a double awareness: that representation itself cannot be taken for granted in terms of a transparent relationship of signifier to signified, sign to referent; and that modernism had always been corrupted from within by its own antitheses—"low" culture or kitsch, the feminine and homosexual, the "primitive" other—while postmodernism embraces these within its purview. To this end, it is crucial to note the importance of feminist, postcolonial, and queer theory in what we call postmodernism: their rupturing of modernism from within by highlighting otherness.

Postmodernism can thus be thought of as a radical critique of the stable, normative, Cartesian subject or the figure of the centered and autonomous "individual" so central to the more conservative variants of modernism. This argument does not deny the potentially reactionary components of postmodern culture. There continues to be a far more negative view of postmodernism, largely articulated by both the Marxian left and the tradition-bound right. While the former has tended to see postmodernism as aiding and abetting the perceived ahistorical, anti-Enlightenment mentality of its theoretical twin, poststructuralism (Habermas, "Modernity versus Postmodernity"), the right has tended to view postmodernism as a threat to the very existence of "quality" and the standards that a more conservative modernism has long upheld. Thus, for cultural theorists such as Clement Greenberg and Allan Bloom, the incursion of otherness into the "autonomous" and pure domain of high modernism could be seen only in a negative light.

The following will excavate these various threads, especially in the visual arts, by examining the following three areas: camp, popular culture, and everyday life (the merging of high and low culture that had its initial impulse with the historic avant-garde); aesthetic and social issues (debates about the political efficacy of postmodernism, originality, authorship, and meaning); and technology, multiculturalism, and the dispersal of the subject. While these three topics are by no means comprehensive, they sum up the major epistemological and cultural shifts that have come to determine the experience we now label "postmodernism."

CAMP, POP CULTURE,
AND EVERYDAY LIFE

The two major world wars of the twentieth century clearly marked a watershed for the hallowed concept of Western civilization as the primary, or only, site of important cultural expression (as in the modernist formalist view). The dismembering of European people, lands, and cultural monuments put an end to the hopeful, progressive, and imperialist notion of Western culture solidified by Enlightenment philosophies of cultural and political change. After World War II, with the United States emerging as the dominant power in the West, the horror of the Holocaust (the incomprehensible fact of the uncivilized behavior of the nation that had nurtured Goethe, Beethoven, Hegel, and Nietzsche) still fresh, and the rise of the cold war and its new, baffling national antagonisms, official Western culture congealed into a mass of ideas resting on the promotion of American-style "democracy" and its notion of the autonomous and centered "individual," claimed by the proponents of the modernist formalism as the linchpin of their conception of artistic autonomy. In the case of the visual arts, American abstract painting was marketed at home and abroad as exemplary of the ideal of personal "freedom" (the expressionist brushstrokes ostensibly serving as visual proof of this freedom).

In the face of the extreme hypocrisies of this period (the marketing of supposedly autonomous high art, the ideological construction on the part of the state of the notion of individual freedom, and so on), writers and artists began to undermine

mainstream ideologies of high culture through an ironic or cynical attitude and the imposition of everyday life into literature and art. Holden Caulfield's cynicism and rebellion, as articulated by J. D. Salinger in his best-selling 1951 novel, *The Catcher in the Rye,* symbolized appropriate attitudes for the disillusioned youth of this period. The Beat writers and their corollaries in the visual arts—the photographer Robert Frank, the New York–based artists Robert Rauschenberg and Jasper Johns, and the California-based assemblage artists Wallace Berman, George Herms, Jess, and others—began making works that deployed elements of popular culture and everyday life to undermine the pretensions of high modernism. Dance and music played a crucial role in this shift: musician John Cage and dancer Merce Cunningham, who worked together during this period, integrated aspects of chance, indeterminacy, and the everyday into their joint produc-

Merce Cunningham in *Summerspace.* A protégé of Martha Graham, Cunningham brought to dance a typically postwar concern with the everyday. Rejecting the restricted dress and movements of both classical and modern dance, Cunningham introduced walking and other mundane movements into his choreography, here with pared-down sets by assemblage artist Robert Rauschenberg and the spare music of Morton Feldman. CUNNINGHAM DANCE FOUNDATION, INC. PHOTO BY JACK MITCHELL

228

tions. Teaching at Black Mountain College in North Carolina in the 1950s, Cage and Cunningham purveyed anti-aesthetic ideas about art that had a great deal of impact on younger artists studying there, including Rauschenberg.

In visual arts discourse the volatile social movements of the 1950s and 1960s—from civil rights to the women's and gay-lesbian rights movements and the antiwar protests—and the rise of identity politics in the 1970s were not always explicitly acknowledged but worked as pressurizing forces in the drawing of battle lines between the modernists and nascent postmodernists. The dominant art critic of the 1950s and 1960s was Clement Greenberg, originally a Marxist thinker, who, like many other American intellectuals, shifted to the right at the beginning of World War II. As early as 1939 Greenberg had excoriated the incursion of popular culture or "kitsch" into the realm of high art in his essay "Avant-Garde and Kitsch," and by the early 1960s this rigid view had solidified. Greenberg's arguments were framed from an increasingly conservative point of view; in essays such as "Modernist Painting" (1960), Greenberg drew on Kantian theory and on the nineteenth-century modernist belief in "art for art's sake" to make claims for the autonomy of high art and its necessary repudiation of narrative and of mass cultural forms and content.

By the late 1960s Greenberg's position had become oversimplified to the point of being almost self-parodic, especially as carried through in the work of followers such as Michael Fried and Hilton Kramer. In a 1982 essay titled "Postmodern: Art and Culture in the 1980s," Kramer explicitly extended the modernist values set forth by Greenberg, pointing the finger at Susan Sontag's important 1964 essay "Notes on 'Camp'" for having defined a dangerous new anti-aesthetic impulse that threatened to destroy the seriousness of the high modernist project: "We are thus reminded [by Sontag] that the origin of Camp is to be found in the sub-culture of homosexuality" and this homosexualized postmodernism brings about a definitive "corruption of standards" (Kramer, p. 39). In "Notes on 'Camp,'" Sontag had indeed described the homosexualized camp aesthete—epitomized for Sontag by Oscar Wilde—as the antithesis of Greenberg's serious, macho abstract expressionist genius (himself a counterpart to the modernist "individual").

Sontag's formulation, expanded upon by art historians such as Calvin Tomkins and Moira Roth, signaled a sea change in the conception of the visual artist. In visual art discourse, modernism had come to be perceived by younger artists and art writers in the 1960s as masculinist, formalist, and Greenbergian—and in dire need of radical revision. In antagonism to this limiting formulation, the younger generation integrated popular culture—which in this context was feminized and homosexualized or "queered"—into "high" art production. Following on the heels of the British Independent Group of artists, writers, and architects, who in the 1950s had embraced American popular culture as part of their work, the American pop artists Andy Warhol, Tom Wesselman, Ed Ruscha, Marisol, and others began around 1960 to produce artworks heavily inflected by mass cultural topics, images, and processes. These included cartoonish renderings of specifically feminine topics (Wesselman's "Great American Nude" series) or female celebrities (Warhol's "Marilyn" series). Too, Warhol's effete self-posing, which he explicitly articulated in his writings as being in opposition to the macho seriousness and angst of the abstract expressionist artists, aligned him with the debased realms of kitsch and camp that Greenberg and Kramer had excoriated as corruptive of high modernism.

Other contemporaneous movements such as Fluxus and Happenings, showing an affinity for the anti-aesthetic philosophies of Cage, Cunningham, and Duchamp, emphasized the embrace of the everyday, producing performances of mundane activities that stretched the boundaries of what could be considered art. While the artists involved in Fluxus and Happenings—including George Maciunas, Alison Knowles, and Allan Kaprow—were not overtly queer or feminized in their attitudes and methods, their performances pushed "high" art into the realm of the popular. (One of the primary goals of this work was to integrate performers with audience so as to merge art with life.) It was peripheral Fluxus works such as Yoko Ono's *Cut Piece* (1964), in which Ono sat on a stage while audience members one by one cut off pieces of her clothing, or Carolee Schneemann's visceral *Meat Joy* (1964), wherein roiling almost-nude male and female bodies and pieces of meat intertwined orgiastically, which more decisively feminized the excessive emotionality of abstract expressionism by tying it to the immanence of desiring and often female bodies.

Not surprisingly, the feminizing/queering—or "camping"—of high culture took its most dramatic form through feminist and gay and lesbian practice. Works from Miriam Schapiro's and Faith Ringgold's quilt "paintings," which integrated women's crafts into high art production, to Robert Mapplethorpe's exquisite photographs explosively merging a modernist formalist photographic style with incendiary homoerotic content, definitively disrupted Greenberg's insistence on a high modernist formalist art practice that evacuated content and focused on the essence of each medium. Paralleling the camping of the visual arts, the Los Angeles–based architect Frank Gehry introduced definitively everyday materials into domestic and large-scale buildings, including his own 1978 house in Santa Monica, with its chain-link diagonals and plywood forms shaped like flying buttresses. These forms "deconstructed" the rigid cubes and "form follows function" aesthetic of modernist International style architecture.

Along with the camping of Greenbergian modernism and International style architecture came a breakdown of the disciplinary boundaries of art history and other traditional fields in the humanities. Cultural studies, developed in Birmingham, England, at the Centre for Contemporary Cultural Studies under the aegis of Raymond Williams, Stuart Hall, and others, argued for the study of culture across traditional boundaries. Cultural studies made the analysis of Disneyland, television sitcoms, comic books, and Madonna as legitimate in the academy as the analysis of abstract painting, novels, and monumental architecture. Cultural studies, drawing from "whatever fields are necessary to produce the knowledge required for a particular project," typifies the postmodern impulse to democratize culture (Grossberg et al., eds., *Cultural Studies*, p. 2).

Postmodernism in this first sense, then, is characterized by a camping of the universalist assumptions of traditional modernism, a camping that, in the visual arts, often drew on the democratizing strategies of the historic avant-garde to radicalize the congealed value systems of modernist formalism. This postmodernism shatters the boundaries staged not only between high and low but also around each separate discipline in the humanities and beyond.

AESTHETIC AND SOCIAL ISSUES

Greenberg and Kramer's approach to postmodernism is deeply colored by their adherence to the notion of aesthetic "quality," in Greenberg's case a notion explicitly supported by recourse to Immanual Kant's aesthetic philosophy. A key aspect of Greenberg's Kantian value system is the notion of the disinterested critic and the corollary concept of the work of art as autonomous from the social realm. The supposedly disinterested critic (implicitly white, male, and well educated) makes judgments that, because of his "objectivity," cannot be questioned and are thus viewed as universal. In the face of the social explosions of the 1960s, which increased the visibility of subjects previously marginalized in United States culture, debates among scholars in the humanities over the canon have thus ultimately rested on the question of whether or not supposedly objective criteria can be found to judge what is worth studying and historicizing and what is not.

Feminism and the gay-lesbian and ethnic rights movements have been crucial forces in the questioning of the modernist belief in objectivity, itself tied closely not only to Kant but to the Enlightenment belief in progress and the superiority of the West, and the privileging of a supposedly disinterested judging or creating subject who in practice was generally white, male, and financially secure. It has been largely up to feminist, antiracist, and gay-lesbian (or "queer") theories and practices to challenge the reactionary components of both modernism and postmodernism, especially in the 1980s with the overheated Reagan-era economy, which extended to the art market and beyond, threatening to engulf every cultural product into the compromised position in support of the machinations of late capitalism. The art world exploded in a struggle between supporters of a revivalist "neo-expressionist" painting (whose practitioners were all white men) and those radical critical theorists calling for a resuscitation of the heroic, confrontational, and anticapitalist strategies of the historic avant-garde.

The latter arguments took their force from the explicit revival of Marxian thinking on the part of British- and New York–based cultural theorists. British theorists from cultural studies and associated with radical film and visual arts journals such as *Screen* and *Block* drew on Bertholt Brecht's theories of distanciation (whereby the mass audiences of art or popular culture products would be shocked into an awareness of the coercive nature of state institutions), Antonio Gramsci's notion of a noncoercive kind of power in capitalism (hegemony replacing institutional power), and Louis Althusser's psychoanalytical expansion of Gramsci's model explaining how, in capitalism, subjects are seduced into becoming a part of the corporate or state belief systems informing the objects and events they view in an insidious process of ideological hailing or interpellation that replaces the brute material force of totalitarianism by insinuating ideological beliefs into the structures of the subject's unconscious. (In this way, it becomes clear that, even in a democracy, we are never as "free" of state or corporate ideological interests as we would like to think we are.)

All of these theories led to a nuanced, critical study of visual, literary, and mass-media culture as inevitably participating in dominant cultural ideologies but also as potentially riven with contradictions—contradictions that have only to be pointed out by the discerning cultural studies scholar to gain a kind of critical cultural force. Thus, the filmmaker and theorist Laura Mulvey pulled these models together, along with Freud's theory of fetishism, in her epochal 1975 essay "Visual Pleasure and Narrative Cinema." Here, Mulvey uses the conflicting mechanisms of dominant Hollywood cinema in order to critique mainstream representations of women. She highlights the contradictory fixation in classic Hollywood films on women's bodies as symbols of male castration anxiety, a fixation that aims to objectify and so disempower the female body to assuage this anxiety but also simultaneously, in its obsessiveness, raises up the woman to the most important position in the male psyche. Mulvey thus calls for the destruction of male viewing pleasure through this kind of cultural analysis as a weapon to challenge the most basic, sexist ideological formations of capitalist culture.

In New York City, a group of art critics and historians founded the journal *October* in 1976, which, along with *Artforum* and institutions such as the New Museum of Contemporary Art, became the dominant sites for the articulation of a critical Left position in art discourse. In the midst of the New York art world's explosive commodification in the Reagan era, writers and curators based in New York solidified a particular avant-garde, Marxian conception of art as either subsumed into dominant ideologies or as oppositional. Peter Bürger's important book, *The Theory of the Avant-Garde* (1974), provided one of the bases for their privileging of work that traced its lineage back to Bürger's "historic avant-garde" of the 1910s and 1920s, including dada, surrealism, and especially Duchamp's readymades, such as his mounted *Bicycle Wheel* of 1913. With the readymade, he argued, the category of "work" is negated and the notion of art cast into question; ultimately, "the act of provocation itself takes the place of the work" (p. 56). With the term "historic avant-garde," Bürger privileged the very artists whom Greenberg and Kramer had dismissed as corruptive to high modernism.

Also crucial to these new avant-gardist arguments were the texts of French poststructuralist philosophy—works by Roland Barthes, Jean Baudrillard, Gilles Deleuze, Jacques Derrida, Michel Foucault, Félix Guattari, Jacques Lacan, and Jean-

François Lyotard, in particular—that were beginning to be translated into English in the 1970s. While their works varied in emphasis and even in disciplinary concern, these major thinkers all articulated incisive models for dismantling the premises of post-Enlightenment Western thought, which in France had been heavily Cartesian. Along with a burgeoning feminist discourse stemming from Simone de Beauvoir's epochal *The Second Sex* (1949) and developing in the writings of Hélène Cixous, Luce Irigaray, Julia Kristeva, Monique Wittig, and others, these theorists articulated a profound critique of the Cartesian subject, with all of the privileges it had sustained in Western culture up to the contemporary era.

Also, the notion of meaning itself (of a signifier being associated in a direct and transparent way with a single meaning, or "signified") was thrown open to question as these theorists developed complex models for how meaning and subjectivity take form. Thus, in a famous 1968 essay, "Death of the Author," Barthes proclaimed that the author as the origin of meaning had dissolved in favor of the reader as the site where meaning is negotiated in relation to the text. In a 1983 article, "The Precession of Simulacra," Jean Baudrillard attacked the very bases of signification itself, privileging as his objects of analysis American cultural icons and sites, such as Disneyland, to theorize the shift from a modernist notion of representation as a mapping or doubling of the real to a postmodernist "generation by models of a real without origin or reality: a hyperreal" (Wallis, ed., *Art after Modernism*, p. 253).

In dominant New York discourses of postmodern visual art in the 1980s, these critical ideas were expanded and applied to cultural practice. In particular, writers in *October* and other New York–based venues argued that the readymades and photography—two processes whereby reproduction results in works of art and the notion of an original slips away—had all but annihilated the modernist cult of originality and the emphasis on the creative self as the centered and autonomous origin of the work of art. For Rosalind Krauss, "modernism and the avant-garde are functions of what we could call the discourse of originality," and postmodernism acts out the discourse of reproductions without originals (as in photographic practice), ultimately "deconstruct[ing] the modernist notion of origin" (*The Originality of the Avant-Garde*, pp. 162, 170).

Other writers, such as Benjamin Buchloh, Douglas Crimp, Hal Foster, and Craig Owens—all students and colleagues of Krauss's—extended the terms of this argument, in some cases reducing postmodern culture to a field of "good" (critical, avant-gardist) versus "bad" (regressive, modernist) objects. Also endemic to this discourse was the tendency to define a neat counterlineage to Greenberg's privileged genealogy, which ran from Picasso and the Paris school to Jackson Pollock and the abstract expressionists. This counter-lineage most often posed Duchamp as the originator of an avant-gardist and ultimately "post-" or "anti-" modern art, paradoxically making these arguments on the part of Buchloh and others rather closer to modernism (with its obsession over origins and lineages) than these writers were able to acknowledge at the time.

Most important, perhaps, dominant New York discourses of postmodern art articulated a cluster of ideas with which that art could be interpreted and understood; within these discourses, appropriation and pastiche were situated as key strategies that linked postmodernism to earlier modernist practices of montage and collage. The works of Barbara Kruger, Sherrie Levine, Richard Prince, and Cindy Sherman were taken as paradigmatic of this kind of appropriation postmodernism, which was posed in opposition to Greenbergian modernism and its emphasis on purity of form and medium. Douglas Crimp's late 1970s exhibition, "Pictures," and his 1979 essay of the same title explicitly privileged this new work, which, he argued, "is not confined to any particular medium" and has a decidedly innovative and conceptual bent (Wallis, ed., *Art after Modernism*, p. 175). Thus, Levine's rephotographed images of Edward Weston's and Walker Evans's photographs call into question the notion of the modernist photograph as an "original" art object as well as challenging the trope of male genius.

The avant-gardist rhetoric that became dominant in New York postmodern art discourse in the 1980s must be contextualized within the explosion of the art market during the Reagan era and beyond and within what Baudrillard in "The Precession of Simulacra," terms the intense "museumification" of culture, which added "one more turn in the spiral of artificiality" (Wallis, ed., *Art after Modernism*, p. 261). With the explosive success of blockbuster exhibitions, gallery ghettos in major cities, museum gift shops, and the construction of massive new art museum complexes (such as the popular ones designed by Gehry [the Guggenheim building in Bilbao, Spain] and Richard Meier [the J. Paul Getty Center, which has been called a pretentious "acropolis" looming over the city of Los Angeles]), the goal of the avant-garde—to democratize culture—has been achieved. Yet, clearly this democratization has led not to the equalization of economic and social relations but to the commodification of

"high" art *as* mass culture, to the deployment of "the arts" as a means of an urban gentrification that exacerbates rather than ameliorates social inequality. With this museumification of culture, by the end of the 1980s and beyond, the Left found itself in an increasingly difficult situation, caught between the Scylla of avant-gardism and the Charybdis of democratization.

Even the "institutional critique" that Peter Bürger had touted, and which became central to 1970s and 1980s postmodern art theory and practice, has been more or less thoroughly incorporated into the institution itself. This incorporation is exemplified in the mounting of large-scale exhibitions institutionalizing conceptualism (Reconsidering the Object of Art: 1965–1975 in 1996) and body art (Out of Actions: Between Performance and the Object, 1949–1979 in 1998) at the Museum of Contemporary Art in Los Angeles. In both of these shows, inevitably, the critical edge of works that had been created to subvert the very premises of the art institution was blunted. Thus, in Out of Actions, body art or performance artworks, in which the artist had performed live for an audience—at least partly in order to thwart the possibility of museumification and commodification—were represented in the concrete forms of objects, videotapes, or photographs. In the light of such phenomena in the 1990s, it became increasingly clear that the avant-gardist position of resisting the lures of commodification and institutionalization was seriously compromised. A different mode of conceptualizing the postmodern was clearly called for.

TECHNOLOGY, MULTICULTURALISM, AND THE DISPERSAL OF THE SUBJECT

By the year 2000, the globalization of capitalism had clearly taken hold—marked by the passage of the North Atlantic Free Trade Agreement (NAFTA), the emergence of the European Community (EC) with a standardized currency, and the blossoming of post-industrial high-tech businesses. With this globalization of capital and the development of Internet communications and "dot com" companies, which challenge the formerly dominant model of corporate capitalism, a concomitant dispersal of power has taken place. At the same time, and linked to this dispersal, the nationalism of the imperial era has also been transformed by a kind of globalization of identity, characterized by the development of localized micro-identities and conflicts based largely on eth-

Guggenheim Museum, Bilbao, Spain, 1997. Frank Gehry's Guggenheim Bilbao symbolizes the shift in postmodern architecture to a more complex, "deconstructive" approach—contorted, nongeometrical, and voluminous. © GUGGENHEIM BILBAO. PHOTO BY ERIKA BARAHONA

nicity rather than nation, from the Falklands conflict to the Persian Gulf War and the war in Kosovo.

These broad shifts encourage some to argue that postmodernism might be far more than simply a set of strategies to dislocate modernist texts. Beginning in the late 1980s and accelerating into the early twenty-first century, a developing subdiscipline of theories of technological change (or "techno-theory") began to examine postmodernism (though, since the early 1990s, the term largely came to be taken for granted and is rarely used explicitly after this point). Pointing to advances in computer and medical technologies and the ways in which these change the understanding of what it means to be human, these theorists have expanded on the poststructuralist recognition of the profound dissolution of modernist truth value—the uncertainty of meaning and the de-centering of the modernist subject, in order to define our current situation as "posthuman" and as marked by vast transformations in social and cultural meaning.

The key manifesto in this area was Donna Haraway's 1985 essay, "A Cyborg Manifesto," with the "cyborg" (part human, part machine) positioned as the symbolic figuring of the destabilized modern individual, of the "boundary breakdowns" that characterize what would earlier have been called postmodernism (Haraway, *Simians,* p. 151). In philosophy, women's studies, and gay-lesbian studies, scholars such as Judith Butler (in *Gender Trouble,* 1990) have begun to theorize sexual and gender identity itself as mutable and performative, or enacted through self-display in engagements of self and other. And in postcolonial and antiracist studies, writers such as Homi Bhabha, bell hooks, Gayatri Spivak, and Trinh T. Minh-ha opened out theories of identity and meaning by insistently contesting what Audre Lorde described as the "white, thin, male, young, heterosexual, Christian, and financially secure" "universal" subject of Western culture (Ferguson et al., eds., *Out There,* p. 282). With theories of the cyborg, the performative subject, and racial and ethnic difference, the coalitional identity politics of the 1950s to the 1970s have mutated into a far more complex set of notions about identity and social positionality as constituted from moment to moment through multiple and often contesting identifications. The multiethnic, polysexual cyborg refuses fixity, proposing identities as "contradictory, partial, and strategic" (Haraway, p. 155). Thus, Renée Cox's monumental silver print *Yo Mama* (1993) crossed over gender and racial codes, portraying a muscular, masculinized yet nurturing and therefore feminine naked black woman holding a lighter-skinned toddler. For Trinh Minh-ha, the "ideology of separatism" that often accompanied 1970s identity politics was subsequently discarded in favor of an embrace of differences, in the plural, to be lived "fearlessly with and within" (*Woman, Native, Other,* pp. 82, 84).

Along with this shift in conceptualization has come a shift in the theorization of the visual arts and architecture away from the prescriptiveness of 1980s discourse to a broader and more fractured set of ideas about postmodernism. The dispersal of cultural power away from New York City has been key to this fracturing in the context of the United States. With the rise of the Internet and of global multinationalism, New York City can no longer claim to be the sole or even the most important site for the production of culture or cultural discourse. In the United States, alternative centers such as Chicago, Miami, and Los Angeles have emerged as vital sites of cultural energy outside of New York.

The rise of new modes of conceptualizing identity have gone hand in hand with the development of even more complex theories of representation, theories that acknowledge the profound changes wrought in our experience of the world by digital technologies. Extending the insights of DeBord and Baudrillard, these new theories point to the dramatic effects of computer technologies, especially the Internet, on how meaning and human subjectivity are experienced. Thus, Katherine Hayles argues that these new technologies of communication have shifted representation away from the analogical (where the sign is in some way physically linked to its mode of expression, as in the grooves cut in an LP album) to the digital (where the sign has no physical relationship to that which it expresses, with patterns of zeros and ones replacing analogical signifiers). The signifier can no longer be understood as a stable marker; rather, a system of pattern and randomness replaces one of presence and absence, the staples of structuralist models of meaning formation.

In the cultural practices at the turn of the twenty-first century these complex ideas are enacted on the level of material or, in some cases, immaterial form (such as artists' web projects). Far from the avant-gardism or revivalism characterizing definitions of postmodernism in the 1980s, this new kind of cultural expression enacts rather than defines postmodern subjectivity as dispersed, multiply identified, and always existing in relation to otherness. In the case of works such as Joe Santarromana and Ken Goldberg's *Telegarden* (1994)—a garden in Los Angeles controlled by a robotic arm activated by an interactive website—not only are Greenberg's concepts of modernist purity violated, but the very structures by which Westerners had long understood human subjectivity in modernism are shattered. Through such works it has become possible to understand, in perhaps the greatest postmodern insight of all, that otherness and dispersal have always been a condition of human experience.

See also **The Design of the Familiar** *(in this volume);* **The Visual Arts; Architecture; Painting; Sculpture; Music; Dance** *(volume 3); and other articles in this section.*

BIBLIOGRAPHY

Barthes, Roland. *Image-Music-Text.* Translated by Stephen Heath. New York, 1977.

Bloom, Allan. *The Closing of the American Mind.* New York, 1987.

Bürger, Peter. *The Theory of the Avant-Garde.* Translated by Michael Shaw. 1994. Reprint, Minneapolis, Minn., 1984.

Butler, Judith. *Gender Trouble: Feminism and the Subversion of Identity.* New York and London, 1990.

Calinescu, Matei. *Five Faces of Modernity: Modernism, Avant-Garde, Decadence, Kitsch, Postmodernism.* Durham, N.C., 1987.

DeBord, Guy. *Society of the Spectacle.* 1967. Detroit, Mich., 1983.

Ferguson, Russell, et al., eds. *Out There: Marginalization and Contemporary Cultures.* Cambridge, Mass., 1990.

Foster, Hal. *Recodings: Art, Spectacle, Cultural Politics.* Port Townsend, Wash., 1985.

Greenberg, Clement. *The Collected Essays and Criticism.* 4 vols. Edited by John O'Brian. Chicago, 1986–1993.

Grossberg, Lawrence, Cary Nelson, and Paula Treichler, eds. *Cultural Studies.* New York and London, 1992.

Habermas, Jürgen. "Modernity versus Postmodernity." In *The Anti-Aesthetic: Essays on Postmodern Culture,* edited by Hal Foster. Port Townsend, Wash., 1983.

Haraway, Donna J. *Simians, Cyborgs, and Women: The Reinvention of Nature.* London and New York, 1991.

Harvey, David. *The Condition of Postmodernity: An Enquiry into the Origins of Cultural Change.* Oxford, 1989.

Hassan, Ihab. *The Postmodern Turn: Essays in Postmodern Theory and Culture.* Columbus, Ohio, 1987.

Hayles, N. Katherine. "Virtual Bodies and Flickering Signifiers." *October* no. 66 (1993): 69–91.

Hutcheon, Linda. *The Politics of Postmodernism.* New York and London, 1989.

Huyssen, Andreas. *After the Great Divide: Modernism, Mass Culture, Postmodernism.* Bloomington, Ind., 1986.

Jameson, Fredric. *Postmodernism, or the Cultural Logic of Late Capitalism.* Durham, N.C., 1991.

Jencks, Charles. *What Is Post-Modernism?* London and New York, 1986.

Jones, Amelia. *Postmodernism and the En-Gendering of Marcel Duchamp.* New York and Cambridge, U.K., 1993.

——. *Body Art/Performing the Subject.* Minneapolis, Minn., 1998.

Kramer, Hilton. "Postmodern: Art and Culture in the 1980s." *New Criterion* 1, no. 1 (1982): 36–42.

Krauss, Rosalind. *The Originality of the Avant-Garde and Other Modernist Myths.* Cambridge, Mass., 1985.

Lyotard, Jean-François. *The Postmodern Condition: A Report on Knowledge.* Translated by Geoff Bennington and Brian Massumi. Minneapolis, Minn., 1984.

Morris, Meaghan. *The Pirate's Fiancée: Feminism, Reading, Postmodernism.* London, 1988.

Mulvey, Laura. *Visual and Other Pleasures.* Bloomington and Indianapolis, Ind., 1989.

Portoghesi, Paolo. *Postmodern: The Architecture of the Postindustrial Society.* New York, 1983.

Sontag, Susan. "Notes on 'Camp.'" In *Against Interpretation and Other Essays.* New York, 1966.

Steinberg, Leo. *Other Criteria: Confrontations with Twentieth-Century Art.* New York and Oxford, 1972.

Trinh, T. Minh-ha. *Woman, Native, Other: Writing, Postcoloniality, and Feminism.* Bloomington and Indianapolis, Ind., 1989.

Venturi, Robert. *Complexity and Contradiction in Architecture.* New York, 1966.

Wallis, Brian, ed. *Art after Modernism: Rethinking Representation.* Boston, 1984.

THE STRUGGLE FOR THE ACADEMY

Ellen Messer-Davidow

Until the early 1990s most Americans had a benign, if somewhat split, perception of universities and colleges. On the one hand, they recognized that these institutions performed the important services of providing students with an education that enhanced their intellectual growth and employment prospects and generating the knowledges that enabled the nation to prosper. On the other hand, they considered them to be ivory-tower retreats where the learned professors meditated and disputed recondite matters that were irrelevant to the gritty challenges that ordinary people faced in getting on with their lives. For Americans used to dismissing these quaint activities with a good-natured shrug, the news that the academy was now the scene of political combat must have come as a surprise.

That news reached the public toward the end of 1990, when feature stories in the *Wall Street Journal, New York Times, Newsweek,* and *Time* announced that something called "political correctness" (or PC for short) was sweeping college campuses. What did that phrase mean? The 1960s leftists had used it in jest to tweak comrades who were overly fastidious in hewing to an orthodox "party line," but conservatives resurrected it to decry what they styled as a fascist regime in the academy. They claimed that "tenured radicals," former 1960s activists now ensconced in faculty and administrative positions, were trashing the achievements of Western culture, indoctrinating their students, and policing their tradition-minded colleagues. Bemused readers probably thought PC was just another insignificant academic flap that the media sensationalized when the real political news was too dull to sell, but they could not have been more mistaken. The conservative movement had hyped PC to the media and thereby the public in order to justify restructuring the higher-education system. To understand why this system was the object of political struggle, it is necessary to go back in time and trace the forces that made it an instrument that could be used to shape the nation.

THE HIGHER-EDUCATION SYSTEM

Before the twentieth century, American higher education could not be called systematic in any respect, institutionally or intellectually. The nation had a motley group of institutions: a few theological, medical, and law schools; mechanics institutes to train skilled workers; female academies to polish young ladies; and, most important, the historic liberal-arts colleges founded by religious denominations to instill a pious and gentlemanly character in the sons of the privileged white classes. These colleges were nothing like the bucolic retreats of learning portrayed by today's cultural conservatives. The facilities were shabby, with heat and food shortages often provoking riots, and the disciplinary measures were harsh. The curriculum, anchored in classical languages and literatures, seldom included the sciences or any other modern knowledge, and the pedagogy stressed oral recitation and written drills. Since most of the college faculty lacked doctoral degrees and decent salaries, they regarded their positions as way stations to securing nonacademic jobs or easing into retirement.

An Initial Transformation The first great transformation occurred between 1870 and 1910, when the modern form of higher education congealed from several innovations in institutional organization and funding. A younger generation of academic leaders founded Johns Hopkins (1876), Clark (1887), and Chicago (1891) and revamped the historic colleges of Harvard, Yale, Princeton, and Columbia. Taking the French *grande école* and the German research university as models, these leaders instituted rigorous research and training at new pedagogical sites—the science laboratory, the graduate seminar, and the undergraduate classroom—and promoted the ideals of *Lehrfreiheit* and *Lernfreiheit* (freedom to teach and learn). To regularize student education, they implemented admissions and graduation requirements, specialized programs of study, and grading. By the early twentieth century, two organizational trends had taken hold. Universities adopted the department system, whereby a group of scholars could grow their discipline, and professional associations sponsored conferences and journals that enabled like-minded faculty from geographically distant schools to share their work. The creation of department-based jobs, the emphasis on research and publication, and the freedom to teach and learn worked together to legitimize the faculty's disciplinary expertise, which in turn was invoked to justify departmental participation in university decision making.

Meanwhile, to provide the nation's economy with home-grown expertise, Congress had passed the Morrill Acts of 1862 and 1890, which allotted federal land to the states for the purpose of establishing public universities that would teach agricultural and industrial knowledge along with the liberal arts. The revenues flowing to land-grant universities had several effects. They multiplied the disciplines by growing the applied sciences, academicizing the practical crafts of pharmacy and home economics, solidifying the nascent social sciences, and sparking the interdisciplinary fields of urban affairs and public health. They engendered new organizational units: professional schools, teaching hospitals, and science institutes housed together in the multipurpose universities dotting midwestern and western states. Finally, they nudged higher education toward democratization by subsidizing low tuition rates that working-class youths could afford and extension services—agricultural stations, teacher workshops, and free medical clinics—that took the fruits of knowledge to the people. The Morrill Acts inaugurated the twentieth-century partnership between government and academe.

A Second Transformation World War II ushered in the second great transformation. Having learned from wartime collaborations that universities could produce military, industrial, and medical knowledge the nation needed, Congress formulated a coherent policy and used federal agencies to pump money into higher education. The grants and contracts paid for the university laboratories, equipment, and personnel that formed the infrastructure of the big sciences—physics, chemistry, biology, aerospace engineering, and computer science—and the overhead costs written into them subsidized

university libraries and facilities. Other congressional legislation, starting with the GI Bill (1944) and followed by federal scholarship programs, financed the waves of students that flowed onto the campuses. To edge the United States past the Soviet Union in the cold war race for techno-political supremacy, Congress primed the academic machinery for nearly two decades with money from old and new grantors, including the National Science Foundation (1950), the Department of Health, Education, and Welfare (1953), the National Endowments for the Humanities and the Arts (1965), and the Pell Grant Program (1965). Cold war revenues produced the academic boom that transformed campuses into conglomerates.

To accommodate their burgeoning educational programs and research projects, academic institutions erected buildings that crowded onto once grassy malls, recruited throngs of talented faculty and graduate students, and mechanized the unwieldy processes of registration, scheduling, and finance. As sedate liberal-arts colleges swelled into bustling universities that administered graduate and professional programs, and universities sprawled into multiversities that managed research parks, medical centers, sports enterprises, and branch campuses in urban and rural areas, they turned to the states for increased appropriations and found that the trade-off was decreased autonomy. By the mid-1970s the states had consolidated public institutions into a three-tiered system of flagship research universities, four-year colleges, and two-year community colleges regulated by a central higher-education office and dependent on the legislature for a large share of their income.

Numbers tell part of the story about how government revenues and institutional reorganization drove the expansion of higher education during these three periods. Between 1870 and 1900 the number of institutions rose from 563 to 977, faculty from 5,553 to 23,868, and students from 52,000 to 238,000, followed by steady increases over the next fifty years. Between 1949 and 1959 institutions grew modestly in number from 1,800 to 2,000, but ballooned in size as faculty jumped from 246,700 to 380,500 and students from 2.6 million to 3.5 million. Over the next twenty years the number of institutions soared to 3,200, faculty to 685,000, and students to 12 million. By 1980 the federal government was spending $4.3 billion on research and $10 billion on student aid, and the states were appropriating $21 billion for institutional operations. Though government largesse had built the world's largest higher-education system, with public institutions now educating 80 percent of the college population, the other part of the story is that expansion had failed to democratize it.

THE 1960s MOVEMENTS AND THE NEW CRITICAL STUDIES

As the nation lurched from World War II into the cold war, it entered what is often, and for good reason, called the decade of eclipse in American democracy. During the 1950s the nation's ruling elites turned against the people: political dissenters were prosecuted, homosexuals were persecuted, racial minorities continued to be oppressed, women who had worked in wartime jobs were redomesticated, public debate was shifted, and social conformity was exacted. Universities and colleges were not innocent bystanders; they fired leftist faculty, continued to impose quotas on Jews and Catholics, tracked women into so-called female fields of nursing, education, home economics, and social work, and closed their doors to racial minorities. Barred from southern white-only campuses and barely tolerated on northern ones, African Americans attended the historically black colleges that enrolled almost 75,000 students in 1950 and close to 100,000 by the early 1960s.

Yet beneath the surface of these calcified patterns of repression, little ruptures began to occur. McCarthyism stirred quiet outrage, reports of fallout sickness provoked questions about atomic-weapons testing, the shining promise of corporate jobs and suburban homes tarnished, the rebel played the hero's role in Beat poetry and Hollywood films, and forbidden images of sexuality bubbled onto magazine pages. The new sociology, much of it available to the public in cheap paperback editions, painted a critical picture of American life, depicting citizen alienation in *The Lonely Crowd* (1950), by David Riesman; the iron grip of the ruling class in *The Power Elite* (1956), by C. Wright Mills; lock-step corporate culture in *The Organization Man* (1956), by William Whyte; and manipulative advertising in *The Hidden Persuaders* (1957), by Vance Packard. The work of European intellectuals—Marxists, existentialists, structuralists, Frankfurt school theorists—trickled onto college campuses, inspiring faculty and students to found leftist journals and clubs. These little ruptures might have gone the way of all passing trends that are ignored by the media and frozen into the footnotes of history books, but something happened.

The Civil Rights Movement The racial protests that erupted in the South during the mid-1950s, rather than combusting spontaneously, were carefully orchestrated by organizations that African Americans had built over the course of a century: churches, schools, colleges, media outlets, and national political organizations. Permeating the grassroots, the National Association for the Advancement of Colored People (NAACP, 1910), Urban League (1911), and Congress of Racial Equality (CORE, 1942) established chapters; the Southern Conference Education Fund (1942) and Southern Christian Leadership Conference (SCLC, 1957) outreached through black college and church networks; and community improvement associations supported local activities. By the time the U.S. Supreme Court finally overturned the doctrine of "separate but equal" education in its ruling on *Brown v. Board of Education* (1954), these organizations were ready to take on the machinery that southern states used to keep the white-supremacist system in place.

What did that machinery do? The black-only state schools that inculcated ignorance or fear in children worked hand in hand with state-enforced segregation of public facilities, state-countenanced oppressive labor practices, state-mandated poll taxes and voter registration tests, and state-condoned vigilante violence to deny African Americans citizen rights, opportunities, and protections. Frustrated by the South's obduracy and the conservatism of the Eisenhower administration, civil rights and black community organizations began employing direct action, which attracted national media coverage and spread the struggle. The ten-day bus boycott in Baton Rouge (1953), the year-long bus boycott in Montgomery (1955–1956), and the battle to integrate Little Rock's Central High School (1957) inspired similar action in Tallahassee, Birmingham, New Orleans, and elsewhere. Then, in 1960, college students joined the fray, initiating the movement protests that would roil the nation for a decade.

That February, four black students sat at a whites-only Woolworth's lunch counter in Greensboro, North Carolina. Within months, fifty thousand students had held sit-ins in hundreds of southern towns, and by fall the leaders had founded the Student Nonviolent Coordinating Committee (SNCC). SNCC moved quickly from confrontational tactics to community organizing in the rural areas and small towns of the Deep South. In 1964 SNCC directed the Mississippi Freedom Summer Project, an ambitious statewide initiative to register black voters in the Mississippi Freedom Democratic Party, build community centers, and sponsor freedom schools. The two thousand youngsters and adults who attended the freedom schools held in black churches and homes were taught by volunteers who had attended a training institute in Oxford, Ohio, to learn techniques that would empower and politicize black communities. The local people learned how to carry on the struggle against the system that oppressed them, and the volunteers, mostly students and young faculty from northern campuses, were politicized by the Summer Project. They returned to their home communities with a sophisticated understanding of systemic oppression, organizational infrastructure, and social-change strategies that they would deploy in the New Left, antiwar, and women's movements.

The New Left   The southern struggle galvanized what would become a nationwide New Left movement. In 1960, after Bay Area students held a mass demonstration against the House Un-American Activities Committee hearings in San Francisco, they began forming campus political clubs and picketing local businesses to support the civil rights movement in its struggle against racism. Pressured by civic authorities, the administration of the University of California at Berkeley responded in the fall of 1964 by prohibiting the student clubs from engaging in political activities on university grounds. What happened next was that the two parties co-scripted an escalating conflict: the administration took disciplinary action, which provoked the student clubs to form a coalition called the Free Speech Movement (FSM) and organize rallies, which elicited more administration crackdowns, which in turn ignited mass demonstrations and building occupations, and so on. Thousands of Berkeley students and faculty, who would not have been roused by the FSM's critique of the multiversity, were radicalized in the hard-knocks school that the administration obligingly conducted by arresting, indicting, and suspending ever-larger numbers of protesters.

Did the university violate the students' right to free speech? "The Issue Was Not the Issue," said an FSM slogan. Rather, the FSM used the free-speech issue to mobilize students behind the big issue: that the multiversity, like a highly efficient factory, was churning out research for the military-industrial complex and fabricating raw student material into the technocrats, managers, and leaders that the establishment needed. Just before a two-day occupation of the administration building, FSM leader

Mario Savio made a statement that typified the New Left's analysis and activism:

> There is a time when the operation of the machine becomes so odious, makes you so sick at heart that you can't take part . . . and you've got to put your bodies upon the levers, upon all the apparatus and you've got to make it stop. And you've got to indicate to the people who run it, to the people who own it, that unless you're free the machine will be prevented from working at all. (Teodori, *The New Left,* p. 156)

The FSM showed students across the nation how to think critically about academic institutions, disrupt business as usual, and prefigure through their collective decision making the democracy they wanted the nation to adopt.

Also, in 1960 a small band of students at the University of Michigan launched Students for a Democratic Society (SDS). In its famous Port Huron Statement (1962), as well as other documents and discussions, SDS presented a wide-ranging indictment of the American system for failing to live up to its professed democratic principles and envisioned a participatory democracy that would, in the words of the evocative slogan SDS borrowed from SNCC, "Let the people decide." Policy makers would have to stop their power brokering and start solving the people's problems, bureaucracies would have to transfer decision making to citizen communities, the economy would have to be regulated by and for the people, and stultifying jobs would have to be redesigned to foster worker creativity and independence. Drawing on civil-rights analysis, SDS criticized educational institutions for their complicity with the state: schools trained students in obedience and tracked them into vocational or college-preparatory programs, while universities supplied the human and intellectual capital needed by the military-industrial complex. Since these relays between power and knowledge excluded "the people," the antidote was to build a student movement that would collaborate with the civil rights, labor, and peace movements on transforming the system.

At first SDS grew slowly, but after conducting political education projects on college campuses and organizing poor communities in northern cities, its 13 chapters and 1,000 members in 1962 increased to 125 chapters and 4,000 members in 1965. When SDS began sponsoring protests against the Vietnam War—in October 1965 some 30,000 people joined a Washington march, 20,000 a New York City parade, and 10,000 a Berkeley march—its membership surged to 100,000 in 1968. But the theory that students could make structural change did not pan out in practice because the New Left lacked the hard infrastructure that had sustained the civil-rights movement. It did not have institutions like the black churches and schools to provide historical continuity, councils like SNCC and SCLC to coordinate systemic initiatives, or professionalized organizations like the NAACP to litigate the nation's laws and policies. Moreover, the New Left often failed to abide by its own participatory ideal: power grabs by old and new movement members, tensions between black-power and white student groups, and sexist insults hurled at female activists hardened antagonisms into schisms.

Women's Movement Feminist ideas had been incubating in civil-liberties organizations, progressive labor unions, and women's club networks for over two decades before several events in the mid-1960s—including New Left sexism, the passage of the Civil Rights Act of 1964, and government truancy in implementing anti-discrimination laws—precipitated the formation of an independent women's movement. By 1971 feminists had built an infrastructure. In the political sector they had established the National Organization for Women (NOW, 1966), the Women's Equity Action League (WEAL, 1968), Human Rights for Women (1968), the National Women's Political Caucus (NWPC, 1971), and the Women's Legal Defense Fund (1971). In the civic sector, they were bringing feminist issues to such voluntary organizations as the League of Women Voters, the Young Women's Christian Association, the National Federation of Business and Professional Women's Clubs, the National Council of Negro Women, and the National Council of Jewish Women. In the academy they had carved out little toeholds—women's caucuses in professional associations, women's centers and courses on campuses, KNOW Press and the Feminist Press—to fight academic sex discrimination and build female studies.

But the primary tool for mobilizing a mass movement across these sectors was the small consciousness-raising (CR) group. First formed in 1969, CR groups had spread to virtually every city and campus town by 1971. As precursors of consciousness raising, the early feminists credited the Chinese peasants' technique of "speaking bitterness," the New Left's criticism–self-criticism meetings, and especially the catalytic organizing in the South. They regarded the CR group as a free space, something like SNCC's freedom schools, where women could share their experiences and assemble the picture they had not been permitted to see: that

their personal problems had social causes and therefore political solutions. The sudden insights, which were called "clicks," fanned their anger, which in turn drove them to take action in their own lives and join their sisters in movement activism.

Many Americans who witnessed 1960s activism from the sidelines were so stunned by the disorder that they could not assess the grievances voiced by the movements. They were horrified by the masses of people marching, occupying, chanting, and taunting, only to be beaten down by government forces, as when Chief Eugene "Bull" Connor's police unleashed attack dogs on black demonstrators at Birmingham in 1963, Chicago mayor Richard Daley's twelve thousand police warred with protesters at the Democratic Convention in 1968, and Ohio governor James Rhodes's state troopers fired on Kent State University students, killing four and wounding nine, in 1970. But other Americans would recognize, at least in retrospect, that these events dramatized the central grievance articulated by the movements which was that the widespread injustices sanctioned by laws, perpetuated by institutions, and enforced by them might bely the official ideology that America was a democracy.

The Critical Studies Building on the movements' insight into American society and education, leftist faculty and students launched the new critical studies—feminist, ethnic, gay-lesbian, cultural, and postcolonial—to study social formations. The critical studies generally followed three courses of inquiry: one was to open the disciplines to the histories and achievements of marginalized peoples; the second was to revise the biased concepts and theories derived from studying elite Western thought and culture; and the third was to analyze the intricated mechanisms of power/knowledge relays. Teachers and students wanted to understand how these mechanisms organized the political, economic, and cultural spheres; how they distributed material and social goods by sex, race, and class; and how they produced and repressed knowledge.

Feminist studies perhaps best exemplifies what has happened, or is happening, to so many of the critical studies; they started as insurgent projects then became scholarly disciplines. The founders of female studies, as it was then called, envisioned a project that would use the academy's wherewithal to produce knowledge of women and oppression that in turn could be deployed in the struggle for social change. In 1970, a year after the first few courses on women were offered at mainstream universities and colleges, the nascent field of female studies consisted of little more than some one hundred courses taught by marginal faculty, conventional literatures written by and about women, and photocopied papers on women's oppression circulated by the movement. By 1996 feminist studies was institutionalized as 630 women's studies programs, feminist subfields within the disciplines, some eighty research centers, hundreds of feminist presses and journals, and such organizations as the National Women's Studies Association and the National Council for Research on Women. Using this apparatus, academic feminists had produced a vast body of knowledge—data, analyses, theories—that spanned the disciplines.

What allowed academic feminists to build the apparatus was the academic trajectory of growth, corporatization, and competition. During the era of expansion, universities and colleges hoisted the faculty publishing requirements to gain an edge over peer institutions in the race for intellectual prestige. Hoping to profit from the growing academic markets, commercial presses issued books in the high-volume paperback format, but as production costs rose and fiscal problems set in, large corporations acquired the presses and retooled them according to business-management principles. The corporations brought commodification to publishing; they packaged and promoted books to attract purchasers and snapped up feminist work because its interdisciplinary scope and bold claims promised lucrative sales. Meanwhile, universities trimmed the subsidies that allowed their presses to publish traditional specialized scholarship, thereby edging the conservative sector of publishing toward the market competition for profitable scholarship. Together the prestige-hungry universities and the profit-seeking presses grew feminist studies, and the discipline, as it became more entrenched in the academy, was transformed from an insurgent project into a scholarly field.

FISCAL CRISES AND CONSERVATIVE DEFEDERALIZATION

Meanwhile, the forces that expanded higher education also set in motion the spiraling problems that would cripple it. Beginning with the OPEC oil crisis in the mid-1970s, the price of campus growth that administrators anticipated was repeatedly compounded by the soaring costs of fuel, building construction, regulatory compliance, and employee health care. Universities and colleges hired experts in corporate management to preside over the fis-

cal and operational complexities that traditional professor-administrators lacked the training to manage. The new managers revamped nonacademic operations and moved on to evaluate academic departments for their productivity, efficiency, and cost-effectiveness. Acting on the market imperatives, each institution scrambled for advantages over peer institutions in the competition for government appropriations and public approbation. But they had difficulty achieving these objectives because they had become more vulnerable to external constituencies.

As recipients of postwar revenues, academic institutions were required to submit project reports to government agencies and private foundations, document their compliance with federal laws, and inform donors of how their gifts were used. Demands for accountability proliferated when American politics was reorganized around interest groups. The social movements called for access to higher education, the states exacted services for support, the corporate partners insisted on applied research, the taxpayers expected better education for less money, the underpaid faculty unionized, and the legislators adopted line-item budgeting. Universities and colleges thus found themselves besieged by a dizzying array of constituency demands that they had too little wherewithal to satisfy. Then conservative government delivered the next series of jolts.

Soon after President Ronald Reagan took office in 1981, the Heritage Foundation, the leading conservative think tank, assembled *Mandate for Leadership* (1981) and *Mandate for Leadership II* (1984) to guide his administration. The "mandate" volumes accused federal education agencies of pandering to special interests because they enforced antidiscrimination laws; funded programs that helped female, minority, and learning-challenged students; and bestowed grants on the new critical scholarship and art. The volumes also contained several policy recommendations. For the Department of Education, the administration should eliminate most of its programs for female, minority, and learning-challenged students and refocus on two tasks: compiling national statistics on education and circulating ideas for educational reform. For other federal agencies, the administration should order them to retrench their civil-rights enforcement efforts to support only uncontroversial arts, traditional scholarship, and science that advanced government interests. Finally, the administration should back away from direct federal funding of education by giving block grants to the states to allocate as they see fit, shifting student aid from college scholarships to loans and instituting a voucher or tax-credit program to skirt the prohibition on public funding of private and religious schools. Critics saw these policy initiatives as a recantation of the federal commitment to ensure that citizens had equal rights, protections, and opportunities. They feared that the retreat from affirmative action and civil-rights enforcement would once again close the doors of higher education to historically excluded groups, that the elimination of programs helping disadvantaged students would widen the disparities between the haves and have-nots, and that the directives on research funding would constrain innovation in the arts, humanities, and sciences.

To win public support for the policy initiatives, the Reagan and Bush administrations referred to them as the defederalization of tax-and-spend government and claimed that defederalization was a trickle-down strategy that, by returning dollars to the states, would enhance services to citizens. Defederalization had the opposite effect because it transferred to the states not only revenues but also expenses, not only programs but also problems. Straining to fund overcrowded prisons, underfinanced schools, services for aging populations, and social programs retrenched by the federal government, the states reduced their appropriations to public universities. Whereas in the 1970s the states supplied public institutions with as much as 50 percent of their revenues, by the early 1990s they furnished between 33 percent and 12 percent. All states pulled back, and over two-thirds carved millions of real dollars out of public university budgets.

When soaring expenses and sprawling accountability collided with sluggish revenues, academic institutions were plunged into deep fiscal crisis. The problems may have been less acute for well-endowed colleges than for public universities with high-overhead medical centers, science laboratories, and technology complexes, but all institutions resorted to the same remedies. To increase income they raised tuitions, launched fund-raising drives with goals that rose from $100 million in the mid-1980s to over $1 billion in the late 1990s, stepped up their grant applications, and formed corporate research partnerships. To reduce expenses they deferred physical-plant maintenance, trimmed extracurricular services, cut library budgets, downsized nonacademic staff, converted full-time faculty lines to part-time instructorships, and even eliminated academic departments. To boost efficiency they instituted work speedups, larger classes, and time-to-graduation standards urging students to complete their degrees more quickly.

Everyone suffered. The money that administrators wrung from departments, libraries, and laboratories crimped education and research. The declining financial aid and rising tuition put college beyond the reach of many students. In 1980 a Pell Grant covered about 80 percent of an undergraduate's tuition at a public university and 40 percent at a private one; by 1994 it had dropped to 35 percent and 15 percent respectively. Most students took on loan debts and jobs that prolonged their time to graduation. The shift to cost-effective employment reorganized the professionalized faculty as an expendable work force. By the mid-1990s, over 50 percent of recent Ph.D.s were unemployed, and 45 percent of employed faculty nationwide held part-time positions as compared with 22 percent in 1970. Faculty working hours lengthened and salaries lagged behind the rate of inflation: on average, the full-timers worked 52.5 hours a week while the part-timers worked 33.8 hours a week for no benefits and substandard pay, 75 percent of them making less than $10,000 per year.

Defederalization completed the fourth great transformation of the higher-education system. Academic institutions had shifted from collegial governance to corporate managerialism, from intellectual inquiry to entrepreneurial research, from education as cultivation to education as commodity, from an era of growth that fueled democratization to an economy of scarcity that fed resentment.

POLITICAL CORRECTNESS
AND POLITICAL ACTION

The Reagan administration launched a public opinion campaign to gain support for restructuring higher education. Officials used their government posts as bully pulpits to proclaim that a gang of leftists—neo-Marxists, feminists, multiculturalists, and theorists—were destroying the academic humanities and, with them, the eternal verities of Western culture. The chairman of the National Endowment for the Humanities (NEH), William J. Bennett, sounded the alarm in a *Wall Street Journal* article ominously titled "The Shattered Humanities" (1982) and an NEH report prescriptively called *To Reclaim a Legacy* (1984). His successor, Lynne V. Cheney, followed suit by issuing several NEH reports: *The Humanities and the American Promise* (1987), *Humanities in America* (1988), *50 Hours* (1989), *Tyrannical Machine* (1990), and *Telling the*

243

Truth (1992). Other conservative officials stirred public qualms about affirmative action. At the Department of Education some declared that it had lowered educational standards, and at the Department of Justice others denounced it for imposing quotas on white men and giving preferences to racial minorities and women.

Taking the campaign into a variety of media markets, conservative intellectuals adopted the term "political correctness" for public consumption in a variety of media markets. They penned articles for conservative readers of the *National Review,* the *New Republic, Commentary,* and the *American Spectator;* business readers of *Forbes* and the *Wall Street Journal;* and general readers of the *Atlantic Monthly* and *U.S. News & World Report.* They wrote books with highly charged titles at the impressive rate of two per year. These included *Profscam: Professors and the Demise of Higher Education* (1988), by Charles Sykes; *Tenured Radicals: How Politics Has Corrupted Our Higher Education* (1990), by Roger Kimball; *Illiberal Education: The Politics of Race and Sex on Campus* (1991), by Dinesh D'Souza; and *Impostors in the Temple: American Intellectuals Are Destroying Our Universities and Cheating Our Students* (1992), by Martin Anderson.

The complaints about higher education spread like wildfires because conservative organizations supplied the kindling and fanned the flames. The Bradley, Olin, and Scaife foundations awarded generous research and promotion grants to many of the authors. The Intercollegiate Studies Institute, the Madison Center for Educational Affairs, and the National Association of Scholars (NAS) hyped stories of political correctness on campus in their journals and newsletters, as did syndicated columnists George Will and Cal Thomas and talk-show hosts Rush Limbaugh, Oliver North, and William F. Buckley Jr. Even think tanks like the Heritage Foundation, traditionally concerned with economic and political issues, sponsored policy papers and conferences on PC. The concerted effort produced results. While the number of print-media articles referring to political correctness soared from 66 in 1990 to 2,672 in 1992, the frequent references to PC in Congress spilled onto the pages of the *Congressional Record* and the *Congressional Quarterly* and into the airwaves of C-Span and the Voice of America.

By the time progressives began to defend the academy's democratized knowledges and policies in the early 1990s, conservatives had reframed the issues. The faculty were "thought police" for pointing out racism, sexism, classism, or homophobia in literature and scholarship; "barbarians" and "Visigoths" for criticizing Western civilization; "multiculturalists" for affirming the achievements of ethnic groups; and "relativists" for acknowledging the diversity of cultural values or the instability of textual meanings. Feminists were "femi-Nazis" for organizing against sex discrimination, and administrators were "the new McCarthyites" for investigating incidents of bigotry on campus. The curriculum was "dumbed down" by teaching popular culture, such as film or rock music; "primitivized" by assigning Alice Walker's novels; and "politicized" by doing critical analysis.

While progressives were busy responding to these claims, conservatives were working the channels of official politics to roll back the democratizing trends. Opposed to the national accrediting associations holding academic institutions to antidiscrimination laws and diversity standards, conservatives orchestrated a double-pronged strategy. As one prong, the conservative National Association of Scholars and Bush administration secretary of education Lamar Alexander pressured the accrediting associations to drop their diversity standards. As the other, the NAS founded the American Academy of Liberal Arts (AALE), a conservative accrediting agency opposed to regulating diversity standards, which the Education Department granted official status. The point of this strategy was not merely to halt democratization but to skirt the federal policy that only accredited schools could participate in student-aid programs; now any AALE-accredited institution could qualify for student aid while ignoring diversity. In a look-alike strategy, the NAS launched the National Alumni Forum (NAF). Besides lobbying against progressive programs and policies, NAF members used dollar power, withholding donations when an institution did not yield to their demands and contributing when it did.

Meanwhile, conservative organizations were masterminding policy initiatives that would dismantle affirmative action. The concepts of discrimination and affirmative action were codified by federal legislation, executive orders, and agency directives issued from 1964 onward. This body of law not only prohibited federally funded organizations from discriminating on the basis of race, sex, religion, and national origin, but also enjoined them to take affirmative measures to provide the protected groups with equal educational and employment opportunities. Conservatives claimed that affirmative-action procedures caused "reverse discrimination" against white men. If a university admissions committee considered a racially diverse student body to be desirable, it was said to give "preferences" to racial minorities. If a department set long-range goals for increasing the number of minority or female faculty, it was said to impose "quotas" on white men.

Emboldened by the conservative sweep of Congress and state offices in 1994 elections, the movement's machinery began grinding away to produce anti-affirmative action initiatives. The NAS searched for complaints of discrimination against whites, and conservative legal centers obligingly crafted the complaints as lawsuits against universities in Maryland, Texas, Michigan, Washington, and other states. Conservative governors, legislators, and regents called for an end to affirmative action in Arizona and California, and NAS members organized a voter referendum to ban affirmative action in California. After its passage, conservative California businessman and University of California regent Ward Connerly founded the American Civil Rights Institute to organize look-alikes in other states. A Washington state referendum passed, while a Florida referendum temporarily stalled when the conservative governor presented a plan for university admissions and hiring that would replace affirmative action.

The conservative argument that affirmative action had already remedied institutionalized discrimination against the protected groups was not, however, supported by the facts, which showed that women had made uneven gains in higher education and racial minorities had made negligible ones. As a proportion of the nationwide undergraduate enrollment, women had edged upward from 52.1 percent in 1988 to 54 percent by the mid-1990s. Yet as the level of education rose, the patterns of sex stratification and segregation became sharper. In 1997, when students from the late 1980s undergraduate cohort were completing their graduate education, women received about 40 percent of the total doctorates but they were still clustered in certain disciplines. Women earned a far higher proportion of total doctorates in the modern languages and feminized fields (e.g., education, social work) than in the sciences and a higher proportion in the qualitative or empirical sciences (e.g., anthropology, sociology) than in the quantitative and theoretical sciences (e.g., economics, physics). Moreover, faculty

women with doctorates were still disproportionately situated in part-time and nontenure-track jobs and still shunted into two-year colleges and the less prestigious four-year colleges and state universities.

During the Reagan and Bush years, the percentage of white high-school graduates enrolling in college rose while the percentages of African American and Hispanic American high-school graduates declined. Although the numbers of minority-group students began to increase in 1995, their proportions remained low: for the 1997 nationwide college enrollment, 0.8 percent were Native Americans, 8 percent were Hispanic Americans, and 10.6 percent were African Americans. At the graduate level, they were lower still: for 1996 doctorates, less than 0.5 percent went to Native Americans, 2.5 percent to Hispanic Americans, and 4.6 percent to African Americans. The gross percentage of doctorates awarded to African Americans is somewhat misleading for two reasons. First, like women, African Americans were not evenly distributed across the disciplines; in 1996 they received 10 percent of all doctorates in education but only 2 percent of all doctorates in many of the sciences and humanities. In English and American literature, a field that awarded nearly 60 percent of its doctorates to (predominantly white) women between 1993 and 1996, African Americans received on average 2 percent of the doctorates awarded during those years. Second, the underrepresentation of African American students in higher education would have been more acute without the historically black colleges and universities that educated the largest share of African American undergraduates who went on to graduate and professional programs. Finally, as academic institutions began taking affirmative action to remedy discrimination during the 1980s, the percentages of racial minorities hired into faculty positions rose slightly. But whites, who held 91 percent of the faculty positions nationwide in 1970, still held 88 percent of those positions in 1991.

The PC debate was not academic business as usual, with ivory-tower scholars bickering about books, sparring over speculations, and warring with words. The adversaries in this struggle did agree on one matter: they regarded academic institutions as the power tools that could be used to shape the nation's future.

BIBLIOGRAPHY

The Higher-Education System

INSTITUTIONALIZATION AND PROFESSIONALIZATION

Bledstein, Burton J. *The Culture of Professionalism: The Middle Class and the Development of Higher Education in America.* New York, 1978.

Clark, Burton R. *The Higher Education System: Academic Organization in Cross-National Perspective.* Berkeley, 1983.

Geiger, Roger L. *To Advance Knowledge: The Growth of the American Research Universities, 1900–1940.* New York, 1986.

Kerr, Clark. *The Great Transformation in Higher Education, 1960–1980.* Albany, N.Y., 1991.

Veysey, Laurence R. *The Emergence of the American University.* Chicago, 1965.

ORGANIZATION OF KNOWLEDGE

Becher, Tony. *Academic Tribes and Territories: Intellectual Enquiry and the Culture's of Disciplines.* Milton Keynes, U.K., 1989.

Klein, Julie Thompson. *Crossing Boundaries: Knowledge, Disciplinarities, and Interdisciplinarities.* Charlottesville, Va., 1996.

Oleson, Alexandra, and John Voss, eds. *The Organization of Knowledge in Modern America, 1860–1920.* Baltimore, 1979.

Shumway, David R., and Ellen Messer-Davidow. "Disciplinarity: An Introduction." *Poetics Today* 12, no. 2 (1991): 201–225.

CONSERVATIVE DEFEDERALIZATION

Docksai, Ronald F. "The Department of Education." In *Mandate for Leadership: Policy Management in a Conservative Administration.* Edited by Charles L. Heatherly. Washington, D.C., 1981.

Covington, Sally. *Moving a Public Policy Agenda: The Strategic Philanthropy of Conservative Foundations.* Washington, D.C., 1997.

Gardiner, Eileen M. "The Department of Education." In *Mandate for Leadership II: Continuing the Conservative Revolution.* Edited by Stuart M. Butler, Michael Sanera, and W. Bruce Weinrod. Washington, D.C., 1984.

Joyce, Michael S. "The National Endowments for the Humanities and Arts." In *Mandate for Leadership: Policy Management in a Conservative Administration.* Edited by Charles L. Heatherly. Washington, D.C., 1981.

Messer-Davidow, Ellen. "Dollars for Scholars: The Real Politics of Humanities Scholarship and Programs." In *The Politics of Research.* Edited by E. Ann Kaplan and George Levine. New Brunswick, N.J., 1997.

THE CONSEQUENCES OF FISCAL CRISES, CORPORATIZATION, AND CONSERVATIVE POLICY

Benjamin, Ernst. "A Faculty Response to the Fiscal Crisis: From Defense to Offense." In *Higher Education Under Fire: Politics, Economics, and the Crisis of the Humanities.* Edited by Michael Bérubé and Cary Nelson. New York, 1995.

Breneman, David W. "The 'Privatization' of Public Universities: A Mistake or a Model for the Future?" *Chronicle of Higher Education,* 7 March 1997, Sec. B, pp. B4–B5.

Lauter, Paul. "'Political Correctness' and the Attack on American Colleges." In *Higher Education Under Fire: Politics, Economics, and the Crisis of the Humanities.* Edited by Michael Bérubé and Cary Nelson. New York, 1995.

Rhoades, Gary, and Sheila Slaughter. "Academic Capitalism, Managed Professionals, and Supply-Side Higher Education." In *Chalk Lines: The Politics of Work in the Managed University.* Edited by Randy Martin. Durham, N.C., 1998.

Slaughter, Sheila, and Larry L. Leslie. *Academic Capitalism: Politics, Policies, and the Entrepreneurial University.* Baltimore, 1997.

Tirelli, Vincent. "Adjuncts and More Adjuncts: Labor Segmentation and the Transformation of Higher Education." In *Chalk Lines: The Politics of Work in the Managed University.* Edited by Randy Martin. Durham, N.C., 1998.

Vest, Charles M. "Research Universities: Overextended, Underfocused; Overstressed, Underfunded." In *The American University: National Treasure or Endangered Species?* Edited by Ronald G. Ehrenberg. Ithaca, N.Y., 1997.

The Social Movements, 1960–1980

THE CIVIL RIGHTS MOVEMENT

Graham, Hugh Davis. *The Civil Rights Era: Origins and Development of National Policy, 1960–1972.* New York, 1990.

McAdam, Doug. *Political Process and the Development of Black Insurgency, 1930–1970.* Chicago, 1982.

Morris, Aldon D. *The Origins of the Civil Rights Movement: Black Communities Organizing for Change.* New York, 1984.

Williams, Juan. *Eyes on the Prize: America's Civil Rights Years, 1954–1965.* New York, 1987.

THE NEW LEFT MOVEMENT

Gitlin, Todd. *The Sixties: Years of Hope, Days of Rage.* New York, 1987.

Heirich, Max. *The Spiral of Conflict: Berkeley 1964.* New York, 1971.

Miller, James. *"Democracy Is in the Streets": From Port Huron to the Siege of Chicago.* New York, 1987.

Teodori, Massimo. *The New Left: A Documentary History.* Indianapolis, Ind., 1969. Combines historical narrative with documents written by movement members.

THE WOMEN'S MOVEMENT

Ehols, Alice. *Daring to Be Bad: Radical Feminism in America, 1967–75.* Minneapolis, Minn., 1989.

Evans, Sara M. *Personal Politics: The Roots of Women's Liberation in the Civil Rights Movement and the New Left.* New York, 1979.

Hartmann, Susan M. *The Other Feminists: Activists in the Liberal Establishment.* New Haven, Conn., 1998.

Hole, Judith, and Ellen Levine. *The Rebirth of Feminism.* New York, 1971.

THE GAY AND LESBIAN MOVEMENTS

Adam, Barry D. *The Rise of a Gay and Lesbian Movement.* Boston, 1987.

D'Emilio, John. *Sexual Politics, Sexual Communities: The Making of a Homosexual Minority in the United States, 1940–1970.* Chicago, 1983.

———. *Making Trouble: Essays on Gay History, Politics, and the University.* New York, 1992. Contains several essays on gays and lesbians in higher education.

THE CONSERVATIVE MOVEMENT

Blumenthal, Sidney. *The Rise of the Counter-Establishment: From Conservative Ideology to Political Power.* New York, 1986.

Gottfried, Paul. *The Conservative Movement.* Rev. ed. New York, 1993.

Himmelstein, Jerome L. *To the Right: The Transformation of American Conservatism.* Berkeley, 1990.

Messer-Davidow, Ellen. "Manufacturing the Attack on Liberalized Higher Education." *Social Text* no. 36 (1993), 40–80.

The New Critical Studies

FEMINIST STUDIES

Boxer, Marilyn Jacoby. *When Women Ask the Questions: Creating Women's Studies in America.* Baltimore, 1998.

Collins, Patricia Hill. *Black Feminist Thought: Knowledge, Consciousness, and the Politics of Empowerment.* Boston, 1990.

CULTURAL STUDIES

Grossberg, Lawrence, Cary Nelson, and Paula A. Treichler, eds. *Cultural Studies.* New York, 1992.

Long, Elizsabeth, ed. *From Sociology to Cultural Studies: New Perspectives.* Malden, Mass., 1997.

GAY-LESBIAN STUDIES

Beemyn, Brett, and Mickey Eliason, eds. *Queer Studies: A Lesbian, Gay, Bisexual, and Transgender Anthology.* New York, 1996.

Foster, Thomas, Carol Siegel, and Ellen E. Barry, eds. *The Gay '90s: Disciplinary and Interdisciplinary Formations in Queer Studies.* New York, 1997.

MULTICULTURAL STUDIES

Goldberg, David Theo, ed. *Multiculturalism: A Critical Reader.* Oxford and Cambridge, Mass., 1994.

Gordon, Avery F., and Christopher Newfield, eds. *Mapping Multiculturalism.* Minneapolis, Minn., 1996.

POSTCOLONIAL STUDIES

Chaturvedi, Vinayak, ed. *Mapping Subaltern Studies and the Postcolonial.* London, 1999.

Moore-Gilbert, Bart, Gareth Stanton, and Willy Maley, eds. *Postcolonial Criticism.* New York, 1997.

Interest-Group Politics and Economics

Barlett, Donald L., and James B. Steele. *America: What Went Wrong?* Kansas City, Mo., 1992.

Danziger, Sheldon, and Peter Gottschalk, eds. *Uneven Tides: Rising Inequality in America.* New York, 1993.

Edsall, Thomas Byrne, and Mary D. Edsall. *Chain Reaction: The Impact of Race, Rights, and Taxes on American Politics.* New York, 1991.

Hunter, James Davison. *Culture Wars: The Struggle to Define America.* New York, 1991.

Steinberg, Stephen. *Turning Back: The Retreat from Racial Justice in America.* Boston, 1995.

Tolchin, Susan J. *The Angry American: How Voter Rage Is Changing the Nation.* Boulder, Colo., 1996.

The Political Correctness Debate

CONSERVATIVE LITERATURE

Anderson, Martin. *Impostors in the Temple.* New York, 1992.

Bloom, Allan. *The Closing of the American Mind.* New York, 1987.

D'Souza, Dinesh. *Illiberal Education: The Politics of Race and Sex on Campus.* New York, 1991.

Kimball, Roger. *Tenured Radicals: How Politics Has Corrupted Higher Education.* New York, 1990.

Smith, Page. *Killing the Spirit: Higher Education in America.* New York, 1990.

Sykes, Charles J. *Profscam: Professors and the Demise of Higher Education.* Washington, D.C., 1988.

——. *The Hollow Men: Politics and Corruption in Higher Education.* Washington, D.C., 1990.

PROGRESSIVE LITERATURE

Booth, Wayne. "A Politically Correct Letter to the Newspaper." *Democratic Culture* 3, no. 1 (1994), 2.

Feldstein, Richard. *Political Correctness: A Response from the Cultural Left.* Minneapolis, Minn., 1997.

Levine, Lawrence W. *The Opening of the American Mind: Canons, Culture, and History.* Boston, 1996.

Newfield, Christopher, and Ronald Strickland, eds. *After Political Correctness: The Humanities and Society in the 1990s.* Boulder, Colo., 1995.

Williams, Jeffrey, ed. *PC Wars: Politics and Theory in the Academy.* New York, 1995.

Wilson, John K. *The Myth of Political Correctness: The Conservative Attack on Higher Education.* Durham, N.C., 1995.

ANTHOLOGIES

Aufderheide, Patricia, ed. *Beyond PC: Toward a Politics of Understanding.* St. Paul, Minn., 1992.

Berman, Paul, ed. *Debating PC: The Controversy over Political Correctness on College Campuses.* New York, 1992.

Flashpoint Issues in the 1990s

AFFIRMATIVE ACTION: CONSERVATIVE VIEWS

Bolick, Clint. *The Affirmative Action Fraud: Can We Restore the American Civil Rights Vision?* Washington, D.C., 1996.

Eastland, Terry. *Ending Affirmative Action: The Case for Colorblind Justice.* New York, 1996.

Kahlenberg, Richard D. *The Remedy: Class, Race, and Affirmative Action.* New York, 1996.

Lynch, Frederick R. *Invisible Victims: White Males and the Crisis of Affirmative Action.* New York, 1989.

Sowell, Thomas. *Preferential Policies: An International Perspective.* New York, 1990.

AFFIRMATIVE ACTION: PROGRESSIVE VIEWS

Bergmann, Barbara A. *In Defense of Affirmative Action.* New York, 1996.

Bowen, William G., and Derek Bok. *The Shape of the River: Long-Term Consequences of Considering Race in College and University Admissions.* Princeton, N.J., 1998.

Edley, Chistopher, Jr. *Not All Black and White: Affirmative Action, Race, and American Values.* New York, 1996.

Lawrence, Charles R., III, and Mari J. Matsuda. *We Won't Go Back: Making the Case for Affirmative Action.* Boston, 1997.

Takagi, Dana Y. *The Retreat from Race: Asian-American Admissions and Racial Politics.* New Brunswick, N.J., 1992.

AFFIRMATIVE ACTION: LAWS AND CONSEQUENCES

Brody, Carl E., Jr. "A Historical Review of Affirmative Action and the Interpretation of Its Legislative Intent by the Supreme Court." *Akron Law Review* 29, no. 1 (1996), 291–334.

Carlson, Scott. "Minority Students Posted Slight Increase in College Enrollments in 1997, Report Says." *Chronicle of Higher Education,* 17 December 1999, Sec. A, p. 53.

Cross, Theodore, and Robert Bruce Slater. "Special Report: Why the End of Affirmative Action Would Exclude All But a Very Few Blacks from America's Leading Universities and Graduate Schools." *Journal of Blacks in Higher Education* 17 (1997): 8–17.

Gerstman, Evan. *The Constitutional Underclass: Gays, Lesbians, and the Failure of Class-Based Equal Protection.* Chicago, 1999.

LaNoue, George R., and Barbara A. Lee. *Academics in Court: The Consequences of Faculty Discrimination Litigation.* Ann Arbor, Mich., 1987.

Magner, Denise K. "The Number of Minority Ph.D.'s Reached an All-Time High in 1996." *Chronicle of Higher Education,* 21 November 1997, Sec. A, pp. 10–11.

FEMINISM: CONSERVATIVE VIEWS

Simon, Rita J., ed. *Neither Victim nor Enemy: Women's Freedom Network Looks at Gender in America.* Landham, Md., 1995.

Sommers, Christina Hoff. *Who Stole Feminism? How Women Have Betrayed Women.* New York, 1994.

FEMINISM: PROGRESSIVE VIEWS

Chamberlain, Mariam, ed. *Women in Academe: Progress and Prospects.* New York, 1988.

Clark, VéVé, et al., eds. *Antifeminism in the Academy.* New York, 1996.

HOMOSEXUALITY: CONSERVATIVE VIEWS

LaHaye, Tim. *The Unhappy Gays: What Everyone Should Know about Homosexuality.* Wheaton, Ill., 1978.

HOMOSEXUALITY: PROGRESSIVE VIEWS

Herman, Didi. *The Antigay Agenda: Orthodox Vision and the Christian Right.* Chicago, 1997.

Gluckman, Amy, and Betsy Reed, eds. *Homo Economics: Capitalism, Community, and Lesbian and Gay Life.* New York, 1997.

Race

CONSERVATIVE VIEWS

D'Souza, Dinesh. *The End of Racism: Principles for a Multiracial Society.* New York, 1995.

Steele, Shelby. *The Content of Our Character: A New Vision of Race in America.* New York, 1990.

Thernstrom, Abigail. *Whose Votes Count?: Affirmative Action and Minority Voting Rights.* Cambridge, Mass., 1987.

Thernstrom, Stephan, and Abigail Thernstrom. *America in Black and White: One Nation, Indivisible.* New York, 1997.

PROGRESSIVE VIEWS

Ansell, Amy Elizabeth. *New Right, New Racism: Race and Reaction in the United States and Britain.* New York, 1997.

Guinier, Lani. *The Tyranny of the Majority: Fundamental Fairness in Representative Democracy.* New York, 1994.

Omi, Michael, and Howard Winant. *Racial Formations in the United States: From the 1960s to the 1990s.* 2d ed. New York, 1994

West, Cornel. *Race Matters.* New York, 1994.

THE BELL CURVE

This book sparked an incendiary debate about race by putting a quantitative spin on the old doctrine of hereditarianism that linked intelligence to race. The authors asserted that data obtained from IQ testing and other sources show that African Americans as a group inherently have a lower intelligence than Asian-Americans and white Americans. See, for instance:

Fischer, Claude S. et al. *Inequality by Design: Cracking the Bell Curve Myth.* Princeton, N.J., 1996.

Herrnstein, Richard J., and Charles Murray. *The Bell Curve: Intelligence and Class Structure in American Life.* New York, 1994.

Jacoby, Russell, and Naomi Glauberman, eds. *The Bell Curve Debate: History, Documents, Opinions.* New York, 1995.

MULTICULTURALISM IN THEORY AND PRACTICE

Nathan Glazer

"Multiculturalism" is a term that describes both a reality and an ideology or program. When it refers to the fact that people may come from many cultures and create many subcultures while living in a common polity, a common society, or indeed a common culture, it would seem on the surface to describe a reality. Of course there are empirical issues of how to describe the degree of multifariousness that the term refers to, and what behavioral consequences follow from it. But when "multiculturalism" refers to an ideology or program, describing how such a society or polity should be organized, or how its culture should be influenced or directed or shaped, it raises great issues of policy, primarily in the field of education. These have been fiercely disputed through the last few decades of the twentieth century, and the disputes continue in the new millennium.

PRECURSORS

The term "multiculturalism" surprisingly sprang into widespread use only at the end of the 1980s and in the 1990s. The word—even the more plainly descriptive "multicultural"—is not to be found in dictionaries much before 1990. The Harvard library catalog lists some 750 books under the subject heading "multiculturalism." Almost none were published before 1990, and of those published earlier, many deal with developments in countries other than the United States. In Canada, multiculturalism became an official term with the Canadian Multiculturalism Act of 1988, "An Act for the preservation and enhancement of multiculturalism in Canada." A Department of Multiculturalism and Citizenship was established in 1991, which promotes multicultural activities. (It became the Department of Canadian Heritage in 1995.)

There is nothing like this official recognition of multiculturalism in the United States, nor is it to be expected. Yet the reality to which the term refers has of course characterized American society since its founding. In 1782, the author of *Letters from an American Farmer* could answer his famous question, "What then is the American, this new man?" with an ethnic miscellany:

> He is either an European, or the descendant of an European, hence that strange mixture of blood, which you will find in no other country. I could point out to you a family whose grandfather was an Englishman, whose wife was Dutch, whose son married a French woman, and whose present four sons have four wives of different nations. *He* is an American, who, leaving behind him all his ancient prejudices and manners, receives new ones from the new mode of life he has embraced, the new government he obeys.... Here individuals of all nations are melted into a new race of men. (Michel-Guillaume Jean de Crèvecoeur, *Letters from an American Farmer,* as in Gleason, 33)

Today, multiculturally sensitive, we note the exclusion or ignoring of native American Indians and African blacks in this listing; that a "melting" rather than a continuance of language and culture is expected; that the "new race" is "of men." But what should arouse special notice in this statement considered in the context of its time is that it was meant to contrast America with the narrower, more restrictive, less open, less welcoming, less "multicultural" societies of Europe. The "new race" is to be created not by a harsh limitation on the continuance of language, culture, religion; rather, it comes into existence because of the openness of a free government allowing people to develop and change as they will. This is what Crèvecoeur wants to tell us.

Similarly with later, more inclusive expressions of how diversity fares in America. So Ralph Waldo Emerson, writing in 1845 in his journal against the Know-Nothings:

> I hate the narrowness of the Native American party. Man is the most composite of all creatures ... as in the old burning of the Temple at Corinth, by the melting & intermixture of silver & gold & other metals, a new compound more precious than any, called the Corinthian Brass, was formed so in this

Continent,—asylum of all nations, the energy of Irish, Germans, Swedes, Poles & (the) Cossacks, & all the European tribes,—of the Africans, & of the Polynesians, will construct a new race, a new religion, a new State, a new literature, which will be as vigorous as the new Europe which came out of the smelting pot of the Dark Ages. (Emerson, *Journals,* 9:299–300, as in Sollors, p. 95)

THE "MELTING POT"

Such early celebrations of American diversity are today noted more to emphasize who is excluded (though Emerson excluded nobody) than who is included, but also to note with multicultural disapproval the expectation of ultimate assimilation. Do not such sentiments celebrate, before the creation of the term itself, the "melting pot," the stark alternative to the continuity of distinctive culture and identity? But in fact there is great similarity in how both ideals have been envisaged historically: Both are considered to be the undirected and freely chosen outcome of life in a free and open society.

This is the case with *The Melting-Pot* itself, the successful play of 1909 by Israel Zangwill from which the term derives. Zangwill's—as Emerson's—idea of the melting pot was inclusive, accepting, resulting in a new and better society. As the hero declaims:

Ah, what a stirring and a seething! Celt and Latin, Slav and Teuton, Greek and Syrian,—black and yellow . . . East and West, . . . the crescent and the cross . . . ! Here shall they all unite to build the Republic of Man and the Kingdom of God. (Quoted in Levine, p. 107)

One may oppose the melting pot even in this expansive formulation. But one must recognize the difference between choosing it and being thrust into it, between a society of forced uniformity and one in which individual choices—as in the case of *The Melting Pot* itself, where the Jewish hero and the daughter of a Russian anti-Semite choose each other—create something new and different and better. The melting pot came in various versions, from the most liberal and the most welcoming to the most crabbed and most restrictive, as is the case too with multiculturalism. In the liberal form of the two contrasting ideals, there was a great deal in common.

CULTURAL PLURALISM

We see this clearly as the first well-known alternative to melting pot ideology emerges during World War I, in the writing of the philosopher Horace Kallen and the journalist Randolph Bourne. They are considered the creators of "cultural pluralism," a concept later coined by Kallen and itself a forerunner of multiculturalism. Cultural pluralism comes close to the multicultural ideal. Consider a speech John Dewey gave to educators in 1916, which Kallen quotes at length in support of cultural pluralism in his *Culture and Democracy in the United States.* The demand for an exclusive loyalty was then at its height, and former president Theodore Roosevelt denounced "hyphenated" loyalty. Dewey responds:

Such terms as Irish-American or Hebrew-American or German-American are false terms because they assume something which is already in existence called America, to which the other factors may be externally hitched on. The fact is, the genuine American, the typical American, is himself a hyphenated character. This does not mean that he is part American and that some foreign ingredient is then added. It means that . . . he is international and interracial in his make-up. He is not American plus Pole or German. But the American is himself Pole - German - English - French - Spanish - Italian - Greek-Irish-Scandinavian-Bohemian-Jew—and so on. The point is to see to it that the hyphen connects instead of separates. And this means at least that our public schools shall teach each factor to respect every other, and shall take pains to enlighten all as to the great past contributions of every strain in our composite make-up. (Kallen, pp. 131–132)

In our age of multicultural alertness, one notes that Dewey refers to Europeans only. But the context of Dewey's speech was a widespread attack on *European* immigrants for putting loyalty to homeland over loyalty to the United States. The necessary task of the times was to teach that no group is to be favored in the American mix. The American identity was being forged, and the newer immigrant groups played as legitimate a role in making it as the earlier ones. Dewey again:

No matter how loudly anyone proclaims his Americanism if he assumes that any one racial strain, any one component culture, no matter how early settled it was in our territory, or how effective it has proven in its own land, is to furnish a pattern to which all other strains and cultures are to conform, he is a traitor to an American nationalism. (Quoted in Sollors, p. 88)

THE ROAD TO MULTICULTURALISM

Cultural pluralism had little impact when it was formulated, on thinking in general or in the area where one might have expected the greatest effect, the schools. They were then busy with the education or socialization or training of the huge numbers of immigrant children, as dominant in the big cities of the 1920s as they are today. The dominant style was Americanization. Jewish and Italian children may have made up two-thirds or more of the schoolchildren in the public schools of New York City, but they heard nothing of Jewish or Italian culture or history, and it took a considerable effort to introduce the teaching of Italian and Hebrew as voluntary foreign language choices into a few city high schools.

With the coming of World War II, and the rising political influence of immigrants and the children of immigrants, the rigorous Americanism that was the pattern of American public school education in the 1920s and 1930s softened. With a new international war looming, ethnic groups (Japanese aside) were no longer to be viewed with suspicion but with solicitude, in order to recruit them in the service of the war effort.

If Hitler preached intolerance, America should preach tolerance. If he taught racism, we should teach that race was a constructed fiction and could not be used to justify a racially hierarchical society. The anthropological work of Franz Boas and his students made this argument, which began to influence the schools. And so another predecessor to multiculturalism emerged, under the name of "intercultural education." Intercultural education had a brief run during and after the war years but then petered out. Its major teaching was tolerance, and its basic theme was that we should learn about and appreciate others. Blacks were now clearly included, along with American Indians and Mexican Americans.

But teaching tolerance, good as it is, did not engage effectively with the realities of racism and discrimination in an America with a built-in racial and ethnic hierarchy. To do so would require a social movement, the exercise of power, and the use of the resources for change that American society and politics made available. With the civil rights upheavals of the 1950s, it was inevitable that American culture and education would change.

CIVIL RIGHTS AND MULTICULTURALISM

There was no necessary connection in logic between the civil rights revolution and the multicultural transformation that flowed from it. Civil rights initially seemed to call for an abstract equality. Blacks demanded for blacks only what whites had: entry into the same schools, the same public accommodations, the same treatment in applying for a job or an apartment, the same treatment in the armed forces and by every branch of government. This was the language of the Civil Rights Acts of 1964 and 1965. It was not at the beginning clear that any implications for culture followed. Would schools and colleges have to be different because blacks entered what were once white schools and colleges? There was no demand by civil rights advocates that they should be: they were asking only for what privileged whites already had.

But it turned out that everything else had to change too. One could ask—many did—why must we now have black or Jewish or Chicano studies, if there were no Jewish or Italian studies when these groups entered public colleges in large numbers? But the expectation that only the color of those learning and teaching would change with the expansion of equal treatment turned out to be false. American blacks were not merely Americans with black skins. There was a distinctive culture or cultures, variably affecting many blacks, and when integration replaced segregation, that fact would have to affect what was taught and how it was taught. The impact on curriculum was also marked as the number of Latino students increased, and as an expanded feminist ideology affected women.

One could have imagined a situation such as prevails in some formerly colonial countries where, despite the enormous differences in culture and climate, the curriculum imposed by the former colonizing power has been retained. But the civil rights revolution was also a revolution in consciousness. So in the elementary and secondary schools and colleges it became evident that something was wrong with curricula and texts in which no blacks appeared. Those in charge might not see a problem, but many black students and teachers and parents did. The political and social movement for racial equality had cultural and intellectual consequences that were not part of its original plan. What concern after all did Thurgood Marshall or Martin Luther King Jr. voice over school curricula?

The stages of the development of multiculturalism can be matched quite directly with the political stages of the civil rights movement: changing demands, changing language, and an expanding consciousness that detected disdain or denial of presence or difference in long-established language and practice—all of these things had curricular consequences.

The story of what happened in education provides the central thread for the account of multiculturalism that is given here, though something

255

that may be called "multiculturalism" was evident and expanding in almost every sphere of life: in entertainment, in business, in fashion, in the mass media. All these sectors responded variously to an expanding and different market, to a changing work force, to new opportunities, as well as to demands from minority groups and to the requirements of law and administrative regulation.

Affirmative action in employment, the explicit mandate to recruit minorities, was one of the major consequences of the civil rights movement—though not something originally intended. It had important bearing on how multiculturalism developed. Formulated in the late 1960s and early 1970s during the Nixon administration, expanded and maintained during subsequent years by federal, state, and city governments, it affected the employment policies of colleges and universities and schools, bringing in more black and other minority and women administrators and teachers. In time, affirmative action in employment hardly depended on legal requirements; it had become part of common practice, part of the necessary culture of schools and colleges. Similarly with affirmative action in college and university and professional school admissions. These affirmative targets or preferences or quotas, however, came under challenge in the later 1990s and were limited by various means—referendum, legal challenge, or political action—in California, Texas, Washington, and Florida. To alarmed defenders of affirmative action this meant the end of diversity, an attack on multiculturalism. But in fact no such consequences followed: the presence of black students in the colleges and universities of these states was not much reduced, nor the strong role of multicultural practices in them.

Similarly, radio and television were changed by regulatory decisions, by the expansion of black and other submarkets, and by the increase in black and minority performers. Newspapers and magazines became more sensitive to their black and other minority markets and to the need to add minority reporters and writers. Along with widened opportunities, greater awareness of markets led to a change in what kind of entertainment and news were provided. There were indeed different cultures and subcultures, and the employment of personnel from a subculture would enlighten administrators to either an opportunity or a necessity in the practice of their business. Thus multicultural consciousness increasingly suffused the culture in the 1980s and 1990s.

All this was the fallout from the civil rights revolution. Rights had consequences for culture. Of course not all minority individuals wanted the same news or entertainment or education or anything different from what was provided before. Not all minorities employed in the schools and colleges and mass media brought a new perspective to their place of work. But with the change in consciousness that was both created and furthered by the civil rights revolution, it was increasingly the case that employees from a new and underrepresented group also meant a new and underrepresented perspective.

Multiculturalism was primarily the consequence of the civil rights revolution. While black Americans launched it to overcome their caste condition, the civil rights demanded and won by blacks were formulated, whether as political demand or realized legislation, in universal terms. There was to be no discrimination on grounds of race—nor on grounds of sex or national origin. The consequences of the demand for equality could not be limited to the one great group that had been deprived of equality from the beginning of English colonization. American racism had not been limited to blacks. And so while the condition of blacks was the primary cause for the wave of antidiscrimination legislation, and their demands the primary motivator of a rising multicultural consciousness, Asian groups, Mexicans, Puerto Ricans, women, and in time homosexuals and lesbians were all included, even if the grounds of deprivation and its scale and weight were very different. In each case, an initial demand for equal treatment rapidly evolved into a demand for the recognition of distinctiveness, a recognition that was expected to reshape institutions. The most affected and vulnerable institutions were the schools and colleges.

COLLEGE AND UNIVERSITY

The impact of multiculturalism in colleges and universities has produced an enormous literature, more one of attack than of defense, and one in which key incidents and conflicts recur again and again. One could tell the story through these conflicts: the battle over a course on Western Civilization at Stanford in 1987–1988; the battle over a required course for all students on ethnic and racial groups at Berkeley shortly thereafter; conflicts over the disciplining of faculty or students who had offended or outraged minority students with comments and assertions in or outside of class at many institutions; conflicts over the establishment of separate living quarters and centers for minority students; conflicts over speech codes; conflicts over the degree to which courses and centers of studies for each group should be created; and the like.

It is impossible to characterize on the basis of comprehensive research the degree to which the huge world of higher education, with its thirty-five hundred institutions of very different types, has been influenced by the rise of multiculturalism. Some titles of the many books dealing with the impact of multiculturalism on the American college and university—*The Closing of the American Mind, The War Against the Intellect, Tenured Radicals, Killing the Spirit, Illiberal Education, The De-Valuing of America, Dictatorship of Virtue: Multiculturalism and the Battle for America's Future, The Menace of Multiculturalism*—suggest that the impact has been enormous, but we do not have the comprehensive research we had during the McCarthy period, or during the student revolt of the late 1960s and early 1970s, that would enable us to answer some of the most important questions.

We know there are black and other ethnic studies centers and women's studies centers almost everywhere; we know there has been a great increase in courses, in both specially created programs and traditional departments, dealing with minority groups and women. But to what extent does the atmosphere on campus inhibit faculty and students in presenting opinions and analyses or even facts that might be considered offensive to these groups? Some intimidation undoubtedly exists. To what degree is this inhibition a proper corrective to a pre-existing insensitivity or crudity in discussing issues affecting these groups? We have strongly felt opinions, but we do not have extensive research on student and faculty attitudes and experience. What research we have, as in faculty surveys and in some partial student surveys, suggests most faculty and students think "diversity" and "multiculturalism" a good thing. These surveys have on the whole been conducted by researchers who agree with this opinion. Other, more skeptical researchers who ask more searching questions might uncover a different story.

Many books view the situation from the perspective of the most widely covered and controversial conflicts. How characteristic these conflicts are is not clear. At the worst, we have a picture of higher education under a pall, in which each group is separated from the other; each is taught, in separate courses and centers, a distorted view of both its own and the general history and culture; and in which faculty and students lie silent under restrictive speech codes and the demands of political correct-

ness. This extreme picture may be realized in some places at some times. But surely one must exempt from the general impact of multiculturalism such fields of study as mathematics, the natural and biological sciences, and some fields of the humanities and social sciences, such as economics, that are little affected by multiculturalism. One wonders also to what extent the most widely studied field in American postsecondary education, business, is affected—and, if it is affected at all, is it not as a result of practical considerations of changing markets and the like?

But the softer social sciences, sociology and anthropology, are certainly affected by multiculturalism, as are the study of literature and some of the preprofessional fields, in particular, education. If the impact is not as extensive as the critics charge and fear, it is substantial. But we must also note that on the other side of the political spectrum there are advocates of a more far-reaching multiculturalism, labeled critical, or transformative, or insurgent, who claim that multiculturalism has been co-opted by the establishment, that it has produced no substantial change at all, and that it is at best a kind of unintegrated "add-on" to what is still primarily a Eurocentric curriculum.

There are at least three key areas in which the development of multiculturalism has raised some important issues for higher and postsecondary education: ethnic studies, "political correctness," and voluntary segregation.

ETHNIC STUDIES

By the late 1960s, the student revolt that had begun in 1964 at the University of California, Berkeley, and whose causes are still debated, had spread to almost all institutions of higher education. Demands connected with civil rights—for more black students, faculty, studies—were widespread, though the nationwide growth of the student revolt was driven primarily by the expansion of the war in Vietnam. Black students formed a separate wing of the student movement on many campuses, pursuing their own demands, with the support of white students. The numbers of black students—and very shortly Mexican American and American Indian students—rapidly increased on hundreds of campuses as a result of special programs of preparation and recruitment. Black studies programs, variously named, were launched on hundreds of campuses.

The first and best-established expression of multiculturalism in higher education was the rise of centers for the study of the experience of American blacks. To these were soon added, where the numbers of such students were large, academic centers for the study of the experience of Mexican Americans, Puerto Ricans, and other groups of Latin American origin; American Indians; and Asians. Almost everywhere, women's studies centers were also established, as a consequence of the rise of the women's movement. These too are generally encompassed under the capacious label of "multiculturalism." In the 1990s, this pattern spread to include a number of centers for gay and lesbian studies, and their numbers will undoubtedly increase. Aside from specifically named centers and departments, courses in traditional departments dealing with all these groups increased greatly. For a while in the 1970s it appeared as if centers for the study of European Americans might also emerge, but this did not happen on any large scale. The only European group for which the institutional base expanded was Jews, and this primarily because of the Holocaust. Jewish studies centers are often but not always Holocaust studies centers.

Almost all of these new academic enterprises raised troubling questions. They were all interdisciplinary, dealing with history, sociology and anthropology, literature, and other areas with traditionally distinct standards and methods. More problematic was the fact that the new programs were clearly centers of advocacy as well as centers of scholarship. The mixture varied, but advocacy was always present, an advocacy at the least for consciousness and recognition of racial or ethnic difference. This was something new in higher education.

Second, it was taken for granted that ethnic studies would be guided by faculty drawn from the ethnic or racial group concerned, even though this was not written into any charter or requirement. When faculty members not of the group were considered for appointment, one could expect resistance by students or faculty members of the group. There were many such cases in the 1980s and 1990s, notably at Harvard, Berkeley, and Queens College.

Third, there were problems of the scholarly competence of appointees. Jewish studies could draw on an extensive Jewish professoriat. But for new and unestablished fields where were faculty to be found, and how were they to be judged? Some strange choices were made in the early history of these centers and departments, providing opponents of ethnic studies with a basis for their attacks for years to come. Thus, the first chairman of Afro-American studies at Harvard had not pursued an academic or scholarly career, but came from a leadership position in a trade union. The first chairman of the black studies department of the City College of New York had a respectable academic degree but was maintained as chairman for two decades while publishing nothing and developing and teaching weird theories. Over time, at least in the larger and better funded institutions, these centers or departments have improved, the scholarship on the whole has become better, and the presence of jobs has led to the creation of programs for scholars to fill them. But all the issues raised at the beginning by ethnic studies centers still persist. Campus multicultural conflict at the end of the 1990s centered around demands for the expansion and upgrading of old centers of ethnic studies and the creation of new centers for emerging groups.

"POLITICAL CORRECTNESS"

"Political correctness" is not an issue of curriculum, but one of tone, atmosphere, quality of life, and freedom of discussion on the campus. The origins of the term are in the old Stalinist Left, but it was co-opted by both conservatives and liberals to protest the increasingly sensitive response to language considered offensive on campus, in or out of class. The issue of offensiveness is a difficult one. Offensiveness is in the eye of the beholder. "Niggardly" is a Norse-derived term having nothing to do with the common American racial slur. But in 1999 a public official was pressured to resign because of his use of it. Is a criticism of racial preference in admission offensive? Does it create a hostile environment for minority students?

On this issue, conservatives, neoconservatives, and liberals—or many of them—came together in criticizing campus policing of language and "speech codes." Free-speech liberals found it necessary to part with minority and female advocates of controls on language. The latter asserted that language alone could produce a hostile and unfriendly atmosphere, harming minority and women students. Political correctness triggered a media multicultural firestorm in the 1990s, with much ridicule of language restrictions on campus. For example, the word "seminal" was attacked for patriarchalism, and no female above the age of twelve could be referred to as a "girl." The language suitable for referring to minority groups was under continual surveillance, and it was difficult to know which terms could be used without offense.

Multiculturalists and their law-professor allies who have argued the case against demeaning or ridiculing or offensive language have not been able to generally institutionalize the policing of language, though there are many individual cases where faculty and students have been charged and even punished. Courts have not been willing to uphold speech codes. One would think private universities would have greater freedom to impose speech codes than public universities, and perhaps to some degree they do. But the lawyer-president of Harvard, Derek Bok, has opposed such a code on the grounds that it would violate the First Amendment. The tradition of freedom of speech, which can be drawn upon to defend even pornography, is too strong to be overcome for controls on speech on campus. But undoubtedly this issue will continue to be tested and contested.

RACIAL AND ETHNIC SEGREGATION

The concentration of minority students in living quarters or social settings to the point where only students of one ethnic group are present reduces one supposed benefit of the multicultural campus, direct personal knowledge of other races, ethnic groups, or religions. Much of this clustering is simply the gathering of students of like interests and backgrounds in lunchrooms and elsewhere. The college and university may do nothing to encourage or facilitate this.

But there are ways in which an institution directly facilitates such clustering. While many students continue to live in integrated settings, on many campuses there are "theme houses," in which black students or Latinos or students of some other group gather for out-of-class socialization and for cultural and political programs. Sometimes these houses are living quarters, containing only black students who select this option because of an interest in or commitment to African American culture, or because they feel more comfortable among other blacks. Should the university encourage this, allow this, or try to break up a minority concentration that has occurred through voluntary choice? If there is a theme house for French language and culture, why not one for Afro-American students, for Mexican American students? But of course the students in the French house are not French—they are only learning or practicing French. And the Afro-American house, even if chosen voluntarily, which it always is, reminds too many of the segregation of black students involuntarily, by law or practice.

This voluntary clustering or segregation by race or ethnicity is a question of concern on almost all campuses. And yet students with common interests, whether an athletic team or a drama production, do spend time together. This clustering becomes visible when it consists of a visible minority. It will also be visible if the clustering is that of men or women. But even multiculturalists will agree there is some legitimacy to a residential living quarter for women alone. Matters become stickier when the issue is whether to take account of homosexuality or lesbianism in making room assignments.

Multiculturalism—the term—does remind us that culture or subculture is involved, it is real, and it has consequences. How is a culture to be maintained except through contact among those who share it? If one accommodates this interest, is one not contributing to a separatism that only extreme multiculturalists—and even few of those—find desirable? Students coming to residential campuses are queried as to their tastes in order to make their lives with roommates more comfortable. Blacks and whites, it is again and again reported, differ in musical tastes. Does one take account of this? Is one being racist in doing so?

This problem is a permanent dilemma of multiculturalism, for despite the common denunciation of multiculturalists as separatists, they too aim at the ultimate common society in which they are fully included. Not many want the clustering to be permanent; it is a means of accommodating interests and establishing comfort levels.

On all these issues, as on others, it is not fully clear how matters stand. Undoubtedly there are community college campuses where the quality of ethnic studies programs is poor, "political correctness" affects classroom discussion and campus life, the degree of concentration of minority students is too high. By the end of the 1990s conflicts over campus life and course offerings seemed to lessen. As the twenty-first century opened, debate centered more on the issue of affirmative action and admissions—on access to college and university.

PUBLIC EDUCATION

The greatest impact of multiculturalism has been in public elementary and secondary education. In the colleges and universities, students can avoid multiculturalism if they so decide, in their studies and generally in their campus life. In public elementary and secondary schools, we deal with fixed curricula, with few or no alternatives, set by state committees and applying to all public schools. The dominant tone, set by teacher's colleges and schools of education, is one of acknowledgment and appreciation of multiculturalism. This means learning about other groups by including in reading materials stories of women and individuals from minority groups and adapting history and social studies guidelines to emphasize the role of minority groups and women. Some multicultural advocates want to go further, to infuse every aspect of the curriculum, from mathematics to physical education, with some multicultural theme.

Different in origin and character from multicultural education was bilingual education, which spread through American schools during the last two decades of the twentieth century on the basis of legislation, court mandates, and federal financial assistance. The steady increase in immigration spurred the spread of bilingual education. It was promoted as a means for rapidly inducting non-English-speaking children into the common curriculum. Thus, state legislation often limited bilingual instruction to a few years, on the assumption that it would be enough for children to join classes in English. But this pragmatic approach was overwhelmed, particularly in the case of children from Spanish-speaking homes, by an ideological commitment, on the part of bilingual teachers and administrators, to the maintenance of the home language and original national cultures of the children's families. In a monolingual America, the maintenance of two languages was certainly a desirable objective. But in California, the state with the largest bilingual program, it emerged that children were retained in Spanish-speaking classes year after year, and that there was considerable resistance by bilingual teachers and administrators to moving them into English-speaking classes. A popular movement led to a state initiative that limited bilingual education to one year.

But the de-emphasis on bilingualism did not affect the grip of multiculturalism on the language and social studies curriculum. The 1980s and 1990s were marked by a series of media explosions on the degree to which the traditional materials of high school reading and history had been replaced by multicultural substitutes. Major conflicts erupted over standards for social studies textbooks in California and over the texts selected by state committees as fulfilling those standards; over an attempt to revise social studies guidelines in New York State about the same time; and over an elaborate federally funded effort to create national history standards for American and world history in the early 1990s.

Critics, some as distinguished as the historians Arthur M. Schlesinger Jr. and C. Vann Woodward and the educational historian and reformer Diane Ravitch, argued that these efforts not only distorted history, which was being skewed to overemphasize the role of minorities and women, but also failed to fulfill a key function of history teaching in elementary and secondary schools, establishing a base of knowledge and appreciation of the unique story of America as a democratic and inclusive society.

There was particular outrage at one variant of multiculturalism, Afrocentrism, which insisted on the contributions of Africa to world civilization, contributions which Afrocentrists believed had been ignored or suppressed. To spread Afrocentrism, teaching materials were prepared by Afrocentrist advocates which were widely deplored for inaccuracy and preposterousness by critics. To what extent these materials were actually used in schools was not known. But in the course of this controversy it became clear that more could be taught about Africa than was offered by most school curricula, and African materials began to be a regular part of social studies curricula.

Controversies over multiculturalism in the public schools had died down by the end of the 1990s, but multiculturalism by that time was well established in schools, particularly in social studies and English teaching. There had been a huge increase in what students were taught about African Americans. How that affected students was not known. Toni Morrison and Alice Walker were now found alongside Shakespeare and George Eliot. The canon, multiculturalists insisted, was an ever-changing one, and the new changes were well within the range of the changes of the past.

There is no agreement on many questions about multiculturalism. Just how much is there in the schools, and in which schools? What is the effect of multiculturalist educational materials on minority students, on majority students? Do they portend permanent bitterness and divisiveness in the United States—or do they rather teach a general tolerance and acceptance? Do they undermine national unity—do they contribute, as one of the most widely read books attacking multiculturalism by Arthur M. Schlesinger Jr. asserts, to the "disuniting of America"—or do they rather serve to teach a more realistic view of American history, American life, and American problems?

MULTICULTURAL THEORY

Multicultural theory is part of that general expansion of theory critical of capitalism and the West which has had a great impact on the teaching of English and the humanities in colleges and universities in the last two or three decades, and which has in varying degrees also affected the social sciences. This kind of advanced theory has had less impact on elementary and secondary schools, where multiculturalism tends to be a response to the practical task of teaching minority students and maintaining order rather than an expression of new theoretical understandings. Multicultural theory is linked particularly to postcolonial theory. The impact of the new varieties of contemporary theory on teaching in the humanities is weakened by their attachment to difficult and abstruse language, which can affect students only in the top layer of colleges and universities, and not many of them.

To traditionalists, multicultural theory is on the whole more alarming than multicultural practice. Indeed, since practice is difficult to know about—it is after all located in a million classrooms—traditionalists generally attack multicultural theory for undermining the notion that truths can be found and exist independent of power and position, and for insisting that power rather than evidence or scientific investigation determines what is taught.

Many multiculturalist theorists, on the other hand, are dissatisfied with the state of multicultural practice. They see it as limited to the teaching of tolerance or understanding, rather than engaging in a radical reordering of how we view our culture and society. To these critics, Eurocentrism and Anglocentrism still hold the center of attention, and multiculturalism becomes an add-on, rather than a transformation of traditional practice and understanding. A few books by minority, third-world, and women writers will be added to the reading lists, but the courses will not thereby become sufficiently critical in examining received wisdom and reconstructing understanding.

Those who want multiculturalism to go further call for a "critical multiculturalism," a "transfor-mative" multiculturalism, an "insurgent" multiculturalism, all ways of attacking existing multiculturalism as insufficient. One sees in these terms and these proposals an effort to make multiculturalism serve as a substitute for radical movements that have failed and that find little response among most people. It is doubtful that multiculturalism can play this role. One cannot make up for the failure of large movements of social transformation by, to adopt a phrase of the sociologist Todd Gitlin, marching on the English department.

On the whole, multiculturalism in practice aims at something more moderate than radical multicultural theory calls for, and that is respect for and acknowledgment of a range of subcultures and groups that are part of American life and culture and are changing it in various degrees. Whether this means a wholesale rejection of assimilation is really not clear. Multiculturalist advocates do not devote any great effort to projecting a picture of how American culture and life will in time evolve. Multiculturalism is a response by minority and other groups to their current sense of deprivation and to what they feel is insufficient recognition and respect. One expects that as deprivations are overcome, as respect for difference becomes more widespread, as American culture—operating through the mass media, the economy, and political activity—affects all groups, the urgency of multiculturalist demands will decline. One reason for the present unease is that the role of schools and colleges in spreading this common culture has declined with the rise of multiculturalism. But was it really the commitment of the common school to Americanization that created the common culture, or was it the larger forces that still operate effectively, even in a multicultural America? Assimilation proceeded though cultural forces far greater than the schools' efforts at Americanization, and these still continue to make a common culture.

See also **Ethnicity: Early Theories; Ethnicity and Race; Race; Class; The Visual Arts; Elite vs. Popular Cultures; Culture for Mass Audiences; Advertising; Memory; Marxist Approaches** *(volume 3).*

BIBLIOGRAPHY

Abramson, Harold J. "Assimilation and Pluralism." In *Harvard Encyclopedia of American Ethnic Groups,* edited by Stephan Thernstrom, pp. 150–160. Cambridge, Mass., 1980.

Berman, Paul, ed. *Debating P.C.* New York, 1992.

Bernstein, Richard. *Dictatorship of Virtue.* New York, 1994.

Gitlin, Todd. *The Twilight of Common Dreams*. New York, 1995.

Glazer, Nathan. *Ethnic Dilemmas, 1964–1982*. Cambridge, Mass., 1983.

——. *We Are All Multiculturalists Now*. Cambridge, Mass., 1997.

Gleason, Philip. "American Identity and Americanization." In *Harvard Encyclopedia of American Ethnic Groups*, pp. 31–58. Cambridge, Mass., 1980.

Goldberg, David Theo, ed. *Multiculturalism: A Critical Reader*. Cambridge, Mass., 1994.

Hollinger, David A. *Postethnic America: Beyond Multiculturalism*. New York, 1995.

Kallen, Horace. *Culture and Democracy in the United States*. New York, 1924.

Kors, Alan Charles, and Harvey A. Silverglate. *The Shadow University: The Betrayal of Liberty on America's Campuses*. New York, 1998.

Levine, Lawrence W. *The Opening of the American Mind: Campus, Culture, and History*. Boston, 1996.

Schlesinger, Arthur M., Jr. *The Disuniting of America*. Knoxville, Tenn., New York, 1991.

Sollors, Werner. *Beyond Ethnicity: Consent and Descent in American Culture*. New York, 1986.

Stotsky, Sandra. *Losing Our Language: How Multicultural Classroom Instruction Is Undermining Our Children's Ability to Read, Write, and Reason*. New York, 1999.

Zangwill, Israel. *The Melting-Pot: Drama in Four Acts*. New York, 1911.

NEW PHILOSOPHICAL DIRECTIONS

Shannon Sullivan

In the 1980s and 1990s, philosophy in the United States developed in a number of new directions, diversifying beyond the concerns and styles of analytic philosophy that dominated the discipline after World War II. These new directions include postmodernism's turn to French and German rather than British philosophy for inspiration; feminist theory's shift from emphasizing women and men's equality to emphasizing their differences, as well as its destabilization of the category of woman by intersecting the concept of gender with those of race, class, and sexuality; the development of queer theory and masculinity studies out of sexuality and gender; the emergence of critical race theory and postcolonial theory out of concerns about racial and colonial oppression; and the revival of pragmatism, America's only homegrown philosophy, after its eclipse by analytic philosophy in the 1950s.

POSTMODERNISM

The perceived sterility of analytic philosophy led some American philosophers in the 1970s and 1980s to search outside of the Anglo-American philosophical scene for alternatives to it. The result was the U.S. import of philosophy from the European continent, particularly that of French philosophy from the 1960s and 1970s. While called "postmodern," the work of European philosophers from this period does not describe itself with this term. Instead the term is a specifically American label for a type of European thought.

"Postmodern" covers so many different forms of philosophy that many European-influenced philosophers in the United States avoid using it because they find it meaningless. Because postmodern philosophies bear a family resemblance to one another, the label is useful nonetheless. Broadly speaking, postmodern philosophy is a form of criticism of modern, Enlightenment thought. Because modern philosophy is characterized by its criticism of eras

that preceded it, postmodern philosophy should be seen as emerging out of modernism, rather than as diametrically opposed to it. Thus, postmodern philosophy does not so much break with modern thought as it transforms it through its extension.

Another helpful way of characterizing postmodernism is as a style of philosophy that rejects grand narratives. A grand narrative provides an account of something—such as action, knowledge, society, or the individual—that legitimates it from a position external to it. For example, one grand narrative that has come under heavy attack by postmodern philosophy is the position that the human pursuit of knowledge is for its own sake and is not driven by particular human interests. Other grand narratives criticized by postmodern philosophy include: the assumption that the self is essentially unified; the idea that facts and values are sharply opposed to one another; and the claim that authorial intention is ultimate in establishing the meaning of a text.

The roots of postmodern philosophy in the United States are found primarily in the philosophy of Jacques Derrida and Michel Foucault. In the late 1960s, Derrida criticized philosophy's reliance upon the grand narrative of a "metaphysics of presence," which holds that meaning is found only in that which is and never in that which is not. Coining the term *différance* on the basis of the French verb *différer,* which means both to differ and to defer, Derrida claimed that meaning presents (presences) itself only by excluding that which is absent. *Différance* then is the difference that is deferred or excluded by Western metaphysics and that must be deferred if Western metaphysics is to maintain its emphasis on presence.

In the late 1970s, Foucault demonstrated how power, knowledge, and discipline are intimately related. Rather than being a thing that the powerful have and wield over those without power—a "vertical" conception of power—power occurs "horizontally" in everyday practices of normalization and self-discipline that are encouraged by medical, psychological, military, educational, and other societal institutions. In these practices, the subject that is supposed to preexist the institution that studies it is brought into existence. For example, while same-sex activities have long taken place, Foucault held that the homosexual subject did not come into existence until nineteenth-century medical and other disciplines created it as a specific type of "deviant" identity. According to Foucault, by seeking knowledge of their sexuality as the truth of who they are, people contribute to and participate in a situation of power that constructs their sexual existence in oppressive ways.

While most contemporary philosophy studied and practiced in the United States remains analytic, postmodernism continues to gain strength. Late-twentieth-century work in "Continental" philosophy, as postmodernism also is called, includes John Sallis's (1986) examination of the claim that metaphysics is at an end. Sallis suggested that the end of metaphysics marks not so much its termination, as its boundaries beyond which other, nonmetaphysical modes of thinking might be possible. Charles Scott (1990) addressed ethics from a postmodern point of view. Putting ethical grand narratives into question, he examined the degree to which ethical concerns produce human suffering in their quest for well-being. Donna Haraway (1991) challenged the construction of scientific knowledge from a feminist perspective. Analyzing the power struggles at work in evolutionary tales, she demonstrated the ways in which nature is socially and culturally constituted as independent of and prior to the social and cultural.

FEMINIST THEORY

Women's Different Voice   In the 1980s, feminist theory shifted away from the arguments for the equality of men and women that marked feminism in the United States in the 1960s and 1970s, and shifted toward arguments for fundamental differences between women and men that make women unique and perhaps even superior to men. "Difference feminism," as it later came to be called, holds that "equality feminism" inadvertently supports women's oppression by conceiving of women's liberation as a process of women's becoming similar to men. According to difference feminists, the fight for women's equality with men operates with a singular model of subjectivity that is masculine rather than gender free. Understanding the concept of the universal as a device by which patriarchy sustains itself, difference feminism insists that eliminating sexism and male bias must take the form of attending to, rather than attempting to erase, the differences between women and men.

Carol Gilligan's *In a Different Voice: Psychological Theory and Women's Development* (1982) helped establish feminist philosophers' focus on the differences between women and men in the 1980s. Gilligan's research on the moral development of young girls and boys demonstrated that while boys tend to resolve moral dilemmas with abstract moral principles, girls tend to be concerned about concrete relationships between people when making ethical decisions. On "standard" measurements of psychological development, which define mature development as the ability to apply universal moral rules to ethical situations, girls thus are judged to be morally and psychologically underdeveloped with respect to boys. Gilligan's work charged such standard measurements with male bias: they ignore the fact that girls and women tend to have a moral sense different from but not inferior to that of boys and men.

In the introduction to *In a Different Voice*, Gilligan stated that "the different voice I describe is characterized not by gender but by theme" (p. 2). Her work generally was and is read, however, as demonstrating that the different moral approaches used by girls and boys are fundamentally gendered (and this reading is supported by Gilligan's research in that it repeatedly links situated reasoning with girls and abstract reasoning with boys). Drawing from Gilligan, difference feminists in the 1980s thus claimed that women speak in a different "voice" than men, which makes possible an ethics of care in contrast to the ethics of justice that characterizes much of traditional Western philosophy. For example, Nel Noddings's work on care (1984) asserted that solutions to moral dilemmas should be generated by attending to the relationships involved in specific situations, rather than applying to a situation abstract ethical rules that were developed wholly apart from it. Similarly, Sara Ruddick suggested that an ethics founded in the practice of mothering is better suited to solving contemporary moral problems than an ethics of justice. In the 1990s, contributions to feminist ethics attempted to demonstrate that an ethics of care and an ethics of justice are not diametrically opposed. Marilyn Friedman argued that concerns about justice often are relevant to situations of caring, such as those found in families and friendships, just as concerns about care can be important to situations of justice, such as those that occur in educational and legal institutions.

Intersecting Gender with Race, Class, and Sexuality

At the same time that some feminists in the 1980s challenged the emphasis upon equality in the 1960s and 1970s by stressing women's differences from men, other feminists in the 1980s challenged both equality and difference feminism by claiming that feminism addressed the problems of white, middle-class, heterosexual women only. Echoing the American reformer Sojourner Truth, bell hooks (1981) asked on the part of black women, "Ain't I a woman?" thus demanding that feminism examine its racist assumptions about who counts as a woman. According to hooks, when white, middle-class feminists write about, for example, the need for women to be free to work outside the home, they ignore the fact that many women of color and poor white women already work outside their homes out of necessity. By claiming that women were oppressed by the demand that they remain at home, feminists dismiss the ways in which many women of color are oppressed by not having the choice to remain at home. hooks argues that by taking up the problems of a small group of women and addressing them as the problems of all women, feminism implicitly declares that only white, middle-class women really are women.

Feminists in the 1980s also demanded that feminist theory tackle its heterosexism. Adrienne Rich (1980) argued that heterosexuality is compulsory in the United States in that women are assumed to be heterosexual and are not allowed to choose a lesbian existence without severe economic and other penalties. According to Rich, compulsory heterosexuality is a problem for all women, not just lesbians, because it functions to keep women dependent on men and to minimize the positive connections that women might have with one another. To the extent that feminists fail to recognize compulsory heterosexuality as a feminist problem, feminism thus furthers the oppression of all women, lesbian and heterosexual alike. To combat compulsory heterosexuality, Rich suggested that all women think of themselves as on a "lesbian continuum," which emphasizes women's connections with one another, ranging from nonsexual friendships and relationships with sisters and mothers to relationships that include sexual intimacy.

Elizabeth Spelman (1988) strengthened feminism's rejection of the homogenization of women by criticizing "additive analyses" of gender and race. Additive analyses suffer from what Spelman called "the ampersand problem": they understand gender and race as separate aspects of the self to be joined or added together. Spelman argued that race and gender are not separate things that then come into connection with one another. For example, a black woman is not divided into being a black person and also a woman who somehow adds her race and gender together. Race and gender help constitute each other such that a black woman and a white woman will experience both their gender and sexism in different ways because of their race. By extension, Spelman's arguments apply not only to a woman's race and gender, but also to her sexuality, class, nationality, and so on. For Spelman, there is no essential woman, since what a woman is varies depending on aspects of her being other than her gender.

Postmodern Feminism

The impact of Judith Butler's *Gender Trouble: Feminism and the Subversion of Identity* (1990) on feminist philosophy and related fields in the United States cannot be overstated. Both drawing from and criticizing Michel Foucault's philosophy, as well as the psychoanalytic theory generated out of Freud's work, Butler argued that gender is performative: it is constituted by the particular styles by which people are compelled to act, dress, speak, think, and move. This does not mean that gender is something superficial that overlays a primary self that is not gendered. Butler's point is just the opposite: performances of gender make up the self that one is. According to Butler, even sex—the biological division of human beings into male and female—is constituted by the gendered performances of femininity and masculinity. For Butler, just as an onion has no core and thus no existence apart from the many layers that compose it, the self has no sexed substratum underlying the layers of gender that constitute it.

Put another way, Butler held that sex is the product, not the cause, of the gendered division of humanity into men and women. Instead of biological differences of sex producing cultural differences of gender, the rigid binary of man and woman presupposes a preexisting biological difference in order to mandate heterosexuality. The heterosexual demand that results is that men and women sexually desire beings on the opposite side of the sex/gender binary only. By calling into question the essential nature of gender and its relationship with sex, Butler sought to destabilize the categories of sex and gender such that they can no longer rigidly bind people into (hetero)sexual roles.

Also drawing from Foucault's philosophy, Susan Bordo argued that the body is not secondary or un-

THE DESTABILIZATION OF SEX AND GENDER

In the following selections, Judith Butler urges feminists to abandon the quest for the true identity of the self by questioning the idea that the human body's sex and gender are fixed by nature, prior to the influence of cultural meaning.

Consider gender, for instance, as *a corporeal style*, an "act," as it were, which is both intentional and performative, where *"performative"* suggests a dramatic and contingent construction of meaning. . . . That the gendered body is performative suggests that it has no ontological status apart from the various acts which constitute its reality.

"The body" itself is a construction. . . . Bodies cannot be said to have a signifiable existence prior to the mark of their gender; the question then emerges: To what extent does the body *come into being* in and through the mark(s) of gender?

It would make no sense, then, to define gender as the cultural interpretation of sex, if sex itself is a gendered category. Gender ought not to be conceived merely as the cultural inscription of meaning on a pregiven sex (a juridical conception); gender must also designate the very apparatus of production whereby the sexes themselves are established. As a result, gender is not to culture as sex is to nature; gender is also the discursive/cultural means by which "sexed nature" or "a natural sex" is produced and established as "prediscursive," prior to culture, a politically neutral surface *on which* culture acts.

It is no longer clear that feminist theory ought to try to settle the questions of primary identity in order to get on with the task of politics. Instead, we ought to ask, what political possibilities are the consequence of a radical critique of the categories of identity?"

Source: Judith Butler. *Gender Trouble: Feminism and the Subversion of Identity Thinking,* pp. 139, 136, 8, 7, ix

important to the "true" self, variously conceived as mind, soul, consciousness, or spirit. Body and mind instead are part of the psychosomatic intertwining that is the self. Bordo focused on women's bodies in particular, demonstrating the ways in which patriarchal power sustains itself through women's self-disciplining activities that aim for feminine ideals of slenderness and beauty. Exploring anorexia nervosa as the crystallization of late-twentieth-century Western culture, Bordo demonstrated the complex way in which anorexia can be understood as a protest against oppressive standards of femininity that limits rather than expands women's capabilities.

Additionally, Bordo challenged the "gender skepticism" that she claimed emerged in the early 1990s from the combination of feminist concerns about racial bias with a postmodern emphasis upon multiplicity and difference. According to Bordo, the combination serves to make feminists skeptical about the possibility of generalizing about gender. If rigid gender binaries are replaced by a complete fluidity of gender and if gender never occurs apart from race and class, then all possibility for focusing exclusively on gender seems to disappear. According to Bordo, skepticism about the value of the category of gender inadvertently operates in service of male privilege because it prevents feminists from exploring and critiquing the gender-based oppression that plagues all women's lives. Bordo held that instead of avoiding all generalizations about women, feminists should recognize both the need for practical spaces in which women are theorized as women and the complexity and fluidity of women's lives. For Bordo, feminist theory must consider the category of women contextually: in some situations, generalizing about gender will be helpful to ending women's oppression, and in other situations, it may not.

Third-Wave Feminism The first wave of feminism in the United States was organized around nineteenth- and early-twentieth-century fights for women's suffrage, and the second wave was born out of the civil rights movements of the 1960s. In contrast, there is no historical event to mark the third wave of feminism, which is why debate occurs over whether third-wave feminism is distinct from or merely an extension of second-wave feminism. However it is considered, most scholars agree third-wave feminism should not be seen as a rejection of earlier feminist movements. Third-wave feminists are the daughters, metaphorically speaking, of second-wave feminists. They grew up with the benefits for women that their "mothers" fought for, as well as with the backlash against feminism that soon followed the civil rights era. As part of Generation X, third-wave feminists explore what feminism might mean in the context of a conservative time that often claims to be "postfeminist," that is, to no longer need feminism because the oppression of women allegedly no longer exists.

No single issue marks third-wave feminism, in part because third-wave feminism seeks to embrace the many contradictions and tensions that diversity amongst women and men generates. The embracing of "lived messiness" thus can be said to characterize the third wave:

> . . . girls who want to be boys, boys who want to be girls, boys and girls who insist they are both, whites who want to be black, black who want or refuse to be white, people who *are* white *and* black, gay *and* straight, masculine *and* feminine, or who are finding ways to be and name none of the above; successful individuals longing for community and coalition, communities and coalitions longing for success; tensions between striving for individual success and subordinating the individual to the cause; identities formed within a relentlessly consumer-oriented culture but informed by a politics that has problems with consumption. (Heywood and Drake, *Third Wave Agenda*, p. 8)

Third-wave feminists attempt to understand the ways in which class, race, sexuality, and nation of origin impact women's lives. Many of them theorize love and family relationships from the particular perspective of having been reared in feminist and lesbian households. Unlike the generation of women ahead of them, who had to fight for the right to birth control, abortion, and other reproductive freedoms, third-generation feminists grew up with many of these rights and freedoms and examine their impact on women's sexuality. The increase in anorexia, particularly for women in their late teens and early twenties, has led many third-wave feminists to analyze how women's attitudes toward their bodies are formed in a social and political context that demands women's powerlessness.

QUEER THEORY

While Judith Butler did not conceive of *Gender Trouble* as spawning a new field, the book is considered one of the founding texts of queer theory. Aligned with postmodernism, queer theory rejects the identity politics that tends to characterize lesbian and gay politics and some strands of feminism in the 1980s. Lesbian and gay politics often assumes that political movements operate in the service of a group of people whose identities can be clearly and unproblematically established. In contrast, queer theory holds that the notion of a coherent identity itself is oppressive and thus should be a site for political activity. Challenging static, rigid notions of sexual identity, queer theorists seek to demonstrate that no one fully embodies the heterosexual ideals of Western culture. In that sense, all people—lesbian, gay, or heterosexual—can be seen as at least somewhat queer and can use their sexual practices to subvert sexual oppression by undermining the stability of sexual identity.

At the same time that it attempts to see a broad number of sexual practices as subversive, queer theory recognizes that the claim that the majority of people are queer is potentially dangerous. It can be taken to mean that no sexual differences between people exist, and in that way erase from view the ways that gay and lesbian people economically and physically suffer from homophobia in ways that heterosexual people do not. Precisely at this point is queer theory's main concern clearest, however. Queer theorists hold that the fight against gay and lesbian discrimination does not and should not depend upon configuring people in rigid sexual identities.

MASCULINITY STUDIES

A small but growing field, masculinity studies is a late-twentieth-century product of feminist theory. It includes two related topics: that of what it means for men to be feminists and how masculinity itself is socially, politically, and culturally constituted. Some disagreement exists about whether men can be feminists or should be said instead to be merely pro-feminist. The issue concerns whether men should be conceived as playing only supportive roles in feminist work so as to prevent them from reinforcing patriarchy by usurping women's authority and power. Whether men are thought of as profeminist or feminist, however, there is growing agreement in feminist philosophy that men have an important role to play in the fight against women's oppression and that ending sexism will require the reconfiguration of not just femininity but masculinity as well.

The attempt to rethink masculinity and men's relationship to feminism has generated new issues for feminist theory that are specific to men. Beginning with a concern related to the pro-feminist/feminist debate, those issues include: managing (pro-)feminist men's potential threat to women's authority in feminist groups and movements; confronting the fear and suspicion of men who claim to be (pro-)feminist (a fear manifested variously, often by sexist men and sometimes by feminist women); determining the extent to which men's fighting patriarchy means fighting themselves and possibly refusing to be a man; negotiating the benefits and disadvantages of men instructors' teaching feminism; examining the role that violence and aggression play in ideals of masculinity; and exploring what sort of transformations are needed in men's attitudes toward institutions and practices such as fatherhood, marriage, sexuality, and pornography (May, Strikwerda, and Hopkins, 1996; Digby 1998).

CRITICAL RACE THEORY

Using the adjective "critical" to distinguish itself from accounts of race that seek to justify racism, critical race theory emerged in the 1990s out of efforts to understand the category of race in antiracist ways. The goal of critical race theory thus is roughly analogous to that of feminist theory, which seeks to theorize the category of gender in antipatriarchal terms. Critical race theory starts from the acknowledgment of biological science's discrediting of the concept of race. Biological, genetic, and physical differences—such as skin color, texture of hair, and body shape—are often more pronounced within a racial group than between members of different groups. There are no differences in blood between racial groups, such as those commonly assumed by the "one-drop" rule that declares that a single drop of black blood makes a person black rather than white. In short, there is no scientific support for the concept of race. Scientifically speaking, races do not exist.

In the face of science's discrediting of race, critical race theorists disagree about whether the concept of race should be retained once people acknowledge that it has no biological necessity. Kwame Anthony Appiah (1992) argued that the concept should be discarded because without any scientific grounding the concept of race can have only a racist meaning. According to Appiah, its continued use promotes racism by encouraging people to think of themselves as racially divided when they are not. Similarly, Naomi Zack (1993) claimed that without any scientific standing, the category of race has racist effects. In particular, Zack charged that continued use of the category of race alienates mixed race people, who cannot classify themselves

racially without contorting or disregarding significant aspects of their identities.

In contrast to Appiah and Zack, Lucius Outlaw (1996) argued that even though race is socially and politically constituted rather than biologically necessitated, the concept of race should be retained. According to Outlaw, different races have different "messages" to give to one another. To dissolve all people into one khaki-colored race thus would eliminate the richness of life that a plurality of races makes possible. In addition, Outlaw suggested that people need ways of grouping themselves with similar people to provide life-sustaining order to their existence. For Outlaw, race is an important way, though not the only one, by which people order their lives and thus should not be abolished.

Charles Mills (1997) likewise claimed that the concept of race should be neither eliminated nor collapsed into the notion of ethnicity because doing so would make invisible the political system of white supremacy that privileges white people over people of color. Mills theorized race as a social contract between white people that allows for their domination over nonwhite people. Although it is not biologically necessary, the racial contract made by white people is real and cannot be dismantled without continuing to theorize the effects of race on people's lives. Since examining the effects of race requires the continued use of the concept of race, the concept is crucial to antiracist projects.

One particular focus of critical race theory is on whiteness, more specifically on understanding how whiteness is constructed and maintained and how white people can work to eliminate racism even as they inevitably benefit from it. In this context, scholars disagree over the value of "white studies" and the attitude toward whiteness that antiracists should take. Noel Ignatiev argued that whiteness must be abolished if racism is to end: "Whiteness is one pole of an unequal relationship, which can no more exist without oppression than slavery could exist without slaves" (*Race Traitor* 10, p. 7). In Ignatiev's view, even though they may be well intentioned, efforts to transform the meaning of whiteness only support white supremacy because they preserve the concept of whiteness, which can mean nothing other than white domination of nonwhite people. In contrast, some scholars hold that while whiteness historically has meant white oppression of people of color, whiteness can and must be transformed into a nonracist category. This is because eliminating whiteness seems to entail white people's thinking of themselves as raceless, which functions to obscure rather than combat their racial privilege (Kincheloe, 1998).

POSTCOLONIAL THEORY

Postcolonial theory is related to critical race theory in that both are concerned with racial oppression and white supremacy. Postcolonial theory focuses on the effects of and efforts to resist European colonization of the non-European world, which overlaps with the domination of white over nonwhite people. A discussion of European colonization includes the ways in which not just Europe, but so-called first world nations settled by Europeans, such as the United States, colonized so-called third world nations. Postcolonial theory also demonstrates how colonization continues to take place today as much economically (for example, through the world capitalism of the International Monetary Fund and World Bank) and culturally (for example, through the expansion of American icons such as McDonald's and Disney World) as it does militarily.

Postcolonial theory can be seen as postmodern in that it exposes many of the founding myths of the Western world as oppressive grand narratives. One such grand narrative is the "discovery" of the "New World" by Christopher Columbus. This myth presents itself as a neutral fact and in so doing camouflages its white, European bias. The "New World" was a new discovery from the perspective of white Europeans, not from the perspective of the native people who inhabited North America long before Columbus arrived. From the perspective of the native tribes of North America, Columbus's voyage began a European invasion of a land rich with history, rather than the discovery of an open wilderness untouched by human beings.

In the late 1970s, Edward W. Said helped establish postcolonial theory by tracing how the Western categories of "Orient" and "Occident" marginalize non-Westerners as exotic inferiors to Westerners. Using a Foucauldian approach, Said argued that European texts on the "Orient" masquerade as objective knowledge when they instead are the products of Western fantasies and fears regarding non-Westerners. For Said, rather than being benign attempts to learn more about the non-Western world, Western studies of the "Orient" are exercises of power that help maintain an oppressive, racist hierarchy of West over East. In a similar fashion, Gayatri Spivak's *In Other Worlds* (1987) criticized the field of "subaltern studies," which attempts to give a voice to marginalized peoples who have been silenced by historical accounts that focus primarily on dominant groups. Drawing on Derrida's concept of *différance,* Spivak argued that while these attempts are well intentioned, they problematically assume that the subaltern has a singular, unified identity that can be contained within Western descriptions of it. According to Spivak, scholars who want to empower oppressed groups must acknowledge their heterogeneity and alterity if they are not to contribute further to the subaltern's oppression.

PRAGMATISM

The perceived sterility of analytic philosophy in the United States led not only to the emergence of postmodern philosophy in the 1980s but also to a resurgence of interest in American pragmatism, including the work of classical American pragmatists in the late nineteenth and early twentieth centuries such as Jane Addams, John Dewey, Charlotte Perkins Gilman, William James, Alain Locke, George Herbert Mead, and Charles Sanders Peirce. In particular, Richard Rorty's *Philosophy and the Mirror of Nature* (1979), a work that criticizes analytic philosophy from a combined pragmatist-postmodern perspective, led philosophers to pay renewed attention to pragmatism. Rorty argued that philosophy should abandon the task of epistemology as traditionally conceived, which is to know the world as it exists apart from human perspectives. Rather than view itself as mirroring nature in the attempt to capture the one true story of the world, philosophy should see itself as facilitating conversations between different groups of people who understand the world in incommensurable ways. According to Rorty, since there is no "real" world or experience apart from the language people use to describe it, philosophy must stop trying to get "behind" language if philosophy is to remain relevant to human life.

While Rorty's is the best-known form of pragmatism in the United States, other important contemporary appropriations and extensions of pragmatism abound. John McDermott (1986) gave pragmatism an existential angle by emphasizing the richness and tragedy to be found in human experience. In *The American Evasion of Philosophy* (1989) Cornel West developed a "prophetic pragmatism" that sought to improve the lives of "the wretched of the earth" by means of critical intelligence and social action. Richard Shusterman (1992) showed how pragmatism can shed new light not only on the academic field of aesthetics, but on the art of living. Scholars working on environmental philosophy (Light and Katz, 1994) demonstrated how pragmatism can offer a helpful alternative to the false dichotomy of anthropocentrism and bio-centrism in environmental movements. Establishing pragmatist feminism as a new field in philosophy, Charlene Haddock Seigfried in *Pragmatism and Feminism* (1996) illustrated how pragmatism and feminism have much in common, as well as much to learn from one another. Pragmatist forays into medical ethics (McGee, 1999) showed how pragmatism can help doctors and others wrestle with moral dilemmas concerning genetic research, cloning, and human enhancement. In various fashions, these ideas all challenge traditional ideas of "applied philosophy" by drawing theory and practice together in ways that make practices more thoughtful, rather than applying theory to practice in a "top-down" fashion.

The new directions that philosophy has taken in the United States in the 1980s and 1990s demonstrate that the field is thriving and complex. At the end of the twentieth century, postmodernism, feminist theory, and American pragmatism were fairly well established in the discipline of philosophy, and interest in queer theory, masculinity studies, critical race theory, and postcolonial theory continues to grow. The further development of these fields in the twenty-first century likely will generate additional, as-yet-unimagined directions for philosophy to take in the future.

See also **Individualism and the Self; Family; Sexuality; Class; The Role of the Intellectual; The Internet and Electronic Communications** (*volume 3*); *and other articles in this section.*

BIBLIOGRAPHY

Postmodernism

Derrida, Jacques. *Speech and Phenomena, and Other Essays on Husserl's Theory of Signs.* Translated by David B. Allison. Evanston, Ill., 1973.

Foucault, Michel. *The History of Sexuality.* Vol. 1. Translated by Robert Hurley. New York, 1980.

Haraway, Donna J. *Simians, Cyborgs, and Women: The Reinvention of Nature.* New York, 1991.

Lyotard, Jean-Francois. *The Postmodern Condition: A Report on Knowledge.* Translated by Geoffrey Bennington and Brian Massumi. Minneapolis, Minn., 1984.

Sallis, John. *Delimitations: Phenomenology and the End of Metaphysics.* Studies in Continental Thought. Bloomington, Ind., 1986.

Scott, Charles E. *The Question of Ethics: Nietzsche, Foucault, Heidegger.* Studies in Continental Thought. Bloomington, Ind., 1990.

Feminist Theory
WOMEN'S DIFFERENT VOICE

Friedman, Marilyn. *What Are Friends For? Feminist Perspectives on Personal Relationships and Moral Theory.* Ithaca, N.Y., 1993.

Gilligan, Carol. *In a Different Voice: Psychological Theory and Women's Development.* Cambridge, Mass., 1982.

Noddings, Nel. *Caring: A Feminine Approach to Ethics and Moral Education.* Berkeley, 1984.

Ruddick, Sara. *Maternal Thinking: Toward a Politics of Peace.* Boston, 1989.

INTERSECTING GENDER WITH RACE, CLASS, AND SEXUALITY

hooks, bell. *Ain't I a Woman? Black Women and Feminism.* Boston, 1981.

Rich, Adrienne. "Compulsory Heterosexuality and Lesbian Existence." In *Blood, Bread, and Poetry: Selected Prose, 1979–1985.* New York, 1986.

Spelman, Elizabeth V. *Inessential Woman: Problems of Exclusion in Feminist Thought.* Boston, 1988.

POSTMODERN FEMINISM

Bordo, Susan. *Unbearable Weight: Feminism, Western Culture, and the Body.* Berkeley, 1993.

Butler, Judith. *Gender Trouble: Feminism and the Subversion of Identity.* Thinking Gender Series. New York, 1990.

THIRD-WAVE FEMINISM

Findlen, Barbara, ed. *Listen Up: Voices from the Next Feminist Generation.* Seattle, Wash., 1995.

Heywood, Leslie, and Jennifer Drake, eds. *Third Wave Agenda: Being Feminist, Doing Feminism.* Minneapolis, Minn., 1997.

Queer Theory

Butler, Judith. *Gender Trouble: Feminism and the Subversion of Identity.* New York, 1990.

Masculinity Studies

Digby, Tom, ed. *Men Doing Feminism.* New York, 1998.

May, Larry, Robert Strikwerda, and Patrick D. Hopkins, eds. *Rethinking Masculinity: Philosophical Explorations in Light of Feminism.* Lanham, Md., 1996.

Critical Race Theory

Appiah, Kwame Anthony. *In My Father's House: Africa in the Philosophy of Culture.* London, 1992.

Ignatiev, Noel. "Abolitionism and the White Studies Racket." *Race Traitor* 10 (1999): 3–7.

Kincheloe, Joe L., ed. *White Reign: Deploying Whiteness in America.* New York, 1998.

Mills, Charles W. *The Racial Contract.* Ithaca, N.Y., 1997.

Outlaw, Lucius T., Jr. *On Race and Philosophy.* New York, 1996.

Zack, Naomi. *Race and Mixed Race.* Philadelphia, 1993.

Postcolonial Theory

Said, Edward W. *Orientialism.* New York, 1978.

Spivak, Gayatri Chakravorty. *In Other Worlds: Essays in Cultural Politics.* New York, 1987.

Pragmatism

Light, Andrew, and Eric Katz, eds. *Environmental Pragmatism.* New York, 1996.

McDermott, John J. *Streams of Experience: Reflections on the History and Philosophy of American Culture.* Amherst, Mass., 1986.

McGee, Glenn, ed. *Pragmatic Bioethics.* Nashville, Tenn., 1999.

Rorty, Richard. *Philosophy and the Mirror of Nature.* Princeton, N.J., 1979.

Seigfried, Charlene Haddock. *Pragmatism and Feminism: Reweaving the Social Fabric.* Chicago, 1996.

Shusterman, Richard. *Pragmatist Aesthetics: Living Beauty, Rethinking Art.* Cambridge, Mass., 1992.

West, Cornel. *The American Evasion of Philosophy: A Genealogy of Pragmatism.* Madison, Wis., 1989.

Part 9

CULTURAL GROUPS

Part 9, *continued*

AFRICAN AMERICANS

Harold Brackman

Over the course of three hundred and fifty years, African Americans have moved from the periphery to the vital center of American cultural and intellectual life. All along the way, black intellectuals and artists have had to contend with what the sociologist W. E. B. Du Bois in *The Souls of Black Folk* (1903) called "double consciousness":

> One ever feels his two-ness,—an American, a Negro; two souls, two thoughts, two unreconciled strivings; two warring ideals in one dark body, whose dogged strength alone keeps it from being torn asunder. The history of the American Negro is the history of this strife,—this longing to attain self-conscious manhood, to merge his double self into better and truer self. In this merging he wishes neither of the older selves to be lost. . . . He simply wishes to make it possible for a man to be both a Negro and an American, without being cursed and spit upon by his fellows, without having the doors of Opportunity closed roughly in his face. (p. 39)

African American cultural and intellectual life is still emerging from "behind the veil" (again Du Bois's words) of historic racism in the twenty-first century.

FIRST IMPRESSIONS

Newcomers to America, but as involuntary rather than voluntary immigrants, African-born slaves underwent a socialization process that in some ways paralleled the "Americanization" process later experienced by European immigrants. In the case of enslaved Africans and their children, acculturation primarily meant learning English and adopting the Christian religion. The uprooting experience of the slave trade made it difficult for Africans to transplant intact to North America their traditional religions, including Islam. Yet Africans in America did not just passively adopt Euro-American culture. They also adapted and changed it. They cultivated attitudes borne of their experience of enslavement and implanted styles of thought and expression carried over from the West African tribal cultures—Akan, Ashanti, Dahoman, Ibo, Yoruba, and others—from which most of them came.

The result was the genesis of a distinctive African American culture that fused or syncretized African with Euro-American elements. Its unique imprint can be seen in black Protestantism's Old Testament orientation and identification with the "Hebrew children" delivered from Egyptian bondage, and in black folklore featuring animal trickster heroes of African origin such as the spider Anansi and Brer Rabbit. The same imprint can be heard in the call-response pattern and "ring shouts" of slave music, and in the Gullah dialect, an early version of "black English," spoken by the residents of the Sea Islands of South Carolina.

Plantation slave culture was not just a product of passive compliance with the master's wishes. It embodied positive coping mechanisms and survival strategies that enabled the young slaves to learn from the wisdom of their elders and for the entire slave community to achieve informally a degree of cultural autonomy for life in the slave quarters.

Starting in slavery times, African American culture also influenced the culture of white Americans. The Great Awakening of the 1730s and 1740s and Second Great Awakening of the early 1800s—the first major religious revivals in American history—displayed a style of emotional religiosity, especially in "back country" camp meetings, that attracted believers across racial lines. African Americans who heard white preachers were "born again," but patterns of influence ran both ways. The emotive spirituality of black religion partly shaped evangelical white Protestantism.

Much of historians' knowledge of these developments derives from observations by white Americans whose vision was often clouded by prejudice. For example, Thomas Jefferson wrote *Notes on the State of Virginia* in the 1780s to give European readers a sense of the emerging culture of the newly independent United States. Regarding African

Americans, he advanced the opinion, though "as a suspicion only," that blacks were mentally inferior to whites. On the basis of his observation of the banjo playing and dancing of plantation slaves, Jefferson credited them with being "more generally gifted than the whites with accurate ears for tune and time" but voiced skepticism about whether "they will be equal to the composition of a more extensive run of melody, or of complicated harmony" (pp. 139–140).

From Jefferson's time onward, African Americans who wanted cultural and intellectual recognition were under great pressure to disprove white presumptions about black inferiority. This was true of the eighteenth century's two most famous creative people of color. Brought to America from Africa as a slave at age eight, Phillis Wheatley was educated and freed by a Boston merchant whose last name she took. She quickly learned English and wrote her first published poem in 1766 at the age of thirteen. Her first book of poetry, published in England in 1773, was conventional sentimental verse in the style of Alexander Pope's couplets. Desperate to show that she could imitate white poets, Wheatley sacrificed her chance for originality. Born free on a Maryland farm, Benjamin Banneker taught himself astronomy by watching the stars and mathematics by borrowing books. In 1791 he was commissioned to help survey the new capital district that became Washington, D.C. His main claim to fame was a series of almanacs, published between 1791 and 1802. Banneker's reputation as "an ebony Benjamin Franklin" was purchased at the price of living in the shadow of his white role model.

The alternative to "crossing over" to win white recognition was to create distinctive institutions that would provide African Americans with their own intellectual and cultural validation. The first important example of this impulse was the independent free black churches founded in the remaining decades of the eighteenth century. Free black worshippers in Philadelphia resisted segregated seating along walls or in balconies ("nigger heavens") and other disrespectful treatment by white congregants. This protest motivated their withdrawal from St. George's Methodist Church in 1787, the same year that America's Founding Fathers were drawing up a new frame of government in nearby Independence Hall. They formed the Free African Society, a benevolent organization devoted to helping free blacks help themselves in much the same way as the black Masonic lodges that also originated during this period.

Then, in 1794, the African Episcopal Church of St. Thomas was organized. The purpose, in the words of the founder Absalom Jones, was to "throw off that servile fear, that habit of oppression and bondage train[ed] up in us" (Berlin, *Many Thousand Gone*, p. 252). Gradually withdrawing from white sponsorship and oversight, black churches in Philadelphia formed the nucleus of an independent black denomination, founded in 1816. Under the leadership of Bishop Richard Allen, the African Methodist Episcopal (AME) Church grew from small beginnings to 296 churches, 776 clergy, and over 17,000 members by 1846. Though denied ordination as ministers, African American women like Jarena Lee were allowed to lead prayer meetings.

Richard Allen and Absalom Jones, both born in slavery, had worked and saved to purchase their freedom. Not ashamed of their ancestral roots, they proudly called themselves "Africans." Paul Cuffee of Boston, a seafaring man, was among the small number of free blacks who went further by becoming colonists to Africa and laying the foundations for the Republic of Liberia. Their motives ranged from escaping American racism, to promoting trade across the Atlantic, to furthering the conversion to Christianity of native Africans. The American Colonization Society, organized in 1816, also encouraged this "back to Africa" movement, but free blacks overwhelmingly opposed the white-run Society as a plot by slaveholders to coerce them into leaving the country.

FROM SLAVERY TO FREEDOM

Independent African American churches, according to the black abolitionist Frederick Douglass, were "the Alpha and Omega of all things"—the vital foundation of free black communities. All eight black founding members of the American and Foreign Anti-Slavery Society, formed in 1840, were ministers. As with the civil rights movement after World War II, the antislavery movement before the Civil War was a spiritual crusade that fused religion and politics. The movement's objective was to end not only slavery but also racism and to empower blacks as members of the culture of freedom. At a time when there were no black higher educational institutions in the United States, decisions by colleges such as Oberlin, founded in Ohio in 1833, to admit African Americans and to expel a white student who called a classmate "a black nigger" helped to define the moral essence of abolitionism.

276

A shining example of the nineteenth-century American ideal of "the self-made man" who rises from humble origins to achieve greatness, Frederick Douglass personified in heroic fashion the transition from slavery to freedom. Born in bondage on Maryland's eastern shore circa 1817, Douglass spent his childhood in Baltimore where he bribed his white playmates on the city's docks to teach him to read. Succeeding in his second attempt to escape to freedom, Douglass arrived in 1838 in New York where he married. At risk of being returned to slavery, he and his family used the Underground Railroad to move to New Bedford, Massachusetts. There, he joined an all-black abolition society and worked as a common laborer until his ability as an antislavery orator was discovered by William Lloyd Garrison, the militant white abolitionist whose battle cry was "immediate emancipation." A champion of the rights of all, Douglass in 1848 delivered the only major speech by a man at the Seneca Falls Convention in New York for women's rights, a cause he supported until his death in 1895.

Douglass's eloquent autobiography, the *Narrative of the Life of Frederick Douglass* (1845), subsequently revised and expanded in many editions, became an international best-seller and the most celebrated of the nearly one hundred such accounts written by escaped slaves. There used to be a tendency by historians and literary critics to treat slave narratives as highly fictionalized accounts, almost on a par with Harriet Beecher Stowe's novel, *Uncle Tom's Cabin* (1852). More recently, the pendulum was swung back toward crediting the factual accuracy of previously suspect works such as *Incidents in the Life of a Slave Girl* (1861), written by Harriet A. Jacobs using the pen name Linda Brent. The first full-length autobiography of the life of an African American woman, the book frankly documents the sexual abuse of female slaves as well as the coping strategies used by slaves to survive the many forms of exploitation.

Frederick Douglass's complement was Harriet Tubman, sometimes called "the Moses of Her People." Also born a slave in Maryland circa 1820, she was the property of a master who refused to allow her parents to legally marry and who beat her as stupid and obstinate. In 1849 she fled but returned to the South at least nineteen times to lead hundreds of other slaves, including ultimately her own parents, to freedom. During the Civil War, she served as a cook and then a scout and sometime spy behind Confederate lines for the Union Army. Afterward, she founded a care facility for needy African Americans in upstate New York.

Declaring "I always tole God, I'm gwine to hold stiddy on to you, an' you've got to see me through," Tubman shared a powerful sense of religious mission with Sojourner Truth, originally named Isabella "Bell" Baumfree by her Dutch master in Kingston, New York (Patterson, in *The Reader's Companion to American History,* p. 1089). Reluctantly freed by a cruel master when New York State ended slavery in 1827, she had to sue to win the freedom of her children. Emancipation also meant spiritual redemption to Bell Baumfree:

> When I left the house of bondage I left everything behind. I wa'n't goin' to keep nothin' of Egypt on me, an' so I went to the Lord an' asked him to give me a new name. And the Lord gave me Sojourner because I was to travel up an' down the land showin' the people their sins an' bein' a sign unto them. Afterward I told the Lord I wanted another name 'cause everybody else had two names; and the Lord gave me Truth, because I was to declare the truth to the people. (*The Narrative of Sojourner Truth,* p. 164)

A powerful if unschooled voice in the antislavery movement, Sojourner Truth also crusaded for women's rights both before and after the Civil War.

Special in their abilities, Harriet Tubman and Sojourner Truth also typified the resilience and flexibility of black women whose fathers and husbands, because of slavery, could not be relied on to protect and support their daughters and wives.

Both free-born blacks and former slaves like Frederick Douglass, Harriet Tubman, and Sojourner Truth actively shaped the new antislavery movement that emerged after 1830. When William Lloyd Garrison began publishing his newspaper, the *Liberator,* in Boston in 1831, blacks were the majority of his subscribers and financial supporters. Four years earlier, John B. Russwurm, America's first black college graduate (Bowdoin College, 1826), launched in New York the nation's first black newspaper, *Freedom's Journal,* which also anticipated Garrison's new militancy. Then in 1829 in Garrison's own Boston, David Walker, a self-taught African American dealer in used clothes, published *David Walker's Appeal,* the most uncompromising demand yet for an immediate end to slavery. When Nat Turner's slave revolt erupted in Virginia in 1831, Walker as well as Garrison were blamed by white southerners for incitement.

In the pre–Civil War antislavery movement, blacks explored both interracial cooperation and racial self-reliance or "going it alone" as group advancement strategies. They cooperated with white allies, yet also organized and acted independently. Many free blacks joined racially integrated abolitionist organizations but others joined all-black auxiliaries. Garrison, though respected by black abolitionists, was not slavishly followed. In 1840, when the abolitionist movement split because Garrison was opposed to participating in conventional party politics, many blacks outside Massachusetts sided with the anti-Garrisonians. In 1843 Garrison's philosophy of pacifism and nonviolent resistance was rejected by Reverend Henry Highland Garnet, who exhorted the South's 4 million slaves to rise up in rebellion against their masters. In 1847 Frederick Douglass also broke with Garrison to found his own independent newspaper, the *North Star.*

During the 1840s and 1850s, African Americans held numerous black conventions to shape their own political agenda. Calling for greater emphasis on black self-help, these conventions also became more receptive to colonization proposals after the African American community was stripped of legal protections by the Fugitive Slave Law, passed by the Congress in 1850, and the Dred Scott decision, handed down by the Supreme Court in 1857.

The philosophy of what later came to be called "black nationalism" was articulated by Martin R. Delany in his political manifesto, *The Condition, Elevation, Emigration, and Destiny of the Colored People of the United States, Politically Considered* (1852). Admitted to Harvard Medical School, though forced to withdraw because of white prejudice, Delany saved many lives as an apprentice physician in Pittsburgh during the cholera epidemic of 1854. A co-founder with Frederick Douglass of the *North Star,* he began to question whether racial justice was possible in America and led an expedition to the Niger River Valley in 1859 to explore the possibility of African Americans expatriating to Africa. The outbreak of the Civil War in 1861 changed Delany's mind. Like Frederick Douglass, who lobbied President Abraham Lincoln in the White House to authorize the use of black troops to help free the slaves, Delany became a tireless organizer of African American support for the Northern war effort. In 1865 he was commissioned as an infantry major, the first black field officer in the history of the U.S. Army. During postwar Reconstruction, he worked with the Freedmen's Bureau in South Carolina and encouraged ex-slaves to become politically active citizens.

SEPARATE AND UNEQUAL

The political gains, including the election of two senators and fourteen congressmen, that southern blacks scored during Reconstruction were rolled back after 1877 by a white backlash. Jim Crow segregation was imposed and the freedmen were reduced to the status of second-class citizens. Yet the cultural impact of Reconstruction was enduring.

The ex-slaves took the opportunity afforded by legal freedom to formalize with marriage licenses and birth certificates the realities of family life that had been recognized only informally during slavery times. No longer subject to laws against teaching slaves to read, black people of all ages flocked to "the freedom schools" staffed by five thousand northern teachers, many of them young women from New England. African American churches, which had been invisible institutions on the slave plantations, now also became visible in the South, as the AME denomination increased its membership threefold to two hundred thousand in ten years. Negro Baptists, numbering a half million by 1870, seceded from white control to form their own independent denomination.

The new system of public education was maintained after the end of Reconstruction, but it was continued on a "separate and unequal" basis, drastically underfunding colored schools, which often were in session irregularly and only part of the year. Even so, public schooling remained a valued institution among southern blacks. African Americans also enthusiastically supported public and private educational institutions—Atlanta University (1865), Fisk University (1866), Morgan State College (1867), Howard University (1867), the Hampton Institute (1868), Dillard University (1869), Alcorn University (1871), Tougaloo College (1871), and the Tuskegee Institute (1881)—offering them secondary and collegiate schooling. Thanks partly to funding provided by northern charitable foundations—the Peabody Education Fund, the John F. Slater Fund, the Rosenwald Fund, and others—illiteracy among southern blacks declined from an estimated 90 percent in 1863 to 30 percent in 1913, while there were two thousand black college graduates in 1900.

The multiplication of African American churches and schools created some new black-white tensions. White ministers and teachers who came South to instruct the black freedmen were often appalled by their emotional style of worship, their unconventional religious ideas, and their failure to speak standard English. Black colleges and seminaries that sought to correct these perceived defects sometimes had the unfortunate effect of alienating from their roots students who were already uncertain about the heritage of slave culture. Ironically, white faculty members at Hampton, Fisk, and

Howard were often more favorable toward the plantation spirituals than their black students who periodically rebelled against music that they viewed as a humiliating vestige of bondage. "I had come to school to learn to do things differently; to sing, to spoke, and to use the language and of course the music, not of colored people but white people," wrote the educator Robert Russa Moton in his autobiography (*Finding a Way Out*, p. 157). This was his explanation of why, as a freshman at the Hampton Institute in 1885, he was disappointed to hear his fellow students singing spirituals. The Fisk Jubilee Singers had demonstrated in the 1870s that there was money to be made performing "sorrow songs" for northern white audiences. Yet the members of the chorus agreed with their white vocal music instructor that the songs needed to be "refined" by smoothing voices, altering grammar, and improving pronunciation. Something of the "soul" of the original music was lost in the process.

African Americans were terrorized into accepting the rigid system of Jim Crow racial subordination, as lynchings of blacks increased from 12 in 1872 to 255 in 1892. Schemes to leave the South for the farmlands of Kansas and Nebraska, or even for Africa, were increasingly talked about beginning in the 1870s. The millions of southern blacks not yet ready to emigrate had to seek other outlets for their anger and frustration. The educator Benjamin E. Mays speculated that his people fought each other "because they were taking out on other blacks what they really wanted but feared to take out on whites" (*Born to Rebel*, p. 26). Southern culture became increasingly violent in the late nineteenth century, with blacks often victimized by other blacks as well as whites.

Another cultural characteristic shared by white and black southerners was the heritage of evangelical Protestantism and its theology. This could result in similar attitudes across racial lines. For example, the novelist Richard Wright noted that southern blacks (like their white Christian neighbors) were notably ambivalent toward Jews, sometimes favorably viewed as God's "chosen people" but other times stigmatized as "Christ killers" (Wright, *Black Boy*, p. 70). Regarding race relations, however, southern whites and blacks typically disagreed about interpreting the Bible. White Biblical Fundamentalists often cited as a justification for black subordination the story in the Book of Genesis of how Noah, disrespected by his son Ham, placed the curse of slavery on Ham's descendants, some of whom the Bible associates with Africa. Black Protestants, on the other hand, pointed out that only

one of Ham's sons, Canaan, was cursed, and that the Bible identifies Ham's other descendants, including the Ethiopians, in a more favorable light. "It must, indeed, be a stimulus to any people to be able to refer to their ancestors as distinguished in deeds of valor," wrote E. A. Johnson in *A School History of the Negro Race in America* (1893), "and particularly so to the colored people . . . a race of people once the most powerful on earth" (Meier, *Negro Thought in America*, p. 53). Such biblical interpretations, which had much in common with today's controversial "Afrocentric history," reinforced the self-esteem of African Americans victimized by racism.

"THE TALENTED TENTH"

The twentieth century opened with the publication of *Up from Slavery* (1900), the autobiography of Booker T. Washington, the most influential person in African American life. Nine years old when emancipation came with the ratification of the Thirteenth Amendment in 1865, Washington never participated in antislavery struggles like Frederick Douglass. He was educated at Virginia's Hampton Institute whose founder, the white general Samuel Chapman Armstrong, taught the virtues of hard work and self-reliance to black students who were trained as primary schoolteachers, farmers, mechanics, and domestic servants. In 1881 Washington carried this gospel to Tuskegee in Alabama where his pledge that blacks would avoid politics and not challenge segregation won him the support of powerful white men in both the South and the North. Building his own empire that included control over schools, churches, newspapers, businesses, and even government jobs, Washington viewed himself with some justification as an African American example of the "rags to riches" success stories dramatized in Horatio Alger's immensely popular dime novels during the era when businessmen like John D. Rockefeller and Andrew Carnegie were building great industrial empires.

Washington's great rival after 1900 was W. E. B. Du Bois. Born during the first post-slavery generation—in 1868, in Great Barrington, Massachusetts—Du Bois attended all-black Fisk University in Tennessee, and then the University of Berlin and Harvard University, where in 1895 he became the first African American awarded a Harvard Ph.D. If Washington's values reflected the late-nineteenth-century era when big businessmen were glorified, Du Bois personified the early-twentieth-century

THE CRUSADE AGAINST LYNCHING

Between 1882 and 1951, 4,730 people were lynched in the United States—3,437 black and 1,293 white. Three-quarters of all lynchings occurred in the South, where 90 percent of the victims were African Americans. Contrary to white supremacist mythology about black men assaulting white women, only one in five of those lynched were even accused of rape. About two-fifths of the victims were accused, often unfairly, of assaulting whites. Most of the rest were lynched for trivial offenses, like disrespecting whites or petty theft, or for no offenses at all. Grisly lynchings, in which the victim was shot, burned, and mutilated as well as hanged, were the white South's way of "keeping the Negro in his place."

Though almost all victims were men, African American women took the initiative in the anti-lynching movement. Ida B. Wells, born in slavery during the Civil War, was orphaned as a teenager and forced to assume parental responsibility for her brothers and sisters. In Memphis, her first career as a teacher ended when she criticized the shoddy condition of black schools. As co-owner and editor of the newspaper, *Memphis Free Speech,* she attacked the mob responsible for lynching three African American shopkeepers who were disliked by their white competitors. In 1892, while she was out of town, the offices of her newspaper were destroyed. She left Memphis, urging other African Americans to do so as well. Continuing her journalistic crusade against lynching in New York, where she wrote for the *New York Age,* she visited President William McKinley in the White House and journeyed to London where she had a great effect on British public opinion. Later, in Chicago, she became a charter member of the NAACP and was appointed as a probation officer in which position she allied herself with Jane Addams in the social settlement and women's suffrage movements.

Reflecting the general trend toward organization in American life around 1900, Wells's individual crusade was taken up by the new black women's club movement. In the 1890s, Josephine St. Pierre Ruffin organized the First National Conference of Colored Women in Boston; Booker T. Washington's wife, Margaret Washington, organized the National Federation of Afro-American Women; and Mary Church Terrell organized the National League of Colored Women. In 1896, the three organizations joined to form the National Association of Colored Women (NACW). The NACW remained the most important women's organization until 1935 when Mary McLeod Bethune, an educator and informal advisor to President Franklin D. Roosevelt, organized the National Council of Negro Women (NCNW), which eventually claimed a membership of 3 million.

After the NAACP was formed in 1909, the black women's club movement collaborated with it in the anti-lynching crusade. White southern opposition in the United States Senate prevented the passage of the Dyer Anti-Lynching Bill during the 1920s, but some states did pass anti-lynching laws. More important, a successful lobbying campaign won the support of the white southern women who organized the Association of Southern Women for the Prevention of Lynching (ASWPL). Together with the Commission for Interracial Cooperation, the ASWPL helped change white southern opinion. Lynchings gradually declined in frequency but continued sporadically until 1955 when Emmett Till, a Chicago teenager visiting Mississippi, is reported to have been the last African American lynch victim in the United States.

Progressive Era when political reformers allied with social scientists were expected to solve America's urban-industrial problems.

Commissioned by the University of Pennsylvania to research and write *The Philadelphia Negro* (1899), his pioneering study of urban race relations, Du Bois moved to Atlanta University where he produced groundbreaking studies of black life in the South. In *The Souls of Black Folk* (1903)—a literary and political manifesto announcing that "the problem of the Twentieth Century is the problem of the color line" (p. 34)—Du Bois challenged Washington's program of racial accommodation, acceptance of segregation, and industrial education. He proposed instead a militant crusade for integration and equality, to be led by the college-educated "Talented Tenth" of African American "leaders of thought and missionaries of culture to their people" (Banks, *Black Intellectuals,* p. 305). In 1905, Du Bois assembled the Niagara Movement, a vanguard of young African American intellectuals, to promote "a new abolitionism." In 1909, a year after whites rioted against blacks in Abraham Lincoln's hometown of Springfield, Illinois, the National Association for the Advancement of Colored People (NAACP) was launched, with Du Bois prominent among its integrated leadership.

Du Bois's new program was made possible by the emergence of the black bourgeoisie. A small but vital class of middle-class African Americans had appeared on the scene by 1900. Included were businesspeople and entrepreneurs serving the growing black population of both southern and northern cities, who often belonged to Booker T. Washington's National Negro Business League. More important in terms of articulate leadership were ministers, teachers, journalists, and other professionals with liberal arts educations. Du Bois articulated what these people were already thinking. Indeed, he borrowed the term "Talented Tenth" from Reverend Henry L. Morehouse, after whom Morehouse College in Atlanta was named. He also owed an intellectual debt to Reverend Alexander Crummell, founder in 1897 of the American Negro Academy (ANA), akin to later "think tanks," an institution whose members included Du Bois as well as Carter G. Woodson, the Harvard-trained historian and originator of Black History Month.

It is impossible to understand American intellectual and cultural life—black or white—around 1900 without using the paradigm of professionalization. In all fields of African American endeavor, "amateurs," such as the slave craftsmen who had produced the first African American art, were being replaced by "professionals." An ex-slave who earned a graduate degree, George Washington Carver, Tuskegee's agricultural research director, became famous for his study of the industrial uses of the peanut, but he considered himself primarily a research biologist. The inventor Granville T. Woods, sometimes referred to by historians as the Black Edison, was a machinist, blacksmith, and railroad engineer, but then studied electrical and mechanical engineering in college before patenting his first important invention in 1884. Daniel Hale Williams, the first American doctor to perform open heart surgery in 1893, followed up a traditional medical apprenticeship with a more rigorous medical education at the Chicago Medical College. The writers Paul Laurence Dunbar and Charles W. Chesnutt wrote poetry and novels for their livelihood. The painter Henry O. Tanner was taught by Thomas Eakins at the Pennsylvania Academy of Fine Arts and by Benjamin Constant at the Académie Julien in Paris, where he stayed and earned a reputation as "the dean of American painters." The sculptor Meta Vaux Warrick Fuller underwent her professional apprenticeship at the Pennsylvania Academy and the École des Beaux-Arts in Paris, where she also studied under Auguste Rodin. The musicologist Harry T. Burleigh studied at the National Conservatory of Music under Antonin Dvořák, whom he introduced to Negro spirituals. The soprano Sissierta Jones, dubbed by her peers the Black Patti (after the Italian soprano Adelina Patti), was classically trained at the New England Conservatory. And the theater professionals Bob Cole, Will Marion Cook, James Weldon Johnson, and John Rosamond Johnson wrote and produced ragtime-era musical comedies for the Broadway stage, where the consummate performer Bert Williams refined old minstrel stereotypes.

African American professionals, whether in science and technology or literature, painting, music, and theater, faced difficulties in living up to Du Bois's ideal of a Talented Tenth that would lead and inspire the black masses. Granville T. Woods was drained by his fight with his former employer, Thomas Edison, who challenged Woods's patent on the steam boiler furnace. Charles W. Chesnutt's novels sold poorly in spite of favorable reviews; he gave up creative writing for a legal career. Henry O. Tanner achieved professional recognition, but as an expatriate in France he abandoned his early interest in black themes (*The Banjo Lesson*) and specialized in religious painting. Sissierta Jones, no matter how serious her classical training, was denied an operatic career because of her race; she became a musical comedy performer starring in Black Patti's Troubadours.

BLACK NATIONALISM

Despite the frustrations of the African American middle class and Du Bois's Talented Tenth, his influence was surpassing that of the Wizard of Tuskegee by the time Booker T. Washington died in 1915. Ironically, the very next year marked the appearance of the man—the black nationalist leader Marcus Garvey—who would challenge Du Bois as harshly as he had Washington.

Born in 1887 in Jamaica, where he first organized his Universal Negro Improvement Association (UNIA), Garvey arrived in the United States as an admirer of Washington's programmatic emphasis on black solidarity and self-help, which he wanted to put in practice on a global scale. With the ambitious goals of "bringing the Negroes of the world in one solid body" and "relieving Africa of Anglo-Saxon domination and oppression," the UNIA manifested a rhetorical militancy that exceeded that of the NAACP (Ottley and Weatherby, *The Negro in New York,* p. 211). A master of theatrics and pageantry, Garvey elected himself "the provisional president of Africa," and appointed his aides as dukes, duchesses, and knights commander of "the Court of Ethiopia." He promulgated his own religion, featuring a black Christ and Virgin Mother, and organized an "African legion" to liberate the mother continent. Dressed in a purple, green, and black uniform with a helmet with a white feathered plume, he marched through Harlem, New York, to the UNIA's Liberty Hall, capable of seating six thousand, where he preached his "Back to Africa" gospel to capacity crowds. Like no leader before or since, he captured the imagination of the black masses, many of them recent migrants to the urban North from the rural South.

Garvey rejected the NAACP's objective of racial integration and challenged the right of the middle-class elite to lead African Americans. He was loathed as a vulgar demagogue by Du Bois who also viewed Garvey's "Black Zionism" as a threat to his own leadership role in the Pan-African movement that sought the end of European colonialism. Garvey, however, denounced the NAACP as an organization led by "light-skinned Negroes" like Du Bois who were "not really black." Their real purpose, he charged, was to intermarry with white people (*The Philosophy and Opinions of Marcus Garvey,* vol. 2, pp. 42, 57).

In the 1920s, Garvey made mistakes that destroyed his movement. Declaring that "potentially, every white man is a Klansman," he entered into a political alliance with white racists that was unpopular in Harlem (Cronin, *Black Moses,* p. 190). He was also convicted of mail fraud, which resulted in a prison sentence followed by his deportation as an undesirable alien. Yet despite and perhaps because of its failings, Garvey's movement cast a long shadow over African America during the jazz age of the 1920s.

THE HARLEM RENAISSANCE

The Harlem Renaissance according to the Howard University professor Alain Locke, the first black Rhodes scholar and editor of *The New Negro* (1925), was the African American contribution to America's "spiritual Coming of Age" (p. 16). The many blossoms of cultural pluralism would bloom as the United States, led by its black creative elite, threw off its Anglo-Saxon hypocrisies and Victorian repressions, and achieved a more honest, spontaneous civilization. The poet Langston Hughes expressed the dominant impulse this way:

> We intend to express our individual dark-skinned selves without fear or shame. If white people are pleased, we are glad. If they are not, it doesn't matter. We know we are beautiful. And ugly too.... We build our temples for tomorrow on top of the mountain, free within ourselves. (Rampersad, *The Life of Langston Hughes,* vol. 1, p. 131)

Ideology aside, the creative output of the Harlem Renaissance is impressive. In writing and the visual arts, it ran the gamut from the folk poetry of Langston Hughes, to the lyric poetry of Claude McKay and Countee Cullen, to the comic novels of Wallace Thurman and Rudolph Fisher, to the social novels of Jessie Redmond Fauset and Nella Larsen, to the experimental fiction of Jean Toomer, to the satiric journalism of George Schuyler, to the folklore studies of Zora Neale Hurston, to the graphic art of Aaron Douglas, to the sculpture of Richmond Barthé.

Yet music and dance were the signature contributions by African Americans to the jazz age. In 1920 Mamie Smith's "Crazy Blues," the first genuine blues recording, was sold as a "race record" on the Okeh label. In 1921 Noble Sissle and Eubie Blake's all-black musical, *Shuffle Along,* introduced jazz to Broadway. In 1923 black jazz performers began to enter the recording industry mainstream as the pianist Jelly Roll Morton played with a white band, the New Orleans Rhythm Kings, and the vocalist Bessie Smith's "Down-Hearted Blues" sold over 1 million copies on the Columbia label. In 1924 the trumpeter Louis "Satchmo" Armstrong completed his odyssey from New Orleans through Chicago to New York where he joined Fletcher Henderson's Band at the Roseland Ballroom. In 1925 jazz went international as Josephine Baker dazzled Paris audiences in *La Revue Nègre*.

Paradoxically, jazz—the revolutionary African American music of the 1920s—was not uniformly embraced by enthusiasts of "the New Negro." On the one hand, W. E. B. Du Bois's musical tastes never evolved beyond the spirituals; James Weldon Johnson preferred ragtime; and Alain Locke considered "hot" music insufficiently inspirational to fulfill the spiritual promise of the movement. On the other hand, Langston Hughes, a younger man who unpretentiously defined himself as a folk artist, made jazz the metaphor for his own poetry in *Weary Blues* (1926).

Another major theme of the Harlem Renaissance—the discovery of Africa as a source of race pride—was also fraught with ambiguity. Langston Hughes un-self-consciously invoked the ancestral connection in his poem "The Negro Speaks of Rivers" (1921). Yet the lyric poet Countee Cullen related ambivalently to stereotypes of African "primitivism." His poem "Heritage" (1925) repeats the skeptical refrain, "Spicy grove, cinnamon tree/ What is Africa to me?" (Huggins, *Harlem Renaissance*, p. 81). Unlike the slave spirituals, modern jazz also did not easily connect with African roots. Bearing "all the marks of a nerve-strung, strident, mechanized civilization," jazz according to the African American cultural critic J. A. Rogers was something that "the African Negro hasn't at all" (Locke, *The New Negro*, pp. 218, 220). European artists and musicians like Pablo Picasso, Henri Matisse, Igor Stravinsky, and Dvořák were often the first to embrace African art and music. In an ultimate irony, a European artist, Winold Reiss, taught the African American sculptor Aaron Douglas to appreciate African design.

Some Harlemites during the 1920s thought that "the race problem had been solved through Art," or so Langston Hughes recalled later. They learned otherwise when white patrons, including the Rosenwald, Guggenheim, and Harmon Foundations, reduced their support of Harlem's creative community after the Stock Market Crash of 1929. The Great Depression, Hughes added, "brought everybody down a peg or two. And Negroes had but few pegs to fall" (*The Big Sea*, pp. 228, 247).

NATIVE SONS

The one-third of a century roughly from the bottom of the Great Depression to the beginnings of the Vietnam War was a period of increasing global engagement for the United States, combined with a heightened American nationalism demanding greater cohesion to meet foreign and domestic challenges. Affected by the same pressures as all Americans, African Americans responded in the intellectual and cultural realm by affirming the American dream of equality at the same time as they protested its denial by racism.

During the New Deal and World War II, music became a metaphor for a society trying to harmonize—economically, militarily, and racially. Benny Goodman experimented with integrating his previously all-white "swing" orchestra with trios and quartets featuring Gene Krupa, Teddy Wilson, and Lionel Hampton as well as singers Ella Fitzgerald and Billie Holiday. The African American bandleaders Fletcher Henderson, Duke Ellington, and Count Basie, despite victimization by Jim Crow, won unprecedented national audiences cutting across racial lines, as did the singers Roland Hayes and Paul Robeson and the composer William Grant Still, whose "Afro-American Symphony" (1931) was the first work by a black composer performed by a national symphony orchestra. The contralto Marian Anderson, whose repertoire mixed arias with spirituals, also powerfully symbolized the moral of music arrayed against bigotry. Denied permission to perform in Adolf Hitler's Berlin and snubbed by the Daughters of the American Revolution who barred her from singing at Constitution Hall in Washington, she gave a triumphant concert on the steps of the Lincoln Memorial on Easter Sunday, 1939.

In sports as well as music, African Americans recorded notable breakthroughs. Jesse Owens gave the lie to Hitler's theory of Aryan supremacy by winning four gold medals at the 1936 Berlin Olympics. The boxer Joe Louis became an all-American hero by knocking out Germany's Max Schmeling in 1938. And, finally, in 1947 Jackie Robinson demolished major league baseball's color line.

Of course, there was also plenty of disharmony on the American scene. Wartime racial tensions spilled over in the Zoot Suit riots in Detroit, Los Angeles, and Harlem during 1943. Black opinion makers articulated the "Double V" campaign (victory over fascism abroad and racism at home). But minority youth, including Hispanics, expressed their frustrations with countercultural trends: the zoot suit (single-breasted jackets with flared lapels and padded shoulders accompanied by pleated trousers with wide knees and tight cuffs, a porkpie hat, and long key chain), the Lindy hop dance, frenetic bebop jazz, and "hep cat" lingo. White youth, especially those in uniform, reacted with an explosive mix of envy and outrage that helped fuel the riots, as did black anger over wartime discrimination.

Before World War II, many young writers, white and black, had worked for the New Deal's Federal Writers' Project, even while writing "protest fiction" in the proletarian mold that rejected failed capitalism. A memorable example is Richard Wright and his pessimistic masterpiece in the naturalistic style of Émile Zola and Theodore Dreiser. Wright's *Native Son* (1940) is the story of Bigger Thomas, a product of Chicago's South Side ghetto, who murders two women, one white and one black, because his potential for moral responsibility has been crushed under the dual weight of class and color oppression. A chauffeur to a rich white girl, he suffocates her out of dread that her drunken murmurs may be mistaken by her mother for cries of rape. This is the crime for which he is punished—not his subsequent sadistic killing of his black girlfriend while a criminal on the run. A "black nationalist" in only the negative psychological sense, Bigger Thomas is wholly consumed by fear and envy of whites:

> Goddamit, look! We live here and they live there. We black and they white. They got things and we ain't. They do things and we can't. It's just like living in jail. Half the time I feel like I'm on the outside of the world peeping in through a knot-hole in the fence. (p. 17)

As documented in *Black Boy* (1945), Wright's memoir of growing up in small town Mississippi, Bigger was an autobiographical metaphor for Wright, though Wright had the will and imagination to escape. Indeed, Bigger was to Wright, as he later explained, a nightmarish African American everyman of universal significance because

> Negro life is [all] life lifted to the heights of pain and pathos, drama and tragedy. The history of the Negro in America is the history of America written in vivid and bloody terms; it is the history of Western Man writ small.... The Negro is America's metaphor. (pp. 108–109)

Wright had no faith in the redemptive power of either Marcus Garvey's version or the Harlem Renaissance's version of the New Negro. The only glimmer of hope in the novel, the one moment of human intimacy, is Bigger's death row conversation with Max, his white communist lawyer—before hope yields again to hate.

Like Richard Wright, the political scientist (and later diplomat) Ralph Bunche and the sociologist E. Franklin Frazier were critics of American society who believed there was little if anything worth preserving in African American culture. Gunnar Myrdal's highly influential *An American Dilemma: The Negro Problem and Modern Democracy* (1944), for which Bunche was a senior researcher, sums up this view of "American Negro culture ... [as] a distorted development, or a pathological condition, of the general American culture" (Southern, *Gunnar Myrdal and Black-White Relations*, p. 45). The problem, according to Bunche, was that "the Negro is an American citizen, but his thinking is more Negro than American" (Banks, *Black Intellectuals*, p. 107). In Frazier's classic, *The Negro Family in the United States* (1939), distinctive African American family patterns were analyzed as unhealthy adaptations to urban-industrial conditions, termed "the House of Destruction." Frazier's solution was to equalize the income of the black poor and integrate them into the white working class. This worthy goal was linked with a denigration of African American culture, not only in Frazier's work, but in an entire generation of social policy studies culminating in Daniel Patrick Moynihan's *The Negro Family: The Case for National Action* (1965), an intellectual cornerstone of the 1960s War on Poverty.

When prosperity returned after World War II, radical criticisms of capitalism were usually rejected or forgotten, but not the subordination of claims to a distinctive African American culture. The transcendent imperative was still the merging of black and white in accordance with Richard Wright's plea in *Twelve Million Black Voices* (1941): "If we had been allowed to participate in the vital processes of American national growth ... [w]e black folk say that America would have been stronger and greater" (p. 145).

Born in Oklahoma, Ralph Ellison had been Wright's friend and comrade in the 1930s. His National Book Award–winning novel *The Invisible Man* (1952) counterpoints the blindness of racism that renders blacks culturally "invisible" to whites with "the infinite possibilities" that American life, despite its flaws, offers African Americans. Ellison's hero finally emerges in the light of day after going underground to escape an apocalyptic race riot sparked jointly by a black nationalist madman and white communists willfully blind to the inhumanity of their own manipulation of blacks in the name of historical necessity.

Ellison in his literary criticism took to task Wright's *Native Son,* not so much for its criticisms of American society, but for its despairing vision of African Americans, personified in Bigger Thomas, as passive victims of circumstances lacking the cultural resources for positive action. In Ellison's view, "white culture" and "black culture" were "vague, racist terms." African Americans have elaborated a rich cultural idiom, through folklore and music, that is an integral part of the American experience. The result has been the creation of a hybrid national culture—"a matter of diversity within unity"—that whites and blacks have collaborated in making (*Shadow and Act,* pp. 254–255). The African American strand of the American cultural mosaic qualifies black writers and artists to speak, not just for their own community, but for all Americans. But the African American cultural idiom is also a resource available to whites, like Mark Twain in *Huckleberry Finn,* willing to "pay dues" and make the imaginative investment required to understand African American history. The "white Negro" persona of rock-and-roller Elvis Presley, emerging from the black blues and gospel musical cultures of the Mississippi Delta and Memphis, provided an Eisenhower-era confirmation of Ellison's intuition.

The son of a Harlem minister, James Baldwin stood alongside Wright and Ellison in the trilogy of mid-twentieth century's most influential African American writers. Baldwin wrote fiction but is better remembered for his essays. In *Notes of a Native Son* (1955), *Nobody Knows My Name* (1961), and *The Fire Next Time* (1963), Baldwin reinforced Ellison's critique of the "protest novel" tradition identified with Richard Wright. He challenged black writers to engage racial injustice, not to dwell on it, but to transcend it through the universalism of art. As the civil rights movement entered a crisis stage in the early 1960s, Baldwin's eloquence became increasingly anguished and angry. In *The Fire Next Time,* he tried to explain to white readers the rage of black militants and separatists such as Malcolm X of the Nation of Islam. Frustrated by the slow pace of racial integration, Baldwin rhetorically asked: "Do I really *want* to be integrated in a burning house?" (p. 108).

BLACK POWER/BLACK ARTS

After World War I, relations between Marcus Garvey's political black nationalism and the creative vanguard the Harlem Renaissance were, at best, strained. A half century later, Black Power politics and the cultural phenomenon known as Black Arts were two faces of the same movement.

In 1965 Malcolm X was assassinated and Watts in Los Angeles exploded in the first of the race riots that swept African American ghettoes. The new political black nationalism rose and fell between 1966 when the civil rights activist Stokely Carmichael (later Kwame Turé) of the Student Nonviolent Coordinating Committee (SNCC) raised the battle cry Black Power and 1975 when the Black Panther Party of Huey P. Newton, Bobby Seale, and Eldridge Cleaver disintegrated. The new militants tried to organize the ghettoes but drew greater strength from the college campuses where the number of black students, the majority attending integrated colleges, more than doubled during the decade.

Their program challenged the mainstream civil rights movement of the NAACP and Reverend Martin Luther King Jr. by rejecting the support of white liberals and demanding community control and black political self-determination. All African Americans were inspired by the freedom movements that won independence for the countries of Africa, beginning with Ghana in 1957. Black Power ideologues went further by embracing the urban guerrilla warfare model of third-world revolutionary movements like that of Vietnam's Ho Chi Minh. Only later, as victims of government repression, did they begin to see the value in the "liberal" values of free speech and association championed by Thurgood Marshall Jr., the NAACP Legal Defense Fund lawyer who made the winning arguments in the historic school integration decision, *Brown vs. Board of Education of Topeka* (1954) and then became the first African American appointed to the U.S. Supreme Court in 1967.

During this same period, black cultural nationalists such as Amiri Baraka (formerly LeRoi Jones), Larry Neal, and Sonia Sanchez articulated an aesthetic of revolutionary protest that complemented the Black Power battle cry. To poet Haki R. Madhubuti (known as Don L. Lee until 1973), founder of Third World Press, cultural and political action were inseparable because "a people without their culture are a meaning without meaning . . . a dead people," but "no poems stop a .38 . . . no stanzas can protect me from a nightstick" (Van Deburg, *New Day in Babylon,* pp. 280, 282).

One word—"soul"—summed up the new black cultural aesthetic. Unlike Ralph Ellison's nonracial conception of the African American cultural idiom, the new "soul" culture was supposed to be an in-group thing open only to blacks—though whites might try to imitate it. Encompassing popular

A TALE OF THREE MARCHES

1941: In the summer before Pearl Harbor, as American defense industries geared up for the possibility of war, white racism shut black Americans out of job opportunities. The African American labor leader A. Philip Randolph decided to organize a mass protest. Born in Florida, the son of a Methodist minister, Randolph moved to Harlem, New York, where he worked as a porter and then devoted himself to socialist journalism and politics as the editor of *The Messenger.* In 1925 he founded the Brotherhood of Sleeping Car Porters, which waged a ten-year struggle to win the right to collectively bargain from the Pullman Palace Car Company. Wedding the trade union movement to the civil rights struggle, Randolph warned the Roosevelt administration that he would peacefully descend on Washington with 100,000 African American supporters unless something was done to curb employment discrimination against blacks in war-related employment.

The threat of an all-black march that would embarrass the federal government both at home and abroad was enough. In June 1941 President Franklin D. Roosevelt created a Fair Employment Practice Committee, with authority not to punish but investigate Jim Crow job practices. Continuing during World War II to demand that anti-bias measures be enacted and enforced, Randolph crusaded after the war for the desegregation of the U.S. military. He also organized the A. Philip Randolph Institute in New York that sought to remedy job discrimination by unions as well as employers. In 1963 Randoph stood beside Reverend Martin Luther King Jr. during King's March on Washington that might never have occurred except for Randolph's precedent-setting action in 1941.

1963: On 28 August 1963, 250,000 Americans, black and white, congregated at the Lincoln Memorial in Washington, D.C., to hear Reverend Martin Luther King Jr. deliver his "I Have a Dream" speech. Born in 1929 into a family of ministers in Atlanta, young King was an exceptional student at Morehouse College in Atlanta, Crozer Theological Seminary in Pennsylvania, and Boston University's School of Theology, which awarded him a Ph.D. Not an original thinker but a brilliant synthesizer, King combined in his political philosophy many strands— the ethical teachings of the Old Testament prophets, the social gospel of the Progressive Era's reform-minded Protestant ministers, the political realism of the neo-Orthodox theologian Reinhold Niebuhr, and the creed of nonviolent protest identified with America's Henry David Thoreau as well as India's Mahatma Gandhi. King was a minister at the Dexter Street Baptist Church in Montgomery, Alabama, when he was catapulted into national prominence by the Montgomery Bus Boycott, ignited on 1 December 1955 when the black seamstress Rosa Parks was arrested for refusing to give up her seat to a white passenger.

Fresh from launching his ultimately successful integration campaign in Birmingham, King came to Washington to galvanize the nation's conscience behind the passage of landmark civil rights legislation. The 1963 March on Washington not only paved the way for the passage of the Civil Rights Act of 1964; it also was the prelude to King's deserved coronation with the 1964 Nobel Peace Prize four years prior to his assassination in Memphis, Tennessee.

1995: On 19 October 1995, a huge throng (estimates vary from a half million to over one million) arrived in Washington, D.C., to participate in the Million Man

CONTINUED NEXT PAGE

March organized by the Nation of Islam (NOI) minister Louis Farrakhan. At the time of King's 1963 March on Washington, Farrakhan, a protégé of Malcolm X, was a rising star in the ranks of the NOI whose leader, Elijah Muhammad, dismissed Reverend King's integrated march as a frivolous waste of time. During the next three stormy decades of NOI history, Farrakhan outlived the assassinated Malcolm X, spurned the leadership claim of Elijah Muhammad's son, and emerged as the leader of the small but passionate Black Muslim movement dedicated to racial separatism. His 1995 "Day of Atonement and Reconciliation," which few observers thought would ever take place, marked Farrakhan's triumphant entry into the African American mainstream as a leader whose influence was often compared to Jesse Jackson and General Colin Powell. At the National Mall, Farrakhan preached a three-hour-long sermon alternating obscure NOI theology and numerology with, in many ways, a conservative gospel of self-help, spiritual renewal, and racial solidarity. This message was well received by men who pledged to return home and redeem their neighborhoods from drugs and crime.

The Million Man March was controversial for its exclusion of women and whites, which made it very different from Reverend King's inclusiveness. Also heatedly debated was whether the message could be separated from the controversial messenger. Widely criticized for harsh rhetoric against whites in general and Jews in particular, Minister Farrakhan long seemed incapable of keeping apart his positive vision of ingroup renewal from his negative attacks on racial "outsiders." Subsequent to the Million Man March, Farrakhan survived a near-fatal illness, an experience that seemed to accelerate his new course of moderation and peacemaking with his critics. Whatever the ultimate verdict on Farrakhan, his Million Man March has won a secure place as a landmark in African American history.

culture as well as the intellectual avant-garde, soul included everything from slang (hip, cool, and Swahili words) to cuisine (soul food), to handshakes (getting and giving "skin"), to hairstyle and clothing (the Afro and dashikis), to music (Aretha Franklin, James Brown), to religion (black theology and the Kwanza holiday), to black studies programs on campus.

The new black cultural militancy influenced white youth culture (the music of Janis Joplin, Eric Burdon, the Righteous Brothers) and even made inroads into the mass media as television began incorporating black characters with a soulful look (Clarence Williams III in *Mod Squad*, Nichelle Nichols in *Star Trek*) and "blaxploitation" films (*Shaft, Superfly*) enjoyed a fad. Without any need to attach their professional stars to "soul," black artists like the opera singer Leontyne Price, the choreographer Alvin Ailey, and the painters Jacob Lawrence and Romare Bearden also thrived during the 1960s and 1970s.

Partly a victim of its success, the Black Arts movement was diluted by imitation and commercialization. The phenomenal success of Alex Haley's novel *Roots* (1976), the winner of both a National Book Award and Pulitzer Prize and the basis of an extremely successful television miniseries, was in part a reflection of how the assumptions about pride in ethnic origins of black "cultural nationalism" had triumphed in the American mainstream. The Black Power movement was also destroyed at roughly the same time by violent internal disagreements and repression by the Federal Bureau of Investigation. Yet seeds planted in the 1960s and 1970s were harvested in the 1980s and 1990s in what scholars have termed the new Black Renaissance.

THE NEW BLACK RENAISSANCE

The last two decades of the twentieth century replicated the achievements of the Harlem Renaissance of the 1920s, but on a much larger scale. Professor Henry Louis Gates Jr. of Harvard's Department of Afro-American Studies put it thus:

It's not that there are black artists and intellectuals who matter; it's that so many of the artists and intellectuals who matter are black. It's not that the cultural cutting edge has been influenced by black creativity; it's that black creativity, it so often seems today, is the cultural cutting edge. ("Black Creativity," p. 74)

Supported by the fourfold increase in the size of the African middle class between 1940 and 1990, the black creative community no longer had to depend so heavily on the financial support of white foundations and institutions. It also benefited from the unprecedented emergence of a supportive cultural infrastructure of black publishers, editors, reviewers, producers, directors, and agents.

Black cultural creativity in the 1990s ran the gamut from the novelists Toni Morrison (the first black woman to win the Nobel Prize in literature) and Charles Johnson, to the playwrights Angus Wilson (a Pulitzer Prize winner for *Fences*) and Anna Deavere Smith, to the poets Maya Angelou and Rita Dove, to the choreographers Bill T. Jones and David Roussève, to the composers Alvin Singleton and Anthony Davis, to the painters David Hammons and Lorna Simpson, to the filmmakers Spike Lee and John Singleton. Cornel West arguably became the first American philosopher since John Dewey to have a broad influence beyond the "ivory tower." And the literary critic Henry Louis Gates Jr., editor (with Nellie Y. McKay) of the *Norton Anthology of African American Literature* (1996) and (with Kwame A. Appiah) of *Africana: The Encyclopedia of the African and African American Experience* (1999), achieved a reputation reminiscent of such earlier cultural arbiters as H. L. Mencken and Edmund Wilson, as he championed a multicultural enlargement of the Western canon of great books to include black and other minority literatures. Like Gates, Houstan A. Baker Jr., also a literary critic, was honored with the presidency of the Modern Language Association, as was the historian Thomas C. Holt of the American Historical Association. African American academic success stories were no longer rarities.

Popular culture, like the avant-garde, continued to show the African American imprint. The singer Michael Jackson marketed himself as a global pop idol, the actors Bill Cosby and Oprah Winfrey became television icons, and—despite continuing black frustration over the slow pace of integration behind and in front of the camera—Spike Lee emerged as the celebrity producer-director of the 30-million-dollar film epic, *Malcolm X* (1992). Terry McMillan's melodrama about the lives and loves of four thirty-something black women, *Waiting to Exhale* (1992), became a runaway best-seller. The crime novels of Walter Mosley and the science

fiction of Otavia E. Butler entered literary realms that used to be all-white preserves. And in the form of *Encarta Africana 2000,* the version for Microsoft of Bill Gates's encyclopedia, the new Black Renaissance entered the realm of virtual culture.

When George C. Wolfe succeeded Joseph Papp as the leader of New York City's Public Theater, race was hardly mentioned. Black themes were dominant in the works of many, but not all, members of the African American creative community. Rita Dove had the self-confidence to move gracefully between racial and nonracial content: "There are times when I am a black woman who happens to be a poet and times when I am a poet who happens to be black" (White, *Time,* October 10, 1994, p. 69). Henry Louis Gates Jr. warned that "the mindless celebration of difference has proven as untenable as the bygone model of monochrome homogeneity" (Levine, *The Opening of the American Mind,* p. 162). He also lauded Toni Morrison for taking on the challenge "to create a fiction *beyond* the color line, one that takes the blackness of the culture for granted, as a springboard to write about those human emotions that we share with everyone else" (Forman, *Partisan Review,* p. 589).

In terms of gender politics, women—Michele Wallace, Alice Walker, Toni Morrison—pioneered the new Renaissance in the early 1980s. Alice Walker's novel, *The Color Purple* (1982), fused black and feminist themes in an unprecedented way. With its impact magnified by Steven Spielberg's 1985 movie version, the novel also brought into the public realm tensions within African American culture over gender status and gay/lesbian identities. The resulting controversy prefigured the ambivalent, divided reactions of African Americans in 1991 when the black law professor Anita Hill accused Clarence Thomas, nominated to succeed Supreme Court Justice Thurgood Marshall, of sexual harassment. Black women in particular, desiring dual liberation from racial and sexual discrimination, often were in a quandary about whether their final emancipation would be in consort with, or in conflict with, that of black men.

Black public intellectuals played a pivotal role in the new multicultural dialogue debating the meaning of race, gender, and class in the American experience. Despite complaints about "political correctness" stifling intellectual diversity on college campuses, the black intellectuals covered quite a wide ideological spectrum. Radicals like Cornell West, Manning Marable, Adolph Reed, and bell hooks were balanced by centrists like Randall Kennedy, William Julius Wilson, and Stephen Carter and conservatives like Thomas Sowell, Shelby Steele, and Glenn Loury. Others like the sociologist Orlando Patterson, the novelist and essayist Ishmael Reed, and the cultural critics Stanley Crouch, Michael Eric Dyson, and Gerald Early defied the usual labels.

The African American community for which the black intellectuals were cast in the role of spokespeople was more diverse than ever before. The black middle class grew, but the black underclass did not shrink, and its cultural dynamism, manifested in rap music, also shaped the new Black Renaissance. Real tensions existed between the style of "buppies" or black urban professionals and "b-boys" or representatives of hip-hop culture. "Gangsta rappers"—the shock troops of hip-hop culture—have become the lightning rod for criticisms of inner-city lifestyles. Incorporating the political message music of the rap group Public Enemy into the score of his film *Do the Right Thing* (1989), Spike Lee tried with some success in this and subsequent films to bridge gaps by exploring color and class prejudices as well as sexism among African Americans.

Paul Gilroy, a black cultural critic born in Great Britain, suggested in *The Black Atlantic* (1993) that music might yet provide a basis for overcoming ideological oppositions between tradition and modernity and for defining a postmodern cultural synthesis uniting Africans with the diaspora peoples of African origin in the United States and throughout the Atlantic world.

A musical marriage between African "roots" and American "routes" was promoted by the white folk musician Paul Simon whose "Graceland" tour and album (1986) introduced the South African vocal group, Ladysmith Black Mambazo, to the American audience. The biographical book and film *Listen Up: The Many Lives of Quincy Jones* (1990) charts Jones's global odyssey—from poverty on Chicago's South Side, through world capitals, to Los Angeles, the television and music capital. Ensconced as an entertainment industry mogul and multicultural oracle, Jones mixed African American rap with Brazilian rhythms, and explained that both derived from the same "traditions of the African griot storyteller" (*Listen Up,* p. 167). Yet Gilroy ultimately doubted that Quincy Jones's celebrity self-promotion and facile musical sleight-of-hand were really harbingers of a postmodern global culture for the twenty-first century.

Around the mid-twentieth century, the protagonist of Ralph Ellison's *The Invisible Man* asked himself, "We, who write no novels, histories or other books. What about us?" More than fifty years later, he would be glad to know that—even if ultimate answers still prove elusive—African Americans were producing books and art of all kinds in an effort to tackle this question.

See also **Africa and America; Race as a Cultural Category; The Black Church: Invisible and Visible; Slavery and Race; Slave Culture and Consciousness; Thought and Culture in the Free Black Community; Antislavery; Gender, Social Class, Race, and Material Life; Racialism and Racial Uplift; The Harlem Renaissance** *(volume 1);* **Race, Rights, and Reform; Resurgent Conservatism** *(in this volume);* **Race; Marxist Approaches** *(volume 3).*

BIBLIOGRAPHY

Anderson, Jervis. *A. Philip Randolph: A Biographical Portrait.* New York, 1973.

Baldwin, James. *The Fire Next Time.* New York, 1963.

Banks, William M. *Black Intellectuals: Race and Responsibility in American Life.* New York, 1996.

Berlin, Ira. *Many Thousand Gone: The First Two Centuries of Slavery in North America.* Cambridge, Mass., 1998.

———. *Slaves without Masters: The Free Negro in the Antebellum South.* New York, 1974.

Blassingame, John. *The Slave Community: Plantation Life in the Antebellum South.* Rev. ed. New York, 1979.

Bone, Robert A. *The Negro Novel in America.* New Haven, Conn., 1958.

Bradford, Sarah. *Harriet: The Moses of Her People.* New York, 1886.

Branch, Taylor. *Parting the Waters: America in the King Years, 1954–1963*. New York, 1988.

———. *Pillar of Fire: America in the King Years, 1963–1965*. New York, 1998.

Butcher, Margaret Just, based on materials left by Alain Locke. *The Negro in American Culture*. New York, 1956.

Butterfield, Fox. *All God's Children: The Bosket Family and the Tradition of American Violence*. New York, 1995.

Carson, Clayborne. *In Struggle: SNCC and the Black Awakening of the 1960s*. Cambridge, Mass., 1981.

Cronin, Edmund David. *Black Moses*. Madison, Wisc., 1968.

Dates, Jannette L., and William Barlow, eds. *Split Image: African Americans in the Mass Media*. Washington, D.C., 1993.

Douglas, Ann. *Terrible Honesty: Mongrel Manhattan in the 1920s*. New York, 1995.

Douglass, Frederick. *Life and Times of Frederick Douglass: His Early Life as a Slave, His Escape from Bondage, and His Complete History; An Autobiography*. 1892. Reprint, New York, 1993.

Du Bois, W. E. B. *The Souls of Black Folk*. 1903. Reprint, edited by David W. Blight and Robert Gooding-Williams. Boston, 1997. Page references in the text are from the reprint edition.

Ellison, Ralph. *Shadow and Act*. New York, 1964.

Erenberg, Lewis A. *Swingin' the Dream: Big Band Jazz and the Rebirth of American Culture*. Chicago, 1998.

Foner, Eric. *Reconstruction: America's Unfinished Revolution, 1863–1877*. New York, 1988.

Forman, Seth. "On Howe, Ellison, and Black Intellectuals." *Partisan Review*, 66, no. 4 (Fall 1999): 587–624.

Gardell, Mattias. *In the Name of Elijah Muhammad: Louis Farrakhan and the Nation of Islam*. Durham, N.C., 1996.

Garrow, David J. *Bearing the Cross: Martin Luther King, Jr., and the Southern Christian Leadership Conference*. New York, 1986.

Garvey, Marcus. *The Philosophy and Opinions of Marcus Garvey*. 2 vols. 1925. Reprint, edited by Amy Jacques Garvey. New York, 1969. Page references in the text are from the reprint edition.

Gates, Henry Louis, Jr. "Black Creativity: On The Cutting Edge." *Time* 144, no. 15 (October 10, 1994): 74–75.

———. "Harlem on Our Minds." *Critical Inquiry* 24, no. 1 (Autumn 1997): 1–12.

Gates, Henry Louis, Jr., ed. *"Race," Writing, and Difference*. Chicago, 1986.

George, Carol V. R. *Segregated Sabbaths: Richard Allen and the Rise of Independent Black Churches, 1760–1840*. New York, 1973.

Gilroy, Paul. *The Black Atlantic: Modernity and Double Consciousness*. Cambridge, Mass., 1993.

Hall, Jacquelyn Dowd. *Revolt Against Chivalry: Jessie Daniel Ames and the Women's Campaign Against Lynching*. New York, 1979.

Harlan, Louis R. *Booker T. Washington: The Making of a Black Leader, 1856–1901*. New York, 1972.

Howe, Daniel Walker. "Frederick Douglass." In *Making the American Self,* edited by Daniel Walker Howe, 149–156. Cambridge, Mass., 1997.

Huggins, Nathan Irvin. *Harlem Renaissance.* New York, 1974.

Hughes, Langston. *The Big Sea: An Autobiography.* New York, 1968.

Hutchinson, George. *The Harlem Renaissance in Black and White.* Cambridge, Mass., 1995.

Jacobs, Harriet A. (Linda Brent). *Incidents in the Life of a Slave Girl: Written by Herself.* 1861. Originally edited by Lydia Maria Child. Reprint, edited by Jean Fagan Yellin. Cambridge, Mass., 1987.

Jefferson, Thomas. *Notes on the State of Virginia.* 1784. Reprint, edited by William Peden. Chapel Hill, N.C., 1995. Page references in the text are from the reprint edition

Jones, Quincy. *Listen Up: The Many Lives of Quincy Jones.* New York, 1990.

Jordan, Winthrop D. *White Over Black: American Attitudes Toward the Negro: 1550–1812.* Chapel Hill, N.C., 1968.

Keiler, Allan. *Marian Anderson: A Singer's Journey.* New York, 2000.

Kelley, Robin D. G. *Race Rebels: Culture, Politics, and the Black Working Class.* New York, 1994.

King, Martin Luther, Jr. *A Testament of Hope: The Essential Writings and Speeches of Martin Luther King, Jr.* Edited by James M. Washington. New York, 1986.

Knupfer, Anne Meis. *Toward a Tenderer Humanity and a Nobler Womanhood: African American Women's Clubs in Turn-of-the-Century Chicago.* New York, 1996.

Lerner, Gerda., ed. *Black Women in White America: A Documentary History.* New York, 1973.

Levine, Lawrence W. *Black Culture and Black Consciousness: Afro-American Folk Thought from Slavery to Freedom.* New York, 1977.

———. *The Opening of the American Mind: Canons, Culture, and History.* Boston, 1996.

Lewis, David Levering. *W. E. B. Du Bois: Biography of a Race, 1868–1919.* New York, 1993.

Litwack, Leon F. *Trouble in Mind: Black Southerners in the Age of Jim Crow.* New York, 1998.

Locke, Alain L., ed. *The New Negro: An Interpretation.* 1925. Reprint, New York, 1968. Page references in the text are from the reprint edition.

Mays, Benjamin E. *Born to Rebel: An Autobiography.* New York, 1971.

Meier, August. *Negro Thought in America, 1880–1915.* Ann Arbor, Mich., 1963.

Morrison, Toni, ed. *Race-ing, Justice, En-gendering Power: Essays on Anita Hill, Clarence Thomas, and the Construction of Social Reality.* New York, 1992.

Moton, Robert Russa. *Finding a Way Out: An Autobiography.* New York, 1969.

Moses, Wilson J. *The Golden Age of Black Nationalism, 1820–1925.* New York, 1988.

Mullin, Michael. *Africa in America: Slave Acculturation and Resistance in the American South and the British Caribbean, 1736–1831.* Urbana, Ill., 1992.

Osofsky, Gilbert, ed. *Puttin' On Ole Massa: The Slave Narratives of Henry Bibb, William Wells Brown, and Solomon Northup.* New York, 1969.

Ottley, Roi, and William J. Weatherby, eds. *The Negro in New York: An Informal Social History, 1626–1940.* New York, 1967.

Patterson, Tiffany R. L. "Tubman, Harriet." In *The Reader's Companion to American History,* edited by Eric Foner and John A. Garraty, 1088–1089. Boston, 1991.

Pearson, Hugh. *The Shadow of the Panther: Huey Newton and the Price of Black Power in America.* Reading, Mass., 1994.

Perry, Bruce. *Malcolm X: The Life of a Man Who Changed Black America.* Tarrytown, N.Y., 1991.

Porter, James A. *Modern Negro Art.* New York, 1969.

Quarles, Benjamin. *Black Abolitionists.* New York, 1969.

Raboteau, Albert J. *Slave Religion: The "Invisible Institution" in the Antebellum South.* New York, 1978.

Rainwater, Lee, and William L. Yancy. *The Moynihan Report and the Politics of Controversy.* Cambridge, Mass., 1967.

Rampersad, Arnold. *The Life of Langston Hughes.* 2 vols. New York, 1986–1988.

Smith, Theophus H. *Conjuring Culture: Biblical Formations of Black America.* New York, 1993.

Southern, David W. *Gunnar Myrdal and Black-White Relations: The Use and Abuse of* An American Dilemma, *1944–1969.* Baton Rouge, La., 1987.

Truth, Sojourner. *The Narrative of Sojourner Truth.* 1878. Reprint, edited by Olive Gilbert. New York, 1968. Page references in the text are from the reprint edition.

Van Deburg, William L. *New Day in Babylon: The Black Power Movement and American Culture, 1965–1975.* Chicago, 1992.

Washington, Booker T. *Up from Slavery.* 1900. Reprint, edited by William L. Andrew. New York, 1995.

Wells, Ida B. *The Autobiography of Ida. B. Wells.* Edited by Alfreda M. Duster. Chicago, 1970.

White, Jack E. "The Beauty of Black Art." *Time* 144, no.15 (October 10, 1994): 66–73.

Wright, Richard. *Black Boy.* New York, 1945.

——. *Native Son.* New York, 1940.

——. *Twelve Million Black Voices.* 1941. Reprint, New York, 1969. Page references in the text are from the reprint edition.

——. *White Man, Listen!* 1957. Reprint, Westport, Conn., 1978.

Yee, Shirley J. *Black Women Abolitionists: A Study in Activism, 1828–1860.* Knoxville, Tenn., 1992.

Zangrando, Robert L. *The NAACP Crusade Against Lynching, 1909–1950.* Philadelphia, 1980.

AMERICAN EXPATRIATE ARTISTS ABROAD

Betsy Fahlman

Expatriation has long been a distinctive aspect of American cultural thought and for many American leading artists and writers represented a complex dynamic of the aesthetic and the psychological. Deeply rooted in America's national history, the concept is a complex one for a country whose first artists were not native-born; and the term addresses the uneasy negotiation between personal and national identity. An artist born in America would always be an American artist by fact of birth, if not by inclination. A counterpoint is provided by Edward Everett Hale in his story *The Man without a Country,* first published in 1863, which addresses the related issues of patriotism and exile.

The realm of arts and letters is rich in examples which highlight the complexity of what is and is not American art. For instance, that icon of American identity, *Washington Crossing the Delaware* (1851), was painted in Düsseldorf by Emanual Leutze, an artist who had been born in Germany but was brought to the United States as a child by his parents. He returned to the country of his birth in 1841, coming back to the United States in 1859, where he remained until his death. Just how well he assimilated American cultural values is evidenced by his mural, *Westward the Course of Empire Takes Its Way* (1862), which was prominently installed in the rotunda of the United States Capitol and which celebrated the agenda of manifest destiny. Throughout the nineteenth century, as political and economic security was consolidated, national identity was increasingly defined as a central issue, and writers and artists sought to locate its discussion within themes inspired by American places and events. The poet William Cullen Bryant urged artists to preserve "that wilder image" of an Edenic America when they traveled abroad. The works of America's first national group of landscape painters, collectively known as the Hudson River school, was led by Thomas Cole. Born in England, Cole did not come to America until he was seventeen, and subsequently returned to Europe for two extended stays.

For a colony, a cultural relationship with a mother country is a given. While America progressed toward independent nationhood, many residents traveled extensively abroad. But a citizen cannot properly become an expatriate from a place that is not yet a country, and therefore expatriatism could not become a concrete issue until independence, though it had been something with which America's early artists had already grappled. The career of John Singleton Copley is neatly split between his work as Boston's leading portraitist of the pre-revolutionary period and his great success in Britain after his departure in 1774. Some, like Benjamin West, who had preceded Copley to London well before the beginning of the Revolution, urged their fellow painters to come to Europe and generously befriended several generations of American art students. Although West benefited from royal patronage, eventually becoming president of the Royal Academy, he remained fascinated by themes drawn from American history. He encouraged John Trumbull to undertake picturing the significant events of the revolution, a subject whose political volatility he could not prudently depict. West's most significant works were executed abroad, but Copley had a decidedly more bifurcated career, enjoying success on both sides of the Atlantic, and he is claimed dually as "American" and "British" school in the museums where his work is displayed.

In fact, some American artists might have done better had they remained abroad, for a lifetime of financial insecurity was often the unhappy fate of those who returned. John Vanderlyn, the first American to enter the École des Beaux-Arts (1796) and the first American to show at the Salon (1804), did not return to the United States until 1815 when he was forty, and his late mural *Landing of Columbus* (1839–1846), which was commissioned for the Capitol, was painted in Paris. Like so many of his fellow artists, he was embittered by the lack of support the arts received in the United States. Whatever their personal feelings, nationhood gave artists and writers more clearly defined choices as to whether to remain at home, to travel abroad, or to leave the country for good. Expatriation could now be a conscious decision.

HISTORIOGRAPHY

The historiography of American expatriate artists is relatively recent and reflects the discipline of American art history as a whole, which developed as a serious field of study only after World War II. The war had made scholarly access to Europe more difficult, a circumstance which served to encourage those graduate students who remained at home to consider the art of their own country as a viable subject for serious research. As the field matured, what was "American about American art" remained a persistent, if ultimately unanswerable, question. Those artists who were perceived as both taking their themes directly from American life and painting them in a straightforward mode without embellishment were regarded as the chief carriers of "American" cultural values, a view which not surprisingly resulted in some decidedly skewed analyses. Those touchstones of pragmatic American realism, notably Thomas Eakins, who received superb training under the French academic artist Jean-Léon Gérôme, and Winslow Homer, who too had spent almost a year in Paris, achieved "master" status within the national canon. Within this construction of culture, the expatriates were largely ignored, as was a good deal else about nineteenth-century art, for stereotypical views of Americanness were not easily reconciled with the worldly vantage of those who chose to live abroad.

In 1976 Michael Quick organized an exhibition entitled "American Expatriate Painters of the Late Nineteenth Century" for the Dayton (Ohio) Art Institute. Bringing together fifty-seven works by thirty-nine artists, it was the first to focus attention on a significant art historical episode. Of those artists presented, only Mary Cassatt, John Singer Sargent, James Abbott McNeill Whistler, Edwin Austin Abbey, Theodore Robinson, and Elihu Vedder had previously been the subject of any serious scholarship. A biography on Sargent had been published in 1955, but most other studies of his work dated from after 1970. Since then, many of the artists included have been the subject of monographs and broader thematic considerations. In his catalogue, Quick gave a definition of what he felt comprised an expatriate artist: "One who spent at least ten years of his best mature period painting abroad." Figures like Frank Duveneck and Edwin Howland Blashfield "who did some of their best work in Europe, but who are primarily identified with an influential teaching role in this country" were not included, nor were artists painting in the Orient or other places outside of Europe.

Clearly a central problem is determining the fundamental nature of the expatriate. How one now positions these artists is a complex differential of their professional maturity at the time they went abroad, how much time was actually spent away from America, their motives for doing so, whether they remained in one place for any length of time, how much they were affected by their newly adopted culture, and, finally, how they regarded themselves. In their commitment to live abroad, artists and writers were governed by multiple impulses. Neither tourists nor exiles, they chose extended residence in major European cultural capitals, an experience which sometimes had the ironic effect of intensifying a sensibility of national identity and roots.

General art historical interest in the late nineteenth century intensified after the mid-1970s and was part of a more general rehabilitation of Victorian art, long disdained by modernists. In painting especially, enthusiasm continues, and by the turn of the twenty-first century there was a surprising resurgence of interest in the academic styles once popular among the expatriates. Still others have been repositioned within an ongoing scholarly dialogue of modernity. Major traveling museum exhibitions organized by institutions both in the United States and abroad throughout the 1990s highlighted the work of Henry Ossawa Tanner (Philadelphia Museum of Art, 1991), Whistler (Tate Gallery, 1995), Cassatt (Art Institute of Chicago, 1998), and Sargent (Tate Gallery, 1998), and contextualized their work within an international art community. Broader studies dealing with Salon, academic training, and the vast international exhibitions held in Paris featuring large installations of American artists have also appeared.

NEOCLASSICAL SCULPTORS IN ITALY

The first identifiable community of American expatriate artists of any size was established in Italy during the middle years of the nineteenth century. United by language, and sometimes sharing patrons, both British and Americans were collectively known as the "inglesi." The Americans established a lively subculture, interacting with Italians largely as servants, studio assistants, or merchants in their roles as providing the support mechanisms for the life the Americans constructed abroad. The sculpture community was an international one, and Italy offered the expatriate sculptor many advantages, including a richly suggestive historic atmosphere of art which spanned the ancient world to Michelangelo, technically skilled studio assistants, and famed marble quarries. Even if an artist did not expatriate more or less permanently, it was still necessary to come to Italy in order to execute the large public commissions they began to receive in America. Themes inspired by literature, history, and religion were typical of the work they executed, and portrait busts also provided a reliable source of income.

If in 1825 Horatio Greenough was the first American-born sculptor to visit Italy, the first to achieve international acclaim was Hiram Powers, famous for his *Greek Slave* (1843). Powers had arrived in 1837, having already been successful as a portraitist in America, and settled into a Florentine villa that would remain his base for the rest of his career. Still others took up residence in Rome, including Thomas Crawford, who came in 1835, and worked there until his tragic early death. William Wetmore Story, the well-educated and cultured son of an associate justice of the United States Supreme Court, gave up a successful law career to go to Rome in 1856. Randolph Rogers arrived in 1848 and achieved fame with *Nydia, the Blind Girl of Pompeii* (1853), inspired by Edward Bulwer Lytton's widely read *The Last Days of Pompeii* (1834).

Women formed a significant part of this group and were collectively known by what Henry James in 1903 dismissively termed the White Marmorean Flock. Pursuing successful careers abroad, most chose not to marry, often maintaining long-term affective same-sex relationships with other women. Harriet Hosmer came to Rome in 1852, and her circle of friends included actress Charlotte Cushman and poets Robert and Elizabeth Barrett Browning. She remained active as a sculptor until the mid-1870s, returning to the United States in 1900. The work of Edmonia Lewis, the first American sculptor of color to achieve international recognition, is an intriguing mix of American Indian and antislavery themes, inspired in part by her racial heritage (her mother was Native American, her father African American). The poetry of Henry Wadsworth Longfellow was also an important source of inspiration for her sculpture.

AMERICANS IN FRANCE AND ENGLAND: THE LATE NINETEENTH CENTURY

The beginning of what could be regarded as the golden age of American expatriation began during the post–Civil War years. While Italy remained popular with many artists—Venice especially provided an exotic locale for visitors well into the twentieth century—France became the destination of choice for artists desiring both modernity and extended residence abroad. A painter like Elihu Vedder, who maintained lengthy periods of residence in Rome, was the exception rather than the rule. Paris was the most alluring art capital, and progressive artists abandoned the atmosphere of the Italian past for the cosmopolitan and forward-thinking environment of Paris.

As advances in transportation made transatlantic travel faster, safer, and more affordable. Europe became accessible to both students and collectors, and it was often cheaper to live abroad than in the United States. Also, buoyed by a new cultural confidence, American artists could finally compete within an international community as sophisticated equals. Americans participated in the apparatus of a formidable art establishment inconceivable back in the United States, one which linked training, exhibition, and patronage in a highly cosmopolitan context.

Expatriation was symptomatic of a larger societal shift and was inextricably linked with a general enthusiasm for Europe. American collectors, including the nouveau riche, were purchasing European art. Large American public museums began to form substantial collections and gave official recognition to the European high culture that was fundamental to the expatriate experience. The expansion of the art market was concurrent with a vigorous era of public philanthropy in the arts which also celebrated this prized European taste.

Despite their comfort within foreign culture, expatriates would always remain in an uneasy limbo of identity for however long they remained abroad; in whatever country they settled Americans would always be regarded as outsiders, and the cultural politics of the day mandated that they could never fully shed their fundamental identity as Americans and be accepted as true Europeans. As the scholar Marc Simpson has astutely observed: "In an age fascinated by the possibility of classification by type, size, shape—the taxonomy of the world—the issue of national identity was of great moment in the 1880s art press. . . . But nationalistic classification also encouraged a hybrid of patriotism and xenophobia to enter the art arena" ("Reconstructing the Golden Age," pp. 40–41).

While American artists might have felt disillusioned with America, they did cultivate extensive contact with other Americans and often sought to form official groups. For instance, an American Art Association and an American Art Students Club were formed in Paris, whereas progressive organizations in America emphasized the French connections of their artist members. After leaving New York, James Gordon Bennett began publishing the English-language *Paris Herald* in 1887, and it was widely read by the international set. Even if they were not overtly patriotic, few were willing to give up their American citizenship. And because many expatriates were Protestant, they could not be fully assimilated into Catholic society in France and Italy. Some of their nationalist networking was economically prudent, for those without the cushion of an independent income continued to receive considerable support from patrons in the United States, who purchased productions by Americans which most resembled European works.

In America, two displays mounted in the late nineteenth century heralded a new consciousness of cultural maturity. The Centennial Exposition held in Philadelphia in 1876 provided the catalyst for an intensive retrospection of both American origins and progress, spurring the colonial revival. But it was the World's Columbian Exposition of 1893 in Chicago that exemplified an international perspective for both artists and audiences. Seen as the highly visible hallmark of the American Renaissance, the embrace of European aesthetic values was no provincial capitulation to a more powerful culture, but rather a bold assertion of the ability of American artists to compete as equals in strength and quality within an international art arena.

For the second wave of expatriates, expanded opportunities for art training initially lured them abroad. Although art study was available in the United States, notably at the National Academy of Design, the Pennsylvania Academy of the Fine Arts, and the Yale School of the Fine Arts, foreign study remained necessary for ambitious American artists if they were to meet the new international thematic and aesthetic standards that provided the solid foundation for a successful career at home and abroad. An earlier generation went to Germany to study under artists in Munich and Düsseldorf, where they absorbed the bravura brushwork, expressive realism, and dark tonalities favored by mas-

ters there. But a large resident expatriate colony was never formed in that country.

Paris was recognized as the world's cosmopolitan art center, and its aesthetic authority set an international art paradigm. France was not just leading Americans, but its cultural hegemony was the standard for all of Europe. A substantial number of expatriates were well off and like their wealthy colleagues in other fields, they traveled Europe extensively. But regardless of class, artistic reasons were the primary impetus for going abroad. Many who eventually became expatriates did so less out of conscious intention than as the result of a gradual process. Most had left America intending to return after they had completed their studies, but found it difficult in the end to leave the subjects of their paintings, the supportive art environment, the sense of community, the well-established systems of training, and the exhibitions that gave them such affirmation and prestige.

The careers of several of America's leading expatriate artists highlight the major issues they had to negotiate. A description of John Singer Sargent demonstrates how he exemplifies this era of hybrids: "He was an American born in Italy, who dressed like a German, spoke like an Englishman, and painted like a Spaniard" (Kenin, *Return to Albion,* p. 116). Born in Florence to American parents from Philadelphia, for most of his life he lived in France and England, while maintaining extensive contact with American patrons, especially Bostonians. But he did not make his first trip to America until 1876 when he was twenty, and it would be another decade before he returned again. He had traveled extensively throughout Europe before beginning formal art studies in the atelier of Carolus-Duran in Paris in 1874, entering the École des Beaux-Arts that same year. Three years later, he made his Salon debut, where he continued to make successful showings, but the aftermath of the scandal caused by his exhibition of *Madame X* (1884) at the 1884 Salon led him to establish London as his permanent home in 1886. From this base, he received considerable patronage not only from the English aristocracy but also from wealthy Americans either traveling or expatriated like himself. For Americans with newly acquired fortunes, a connection to the British elite class permitted them to legitimize their recently achieved social position. It would be hard to overestimate the social cachet of a title, and such connections were further strengthened when several prominent American heiresses married high-profile Britishers of impeccable lineage. For both groups, the portrait painted by Sargent became an icon of their status within the hierarchy of Anglo-American society.

One of the leading expatriate painters was a wealthy American aristocrat herself. Mary Cassatt, whose family's fortune came from the Pennsylvania Railroad, went abroad in 1872. Joined by her family in 1877, except for two short visits (the first more than twenty years after she first left), she never returned to America, though her mural was prominently featured at the Columbian Exposition. In an essay entitled "How Cassatt became an American Artist," Kevin Sharp explored the problematics of national identity. Despite her having come to artistic maturity in Europe and her participation in official impressionist exhibitions as early as 1879, her prints were excluded from an 1891 exhibition held at Durand-Ruel's gallery open only to artists born in France (a limitation that affected her friend Camille Pissarro as well). Yet not until 1895 would she have a solo show in the United States. Cassatt's taste exerted a broad cultural influence, as seen in her friendships with several well-born and well-married wealthy women collectors, including Louisine Waldron Havemeyer, Bertha Honoré Palmer, and Sarah Choate Sears. Based on her advice, with their husbands they formed substantial art collections, which when they entered public collections by gift or bequest, deepened public appreciation of French culture in America.

While bound by more social restrictions than their male counterparts, women found that residence abroad still offered many apparent freedoms not available to them at home. But although artist life in Paris was intellectually liberating, women had to comply with a more rigid code of public and private behavior within a carefully ordered structure of social discourse. Female expatriates negotiated their careers within a matrix of gendered expectations, and women could never be as free as their male counterparts, needing to remain vigilant regarding expected proprieties. Sexual scandal—which was the only kind that really mattered—was far more damaging to female transgressors in a sensitized atmosphere where rumors could be as destructive to a reputation as the truth. An independent income provided some protection, but unmarried women were even more socially vulnerable than their married counterparts. The novelist Edith Wharton, whose own lineage was eminent, was keenly attuned to such nuances in her writings. Like James, Wharton often considered the position of Americans in relation to European culture.

Several careers provide instructive examples. Both Cecilia Beaux and Elizabeth Nourse studied in Paris in the 1880s and fully mastered figure painting—Beaux specialized in portraits, Nourse in scenes of peasant life—but pursued their careers from an American base. Several others became expatriates, establishing close connections to French painters. Lucy Lee-Robbins, a favored protégée of her teacher Carolus-Duran, with whom Sargent also studied, remained in France. Despite her independent means, the notorious reputation of her instructor meant she was subject to considerable innuendo. Though women were permitted to study from the female nude, they could not attempt such a subject for large exhibition pictures. Elizabeth Gardner (later Bouguereau) actually married her teacher Adolphe-William Bouguereau in 1896 but only after an engagement of twenty years (his mother disapproved of her); she was fifty-nine, he seventy-one years old when they finally wed. Anna Elizabeth Klumpke, part of the Parisian expatriate community for over forty years, became the companion of Rosa Bonheur in 1898, inheriting the French painter's estate at her death the following year.

Race is another intriguing facet of expatriation. The family of Henry Ossawa Tanner, the son of a minister, moved to Philadelphia from Pittsburgh in 1868. He began study at the Pennsylvania Academy of the Fine Arts under Thomas Eakins in 1879, continuing there sporadically until 1885, making his exhibition there in 1880, and at the National Academy of Design in 1885. Despite his evident talent, because he was African American his career developed more slowly, and not until 1891 was he finally able to go to Europe. After study at the Académie Julian, he made his Salon debut in 1894. His marriage to a white American woman in 1899 meant that if he had seriously thought about returning, his new status as part of a rare biracial couple would make it advisable for him to remain abroad. His early canvases presented African American genre scenes, but he achieved international fame as a painter of ambitious biblical subjects, which appealed to a much broader audience. The historian Dewey Mosby noted the irony of a career that "was heralded both in his native America and in his adopted France, yet paradoxically, in the United States he tended to be seen as an expatriate absorbed into French culture, and in France, he was always 'citoyen américain'" (*Henry Ossawa Tanner*, p. 15).

Architects faced different challenges. The first American to be admitted to study architecture at the École was Richard Morris Hunt, who entered in 1846. But the portability of painting that broadened American artists' patronage and exhibition base was not possible in architecture, which was bound by site, though Americans would occasionally find employment or receive commissions abroad. For instance, Hunt worked in the Paris office of Hector Martin Lefuel, assisting him in the Louvre expansion before returning to the United States in 1855. Henry Hobson Richardson, who in 1860 was the second American to enter the École in architecture, at the end of his career designed "Lululand" for the British painter Hubert von Herkomer, who had executed portraits of several Americans. In contrast to painters, architects had little choice but to return to America after their training, and there was not a significant expatriate architectural community. But an extensive familiarity with European buildings was essential for a revivalist architect, and prizes were established in American architectural schools to support student travel to Europe during the summer. Established in 1894, the American Academy in Rome provided its architect fellows with a three-year residency, and this institution played a leading role in maintaining the vitality of the Beaux-Arts style well into the twentieth century.

Historical ties of language and literary culture made England another attractive place for American expatriates to reside. One of the most visible was James Abbott McNeill Whistler. Born in Lowell, Massachusetts, he moved with his family to Russia where his father was employed as a civil engineer, but at his father's death, his mother brought the family back to the United States in 1849. After flunking out of the United States Military Academy at West Point, Whistler left for France in 1855, never to return to America, moving to London in 1859. Although he would travel extensively on the continent, England would remain thereafter his most consistent base. Like Sargent, he bridged two art communities, showing both at the Royal Academy in London and at the Salon in Paris. Although Whistler never returned to the country of his birth which he had left in his twenties, like many of his own countrymen, he long thought of America as "home," though this was for him more a personal rather than an artistic sensibility.

Anglo-American enthusiasm was at its peak during the 1880s and 1890s. Edwin Austin Abbey, who settled in England in 1878, was the social center of a community of expatriate artists centered on the charming Worcestershire village of Broadway in the late 1880s. Deeply assimilated into the life of the country he had adopted, he helped to foster the popularity for a "Cotswolds picturesque," and he and his compatriots Frank Davis Millet, Sargent, and others, led a highly constructed existence, one that was dually self-conscious about literature and history, as they appropriated English culture as their own. These artists remained strongly identified with England, but traveled widely on the continent, exhibiting both in England and America, and remaining dependent on American patronage. George Henry Boughton, who had actually been born in England, but was raised in the United States, also specialized in themes inspired by the British Isles. Already successful, he settled in London in 1862 after two years of study in Paris.

Those who chose not to become expatriates participated in an extensive network of summer art colonies that formed near the subjects they favored. Throughout the 1880s and 1890s, when paintings of peasants were internationally popular, American artists sought locales relatively easy of access from the cities where most of them lived. The villages they chose were seemingly untouched by modern life and steeped in history, and the themes they inspired contrasted sharply with the urbanization and industrialization typical of the contemporary city life they knew. The scenes of rural existence that so fascinated them could not be found at home, and the American farmer laboring in his field found no comparability with the European peasant.

In France, Brittany and Normandy were popular with painters, and by the 1890s, impressionism, whose subject matter could now be broadened beyond what was available only in Europe, had become widely accepted. Giverny, since 1883 the home to the impressionist Claude Monet, served as the base for a substantial seasonal American colony. Prominent members of this community included Theodore Robinson, who spent ten summers there, and Lilla Cabot Perry, who left fascinating reminiscences of her twenty-year friendship with Monet.

Some countries were significant tourist destinations for artists but did not become the site of either seasonal or permanent resident colonies. Hispanism, an international enthusiasm for anything Spanish, was widespread, but while Spain attracted many visitors, especially those eager to view the work of the baroque realist Diego Velázquez, artists did not linger. Those desiring to see paintings by Frans Hals traveled to Holland, whose small rural towns bustled with art visitors during the warmer months. Painters like George Hitchcock produced nostalgic, anti-industrial views comparable to the rural French subjects popular at the Salon.

Although painters were the most visible expatriates in the visual arts during this period, artists in graphic media shared many common concerns, and printmaking was another medium actively pursued by American artists abroad. Its portability was linked with the fashion for picturesque travel, and the etching revival flourished during the last two decades of the nineteenth century. The movement was inspired by Whistler's handsome Venetian etchings, produced following his highly publicized trial with the British critic John Ruskin and subsequent bankruptcy. A whole generation of graphic artists were strongly influenced by Whistler, who had begun his career as an etcher, including Joseph Pennell, who was a friend of the artist. Pennell moved to London in 1884, and remained in Europe until 1917, making attractive prints of handsome old European buildings, but also modern skyscrapers and technological achievements and industry, publishing his images of "the wonders of work" in a series of books.

Photography provided another connection for American expatriates. Born in Boston, Alvin Langdon Coburn was a member both of Alfred Stieglitz's Photo-Secession in New York, as well as its British counterpart, the Linked Ring, in which he was one of the few American members. Through his gallery, 291, his publication *Camera Work*, and the formation of his own personal collection, Stieglitz participated in an international network of pictorialist photographers, and of all the Americans, Coburn had the strongest connections to England. The artist made his first visit in 1899 when he went to London to make photographs of leading British artists and writers, images subsequently published in his books, *Men of Mark* (1913) and *More Men of Mark* (1922). One of his portrait subjects was the novelist Henry James, and Coburn produced photogravure frontispieces that were published in each of the twenty-four volumes of *The Novels of Henry James* (1909). In 1909, the photographer established permanent residence in London, and after 1912 never returned to America again, though he did not become a British citizen until 1932. His platinum prints of Venice and England have an evocative romanticism comparable to Whistler's etchings. In 1916, he made a series of Vortographs as well as abstract photographs of the poet Ezra Pound.

THE MODERNIST EXPATRIATE: THE TWENTIETH CENTURY

Although Parisian art study remained an attractive option for American artists, as modernist modes replaced academic ones in the twentieth century, the character of the American expatriate was once again transformed. By this time there were more viable options for art training available in the United States, but with the rise of the avant-garde, Paris was now the venue for seeing the newest art forms that were scarcely exhibited in America before the Armory Show, held in New York in 1913. A dramatic cultural and social shift radically changed the conservative values of the art establishment which supported the expatriates throughout the 1880s and 1890s, and the first two decades of the twentieth century witnessed a steady stream of American artists encountering cubism, fauvism, and their variants in Paris, Berlin, and Munich. Most of these early moderns returned home (with some irony, many immigrants themselves). Those who remained included Morgan Russell, who lived abroad between 1906 and 1946, and who with his fellow countryman Stanton Macdonald-Wright had invented the colorful style synchromism in the mid-teens. The sculptor John Storrs also spent much of his career in France.

Expatriates became even more notable during the 1920s. Paris remained the center of an unparalleled cultural and creative concentration of writers and artists, and their lively public life flourished in Left Bank cafés. The city embodied a rich cultural geography, serving as the nexus of "creative freedom, intellectual stimulation, and personal liberty." Immersed in a culture perceived to be less puritan than the one they had fled, with a favorable exchange rate making possible an intellectually and economically comfortable life, they relished residence in a city decidedly more supportive of the arts and less materialistic than any they had encountered. In his memoir *Days of the Phoenix: The Nineteen-Twenties I Remember* (1957), the cultural historian Van Wyck Brooks observed that the nature of the term "expatriate" assumed new meaning in the 1920s: "No European could understand this constant American talk of roots, or why it was that expatriates discussed expatriation—a word that scarcely existed in any other country" (pp. 2–3).

The historian Wanda Corn has identified a new kind of cultural traveler, the "*transatlantique*," a type whose presence enriches discussions of Americans abroad. Their characteristics were different from those of the expatriates "who abandoned their home culture to live in another, never intending to return to their native land. Expats maintained permanent homes abroad and more or less assimilated to their adopted countries. They often expressed deep alienation from their country of birth. *Transatlantiques,* in contrast, were migrant artists, moving back and forth across the Atlantic, carrying the ideas and values of one culture into the heart of another. Even when they stayed abroad for a number of years, they continued to fashion themselves as non-nationals; they did not renounce their birthplace and assumed that they might someday go home again" (*The Great American Thing*, pp. 91–92).

Though characterized by the novelist Ernest Hemingway as "the lost generation" in *The Sun Also Rises* (1926), expatriates were truly neither personally nor aesthetically lost. Foreign residence offered conspicuous pleasures and freedoms, but a sense of alienation from cultural norms and an implicit criticism of America is characteristic of the twentieth-century expatriate, who both rejected home and found acceptance if not assimilation into a new place. Those who had felt stifled in America were liberated by their new circumstances, the change of place constituting as much a mental relocation from a dissonant present as was their physical removal from the country of their birth.

Two expatriate salons enlivened the Parisian artistic and literary world of the 1910s and 1920s, though their circles did not intersect. The most famous was that presided over by Gertrude Stein, who arrived in Paris in 1903, eventually taking up residence with Alice B. Toklas in an art-filled apartment at 27 rue de Fleurus in the city's Latin Quarter. Making only one return trip to the United States in 1934, their gatherings served as a touchstone for a whole generation of American artists and writers who regularly sought her out (Ernest Hemingway was a regular, if ultimately ungrateful, visitor). With her brothers Leo and Michael, and the latter's wife Sarah, they formed substantial collections of the work of Paul Cézanne, Pablo Picasso, and Henri Matisse. Together they were the most notable patrons of modern art during their period, and Stein's *Autobiography of Alice B. Toklas* (1933) gives an engaging account of expatriate life.

The number of remarkable and independent women in Paris noticeably increased during the 1920s, and the city became the base for a substantial lesbian community. Throughout the next several decades, the salon at 20 rue Jacob established by the heiresses Romaine Brooks and Natalie Clifford Barney, her companion of more than fifty years, provided a stimulating focus for the many gay women who had moved to Paris. Notable were Janet Flanner, who settled in Paris in 1922 and between 1925 and 1975 wrote a fortnightly "Letter from Paris" for the *New Yorker* under the name "Genêt," and Djuna Barnes, who also arrived in Paris in the 1920s. Painted portraits by Brooks and photographs by Berenice Abbott, who lived in Paris between 1921 and 1929, record many of its luminaries and comprise a expatriate visual history of this community.

Between the world wars, many expatriates were involved with private presses and little magazines, which published modernist works not favored by mainstream houses, and a significant number of these figures were women, including Margaret Anderson and Jane Heap, the leading forces behind the *Little Review*. One of Abbott's photographs records the features of Sylvia Beach, who in 1919 established Shakespeare and Company. Famed for the publication of James Joyce's *Ulysses* in 1922, the shop sold and lent English and American books, becoming a major focus of literary activity for the expatriate community.

The wealthy American Gerald Murphy and his wife Sara arrived in Paris in 1921. Taking his first art lessons from the Russian painter Natalia Goncharova, his circle of friends soon numbered many leading artistic figures, including Fernand Léger, Igor Stravinsky, Pablo Picasso, John Dos Passos, Archibald MacLeish, and Cole Porter. By 1924, his family was installed in the south of France at Antibes at a house he called the "Villa America." The Murphys remained on the Mediterranean until 1929 when family and business concerns forced Gerald's return to the United States. He never painted again. Although Murphy produced fewer than fifteen finished works, his personal style and artistic themes became emblematic of 1920s expatriate life, and serve as analogues to musical works such as George Gershwin's *An American in Paris* (1928).

Some Americans produced some of their most significant work abroad, though they were not exactly expatriates. Alexander Calder, whose father and grandfather were noted Philadelphia sculptors, began the first of a series of extended Paris sojourns in 1926. It was there he devised the first pieces of his now-famous *Circus* (1926–1931), a kinetic work which introduced him to the French avant-garde. He became increasingly nonobjective, developing his mobiles and large-scale abstract stabiles throughout the 1930s. Dividing his time between the United States and France, he would not actually purchase property there until 1953. Man Ray, also born in Philadelphia, was a more typical expatriate. He arrived in Paris in 1921 and lived abroad for much of his career. His paintings, photographs, films, and enigmatic sculptural compositions link the early American moderns, the dada, and surrealist movements. He returned to the United States in 1940 with the German occupation of Paris. Settling in Los Angeles, he did not return to Paris until 1951.

As they had during the nineteenth century, African Americans came to escape America's overt racism and discrimination in a more artistically and socially tolerant country. Among the most famous was jazz singer Josephine Baker, the subject of a series of wire sculptures by Calder. She was tremendously popular in Paris and served as the lively center of a vibrantly sexy jazz culture. Getting her start in vaudeville, she arrived in Paris from New York in 1925 with La Revue Nègre. With her considerable theatrical and comic skills, Baker was a sensation in an era of hot jazz and sexual freedom, and performing in a costume composed mostly of bananas and a G-string, her energetic dancing thrilled her audiences. She became a French citizen in 1937.

DENOUEMENT

With the stock market crash of 1929 and resultant international economic depression, the funds which had sustained many Americans abroad dramatically dwindled, forcing them to either reconsider a lifestyle under reduced circumstances or return home. Although Americans continued to flock to Europe, the direction of travel changed noticeably, with the numbers of Europeans coming to the United States throughout the 1930s and 1940s increasing substantially. Political instability and the concurrent rise of Nazism and fascism further destabilized what had sustained the expatriate community for the past century, and many foreign artists fled to New York. America's intellectual relationship to Europe continued to transform itself following World War II in an atmosphere of social conservatism and cold war ideological polarization. Cross-cultural dialogue continued between France and the United States, as America achieved international cultural recognition, and with the rise of abstract expressionism New York replaced Paris as the new center of the art world.

See also **Franco-American Cultural Encounters and Exchanges; Countercultural Visions; Vietnam as a Cultural Crisis** (*in this volume*); *and other articles in this section.*

BIBLIOGRAPHY

Barter, Judith A., with essays by Erica E. Hirschler, George T. M. Shackelford, Kevin Sharp, Harriet K. Stratis, and Andrew J. Walker. *Mary Cassatt: Modern Woman.* Chicago, 1998.

Blaugrund, Annette. *Paris 1889: American Artists at the Universal Exposition.* Philadelphia, 1989.

Boone, M. Elizabeth. *España: American Artists and the Spanish Experience.* New York, 1999.

Bruccoli, Mathew J., and Robert W. Trogdon, eds. *American Expatriate Writers.* Vol. 15 of *Dictionary of Literary Biography Documentary Series: An Illustrated Chronicle.* Detroit, Mich., 1982.

Corn, Wanda M. *The Great American Thing: Modern Art and National Identity, 1915–1935.* Berkeley, Calif., 1999.

Dorment, Richard, and Margaret F. MacDonald. *James McNeill Whistler.* London, 1995.

Fink, Lois Marie. *American Art at the Nineteenth-Century Paris Salons.* Washington, D.C., and New York, 1990.

Fischer, Diane P. *Paris 1900: The "American School" at the Universal Exposition.* New Brunswick, N.J., 1999.

Fitch, Noel Riley. *Sylvia Beach and the Lost Generation: A History of Literary Paris in the Twenties and Thirties.* New York, 1983.

Fortune, Brandon Brame. "'Not Above Reproach': The Career of Lucy Lee-Robbins." *American Art* 12, no. 1 (spring 1998): 40–65.

Gerdts, William H. *Monet's Giverny: An Impressionist Colony.* New York, 1993.

Hansen, Arlen J. *Expatriate Paris: A Cultural and Literary Guide to Paris of the 1920s.* New York, 1990.

Kenin, Richard. *Return to Albion: Americans in England, 1760–1940.* Washington, D.C., 1979.

Kilmurray, Elaine, and Richard Ormond, eds. *John Singer Sargent.* London, 1998.

Levenstein, Harvey. *Seductive Journey: American Tourists in France from Jefferson to the Jazz Age.* Chicago, 1998.

Lovell, Margaretta M. *A Visitable Past: Views of Venice by American Artists 1860–1915.* Chicago, 1989.

———. *Venice: The American View, 1860–1920.* San Francisco, 1984.

Mosby, Dewey F. *Henry Ossawa Tanner.* Philadelphia, 1991.

Parrott, Sara Foose. "Expatriates and Professionals: The Careers in Italy of Nineteenth-Century Women Writers and Artists." Ph.D. diss., George Washington University, 1988.

Pizer, Donald. *American Expatriate Writing and the Paris Moment: Modernism and Place.* Baton Rouge, La., 1996.

Plante, Michael David. "The 'Second Occupation': American Expatriate Painters and the Reception of American Art in Paris, 1946–1958." Ph.D. diss., Brown University, 1992.

Quick, Michael. *American Expatriate Painters of the Late Nineteenth Century.* Dayton, Ohio, 1976.

Sellin, David. *Americans in Brittany and Normandy, 1860–1910.* Phoenix, Ariz., 1982.

Simpson, Marc Alfred. "Reconstructing the Golden Age: American Artists in Broadway, Worcestershire, 1885–1889." Ph.D. diss., Yale University, 1993.

Simpson, Marc Alfred, Richard Ormond, and H. Barbara Weinberg. *Uncanny Spectacle: The Public Career of the Young John Singer Sargent.* New Haven, Conn., 1997.

Stebbins, Theodore. *The Lure of Italy: American Artists and the Italian Experience, 1760–1914.* Boston, 1992.

Stott, Annette. *Holland Mania: The Unknown Dutch Period in American Art and Culture.* Woodstock, N.Y., 1998.

Stovall, Tyler. *Paris Noir: African Americans in the City of Light.* Boston, 1996.

Turner, Elizabeth Hutton. *American Artists in Paris, 1919–1929.* Ann Arbor, Mich., 1988.

Turner, Elizabeth Hutton, Elizabeth Garrity Ellis, and Guy Davenport. *Americans in Paris, 1921–1931: Man Ray, Gerald Murphy, Stuart Davis, Alexander Calder.* Washington, D.C., 1996.

Vance, William L. *America's Rome.* 2 vols. New Haven, Conn., 1989.

Volk, Mary Crawford. *John Singer Sargent's El Jaleo.* Washington, D.C., 1992.

Weinberg, H. Barbara. *The Lure of Paris: Nineteenth-Century American Painters and Their French Teachers.* New York, 1991.

Weintraub, Stanley. *The London Yankees: Portraits of American Writers and Artists in England, 1894–1914.* New York, 1979.

Wiser, William. *The Great Good Place: American Expatriate Women in Paris.* New York, 1991.

ARTISTIC, INTELLECTUAL, AND POLITICAL REFUGEES

Claus-Dieter Krohn

Immigration as a key element of modern American society and culture constitutes one of the classical topics of social and historical sciences. However, the statistics on immigration do not distinguish between refugees—those who were expelled from their home countries for religious, political, ethnic, "race-related," or other reasons—and ordinary immigrants. Accordingly, scientific research has refrained from further differentiations. Thus, for instance, the immigration historian Maurice Davie, in defining emigration from the mother country, puts economic, political, and religious reasons on one and the same level.

Economic incentives and a need to escape religious persecution may have carried equal weight in the motivations of immigrants to America during the colonial era—for example, the Puritans, French Huguenots, Scots-Irish Catholics, and others. But during subsequent eras of immigration the social and mental profiles of refugees and immigrants diverged. The nineteenth and early twentieth centuries witnessed a period of mass immigration for economic reasons, with only small groups that might be considered refugees; these were mostly for political reasons—for example, the forty-eighters who fled Germany after the 1848 revolution there, or eastern European Jews, after the pogroms in tsarist Russia and in Romania.

Only after the end of World War I can refugees to the United States clearly be distinguished as such, although they continued to be neglected in the statistics. These newcomers stood out against the previous immigrants not only in the reasons that impelled them to leave their home countries but also because they belonged to the well-educated social and intellectual elites of their native societies. These refugees were the victims of totalitarian and authoritarian European regimes. In their intellectual luggage they brought with them cultural impulses that met with a positive response in the United States—a country that had withdrawn from world politics (after the failed peace efforts proposed by President Woodrow Wilson at the Paris Peace Conference in 1919), but was simultaneously undergoing an internal change from being a relatively business-oriented country to becoming a modern cultural nation. Despite the United States' political isolationism and the introduction of rigid national quotas by the immigration law in 1921, these "new" refugees were received with open arms; the immigration quota did not apply to either intellectuals or scientists, and numerous philanthropical foundations as well as newly founded relief organizations strove for their smooth integration into American life.

The arrival of the refugees coming from Germany after Adolf Hitler's rise to power and from Austria after the Anschluss of 1938 coincided fortuitously with the tenure of President Franklin D. Roosevelt and with the era of Roosevelt's massive new government program, the New Deal, which not only initiated unprecedented economic and social measures but also stimulated a scientific debate about the nature of modern society. The effects of this debate on the entire intellectual culture of the United States can hardly be overestimated, and the involvement of the newly arrived refugee intellectuals was crucial. Thereafter, when social scientists and historians directed their interests to special aspects of immigration, refugee research was treated as an independent topic that focused on the singular quality of refugee arrivals.

NATIONS OF ORIGIN OF INTELLECTUAL REFUGEES

The German refugee group included a number of Russian émigrés, who had fled their home country either after the October revolution of 1917 or the civil war of 1920–1921. The majority of these Russians first resettled in European centers such as Berlin, Vienna, or Paris. In the 1930s, those of Jewish family background or with democratic inclinations were once again uprooted and started their second exile in the United States after the Nazi takeover, together with the German-speaking émigrés. Refugees from Poland and Hungary may also be considered as part of these groups, but a clear classification is difficult because they often received their education in either Germany or Austria, where they then also lived before their emigration to the United States. Intellectual refugees from fascist Italy, with a few exceptions, only appeared after 1938, once Benito Mussolini had adopted the anti-Semitic laws from Germany.

The refugee intellectuals from Germany and Russia exerted the most lasting influence on American culture during the two decades from 1920 to 1940. After 1945 other groups of refugees of the modern antitotalitarian type came to the United States from countries ruled by communist regimes, and during the cold war they played an important role as experts in the ideological battle. Their cultural importance, however, was limited, except for a few individual cases.

Of the 1.5 to 2 million exiles from post-tsarist Russia, about 16,000 fled to the United States after 1920; the number of those who came via third countries after 1933 is unknown. Of the 500,000 German-speaking refugees from the Nazi state, on the other hand, about 130,000—that is, more than a third of all German refugees—found refuge in the United States. Of the total of the European refugees who came to the United States from 1920 to the end of the 1940s, the Germans constituted the vast majority with 53 percent, followed by the Poles (11.1 percent), the Italians (8.9 percent), the Russians (3.4 percent), the French (2.7 percent), and the Hungarians (2.2 percent), to mention only the most important national groups, with the German and the Russian groups comprising the highest percentage of cultural elites. The total cultural migration from Europe during this period is estimated at a total of 22,000 to 25,000 persons.

Compared with intellectual and artistic refugees, political refugee groups were of less importance among this exodus to the United States. The Russian refugee population included representatives of different political parties persecuted in their home countries—for example, the old tsarist nobility or the Mensheviks—who kept to themselves after immigrating and assimilated slowly to the American way of life. Of the German politicians, from prominent representatives of the Weimar Republic down to simple members of the different democratic parties, on the other hand, only a small number initially fled to the United States. Most of them immigrated to the United States with emergency visas after the Nazis invaded their European countries of exile in 1940. The fact that they joined forces in an attempt to establish a United States–based movement for a democratic Germany produced no effect. This was above all true after Roosevelt and Churchill had, in Casablanca in January 1943, agreed upon the demand for unconditional surrender of the Axis powers, a demand that left no room for postwar plannings by German political refugees. Similarly, the Mazzini Society, founded by Italian émigré antifascists in 1940, had no success with comparable plans for a democratic Italy in the future.

The majority of the American public ranged from skeptical to negative in its attitude toward the refugees, suspecting many of the Russians of being Bolsheviks (the United States had only recognized the Soviet Union diplomatically as late as 1933) and fearing that the Germans might become an unwelcome competitor on the labor market in view of the worldwide economic crisis. Anti-Semitic feeling also ran high in the United States. But intellectuals who were more farseeing were well aware of the cultural benefits to be gained from the academic excellence embodied by the Russian and German refugees. Against the background of the traditional American appreciation of the German educational system (many universities had been founded on the German model and, even during the first decades of the twentieth century, the leading American representatives of most disciplines had studied in Germany) American intellectuals were generally eager to bring such intellectual potential into the United States, even while other countries were refusing to offer these refugees asylum.

ORGANIZING AID FOR EXILES

As early as 1921, the Russian Student Fund had been founded by Stephen Duggan, the director of the Institute of International Education at New York. With $600,000, the fund had enabled more than five hundred young Russians to complete their academic education in the United States. In 1933, Duggan founded the Emergency Committee in Aid of Displaced Foreign Scholars, which, together with the Rockefeller Foundation, made possible the placing of almost six hundred scientists from Germany and, later, from other European countries. These two institutions paid for half of the university salary of any refugee in the program, for up to several years, if the university in turn agreed to budget in order to keep the scholars on the faculty beyond the initial subsidized period (Duggan and Drury).

In addition, the Rockefeller Foundation developed its own relief program with a total of $1.4 million. This foundation was probably the most important agency for the winning of refugee scholars. At the time of its formation in 1911, it had focused on medical and natural science research. During the 1920s, and against the background of the unsolved social and economic problems following World War I, the social sciences were added to its mission. Because its sponsorship in these fields was international, the foundation had precise insight into research standards in Europe and was acquainted with almost all of the scientists in the individual countries. On the basis of this knowledge, it managed to win for the United States (from among the refugees specifically) Europe's most important scholars, many of whom it had been supporting before 1933. The Rockefeller Foundation thus continued sponsorship of more than three hundred professors after financial support in Nazi Germany was suspended. The foundation had not been active within Soviet science.

In New York City, Alvin Johnson, the director of the New School for Social Research, raised the financial means to found, in the summer of 1933, an entire "University in Exile." As co-editor of the *Encyclopedia of the Social Sciences* that had been published in the 1920s, he also knew most of the European scientists who had contributed articles to that multivolume enterprise. As a committed New Dealer, he was especially interested in attracting German thinkers who he felt confident would contribute to the theoretical substantiation of the program initiated by Roosevelt. From 1933 to 1945, more than 170 scientists from Germany and other European countries were to teach at the unique University in Exile, which later became the Graduate Faculty of Political and Social Science of the New School. For many of these scholars the New School became the stepping-stone to other universities. In 1940, a French university in exile was founded at the New School, but its members, who had belonged to the France Libre movement, went back to France after World War II. The Black Mountain College in North Carolina, founded in 1933, also became a launching pad into an American career for refugee artists, in particular, and proved to be of fundamental importance to different avant-garde movements after 1945.

A number of relief committees were founded for specific academic professions. Other foundations provided large sums that enabled two-thirds of the roughly three thousand scientists expelled from Germany—representing 20 percent of all German university teachers—to be admitted to the United States. The art historian W. S. Cook, director of the Institute of Fine Art at New York University, coined a slogan: "Hitler is my best friend. He shakes the tree and I collect the apples" (quoted in Fermi, p. 78). Others declared that the rescue of the intellectuals was neither philanthropy nor a form of protest against National Socialism but, rather, corresponded with the national interest of the United States; the calculation even took into account the education costs saved through this gratuitous gain of highly qualified scholars. In fact, the refugees contributed in important ways to nearly all disciplines: for instance, to the modern social sciences, which had only just begun their professionalization during the 1920s; to the history of art; and also to the different new subdisciplines of natural sciences, such as nuclear physics or biochemistry. At the same time, this professional success hastened the integration of refugees into the American community of science, so that many of the exiles hailed the learning process enforced by their emigration in spite of all the emotional and psychic problems of dislocation. American science thus achieved a tenacious hold on international leadership, and the refugees also flanked the victory over traditional American isolationism with their scientific contributions to the war effort, which aimed at Europe's and Asia's liberaton from the totalitarian regime of the Axis powers.

PREEMINENT FIGURES AMONG THE INTELLECTUAL REFUGEES

The list of former refugee intellectuals reads like a *Who's Who* of the American community of science. Among the Russian scholars who found a position at a university were the economists Wassily Leontief (Harvard), Paul Studenski (New York University), Paul W. Haensel (Northwestern), and Simon Kuznets (National Bureau of Economic Research and the University of Pennsylvania). Leontief—who had initially worked in Germany after fleeing the Soviet Union, obtaining his Ph.D. at Berlin in 1928, and coming to the United States in 1931—received a Nobel Prize in 1973 for his input-output analysis, published in 1941. Kuznets, in the United States since the early 1920s and sponsored by the Russian Student Fund, is considered one of the pioneers of the national income analysis, which was a new field in economic theory during the 1930s. He, too, was awarded a Nobel Prize (1971) for his achievement, and his expertise was tapped by naming him planning director of the War Production Board during World War II.

Besides Leontief other exceptional Russian economists worked in Germany during the 1920s and came to the United States with the refugee exodus after 1933; these included Jacob Marschak, George Garvy, and Wladimir Woytinski. With his work on the mathematical analysis of the information and decision theory and as long-standing director of the Cowles Commission for Research in Economics in Chicago, Marschak was one of the major initiators of modern econometrics. Under his guidance, a circle of young Americans worked in Chicago—among them Kenneth Arrow, Lawrence Klein, and Herbert Simon—together with numerous young refugee scholars such as Oscar Lange from Poland, Trygve Haavelmo from Norway, Tjalling Koopmans from Holland, and Franco Modigliani from Italy. All received the Nobel Prize in later years.

The striking mathematical orientation of the Russians may perhaps be explained by the fact that this field represented the only form of unsuspicious scientific activity open to the young committed economists in reactionary tsarist Russia. Other refugees with a genius for mathematics made trailblazing achievements in, for instance, the fields of mechanics or engineering in the United States. Well known is the invention of the helicopter by Igor Sikorsky, while Vladimir K. Zworykin developed the first television broadcast for Westinghouse. The same trend manifests itself among former refugees from Poland, who—with Alfred Tarski, Stanislaw Ulam, Antoni Zygmund, and others—provided as many as seven of the fifty-two members of the mathematics class of the National Academy of Science in the 1960s.

In other fields, too, Russians attained celebrity. The writings of the sociologist Pitirim Sorokin at Harvard University and of the historian Michael Rostovzeff at Yale have been translated into several languages; at Johns Hopkins University the medical historian Owsei Temkin was awarded numerous honors. In the field of the arts, the composer Igor Stravinsky, the pianist Sergey Rachmaninoff, and the conductor Serge Koussevitzky, to name a few, rose to international fame from their exile in the United States, as did the choreographer George Balanchine, who had immigrated into the United States in 1933 and whose school of "American ballet" had worldwide impact. The visual artist Marc Chagall and the writer Vladimir Nabokov both

came from France as refugees in 1940. Although Nabokov was the only Russian refugee writer of international rank in the United States, he contributed rather more to American than to Russian literature.

While the refugee scientists and artists from Russia and from other European countries immigrated either as individuals or in small groups, entire academic schools and artistic movements emigrated from Germany after 1933. Indeed, representatives of the "Weimar culture" (a term coined by the historian Peter Gay, himself a refugee from Nazi Germany)—renowned as the avant-garde of modern art, literature, and science—transferred a whole culture. They supported the first German democracy after 1918 and were accordingly persecuted for political and—as far as they were intellectuals of Jewish origin—"racial" reasons as non-German by the adherents to the "blood and soil" fanaticism of the Nazis. Not without reason has this transfer repeatedly been compared with the exodus of the learned men from Byzantium after the fall of Constantinople and the Eastern Roman Empire in 1453—men who contributed considerably to the flourishing of the Renaissance in Italy and in western Europe.

About seven thousand literary and artistic emigrants had come to the United States up to 1940 or 1941; among them were those who, like Thomas Mann or Lion Feuchtwanger and others, were already known in the United States through translations of their work. Most of the writers, who were dependent upon their mother tongue, did not contribute directly to the progress of the American culture; however, with their literature they drew attention to the antifascist struggle of the "other Germany." Hollywood was at the receiving end of more than eight hundred immigrants, including scriptwriters (Bertolt Brecht, George Froeschel, Anna Gmeyner, Frederick Kohner), producers (Alexander Korda, Erich Pommer), directors (Fritz Lang, Otto Preminger, Douglas Sirk [Detlef Sierck], Robert Siodmak, Billy Wilder, Fred Zinnemann) and actors (Marlene Dietrich, Paul Henreid, Lotte Lenya, Peter Lorre, Conrad Veidt), who not only created the genre of the anti-Nazi film but who also had a strong impact on the American cinema with their comedies, horror movies, and contributions to film noir.

In the field of fine arts, the artists (for example, László Moholy-Nagy, Josef Albers, Lyonel Feininger) and architects (Walter Gropius, Mies van der Rohe, Marcel Breuer, and Erich Mendelssohn) of the German Bauhaus school had a style-forming impact with their vision of a *Gesamtkunstwerk,* in which aesthetics and technique, rational form and artistic design, converged to form a unit. In this, the influence of Frank Lloyd Wright upon the Bauhaus architecture of the 1920s and the Bauhaus ideas of the 1930s merged into a so-called International style that remained valid decades later. The success of the former Bauhaus members at Black Mountain College, the Harvard Graduate School of Design, or the "New Bauhaus" (now the Institute of Design) at the Illinois Institute of Technology in Chicago was also fostered by the fact that the educational ideas associated with the Bauhaus school were largely identical to the principles of American pragmatism and John Dewey's theory of "learning by doing" that were enjoying academic enthusiasm in America.

In the academic professions, the refugee social scientists and, in particular, economists with new intellectual messages were the most successful. The worldwide economic crisis after 1929, which was of such proportions that it could hardly be fought with the self-healing powers of the market (as was claimed by mainstream economics), had led to a swing to the left among the intellectuals of the Western industrial countries. Their demand for a realistic theory of crises initiated the fundamental change in paradigms of the 1930s, which was to become known as the Keynesian revolution and of which the New Deal was also a symptom. Economists from Germany, in particular, coming from a country where traditions of market interventions through government incentives prevailed, contributed to economic theory in ways that went far beyond the merely cyclical model developed by the British economist John Maynard Keynes because, in their analysis, they also took into account the economic structures and the development of modern technology with its labor-displacement effects. They thus enriched the theories of trade cycles and growth with new ideas, and they established financial theory, which represented but a marginal field in American economics, as a subdiscipline in its own right. This trend is represented by economists who worked at the University in Exile such as Emil Lederer, Adolph Lowe, Hans Neisser, or Gerhard Colm. Colm left the New School for a breakneck career in Washington, where he joined Roosevelt's team of advisers and became one of the initiators of the Full Employment Act of 1946. Richard Musgrave, who had come to Harvard from Heidelberg in 1933 as a student, is another of the financial scientists who became internationally known.

While most of the Germans had come as committed New Dealers, a not inconsiderable number of neoclassical theorists who originally had their stronghold in Austria arrived in America as vehement anti–New Dealers. They were above all accommodated by the conservative universities of the Ivy League; for instance, Joseph Schumpeter and Gottfried Haberler found places at Harvard and Fritz Machlup and Oskar Morgenstern at Princeton. Morgenstern gained pioneer importance for the sophistication of his free-enterprise analysis in *Theory of Games and Economic Behavior* (1944), which he developed together with another immigrant, the mathematician John von Neumann.

Refugee scholars furthermore contributed to the formation of the young disciplines of sociology and political science. The representatives of the former Frankfurt Institute of Social Research—with men like Max Horkheimer, Franz Neumann, Herbert Marcuse, and others—found refuge at Columbia University as an intact group. To this field also belong Sigmund Neumann, Hannah Arendt, Karl W. Deutsch, Hans Morgenthau, Waldemar Gurian, Lewis Coser, and Hans Gerth. Arendt and Marcuse figured among the most often quoted social scientists of the 1960s and 1970s. On the basis of their German experiences, they had sharp eyes for modern mass society and mass culture, and the threats to democracy in social and economic crises—a problem that was hardly discussed by their American colleagues in view of the deeply rooted democratic development of the United States. The theory of totalitarianism, which was to become an important paradigm in the East-West confrontation of the cold war, traces back to this circle of scholars. They also contributed to the enrichment of the empiricist-behaviorist orientation of American social science through their theoretical systematizations and Weltanschauung. Just as the economists in diverse new administrative bodies took part in the war effort, many of these scholars cooperated in the planning of the American war strategy and of the European postwar organization, for instance in the Office of Strategic Services.

Countless examples could be listed concerning the contribution of German refugees to the development of other disciplines. Thus, for instance, in the fields of psychology and psychoanalysis there are Erik H. Erikson, Karl and Charlotte Bühler, Erich Fromm, Kurt Lewin, and Bruno Bettelheim; of the psychology of advertising, George Katona; of empirical social research, Paul Lazarsfeld; of legal sociology, Hans Zeisel; of the theory of science and in philosophy, Rudolf Carnap, Herbert Feigl, Ernst

Cassirer, Leo Strauss, and Erich Kahler; or in the history of art, Erwin Panofsky and Richard Krautheimer. The field of Judaic studies, a peculiarity of German-Jewish culture, was also transferred by refugees (Ismar Elbogen, Eugen Täubler). Instead of rabbinical learning this discipline aimed at the scientific research of all aspects of Jewish life in the tradition of enlightenment. Refugee scholars in the field of legal science had the choice of either studying this law anew (in view of the differently oriented legal system of the United States) or switching to other fields. Many chose the second path and thus became the founders of international comparative law (Hans Kelsen, Heinrich Kronstein, Max Rheinstein, John H. Herz). However, in this intellectual influx the historians were underrepresented, despite scholars such as Hajo Holborn, Felix Gilbert, or Hans Rothfels. In Germany, history was a conservative, national profession that represented more or less a private party, and to which Jews or democrats had hardly been given access, so only a few of its members were expelled in 1933. In this field, only representatives of the second generation (including, among others, Peter Gay, George Mosse, Carl Schorske, and Fritz Stern) contributed after 1945 to the contours of the field in the United States. Exceptional, however, was Ernst Posner, who laid the foundations for the professional training of archivists.

For the natural sciences, finally, the physicists who cooperated in the Manhattan Project at Los Alamos, New Mexico, during the war may serve as an example. An indicator of the significance of refugees in this discipline is the awarding of the Nobel Prize. Albert Einstein and James Franck had already been awarded the prize before their arrival in the United States (1921 and 1925); Victor Hess (1936), Otto Stern (1943), Felix Bloch (1952), Eugene Wigner (1963), and Hans Bethe (1967) were to receive it as American citizens. To these prizewinners may be added the Italian refugees Enrico Fermi (1938) and Emilio Segrè (1959). A similar picture presents itself with the chemists, among whom also figured several later Nobel Prize winners and internationally famous scholars, such as Erwin Chargaff, who laid the foundation for the modern genetic analysis. Of the more than one hundred mathematicians expelled from Germany, more than sixty came to the United States, among them Richard Courant, Abraham Fraenkel, Kurt Gödel, Emmy Noether, John von Neumann, and others.

The mass emigration of the intellectual and cultural elites expelled from Germany, which have been sketched only roughly and insufficiently with the names mentioned here, easily hides that no less important scholars had come from other countries, too. With Modigliani, Fermi, and Segré, refugees from Italy already have been named. To this circle of Italians also belonged the historian Gaetano Salvemini, the political scientist Max Ascoli, the literary critic Guiseppe Antonio Borgese, and others, while the conductor Arturo Toscanini is representative of the fine arts. From Hungary came, for example, the physicists Leo Szilard and Edward Teller, the Bauhaus designer Moholy-Nagy, and the composer Béla Bartók. The majority, however, came (as has already been suggested) as individual persons; and, in the case of the Hungarians, it is furthermore questionable to take the place of birth as a point of orientation because, as a rule, they had worked either in Germany or in Austria until 1933 or 1938.

Not without reason a vivid discussion on the significance of those intellectuals who had immigrated in the 1930s flared up in the 1980s, during the era of Ronald Reagan's presidency. This debate found its climax in the publication of the 1987 bestseller *The Closing of the American Mind,* written by the philosopher Allan Bloom, oddly enough himself a disciple of the emigrated conservative philosopher Leo Strauss. In this curious manifest of nativism, the author settles with the supposedly disastrous influence of that intellectual "German connection" of former emigrants who, with their methods of social and ideological critique, ostensibly spoiled the younger generation, thus destroying the foundations for understanding the great liberal and Christian values of America. Due to this influence, American culture had been turned into a sort of "Disneyland version of the Weimar Republic" (Bloom, p. 141ff). Others voice the opinion that the United States would have become a leading power in science without the emigrants, simply due to its material resources. That may be so, but it does not refute the fact that the "brain drain" represented by the dispersal of German and European refugees was absorbed by the United States at a time when that country had only just started on its way to becoming a leading intellectual power.

See also **The Arts in the Republican Era; Popular Intellectual Movements: 1833–1877; The Artist and the Intellectual in the New Deal** *(volume 1);* **Franco-American Cultural Encounters and Exchanges; Countercultural Visions; Vietnam as a Cultural Crisis; Interna-**

tional Relations and Connections; Anti-Statism *(in this volume); and other articles in this section.*

BIBLIOGRAPHY

Bloom, Allan. *The Closing of the American Mind: How Higher Education Has Failed Democracy and Impoverished the Souls of Today's Students.* New York, 1987.

Coser, Lewis A. *Refugee Scholars in America: Their Impact and Their Experiences.* New Haven, Conn., 1984.

Davie, Maurice R. *World Immigration: With Special Reference to the United States.* New York, 1936.

Davie, Maurice R., et al. *Refugees in America: Report of the Committee for the Study of Recent Immigration from Europe.* New York, 1947.

Duberman, Martin. *Black Mountain: An Exploration in Community.* New York, 1972.

Duggan, Stephen, and Betty Drury. *The Rescue of Science and Learning: The Story of the Emergency Committee in Aid of Displaced Foreign Scholars.* New York, 1948.

Fermi, Laura. *Illustrious Immigrants: The Intellectual Migration from Europe, 1930–1941.* Chicago, 1968.

Fields, Harold. *The Refugee in the United States.* New York, 1938.

Fleming, Donald, and Bernard Bailyn, eds. *The Intellectual Migration: Europe and America, 1930–1960.* Cambridge, Mass., 1969.

Fosdick, Raymond B. *The Story of the Rockefeller Foundation.* New York, 1952.

Hughes, H. Stuart. *The Sea Change: The Migration of Social Thought, 1930–1965.* New York, 1975.

Krohn, Claus-Dieter. *Intellectuals in Exile: Refugee Scholars and the New School for Social Research.* Translated by Rita Kimbler and John Kimbler. Amherst, Mass., 1993.

Speier, Hans. "The Social Conditions of the Intellectual Exile." In *Social Research* 4, no. 3 (September, 1937): 316–328.

ASIAN AMERICANS

Henry Yu

The intellectual and cultural history of Asian Americans has been dominated by Orientalism, a structure of ideas and representations that has defined Asia as an exotic place that is antithetical in every way to the United States. As a direct result, Americans whose ancestors have come from Asia have been seen as perpetual foreigners, marked because their bodies are considered different from other Americans. Orientalism can be found in important American social theories and in cultural representations such as movies, television, and literature. More than just a set of representations, however, Orientalism as a relationship of unequal power has structured the way that Asian Americans have struggled to live in the United States, marginalizing them and constraining their ability to find a meaningful place for themselves in America.

Between 1860 and 1945 Asian Americans were regarded as a threat to a united white America, an "Oriental problem" that needed to be solved. Ironically, in the last four decades, Asian Americans have increasingly come to be seen as a "model minority," the exemplary solution to the racial problems of America. However they are viewed, Asian Americans have been treated as different, at worst as foreign invaders and at best as exotic Americans who are not quite the same as everyone else.

Unlike European immigrants who blended into whiteness, Asian Americans, like African Americans, have always been valued and denigrated for what was assumed to be unique about them. Tracing ancestry to a wide variety of geographic origins all around Asia and the Pacific Islands, Asian Americans have little to unite them in the United States except for parallels in oppressive treatment by whites. The very designation of "Asian Americans" as single group has been created out of sense of a shared history of being treated in a similar manner throughout America's history. The very idea people migrating from the continent of Asia were somehow connected to each other and should be treated

similarly was the consequence of the concept of Orientalism. Similar to, yet different than, longstanding European representations of the inhabitants of what is now known as the Middle East, American conceptions of the Orient in the nineteenth and twentieth centuries focused more on China and Japan. Although biblical scholars of the late nineteenth and early twentieth century also referred to the Near East as the Orient, most Americans understood the term "Oriental" to mean the Far East. The very conception of Asia as a singular place has been derived from definitions of the monolithic Orient. Therefore, who can be understood to be Asian American both in the present and in the past is open to debate, having been powerfully affected by changing ideas about who and what was Oriental.

ORIENTALISM

Long before Asian immigrants came in significant numbers to the shores of the United States, the cultural meanings of a mythical Orient had shaped American history. The Americas as a dominion of Europe was an accidental creation, founded on the desire Europeans held for goods from the Orient. The first European explorers accidentally arrived at the "New World" while searching for a new trade route to Asia. As an imagined locale, the exotic Orient had been one of the foundational ideas of European exploration and, subsequently, American definitions of the larger world. At various moments, East Asian civilizations in China, Japan, and Korea have been lumped together as Oriental, and at other times South and Southeast Asian societies in the subcontinent of India and Indochina (the present-day nations of Vietnam, Cambodia, and Laos) have also been defined as Oriental.

From the United States' first moments as a nation, the cultural and spiritual life of white Americans has been marked by a fascination for the

Orient. During the period of British colonization of North America, merchants in the colonies were not allowed to trade directly with China, and so one of the first significant acts of national economic independence in the 1790s for the new American republic was participation in the lucrative China trade. It was the desire for the luxurious goods of the Orient—spices, silk, tea, and porcelain—that built the wealth of many early American merchants in New England.

Early elites such as George Washington carefully cultivated an ideal of themselves as cultured by proudly decorating their homes with porcelain tea sets and tasteful chinoiseries, and the exotic cachet of Oriental objects has been a crucial element of class distinction in the United States ever since. In the 1890s and 1920s, Japanese art objects were eagerly sought by American collectors, and since the 1980s automobiles and electronics produced in Asia and bearing the brand names of Toyota and Sony have come to dominate American consumption patterns.

MISSIONARIES AND ASIAN AMERICANS

Like the desire created by Oriental goods, the spiritual call to save lost Asian souls has been a constant pull for American missionaries. Protestant missions to Asia and the Pacific Islands began by the 1820s, marking a long-term obsession with converting "heathens" across the Pacific. By the twentieth century, China and Japan had become the two most significant destinations for American missionaries, and South Korea became one of the most successful conversion projects in American evangelical history. Christian ideas, along with theories about science and modernity that placed Asia behind Europe and the West in the progress of civilization, were often appropriated by Asian students and intellectuals searching for a synretic set of beliefs to respond to intrusions into their home countries by Europeans. Many of these students migrated between Asia and the United States under the auspices of American Protestant missionary organizations that set up schools in China and Japan. After the Boxer Rebellion of 1900, when a group of Chinese revolutionaries tried unsuccessfully to expel Americans and Europeans from China, the indemnity fund paid the United States by the Chinese government became the most prominent source of funding for Chinese students traveling abroad. For the next three decades, hundreds of Chinese students, most of them converted Christians initially trained in missionary

schools, came to the United States for college degrees. Some of them stayed after their schooling, forming the first significant group of Asian American intellectuals.

Conversely, religious traditions associated with Asia such as Buddhism have been embraced by many Americans searching for alternative forms of spirituality. Such a longing for the seemingly mystical aspects of Eastern spirituality was evident during the 1890s but has become particularly prominent since the late 1960s. The hunger of non-Asian Americans for exotic Oriental traditions such as martial arts has often been a distinguishing feature of their dissatisfaction with what they understand to be American culture.

EARLY HISTORY: CHINESE AMERICANS

The cultural and intellectual history of Asian Americans has been dominated by the idea that Orientals are forever foreign, and immigrants from Asia as well as those born in the United States have constantly struggled to define a place for themselves within America. When Chinese males migrated to the gold fields of California in the 1850s and became the first significant group of Asians to reside in the continental United States, cultural representations of the Orient had already marked them as alien and exotic. Labor conflicts with ethnic white workers, particularly Irish migrant laborers competing for the same work, fueled anti-Chinese violence, and during the 1870s organized lynching and arson drove most Chinese out of small towns in the West and into urban ghettoes like San Francisco's Chinatown. White supremacist organizations such as the Ku Klux Klan, and labor organizations such at the Workingman's Party, agitated for the complete exclusion of Chinese from the United States, arguing that Asians were impossible to assimilate into America.

Beginning in 1870, when naturalization as an American citizen was restricted to "white persons and persons of African descent," the idea of Asians as alien to America was enshrined in a series of legislative acts. On the state level, anti-miscegenation laws in the 1870s and 1880s made it illegal for Asians to marry whites in most western states, and in the 1910s and 1920s, several states made it illegal for alien Asians to own land. Legally excluded by the Chinese Exclusion Act, an act of Congress in 1882, Chinese laborers were cut off from further migrations to the United States, and though merchants and students were still allowed, the number of Chinese in America steadily declined from around 100,000.

JAPANESE AMERICANS

Between 1880 and 1924, large numbers of Japanese immigrants came to the West Coast, but anti-Oriental organizations decrying a "Yellow peril" and an "Oriental problem" transferred onto them the political rhetoric and cultural representations used to exclude the Chinese. The popularity of pulp fiction novels such as Sax Rohmer's Fu Manchu series used the threat of a Chinese genius to encapsulate and promote a fear of "Asiatics" in general. Asian men were portrayed in images and in prose preying on helpless white women, in particular using opium to drug them into submission. Representations of Asian women were dominated by characterizations as prostitutes. Altering between the stereotype of the "Dragon lady," who was sexually dominant, and of the "China doll" or geisha, who was compliant and submissive, Asian women existed as sexual slaves for white men. Theories about the higher birth rate of Orientals plugged into nightmares about the overwhelming of European culture by the primitive fecundity of nonwhite people.

By 1924, anti-Asian agitation had succeeded in eliminating Japanese immigration to the United States. The Immigration Act of 1924 had a formative effect on the United States, ending decades of massive migration from southeastern Europe, but it merely continued a longer history of anti-Asian exclusion. Smaller streams of Korean and East Indian immigrants were also cut off, and significant Asian immigration did not resume until reforms of immigration law in 1965.

COLONIZATION OF THE PHILIPPINES

The inequities in power that contribute to the definitions of Orientalism are best exemplified by the role of the U.S. military in Asian American history. From the gunboats that forced the opening of Japan to foreign trade in the middle of the nineteenth century, to those that annexed Hawaii and the Philippines and enforced the territorial rights of American citizens in China in 1900, American military presence has been a factor in how Americans have treated Asians at home and abroad, and how Asians have experienced life both in and as emigrants from their home country.

The American annexation of the Philippine islands after the Spanish-American War of 1898 is a prominent example of the centrality of the U.S. military in Asian American history. Philippine nationalist forces had done much of the fighting to defeat the Spanish during the war, but despite promises that they would be granted independence if they allied with the United States, the American army spent almost five years in a bloody campaign to wipe out forces opposing American rule. Estimates vary, but it is probable that hundreds of thousands of Philippine civilians were killed or died from the deliberate starvation policies that the U.S. Army used to pacify resistance. Importantly, the military had learned these techniques in genocidal campaigns against natives in the American West.

The similar treatment of Native Americans and Philippine nationalists by the U.S. military highlights a parallel that has distinguished the treatment of Filipino Americans from the forms of American Orientalism that affected the Chinese and Japanese Americans. Serving the needs of military power and the hierarchies of violent American colonial rule, social theories and cultural representations of Philippine citizens were dominated by the portrayals of natives as primitive. Unlike the seemingly positive valuations of exotic civilization that Orientalist definitions often bestowed upon China and Japan, American representations of Philippine natives were characterized by the language of anthropology, describing them in a manner parallel to Native Americans. Civilization and modernity laid with the acceptance of American ideals and political rule, and the retention of native culture was defined as atavism at the same time that it signified disloyalty to the United States.

Even American missionaries, who had fought against anti-Chinese and anti-Japanese agitation in the United States by extolling the accomplishments of thousands of years of Oriental civilization, did not extend such arguments to the Philippines. Against American imperialism by principle, many missionaries opposed annexation, but at the same time believed that the predominantly Catholic Philippines needed the civilizing influence of American Protestants.

FILIPINO AMERICANS

Almost immediately after the American annexation of the Philippines, An American-controlled education system was instituted in the islands, inculcating a pro-American ideology that controlled the Philippines even after formal independence at the end of World War II. Elite, educated students came to the United States from the Philippines to attend college, but often found that despite their privileged, educated backgrounds they were, at best, treated as civilized savages.

In the 1920s and 1930s, the growing demand for agricultural labor created a migrant work force of male Filipino workers on the West Coast. Filipinos were exempt from the 1924 laws that excluded Asian immigrants because they were technically American subjects living in a U.S. territory, even if they had no rights as citizens. Like the Chinese and Japanese, Filipino immigrants met with violence from whites, and further migration was cut off in 1935 when Filipinos were declared no longer to be American subjects. The Repatriation Act offered one-way tickets to the Philippines to resident Filipinos, under the condition that they agree not to return to the United States.

The hypocrisy of American ill-treatment of Filipino workers in the 1930s was immortalized by the Filipino American writer Carlos Bulosan's *America Is in the Heart*. Bulosan, like many of his friends and colleagues, had been educated in the Philippines in an American school system. He described how Filipinos coming to the United States had already been taught to love the ideas of democracy and fair play that America seemingly represented, but the harsh realities of racism and the difficult life of migrant agricultural work constantly undermined such ideals.

A scathing indictment of American racism, Bulosan's work also captures the dynamic that almost all Asian American writers faced for much of American history: the juxtaposition between endemic racial practices in the United States and ideal principles of democracy and equality that promised a better world. By the 1920s, a sizable second generation of Chinese Americans and Japanese Americans had begun to come of age, and unlike their parents who were not legally allowed to become naturalized Americans, they were citizens born in the United States. Educated in American schools, they fought for the hope contained in American political rhetoric. For most Asian American intellectuals between 1920 and 1970, the only hope for improving the situation of Asians in America was to champion those idealistic promises and to challenge the racial exclusion of Asians as un-American. In the words of the title of Bulosan's novel, "America is in the heart," and it was particularly in the hearts of those Filipino American immigrants who suffered at the hands of white Americans and yet remained truer to American ideals than their tormentors.

ORIENTALISM AND ASIAN AMERICAN IDENTITY

American Orientalism has structured the manner in which European Americans have dealt with ideas, goods, and immigrants from Asia; however, it has also had a profound effect on Asian American's concepts of themselves. Because white Americans treated them as exotic foreigners, second-generation Chinese Americans and Japanese Americans often tried to erase any connections to their Asian parentage. Chinese Americans and Japanese Americans were lumped together as Orientals, and because they were treated in similar ways, their reactions were similar. Perpetually questioned as to how American they could be, they constantly tried to prove that they were 100 percent American.

However, even though Chinese Americans, Japanese Americans, and Filipino Americans were excluded by white racism from most neighborhoods, and thus forced to live in neighborhoods bordering on each other, their social lives and self-identification were often with their individual communities. A history of conflicts between China and Japan during much of the early twentieth century, culminating in warfare between 1933 and 1945, resonated in Chinese American and Japanese American enclaves; the Japanese invasion of the Philippines during World War II led to incidents of Filipino American violence against Japanese Americans, and Japanese colonization of Korea between 1910 and 1945 created a legacy of animosity between Korean Americans and Japanese Americans.

Since the knowledge of white Americans about Asian Americans was structured by the linking together of them as Orientals, the self-understanding of intellectuals who entered American institutions of scholarship reflected this structure. For instance, at the most important institution producing knowledge about Asian Americans during the period between 1920 and 1965, the University of Chicago's Department of Sociology, Chinese American and Japanese American students were recruited to study what the white sociologists considered the "Oriental problem": the question of whether Orientals could be assimilated into American society. Drawn into academic institutions that were overwhelmingly white and male, these students created knowledge that answered the interests of their colleagues, and at the same time came to understand themselves through the social theories that they learned.

Under the leadership of social theorists such as Robert E. Park, William I. Thomas, Ernest Burgess, and Louis Wirth, social scientific research at Chicago and at a number of universities on the West Coast and in Hawaii were dominated by University of Chicago–trained social scientists. These sociologists, who created the foundation for much of American social scientific theory on culture, urban studies, labor relations, family life, race relations, and immigration, began a research program that focused upon those they termed "Oriental Americans." They were specifically interested in the possibilities of cultural assimilation, the wholesale adoption by American-born Orientals of American culture to the extent that they were culturally identical to white Americans. Having already studied the cultural assimilation of immigrants for Europe, the Chicago sociologists were hopeful that Asian-Americans, as immigrants and racial minorities, offered a link between these studies and research on African Americans.

The white sociologists found that second-generation Chinese American and Japanese American students not only made perfect researchers, but that they were the ideal subjects for research. Proving that cultural assimilation was possible, these second-generation Oriental Americans were American in every sense except their skin color. In the words of Robert Park, they were like Americans in exotic Halloween masks, identical in behavior, speech, and ideas to white Americans.

The Chicago sociologists' theories drew extensively upon the experiences described by their Chinese American and Japanese American subjects. For instance, in 1924 a young Japanese American student named Kazuo Kawai gave a long interview on the difficulties he had experienced being accepted as an American in the United States, and also as a Japanese in Japan. The Chicago sociologists used his testimony, and many others like his, to generalize social theories about marginalization. The American-born students saw themselves caught between two worlds, alien to the Asian cultures of their parents, and yet denied entrance into the white American culture that they had learned in school. Interestingly, when other students of Chinese and Japanese heritage came to study at the University of Chicago and at the numerous American universities that taught Chicago social theories, these students came to understand themselves with the help of the definitions they found in these theories.

DIVIDED IDENTITY

One of the most important Chicago-trained sociologists to study Asian Americans was the Chinese American sociologist Rose Hum Lee. Receiving her Ph.D. in sociology from the University of Chicago in 1947, Lee became committed to the project of assimilating Chinese Americans into mainstream American society. Her research work directed anger at any obstacle to the integration of Orientals, whether is was Chinatown organizations that sheltered Chinese Americans and thus kept them apart from whites, or white Americans who hypocritically claimed their lack of racism while simultaneously excluding Asians from their neighborhoods and workplaces. One of the most interesting qualities of Lee's research and life was how her theories regarding cultural assimilation reflected her own difficulties as a Chinese American woman. Much of Lee's commitment to American assimilation was derived from her belief that American culture offered modern gender roles to women, and that traditional Chinese culture denied women the freedom to accomplish what she herself had managed.

Within Lee's theories, the opposition between what was Chinese and what was American was stark. Her existence within American society could only make sense if some traits of her life were associated with American culture, and other parts were associated with a traditional China that was exotic and different. It was telling that those cultural elements that her white American colleagues and friends found most acceptable, such as ancient Chinese philosophy, religion, calligraphy and painting, were also the ones Lee valued, and those that were viewed in a negative light were those that Lee herself wanted Chinese Americans to eradicate.

In a very different manner, the Chinese American novelist Maxine Hong Kingston's *Woman Warrior* (1978) expresses the tensions involved in definitions of identity that attempt to extricate what is American and what is Asian. Through its metaphor of ghosts, Kingston's novel exemplifies the haunting ephemeral quality of ethnic identity. As a memoir about childhood in the United States, it shows how the meaning of what exists in America and the memories of what was there in China are impossible to distinguish.

American readers responded favorably to Kingston's descriptions of an exotic and haunting Chinese past, and the popular reception and continuing sales of her book point to her powerful lyric prose style, but also to the continuing desire for the exotic that her text fulfills. Like Rose Hum Lee's need to calculate what were desirable and undesirable Chinese traits in the context of American colleagues who valued her for being Chinese, Kingston and other Asian American writers face a market for cultural representations of Asian Americans that commodifies the exotic. Regardless of the intentions of Asian American writers and artists, the reception of their work by a larger public often reflects this desire for what is uniquely Oriental about them.

HISTORY, MEMORY, AND ASIAN AMERICAN IDENTITY

The haunting presence of the past, in particular memories passed down of ancestors' lives, is a narrative of ethnic identity that extends beyond Kingston's metaphor of ghosts from a faraway land. The presence of the past within present Asian American identity has also been powerfully demonstrated by memories of the forced internment of over 120,000 Japanese Americans during World War II. Although almost two-thirds were American citizens by birth, Japanese Americans were treated as foreigners without constitutional rights, and the traumatic effects of being stripped of their possessions and exiled to barbed-wire camps far from their homes left a lasting effect on their identity as Japanese Americans. Sansei, or third-generation Japanese Americans growing up in the 1970s, discovered in their own lives the lingering effects of what had happened to their parents and grandparents. Pushing for some form of redress for internment, Japanese Americans of all ages underwent a process of rediscovering the power and meaning of the past, joined by other Asian Americans who recognized that it might have easily been themselves who were interned.

The development of Asian American studies, and other forms of ethnic studies that came into being in the 1970s, was a direct reaction to the exclusion and exoticization of Asians in America. The very term "Asian American" was coined by activists and intellectuals in the 1960s and 1970s as a reaction to the exotic connotations of the term "Oriental." Valuing a past that had its roots in Asia, yet emphatically sounding a right to be treated as Americans, Asian American activists turned Orientalism on its head. The pursuit in Asian American studies arose as part of a larger political challenge to the oppression and marginalization of Asians in the United States and around the world, in particular in light of the racism displayed during American wars in Southeast Asia. Many of the proponents of Asian American consciousness were American-born Chinese and Japanese Americans, but they joined with recent immigrants and with other people of color everywhere against racism. Historians such as Him Mark Lai, Yuji Ichioka, Sucheng Chan,

and Ronald Takaki recovered the lost history of Asian migrants to the United States, and filmmakers such as Renée Tajima, Christine Choy, Spencer Nakasano, Loni Ding, and Arthur Dong have created remarkable documentaries about the history of Asian Americans. The commercial and critical success of Asian American novelists and writers such as Amy Tan, David Wong Louie, and Chang-rae Lee in the 1980s and 1990s highlighted the important work of (and the difficulties encountered by) earlier pathbreaking authors such as Maxine Hong Kingston, Frank Chin, Hisaye Yamamoto, and Carlos Bulosan. The need to document and describe the little known lives and histories of Asian Americans drove much of the scholarship and fiction of early Asian American writers.

By the 1970s, changes in immigration had transformed American society. For the first time since the 1920s and 1930s, immigrants from Asia were entering the United States in large numbers. New legislation in 1965 replaced immigration laws that had barred Asians for over forty years. Though the framers of the legislation had anticipated only a small number of Asian immigrants as a result of the reform, the laws proved pivotal in allowing new and significant numbers of Asian immigrants. By the 1970s, immigrants from the Philippines, Taiwan, Korea, and India began to emigrate to the United States to fill jobs in the burgeoning economy. This generation of immigrants was different from earlier waves of mostly male laborers. Often coming over as family units, large numbers of highly educated and skilled economic immigrants proved a boon to the U.S. economy, sometimes transforming high-tech industries. The majority of Asian immigrants were unskilled workers, but the high-profile professionals joined a growing number of second- and third-generation Chinese and Japanese Americans in white-collar jobs that previously barred Asians.

THE MODEL MINORITY MYTH

The high levels of education among recent Asian immigrants, combined with the drive for success shown by many children of immigrants, has led to a new characterization of Asian Americans as a "model minority." The seeds of the description of Asian Americans' exemplary status had been planted during the internment of Japanese Americans in 1942. Forced to prove their loyalty, Japanese Americans evinced a super-patriotism that allowed for little dissension, and was marked by the demand for overachievement. The 442nd Regiment, a

316

Manzanar Concentration Camp, California, c. 1944. Some 120,000 Japanese Americans were interned during World War II. © HULTON-DEUTSCH COLLECTION/CORBIS

segregated Japanese American unit that suffered horrendous casualties during World War II, was lionized for its sacrifice and used as an example to prove the unquestionable loyalty of Japanese Americans. Such extolling of the achievements of Japanese Americans continued after the war, as Japanese American intellectuals and those who had supported them, including many social scientists at the University of Chicago, produced studies that argued that the Confucian culture of Japanese Americans had helped them achieve success in the United States.

By the late 1960s and during the 1970s, the exemplary status of Japanese Americans was extended to other Asian American groups, and the myth of a model minority was accepted by many Asian Americans, as well as those white Americans who argued that African Americans and other groups that had suffered racism should follow the lead of Asians. Rather than ascribing success to hard work and sacrifice, much of the rhetoric of the model minority has explained Asian American achievement as the result of some unique Asian quality such as Confucianism, an exoticization that has continued to define Asian Americans as essentially foreign. In addition, the pitting of Asian Americans against other racial minorities has had divisive effects to this day.

WAR AND ASIAN AMERICANS

The impact of war has also continued to be central to the history of Asian Americans since 1965. By the 1980s, two of the most significant groups of Asian immigrants were from the former American colony of the Philippines and from South Korea, the latter of which has had a significant American military and cultural presence since the Korean War of 1950 to 1953. As a result of the Vietnam War that ended in 1975, tens of thousands of former allies from South Vietnam, Cambodia, and Laos came as refugees. Hmong and other nomadic tribes recruited by the Central Intelligence Agency to fight secretly against the North Vietnamese have had the most difficult time in the United States. Thrust suddenly into urban America, these refugees of American wars have found their exile to an unwelcoming United States particularly difficult. A sizable portion still live in poverty, and they continue to struggle in their adjustment to a new home.

As with the colonization of the Philippines, American military presence has continued to be a major factor in the cultural representations of Pacific Islanders. Residents and immigrants from Samoa, Guam, and other Pacific islands dominated by the United States since World War II share the characterizations that have marked native Hawaiians and Filipinos. Often portrayed through the lens of sexual recreation for American servicemen, Pacific Islanders, in particular women, have been viewed as sexually available and ascribed with primitive sexuality.

DIFFERENT FORMS OF ORIENTALISM

The label of primitive that was applied to Filipino Americans at the beginning of the twentieth century has continued to place all Pacific Islanders in a hierarchy of civilization that reduces them to a third world, underdeveloped status. This "Polynesian" variant of Orientalism has served to separate Pacific Islanders from other Asian Americans because of the different way they have been treated. For instance, even though there has been an enormous influx of highly educated Filipino immigrants since the 1970s, particularly in the medical professions, Filipino Americans are seldom envisioned as model minorities in the same way most East Asian immigrants are.

The variations between the forms of Orientalism that have defined differing groups of immigrants from Asia and the Pacific have had important results. The question of who is Orientalized and in what ways has affected which immigrant groups are even present in cultural representations of Asian Americans. Korean Americans and for the most part Vietnamese Americans have found themselves linked with Chinese Americans and Japanese Americans, suffering and benefiting from Orientalist definitions that grant them an exotic, civilized culture.

Left out have been Pacific Islanders and South Asians. Earlier migrations of laborers from India, in particular from the Punjab, went in significant numbers to Canada and other British colonies, and some made their way to the United States, but they have rarely been considered by Americans as Oriental in the same manner as the Chinese and Japanese. Especially in comparison to the massive Orientalist discourse concerning India that marks British cultural history, South Asians in the United States have been completely ignored. Recent South Asian immigrants have faced the question of whether to identify with other Asian Americans, in particular in response to the effects of a model minority characterization that has divided highly educated South Asian immigrants.

In a similar manner to successful professionals among other Asian American groups, South Asian Americans have had to choose between identifying themselves with white Americans who have applauded their achievements and granted them honorary white status, or retaining an awareness of the continuing effects that Orientalism has had on not only themselves but also other less successful Asian American groups. One of the arguments for an Asian American pan-ethnicity is that different strains of Orientalism, in particular the "primitive Polynesians" and "civilized Orientals," have had much in common.

For the last seventy years, Asian American intellectuals and artists have been caught between the need to create knowledge and cultural representations that are valuable within a market dominated by the desires of whites, and a need to help, through their knowledge, others who have been similarly treated as Orientals. Asian Americans have been commodified for being exotic and different at the same time that they have been marginalized for the same reasons. Always tied to some other faraway place, and marked with the desire for and abhorrence of the foreign that suffuses the use of the term Oriental, Asian Americans continue to struggle to define themselves as part of the American social body.

See also **Racialism and Racial Uplift** (volume 1); **San Francisco Bay Area** (in this volume); **Ethnicity: Early Theories; Ethnicity and Race; Race** (volume 3).

BIBLIOGRAPHY

Primary Sources

Bulosan, Carlos. *America Is in the Heart*. Seattle, Wash., 1997.

Gulick, Sidney L. *The American Japanese Problem: A Study of the Racial Relations of the East and the West*. New York, 1914.

Kingston, Maxine Hong. *Woman Warrior: Memories of a Childhood Among Ghosts*. New York, 1995.

Lee, Rose Hum. *The Chinese in the United States of America.* Hong Kong, 1960.

Miyamoto, Shotaru Frank. *Social Solidarity among the Japanese in Seattle.* Seattle, Wash., 1939.

Rohmer, Sax. *The Insidious Dr. Fu-Manchu.* New York, 1913.

Park, Robert. *Race and Culture.* Edited by Everett C. Hughes, et al. Glencoe, Ill., 1950.

Siu, Paul Chan Pang. *The Chinese Laundryman: A Study of Social Isolation.* Edited by John Kuo Wei Tchen. New York, 1987.

Secondary Sources

Asian Women United of California, eds. *Making Waves: An Anthology of Writings by and about Asian American Women.* Boston, 1989.

Chan, Sucheng. *Asian Americans: An Interpretive History.* Boston, 1991.

Daniels, Roger. *Asian America: Chinese and Japanese in the United States since 1850.* Seattle, Wash., 1988.

Espiritu, Yen. *Asian American Pan-Ethnicity.* Philadelphia, 1994.

Freeman, James. *Hearts of Sorrow: Vietnamese-American Lives.* Stanford, Calif., 1989.

Ichioka, Yuji. *Issei: The World of the First Generation Japanese Immigrants, 1885–1924.* New York, 1988.

Lee, Robert. *Orientals.* Philadelphia, 1998.

Lowe, Lisa. *Immigrant Acts.* Durham, N.C., 1996.

Moy, James S. *Marginal Sights: Staging the Chinese in America.* Iowa City, Iowa. 1993.

Okihiro, Gary. *Margins and Mainstreams.* Seattle, Wash., 1994.

Said, Edward. *Orientalism.* New York, 1978.

Takaki, Ronald. *Strangers from a Different Shore.* New York, 1989.

Tchen, John Kuo Wei. *New York before Chinatown: Orientalism and the Making of American Culture, 1776–1882.* Baltimore, 1999.

Welaratna, Usha. *Beyond the Killing Fields.* Stanford, Calif., 1993.

Yu, Henry. *Thinking Orientals: Migration, Contact and Exoticism in Modern America.* New York, 2000.

Yung, Judy. *Unbound Feet: A Social History of Chinese Women in San Francisco.* Berkeley and Los Angeles, 1995.

EVANGELICAL PROTESTANTS

D. G. Hart

On the surface, Jonathan Edwards and Henry Alline did not have much in common. Edwards, steeped in the doctrinal rigor of eighteenth-century New England Puritanism, was as gifted a theologian and philosopher as America has produced. Compared to Edwards, Alline, a Free Will Baptist who preached to poor and illiterate folk in Canada's Maritime Provinces and gained a reputation as Canada's George Whitefield, was like a shooting star, aflame with a radical message and charismatic demeanor. And yet, for all of their cultural and personal differences, Edwards and Alline had both experienced the work of divine grace. In fact, when each man wrote about that experience, the Ivy League–trained preacher and the backwoods itinerant used remarkably similar words.

For Edwards that experience came while he was an undergraduate at Yale College. After a bout with illness during which he questioned the authenticity of his faith as a boy, Edwards sensed the serenity and joy that would become the benchmark of evangelical piety. As he meditated particularly on the beauty of Jesus, Edwards wrote that he felt:

> a calm, sweet Abstraction of Soul from all the Concerns of this World; and a kind of Vision, or fix'd Ideas and Imaginations, of being alone in the Mountains, or some solitary Wilderness, far from all Mankind, sweetly conversing with Christ, and wrapt and swallowed up in GOD. The Sense I had of divine Things, would often of a sudden as it were, kindle up a sweet burning in my Heart; and ardor of my Soul, that I know not how to express. (Hopkins, *Life and Character*, p. 23)

Alline did not enjoy the benefits of a Yale education. Nor had he been steeped in the doctrinal precision of New England Calvinism. But at the age of twenty-seven, he underwent an experience very similar to Edwards's. Alline feared for his life and plummeted to the depths of morbid introspection, only to be lifted to the certainty of God's favor. As Alline described his own experience of the new birth:

> O the infinite condescension of God to a worm of the dust! for though my whole soul was filled with love, and ravished with divine ecstasy beyond any doubts or fears, or thoughts of being deceived, for I enjoyed a heaven on earth, and it seemed as if I were wrapped up in God. (Rawlyk, *Ravished by the Spirit*, p. 5)

For Edwards and Alline, the experience of divine grace that transformed tortured and sorrow-ridden souls into ones assured of God's love thanks to a direct tasting and touching of divine beauty and majesty was the centerpiece of true Christianity. In turn, the conversion experience became the defining mark of evangelicalism. And the enthusiasm and fervor that characterized genuine conversion shaped the intellectual pursuits and cultural expressions of evangelicals in the United States.

DOCTRINAL CONCEPTS OF EVANGELICALISM

Conversion Typically, historians have defined evangelicalism by its doctrinal affirmations. One common list includes: (1) the authority of Scripture; (2) the real historical character of miracles; (3) salvation through faith in Christ alone; (4) a commitment to evangelism and missions; and (5) a spiritually transformed life. Another set of doctrines includes a stress on the sacrifice of Christ upon the cross. But these definitions read late-twentieth-century developments back into the entire history of evangelicalism, thereby distorting the movement's basic impulse.

What makes better sense of evangelicalism throughout its history and across its varied expressions is the recognition of the centrality of religious enthusiasm and its implications for the lives of individuals and the ordering of society. Indeed, conversion helps to explain a number of evangelicalism's other features that are seemingly unrelated to the theological affirmations that supposedly define the movement. Most obviously, the intimacy and subjectivity of conversion makes evangelicalism individualistic in orientation. For this reason, corporate expressions of Christian faith, such as creeds, liturgy, or church government, matter much less than do the personal experiences of individuals. This individualism extends even to the hallowed evangelical institution of the family. Unlike historic Christian traditions that cultivate a sense of passing on the faith from one generation to another through means administered by the church, evangelicals put great stock in the power of individuals to choose their own religious identity. In fact, religious faith that is received on the basis of tradition is suspect.

Bound up with its inherently individualistic spirituality is evangelicalism's conception of God's dealings with men and women. Because conversion is the direct work of God upon the individual, evangelicals seek to eliminate any interference between the divine and the human. This hostility to mediation helps to account for evangelicalism's distrust of creeds, rites, or offices as human creations. Instead of recognizing the legitimacy of means, evangelicals typically regard the churchly aspects of Christianity as impediments to the free and sovereign operation of the spirit. Evangelical antiformalism takes its most prominent expression in anticlericalism and anticreedalism. But it also exalts the faith and experience of ordinary people. Thus, evangelicalism dissolves all religious hierarchies, giving equal weight to the catechized and uncatechized, the ordained and laity, the baptized and unbaptized.

A Transformed Life　One last aspect of evangelicalism that flows from the centrality of conversion is an eschatological vision of the Christian life that emphasizes holy living not just for individuals but also for society. Because the born-again experience results in a complete reorientation of the individual, believers naturally reflect their new identity in visible ways. Consequently, evangelicals look for evidence of conversion in a variety of behavioral norms. Sometimes these regulations may be as simple as the Ten Commandments. But more often evangelicalism's moral compass points away from any kind of activity deemed worldly.

But holy living is not simply for individuals. Evangelicals have historically been involved in a variety of efforts to reform society. To be sure, evangelical activism begins with the individual. But as much as evangelical piety might encourage an antiworldly attitude toward existing cultural norms, evangelicalism is still a world-affirming faith. For

this reason, the desire to see other people converted is never far from a wish for a more righteous social order. Sometimes conversion of individuals may sound like only a means toward the end of a moral society. But this stems from the close connection between conversion and holy living. Conversion is never simply a way to escape eternal damnation. It is also the first step toward a new way of life that will be marked by holiness, both for individuals and nations.

Because the conversion experience involves not only the direct intervention of God into the soul of the believer but also the filling of that soul with the presence of the Holy Spirit, evangelicals sometimes speak of perfection. So intimate and all consuming is the change wrought in conversion that evangelicals have often looked in this life for the sorts of blessings typically reserved for life after death when believers will be free from all temptation and sin. In other words, evangelicalism has nurtured millennial expectations about the kind of holiness that individuals and societies will exhibit. This is why evangelicals have been prone to various kinds of utopian schemes. Accompanying millennial hopes is disappointment if such dreams are unrealized. Evangelical piety, then, typically runs from the extreme of grand plans and expectations to despairing about the woeful state of society or the church.

Evangelicalism, then, is a form of Protestant Christianity that is not identifiable with one particular denomination. As Donald A. Mathews has argued, "evangelical" is most properly an adjective, instead of a noun, and is most appropriately associated with movement, innovation, and popular appeal (antistructure) than with institutions, organization and elites (structure) (Stout and Hart, *New Directions*, p. 103). Because of its innovative ways and populist appeal, evangelicalism has thrived in modern settings like the United States where churches have been disestablished and religion's success depends on popular support. Still, evangelicalism manifests specific characteristics that make it different from other forms of Christianity. Of overriding importance is the conversion experience. Without it an individual cannot be an evangelical, and from it stems the several notable strands of evangelical piety. The immediate and supernatural character of conversion makes evangelicals suspicious of all forms or institutions that presume to mediate salvation. Moreover, because of the change that conversion initiates, evangelicals expect converts to exhibit markedly holy ways of living that set them apart from the world and result in a better society. Bound up with this expectation for holiness

322

is a view of the history of salvation that sees the beginning of God's earthly reign, not in some distant time, but here and now in the routine activities of individuals, families, nations, and civilizations.

SEVENTEENTH- AND EIGHTEENTH-CENTURY ROOTS

Pietism and Puritanism The kind of piety that has become characteristic of American evangelicalism first surfaced in the seventeenth century among German pietists and English Puritans. In both instances, church leaders and laity, in reaction to a perceived formalism, ritualism, and rationalism in the state churches, touted the importance of the heart or will as the source of true religion. Puritanism was especially significant for religious developments in the North American British colonies. Unlike pietism, which opposed the theological formulations of the universities and their attendant corruption of prospective ministers, Puritanism combined theological rigor with a concern for heartfelt devotion. This combination of head and heart was particularly evident in the Puritans' scholarly analysis of the stages of conversion. Not only did Puritan theologians discuss at length the nuances of spiritual emotions, but pastors preached sermons that encouraged self-examination for the purpose of discerning emotional states that reflected the movement of the Holy Spirit. In early-eighteenth-century New England, Cotton Mather and Solomon Stoddard began to preach the terrors of the law and damnation to drive anxious hearers to Christ for salvation.

Revival and Awakening The combined influences of pietism and Puritanism came together vigorously during the period from 1729 to 1745, sometimes called the First Great Awakening. For the first decade, this early flowering of evangelical religion was primarily local. In the middle colonies, Theodore Jacobus Frelinghuysen, a Dutch Reformed minister in New Jersey, brought pietistic theology and practices to the New World. He not only deviated from Reformed liturgy in worship and preached sermons designed to lead to conversion, but Frelinghuysen also advocated standards for church membership that required the experience of the new birth. His message and methods spread to nearby Presbyterians through the work of the Tennent family, whose patriarch, William Tennent Sr., had established the Log College in Ne-

shaminy, Pennsylvania, to train ministers in evangelical ways, and whose most influential member, Gilbert Tennent, led revivals as a Presbyterian minister, first in New Jersey and later in Philadelphia.

A few years later, New England experienced a similar awakening through the ministry of Jonathan Edwards, the grandson of and successor to Solomon Stoddard in Northampton, Massachusetts. Here the conversionistic impulse within Puritanism was clearly evident as Edwards preached a series of sermons from 1734 to 1735 on the doctrine of justification, which reminded hearers of their need to convert. Edwards eventually interpreted Northampton's revival in *A Faithful Narrative of the Surprising Work of God* (1737), a work that featured the introspective piety of converts and their subsequent commitment to lead holy lives, and that provided inspiration and directions for future revivals. Edwards emerged as the most thoughtful interpreter of religious experience in works like *A Treatise Concerning Religious Affections* (1746), while at the same time making conversion, holy living, and the reform of civic life the signs of genuine Christianity, as well as the firstfruits of the millennium.

Evangelicalism became a transatlantic phenomenon with George Whitefield's arrival in 1739 to preach throughout the middle colonies. A graduate of Oxford University and ordained priest in the Church of England, Whitefield had already participated in revivals in Great Britain. In North America he achieved celebrity status through sermons on sin, hell, the atonement, and assurance; a manner of speech that abandoned technical language for vivid and colloquial expressions; and methods that took advantage of newly emerging forms of publicity and commerce. The overall effect of his first tour in America was to consolidate the various local expressions of evangelical zeal and preaching into a movement that was identifiably different from the existing forms of Protestant Christianity.

Signs of that difference were evident during Whitefield's tour. The evangelist became a litmus test among various groups of Protestants. For instance, among Presbyterians in the middle colonies, Whitefield's preaching precipitated a controversy that had been festering for two decades, resulting in a split from 1741 to 1758 between pro- and anti-revival parties (New and Old Side Presbyterians, respectively). In New England, similar divisions occurred, especially with the Standing Order of Congregationalist churches, with Old Lights opposing evangelicalism for subverting the authority of established clergy and undermining the reasonable nature of genuine piety. New Lights, like Edwards, however, supported the revivals, though he also denounced their radical elements.

In both cases, evangelicalism did not start a new church but instead was a leaven within an existing communion. Time eventually healed these divisions so that evangelicalism and its revivalistic piety became a respectable part of American Protestantism. Instead of being perceived as a threat to particular denominations, evangelicalism emerged as the way to be a more devout Presbyterian, Congregationalist, or Episcopalian. As such, historic Protestant traditions that were more formal or liturgical, accommodated the individualism, antiformalism, and enthusiasm of evangelicalism. The legacy of this accommodation has been a tension, played out in various denominational settings, between the zeal of evangelical religious life and the traditionalism required for institutional stability and order.

THE METHODIST AGE OF
AMERICAN CHRISTIANITY

Groups that benefited from the 1740s revivals generally experienced a phase of institutionalization afterward so that evangelical fervor died down in the decades before the Revolutionary War. Baptists, however, who had assisted the revivals in New England, took the evangelical message to the South and during the 1750s established churches in Virginia and North Carolina. Methodists did not become a denomination until 1784, but through the local societies and system of itinerant ministers they established churches in the latter half of the eighteenth century, especially in the western parts of the South. In fact, the newly settled environment of the southern frontier would prove to be a hotbed for the religious zeal upon which evangelicalism thrived, the 1801 camp meeting of Cain Ridge, Kentucky, being one of the best examples of evangelicalism's conversionist fervor. There evangelical Methodists, Baptists, and Presbyterians came together to lead a revival of unprecedented size with even more spectacular forms of religious fervor (including swooning, barking, dancing, and laughing).

Revival and Religious Disestablishment Because evangelicalism resisted conformity to churchly forms, and because of its populist appeal, historians have sometimes speculated on the links between revivalism and the American Revolution. To be sure, certain similarities appear to unite the religious and political upheavals of the British colonies in North America. Aside from undermining patterns of re-

ligious deference, encouraging an individualistic piety, and promoting greater lay participation in church life, evangelicalism also affected the Revolution in more direct ways. Puritanism's opposition to religious tyranny proved a ready ally to Whig political ideology which rejected all forms of centralized authority. Evangelicalism also bred suspicion of the Church of England and all efforts to expand its influence. What is more, evangelicalism's heightened millennialism readily fed dissenting Protestant fears about foreign conspiracies and fostered Manichaean conceptions of America's righteous cause against the satanic ways of England. Nevertheless, evangelicalism was not solely responsible for the rise of revolutionary sentiments that emerged from nonreligious sources as well, and was not evident in all evangelicals.

No matter what the connection between revivalism and revolution, the social environment of the new nation was particularly conducive to evangelicalism. What was especially important for evangelical success was religious disestablishment. Its result was deregulation of the religious world and the consequences were far reaching. Churches that had previously been assigned parishioners in a particular locale were now forced to compete for adherents. The separation of church and state, in effect, engendered a religious market. Churches looking for ways to appeal to individuals logically looked to evangelical techniques, which offered a direct and ardent faith.

In this setting the churches that grew fastest, Baptists and Methodists, were the ones least encumbered by tradition and learning and most open to revivals. For instance, Congregationalists and Presbyterians at the time of the American Revolution accounted for approximately 40 percent of religious adherents in the United States (20 and 19 percent, respectively), while Baptists and Methodists were only half the size in 1776 (17 and 3 percent, respectively). But after religious disestablishment, Methodists and Baptists put a great statistical distance between themselves and other Protestant denominations. By 1850 Methodists were the largest denomination, accounting for 34 percent of American Protestants, and Baptists were second with 20 percent. In contrast, Congregationalists were down to 4 percent and Presbyterians to 12 percent. Lots of factors go into explaining these changes. But the antiformalist ways and individualistic faith of evangelicalism were significant factors.

Revival and Reform As these statistics indicate, evangelicalism not only altered the denominational landscape of the new nation but also offered a conception of the relationship between faith and society that had far-reaching consequences. Because genuine conversion naturally led to holy living, nineteenth-century evangelicals sponsored a host of social reforms that indelibly stamped the United States and provided much of the organization necessary for social order. Commonly referred to as the "Benevolent Empire," evangelicals founded an array of voluntary societies, the task of which was to purge America of sinful behavior and establish a righteous society. To be sure, many of these societies were explicitly religious in character, such as the American Bible Society (1816), the American Tract Society (1825), and the American Board of Commissioners for Foreign Missions (1810), an agency that extended evangelical influence beyond the United States. But many of these voluntary societies were explicitly social in purpose, such as the American Colonization Society (1817), the American Society for the Promotion of Temperance (1826), and the American Sunday School Union (1824), in addition to numerous other efforts devoted to women's rights, penal reform, antislavery, sabbath observance, and antismoking.

The moral imperatives synonymous with evangelicalism always tamed the radical egalitarian side of the new birth and over time would give the movement a high degree of respectability. For this reason, although Presbyterians and Congregationalists led in the establishment of the Benevolent Empire, Baptists and Methodists were quick to follow. One of the best examples of evangelical respectability came in the nineteenth century with the proliferation of denominational colleges. Here the moral rigor of evangelical piety received curricular embodiment in the senior-year course in moral philosophy, usually taught by the college president, which integrated the undergraduate course of study into a devout and practical whole. The importance of education was not simply a concern of the older Protestant denominations such as the Congregationalists and Presbyterians, but it also beckoned Baptists and Methodists to found their own institutions that provided a similar course of instruction that would impart Christian truths about all of life and train the next generation of social leaders.

But the greatest of all evangelical efforts in social reform came in the sectional controversy that led to the Civil War. To be sure, a variety of political and economic issues played into the conflict between North and South. But the moral implications of slavery were also crucial and very much stemmed from the success of evangelicalism. Especially in the North, revivalism unleashed in the 1830s an aggressive campaign that concluded slavery was sinful and that the United States could not advance the kingdom of God if it condoned the evil institution. Evangelicalism also fed discontentment with efforts to reform slavery gradually. Revivalists insisted that slaves be freed as immediately as individuals decided to follow Christ and as quickly as believers exhibited holy living. What is more, in the fifteen years before the Civil War slavery divided Baptists, Methodists, and Presbyterians into northern and southern branches, divisions that set into motion the secession of the South from the Union. Not all evangelicals opposed slavery. Southern evangelicals especially went from ambivalence to an outright defense of the institution as necessary to domestic tranquility and social order. But evangelicalism was such an important factor in the conflict that it is possible to speak of the Civil War as the last chapter in the Second Great Awakening.

EVANGELICALISM SHAKEN

Modernists and Fundamentalists Ironically, a war that many evangelicals regarded as a victory for the forces of righteousness also turned out to be a threat to evangelical success. The war effort unleashed a variety of political and economic forces that transformed the United States from a country dominated by republican virtue and small-town Christian morality into a large centralized and secular nation. The war spurred new industries, which in turn increased the size of cities as workers migrated from farms and other countries to take new jobs, which in turn generated greater concern for economic and political efficiency in large bureaucratic organizations. In the face of these profound changes, evangelicalism did not so much become marginal as lose some of its luster. Some Protestants were particularly concerned that evangelicalism's individualistic ethic did not offer spiritual resources for the new urban-industrial order. This prompted the largest Protestant denominations to establish denominational agencies and interdenominational institutions to work for greater social harmony and goodwill throughout all phases of American life, but especially between labor and capital. The most important and visible institution was the Federal Council of Churches (renamed the National Council of Churches in 1950), established in 1908.

Other Protestants, who adhered more closely to the revivalist tradition of evangelicalism, became critical of such social endeavors, not so much because they disagreed with the policies, but because they conceived the gospel in individualistic rather than corporate categories. This tension within mainstream Protestantism was largely responsible for the Fundamentalist-modernist controversy of the 1920s. Fundamentalists and modernists quarreled within America's largest Protestant denominations over a variety of matters, but their debates mainly revolved around whether genuine Christianity involved the conversion of individuals or the redemption of society. Fundamentalists came down on the side of the former and accused modernists of abandoning the gospel. In keeping with their individualistic theology, Fundamentalists eventually lost the battle for the denominations. The mainstream Protestant churches emerged from the 1920s and 1930s committed to a form of social Christianity that presupposed America's Protestant cultural identity. Fundamentalists in turn kept alive the revivalist tradition and thrived in a religious subculture that made soul-winning, both in America and around the world, the essence of biblical faith.

Urban Parachurch Revivalism In some respects, Fundamentalist losses within the denominational conflicts of the 1920s was a foregone conclusion, not only because of evangelicalism's discomfort with institutional expressions of Christianity but also because of the way that the evangelical movement took shape after the Civil War. Beginning with Dwight L. Moody, evangelicalism found an organizational home outside the Protestant denominations. Until Moody, evangelicalism existed within the churches and depended on the clergy's support. But with Moody parachurch evangelicalism took on a momentum of its own. He was a successful Chicago businessman who gave up sales for salvation in the 1860s. His revivals, in fact, turned into a big business, attracting crowds in urban centers greater than the capacity of the largest churches, and relying upon an organization that planned and executed Moody's campaigns. To be sure, he received the approval of the largest Protestant denominations. But his genius was to bring the message of individual conversion and holy living to a rapidly urbanizing environment, free from the red tape of church bureaucracies.

Moody set the pattern for twentieth-century evangelicalism. Billy Sunday, like Moody, achieved success outside religious work, in his case as a professional baseball player. But after his conversion in 1887, Sunday gave up the big leagues for big crowds who would come forward at the end of his speaking and shake the revivalist's hand, a gesture that indicated the convert's decision to follow Jesus. Sunday started his evangelic work in smaller towns throughout the Northeast and northern Midwest, but by the 1910s started a series of engagements in America's largest cities. In the process, he received the endorsement of church leaders, businessmen, and politicians. Sunday was technically ordained by the northern Presbyterian Church (PCUSA) as an evangelist. But his Presbyterian credentials were peripheral to his message, organization, and fame.

The greatest example of twentieth-century evangelicalism is Billy (William Franklin) Graham, who adapted the simple call for conversion and the organizational techniques of urban revivalism to build a large parachurch ministry, the Billy Graham Evangelistic Association, which promotes evangelicalism not simply through revivals but also through an array of media that include weekly radio broadcasts, television shows, and even feature films. After graduating from Wheaton College in 1943, Graham worked as a pastor and Bible college president. He made his mark in 1949 with the Los Angeles crusade where the newspaper publisher, William Randolph Hearst, instructed his correspondents to "puff" the youthful and handsome evangelist, thanks largely to Graham's anticommunist stance. Hearst's publicity fanned the Los Angeles revivals, and news of Graham's success spread. It also followed him as he continued to speak to large crowds in major metropolitan areas throughout the 1950s. His persistence and the simplicity of his message, combined with his obvious integrity and the savvy instincts of his handlers, made Graham a religious hero. More than four decades later, opinion polls continued to rate him as America's most respected man.

Early on in his career, Graham was closely associated with the neo-evangelical movement, a wing of fundamentalism that craved less belligerency and greater engagement with American society. Crucial to the neo-evangelical outlook was an aversion to fundamentalists' complete disavowal of the mainline Protestant denominations as liberal. Neo-evangelicals conceded that the mainline churches did harbor theological liberalism, but they would not refuse to work with American Protestant leaders to spread the evangelical faith. Graham was especially important to the neo-evangelical strategy. In 1957 at the New York City crusade, Graham invited mainline congregations to cosponsor his meetings, at which point he lost the support of fundamentalist leaders. By cooperating with the Protestant mainstream, Graham culminated evangelicalism's his-

Billy Graham at Madison Square Garden, 1970. More than 20,000 people attended Graham's revival meeting, the first of a series held throughout the country in 1970. © BETTMANN/CORBIS

toric effort to transcend formal differences (whether ecclesiastical or creedal) and make the gospel bigger than any particular strand of the Protestant church. Graham also singlehandedly solidified the link between evangelicalism and the religious sensibilities and pragmatic instincts of parachurch revivalism. Prior to World War II all Trinitarian Protestants spoke of themselves as evangelical, in the sense of the sixteenth-century Protestant Reformation's recovery of the gospel (or *evangelion,* in Greek). But thanks to Graham's high visibility and remarkably lengthy tenure, evangelicalism now refers narrowly to Christians who believe that a personal decision for Christ and moral living, not creed, church membership, or sacraments, are essential to genuine Christian faith. For that reason, even though evangelicals lost the battle for the Protestant denominations earlier in the twentieth century, they wound up winning the war for the soul of popular American religion by following the methods and appeal honed by urban revivalists such as Moody, Sunday, and Graham.

EVANGELICALISM AND POPULAR AMERICAN RELIGION

The results of public opinion polls in the United States and Canada consistently demonstrate evangelicalism's triumphant resurgence since World War II. At the same time that denominational statistics indicate decline in church membership, answers to pollsters show the pervasiveness of evangelical beliefs and attitudes. Some estimate the number of evangelicals in the United States to be as high as 38 million. Others put the figure more around 20 million. But with Presbyterians representing only about 3 million church members, Lutherans accounting for roughly 8 million, and Southern Baptists—America's largest Protestant denomination—comprising 15 million, clearly evangelicalism is a force in America's religious life. What is more, the questions that social scientists typically ask about religious identity reflect the degree to which evangelicalism has shaped perceptions about religion in the United States. Instead of questions about the two natures of Christ, the three persons of the Trinity,

327

the number of sacraments, or the authority of church officers, pollsters regularly ask about the inerrancy of the Bible, the goodness of human nature, and personal commitment to Jesus Christ. However much opinion polls might favor the kind of answers evangelicals would be inclined to give, the surveys continually show the United States to be a place where religion matters far more than in any other Western democracy, contrary to conventional wisdom about the effects of modernization on religion. Explanations for America's unusual religiosity typically point to evangelicalism's populist appeal, the downside of which is that the movement has little influence upon government, universities, the arts, and the mainline churches.

Whatever the explanation for America's religious vitality, evangelicalism has clearly left a mark upon the United States. According to the sociologist of religion David Martin, evangelical forms of religion go a long way toward explaining the character of American culture. While English culture stresses formality and privacy, the United States cultivates sincerity and openness. According to Martin, enthusiasm "of all kinds" became endemic in America but in England was little more than a mild curiosity.

These differences can be attributed to the success of evangelicalism, combined with the social arrangements that have given the movement such freedom to develop and evolve (*Tongues of Fire*, p. 21). From a different discipline comes a similar assessment. The literary critic Harold Bloom has argued that evangelicalism is virtually synonymous with American religion. "Revivalism," he wrote, "tends to be the perpetual shock of the individual discovering yet again what she and he always have known, which is that God loves her and him on an absolutely personal and indeed intimate basis" (*The American Religion*, p. 17).

The experience of which Bloom writes may be a long way from what Jonathan Edwards or Henry Alline thought they were describing when they wrote about their own experiences. But whatever Edwards and Alline intended by their preaching and counsel, or thought about what God was up to in the revivals they promoted, the intimate conversions they experienced have after almost three centuries of development set the standard for religious life in America. Whether evangelicalism's popularity stems from the genius of the movement or the nature of American institutions, its pervasiveness is a reality that cannot be denied.

See also **Anglo-American Religious Traditions; The New England Theology from Edwards to Bushnell; The Transformation of American Religion, 1776–1838; Evangelical Thought** *(volume 1);* **Organized Religion; Hermeneutics and American Historiography** *(volume 3).*

BIBLIOGRAPHY

Bebbington, David. *Evangelicalism in Modern Britain: A History from the 1730s to the 1980s.* Grand Rapids, Mich., 1989.

Bloom, Harold. *The American Religion: The Emergence of the Post-Christian Nation.* New York, 1992.

Butler, Jon. *Awash in a Sea of Faith: Christianizing the American People.* Cambridge, Mass., 1990.

Carwardine, Richard J. *Evangelicals and Politics in Antebellum America.* New Haven, Conn., 1993.

Carpenter, Joel A. *Revive Us Again: The Reawakening of American Fundamentalism.* New York, 1997.

Hatch, Nathan O. *The Democratization of American Christianity.* New Haven, Conn., 1989.

Hatch, Nathan O., and Harry S. Stout, eds. *Jonathan Edwards and the American Experience.* New York, 1988.

Heyrman, Christine Leigh. *Southern Cross: The Beginnings of the Bible Belt.* New York, 1997.

Hopkins, Samuel. *The Life and Character of the Late, Reverend, Learned, and Pious Mr. Jonathan Edwards.* Boston, 1765.

Lambert, Frank. *"Pedlar in Divinity": George Whitefield and the Transatlantic Revivals.* Princeton, N.J., 1994.

Marsden, George. *Fundamentalism and American Culture: The Shaping of Twentieth-Century Evangelicalism, 1870–1925.* New York, 1980.

Marsden, George, ed. *Evangelicalism and Modern America.* Grand Rapids, Mich., 1984.

Martin, David. *Tongues of Fire: The Explosion of Protestantism in Latin America.* Cambridge, Mass., 1990.

Martin, William. *A Prophet with Honor: The Billy Graham Story.* New York, 1991.

Noll, Mark A., David W. Bebbington, and George A. Rawlyk, eds. *Evangelicalism: Comparative Studies of Popular Protestantism in North America, the British Isles, and Beyond, 1700–1900.* New York, 1994.

Rawlyk, G. A. *Ravished by the Spirit: Religious Revivals, Baptists, and Henry Alline.* Kingston and Montreal, Canada, 1984.

Schmidt, Leigh Eric. *Holy Fairs: Scottish Communions and American Revivals in the Early Modern Period.* Princeton, N.J., 1989.

Smith, Christian. *American Evangelicalism: Embattled and Thriving.* Chicago, 1998.

Smith, Timothy L. *Revivalism and Social Reform: American Protestantism on the Eve of the Civil War.* Baltimore, 1980.

Stout, Harry S. *The Divine Dramatist: George Whitefield and the Rise of Modern Evangelicalism.* Grand Rapids, Mich., 1991.

Stout, Harry S., and D. G. Hart, eds. *New Directions in American Religious History.* New York, 1997.

Sweet, Leonard I., ed. *The Evangelical Tradition in America.* Macon, Ga., 1984.

GAYS AND LESBIANS

Susan E. Myers-Shirk

People have engaged in sexual relations with partners of the same sex since the beginning of recorded history (and probably before that, too). But prior to about the middle of the nineteenth century, few of those who did so would have seen their choice of sexual partner as a marker of identity. Sex was something they did, not something they were. Even the church and the courts saw same-sex relations as one sin among many, not something special to be singled out. Thus, in colonial America, where legal and religious concerns revolved around procreation, sodomy was defined as any nonprocreative behavior and was punished with equal enthusiasm whether the perpetrators were of the same or different sex.

Sometime after the Civil War, however, the meaning of same-sex relations changed. The change was fueled by medical discourse and the emergence of a community of individuals who engaged in same-sex relations, preferred the company of same-sex partners, and who referred to themselves by a variety of terms including homosexual, invert, fairy, queer, gay, or lesbian. It was in this context that the idea arose that individual identity derived from sexual behavior and sexual desires. It was a distinctly modern idea with wide-ranging implications. This essay illustrates the way in which the concept of sexual identity sustained the growth of a gay and lesbian community in the twentieth-century United States.

A WORD ABOUT WORDS

In the colonial and Early Republic periods, those who engaged in same-sex relations were described legally in terms of their actions. Thus, charges were brought against "the sodomite" or "the adulterer" or "the fornicator." In the mid- to late nineteenth century, new terms emerged. Within the intellectual community, medical and academic researchers who concerned themselves with the study of sex (called

sexologists) used terms such as "homosexual" or "invert" to classify these groups in a larger class of what those same doctors called "perverts" and "degenerates." Within the community of individuals who engaged in same-sex relations, the terms were quite different, sometimes varying by region. In turn-of-the-century New York City, the term "fairy" was used to refer to effeminate men who pursued same-sex relations and "queer" was used to refer to any person, regardless of gender characteristics, who preferred same-sex relations. There were also a whole range of terms used to refer to men who engaged alternately in both same-sex and different-sex relations. Eventually "gay" replaced queer, especially among men, and the term "lesbian" became more common for women. In fact, the terms "gay" and "lesbian" did not come into common usage until the 1930s and 1940s. When those words appeared they did so with a fairly specific meaning. Eventually, they were used to identify those who engaged exclusively in same-sex relations.

So do historians and scholars begin their discussion of gays and lesbians at the historical moment in which those two words appeared? Most historians have not. Instead, they have begun much earlier and have explored a much broader spectrum of same-sex love and sexuality. The history of same-sex love and sexuality has included individuals who organized their affectional lives around the same sex but who did not self-identify as lesbian or, as far as it is recorded, engage in sexual activity. In her 1999 survey of same-sex love and sexuality, historian Leila Rupp described the lives of a number of middle-class, educated, white women who, in the late nineteenth century, participated in long-term, committed relationships with other women but resisted seeing themselves as lesbians. The history of gays and lesbians has also included individuals who have engaged in same-sex sexual activity but who have not self-identified as gay or lesbian. Scholars Elizabeth Kennedy and Madeline Davis, in their study of Buffalo, New York, in the mid-twentieth century, demonstrated that some women spent part of their lives with female partners, moved out of the community to live with male partners and bear children, and eventually returned to same-sex partnerships. Still others sustained same-sex and different-sex relationship simultaneously.

This article follows the pattern of other scholars who include the broader spectrum of same-sex love and sexuality in their discussions of gay and lesbian history. Hence, it addresses in particular the emergence of a community of people who organized their affectional and sexual lives almost exclusively around the same sex and who self-identified first as fairies and queers, or even inverts, and later as gays and lesbians. But it also explores the lives of those individuals who, at some point in their lives, may have organized either their affectional lives or their sexual lives around the same sex but who did not self-identify as queer or gay. Thus, in the context of this article, the term "gay people" or "gays and lesbians" refers to a subculture of individuals who self-identified as such in the larger world of same-sex love and sexuality.

NINETEENTH-CENTURY GENDER IDEALS AND THE SEXOLOGISTS

The way that sexologists interpreted same-sex love and sexuality derived directly from their views on gender. In nineteenth-century thought about sexuality, gender and sexuality were conflated. That is, individuals with female organs were expected to behave within certain prescribed parameters. In general, they were characterized as passive, naturally domestic, given to emotion (rather than intellect), and morally superior to men as a result of their supposedly greater ability to control their sexual desires. Men, in contrast, were characterized as aggressive, naturally given to pursuits outside the home, rational creatures but morally disadvantaged because of their strong—and sometimes barely controlled—sexual desires. Because most sexologists assumed such a direct connection between sexual organs and gender behavior, their explanation for the behavior of those who engaged in same-sex relations or sexually desired a member of the same sex featured gender transgression as a key element.

One such explanation that held sway in the late nineteenth and early twentieth centuries was "sexual inversion," a term first used in English by the medical doctor and sex reformer Havelock Ellis. In this theory, the sexual invert inverted the so-called natural desire of man for woman and woman for man. Because of what most sexologists believed about the link between gender and sex, they assumed that inverts adopted the gender characteristics of the opposite sex as well as its object of desire. Hence, the male invert assumed feminine characteristics and desired men, while the female inverts took on masculine characteristics and desired women.

Whether sexologists used the term sexual inversion, contrary sexual instinct, or homosexual, many shared the assumption that homosexuals were deviant, diseased, pathological, or abnormal because they challenged gender ideals. German psychiatrist Richard von Krafft-Ebing viewed homosexuality as a modern disease of the nervous system that spawned a downward spiral of degeneracy and immorality. Some doctors, such as Havelock Ellis, resisted the idea that homosexuality was a vice, arguing instead that homosexuality resulted from a "congenital predisposition" and deserved tolerance and sympathy. On the whole, however, Ellis resorted to the same sort of language of pathology as his colleagues did.

Most early sexologists assumed, too, that homosexuality was constitutional and that homosexuals were born rather than made. Sigmund Freud, a Viennese doctor who originated the theory and practice of psychoanalysis, was among the first to offer a psychogenic explanation for same-sex love and sexuality. Two of Freud's theories exercised a particular influence on how Americans viewed homosexuality. First, Freud saw homosexuality as a stage in normal childhood development and as one among many possible perversions of adult sexuality. As a result, his theory was used to interpret homosexuality as arrested development and to suggest that only mature (or normal) sexuality was heterosexual. Freud was also the first to seriously challenge the unquestioned link between sex and gender characteristics. Freud suggested that sexual desire should really be understood in terms of aim and object. That is, the aim of the individual's desire might be to play the passive role or to engage in anal sex while the object of desire could be either male or female. Sexologists who promoted a theory of sexual inversion did not distinguish between aim and object. Hence they theorized that the individual whose object of desire was a member of the same sex had a corresponding sexual aim. Men could only desire men if one played the passive role (feminine) and the other played the active (masculine). In this theory, the true invert was the man who played the feminine role. Freud's theory, by dividing aim and object, helped to explain the existence of men who engaged in same-sex relations but did not exhibit feminine characteristics. Interestingly, Freud resisted the division of aim and object in his discussion of female homosexuals and persisted in the language of inversion.

If much of the medical discourse was intended to explain, classify, and control the behavior of sexual inverts, it ended up serving other purposes. Gays and lesbians participated in shaping medical discourse and made use of it for their own ends. For one thing, homosexuals played a key role in defining homosexuality. In the 1860s the German lawyer Karl Heinrich Ulrichs offered one of the first scientific theories of homosexuality and the German-Hungarian writer Karoly Maria Benkert coined the word "homosexuality." In the face of sexological theories that conceptualized homosexuality as pathology, German physician and reformer Magnus Hirschfeld portrayed the phenomenon as a "benign variation" in sexual behavior. Each of these men was attempting to provide a rationale for homosexuality as a defense against increasingly restrictive laws in Europe, but their contributions had important implications for the American understanding of homosexuality.

THE WORLD OF SAME-SEX LOVE AND SEXUALITY, 1890–1940

It would be a mistake to say that sexologists, sympathetic or otherwise, somehow "invented" homosexuality. It is more accurate to see them as engaged in describing a phenomenon that was increasingly visible as the century wore on. A visible gay community had begun to appear as early as the 1880s in some urban areas, particularly in the red light and furnished room districts. In fact, society's liminal spaces provided a place for homosexuals to find one another. Places such as transvestite clubs, waterfront areas, boardinghouses, and the Young Men's Christian Association (YMCA) permitted a way of life that small-town America would not tolerate. It is important to note, however, that differences in gender ideals for men and women shaped the experience of same-sex love and sexuality. Members of this community understood themselves in terms of conventional gender ideals similar to those promoted by sexologists. Additionally, in the early twentieth century, gender determined one's access to public space. As a result, the trajectories of the gay and lesbian community were somewhat different and, hence, must be explored separately.

FAIRIES, QUEERS, AND TRADE

Quite simply, both middle- and working-class men had greater access to public space and so their community emerged in this public context. Historian George Chauncey showed the extent to which the gay community followed the contours of working-class culture in New York City and has suggested that middle-class men had easy access to this same space. "Fairies," men who exhibited some of the gender characteristics usually associated with women, were the most visible, although not the only, members of these communities. In the 1920s, places such as New York City's Greenwich Village and Harlem provided a space where homosexuals could congregate with relative impunity.

Young men new to New York frequently found housing, upon arrival in the city, at places such as the YMCA. Middle-class reformers originally established the YMCA as an inexpensive alternative to the boarding- and flophouses. Reformers wanted to create a space that would preserve a high moral tone for young men living on their own. The Seamen's Institute was established for similar reasons. Ultimately, however, both the YMCA and the Seamen's Institute became centers of gay community and allowed young men to find their way into the male gay world of New York. Gay men congregated in the speakeasies and clubs of the Village and Harlem, at the cafeterias and automats, and in the bathhouses that catered specifically to a same-sex clientele. The proprietors of the bathhouses had originally proposed to provide a service to working-class people who did not have access to bathing facilities in their homes, but the baths quickly became a popular gathering spot for gay men.

Prior to the 1930s the boundaries of the gay world were permeable. First, men who did not consider themselves gay or queer frequented the areas such as the Bowery, the Village, and Harlem and engaged in sexual relations with other men. The most telling example of this kind of relationship is the story of Loop-the-loop, a well-known Bowery fairy who was in a long-term relationship with a man whom Loop-the-loop referred to as his husband and who did not consider himself gay or queer. Up until about the 1930s a remarkable number of men, primarily working class but also some of the middle class, engaged in same-sex relations and did not consider themselves queer as long as they played the masculine or insertive role. This way of thinking resulted from the emphasis on gender characteristics rather than sexual object choice. There was even a word for these men in New York

City; at one point, they were known as "trade." Although the meaning of the word changed over time and in different contexts, it referred generally to a "straight" man who would accept the advances of the fairies or queers.

Another factor that gave the impression of a world with permeable boundaries was the presence of both men and women of the middle class who frequented Village and Harlem clubs in search of excitement and a vicarious thrill. They called it "slumming," but whatever they called it, it resulted in a mix of gay and straight, middle and working class, and, in Harlem, black and white. The most spectacular example of this interaction was the Hamilton Lodge Drag Ball that attracted contestants from all ethnic and racial groups and drew mixed crowds of up to nine thousand.

The social and cultural anxiety precipitated by the economic crisis of the 1930s led to a crackdown on the gay community and considerably reduced its visibility. Reformers who were concerned that the end of Prohibition would mean a return to the pre-Prohibition days of saloons moved to establish state regulation of both the sale of alcohol and the public spaces where alcohol was sold. Attempts to create what these reformers saw as "orderly" spaces (as opposed to the disorderly saloons of an earlier era and the completely unregulated clubs and speakeasies of the 1920s) provided the rationale for the removal of gay patrons from bars and clubs. Any gay man who was visibly so was subject to arrest for "disorderly conduct." Club and bar owners who permitted the presence of these gay men risked prosecution and even being forced out of business. Gay men, in turn, were forced to maintain a less visible presence in these public spaces, as they did, for instance, at the famous Astor Hotel, or to socialize in private parties. For middle-class men, opera and dance performances provided opportunities to socialize. Likewise, some clubs continued to cater to gay patrons exclusively, but those clubs inevitably were short lived under the new laws.

The film and theater industry witnessed a similar effort to make gays and lesbians less visible. As early as 1927 the New York State legislature passed the Padlock Law prohibiting the portrayal on stage of sexual perversion or degeneracy, partly in response to the high-profile play *The Captive*. The play frankly portrayed a lesbian relationship and drew large audiences. In the 1930s Hollywood followed suit. At the beginning of the decade, fearing censorship from outside, the studios adopted a production code intended to allow them to self-regulate. The code prohibited the portrayal of so-called im-

moral behavior unless it was portrayed as wrong and prohibited absolutely the portrayal of homosexuality. In 1934, again fearing censorship, Hollywood studios established the Production Code Administration to enforce the terms of the code.

ROMANTIC FRIENDSHIPS, BULLDAGGERS, BUTCHES, AND FEMS

Women's experience in the years between 1880 and 1940 differed significantly from men's. And among women, class and race also made a significant difference in experience. When sexologists first began to think about the nature of inversion among women, they looked first to the working class. They did so to a large extent because it was there that they found the examples that best fit their understanding of inversion. For instance, working-class women were more likely to dress and attempt to pass as a man. They had good economic reasons for doing so. For the most part, women earned significantly less than men and it was virtually impossible to support themselves on those wages. Women who passed did so because it was to their economic and social advantage, and some women said so explicitly. Ralph Kerwinieo, a Native American woman who passed for years as a man, framed his choice in these terms:

> This world is made by man—for man alone.... In the future centuries it is probable that woman will be the owner of her own body and the custodian of her own soul. But until that time you can expect that the statutes [concerning] women will be all wrong. The well-cared for woman is a parasite, and the woman who must work is a slave.... Do you blame me for wanting to be a man—free to live as a man in a manmade world? Do you blame me for hating to again resume woman's clothes? (Faderman, *Odd Girls and Twilight Lovers,* p. 44)

These women belong in a discussion of sexual inversion, but do they belong in a discussion of same-sex love and sexuality? The answer for some of these women is yes. Some women who passed as men took other women as lifelong partners, while others took the road of gender transgression as a means to earn more money, fight in wars, move about the country freely, and receive the respect and admiration typically reserved for men.

For most working-class women the opportunity to pursue same-sex relations occurred in an urban setting and most typically in the red light and furnished room districts of those cities. Once again economics were a key factor. Even the wages of two women was seldom sufficient to support both. Frequently, one of the women sold her services as a prostitute while maintaining a relationship with, and many times supporting, a female partner. Some historians have suggested that women found an intimacy and nurturing environment with other women that served as an antidote to their relationships with men.

In the gay male world working and middle classes intermingled. But because of Victorian gender ideals, women of different classes were much less likely to associate with one another. Because of Victorian gender ideology, middle-class women who consorted with working-class women and frequented forbidden public spaces—other than in the context of reform work—risked their reputation. As a result, middle-class women's experience of same-sex love and sexuality differed significantly.

For middle-class women same-sex bonds were forged as they pursued higher education and reform work together. Same-sex emotional intimacy or "romantic friendships" were encouraged in the eighteenth and early to mid-nineteenth centuries. The ideology of separate spheres in which women were perceived as governing the domestic sphere and men the public fostered two distinct same-sex cultures. Ultimately, some of these young women pursued higher education at the elite eastern women's colleges and there formed even more intense relationships. A wealth of letters, diaries, and school newspapers confirm that "smashing" and "crushes" among the girls were relatively common and openly acknowledged, as upperclasswomen pursued and won the affection of first-year girls. Some of these women pursued professional careers; others, such as Jane Addams, took their family fortunes and entered into reform work with the poor and working classes. Most believed they could not marry and pursue a career, but they did not hesitate to form long-term committed relationships with other women that mirrored different-sex marriages and were commonly known as Boston marriages because of their prevalence in that community.

Historians have struggled with the question of whether these relationships can properly be understood as lesbian, as that term is currently used. To answer that question, they have tried to determine the extent to which the love of these women for each other found genital expression, but the record, as might be expected, is difficult to decipher. What is true is that most of these women, even when they engaged in sexual or erotic behavior, did not necessarily perceive themselves as lesbian and felt constrained to defend themselves as the literature of sexology became more available to the average reader. For instance, the writer Mary Casal in her autobiography indicated that she and her longtime partner, Juno, had engaged in "sexual intercourse," but Casal did not consider herself or her partner lesbian because they did not engage in sexual relations frequently. Like the sexologists, Casal associated hypersexuality (a distinctly masculine characteristic) with true inversion. Since she did not perceive herself or Juno as hypersexual or masculine, she concluded they could not be lesbians. Other women who had enjoyed long, happy Boston marriages felt constrained to take an aggressively antilesbian stance.

While romantic friendships and Boston marriages probably do not belong in a discussion of lesbianism (with that term understood in its contemporary sense), they do belong in a discussion of same-sex love and sexuality. A consciously lesbian culture among middle-class women first appeared in the context of New York's Greenwich Village with its nascent bohemian culture. Here women were encouraged to "experiment" with their sexuality. One group in particular linked their experimentation with a feminist sensibility. The Heterodoxy Club organized by the suffrage leader and minister Marie Jenney Howe included many prominent feminists and reformers of the time who broached a significant challenge to the Victorian ideal of marriage. When sexologists finally discovered the female invert among middle-class women, they linked inversion to feminism claiming that it fueled a desire to be masculine and to claim the objects of masculine desire.

Lesbian culture also thrived in Harlem during the 1920s. A significant number of prominent female blues singers openly engaged in same-sex (and different-sex) relations. Ma Rainey, Bessie Smith, and Alberta Hunter even sang about the delights of same-sex love. In Harlem the term "bulldagger" (also "bulldiker") was used to refer to the mannish woman who preferred the company of other women. The relative tolerance of gay and lesbian life in Harlem even permitted the occasional same-sex wedding complete with all of the accoutrements. There was, of course, some ambivalence, particularly among middle-class, civil rights activists who feared the white community would use black tolerance of gays and lesbians as an excuse to further limit black upward mobility. W. E. B. Du Bois, for instance, looked with great disapproval upon homosexuality, as did conservative black churches. On the whole, however, gays and lesbians enjoyed greater tolerance in Harlem than they did most other places.

The idea of a distinctive lesbian identity was fostered in the 1920s by literature, theater, and the high profile of literary figures such as expatriate Gertrude Stein. Other prominent literary figures such as Ernest Hemingway and Sherwood Anderson included lesbian characters in their stories. The 1920s saw, too, the publication of Radclyffe Hall's landmark work, *The Well of Loneliness* (1928). On stage several plays took up the theme of lesbianism, including *The Captive,* the story of a young woman who could not be happy in her marriage because of her desire for a woman.

The end of the Jazz Age came as a particular blow to this emerging lesbian culture. Because women's access to public space had been so limited to this point, they had enjoyed little of the time and context necessary to develop the sorts of spaces and networks gay men had established. Hence, the efforts in the 1930s to eradicate mention of gays and lesbians from public discourse left lesbians particularly isolated. An economic environment that discouraged women's economic independence left women, once again, dependent on men. Some women who would have preferred to remain exclusively with same-sex partners chose to marry men and maintain their same-sex relationships on the side. The diary of a middle-class, African American clubwoman named Alice Dunbar-Nelson reveals a network of women who chose this path. The autobiography of a hobo named Boxcar Bertha suggests that among working-class and poor women who were displaced by the economic distress the world of transients provided a community for women seeking same-sex companions.

WORLD WAR II AS A PIVOTAL MOMENT

If the 1930s witnessed a crackdown on the gay community, World War II provided the context for its resurgence. At this point the stories of gay men and lesbians come together, in part, because of the way World War II transformed gender roles and changed women's access to public space. Young men and women who left small town lives to fight in the war or go to the city to work in wartime industries discovered a life very different from the ones they left behind as they entered the military or sex-segregated jobs. There they found others who were interested in same-sex love and sexuality. Both lesbians and gay men thrived in the military. Gay men, much to their delight, frequently found themselves responsible for staging elaborate drag shows intended to raise the morale of soldiers deprived of

female company. Because of the tremendous need for personnel, the military brass ignored allegations of homosexuality. One former Women's Army Corps member recalled her desperate efforts to convince her commanding officer that she was a lesbian so that he would discharge her from the army and she would be able to join her lover who had been transferred. Much to her dismay, he steadfastly refused to believe her. After the war, the situation changed dramatically.

In the postwar era, gays and lesbians were ferreted out and dishonorably discharged in significant numbers. Part of the enthusiasm for these witch-hunts stemmed from the anti-Communist fervor. The junior senator from Wisconsin, Joseph McCarthy, and his secretly gay sidekick, Roy Cohn, explicitly linked Communism and homosexuality. They argued that gays were a weak link in the fight against Communism because their secret, closeted lives made them susceptible to blackmail by Communist agents and potentially prone to yield up important state secrets. They also argued that the United States needed strong, masculine men to win the cold war and that gay men were not, by definition, masculine. This kind of rhetoric led to widespread persecution of gays and lesbians including—but not limited to—efforts to purge them from government jobs. In order to avoid losing their jobs, many middle-class gays and lesbians chose to hide their sexual preference and "stay in the closet."

It is important, however, not to overstate the repression of the 1950s. Gays and lesbians made real gains as a result of World War II and continued to build on those gains by moving toward a stronger sense of gay and lesbian identity. Several factors helped to build gay identity in the postwar era. In the late 1940s and early 1950s, Alfred Kinsey published his reports on human sexuality in which he suggested that same-sex relations were more common than most Americans imagined. One unlikely source of lesbian identity emerged with the publication of lesbian pulp fiction. The novels were intended for a male heterosexual audience and always ended with the man winning the woman away from her female partner. But the books also contained explicit descriptions of female, same-sex relations. For young women who felt they had no real lesbian community these novels provided a point of contact. At the same time, the emerging Beat culture celebrated both homosociality and homosexuality as, for instance, in the poetry of Allen Ginsberg, whose poem "Howl" (1956) caused a tremendous stir in middle America. Elsewhere drag balls enjoyed a season of resurgence and, at Cherry Grove in Fire

The Castro District, San Francisco. Though San Francisco had long fostered a gay and lesbian subculture, in the early 1970s the Castro became a popular open community. This transition was not without its struggles: California's first openly gay elected official, the popular Castro resident Harvey Milk, was assassinated in 1978 by a fellow member of the Board of Supervisors. © ROBERT HOLMES/CORBIS

Island, New York, gays and lesbians could experience a sort of Greenwich Village revival. For working-class women the 1950s marked the heyday of the bar culture. World War II made it possible for women to frequent public places like bars in ways previously closed to them. In the context of bar culture, working-class women carved out a new kind of lesbian identity based on butch-fem roles. The butch dressed like a man or in men's clothing, adopted masculine attributes, and was responsible both for protecting the fem and for taking the dangerous position of being visible to the straight community. Her partner, the fem, took her cues from conventional postwar femininity. Middle-class gays and lesbians looking for alternatives to bar culture ultimately formed groups such as the Mattachine Society for gay men and the Daughters of Bilitis for lesbians. Both published newsletters and became active in lobbying for gay rights, while staying well within the parameters of respectable, middle-class society while they did so. The emerging civil rights movement provided them with a model for activism

and the rising social tensions of the early 1960s fueled greater activism.

A SEXUAL REVOLUTION AND THE GAY CIVIL RIGHTS MOVEMENT

In the summer of 1969, the struggle for gay rights became much more visible when patrons at a Greenwich Village gay bar, the Stonewall Inn, resisted the nightly police raid and touched off rioting throughout the city. Stonewall provided the starting point for a highly visible gay liberation movement that received media attention and, for many gays and lesbians, made "coming out of the closet" a possibility. In the wake of Stonewall, the Gay Liberation Front formed. Many lesbians, however, found themselves facing a dilemma. Like female civil rights workers who ended up making coffee and typing, many lesbians questioned their place in a gay liberation movement which seemed male dominated. In fact, the feminist movement pro-

337

vided a much more inviting space for lesbians who ultimately played a crucial role in the construction of feminist community and theory. Lesbian feminists played a crucial role in the development of a woman-identified record industry. Collectives such as Olivia Records brought the music of lesbian artists to a wider audience not only through the sale of record albums but by sponsoring annual music festivals. Lesbian feminists played a similar role in creating newspapers, magazines, and publishing houses.

The relationship between lesbians and feminists was not without complications. Betty Friedan, a key figure in the feminist movement and the founder of the National Organization of Women, attempted to distance the organization from lesbians. In the mid-1970s, however, a lesbian separatist movement coalesced typified by the "radicalesbians" who called for an end to heterosexual relations and the gender roles associated with those relations. These lesbian feminists understood themselves as woman-identified women and suggested that it was possible to choose lesbianism as political strategy. They expressly challenged the idea of modeling lesbian relationships on the heterosexual order. Older working-class lesbians who perceived their sexual preference as a biological fact and who had come of age in the era of the butch and fem were puzzled and alienated by such assertions.

TWO FORCES FOR CHANGE: AIDS AND THE RELIGIOUS RIGHT

Indeed, in the early 1980s it seemed that even as gay men and lesbians self-identified by their sexual object choice, their gender characteristics became increasingly important. Among women this was the era of the butch-fem revival. Among gay men, this was the era of the clone, where gay men assumed a hypermasculine persona that included a hypersexuality that was almost hostile to relationships. By the mid-1980s two forces, in particular, reshaped the gay and lesbian community: one was AIDS and the other was the religious Right. Both served to unify gays and lesbians against a common enemy. AIDS devastated the gay male community even as it precipitated both local and national efforts to care for the sick and dying, including everything from lobbying for government action to campaigning for safe sex. Gays and lesbians were forced to mobilize in similar ways against the efforts of the religious Right to limit gay and lesbian civil rights.

QUESTIONS ABOUT IDENTITY: WHERE DO WE GO FROM HERE?

In some ways, groups such as ACT-UP (AIDS Coalition to Unleash Power), Queer Nation, and Lesbian Avengers emerged in the early 1990s as attempts to address these assaults with a kind of in-your-face style that included the "outing" of prominent "closeted" gay people. These groups illustrate the kind of changes that had occurred in the course of one hundred years.

The idea that individual identity derived from sexual desire and behavior had become firmly entrenched and, for gay and lesbian Americans, served as a starting point for building community and organizing politically. Ironically, at the very historical moment when this idea reached its zenith, it was already on the wane. A variety of factors undermined the possibility of using sexual identity effectively as a tool for political organization. First, one of the consequences of a politics constructed around sexual identity was that those who self-identified as gay or straight tended to talk as if there were only two choices—gay or straight. In reality, sexual desire and behavior continued to defy such easy dichotomies and increasingly gay and lesbian activists found themselves forced to consider the needs and desires of people who self-identified as something other than gay or straight—such as bisexual or transgender[ed]. The poet, scholar, and gay activist Minnie Bruce Pratt and her partner the author/activist Leslie Feinberg were among those who led the way in challenging a dualistic understanding of sexual identity through their writing and public speaking

A second factor that undermined the possibility of using sexual identity as a starting point for political organization was that many of the gay intelligentsia disagreed fundamentally about what it meant to be gay, lesbian, or transgender[ed] and, by extension, about the nature and purpose of gay activism. On the one hand were those folks who saw sexual and gender transgression as central to their perception of themselves as gay people and who highlighted the importance of a liberationist view. People such as the playwright and ACT-UP founder Larry Kramer, activist Urvashi Vaid, author of *Virtual Equality* (1995), and Michael Bronski, author of *The Pleasure Principle* (1998), argued that gays, lesbians, and transgender people were uniquely qualified to lead the way in transforming (not reforming) sexual and gender values. In contrast, people such as the poet and literary critic Bruce Bawer, best known for his book *A Place at the Table* (1993), and the journalist Andrew Sullivan, who was for a number of years editor of the the *New Republic* and author of the *Virtually Normal* (1995), pursued a more integrationist (their opponents called it assimilationist) position. They argued that gay activists ought to focus on achieving basic civil rights including equal protection under the law. Those with views similar to Kramer's tended to see Bawer and Sullivan as "conservative" and "sex-negative." While those who shared the views of Bawer and Sullivan tended to see liberationists as extreme and likely to alienate straight allies. Gay pride marches and rallies that inevitably included the more flamboyant representatives of the gay community were a particular point of contention. No simple dichotomy existed. Equally controversial were Gabriel Rotello, author of *Sexual Ecology* (1997), whose book critics saw as a challenge to the idea that promiscuity was central to gay male identity, and cultural critic and self-proclaimed "all-around provocateur" Michelangelo Signorile, both of whom drew fire from a variety of sources.

The divisions within the gay community were most clearly in evidence in the debate about gay marriage. The 1990s saw the religious right mobilize to convince state and federal legislators to pass Defense of Marriage Acts (DOMA) that outlawed same-sex marriage and reaffirmed the idea that marriage must be between a man and a woman. Bawer and Sullivan saw resistance to DOMA and the pursuit of the right to marriage as a legitimate, necessary, and worthwhile goal of the gay activists. In contrast, people like Kramer and Michael Warner, scholar and author of *The Trouble with Normal* (1999), saw the pursuit of marriage rights as perpetuating social inequalities for anyone who chose not to marry and betraying the ideal of sexual liberation. When the Vermont legislature voted in the spring of 2000 to permit same-sex couples to enter civil unions, gay activists responded accordingly. Some saw it as much needed step toward greater equality and civil rights. Others saw it as an effort to create second-class citizenship for gays and lesbians. Still others dismissed it entirely as unworthy of their attention or efforts.

One other factor that potentially undermined the effectiveness of organizing politically around sexual identity was the increased visibility of gay and lesbian people in all walks of public life. This inevitably challenged the idea that the gay community was somehow homogenous or that gay people were easily identifiable based on certain stereotypical characteristics. In general, gay, lesbian, and transgender people enjoyed increased visibility in the

1990s in arenas ranging from television, movies, and theater to politics and journalism.

One of the most talked about events occurred on television. In 1997 Ellen DeGeneres "came out" along with her character Ellen in the television series of the same name. DeGeneres and her partner Anne Heche were one of Hollywood's most visible lesbian couples. Nor did gay characters disappear from television after *Ellen*. The late 1990s saw a successful television series called *Will & Grace* in which one of the main characters was a gay man. At the same time, an increasing number of films about gay and lesbian relationships appeared, many of them aimed at a mainstream audience. Some of these films, most notably *Longtime Companion* (1990), attempted to dramatize the tragedy of AIDS. Others, however, sought to depict the joys and sorrows of gay and lesbian relationships, including films such as *Desert Hearts* (1985), *Birdcage* (1996), *Bent* (1997), and *Better Than Chocolate* (1999). A few films addressed race issues, including *Tongues Untied* (1989) and *Paris Is Burning* (1990). The latter also addressed transgender issues, as did a number of other films. *To Wong Foo, Thanks for Everything! Julie Newmar* (1995) followed the escapades of three drag queens on their way to a beauty contest. In a more serious vein the 1999 release *Boys Don't Cry* told the story of Brandon Teena who was brutally raped and murdered by his "friends" when they discovered he had begun life as a woman.

In addition to television and movies, prominent openly gay people contributed to the visibility of the gay community. Andrew Sullivan's position as editor of of the *New Republic,* a respected journal of politics and culture, allowed him to maintain a relatively high profile. The novelist, playwright, and activist Sarah Schulman was one among a number of gay artists and authors that gained a greater share of the market. In politics, two openly gay congressional representatives—Democrat Barney Frank and Republican Steve Gunderson—led the way for their respective parties. Both Melissa Etheridge, who came out in the nineties, and the folk/rock artists Indigo Girls, had a strong market share among both gays and straights. At both the national and local level activist groups such as Human Rights Campaign, Lambda, and ACT-UP kept gay issues in the public forum.

Not all of the visibility was a good thing. The debate about gays in the military put homosexuals center stage but resulted in a "don't ask, don't tell" U.S. military policy, in which American soldiers were warned to keep their sexual orientation a secret or risk punishment. The brutal murders of three young gay men in three separate incidents garnered national attention at a terrible price. Matthew Shepard, Billy Jack Gaither, and Private Barry Winchell all died at the hands of anti-gay attackers. And the efforts of those who opposed same-sex marriage led to legislation at the federal and state level that limited marriage to different-sex couples. Thus, while gays, lesbians, and transgender people gained greater visibility, they did so in the context of continuing and vocal resistance to full rights, privileges, and protection under the law. The opening of a new century saw the gay and lesbian community continuing to struggle with questions about the nature of sexual identity and its political implications, the ongoing AIDS crisis, and a new awareness of the importance of recognizing and addressing differences of class and ethnicity.

See also **Countercultural Visions; Multiculturalism in Theory and Practice** *(in this volume);* **Sexuality** *(volume 3).*

BIBLIOGRAPHY

General

Bérubé, Allan. *Coming Out under Fire: The History of Gay Men and Women in World War Two.* New York, 1990.

D'Emilio, John, and Estelle Freedman. *Intimate Matters: A History of Sexuality in America.* 2d ed. Chicago, 1997. This work provides a general overview of the history of sexuality beginning with colonial America and concluding with the AIDS crisis. This book locates the story of same-sex love and sexuality in a larger context.

Faderman, Lillian. *Odd Girls and Twilight Lovers: A History of Lesbian Life in Twentieth-Century America.* New York, 1991.

Rupp, Leila. *A Desired Past: A Short History of Same-Sex Love in America.* Chicago, 1999. This work provides an overview of same-sex love and sexuality from colonial times to the present. It is very readable and provides an excellent bibliography.

Smith-Rosenberg, Carroll. *Disorderly Conduct: Visions of Gender in Victorian America.* New York, 1985. This is the classic work on middle-class female sexuality and gender identity and is crucial to understanding middle-class women's same-sex relationships. Smith-Rosenberg's conclusions have shaped much of the subsequent scholarship.

History

Chauncey, George. *Gay New York: Gender, Urban Culture, and the Making of the Gay Male World, 1890–1940.* New York, 1994.

D'Emilio, John. *Sexual Politics, Sexual Communities: The Making of a Homosexual Minority in the United States, 1940–1970.* 2d ed. Chicago, 1998.

Duberman, Martin B. *Stonewall.* New York, 1993.

Kennedy, Elizabeth Lapovsky, and Madeline D. Davis. *Boots of Leather, Slippers of Gold: The History of a Lesbian Community.* New York, 1993.

Intellectual History

Bland, Lucy, and Laura Doan, eds. *Sexology in Culture: Labelling Bodies and Desires.* Chicago, 1998. This edited collection focuses primarily on Great Britain, but is useful for understanding the basic ideas of sexologists.

———. *Sexology Uncensored: The Documents of Sexual Science.* Chicago, 1998. This collection of primary materials includes excerpts from the works of a wide variety of sexologists.

Katz, Jonathan Ned. *The Invention of Heterosexuality.* New York, 1995. This work makes a convincing argument for the socially and culturally constructed nature of heterosexuality and, simultaneously, illuminates the social construction of homosexuality by demonstrating the connection between the two.

Robinson, Paul A. *The Modernization of Sex: Havelock Ellis, Alfred Kinsey, William Masters, and Virginia Johnson.* New York, 1976.

Terry, Jennifer. *An American Obsession: Science, Medicine, and Homosexuality in Modern Society.* Chicago, 1999.

GERMAN SPEAKERS

Marianne S. Wokeck

Over the course of almost four centuries speakers of German were part of the European colonization and settlement of the North American continent. Well over 7 million German-speaking immigrants have played roles in shaping American society and culture. Like other immigrants who have developed into ethnic groups and who have become hyphenated Americans, their contribution—as individuals rather than as one group—has largely depended on who came to America, when, and on where they settled and under what circumstances. While the ultimate success of German speakers in North America is aptly demonstrated by their complete integration into the fabric of American life, tracing their cultural imprint is complicated and interpreting its diffused impact is rarely unequivocal.

IMMIGRATION

The flow of German-speaking immigration was diverse in its composition and unevenly distributed over time. It drew from a great variety of localities in Europe that were home to speakers of different kinds of German, stretching from regions west and south of the Rhine to districts in Russia and areas bordering the English Channel and the Baltic Sea. Comparable to this diversity of geographic backgrounds was the variety of religious affiliations among the immigrants. Many belonged to the three Christian faiths established in continental Europe, Catholicism, Lutheranism, and Reformed Protestantism; others associated in smaller churches and sects such as the Moravians, Schenkfelders, and Mennonites, or were members of other beliefs, like the Jews; and others rejected authority and organization in matters of religion altogether, as did the Freethinkers. Although the vast majority of German-speaking immigrants were of moderate means, even poor, the migrants overall represent a broad spectrum of wealth and social status, educa-

tion and skills, and professions and occupations. More often than not they emigrated from rural places and usually they were part of intricate migration networks that linked kin and neighbors and that included sizable proportions of single men and women. Among the voyagers young and middle-aged German speakers were predominant. Their reasons for immigrating to North America ranged widely from fleeing religious and political persecution to seeking fortune and adventure. Thousands of individual decisions combined to create distinct fluctuations in the migration stream. In very general terms, however, it swelled when local circumstances that made life at home excessively hard or dangerous were combined with expectations of safety or hopes for a better life across the Atlantic, and also with concrete opportunities for making the move; it waned when prospects close to home seemed comparable or superior to promises overseas or when war made travel over long distances hazardous and expensive or impossible.

In the seventeenth century, migration was sporadic and small. In 1683, with the settlement of Germantown in Pennsylvania by thirteen Quaker and Mennonite families from Krefeld led by Francis Daniel Pastorius, the nature and pace of the immigration changed in fundamental ways in that transatlantic networks formed among relatives, coreligionists, and compatriots, which drew and channeled more migrants to relocate in the American colonies. As a consequence, the numbers of newcomers in the eighteenth century increased to a total of more than 111,000 and peaked impressively around 1750. The flow of German speakers ebbed after the French and Indian War, ceased during the Revolutionary War, and regained only little strength in the Early Republic. When the tide of German-speaking migration rose next around 1820, the level increased tremendously to close to 6 million immigrants for the nineteenth century—the classic age of mass migration to the United States. The first surge occurred in the 1830s, made up in part of

FRANCIS DANIEL PASTORIUS

Francis Daniel Pastorius was an early but an ordinary colonist whom German-speaking immigrants and their descendants in the nineteenth and twentieth centuries made into a cultural icon.

Pastorius was born in 1651 as the oldest son of a prominent municipal official in Franconia, Germany, and received the traditional classical education of a continental gentleman. He attended Latin school and studied law, French, and Italian at universities in Altdorf, Jena, Regensburg, Strasbourg, and Basel (from 1668 to 1676). He first practiced law in Windsheim, then in Frankfurt am Main, after which he accompanied a young nobleman on his grand tour through the Netherlands, England, France, Switzerland, and Germany. Pastorius became disenchanted with European society and upon his return in 1682 associated himself with a group of educated men and women influenced by mystic and separatist currents of religious thought. They became investors in William Penn's "holy experiment" and made Pastorius their agent. He undertook the transatlantic voyage in the ship *America,* which landed in Philadelphia in August 1683.

Together with thirteen Quaker and Mennonite families from Krefeld, who arrived on the *Concord* in October, he convinced the proprietor to grant them two German townships to lead a "quiet, godly & honest life in a howling wilderness." Pastorius worked with the Quaker families to lay out Germantown in 1684. He reported the progress of the settlement regularly to his father and to the German investors. Several of those accounts were incorporated in the 1700 publication of his "detailed description of Pennsylvania," that helped establish and promote the solid reputation of Penn's colony in Germany.

Pastorius stood out from his Dutch and German neighbors because of his work as magistrate, scribe, lawyer, teacher, and organizer of Germantown, whose administration and court system were modeled after Old World municipalities. The sincerity of his commitment to reside in Pennsylvania, which found an early expression in his mastering of the English language, was coupled with his desire to ensure the preservation of certain ways of German life and culture. As his responsibilities as agent of the Frankfurt land company were coming to an end around 1700, he taught briefly at the Penn Charter School in Philadelphia and then he became a teacher at the newly chartered (1702) Germantown school, a position he held until shortly before his death and in which he used the English primer he wrote and published in 1698.

Pastorius took an active part in the religious affairs of Delaware Valley Friends. His commitment to Quakerism seems to have been a combination of his early pietist convictions grafted upon a Lutheran upbringing, and his friendship with Germantown and Philadelphia Quakers. During the first decade of his life in the New World he became involved in important issues the Quakers faced in the early years of Penn's colony. On 18 April 1688, Pastorius, together with Gerret Hendricks, Dirck op den Graef, and Abraham op den Graef, drew up a protest against slavery—the first such document in America.

In addition to his official responsibilities, Pastorius was a prolific writer of prose and verse. In keeping with the traditions of his time and education, he collected his literary materials from a wide range of sources, including the writings of

CONTINUED NEXT PAGE

classical authors, the testimony of Quakers, and mundane facts and figures about husbandry and life in Pennsylvania. The books in his library and the references in the various compendia of cumulative knowledge he compiled attest to his breadth of reading and his love of traditional learning. Although Pastorius had few kind words about European university education, he himself maintained the habits of bookish learning from which he derived so much pleasure. He passed the fruits thereof on to his sons, whose education as weaver and shoemaker were much more oriented toward practical pursuits than his own. In his later years, when his official duties were few and his service as scribe much in demand, he spent his spare time tending his vines, his bees, and his garden.

exiled reformers and liberal and patriotic intellectuals who supported and led emigration societies. The second and second largest wave crested in 1854, carrying with it Carl Schurz and other members of the bourgeois elite who became political refugees after the failure of the German revolution of 1848. The greatest flood of immigrants occurred in the decade before the turn to the twentieth century, which included Catholics and radical social democrats expelled by reforms in imperial Germany among large numbers of working-class men and women. The turn to the twentieth century signaled a change to a relatively much more reduced number. After legislation affected a decrease in immigration overall, German-speaking newcomers declined to about 1 million, with notable immigration peaks after each of the world wars and with significant numbers of refugees (about 200,000, half of them Jews) and of displaced persons, among them numerous high-profile immigrants, including Albert Einstein.

In comparison to the millions of German-speaking immigrants in the eighteenth and nineteenth centuries, the thousands who relocated to North America before the American Revolution seem insignificant. Yet in proportionate terms they made up a sizable part of the resident population during the formative stage of American society, and because many of them came with kin their numbers increased considerably in the second, third, and subsequent generations and thus augmented the impact of the early tide of German-speaking immigrants. Since the proportion of families among nineteenth-century immigrants was also high, the growth of Americans with roots in German-speaking communities and cultures continued to rise, which accounts for the large number of citizens in the 1990 U.S. census who marked their origin as German.

Timing and numbers are not the only critical differences between German-speaking settlers in the colonial period and those who came after the birth of the nation. Issues concerning national identity and loyalty distinguished them, too. Before the creation of the nation-state, religion, regional, and occupational or status-linked cultures defined people and determined their sense of belonging. After "nationality" had emerged as a distinguishing characteristic, all German speakers in North America were lumped into one category, with little or no regard to historical divisions and changing borders and to cultural differences and shadings. In the eighteenth century, German-speaking immigrants were indiscriminately labeled "Palatine" or "Dutch"; in the nineteenth and twentieth centuries they were simply "German," even if they originated from homelands in Switzerland, Austria, France, or Russia. In the twenty-first century, the term "German speakers" reflects a more inclusive understanding of the multicultural nature of American society and also underscores the cultural dimension of origins in a European world with complex and changing political realities.

When North America first became a regular destination for emigrants in the eighteenth century, it was a small minority of German speakers who turned westward and braved the Atlantic in their search for freedom and a decent living. Most of those emigrants came from lands along the Rhine, an important artery for international traffic, trade, and communication. Following disastrous harvests and political upheaval that marked the beginning of the nineteenth century, migrants from those traditional areas of outmigration continued to relocate overseas. Yet migrants from other German-speaking lands opted increasingly to move to the United States, too, as difficulties mounted in reaction to efforts to unify German territories, as economic

CARL SCHURZ

Carl Schurz, the most prominent German American among the "forty-eighters" (political refugees of the failed 1848 revolution), modeled that it was possible to combine love for Germany with loyalty to the United States. At a time when national identities were often defined in terms of exclusive political rights, Schurz demonstrated convincingly that concern with moral goals was not the prerogative of a single nation but an important aim for all humankind.

Schurz was born in 1829 near Cologne, Germany, and was a student at the University of Bonn when he joined what would become the German revolutionary movement in 1848. Since he participated in the rebellions in the Rhineland, the Palatinate, and Baden, he was forced to flee. After escaping from Germany to Strasbourg, France, he made his way via Switzerland, Paris, and London to America. He arrived in New York in 1852 together with his wife, Margarethe Meyer Schurz, whose family were Jewish merchants in Hamburg. After a period of intensive study of the English language and about the United States, they settled as farmers in Watertown, Wisconsin, in 1855 where Meyer Schurz opened the first American kindergarten (1856) in accordance with the ideas of the German reform educator Friedrich Fröbel, and where her husband practiced law.

Schurz became a dedicated supporter of the Republican Party and campaigned for Abraham Lincoln in those states where German-speaking immigrants and their descendants clustered. The first defeats of the Union army in the Civil War prompted his return from Spain where President Lincoln had sent him as envoy of the United States. Schurz played an active role as Union general in the war against the Confederacy and in the struggle for emancipation of enslaved Americans.

After the war, Schurz worked as a correspondent for the *New York Tribune,* then as editor-in-chief of the *Detroit Post,* and after 1867 as co-editor and part owner of the German-language *Westliche Post* in St. Louis, Missouri, his new home state. At the age of forty he was elected senator from Missouri (1869–1875), a remarkable achievement for a political refugee. He continued his political career by serving as secretary of the interior under President Rutherford B. Hayes (1877–1881), a post that allowed him to pursue civil service reform and improvements in the Bureau of Indian Affairs.

Upon completion of his service in the cabinet, Schurz continued to speak out on questions of American domestic politics. He undertook new journalistic endeavors and extensive lecture tours. German clubs around the country wanted him as a speaker because he portrayed self-confident German Americanism. He supported "healthy Americanization," which he understood to mean that German speakers in the United States should not reject their heritage but combine the best of the German character with the best of the American character in order to best serve the American people. Schurz's idea about the contribution of German culture for the advancement of American civilization was very different from the conviction of many of his German American contemporaries who extolled German cultural superiority with disastrous effects when Germany and the United States faced each other in World War I.

Carl Schurz, c. 1877. Portrait, Mathew Brady.
© BETTMANN/CORBIS

instability developed into an accompanying feature of the industrial revolution, and as transportation to Bremen and other overseas ports became more readily available and affordable. By the end of the nineteenth century America had become the first choice of the vast majority of migrants who left home for faraway places—a development that expanded and extended the networks that connected German speakers on both sides of the Atlantic. In the twentieth century this diversity of geographic origin persisted and was complicated in terms of concentrating particular migration flows according to religious and occupational criteria in addition to those that occurred in the wake of destruction and displacement caused by two world wars.

SETTLEMENT PATTERN

In America, German-speaking newcomers settled where opportunities for making a living seemed promising. Whether they sought work, land, or investment possibilities the pattern of their settlement is closely tied to the development of the United States as a whole. Before the Revolution, German-speaking colonists were well distributed along the eastern seaboard, many of them concentrated in backcountry areas that opened for European settlement at the time of the immigrants' arrival. Since most of the eighteenth-century colonists landed in Philadelphia, settlement of German speakers clustered there, in Penn's colony, and in territories linked to the main roads of western expansion and south into the Great Valley region that stretched from Maryland to the Carolinas. By the time new waves of German-speaking immigrants landed on American shores, Baltimore and especially New York were the major ports of entry. Many of those who moved on settled in the Midwest, where they competed with native-born Americans and other immigrants to make a living on farms and in frontier cities. Wisconsin, Minnesota, and Illinois had the highest concentration of recently arrived German speakers and German neighborhoods were characteristic not only of nineteenth-century New York, Philadelphia, and Baltimore but also of Chicago, Cincinnati, Louisville, Milwaukee, and St. Louis. Together with other Americans and immigrants, German speakers were also lured to the West by promises of gold and for a better life, which meant they had a significant presence there, too. Only the South attracted few German-speaking immigrants before the Civil War, excepting New Orleans and Texas. When the last and greatest wave of German speakers occurred just before the turn to the twentieth century, newcomers increased and reinforced earlier settlements in the "German belt" that stretched from Ohio to Nebraska and Missouri to Wisconsin with a disproportionately large number of them channeled into the industrializing cities. In the twentieth century, when the numbers of German-speaking immigrants were relatively much smaller, their settlement had been widely dispersed across all of the United States.

COMMUNITIES

The settlement pattern of German speakers provides the context for immigrant communities that developed distinctively ethnic ways. Although always intensely personal in nature, the transformation of immigrant strangers into Americans played out locally, often over the course of more than one generation. German American communities that differed in their organization and view of family, religion, work, and leisure from those common to their American or immigrant neighbors could bring Old World heritage, experience, values, and convictions to bear in places where newcomers presented no threat to those already settled and at times when

ALBERT EINSTEIN

Albert Einstein was born in 1879 to Jewish parents in Ulm, Germany, but he has come to symbolize the new age in which modern science and globalization play critically important roles.

Einstein spent his youth in Munich where his father and uncle established an electrical engineering firm. His formal and informal boyhood education was eclectic, including private tutoring, attendance at a Catholic primary school, acceptance to the Luitpold Gymnasium (high school), Jewish religious instruction, and mentoring by Max Talmud, a Jewish medical student who ate dinner regularly with the Einsteins, who acquainted him with scientific and philosophical writings. Drawing on those experiences and readings, Einstein formed his own ideas about laws governing nature and governing society, questioning authoritarian doctrine, and distrusting authority.

Following his parents to Milan before he graduated from high school, he applied to the Federal Polytechnic Academy in Zurich, Switzerland, and began his studies there in 1896, the year of his release from Württembergian (German) nationality. His professors in Zurich did not recognize his genius; nor did his colleagues at the Swiss patent office in Bern, where Einstein was employed when he worked out the special theory of relativity and the hypothesis of light quanta around 1905, which earned him a Nobel Prize in physics in 1921.

The scientific revolution of the 1920s that began with Einstein signaled a new epoch of human thought. Einstein's general theory of relativity made radically new statements about the universe and his quantum theory changed the concept of the atom. The debate about the new theories that forced a paradigm shift in physics was not only heated among the specialists but also caused a considerable public stir at a time of political upheaval. Anti-Semitism was widespread, and as the Jews in general were blamed for the ills that befell Germany after World War I, so were Einstein's ideas branded as destructive to sound scientific thought. Such political resentment notwithstanding, Einstein became the legendary "pope of physics," was appointed professor at several European universities, elected a member of the Prussian Academy of Science in Berlin, and sought after as lecturer worldwide.

When the Nazis seized power in 1933, Einstein was in the United States. He refused to return to Germany, resigned from the Prussian Academy of Science, and severed all ties with official German institutions. He was undoubtedly the most famous among the exiles who escaped from the Nazis and became a United States citizen in 1940 (he had obtained Swiss citizenship in 1901). His migration to the New World was significant in that it signaled the passing of the world leadership in physics from Germany to the United States where it since has attracted many young physicists from all over the world which, in turn, has led to making the field broadly international.

Einstein recognized long before his fellow physicists that in principle energy could be produced through nuclear reaction. When, on the eve of World War II, the discovery of how to split the atom proved the technical feasibility of nuclear reaction, Einstein warned President Franklin D. Roosevelt of the dangers then threatening the world. It is ironic that Einstein, a dedicated pacifist, who rightfully

CONTINUED NEXT PAGE

dreaded the hubris of the German National Socialists, gave the impetus for developing the bomb that ushered in the nuclear age. After the first atomic bomb was dropped on Hiroshima, Japan, Einstein—fiercely committed first to arms control and then to disarmament—assumed the chair of the Emergency Committee of Atomic Scientists and publicly championed a world government. Three years before his death in 1955, he declined the offer to become president of Israel and continued his work in physics and for world peace from his home base at the Institute for Advanced Study in Princeton, New Jersey.

Albert Einstein, c. 1943. © BETTMANN/CORBIS

native-born Americans did not fear competition for land, jobs, and investment. Germantown in early Pennsylvania and nineteenth-century Milwaukee are two very different examples that show marks of such charter groups. The ethnic character of many pioneering communities changed, however, quite radically and fast as the children and grandchildren of German-speaking immigrants moved in search of farms, different kinds of jobs, and better housing. New waves of immigrants sometimes slowed the pace of that change by revitalizing the use of the German language, reestablishing connections to the homeland, and invigorating community institutions; other times recent immigrants were the rea-

son for accelerating the Americanization of those already in place who felt threatened in their position.

FAMILY

For many German speakers the private spheres of family and home represented unquestioningly the core of traditional customs and values that distinguished them from others in their country of choice or exile. Many rural settlers subscribed to the unsentimental conception of family and of marriage as a cooperative enterprise serving economic needs. The urban middle class accepted the romanticized and sentimentalized sexual views of the Victorian era but retained the patriarchal orientation. Both views limited the role of women to a close circle of family and friends, a critical position for preserving language and traditions.

RELIGION

Rituals of worship, celebrations of important life cycle events, and some public ceremonies were cultural expressions that served to demonstrate and cement common bonds among religious German speakers. But religion was also a major source for division among them because competition among denominations prompted some churches and sects, like the Amish, Hutterites, and Old Lutherans, to adopt strategies of exclusion.

All denominations of German speakers, however, agreed that if they were to carry on Old World traditions that were language specific such as professing the faith to their respective congregations, instructing children, and training priests, pastors, or rabbis, they had to establish their own schools and seminaries. Both kinds of institutions played crucial roles in maintaining and redefining ethnic identities and in providing important community-based leadership.

ASSOCIATIONS

The so-called church or soul Germans (their lives revolved around church as the central social function) remained usually distinct and separate from the club Germans (their lives centered on clubs, associations, or organizations) but they were largely united in their opposition to the American leisure ethic, which preached against breaking the Sabbath and alcohol consumption. German speakers and their descendants counted conviviality on Sundays among their personal liberties. It was one of the few issues they fought in the arena of electoral politics as a bloc, warding off prohibition in some states in the nineteenth century but not in the nation in the 1920s when distrust of and contempt for German Americans was strong. The diversity of club life was especially rich and vibrant in cities with high concentrations of German speakers and the continued influx of new immigrants. This phase of extraordinary energy and engagement in community affairs extended from the 1830s to the 1920s. It began with the arrival of the first group of exiled reformers, who prepared the ground for the activism of the second wave of reform-minded "forty-eighters" (political refugees of the failed 1848 revolution) to take hold and flourish; it began to wane around 1900 and came to an early and abrupt end, when, in reaction to American loathing for all things German, many associations ceased to exist or redefined their focus.

LANGUAGE

Central to the transfer and maintenance of Old World values and cultural traditions was the use and preservation of the German language. Speaking German helped immigrants to identify friends and support that were vital in coping with and overcoming the difficulties inherent to life in a strange country, especially at times when nativist resentment against newcomers ran high, as in the 1850s. Yet vernacular and dialect forms of the German language could also underscore differences among German speakers along lines of religion, class, and regional origins, creating dissention and division in German-speaking communities locally, and especially in the context of electoral politics on the state and national levels.

The use and knowledge of German that distinguished immigrants and many of their children rarely survived into the third generation of German Americans who used English as their first language. Most often the transition from German to English began with the passing of the immigrant generation, and was a result of a strong commitment to bilingual education as the best way for improving the chances of success for the second generation. Under those circumstances, institutions and mechanisms that sustained the vitality of German were key if language-specific traditions were to survive. A continued influx of new immigrants contributed much to the preservation and revitalization of language and European customs. It was the most crucial link of the intricate networks of contact and communication that bound German speakers on both sides of the Atlantic and cross-fertilized their respective cultures; other important connections were forged—privately as well as officially—through letters, visits, many different kinds of print materials, and, during the twentieth century, by telephone and electronic means.

Similarly important were the roles the German-language press and educational and cultural institutions played locally. The significance of the press and the schools for the preservation of the German language cannot be overemphasized. In its golden period (1850–1900), the German immigrant press was particularly rich in its diversity and reach compared to the print media in Germany, as well as to that of other immigrant groups. Daily and weekly papers served German speakers in counties and cities, distributed news and commentary on everything from politics to art and entertainment, offered readers a wide variety of editorial positions, which included distinct denominational and party perspectives, labor and union, socialist and anarchist points of view, and provided a platform and work for many prominent, well-educated, and professionally trained immigrants. While the editors of the larger German immigrant press tended to define their goals in terms of the preservation of traditional values, the editors of the German American radical press were committed to the principle of Americanization, which they considered inseparable from their socialist mission and from the self-imposed charge of warding off decline of classical German literary culture. Therefore German-language writing, encompassing essays, novels, short stories, poems, and plays, were widely disseminated in periodicals, which was an essential feature for a healthy German-language book market.

In regard to education, religious and labor leaders as well as other exiled reformers brought with them a culturally based understanding of learning and instruction that they translated into an institutional framework that served the German ethnic community and also the society at large. Their ideas and innovations extended from early childhood education to the production and transmission of knowledge at the university level. Especially noteworthy are the introduction of kindergarten for the youngest among the immigrants; the support of bilingual education at all instructional levels as a way of preserving the native culture and preparing immigrant children to become free American citizens; the development of confessional education (led by the Catholic religious orders and the Lutherans) as an alternative to public schooling to which German-speaking immigrants were strongly committed; the adoption of the German system of continuation schools for vocational education; and the power of the spirit of *Wissenschaft* (scholarship) that affected curricula and conventions in academia.

Other cultural institutions and organizations supported and complemented the German-language preservation efforts of formal education establishments. Most often they were community based rather than statewide or national in terms of structure and membership. Since selectivity, even exclusivity, along lines of religion and class commonly divided German-speaking immigrants and German Americans, those distinctions also affected the ways in which voluntary associations understood their role of preserving and promoting Old World heritage. Protestant, Catholic, and secular ideologies and cultures did not mix, nor did those of the elite and working class. As a result, parallel claims to the guardianship of classical culture developed and found their expression in different forms of art and entertainment. Music is a case in point: virtually all German speakers considered it an important part of their heritage, but they differed in what kinds of music they appreciated and practiced, some celebrating the traditions of church music, others enjoying traditional folk music and song, and yet others deriving pleasure from the classical repertoire.

CULTURAL LEGACIES

Many German-speaking immigrants came with a keen consciousness of their cultural heritage and often with a strong desire to hang on to it. Since much of the Old World culture was tied to the use and knowledge of the German language, the virtu-ally universal acceptance of English as the first language of communication in the community at large meant that the decline of German even as a second language became inevitable among third and subsequent generations. Without German, the press, belles lettres, theater, and all other language-specific expressions were bound to become insignificant for the vast majority of Americans. After the turn to the twentieth century, when the number of new immigrants fell, even the cultural chauvinism of the descendants of the nineteenth-century German Americans could not hold off that development. To the contrary, their actions in the name of German cultural superiority, symbolized by the National German-American Alliance (1901–1918), had just the opposite effect: with the entry of the United States into the war against Germany in 1917 American sentiment turned aggressively and lastingly against German Americans and things German.

German speakers left an enduring legacy, however, which can be divided into four broad categories. The first one includes all those institutions and associations that have been completely accepted and transformed into American structures and establishments such as the kindergarten, parochial schools, symphony orchestras, and athletic clubs.

The second category covers scholarly inquiry into and interpretation of the Americanization process of German speakers. While historians and other social scientists have diverse interests in exploring how and why American culture and society formed and changed over time, their goal is a better understanding of the circumstances and forces that make up the complexity of the modern world. Their work looks at the total immigrant experience, investigates the role of ethnic groups, and deals with conflicts that pit immigrant and ethnic groups in the minority against the majority of the dominant society. Politicians and German Americans and their descendants make selected use of the historians' findings to further their own goals, gaining respect and especially votes from ethnic Americans and, respectively, proudly retelling the story of German speakers in the United States as one of definite success and of appealing heritage.

The third type of legacy comprises stereotypical and highly stylized expressions of folk and popular culture that once were exclusively identified with German speakers or German Americans but that have gained broad recognition and general acceptance as manifestations of American cultural diversity. They include often romanticized and quaintly redefined customs and rituals of conviviality, especially food and drink, festivals and pageants. Santa

Claus, beer, sausages, Oktoberfests, and von Steuben parades are just some of those non-language-specific German things that all Americans are familiar with, even enjoy, and that have become the rather narrow focus of many celebrations of ethnic pride and achievement.

Yet most often admiration for things German stems from the extraordinary success of individual German speakers—the fourth category of the cultural legacy that survived well beyond the immigrant generation. All ethnic groups like to claim as theirs those who changed the world for the better, and since the number of German immigrants and German Americans is huge, those exceptional people make up a large and varied lot.

The following is a sampling of German Americans' spectacular and lasting role in shaping the American fabric of life: Marlene Dietrich, actress; Walter Gropius and Ludwig Mies van der Rohe, architects; Lyonel Feiniger, John Lewis Krimmel, and Thomas Nast, artists (painters and cartoonists); George Herman (Babe) Ruth and Johnny Weissmuller, athletes; Bertolt Brecht, Thomas Mann, and Charles Sealsfield, authors; Arnold Schoenberg and Kurt Weill, composers; Leopold Damrosch, Otto Klemperer, and Bruno Walter, conductors; John Augustus Roebling, engineer and bridge builder; John Jacob Astor, Henry John Heinz, Henry Engelhard Steinway, Levi Strauss, Henry Villard, and George Westinghouse, entrepreneurs; Fritz Lang, Ernst Lubitsch, Otto Preminger, and Billy Wilder, film directors; Charles Proteus Steinmetz, inventor; Friedrich Wilhelm von Steuben, Friedrich Hecker, and Franz Sigel, military men (the American Revolution and the Civil War, respectively); Henry Louis Mencken, journalist; Henry Kissinger, Jacob Leisler, and John Peter Gabriel Muhlenberg, politicians; and Theodor Adorno, Hannah Arendt, Herbert Marcuse, Max Horkheimer, Hans A. Bethe, Wernher von Braun, David Rittenhouse, Albert Bernhardt Faust, Franz Lieber, Philip Schaff, and Paul Tillich, scholars.

See also **Ethnicity: Early Theories; Ethnicity and Race; Marxist Approaches** *(volume 3).*

BIBLIOGRAPHY

General and Reference Works

Americans and Germans: A Handy Reader and Reference Book with 258 Illustrations. Gradelfing vor München, Germany, 1986.

Miller, Randall M., ed. *Germans in America: Retrospect and Prospect: Tricentennial Lectures Delivered at the German Society of Pennsylvania in 1983.* Philadelphia, 1984.

Moltmann, Günter, ed. *Germans to America: 300 Years of Immigration, 1683–1983.* Stuttgart, Germany, 1983.

Reichmann, Eberhard, LaVern J. Rippley, and Jörg Nagler, eds. *Emigration and Settlement Patterns of German Communities in North America.* Indianapolis, Ind., 1995.

Rippley, LaVern J. *The German-Americans.* Lanham, Md., 1984.

Schultz, Arthur R., ed. *German-American Relations and German Culture in America: A Subject Bibliography, 1941–1980.* Millwood, N.Y., 1984.

Thernstrom, Stephan, et al., eds. *Harvard Encyclopedia of American Ethnic Groups.* Cambridge, Mass., 1980. Includes articles by Kathleen Neils Conzen and Don Yoder.

Tolzmann, Don Heinrich. *The German-American Experience.* Amherst, N.Y., 2000.

Trommler, Frank, and Joseph McVeigh, eds. *America and the Germans: An Assessment of a Three-Hundred Year History.* 2 vols. Philadelphia, 1983.

Wust, Klaus von, and Heinz Moos, eds. *Three Hundred Years of German Immigrants in North America, 1683–1983: Their Contributions to the Evolution of the New World: A Pictorial History with 510 Illustrations*. Baltimore, Md., 1983.

Yearbook of German-American Studies. Lawrence, Kans.

Immigration and Settlement; Communities and Associations

Engle, Stephen Douglas. *The Yankee Dutchman: The Life of Franz Sigel*. Fayetteville, Ark., 1993.

Johnson, Charles Thomas. *Culture at Twilight. The National German-American Alliance, 1901–1918*. New York, 1999.

Kamphoefner, Walter D., Wolfgang Helbich, and Ulrike Sommer, eds. *News from the Land of Freedom: German Immigrants Write Home*. Translated by Susan Carter Vogel. Ithaca, N.Y., 1991.

Pickle, Linda Schelbitzki. *Contented among Strangers: Rural German-Speaking Women and Their Families in the Nineteenth-century Midwest*. Urbana, Ill., 1996.

Shaw, Stephen J. *The Catholic Parish as a Way-station of Ethnicity and Americanization: Chicago's Germans and Italians, 1903–1939*. Brooklyn, N.Y., 1991.

Struve, Walter. *Germans and Texans: Commerce, Migration, and Culture in the Days of the Lone-Star Republic*. Austin, Tex., 1996.

Language; Education; Press

Arndt, Karl John Richard. *German-American Newspapers and Periodicals, 1732–1955*. Heidelberg, Germany, 1961.

Geitz, Henry, ed. *The German American Press*. Madison, Wisc., 1992.

Geitz, Henry, Jürgen Heideking, and Jurgen Herbst, eds. *German Influences on Education in the United States to 1917*. Washington, D.C., 1995.

Lehmann, Hartmut, and James Sheehan, eds. *An Interrupted Past: German-speaking Historians in the United States after 1933*. Washington, D.C., 1991.

Shore, Elliott, Ken Fones-Wolf, and James P. Danky, eds. *The German-American Radical Press: The Shaping of a Left Political Culture, 1850–1940*. Urbana, Ill., 1992.

Arts; Letters; Science; and Popular Culture

Cazden, Robert E. *A Social History of the German Book Trade in America to the Civil War*. Columbia, S.C., 1984.

Keil, Hartmut, ed. *German Workers' Culture in the United States, 1850–1920*. Washington, D.C., 1988.

Merrill, Peter C. *German Immigrant Artists in America: A Biographical Dictionary*. Lanham, Md., 1997.

Pochmann, Henry A. With the assistance of Arthur R. Schultz and others. *German Culture in America: Philosophical and Literary Influences, 1600–1900*. Madison, Wisc., 1957.

Pumroy, Eric L., and Katja Rampelmann, comps. *Research Guide to the Turner Movement in the United States*. Westport, Conn., 1996.

Stuecher, Dorothea Diver. *Twice Removed: The Experience of German-American Women Writers in the Nineteenth Century*. New York, 1990.

Ward, Robert Elmer. *A Bio-bibliography of German-American Writers, 1670–1970*. White Plains, N.Y., 1985.

IRISH AMERICANS

Jay P. Dolan

THE COLONIAL ERA

The Irish were part of the Great Migration of European peoples that took place in the post-1600 period. The vast majority of these migrants journeyed to America; the Irish sent a larger proportion of their population to the New World than any other country. Ireland had undergone a radical transformation in the seventeenth century that resulted in an upsurge in emigration, which marked the beginning of the decline of Gaelic political power in Ireland. Symbolically, it began with the Flight of the Earls in 1607 when the leaders of Gaelic Ireland, defeated in battle, fled the country. Their lands were confiscated and handed over to English and Scottish newcomers. More confiscation of land took place during the Commonwealth era of Oliver Cromwell when his army ravaged the countryside of Ireland, forcing Catholic landowners to give up their land. Dispossessed of their land and considered outcast because of their religion, Irish Catholics began to migrate to colonial America. Other Irish came as convicts or as indentured servants—individuals who were sold into service for a number of years upon their arrival in the colonies. By the late 1600s the number of Irish Catholic immigrants was large enough that several colonies passed laws restricting the immigration of "Irish papists."

Despite such restrictions, Irish immigration to colonial America increased in the eighteenth century. During this period the profile of the Irish immigrant changed. The majority of these immigrants were Presbyterians from Ulster. The main reason so many Presbyterians left Ulster was an economic one: poor harvests, famine, and high rents persuaded many people to emigrate in the hope of bettering themselves in colonial America. Religion also entered into the equation. Since the Church of England was the established church in Ulster, Presbyterians often suffered discrimination at the hands of the Anglican rulers. Penalized because of their religion and facing a life of poverty, large numbers

of Ulster Irish abandoned their homeland. The majority of them settled in Pennsylvania and the Cumberland Valley. From here they migrated south to Virginia, the Carolinas, and Georgia. Settling along the frontier, the Ulster Irish acted as a buffer against hostile Indian raids. Known for their fighting prowess, they would come to play an important role in spearheading westward expansion.

Irish Catholics migrated to the colonies for the same reasons as the Presbyterians: economic opportunity and religious freedom. Coming from the south and west of Ireland, most traveled as indentured servants and settled in Maryland, where they worked on the farms of Catholic landowners. Pennsylvania was another favorite destination. Philadelphia was the hub of a significant trading network between Ireland and the American colonies, and this accounted for a sizable number of Irish merchants and artisans. By the end of the eighteenth century, Philadelphia's Irish numbered about six thousand. New York also had a large Irish community comprised of merchants, tavern keepers, artisans, laborers, and sailors.

By 1790, when the first national census was taken, the Irish population in the United States numbered between 400,000 and 500,000, or 13 to 16 percent of the white population. In terms of occupation and religion, the Irish were as diverse as the rest of the American population. Charles Carroll of Carrollton in Maryland was one of the wealthiest individuals in the new nation. The grandson of a seventeenth-century immigrant, Carroll distinguished himself during the American Revolution as a champion of independence. He was also present at the First Continental Congress in 1774. Two years later he fixed his signature to the Declaration of Independence. His cousin, John Carroll, became the first Roman Catholic bishop in the United States; most of the clergy who served with John Carroll were also Irish. Another prominent Irishman, Mathew Carey, emigrated to Philadelphia in the early 1780s and, by the turn of the century, established himself as a leading citizen in Philadelphia. A book publisher and prolific writer, he founded an emigrant aid society for the Irish in 1790. One of Philadelphia's leading merchants was the Irish Presbyterian, Blair McClenachan.

New York also had its share of prominent Irish. Waddell Cunningham and Thomas Greg were two of the city's most successful merchants. Samuel Clossy, a graduate of Trinity College in Dublin, was a well-respected physician. Joseph Murray had a distinguished career as an attorney and was a major benefactor of Kings College. Though there were numerous prominent Irish in colonial America, most Irish could be found at the bottom of the social ladder, crowding the city jails in New York and in Philadelphia, or working as porters, day laborers, or sailors. In terms of religion, the Irish were also very diverse. The New York Irish supported Anglican, Catholic, and Presbyterian congregations. Irish Catholics founded parishes in Philadelphia, Boston, and Charleston. Irish Presbyterians were prominent in New Jersey, Pennsylvania, and along the frontier, where they sparked a revival of religion in the 1790s. Irish Quakers could be found in Pennsylvania, Delaware, Virginia, and South Carolina.

By the middle of the eighteenth century, the Irish began to manifest a sense of ethnic identity. This was most evident in cities like Philadelphia and New York, where they founded benevolent societies to assist Irish immigrants in need. In these cities the Irish celebrated St. Patrick's Day with dinners, toasts, and parades—a tradition that has continued to the present day. In rural Maryland Irish Catholics bonded together in tightly knit communities. They acted as sponsors at the baptisms of other Catholic families, cared for orphans in the community, entered into business partnerships with one another, and supported and socialized with the clergy who ministered to them. Religion as well as ethnicity was the cement that bound this community together.

THE IMMIGRATION ERA: 1820–1920

In the early years of the nineteenth century, the decades prior to the Great Famine in Ireland (1845–1849), Irish America had already acquired those distinctive features that would set it apart from other ethnic groups for much of the nineteenth and twentieth centuries. Supporters of Republican politics in the Jefferson era, the Irish became enthusiastic Jacksonian Democrats by the late 1820s. Their allegiance to the Democratic Party would intensify in later years. Immigration from Ireland continued in these prefamine years, with the majority of newcomers arriving from Ulster. Large numbers of them settled in the cities along the northeast coast, where Irish communities were already well established. The religious tranquillity that marked the Irish in the colonial era slowly began to erode during these years. The rise of sectarian politics in Ireland during the campaign for Catholic emancipation set the tone for the rest of the century. Religious differences acquired an importance in nineteenth-century America that was not so noticeable in the Early Republic. Such differences often led to severe social conflict and sparked a Protestant crusade against Catholics in the 1830s and 1840s which was marked by the burning of convents and churches and the publication of numerous anti-Catholic, anti-Irish tracts.

IMMIGRATION AND SETTLEMENT

The Great Famine was a defining moment in Irish history and its impact on Irish America was also decisive. More than 1 million Irish men and women fled Ireland during these famine years. Because of the famine and the economic devastation it caused, emigration now became an accepted feature of Irish life. No other country in world history lost such a high proportion of its population to emigration in the United States. By 1900 the number of first- and second-generation Irish exceeded 3.3 million. Unlike prefamine Irish emigrants, the vast majority of Irish who came to the United States during and after the famine era were Catholic. They came from the desperately poor regions of the south and west of Ireland where a peasant, Gaelic culture still existed. Barely influenced by the modern industrial era, they carried few marketable skills with them. Mostly laborers or servants, they were young in age, in their teens or early twenties. As many women emigrated as men.

When these newcomers arrived, they settled in the cities where the Irish had already established their communities. By 1850 New York had emerged as the capital city of Irish America, and it maintained that distinction throughout the immigrant era. Philadelphia and Boston also had sizable Irish communities. Even though most Irish settled in cities along the northeast coast, large numbers of Irish could be found in Chicago, St. Louis, and San Francisco. They also established communities along the mining frontier of the West and Southwest. One of the most Irish communities in the country was Butte, Montana, the site of the Anaconda Mining

Company founded by the Irish immigrant laborer Marcus Daly in 1891. Daly not only amassed an enormous fortune, but his fame attracted numerous Irish to work in the Butte mines. By 1900 one of four people in Butte was Irish, a higher percentage of Irish than in any other American city at this time. Wherever they settled, the Irish established their own distinctive neighborhood enclaves known by such names as Dublin, Gulch, or Corktown. Although people of different ethnic backgrounds may have lived in these neighborhoods, the major cultural institutions in these locales were Irish. The Catholic Church was a physically imposing presence with its complex of structures—church, school, convent, and rectory—often occupying an entire city block. The saloon was another key neighborhood institution, along with the political club. Irish fraternal organizations also had their offices in these neighborhoods. One visitor noted that the urban Irish as well as other immigrant groups "create for themselves distinct communities, almost as impervious to American sentiments and influences as are the inhabitants of Dublin or Hamburg" (Dolan, *The American Catholic Experience*, p. 195).

CATHOLICISM AND NATIONALISM

For all practical purposes, to be called an Irishman or -woman in America during the immigrant era meant that you were also Roman Catholic. By this time the Ulster Irish, the vast majority of whom were Presbyterians, had sought to set themselves apart from the ragged masses of Catholic immigrants who came during and after the famine. In order to achieve this, they took on an identification as Scotch Irish and proceeded to participate in the anti-Catholic, anti-Irish crusade of the antebellum era. The establishment of the Orange Order in the United States in the early nineteenth century fostered this separation between Catholic and Protestant Irish. A fiercely anti-Catholic political organization founded in Ulster in 1795 to maintain the Protestant ascendancy in Ireland, and later imported to America, the Orange Order helped to perpetuate anti–Irish Catholic prejudices for much of the nineteenth century.

For Irish Catholics, religion was clearly a defining element of their culture. For more than two centuries Catholics in Ireland had suffered persecution and discrimination because of their religion. Even though they comprised the majority of the population, Irish Catholics suffered at the hands of their Protestant rulers and landlords. The nineteenth cen-

tury witnessed the revival of Irish Catholicism. Militantly sectarian, Catholicism in the mind of its followers became identified with the destiny of Ireland. This was the religion that the immigrants carried with them. Whether they were regular churchgoers or not, Irish immigrants remained loyal to their Catholic heritage. As a result, the church became one of the most important institutions in their community.

The Irish reshaped Catholicism in the United States during the nineteenth century. In the republican era Catholicism had a distinctive democratic ethos that was evident in local parish communities. It also nurtured a humanist religion centered on the person of Jesus and was tolerant of other religions. This all changed over the course of the nineteenth century, during which Catholicism became very sectarian. It emphasized clerical control and authoritarianism more than democracy. An Irish Puritan ethos, manifested in a stern moralism and nurtured by an elaborate popular devotionalism, shaped the religion of the people. The Irish clergy were the principal promoters of this Irish brand of Catholicism. Like the lay people, large numbers of Irish priests and nuns immigrated to the United States over the course of the nineteenth century, carrying the Irish brand of Catholicism with them. In some cities as many as half of the male clergy were Irish and well over half of the sisters were of Irish descent. By 1900, two out of three bishops in the United States were Irish—a dominance that would continue through the early part of the twentieth century. These were the leaders of the Catholic reform that took shape in the nineteenth century.

A defining feature of Irish Catholicism was the parish. More than just a church building, it was a center for the social and recreational life of the people. Modeled on the great Romanesque and Gothic churches of Europe, the church defined the neighborhood. The Irish valued education and supported a vast network of parochial schools, staffed by women religious recruited from Ireland. The school was the cornerstone of the parish and the principal institution responsible for handing on the faith to the younger generations. In addition to church and school, the Irish supported hospitals, orphanages, and other institutions devoted to the welfare of an immigrant population, which were founded and staffed by Irish women religious. On a regional level Irish Catholics supported many institutions of higher learning, thereby establishing the foundation for an expanding network of Catholic colleges for men and women.

Many of the more charismatic leaders of the immigrant church were of Irish descent. As bishop and later the first archbishop of New York (1850), the Irish-born John Hughes led the campaign for parochial schools and laid the cornerstone of St. Patrick's Cathedral. He ruled the New York clergy with an iron hand. When the clergy dared to challenge his authority, he threatened to "send them back to the bogs from whence they came" (Dolan, *Immigrant Church,* p. 164). As for the lay people, he never ceased to remind them that "Catholics did their duty when they obeyed their bishop" (ibid). Another Irish bishop, James Gibbons, was cut from a different cloth. As the archbishop of Baltimore from 1877 to 1921, he became the second Roman Catholic cardinal of North America, an honor reserved for only the most distinguished members of the hierarchy. More irenic and tolerant than Hughes, Gibbons often acted as a lobbyist with church authorities in Rome, helping them to understand more fully the special nature of Catholicism in the United States. A supporter of the workers' union the Knights of Labor, he convinced Pope Leo XIII to support this union by endorsing the right of workers to organize.

A contemporary of Gibbons was the Irish-born John Ireland, the archbishop of St. Paul, Minnesota. An eloquent orator, he was an advocate of a more American, progressive style of Catholicism. He wanted the immigrant Catholics to become more American and encouraged them to cooperate with the nation's public school system by joining together to form Catholic public schools. His desire was to have "church and age unite" so that Catholicism would be better able to shape and refashion American culture. Like John Carroll, he praised American democracy and the separation of church and state.

As religion shaped the Irish soul, the dream of a free and independent Ireland inspired it. The immigrants carried this spirit of nationalism with them to the United States and remained very involved with the struggle for Irish independence. Irish American nationalism intensified during the famine era. Famine immigrants carried with them a strong sense of exile and a bitter dislike of British rule, which many blamed for the human devastation caused by the famine. They channeled these sentiments into clubs and organizations whose only purpose was to support the crusade for an independent Ireland. The Fenians, an Irish nationalist society founded in New York City in 1858, championed a revolutionary nationalism. In Ireland its counterpart, the Irish Republican Brotherhood, was established at the same time. By the 1860s, Fenian organizations could be found in most Irish communities. Many of their members were Civil War veterans. As enthusiasm for an armed rebellion in Ireland waned, the Fenians declined in importance.

New York City was the site for the founding of another revolutionary organization, the Clan na Gael. Founded in 1867, it was a secret organization that maintained close ties with the Irish Republican Brotherhood. Like the Fenians, it advocated the violent overthrow of British rule. Though the Clan never attracted many members, it fueled the flames of Irish American nationalism, and provided financial and political support for the Irish Republican Brotherhood in the armed Easter Rising of 1916.

Another more moderate strain of nationalism also existed among Irish Americans. It endorsed the idea of constitutional, legislative reform through the British Parliament rather than the violent overthrow of British rule. The Home Rule movement in Ireland in the late nineteenth and early twentieth centuries was the principal expression of this idea of reform. Led by the Irish members of Parliament Charles Stewart Parnell and later John Redmond, it sought a political solution to the cause of Irish independence. Both Parnell and Redmond made speaking tours of Irish America, raising substantial funds for the Home Rule movement. After the failure of the Easter Rising in 1916 and the execution of its leaders, the people of Ireland began an armed struggle for independence. Irish Americans contributed millions of dollars to support Irish freedom. They also lobbied the American government to put pressure on England to grant Ireland independence. With the establishment of the Irish Free State in 1922, Irish American nationalism subsided, only to be rekindled by the civil rights movement in Ireland in the 1960s and 1970s.

POLITICS, LABOR, AND LITERATURE

Early in their history, the Irish were actively involved in politics. In Ireland the Catholic campaign for emancipation, or the right to be an elected member of Parliament, was a popular crusade in the 1820s. Thousands of people cheered the campaign's leader, the Irish lawyer and orator Daniel O'Connell, and such popular support persuaded the British government to allow Irish Catholics to have representatives in Parliament. Schooled in the political process of this campaign and others like it throughout the course of the nineteenth century, Irish immigrants carried with them a taste for politics. Their ability to speak English and the timing of their arrival, just when the political machine and mass party politics was taking shape in America, enabled the Irish to take advantage of the opportunities offered by the changing political climate.

While the Irish did not invent the political machine, they soon mastered it. In New York they became closely identified with the notoriously corrupt "Tweed Ring" that ran the city in the 1860s. Led by the rotund politician William Marcy Tweed, the ring included Peter Barr Sweeny, the county treasurer, and Richard Connolly, city comptroller, both Irish immigrants. The Irish also ruled Tammany Hall, the executive committee of New York City's Democratic Party that controlled the city government from 1854 to 1934. William Grace, an Irish immigrant who became a shipping magnate, became the city's first Irish Catholic mayor in 1880. Richard "Boss" Croker was another Irish immigrant who used politics as the avenue to success, and as the leader of Tammany Hall in the 1880s he amassed an estate valued at 8 million dollars.

Boston, one of the most Irish cities in the nation, was another city where the Irish were politically powerful, although, unlike New York, there was no single political machine in Boston that ruled city politics. The Irish gained political clout as local ward or neighborhood bosses. They elected Boston's first Irish Catholic mayor, Hugh O'Brien, in 1884, who was reelected three more times. Prior to 1920 Boston would have four more Irish mayors. John Fitzgerald, born in Boston, was affectionately known as "Honey Fitz." After serving in Congress for three terms he returned to Boston to become mayor from 1906 to 1907 and again from 1910 to 1913. His oldest daughter, Rose, married Joseph P. Kennedy, and their son, John, later became president of the United States.

Surely one of Boston's most colorful political figures was James Michael Curley. He became mayor of Boston in 1914 and would serve three more terms, serving part of his last term in federal prison following a conviction for mail fraud. He also served as governor of Massachusetts from 1935 to 1937. When he died in 1958, 1 million people lined the streets to mourn his passing. In addition to Boston and New York, in the 1890s Irish politicians ruled in Chicago, San Francisco, Pittsburgh, St. Louis, New Orleans, and Buffalo, New York. As one writer put it in 1894, they "have a genius for municipal government—at least for getting municipal offices."

Another arena that attracted the Irish was the labor movement. As in politics, the timing of their arrival was crucial. Large numbers of Irish came when the organized labor movement was beginning to take shape. Working class and speaking English, the Irish were ideal candidates to become members and leaders in the union movement. No other ethnic group would match them for union activism in the nineteenth and twentieth centuries. The first major labor organization, the Knights of Labor, was overwhelmingly Irish. In 1879, Terence V. Powderly, the son of Irish immigrant parents, became head of the Knights. During his fifteen-year tenure as Grand Master Workman of the Knights, Powderly successfully gained the approval of the Catholic Church for the union and opened up the union to all occupations, nationalities, and races (except Chinese), as well as to women. With the rise of the American Federation of Labor and trade unions in the 1890s, the Irish continued to take on leadership roles. By the first decade of the twentieth century, more than fifty of the 110 unions in the American Federation of Labor had an Irish person as president.

In the second half of the nineteenth century the best-known women labor activists were Irish. The Irish-born Elizabeth Rodgers was not only the mother of eight children, but the head of the Knights of Labor in the Chicago district, whose membership numbered 50,000. The immigrant Leonora Barry (also known as Mother Lake) was a key organizer for the Knights of Labor in Amsterdam, New York, and headed up the Knight's Department of Women's Work. Margaret Haley, a teacher in Chicago's elementary schools, was the major force behind the organization of the Chicago Teachers' Federation, the first teachers union in the United States.

Ideologically, Irish involvement in the labor movement covered the spectrum from conservative to radical. The Molly Maguires, a clandestine organization of coal miners in the anthracite region of Pennsylvania, terrorized the coalfields of Pennsylvania from 1862 to 1875. Accused and convicted of a series of assassinations, twenty Irishmen were hanged between 1877 and 1879. The Irish-born Mary Harris Jones became known as the "Joan of Arc" of the coalfields. She was a strong supporter of Terence Powderly and the Knights of Labor. Called "the greatest woman agitator of her time," she would appear at major strikes throughout the country and with uncommon eloquence rally the workers. She earned the title of "Mother Jones" because she cared for striking workers injured in battles with police. In addition to her work with the United Mine Workers union, she was also one of the founders of the Social Democratic Party in 1898 and of the Industrial Workers of the World in 1905.

Mother Jones (1830–1930). Born in Cork in 1830, Mary Jones came to America with her family in 1835, after her activist father had been forced to leave Ireland. Her grandmotherly appearance belies her incendiary nature. © UNDERWOOD & UNDERWOOD/CORBIS

Politics and the labor movement proved to be an economic escalator for large numbers of Irish. They gained jobs in various trades where the Irish held leadership positions. In the cities politically dominated by the Irish, patronage flourished. As many as one in three municipal workers in these cities were Irish. Such opportunities enabled the children of the immigrants to move into the lower middle class. As they journeyed from rags to respectability, the Irish gained greater acceptance in American society. By World War I the Irish Paddie of the famine era had become the American Patriot.

Another very important dimension of the Irish American experience was its literary tradition. The first generation of Irish American writers in the pre-famine era was a sophisticated, confident generation who were at home in the new American culture. Satire and comedy were defining features of their work. With the famine generation such laughter ceased. More sober, this generation of writers wrote fictional tracts that sought to educate the newcomers. Three themes were dominant: how to keep the faith in Protestant America; how to get along in a new homeland; and how to have a spirit of nationalism. The most prolific writer at this time was the Irish-born Mary Anne Sadlier. Married and the mother of six children, Sadlier published more than sixty volumes of literature in a career that lasted throughout the second half of the nineteenth century. Her writings are moralistic tales that provide a valuable insight into immigrant culture.

By 1900, a sizable number of Irish, perhaps as many as 20 percent of the population, had moved into the middle class. The writers of the 1890s and early twentieth century reflected this transition. Finley Peter Dunne of Chicago best represents this generation of writers. Charles Fanning described Dunne as "Irish American literature's first genius" (p. 214). The American-born Dunne was at home in the United States. His writings exhibited a self-confident and, at times, critical view of American society. He created the fictional Mr. Dooley, a memorable character whose homespun philosophy on life in Irish America charms his readers. Like Mark Twain's Huck Finn, Dunne created Mr. Dooley, a saloonkeeper on Chicago's South Side, to speak in a unique Irish dialect. His monologues, delivered to his customers in the saloon, and printed each week in the Chicago newspapers, are still read today for their valuable insights into the character of the American Irish at the turn of the century.

By the 1920s the Irish American literary tradition had reached a nadir. This generation of writers, best illustrated in the writings of F. Scott Fitzgerald, were ambivalent about their Irish heritage. American born and middle class, they rejected the ethnic Irish literary tradition and focused on themes not peculiar to Irish culture. This would all change in the 1930s with a new generation of writers.

THE AMERICANIZATION OF THE IRISH: 1920–2000

Though the Irish began the process of Americanization the moment they landed on the nation's shores, the twentieth century was the period in which the descendants of the immigrant generation acquired a decidedly American identity.

After a large influx of about 210,000 immigrant Irish in the 1920s, immigration rapidly declined. In fact, more Irish returned to Ireland in the 1930s than emigrated to the United States. The new immigration legislation passed by Congress in 1965 did not favor the Irish. In the 1980s, however, lobbying by the Irish government and Irish American organizations secured favored treatment for the Irish. As a result, the number of Irish immigrants increased in the 1980s, and in the 1990s more than 60,000 Irish came to the United States, the highest number of immigrating Irish since the 1920s. In the 1990s, Ireland experienced an economic surge, largely because of American investments. Due to this prosperity, immigration from Ireland declined, and large numbers of Irish Americans returned to their homeland.

For much of the twentieth century the defining features of the Irish immigrant era remained strong. The Irish continued to have a strong presence within the Catholic Church. Even as late as 1970, half of the Catholic hierarchy and one out of every three priests was of Irish descent. A similar numerical dominance among women religious was also present. The Irish Catholic ethos, fashioned in Ireland and transplanted to the United States, continued to influence generations of Catholics. Changes within the church since the 1960s and the influx of new Catholic immigrants from Asia and Latin America had begun to remake American Catholicism. As this developed the Irish influence on American Catholicism started to diminish.

The 1920s was the heyday of the Irish political machine. Irish bosses controlled New York City, Jersey City, Kansas City, Chicago, Pittsburgh, Boston, and Albany, New York. Alfred E. Smith, the four-time governor of New York and a beneficiary of Tammany Hall's political clout, was the Democratic candidate for president in 1928. The first Roman Catholic to run for the U.S. presidency, he lost in an election noted for its anti-Catholic, anti-Irish tenor. During the presidency of Franklin D. Roosevelt, many Irish men and women rose to political prominence at the national level. Thomas G. Corcoran, James A. Farley, and John W. McCormack were three of the most distinguished of this group. The Irish rise to political prominence at the national level reached its zenith in 1960 when John F. Kennedy was elected president. As the Irish moved into the middle class in large numbers in the post–World War II era, they left the city for the suburb. Such a shift signaled the demise of the Irish political boss, with the exception of Chicago, where Mayor Richard J. Daley and his Irish machine ruled the city from 1955 until his death in 1976.

Throughout the twentieth century the Irish continued to have a significant presence in the labor movement. At the national level the American labor leader Philip Murray was a major figure in the United Mine Workers from the 1920s to the 1940s. In 1940 he became president of the Congress of Industrial Organizations (CIO) and remained in office until his death in 1952. George Meany was another major labor leader, who became president of the American Federation of Labor (AFL) in 1952. When it merged with the CIO in 1955, he was chosen president and remained its head until 1979. As the Irish moved out of the working class in the post–World War II era, their membership and leadership in the labor movement waned. The election of John J. Sweeney, the son of Irish immigrants, to the AFL-CIO presidency in 1995 suggested that the Irish presence in the American labor movement still remained significant at the end of the twentieth century.

The 1930s witnessed the arrival of one of Irish America's great literary geniuses, James T. Farrell. His famous *Studs Lonigan* trilogy has become an American classic. Set in Chicago in a lower-middle-class Irish neighborhood, it examines the social and moral failings of Irish American culture. As the most illustrious of a generation of writers who wrote about Irish America in the 1930s and 1940s, his writings fill over fifty volumes. In the 1950s another acclaimed writer, Edwin O'Connor, emerged on the literary scene. His novel about Irish politics, *The Last Hurrah* (1956), immortalized the career of Boston's James Michael Curley. Another novel, *The Edge of Sadness* (1961), focuses on religion and complacency in a parochial Irish world. It earned O'Connor the Pulitzer Prize in 1962. With the rise of ethnic consciousness in the closing decades of the twentieth century, a new wave of Irish writers emerged, the more notable of whom included William Kennedy, Alice McDermott, and James Carroll.

Irish American nationalism, dormant since the creation of the Irish Free State in 1922, reappeared in the 1960s and 1970s as a civil rights movement transformed Northern Ireland. Together with such Irish American politicians as Senators Edward Kennedy and Daniel Patrick Moynihan, many Irish Americans were able to persuade the American government to become involved in the Ulster peace process. In the 1990s, President Bill Clinton and Senator George Mitchell, both of Irish heritage, played key roles in this search for peace in Northern Ireland. The journey of the Irish from the shanty-towns of urban America to the White House is one of the great American success stories. Their long and varied history has touched all aspects of American life.

See also **Ethnicity: Early Theories; Ethnicity and Race** *(volume 3); and other articles in this section.*

BIBLIOGRAPHY

Blessing, Patrick J. "The Irish." In *Harvard Encyclopedia of American Ethnic Groups,* edited by Stephan Thernstrom. Cambridge, Mass., 1980.

Diner, Hasia. *Erin's Daughters in America: Irish Immigrant Women in the Nineteenth Century.* Baltimore, 1983.

Dolan, Jay P. *The Immigrant Church: New York's Irish and German Catholics, 1815–1865.* Baltimore, 1975.

Emmons, David M. *The Butte Irish: Class and Ethnicity in an American Mining Town, 1875–1925.* Urbana, Ill., 1989.

Erie, Steven P. *Rainbow's End: Irish Americans and the Dilemmna of Urban Machine Politics, 1840–1985.* Berkeley, 1988.

Fanning, Charles. *The Irish Voice in America: Irish American Fiction from the 1960s to the 1980s.* Lexington, Ky., 1990.

Glazier, Michael, ed. *The Encyclopedia of the Irish in America.* Notre Dame, Ind., 1999.

Handlin, Oscar. *Boston's Immigrants 1790–1865.* Cambridge, Mass., 1941.

Knobel, Dale T. *Paddy and the Republic: Ethnicity and Nationality in Antebellum America.* Middletown, Conn., 1986.

Levine, Edward M. *The Irish and Irish Politicians: A Study of Cultural and Social Alienation.* Notre Dame, Ind., 1966.

Miller, Kerby. *Emigrants and Exiles: Ireland the Irish Exodus to North America.* New York, 1985.

O'Connor, Thomas H. *The Boston Irish: A Political History.* Boston, 1995.

Potter, George W. *To The Golden Door: The Story of the Irish in Ireland and America.* Boston, 1960.

Shannon, William V. *The American Irish.* New York, 1967.

Thernstrom, Stephan. *Poverty and Progess: Social Mobility in an American City.* Cambridge, Mass., 1964.

ITALIAN AMERICANS

Thomas J. Ferraro

MIGRATION, MOBILITY, AND THE SOCIOLOGISTS

From the time of the Great Migration of the 1880s to the prejudicial immigration restriction laws that were implemented by 1924, the representation of Italians in the United States fell by default to non-Italians. The exception was a fragile Italian language press that addressed the comparatively few immigrants who were literate in standard written Italian. The majority of Italians who emigrated to the United States—at least 5 million of them—were *contadini* (peasants) from south and east of Naples, rarely skilled and less often literate. They arrived as transient labor, for years shuttled money and themselves back and forth to Italy, and only subsequently settled down, with increasing numbers of emigrant women and children, to stay. As early as 1872, with Charles Loring Brace's *The Dangerous Classes of New York,* the men who would be most exploited to build the industrial cities (Thomas Kessner cites that by 1890, 90 percent of all labor on New York City Public Works projects was Italian) were already serving as scapegoats for what the American majority feared about those cities: filth, ignorance, crime, and cultural difference. In the work of cartoonists such as Thomas Nast, Italians were portrayed as dark-skinned, misshapen, sinister stiletto-wielders—"guineas," "dagos," and "wops"—whose simian features were shared with other racially suspect peoples. Progressivist reformers and social workers of goodwill (including Jacob Riis, Jane Addams, and Ernest Poole) addressed serious concerns—tenement housing, infant mortality, child labor—but in their reports it was sometimes difficult to distinguish between humane empathy and nativist anxiety. Jacob Riis responded to Italian foodstuffs with the kind of ignorant disdain—"slimy, odd-looking creatures . . . that never swam in American waters," "big, awkward sausages, anything but appetizing"—that greeted the immigrants themselves (p. 50).

Italian America had its antecedents among a people disenfranchised from the great intellectual, artistic, and sociopolitical legacies of northern Italy; a people who, for good reason, were notoriously suspicious of government and business, of the Roman Catholic Church, and of elite education, and who therefore held their young people emotionally and culturally close, making "the family" and immediate community, first defined by dialect and region, the principal means and thus the only logical ends of their existence; a people attached to "*la via vecchia*" and reluctant to embrace change, telling themselves "*Chi lascia la via vecchia per la nuova, sa quel che perde e non sa quel che trova*"—"Whoever forsakes the old way for the new knows what he is losing but not what he will find." The southern Italian "domus" was *the* center of an ethnic, predominantly but not exclusively working-class subculture that was "home smart" *and* that admired both street savvy and technical expertise, *but* that feared characteristically American forms of self-determination, including liberal education, exogamy, and geographic mobility. The clash of values was epitomized by a proverb common to Italian Americans not to educate one's daughter, as the scholar Jerre Mangione noted, "because she'll write letters to her boyfriend." Although a sorority was founded at Barnard College in the early 1920s to accommodate Italian American women (whom the established sororities would not admit), Italian American women would remain significantly underrepresented in many professions late into the twentieth century, not in small measure by their own design (as the St. John's University School of Law professor Rosemary Salomone has shown).

In the flashback section of the 1974 film *The Godfather, Part II,* which narrates the early adulthood of the crime boss Vito Corleone, the film's director Francis Ford Coppola created a suggestive glimpse of what sufficed as "cultural and intellectual life" among the vast majority of Italian immigrants and their children. At the center of concern is the family—a unit of both ultimate religious value *and* economic last resort that was extended, in better times, by neighborhood institutions of symbolic kinship (adults standing godparents to each other's children), men's networks (café, clubs, and light-opera theaters), and women's networks (centered on kitchen and stoop). The June Fiesta of San Rocco in Greenwich Village that the film features is one of the many that functioned over time, however reminiscent of local Italian hilltown celebrations, to forge disparate village and regional identities into a (pan) Italian American ethnicity. The fiesta functioned as a catharsis for filial guilt and parental anger at inevitable change, and it did so by reasserting the values of home, food, and sacrifice—a "theology of the streets"—in the face of increasing opportunities for social mobility and cultural assimilation.

Concentrated conspicuously in the industrial Northeast and Midwest, the American offspring of Italians enacted a slow yet steady transformation from the unskilled underclasses to the solid blue-collar ranks—a demographic shift signaled as early as the late 1920s, set back by the Great Depression, and then secured at midcentury, with the relaxing of once-virulent prejudice (in 1942 President Franklin D. Roosevelt removed Italians from the "suspect aliens" list and closed the internment camps), the coming of postwar prosperity, and the lasting force of the GI Bill. Yet it was during this period, from the 1920s through the late 1950s, that Italian American family culture became of grievous concern to social workers and cultural arbiters who, with Eastern European Jewish trajectories in mind, held the "fatalistic" ethos of Italian American "peer-group sociability" responsible for the group's "retarded" progress. The Harvard sociologist Edward Banfield in *The Moral Basis of a Backward Society* (1958), traced the endemic problems of the Italian South to a single institution—which he called, pointedly, its "amoral familialism." To read Banfield, or the Yale psychologist Irvin Long Child (*Italian or American?*, 1943), is excruciating now, yet the same moment also produced empathetic, incisive, if at times condescending accounts of the Italian American experience: the intermittent essays of the Bronx educator Leonard Covello, a domus veteran; *South Italian Folkways in Europe and America* (1938) by Phyllis Williams, a researcher in sociology at Yale University; William Foote Whyte's *Street Corner Society* (1943), which portrays the "social structure of racketeering" (including police sanction) seriously; and Herbert Gans's portrait of Boston's West End on the eve of its elimination, *Urban*

Villagers (1962), a transitional work that culminates midcentury sociology and anticipates the turn to the new social history.

REALIST FICTION IN THE BLUE-COLLAR ERA

It was also during the blue-collar period that the Italian American family produced its first professionals, at times by alienating the ambitious young, at other times by supporting them, corporately and proudly. Along with the boxers and ballplayers, the orchestral and band musicians, the mayors and ward heelers whom the nation vividly recalls (Joe DiMaggio, Fiorello La Guardia, and Frank Sinatra), came a coterie of novelists, journalists, and professors who are little remembered now, but whose autobiography, historical fiction, and autobiographical fiction constituted the Italian American beachhead into "American intellectual history." First cataloged by the librarian Olga Peragallo in 1949 in her *Italian-American Authors and Their Contribution to American Literature,* the Italian American literary risorgimento was nuanced where the sociology of the same period was characteristically reductive, and corrective where the sociology was often wrong—but only, as it were, in passing. For the primary purpose of the genre was to enable, either through a direct restaging or through allegorical inference, the writer's passage from immigrant enclaves to the polyethnic world of letters—in which the double curse of the immigrant writer (guilt for abandoning the past and anxiety over inadequate cultural capital) are cross-interrogated if not mutually exorcised. In the best of the works, produced in the late 1930s and early 1940s, thick realistic description courts mythic power.

In the 1920s, some attention in literary circles was paid to a series of "from alien to citizen" autobiographies—most notably by the sociologist Constantine Panunzio (*The Soul of an Immigrant,* 1921) and the "pick and shovel poet" Pascal (born Pasquale) D'Angelo (*Pascal D'Angelo, Son of Italy,* 1924). Honorable mention also goes to Louis Forgione's novelization of the famous 1906 Cuocolo murders, *The Men of Silence* (1928), which documents the investigation and prosecution of the Camorra (a mafia) in Naples by the remarkable Joseph Petrosino—a New York City police detective of Neapolitan descent who, in 1895, as a near-rookie, helped Maria Barbella escape being the first woman executed in the electric chair, and who was brought onto the Cuocolo case at the behest of the Italian government. The publication of *The Men of Silence* confirmed crime as an Italian problem, yet portrayed Italian America as integral to its solution: it was a potential force in the wake of the resurgence of anti-Italian sentiment surrounding the case of the Italian anarchists Sacco and Vanzetti, and also a harbinger—one year before the publication of Dashiell Hammett's *Red Harvest*—of the hard-boiled detective novel.

The first work of Italian American literature to reach a national audience was a short story, "Christ in Concrete," which appeared in *Esquire* in 1937. On Good Friday, a bricklayer who is also supervisor to his small work crew, is buried alive when a retaining wall, which the contractor refuses to build to legal specifications, collapses. In "Christ in Concrete," Pietro Di Donato fashioned a rough lyric vernacular to give the effect, in English, of the dialect sensibility of preliterate skilled laborers, earthy and articulate in ungenteel yet warm ways; the story foregrounds a man of fierce husbandly and paternal dedication, fixated upon the culmination of twenty years of work to buy a modest house, about to be trapped (literally) in capitalism's contradictions; and the story is laced not only with a Christic protest idiom—his hero sacrificed at the altar of American greed—but with a "pagan Catholic" or Marian sense of sacramental materiality toward food and connubial sexuality especially. So strong was the literary reception that Di Donato felt compelled to continue the story; in 1939, the Book-of-the-Month Club made *Christ in Concrete* its main selection, at the expense of first alternate, John Steinbeck's *The Grapes of Wrath*. Over the course of a long lifetime, Di Donato continued to write fiction and nonfiction, including a history (1960) of Mother Cabrini, the first "American Saint."

Jerre Mangione, the national coordinating editor of the Federal Writers' Project, and its major historian (*The Dream and the Deal*, 1972), was the scion of a Sicilian family of bricklayers. Born and raised in Rochester, New York, educated at Syracuse University, and employed as a professor of English at the University of Pennsylvania, Mangione was also uncle to the accomplished jazz trumpeter, Chuck Mangione. In 1943, Jerre Mangione produced a set of autobiographical sketches that, at the publisher's insistence, was repackaged into "a fictional memoir"—*Mount Allegro*—and focused on the conviviality of Mangione's extended family. As the scholar Werner Sollors has observed, *Mount Allegro* provides an anthropological "folklore" corrective (albeit featuring a strong comic component) to the despairing sociological portrait of *Christ in Con-*

crete: a difference in approach sponsored, in part, by the economic conditions distinguishing metropolitan New York at the height of the Great Depression from the smaller industrial cities of upstate New York during Mangione's youth in the 1920s. In the course of a long career, Mangione wrote several novels and many books on a wide range of topics—on his own experiences as the honorary Italian among the "New York Intellectuals" (*Ethnic at Large*, 1978); on the famed Sicilian socialist and social worker Danilo Dolci (*A Passion for Sicilians*, 1968); and on five hundred years of Italian American history (*La Storia*, 1992, with Ben Morreale).

Of more concentrated ambition as a novelist was John Fante, who was raised in Colorado and sporadically educated at the University of Colorado and Long Beach Junior College. Fante's best-known novel, *Wait Until Spring, Bandini* (1938) attempts psychological realism within a second generation setting: a son's effort to deal with the tension between his mother's devout Catholicism and his father's philandering ways, against the backdrop of labor, poverty, and prejudice in the stone-cutting industry of the Colorado Rockies. Three novels later, Fante turned *Wait Until Spring, Bandini* into the first book of a tetralogy, *The Saga of Arturo Bandini*. A half century later, in the wake of a republication of Fante's corpus, an Italian-French-Belgium production company produced quite a faithful film adaptation of *Wait Until Spring*, with the actor Joe Mantegna portraying Arturo's father.

Less well known are two stronger novels manifesting marked empathy for women. Michael De Capite's *Maria* (1943), rendered in spare reminiscent naturalist prose, tells the story of a second generation woman in Cleveland, who is married at the behest of her family, bears several children in rapid sequence, and then is abandoned to poverty when the husband cannot face the shame of his financial stupidity. With inarticulate intensity, De Capite's title character learns to fight on behalf of her children, bouncing between factory lines and relief lines during the Great Depression, securing a stepfather who again proves improvident, and finally finding the ethical courage (in a devastating turn of events) to have an untimely pregnancy aborted. Mari Tomasi's second novel and the first significant work of Italian American fiction by a woman, *Like Lesser Gods* (1949), is told over the shoulder of an immigrant schoolteacher with a resolutely Franciscan sensibility. It examines the pleasures and dangers of the Vermont granite industry, where cutters from the Piedmont make art of stone, yet in doing so risk death from a lung disease specific to granite (unknown in Italy). The characters put their wives in the untenable position of having to mediate between a vocation of sacred force (the cutters being "like lesser gods") and its threat to life, love, and security (ultimately ameliorated by advances in safety technology).

The publication of serious fiction continued into the 1960s, with particularly accomplished contributions by Raymond De Capite (Michael's brother), in his *The Coming of Fabrizze* (1960), whose protagonist is, as the scholar Rose Basile Green summarized, "a folk-hero of the Italian-American zest for life"; and, alternatively, Rocco Fumento's *Tree of Dark Reflection* (1962), whose lyrical yet ominous title invokes the psychological dynamics of second generation cultural re-formation. In 1964, just at the moment when the immigration restriction laws were finally stripped of their pro-northern European biases, Mario Puzo—a virtual unknown from Hell's Kitchen via postwar Germany—published an autobiographical novel focused on his mother. At once the most specifically Southern Italian and most generically ethnic achievement in American immigrant fiction, Puzo's *The Fortunate Pilgrim* portrays the twice-abandoned matriarch of an impoverished family who, after much struggle, achieves security, only to have to ask for mercy (within the framework of the most unforgiving of social mores) for having alienated her children from her heritage—and herself.

INTELLECTUALS AND THE NEW ETHNIC CONSCIOUSNESS

In terms of intellectual history proper, the breakthrough decade for Italian Americans was, beyond debate, the 1970s. Coincident with the rise of the new ethnic consciousness nationwide was Italian America's first significant steps into the professions, a demographic shift that included the first of what the historian Antonio Gramsci called "organic intellectuals": predominantly sociologists and historians, mainly but not hermetically academic, working across the minority-majority line. These Italian American intellectuals produced "thick descriptions" (in the anthropologist Clifford Geertz's sense) of what the people already knew: the reciprocal interplay between the family and capitalism; the special role of a de facto matriarchy in mediating cultural reproduction; and the contributions of the U.S. industrial city to putatively Italian forms of enterprise, class mobility, and group identity. By 1983, the striking, apparently sudden presence of Italian

American leaders in government, business, and the professions prompted the journalist Stephen S. Hall to title his cover story for the *New York Times Sunday Magazine*, "Italian Americans Coming into Their Own."

In 1964, the historian Rudolph J. Vecoli wrote a short, blistering critique of Oscar Handlin's *The Uprooted* (1951), which not only initiated massive reconsideration of Italian Americans over the next two decades—by Humbert Nelli, Virginia Yans-McLaughlin, John W. Briggs, Thomas Kessner, Judith Smith, Andrew Rolle, Francis Ianni, Victor Greene, and others—but almost single-handedly put the family inflection (as opposed to labor and women's foci) in what would be called "the new social history" as it arrived on the national academic agenda, and which was codified after a quarter-century of research in John Bodnar's *The Transplanted* (1985). By 1975, Richard Gambino had produced *Blood of My Blood*, which systematized "the old ways" for a popular as well as academic audience; Wayne Moquin had given *A Documentary History of the Italian Americans*; Francesco Cordasco and Eugene Bucchioni had written *The Italians: Social Backgrounds of an American Group*; Rose Basile Green had cataloged Italian American literary production, on the heels of Olga Peragallo; Luigi Barzini produced his best-seller, *The Italians* (1964), while Ann Cornelisen had followed up *Torregreca* (1969) with *Women of the Shadows* (1976); the journalist Gay Talese (1971), the sociologist Francis Ianni (1972), and the historian Humbert Nelli (1976) had produced works on syndicate crime; and Marcella Hazan had produced a wonderful cookbook and cultural guidebook, *The Classic Italian Cook Book* (1973). The American Italian Historical Association would be founded in 1967, producing its own journal devoted to Italian American history, sociology, and the arts.

In the years since 1975, the "new" ethnic history has been consolidated with the work of another generation, inspired in part by Werner Sollors's seminal work, which paved the way for moving "beyond ethnicity," meaning, in part, beyond ethnic essentialism. Increasing attention was paid to the relation of culture persistence and the urban economy (the Bodnar/Simon/Weber consortium *Lives of Their Own*); to the emergence of racial consciousness (in the works of Jonathan Rieder and Robert A. Orsi); to the "twilight of ethnicity" among third and fourth generation suburbanites (in the works of Richard Alba and Mary Waters); and to the varieties of ethnicity experienced among rural, often Protestant, often Northern Italian settlements (in the works of Micaela di Leonardo and Donna Gabaccia). In *The Madonna of 115th Street* (1985), Robert A. Orsi analyzed the East Harlem devotion to the Blessed Virgin in terms of immigration and mobility—thereby partially secularizing immigrant religious expression while also formulating, in his authorial compassion for the immigrant women, a Marian interpetive sensibility.

Although Peragallo and Basile Green pioneered the cataloging of Italian American literature, the first steps to thinking imaginatively about it appeared in the early 1980s from the comparativist Robert Viscusi, whose essays spin a transatlantic genealogy; and, an ocean apart, from Americanist William Boelhower, who applied semiotics to demystify ethnic representation as an Americanizing genre. Helen Barolini followed up her own successful *Umbertina* (1979), a multigenerational autobiographical novel, with an alertly introduced anthology, *The Dream Book* (1985), generously inclusive, that features occasional gems, including several poets and excerpts from her contemporary Tina de Rosa's novel, *Paper Fish* (1980). Working at the intersection of these pioneering efforts, a triumvirate of Chicago-area scholars, Fred L. Gardaphé, Paolo A. Giordano, and Anthony Julian Tamburri, combined critical essays and creative writing in an anthology, *From the Margin* (1991), uncannily answering the long-standing question "Where are the Italian American novelists?" before the senior statesman Gay Talese notoriously reuttered it in 1993.

Gardaphé's *Italian Signs, American Streets* (1996) draws upon the Italian philosopher Giambattista Vico's mythic historiography to offer the first comprehensive interpretation of Italian American narrative—from Constantine Panunzio and Pietro Di Donato through its contemporary prophetic turn in the postmodernists Gilbert Sorrentino and Don DeLillo. In 1998, the first Gay Talese Prize was given to the English professor Louise DeSalvo for her critical autobiography, *Vertigo,* in the genre visited variously by myriad others, including several contributors to *Beyond the Godfather* (1998): Sandra M. Gilbert, Frank Lentricchia, Marianna Torgovnick, and Jay Parini.

THE MEDIA ARTS: FILM, PAINTING, POP MUSIC, AND VIDEO

In the late 1990s, Pellegrino D'Acierno, a comparativist, screenwriter, and theoretician of architecture and film, led a prodigious effort to consider the entire span of Italian aesthetic production, in his *The Italian-American Heritage: A Companion to Literature and the Arts,* an exemplar of its kind, hugely informative, smart, provocative, and beautifully illustrated. While the work by diverse scholars in the volume pays testimony to the consolidation of a formidable Italian American intelligentsia, what the pages themselves reveal is a simple, paradoxical, yet elegant fact: in the final analysis, Italian America has had its most lasting cultural, and hence "intellectual," impact on mainstream culture not through intellectual work proper but rather via aesthetic form—not only the novel and self-reflective essay, but also, indeed principally, through popular and classical music, vanguard and amateur painting, architecture as well as construction, and, above all, independent auteur and Hollywood studio filmmaking. This is a message America at large still needed to hear: in the director Spike Lee's film *Do the Right Thing* (1989), for instance, the vaunted "wall of fame" in Sal's Pizzeria invokes the Italian American iconographic practice accurately enough, but the black and white photographs (chosen for the film) possess shockingly little aesthetic power— they pale, literally, in comparison to the colorful vibrancy of the street Lee brilliantly re-created, and are meant as whipping boys for racial resentment— yet ironically the figures depicted are, without exception, performers in diverse media of nonpareil virtuosity. At least two of them (Al Pacino, Frank Sinatra) remain lodged in the national imagination, however contrarily, including, as the cultural historian John Gennari has shown, the African American imagination.

Impatient of ethnic apologetics, ghetto sensibilities, and the banalities of cultural relativism, the Italian American intelligentsia has nonetheless been interested in recovering and debating the persistence and reemergence of *Italianita* in those who have taken the major stage—a process that the D'Acierno encyclopedia mightily codifies but does not monopolize. A crucial recognition, partially theorized but, more importantly, *enacted* by the literary intellectuals Camille Paglia (on the image, in *Sexual Personae,* 1990) and Frank Lentricchia (on the "drama" of everyday life, in *The Edge of Night,* 1994) demonstrates the persistence even within formal literary writing of visual and oral forms— bridging the gap between folk culture and intellectual history, as well as the gap between minority and majority representation. Although the British literary critic Paul Giles has protested the easy reliance upon ethnic essentialism, Giles's own analysis of the director Martin Scorsese's 1991 remake of J. Lee Thompson's film *Cape Fear* and his 1993 film version of Edith Wharton's novel *The Age of Innocence* makes a convincing case for Scorsese's Italian Catholic sensibility, especially his refocusing of *Cape Fear* onto the villain as "a dark agent of redemption" and his transfiguring of Wharton's scorn for ritual (as the epitome of corruption) into cinematic luxuriousness. Giles had been among the first to press, beyond the small Italian American journals, for a consideration of the effect of immersion in an iconic culture—Catholic, yet in a very Italian way—on putatively secular arts, the visual and performing arts especially. What emerges is an extraordinarily *material* aesthetic sensibility, in which various modes of written signification (screenplays, song lyrics, rock performance) are channeled into the visual and performing arts, which in turn inform more strictly literary productions (novels that read like films, literary criticism that is highly theatrical, videos produced from songs, and so forth).

When "intellectual history" is reconceived to accommodate Italian American performance, several trajectories emerge that are worthy of full-length treatments of their own. The first and least surprising is the sacralizing of the family. Debated as to whether it serves as a means or a threat to upward mobility, the sense of family is also crucially *performed,* in the fiction and in the sociology, in the direction, writing, and acting of film producers. It is not happenstance that the rise of Italian American intellectualism was accompanied by, arguably inspired and instigated by, the astonishing breakthroughs of Italian Americans in major populist media, including works that stand the tests of aesthetic value and time. In 1969, in the wake of *The Valachi Papers* (1968; based on Senate hearings during the mid-1960s), Mario Puzo, exhausted by his obscurity and poverty as a serious writer, published *The Godfather* which rapidly proved to be the best-selling, and probably the most widely read, novel in history. *The Godfather* cut into the national consciousness a model in which ethnic family values support, rather than destroy, however "illegitimately," upward mobility under capitalism. Once the genre of the frustrated loner, the gangster film was reborn as a debate over the fate of the ethnic patriarchal family in the face of corporate aggrandizement, masculine street glamour, and female self-determination—from Coppola's screen renditions *The Godfather* (1972) and *The Godfather, Part II* to several dozen films involving directors as distinguished as John Huston, Norman Jewison, Sergio Leone, and the Coen brothers. The most blistering response was issued by a then-unknown graduate of Greenwich Village's Little Italy and New York University's Film School, Martin Scorsese, whose 1973 film *Mean Streets* was the harbinger of Robert DeNiro–centered masterpieces—*Taxi Driver, Raging Bull,* and *Goodfellas*—that would redefine cinematic art in the 1980s. Although given courage by the new ethnicity, and as importantly bolstered by the initial registering of a demographic shift, Italian American self-representation distinguished itself in several ways that are traditional to strong ethnic literature—not the least of which was its refusal of the renewed mandates to claim victimization, refute stereotypes, and mobilize politically. It would take the writer John Patrick Shanley and the director Norman Jewison to produce the cartoonish cuckoldry of *Moonstruck* (1987). The writer Richard Condon and the director John Huston to produce the capitalist pastiche of *Prizzi's Honor* (1985), and the director Jonathan Demme (with a couple of non-Italian writers) to produce the feminist comedy *Married to the Mob* (1988). What Coppola and Scorsese gave viewers was the twin stereotypes used against Italian Americans (the crime charge going back to the 1870s, the family charge going back to the 1920s), mythically reinvigorated, made sociologically responsible, and subjected to critique.

Of the several media in which it would excel, popular film was to be the paramount mode not only for the representation of America by Italians—the director Frank Capra in the 1930s, the director Vincente Minnelli in the 1950s, and the contemporary directors Brian DePalma and Michael Cimino—but for Italian American self-representation. Coppola's *Cotton Club* (1984) and *The Godfather, Part III* (1990), Scorsese's *Goodfellas* (1990), DePalma's *The Untouchables* (1987), and a spate of independent films by the director Abel Ferrara (*China Girl,* 1987; *The Bad Lieutenant,* 1992; and *The Funeral,* 1996) continue the mob-focused end of the conversation. The discourses of family, *fésta,* and romance, given early cinematic birth in *Love with a Proper Stranger* (1963) and *Lovers and Other Strangers* (1970), are revisited from women's perspectives in the director Nancy Savoca's *True Love* (1989) and *Household Saints* (1993) and from a gastronomic aesthete's perspective in the directors Stanley Tucci and Campbell Scott's *Big Night* (1995). As late as 1972, it was a measure of the limits of what Coppola felt the American public could handle that he excised from *The Godfather* the brilliant and shocking ending to Puzo's book, wherein, crime boss Michael Corleone's wife, Kay, with full knowledge of the mafia's evil and her husband's complicity, converts to Catholicism, better to pray, daily "for the soul of Michael Corleone." Instead, in a stroke of audience-receptive genius,

Coppola ended his *Godfather* by closing the door to Michael's study in the face of Kay, with whom the audience is encouraged to identify, and who as an autonomous woman of conscience (still very much a Protestant) is left out in the cold.

For all the force of family-and-crime narrative, Italian Americans have weighed in heavily in other matters, dramatically enough to have been recognized without having been thoroughly or, at times, adequately understood, at least within the academy proper (where both the humanist and Marxist traditions shy away from the body, spectacle, and lower-middle-class taste). Surely the earliest impact involves identifying and embracing "the urban sublime"—in which the industrial cityscape (bridges and tunnels, factories and skyscrapers, alleyways and amusement parks), including the ultimately abandoned industrial cityscape, is rendered sacred and prophetic—the focus of terror and wonder simultaneously, the kind of doubly layered emotion that Italians live by, in faith and daily praxis. The urban sublime is a discourse that reaches its first crescendo in the immigrant Joseph Stella's futurist oils (the *Coney Island* series of 1913 to 1914, the *Brooklyn Bridge* and *New York Interpreted* paintings of 1920 and 1922) as well as his charcoals for the Pittsburgh *Survey* (1918–1924). It is a discourse that continues less experimentally but at least as iconically in the city canvases of the activist and gas station attendant Ralph Fasanella. It serves as the habitus of both the naturalist immigrant novels (*Christ in Concrete, Maria, The Fortunate Pilgrim*) and postmodern, postethnic novels (Don DeLillo's *Underworld*, 1997; Frank Lentricchia's *Johnny Critelli; and, The Knifemen*, 1996). And it reaches its most influential incarnations in the singer-songwriter Bruce Springsteen's song-cycles, which focus on the New Jersey shore and the industrial heartland; and in the mean-streets cinema of Coppola, Cimino, Scorsese, and Ferrara.

Although film remains the primary vehicle of Italian American self-representation, popular music rivals film in terms of a less explicit but no less powerful "Italianization" of mainstream U.S. culture. At stake here is not only recovering the reciprocal importance of Italian Americans and genres of popular music to each other, but charting how Italian American styles of vocalization, presentation, and authorial vision have incised themselves into the national psyche. Witness Harry Warren (born Salvatore Guaragna), one of the great Tin Pan Alley songwriters; Eddie Lange (born Salvatore Massaro), the major force behind jazz guitar; the dominant Italian composition of Benny Goodman's

FRANK SINATRA

Frank Sinatra (1915–1998). One of the most popular entertainers of the twentieth century. © BETTMANN/CORBIS

big band, and the centrality of South Philly and similar enclaves to white soul and doo-wop.

Dating back to the 1930s with Russ Colombo and moving forward to the 1990s with John Pizzarelli, the litany of Italian American mainstream pop vocalists at midcentury alone is legion, including Jerry Vale, Vic Damone, Tony Bennett, Dean Martin, Al Martino, Frankie Laine, Connie Francis, Keely Smith, Bobby Darin, Louis Prima, Julius LaRosa, and many others—among whom Frank Sinatra is a colossus rivaled only, in the history of entertainment, by his musical godfather Louis Armstrong. The first master of the microphone, Sinatra reinvigorated once-exhausted Tin Pan Alley lyrics (many originally written for women), giving them "swing" as well as dramatic bite, with the listener serving as love object, coconspirator, sympathizer, or ephebe. He personified an Italian male bravado—at once confident and vulnerable, nonchalant and defensive, broken and expectant—with his spoken New Jersey vernacular qualifying and at times poking through the elegant Park Avenue accent of his enunciation when singing. And, over time, he became increasingly adept at deploying song as self-commentary, projecting wisdom commensurate with the roughening and ultimately weakening of his voice, in the end dramatizing how a man of force ages in a youth culture of planned obsolescence and Oedipal displacement.

The rock guitarist Steve Van Zandt of the E Street Band once quipped that "to sound that black and be white, you have to be Italian"; what he had in mind were the doo-wop and related groups of the late 1950s and early 1960s: the Rascals featuring Felix Caviliere, Dion DiMucci, Frankie Valli and the Four Seasons, and a host of others. When CBS sent Bruce Springsteen (whose mother's name was Zirilli and who referred to Van Zandt as "mio fratello") into the studio in the early 1970s, it was the "next Bob Dylan" they had in mind, but Springsteen would not take his place as one of the greatest live performers in rock history until he reclaimed the serenade form of Frank Sinatra. Of course he was also reclaiming, with the help of the E Street Band, the legacy of rock'n'soul, including the power-pop of Mitch Ryder (William Levise Jr.) and the Detroit Wheels, a legacy that reached its apotheosis in the mid-1980s, with the record-setting *Born in the U.S.A.* stadium tour.

The mid-1980s also marked the professional coming of age of another epoch-making charismatic songster, Madonna, whose name is not a media handle but her actual first name (like that of her mother before her). By the late 1990s, Madonna's chameleonesque reinventions in the American romantic tradition may have begun to grow thin, but her combination of intoxicating dance pop and stage presence produced a beloved icon worthy of early power feminism, beginning with the ingratiating "material girl" of the director Susan Seidelman's film *Desperately Seeking Susan* (1985). Sardonically self-reflective, the videos of the mid-1980s dominated the dissemination of MTV and have withstood the test of time—as has the concert footage of the *Blonde Ambition* and *Ciao, Italia* tours, which demonstrate a Broadway or Las Vegas stage master at work who knows, in addition, how to turn Catholic aesthetics against conventional mores (the *Blonde Ambition* set designed by her brother, Christopher Ciccone).

Of the young feminist singer-songwriters of the 1990s, who chant a powerful retort both to misogynistic rock and the 1990s backlash, perhaps none is more respected than Ani DiFranco. DiFranco's cynical savvy may, like Madonna's, have more than a touch of the female experience of what the literary journalist Barbara Grizzuti Harrison called "the domestic guerilla warfare" of Italians. The establishment of her own label, to wrestle artistic as well as economic control of her destiny from the conglom-

erating industry houses, is reminiscent of nothing so much as Frank Sinatra's founding, in 1960, of his own record company, Reprise Records.

The genteel commentators who adore the suave, mannered Sinatra of the Rogers and Hart and Cole Porter songbooks tend to be put out by the Ring-a-Ding swagger of the Chairman years. Yet Springsteen spoke in affirming recognition of Sinatra's recurring belligerence: "It was a voice filled with bad attitude, life, beauty, excitement, a nasty sense of freedom, sex, and a sad knowledge of the ways of the world. Every song seemed to have as its postscript 'And if you don't like it here's a punch in the kisser'" (Lahr, p. 94). Springsteen might as well have been speaking of Madonna or DiFranco—or, indeed, of Italian American creativity writ large, in the context especially of what is regarded as "intellectual history."

Italian immigration to the United States peaked in 1907. Almost a century later, during the television season of 1998–1999, a merry band of Northeasterners led by David Chase (né Cesare) took the American imagination by storm with a black comedy about the Jersey mob entitled *The Sopranos*. In print and especially on the Internet, some Americans of Italian ancestry complained bitterly that here was the old formula, Italians are (just) gangsters, all over again. Yet the complaints sound hollow given the ferocious self-knowing and sardonic grace of Chase's actors, writers, and design crew. The first year of *The Sopranos* played less like a television series than a serial novel that the nineteenth-century Londoner Charles Dickens might have written had he grown up a "guido" in New Jersey. The story it told, satirizing upscale suburban domesticity by revealing its entanglement in the enterprise zones of postindustrial crime, placed Italian Americans as a group in the suburbs for the first time, living cheek by jowl with dentists and CEOs, while portraying their particular forms of ethnic self-conflict as fundamentally American. When the midlife performance anxiety of lead mobster Tony Soprano is held accountable to a trinity of formidable women (his mother, his wife, his psychiatrist), something new and wondrous has taken place in the national imagination: the icon of the mafia family, which under Puzo and Coppola's regime played out as entirely male, has been corrected for gender bias, not in generic feminist fashion, but in a way that holds our understanding of the sexual dynamics of masculine achievement under capitalism accountable to one hundred years of Italian American social history, to that very history best known through the archive of self-reflexive performance this essay has just surveyed.

See also **Ethnicity: Early Theories; Ethnicity and Race** *(volume 3); and other articles in this section.*

BIBLIOGRAPHY

Sociology and Social History

Bodnar, J., R. Simon, and M. Weber. *Lives of Their Own: Blacks, Italians, and Poles in Pittsburgh, 1900–1960.* Urbana, Ill., 1982. Comparative statistical history, showing why those of Italian extraction fared better, eventually, than African Americans and Polish Americans.

Cornelisen, Ann. *Women of the Shadows.* Boston, 1974. On poverty, subsistence, and women's control in Marian Catholic Southern Italy; gorgeously written.

di Leonardo, Micaela. *The Varieties of Ethnic Experience: Kinship, Class, and Gender among California Italian-Americans.* Ithaca, N.Y., 1984. Northern Italians who settled in rural California.

Gambino, Richard. *Blood of My Blood: The Dilemma of the Italian-Americans.* New York, 1975. A codification of Italian American family values that was also a clarion call, at the height of the new self-consciousness, for ethnic retrenchment.

Gans, Herbert. *The Urban Villagers: Group and Class in the Life of Italian-Americans.* A testament to Boston's West End on the eve of its razing, in which Gans takes the measure, in sociological terms, of a distinct Italian American subculture.

Kessner, Thomas. *The Golden Door: Italian and Jewish Immigrant Mobility in New York City 1880–1915.* New York, 1977. Comparitive statistical history, showing why the Italians in the early years did not fare as well as the Jews.

Mangione, Jerre, and Ben Morreale. *La Storia: Five Centuries of the Italian American Experience.* New York, 1992. An effort to synthesize Italian American history.

Nelli, Humbert S. *Italians in Chicago, 1880–1930: A Study in Ethnic Mobility.* New York, 1970. In implicit dissent from Vecoli: economic and cultural mobility among the paesans of Chicago.

Orsi, Robert A. *The Madonna of 115th Street: Faith and Community in Italian Harlem, 1880–1950.* New Haven, Conn., 1977. A major crossover study of beguiling empathy, where second generation experience, women's history, and popular religious devotions meet.

Pucci, Idanna. *The Trials of Maria Barbella: The True Story of a 19th Century Crime of Passion.* Translated by Stefania Fumo. New York, 1996. An incisive, withering reconstruction of how an Italian seamstress was sentenced, in 1895, to become the first woman in history to be put to death by the electric chair.

Riis, Jacob. *How the Other Half Lives: Studies Among the Tenements of New York.* New York, 1971. What New York's Italian East Side looked and "felt" like to the majority culture, 1892.

Vecoli, Rudolph. "*Contadini* in Chicago: A Critique of *The Uprooted.*" *Journal of American History* 51 (Dec. 1964): 404–417. Culture persistence among the paesans of Chicago, by the dean of the new Italian American social history.

Whyte, William Foote. *Street Corner Society: The Social Structure of an Italian Slum.* Chicago, 1943. A sociologist looks at gang life in the second generation inner city.

Williams, Phyllis. *South Italian Folkways in Europe & America: A Handbook for Social Workers, Visiting Nurses, School Teachers, and Physicians.* New Haven, Conn., 1938. One social worker who cared about immigrant offspring—and knew what she was talking about.

Yans-McLaughlin, Virginia. *Family and Community: Italian Immigrants in Buffalo, 1880–1930.* Ithaca, N.Y., 1977. The study that brought rigor and female focus to Vecoli's groundbreaking "*Contadini*" argument.

Arts and Letters

Barolini, Helen, ed. *The Dream Book: An Anthology of Writings by Italian American Women.* New York, 1985. A generous primer on writing by women, with a seminal introduction.

Boelhower, William Q. *Immigrant Autobiography in the United States: Four Versions of the Italian American Self.* Verona, Italy, 1982. The first full-length scholarly treatment of Italian American autobiography.

Ciongoli, A. Kenneth, and Jay Parini, eds. *Beyond the Godfather: Italian American Writers on the Real Italian American Experience.* Hanover, N.H., 1997. A collection of autobiographical and critical pieces, with some especially nice turns by a younger generation of women.

D'Acierno, Pellegino, ed. *The Italian-American Heritage: A Companion to Literature and the Arts.* New York, 1998. An indispensable introduction to the representation, self-representation, and general contributions of Italian Americans in U.S. literature, film, classical and popular music, architecture, painting, and sculpture.

Ferraro, Thomas J., ed. *Catholic Lives, Contemporary America.* Durham, N.C., 1997. With pertinent contributions by Robert A. Orsi, Frank Lentricchia, Camille Paglia, Paul Giles, James T. Fisher, and the editor.

Gardaphé, Fred L. *Italian Signs, American Streets: The Evolution of Italian American Narrative.* Durham, N.C., 1996. The first synthetic scholarly treatment of Italian American writing.

Gennari, John. "Passing for Italian." *Transition* 36 (winter 1997): 36–37. A deft introduction to African American identifying and with Italian American icons and vice versa.

Green, Rose Basile. *The Italian-American Novel: A Document of the Interaction of Two Cultures.* Rutherford, N.J., 1974. A cataloging focused on the novel and updated at the height of the "new ethnic consciousness."

Haskell, Barbara. *Joseph Stella.* New York, 1994. An overview of the first major Italian presence in U.S. high culture, the famous futurist who was also an immigrant realist and Marian primitivist.

Lahr, John. *Sinatra: The Artist and the Man.* New York, 1997. An excellent place to be introduced to writing about Sinatra, and to photographs of him.

Lentricchia, Frank. *The Edge of Night.* New York, 1994. Brilliantly written challenges to multiculturalist essentialism and theoretical anti-aestheticism, in an essay idiom all its own, at once autobiographical and critical, derived from T. S. Eliot and ethnic vernacular.

Paglia, Camille. *Sex, Art, and American Culture.* New York, 1992. Occasional pieces, including the MIT lecture, *Arion* essay, and short takes on the pop star Madonna, through which Paglia called anti-aestheticism, Foucault-influenced cultural studies, and feminist self-delusion to account, in bitingly imagistic prose.

Peragallo, Olga. *Italian-American Authors and Their Contribution to American Literature.* New York, 1949. The earliest cataloging.

Puterbaugh, Parke, and the editors of *Rolling Stone. Bruce Springsteen: The Rolling Stone Files.* New York, 1996. Occasional pieces constituting the strongest writing yet to appear on the bard who gave American romanticism a Jersey Shore accent.

Talese, Gay. "Where Are the Italian-American Novelists?" *New York Times Book Review* (14 March 1993), 1, 23, 25, 29. A controversial essay that presumes and explains the absence of Italian American writers.

Tamburri, Anthony Julian, Paolo A. Giordano, and Fred L. Gardaphé, eds. *From the Margin: Writings in Italian Americana.* West Lafayette, Ind., 1991. A potpurri of creative and critical works.

Watson, Patrick. *Fasanella's City: The Paintings of Ralph Fasanella with the Story of His Life and Art.* New York, 1973. The only illustrated account of the gas station attendant and activist who painted second-generation Italian New York with a "primitive realism" that was actually sacralizing and iconographic.

JEWS

Stephen J. Whitfield

Although all Americans are descendants of people who came from somewhere else, the history of Jews is especially prone to the demarcations of immigration and settlement. The first group of Jewish settlers to reach the future United States fled from the Inquisition in Portuguese Brazil and in 1654 were permitted to land in New Amsterdam. Since then transplantation to the New World has been almost continuous. In 1790 the first federal census located only two thousand Jews, who could not have foreseen that they and the coreligionists, who would eventually join them in the United States, would form the largest population of Jews since Abraham left "Ur of the Chaldees" for the land of Canaan (Genesis 11:31). Immigration to the new republic began to swell shortly before and after the Civil War, and about a quarter of a million Jews were living in the United States by 1880. Then the increase of refugees from eastern Europe became enormous. The third wave of immigration took place from 1882 until 1924, when over 2.3 million Jews swelled the Jewish population in America to 4.2 million. The combination of immigration restriction in the 1920s, the ravages of the Great Depression of the 1930s, World War II, and the destruction of two-thirds of European Jewry reduced the flood to a trickle, and only a little more than half a million Jews arrived from the 1920s to the 1970s. Beginning in the 1970s, emigration from the Soviet Union, Iran, and even Israel helped to bring the U.S. Jewish population to about 5.5 million by the end of the twentieth century.

The influx of new immigrants was decisive in the evolution of the Jewish community in America. The diversity of origins also affected its character. Jews came from widely differing (though overwhelmingly European) societies, where they had experienced disparate conditions. Although Jewish immigrants shared Hebrew as the language of worship, their vernacular tongues differed. The twenty-three Jews who landed in New Amsterdam in 1654 were Sephardim whose ancestors had flourished in the Iberian Peninsula. Only after the first third of the nineteenth century did large numbers of Jews come from the German-speaking areas of central Europe and from Russian Poland. These people, known as Ashkenazim, spoke Yiddish, a language formed primarily from medieval German, with accretions from Hebrew, Aramaic, and other tongues. By the last decades of the nineteenth century, other Yiddish-speaking Jews came from Poland, Lithuania, Ukraine, Galicia, Hungary, and Romania. In the twentieth century, immigrants from the disintegrating Ottoman Empire usually spoke Ladino (Judeo-Spanish) or Arabic, and refugees from Nazi terror spoke a variety of tongues, especially German and Yiddish.

The sheer scale that the newer immigrant concentrations represented also deepened the divisions within Jewry. The eastern Europeans had often come from tiny villages in the confinements of the Pale of Settlement, which consisted of what became Belorussia, Lithuania, Ukraine, and much of eastern Poland. The newcomers brought to the New World not only local customs and parochial suspicions but also the intensities of ideological struggles that had permeated tsarist Russia. Such conflicts centered on the religious traditions that were cracking under the pressure of modernity and on the socialism that was the proposed remedy for appalling impoverishment. These conflicts were often transferred to the New World. Those who escaped from or who had survived Nazi-occupied Europe, though less numerous than the third wave of immigrants, constituted a diverse new stratum. Often well-educated, they had little in common either with the descendants of those who had come from the Germanic principalities a century earlier or with the insular, ultra-Orthodox survivors—especially from Poland—who kept themselves apart even from other observant Jews.

Social and cultural differences can be exaggerated, however. Imagining themselves as engaged in a collective destiny, the immigrants were likely to share distinctive beliefs, like that of ethical monotheism, which bound them historically through a covenant to a single powerful deity which demanded of them righteous acts. Those beliefs were also characterized by some important binary lines—for example, divisions that separated the Sabbath from the rest of the week and distinguished food that was fit to eat under kosher regulations from "unclean" food. Another sort of division was common: only by insulating Jews from Christians might these particular practices and rituals be honored and perpetuated. However varied, their experiences could be seen as continuing a corporate existence inaugurated by the biblical Hebrews. They formulated a set of ethical principles that was supposed to be of universal applicability. But the Jews had remained a tribe, and their Bible was not only the basis of their faith but also a historical account of a nation, which had been dispersed and, in the bitterness of exile, awaited redemption. The Judaism that the rabbis revised in the Diaspora therefore made survival an obligation that could not be evaded. Thus, external oppression and an internal dynamic kept Jews intact until the corrosive effects of the Enlightenment and Emancipation.

Beginning in the eighteenth century in parts of western Europe and spreading to central and eastern Europe in the nineteenth century, the medieval walls that had tied Jews to ghettos came tumbling down, and the opportunity to live freely in burgeoning cities like Berlin, Vienna, Budapest, and Prague beckoned. Jews no longer had to live as pariahs, behind gates that were locked at night. Instead, what was offered were the rights of citizens in the new states and transnational empires that had to reckon with the humanitarian, nationalist, and republican ideals projected by the French Revolution. As Jews increasingly sought to become absorbed into the communities that consisted of Frenchman and Germans, Italians and Hungarians, Austrians and Czechs, the historic sense of peoplehood—reinforced by centuries of Christian persecution—weakened. In the nineteenth century in particular, Jewish identity increasingly jostled with civic consciousness by a yearning for political and social equality. Jewish observance could also not long evade the challenge of the rationalism that was so central to the Enlightenment, which also left as its legacy a faith in progress and benevolence and in the blessings of scientific advance and secular education.

Although an unascertainable proportion of immigrants to the United States were already affected by the secular ideologies that were disrupting the religious cohesiveness of European Jewry, nearly all who arrived could at least remember a rather stable traditional order. The claims of the past were not utterly abandoned, and the sense of a common Jewish fate, as well as the responsibility to aid beleaguered brethren, affected even the most acculturated. Tradition may have been imperiled, and the lure of a relatively open society that promised material rewards to the industrious and the enterprising was powerful. But the vestiges of a historical religious outlook were still durable enough to distinguish Jews from other immigrants. The republic posed a new challenge: How could the claims of a religion that defined the American condition as exilic be reconciled with the temptations of personal fulfillment and social integration? Unprecedented opportunities would raise doubts about the continuity of a group presumably awaiting a messianic End of Days. A society that encouraged the pursuit of happiness invited questions about the meaning of Jewish history itself.

SEPHARDIM AND ASHKENAZIM

Such dilemmas were hardly apparent at first. When America was still British, the Sephardim hovered along the Atlantic coast, links in a chain of Jewish settlements that included the Dutch and British West Indies, emanating from Amsterdam and London. Some Ashkenazim also settled in North America, but their numbers were so sparse that the two Jewish populations easily fused together. Homogenization was smoothed by a similar occupational pattern (since males tended to be merchants and tradesmen) and the absence of religious strife, despite differences in Sephardic and Ashkenazic rites. In addition, friction may have been reduced because it was not until the 1840s that ordained rabbis came to America. The small number of Askenazim and Sephardim also eased integration into a fluid society, which imposed few barriers to economic advancement. Jews were one religious minority among many—and could not easily be stigmatized as pariahs. Jewish and Christian children attended the same schools, and religious identity rarely determined eligibility for citizenship. The explicit assurance that George Washington sent to synagogues in Newport, Rhode Island, and elsewhere—that the new government would "give to bigotry no sanction, to persecution no assistance"—was credible. In Europe a structure of rabbinical authority had been maintained even after ghetto walls crumbled. But in an every-man-for-himself democracy, no consensual discipline could be imposed; religious belief was subject to freedom of choice. Within a decade of the founding of the nation's most famous Reform synagogue, Temple Emanu-El, in 1845, ten Jewish congregations were flourishing there.

Variations in Judaic expression coincided with geographical dispersion. Jewish immigrants from the German states gravitated toward the agrarian South and Midwest as well as the Far West. These newcomers were not very distant from medieval Judaic practices. But they had usually emancipated themselves from the separatism that legal codes dictated and did not shrink from overwhelmingly Gentile settings in America. It was not until 1899 that federal immigration data distinguished Jews from others who arrived from the same countries, and such blurring is apt when considering the German-speaking migration. Despite the religious rift between Jews and other Germans and the legacy of anti-Semitism, Jews were shaped by the social and cultural ambience from which they had fled. Indeed *Kultur* enjoyed such prestige that one Chicago rabbi, Bernhard Felsenthal, acknowledged a "triple loyalty." "Racially, I am a Jew," he proclaimed in 1901, "for I have been born among the Jewish nation. Politically I am an American as patriotic, as enthusiastic, as devoted an American citizen as it is possible to be. But spiritually I am a German, for my inner life has been profoundly influenced by Schiller, Goethe, Kant and other intellectual giants of Germany." Felsenthal added, "with a certain pride, in thought and feeling I am German" (p. 19).

Although business opportunities largely inscribed the map of Jewish migration and settlement, the arrival of rabbis—most educated in universities in central Europe—also began to alter the character of communal life. Reform Judaism held that encrusted medieval rituals and restrictions could not be squared with rational thinking. Many of the immigrant rabbis opposed the separatist rigidity of orthodoxy, which is why America was so attractive. The rabbi's vocation became Americanized when the model of the Protestant minister was adopted: effectiveness in preaching of sermons superseded the traditional responsibility to interpret Judaic law, and pastoral concern became more valued than devotion to the study of the legal texts. Reform Judaism went its own way by creating a denominational nexus under the leadership of Isaac Mayer Wise of Cincinnati. The Bohemian-born rabbi was not much of a scholar, but he was a master builder who exhibited pragmatic flexibility, plus organizational energy in overdrive. In 1873 Wise organized liberal synagogues into the Union of American Hebrew Congregations. Two years later he created the Hebrew Union College, the nation's first rabbinical seminary, in Cincinnati and became its president. Another institution that bore his imprint was a national organization of Reform clergy, the Central Conference of American Rabbis. The measure of Wise's managerial skills and practical vision was that, by 1880, nearly all houses of worship (except for small synagogues where newly arrived immigrants from eastern Europe prayed) were Reform.

EASTERN EUROPEANS

The rapid ascent to respectability of German-speaking Jews and their children was threatened by the mass immigration of conspicuously observant, wretchedly poor, Yiddish-speaking Jews from tsarist Russia and eastern Europe. Jews who had already proven their civic worthiness feared too close an association with an influx from eastern Europe that proved to be unstoppable until the U.S. Congress placed restrictions on immigration in 1921 and 1924. By 1920 these newcomers and their children constituted about five-sixths of American Jewry. Religious persecution, economic deprivation, and relentless demographic pressure impelled one out of every three eastern European Jews to emigrate during 1880–1920—and, despite their prayers for a restored Zion, more than 90 percent of them participated in the exodus to America rather than to Palestine. Never before (and never again) in Jewish history had so grand a population movement occurred, and the profile of this minority in the United States was permanently altered.

The eastern European Jews remained in the packed cities of the East Coast and the large midwestern cities. The stretch of coastline from Boston to Baltimore probably contained three-fifths of all Jews in the United States, and the largest cities of the Midwest harbored another third. In the three decades after 1881, almost 1.5 million Jews landed in New York, and about two-thirds stayed there, making the 1.5-square-mile area of the Lower East Side of Manhattan (where more than half a million Jews resided) into one of the most densely packed spots on earth. In other ethnic enclaves, such as the North End of Boston, South Philadelphia, and the West Side of Chicago, were the workshops of the garment trade and small synagogues, cafés, and saloons frequented by Jews. Jostling against one another were workers, labor organizers, intellectuals, pious men, prostitutes, and gangsters. The immigrants were not on their own. The literary critic Alfred

Kazin, whose parents had emigrated from Poland, recalled that the most terrifying Yiddish word in their Brooklyn, New York, neighborhood was *aleyn* (alone). Those Jews who emigrated from the same town banded together into associations called *landsmanshaften,* which were created to solve problems of adjustment through mutual aid and by providing interest-free loans, sickness benefits, life insurance, and burial rights. By 1917 more than one hundred thousand immigrants in New York belonged to about one thousand *landsmanshaften.*

Work on Saturday (the Sabbath day) was expected in the garment trades, which attracted the plurality of immigrant workers, thus inevitably reshaping Judaism. Religious observance was soon recognized as voluntary and revocable, not a communal way of life. Because orthodoxy was no longer obligatory, because its power to compel assent and observance receded, no authoritative religious leadership could be recreated to match the role that the rabbinate played in eastern Europe. In 1893, when the rabbi Hayim Vidrowitz arrived from Moscow and erected a sign identifying himself as the "Chief Rabbi of America," he was asked by whose authority he held that position and was obliged to admit, "the sign painter's." The learning that was applied in the Old World to elucidating Judaic codes of conduct was of little use in the New World. The rabbinate was characterized by low wages, no job security, and minimal authority over the lives of congregants. Thus the duties of clergy either atrophied or were eliminated.

Mandatory—and free—public education offered the allure of escape from the ghetto through the process of Americanization; the contrast of such schools with traditional forms of primary Jewish education made the *heder* (an elementary Jewish school that taught boys to read the Torah) look dreary, punitive, and irrelevant. Public schools encouraged integration into the larger society by showing how economic and personal advancement might be achieved. After the last afternoon bell rang in the public schools, the *heder* was reduced to providing supplementary education for children whose families wanted Jewish continuity. But resources were meager. Between the dream of individual success in a seemingly open and fluid society and the traditional claims of an Old World religious culture, the playing field was not level. The most observant segment of the community lacked the members, the money, or the will to transmit to another generation the intricacies of traditional Judaism. In crossing the Atlantic, orthodoxy had surrendered its hegemony.

The reorganization of the Jewish Theological Seminary of America (JTS) in New York City was crucial in providing children of the eastern European immigrants in particular with an alternative to both Reform Judaism (which seemed alien and forbidding) and Orthodox Judaism (which seemed a relic of the Old World). Aiming to train rabbis for the Conservative denomination, the JTS, founded in 1886, was headed from 1902 to 1915 by Solomon Schechter, an observant, Romanian-born scholar. Schechter brought to the United States outstanding scholars to staff the faculty, which tried to equip future rabbis with the adroitness to reconcile the imperatives of tradition with the appeal of Americanization. In 1913 he also created an umbrella organization, the United Synagogue of America, for houses of worship that expected to serve social and cultural needs as well. By the end of World War II, Conservative Judaism had become the largest denomination in American Judaism.

Also influential in the public culture of American Jewry were labor organizations, of which the most powerful were the International Ladies' Garment Workers' Union (ILGWU), organized in 1900, and the Amalgamated Clothing Workers Union (ACWU), formed in 1914. Influenced by Russian radicalism, these unions also enjoyed the enthusiastic support of the most widely read Yiddish newspaper in the world, the *Jewish Daily Forward;* indeed, the *Forward* was the most widely read foreign-language daily in the United States. Founded in 1897 in New York City, the newspaper reinforced the radical consciousness of the Jewish proletariat. The editor and founder Abraham Cahan wanted to implement the militant credo of the French Revolution by hurtling "the workingmen's organ in their every righteous fight against their oppressors; this struggle is the body of our movement. But its soul is the liberation of mankind—justice, humanity, fraternity" (in Rischin, p. 160). Yet he also sanctioned acculturation by publishing advice columns and explanations of the intricacies of baseball and by incorporating English vocabulary into a Yiddish that sought to reproduce the colloquial patterns of the streets. The *Jewish Daily Forward* was not, however, the only interpreter of American life. Between 1908 and 1918 Cahan had to compete with four other Yiddish-language dailies—all of them sympathetic toward the Jewish labor movement.

Although only twelve thousand members could be claimed by the Zionist movement in 1914, its significance exceeded its membership list. This primarily secular movement, born in central and eastern Europe, injected vigor into Jewish communities

First Issue of the *Jewish Daily Forward*, 22 April 1897. The *Forward* published nearly every master of Yiddish literature. In 1990 it became an English-language paper, while maintaining the Yiddish *Forverts* publication separately. The *Forward* launched a Russian-language edition in 1995, fostered in part by New York's growing Russian Jewish community. FORWARD ASSOCIATION

by seeming to transcend the parochialism of the particular nations in which Jews happened to reside. The image of a redeemed and restored homeland in Palestine offered the hope of refuge from persecution and the reassurance of Jewish continuity. Zionism served as an alternative not only to limited and denominational definitions of Judaism but also to the perils of secular modernity and assimilation in the Diaspora. Even when the prospects of integration into open societies like the United States were alluring, this movement appealed to both working-class Jews from eastern Europe and to progressive, middle-class intellectuals whose pedigrees and professional credentials enabled them to gravitate to the leadership of American Zionism.

How to forge an identity that made ethnicity congruent with citizenship became the concern of several prominent religious and secular thinkers during World War I. They worried about the alienation of young Jews from their own heritage and the depletion of the cultural resources that had sustained their ancestors during centuries of adversity. Such assimilation was neither decent nor beneficial to a nation that would by enriched by diversity. Horace M. Kallen, the secularist son of an immigrant rabbi, provided a concept in 1915 he called "cultural pluralism." To deny one's grandfather was not desirable, he insisted, nor was it even possible, since genealogy is immutable. Mandatory blending into a general populace in which differences had been expunged was an ineffective policy. He called the Jewish contribution to the American kaleidoscope "Hebraism," by which he meant the entire

historical experience—and not merely the religious ideas and practices—of the Jewish people. The Zionist tribune and Supreme Court Justice Louis D. Brandeis concurred. The liberal credo, he believed, entailed the obligation of every minority to cultivate its own unique legacy, a kind of experimental method that would invigorate the nation.

AMERICANIZATION

Quite strikingly, American Jews were also legatees of a culture that cherished learning. No other ethnic group so conceived of education as the escape route from the working class or so invested its savings and hopes in the possibility of professional careers. By 1905 Jews constituted the majority of students at the tuition-free City College of New York. Ten years later about one-quarter of U.S. medical students were Jews. Thinking that Gentiles might make disagreeable employers or refuse to hire Jews at all, American Jews saw the independence that a professional career promised as an additional advantage, justifying the financial sacrifices that years of education and training required. That is why so many immigrant Jewish parents, who appreciated the cultural meaning and practical benefits of education, encouraged their children to remain in school and to graduate from universities—more so than any other ethnic group. The effects of such encouragement were palpable. In 1937 Jews constituted one-quarter of the population of New York City, but they made up two-thirds of its attorneys and judges and more than half the city's doctors. The proportions in other cities were also notable.

When the Great Depression began, the narrowing of both the social and geographical gaps among Jews became obvious. In 1930 those who could trace their roots to eastern Europe already comprised half the membership of Reform synagogues, and some of the most acculturated Jews were being admitted to the clubs that German Jews had founded and serving as officers of charitable organizations. Although ten Yiddish dailies were being published in the United States in 1920, and almost half of American Jews told census takers that Yiddish was their mother tongue, that proportion of Yiddish-speaking people was already beginning its slow decline into near extinction. Two decades later barely more than one-third could make the same linguistic claim, and the Holocaust doomed the prospect of a revival of Yiddish as a living language in the United States.

More than half a million American Jews served in the military during World War II, and those who returned found fellow citizens far more aware than before the war of the consequences of racial and religious discrimination. In the immediate postwar years Jews became almost fully integrated into a nation that enjoyed unprecedented affluence. Huge demand for a cornucopia of goods and services made businessmen and professionals the special beneficiaries of prosperity. In educational credentials and income levels, Jews equaled or surpassed the religious and ethnic groups that had founded the nation two centuries earlier. Yet despite acculturation, the community managed to sustain its cohesiveness and to exhibit a degree of separateness from other Americans. Nevertheless, a low birthrate and the virtual cessation of immigration meant that the percentage of Jews in the U.S. population declined from a high of 3.7 percent in 1937, hovering in the second half of the twentieth century at barely more than 2 percent. The total U.S. general population grew by more than two-thirds, but its Jewish minority by only one-fifth. No major ethnic group reproduced itself so wanly, despite an influx of Soviet Jews beginning in the 1980s. Dispersal to the Sunbelt states also resulted in new geographical and cultural configurations. Los Angeles became the second most populous Jewish community, and Miami, Florida, became almost as significant, while the Rustbelt cities such as Chicago, Cleveland, and Detroit showed depletion. The ghettos of the early century almost disappeared, to be replaced by suburbs, where only the very elderly and the very poor were absent.

Following World War II, Jews were employed as managers or administrators at three to four times the rate of the rest of the U.S. population; the proportion of Jews of university-age attending an institution of higher learning was close to 90 percent; and the proportion of Jews belonging to labor unions in the garment trades declined much more sharply than the percentage of Jews who remained as their employers (or indeed, as union officials). The son of Sol C. Chaikin, a postwar president of the International Ladies' Garment Workers' Union, became a dress manufacturer. By coincidence, two rival fashion designers of the late twentieth century, Ralph Lauren and Calvin Klein, grew up in the same neighborhood in the Bronx, New York. The most innovative builders of suburban housing in the immediate postwar era were Abraham Levitt and his sons, William and Alfred, who constructed housing communities called Levittown on Long Island, New York, and near Philadelphia; other Jewish realtors and builders were responsible for shopping centers and office complexes throughout the nation. Jews also pioneered in radio and television. David Sarnoff created the National Broadcasting Company (NBC), and William Paley built its chief rival, the Columbia Broadcasting System (CBS). When Leonard H. Goldenson became president of the American Broadcasting Company (ABC) in the 1960s, all three commercial networks were headed by Jews. Leading publishing houses—such as Alfred A. Knopf, Random House, Viking, and Simon and Schuster—also bore the imprint of Jewish management and editorial taste. Elite daily newspapers such as the *New York Times* and later the *Washington Post* also registered the impact of editors, reporters, and columnists of Jewish descent.

Talented Jews catapulted themselves out of the slums and into mass entertainment early in the twentieth century. All the major Hollywood studios—Metro-Goldwyn-Mayer, Paramount, Universal, Columbia, Twentieth Century–Fox and Warner Brothers—had been built by Jews (or the sons of Jews) who had been born within a radius of a few hundred miles of Warsaw. These rambunctious and ambitious entrepreneurs seized the film market from France, which in 1912 produced 90 percent of the movies exhibited internationally. By 1918, 85 percent of the world's films were American; and by the mid-1920s more than two-thirds of the movies shown in France had come from Hollywood. Broadway—the glamorous and brightly lit Manhattan theater district—was also heavily Jewish; the most creative figures in the evolution of the Broadway musical were Jewish composers and lyricists such as Irving Berlin, Jerome Kern, Oscar Hammerstein II, George and Ira Gershwin, Richard Rodgers, Leonard Bernstein (the conductor of the New York Philharmonic as well), and Stephen Sondheim. Many professional comedians since the beginning of the twentieth century have been Jewish; among those who achieved an international reputation were the Marx Brothers and one of their later admirers, Woody Allen. Serious Jewish dramatists were somewhat less influential, but the plays of Lillian Hellman, Clifford Odets, Arthur Miller, and David Mamet offered searing criticism of the corrupting influences of American society.

The postwar era was also unprecedented in the collapse of academic barriers to Jewish advancement. Because the cold war helped to enfeeble a native tradition of anti-intellectualism, scientific and technological research in particular fueled the growth of colleges and universities and encouraged a notion of individual merit rather than pedigree in judging the credentials of faculty. By 1970 the proportion of U.S. professors who were Jews was more than three times their percentage in the overall population and was even higher in the institutions considered the most advanced in research and the most intellectually demanding.

Whether a distinctive American Jewish culture had emerged in the twentieth century is a question that cannot be satisfactorily resolved. But the impact of Jews upon art and thought in the United States was by any criterion extraordinary. That influence has proved to be far too variegated and extensive to yield to any firm generalizations, but some creative figures might be mentioned here. Henry Roth's novel of a Lower East Side childhood, *Call It Sleep* (1934), was neglected upon its publication, and its author stopped writing for about another half-century, awaiting the belated discovery of his masterpiece of Joycean subconscious fury, played out within the dynamics of a desperate and impoverished immigrant family. *Call It Sleep* became the most admired novel ever written by an American Jew. But other works approximated the literary power that Roth achieved. For example, the intellectual rigor and emotional turmoil of *Herzog* (1964) and *Mr. Sammler's Planet* (1970) helped earn Saul Bellow a Nobel Prize for literature in 1976. Philip Roth produced a remarkable shelf of novels, ranging from the Rabelaisian satire of *Portnoy's Complaint* (1969) to an oscillating record of American Jewish attitudes toward Israel in *The Counterlife* (1987) to a terrifying exposé of the national ideal of success in *American Pastoral* (1997).

Beginning in the 1960s, American Jews stared into the abyss of the Holocaust and tried to discern meaning from that catastrophe (or at least to memorialize the two out of three European Jews whom the Nazis murdered). No one was more prominent (or more subtle) in that effort at understanding and commemoration than the Romanian-born novelist and essayist Elie Wiesel, who became the first commission chairman for the U.S. Holocaust Memorial Museum in Washington, D.C. No theologian was more willing to address the inadequacy of historic Judaic thought, in the shadow of the Holocaust, than the rabbi Richard Rubenstein, best known for *After Auschwitz* (1966). Nor was there a more surprising creative response than that of the cartoonist Art Spiegelman. His two-volume *Maus* (1986, 1991) was a history of the Holocaust told largely through the fate of his own father, who managed to survive, and of their relatives, who perished. Depicting Jews as mice and Germans as cats, *Maus* won a special Pulitzer Prize in 1992 and strikingly demonstrated

how a Jewish perspective might be injected into American popular arts to enrich the nation's Jewish culture.

The politics of nineteenth-century Jewry tended to be centrist and moderate and did not shift to the left until the arrival of eastern European immigrants. Their socialism usually ran its course into the liberal wing of the Democratic Party, where Jewish voters have felt most comfortable, beginning with the New Deal. Unlike the other minorities constituting the Franklin D. Roosevelt coalition, Jews subscribed to progressive stances on all political, social, and economic issues—from civil rights to civil liberties, from the formation of a welfare state to an internationalist perspective in foreign policy. Nominally socialist in ideology, labor leaders such as David Dubinsky of the ILGWU and Sidney Hillman of the ACWU, along with Cahan's *Jewish Daily Forward,* helped direct the energies of immigrant radicalism into the reformist wing of the Democratic Party. No other constituency was so unswerving in its devotion to the comprehensive liberal legacy represented by the New Deal. Bourgeoisification did not exercise the same effect on Jewish voters as on other ethnic groups, which became more Republican and defined their interests far more in terms of class. Jews remained issues-oriented and usually did not equate their values with conservative policies or candidates. Consistent loyalty to the Democrats— and to policies aimed at helping the neediest— made Jews the most eccentric voters in the republic.

DESTINY

Since the 1960s, the peculiarity of Jewish voting patterns did not prevent many communal spokesmen from warning that the security and prosperity that cushioned Jewish life endangered continuity and that a distinctive identity was being eroded because social integration had become so complete. As the Old World and the immigrant experience receded over the horizon of memory and then into oblivion, the sociologist Will Herberg argued in 1955 that Jews were inclined to define themselves in religious rather than ethnic terms. Theirs was a common faith; tribal instincts could no longer be easily tapped. As a former Marxist and self-taught theologian, Herberg elevated the status of Judaism, which was associated with only about one out of thirty-three Americans, to a level equivalent to Protestantism and Catholicism. Once disparaged for denying the resurrection of Jesus Christ, Judaism became one of the three ways of identifying as an

American. Much of Herberg's theory was unconvincing; he certainly soft-pedaled the secularism of so many of his fellow Jews, of whom only about half belonged to synagogues (although some of those who weren't members had been at one time). But he was right to emphasize how quickly the world of secular Yiddish culture was vanishing, while the birth of Israel was siphoning off many who took Zionism most seriously. That left the synagogue standing as the dominant institution in Jewish life.

Indeed, the suburban house of worship was expected to assume tasks it had never borne in the remote past. The synagogue was asked to do virtually everything: to transmit the Judaic knowledge that once was the responsibility of the family, to satisfy the social and cultural needs even of the alienated and the disaffiliated, and, above all, to convey the value of Jewish identity to the young. Employees of synagogues—rabbis, cantors, teachers, and administrators—were obliged to be the main conduits of tradition and learning. Yet few of those who belonged to synagogues attended services regularly—perhaps about 15 percent in the final decades of the twentieth century (which is a strikingly low figure, since about one-tenth of American Jews considered themselves Orthodox). Motivations may have been more social than theological because smaller communities enjoyed higher rates of synagogue membership. In the final decades of the century, Reform Judaism forged slightly ahead of Conservative Judaism in attracting the most Jews.

No change in the religious culture following World War II was more pervasive than enhanced roles granted to women, whose pleas for equality within Judaism coincided with the rise of American feminism in the 1960s. Of the three main denominations, Reform Judaism was the most committed—at least in principle—to female equality. At Hebrew Union College in 1972, Sally J. Priesand became the first woman in all of Jewish history to be ordained a rabbi. The Philadelphia seminary of the tiny Reconstructionist movement, founded by JTS's Mordecai M. Kaplan, accepted female rabbinical candidates from its founding in 1968 and ordained Sandy Eisenberg Sasso in 1974. Claiming greater respect for the obligations of Judaic law, the Conservative denomination moved much more cautiously, and ordained Amy Eilberg in 1985. In some Orthodox congregations, women conducted prayer meetings and participated in several ceremonies equivalent to rituals that only men were expected to perform. Even as the axis of Orthodox Judaism shifted to the right, feminist claims could not be spurned. Women were increasingly visible and vocal as officers in non-Orthodox synagogues and in national as well as local philanthropic and other communal organizations.

Although the prestigious Ivy League institutions had earlier restricted Jewish enrollment, they and hundreds of other secular colleges and universities began in the 1970s to offer courses in Jewish studies. The Association for Jewish Studies, founded in 1969, helped to legitimize the scholarly excavation of the Jewish heritage. In the last decades of the century, about fifty local communities were publishing weekly newspapers, and among the approximately three dozen magazines aimed explicitly at Jewish readers, *Commentary,* a monthly subsidized by the American Jewish Committee, was preeminent for its acute analyses of political and cultural affairs. But the Yiddish-language *Jewish Daily Forward* became a weekly as readership fell and then—beginning in 1990—managed to keep subscribers only by publishing a weekly edition in English.

No issue bedeviled the Jewish community more poignantly or affected its will to survive more vexingly than exogamy. Until the 1960s the intermarriage rate was too low to be noticeable, reaching about 6 percent. In the first half of that decade, the rate suddenly tripled. One-third of Jews who married between 1966 and 1972 married non-Jews, and then the percentage reached and then exceeded one-half, as parental opposition to such unions largely collapsed. The conversion rate remained far below the intermarriage rate, and perhaps only one-fifth or one-fourth of such families raised children who defined themselves as Jewish. The belief in the compatibility of American ideals and Jewish continuity faced its most delicate challenge on the issue of intermarriage. An inalienable right to self-satisfaction was trumping a collective commitment to Jewish preservation. This was a dilemma that a community consecrating itself to a synthesis of citizenship and peoplehood, modern values and group allegiances, was ill-equipped to resolve.

For most of its history, American Jewry occupied an outpost on the periphery of the Jewish world. By the late twentieth century, however, the Holocaust had traumatically cast American Jewry as the most important community in the Diaspora. About two out of every five Jews in the world have lived in the United States, and the rest—including those who are citizens of Israel—depend on the resources, sense of solidarity, and leadership of American Jewry. In the millennia of the Diaspora, perhaps no community had adjusted so brilliantly to a national environment, or shown how harmonious Judaism might be with democratic pluralism.

And because an ancient covenant required survival as a distinct and vibrant group, perhaps no minority in the United States, with a population of over five million in 1990, was bearing such heavy responsibilities—or seemed so implicated in a larger destiny.

See also **Ethnicity: Early Theories; Ethnicity and Race; Organized Religion; Marxist Approaches** *(volume 3); and other articles in this section.*

BIBLIOGRAPHY

Antler, Joyce. *The Journey Home: Jewish Women and the American Century.* New York, 1997.

Auerbach, Jerold S. *Rabbis and Lawyers: The Journey from Torah to Constitution.* Bloomington, Ind., 1990.

Biale, David, Michael Galchinsky, and Susannah Heschel, eds. *Insider/Outsider: American Jews and Multiculturalism.* Berkeley, 1998.

Bloom, Alexander. *Prodigal Sons: The New York Intellectuals and Their World.* New York, 1986.

Cohen, Naomi W. *Jews in Christian America: The Pursuit of Religious Equality.* New York, 1992.

Eisen, Arnold M. *The Chosen People in America: A Study in Jewish Religious Ideology.* Bloomington, Ind., 1983.

Erens, Patricia. *The Jew in American Cinema.* Bloomington, Ind., 1984.

Feingold, Henry L., ed. *The Jewish People in America.* 5 vols. Baltimore, 1992. Vol. 1, *A Time for Planting: The First Migration, 1654–1820,* by Eli Faber. Vol. 2, *A Time for Gathering: The Second Migration, 1820–1880,* by Hasia R. Diner. Vol. 3, *A Time for Building: The Third Migration, 1880–1920,* by Gerald Sorin. Vol. 4, *A Time for Searching: Entering the Mainstream, 1920–1945,* by Henry L Feingold. Vol. 5, *A Time for Healing: American Jewry Since World War II,* by Edward S. Shapiro.

Felsenthal, Emma. *Bernhard Felsenthal: Teacher in Israel.* New York, 1924.

Fishman, Sylvia Barack. *A Breath of Life: Feminism in the American Jewish Community.* New York, 1993.

Gabler, Neal. *An Empire of Their Own: How the Jews Invented Hollywood.* New York, 1988.

Glazer, Nathan. *American Judaism.* 2d ed. Chicago, 1989.

Goren, Arthur A. *The American Jews.* Cambridge, Mass., 1982.

Herberg, Will. *Protestant, Catholic, Jew: An Essay in American Religious Sociology.* Chicago, 1983.

Howe, Irving. *World of Our Fathers.* New York, 1976.

Joselit, Jenna Weissman. *The Wonders of America: Reinventing Jewish Culture, 1880–1950.* New York, 1994.

Klingenstein, Susanne. *Jews in the American Academy, 1900–1940: The Dynamics of Intellectual Assimilation.* New Haven, Conn., 1991.

Rischin, Moses. *The Promised City: New York's Jews, 1870–1914.* Cambridge, Mass., 1962.

Sarna, Jonathan D. *JPS: The Americanization of Jewish Culture, 1888–1988.* Philadelphia, 1989.

Sarna, Jonathan D., ed. *The American Jewish Experience.* 2d ed. New York, 1997.

Shechner, Mark. *After the Revolution: Studies in the Contemporary Jewish-American Imagination.* Bloomington, Ind. 1987.

Sklare, Marshall. *Observing America's Jews.* Hanover, N.H., 1993.

Whitfield, Stephen J. *American Space, Jewish Time.* Hamden, Conn., 1988.

——. *Voices of Jacob, Hands of Esau: Jews in American Life and Thought.* Hamden, Conn., 1984.

LATINAS AND LATINOS IN THE UNITED STATES

Eduardo Obregón Pagán

Although the histories of Mexican Americans, Puerto Ricans, Cubans, Dominicans, and Central Americans in the United States have important distinctions and characteristics that merit individual consideration, there are three critical periods in Latino history that mark important commonalities shared by these communities. The first period coincides with the age of American expansion into Latin American provinces, from 1848 to 1898. The second period begins in the late 1960s with the rise of ethnic nationalism among Chicanos and Puerto Ricans and ends by the mid-1970s, ironically before the so-called Decade of the Hispanic of the 1980s. The third period begins with the phenomenal growth of Latino communities in the United States after the 1980s and into the twenty-first century.

American imperialist expansion that resulted in war with Mexico in the mid-nineteenth century and with Spain at the end of the nineteenth century brought Americans into direct contact with and occupation of Latino peoples and communities. The Latino populations of the American Southwest, Cuba, and Puerto Rico were relatively small and sparse outside urban centers, and growth rates among these communities remained slow for much of the nineteenth century. Mexican Americans in the American Southwest were furthermore overwhelmed by European migration, and all of the Latino communities endured the slow and steady process of structural and cultural subjugation to Anglo-Americans.

The second period coincides with the rise of racial and ethnic assertiveness at the end of the civil rights movement in the United States. With the articulation of racial pride through black power among African Americans came a greater attention among black Puerto Ricans to their own ethnic heritage. Mexican Americans were also deeply affected by the revolt against assimilation, and, at the same time with Puerto Ricans, challenged dominant assumptions of Anglo-American supremacy. Latino activists championed community renewal programs, bilingual education, instructing the young about their native culture, fostering racial pride, and reexploring connections with and the meanings of their indigenous heritage. The Chicano movement and the Puerto Rican movement fell apart by the mid-1970s without developing strong organizational, philosophical, or communicational ties between Chicano and Puerto Rican communities. Both Chicano and Puerto Rican movements furthermore lacked consensus on objectives, strategies, and procedures within their own communities, and some of the more militant groups like the Young Lords Party (Puerto Rican) and the Brown Berets (Chicano) espoused inchoate and sometimes unobtainable goals of liberation. The structural changes in the U.S. political and economic systems that were furthermore necessary to empower these politically and economically disfranchised communities were slow in coming.

Latinos have been a growing presence in the United States since the 1980s and will no doubt impact upon the political and social landscape of the twenty-first century. This change has occurred not so much by the success of ethnic nationalist movements but by global and historical forces that have shifted demographics. Geographic contiguity, as well as technological innovations in transportation, communication, and the Internet, have facilitated personal and cultural contact with Latin America in ways that immigrants of other times and from other places could not sustain. At the same time, technology also serves to expand the pervasiveness of American culture into the homes of Latinos in the United States and in Latin America through television, movies, advertising, and commerce.

Despite different national histories and experiences, Latinos also share common cultural and structural experiences in the United States. Many Latinos are bilingual and bicultural in being able to bridge differences between their home communities and the dominant American culture. Although some Latinos have attained a measure of socioeconomic advancement in certain fields, Latinos are overrepresented among the unemployed, undereducated, and the imprisoned. Latinos furthermore contributed to 33 percent of the nation's growth between 1992 and 2000, and they are projected to contribute 37 percent between 2000 and 2010. Demographic forecasts estimate that Latinos in the United States will become the largest racial minority in the United States early in the twenty-first century. Indeed, some forecasts predict that by the year 2050 almost one out of every four Americans will be Latino. Their projected numeric strength could result in greater political power than exists at the beginning of the twenty-first century.

TERMS OF IDENTITY

The use of pan-ethnic terms of identity such as "Latino," "African," or "Asian" at best presumes that people from the same geographical region share important commonalities in history, heritage, and culture. At worst it conflates national differences and elides how ethnic communities understand and distinguish themselves from their neighbors. Although there is a measure of truth to the assumption that Latinos share a common history, language, and culture, such commonalities do not always lend to ethnic accord or unanimity. Indeed, Americans of Spanish-speaking origin are often as different as they are similar.

As an umbrella term for a culturally, racially, and historically diverse population of Spanish-speaking Americans, "Latino" is relatively new. Until the close of the nineteenth century when, in addition to seizing Mexico's northern territory in 1848, the United States acquired Puerto Rico, Cuba, and the Philippines from Spain, European Americans had little practical need to utilize a pan-ethnic term of identity for Americans of Latin American origin. Earlier generations of the twentieth century preferred to use terms such as "Latin American," "Spanish American," or even "Spanish" in collective reference to people from the former Mexican territories in the Southwest, Mexico, Cuba, and Puerto Rico. In the post–World War II period, some Latino groups utilized a hyphenated name to emphasize both their heritage and their citizenship status. Americans of Mexican origin preferred "Mexican-American" and American-born Cubans preferred "Cuban-American." Since the rise of cultural nationalism in the mid-1960s various Latino groups have embraced indigenous terms of identity as a

way of locating their politics and cultural affiliation against assimilated and acculturated Latinos. *Chicano* or *Xicano* derives from the Nahuatl name *Mexica,* from which Mexico gets its name. Some Puerto Ricans on the mainland and the island use the term *Boriquas,* which comes from the Taino name for the island of Puerto Rico, *Borinquen,* and some Dominicans refer to themselves as *Quisqueyanos,* which comes from *Quisqueya,* the Taino name for that island.

Latino is a category of identity that carries significance largely within the United States. There exists no bona fide sense of pan-ethnic identity within Latin America and most Americans of Latin American cultures and communities identify first and foremost by their country of origin. Thus, on the one hand, Latino is a term of identity imposed by the political majority within the United States to differentiate themselves from Spanish-speaking Americans. On the other hand, it is a term increasingly embraced by Spanish-speaking Americans in an effort to recognize historical and cultural similarities as well as to promote common economic and social concerns within the United States.

At the same time, Latino is not the only pan-ethnic term utilized by Spanish-speaking Americans. "Hispanic" is the term officially adopted by the United States government and embraced by many Spanish-speaking Americans. However, there are sharp divisions among Spanish-speaking Americans as to which term is more appropriate. Critics of the term "Hispanic" argue that it applies to and includes Spaniards, and that the term privileges European culture over native and mestizo cultures in the Americas. Proponents of the term "Latino" argue that it makes more specific reference to the people of the Americas, although critics of this term point out that "Latino" derives from the term "Latin" and is no more representative of American peoples and cultures than the term "Hispanic." What further complicates the argument is that younger Spanish-speaking Americans across the country are increasingly using the term "Latin" in self-reference. There is no consensus regarding which term is the most appropriate, although by popular usage Hispanic tends to be used more frequently west of the Mississippi (with some notable exceptions) and Latino tends to be used more frequently east of the Mississippi.

Regardless of which term is the more appropriate, the common consensus is that not all Latin Americans are part of the Latino community. The term Latino, in current usage, applies to Americans whose origins come from Latin American countries with long historical, economic, political, and cultural ties to the United States. The implication is that Latinos tend to be bicultural and bilingual in retaining a strong sense of their cultural and linguistic heritage while also identifying themselves as citizens of the United States and readily participating in the production and consumption of American culture. Thus Latino applies primarily to Mexican Americans, Puerto Ricans, and Cubans, although increasingly so to immigrants from Central America and the Dominican Republic as well.

There are other important terms of identity utilized among Latino groups that identify one by region, generation, or ideology. When referring to their own or to other Latino nationalities, Latinos often use Spanish terminology. Puerto Ricans are *Puertorriqueños,* Cubans are *Cubanos,* Dominicans are *Domenicanos,* and so forth. Traditionally, Latin Americans have also identified by their place of birth, or *patria chica,* and some Latino groups in the United States have continued with this custom. Texan-born Mexican Americans refer to themselves as "Tejanos," New Mexicans call themselves "Hispanos," and Californians refer to themselves as "Californios." Those born in Arizona and Colorado use "Hispanic" or "Chicano" interchangeably, depending largely upon generation and political orientation. In a similar manner, Puerto Ricans born and raised in New York City identify as "Nujorican" as opposed to the island-born Puerto Ricans. There are some notable exceptions to the *patria chica* custom, however. Neither Cubans, Dominicans, nor Central Americans born in the United States have followed this custom. In the Midwest, primarily around the Chicago area, the Mexican-origin population prefer *Méxicano* to any of the other current terms used by Mexican Americans.

DEMOGRAPHIC DIVERSITY

Mexican Americans are at once the oldest and youngest of the Latino subgroups. When the United States acquired Mexico's northern territory after invading Mexico City in 1848, the Mexican citizens living primarily in New Mexico, Texas, and California became naturalized by the Treaty of Guadalupe Hidalgo. Despite these political changes, social, economic, and cultural relations continued uninterrupted along the border and migration between the two countries was common until the 1920s. During the Mexican Revolution of 1910, an estimated 10 percent of the Mexican population fled to the United States as refugees of war and many relocated

in El Paso and Los Angeles. Although a significant number returned after the revolution ended, and many more were deported during the early years of the Great Depression, the United States government formally recruited Mexican labor through the Bracero Program during World War II to assist in agribusiness and other industries. Although the program formally ended years later, many American businesses continued to recruit Mexican laborers. Thus Mexican Americans are the largest Latino group, making up almost two-thirds of the Latino population in the United States. They are concentrated most strongly in Colorado, Texas, New Mexico, Arizona, and California, although many live throughout the western states. Large concentrations of Mexican Americans are also found in Illinois, Washington, and in the regions of agricultural production in the Midwest, Northeast, and South.

Puerto Ricans are the second oldest group of Latinos in the United States. The United States acquired both Puerto Rico and Cuba in the Spanish-American War in 1898. While Cuba gained its formal independence in 1902, Puerto Rico is a commonwealth in free association with the United States. Thus Puerto Ricans, who were naturalized in 1917, began a long history of migration from the island to the mainland in ways that never developed for Cubans. About one out of every ten Latinos on the United States mainland is Puerto Rican. The mainland Puerto Rican population is among the most urban of the Latino communities, with numbers concentrating more in major cities in New England, the mid-Atlantic states, and in Chicago. Indeed, New York City has the highest concentration, where an estimated one out of every four children attending public school is Puerto Rican. Puerto Ricans have also migrated to Hawaii. American plantation owners in Hawaii recruited heavily among Puerto Rican laborers in the late nineteenth and early twentieth centuries, and about 8 percent of Hawaiians today identify as Puerto Rican (including children of intermarriage). The experiences of Puerto Ricans in the mainland United States are one of the great paradoxes of the Latino experience. While Puerto Ricans have had the benefit of United States citizenship for most of the twentieth century, they have the highest rates of poverty (38 percent), unemployment (11 percent), and households headed by single females (41 percent) among Latinos.

Cubans came to the United States in three successive waves, each in response to international crises. The first wave lasted from 1959 to 1962 when Fidel Castro overthrew the military dictatorship of

Fulgenico Batista, and hundreds of thousands of Cubans relocated in the Miami area. The United States government warmly welcomed the Cuban refugees and offered financial assistance and automatic legal residency. The second wave occurred during the Mariel boatlift in 1980 when close to 125,000 Cuban refugees, many of whom had been jailed by Castro, came to the United States from the Cuban port of Mariel. Despite popular opinion to the contrary, President Jimmy Carter accepted most of the refugees. Close to 2,500 were declared "excludable" and held in American prisons. Fourteen years later, in 1994, more than 30,000 Cubans fled the rising food costs and increasing poverty in Cuba and sailed to Florida. President Bill Clinton allowed only 12,000 refugees to be processed for admission into the United States at Guantánamo Bay Naval Base. As a consequence of these waves of immigration, Cubans constitute about one-fifth of the Latino population with concentrations strongest in southern Florida, and growing numbers in New York and New Jersey.

Between 1965 and 1980, almost one out of every ten Dominicans (roughly 400,000) migrated from the Dominican Republic to the United States for economic reasons. On the mainland United States, the Dominican population is largest in the metropolitan centers in New York, New Jersey, and Massachusetts, although substantial numbers of Dominicans live in Florida and Puerto Rico.

During the 1980s and 1990s Central and South Americans fled political instability and war in their home countries of El Salvador and Guatemala, Colombia, Ecuador, and Peru. Although they are among the newer groups of Latinos in the United States, they have quickly outnumbered Cubans and Dominicans to become the fourth largest subset of the Latino population. Central and South Americans make up about 14 percent of Latinos in the United States and the majority reside in the greater metropolitan area of Washington, D.C., which includes portions of Maryland and Virginia. Significant numbers of Central Americans have also relocated to Miami, Houston, and Los Angeles.

RACIAL DIVERSITY

The racial diversity of Latinos in the United States reflects the legacy of Spanish colonial policy, settlement patterns, and economic relations. Although Spain initially laid claim to the Western Hemisphere, the number of Spaniards who colonized New Spain was never great relative to the larger in-

digenous population. Spanish authorities and colonizers furthermore tended to concentrate in the urban centers already established by the Indian empires of Mexico and Peru, leaving large numbers of indigenous communities in the hinterlands intact.

Centuries of acculturation, structural assimilation, and intermarriage have created populations of mixed ancestry. The majority of Mexican citizens, about 60 percent, are *mestizo*, or of mixed Spanish and Indian ancestry. About 24 to 30 percent of Mexicans come from indigenous communities, and Mexicans who are "white," or European in ancestry, range from 9 to 15 percent. The majority of Central Americans also tend to come from indigenous or mestizo communities.

In Brazil and the Caribbean, where the devastation from European pathogens was greatest during the early colonial period, Spaniards imported enslaved West Africans to replace the labor supply, many of whom intermarried with most of the surviving natives there. Latinos from the Caribbean reflect the diversity of this history. Puerto Ricans are "the rainbow people," according to some scholars, because they range in appearance from light-skinned Spaniards to mid-toned trigeños to dark-skinned mixtures of Taino, West African, and Spanish ancestry. The majority of Dominicans, about 73 percent, are of mixed African and European ancestry. Only about 11 percent of Dominicans are "black" or of West African ancestry, and only 16 percent are "white," or of Western European ancestry.

The Cuban population also reflects this same racial diversity, although the distribution is different from the Dominican Republic in some important ways. Fifty-one percent of Cubans are mulatto, and an estimated 37 percent are "white." About 11 percent classify as "black" and 1 percent are of Chinese descent. Furthermore, Cubans who came to the United States after the Castro revolution tended to be more European in appearance and middle class in education, attainment, and cultural orientation. Cubans from the Mariel boatlift tended to be more working class and of mixed or African ancestry. Because Latinos from the Dominican Republic and from the Mariel boatlift have higher concentrations of West African ancestry, they are often confused in the United States for African Americans.

Although Spaniards were the dominant European group in Latin America, large numbers of French, Italians, Germans, Irish, and Jews also settled in various parts of Latin America and left their distinctive cultural and ethnic legacies on the population. So too have a number of Chinese, Japanese, and East Indians settled in various parts of Latin America and the Caribbean.

LINGUISTIC DIVERSITY

Although Latinos are commonly referred to as "Spanish-speaking Americans," not all Latinos in the United States speak Spanish as their primary language. English instruction in Puerto Rican schools is common, and generations have grown up bilingual since the United States acquired Puerto Rico from Spain. Mexican Americans in the Southwest have also had long contact with United States culture and language. Indeed, as a whole, Latinos living in the United States tend to achieve English proficiency faster than other immigrant groups. Studies show that fluency in English has a direct correlation to socioeconomic mobility and English increasingly becomes the primary language spoken in Latino households among the second and third generations living in the United States.

The Spanish that many Latinos speak reflects the diverse histories and demographics of their respective native countries. Spanish in Puerto Rico and Mexico, for example, contains many words borrowed from their respective indigenous communities and from neighboring countries like the United States. Thus there are appreciable differences in the vocabulary used by Mexicans, Puerto Ricans, Cubans, and Dominicans, and the Spanish spoken by all of these communities is qualitatively different from the language of Castile. These grammatical and vocabulary differences are more or less equivalent to the differences between the Queen's English, American English, and Australian English.

In addition, many Latin Americans have developed their own unique patois, or slang, which continues to grow and adapt to new contexts and environments in the United States. Latinos in the United States have Hispanicized American terms and created a hybrid Spanglish. Words such as "computer" become *compuder* or *compudora,* the verb "to park" becomes *parquear* rather than *estancionar,* and the word "lunch" becomes *lonche* rather than *almuerzo.* At the same time, some Latinos engage in code switching, or a shifting back and forth between Spanish and English, such as "no me gusta pickles con my Big Mac." Americans have likewise embraced (and often Americanized) Spanish words. Terms traditionally utilized in the American cattle industry come from Mexican Spanish (lasso, ranch, corral). Spanish words that are quickly becoming part of the American fast food diet come primarily from Mexican foods or their derivatives, such as *burritos, fajitas, nachos,* and *quesadillas.*

Some of the Latino dialects are more arcane, such as the Pachuco argot called *Caló.* The origin of Pachucos and their language is shrouded in the unrecorded past. As a linguistic and cultural form *Pachuquismo* has been utilized most often among the laboring class of Mexican Americans, although certain phrases from Caló have gained widespread usage among Mexicans and Mexican Americans, such as *orale* (depending upon context it is equivalent to the salutation "hey" or the approbation "okay"), *chale* ("no"), or *la migra* (the Immigration and Naturalization Service). Caló has continued to develop a unique vocabulary within the American prison complex.

Recent arrivals from southern Mexico, Guatemala, and El Salvador, where indigenous communities thrive in significant numbers, further diversify the linguistic possibilities of Latinos in the United States. Studies estimate that one out of every three Mexicans does not speak Spanish as a primary language, but a native dialect instead. Thus the economic and political refugees from these regions, who often work as migrant laborers in the United States, are often trilingual in speaking Spanish as a secondary language and English as a tertiary language.

RELIGIOUS DIVERSITY

The effort to convert Native Americans to Christianity followed the European conquest of the Americas quite closely, and Roman Catholicism has played a dominant role in much of the history of Latin America. Indeed, an estimated 95 percent of all Latinos are Roman Catholic. Popular expression of piety among Latinos, however, tends to display such a remarkable degree of native thought and practice that Latino spirituality cannot be adequately summarized merely as "Christian." In the competing efforts to promote conversion and resist it, both Roman Catholic missionaries and converts within indigenous communities reached a syncretism of belief and behavior through formal and informal means that accommodated complimentary modes of thought and worship.

Dia de los Muertos (Day of the Dead) is a holiday observed by Roman Catholics both in Europe and in Latin America to remember departed relatives. Although celebration of this day varies greatly within and between European and Latin American countries, there are unique ways in which the day is celebrated in the Americas that derive from native practices. Cemeteries in Mexico and in Central America are decorated with flowers and *papel picado* in anticipation of the spiritual return of the dead to visit their families between October 31 and November 2. Living families often gather to make altars and place offerings of food, candles, incense, yellow marigolds, and a photo of the departed.

The unique features of this celebration can be traced to ritual festivities dedicated to remembering the dead during the reign of the Aztec empire. In an effort to Christianize this celebration Spanish priests moved the holiday, traditionally celebrated during the ninth month of the Aztec calendar, Tlaxochimaco ("Birth of Flowers"), also known as Miccaihuitontli ("Little Feast of the Dead"), to coincide with the Christian holiday of *Día de Todos Santos,* or All Saints' Day and All Souls' Day. Latinos now celebrate the Day of the Dead during the early fall rather than at the beginning of summer.

Latinos from the Caribbean also brought to the United States syncretistic belief systems that blended Christian traditions with beliefs and practices originating among the Yoruba of West Africa. The spiritual traditions of the Yoruba people transformed in the Americas where Christianized Africans were most highly concentrated, to produce the new religious traditions of *Santería* in Cuba, *vodun* (also known as voodoo) in Haiti, and *Candomblé* and *Umbanda* in Brazil.

These religious traditions that flourished in the Americas share elements of Roman Catholic and Yoruba beliefs in the way they conceptualize the existence and nature of the divine, the proper relationship that mortals should have with immortal beings, and how one accesses divine power. Although a supreme being exists, mortals have a more intimate relationship with a group of minor deities collectively known as saints or *orishas*. The orishas are like mortals in character and personality, yet each possesses powers associated with a particular force of nature. The orishas are also known by both their Yoruba and Roman Catholic identities: the Virgin Mary is *Iemaná,* St. Peter is interchangeably associated with *Ogun* or *Eshu-Eligba,* St. Raphael is *Osanyin,* and Sta. Barbara, or at times John the Baptist, is associated with *Xango.*

Devotion to the orishas includes ritualized drumming, dancing, offerings of food, and animal sacrifice. Those who minister divine power possess *ache,* the power of the orishas, and are known as *santeros.* Ache allows santeros to access divine power through trances in order to determine the causes and cures of health or social problems. Fol-

lowers of Santeria also believe that a particular orisha can at times intervene on one's behalf or even enter into one's body and meld with one's personality.

Despite the predominance of Roman Catholicism and syncretistic traditions within Latino histories and cultures, Protestant evangelical religions have made significant inroads among Latinos, as well as Jehovah's Witnesses and Mormons. Indeed, Mormon proselytizing within Latin America and within Latino communities has been so successful that Spanish is projected to be the most commonly spoken language within the Mormon Church in the twenty-first century.

CULTURAL DIVERSITY

Music and Dance Toward the end of the eighteenth century, black musicians in Cuba, and to some extent in Haiti and the Dominican Republic, created a number of distinctive musical styles in artfully blending the musical instruments and traditions of Europe and Africa in a variety of combinations. In reproducing European style harmonies and melodies in thirds, black musicians utilized "blue notes" derived from the West African musical scale, and added the responsorial form (where the lead singer alternates with a choral response), with polyrhythms and syncopation (off-beat accents). The African influence was especially strong in the rhythm and instrumentation of Caribbean music. Black musicians employed a variety of percussion instruments such as drums, scrapers, gourd rattles, bells, and handclaps to maintain an unchanging, repetitive rhythmic pattern known as the African timeline. It survives in the *clave* rhythms common to Afro-Caribbean music.

Musicians in the Caribbean also combined European and African instruments in a variety of ensembles while performing in certain musical genres. In the late nineteenth century, Cuban musicians playing the *danzon* formed *charanga* orchestras that included the flute, piano, violins, and timbales (an Afro-Caribbean percussion instrument). In the early twentieth century small *conjuntos* in Havana popularized the *son,* which was a rural song genre and a secular dance form originating in eastern Cuba, by adding trumpet and bass to guitar and percussion.

Much of the music popular among twenty-first-century Latinos is derived from musical trends developed in Havana. Musicians in late-eighteenth-century and early-nineteenth-century Havana added

African musical styles and instrumentation to the English country dance, or contra dance, and created the *contradanza* that eventually became popular throughout the Caribbean. In the early nineteenth century, black musicians of the Dominican Republic and Haiti also experimented with combining European dance music with African drum rhythms and created *merengue.* In the late nineteenth century, charanga orchestras popularized the danzon, and by the 1930s the son overtook the danzon in popularity.

The son, which is characterized by a vocal melody independent of the percussive rhythm and traditionally performed by a *tres,* a *bojita,* and a *marimbula,* grandfathered a number of popular musical styles and dances of the twentieth century. From the son came the *rumba,* which became a ballroom dance of Afro-Cuban folk-dance origin where the basic movement was to step back, step front, close and hold in 4/4 time. From the rumba came the *mambo,* which is essentially an offbeat rumba, where a step taken on the last beat of music in 4/4 time is held through to the first beat of the following measure. Mambo foot patterns are essentially the same as in the rumba, but couples more often abandon the standard ballroom embrace position and dance holding one hand or without touching. The *cha-cha* is a faster, rhythmic dance invented around 1948 by the Cuban violinist and bandleader Enrique Jorrín. The cha-cha is derived from rhythmical innovation to the mambo, in which a quick change of step is done on the last two beats of the measure.

The big-band arrangements of Perez Prado helped popularize the mambo in Latin America and the United States. Arsenio Rodriguez gave birth to modern Cuban dance music called *salsa* through his innovations to the mambo. The Cuban bandleader (and later television star and producer) Desi Arnaz played a key role in popularizing the Caribbean sound in big band music. The Puerto Rican musicians Cesar Concepcion and Rafael Cortijo further incorporated the *plena* and *bomba* into the salsa repertoire during the 1940s and 1950s. Salsa dominated Puerto Rican popular music, both on the island and in United States urban areas—especially in New York City by Tito Puente and Machito.

The United States embargo of the Castro revolution included a censorship of Cuban music in the United States, and Cuban and Puerto Rican musicians in the United States recontextualized the genre in America's barrios. "The lyrics of salsa," according to the ethnomusicologist Frances Aparicio, "have documented the *vision de mundo* of the Latino working-class sector the immigrant, working-class

. . . its lyrics continue the traditional role of the Puerto Rican plena, the Cuban son, the Colombian vallenato, and the Mexican corrido—the role of narrating historical events, local situations, and stories from the point of view of the marginalized."

The Cuban diaspora also ensured the musical growth and commercial popularity of salsa in the United States. Johnny Pacheco, Celia Cruz, Eddie Palmieri, and Willie Colon established themselves as key salsa artists. Panamanian-born Ruben Blades further contributed to the growth of salsa by introducing synthesizers and using more complex arrangements and socially conscious lyrics. During the 1980s, the Dominican merengue tended to dominate salsa among Puerto Ricans and Central Americans. In contemporary salsa music, the merengue is characterized by duple meter (two-beat measure), fast tempos, and saxophone arrangements employing fast-note passagework. Among the stars of the 1980s merengue were performers Johnny Ventura and Wilfredo Vargas.

Around the same time that Americans began to discover rock and roll, Latino musicians began experimenting with a fusion of American rock with salsa and Tejano swing that eventually became Latin pop. From the 1950s to the late 1960s Mexican American artists like Ritchie Valens (born Ricardo Valenzuela), Linda Ronstadt, and Trini López tended to dominate Latin pop. Mexican American musicians also recorded a number of hit songs with Herb Alpert and the Tijuana Brass Band in a pop *mariachi* style dubbed "Ameriachi." Carlos Santana of Santana experimented with fusion sounds of rhythm and blues and Latino rock, and, to a lesser extent, Jerry Garcia of the Grateful Dead reflected the influence of Tejano swing in the Grateful Dead's countercultural music.

During much of this period, Latino artists also recorded and performed in English for American popular tastes and Latin-styled music performed in Spanish largely remained a novelty. However, it was not until the black power movement shifted the focus of the civil rights movement toward the end of the 1960s that Latino artists began to assert a stronger ethnic identity in their music and public personas. In the process, Latino musicians and recording artists created a unique fusion of rhythm and blues, Latin jazz, and traditional Mexican and Caribbean music.

Since the 1980s Cuban and Puerto Rican artists have gained increasing popularity in the American pop market with Latin pop and Spanish-language recordings. The folk singer Joan Baez was an active presence early in the civil rights and antiwar movements, and the Puerto Rican guitarist Jose Feliciano pioneered crossover recordings with Latino-styled music and Spanish lyrics. It was not until the success of the Miami Sound Machine in the early 1980s, however, that Latin pop took on a distinctive Caribbean influence. Founded by the Cuban-born bandleader Emilio Estefan, the Miami Sound Machine crossed over musical genres with their 1985 hit "Conga," featuring Estefan's wife Gloria Maria Fajardo. Since that time Gloria Estefan has gone on to a solo career, recording numerous international hits and earning acclaim for her Cuban-based music around the world. Emilio Estefan has taken to producing his wife's work as well as encouraging the talents of other Latino singers, including Jon Secada and Ricky Martin.

In the early 1990s the rerecording of Ritchie Valens's "La Bamba" by the east Los Angeles band Los Lobos for the movie of the same title precipitated the resurgence of Chicano rock. Los Lobos' success opened the way for a number of Latino recording artists to cross over from Latin American markets into mainstream American markets. Tejana performing sensation Selena recorded songs in both English and Spanish, and her untimely death at the hands of a crazed fan cut short what promised to be a successful career.

By the end of the twentieth century the crossover successes of Latino recording artists already popular in Latin America prompted a number of non–Latino American artists and groups to market albums specifically for Latin American consumption. Puerto Rican and Cuban artists continued to dominate Latin pop at the end of the twentieth century with Marc Anthony, Ricky Martin, Jon Secada, and Jennifer Lopez. Although Martin was born in San Juan, Puerto Rico, Anthony in Spanish Harlem, and Secada in Havana, all were influenced by American and Caribbean musical styles. Anthony brings more of an accomplished Caribbean sound to Latino pop, having sold more records throughout the world than any other salsa singer, whereas Martin, Secada, and Lopez perform in more of a Latinized funk-rock style. The music of newcomer Christina Aguilera, of Ecuadoran descent, shows stronger influences of rhythm and blues and hip-hop.

Literature The literature of Chicano, Puerto Rican, and Cuban writers is vast and varied, and can only be summarized broadly in this essay. Latino literature tends to explore life in Latino communities and on the margins of American social life. Like the literature of other immigrant groups Latino writing explores questions of cultural preservation in the face of structural assimilation. Unlike other immigrant groups, however, Latino writers within these communities have also recognized the revolutionary power of language and have been experimental and political in their usage of their distinctive idioms. While some Latinos have written entirely in Spanish and others entirely in English, still others have combined both languages in a variety of ways. Both Chicanos and mainland Puerto Ricans in particular have written in their own barrio slang that combines English and Spanish.

For this discussion, the history of Mexican American and Chicano literature begins in 1910, when hundreds of thousands of refugees fled the devastation of the Mexican Revolution, and the Mexican nationals who resettled in the urban centers in the American Southwest reinvigorated the Mexican American communities already established there. The political exiles and refugees, who anticipated returning to Mexico with the cessation of hostilities, took seriously the responsibility of reeducating Mexican Americans in Mexican ways. They established Spanish-language newspapers and small presses to publish their works within the Mexican communities *de afuera*. The writings of Mexican exiles of this period included humorous novels, satirical sketches of Mexican daily life, and collections of Mexican tales and legends. The behavior and speech of the *pocho*, the Mexican American who lost his cultural connections to Mexico, received particular attention by the Mexican intellectuals in exile.

At this same time a group of Mexican American writers, trained at American colleges or in the styles of Anglo-American authors, began to emerge. Writers such as Vicente J. Bernal, María Cristina Mena Chambers, Josefina Niggli, Luis Pérez, Fray Angélico Chávez, and Mario Suárez were of Mexican descent or nationality (as in the case of Josefina Niggli who was born in Monterrey, Mexico, of Scandinavian American parents) and were born in or had relocated to the United States at an early age. They wrote in English, at times bilingual, and often in a romantic style about pre-revolutionary Mexico. Only occasionally and with great subtlety did they address the issues they faced as racialized minorities in the United States.

José Antonio Villarreal's *Pocho* (1959) signaled a transition from the insular and relatively innocuous Mexican American writings of earlier generations to the radical and leftist works of the Chicano period. Written in the third person, the story of *Pocho* closely parallels the life of Villarreal as it explores the meaning of growing up as an Americanized Mexican in California. Although Villarreal's story never really develops a keen sense of ethnic pride or awareness, his work anticipates the themes and issues of the Chicano generation.

A solid corpus of Chicano literature emerged in the 1970s with Rudolfo Anaya's *Bless Me, Ultima* (1972), Tomás Rivera's *... And the Earth Did Not Part* (1971), Estela Portillo Trambley's *Rain of Scorpions and Other Writings* (1975), and Rolando Hinojosa's *Klail City and Its Surroundings* (1976). The writers of this generation eschewed the hyphenated identity implied by the term "Mexican American" in favor of the more indigenous implications of the term "Chicano." Chicano activists and intellectuals were greatly influenced by the *indigenismo* movement of Mexican literature of the post-revolutionary period, and the American writers who identified as Chicano explored in their works the more native aspects of Mexican culture. Both Anaya and the poet Alberto Alurista furthermore experimented with magic realism, a literary technique combining the real with the unreal (or at least, reality not understood through empiricism) in blending traditional native myths and legends with current social issues and contexts.

From works as diverse as Oscar Zeta Acosta's *Autobiography of a Brown Buffalo* (1972), Rodolfo "Corky" Gonzales's poem *I Am Joaquín/Yo Soy Joaquín* (1967), and Armando Rendon's *Chicano Manifesto* (1971), Chicano intellectuals explored the meanings of Chicanismo itself and attempted to define a philosophy that united a population historically divided by color, class, and citizenship. Although most Chicano writers of this period agreed that liberation was the goal and assimilation was the foe, they could find no consensus on what either term meant or how they were to be actualized. Other Chicanos wrote to document the sufferings and struggles of Mexican Americans, to protest social injustices, combat stereotypes, critique cold-war society and American materialism, examine the relationship of Mexican Americans to Anglo-American culture, and to promote bilingualism, cultural nationalism, and folk customs.

In the 1980s and 1990s, a generation of post-Chicano writers turned their attention toward personal liberation and explored the borderland as a metaphor for multiple sites of identity. Chicana writers further pushed beyond the paradigm of Chicano liberation to explore topics and issues altogether ignored by the Chicano movement, such as sexuality, gender, race, and the politics of the body. In the process Chicana writers such as Sandra Cisneros's *Loose Woman* (1994), Ana Castillo's *So Far*

from God (1993), Gloria Anzaldúa's *Borderlands: The New Mestiza* (1987), and Cherríe Moraga's *Loving in the War Years* (1983) have entirely reinvented the meaning of "Chicano/a" identity.

Puerto Rican literature in the United States has an interesting history, dating back to the late nineteenth century when Puerto Rico became an American colony. Yet mainland Puerto Rican writings from that time up until the 1960s were not substantially different from the literature produced on the island of Puerto Rico, either aesthetically or thematically. It was not until the second half of the 1960s that Puerto Ricans living in the United States expressed a consciousness and perspective different from that of their island relatives. While Puerto Rican writers on the mainland retained memories of Puerto Rico and even mythologized Puerto Rico as an island paradise, they nonetheless increasingly explored the meaning of their history and place in New York City as urban Nuyoricans. Since the 1980s a number of writers have explored a post-Nuyorican paradigm in seeking to embrace the commonalities shared with other peoples and cultures.

Because of Puerto Rico's status as a commonwealth of the United States, and because Puerto Ricans have been citizens of the United States since 1917, Puerto Ricans in both venues have addressed many of the same issues. However, Puerto Rican literature written in and about the island of Puerto Rico has generally been critical of American imperialism and revolves around the political status of Puerto Rico. Nuyorican writers, on the other hand, have addressed experiences on the mainland contextualized more specifically by ethnic identity and racial status in the United States.

Most of the Nuyorican writers were transplanted to the United States as a result of the mass emigration from Puerto Rico starting in the 1940s. Unlike the "canonical" elite of intellectuals still living in Puerto Rico, Nuyoricans came as a class of laborers drawn by wartime production and the promises of better standards of living and opportunities. Their literature, often through autobiographical works, addresses the strains of adaptation to life in the urban jungle, and to being immigrants with secondary social, political, racial, and economic status in the United States. The street and the barrio framed the worlds of Nuyorican writers of the late 1960s and 1970s, and their works became chronicles of the promise and pain of barrio life. Piri Thomas's classic work *Down These Mean Streets* (1967), follows the life of a dark-skinned boy growing up in Spanish Harlem who is often mistaken by whites as an African American and who suffers the consequences of his color. It is also the tale of an epic struggle against the relentless tide of street drugs, crime, and gangs, and of his eventually finding redemption through his art of writing. Nicholasa Mohr's *Nilda* (1973) also described life in the barrio but with a different and more feminist perspective as she traversed the social space occupied by women as mothers and wives in a patriarchal Puerto Rican world to find greater freedom in a career in the capitalist world. Works such as these affirm the cultural difference mainland Puerto Ricans have from Puerto Rican islanders, as well as their survival in very difficult circumstances.

With the social upheavals of the late 1960s in the United States, Puerto Ricans began to assert more forcefully their ethnic identity and difference through literature. Puerto Rican writing from this period is a literature of resistance that invites readers to question the assumptions of political, cultural, and social institutions that allow discrimination, widespread poverty, and the lack of educational and economic opportunities for Puerto Ricans in the United States. Some writers have written to expose and condemn the socioeconomic conditions experienced by mainland Puerto Ricans. Others have written in critique of the materialism of the American Dream, and still others have written to explore and celebrate cultural nationalism in themes of cultural resistance, assimilation, and ethnic identity.

Post-Nuyorican writers from the 1980s onward, like the poet Victor Hernández Cruz, Tato Laviera, and others, have written beyond a specific Puerto Rican paradigm to embrace multiculturalism and multilingualism. A number of mainland Puerto Ricans have explored commonalities and shared experiences with other American minority groups, and have especially emphasized their ties to African cultures. Post-Nuyorican writers, rather than mourning the loss of an imagined essential Puerto Ricanness, celebrate the creation from many influences of a new identity. At the same time, Puerto Rican women writers, like Chicana writers, have come to the fore in seeking to redefine the roles of Puerto Rican women within home and community, and the explicit patriarchy of traditional Puerto Rican culture. A number of female Puerto Rican writers continue to face the challenge of helping preserve their culture in the face of Anglo-Americanism while also calling for sweeping changes in the culture to end sex discrimination.

Cuban literature is the latest of the Latino literatures to develop in the United States. It was not until the Castro revolution, when many Cuban professionals and intellectuals fled the island, that Cubans lived in the United States in substantial numbers. The Mariel boatlift added substantial refugees to the Cuban population in exile and hastened a growing realization on the part of many Cuban Americans that there was no hope of returning home.

The historic and political contexts of Cuban experiences in the United States have shaped Cuban literature in exile in fundamental ways. Early Cuban writing dwelled less on the relationships between Anglos and Latinos than that of Chicanos and Puerto Ricans, and lacked the leftist critiques of American society and revolutionary positions embraced by Puerto Rican and Chicano writers of the 1960s and 1970s. Instead, Cuban writers of the first generation focused their writings on the revolution in Cuba and the home they had lost. Writers like Lydia Cabrera and José Sánchez-Boudy wrote nostalgically of the customs and folklore of old Cuba. Like the literature of other immigrant communities, Cuban literature also reveals feelings of isolation and loneliness in a strange land, the seeming vacuity of their present lives, and a mourning for the loss of the traditional values and cherished ways of life. Some writers in exile, in retelling their violent and dramatic escapes from Cuba, explicitly express strong anti-Castro, anti-Communist, and counter-revolutionary views.

With the coming of so large a body of refugees from the port of Mariel, Cuban exiles have increasingly embraced the view that they will remain in the United States. A newer generation of writers, who do not identify as Cuban but as Cuban Americans and who do not remember the lost island, have turned inward for their inspiration and source material. Cuban Americans like the author Celedonio Gonzales and the playwright and poet Omar Torres began to more fully explore the tensions of making a new life in the United States *as* immigrants, and in trying to preserve their cultural identities while structurally assimilating in a land dominated by an Anglo-American culture. Some authors of the Cuban American generation, like the playwright Dolores Prida, have articulated more direct criticism of the United States rather than Castro's Cuba. Others, like Roberto Fernandez and Ivan Acosta, have explored tensions and contradictions within the Cuban American community itself as a mixture of both Cuban and North American culture. Oscar Hijuelos, who won a Pulitzer Prize for his 1989 novel *The Mambo Kings Play Songs of Love,* has been

Puerto Rican Day Parade, New York City, June 1985. The parade began in New York in 1958, becoming a nationwide event in 1995. It draws millions of people from many different ethnicities. © OWEN FRANKEN/CORBIS

the most successful of the Cuban American writers in receiving mainstream attention.

LATINISMO IN THE UNITED STATES

So much diversity exists among the Latino population that one can justifiably question whether any unity exists. There has yet to develop a political agenda that coheres to any sense of Latinismo among the different Latino subgroups. Cubans of the first and second generation tend to be the most economically and politically integrated of all Latinos, and their politics run toward conservative Republicanism. They ardently supported cold-war policy and they continue to strongly support American policies that oppose Castro. Mexican Americans, Puerto Ricans, and Dominicans as a whole tend to be more liberal and vote Democratic, and opposed American cold-war policy particularly in Central America. Some community activists among Chicanos and Puerto Ricans lean toward socialist philosophy, and strains of libertarianism run throughout the politics of

Central Americans in their distrust of strong centralized government.

At the same time, there are commonalities of Latino experiences in the United States, both historical and present day, that may provide fertile ground for a more developed sense of Latinismo. The increasing numbers of multiracial Latinos may challenge what is all too often a binary discourse of race in America. Latinos tend to occupy a cultural and intellectual middle ground in being bilingual and bicultural, and may add new life to the discourse on multiculturalism.

The growing population of Latinos in the United States constitutes one of the most dramatic demographic shifts in American history. In some cities like Laredo and Brownsville, Texas, Latinos (mostly Mexican American) constitute 80 to 95 percent of the population. In California, Latinos make up 30 percent of the state's population and they are projected to outnumber non-Latino whites by the year 2020. In New York City, Puerto Ricans, Dominicans, Central Americans, and Cubans have increased the number of Latinos to 3.6 million. In Chicago Latinos are approximately 27 percent of the population. Chicago presently ranks second in the number of Puerto Ricans, fourth in the number of Mexicans, and third in the number of Central Americans in the United States. In Miami, Latinos (mostly Cuban) make up about 60 percent of the population.

There are also signs that Latinos are growing in political and economic strength, despite an array of social issues that continue to challenge the Latino population. A recent survey in *Latino Business* found that eighty Latinos in the United States are worth $25 million or more—40 percent of whom are Cuban. Coalitions between Latinos have developed in major cities around particular social issues and concerns, and public Latino celebrations that were once specific to a particular nationality are beginning to synchronize with other Latino groups. Latinos' history of syncretism and *mestizaje* may add new life to the national discourse on race, identity, and culture.

See also **The Southwest; Borderlands; Southern California** *(in this volume);* **Ethnicity: Early Theories; Ethnicity and Race** *(volume 3); and other articles in this section.*

BIBLIOGRAPHY

Acosta-Belén, Edna, and Barbara R. Sjostrom, eds. *The Hispanic Experience in the United States: Contemporary Issues and Perspectives.* New York, 1988.

De la Garza, Rodolfo O. *Latino Voices: Mexican, Puerto Rican, and Cuban Perspectives on American Politics.* Boulder, Colo., 1992.

Fox, Geoffrey. *Hispanic Nation: Culture, Politics, and the Constructing of Identity.* New York, 1995.

Gann, L. H. *The Hispanics in the United States: A History.* Boulder, Colo., 1986.

Kanellos, Nicolas. *Hispanic Firsts: 500 Years of Extraordinary Achievement.* Farmington Hills, Mich., 1997.

López, Antoinette S., ed. *Historical Themes and Identity: Mestizaje and Labels.* New York, 1995.

Meier, Matt S. *Notable Latino Americans: A Biographical Dictionary.* Westport, Conn., 1997.

Oboler, Suzanne. *Ethnic Labels, Latino Lives: Identity and the Politics of (Re)Presentation in the United States.* Minneapolis, Minn., 1995.

Shorris, Earl. *Latinos: A Biography of the People.* New York, 1992.

Stavans, Ilan. *The Hispanic Condition: Reflections on Culture and Identity in America.* New York, 1995.

Torres, Rodolfo D., and Antonia Darder, eds. *The Latino Studies Reader: Culture, Economy, and Society.* Malden, Mass., 1998.

Toucan Valley Publications Research Staff. *Hispanic Databook of U.S. Cities and Counties.* Milpitas, Calif., 1994.

NATIVE AMERICANS

Robert Warrior

Native American people and tribal groups have participated in virtually every aspect of the social and intellectual life of the Americas for longer than any other group, but that participation has all too often been understood only in military terms or, worse, ignored. Current work in historical, literary, and cultural studies allows a deeper appreciation for the nuanced ways in which American indigenes have provided some of the foundations for North American intellectual and social life and have responded to the settlement of their lands by successive waves of immigrants, first from Europe, then from every corner of the globe.

At times throughout history, especially in the first two centuries of colonization in the Americas, American Indians have been the central focus of hemispheric life as adversaries and impediments rather than as partners in the creation of a new set of cultural and social conditions on the continent. In the twentieth century, American Indians made important contributions to contemporary social and intellectual life as public figures, authors, musicians, artists, and politicians. Perhaps the most neglected aspect of life for Native Americans has been the largely overlooked but still vital work of ensuring a future for indigenous cultural life in the centuries since the arrival of Europeans on American soil. Each of these areas is important in developing an understanding of how indigenous peoples have responded as historical agents to the changes that have taken place under modernity.

AMERICAN INDIGENES BEFORE 1492

Thousands of years ago, indigenous groups in the Americas began organizing themselves and developing into recognizable societies. Along with the Mayan and Aztec civilizations that were still intact when Europeans arrived in Mesoamerica in the sixteenth century, North America had seen a series of cultures that had settled in various areas. By 1500 B.C., traders from present-day Mexico and Central America had introduced corn to their northern neighbors. One of the earliest North American settlement sites is Poverty Point, in present-day Louisiana. At that major mound site, there is some evidence of pottery making and some signs that people had banded together in centralized political arrangements.

Several centuries later, a more developed culture emerged in the central Ohio River valley. These people, named the Adena, also built mounds, including the 1,254-foot-long serpentine mound in present-day southern Ohio. Adena people lived in villages of around ten houses and gathered together at their ceremonial mounds in an annual cycle of rituals. From the Adena culture came the Hopewell culture, which existed from around 100 B.C. to A.D. 800 in present-day Illinois. The Hopewell provide the strongest early evidence for the extent of trading networks between indigenous groups in the Americas; among funeral objects in Hopewell mound sites are objects from as far away as Montana, North Dakota, and Florida. Hopewell and the nearby Marksville culture began to decline around A.D. 400, perhaps because of an increased population creating pressures on the local environment or the introduction of bows and arrows.

The next major culture to emerge in North America was the Mississippi, which was the first North American culture to feature heavy reliance upon agriculture and a highly stratified social order. Mississippi culture began around 700 and lasted until the advent of European colonization in the Mississippi Valley around 1600. The largest of the Mississippi mound cities was Cahokia, across the Mississippi River from present-day St. Louis. Cahokia had as many as 30,000 residents. Some evidence there suggests strong trading ties to groups in Mexico. Epidemics introduced by Europeans in the 1500s brought quick demise to Mississippian culture. European explorers reported abandoned

Ruins of Pueblo Bonita, Chaco Canyon, New Mexico. During the heyday of the Anasazi (900 to 1130 A.D.), Pueblo Bonita sheltered over 1,000 people. ©DEWITT JONES/CORBIS

villages, and some archaeologists argue population loss in the period was as high as 90 percent.

While these various mound-building cultures were developing along the Ohio and Mississippi Rivers, another horticultural society was emerging in the Southwest. The Hohokam came from Mexico around 300 and settled along the Gila River. The Hohokam brought with them features of Mexican society and culture, including a heavy reliance on growing corn and ceremonial ball games on large courts. The Hohokam, in turn, influenced other loosely organized groups around them and contributed to the emergence of the Anasazi, who left extensive cliff dwellings before their decline in the thirteenth century. The largest of these sites is Pueblo Bonita in Chaco Canyon, which consists of over eight hundred rooms arranged around thirty-five underground ceremonial kivas.

These kivas closely link the Anasazi to the present-day Pueblo people, who began developing as a distinct people around 900. With trading ties to Mexico and to California tribes, the Pueblos developed large town sites and extensive irrigation systems. Drought in the thirteenth century caused the

Pueblo people to move to sites along the Colorado River, where they came to be known as the Hopi, and along the Rio Grande, where as many as forty villages once existed.

On the other side of the continent, in the Northeast, the Iroquois developed yet another style of culture and governance. Sometime between 1000 and 1450 the Mohawk, Cayuga, Onondaga, Oneida, and Seneca nations formed a confederacy, known as the Iroquois League, in hopes of ending a wave of violent conflict among themselves. The main seat of the confederacy was at Onondaga, where a robust ceremonial culture was structured around clans. These clans had chiefs to lead them, and the chiefs were selected by clan mothers. This custom created a system of power sharing between men and women that has few parallels in early human history.

These are but a few examples of the hundreds of indigenous societies that were in various stages of development in North America before the arrival of Europeans in the sixteenth century. Far from static groups of nomads with little knowledge of each other, these groups had already created major trade routes and developed their own cultural identities before laying eyes on European explorers and settlers.

THE MODERN PERIOD

The arrival of Europeans in the Western Hemisphere was nothing short of a disaster for indigenous people. Even before encountering the new arrivals, natives were introduced to a new set of diseases against which they had no biological defense. Successive waves of smallpox and other epidemics decimated many tribal groups and saw severe population declines among nearly every indigenous group on the North American continent. Those fleeing their villages during these epidemics often carried these diseases to the nearby villages to which they fled. These waves of disease plagued native communities for four centuries and were a major reason for a population decline from as many as 15 million indigenes north of the Rio Grande in 1500 to a nadir of 250,000 in 1900.

The combination of deadly diseases, the introduction of alcohol, missionization attempts, and military conflict has made the history of indigenous people in the Americas infamous worldwide. In the midst of these stunning changes, it is easy to focus at the macro level on the massive wave of change and destruction that decimated so many native people. But doing so has effectively silenced the many voices of American Indian people who have responded successfully to the challenges of the new conditions, left records of their own experiences, and interpreted their realities in various ways. Far from mere victims in the wave of history, the indigenous peoples of North America have been creative agents of their histories. And, at times, natives have provided the basic model for intercultural change.

One of the most impressive ways in which American Indians influenced the development of North American society is in the tradition of diplomacy and negotiation that developed in the Northeast. The strength of the tribal groups from the east coast to the Ohio River valley forced the colonists to adapt themselves to the style of negotiation that predated their arrival. This tradition centered on an elaborate system of beaded wampum belts. Historians agree widely that the exchange of wampum belts had its origins in gift exchanges that took place between families and between tribes at funeral ceremonies. Deaths of prominent leaders created opportunities to shore up alliances and mend wounded relationships.

The Iroquois came to prefer giving beaded belts that they made from materials found in the coastal areas. Natives in present-day Long Island, New York, and in the Connecticut River Valley produced spiralled columella of periwinkles, knobbed whelks, and channeled whelks, along with purple beads that came from the shells of mollusks from the Long Island Sound. The white and purple beads together became the basis for the beaded belts on which Iroquois beaders told stories of how people of differing cultural backgrounds achieved peace among themselves.

These beaded belts ranged from simple, personal belts little more than the size of a lanyard key chain an American child produces at summer camp to several-foot-long pieces that are prized in museums (Iroquois communities continue to produce wampum for use in contemporary life). Each belt served a function, from announcing a condolence ceremony commemorating the death of an important chief to the simple announcement of a group's identity. The makers of these belts devised elaborate systems for identifying the authenticity of these beaded belts; makers memorized the numbers of knots between beads. If any question arose about the identity of someone wielding a wampum belt, the makers could always disassemble a belt and determine its origin. This level of watchfulness testifies to the level of suspicion that the colonization period inspired among the Iroquois.

Settlers arriving in New England soon realized that wampum provided the basis for the region's economy and began to acquire them and use them to negotiate with native groups. Factories dedicated to the production of wampum eventually flourished in New England, the last one closing in 1880. The historian Richard White called this world, in which both sides worked to find new ways of relating to one another, the middle ground:

> The middle ground depended on the inability of both sides to gain their ends through force. The middle ground grew according to the need of people to find a means, other than force, to gain the cooperation or consent of foreigners. To succeed, those who operated on the middle ground had, of necessity, to attempt to understand the world and the reasoning of others and to assimilate enough of that reasoning to put it to their own purposes. Particularly in diplomatic councils, the middle ground was a realm of constant invention, which was just as constantly presented as convention. Under the new conventions, new purposes arose, and so the cycle continued. (*The Middle Ground,* p. 52)

The diplomatic tradition of the Iroquois became an adapted, middle ground way for Native Americans and settlers to negotiate their differences and make and break alliances. That middle ground, of course, shifted more and more to favor the various immigrant cultures and societies that were arriving in North America and developing into the European-American dominated culture that would come to prevail on the continent. Still, indigenous groups continued to respond, sometimes by resisting, sometimes by withdrawing, and sometimes by accommodating.

New England and northeastern natives, for instance, not only engaged in military negotiation and resistance against English, French, and other settlers but also learned to adapt to the new situation they faced. Men from coastal groups became part of the labor pool for the whaling industry, many of them using tribally derived skills to make their marks as harpooners. Some became Christians and even missionaries. And, as the skyscraper landscape of Manhattan and other eastern seaboard cities began to take shape in the nineteenth century, a robust tradition of steelworking flourished among the Iroquois. That tradition continues to the twenty-first century and is one of the strongest threads of potential American Indian entrepreneurship, as Iroquois workers bring their skills home to reservations and begin their own businesses.

THE PUEBLO REVOLT

From New England to Georgia to California to the northern Plains, the process of creating a new, different set of social conditions and historical realities continued across the continent. The Pueblo peoples of the Southwest did their share of resisting, withdrawing, and accommodating. Upon the arrival of Mexicans and Spaniards to settle and occupy the Rio Grande valley at the end of the sixteenth century, the various Pueblos were already suspicious of the Spaniards, having had their food stores expropriated by the Spanish explorer Hernando Cortés during his explorations in the 1540s. From 1692 until 1780, the Pueblos existed under the Spanish *encomienda* system, in which native food and labor were exploited under the dictates of Spanish imperial law.

The colonists introduced missionaries and a disdain for traditional religious ceremonies and traditions. In response, for religious sanctity, Pueblo religious leaders had to rely on the underground kiva structures where they had practiced religious ceremonies since the time of the Anasazi. The Spaniards at times violated these sacred structures, but

Pueblo religious leaders managed to hold onto their ceremonies, making them even more secret than before.

In 1680, Pueblo leaders made a concerted effort to wrest control of their own affairs back from the Spanish. Under the leadership of a kiva priest from San Juan, Popé, the Pueblos drove the Spanish out. For twelve years, they lived under a system of self-rule adapted from their own traditions and the new economic ways they had learned by force under the Spanish. The colonists returned in 1692 and regained control of the Pueblos but were more tolerant of native religion and culture.

Since the Pueblo revolt, the Pueblos have come to be famous for a different sort of metalworking than the Iroquois steelworkers; many Pueblo families have relied on silversmithing for their livelihood. Indeed, throughout the Southwest, American Indian jewelry, pottery, and weaving have come to be famous around the world. And through the late nineteenth and early twentieth centuries, Pueblo people themselves had taken progressively more economic control over their own arts and crafts industry. That is, instead of a trader coming and paying low prices for bulk goods and taking them to market in the East, Pueblo and other southwestern people managed to reserve a healthy part of the market for themselves in their own galleries, at roadside stands, and at the annual Indian Market in Santa Fe, New Mexico, and other Native American arts shows. This process continues in the twenty-first century.

Though far from being as economically developed as it could be, the world of contemporary American Indian arts and crafts provides an excellent example of how native people have managed to create a synergistic relationship between resistance, withdrawal, and accommodation. Within a single extended family, one person might remain firmly committed to preserving cultural traditions while another embraces Western-style education, while yet even another staunchly opposes the economic dependence of tribal groups on U.S. government assistance. All of these factors can come together in a successful family business, where one person provides a marketable set of goods to trade, another the knowledge of how to participate in the world of the market economy without as many middlemen as was the case in earlier generations, and still another strong presence argues for the justified continuing independence of the tribal group and its cultural and intellectual past. More important, southwestern people through their economic development of their own cultural ways have continued to contribute to the development of their region over the centuries, another trend that continues in the twenty-first century.

AFTER THE VANISHING INDIAN

Native American cultural, intellectual, and economic development has taken place against a background in which the voices of prominent politicians and cultural leaders have predicted the disappearance of indigenous peoples and native cultures. Indeed, along with all the other social, cultural, and economic challenges American tribal groups have faced in ensuring themselves a future, facing down the widespread expectation of their own disappearance has also been a major challenge.

Finding the myriad instances of how native people have done just that throughout history is not always easy. Though thousands of books have appeared on every side of most native issues, too often the loudest voices have been those of outsiders representing native life to other outsiders. Early European travelers' accounts testify to the existence of oddly colored grotesque beings peopling the Western Hemisphere, and most of the time what operates in those accounts is a none-too-subtle attempt to win a political argument raging in Europe between the various colonial powers. Seventeenth-century English publishers, for instance, were only too happy to print translations of pro-Indian tracts from Spain in order to create anti-Spanish sentiment in England.

Similarly, sensationalist writers have opportunistically used the isolation of their readers to create misapprehensions about Native American life in a gullible audience far away from the indigenous world. From supposedly accurate firsthand accounts of the early travels of missionaries to the dime novels of the Wild West to the obvious inaccuracies of Hollywood portrayals of native people, American Indians have struggled to have their own voice represent native points of view to a modern public.

Though not as well known as the African American writers who have chronicled the experiences of that group in the Americas, a smaller number of native writers have also sought to add their voices to intellectual and cultural history. Starting in New England, a steady progression of native writers has provided the public with an alternative to the standard history of indigenous "victimry," valiance, and disappearance.

Though preceded by important figures such as Samson Occum (a Mohegan contemporary of the African American poet Phillis Wheatley) and Joseph Johnson, William Apess gave perhaps the fullest voice to the New England Indian experience. Having grown up in poverty and in foster homes in the Connecticut River valley, Apess eventually turned to Methodism and became a minister. His first and most famous book, *A Son of the Forest* (1829), gives voice to what it meant to have lived through life poverty stricken in a tribal group that had been decimated in the 1630s and all but ignored afterward. Apess was apparently self-schooled and published and marketed his five books with little apparent help from anyone.

After helping lead a revolt of Mashpee Indians whose lumber was being expropriated against the law, Apess apparently left the ministry and lived in New York before dying of alcoholism sometime around 1840. One of Apess's major messages to his New England readers was to call white Christians to task for condemning white southerners for slavery and the removal of indigenous groups from the Southeast, while virtually ignoring what was happening to tribal people in New England. His scathing critiques of white Christians, in essays like "An Indian's Looking Glass for the White Man" (1833), sound as though they could have been written as easily by a late-twentieth-century radical writer and testify to the similarity of the American Indian intellectual struggle over the course of centuries.

Those southeasterners had an emerging set of writers who made important contributions to the resistance against removal, many of whom were educated in New England. Perhaps the most important of these figures was John Ross, who led the large Cherokee traditional majority against the much smaller faction of the tribe that advocated capitulation to white settlers and removal to lands west of the Mississippi River. Ross, whose family had long placed its destiny in accommodating the new realities that came with the European settlement of North America and who was one of the most educated men in the tribe, nonetheless sided with the most conservative and traditional elements of the Cherokee in standing against removal. Even once removal became a reality, Ross led his people both across the infamous Trail of Tears and into their new life in Indian Territory. In his pleas to the U.S. Congress, exhortations to his own people, and his correspondence with a wide range of people in American cultural and political life, Ross demonstrated an acute intellect and an unbending support for his Cherokee people. And, though they were reduced from 14,000 people to less than 10,000, Ross and others began the grueling task of rebuilding. Twenty-first-century Cherokees continue to count him as a national hero.

The tradition of public and political writing that saw such an important turning point in the 1830s continued through the nineteenth and twentieth centuries and into the twenty-first. Virtually every generation saw a stream, sometimes narrow, sometimes broad, of engagement by American Indian writers with the issues of their day and the contours of their lives. By the latter half of the nineteenth century, American Indian women were clearly a part of this native public voice, with figures such as Susette LaFlesche Tibbles, Sarah Winnemucca, and Canada's poet laureate E. Pauline Johnson vigorously participating in national life. These women often adapted the sentimental women's voice of their day to their work as American Indian women, but their own commitment to the furthering of American Indian life in a just, robust manner was anything but sentimental.

THE TURN OF THE TWENTIETH CENTURY AND BEYOND

The early years of the twentieth century witnessed the first discernible emergence of a national Native American intellectual voice. Coming mainly from educated backgrounds, these writers were also normally involved in local, regional, and national American Indian politics. Charles Eastman, who authored several best-selling books and worked closely with the Boy Scouts of America in developing their American Indian scouting material, was perhaps the most famous of these figures. Having grown up in the traditional hunting culture of the Sioux in the Dakotas, he came to be involved in Christianity and Western education after his father converted to Episcopalianism in the mid-1860s. Eastman went on to attend Dartmouth College and studied to become a physician at Boston University. He returned to the Dakotas to work as a physician in the Indian Service just in time to witness the aftermath of the carnage of the Wounded Knee Massacre in December 1890.

In the prime of his life, he and his educated, middle-class native contemporaries believed that the Indian world needed Indian leadership to propel native people into the modern world. Eastman and his generation of writers, who eventually came together in an organization called the Society of American Indians, from which they pursued their

John Ross, Cherokee Chief (1790–1866). Although Ross and roughly a thousand other Cherokees had fought with Andrew Jackson in the Creek War (1813–1814), Jackson, as president, signed the Indian Removal Act into law. Ross protested and the Cherokees won two cases in the Supreme Court, but Jackson ignored the decisions and sanctioned further pillaging of Cherokee land. © CORBIS

causes, are often justifiably associated with the assimilative ideologies of their time (notably boarding school education for American Indian children and the allotment of tribal lands into individual holdings).

Carlos Montezuma, an Apache who like Eastman had become a physician, believed, for instance, that American Indian people should be spread, one per county, to assist the process of assimilation. Gertrude Bonnin was a leader in the effort to ban natives from worshiping in the Native American Church (NAC), in which the hallucinogen peyote is used in a ritual fashion; her opposition stood in stark relief to constitutional promises of freedom of religion and to the fact that the Native American Church had proven itself the most effective alternative to mounting alcoholism in many native communities. Yet, in spite of their often frustrating positions vis-à-vis the traditional elements in their own tribes, these figures were also deeply knowledgeable about the native world and its people in a way that many Native American scholars of the twenty-first century are not.

Nearly half a century later, a watershed occurred in the intellectual world of American Indians. In 1969, N. Scott Momaday won the Pulitzer Prize for fiction for his masterful novel *House Made of Dawn,* marking the beginning of a wave of Native American fiction writing that includes the phenomenal achievements of James Welch, Leslie Marmon Silko, Gerald Vizenor, Louise Erdrich, and scores of others. Hundreds of American Indians published poetry in the same period, led by the signal efforts of such poets as Joy Harjo, Simon J. Ortiz, and Ray Young Bear. And Native American intellectual achievement transcends fiction and poetry: Vine Deloria Jr., with his incisive analytical power and sharp-edged humor, has been one of the most important native writers of his time; and the contributions of Native American journalists and newspaper publishers that grew alongside contemporary fiction and poetry have been just as important as any novel to the growth of Native American intellectualism. And many writers, such as the Crow Creek novelist, poet, essayist, editor, and publisher Elizabeth Cook-Lynn, have worked successfully across the grain of all genres.

It was not until the late twentieth century that scholars began to appreciate the great achievement of writers like John Joseph Mathews of the 1930s and 1940s, Ella Deloria of the 1940s, and even the Cherokee playwright Lynn Riggs, for whom a lack of Native American subject matter makes their work seem more an example of assimilation than survival. Clearly, scholars have begun to realize that categorizing American Indian writers into neatly labeled categories would obscure the outlines of native existence more than it would illuminate them. And though the history of the first centuries of American Indian public intellectual writers is skewed toward people who converted to Christianity, adopted Western ideas, or otherwise turned away from particular American Indian traditional values, that history has become more balanced and more often reflects the real world of American Indian people living in real time.

INTELLECTUAL LIFE BEYOND THE WORD

Not just as writers but also as artists, entertainers, and public figures, American Indians have participated and contributed to twentieth-century life. The Cherokee entertainer Will Rogers was the first person to address the entire United States by radio and was a central figure in the emergence of the film industry. Another Oklahoman, the Sauk and Fox athlete Jim Thorpe, won both the decathlon and pentathlon at the 1912 Stockholm Olympics and then went on to a spectacular career as a professional football and baseball player. Indeed, Thorpe was the first president of the American Professional Football Association (later the National Football League) and is commemorated in a larger-than-life bronze statue in the entrance to the Pro Football Hall of Fame in Canton, Ohio.

Still another Oklahoman, Maria Tallchief, emerged from the small town of Fairfax on the Osage Reservation to become one of the most celebrated ballerinas of her generation. Praised around the world as the first American ballerina to match the skills and talent of her European counterparts, she thrilled audiences around the world as the famed choreographer George Balanchine's muse during one of his most fertile phases.

Rogers, Thorpe, and Tallchief were far from anomalies. Rogers had plenty of Indian company among actors in Hollywood, even if most of the others struggled in obscurity in small roles or as extras. Though not as famous or successful, other American Indians competed as professional baseball players, football players, and Olympic-level athletes (including the Lakota athlete Billy Mills, who managed to win the 10,000 meters at the 1964 Tokyo Olympics even after stumbling early in the race). Oklahoma boasted of several more highly successful ballerinas following Tallchief, and scores if not hundreds of others have made careers as dancers, actors, and singers.

American Indians also played a crucial role in World War II as "code talkers." Starting in World War I, radio operators in the field realized that they could put two American Indians speaking their own native languages on either end of a radio and virtually ensure that vital information would not be intercepted. In World War II, military intelligence developed this basic idea by having a group of Navajo soldiers develop a code using their tribal language. The resultant code completely confounded the Axis Powers and has been widely cited as a primary reason for successful intelligence and communication throughout the war.

In conclusion, the social and intellectual history of Native American people has been a long, impressive, and sometimes harrowing one. They have been called military adversaries from 1600 to 1900, crucial bearers of sensitive information in World War II, impediments to nationalist designs, and innovators and leaders in entertainment and the arts. Once the doomed victims of another people's destiny, tribal peoples are now grasping toward their own future, paving the way for yet another era and struggling toward a future. Whether the twenty-first century will have indigenous people suffering from the marginalization and invisibility they experienced in centuries past, only time will tell. But if the past is any augur of the future, society can expect to see new ways for Native Americans to participate in their own social and intellectual world through new discourses and in creative places, including film, music, renewed traditions, educational programs—even casinos.

See also **European and Indigenous Encounters; Prophetic Native American Movements; Expansion and Empire; Racialism and Racial Uplift** *(volume 1);* **The Ideal of Spontaneity; Race, Rights, and Reform; The Frontier and the West; The Southwest; Borderlands** *(in this volume);* **Myth and Symbol** *(volume 3); and other articles in this section.*

BIBLIOGRAPHY

Armstrong, Jeannette, ed. *Looking at the Words of Our People: First Nations Analysis of Literature.* Penticton, British Columbia, 1993.

Berlo, Janet Catherine, and Ruth B. Phillips. *Native North American Art.* Oxford, U.K., 1998.

Champagne, Duane, ed. *Chronology of Native North American History: From Pre-Columbian Times to the Present.* Detroit, Mich., 1994.

——. *Native America: Portrait of the Peoples.* Detroit, Mich., 1994.

——. *The Native North American Almanac: A Reference Work on Native North Americans in the United States and Canada.* Detroit, Mich., 1994.

Deloria, Vine, Jr., and Raymond J. DeMallie. *Documents of American Indian Diplomacy: Treaties, Agreements, and Conventions, 1775–1979.* Norman, Okla., 1999.

Harjo, Joy, and Gloria Bird. *Reinventing the Enemy's Language: Contemporary Native Women's Writings of North America.* New York, 1997.

La Flesche, Francis, and Garrick A. Bailey, eds. *The Osage and the Invisible World: From the Works of Francis La Flesche.* Norman, Okla., 1995.

Peltier, Leonard, with Harvey Arden. *Prison Writings: My Life Is My Sun Dance.* New York, 1999.

Smith, Paul Chaat, and Robert Allen Warrior. *Like a Hurricane: The Indian Movement from Alcatraz to Wounded Knee.* New York, 1996.

Warrior, Robert Allen. *Tribal Secrets: Recovering American Indian Intellectual Traditions.* Minneapolis, Minn., 1995.

Weaver, Jace. *That the People Might Live: Native American Literatures and Native American Community.* Oxford, 1997.

White, Richard. *The Middle Ground: Indians, Empires, and Republics in the Great Lakes Region, 1650–1815.* New York, 1991.

Womack, Craig S. *Red on Red: Native American Literary Separatism.* Minneapolis, Minn., 1999.

ROMAN CATHOLICS

Patrick Allitt

About one-third of the American population is religiously identified with Roman Catholicism. Americans of Irish, Italian, Polish, south German, French, and Hispanic descent are most likely to be Catholic, but members of many other ethnic groups have become Catholic too, through intermarriage and conversion. The Catholic presence in America, slight until the early nineteenth century, increased rapidly owing to immigration after 1830. Suspected by Protestants of dual loyalties to the autocratic pope as well as the democratic nation, Catholics strove through the nineteenth and early twentieth centuries to demonstrate that they could be good American citizens. At the same time they took pride in believing that theirs alone was genuine Christianity and that Protestants were heretics.

American Catholicism lacks a distinguished intellectual history. A largely working-class community and one preoccupied with defending its faith against external challenges, it gave rise to few noteworthy authors or intellectual movements prior to the mid-twentieth century. American Catholic literature was confined largely to apologetics and controversy with Protestants and seasoned with a didactic popular literature of heroic suffering and saintliness. Several American novelists, including Theodore Dreiser, F. Scott Fitzgerald, and Mary McCarthy, were lapsed Catholics who wrote critical accounts of their childhood church and contributed to its low esteem in other Americans' eyes. Since the Second Vatican Council (1962–1965), however, American Catholic intellectuals have been less confrontational, have developed a more ecumenical outlook, and have contributed more broadly to American intellectual life.

ORIGINS

The Catholic presence in America began with the foundation of the colony of Maryland in 1632 by Caecilius Calvert, a Catholic nobleman and favorite of King Charles I of England. The first Catholic colonists, arriving on the *Ark* and the *Dove*, later played a similar role in American Catholic mythology as did the *Mayflower* settlers for Protestants. The Catholic presence in Britain's American colonies remained small throughout the colonial era, however, and its intellectual achievement slight. Just one signer of the Declaration of Independence, Charles Carroll, was a Roman Catholic. His brother, John Carroll, was the first Roman Catholic bishop in the United States and the first archbishop of Baltimore.

Irish migration to America began on a large scale in the 1830s and swelled with the Great Irish Famine of the mid-1840s. It transformed American Catholicism, particularly in the Northeast and the middle states, where the old Catholics of English origin were soon outnumbered. Irish Catholicism was austere. Influenced by Jansenism, an earlier Catholic reform movement, it emphasized the power of sin, the need for sexual self-mortification, and the heroism of suffering and martyrdom. The Irish influence was tempered by the presence of French Catholics, however, who were influential educators and founders of some of the better Catholic colleges, including Notre Dame near South Bend, Indiana, and Holy Cross in Worcester, Massachusetts. Immigrants from Italy, Germany, Poland, and Hungary arrived later in that century and the next, until immigration reforms of the 1920s restricted the flow.

INTELLECTUAL RESTRICTIONS

Priests were often the only educated members of immigrant Catholic communities. They studied not in the vernacular but in the traditional liturgical language, Latin. Few were so proficient in Latin that they could be creative in theology, and none in America showed the intellectual flair of the early church fathers, the medieval Scholastic innovators,

Sanctuary of St. Patrick's Cathedral, New York City.
Designed by James Renwick, St. Patrick's (1858–1879) is
among the most visible symbols of Irish American
Catholicism. © BOB KRIST/CORBIS

The Vatican's *Syllabus of Errors* (1864) enumerated and condemned many political and intellectual innovations of the nineteenth century: democracy, liberalism, religious tolerance, and modern civilization in general. American Catholic bishops of the era, administrators rather than profound thinkers, raised no complaint and did little to cultivative intellectual life, especially if it was going to raise nettlesome problems for the ordinary immigrant in the pew. Irish American archbishops, such as Francis Kenrick of Philadelphia and John Hughes of New York, wanted to prevent members of their flock from being tainted (as they saw it) by America's pervasive cultural Protestantism. In long-running disputes through the middle decades of the nineteenth century they criticized the use of the Protestant King James translation of the Bible in public schools and fought polemical wars with such zealous Protestant spokesmen as Samuel Morse.

ANTI-CATHOLICISM

Catholics, in the eyes of Morse and other militant Protestants, were unassimilable. Most of them, said the Protestants, were filthy, illiterate Irish peasants who lacked the independence of character and the civic virtues necessary to citizens of a republic. Catholics, after all, followed the teaching of a foreign monarch, the pope (whom the Protestants perceived as the Whore of Babylon or the Antichrist foretold in the book of Revelation). Lyman Beecher, one of the leading Protestant intellectuals of his day, preached in 1834 that "the Catholic Church holds now in darkness and bondage nearly half the civilized world. . . . It is the most skillful, powerful, dreadful system of corruption to those who wield it, and of slavery and debasement to those who live under it" (Hennessey, p. 119).

A lurid anti-Catholic popular literature circulated widely, alleging that Catholic convents were brothels, the nuns mere whores at the mercy of lecherous priests, their children bastards who were baptized then strangled and buried in secret. Maria Monk's *Awful Disclosures* (1836) was a popular classic of this genre. Later in the century the Protestant cartoonist Thomas Nast produced a series of brilliant pictorial renderings of the anti-Catholic case. In one, a greedy pope on the dome of St. Peter's in Rome, surrounded by sleek, fat, and cynical cardinals, gazes through his telescope at America and lays his plans for conquest. In another, cardinals, their miters disguised as the fearsome mouths of croco-

or the theorists of the Counter Reformation. Most accepted, instead, a digest of Scholastic philosophy and theology coupled to a faith in natural law. In this system the family, not the individual, was the basic unit of society, and each person lived in a dense web of mutual responsibilities. Society was naturally hierarchical, not egalitarian, an organic entity with successive levels of organization and authority. God presided over the world just as the pope presided over the church, the priest over his flock, and the father over his family. The principle of "subsidiarity" dictated that problems should be dealt with at the lowest possible level of the social hierarchy, rather than being deferred to higher ones such as the state. Freedom meant the proper orientation of the self to the natural order, rather than liberty to act independent of external restraints. Rules of proper conduct governed every moral contingency.

diles, stalk out of a river to bite innocent Protestant children.

The argument that Catholicism was inimical to American notions of liberty persisted well into the twentieth century. Anti-Catholicism flared, especially in the Deep South, against the Democrat Party candidate Al Smith in the presidential election campaign of 1928. The scholar Paul Blanshard warned, in *American Freedom and Catholic Power* (1949) and a string of sequels, that the Roman Catholic Church had the same kind of centralized authority and hatred of freedom as America's other great enemy of the day, international communism. As late as the election of 1960, respectable Protestant ministers such as Norman Vincent Peale campaigned against the Democratic Party candidate John F. Kennedy because of his Catholicism. Only after Kennedy's assassination and the Second Vatican Council did such ideas lose their traditional hold.

INTELLECTUAL CONVERTS

In the 1840s two influential American writers, Orestes Brownson and Isaac Hecker, converted to Catholicism after restless early lives among denominational Protestants and the Transcendentalists. The Catholic authorities were glad to welcome them but became fearful at the newcomers' intellectual adventurousness. Hecker's *Aspirations of Nature* (1857), for example, was designed as a vindication of Catholicism, but it antagonized the Redemptorists by minimizing the power of the doctrine of Original Sin and emphasizing the natural goodness of man. Hecker, a skillful rhetorician, disposed of the familiar anti-Catholic arguments one by one. For example, he depicted the secrecy of confession not as a form of mind control (the Protestant view), but as a superior alternative to the American vogue for titillating popular literature, which publicized the "filthy and disgusting details" of sin (p. 184). The incongruous Americans, said Hecker, were the Protestants, not the Catholics. After all, the Protestant theologian John Calvin had taught that men were so utterly depraved and darkened by sin that only God's mercy kept instant catastrophe at bay. How could such men hope to maintain a republic that required them to show virtue and self-restraint? Catholics, by contrast, with their more optimistic view of the natural man, found their faith consonant with the American experiment.

At odds with his superiors over these writings, Hecker founded his own order of priests, the Paulist Fathers, in 1858, a diocesan organization for mis-

sionary work whose early members were all converts, too. Their journal, the *Catholic World,* and their fellow convert's *Brownson's Quarterly Review,* were self-consciously highbrow attempts to stake a Catholic claim to participation in American intellectual life. Progress was difficult, however; the vast majority of American Catholics remained too poor and undereducated to take an interest in such projects. If they read at all, it was in devotional literature and hagiography.

CATHOLIC EDUCATION

An important turning point for American Catholicism was the decision, taken at the third Plenary Council of Baltimore in 1884, to create a separate educational system for Catholic children, beginning with grade schools but aiming eventually at a system stretching from kindergarten to graduate school. New settlements of Catholics throughout America rose to the challenge, devoting their resources first to schools and only later to building churches. By the second and third decades of the twentieth century, the ideal of an educational system parallel to public schools was becoming a reality in many American cities.

The system created an immense demand for teaching sisters, and the teaching orders were a leading source of careers for Catholic women. They outnumbered contemplatives (cloistered nuns) in America throughout the nineteenth and twentieth centuries. Stock figures in Catholic and ex-Catholic literature, the sisters varied widely in their attitudes and attainments, some being weak and tyrannical, others learned and conscientious. Mary McCarthy recalled her rigorous 1920s Catholic education in *Memories of a Catholic Girlhood* (1957). In addition to the usual gossip, scandal, and intrigue of boarding school life, she wrote, "there sounded in the Sacred Heart convent heavier, more solemn strains, notes of a great religious drama, which was also all passion and caprice, in which salvation was the issue and God's rather sultanlike and elusive favor was besought, scorned, despaired of, connived for, importuned" (p. 92). Her work draws a vivid picture of the way religious and secular learning crisscrossed at the school and shows how they contributed to McCarthy's teenage crisis of faith. Michael Harrington, later a prominent democratic socialist, studied at an excellent Jesuit school in St. Louis, Missouri, in the 1930s and 1940s, and also attested to the rigorous teaching and strenuous curriculum of the Jesuits' *ratio studiorum.*

But the Catholic educational system was not an unmixed success. It worked in terms of preserving the Catholic faith of most pupils and Americanizing generations of new immigrants, but its defensive approach to key issues in modern intellectual life made it incapable of cultivating distinguished thinkers. Faculty in the Catholic colleges rarely enjoyed academic freedom or the tenure-track career paths secured by their counterparts in secular education. The colleges and universities remained in the hands of the religious orders that had founded them. Competition among the teaching orders meant that there were too many colleges, all underfunded, for the available student population, the standards were too low, and bankruptcy was always looming on the horizon. By the 1950s their mediocrity had created a mood of widespread soul-searching and internal self-criticism, which crystallized in an outspoken appeal for reform by Father John Tracy Ellis, *American Catholics and the Intellectual Life* (1956).

MODERNISM

The Catholic colleges' practical problems were aggravated by their church's intellectual timidity. In 1899 Pope Leo XIII warned against a tendency that he named "Americanism." Never a coherent movement, Americanism was the view, espoused by Isaac Hecker and such pro-assimilation bishops as John Ireland of St. Paul, Minnesota, that the separation of church and state was a positive good rather than a tolerable evil and that the American republic was the ideal setting for Catholicism to flourish.

The warning against Americanism was followed in 1907 by a sweeping condemnation of "modernism" by Pope Pius X. His encyclical letter *Pascendi Dominici Gregis* (Feeding the Lord's flock) of that year made it impossible for Catholic scholars to teach evolutionary biology, comparative religion, modern biblical criticism, psychology, or philosophical vitalism. Adventurous scientists, such as John Zahm, a professor of biology at Notre Dame and the author of a pioneering study of evolutionary theory, *Evolution and Dogma* (1896), were forced to retract their findings. No wonder that over the following decades Catholic scholarship became in many respects a backwater, regarded with pity or contempt by scholars in the American academic mainstream.

THE CATHOLIC REVIVAL

Pope Leo XIII's encyclical letter *Aeterni Patris* (Eternal Father) of 1879 had, however, stimulated a re-

vival in Scholastic philosophy, sending scholars back to the original medieval texts rather than to the arid abstracts of later medieval schoolmen. This neo-scholastic revival was, said the historian Philip Gleason, "unmistakably anti-modern from the outset," part of a "counteroffensive against some of the most powerful movements of the day: nationalism and liberalism in politics, and rationalism, skepticism, and agnosticism in the realm of ideas and religion" (*Contending with Modernity*, p. 107). It was also the intellectual basis of a limited Catholic revival in the interwar years. It drew admiring glances from such non-Catholic scholars as Mortimer J. Adler and Robert M. Hutchins at the University of Chicago, but it failed to make broad inroads into an increasingly secular and pragmatic American intellectual world.

A handful of Catholic intellectuals in the generation after *Pascendi* tried to create for their faith a dignified position in American intellectual life by building on the neo-scholastic revival. The Jesuits' journal *America,* begun in 1909, and the lay-run *Commonweal,* founded in 1924 by Michael Williams and George Shuster, presented themselves as broad-minded Catholic rivals to such secular journals as the *New Republic.* The Catholic publishers Frank Sheed and Maisie Ward, meanwhile, popularized in America the work of European Catholic writers, notably Jacques Maritain, Charles Péguy, François Mauriac, and Léon Bloy. But Sheed, an immigrant from Australia, found little to cheer. He wrote that "the absence of a Catholic reading public was our continuing problem" and that as a publisher he found it very difficult to create one. "Like all intelligent parasites," he added, "we studied the plant to which we had attached ourselves and found it depressingly weedy" (in Allitt, *Catholic Converts,* p. 198).

Another potential source of vitality for American Catholic scholarship was the arrival of a steady stream of adult converts in the tradition of Hecker and Brownson. Attracted by neo-scholasticism, by Catholicism's doctrinal certitude, and by its apparent ability to offer a sure moral guide to every vexing question, they saw it as a welcome alternative to the self-doubting liberal Protestant denominations. Among Catholic historians, converts played a central role in raising scholarly standards. Carlton Hayes, Ross Hoffman, Parker T. Moon, Marshall Baldwin, and Gaillard Hunt, all of them convert historians and all elected presidents of the American Catholic Historical Association in the interwar years, rejected the old clichés of Catholic hagiography and insisted on rigorous, impartial analysis of evidence, even for the study of such religiously

408

sensitive areas as Reformation-era history. The writing of English converts was particularly influential for this revival generation in America, especially that of Cardinal John Henry Newman and Gilbert Keith Chesterton.

SOCIAL TEACHING

American Catholicism was never so rural as its European counterpart, and Catholic farmers, though numerous among German American groups in the Midwest, were always a small minority of the Catholic people. In the cities, Christian social teaching had to be adapted, in the nineteenth century, to the wrenching changes of the industrial revolution. Pope Leo XIII's encyclical letter *Rerum Novarum* (1891; On the new order of things) warned Catholics against the soulless character of industrial capitalism but also forbade them to join the socialist movement. One of the first American Catholics to take up the challenge of finding a third alternative was John Augustine Ryan, a Minnesota priest. His book *A Living Wage* (1906), following *Rerum Novarum,* insisted that employers had a duty to provide their workmen with money sufficient to care for their wives and children in decent surroundings, to buy small properties of their own, and not to let impersonal market forces dictate wages and prices. Nonviolent strikes and orderly labor unions should be permitted, and a spirit of justice and charity should prevail in the workplace. Ryan hoped that medieval guilds might revive to guide the fortunes of each industry as they had in the era of Thomas Aquinas.

Ryan was a member of the National Catholic War Council, which mobilized Catholic patriotism and fund-raising during the First World War. He presided over its mutation into the National Catholic Welfare Conference after the war and persuaded the bishops to adopt his radical Program for Social Reconstruction (1919), which argued for a national minimum wage, national health insurance program, equal pay for women, and the abolition of child labor. In practice, however, he found them reluctant to lobby politically for such bold measures. He approved of President Franklin D. Roosevelt's New Deal plan for business, the National Recovery Administration (1933), construing its industry councils as a modern version of the medieval guilds.

Ryan was popular with the secular Democratic Left, but it is misleading to think of his theories as belonging either to the right wing or the left wing.

To a striking degree, then and throughout the twentieth century, Catholic ideas have not coincided with positions on the American political spectrum. After all, Charles Coughlin, the Detroit "radio priest" who at first supported the New Deal but later turned against Roosevelt's innovations, admired Italian fascism, but he too claimed, plausibly, the guild and corporatist heritage of *Rerum Novarum* and its successor, *Quadragesimo Anno* (1931; In the fortieth year). On Catholic principles Ryan and Coughlin were in close accord. Only in applying them to the world's industrial societies in the crisis of the Great Depression did they differ.

CATHOLIC RADICALS

The more radical implications of Catholic social teaching were taken up not in archdiocesan chanceries but among a handful of advocates for the poor, of whom the most famous was another convert, Dorothy Day (1897–1980). Day, born into a working-class Protestant family, worked as a radical journalist in Greenwich Village during its bohemian heyday in the teens of the twentieth century and briefly for the Communist Party after the Russian Revolution. She horrified her Marxist friends by converting to Catholicism in 1927. With the help of a homeless French philosopher, Peter Maurin, she founded a radical and pacifist newspaper, the *Catholic Worker,* in 1933, and a slum shelter, the House of Hospitality, for the homeless unemployed. From then until her death in 1980, she persisted with both ventures, insisting on the incompatibility of Catholicism and American commercial capitalism. Sympathetic to communist actions but not to the philosophy that underlay them, she, even more than Ryan, sought to put the Gospel and the Catholic tradition into action and was meticulous in her orthodoxy.

Her charismatic equal was Thomas Merton (1915–1968), the most famous monk in American history. He too was a convert, who took vows of perpetual silence at a Trappist monastery in Kentucky. His spiritual autobiography, *The Seven Storey Mountain,* became a surprise best-seller in 1948 and made his name famous within and beyond the Catholic community. It juxtaposed a decadent Western world in which he had misspent his youth with a militantly dogmatic Catholicism that he claimed offered salvation not just to individuals but to a society floundering in its excesses of greed, materialism, and war. Dozens of young men flocked to the Trappists' gates over the following decade, and

Dorothy Day, 1916. The Catholic Worker movement that Day founded continues today in over 175 Catholic Worker communities. © BETTMANN/CORBIS

the order had to open more monasteries to deal with the rush Merton had inspired. Merton later became a shrewd observer of American political and social life, bringing uncompromising Catholic principles to bear on the nuclear arms race, southern racial injustice, and other social problems. Day, Merton, and a handful of contemporaries who tried to live according to Catholic precepts at their most strenuous, formed the nucleus of what the historian James Fisher called the Catholic counterculture.

PRECONCILIAR CHANGES

John Courtney Murray S.J. (1904–1967) was a social and economic conservative, but his eventual impact on American Catholicism was as dramatic as that of his contemporaries Merton and Day. Taking up in the 1950s the still controversial issue of whether Catholicism could be blended with the American identity in theory as well as in practice, Murray argued in a long succession of articles and a brilliant book, *We Hold These Truths* (1960), that the American civil tradition was based on Catholic

sources, including St. Augustine, St. Thomas Aquinas, and St. Robert Bellarmine. It could trace as many of its philosophical and political antecedents to Catholic Europe as to the Reformation, he believed. An urbane and worldly priest, he enjoyed the company of educated men from other traditions and seemed to his Jesuit superiors a suspiciously ecumenical figure. For a time in the mid-1950s, they prevented him from publishing articles on political theology but continued to recognize him as an exceptional teacher and writer.

Murray's political views were in fact similar to those of the great Protestant theologian of his era, Reinhold Niebuhr. Both had supported America's active role in the Second World War and both believed, in the late 1940s, that the Soviet Union and militant communism were threats to be met by force or the threat of force, including nuclear weapons. In the cold war era Murray's style of aggressive Catholic anticommunism was far more widespread than Day's pacifism; the Wisconsin senator Joseph R. McCarthy embodied it in extreme and vulgar form. William F. Buckley Jr., a rich young writer from Connecticut, voiced an equally intense but more intelligent version of Catholic anticommunism. His first book, *God and Man at Yale* (1951), argued for the compatibility of Christianity and free-market capitalism, adding that his alma mater, Yale, had disgraced itself by showing precious little respect for either. Buckley went on to co-author a defense of McCarthyism, *McCarthy and His Enemies* (1954), and then to found a conservative journal, *National Review* (1955). This journal and *Modern Age,* its companion in the new conservative movement of the 1950s, both exhibited a strong Catholic influence: *Modern Age*'s editor Russell Kirk was another convert to Catholicism. Both journals argued that the cold war was not a pragmatic struggle between materialist giants but rather an apocalyptic ideological struggle between "godless communism" and the Christian West.

Catholic Americans split sharply in the 1950s over this issue. Nearly all agreed that communism was both threatening to the West and intrinsically evil, but the liberal Catholics John Cogley, Joseph Cunneen, Edward Skillen, and Donald Thorman gathered around their respective journals *Commonweal, Ave Maria,* and *America,* to repudiate Buckley's militant defense of the free market. Children of the New Deal, respectful of Franklin Roosevelt's legacy, and under the influence of Ryan, Day, and Merton, they argued for a welfare state and what they saw as a more humane political economy based on the social encyclicals.

410

VATICAN II

The Second Vatican Council had profound implications for American Catholics. John Courtney Murray accepted an invitation to draft the council's Declaration on Religious Freedom, *Dignitatis Humanae,* which was particularly important to Catholics in religiously diverse nations such as the United States. Catholics were now urged to treat Protestants and other Christians not as heretics but as "separated brethren" in the larger Christian family. The council also specified a change in the liturgy and in theological education, into vernacular languages and away from Latin. This reform changed the quality of church life for all, replacing what to most parishioners was an unknown, mysterious, and time-honored language with familiar words, in a sometimes jarring and incongruous way. It also encouraged radical speculation among theological students, who felt the weight of clerical censorship lifting. As the commentator Garry Wills wrote, Vatican II was more radical in its sum than in its parts because it "let out the dirty little secret . . . that the church changes" and so paved the way for further changes (*Bare Ruined Choirs,* p. 21).

Coinciding with the social and political upheavals of the 1960s, the aftermath of Vatican II was dramatic. Many priests and sisters, no longer encouraged to mortify their desires, abandoned their vocations, and a long decline set in, creating a severe shortage by the 1990s. It was an era of lay assertion in many areas, partly from necessity, as priests and nuns were no longer available (as teachers in Catholic schools, for example), partly from a desire to see Catholic organizations run on more businesslike and professional lines. A bitter 1966 strike at St. John's University in New York, hitherto run autocratically by the Vincentian fathers, led to the replacement of clerics by lay trustees and administrators in many Catholic colleges.

Vatican II's pastoral constitution *Gaudium et Spes* (On the church in the modern world) encouraged Catholics to be attentive to such events in the world around them as the civil rights movement and the Vietnam War. Among the new activists Daniel and Philip Berrigan, the first a Jesuit and the second a Josephite priest, both poets and polemicists, staged dramatic, pseudoliturgical actions against the war. They staged symbolic attacks on Baltimore's military draft centers with blood and homemade napalm. Daniel Berrigan, convicted for his role in these affairs, went "underground" rather than submit to prison and became a hero of the antiwar Left as he mocked the efforts of police and the Federal Bureau of Investigation to arrest him. Philip, whose order had specialized in converting African Americans to Catholicism, led Catholic demonstrations against racial and residential segregation in northern cities.

Catholic theology, meanwhile, now in the vernacular, took a worldly turn. Vatican II had replaced a hierarchical model of the church with a fraternal notion, "the people of God," which began to find expression in theological writing. Forsaking the neo-scholastic style, Catholic theologians began to make personal experience the starting point of their work. For example, Mary Daly's *The Church and the Second Sex* (1968) argued that Catholicism was patriarchal and repressive of women. She proposed sweeping changes in Catholic gender relations and contributed to a movement for the ordination of women, a reform that a succession of popes refused. Daly, the first woman to teach theology at the Jesuits' Boston College—and in a thoroughly unorthodox way—was the subject of a bitterly controversial and widely publicized tenure case. She tried to ban men from her classes altogether and in later books, such as *Beyond God the Father* (1973) and *Gyn/Ecology* (1978), abandoned Christianity completely as inherently abusive toward women. More temperate but equally gifted women theologians, notably Rosemary Ruether, stayed within the Catholic fold, arguing for women's ordination and a less hierarchical, more consensual, approach to Catholic gender relations. Other women, including Sidney Callahan and Margaret O'Brien Steinfels, rose to editorial positions in Catholic journals and became influential commentators.

SEXUALITY

Sex, like race, war, and feminism, was one of the 1960s great causes. In a 1930 encyclical letter, *Casti Conubii* (On Christian marriage), Pope Pius XI had prohibited Catholics from using modern artificial contraceptives, reasoning traditionally that any deliberate separation of sex from procreation violated the natural law. In a speech to Italian midwives in 1951, however, his successor Pope Pius XII had approved Catholic use of the rhythm method of birth control, which appeared to open the door to the idea of permitting sexual expression in marriage while avoiding conception. The rhythm method was not reliable, however, and often led to unexpected births. Big families, once common throughout America, were by the 1950s and 1960s a special mark of Catholicism. Economic, health, and over-population concerns prompted growing numbers of Catholics, lay and clerical, to press for a change in their church's teaching in the 1960s.

Pope Paul VI, reacting to this pressure, convened a pontifical commission in 1966 to debate the issue and make recommendations. Among its members was John T. Noonan Jr., a brilliant Catholic lawyer and professor at the University of California's Boalt Hall School of Law. His *Contraception* (1965) showed that there had been many changes in the church's sexual teaching throughout Christian history, and he endorsed the commission's majority report, urging Catholic approval for artificial contraceptives. The pope, however, decided against this report and his 1968 encyclical letter *Humanae Vitae* (On human life) upheld the old teaching.

Catholics had accepted *Casti Conubii* meekly in the 1930s, but the spirit of Vatican II had aroused a more militant and articulate mood, so *Humanae Vitae* was greeted with protests, angry editorials, denunciations of the pope, and widespread pledges not to follow its teaching. Charles Edward Curran, a theology professor at the Catholic University of America in Washington, D.C., defied his archbishop on the issue and led a protest movement. The bishop retaliated by suspending fifty-one priests until they recanted. Only die-hard traditionalists, such as the writers gathered around *Triumph* magazine and *The Wanderer,* spoke up in favor of the encyclical. The prolific Catholic sociologist Andrew Greeley found by the mid-1970s that married Catholics were using contraceptives at about the same rate as other Americans and that the venerable big Catholic family was disappearing.

Abortion soon replaced contraception as the flashpoint of sexual controversy. Liberalized abortion policies in several states were boosted in 1973 by the Supreme Court's pro-choice decision in *Roe v. Wade.* Most Catholics who had favored contraceptive reform were shocked by the decision, which they interpreted as an attack on prenatal human life itself, analogous to the Nazi attack on entire categories of the human population. John Noonan again figured prominently in the debate, arguing in a series of impassioned books and articles that protection of the unborn, "an almost absolute right" through Christian history, was now jeopardized. James McFadden, who became the editor of a leading antiabortion journal, the *Human Life Review,* opposed both contraception and abortion, arguing that the one actually led to the other. A couple using contraceptives, he reasoned, had already made the decision to separate sex from procreation, so they would treat a fetus as an unwanted by-product of their act rather than as its natural culmination. In a memorable phrase he declared that "contraception is the John the Baptist to the Antichrist of abortion."

POSTCONCILIAR DIVISIONS

Cardinal Joseph Bernardin of Chicago tried to unify and explain the social policies of his church in the 1980s with the metaphor of a "seamless garment." Reverence for life, he explained, was in every instance the guiding principle, so that there was no contradiction between Catholic condemnation of abortion, condemnation of capital punishment, and support for a welfare state and basic economic rights for all citizens, even if these policies rarely showed up together in other Americans' views.

Bernardin and his fellow bishops undertook an experiment in public theology in the early 1980s by writing pastoral letters through open consultation with interested Catholics. Initial drafts (by Bryan Hehir on nuclear weapons and by David Hollenbach S.J. on the economy) were subjected to public hearings at which Catholics of all sorts commented and proposed changes. In both instances an initially radical proposal came under heavy fire from Catholic neoconservatives, including Michael Novak, George Weigel, and William Simon, and was modified in light of their criticisms. In the case of the nuclear weapons letter, pro- and antinuclear advocates all drew on Catholic Just War teaching, a set of principles first developed in the Middle Ages to temper the ferocity of combat between Christians. A rich tradition, it provided each group with materials sufficient to claim that its own policy fulfilled the tradition, even though in Hehir's hands that amounted to a virtual ban on the weapons, and in Novak's it was somewhere close to full endorsement. Unlike such peace churches as the Mennonites and Quakers, however, the existence of Just War teaching clearly denied Catholic pacifists the claim that theirs was an intrinsically antiwar branch of Christendom.

By the 1980s it was clear that on many issues Catholic conservatives had more in common with Jewish and Protestant conservatives than with Catholic liberals and radicals and also that the rich Catholic patrimony could provide texts and principles to suit both. This cleavage within Catholicism and the other major religious groupings, so different from the stark Catholic-Protestant antagonism of earlier eras, was demonstrated by the Princeton sociologist of religion Robert Wuthnow in his influential book *The Restructuring of American Religion* (1988). Where once Catholic difference from the rest of America had been the great issue, by the 1990s Catholic assimilation into the mainstream of American life had gone so far that Notre Dame and

other Catholic colleges began taking steps to reassert at least a few elements of their Catholic distinctiveness before they disappeared completely. By then there was no unitary "Catholic view" on any subject. Catholic intellectual life in America had become richer and more diverse, but less distinctive than ever before.

See also **The Struggle over Evolution** *(volume 1);* **Ethnicity: Early Theories; Ethnicity and Race; Organized Religion** *(volume 3); and other articles in this section.*

BIBLIOGRAPHY

General Histories

Bellah, Robert N., and Greenspahn, Frederick E., eds. *Uncivil Religion: Interreligious Hostility in America.* New York. Part II deals entirely with Protestant-Catholic animosities.

Bokenkotter, Thomas. *A Concise History of the Catholic Church.* Garden City, N.Y., 1979. A useful summary of the European and Vatican background to American Catholicism.

Dolan, Jay P. *The American Catholic Experience.* Garden City, N.Y., 1985. Particularly good on Catholic social history.

Hennesey, James, S.J. *American Catholics: A History of the Roman Catholic Community in the United States.* New York, 1981. Good on Catholic institutional history.

Moore, R. Laurence. *Religious Outsiders and the Making of Americans.* New York, 1986. Chapter 2, "Managing Catholic Success in a Protestant Empire," explains the benefits as well as the drawbacks for Catholics of being "outsiders."

Morris, Charles R. *American Catholic: The Saints and Sinners Who Built America's Most Powerful Church.* New York, 1997. The best one-volume history of American Catholicism.

Published Primary Sources

Blanshard, Paul. *American Freedom and Catholic Power.* Boston, 1949. Post–World War II anti-Catholic tract.

Daly, Mary. *The Church and the Second Sex.* Boston, 1968. Early statement of Catholic feminist theology.

Ellis, John Tracy. "American Catholics and the Intellectual Life." *Thought* 30 (autumn 1955): 351–388. Famous lament about the low quality of Catholics' intellectual attainments.

Harrington, Michael. *Fragments of the Century.* New York, 1973. Early chapters vividly evoke his Jesuit education.

Hecker, I. T. *Aspirations of Nature.* New York, 1857. A nineteenth-century American convert's defense of Catholicism.

McCarthy, Mary. *Memories of a Catholic Girlhood.* New York, 1957. Entertaining and insightful memoir of her Catholic schooling.

Merton, Thomas. *The Seven Storey Mountain.* New York, 1948. Best-selling spiritual autobiography of the Trappist monk.

Monk, Maria. *Awful Disclosures of the Hotel Dieu Nunnery of Montreal.* New York, 1836. A lurid anti-Catholic tract, a best-seller in its day.

Murray, John Courtney, S.J. *We Hold These Truths: Catholic Reflections on the American Proposition.* New York, 1960. Theoretical justification of Catholic adaptation to the American polity.

National Conference of Catholic Bishops. *The Challenge of Peace: God's Promise and Our Response.* Washington, D.C., 1983. The first of the bishops' public pastoral letters.

Noonan, John T., Jr. *Contraception: A History of Its Treatment by the Catholic Theologians and Canonists.* Cambridge, Mass., 1986.

Novak, Michael. *Moral Clarity in the Nuclear Age.* Nashville, Tenn., 1983. A Catholic neoconservative rebuttal to the pastoral letter *The Challenge of Peace.*

Intellectual History Studies

Allitt, Patrick. *Catholic Intellectuals and Conservative Politics in America: 1950–1985.* Ithaca, N.Y., 1993. Explains Catholic prominence in American Conservatism since 1950.

——. *Catholic Converts: British and American Intellectuals Turn to Rome.* Ithaca, N.Y., 1997. Describes and explains the dominance of converts in Catholic intellectual life.

Appleby, R. Scott. *"Church and Age Unite!": The Modernist Impulse in American Catholicism.* Notre Dame, Ind., 1992. On the condemnation of Americanism and modernism.

Blantz, Thomas. *George Shuster: On the Side of Truth.* Notre Dame, Ind., 1993. A biography of the founder of *Commonweal.*

Broderick, Francis L. *Right Reverend New Dealer.* New York, 1963. Biography of the priest, author, and activist.

Fisher, James Terrance. *The Catholic Counter Culture in America, 1933–1962.* Chapel Hill, N.C., 1989. On Day, Merton, and other Catholic radicals.

Gleason, Philip. *Contending with Modernity: Catholic Higher Education in the Twentieth Century.* New York, 1995.

Halsey, William M. *The Survival of American Innocence: Catholicism in an Era of Disillusionment, 1920–1940.* Notre Dame, Ind., 1980.

O'Brien, David J. *Isaac Hecker, An American Catholic.* New York, 1992. Excellent intellectual biography of the Paulists' founder.

Ryan, Thomas P. *Orestes Brownson: A Definitive Biography.* Huntington, Ind., 1976. Immense biography of a prominent nineteenth-century convert intellectual.

Sparr, Arnold. *To Promote, Defend, and Redeem: The Catholic Literary Revival and the Cultural Transformation of American Catholicism, 1920–1960.* Westport, Conn., 1990. This book and Halsey's, noted above, explain the interwar years of Catholic revival.

Weigel, George. *Tranquillitas Ordinis: The Present Failure and Future Promise of American Catholic Thought on War and Peace.* New York, 1987. Thorough history and analysis of Catholic Just War theory.

414

Wills, Garry. *Bare Ruined Choirs: Doubt, Prophecy, and Radical Religion.* Garden City, N.Y., 1972. Part memoir, part analysis of the dramatic changes wrought by Vatican II.

Wuthnow, Robert. *The Restructuring of American Religion.* Princeton, N.J., 1988. Explains the alignment of religious Americans by political rather than denominational allegiance.

WHITES AND THE CONSTRUCTION OF WHITENESS

Noel Ignatiev

For most of the seventeenth century the English colonies in America contained no white people. It was decades before English, Scottish, Irish, and other colonists from Europe were made into "whites." As a biological category, "white" is so imprecise that natural scientists discarded it long ago, along with the whole notion of race. Nor does the term describe an ethnic group; there is no "white" language, religion, music, or any of the other cultural belongings normally associated with nationality or ethnicity. So for the purposes of this essay, "white" will be used to describe a social formation, like "aristocracy."

In Virginia, the largest and most commercially important of the English mainland colonies, people from England and people from Africa labored together almost from the beginning. The characteristic form of labor exploitation was indentured servitude, a status somewhere between freedom and slavery; laborers were held in bondage for a stipulated number of years, after which they would in theory become free and even owners of land. The distinction between those laborers who were captured and sold and those who sold themselves was of little importance. Notwithstanding their diverse origins, laborers from Europe and Africa played, intermarried, ran away, and occasionally rebelled together. The most striking division in society was between masters and servants, and there were people from Africa and people from England on both sides of the line. The term "white" was hardly used to describe human beings, and while people from Africa were identified as "black" or one of its variants, it was a *national* designation, parallel to "English" or "French." From a *racial* standpoint America was probably freer than it has been at any time since.

THE ESTABLISHMENT OF SLAVERY

Around midcentury the tobacco planters, facing an extreme labor shortage, discovered the virtue of life-

time servitude, or slavery, which previously had not existed in English law. In part they were motivated by an increase in life expectancy that made lifetime servants "cost effective" even though their initial purchase price was higher than that of term servants. If the decision to adopt this new form of labor exploitation was based purely on profit considerations, the choice of *whom* to enslave was political. To enslave for life poor English would deter others from coming, thereby intensifying the labor shortage the measure was intended to relieve. To adopt a general policy of enslaving the natives would bring about general warfare along the frontier and induce the natives to offer sanctuary to fugitive servants, further aggravating the problem. Africa, however, was an inexhaustible source of laborers with none of the drawbacks attached to the alternatives: extending the term of service of people from Africa would not deter them from coming since they had come involuntarily in the first place, nor could it effect frontier security in the colonies. By a process of elimination, therefore, they were selected to fill the slave-labor slot. Once the status of lifetime slave was assigned exclusively to people from Africa, the black skin became the badge of slavery.

Although the first law in favor of slavery in the colonies was enacted in Massachusetts in 1641, it was in the plantation colonies that slavery became the basis of the economy and was perfected as a system. Virginia made it hereditary in 1661 by decreeing that a child follow the condition of his or her mother. This was followed by laws defining a slave as property with no right to own anything, travel, engage in trade, gather in large groups, or marry, without the consent of the master. The next step was to define slavery on a racial basis; this was done by repealing the laws that exempted baptized Christians of African descent from enslavement. It was also necessary to discipline English who might have been tempted to demonstrate sympathy for the slave; toward this end the right of the master to free or educate his slaves was curbed or eliminated, and severe penalties were imposed on English servants who befriended, married, or had children with slaves, or ran away from bondage with them. The last step in the process of defining slavery was to strip away the rights of free persons of African descent and make the "free Negro" an anomaly. The reduction of all persons of African descent to a status beneath that of any person not of African (or Native American) descent marked the birth of the "white race."

CATEGORIZING NATIVE AMERICANS

There were conflicts between English settlers and indigenous people from early on, but not until the era of Andrew Jackson did the United States embark on a definitive policy of treating the native peoples as an undifferentiated group, turning them into "redskins," and not until after the Civil War was the policy fully implemented. While people from Africa served as the main foil against which the white race developed as a social formation, white people formed an image of themselves in opposition to "Indians" as well as to "Negroes." If black people were a part of commodity society, like the ox, the indigenous people were largely outside of it, like the timber wolf. In addition to meaning free in contrast to slave, "white," therefore, came to mean "civilized" in contrast to "savage."

White was more than a way of saying nonslave, non-Indian: it was a social formation whose every member was by racial definition an enforcer of the oppression of those defined as nonwhites. This function was made clear by the 1790 law limiting naturalization to "free white persons" and the 1792 law decreeing militia service for all white males. The two measures were linked: "Citizen" meant "white," and "white" meant someone who could be counted on to put down slave uprisings or take part in Indian wars. The so-called White Republic at first presented few problems of definition, since most "white" persons in the country were of English, Scottish, or Irish Protestant descent.

REFINING THE DEFINITION OF WHITE

This definition changed in the mid-1840s with the increase in the number of people coming to America from Ireland and Germany. The Irish in particular posed a problem for existing whites, since not only were they now in their majority Catholic, they were in their homeland regarded by the dominant Protestants very much as persons of color were regarded by whites in America. They faced widespread discrimination in the new country and were often thrown together with slaves and free Negroes, while nativists, gathered in the American Party (called the Know-Nothings) and other formations, sought to restrict their access to citizenship. For their part, the Irish waged a protracted, determined, and often violent battle against both nativists and Afro-Americans, whom they resented for presuming to be in a position of equality with them. Their actions, which reached a peak in the 1863 New York draft riot, resulted ultimately in the Irish securing their citizenship and civil rights, and were a major factor in the denial of those rights to black people. The Irish were aided in their efforts by the slaveholder-controlled Democratic Party, which supported them in return for Irish support at the polls.

POST-EMANCIPATION RACE THEORIES

The end of slavery called into question the meaning of whiteness, but the overturning of the Reconstruction governments of the southern states, symbolized by the Tilden-Hayes Agreement of 1877 and the withdrawal of federal troops from the South, restored the color line on a new basis, as the freedpeople were made into nonvoting, semi-feudal sharecroppers and servants. Industrial growth stimulated a new wave of immigrants, this time from southern and eastern Europe; "foreigners" once again made up the bulk of the unskilled industrial labor force. The years between 1877 and 1920 were years of intense class struggle in industry; the banker Jay Gould declared that he could "hire one half of the working class to shoot down the other half," and leading elements of society, still mostly Protestant English, denounced "anarchists" and strikers in racial terms. The once-monolithic white race, already shaken by the Irish and German "invasions," was subdivided into distinct *races*: Celts, Teutons, Slavs, Hebrews, Mediterraneans, Nordics, and so forth. "Race" theories flourished, and "science"—represented by the work of Arthur de Gobineau, Samuel G. Morton, and Louis Agassiz, as well as the new theories of eugenics—was enlisted in the service of Anglo-Saxon supremacy; some immigrant groups, most notably Italians, were targets of violent nativist attacks, and all were to one degree or another victims of discrimination. Yet even as their own racial standing was in many cases being questioned, working-class immigrants of European

418

descent mobilized along white lines to drive Chinese workers out of industry, and they were able with the Chinese Exclusion Act in 1882 to bring about a total ban on Chinese immigration and maintain it in force until 1943.

The 1911 report of the joint House-Senate Committee on Immigration, chaired by Senator William P. Dillingham, enumerated thirty-six different "races" indigenous to Europe, and ranked them in order of desirability, with the Anglo-Saxon "race" at the head. Anglo-Saxon racialism achieved its greatest triumph with the Immigration Act of 1924, which drastically reduced overall immigration and assigned new quotas favoring the countries of northern and western Europe. It persisted as a force until the Great Depression, but the labor upsurge and triumph of the Congress of Industrial Organizations led once again to the recomposition of whiteness, as immigrants from eastern and southern Europe (and their children) repeated the experience of the Irish of the previous century. Key to their inclusion in the white category were various New Deal measures and agencies including unemployment compensation, Social Security, and the Federal Housing Authority. These measures, as enacted by a coalition of northern New Dealers and southern segregationist Democrats, largely excluded Afro-Americans from coverage, deepened the gap between them and those covered, and stamped "white" on the birth certificate of the welfare state. World War II underscored it with the GI Bill and the Veterans Housing Authority. The election of the Irish Catholic John F. Kennedy as president of the United States in 1960 and the son of Greek immigrants Spiro Agnew (Anagnostopoulos) as vice president in 1968 showed that all those of presumptive European descent had found their place in the White Republic.

CHALLENGES TO WHITE PRIVILEGE

Even as the United States celebrated the new inclusivity, a number of developments, both structural and political, were transforming race. Beginning in the late 1960s, U.S. economic strength declined relative to that of other world centers, and transnational corporations supplanted U.S.-based corporations within a new, global economy. The New Deal compact, on which the privileged position of white labor rested, became more expensive to the owners of capital just as it was becoming less strategically important to them. The civil rights movement, taking advantage of East-West competition, toppled legal segregation and discrimination. Finally, there was an influx of people from Asia, Africa, the islands of the sea, and the Western Hemisphere south of the Rio Grande. The symbolic moments are the Civil and Voting Rights Acts of 1964 and 1965, the immigration legislation of 1965, and the United States defeat in Vietnam. By the end of the century it was clear that whiteness was evolving in two directions simultaneously:

1. Some traditionally nonwhite groups, of whom Chinese Americans were the most notable example, surpassed whites of European ancestry in income, education, and other measures of status. Multiculturalism and diversity became the official ideologies of white recomposition, and ethnicity became the new formula for whiteness. The line between whites and "people of color" gave way to a line between African Americans and *everyone else.*

2. At the same time the white race was being recomposed, its value, and therefore its very existence, was being called into question by the emergence of new black professional and entrepreneurial strata based in mainly white institutions and by the erosion of the privileges that had guaranteed the most degraded white status above that of *any* black.

In response to the perceived decline in their status, traditional whites launched a counterattack against civil rights. A component of this so-called white backlash was the appearance of a novel "ethnic" consciousness among many who up until then had been pleased to regard themselves as white and who now sought to recover or reinforce their racial privileges by denying they had ever possessed them. One wing of this rediscovered ethnicity shades over into and merges with white power circles; the other wing makes up part of the field of white studies.

The white race is a club that enrolls certain people at birth, without their consent, and brings them up according to its rules. For the most part members go through life accepting the benefits of membership, without thinking about the costs. The club operates by the blackball system, which gives every member a veto power over new candidates for admission; it does not require that all members be strong advocates of white supremacy, merely that they defer to the prejudices of others. Moreover, it does not like to surrender a single member, so that even those who step out of it in one situation find it difficult not to be pulled back in later, if for no reason other than the assumptions of others. Like royalty, it seeks to regulate human society according to the laws of animal breeding, excluding certain people from the universe of possible lovers, even comrades, of others.

WHITE STUDIES

Nonwhite Perspectives As a matter of their own survival, the direct victims of whiteness have always studied it. Moreover, among black Americans in particular there has long existed a popular understanding, manifest positively in the phrase "blue-eyed soul brother" or negatively in the term "oreo," that the white race is not a natural but a peculiar sort of social formation, one that depends on its members' willingness to conform to the institutions and behavior patterns that reproduce it. Nella Larsen and James Weldon Johnson wrote novels in the 1920s on the artificiality of American race categories, and George Schuyler's 1931 novel, *Black No More*, is a biting satire on that theme. In *If He Hollers Let Him Go* (1945), Chester Himes wrote of whiteness as a thing apart from the individual, as in "the white folks sure brought their white to work with them." W. E. B. Du Bois wrote of the public and psychological wage attached to whiteness. James Baldwin declared flatly that "no one was white before he/she came to America," and that people from Europe "became white: by slaughtering the cattle, poisoning the wells, torching the houses, massacring Native Americans, raping Black women." Lerone Bennett Jr. wrote of whiteness as a "deliberate invention," and declared that John Brown transcended race. Malcolm X spoke of having met people who looked white but who had shed their whiteness. In the 1990s, Barbara J. Fields analyzed whiteness as "ideology," Cheryl Harris analyzed it as a form of property, and Toni Morrison, Cornel West, Michael Dyson, and others wrote on its social meaning.

Academic Perspectives Following the black writers' lead, a number of other scholars, mainly in academia, began to examine whiteness as a social phenomenon tied to privilege. By the 1990s their efforts had given rise to what some called a new field of study, critical race theory or white studies, and what others saw as simply a new look at the past and present. As of this writing there are at least five college readers on whiteness. At least three universities have sponsored conferences on the topic, and there are courses on a number of college campuses. New books are coming out constantly, and the dissertation mill is operating around the clock. Nu-merous articles have appeared in the mainstream press, reporting, often ironically, the "discovery" that white people have race. Any subject of study linked to power and privilege is bound to be politicized; among those who study whiteness there have appeared two schools: the preservationists and the abolitionists.

Preservation and Abolition For the most part the preservationists seek to identify aspects of whiteness that do not depend on racial oppression and privilege for their existence and that can be maintained without reproducing these things. Many work at excavating elements of a white culture analogous to black culture; but while they may, if they search diligently, find aspects of American life where Afro-American influence is absent or relatively unimportant, they have difficulty explaining that absence by anything other than white supremacist exclusion. Other preservationists acknowledge that whiteness is the product solely of privilege but hold that it is too deeply imbedded in the social structure to be done away with, and therefore argue, on political grounds, that it shall have to be "reframed" or "rearticulated" to remove its oppressive aspects. They, too, have a hard time specifying what would be left of it if the oppression were removed. Grouped with the preservationists are white racial awareness trainers and professional diversity consultants, pursuants of occupations that assume the existence of a valid white identity as a condition for carrying out their tasks. While at present nearly all of those within academia and the associated professions who seek to "rearticulate" whiteness claim to be antiracist, it can be difficult to differentiate their pronouncements from those of some white power advocates, who also promote racial consciousness while denying any intent to subjugate others.

The abolitionists hold that whiteness is based solely on oppression and that it could no more exist without white supremacy than slaveholding could exist without slavery. Hence they propose not to "deconstruct" or "rearticulate" the white race but to abolish it as a social category by doing away with the privileges of whiteness. They focus their attention on the institutions and behaviors that reproduce these privileges: the criminal justice system, historically determined racialized job reference networks, school segregation both geographical and test based, and home-buying and home-improvement loan discrimination; in every case they seek to discover and expose how these institutions operate to perpetuate white supremacy, and to challenge their operation. The abolitionists include people of varying opinions on a range of issues, including the "whitening" of the new immigrants, tactics, estimates of trends in the United States, and so on.

LOOKING FORWARD

Projecting from current population trends, some observers have predicted that by some proximate future date whites will be a minority in the United States. That prediction is based on the mistaken assumption that the white race is a natural grouping whose boundaries cannot be redefined. At this point the future of the white race is uncertain. Whites may maintain or even expand their numerical preponderance by incorporating new groups; people of exclusively European descent may adopt and impose on America a "restricted" definition of the white race, which would entail minority rule, population transfers, and genocide; or the white race may cease to exist, opening the way to a world without race.

See also **Race as a Cultural Category; Racialism and Racial Uplift** *(volume 1);* **Anthropology and Cultural Relativism** *(in this volume);* **Race** *(volume 3).*

BIBLIOGRAPHY

Allen, Theodore W. *The Invention of the White Race.* 2 vols. New York, 1994.

Brodkin, Karen. *How Jews Became White Folks and What That Says about Race in America.* New Brunswick, N.J., 1998.

Delgado, Richard, and Jean Stefancic, eds. *Critical White Studies: Looking behind the Mirror.* Philadelphia, 1997. A useful compendium.

Haney-Lopez, Ian F. *White by Law: The Legal Construction of Race.* New York, 1996.

Ignatiev, Noel. *How the Irish Became White.* New York, 1995.

Ignatiev, Noel, and John Garvey, eds. *Race Traitor.* New York, 1996. An anthology of abolitionist writings.

Jacobson, Matthew Frye. *Whiteness of a Different Color: European Immigrants and the Alchemy of Race.* Cambridge, Mass., 1998.

Mill, Charles W. *The Racial Contract.* Ithaca, N.Y., 1997.

Roediger, David R., ed. *Black on White: Black Writers on What It Means to Be White.* New York, 1998. Includes commentaries since 1830.

——. *The Wages of Whiteness: Race and the Making of the American Working Class.* New York, 1991.

WOMEN

Louise L. Stevenson

In an immediately influential and now-famous 1986 article, the historian Joan Scott explained how use of the term "gender" could deepen historical analysis. She proposed deployment of gender as a substitute for what she perceived as the limiting analytical category of women. She argued that gender analysis would permit historians to move beyond the study of women, thereby providing several new benefits, including an inclusion of how identities are constructed and the interaction between male and female gender categories. Indeed, Scott's predictions have proven extraordinarily useful for United States social history since the mid-1980s. Because her recommendations were based on her knowledge of social history, she never considered the analytical usefulness of the term "women" for intellectual historians. Thus, her article can serve as a launching pad for investigation of how the term "women" has and has not proved useful in the writing of American intellectual and cultural history. In this essay, the term "intellectual history" comprises the history of intellectuals, the history of ideas, and the history of intellectual life. It excludes discussion of historians and histories who use analysis of ideas to understand their topics, such as the ideas of the working class, of woman's suffrage, or of social reform. This essay's task is to see as much as possible the uses to which pre–women's movement intellectual historians put the term "women," to understand the role that women played in their histories, and to see what intellectual history has come to look like as a result of the women's movement and the rise of women's history.

Most intellectual historians of the first half of the twentieth century were men: Vernon Parrington, Ralph Henry Gabriel, Merle Curti, and Perry Miller, to name a few. Women historians usually specialized in social or educational history, as did the historian of colonial America Alice Morse Earle. The publications of these men's writings rarely contain women as a category of analysis and barely consider women as shapers of national discourse. When doing intellectual history, these writers took for granted that women did not merit study. Thus, men historians apparently never recognized the need to justify exclusion of women from their histories, since common knowledge supposedly said that few women had been intellectuals as they defined an intellectual. Examples of this assumption abound, and can be seen in a 1955 article by Merle Curti about the rise of scholarship in America. The article lists significant American scholars of the early twentieth century and names only men with academic positions.

Of course, it was not just women whom intellectual historians excluded. A list of all the people that intellectual history did not comprise includes African Americans and working people. Historians relied upon disciplinary subfields—African American history, women's history, and social history—to deal with the people whom they excluded. Still other conventions narrowed the subject matter of intellectual history further and made inclusion of women even less likely. Historians acted on the assumption that voices from academia, the pulpit, the printed page, the lectern, and the halls of government spoke for Americans. Social exclusion of minority groups and women from these public forums meant their exclusion from intellectual history. Further, intellectual historians assumed that intellectual history resided largely in public life. They sought to recapture the history of the United States that occurred as thinkers tried to influence national debate or the development of their profession. Unless a person had public stature as did the theologian Jonathan Edwards, the philosopher Ralph Waldo Emerson, or the educator James Conant, intellectual historians deemed his or her diaries and letters—all private documents—largely irrelevant.

With its emphasis on public affairs, and intellectual life as defined by professionals (ministers, editors, academics) few women stood a chance of inclusion in the canon of American intellectuals. For until the twentieth century, these professions included fewer than 5 percent women and these few women encountered obstacles in their pursuit of knowledge, including exclusion from higher education, professional associations, and publication outlets. The few who have been included—Ann Hutchinson, the seventeenth-century Antinomian; Harriet Beecher Stowe, the author of *Uncle Tom's Cabin;* and Margaret Fuller, the New England author and educator, for instance—often suffered trivialization. Hutchinson gained admiration more for her rebellion against authority in seventeenth-century Massachusetts than for her ideas, Stowe was notable for her undergarments in Robert Forrest Wilson's *Crusader in Crinoline* (1941), and Fuller appeared as an unfortunate, ugly appendage to the Transcendentalist movement. Rather than seeing women as playing a role in major literary movements, such as late-nineteenth-century realism, literary scholars assigned women like Stowe, the Maine novelist Sarah Orne Jewett, and others to the lesser category of local colorists. If women were allowed to speak in intellectual histories, they often commented on other women only, while authors allowed men to speak on the whole human race. To illustrate a point, in *The Crisis of the Negro Intellectual* (1967), Harold Cruse mentioned women almost exclusively in laundry lists of intellectuals. The one woman whom he discussed at some length, the Harlem Renaissance playwright Lorraine Hansberry, he used as an illustration of the tendency of accommodation to middle-class ethics. In these histories, if women have any power to effect change, it has been interpreted in the negative. In the past two centuries, popularity of women writers has frequently been held culpable for the feminization of American culture as in Fred Lewis Pattee's *The Feminine Fifties* (1940).

Marginalized and trivialized are the adjectives that describe women in intellectual history before the changes inspired by the women's movement of the late 1960s and 1970s. The movement brought changes in four ways to the almost nonexistent subfield of women's intellectual history. The first was the discovery or reinterpretation of women who deserved to be called intellectuals. Literary scholars started by rediscovering little-known authors such as the late-nineteenth-century author Kate Chopin, and by reinterpreting well-known authors such as Margaret Fuller and the early-twentieth-century novelist Willa Cather. By analyzing the diaries of someone who never published and rarely left her home—Alice James, the sister of novelist Henry James and psychologist William James—the biographer Jean Strouse showed that unpublished ma-

terials written by people without public significance might reveal much about family, gender conventions, and highbrow intellectual culture. With *Beyond Separate Spheres* (1982), Rosalind Rosenberg not only recovered a lost generation of women social scientists, including Mary Roberts Coolidge, Marion Talbot, and Elsie Clews Parsons, but demonstrated how in the first years of the twentieth century these social scientists conducted research about women, their intellects, and sexual natures that countered prevailing scientific ideas with no empirical basis. In the field of the history of the natural sciences, Margaret Rossiter looked beyond the walls of academia and so was able to recover the record of early women scientists with her *Women Scientists in America: Struggles and Strategies to 1940* (1982).

Second, women historians of the 1970s and 1980s had learned from the women's movement that the personal was vital to understanding women's lives. By applying lessons drawn from feminism to scholarly practice, they began to see that understanding the private-public relationship enriched and complicated their understanding of women's experiences. Nancy Cott broke the trail with her *Bonds of Womanhood: "Woman's Sphere" in New England, 1780–1835* (1977), which lays out the rich life that New England women enjoyed in their domestic sphere. In *Private Woman, Public Stage* (1984), Mary Kelley analyzed the careers and writings of the best-selling authors of the nineteenth century, including Caroline Lee Hentz, Harriet Beecher Stowe, and Sara Payson Willis Parton (Fanny Fern). While providing authors with subject matter, Kelley observed, women's domestic lives often hindered their professional aspirations. Underneath the supposed glorification of home and family, Kelley found persistent criticism of the precariousness of family life, its hazards to intellectual productions, and the confines women experienced. These women displayed the strength and self-reliance of their heroines as they negotiated with editors and publishers to publish and earn money vital for the support of their families.

Third, the opening up of private life allowed historians to appreciate how female-female friendships and women-centered institutions had supported and sustained the life of the mind for women intellectuals. Comparison of Allen F. Davis's *American Heroine: The Life and Legend of Jane Addams* (1973) with late-twentieth-century books on social reformers that foreground women's communities and female friendships as sustenance for productive public lives reveals the concerns of the new history. Kathryn Sklar's 1995 biography of Florence Kelley shows the key role of the social reformer Jane Addams's Hull-House as an intellectual, social, and emotional community of women. With the support of its residents in raising her children and in educating her about sweatshop conditions, Kelley gained the strength and insight to apply her mind to conceptualizing reforms.

Last, and perhaps most significant for the recovery of women's intellectual history, the women's movement encouraged an appreciation of women's institutions. For intellectual historians, the most important were women's educational institutions, which included both schools and colleges and institutions of informal education such as clubs and reading groups. Scholars who study women's schools and colleges received impetus to analyze anew women's colleges and coeducation. The new social history and feminism inspired a discovery and reconsideration of the histories of Mt. Holyoke College, the Troy Female Seminary, Miss Porter's School, and Wellesley College, to name a few institutions. The new works described students' lives and friendships, teacher-student relationships, and career trajectories of graduates. The historian Anne Firor Scott of Duke University pioneered this recovery with her revelation of the impact of the Troy Female Seminary on its students' lives and on ideas about women's education. Kathryn Sklar's masterful 1973 biography of the educator Catharine Beecher reveals the tenets and intellectual roots of Victorian domestic education. Also, it uncovers how a woman might play the role of a public intellectual and fashion a career for herself by drawing on the ideals of true womanhood as well as networks of family connections and friends. Further, the impetus to study women led to the recovery of women's areas of learning that had been marginalized, such as the new disciplinary field of domestic science as promoted by Massachusetts Institute of Technology professor and scientist Ellen Swallow Richards.

From studying women's educational institutions, historians began to argue that in many cases, and at some time periods, coeducation had not meant an equal education. Coeducation was not necessarily progress, they argued. Separate women's education often had meant a superior education. Additionally, historians of education began to adopt analytical strategies from social historians of education and women's cultural historians. They saw that women's educational institutions were notable for the social life they provided women, and that this social life nurtured a rich intellectual life. In the scholar Carroll Smith-Rosenberg's words the extra

curriculum and social life of these schools often belonged to what she had termed the "Female World of Love and Ritual." An all-girl school or college allowed female friendships to flourish and students to express themselves in ways that would have been censored in coeducational settings. Social ostracism and limitations on academic lives that women suffered in coeducational institutions often jeopardized the intellectual advances promised by women's admission into those same institutions.

While in this essay the discussion of the prescription on women's behavior follows the discussion of other changes in intellectual history, in the real world it actually preceded these and initiated a new era of women's history writing in the late 1960s. Then, the historian Barbara Welter wrote a series of influential articles partially in response to Richard Hofstadter's *Anti-Intellectualism in American Life* (1963). She analyzed the prescriptive literature of the antebellum period to determine how it had shaped American attitudes toward women and their intellectual achievement. Her "The Cult of True Womanhood, 1820–1860" (1966) became the most anthologized and quoted article of the 1970s and 1980s. By categorizing and explicating the prescriptive norms—piety, purity, domesticity, submissiveness—that had limited middle-class women's lives in the antebellum period, Welter revealed the norms that had defined ideal nineteenth-century middle-class womanhood. Almost immediately, historians committed to the new social history of womanhood began to attack Welter's analysis, which drew on literary sources. They pointed out that prescriptions of womanhood had been directed at middle-class women, and that prescriptions often did not describe life as lived. Moreover, these prescriptions described neither the lives of working and minority women nor the prescriptions applied to their class and race.

A more serious criticism of Welter's arguments came in the 1970s. Then, historians were learning from anthropologists, most notably Clifford Geertz, how to develop a more complex understanding of culture. The new anthropologically informed historians appreciated that culture and its prescriptions applied to all people in a culture, though in different ways depending upon factors such as sex, race, and class. In Welter's articles, prescription usually implied limitation. Because of the cult of true womanhood and anti-intellectualism, she had argued, antebellum women had had their ability to participate in American culture limited. Starting with the works of Cott and Sklar in the 1970s, historians began to understand that the prescriptions of true womanhood might also serve as bases for productive domestic lives or as springboards for engagement in public life.

Still, Welter's "True Womanhood" and "Anti-Intellectualism and the American Woman" (1967) deserve notice. Both articles helped a generation of historians talk about womanhood as a category of cultural analysis and pointed out the general predispositions in American culture working against an appreciation of women's intellectual achievements. Welter's great achievements, though no historian identified them as great at the time, were the revelation and identification of the gender conventions governing the activities of middle-class womanhood. Though the scholarly vocabulary in the late 1960s did not contain the concept of cultural construction, Welter had revealed the cultural construction of womanhood. By isolating and revealing the gendered terms applied to women, Welter had performed the intellectual exercise that often lies at the beginning of a field, namely identification and classification. In the 1990s, Lora Romero's very smart analysis of the category of domestic fiction in the antebellum period takes Welter's original findings to a new level. Romero argued the complicity of contemporary scholars with the prejudices of the antebellum era in marginalizing women's literary production.

Ironically, while social historians moved to gender analysis after starting to recover the history of women, cultural and intellectual historians such as Welter worked at the task of gender analysis first. If Joan Scott had been an intellectual historian, she would have recommended that fellow historians enrich their gender analysis with a history of actual women's intellectual lives.

Though covering only the antebellum years and admittedly dealing exclusively with prescriptive literature, Welter's articles raised to visibility the major way that the term "women" has been a useful category for intellectuals and intellectual historians. Both have used women to help them define what was wrong or weak in American thought: its distrust of the overly rational and reliance upon the intuitive; its inability to reach hard judgments, to imagine evil, its nicey-nice veil over sex. Though each historical era from the seventeenth century to the present called upon different metaphors and associations to express itself, each has used the discussion of women to express, on the one hand, cultural discomfort and fears, and on the other hand, a yearning for cultural stability. Criticism runs from the colonial period in the president of Yale College Timothy Dwight's *Morpheus* (1801–1802), a dia-

tribe against the overly intellectual Enlightenment author Mary Wollstonecraft, to the 1940s author Philip Wylie's anger at women expressed in his *Generation of Vipers* (1942). Similarly, little encouragement can be found in the Puritan's praise for the biblical Bathsheba to the conservative national leader Phyllis Schlafly's explanation of the effects of the Equal Rights Amendment.

Until the late 1980s, it was unclear that the women's movement and the historical writing resulting from it would influence the established field of intellectual history. In the 1970s, social history monopolized the excitement of innovation in the academy with its promise to write a new history founded on the experiences of minority and working-class Americans. In response, intellectual historians regrouped, and by the end of the decade announced the arrival of their own new history. In a decade of extraordinary ferment, especially of feminist thought and criticism, the intellectual historians John Higham and Paul K. Conkin assembled an anthology, *New Directions in American Intellectual History* (1977). It includes only one article by a woman and none about women. In the late 1980s and 1990s, it seems historians had left these exclusionary ways behind. Whether women play a major role in their stories or not, historians acknowledged the presence of women, and stated whether women had or had not had similar experiences to those of men. In the 1940s, women or the female gender were not even topics for the Harvard historian Perry Miller. He mentioned but two women, the poet Anne Bradstreet and the religious dissident Anne Hutchinson, in his *New England Mind: The Seventeenth Century* (1939). Fifty years later, in *Worlds of Wonder* (1989), David D. Hall took care in explaining why he did not consider women as a separate category in his history of the seventeenth century. In the introduction to *Worlds of Wonder,* he explained that he understood women and men experiencing the supernatural in New England in similar ways. In contrast, in intellectual histories of the past forty years, women have taken a vital role. In his *The Postmodernist Turn: American Thought and Culture in the 1970s* (1996), the historian J. David Hoeveler created a chapter entitled "Writing Feminist," which explicates relationships between 1970s feminist literary scholarship, French feminism, and the developing scholarly debate centered on Marxism, poststructuralism, and psychoanalytic theory. Hoeveler admitted that he approached the cultural and intellectual history of the 1970s women's movement with humility since, he observed, not even an entire book could encompass the complete record of feminist scholarship. Starting in the 1970s, it caused, he argued, every social science and humanities discipline to experience an upheaval in its methodology and content.

In addition, books and articles published in the 1990s reconsider how American women have fashioned themselves as intellectuals. Linda Kerber has devoted considerable attention to women's becoming included in academia and published these articles in *Toward an Intellectual History of Women* (1997). For many years, Kerber had been analyzing the meaning of central terms in American political discourse, namely republicanism and individualism, when they are applied to women.

Today's biographers of women use their subjects to illuminate major topics in intellectual and cultural history. Joan Hedrick's authoritative biography *Harriet Beecher Stowe: A Life* (1994) redeems Stowe from being merely a wearer of crinoline and tells several important stories, among them how domestic experience provided fodder for the national political novel, and how the advent of the professional author and criticism in the late nineteenth century resulted in the marginalization of women authors. Instead of commenting on Margaret Fuller's physiognomy as *New England Mind* does, Charles Capper's 1992 biography of Margaret Fuller treats her as the overpowering intellect that she was and shows her relationship to major national and European intellectual sources and political events, including nineteenth-century liberalism. Daniel Horowitz performed similar work by having considered Betty Friedan's *The Feminine Mystique* (1963) as a revealing work of American cultural and intellectual history with roots in the American postwar discourse of the Left and about consumption in his *Betty Friedan and the Making of the Feminine Mystique* (1998).

A review of Joan Scott's article might urge intellectual historians toward at least one more task. Scott identified the modification of historical paradigms as one of the major benefits promised by the deployment of gender analysis. So, women's intellectual history might also go one step further and inspire a rethinking of the labels and periodization that currently rule. Instead of asking what women fit into existing conceptions of intellectual history, scholars might ask how women's inclusion reshapes intellectual history. For example, a dominant paradigm in the history of higher education labels the most significant intellectual changes of the late nineteenth-century—the rise of the research-oriented university. With few exceptions, men have the leading roles in this story. But focus on the university not only veils the multifold advances then being made at small liberal arts colleges, but overlooks the founding of women's educational institutions and the admission of women to state universities and historically black colleges. Certainly, that half the American population gained access to higher education should affect the accepted trajectory of nineteenth-century college university development. The age of the university was also the age of inclusion for American higher education; the age when higher education no longer implied the education of white men exclusively.

Focus on women can be a useful strategy for intellectual historians for some time to come. Many scholars contend that intellectual and cultural historians have to continue the work of biographers such as Hedrick and Capper and of intellectual historians such as Kerber. There are many women intellectuals who need redemption from the marginal positions where previous generations of historians have put them. The work of appreciating women's role in shaping thought about crucial American terms, including progressivism, liberalism, and pragmatism, and the meaning of these terms to each gender, needs to continue.

The challenge of inclusion should continue to redefine and enlarge the province of intellectual history. Rosalind Rosenberg's and Margaret Rossiter's revelations about women social scientists and scientists should push historians to look for intellectual ferment and influence beyond academia, perhaps in the lives and ideas of women marginalized by the established academic community. With historians' new interest in public intellectuals, they might start to rethink the demeaning role of popularizer as previously assigned to writers and intellectuals such as Mary Baker Eddy, Margaret Mead, Ayn Rand, and Rachel Carson. Peter Conn did this in his 1996 biography of the novelist Pearl Buck.

As scholars explore the research possibilities of all the women educators, scientists, and writers who have thus far been ignored, trivialized, or marginalized, the drive toward inclusion impels them in new directions and encourages deployment of fresh analytical strategies. If scholars presume that enlargement of the reach of intellectual history to encompass more women is a good thing, then they can attempt to leave behind one of the limitations of the intellectual histories of the past. From the time of Welter's articles to the present, the term "women" has usually meant a history of literate women who could afford the time and situation necessary for conduct of an intellectual life. So intellectual historians might start employing new approaches that permit them to reach for new subjects for analysis. David Hall's borrowing of historical methods derived from European historians of popular culture and popular religion expanded the boundaries of intellectual history for seventeenth-century New England. His history of popular religion recovers the beliefs of lay Protestants as they expressed them in folk stories, diaries, and court testimony. Nell Irvin Painter's *Sojourner Truth: A Life, a Symbol* (1996) suggests another way. Painter analyzed visual images, narratives, and accounts of Truth's presentations to recapture her intellectual presence and cultural meaning.

Historians of readers and reading have blazed still another promising path. Though studies of women's reading of the late twentieth century initially took for their subjects primarily upper- and middle-class people and groups, the work suggests that an intellectual history centered on individuals possesses potential to illuminate an everyday dimension of intellectual life and individuals' agency in making it. Person-centered histories of thought and careful tracking of their movement through society will allow historians to root their histories more deeply in actual experience. Though pioneered by historians of women and their reading, these changes should enrich the writing of intellectual histories about both women and men.

See also **Conflicting Ideals of Colonial Womanhood; Women in the Public Sphere, 1838–1877; Domesticity and Sentimentalism; Gender, Social Class, Race, and Material Life; Gender and Political Activism** *(volume 1);* **Women and Family in the Suburban Age; The Struggle for the Academy; Second-Wave Feminism** *(in this volume);* **Family; Sexuality; Gender** *(volume 3);* and other articles in this section.

BIBLIOGRAPHY

Capper, Charles. *Margaret Fuller: An American Romantic Life.* New York, 1992.

Conn, Peter J. *Pearl S. Buck: A Cultural Biography.* New York, 1996.

Cott, Nancy F. *The Bonds of Womanhood: "Woman's Sphere" in New England, 1780–1835.* New Haven, Conn., 1977.

Curti, Merle. "The Setting and the Problems." In *American Scholarship in the Twentieth Century,* edited by Merle Curti. Cambridge, Mass., 1955.

Hall, David D. *Worlds of Wonder, Days of Judgment: Popular Religious Belief in Early New England.* New York, 1989.

Hedrick, Joan D. *Harriet Beecher Stowe: A Life.* New York, 1994.

Hoeveler, J. David. *The Postmodernist Turn: American Thought and Culture in the 1970s.* New York, 1996.

Horowitz, Daniel. *Betty Friedan and the Making of the Feminine Mystique: The American Left, the Cold War, and Modern Feminism.* Amherst, Mass., 1998.

Kelley, Mary. *Private Woman, Public Stage: Literary Domesticity in Nineteenth-Century America.* New York, 1984.

Kerber, Linda K. *Toward an Intellectual History of Women.* Chapel Hill, N.C., 1997.

Painter, Nell Irvin. *Sojourner Truth: A Life, a Symbol.* New York, 1996.

Romero, Lora. *Home Fronts: Domesticity and Its Critics in the Antebellum United States.* Durham, N.C., 1997.

Rosenberg, Rosalind. *Beyond Separate Spheres: Intellectual Roots of Modern Feminism.* New Haven, Conn., 1982.

Rossiter, Margaret W. *Women Scientists in America: Before Affirmative Action, 1940–1972.* Baltimore, 1995.

———. *Women Scientists in America: Struggles and Strategies to 1940.* Baltimore, 1982.

Scott, Ann Firor. "The Ever Widening Circle: The Diffusion of Feminist Values from the Troy Female Seminary, 1822–1972." *History of Education Quarterly* 79 (1979): 3–25.

——. "What, Then, Is the American: This New Woman?" *Journal of American History* 65 (1978): 679–703.

Scott, Joan Wallach. "Gender: A Useful Category of Historical Analysis." In her *Gender and the Politics of History.* New York, 1988.

Sicherman, Barbara. "Reading *Little Women:* The Many Lives of a Text." In *U.S. History as Women's History: New Feminist Essays,* edited by Linda K. Kerber et al. Chapel Hill, N.C., 1995.

Sklar, Kathryn Kish. *Catharine Beecher: A Study in American Domesticity.* New Haven, Conn., 1976.

——. *Florence Kelley and the Nation's Work.* New Haven, Conn., 1995.

Solomon, Barbara M. *In the Company of Educated Women: A History of Women and Higher Education in America.* New Haven, Conn., 1985.

Stevenson, Louise L. *The Victorian Homefront: American Thought and Culture, 1860–1880.* Boston, 1991.

Strouse, Jean. *Alice James, a Biography.* Boston, 1980.

Welter, Barbara. *Dimity Convictions: The American Woman in the Nineteenth Century.* Athens, Ohio, 1976.

WORKING CLASS

Jefferson Cowie

CULTURE AND THE STUDY OF CLASS IN THE UNITED STATES

Beginning in the 1960s, historians of the American working classes found their way toward a "rediscovery of class through culture," as Richard Johnson has aptly stated it, and labor history has been tightly linked to the study of cultural trends ever since. Indeed, the very definition of "labor history" has expanded well beyond trade unions, economics, and the state and probed deeply into the communities, the plantations, the shop floor, the domestic sphere, the pre-industrial work habits, and on into consumerism, commercial entertainment, and artistic representation of workers. Scholars who emphasize the problem of cultural identity of American workers have typically approached the issue via the intersection of broad economic forces of society and the lived experience of the ordinary worker at the local level. There is, of course, no single "working-class culture," and arguably not a single working class about which scholars can speak. What is evident from scholarship of the last several decades of the twentieth century is that evolutions in a rich spectrum of working-class cultures are tightly linked to the changing economic structure in which they are embedded. Workers' culture, from the slave plantation to the postwar assembly line, is simultaneously a product of powerful economic structures as well as a formidable set of tools to resist and shape those same seemingly uncontestable forces.

This "culturalist" approach to working-class history has not always been the center of historiographical discussion. To understand the culturalist thrust of what is dubbed the "new labor history" one must turn, simply enough, to an understanding of the "old labor history." In an earlier generation of studies, particularly the work of John R. Commons and his student Selig Perlman, workers were understood first and foremost through their trade unions and interactions with the state. Perlman created the cornerstone upon which the rest of class studies would take place with the publication of his *Theory of the Labor Movement* (1928). There he proclaimed that American workers were uniquely pragmatic beings who wisely eschewed the advice of left-wing intellectuals, remained self-interested, relatively apolitical and certainly not radical, and focused on incremental and not fundamental transformations of the capitalist order. The "culture," if that term can be used to describe Perlman's theory, of the American working class was simply "job conscious"—a term he used to explain the largely apolitical, limited purview of workers in the United States. "The solidarity of American labor," wrote Perlman, "is a solidarity with a quickly diminishing potency as one passes from the craft group—which looks upon the jobs in the craft as its common property for which it is ready to fight long and bitterly—to the widening concentric circles of the related crafts, the industry, the American Federation of Labor, and the world labor movement" (p. 136). In sum, if American workers were somewhat parochial and apolitical, especially in contrast to their European brothers and sisters, they were nonetheless capable of clinging tenaciously and militantly to what they regarded as the sacred bond between worker and job.

The Commons-Perlman school dominated much of the thinking on the history and culture of American workers well into the middle of the twentieth century. The "job-conscious" formulation melded neatly with the eclipse of Progressive history and the rise of consensus history after World War II, since it was a quick jump to see working-class culture and consciousness in the age of Eisenhower as largely liberal and committed to the capitalist order. Louis Hartz, in his *The Liberal Tradition in America* (1955), for instance, believed that workers were imprisoned within the confines of Lockean liberalism and those confining walls prevented workers from having the vision necessary to imagine political alternatives. This was an old problem. The suggestion that the United States had an "exceptional" working class in that it did not have a sustained tradition of opposition was at least as old as the question posed by the German sociologist Werner Sombart at the dawn of the twentieth century: "Why is there no socialism in the United States?" Sombart's question is even broader than it appears: Why have American workers not been more class conscious, more aware of themselves as a class?

The publication of E. P. Thompson's monumental *The Making of the English Working Class* (1963) pulled historians from the horns of the many dilemmas in their understanding of class by opening the door to cultural approaches to the subject. Class is not a structural determinant of social behavior, argued Thompson, it is, instead, a cultural awareness with multiple meanings that appears at different times, places, and is a product of different experiences. "Class consciousness is the way in which these experiences are handled in cultural terms: embodied in traditions, values systems, ideas, and institutional forms," proclaimed Thompson. In sum, he argued that "class is as much a cultural as an economic formulation" (p. 10). This breakthrough released scholars from the vise into which Sombart, Perlman, and the consensus historians had placed their subject. Scholars of the American working class no longer had to account for the alleged absence of socialism and class-based ideologies, and they were freed from the narrow job consciousness emphasized by Perlman. Liberated from the normative call of traditional Marxist modes of analysis and the stifling confines of the stodgy institutions of American labor studies, the "new labor history" sought out a fresh agenda: to study working people in their communities, their homes, their workplaces, and to examine their immigration patterns, their race and gender relations. The goal became to write, in short, a new history "from the bottom up." As Ira Berlin summarized it, the basic formulation was "workers' power, workers' culture: one could not be understood without the other" (Gutman, *Power and Culture*, p. 23). Two generations of historians have now made this cultural approach their own and what follows is hardly an exhaustive account of their endeavors. Rather, it will hopefully serve as an introduction to a few of the important themes, including political, commercial, racial, social, and artistic approaches to the problem, in some of the key periods in which working-class culture has been so richly revealed.

THE ARTISANS' REPUBLIC

The greatest inheritance pre-industrial workers received was directly tied to the political culture of the American Revolution. The story of the American Revolution is often told as one of great leaders, such as the merchant John Hancock, but also, thanks to social historians, of more obscure characters such as the shoemaker George Robert Twelves Hewes, who not only fought the British but also began to question social relations at home. Although the Revolution was not an actual revolt of the have-nots, it could not have proceeded without the wide support of various plebian groups. The revolutionary coalition emerged in the major seaports—the bulwarks of popular resistance, what Gary Nash has called "the urban crucible." There, small traders, artisans, and mechanics marched in costumes, burned and hanged colonial authorities in effigies, and slowly began to question deference and hierarchy within the new United States. The many parades, bonfires, and confrontations with the British military gave the imperial crisis a public dimension and led revolutionary elites to depend upon members of this coalition to gather up a mob and then control it. In the long run, the nation's republican experiment came to be defined by the participation of artisan classes who made the idea of liberty, infused with a high degree of equality, their own sacred language.

The Revolution brought artisans into prominent public roles, and politically they would be at the center of the post-revolutionary political culture during the eras of Thomas Jefferson and Andrew Jackson. At the core of this was the development of a republican political culture that fought all forms of monarchy, deference, and authority. "The word republic," wrote Thomas Paine, whose *Common Sense* resonated so deeply with the commoner, "means the public good of the whole, in contradistinction to the despotic form which makes the good of the sovereign, or of one man, the only object of government." This was not an easy or quick conclusion to reach, as the colonists had previously celebrated their position as Englishmen and fought to restore their rights as Englishmen against what they regarded to be a conspiracy against them. The artisans and workers who claimed citizenship under the revolutionary mantle also sought to control the concentration of power in all of its forms and maximize liberty through relatively equal access to property and the simple honesty and civic-mindedness of "republican virtue." For the entire system to work, political equality had to be guaranteed, and the de-

432

gree to which this would be applied would be the contest that would be played out in the Jacksonian era as the spreading market revolution upended the quiescence of a once limited market society.

The politics of the Jacksonian era can in large part be explained by placing this republican political culture (often overly pristine in both the rhetoric of the times and many historians' accounts) against the upheavals sponsored by an expanding "market revolution." As entrepreneurs sought the special privileges of corporate charters and tariff protections, as the factory system began to create European-like class relations, and as ethnic and cultural diversity and heightened geographic mobility tossed strangers into conflict, the virtue of the republican experiment appeared in jeopardy. While Americans may have lacked a Marxist brand of class consciousness, class expression, as Sean Wilentz has shown, did come in the form of a militant Americanism embodied in Andrew Jackson's presidency and the rise of the workingmen's parties of the era. Anxieties over rising class distinctions sponsored by an expanding market took many forms, including religious revivalism, anti-masonry, vibrant party politics, and the political symbol of the renewal of the Bank of the United States; but it was in the short-lived workingmen's parties that we see the republican political culture marshaled most directly against the encroachments of the marketplace. As the wage relationship replaced the master-apprentice system, class hierarchies were challenged as a betrayal to the revolutionary heritage. As the General Trades Union of the city of New York proclaimed:

> We the journeymen artisans and mechanics of the City of New York and its vicinity, therefore, believing as we do, that in proportion as the line of distinction between the employer and employed is widened, the condition of the latter inevitably verges toward a state of vassalage while that of the former as certainly approximates towards supremacy; and that whatever system is calculated to make the many dependent upon, or subject to, the few, not only tends to the subversion of the natural rights of man, but is hostile to the best interest of the community as well as to the spirit and genius of our government. (Wilentz, *Chants Democratic*, p. 247)

Similarly, some of the first factory workers in the United States, the Lowell girls, who labored on the textile mills in Massachusetts, asserted their rights as "the daughters of free men." While still embedded in a gender hierarchy, these young women called upon a culture of revolutionary rights that remained a potent form of resistance well through the nineteenth century.

SLAVERY AND WAGE SLAVERY

As the historian Edmund S. Morgan has so brilliantly shown, so many forms of American "freedom" have rested upon the enslavement of Africans. Indeed, the history of working people prior to the Civil War is, in the broadest terms, a history of competing labor systems, slave and free, that had a tremendous impact upon the way struggles to ameliorate social stratification and the wage relationship took place. For instance, the militancy of the Jacksonian free laborers evolved hand in glove, according to David Roediger, with a distinctive culture of "whiteness." As much as class formation is a cultural project—E. P. Thompson's primary point—it evolved in a context in which the status of whiteness could function as a "wage" for white workers that helped soften, psychologically, the blows delivered by the new factory system and the decline of the small independent producer. In essence, status and privileges conferred by race could be used to make up for alienating and exploitative class relationships, both North and South. Thus the culture of white wage earners was filtered through the fear of slavery and, by not-so-distant association, the fear of blackness. Dignity and meaning could be found in the dependency and denigration of the new wage relationship, since a simplistic form of republican freedom and dignity remained; wage slavery was more acceptable because chattel slavery existed. The much celebrated political culture of republicanism, then, was, at root, a *Herrenvolk,* or master race, republicanism in which a fraternity of equals is based on the oppression and exclusion of other groups.

If a culture of "whiteness" helped alleviate the denigration of the new order for free laborers, slaves developed their own vibrant and sophisticated form of cultural opposition to the system that exploited them. As Eugene Genovese and others have convincingly argued, slavery in the United States was more "paternalistic" and less severe than in other parts of the world, in that it left some room for resistance and bargaining between slave and master. It was nonetheless a wickedly oppressive system, one that bred a sophisticated culture of opposition. Lawrence W. Levine's magisterial *Black Culture and Black Consciousness* (1977) traces the folk culture of African Americans through slavery and emancipation by examining everything from their folktales to their riddles. Levine argues forcefully that "upon the hard rock of racial, social, and economic exploitation and injustice black Americans forged and maintained a culture: they formed and maintained kinship networks, made love, raised and socialized children, built a religion, and created a rich and expressive culture in which they articulated their feelings and hopes and dreams." (p. xx)

CULTURE IN AN INDUSTRIAL SOCIETY

A culture of republican traditionalism, local solidarity, and producerist ideology continued to challenge the rising industrial order well after the Civil War and into the Gilded Age. Here historians have turned their attention to the shop floor, working-class communities, and local and national politics for clues to working-class customs, patterns, and behavior. Herbert Gutman made his most profound contributions to the new labor history by placing culture at the center of the analysis. Far from seeing immigrant working people as acquisitive Lockean individualists, Gutman's innovative use of new sources, and the posing of new questions to old sources, shows how workers viewed the new industrial regime with a fundamental ambivalence, often militant opposition, which they expressed through religious and cultural traditions, ethnic institutions, and rituals of all kinds. The question of class was not merely one of wages and hours as Perlman has suggested, nor a problem of socialist agency as Marxists posited. Rather, the Gilded Age could be understood as a battle over the very culture of society. It was in the communities, the churches, the oratory, and the propinquity of place that workers expressed their common opposition to the new industrial world and their struggle to preserve the solidarity that lay at the core of the old world traditions. Within their values, customs, and communities, new workers found the tools that allowed them to make their claims for a different set of morals and a deeper notion of justice. In their cultural resources, they may not have found a hard-boiled analysis of the political economy, but they had found the "legitimising notion of right" in Thompson's terms that would provide the tools necessary to take their stand against the powerful might of a rapidly and unevenly industrializing society.

The Knights of Labor drew together many of the strands of a Gilded Age producerist culture. As Leon Fink has demonstrated, the Knights showed wide-ranging "cultural imperatives toward productive work, civic responsibility, education, a wholesome family life, temperance, and self-improvement" (*Workingmen's Democracy,* p. 8). Most important, the Knights' labor theory of value remained a constant defense of "nobility of toil" in the face of a

labor market that threatened not just traditional craft skills but inherited visions of citizenship as well. The Knights, unlike many succeeding labor organizations, contained within it a vibrant movement culture that included picnics, festivals, oratory, novels, fusion politics, temperance campaigns, reading rooms, parades, and a host of material cultural forms. Noted for their inclusion of blacks, immigrants, factory hands, and working-class women, Knights members sought solidarity out of the fragmentation of an industrializing world under the banner, "An injury to one is an injury to all." Rather than a sharply defined class consciousness that has always been elusive in the American experience, the Knights developed a fuzzy if potent ideology of producerism and against the forces of idlers and parasites (mostly lawyers, bankers, and liquor dealers). "We declare an inevitable and irresistible conflict between the wage-system of labor and republican system of government," declared the Knights' constitution. Even when a distinctly class-based political culture did emerge, as manifest in the Socialist Party of America, according to Nick Salvatore, it has shown the continuity in the republican tradition. Debsian socialism rose in response to the ways in which the wage system and concentration of capital violated such cultural norms as individual autonomy, manliness, and republican liberty.

Placing the focus on second and third generation workers, David Montgomery has shown how a fascinating occupational culture emerged in some of the skilled occupations. Rather than examining how people new to the industrial regime used traditional social codes to soften the individualism and exploitation of the New World, as Gutman had, Montgomery explored how a series of craft work rules and mutual support systems helped to preserve workers' control over production. A moral code developed among skilled workers that demanded that workers limit their output to a quota set by the workers themselves—not the boss. This was, after all, still an era, in Big Bill Haywood's telling, in which "the manager's brain" was "under the workman's cap." Skilled craftsmen were also expected to demonstrate a "manly bearing toward the boss" in order to preserve the dignity and defiant egalitarianism of their occupational domain (*Workers' Control in America,* p. 13). Co-workers were expected never to undermine the labor of their brothers nor attempt to get ahead at the expense of others. As one employers' journal satirized the accommodation necessary to workers' habits and desires:

Run your factories to please the crowd. . . . Don't expect work to begin before 9 A.M. or to continue after 3 P.M. Every employee should be served hot coffee and a bouquet at 7 A.M. and allowed the two hours to take a free perfumed bath. . . . During the summer, ice cream and fruit should be served at 12 P.M. to the accompaniment of witching music. (Gutman, *Work, Culture*, p. 38)

Many of these forms of occupational culture and resistance would come under direct assault by the principles of scientific management around the turn of the twentieth century, which would, in turn, help to create a new culture—that of the "mass" worker.

COMMERCIALIZATION OF CULTURE AND LEISURE

As much as the political arena, the workplace, and the community were sites of conflict in the industrial age, so were recreation, play, and leisure equally important contested realms. Roy Rosenzweig's *Eight Hours for What We Will* (1983) offers a sophisticated understanding of working-class culture and the commercialization of leisure. Within the workers' saloons, he argues, could be found a culture that was not necessarily one in direct opposition to the dominant culture but one—like Gutman's immigrants—that was certainly an alternative to the dominant trend toward acquisitive individualism. Or, in the case of Fourth of July celebrations, a day with particular Paine-ite significance for turn-of-the-century workers, the lower classes often affirmed mutuality and community but did so fragmented along religious or ethnic lines, which prevented a broader culture capable of unifying workers under a single banner. Moreover, many middle- and upper-class people were horrified by the rowdy and tawdry forms of fun workers found for themselves in their saloons and festivals and countered these with their own campaigns to reform or restrict working-class leisure. Proper decorum and uplift became part of the "civilizing" project of genteel reformers as they launched museums, libraries, and parks in a joint project to separate themselves from the crowd and provide uplift for the toiling masses.

Ironically, neither the genteel reformers nor the rowdier immigrant laboring classes won the turn-of-the-century culture wars, as amusement fell to the same forces as artisan production: commercial production and the market. Working people spent less time creating their own amusement by the dawn of the twentieth century and more purchasing mass-produced fun in the form of movie houses, professional sports, dance halls, amusement parks, and other cheap forms of recreation. The nickelodeon, in particular, was known as the "poor man's amusement" or the "academy of the working man." As Steven Ross has shown in his *Working-Class Hollywood* (1998), even the content of the mass-produced imagery available at the "flickers" was the product of a contest between small-scale, labor-oriented producers in the early years of relatively fluid economic and artistic times, and the centralized studio system that foreclosed the political and thematic diversity available on the silver screen. In between, according to Ross, was "one of the greatest power struggles in American history—a struggle for the control of American consciousness" as broad economic and political forces shaped the very picture of the American working class on the screen (p. 10).

Although the studio system clearly won the battle of images, the commercialization of leisure and the expansion of consumerism into working-class neighborhoods offered an interesting, if unintended, consequence: it helped to break down the barriers of ethnicity and shape the agenda of an expanded living wage for American workers. Throughout the early decades of the twentieth century, divisions among workers by ethnicity, skill, religion, race, and neighborhood undermined intraclass solidarity. As Lizabeth Cohen wrote, however, this changed as mass culture replaced the ethnic cultures celebrated by Gutman. By the 1920s and 1930s, argued Cohen, workers "were more likely to share a cultural world, to see the same movies and newsreels in the same chain theaters, shop for the same items in the same chain stores, and listen to the same radio shows on network radio, a situation very different from that of 1919 when workers lived in isolated cultural communities" (*Making a New Deal*, p. 325). Many groups, most obviously the Industrial Workers of the World (or Wobblies) and the Socialist Party, had tried to unite people across the many divisive boundaries within the U.S. working class, but it is ironic that the means to that elusive "culture of unity" came from the very market forces they so often tried to tame. This common ground created by mass production, mass consumption, and the commercialization of leisure helped lay the groundwork for one of the fundamental turning points in the history of working people, the Great Depression.

THE NEW DEAL ORDER

The organizational forms of American working people had, since the late 1880s and the end of the

Knights, revolved around the skilled, largely white, largely male, workers of the American Federation of Labor (AFL). The historical landscape is scarred by failed attempts to expand that realm, including strikes at Homestead (1892), Pullman (1894), Lawrence (1912), Ludlow (1914), and Chicago (1919), but, constrained by the limited purview of "pure and simple unionism" of the AFL and the long arm of state mechanisms that had often been violently turned against workers, the organizational realm of the American working class remained limited. Much of this changed during the Great Depression as the National Labor Relations Act (1935) granted unions the right to organize. The Congress of Industrial Organizations (CIO) seized upon the opportunity and, backed by the new strategy of the sit-down strike, launched aggressive organizing campaigns across the nation. This delivered over one-third of the nonagricultural labor force into unions, recast the discussion about workers, and thrust it onto the national stage.

Indeed, if ever there was an era in which the national culture turned on the working people, it was the 1930s. The depression decade is readily defined in the popular imagination by the imagery of working people; in fact, to think of the Great Depression is to conjure up a series of iconic figures from the proletarian fiction of John Steinbeck and Jack Conroy, the plays of Clifford Odets, the murals of Thomas Hart Benton, the documentary images of the Farm Security Administration photographs of Dorothea Lange and Walker Evans, and the lyrics of the laborite Woody Guthrie. These added up to an aesthetic insurgency, a "cultural front" in the historian Michael Denning's term, that sought to create a mass proletarian culture to match the depth of the economic crisis. Indeed, the labor Left probably had more cultural influence during this period than in any other time in American history as workers' theater, proletarian fiction, journalism, photography, and poetry were brought to political, pro-labor ends. Although the Communist Party is often understood to be a cornerstone of these efforts, Denning urged caution, as formal party affiliation was very fluid and far from central; the cultural front was, he suggested, supported by a national culture of collective working-class awareness.

Or was it? Lawrence Levine, in fact, suggests the opposite. "Until relatively recently," wrote Levine in "American Culture and the Great Depression," "we have spoken and written as if the political culture of the 1930s represented all of American culture; as if Franklin Roosevelt and his advisers spoke for the vast majority of Americans; as if one could under-

stand the impact of the depression upon American consciousness by comprehending the reform impulse of the 1930s" (*Yale Review* 74, p. 196). Rather than pointing to the collective insurgencies of the 1930s, Levine pointed to how people internalized the economic calamity of the Great Depression, blaming themselves and searching for ways to improve themselves as a way out a structural crisis. "The remarkable thing about the American people before reform did come was not their action but their inaction, not their demands but their passivity, not their revolutionary spirit but their traditionalism" (p. 198). This internalization of the systemic crisis of the 1930s often exploded outward after it was given national legitimacy during President Franklin D. Roosevelt's New Deal government, suggesting that the individual and collective responses to the depression related to the rise of a more national political culture.

Working-class religious expression is another rich arena for the exploration of labor's cultures and an important way to understand the ways in which workers survived the Great Depression and other economic upheavals. For a direct link between mass culture and working-class religion, one can turn to Alan Brinkley's examination of Detroit's Father Coughlin, the "radio priest," in his *Voices of Protest* (1982). There, the role of populism and Catholic reformism mixed with the mass audience of radio and, particularly later in his career, demagoguery in a fascinating amalgam of class, politics, national crisis, and populist behavior. Although a political historian, Brinkley, like many labor and working-class historians dating back to Gutman himself, never actually explored religious values, choosing instead to study faith and religion as aspects of resistance and accommodation. Others, however, have sought out religious practice not to understand the politics of class but simply to understand what it tells society about devotion and adaptation to life in the United States. Robert Anthony Orsi's wonderful *The Madonna of 115th Street* (1985) studies the religion of the streets through the annual *festa* of the Madonna of Mount Carmel in New York City—a "troubled, poor, constantly changing, culturally isolated and neglected community in Italian Harlem" (p. xiii). Religion in Orsi's hands is not about protest but a search for a more transcendent meaning of working-class culture. It was in poor and working-class Italian religious practices, he argued, that "immigrants' deepest values, their understanding of the truly human, their perceptions of the nature of reality were acted out; the hidden structures of power and authority were revealed" (p. xxiii).

For a complete portrait of the rise of the New Deal period, historians need to pull together the solidarity and militancy in the shops, the search for economic security through what John Bodnar called "working-class realism," and the breakdown of ethnic isolation in the face of the growing homogenizing forces of mass culture. In the process, a limited, perhaps, timid place for workers in the national culture emerged from the crises of the Great Depression and World War II. The role of the state in workers' lives—from the National Labor Relations Board to the Social Security Adminstration—was indefinitely secured in the postwar era. Indeed, the industrial relations scholar Sumner H. Slichter suggested after World War II that "the United States is gradually shifting form a capitalistic community to a laboristic one—that is, to a community in which employees rather than businessmen are the strongest single influence" (Brody, *Workers in Industrial America,* p. 158). Although Slichter severely overestimated the changes in the national culture that had typically denied a place for working people, his words do suggest the profundity of the changes during the New Deal era and beyond.

END OF CLASS?

The homogenizing forces of the market, the pull of the consumer nexus, the suburbanization of the nation, and the expanded role of the state all undermined or displaced much of working-class culture as an oppositional tool in the postwar era. This led many observers in the 1950s to speak of everything from the "end of ideology," to the "affluent" society, to the exceptionally "classless" United States. Even if class had once existed in American history, many commentators argued that the "labor question" had been solved by the twin pillars of affluence and intelligent application of sophisticated industrial relations strategies. As the labor historian Leon Fink has suggested, unlike the working-class culture of earlier periods, that of the twentieth century—especially the latter half—"is used less to account for *capacity* or *empowerment* than for *somnolence* or *passivity.*" While this may appear to be the case on the surface, others such as George Lipsitz's broadbased analysis of the 1940s and Jack Metzgar in his memoir-analysis of the steel strike of 1959, argued for the existence of a "culture of unionism" or a "labor culture" in the postwar era. Although relations between the rank and file and the increasingly bureaucratic leadership strained this "culture," workers understood on a profound level that class had not been eliminated from society and that their

union was what separated them—by one slender generation—from toiling in poverty.

Nonetheless, as the civil rights and antiwar protest movements swept across the United States in the 1960s and 1970s, the issue of working-class culture certainly seemed to be, if not gone, in eclipse as the nation focused on race, gender, and, by the 1970s, disillusionment with the state. Many of the major forms of working-class culture explored by the new labor historians seemed weakened, if not beyond repair. As Jefferson Cowie argued, culture and community may have still been sources of power and resistance in the postwar era, but they were nonetheless greatly weakened tools in the face of capital mobility and globalization. Similarly, two heartbreaking, if comic, memoirs demonstrate the breakdown of other cultural patterns. The shop floor, once the skilled workers' domain, had been so completely taken over by the latter-day incarnations of scientific management as to make life on General Motors' shop floor, in Ben Hamper's hilarious evocation of the assembly line, a constant battle for humanity and a sense of self through a madcap series of strategies to destroy time and preserve sanity in a world controlled by management and machines. Similarly, according to Thomas Geoghegan, the once vital "union culture" had been sucked dry by the legal and economic forces in the land. "This is post-strike America: the rank and file stay home and send out their lawyers," exclaimed Geoghegan in his reminiscences of life as a labor lawyer. Turning to popular culture, if the troubling "labor question" once threatened the social order, that issue had certainly been tamed by the popular television characters in shows such as *All in the Family, The Simpsons,* and *Roseanne,* in which the question of class was simply a problem of bad taste and buffoonery.

By the 1980s, the culturalist approach to the study of the working class had fallen on hard times. In 1984 a group of prominent labor and working-class historians gathered at a conference to explore the possibility of building a synthetic narrative out of a field that had succumbed to what many believed was the balkanizing effect of an overemphasis on culturalism in the study of the American working class (see Moody and Kessler-Harris, *Perspectives on American Labor History*). The approach led to too much fragmentation, too much romanticism, and was far too removed from larger macroeconomic structures, argued many, to offer a usable synthetic portrait of the American working class. Others, such as Geoff Eley and Keith Nield, looked back on the political and economic changes in the

1980s and 1990s, and questioned traditional conceptualizations of the idea of class all together. Leon Fink, in contrast, arguing for the continued vitality of the "new labor history" tradition, countered that "for labor historians, the study of culture always begins with the study of possibility, with the assumption that there is 'life below.' Rather than bring down the final curtain on culturalism, let us instead have the second act" (*In Search of the Working Class*, p. 194). If there is going to be a second act, it may well come from the new immigrant working classes in which historians found the study of culture originally so engaging. As the new waves of immigrants arrive from Asia, Latin America, and the Caribbean to do the difficult, strenuous, and low-paying work in the U.S. economy, the study of culture and class will certainly begin anew as these workers tap into their own cultural heritages in a struggle for accommodation and resistance to working-class life in the United States.

See also **Mercantilism; Industrialism and Its Critics; Radical Alternatives** *(volume 1);* **The Culture of Self-Improvement** *(in this volume);* **Success; Technology; Consumerism; Class; Marxist Approaches; Weberian Approaches** *(volume 3); and other articles in this section.*

BIBLIOGRAPHY

The Artisans' Republic and Slavery and Wage Slavery

Genovese, Eugene. *Roll Jordan Roll: The World the Slaves Made.* New York, 1974.

Levine, Lawrence W. *Black Culture and Black Consciousness: Afro-American Folk Thought from Slavery to Freedom.* New York, 1977.

Morgan, Edmund S. *American Slavery, American Freedom: The Ordeal of Colonial Virginia.* New York, 1975.

Nash, Gary B. *The Urban Crucible: The Northern Seaports and the Origins of the American Revolution.* Cambridge, Mass., 1986.

Roediger, David R. *The Wages of Whiteness: Race and the Making of the American Working Class.* New York, 1991.

Wilentz, Sean. *Chants Democratic: New York City and the Rise of the American Working Class, 1788–1850.* New York, 1984.

Young, Alfred F. *The Shoemaker and the Tea Party: Memory and the American Revolution.* Boston, 1999.

Culture in an Industrial Society

Clark, John, C. Clither, and Richard Johnson, eds. *Working-Class Culture: Studies in History and Theory.* New York, 1979.

Commons, John R. *History of Labour in the United States.* 4 vols. New York, 1918–1935.

Fink, Leon. *Workingmen's Democracy: The Knights of Labor and American Politics.* Urbana, Ill., 1983.

Gutman, Herbert G. *Work, Culture, and Society in Industrializing America.* New York, 1966.

———. *Power and Culture: Essays on the American Working Class.* Edited by Ira Berlin. New York, 1987.

Hartz, Louis. *The Liberal Tradition in America.* New York, 1955.

Montgomery, David. *Workers' Control in America.* New York, 1979.

Perlman, Selig. *Theory of the Labor Movement.* New York, 1928.

Salvatore, Nick. *Eugene Debs: Citizen and Socialist.* Urbana, Ill., 1982.

Thompson, E. P. *The Making of the English Working Class.* New York, 1963.

Commercialization of Culture and Leisure

Glickman, Lawrence B. *A Living Wage: American Workers and the Making of Consumer Society.* Ithaca, N.Y., 1997.

Peiss, Kathy Lee. *Cheap Amusements: Working Women and Leisure in New York City, 1880–1920.* Philadelphia, 1986.

Rosenzweig, Roy. *Eight Hours for What We Will: Workers and Leisure in an Industrial Town, 1870–1920.* New York, 1983.

Ross, Steven J. *Working-Class Hollywood: Silent Film and the Shaping of Class in America.* Princeton, N.J., 1998.

The New Deal Order

Brinkley, Alan. *Voices of Protest: Huey Long, Father Coughlin and the Great Depression.* New York, 1983.

Brody, David. *Workers in Industrial America: Essays on the Twentieth-Century Struggle.* 2d ed. New York, 1993.

Cohen, Lizabeth. *Making a New Deal: Industrial Workers in Chicago, 1919–1939.* New York, 1990.

Denning, Michael. *The Cultural Front: The Laboring of American Culture in the Twentieth Century.* New York, 1997.

Levine, Lawrence W. "American Culture and the Great Depression." *Yale Review* 74 (January 1985): 196–223.

Orsi, Robert Anthony. *The Madonna of 115th Street: Faith and Community in Italian Harlem, 1880–1950.* New Haven, Conn., 1985.

End of Class?

Eley, Geoff, and Keith Nield. "Farewell to the Working Class?" *International Labor and Working-Class History* 57 (spring 2000): 1–30.

Fink, Leon. *In Search of the Working Class: Essays in American Labor History and Political Culture.* Urbana, Ill., 1994.

Geoghegan, Thomas. *Which Side Are You On?: Trying to Be for Labor When It's Flat on Its Back.* New York, 1991.

Hamper, Ben. *Rivethead: Tales from the Assembly Line.* New York, 1986.

Lipsitz, George. *Rainbow at Midnight: Labor and Culture in the 1940s.* Urbana, Ill., 1994.

Moody, J. Carroll, and Alice Kessler-Harris. *Perspectives on American Labor History: The Problems of Synthesis.* DeKalb, Ill., 1989.

Part 10

GEOGRAPHY AND CULTURAL CENTERS

Part 10, *continued*

THE CITY

Stuart M. Blumin

"The towns," wrote the great French historian Fernand Braudel, "are so many electric transformers. They increase tension, accelerate the rhythm of exchange, and ceaselessly stir up men's lives" (p. 373). This expression nicely captures the transforming role that towns and cities have played in the histories of many nations, and suggests something of the feelings these energetic centers have generated among people, urban and rural, whose lives have been shaped in some way by the functioning of—one might say the "electric discharge" from—nearby or distant urban concentrations. Electrical power is at once beneficial and dangerous (and is generated by the means of the mutual repulsion of positive and negative forces), and so Braudel's metaphor also serves well to convey the complexities, and even the contradictory nature, of feelings about the city. In their influential book, *The Intellectual versus the City,* Morton and Lucia White discussed the predominantly anti-urban strain of thinking that seemed characteristic of selected American writers of philosophy, fiction, and political economy (and of America's most influential architect, Frank Lloyd Wright). But as the Whites themselves understood, the force of the city in American thought and feeling cannot be captured by so simple a formulation and so restricted a survey as they presented. Quite apart from the need to examine a much broader range of voices, "high" and "low," the positive expressions these voices convey must be taken as seriously as the negative; indeed, attraction and repulsion frequently must be understood as simultaneous and mutually reinforcing parts of responses more complex than mere approval or disapproval. Nor can any consideration of the city in American culture be ahistorical. The city as a place and community and the role it has played in American economic and social life have changed enormously over the course of American history. The character and strength of cultural responses to the city have changed as well, and perhaps to an equal degree.

Even a broad chronological division conveys the importance of historical change in shaping the presence of cities in American culture.

THE CITY IN COLONIAL AMERICA AND IN THE NEW AMERICAN REPUBLIC

The initial English and Dutch settlements on land that would later become the first states of the new American republic were generally centered on towns, and in some cases—Boston, New Amsterdam, Charles Town, Philadelphia—the towns created by the first settlers retained and enhanced their role as regional centers while growing more or less rapidly into communities comparable in size and appearance to European provincial cities. The planting of towns on North American soil was a deliberate act, reflecting the need for defense, administrative control, and the facilitation of trade and continuing settlement; it also, in several notable instances, expressed the exalted, even utopian, visions of colonial leaders regarding the societies they were creating in the New World. In his famous lay sermon aboard the ship that brought the first Puritan settlers of Massachusetts Bay, John Winthrop spoke of founding a "Citty upon a hill," an image easily joined by his fellow dissenting Anglicans to biblical notions of a New Jerusalem. Two generations later the nondissenting proprietors of Carolina and the Quaker founder of Pennsylvania would draw upon a post-Restoration wave of embellishments to English provincial cities in carrying out elegant plans for Charles Town and Philadelphia, both of which expressed the central role each town was expected to play in the construction of a superior New World society. "Wee shall avoid the undecent and incommodious irregularities," wrote one of the Carolina proprietors, "which other Inglish Collonies are fallen unto for want of ane early care in laying out the Townes" (Reps, p. 225). And a few years later in Virginia and Maryland, where initial town centers had been allowed to wither into insignificance within a rapidly spreading landscape of large and small farms, this baroque conception of the civilizing effects of a grand and orderly urban environment yielded impressive plans for the capital cities of Williamsburg and Annapolis.

However, none of these images or plans (nor the still later plan of Savannah, Georgia) expressed a specifically urban vision of the good society, and none of the towns that developed in America was invested with sacral significance, either by its founders or by subsequent inhabitants. Winthrop's exemplary "Citty" was the whole of Massachusetts Bay (to be built upon the "lawe of nature"), which he and other leaders quickly understood as a predominantly rural society of gentlemen and village-dwelling farmers, not as a walled Jerusalem or even a modern English town. Similarly, William Penn intended his Philadelphia to be a "greene Country Towne," essentially a seasonal social center (much like the emerging and still relatively rustic West End of Restoration London) for the rural gentlemen he hoped to attract to Pennsylvania with inexpensive sales of large tracts of land. As the historian Sylvia Doughty Fries has explained, both Boston and Philadelphia grew into commercial cities "in spite of, rather than because of, their founders' expectations. Those expectations had been for the recovery of a traditional rural society in which the new towns on the Charles and the Delaware rivers would serve only limited roles as regional trading centers and loci of moral and political authority in the midst of an agrarian landscape" (*The Urban Idea in Colonial America*, p. 108). As both cities exceeded these limited roles, as they prospered, and as they reached out to and even brought to their docks elements of the polyglot maritime world of the North and South Atlantic, they threatened the founders' visions with new and not always welcome influences, and within a decade of each colony's founding there were important political conflicts suggestive of a sharpening antagonism between town and country. Rural-urban antagonism may have been developing on a popular level, too, beyond the visible conflicts between merchants and magistrates over enriching or corrupting commerce.

However, urban animus was limited by the small size of America's cities. In 1700 Boston was a town of no more than 7,000 inhabitants, and despite the vast eighteenth-century expansion of commerce flowing through the handful of ports, no American city was larger than Philadelphia's 42,000 at the time of the first national census in 1790. The major American cities had continued to advance in many ways as regional centers, but the definitive city for all Anglo-Americans was London, and there was nothing in America that compared even remotely in size, influence, grandeur, squalor, or any other urban attribute with the British metropolis. America, indeed, had no metropolis, and the proportion of Americans living in its largest city (about one in a hundred) was but one-tenth of the proportion of English living in London. London's standard limited the extent to which rural Americans of the seventeenth and eighteenth centuries could conceive of Philadelphia, Boston, and New York—or still smaller regional centers such as Charleston, Baltimore, and Newport, Rhode Island—as alien places that threatened the larger culture. Morton and Lucia White have pointed out that eighteenth-century America's most prominent city dweller, Benjamin Franklin, paid no special attention to either the vices or the virtues of urban life in his written descriptions of American society. Even more strikingly, its most eloquent spokesman for rural life, J. Hector St. John de Crèvecoeur, wrote appreciatively of American cities as centers of a pleasant and edifying urbanity that was not at odds with the culture of country people (*Intellectual versus the City*, pp. 9–12). Crèvecoeur, indeed, was one of a number of American writers who appreciated American cities with a pastoral sensibility that, according to James Machor, substituted for the rural-urban dichotomy "an opposition between the overcivilized city, cut off from nature, and the organic city that maintains contact with pastoral values." Lacking a sprawling, squalid, and overpowering metropolis, Americans of the eighteenth century could perceive a "'middle' realm in which the city blends harmoniously with the countryside or contains within its own boundaries urbanity, complexity, and sophistication combined with the physical and social attributes of simple rusticity" (*Pastoral Cities*, p. 14).

There were, of course, negative voices, most notably that of Thomas Jefferson, who posited the city as a threat to political virtues that were best grounded in agrarian life. But even Jefferson's most forceful and most frequently cited anti-urban statement must be understood against the backdrop of this more inclusive pastoralism and the shaping influence of a very distant metropolis. "The mobs of great cities add just so much to the support of pure government, as sores do to the strength of the human body," he wrote in his *Notes on the State of Virginia* (p. 171). It is too seldom noticed that Jefferson wrote here only of "great" cities, of which America (and Virginia in particular) had none in its present or its foreseeable future, or that his statement about mobs and politics proceeded as much from the logic of his Whiggish political philosophy as from any immediate and tangible fears of extant American cities. That Jefferson did not expand upon this indictment accords well with his later somewhat grudging concession to the need for American cities (though not mob-ridden "great" cities) as centers for the kind of manufacturing that would gain for the young nation a healthy economic independence from Europe and its crippling wars. Most important, this post-Napoleonic Jefferson could look about him and still not see cities that threatened to infest the larger body politic.

THE NINETEENTH-CENTURY URBAN REVOLUTION

Thomas Jefferson died in 1826. Had he somehow lived another twenty or thirty years he would have had good reason to revive his old fears of the great city on American shores. The rapid industrial and general economic development that began during Jefferson's final years was both cause and effect of a striking increase in the number and size of American cities, and of a transfer of population from rural to urban environments that continued without interruption until the Great Depression of the 1930s. When Jefferson was elected to the presidency in 1800, the largest American cities were Philadelphia and New York, each with a population of some 60,000, and the inhabitants of all cities and towns larger than 2,500 amounted to only 5 percent of the total population. On the eve of the Civil War sixty years later, New York was an indisputably "great" city with a population of more than 800,000 (one can identify as well a larger New York metropolitan area, including the booming city of Brooklyn, that numbered more than 1 million), Philadelphia's population exceeded 500,000, and there were in the expanding United States at least a dozen other cities that were larger than any had been in the early 1800s. A much larger minority of the population, 20 percent, lived in the four hundred cities and towns that now spread inland to the most distant frontier, many of them along the new transportation networks that linked much of each region's town and country people to its largest urban center, and each region to the major eastern ports. This was an urban revolution of considerable proportions and effects, and it would continue into the twentieth century. By 1900, 40 percent of the American population, and by 1920 a majority, resided in cities and towns, and the nation was dotted with metropolitan

centers numbering hundreds of thousands (and in three cases, New York, Philadelphia, and Chicago, millions) of inhabitants.

The effects of this urban revolution reached well beyond the borders of the major cities. City life was transformed in many ways, even in the earliest decades of rapid urbanization, and if Jefferson dismissed the city (more accurately its "mobs") as a sore, nineteenth-century observers magnified it into a powerful, living organism, whose avenues and streets were arteries and veins, and whose parks and squares were lungs. Similarly transformed, and sometimes similarly expressed in organic terms, were the relations between cities and the larger society and culture. "In civilization," wrote the *New York Tribune* city reporter George G. Foster in 1849, "every powerful nation must have one intellectual centre, as every individual must have a brain, whose motions and conceptions govern the entire system. In the United States, New York is that centre and that brain" (*New York in Slices,* p. 63). This kind of statement was typical of a generation that sensed not only the growing dominance of New York with respect to other cities, but also the "governing" role of cities in a rapidly changing society. Most obvious was the role cities were playing in the flow of agricultural and industrial goods and of investment capital across vast areas of space. Less tangible but equally significant was their role in the flow of information and ideas. The geographer Allan Pred has fleshed out Foster's image of an urban-centered nervous system with fascinating tabulations of the numbers of letters handled by the post offices of major cities. According to Pred, more than 22 percent of the nation's mail passed through the New York City post office in 1852, a figure fully ten times the proportion of New York City residents to the national population. Boston, with less than 1 percent of the nation's people, handled nearly 8 percent of its mail. New Orleans handled 4 percent. Americans sent just under five letters per capita in 1856. Southern "country districts" sent 1.6, and northern "country districts" 3.5 letters. Businesses and residents of Boston, New York, and New Orleans sent forty, thirty, and twenty letters, respectively (*Urban Growth and City-Systems,* pp. 224–225).

America's biggest cities were increasingly the source of published as well as private messages. Cities had always printed a disproportionate share of the nation's books, newspapers, and magazines, but the industrial transformation of printing during the middle decades of the nineteenth century vastly increased both the total output of publications of all kinds and the concentration of publishing in big cities. The age of popular print culture began then, and it was a decidedly urban phenomenon. Before 1842, according to John Tebbel's estimate, only about one hundred books were produced each year by American publishers, and as late as the decade between 1810 and 1820 about half of the books of fiction were published outside the three major publishing centers of New York, Boston, and Philadelphia. By 1855 more than a thousand books were being produced each year, and fully 92 percent of the country's fiction books were published in these three cities (*A History of Book Publishing in the United States,* vol. 1, pp. 206, 221). Magazine publishing had been a small-scale and ephemeral affair before the 1830s, when several enduring literary and fashion monthlies set the stage for the emergence of mass-circulation magazines such as *Harper's New Monthly, Harper's Weekly,* and *Frank Leslie's Illustrated Newspaper* in the 1850s. All of the successful magazines were published in big cities, and the most widely circulating ones were all published in New York. Even newspaper publishing was becoming urbanized, despite the enormous expansion of the small-town, four-page, weekly press. In 1800 there were fewer than 200 newspapers in the United States, but by 1840 there were more than 1,400, and by 1860 there were 3,700, most of which were partisan county papers published in small cities and towns all across the country. The largest gains in circulation and influence, however, were by the big-city papers, and in particular by the cheap dailies such as the *New York Sun* and the *New York Tribune.* In 1800 there had been five daily papers in New York City, with a total circulation of some 2,500. By 1850 there were fourteen dailies with a vast circulation in and beyond the city that historians have estimated as high as 150,000. Pred has recorded a lower figure for New York, but tabulated some 43 percent of the nation's total newspaper production in the three great publishing centers (*Urban Growth,* pp. 222–223).

Big-city publications brought urban ideas, styles, and living standards to the majority of the population that still lived in small towns and on farms three or four decades before the mail-order catalogs of Montgomery Ward & Co. and Sears Roebuck and Company offered rural Americans a cornucopia of mainly city-designed consumer goods. The historian Richard L. Bushman detailed the diffusion of what he aptly called "vernacular gentility" from the cities to country people, mostly through the influence of the fashion magazines and other widely circulating publications of the pre–Civil War era. The prosperity produced by the antebellum "market revolution" manifested itself most clearly in the rising living standards of many middling city dwellers who could, for the first time, pattern their lives according to the more refined styles that formerly were available only to the wealthy. Out of this downward diffusion of gentility emerged a middle-class way of life that seemed also distinctly urban. " 'City' and 'country' were the words used to designate the broadest cultural regions" within what Bushman called "a geography of refinement" in the sensibilities of antebellum Americans. "The terms divided the world in half, implying refinement and polish in the city and coarseness in the country" (*The Refinement of America,* p. 353). This usage, though, expressed only the flow of influence, not the real geography of elevated material life or genteel aspiration. Small-town and country people could and did adopt city styles in clothing, home furnishing, and personal demeanor, and to the extent that they did so altered the "geography of refinement" in fact if not in general perception. In this way—as country people took up "city ways"—the city exerted a tangible and powerful force on the larger society and culture.

The city's influence on the style and tone of national life derived not only from the circulation of published words and images, but also from the direct experience of the city by rural people. As cities grew, and as they developed institutions such as elegant hotels, department stores, museums, theaters, restaurants, and pleasure gardens, they became more attractive as centers of both business and tourism. It is impossible to specify how many small-town and rural Americans came to the city as part-time or full-time tourists, but the numbers of temporary visitors grew enormously with the continuing expansion of railroad, steamboat, and other lines of transportation that led to each region's major cities. Travelers to seven Midwestern cities in 1850 greatly outnumbered each city's permanent population, according to Pred's calculations, and in sheer volume the draw of the great eastern metropolises must have been much greater. New York was surely one of the most attractive tourist destinations, and the names of its most popular sites and institutions—Broadway, Barnum's American Museum, Stewart's Marble Palace, to cite the best-known cluster—were part of the national language. To experience these places was to partake of the exciting and increasingly "modern" life that was taking shape in the cities. One historian of New York observed that many rural visitors first experienced such modern conveniences as indoor plumbing, steam heat, and gaslight by staying in a city hotel (Spann, *The New Metropolis,* p. 98).

If all of these influences seem positive, it must be noted that this was also the period in which the growing urban environment was becoming more daunting to small-town and rural people, and in which the image of the "wicked city" was growing more pervasive in American culture. For some time there had been a substantial if mostly underground European literature laying bare the evils of the big city, but there is little evidence that this genre of writing was influential or even read in America before the appearance of Pierce Egan's *Life in London* in 1821. Egan's sketches of London's high and low life were enormously popular in England, and, in part because of the relative dearth of American popular writing at the time, were read in America as well. The most impressive offerings of the wicked city theme to American readers, however, came only in the 1840s, after the translation into English of Eugène Sue's highly successful *Les Mystères de Paris.* Sue's complex tale of urban poverty, prostitution, crime, and redemption was extremely popular in the United States, and inspired a long list of American imitations promising to reveal the "mysteries and miseries" of New York, Philadelphia, Cincinnati, St. Louis, New Orleans, San Francisco, and even several smaller industrial towns such as Lowell and Worcester, Massachusetts, and Troy, New York. Only a few of these books were well grounded in the real life of emerging metropolises or industrial cities, most notably the widely read sketches of New York and Philadelphia written by George G. "Gaslight" Foster in the late 1840s and early 1850s. Even Foster's work, however, cultivated wicked-city motifs—prostitution and other crimes and debaucheries, mostly at night, dimly and eerily illuminated by artificial gaslight—that went far beyond dispassionate reporting of the conditions of urban life. For Foster and all these popular writers (and for the authors of more complex fictions and essays such as Nathaniel Hawthorne, Herman Melville, and Ralph Waldo Emerson), the city had become the plausible setting for the exploration of issues created by unsettling real-life changes associated with rapid and irreversible economic, technological, and institutional development—the railroads, factories, and new social configurations of wealth and poverty that threatened both the American "middle landscape" and the customary pace of history. Where does true value lie in a more impersonal, market-oriented world? What would and should endure in a world that is changing so rapidly? How do people in this world sort out truth and falsity, authenticity and

deception, in the marketplace and in human affairs? It was the "great city" that focused these questions in ways that smaller and more slowly changing communities did not. Rural innocence, wrote the Reverend Edwin Chapin in the mid-1850s, is simply less relevant to the modern world; it is in the city that one must search for "the moral ends of being" (*Moral Aspects of City Life,* p. 14).

The inescapable pertinence of city life forced an expansion of the genres of urban analysis in the decades following the Civil War. The titillating "mysteries and miseries" novels of the prewar period evolved into a more substantial and reportorial genre of books depicting the "lights and shadows" of cities increasingly conceptualized in terms of the polar opposites of wealth and poverty, beauty and squalor, virtue and vice, hope and despair. "These chapters have been written," explained one author, "to represent the outer and inner life that makes up the beauty and deformity, the good and evil, the happiness and misery [of the] great metropolis" (Browne, *The Great Metropolis,* preface). Serious writers of American fiction, most notably William Dean Howells, Edith Wharton, and Stephen Crane, turned increasingly to urban life to probe the moral and material hazards of modern life, as did the painters who followed Robert Henri away from rural pastoralism to the urban tableaux that earned them the sobriquet "Ashcan School." Social and political reformers wrote investigative reports on a variety of urban issues, such as slum housing, sanitation, and city administration, stimulating and feeding emerging movements of city planning and municipal reform. By the end of the century it was almost inevitable that the great Chicago exposition celebrating the quatricentennial of the European discovery of America should be conceived of as an ideal "White City," planned in a grandly obsolescing neo-baroque style that nonetheless proclaimed the urban future of this former wilderness and frontier nation.

The irony of the design of the Columbian Exposition of 1893, and the palpable contrast between the artificial "White City" and the real Chicago that lay just to its north, accords well with the tensions inherent in all these forms of urban depiction. Even in those that do not explicate polarities there exists a mutually intensifying allure and revulsion that belies simple oppositions of pro- and anti-urbanism. Many of those writers, thinkers, and painters who celebrated the city were attracted in part by the disorderly variety and moral conundra that impelled others to a more critical view, while many of the latter conceded the necessity, the inevitability, and even the achievements and the excitement of cities, even while they fantasized or planned a brighter—and usually urban—future. In any case, celebration and condemnation drew upon the same perception of the relentlessly rising significance of the city in American life. To ignore or blandly appreciate the city was no longer possible, as it was in the century of Franklin and Crèvecoeur.

THE TWENTIETH-CENTURY METROPOLIS

If it is difficult to separate pro-urban from anti-urban voices, it is nonetheless possible to claim that the former grew louder and more confident in the early decades of the twentieth century. Progressive reformers and planners were confident in their struggles against the slums, the bosses, and urban disarray, and in 1905 one of them, Frederic C. Howe, expressed this confidence by declaring in the subtitle of a well-known book, that the city (contra Jefferson) is "the hope of democracy." To others less inclined to politics the city was the hope of personal and cultural liberation. Parallel to the great body of urban writing in the late nineteenth and early twentieth centuries was a smaller but powerful array of indictments of small-town and rural America as hopelessly retrograde, confining, and deadening to the human spirit. This critique, which can be traced back at least as far as the writings of E. W. Howe and Hamlin Garland in the 1880s and 1890s, sharpened in the new century, culminating during the 1920s in the novels of Sinclair Lewis, at just the moment when metropolitan culture seemed to reach its apogee in a variety of "highbrow" and "middlebrow" testimonies to urban liberation. The sudden popularity of Sigmund Freud's theories about neurosis and repression (which eager young modernists could associate with traditional small-town mores), the white discovery of African American jazz, the creation of the "flapper" as a style and demeanor that challenged traditional notions of female propriety, and other fads of the "jazz age" (the journalist Frederick Lewis Allen added "faddism" itself) were primarily urban phenomena that helped identify the city as the locus of specific new modes of modern life that, more than in earlier generations, rejected rural tradition.

The year 1925 offered several events emblematic of this renewed association between the city—more accurately, the metropolis—and "modernism." Most obvious was the widely followed trial in Tennessee of the high school teacher John Scopes, who had been indicted for violating a new state law prohibiting the teaching in public schools that human beings evolved from other forms of life. Leading Scopes's defense was the prominent Chicago lawyer Clarence Darrow, while the local prosecutor was assisted by the nation's most famous spokesman for rural America, William Jennings Bryan. More importantly, the trial was covered by H. L. Mencken of the *Baltimore Sun,* whose dispatches constantly mocked the hopelessly backward and narrowminded "hicks" who persecuted "the infidel Scopes," and made the Scopes trial a battleground between rural tradition and urban modernism. A second such event of 1925 was the founding of a magazine, the latest in a string of new publications designed for a sophisticated urban readership. This latest imprint was to be called, simply and without apology, *The New Yorker.* Its introductory issue proclaimed (in what remains as a famous testimony to New York's special place in American urban culture), that the new magazine "is not edited for the old lady in Dubuque." Its purpose would be to "reflect metropolitan life," a phenomenon the editors clearly, and with no little arrogance, placed in opposition to rural and small town experience and culture (p. 2). Two other emblematic events of 1925 also occurred in publishing. One was a collection of essays, stories, poems, and plays, written mostly by African American authors, and edited by Alain Locke under the title: *The New Negro: Voices of the Harlem Renaissance.* The extraordinary flowering of black music and literature was specifically an urban renaissance, Locke explained, a consequence of the freedom, the "great race-welding," and the artistic cross-fertilization that followed upon the massive, continuing migration of black people from the rural South to the northern metropolis. "Harlem has the same role to play for the New Negro," he wrote, "as Dublin has had for the New Ireland or Prague for the New Czechoslovakia" (p. 7). The other was a quite different book, F. Scott Fitzgerald's *The Great Gatsby,* the first American novel to be set deliberately and significantly in the suburbs (and to a lesser extent the urban center) of the metropolis, and to probe in that setting the possibilities and the perils of modern metropolitan life. Unlike *The New Negro,* it is the perils that prevail, and the novel concludes on a note of poignant futility: "So we beat on, boats against the current, borne back ceaselessly into the past." It is an explicitly rural past that *The Great Gatsby* evokes here—no less so than did Mencken in Tennessee, the editors of *The New Yorker,* and the writers of the Harlem Renaissance—away from the "inessential houses" of the metropolitan suburbs, and away from the metropolis itself, "somewhere back in that vast obscurity beyond the city, where the vast fields of the republic rolled on under the night." This image resides somewhere between the validity of the rural past and the tragedy of Gatsby's hopes, but it is the latter, set essentially within those "inessential" suburban houses, that is the burden of this most modern of American novels.

Scholars continue to ascribe a specific character to the 1920s, in part because of the decade's sharp contrast with the fifteen years of depression and war that immediately followed. During the 1930s, the confidence in modern life that had characterized at least the more prosperous of urban Americans eroded significantly, and the massive cityward migration that had been steadily reshaping the nation since the early nineteenth century slowed to a near halt. This migration resumed with the return of prosperity, and in particular with the return to civilian life of millions of young World War II veterans. But it differed from the migrations of earlier eras, as did the mix of values and ideas that Americans seemed to bring to urban life. The rural proportion of the population shrank to less than one-quarter during the postwar decades, but within the rising urban majority there was a dramatic increase in more localized migrations from city to suburb. Postwar suburbanization was without precedent in its scale, and though the new suburbs of the 1940s and 1950s reflected in part the special needs of newly forming families in the immediate aftermath of fifteen years of depression and war, the momentum of urban deconcentration has continued into the twenty-first century. The effects on the shape of the city have been enormous. As early as 1950 the Census Bureau recognized the need to track the metropolitan as well as the urban population, and by 1970 found that more Americans were living in suburbs than in cities. By the last decade of the twentieth century the suburb had become the most characteristic form of American community, and significant and increasing numbers of Americans were living in sunbelt suburbs that spread vastly outward from small cities that functioned only minimally as metropolitan centers. Urban analysts today search for new names—"conurbation," "technoburb," "multicentered urban region," and "decentered urban field"—to describe this new way of inhabiting the earth.

Both continuing urbanization and new patterns of urban deconcentration have affected the place of the city in American culture, especially with regard to the propensity to associate the city with an influence that advances or threatens the larger society. If the city is everywhere, but is nearly everywhere decentered and diffuse, it is difficult to define its specific space within the larger cultural field—in effect, if everything is urban, then the meaning of urbanity can no longer be isolated, and the very idea of the city loses force. In fact, cultural innovation and influence are still significantly urban centered, as are powerful institutions of many kinds; indeed, there are tangible day-to-day evidences of this continuing disparity of influence even with respect to the locality-transcending electronic messages that seem to define a new, less urban-centered age. The mid-metropolitan location of the major television networks is tangibly reinforced each day on the popular morning programs, and on nightly news telecasts, whose studio sets of visibly massed communications equipment perpetuate the old idea of the big city as the brain and nerve center of the nation and the world. To be sure, there are still newer communications media—most notably at this writing, the Internet—that are more genuinely transcendent of place, and that promote or at least permit an understanding of influence that is even more decentered than the contemporary human landscape. And it is significant that the majority of people who do not live in cities are suburbanites who stand in a very different relation to the city than did the rural majority of earlier centuries. It is likely that the city is, after all, losing both its positive and negative force in American culture, and that goodness, wickedness, and other such qualities of collective hope and fear will more and more frequently be ascribed to things that have little to do with place. If cities continue in many ways to be the "electric transformers" of American society and culture, they are in this respect being dismantled and replaced by a more uniform grid, within which the lines of force are everywhere, and of physical origin irrelevant or unknown.

See also **Urban Cultural Institutions** (*volume 1*); **The Culture and Critics of the Suburb and the Corporation** (*in this volume*); **Salons, Coffeehouses, Conventicles, and Taverns** (*volume 3*); *and other articles in this section.*

BIBLIOGRAPHY

Barth, Gunther. *City People: The Rise of Modern City Culture in Nineteenth-Century America.* New York, 1981.

Bender, Thomas. *New York Intellect: A History of Intellectual Life in New York City, from 1750 to the Beginnings of Our Own Time.* New York, 1987.

———. *Toward an Urban Vision: Ideas and Institutions in Nineteenth-Century America.* Lexington, Ky., 1975.

Braudel, Fernand. *Capitalism and Material Life: 1400–1800.* Translated by Miriam Kochan. New York, 1973.

Browne, Junius Henri. *The Great Metropolis: A Mirror of New York.* Hartford, Conn., 1869.

Brownell, Blaine A. *The Urban Ethos in the South, 1920–1930.* Baton Rouge, La., 1975.

Bushman, Richard L. *The Refinement of America: Persons, Houses, Cities.* New York, 1992.

Chapin, Rev. E[dwin] H. *Moral Aspects of City Life.* New York, 1853.

Cronon, William. *Nature's Metropolis: Chicago and the Great West.* New York, 1991.

Foster, George C. *New York in Slices: By an Experienced Carver.* New York, 1849.

Fries, Sylvia Doughty. *The Urban Idea in Colonial America.* Philadelphia, 1977.

Howe, Frederic C. *The City: The Hope of Democracy.* New York, 1905.

Jefferson, Thomas. *Notes on the State of Virginia.* 1785. Reprint, New York, 1999.

Locke, Alain, ed. *The New Negro: Voices of the Harlem Renaissance.* New York, 1925.

Machor, James L. *Pastoral Cities: Urban Ideals and the Symbolic Landscape of America.* Madison, Wisc., 1987.

Pred, Allan R. *Urban Growth and the Circulation of Information: The United States System of Cities, 1790–1840.* Cambridge, Mass., 1973.

———. *Urban Growth and City-Systems in the United States, 1840–1860.* Cambridge, Mass., 1980.

Reps, John W. *Town Planning in Frontier America.* Princeton, N.J., 1969.

Rutman, Darrett B. *Winthrop's Boston: A Portrait of a Puritan Town, 1630–1649.* Chapel Hill, N.C., 1965.

Sharpe, William, and Leonard Wallock, eds. *Visions of the Modern City: Essays in History, Art, and Literature.* New York, 1983.

Siegel, Adrienne. *The Image of the American City in Popular Literature: 1820–1870.* Port Washington, N.Y., 1981.

Spann, Edward K. *The New Metropolis: New York City, 1840–1857.* New York, 1981.

Stout, Janis P. *Sodoms in Eden: The City in American Fiction before 1860.* Westport, Conn., 1976.

Susman, Warren I. "The City in American Culture." In *Culture as History: The Transformation of American Society in the Twentieth Century,* edited by Warren I. Susman. New York, 1984.

Taylor, William R. *In Pursuit of Gotham: Culture and Commerce in New York.* New York, 1992.

Tebbel, John. *A History of Book Publishing in the United States.* 4 vols. New York, 1972–1981.

White, Morton, and Lucia White. *The Intellectual versus the City: From Thomas Jefferson to Frank Lloyd Wright.* Cambridge, Mass., 1962.

PASTORALISM AND THE RURAL IDEAL

Susan Sessions Rugh

Pastoralism and the rural ideal can be defined as an affinity for land and farming as a way of life. The pastoral is a middle landscape between nature and civilization, often represented in the symbols of the garden and the machine. The pastoral ideal is borrowed from the literary tradition of the pastoral, with its images of sylvan meadows and the rural life as havens from the dangers of the world. The rural ideal envisions the countryside as a source of life, peace, innocence, and simple virtue, a refuge from the modern world. Pastoralism is a cultural alternative to the idea of the city as a place of noise, corruption, and alienation. Various strains of pastoralism have been identified as pragmatic versus romantic, but its lasting power lies in its conceptual malleability. Pastoralism and the rural ideal are associated with agrarian ideology, which is rooted in the Jeffersonian belief that independent ownership of land by the virtuous yeoman farmer was essential to the safety of the Republic.

The ideals of pastoralism have had a pervasive influence on American politics, society, and culture. Despite the bolder historical narrative of America's urban and industrial modernization, the rural ideal continues to exert a surprisingly strong hold on national consciousness. In the early twenty-first century, as we contemplate the virtual disappearance of the family farm, pastoral ideals still guide public policy and serve as a touchstone by which we measure the modern against the traditional. Furthermore, pastoralism surfaces in many forms of contemporary culture that manifest its lingering power in American life.

NINETEENTH-CENTURY PASTORALISM

Government Policies Thomas Jefferson argued that the nation should develop its agrarian interests because independent land ownership allowed the farmer to possess the virtue unavailable to those who owed their livelihood to others. Belief in an independent farm, a place to raise one's family and earn one's daily bread, powered government policies that opened the national domain for sale to individual freeholders, built roads and canals to move settlers westward, and opened domestic and international markets for American produce. Pastoralism was central to the expansion of the core of the U.S. population onto freehold farms in its newly acquired territories, and to the simultaneous displacement of Native American populations.

Belief in the agrarian way of life underlay the nation's acquisition of territory and the land policy that set the terms for the survey and sale of land to the nation's citizens. The Louisiana Purchase in 1803 doubled the size of the nation, and the Mexican War (1846–1848), and negotiations with the British for the Northwest effectively created the boundaries of our present continental nation by 1850. Land policy was likewise predicated upon a pastoral vision of the family farm. The terms of the Northwest Ordinance of 1787 favored the large landholder and speculator; the Jeffersonian revolution transformed them to favor the smallholder. Successive revisions of land policy carried out this vision, reducing the minimum purchase requirement and the price of land, offering credit, and legitimating claims by squatters. The result was a massive migration of farm families seeking to replicate the pastoral ideal in the West. Their migration was aided by the construction of extensive transportation networks, from turnpikes to canals to railroads, subsidized in large part by state governments hoping to reap the rewards of agricultural prosperity.

Pastoralism motivated the hunger of white settlers for farmland, thus providing a rationale for removing native peoples from their habitats. From the removal and forced march of the Cherokees in 1838, to the wars of extermination against Plains Indians after the Civil War, the government effectively subdued native populations by depriving them of claims to ancestral lands. Policy makers designed programs of settlement and civilization to convert Indians into yeoman farmers and farm families, complete with gendered roles of farm life. The Dawes General Allotment Act of 1887 is evidence of the power of rural ideals, as the government carved up arid land into farmsteads in the hopes that the pastoral life would "civilize" the Indians. For a variety of reasons such programs failed; the insistence on the pastoral ideal without adequate resources rendered some native tribes economically marginal and perpetually dependent upon the government.

Myth of the Garden   Henry Nash Smith has argued for the potency of the myth of the Garden of the World in the nineteenth century, "a cluster of metaphors expressing fecundity, growth, increase, and blissful labor in the earth, all centering about the heroic figure of the idealized frontier farmer" (*Virgin Land*, p. 123). Drawing upon the writings of Thomas Jefferson and J. Hector St. John de Crèvecoeur (*Lettters from an American Farmer*, 1782), writers in the post-Revolutionary era applied the myth of the garden to the vast trans-Allegheny region. Politicians and ordinary settlers alike realized that the huge quantity of land in the American West offered the promise of the fulfillment of the pastoral myth on an unprecedented scale.

Pastoralism was publicly expressed in nineteenth-century landscape painting, notably that of the Hudson River school. Landscape painting depicted the pastoral myth in scenes of wilderness undergoing civilization, as in the Course of Empire series by Thomas Cole. Later painters pictorially reconciled the civilization of the garden by featuring small figures at ease in the landscape. However, their ambivalence about civilizing the garden can be seen in the pictures of stumps of trees felled by the destructive ax, and the remote and insignificant trains camouflaged by the landscape (for example, George Inness, *Lackawanna Valley*, 1855). The tentative presence of both symbols in the landscape signifies the difficulty of reconciling the myth of the garden with the inherently destructive nature of the machine, which Leo Marx argued stood as a symbol of technology and progress (*The Machine in the Garden*, 1964).

Nineteenth-century pastoral literature likewise contemplated the tensions between nature and civilization. Natty Bumppo, the hero of James Fenimore Cooper's Leatherstocking novels (1823–1841), rejected civilization for the wilderness. Adherents of Transcendentalism embraced the pastoral myth in their affinity for nature, and some members of the group created their own pastoral environment in the short-lived Brook Farm (1841–1847) in Massachusetts. Henry David Thoreau's famous retreat to Walden made clear his belief that one could not completely escape the commercial spirit, but could occasionally seek refuge in nature. Thoreau and Ralph Waldo Emerson paid homage to the farmer in their essays on nature, as did Edward Eggleston and E. W. Howe, whose novels captured the local color and primitive nature of midwestern agrarian folk culture.

Southern Pastoralism   The nineteenth-century myth of the garden was inherently problematic for several reasons. Prime among them was the linkage between pastoralism and the independent yeoman farmer, a linkage that resulted in a philosophical split between North and South around 1830. Southern pastoralism idealized the civilized gentility of the established plantation, as evident in John P. Kennedy's *Swallow Barn* (1832), a novel featuring the orderly social relations of the old plantations of the Atlantic seaboard. Politicians in the South, notably John C. Calhoun, labored to retain control of western settlement, but the effort failed and by mid-century proslavery advocates resorted to defending the system on the basis of constitutional rights. The inability of southern pastoralism to accommodate the West, and the Union victory in the Civil War, allowed the myth of the yeoman to be transplanted into the trans-Mississippi West, where it continued to hold sway.

The Machine in the Garden   Powered by pastoralism, the spread of settlement in the West quickly posed a further contradiction: the threat of technology and civilization to the pastoral ideal. The market infrastructure of banks, railroads, and middlemen transformed independent family farming into commercial agriculture, resulting in a rapidly urbanizing West. The Republican Party included a homestead plank in the 1860 platform (160 free acres for settlers) that garnered the votes of farmers and German immigrants. According to Henry Nash Smith, the appeal of the homestead system "lay in the belief that it would enact by statute the fee-simple empire, the agrarian utopia of hardy and virtuous yeomen" (*Virgin Land*, p. 170). The homestead program was promoted as an outlet for discontented industrial workers in the East's crowded cities, but it failed because few laborers had the resources or inclination to go west. Instead, railroads and speculators acquired much more land than did homesteaders who faced increasing rates of tenancy. Nevertheless, the myth of the garden retained enough power to dictate a land policy that failed to recognize the aridity of the West, resulting in disaster for small family farms.

The widening disparity between pastoralism and emerging corporate industrialism began to weaken belief in the pastoral ideal, resulting in bitter agrarian protest by the agricultural classes from the 1870s to the 1890s. Told they were independent lords of the earth, farmers felt they were in thrall to railroad directors, bankers, and middlemen who controlled the market systems. The natural disasters of the period, including drought, an infestation of grasshoppers on the northern Great Plains, and a sequence of unusually severe winter weather in the late 1880s, made farmers feel as if nature itself had turned against them.

The fiction of Hamlin Garland, who witnessed the decline of the farmers' fortunes at the end of the century, sympathetically expressed disenchantment with the rural ideal in *Main-Travelled Roads* (1891). "Under the Lion's Paw" tells the story of a poor farmer desperately in debt to an unscrupulous landlord, while other stories depict the crude living conditions and arduous labor of the farming life. In Garland's view, the farmer was no longer a hero but a mere human struggling with nature and the forces of big business to survive. Garland's story "Rose of Dutcher's Coolly" and Theodore Dreiser's *Sister Carrie* (1900) dramatized the exodus of farm children to the city in search of the urban ideal. In *The Octopus* (1901) novelist Frank Norris wrote about independent farmers crushed under the wheels of industrial capitalism, conveying the frustration of the yeoman ideal.

No longer regarded as virtuous and independent yeomen tending a bounteous garden, farmers by the end of the nineteenth century were disillusioned with the pastoral ideal. From a position of philosophical dominance in the early republic, pastoralism as a system of beliefs faded in importance because it simply could not accommodate the changes associated with urban industrialism.

THE RURAL IDEAL IN THE TWENTIETH CENTURY

Rather than a mainstream current of American culture, the pastoral strain in the twentieth century was a powerful undercurrent that episodically surfaced in times of stress, notably during the Great Depression of the 1930s. Pastoralism took its strongest form in regional movements of art and literature identified with the Midwest and the South. Commitment to pastoralism and the rural ideal underlay social movements and provided a powerful impetus to formulating government policy.

Pastoralism Regionalized The Midwest has long been associated with the ideal of pastoralism, and geographer James A. Shortridge has argued that the region has even come to symbolize pastoralism. The regional identification of the Midwest occurred after the Civil War, and the linkage was completed by 1912 when the term Midwest was applied to the region. The pastoralism of the early twentieth century was optimistic, prosperous, and egalitarian, seen as setting a national moral standard. In the 1920s the pastoral image of the sturdy yeoman gave way to the idea of the farmer as hapless victim beset by hard times in the agricultural depression and drought. That disgust with rural society is best expressed in Sinclair Lewis's *Main Street* (1920), a novel about the stultifying aspects of village life, its pastoral ideals tainted by a rush to materialism.

The rural ideal in the Midwest was revived in the 1930s as the hardships of the Great Depression caused Americans to reassess national values. Two artistic movements represent this resurgence: a spate of midwestern farm novels that portrayed the virtues of rural life, and the regionalist movement of painters. Farm novels like those by Bess Streeter Aldrich relied on details of vernacular scenes to reflect the wholesomeness, individualism, and conservatism of rural life. Regionalist painters, disillusioned by the rise of European modernism, returned to the rural ideal as their subject to create a wholly distinctive American art. The "Big Three" midwestern painters—Grant Wood, Thomas Hart Benton, and John Steuart Curry—focused on pastoral scenes from the Midwest because they believed they so strongly evoked American character. Images like Curry's evocative vistas of harvesting in a thunderstorm or the dour couple in Wood's *American Gothic* (1930) symbolized for many Americans the central place of pastoral virtues in American identity. Regionalist painters became widely recognized and treated as celebrities, written up in popular magazines like *Time* and *Life*. However, by the 1950s their art was seen as parochial and primitive, and modernist art had become dominant in American painting.

The Nashville Agrarians, a group of intellectuals from Vanderbilt University, were responsible for the resurgence of pastoral ideals in the South. Led by John Crowe Ransom, Allen Tate, and Donald Davidson, the movement culminated in the publication

Grant Wood, *American Gothic.* Oil on beaver board, 29⅞ × 24⅞ in., 1930. © Bettmann/corbis

of *I'll Take My Stand* (1930). A collection of prose and personal essays, *I'll Take My Stand* spoke out against industrialism as harmful to religion, the arts, and society. Calling up images of the Old South, they advocated pastoralism as an alternative to the dominant industrial order. The book was surprisingly well received, although its critics noted how it avoided the mention of slavery by blurring the yeoman ideal with planter society.

Country Life Movement   The first widespread effort to address rural issues was the Country Life movement, a campaign to improve the quality of rural life. Motivated in part by rural nostalgia and belief in the yeoman ideal, Country Life reformers feared that the growing tide of rural-to-urban migration would result in economic stagnation, intellectual decline, and social deprivation in the countryside. Ironically, the urban professionals and academics who led the movement wielded the ideals of pastoralism to justify imposing urban standards of living on country people.

President Theodore Roosevelt (1901–1909) legitimized the movement in 1907 when he established the Country Life Commission, naming Cornell University horticulturalist Liberty Hyde Bailey as chair. The commission undertook a study of rural society, achieving a visibility that allowed the members to widely promote their recommendations. The reformers focused on the rural school, which they believed should revise its curriculum to include more vocational education in agriculture and domestic science.

Understandably, rural people resented the efforts of outsiders to remake their society in the urban image, particularly their suggestion to consolidate schools, the heart of rural community. Rural resistance to Country Life reformers limited the success of the movement, which diminished after World War I, but its effort to spread knowledge was carried out by a network of extension agents funded by philanthropists and, with the passage of the Smith-Lever Act in 1914, the federal government. Stronger resistance was offered to the school consolidation movement, which did not achieve momentum until after World War II, with the predicted consequences of weakening rural community. Ultimately, the movement failed because the reformers were unrealistic about sustaining agricultural ideals in the face of industrialism.

Back to the Land Movements   During agriculture's "golden age" in the early twentieth century, the back-to-the-land movement arose from Malthusian concerns that the growth of the population was exceeding the food supply. Philanthropists and industrial magnates like Henry Ford funded the migration of European immigrants to the countryside, where they established small agricultural colonies because it was thought farming offered the best chance of self-sufficiency.

The depression revitalized the back-to-the-land movement, and the government funded irrigation communities and relocated farmers to better land. Ralph Borsodi spread the pastoral gospel in *This Ugly Civilization* (1929) and *Flight from the City* (1933), an account of his flight from Manhattan in 1920 to farm in rural New York. He and his wife carved out a homestead, where they supported themselves through their own labor, even making their own cloth and furniture. Even more radical was the philosophy of Scott and Helen Nearing, who rejected machine technology in their quest for self-sufficiency on a Vermont farm beginning in 1932, as retold in *Living the Good Life* (1954). The Catholic Rural Life movement of the Midwest, which promoted farm ownership, was a more widespread approach to living on the land as a remedy during the depression but was only mildly successful. Building on the tradition of the back-to-the-land initiatives, in the 1960s a segment of the hippie culture sought refuge from the constraints of urban society in rural communes. Most rural communes failed because farming was too demanding and required a commitment the social dropouts were unwilling to make. Nevertheless, the idea of adopting the habits of the simple life to combat modern alienation spread widely, making *Living the Good Life* newly popular.

New Deal Farm Policy   Pastoralism and the rural ideal had its most significant impact on government policy in New Deal farm programs of the 1930s. Part of President Franklin D. Roosevelt's program of national economic recovery from the depression, agricultural policy made sweeping changes in agricultural production and rural society. The most influential policy maker was Henry A. Wallace of Iowa, secretary of agriculture and a strong supporter of the value of farming for the nation as a whole. To ensure a supply of affordable food and provide farmers a stable income, the government established programs that offered credit, established a system of pricing subsidies and production control, and encouraged agricultural cooperatives.

While predicated to some extent on the pastoral ideal, government farm policy benefited large operations more than the small family farm of

Jeffersonian agrarianism. In the late 1930s, stung by criticism that farm programs were not helping the rural poor, the government relocated farmers hit by environmental disaster to more fertile lands and established camps for migratory farm laborers. But these were short-lived and poorly funded attempts that did little to alleviate the problems of those at the bottom of rural society. The New Deal's broadest impact on the quality of rural life was electrification, an initiative spurred by Roosevelt's commitment to rural America.

Despite a severe farm crisis in the 1980s that resulted in the foreclosure of large numbers of family farms, New Deal farm policy remained essentially unchanged until significant revisions in 1996 severely reduced government support for farming. Nevertheless, government policy continues to subsidize the farmer more than it does other groups that have become economically marginal. Some have argued that this results from our attachment to the agrarian ideal, a sense that we will lose our civic virtue and weaken democracy if we let the family farm die.

PASTORALISM IN POPULAR CULTURE

Popular pastoralism in the late twentieth century was largely nostalgic, concerned less with democracy and more for the virtues of a rustic life as refuge from the modern world. American music, film, and television have drawn upon, and perpetuated, the pastoral ideal for most of the twentieth century.

Country Music   Country music, more than any other musical form, has been identified closely with pastoralism. An amalgamation of nineteenth-century stage entertainment, the folk music tradition, and "old time religion," country music has long embodied the simplicity and strong ties to a redeeming land characteristic of pastoralism. Country music tended to shift the focus of these pastoral characteristics from a strictly farm-based context to the more exciting environment of the cowboy. As early as 1908, cowboy songs gained popularity, especially Nathan Howard Thorp's *Songs of the Cowboys* (1921) and John A. Lomax's *Cowboy Songs and Other Frontier Ballads* (1910). Record companies and radio promoters tapped into this desire, and in the 1920s aggressive promotion of cowboy music came into full flower. Acts like Jimmie Rodgers and Billy McGinty's and Otto Gray's Oklahoma Cowboys achieved national status, but the pastoral imagery of cowboy music did not make a significant

impact upon American culture until the next decade.

During the 1930s it became clear that a significant audience existed for country music. Radio shows such as *The National Barn Dance* (1924) and *The Grand Ole Opry* (1925) drew millions of listeners each week. Gene Autry (1907–1998) stood at the head of the "singing cowboy" movement that became wildly popular in the 1930s. In 1934 he moved to Hollywood and claimed the title of "nation's number one singing cowboy." His films, including *In Old Santa Fe* (1934) and *Tumbling Tumbleweeds* (1935), all served to popularize the romantic myth associated with the virtues of rustic life.

This trend in country music continued until after the end of the Second World War. During this period country music's focus began to shift once again. Artists became more concerned with "real life" themes of jobs, divorce, and general disillusionment. A new style known as honky-tonk emerged, and with melancholic ballads like "Your Cheatin' Heart," "Honky Tonk Blues," and "Lovesick Blues," Hank Williams Sr. took up the role as the genre's standard-bearer. These tunes represented a shift away from the pastoral ideal for the first time since commercial country music had become popular in the 1930s.

The social turmoil of the 1960s resulted in a similar flowering of pastoral expression. Country star Porter Wagonner's popular musical television show celebrated the simple virtues and pleasures of rural life, as did Buck Owens's long-running series *Hee-Haw* (1969–1992). During the next decade the pastoral elements of country music became even more pronounced in the work of John Denver, the Nitty Gritty Dirt Band, George Jones, and Hank Williams Jr. These artists gave voice to the widespread longing on the part of many Americans to escape their complex urban and suburban lives and travel to the safety of the pastoral dream. In the 1980s several rock acts responded to the farm crisis and the urban economic difficulties of the Reagan years by performing music with pastoral themes. For example, John Cougar Mellencamp's "Scarecrow" (1985) set forth in stark imagery and haunting melodies the emotionally wrenching process of losing the family farm and the attendant way of life.

In the 1990s country music ascended to new heights of popularity as many singers crossed over to more popular music forms. Along with this shift came a conscious effort on the part of the most popular country acts to distinguish themselves from the twangy, down-home sound of the previous decades. The music lost much of its pastoral flavor in the drive to attract young listeners; however, songs like Tim McGraw's "Where the Green Grass Grows" and the Dixie Chicks' "Wide Open Spaces" indicate that the pastoral impulse still survives in country music.

Television Television did not fully embrace the rural themes of pastoralism until the 1960s, when their popularity soared. *Green Acres* (1965–1971) communicated the complex realities of the effects brought on by confronting, and ultimately dismantling, the pastoral ideal. The series featured a Manhattan couple who move to the country in pursuit of the age-old pastoral dream but discover that farmwork is oppressively difficult and that human nature remains the same, whether it is clothed in a business suit or muddy overalls. Western-themed shows like *Bonanza* (1959–1973), while not about farming, did feature pastoral ideals of independence and virtuous manual labor.

The Waltons (1972–1981) and *Little House on the Prairie* (1974–1983) aired somewhat later and carried a different message. These shows, produced in the wake of the sexual revolution and the drug-saturated counterculture of the 1960s, allowed Americans to indulge their desire for escapism based on the pastoral ideal. Although the lives of the characters in these programs are often depicted as difficult, they also exuded a sense of inner peace. The characters in these shows battle nature and the occasional urban intruder but never face crime, pollution, riots, drugs, or other problems that plagued America during the 1960s and 1970s. Especially prominent in these programs is the pastoral concept of close, traditional families working together to succeed under difficult circumstances. Although during the 1980s and 1990s some television programs with pastoral themes appeared, none achieved the success or longevity enjoyed by the earlier shows, many of which continue in syndication.

Film Moviemakers in America found early and phenomenal success with westerns, which placed a strong emphasis on rural values prominent in more traditional pastoral works. Will Rogers, the first true star of western-themed films, embodied the American ideal of the pastoral man. He starred in three films directed by the legendary John Ford that showcased his down-home wit and wisdom and his benign contempt for things urban. *Doctor Bull* (1933), *Judge Priest* (1934), and *Steamboat 'Round the Bend* (1935) took place in small southern towns in the late nineteenth century. Ford's most realistic look at pastoralism is his 1940 adaptation of John Steinbeck's novel *The Grapes of Wrath,* about refugees from the Oklahoma Dust Bowl. In this highly popular work, Ford brings the Joads to life and we watch as they find hardship and resolve to conquer it by virtue of their standing as "little people."

Comparable characters can be found in the works of director Frank Capra. Although not rural in setting, many of Capra's films feature important elements of the pastoral ideal. In *Mr. Smith Goes to Washington* (1939) and *It's a Wonderful Life* (1946), Capra explores the fundamental belief held by many Americans that a meaningful sense of self may be established in the shadow of the towering, impersonal facade of a modern, urban, hierarchical society. These characters represent, in fact, the lone believer in the pastoral dream, fighting for the values cherished by Americans against an unfeeling world.

While Capra and Ford took the idealistic route, other directors took a more realistic look at the pastoral ideal during this period. In King Vidor's *Our Daily Bread* (1934) a group of struggling farmers finds redemption through cooperation and labor in the healing American soil. In *The Southerner* (1945) French director Jean Renoir also explores the pastoral theme of redemption through land ownership. He tells the story of a drifting southern family who find employment in seasonal agricultural jobs. It is not until they settle their own land and work against natural disasters that they find the satisfaction and independence they had been seeking. In both of these films, the characters ultimately realize at least part of the pastoral dream, but this is tempered with the knowledge that the dream is neither fully attainable nor easily possessed.

In the midst of the farm debt crisis in the 1980s, farm films such as *The River* with Sissy Spacek, Sam Shepard's film *Country,* and *Places in the Heart* with Sally Field (all three released in 1984) displayed the frustrations of those who followed the pastoral dream. The main sources of difficulty for these farm families are natural disasters and predatory creditors, reflecting both the traditional hardships associated with farming as well as the contemporary financial crisis. The Chevy Chase feature *Funny Farm* (1988) and John Candy's film *The Great Outdoors* (1988) explored the same themes, but within a comedic, rather than a tragic, context, belittling the pastoral ideal.

NOSTALGIC PASTORALISM

The attractions of the urban life and the increased efficiency of agricultural production combined to power a great out-migration of rural people that accelerated after World War II. The loss of population, especially young people, endangered long-standing institutions of rural community, like churches and schools, and devastated Main Street in countless small towns. The pastoral image suffered a similar decline; the countryside, particularly the Midwest, was viewed as backward and outmoded. Adherence to the rural ideal waned as the reality of rural life took a downward trajectory, speeded by the farm crisis of the 1980s. By 1990 fewer than 2 percent of Americans lived on farms.

In the absence of an authentic experience on a farm, in the 1970s Americans created an idealized version of agrarian life that can be labeled nostalgic pastoralism. Rural America, particularly the Midwest, was seen as the home of traditional values, such as simplicity, patriotism, self-reliance, decency, and sensitivity to nature. Nostalgic pastoralism was a symptom of the general nostalgia of the period, which historian Michael Kammen has argued arose in response to an alienation from the problems of modern life (*Mystic Chords of Memory,* 1991). The backward look signaled a desire for a national heritage, a constructed past to provide solace in an age of cultural anxiety. Tourism to historic farms and villages skyrocketed as Americans sought to affirm traditional ideals in the supposed simplicity of the pre-industrial past. The opening of Disneyland in 1955 with its small-town Main Street symbolized this yearning for a golden age of community attached to the rural ideal. Nostalgic pastoralism involves not only visiting living farms and reconstructed villages but also collecting items of vernacular culture, such as folk art or antique furniture.

Pastoralism became commercialized in the 1980s in restaurants that featured country cooking and decor, country-themed magazines, and the revival of country crafts like quilting and woodworking. The fantasy version of country life had little to do with the realities of living in rural America, where farms were being foreclosed in large numbers. Reflecting their disillusionment with city life, Americans surrounded themselves with symbols that evoked country life, such as spotted cows and straw baskets. This romanticized pastoralism attempted to soften the edges of modern technology and preserve a notion of traditional American heritage in the countryside. Tied to the yearning for tradition were a conception of the old-fashioned family and a small-town community of commitment and caring.

Evidence of the nostalgic pastoralism in the 1980s was the popularity of Garrison Keillor's radio show, *Prairie Home Companion,* which attracted three to four million listeners. His companion book, *Lake Wobegon Days,* was the best-selling hard-cover fiction of 1985, selling 1.2 million copies. In his mythic fictional town of Lake Wobegon, Minnesota, Keillor created a sense of community and old-time values characteristic of small-town, middle-class America. Indeed, his sentimental pastoralism created a media community of listeners who not only identified with Lake Wobegon but also felt a sense of solidarity with other listeners. The escapist nature of Keillor's nostalgia, and its grounding in white middle-class culture, confirms it as part of the twentieth-century American pastoral tradition.

A narrower spectrum of society promotes romantic pastoralism by advocating a return to the small, independently owned farm as a solution to society's ills. The leading proponent is Wendell Berry, who in *The Unsettling of America* (1977) condemns industrial capitalism, blaming it for the "mentality of exploitation" that he believes afflicts society (p. 7). Berry argues for a holistic culture attached to land "by the investment of love and work, by family loyalty, by memory, and tradition" (p. 13). Farmer-scholars like Victor Davis Hanson (*Fields without Dreams: Defending the Agrarian Idea,* 1996) and David Mas Masumoto (*Epitaph for a Peach: Four Seasons on My Family Farm,* 1995) reaffirm the pastoral ideal as a safeguard to democratic liberties and as beneficial to family and community. Pastoral ideals motivate the sustainable agriculture movement that rejects industrial farming, especially the use of pesticides and low-paid immigrant labor. The idea of the family farm still tugs at the heartstrings of Americans, and the power of pastoralism and the rural ideal suggests a widespread belief that the agrarian way of life must be preserved to preserve American identity.

See also **Agrarianism and the Agrarian Ideal in Early America; Transcendentalism** (*volume 1*); **The Discovery of the Environment; The Natural World** (*in this volume*); *and other articles in this section.*

BIBLIOGRAPHY

Primary Sources

Bailey, Liberty Hyde. *The Country Life Movement in the United States.* New York, 1911.

Berry, Wendell. *The Unsettling of America: Culture and Agriculture.* 3rd ed. San Francisco, 1996.

Borsodi, Ralph. *Flight from the City: The Story of a New Way to Family Security.* New York, 1933.

Garland, Hamlin. *Main-Travelled Roads: Six Mississippi Valley Stories.* 1891. Reprint, New York, 1962.

Hanson, Victor Davis. *Fields without Dreams: Defending the Agrarian Idea.* New York, 1996.

Keillor, Garrison. *Lake Wobegon Days.* 1985. Reprint, New York, 1995.

Masumoto, David Mas. *Epitaph for a Peach: Four Seasons on My Family Farm.* San Francisco, 1995.

Nearing, Scott, and Helen Nearing. *Living the Good Life: How to Live Sanely and Simply in a Troubled World.* 1954. Reprint, New York, 1970.

Thoreau, Henry David. *Walden; or, Life in the Woods.* 1854. Reprint, New York, 1995.

Twelve Southerners. *I'll Take My Stand: The South and the Agrarian Tradition.* New York, 1930. Reprint, Baton Rouge, La., 1977.

Secondary Sources

Bowers, William L. *The Country Life Movement in America, 1900–1920.* Port Washington, N.Y., 1974.

Conkin, Paul K. *The Southern Agrarians.* Knoxville, Tenn., 1988.

Danbom, David B. *Born in the Country: A History of Rural America.* Baltimore, 1995.

Inge, M. Thomas, ed. *Agrarianism in American Literature.* New York, 1969.

Kammen, Michael G. *Mystic Chords of Memory: The Transformation of Tradition in American Culture.* New York, 1991.

Lewis, David Rich. *Neither Wolf nor Dog: American Indians, Environment, and Agrarian Change.* New York, 1994.

Malone, Bill C. *Country Music, U.S.A.* Rev. ed. Austin, Tex., 1985.

Marx, Leo. *The Machine in the Garden: Technology and the Pastoral Ideal in America.* New York, 1964.

Nash, Roderick. *Wilderness and the American Mind.* 3rd ed. New Haven, Conn., 1982.

Novak, Barbara. *Nature and Culture: American Landscape and Painting, 1825–1875.* Rev. ed. New York, 1995.

Sarver, Stephanie L. *Uneven Land: Nature and Agriculture in American Writing.* Lincoln, Neb., 1999.

Shi, David E. *The Simple Life: Plain Living and High Thinking in American Culture.* New York, 1985.

Shortridge, James R. *The Middle West: Its Meaning in American Culture.* Lawrence, Kans., 1989.

Smith, Henry Nash. *Virgin Land: The American West as Symbol and Myth.* 1950. Reprint, Cambridge, Mass., 1978.

Williams, Raymond. *The Country and the City.* New York, 1973.

REGIONALISM

Wilbur Zelinsky

THE REGIONAL CONCEPT

Before one can begin grappling with the nature and meaning of regionalism or its evolution and significance in American life, it is essential to elucidate the regional concept. Intertwined though they obviously are, *region* and *regionalism* are notions that are far from being synonymous.

The recognition of the region as an objective, or subjective, reality, or as a topic worthy of scholarly or administrative pursuit, did not materialize until the mid-nineteenth century. In earlier eras, the mapping and designation of portions of the earth's surface was relatively imprecise and casual. Within whatever major political entities may have existed, boundaries were fluid, contested, or unmarked, and the names of subordinate jurisdictions or general physical features would suffice for all practical purposes. But with the advent of sizable, increasingly centralized nation-states from the seventeenth century onward; the widening of the traveler's and reader's gaze with improved modes of mapping, transport, and communication; and the genesis of the rational, modern scientific mind with its compulsion to classify everything, it began to make sense to think about slicing sovereign states or entire continents into relatively homogeneous parcels in order to bring some rational order into an obviously terribly complicated world. Thus the birth of the region. In simplest terms it is the designation applied to an area of whatever size throughout which there is some sort of homogeneity or internal interaction as specified by the criteria used to define it.

Serious theorizing about regions and empirical efforts to delineate them did not come about until the maturation of professional geography and allied fields from the mid-nineteenth century onward. Throughout its modern history, the discipline has remained fixated on the regional concept (as it has on the equally pivotal notion of landscape) as one of its central concerns: how to define, describe, bound, classify, evaluate, and subdivide regions and set them within hierarchical systems, or deal with their dynamics. The technical details of this discourse are too complex for summarization here. (But see James 1972; Jordan 1978; Minshull 1967; and Steiner and Mondale 1988 [pp. 141–169].) Although geographers may have dominated the regional arena, the concept was adopted by a number of other practitioners in the physical, biological, and social sciences.

For a period during the early twentieth century, geographers envisioned as a kind of Holy Grail the possibility of identifying a set of total geographic regions within a given territory, that is, areas with definable borders within which all terrestrial phenomena—the physical, biological, economic, social, and cultural—nested together in reasonably close spatial concordance. But as it happened, this goal was soon shown to be all too illusory on both theoretical and practical grounds. Although the regional conformation of a given variable might resemble that of another in scattered instances, the much more general situation was for each type of phenomenon to adhere to its own peculiar spatial logic. Piling several sets of specific regions atop one another simply yielded cartographic chaos.

THE REGIONS OF AMERICA

In terms of practical results, the regional approach has generated some interesting and useful schemes in the United States and other countries. Thus it was feasible to reach general consensus by the 1930s concerning the identity and extent of the various physiographic regions of the United States and their subdivisions. In similar definitive fashion, geographers and their allies in other fields have mapped the country's geological, soil, climatic, and vegetational regions. With somewhat less assurance, largely because of the inherently transitory character of the phenomena, geographers have plotted the regional attributes of the American economy and

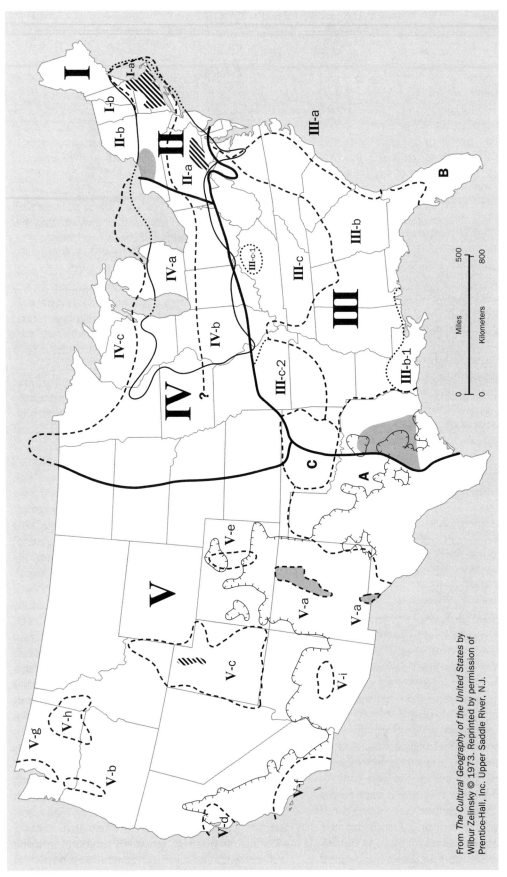

From *The Cultural Geography of the United States* by
Wilbur Zelinsky © 1973. Reprinted by permission of
Prentice-Hall, Inc. Upper Saddle River, N.J.

First-order cultural boundary

Second-order cultural boundary

Third-order cultural boundary

Documented core area

Presumed or incipient core area

Boundary of Socioeconomic Core region of
North America, ca. 1970

Northern boundary of significant Hispanic-American
settlement (after Nostrand)

Miles   0   500

Kilometers 0   800

REGION	APPROX. DATES OF SETTLEMENT AND FORMATION	MAJOR SOURCES OF CULTURE (listed in order of importance)
I. NEW ENGLAND		
I-a Nuclear New England	1620–1830	England
I-b Northern New England	1620–1750	England
	1750–1830	Nuclear New England; England
II. THE MIDLAND		
II-a Pennsylvanian Region	1682–1850	England & Wales; Rhineland; Ulster; 19th-century Europe
II-b New York Region, or New England Extended	1624–1830	Great Britain; New England; 19th-century Europe; Netherlands
III. THE SOUTH		
III-a Early British Colonial South	1607–1750	England; Africa; British West Indies
III-b Lowland, or Deep South	1700–1850	Great Britain; Africa; Midland; Early British Colonial South; aborigines
III-b-1 French Louisiana	1700–1760	France; Deep South; Africa; French West Indies
III-c Upland South	1700–1850	Midland; Lowland South; Great Britain
III-c-1 The Bluegrass	1770–1800	Upland South; Lowland South
III-c-2 The Ozarks	1820–1860	Upland South; Lowland South; Lower Middle West
IV. THE MIDDLE WEST	**1790–1880**	
IV-a Upper Middle West	1800–1880	New England Extended; New England; 19th-century Europe; British Canada
IV-b Lower Middle West	1790–1870	Midland; Upland South; New England Extended; 19th-century Europe
IV-c Cutover Area	1850–1900	Upper Middle West; 19th-century Europe

REGION	APPROX. DATES OF SETTLEMENT AND FORMATION	MAJOR SOURCES OF CULTURE (listed in order of importance)
V. THE WEST		
V-a Upper Rio Grande Valley	1590–	Mexico; Anglo-America; aborigines
V-b Willamette Valley	1830–1900	Northeast U.S.
V-c Mormon Region	1847–1890	Northeast U.S.; 19th-century Europe
V-d Central California	(1775–1848)	(Mexico)
	1840–	Eastern U.S.: 19th-century Europe; Mexico; East Asia
V-e Colorado Piedmont	1860–	Eastern U.S.; Mexico
V-f Southern California	(1760–1848)	(Mexico)
	1880–	Eastern U. S.; 19th- & 20th-century Europe; Mormon Region; Mexico; East Asia
V-g Puget Sound	1870–	Eastern U.S.; 19th- & 20th-century Europe; East Asia
V-h Inland Empire	1880–	Eastern U.S.; 19th- & 20th-century Europe
V-i Central Arizona	1900–	Eastern U.S.; Southern California; Mexico
REGIONS OF UNCERTAIN STATUS OR AFFILIATION		
A Texas	(1690–1836)	(Mexico)
	1821–	Lowland South; Upland South; Mexico; 19th-century Central Europe
B Peninsular Florida	1880–	Northeast U.S.; the South; 20th-century Europe; Antilles
C Oklahoma	1890–	Upland South; Lowland South; aborigines; Middle West

settlement landscape, and, in the process, have sometimes coined terms, such as Corn Belt, Manufacturing Belt, and megalopolis, that have passed into general parlance.

Application of the regional strategy has also produced relatively sturdy maps and analytical commentary in the realm of individual cultural and social items. The most conspicuous successes have been scored in the regionalization of American dialects and subdialects (Carver, Cassidy) and place-names. It has also been possible to set forth the religious regions of the country and to do the same for folk and vernacular architecture, the design of dwellings and barns, folk and popular music, sports (Rooney and Pillsbury), and, even, though rather fuzzily, foodways (Shortridge and Shortridge).

But there is one particular species of region that is especially relevant to any discussion of regionalism: the cultural. At a superficial level it might be regarded as no more that a territorial sandwich of individual cultural elements that happen to coincide spatially, at least more or less. But, using a more meaningful anthropological or sociological definition, the cultural region, or area, is a tract of land whose inhabitants are perceived by themselves and/or external observers to be participants in a specific, shared cultural system peculiar unto themselves. That is to say, these are human beings whose cultural attributes, traditions, and practices are believed to have closer kinship among themselves within the given territory than with the cultural attributes of any other community. Drawing acceptable boundaries around such parcels of humanity, deciding where a specific culture area gives way to its neighbors, and establishing cultural subregions within the larger entity, all these are challenging projects, but the general principle of relative uniformity within the posited regions stands as the core idea.

It is generally agreed that the United States contains five major culture areas: New England, the Midland, South, Midwest, and West (Zelinsky, *Cultural Geography*, pp. 118–119). It is hardly a simple picture. Each of the five primary regions contains a second, or even third, layer of subregions. Although depicted with unequivocal solid lines, almost all the interregional boundaries are subject to qualification and might be better shown as zones of transition. Moreover, a two-dimensional drawing cannot do justice to the dynamics of a constantly evolving system. The late-twentieth-century emergence of southern Florida and southern California, or the recognition of Louisiana's Acadiana, are not readily mappable. Neither are the relentlessly evolving personalities of all the culture areas.

Of the five major culture areas outlined in the accompanying map, perhaps the South comes closest to the ideal example of regionalization. Its cultural integrity and distinctiveness are universally acknowledged by both insiders and outsiders; the key characteristics—speech, religion, historical tradition, music, foodways, settlement landscape, pastimes, folklore—all tend to coincide snugly. However, the South does lack one desirable feature of the fully perfected, the truly ideal culture area: operation as a functional region, one focused upon a central commanding core surrounded by rings of outlying zones within which the purity of the regional character and degree of interaction with the core weakens with distance (Meinig, "Mormon Culture Region"). Such a pattern clearly prevails only in New England, and in the Pennsylvanian and Mormon subregions.

Three of the other macroregions—New England, the Midwest, and the West—are also recognized by scholars and laypersons alike. The strange exception is the Midland, and particularly its Pennsylvanian subregion. Although it has existed for nearly two centuries, and the set of Pennsylvanian cultural attributes are even more tightly packaged areally than the southern, its residents, and Americans in general, seem rather oblivious to its particularity, and academics have only since the 1960s ascertained its existence and significance.

But what may be most troublesome about the combined academic and popular wisdom is its acknowledgment of the presumed existence of the Midwest and the West as genuine culture areas. By any reasonable definition the Midwest is found wanting. Within the designated space there is a major diversity going from east to west or south to north. There is little semblance of uniformity in terms of ethnic composition, religion, language, or cuisine—or in economic patterns for that matter. Its inhabitants display only a weak level of regional awareness or pride or much sense of difference between their turf and the rest of the world. The Midwest's claim to regional status rests mainly on what it is not, an expanse that is non-East, non-South, and non-West. Its distinctiveness may be an absence of individuality, serving as it does as the middle, or modal, America.

The case for western regional cohesiveness is even more difficult to substantiate. Can there be two portions of the nation less alike than the Pacific Northwest and the Southwest, now widely seen as culturally distinctive (both shown in the map as pairs of subregions), yet both tucked into what Americans perceive to be the West? What does the Mormon subregion have in common with the southern Californian, or with the burgeoning Nevada subregion that would have to be added to an updated map? The West would seem to be the creature of myth and the vagaries of historic process. Any resemblance to the classic culture areas of the Atlantic seaboard or those of the Old World is purely fanciful. Yet, notwithstanding the facts on the ground, the stubborn reality is that both the Midwest and especially the West must be accepted as major subnational culture areas simply because that is what they are perceived to be by virtually everybody. Collective perception is what counts.

The South, the West, and the Midwest all belong to a category of regions that can be labeled "vernacular," a subspecies that can be defined as "those perceived to exist by their inhabitants and other members of the population at large. . . . Rather than being the intellectual creation of the professional geographer, the vernacular region is the product of the spatial perception of average people" (Jordan, "Perceptual Regions," p. 295). But in some instances, as with the South or New England, popular perceptions are ratified by scholarly investigation. A few vernacular regions—most notably such examples as the spatially vague Sun Belt and Bible Belt—have achieved general currency but have questionable claims to cultural validity.

Another mechanism for fabricating a vernacular region that can acquire a vigorous life of its own is through a combination of literary artifice and administrative fiat as occurred with Appalachia. The tract so designated occupies much of the eastern portion of the Upper South, a genuine cultural subregion, but also extends into sections of Pennsylvania and New York whose southern affinities are extremely problematical.

It is worth noting that cultural or quasicultural regions, including the vernacular and the spurious inventions of local boosters, come in all sizes and shapes. What the map does not reveal is the existence toward the lower end of the spatial scale of such genuine cultural islands as the Dutch American area in southwestern Michigan, the distinctive black-dominated Sea Islands of South Carolina and Georgia, the Amish enclave in northeastern Indiana, the Native American clusters in the Dakotas and elsewhere, or the many well-defined, self-conscious ethnic/racial neighborhoods in the larger metropolises.

THE BIRTH AND ADOLESCENCE OF REGIONALISM

The cultural diversity of the British North American colonies was apparent to local and foreign observers long before the American Revolution. Each of the thirteen eventually-to-be-united, rather arbitrarily bounded, states had a personality of its own, a distinctive mix of ethnic, religious, economic, and political components. Furthermore, the majority of them, most obviously Virginia, Maryland, Pennsylvania, and New Jersey, were characterized by decided internal diversity. In fact, the severing of West Virginia in 1863 from the grossest of the original colonies was a logical bit of applied cultural geography.

Alongside the more localized complexities, sectional differences had arisen by the mid-eighteenth century: the broad conflicting economic, and ultimately political, interests of the northern (New England and middle Atlantic) colonies versus those of the southern. Later, of course, this clash of materialistic mind-sets was fleshed out in mappable fashion by the compromise siting of the national capital in a neutral zone between the two sections. Not to be confused with regionalism, sectionalism remained alive and vigorous throughout the nineteenth century and is still a force to be reckoned with today. It involves blocks of states, usually northern, southern, and western, pursuing their individual economic and political goals in the halls of Congress or in Washington's administrative agencies. Such activity has only the most remote relationship to cultural realities or authentic regionalism.

Are the individual fifty states repositories of regional sentiment? Weakly or not at all. (What does it mean to be a Marylander or an Illinoian?) But there is one notable exception. In large part because of their unique political history, Texans revel in their Texanness and go to some lengths to make the rest of the world aware of their distinctiveness (Francaviglia). This in spite of the fact of the considerable internal cultural variety within the Lone Star State. Residents of other states do acknowledge their addresses, of course, and may take some pride in the affiliation in question, and state-specific laws and regulations do make for certain interstate differences in behavior, but as regionalism began to flourish, it pretty much ignored state boundaries.

The earliest inklings of a meaningful regional movement can be detected in the local color literature that became popular in the 1880s and 1890s, as well as in the fiction, humor, and verse initially exploiting mostly New England and the South, and later the West. With few exceptions, the literary quality of this initial wave of regional writing was not outstanding, seldom attaining the level of Ellen Glasgow or Edith Wharton, in contrast to what was to come later.

Scholars can date the emergence of that latter-day "ism" they call regionalism to the 1920s. How to define it? It is that mode of thinking and feeling that envisions the region as something to be sought out, studied, nurtured, cherished, and celebrated because of its intrinsic virtue and value in human affairs. Not just any region, but the whole array of them. Thus this generic sentiment does not confine itself necessarily to promoting the particular locality and need not be some type of parochial chauvinism.

Among the more zealous apostles, such as the bioregionalists or such scholar-advocates as Benton Mackaye, Lewis Mumford, and Patrick Geddes, regionalism became a cause akin to a religious faith, a utopian formula for optimizing social and ecological salubrity (Dorman, Wilson). It is worth noting that, except for the fervent few, regionalism did not consciously, overtly displace other isms such as nationalism, politicalism, or the standard theologies, such as Protestantism. It was usually something superimposed upon other greater or lesser enthusiasms.

The fact that the regionalist ideology materialized when it did was not mere happenstance: "the regionalist movement appear[ed] as a result of 'a pervasive sense of malaise, of cultural crisis' that began in the 1920s. The broad sources of the crisis included the work of Freud, Einstein, and Nietzsche, and the social byproducts of modernization, especially consumerism" (Wilson, p. x). And, of course, other factors were involved, not all necessarily proximate, among them the aftereffects of World War I and its disillusionments, a chronic farm crisis, the weakening hold of the mainline religions, disenchantment with the growing cities, the cynicism of much nonregional fiction, and a debunking fad in historical scholarship.

The initial phase of American regionalism reached its climax during the prolonged depression of the 1930s. Numerous regionally flavored novels began to appear, some of the more successful artists produced canvases drenched with regional themes, and various programs sponsored by the New Deal agencies generated much in the way of regionally oriented publications, murals, and drama. The notion of regional planning, largely under federal auspices, came under serious consideration and was perhaps most fully realized in the Tennessee Valley Authority. Not too coincidentally, this was also the decade when folklore studies began to become academically respectable. Within the sociological realm, the regional creed was cultivated with special fervor by Howard Odum and his colleagues at the University of North Carolina at Chapel Hill. The 1930s also brought about the first serious stirrings of interest in ethnic topics in scholarly circles. And, of course, in many ways the ethnic theme is the sibling of the regional. This was also the period when regional theses, books, and articles, most of them quite formulaic and undistinguished, had become one of the more dominant modes of activity amid the still small community of academic geographers.

If the trends set in motion before World War II continued through the 1940s, there was a decided falling off during the flush 1950s and 1960s. It may have been the result of material abundance, the absolute triumph of consumerism, and a preoccupation with national and international issues during the cold war. Regionalism did not vanish, it had simply lost much of its original appeal. Interestingly enough, this was the time when the regional approach fell into serious disrepute among professional geographers as the so-called Quantitative Revolution engulfed the discipline.

THE GOLDEN AGE OF REGIONALISM

Beginning in the 1970s and continuing into the twenty-first century, Americans have witnessed a resurgence of regionalism or what some have styled the new regionalism. This was not a chance occurrence; it was one of several aspects of an unprecedented zeitgeist, being associated as it was with several other novel developments. Moreover, it was a phenomenon that transcended American borders. There has been a concurrent rise in ethnic/regional movements and activity in France, Great Britain, Spain, Italy, and elsewhere in western Europe, presumably activated by the same general causes, quite apart from the chronic restiveness of all manner of aggrieved ethnic communities in the remainder of Eurasia and in Africa and Latin America. The western European (and Canadian) situation is one in which all available forms of cultural assertion are mobilized, but departs from the American case by virtue of the frequent salience of the political factor, the quest for some degree of autonomy or even outright independence. Unlike their New World brethren, the localities in question may claim primordiality, centuries-long retention of regional peculiarity, and perhaps some past measure of self-determination. In the United States, on the other hand, however lively the drive for recognition and admiration, the region nurses no dream of breaking away from the national polity. (The causation of the Civil War is too complex a matter to be ascribed solely to the pressures of regional culture).

The most solid evidence for the vitality of the new regionalism is its institutionalization. Quite apart from various official and quasi-governmental bodies that address regional or multi-state issues today, there are quite a few universities, beginning with the University of Nebraska's Center for Great Plains Studies founded in 1976, that house regional research and study centers, as well as the founding of regional, along with state, museums. Too numerous to be listed are the campus-based presses that pursue a regional mission, evidently finding a responsive market for their wares. The most ambitious of these publications are the regional encyclopedias, the occasional atlas, and other such reference works, including the exemplary *Encyclopedia of Southern Culture, Oxford History of the American West,* and the forthcoming encyclopedias for New England and the Great Plains. Trade publishers are not far behind as they feature regional fiction, history, travel accounts, photography, cookbooks, and other varieties of nonfiction in substantial volume. Then, despite their shakier fiscal status, the current era has seen more regional literary magazines than ever before. Also not to be overlooked is the recent vigor of regional theater.

The tradition of writing worthy, sometimes truly exceptional, regional fiction that began early in the twentieth century has continued and strengthened with the passage of time, and keeping in stride with the same has been the profusion of critical analysis and commentary (Steiner and Mondale, pp. 333–378). Few would argue with the proposition that the South retains primacy as the heartland of great regional writing with its veritable galaxy of novelists, essayists, and others who command national and international attention, although other regions can boast of their literary stars.

A notable addition to the older roster of regions is the Southwest, with a recent efflorescence of highly readable items based within that corner of the nation, a development paralleling the successes of southwestern visual art and crafts. Straddling the tenuous boundary between the regional and the ethnic have been the many Latino, African American, Asian American, and Native American practitioners of fiction, verse, film, and drama who have earned critical acclaim.

Still within the confines of the scholarly world is another development or genre diagnostic of the vigor of the new regionalism: the in-depth geographic/anthropological/historic treatise; these are many-sided works that deal with their territories in a nuanced, sophisticated manner. Following the pioneering efforts of Walter Prescott Webb, there are such outstanding examples as William Cronon's studies of New England and the Midwest, Josh Shelton Reed's many treatments of an enduring South, and Paul Starrs's diagnosis of an evolving West.

Notable in the output of these and other such scholars is a sensitivity to the temporal aspect. Theirs are constantly, complexly changing entities, a far cry from the static places of popular myth. Still another clue to the altered temper of the contemporary scene is the revival of the once-reviled regional theme among the avant-garde of twenty-first-century geographers. They have discovered the urgency of "sense of place" and have been experimenting with new approaches to regional analysis while invoking all the fashionable shibboleths of current social theory.

But the truly compelling evidence of the potency of new regionalism lies everywhere in the world of popular culture. A glance at the magazine rack operated by any respectable news vendor reveals the existence of such highly profitable enterprises as *Southern Living, Sunset, Yankee,* and *Arizona Highways.* In a related development, there is scarcely a town of any size left in the United States today that does not boast of one or more periodicals devoted to the city and its environs.

Few activities attract more devotees or dollars than spectator sports, and it is noteworthy that regional leagues continue to sustain their vigor, especially in the collegiate realm (Rooney and Pillsbury). But competitive numbers are being rung up by the increasingly popular regional festival. These affairs, usually annual in frequency, and often with ethnic overtones, have proliferated remarkably in recent years, offering the patron an enticing array of local and regional music, dance, costume, crafts, doodads, and, above all, food. One need not travel to the region to relish its cuisine. In concert with the related boom in ethnic items, there exists an extraordinary profusion of eating places, many of them franchise operations that feature southern, New England, Cajun, western, and southwestern items, as do some of the food programs on television. The supermarkets have followed suit of late with ample shelf space for regional as well as ethnic specialties, while every well-stocked bookshop can supply the adventurous customer with quite an array of regional cookbooks. We can all be vicarious regionalists.

For the average American no financial decision is greater than the building of a new home or purchase of an existing one. And one of the crucial elements in that decision is the appeal of the architectural design. In some instances, as in the Pacific Northwest and portions of California, it is a freshly evolved regional style that wins over the home buyer. Or, as happens in the more conservative parts of Pennsylvania and Maryland, the residents are happy enough with modestly updated versions of house types with deep, continuous roots in the immediate landscape. But when one considers the various spots in Louisiana's Acadiana, the suburbs of almost any Deep Southern city, any of the burgeoning towns or exurbs of the Southwest, or the German American tracts of central Texas, the retro trend is unmistakable: the mimicking and updating of old indigenous building styles. The practice also applies to commercial construction. There may be no other example so extreme or archaeological as Santa Fe, New Mexico, but similar gestures are not rare elsewhere. Even such usually highly standardized franchises as McDonald's have found it expedient to clamber aboard the regional bandwagon in some localities in their choice of outer and interior decor.

LARGER IMPLICATIONS

Such large, complex social-psychological phenomena as regionalism do not come to pass by chance or as isolated affairs. As already suggested, regionalism is associated with other recent developments and can be regarded as one of many manifestations of a late phase of modernism or, as some people believe, postmodernism.

At a superficial level, one might consider regionalism to be just one of a wide array of casual amusements in an age when mobile, distraction-seeking Americans, equipped as they are with all the latest electronic modes of verbal and visual communication, are able to flit hither and yon with ease. Seen as such, it becomes an aspect of tourism, an industry, incidentally, which has recently reached topmost rank worldwide in dollar terms. And the hedonist need not actually enter the region to savor its delights. Its particularities are portable via the printed word, video, compact disc, boutique, gift shop, and restaurant.

But regionalism as a good thing has subsurface connections with other rather less frivolous developments. Its kinship with ethnic movements in the United States and elsewhere is too obvious to call for explanation. But it is interesting to note that these two ways of expressing collective angst are not altogether in sync. Although regionalism had made itself conspicuous by the 1920s, ethnic issues in the United States did not enter general discourse until the 1960s and 1970s. Indeed the concept, the very term "ethnicity," failed to attain general currency until those recent decades. Perhaps it required the black pride and civil rights movement that began in the 1950s and the great postwar influx of nontraditional immigrants to catalyze national sensitivities toward the other.

The close emotional interrelationship between the new regionalism and the environmental movement is clear and unequivocal. In this instance, the two developments are synchronous, both feeding off a deep anxiety over the health and viability of places. And if environmental concerns do persist or even intensify, as seems all too likely, then such worries will probably help perpetuate regional sensibilities.

Quite possibly the most fundamental of all the grander associations between regionalism and other latter-day social developments has to do with what might be called the nostalgia syndrome. At some point during the final third of the twentieth century there came about a profound reversal in the chronological gaze of first-world populations. No longer did Americans and others, as devout disciples of the modernist doctrine of perpetual progress, peer forward eagerly toward a future laden with ever greater wonders and delights. Instead the mood has gradually turned sour as frustrations mounted over what material progress has actually delivered in terms of alienation, all manner of free-floating anxieties, urban ruination, environmental havoc, social tensions, and the perception of the hollowness of the consumerist vision. The reaction has been to seek refuge in the past. Thus the vogue for antiques, replicas, historical pageants, parks and museums, reenactments of battles and other events, and the new fashionableness of "old-timey" personal names, especially of the biblical variety. The resurgence of fundamentalism among adherents of the Christian, Jewish, Islamic, and other faiths may also be symptomatic of the trend.

But perhaps the most revealing of all such items has been the boom in genealogical activity. Never before have so many families and individuals begun searching for their ancestral roots. And clearly allied to this passion for some grounding in the real or imagined verities of ages past is a collective rootlessness that impels the larger society to find solace in real or imagined regions. It is part of the quest for identity in an ever-more-bewildering, disorienting world. Furthermore, in a world in which Americans find themselves ever more reliant upon vast global economic and social dealings, the region represents a spatial as well as temporal reversion. The global and the regional, or local, Americans have begun to realize, interact dialectically; the homogeneity and blandness of the former engendering new, intimate kinds of spatial uniqueness.

What are the future prospects for regionalism? It is both foolish and impossible to hazard forecasts about anything so complex and also contingent upon so many other factors beyond reckoning. All that one may safely guess is that as long as current conditions, or something like them, prevail, regionalism will sustain its vitality. But, given the rapidity and profundity of twenty-first-century change, such stasis seems improbable.

BIBLIOGRAPHY

Carver, Craig M. *American Regional Dialects: A Word Geography.* Ann Arbor, Mich. 1987. The best tableau and analysis to date of the regional dialects of American English.

Cassidy, Frederic G., ed. *Dictionary of American Regional English.* 3 vols. Cambridge, Mass., 1985–1996. Covering *A* to *O* thus far, this monumental repository of information deals with virtually every aspect of regional usage of the language.

Coan, Otis W., and Richard G. Lilliard, eds. *America in Fiction: An Annotated List of Novels That Interpret Aspects of American Life in the United States, Canada, and Mexico.* Palo Alto, Calif., 1967.

Cronon, William. *Changes in the Land: Indians, Colonists, and the Ecology of New England.* New York, 1983.

———. *Nature's Metropolis: Chicago and the Great West.* New York, 1991.

Dorman, Robert L. "Revolt of the Provinces: The Regionalist Movement in America, 1920–1945." In *The New Regionalism,* edited by Charles Reagan Wilson, pp. 1–17. Jackson, Miss., 1998.

Francaviglia, Richard V. *The Shape of Texas: Maps as Metaphors.* College Station, Tex., 1995. The Lone Star symbol as a potent expression of Texas pride both locally and throughout the world.

Garreau, Joel. *The Nine Nations of North America.* Boston, 1981. A highly readable account of "the way North America really works," at least in regional terms.

James, Preston E. *All Possible Worlds: A History of Geographical Ideas.* Indianapolis, Ind., 1972.

Jenson, Merrill, ed. *Regionalism in America.* Madison, Wis., 1951. An indispensable summation of American regional theory.

Jordan, Terry G. "Perceptual Regions in Texas." *Geographical Review* 68 (1978): 295–307. An exemplary study of vernacular regions and their complexities.

———. "The Concept and Method." In *Regional Studies,* edited by Glen E. Lich, pp. 8–24. College Station, Tex., 1992. A most informative guide to the ways in which geographers deal with the recognition and delineation of regions.

Meinig, Donald W. "The Mormon Culture Region: Strategies and Patterns in the Geography of the American West, 1847–1964." *Annals of the Association of American Geographers* 55 (1965): 213–217.

——. *The Shaping of America: A Geographical Perspective of 500 Years of History.* Vol. 3, *Transcontinental America 1850–1915.* New Haven, Conn., 1998. Among other matters this volume treats "The Emergence of American Wests" in magisterial fashion.

Minshull, Roger. *Regional Geography: Theory and Practice.* Chicago, 1967. An effective, clearly written introduction to the intricacies of European and American regional theory.

Reed, John Shelton. *The Enduring South: Subcultural Persistence in Mass Society.* Lexington, Mass., 1972.

Rooney, John F., Jr., and Richard Pillsbury. *A Geography of American Sport.* New York, 1992.

Shortridge, Barbara G., and James R. Shortridge, eds. *The Taste of American Place: A Reader on Regional and Ethnic Foods.* Lanham, Md., 1998.

Shortridge, James R. *The Middle West: Its Meaning in American Culture.* Lawrence, Kans., 1989.

Starrs, Paul F. *Let the Cowboy Ride: Cattle Ranching in the American West.* Baltimore, 1998. More than the title suggests, an excellent account of the evolution of the West in both myth and actuality.

Steiner, Michael, and Clarence Mondale. *Region and Regionalism in the United States: A Source Book for the Humanities and Social Sciences.* New York, 1988. A superb annotated guide to the literature.

Whittlesey, Derwent. "The Regional Concept and the Regional Method." In *American Geography: Inventory and Prospect,* edited by Preston E. James and Clarence F. Jones, pp. 19–68. Syracuse, N.Y., 1954.

Wilson, Charles Reagan. "Introduction." In *The New Regionalism.* Jackson, Miss., 1998.

Zelinsky, Wilbur. *The Cultural Geography of the United States.* Englewood Cliffs, N.J., 1992. Chapter 4 (pp. 109–140) deals with the regional dimensions of the American cultural system.

——. "The Changing Character of North American Culture Areas." In *Regional Studies,* edited by Glen E. Lich, pp. 113–134. College Station, Tex., 1992.

NEW ENGLAND

Thomas J. Brown

New England has often—doubtless too often—served as the focal point for overviews of American cultural and intellectual history. This centrality partly reflects the undeniable importance of the regional experience. New England was the American stage for such vital movements as Puritanism and Transcendentalism and a pivot in the American Revolution, the industrial revolution, the emergence of radical abolitionism, and other crucial developments. Its prominence in interpretations of American thought also reflects the frequency with which these assessments have emanated from New England. Many observers have pointed out ways in which the tendency to see New England as a synecdoche for the United States distorts understanding of the country. The same tendency to see regionalism in the South or the West but to find America in New England also neglects the construction of a regional identity that has sometimes but not always converged with local visions of the nation.

Representations of New England, framed by outsiders as well as residents, only partly illuminate the regional culture. Elites often used ideas about New England to exclude religious dissidents, immigrants, and other groups. Within the most powerful traditions, moreover, self-definition was merely one mode of thought. The invocation of a divine covenant with New England, for example, was a single strand of the complex Puritan cosmology. The regional image offers only a limited view of the regional imagination; localism is in some ways a highly misleading key to New England culture. Perhaps the most dynamic feature in the making of a creative tradition was the readiness to look outward, from participation in the continuing Reformation to the systematic promotion of European travel and study during the nineteenth century. Emphasis on the definitions of New England understates the continuities that linked the Puritan theologian Jonathan Edwards's wrestling with Newtonian physics, the Transcendental leader Ralph Waldo Emerson's fascination with Eastern religions, and the intricate network of transatlantic relationships that made the poet-essayist James Russell Lowell the godfather of the British author Virginia Woolf.

Provincialism has often been a cosmopolitan strategy, however, and the self-constructions of New England suggest the different intellectual movements that have most characterized the region. The phases of this development are not entirely separate; they overlap and interact. They are also connected by a variety of institutions, another hallmark of New England culture in this essay that is traced only in forms that directly sustained arguments about regional identity, such as publishing ventures, without addressing some initiatives that were arguably more typical and innovative, such as hospitals. The layering of its self-representations and the strength of its institutions have made New England a powerful if protean idea in American history and heightened the self-awareness of those who, as the poet Emily Dickinson put it, "think New-Englandly."

NEW ENGLAND AS A RELIGIOUS CONCEPT

A decentralized movement that demanded rigorous independent examination of religious propositions, Puritanism was less an orthodoxy than a long-running debate over strategies for perfecting the English Reformation. The most important arguments had matured long before the colonization of New England, and although migration offered an opportunity to implement ideas suppressed in England, the colonists remained keenly aware of their participation in a transatlantic community. Their need to explain their initiatives within this framework intensified sharply after the outbreak of the Civil War in England. That conflict and its aftermath obliged colonists to justify the New England enterprise during the Puritan struggle for power in England and to reassess their course in light of

Old Harvard Yard, Cambridge, Massachusetts. Facsimile of an old engraving in the collection of the Massachusetts Historical Society. From left to right, a view of First Harvard Hall (1682), First Stoughton Hall (1700), and Massachusetts Hall (1720). © BETTMANN/CORBIS

growing religious toleration, the expulsion of Puritans from the Church of England, the imperial attempt to reorganize the American colonies, and the Glorious Revolution. As colonists responded to these challenges, they identified New England not merely as a place of refuge but as a part of the divine plan of the universe. Adapting principles previously introduced into Puritanism, the religious concept of New England became a foundation for regional self-interpretation.

New England entered Puritan vocabulary in part through efforts to establish unity around the congregational polity known to contemporaries as "the New England Way." This pattern vested control of parishes in covenanting members who recognized in each other a common experience of saving grace that followed careful study of the Scriptures, meditation upon preaching, and prayer, which a candidate described in a public narrative. The elect not only decided on the admission and discipline of members; they also called and discharged ministers for the congregation. Church and local governance were carefully interwoven. Town funds sustained the parish and minister, and laws enjoined all residents to attend Sabbath services. Only full members

of the church, however, could vote in the town meeting.

This integrated regime drew on a variety of representative New England institutions in addition to the church and the town. Because conversion depended on reading the Bible and contemplating possible interpretations, literacy and education were crucial concerns. New England towns quickly organized public schools, and Massachusetts (1647) and Connecticut (1650) soon required all towns of fifty families to employ a teacher and all towns of one hundred families to maintain a grammar school that taught Latin. "Dreading to leave an illiterate ministry to the churches when our present ministers shall lie in the dust," New Englanders sought to match the training provided at Cambridge University, the intellectual font of Puritanism, by founding Harvard College in 1636. To facilitate the circulation of Bibles, sermons, and other materials central to the religious culture of Puritanism, the first printing press in British North America began operations in Cambridge, Massachusetts, in 1638. By the 1670s, Boston had nine bookstores. The "Great and Thursday Lecture" instituted by the Puritan clergyman John Cotton in 1633, a tradition

474

that would continue for more than two hundred years, was one of many weekday lectures and meetings that supplemented Sabbath preaching.

The New England Way established its boundaries in a series of controversies. The clergyman Roger Williams argued that the Puritans should sever ties with the corrupt Church of England and criticized the New England integration of church and state for authorizing reprobate civil officials to supervise matters of divine law. After a sojourn in the separatist colony at Plymouth, he became the founder of Rhode Island, which the New England colonies of Massachusetts Bay, Plymouth, New Haven, and Connecticut disdained for its religious toleration and excluded from the United Colonies of New England, a confederation formed in 1643. During the Antinomian controversy, the Puritan radical Anne Hutchinson's gatherings of Boston laity to discuss religious experiences and principles became the nucleus for a protest—that the ministry tended to recognize morality rather than an indwelling of the Holy Spirit as the test of grace. Excommunicated after she declared that she communicated with God through "immediate revelation," Hutchinson was exiled for sedition in 1638. Like Williams and Hutchinson, the missionaries who sought to witness the new Quaker faith in the late 1650s could trace intellectual antecedents in Puritanism, but Massachusetts identified their claim to divine inspiration as a dangerous heresy and executed four of them after they defied banishment. Although it never achieved uniformity, New England had become an engine of exclusivity within Puritanism.

Even more important to the religious meaning of the region were the convulsions across the Atlantic. As New Englanders reversed the flow of migration during the 1640s by leaving to join in the epic struggle, the remaining colonists increasingly highlighted the distinctiveness of their role in the Puritan vision of redemption. Peter Bulkeley, an ancestor of Ralph Waldo Emerson, articulated in his expanded second edition of *The Gospel-Covenant,* published in 1651, the idea that the New England Way consisted not only of covenants among elect saints but also of an overarching covenant between God and the people of New England. Making more expansive use of an image that is familiar to Americans primarily through the Puritan founder John Winthrop's "A Modell of Christian Charity," (1630), Bulkeley declared that "we are as a city set upon an hill, in the open view of all the earth; the eyes of the world are upon us because we profess ourselves to be a people in covenant with God."

This self-image deepened after 1662, when the restored Stuart monarchy purged Puritans from the Church of England. Now the center rather than the periphery of the Puritan movement, New England ministers found biblical expression of the regional destiny through their typological interpretation of the Scriptures, which identified Old Testament foreshadowings of the Christian dispensation. New England was the New Israel, the chosen people of God and the divine instrument for inauguration of the millennium.

One important application of this premise was the jeremiad, which echoed the prophet Jeremiah in lamenting a decay of faith that had brought chastisements from the Lord and would result in annihilation if reform did not take place soon. Some scholars have argued that the increasing prevalence of these themes in works such as Michael Wigglesworth's poem "God's Controversy with New England" (1662) reflect a declension of piety as commercial values gained ascendancy and the Puritan cause in England faded. The Half-Way Covenant endorsed by a New England synod in 1662, which authorized the baptism of full members' grandchildren even if their baptized children had not made a profession of grace, underscores the generational dimension of the perceived crisis of faith. Recent scholars have generally doubted that such a decline took place and pointed to other elements of the context in which the jeremiad flourished. Ministers pointed more decisively to divine chastisements—and claimed authority to prescribe more specific remedies—amid social traumas that included the bloody King Philip's War of 1675–1676, the tightening of imperial control and resulting revocation of the Massachusetts charter, and the campaign of the royal governor Sir Edmund Andros to undermine Puritanism.

The double edge of the New England jeremiad—its assertion of divine favor and its anxieties about decline and punishment—helped to make the study of history central to the intellectual identity of the region. Biographies of the founding generation exemplified the standards by which New Englanders would be taught to measure themselves in vain. Collection and analysis of potential clues to providence was one of the chief undertakings of such writers as Increase, Samuel Sewall, and Thomas Prince. The masterpiece of this genre was Cotton Mather's *Magnalia Christi Americana* (1693–1702), which declared that "whether *New England* may Live any where else or no, it must *Live* in our *History!*" Challenges to these historical interpretations only intensified the focus of debate on the New England past, as when the Congregational clergyman-historian William Hubbard's *Narrative of the Troubles with the Indians in New-England* (1677) disputed the suggestion that God had ordained King Philip's War to chastise New England.

The institutional underpinnings of the New England Way proved more vulnerable than the idea of a covenanted nation. The revocation of the Massachusetts charter broadened religious toleration for Anglicans and expanded the franchise beyond the circle of church members. The Brattle Street Church in Boston, founded by an influential faction in 1699, discarded many important principles of organization, including the admission of members on the basis of a personal narrative. The same faction also gained control of Harvard, which led to the founding of Yale College (1701), but the Brattle Street faction tended to ignore the ecclesiological debates that had sustained Puritanism. Despite efforts in Connecticut to redefine a uniform church polity, the trend toward fragmentation continued until the Great Awakening thoroughly splintered the New England religion into a wide range of competing sects.

If New England was no longer a coherent religious idea in institutional terms by the middle of the eighteenth century, it retained an extraordinarily dynamic religious life, a set of educational institutions that fostered continuing intellectual and cultural influence, and an inherited reform mission. New Englanders would carry this sense of duty—and entitlement—to lead Christian regeneration well beyond the Northeast in the years ahead, creating enclaves that resembled New England in some places and informing a broader regional confrontation with the trajectory of America and the world.

NEW ENGLAND AS A POLITICAL CONCEPT

In America as in England, Puritanism was a political as well as a religious movement, fraught with implications for the governance of the local community and the British empire. Enlightenment successors to this intellectual tradition would recognize that New England shaped their work; the politician and political theorist John Adams observed that his 1768 *Dissertation on the Canon and Feudal Law,* a landmark of Revolutionary ideology, might have been entitled "An Essay on Forefathers' Rock." In the eighteenth century, New Englanders also emerged as a distinct social type in the Anglo-American imagination, a process that did not simply describe reality but reflected the values of the region and the perceptions of outsiders. This vision of New England would contribute significantly to early expressions of American nationalism, but it would also lend momentum to the first effort to divide the United States.

Connecticut, and particularly Yale, was the home of the most ambitious attempts to articulate the meaning of New England and present it as a model for America. The most influential figure was the theologian Timothy Dwight, the grandson of Jonathan Edwards, a student and tutor at Yale, and the president of the college from 1795 to 1817. Dwight's epic poem *Greenfield Hill* (1794) and his *Travels in New England and New York* (1821) describe a paradise of pastoral beauty, personal virtue, and social harmony that contrast sharply with the corruption and decay of early-nineteenth-century Europe. A host of Yale graduates and other sympathizers would answer Dwight's call to Connecticutize the country, fanning out across America to reproduce the supposed New England social order. This effort drew not only on Puritan civic ideals but on the inherited apparatus of churches, towns, schools, and colleges; the proliferation of these institutions created many outposts of New England influence. In addition, newer forms of voluntary associations updated the direct confrontation between congregation and sinner, organizing to promote temperance, respect for the Sabbath, and other dimensions of morality during the late eighteenth and early nineteenth centuries. The resulting New England institutional matrix was perhaps best illustrated by the family of Dwight's former student Lyman Beecher, a leading evangelical preacher, a champion of Sabbatarianism and other moral reform movements, and the father of the educator Catharine Beecher, the minister Henry Ward Beecher, and the novelist Harriet Beecher Stowe.

Dwight's solid, hardworking yeomen of Connecticut, the land of steady habits, found comic counterparts in Yankee Doodle, circulating in song by the 1760s, and Brother Jonathan, represented on stage, in cartoons, and in humorous literature beginning in the 1770s. Both icons parodied outsiders' perceptions of New England farmers as country bumpkins. Like more learned celebrations of rural New England, this vein of humor identified Yankee naivete as a source of strength, for Brother Jonathan's energetic common sense often defeated his sophisticated adversaries. Rustic simplicity also served Jonathan well in a more ambiguous way by masking his shrewdness. In this respect, the wily fool tended toward the negative regional stereotype of the Connecticut peddler, a ubiquitous, duplicitous embodiment of scheming acquisitiveness that would be realized to a considerable degree by the Connecticut-born showman P. T. Barnum. While satirists long used Brother Jonathan to personify America without indicating that his New England origins implied any comparisons among regions, critics of New England would often caricature the Yankee peddler as sectional frictions intensified, a theme that the novelist Mark Twain would take up in *A Connecticut Yankee in King Arthur's Court* (1889).

Like other tricksters, Brother Jonathan testified to the strength of the hierarchy that he parodied. Patterns of deference to educated elites remained powerful in the Early Republic and helped to make New England the bastion of the Federalist Party. The clergy, experimenting with new forms of social activism while clinging to a constitutional establishment of religion that persisted in Connecticut until 1818 and Massachusetts until 1833, typified the tendency of traditional leadership groups to identify the meaning of New England with their continued authority. Secular elites were equally resourceful. The development of Beacon Hill by the architect Charles Bulfinch and a syndicate of investors represented their New England political ideal on the landscape of the regional metropolis. Unlike the American capitals in Washington, D.C., Harrisburg, Pennsylvania, Albany, New York, and other cities that separated the seat of government from the influences of commerce and high society, Boston remained a capital on the European model, a convergence of political, economic, and intellectual lines of force. Looking down from Beacon Hill, expecting deference, were the elegant Massachusetts State House designed by Bulfinch and built from 1795 to 1798 and the neighboring mansions Bulfinch designed for the presumptive leaders of the unified society.

Conspicuous in its commemoration of the American Revolution, Beacon Hill resembled *Greenfield Hill* in advancing a model for the nation while expressing New England distinctiveness, but that balance became more difficult to sustain after the election of Thomas Jefferson as president. In addition to its cultural peculiarities, the economic interests of the region—especially its disproportionate dependence on maritime trade—had made New England a singularly troublesome part of the Union since the first Congress, when members' references to New England outnumbered the references to any other region although it comprised less than 25 percent of the American population in the 1790 census. After the Louisiana Purchase promised to accelerate the westward shift of American attentions, small circles of New England Federalists called for disunion. Discontent intensified dramatically with the economic devastation brought by the Jeffersonian embargo and the War of 1812. Sectional identity became the explicit basis of popular politics, as Federalists denounced the diplomatic policies and entrenched dominance of the Virginia dynasty and the religious and social vision of Jeffersonian democracy. A substantial New England secessionism marked a climactic stage in regional representation only in time to explode, for although the Hartford Convention of 1814 sought to rein in the separatist movement, the Treaty of Ghent and American victory in the Battle of New Orleans shattered the Federalist Party and made New England political self-consciousness synonymous with treason. Subsequent New Englanders would necessarily turn to different strategies to define the region and its relationship to the nation.

NEW ENGLAND AS AN ARTISTIC CONCEPT

To suggest that New England flourished primarily as an artistic idea during the century after 1815 is not to deny the artistry in earlier views of New England, nor to neglect the religious striving and political engagement that marked many of the great works of the later phase. For the so-called New England renaissance and its aftermath, however, New England primarily served not as a corporate element of the divine plan or an exemplary social order but as a self-conscious cultural tradition and a field for representing the vision of the individual artist. The religious and political aspects of this vision tended to dissipate during the second half of the nineteenth century, as a new institutional infrastructure developed to sustain New England art for its own sake.

The first institutional innovations contributing to new views of New England drew upon educational and religious precedents. The lyceum movement, launched by the lecturer-teacher Josiah Holbrook in 1826, extended the zeal for schools to create a popular form of adult education and establish an institutional framework for public lectures—strongest in New England but extending throughout the United States—that would provide a financial base for speakers such as Emerson, the educator Horace Mann, the abolitionist crusader Wendell Phillips, and the suffragist Lucy Stone.

Another fertile source of institutional development was the evolution of liberal Congregationalism into Unitarianism, which one polemicist disdainfully called the "Boston religion" because it claimed many of the pulpits of eastern Massachusetts and positions at Harvard. This theology described conversion as a gradual process of character formation, or what the clergyman William Ellery Channing called "self-culture," in which the secular arts might play an important role. Liberal ministers and other like-minded Harvard graduates established a literary magazine, the *Monthly Anthology,* and a valuable library and art collection, the Boston Athenaeum. Although the *Monthly Anthology* lasted only from 1803 to 1811, it gave rise to the *Christian Disciple* (1813 to 1823), later renamed the *Christian Examiner* (1824 to 1869), and the *North American Review* (1815). Adapting the pattern of British quarterlies, these journals became the key publishing organs of the liberal Boston establishment. Orthodox critics responded by founding competing institutions like the Andover Theological Seminary (1807), which trained legions of missionaries and reform leaders, and competing journals, like the Congregational minister Jedidiah Morse's *The Panoplist* (1805 to 1820).

Religious conflict helped to reinvigorate historical representations of New England. The patterns of praise and criticism for liberal Hannah Adams's *Summary History of New England* (1799) and Jedidiah Morse and Elijah Parish's *Compendious History of New England* (1804) typified the rivalry. Lydia Maria Child's romance *Hobomok* (1824) and Catharine Sedgwick's *Hope Leslie* (1827) express Unitarians' ambivalent attitudes toward Puritanism and helped to popularize early New England as a focus of fiction and poetry, a project that would soon attract John Greenleaf Whittier, Henry Wadsworth Longfellow, Harriet Beecher Stowe, and Nathaniel Hawthorne, among other authors. The example of the early settlers remained a powerful theme in evangelical exhortation, particularly in Forefathers' Day addresses commemorating the founding of Plymouth.

Massachusetts Whigs, who long dominated state politics and sought with mixed success to achieve national leadership, similarly depicted New England as distinguished by its historical inheritance. Daniel Webster's addresses at Plymouth and at Bunker Hill, seconded by Edward Everett, Robert Winthrop, Rufus Choate, and other Whig orators, powerfully asserted a regional claim to precedence in the formation of the nation and credit for much of its progress. The Whigs' radical critics, most notably Wendell Phillips and fellow abolitionist Theodore Parker, often fought the conservatives on the historical ground they had chosen and drew different lessons from the regional past. But both sides agreed with the French historian and political writer Alexis de Tocqueville's impression, "I think I can see the whole destiny of America contained in the first Puritan who landed on those shores," a view that infuriated observers elsewhere in the United States. The politics of regional history remained sharply contested throughout the nineteenth century, particularly in disputes over the Boston landscape. For example, the controversial placement of a monument on Boston Common in 1888 to commemorate the Boston Massacre marked a triumph for African Americans who had honored Crispus Attucks as a patriotic martyr since the antebellum crusade against slavery and racism; after Irish Americans gained control of the city government, they needled the traditional elites, often called Boston Brahmins, by commissioning a statue of the apostate aristocrat Wendell Phillips.

The strenuous efforts to define New England through history helped to propel the protest that Ralph Waldo Emerson delivered in the first sentences of *Nature* (1836). As in the elaboration of regional traditions, liberal religion played a key role in reimagining the region through landscape. One of the sites most proudly shown to mid-nineteenth-century visitors and most widely emulated around the country, Mount Auburn Cemetery offered a Unitarian vision of death as reintegration into a beneficent, harmonious nature. Picturesque streams and rocky coastlines became staple metaphors for the region during the first half of the nineteenth century. Henry David Thoreau's transformation of this literature dramatized the religious energy underlying the Transcendentalist exploration of New England as an artistic idea and also underscored the contrast between prevailing artistic representations of the New England landscape and the reality that the region was the most urbanized and industrialized section of United States, a place where the railroad was rapidly making Concord a thriving market town and a suburb of Boston. The site in the region most inevitably shown to foreign visitors in the second quarter of the nineteenth century was probably Lowell, Massachusetts, the vanguard of the American factory system. But despite its cotton mills and densely populated cities, New England did not produce many gritty self-representations of urban diversity and conflict even after the disintegration of the textile entrepreneurs' early hopes to contain industrialization within a pastoral framework.

478

New England figured most prominently as a symbol of modernization in the sectional conflict over slavery and the debates over feminism that abolitionism stimulated. Defenders of slavery often protested that New England was destroying the traditional foundations of society by abandoning workers to a grim dependence on wages, which fostered class conflict; encouraging free thought, which undermined religious authority; and enabling women to fashion independent roles of public engagement and leadership, which eviscerated family structure. The response to these claims tended to be less specifically concerned with New England. Support for free labor revolved instead on a broader contrast between North and South that typically pictured American society as preindustrial. Although the faction of radical abolitionists led by William Lloyd Garrison, editor of *The Liberator,* frequently called on Massachusetts to leave the Union, their secessionist program similarly stressed separation from slaveholders rather than local identity. Unlike the Federalists who had favored secession, Garrisonians did not portray an ideal social order in New England; to the contrary, they fiercely criticized the local elites and immigrant workers whom they considered tools of the slaveholding interest. In many cases an expression of broader anarchism, their secessionism was less a practical strategy than an example of the rhetorical art of abolitionism.

The influx of wealth that accompanied industrialization brought changes to the institutional framework supporting intellectual and cultural representations of New England. After lagging behind Philadelphia and New York for decades, Boston moved to the first tier as a publishing center during the 1850s behind the lead of the firm Ticknor and Fields, which sold the works of such regional authors as Emerson, Longfellow, Stowe, Whittier, and Hawthorne. With the founding of the *Atlantic Monthly* in 1857 (also referred to as the *Atlantic*), the region established a literary magazine with the long-term stability that had eluded *Massachusetts Magazine* (1789–1796), the *Monthly Anthology* (1803–1811), *New-England Magazine* (1831–1835), and the *Dial* (1840–1844). Like the *North American Review* and the *Christian Examiner,* the *Atlantic* was dominated by New England contributors, many of whom also met regularly in social organizations like the Saturday Club. In building around these authors, the new publishing initiatives vastly expanded the market outlets for exploration of New England as a literary theme.

From the end of the Civil War until the First World War, the main avenues of this exploration remained regional history, rural and coastal imagery, and the social world of the New England village. As the religious and partisan controversies underlying historical representation waned, early New England served new purposes. English settlers became prototypes of American martial energy in John Quincy Adams Ward's statue *The Pilgrim* and Augustus Saint-Gaudens's *The Puritan,* both unveiled in 1885. Absorption in New England history through organizations like the Massachusetts Society of Mayflower Descendants, founded in 1896, also correlated with Yankee antagonism to immigrants and frustration over declining political power in cities. The Society for Preservation of New England Antiquities (1910) connected this social exclusivity to the innovative momentum for historic preservation and other forms of land-use regulation. A similarly beleaguered spirit suffused images of the New England town and landscape, often presented as a desolate, autumnal world that mirrored personal isolation. The paintings of Winslow Homer and the fiction of Sarah Orne Jewett and Mary E. Wilkins Freeman suggest that this solitude offers considerable opportunities for renewal, but such darker works as Edith Wharton's *Ethan Frome* (1911) and *Summer* (1917) and the poetry of Edwin Arlington Robinson reflect the increasingly common use of barren New England settings to evoke desperation. The reaction to this trend helped pave the way for the success of the poet Robert Frost, whose measured appreciation for rural New England would make him the most popular literary voice of the region in the decades following the American publication of his *North of Boston* (1914).

Compared to the contemporary artistic fascination with Chicago and New York, Boston remained relatively underdeveloped in representations of New England. The authors of the most sophisticated experiments in city fiction both moved elsewhere. William Dean Howells, who profiled Boston in *The Rise of Silas Lapham* (1885) and *The Minister's Charge* (1886), left his position as editor of the *Atlantic Monthly* to move to New York. Henry James kept up an engagement with New England innocence, moralism, and ambition that lasted from the publication of his *Roderick Hudson* (1875) through *The Bostonians* (1886) to *The Ambassadors* (1903), but his bemusement reflected impatience with the provincialism of the region. T. S. Eliot, a member of a prominent Boston family transplanted to St. Louis, made the most withering

THE
ATLANTIC MONTHLY

DEVOTED TO

Literature, Science, Art, and Politics

VOLUME XLVIII.—NUMBER 289

NOVEMBER, 1881

CONTENTS

BOSTON
HOUGHTON, MIFFLIN AND COMPANY

NEW YORK: 11 EAST SEVENTEENTH STREET

The Riverside Press, Cambridge

The *Atlantic Monthly,* November 1881. The *Atlantic* published works by New England natives, including Henry Wadsworth Longfellow, Ralph Waldo Emerson, Sarah Orne Jewett, and James Russell Lowell, who was the magazine's first editor. It also published many writers born outside the region, such as Ernest Hemingway, Louise Erdrich, Mark Twain, Martin Luther King Jr., and Henry James. © COURTESY OF THE ATLANTIC MONTHLY cosmopolitan rejection of the city and the region as a home and as an artistic concept. Rather than struggling with the theme, he shrugged it off in a few early satirical poems that seemed to end the tradition not with a bang but with a whimper.

NEW ENGLAND AS A MARKETING CONCEPT

The continuing significance of New England drew considerable debate after World War I. *The Education of Henry Adams,* privately printed in 1907 and published in 1918, cast its expatriate author as the embodiment of a culture that had reached a dead end, an argument that would be echoed by George Santayana's *The Last Puritan* (1935) and John P. Marquand's *The Late George Apley* (1937). The irreverent popular culture of the 1920s found its antithesis in H. L. Mencken's dismissal of Puritanism as the "fear that someone, somewhere, may be happy," and the phrase "banned in Boston" became a titillating recommendation. The Sacco-Vanzetti case—the most politically charged legal drama in the region since the fugitive slave cases of the 1850s—seemed to many observers to dramatize the ethnic stalemate in New England, the rigidity of the Brahmin elite, and the impotence of the intellectuals who mobilized in support of the defendants. The first issue of the *New England Quarterly* (1928) admitted that the importance of the region had often been exaggerated and timidly suggested that the topic had not yet been exhausted. For a region characterized in terms of decline and loss since William Bradford's *Of Plimouth Plantation* (1630–1650), the debate partly indicated cultural durability. New England remained a familiar icon of spiritual isolation in the plays of Eugene O'Neill and the paintings of Edward Hopper, a tradition that would be carried forward in poetry by Robert Lowell and in fiction by Andre Dubus. But the shifting spotlight was not an illusion; New England would attract less attention during the twentieth century than it previously had in comparison to other parts of the United States.

To be sure, the changing cultural marketplace incorporated familiar representations of New England, if often in a diluted form. Entrepreneurs had traded successfully in New England identity since the mid-nineteenth century, not only through the publishing industry but also through tourism, and these efforts redoubled with the opening of Mystic Seaport, a museum-village in Mystic, Connecticut (1930), Old Sturbridge Village in Sturbridge, Mas-

sachusetts (1947), Plimoth Plantation in Plymouth, Massachusetts (1947), the Shelburne Museum in Burlington, Vermont (1947), and Historic Deerfield in Deerfield, Massachusetts (1952). In promoting history as a public nostalgia, the installations matched the regional image presented in Norman Rockwell's popular artworks and Thornton Wilder's *Our Town* (1938), which made Grover's Corners, New Hampshire, as emblematic of New England as Greenfield Hill had once been.

Hollywood similarly associated New England with emotional repression and wistful reconciliation in films from *Now, Voyager* (1942) through *On Golden Pond* (1981), and these sentimental stereotypes provided a backdrop for the opposite formula of Grace Metalious's best-selling *Peyton Place* (1956), which updated the regional gothic tradition to detail the sordid private world of a seemingly placid New England village. Comic variations on this contrast focused on the eccentricities of staid Yankees.

Regional representations after World War II also saw several noteworthy transformations of the village setting. Such novels as John Cheever's *The Wapshot Chronicle* (1957) and *The Wapshot Scandal* (1963) and John Updike's *Couples* (1968) made clear that the New England town had become a suburb. The city received more direct and more affectionate attention as the Irish Catholics of Boston increasingly became the social group most widely identified with the region through the radio performances of Fred Allen, the political careers of John F. Kennedy, Edward M. Kennedy, and Tip O'Neill, and the fiction of Edwin O'Connor and James Carroll. Despite the persistence of class, ethnic, and racial tensions demonstrated by the school desegregation controversy of the 1970s, the most popular portrait of the city during the last quarter of the twentieth century was the television series *Cheers* (1982–1993), a comedy about a neighborhood bar where, as the theme song emphasized, "everybody knows your name."

As images of the regional metropolis absorbed traditional images of the New England town, the motif of pastoral seclusion increasingly centered on academic settings, a local specialty in fiction since Hawthorne's *Fanshawe* (1828). In such works as John Knowles's *A Separate Peace* (1959) and Edward Albee's *Who's Afraid of Virginia Woolf?* (1962), the campus became the equivalent to the isolated, inward-looking New England village that William Bradford, Timothy Dwight, Harriet Beecher Stowe, Thornton Wilder, and other authors and artists had made one of the classic images of America. In evoking the perceived distance between the academy and the wider community, this development paralleled the fate of New England in national intellectual and cultural currents. The cosmopolitan style of the twentieth century had established itself in part by repudiating New England; Plymouth Rock, a national icon of considerable force in the nineteenth-century, was widely considered kitsch by the mid-twentieth century. But if retreating in popular culture, New England at the same time became the focus for a remarkable outpouring of scholarship, beginning with Perry Miller's two-volume *The New England Mind* (1939, 1953). After successfully marketing itself as a home of schools, New England had become a concept that tended to receive its fullest consideration in schools. The relationship between schools and the wider culture, one of the building blocks of New England, would in large part determine the vitality of the regional image in the years ahead.

See also **Puritanism as a Cultural and Intellectual Force; The New England Theology from Edwards to Bushnell; Transcendentalism** (*volume 1*); *and other articles in this section.*

BIBLIOGRAPHY

Abzug, Robert H. *Cosmos Crumbling: American Reform and the Religious Imagination.* New York, 1994.

Bercovitch, Sacvan. *The Puritan Origins of the American Self.* New Haven, Conn., 1975.

Brooke, John L. *The Heart of the Commonwealth: Society and Political Culture in Worcester County, Massachusetts, 1713–1861.* Cambridge, Mass., 1989.

Brown, Dona. *Inventing New England: Regional Tourism in the Nineteenth Century.* Washington, D.C., 1995.

Buell, Lawrence. *New England Literary Culture from Revolution through Renaissance.* Cambridge, Mass., 1986.

Capper, Charles, and Conrad Edick Wright, eds. *Transient and Permanent: The Transcendentalist Movement and Its Contexts.* Boston, 1999.

Cayton, Mary Kupiec. *Emerson's Emergence: Self and Society in the Transformation of New England, 1800–1845.* Chapel Hill, N.C., 1989.

Committee for a New England Bibliography. *Bibliographies of New England History.* 9 vols. Boston and Hanover, N.H., 1976–1995.

Cowley, Malcolm. *New England Writers and Writing.* Edited by Donald W. Faulkner. Hanover, N.H., 1996.

Dowling, William C. *Poetry and Ideology in Revolutionary Connecticut.* Athens, Ga., 1990.

Field, Peter S. *The Crisis of the Standing Order: Clerical Intellectuals and Cultural Authority in Massachusetts, 1780–1833.* Amherst, Mass., 1998.

Foster, Stephen. *The Long Argument: English Puritanism and the Shaping of New England Culture, 1570–1700.* Chapel Hill, N.C., 1991.

Fredrickson, George M. *The Inner Civil War: Northern Intellectuals and the Crisis of the Union.* New York, 1965.

Gilmore, William J. *Reading Becomes a Necessity of Life: Material and Cultural Life in Rural New England, 1780–1835.* Knoxville, Tenn., 1989.

Hall, David D. *Worlds of Wonder, Days of Judgment: Popular Religious Belief in Early New England.* New York, 1989.

Hoopes, James. *Consciousness in New England: From Puritanism and Ideas to Psychoanalysis and Semiotic.* Baltimore, 1989.

Howe, Daniel Walker. *The Unitarian Conscience: Harvard Moral Philosophy, 1805–1861.* Cambridge, Mass., 1970.

Jacobs, Donald M., ed. *Courage and Conscience: Black and White Abolitionists in Boston.* Bloomington, Ind., 1993.

Morgan, Winifred. *An American Icon: Brother Jonathan and American Identity.* Newark, Del., 1988.

Nissenbaum, Stephen. "New England as Region and Nation." In *All Over the Map: Rethinking American Regions,* edited by Edward Ayers, pp. 38–61. Baltimore, 1996.

O'Connell, Shaun. *Imagining Boston: A Literary Landscape.* Boston, 1990.

Perry, Lewis. *Radical Abolitionism: Anarchy and the Government of God in Antislavery Thought.* Ithaca, N.Y., 1973.

Peterson, Mark A. *The Price of Redemption: The Spiritual Economy of Puritan New England.* Stanford, Calif., 1997.

Sedgwick, Ellery. *The Atlantic Monthly, 1857–1909: Yankee Humanism at High Tide and Ebb.* Amherst, Mass., 1994.

Seelye, John. *Memory's Nation: The Place of Plymouth Rock.* Chapel Hill, N.C., 1998.

Shand-Tucci, Douglass. *Boston Bohemia, 1881–1900: Ralph Adams Cram: Life and Architecture.* Amherst, Mass., 1995.

Sheidley, Harlow W. *Sectional Nationalism: Massachusetts Conservative Leaders and the Transformation of America, 1815–1836.* Boston, 1998.

Simpson, Lewis P. *Mind and the American Civil War: A Meditation on Lost Causes.* Baton Rouge, La., 1989.

Truettner, William H., and Roger B. Stein. *Picturing Old New England: Image and Memory.* New Haven, Conn., 1999.

Von Frank, Albert J. *The Trials of Anthony Burns: Freedom and Slavery in Emerson's Boston.* Cambridge, Mass., 1998.

Warner, Sam Bass, Jr. *Province of Reason.* Cambridge, Mass., 1984.

Westbrook, Perry D. *The New England Town in Fact and Fiction.* Rutherford, N.J., 1982.

Young, Alfred F. *The Shoemaker and the Tea Party: Memory and the American Revolution.* Boston, 1999.

THE FRONTIER AND THE WEST

Mark David Spence

Historians of the American West have long debated whether it is best to understand western history in terms of process or place. As a process, the West refers to the frontier regions where Europeans, Euro-Americans, East Asians, African Americans, and native peoples have interacted and conflicted with the environment and each other. In this sense, the Chesapeake, Kentucky, the Great Lakes, the Upper Rio Grande Valley, and the Sierra Nevada all represent complex frontier situations (or "Wests") from the seventeenth to the nineteenth centuries. As a place, the West has come to be known as the area west of the Mississippi River—an environmentally diverse region with a rich and varied human history that stretches back for thousands of years.

Both conceptions of the West have particular merits and faults, but neither approach is easily reconciled with the other. Emphasizing frontiers gives a powerful narrative structure to western history, but it tends to overlook historical developments that either preceded or followed a certain frontier experience. Of course, viewing the frontier in terms of a compass direction also tends to ignore the perspectives of "non-westering" peoples. Presenting the West in distinctly regional terms does address both of these shortcomings; all people and all time periods are potential subjects of study when the conceptual limitations of frontier history are dropped. How one defines the historical or spatial boundaries of the region then becomes a matter of great import and disagreement. Without an identifiable set of qualities or characteristics, the history of the West begins to lose definition. Any attempt to explain what makes it distinctly "western" will necessarily bog down into a set of essentialist arguments about environment, cultural diversity, or economic development that echo the singular claims of frontier historians.

One way to resolve these disagreements and shortcomings is to see the West as a historical construction, a distinct region of the United States that has its origins in powerful myths about national destiny. Consequently, any effort to define or locate the temporal and geographic boundaries of the American West must begin in the realm of fantasy and collective imagination. In the simplest terms, the West was created through conquest and annexation. The straight lines of the region's northern and southern boundaries clearly reflect the objectives of territorial expansion and imperial competition that defined the processes of nation building in North America during the nineteenth century. But these straight lines also demonstrate the power of ideas to both invent and define a distinct geographic region. The West is more than a composite of particular cultural, political, or geomorphic qualities, and it is certainly not just the inevitable result of a unidirectional process of expansion and settlement. Rather, the West is built on the ideas and stories that link popular conceptions of the frontier with the political boundaries of a nationally defined region.

Often portrayed as a place of stalwart independence, gritty convictions, and broad vistas, the very idea of the West represents a wellspring of American characteristics to people throughout the United States and around the world. While such ideas often shape the perceptions of outsiders and recent migrants to the region, the sense of special connection to place they inspire also shape the personal and collective identities of many long-term residents. This is hardly a universal experience in the region. Not everyone has seen themselves as western, or even American, and many individuals and groups have long sought to subvert or contest such regional identities as they dealt with the ongoing implications of conquest and incorporation into the United States. Whether contested or actively perpetuated by residents of the region, the ideas and cultural attitudes that informed the region's creation have always remained central, defining features of the West.

THOMAS JEFFERSON AND THE
EMPIRE OF PROPERTY

Though he never traveled beyond the Blue Ridge Mountains, the West's first great visionary was certainly Thomas Jefferson. Long before he assumed the presidency, Jefferson looked to the West as the region that would define the United States and guarantee its future. In a much quoted passage from his "Notes on the State of Virginia" (1787), a work as much about Jefferson's home state as the western portions of North America, he declared, "Those who labour in the earth are the chosen people of God, if ever he had a chosen people, whose breasts he has made his peculiar deposit for substantial and genuine virtue" (p. 280). Such qualities were necessary for the right governance of a republic, a notion which supposedly explained the impending social and economic disintegration of Europe—where "the lands are either cultivated, or locked up against the cultivator" (p. 279). Through geographic expansion, Jefferson was convinced that the United States could ensure the virtue of the nation's citizenry and thus avoid the necessary fate of all empires. Jefferson assumed that, like ancient Rome before, and Europe in the late eighteenth century, all societies were doomed to violent collapse when they turned from their agrarian origins. Urbanization and dependence on manufacturers created gross inequities in wealth and living standards; this in turn would only lead to political corruption, social discord, anarchy, and eventual collapse. Jefferson was convinced that expanding westward could allow the United States to postpone, if not escape, this cruel inevitability. As he wrote James Madison in 1787: "Our governments will remain virtuous for many centuries, so long as they are chiefly agricultural; and this will be as long as there are vacant lands in America" (Boyd, vol. 12, p. 442).

For Jeffersonian Americans, the West also seemed to promise a resolution to the intractable problems that threatened to destroy the young republic at the outset; namely, competition from imperial rivals, conflicts over Indian lands, and slavery. In concluding the Louisiana Purchase in 1803 and then organizing the Lewis and Clark expedition, Jefferson hoped to achieve several immediate goals that would defuse these potential threats and guarantee the long-term health of the nation. Opening up relations with the Indians of the Upper Missouri River not only drew the valuable fur trade away from the British in Canada, but also established the young nation's presence in a region coveted by the French and Spanish as well as the English. Staving off the claims of imperial competitors was only a beginning, however. Establishing trade relations with the Missouri River Indians was deemed a necessary precursor to later acquisition of their lands. This was effected almost immediately among the groups along the lower stretches of the Missouri which had recently suffered through devastating epidemics. These lands provided areas for the removal of eastern tribes to the West, a duplicitous and often violent policy that nevertheless opened up lands in the South and Midwest for the continued development of new American farms and towns.

The planned settlement of the lands to be vacated by the removed eastern tribes had already been provided for in the Northwest Ordinance of 1787, which also banned slavery in the newly organized territories north of the Ohio River. Jefferson drafted the first proposal for the Ordinance, and established the grid pattern of farms and towns that mark the landscapes of the American West. Laying out the squares that would shape the states, counties, farms, forests, and towns of the region, Jefferson and many of his contemporaries apparently saw the Northwest Ordinance as a social template for a culturally and racially homogenous nation. Though no one was ever explicit on how this would be achieved, few doubted that westward expansion would somehow erase the troublesome presence of both Indians and slaves. Jefferson stated as much during the first year of his presidency: "However our present interests may restrain us within our own limits, it is impossible not to look forward to distant times, when our rapid multiplication will expand [over] the whole . . . continent, with a people speaking the same language, governed in similar forms and by similar laws; nor can we contemplate with satisfaction either blot or mixture in that surface" (Lipscomb and Bergh, vol. 11, p. 296).

As a politically and historically defined region, the American West might be said to have begun with the Louisiana Purchase. However, its development and further national expansion would depend on the continual reformulation of Jeffersonian ideals. Charged with so much hope, necessity, and expectation, American visions of the West took resident peoples and their homelands as virtual blank slates for the creation of an agrarian empire. As in Jefferson's sweeping ideas about the "rapid multiplication" of American farmers, the West represented a place that was as empty of consequences as it was full of compelling possibilities. Such visions provide the materials for self-fulfilling prophecies, and territorial expansion became the central maxim of a powerful tautology: Americans had to move west because this empty and unused land required their presence to make both the region and the nation achieve its full potential. The term "manifest destiny" would not be coined until the early 1840s, in the midst of the jingoism that preceded the American invasion and conquest of northern Mexico, but the sentiments of that phrase clearly served as an extension of Jefferson's faith in personal and national regeneration through westward expansion.

AMERICAN ROMANTICISM AND THE WEST

The sense of destiny and hopefulness that informed the rhetoric of national expansion was central to the development of American arts and letters in the first half of the nineteenth century. In both word and image, depictions of western landscapes and an idealized agrarianism became the basis for a self-consciously American aesthetic. Mirroring the claim that westward expansion would deliver the United States from the fate of Old World empires, the nation's frontier origins often served as an important tool for patriotic apologists who felt compelled to reject the subjects of European arts and letters. This sentiment was best expressed by Thomas Cole, the leading figure in the Hudson River school of landscape painters and one of the most influential artists of the antebellum era. As Cole wrote in 1833, the American artist needed to focus on his "own land; its beauty, its magnificence, its sublimity—all are his; and how undeserving of such a birthright, if he can turn towards it an unobserving eye, an unaffected heart!" (p. 11). Cole's own paintings demonstrated that one of the most distinctly American aspects of this landscape was the rough beauty of the agrarian frontier, a subject he returned to in several of his most famous paintings, including *View from Mount Holyoke, Northampton, Massachusetts, after a Thunderstorm (The Oxbow)* (1836), *The Hunter's Return* (1845), and *Home in the Woods* (1847).

Cole and his contemporaries were largely interested in depicting a simple frontier past, and used these images to impress upon the viewer a sense of reverence for the idealized historical origins of places that were fast becoming urbanized marketplaces. The generation of artists that followed Cole looked farther west for their subject matter, a move that reflected a desire to paint contemporary subjects as well as celebrate the conquest of northern Mexico and the geographic enlargement of the United States. Finding lessons in the frontiers along the Mississippi and lower Missouri Rivers, George Caleb Bingham created didactic scenes that portrayed the continuing vitality of Jeffersonian ideals. In paintings like *Country Politician* (1849), *The Squatters* (1850), and *The Verdict of the People* (1854–55), Bingham sought to demonstrate how westward expansion fulfilled the expectations of earlier generations and still set a pattern for the future. This was clearly evident in Bingham's most famous painting, *Emigration of Daniel Boone* (1851), which pictures Boone crossing the Cumberland Gap. Boone was a subject of much popular interest at the time, and the painting captures how this historical hero embodied a celebrated ethos of ongoing expansion and regeneration. These sentiments would find their fullest expression in Emanuel Leutze's 1862 mural for the Capitol rotunda in Washington, D.C., *Westward the Course of Empire Takes Its Way [Westward Ho!]*. In depicting a gathering mass of westward-bound settlers pouring on to a mountainous rampart and looking toward the territories recently won from Mexico, Leutze created a powerful visual allegory for the significance of the West as a place open to the realization of personal and national dreams.

Western and frontier subjects also figured prominently in American letters during the antebellum era, and many writers conflated the nation's political and cultural identity with the West. Like their counterparts in the visual arts, poets, essayists, and novelists self-consciously based their work on American subjects in an effort to create a national aesthetic. Indeed, almost the entire canon of early nineteenth-century American literature consists of authors who, along with Ralph Waldo Emerson, insisted that "we have listened too long to the courtly muse of Europe" and must turn instead to uniquely American subjects for inspiration (p. 69). Perhaps as a result of Emerson's exhortation, the works of Washington Irving, Nathaniel Hawthorne, James Fenimore Cooper, Henry Wadsworth Longfellow, and Herman Melville all focused on American subjects, and each author ruminated at great length on western frontiers in their most famous works.

Though outside the canon of American arts and letters, upper-middle-class women in the Northeast not only shared the aesthetic and nationalistic concerns of their male counterparts, but were largely responsible for the dissemination of these ideas through essays and poems in nationally distributed journals. Poets like Lydia Sigourney and Lucretia Davidson were widely read, and their poems about imagined western landscapes and frontier life were collected and reprinted in numerous editions.

487

Colonial frontiers were also central to the novels of Catharine Sedgwick, including her enormously popular *Hope Leslie* (1827). As the primary readers of early-nineteenth-century novels, women determined many of the popular trends in American literature, and their literary tastes inspired the long slew of stories and novels about historical frontiers or life in the western territories that flooded the American market in the antebellum era.

The fascination with peculiarly American themes and subjects was not limited to an elite circle of men and women in and around Boston and New York City, nor did it stem entirely from romantic sensibilities. In many respects, the literary and artistic popularity of historical frontiers and western landscapes derived from the ability of these subjects to capture a widespread sense of dissatisfaction with American politics and society. As nascent industrial and urban growth, increased immigration, and bitter political campaigns altered established patterns of work and community, public opinion often reflected a pervasive sense of national uncertainty and self-criticism. Furthermore, the growing rift between North and South, the persistence of slavery, and increasingly pronounced divisions between ethnic and religious groups undermined any sense of national unity and deflated the egalitarian rhetoric of political leaders. Together, these profound changes inspired a number of religious and secular reform movements to purify American society, and at times public debate often degenerated into a cacophony of local and national criticism. Not surprisingly, the idealization of historical or contemporary frontiers provided foil for social critics who used it as a corrective symbol of all that was wrong with America.

If the past could be used to criticize the present, it could also serve as a hopeful model for the future. In this context, the West truly represented a landscape of national salvation. "All the past we leave behind," Walt Whitman declared in his poem "O Pioneers!": "We debouch upon a newer, mightier world, varied world, / Fresh and strong the world we seize . . . / All the pulses of the world, Falling in, they beat for us, with the western movement beat" (pp. 183–185). By the time Emanuel Leutze had begun his painting for the Capitol, the supposed necessity of westward expansion was so tied to the expectation of personal and social redemption that "westering" itself had acquired the sanctions of natural law. Such attitudes had already allowed many to excuse the invasion of Mexico as a necessary corollary to a divine exhortation to expand the boundaries of the United States.

The idea that the West was an empty landscape, awaiting improvement, offering redemption and regeneration, and symbolizing an ever-greater future, was at least as old as the nation itself. When the present boundaries of the American West were defined and the process of fully integrating the region into the United States had begun in the mid-nineteenth century, these ideas had already established the basic elements for a distinctive sense of regional identity. Moreover, they defined the terms that outsiders would use to imagine the West and its inhabitants for more than a century and a half.

THE FIRST NATIONAL REGION

Early hopes that Indians and slaves would somehow disappear through the process of westward expansion proved terribly wrong. The acquisition of new territories was always predicated on violent dispossession of native communities, and the process of settling their lands only led to increased debates over whether or not the West would be open to slavery. Five years of Civil War and the subsequent reconstruction of the South would largely decide the latter issue, and allowed the U.S. Army to give its undivided attention to ending the so-called Indian threat in the West. With the Union restored and native peoples confined to reservations, the West was opened to rapid exploitation by northern and European capital. The booms and busts of railroad development and resource extraction would help trigger massive swings in the American economy, but they also fueled an era of tremendous economic growth and concentrated wealth. In ways that Thomas Jefferson never imagined, but investors in the East and across the Atlantic nonetheless celebrated, the New West was a place of tremendous opportunity that literally drove the economy of the United States.

The rapid industrial exploitation of natural resources in the decades following the Civil War made the trans-Mississippi West into a region of central importance for the rest of the nation. With such development, the West also became a meeting ground for people from all parts of the United States. Their encounters with each other, as well as with native peoples and immigrants from various points around the globe, would lead to a heightened sense of regional identity based on certain nationalistic ideals. In this sense, the West came to represent the most American part of the United States. Native homelands, Mexican landholdings, and immigrant communities from overseas were incorporated into a larger regional designation that now defined them as part of the American West, but their presence did not sit well with newcomers from the East who sought to define the region according to terms established throughout the first half of the nineteenth century.

Often sharing the older dream of personal and national regeneration through geographic movement, U.S. citizens who went to the West also sharply defined themselves in terms of race, class, gender, and ethnicity. This was hardly unique to the West, but it took on greater intensity as migrants sought common terms on which to define themselves and their communities. Concerns about racial differences were heightened by the presence of Native, Chinese, and Mexican communities that could lay equal or stronger claims to the land and its resources. A common "white" identity that transcended some ethnic distinctions allowed newcomers from "the States" to distinguish themselves from non-Americans, and inspired a particularly virulent form of racism in the West. Indian massacres by citizen groups, anti-Chinese riots, lynchings, usurpation of Mexican land claims, and the violent quelling of immigrant labor organizations all reflected at some level a need for relative newcomers to define their presence in terms of race and national origin. To angrily claim the region as a "white man's country" was central to most nineteenth-century efforts to define an American West and its residents, but this echo of Jefferson's old concerns about "blot or mixture" only demonstrated how tenuous this claim could be.

Defining the West in such exclusive terms has never gone unchallenged. If anything, the diverse and contested nature of western identities remains central to what the historian Patricia Nelson Limerick aptly called the region's ongoing "legacy of conquest." This is often manifest in efforts to claim a place in the West through a subaltern incorporation, or subversion, of the ideas that informed national expansion: opportunity, regeneration, and escape from social or economic strictures. This is evident in the "Exoduster" migrations of the late 1870s, when some twenty-five thousand blacks fled the brutal conditions of Jim Crowism in the South to create new lives in Kansas. Likewise, the successful efforts of early suffragists to win the vote in several western states before 1900 was also rooted in ideas about the West as a place to remake American society.

Attempts to create new communities that were free of discriminatory laws and practices, and thus open the region to a wider set of opportunity seekers, were always difficult propositions at best. When efforts to organize miners in the Rocky Mountains helped to unite people of various ethnic backgrounds, for instance, their demands were met with state violence. Throughout the West, government authority protected the interests of eastern capital while older ideas about a homogenous rather than a diverse West continued to shape the region and its development. This was clearly evident when Congress banned Chinese immigration in 1882 or passed laws that opened tribal lands to railroad developers and white settlement. Such authority sharply circumscribed the rights of nonwhites in the American West, but it did not end the ongoing desires of various groups to seek new opportunities or retain some control over their place in the region. Nevertheless, all were forced to contend with regional power structures that were grounded in the ideas that had first created the American West.

In the contests to limit or enlarge the benefits of western development, white residents of the region could always draw on a growing national interest in the West throughout the second half of the nineteenth century. Whether through news stories, travel accounts, promotional literature, personal correspondence, or the rapid proliferation of dime novels about western villains and heroes, Americans in the Northeast, the South, the Midwest, and all points in between took a personal interest in the West and its development. In the popular imagination, the West came to exemplify adventure and new beginnings. The people who lived there certainly gave the region a unique cast, and eastern visitors never failed to comment on the strange ways of Mormons in Utah, or denigrate the customs of residents who lived in the region's many Chinatowns, barrios, and Indian reservations. On the other hand, the unfamiliar but spectacular landscapes of the region had great appeal to eastern visitors. All seemed to define the region as a special place, as if its physical nature made it different from all other regions yet augmented and completed the nation as a whole.

As the only region of the United States that drew regular attention from people in all parts of the nation, the landscapes of the West proved a highly profitable artistic subject for many decades. The aesthetic appeal of the West reflected many of the same Romantic sensibilities espoused by earlier artists and writers like Thomas Cole and James Fenimore Cooper, but now Americans could boast of towering mountains, giant trees, and stupendous waterfalls that surpassed anything in the known world. Areas that only shortly before had been parts

***The Mountain of the Holy Cross* (1875) by Thomas Moran.** In 1871, Moran traveled west with a government-sponsored expedition and produced numerous field studies. From these studies came three of his major works, including this painting and *Grand Canyon of the Yellowstone* (1872) and *Chasm of the Colorado* (1873–1874). © GEOFFREY CLEMENTS/CORBIS of Mexico, or "undiscovered" Indian lands, became national natural monuments that glorified a new continental empire. These sentiments are clearly evident in Thomas Moran's *Mountain of the Holy Cross* (1875), which depicts a famous site in the Rocky Mountains. Marked by two perpendicular channels that captured and held winter snows, the upper face of the mountain presented a pure white cross through much of the year that seemed to represent divine confirmation of the nation's manifest destiny. Like the snow-white cross in the wilderness, the spectacular landscapes of the New West were more than artistic subjects; they also became popular pilgrimage sites for eastern tourists who found in places like Yellowstone or Yosemite a chance to share their national identity and an appreciation for natural beauty. Indeed, as Samuel Bowles declared in a widely read travel memoir, visiting the West was to immerse oneself in "the center of the central life of America" (p. 35).

POST-FRONTIER ANXIETY AND THE MILLENNIAL WEST

When Frederick Jackson Turner gave his paper "The Significance of the Frontier in American History" at the World's Columbian Exposition in Chicago in 1893, he was doing more than formulating a theory for interpreting the history of the United States. For Americans living at the end of the nineteenth century, Turner believed the great significance of the frontier lay in its closing. "Up to our own day," he proclaimed, "American history has been in a large degree the history of the colonization of the Great West. The existence of an area of free land, its continuous recession, and the advance of American settlement westward, explain American development" (p. 1). Freighted with a history of powerful cultural biases, Turner's Victorian language sanitizes an often brutal form of conquest in terms that reflected older conceptions of the West as a sort of national tabula rasa. While this sentiment has attracted the most attention from Turner's critics, and certainly reflects the common assumptions of his contemporaries, his argument also proved so compelling because of the sense of alarm it implied in its conclusion:

> What the Mediterranean Sea was to the Greeks, breaking the bond of custom, offering new experiences, calling out new institutions and activities, that, and more, the ever retreating frontier has been to the United States directly. . . . And now, four centuries from the discovery of America, at the end of a hundred years of life under the Constitution, the

frontier has gone, and with its going has closed the first period of American history. (p. 35)

If the frontier explained American development, and the frontier was closed, then what could provide the model for future national development?

A kind of post-frontier anxiety troubled many turn-of-the-century intellectuals, who believed that immigration, industrialization, and urbanization were destroying the fabric of the United States. Fears that America would become another Europe, riddled by class wars and social chaos, echoed the concerns that had once inspired Thomas Jefferson, but were met with a new faith in technological innovation and managerial expertise. As the place of the frontier's recent closing, the West still represented the hope for the nation's future—where active federal management of natural resources could perpetuate the conditions on which the nation was built. Through conservation of forests and grasslands, development and reclamation of rivers and crop lands, and the preservation of scenic frontier "vignettes" in national parks, the West could still fulfill the promise of a nation long predicated on ideals about regeneration and personal liberation.

Perhaps no one better embodied these concerns and hopes than President Theodore Roosevelt. In his annual message to Congress in 1907, he declared that "The conservation of our natural resources and their proper use constitute the fundamental problem which underlies almost every other problem of our national life. . . . As a nation we not only enjoy a wonderful measure of present prosperity but if this prosperity is used aright it is an earnest of future success such as no other nation will have." Because this prosperity was based on a wealth of natural resources, Roosevelt believed that national collapse would ensue if the reckless and wasteful exploitation of the West continued unabated. Conservation and management of the region's natural resources was urgently needed, and this could only be accomplished when government experts could "substitute a planned and orderly development of our resources in place of a haphazard striving for immediate profit" (*Works,* vol. 14, p. 112).

Roosevelt was as much concerned about how the closing of the frontier might threaten the economic strength of the United States as he feared its effects on national character. As he wrote in his popular book *The Wilderness Hunter* (1893), Americans required contact with a wilderness frontier to "cultivate that vigorous manliness for the lack of which in a nation, as in an individual, the possession of no other qualities can possibly atone" (p. xxxi).

Along with conservation of natural resources, the federal government needed to preserve scenic locales where Americans could experience the essential qualities of western frontiers. Such contact with the "strenuous life," as Roosevelt termed it, would allow urbanized Americans to incorporate the supposed virtues of a homogenous frontier in an increasingly diverse nation. This was most readily accomplished in the establishment of national parks and monuments, but Roosevelt's concerns were echoed in the fields of history, anthropology, literature, and art. While scholars like Turner sought to explicate the essential characteristics of national development, anthropologists worked to preserve in museums and books the "last remnants of the savage race" that had tested and shaped the nation's frontier character. Artists like Frederic Remington and Charles Russell, as well as writers like Zane Grey and Mary Austin, also sought to preserve the frontier in paint and prose, and all modeled their personal lives in atavistic tribute to a Romantic past. Through active cultivation of the qualities that had created the West, the frontier itself could be conserved and preserved to shape the character of future generations.

While artistic, academic, and political concerns kept the frontier and the West at the center of national discourse, this was greatly augmented by more popular approaches to the subject and the region. Wild West shows, cheap lithographs, popular fiction, and the new medium of moving pictures all helped to perpetuate the vitality of western themes in the early twentieth century. Pioneer societies in western counties and states also sought to make frontier stories central to the continuing development of communities as diverse as Helena, Montana, and Santa Cruz, California. The death of each society member became a matter of public concern, in which the funeral and obituary became a ritualized retelling of creating homes in the midst of a savage wilderness.

Such memorializing served to sanitize conquest and ignore the persistence of nonwhite communities. As the twentieth century progressed, however, growing numbers of eastern migrants developed a Romantic nostalgia for a pre-American West. Stories about lone individuals hacking out a competence in the wilderness simply did not fit the reality of a region that had long been the most urbanized part of the United States, with a far higher percentage of its residents living in cities than rural areas. Nor did frontier stories adequately capture their western experience of suburban growth in the 1910s and 1920s. In an effort to become localized

to new surroundings, it seemed better to focus on the West as an established home rather than a new frontier. This sentiment led to a sort of cultural cannibalism, in which the perceived spirit of the conquered is allowed to persist in new cultural forms. Thus a faux Spanish style came to define southern California in myriad ways, including pageants, tourist promotions, and, most significantly, new architectural styles. The complete rebuilding of Santa Barbara in the wake of a devastating 1925 earthquake was probably the most extreme expression of this new identification with a distinct regional history. Supported by the University of California professor Herbert Bolton, who built his career on arguing for the cultural and historical distinctiveness of what he called the Spanish Borderlands, the city developed an architectural review board that required all new construction in the downtown core to use white stucco exteriors and red tile roofs.

Bolton's historical aesthetic was greatly augmented by the interests of the *Los Angeles Times* publisher Charles F. Lummis and others, who also championed the development of a "Southwestern style" in northern New Mexico. Mimicking pueblo designs and assuming Spanish imperial airs, the newly designated "Land of Enchantment" attracted a rich mix of artists and intellectuals who found a unique authenticity in the region's reconstructed past. Other areas of the West did not have the same architectural legacy to exploit, but a sense of regional distinctiveness developed on similar lines. Urbanites in the Pacific Northwest, for instance, sought to make connections to their new homes by collecting native artifacts while residents in the Rocky Mountain and Plains states used images of cowboys and the memory of Indian wars to promote and distinguish their towns and cities. This repackaging of the past was always a markedly one-sided affair and never actually included the people whose cultures it supposedly emulated. In this respect, the search for regional distinctiveness did not so much challenge older frontier narratives as reconstitute them in ways that explained new patterns of growth and settlement in the West.

THE WILD NEW WEST

Urban fantasies about a stylized pre-western past and a passion for constructing a certain "spirit of place" continues to define the region for residents and visitors alike. Nevertheless, it is the wide-open spaces that seem to best embody old notions about regeneration and personal freedom. Because the federal government controls a vast public domain that constitutes 50 percent of all land in the West, the allure of the region and its past has taken on a certain Janus-faced quality that reflects broader historical changes. On the one hand, the personal freedoms associated with the western landscape are only possible because of Washington's active management of these lands. The injection of huge amounts of federal money also fostered an explosion in the growth of urban areas. Founded on a broad but potentially antagonistic set of developments, this new federal West would be plagued by competing visions of the frontier and the meaning of the West throughout the second half of the twentieth century. In many respects, these changes reflected just another manifestation of the West as the nation's region. Rapid economic growth also revitalized older ideas about the West as a blessed land of opportunity. Based on the availability of relatively cheap real estate, compounded with government subsidies for water, electricity, and transportation, the West also developed in brand new ways. Sprawling industrial complexes, many of them defense related, were surrounded by vast stretches of suburban neighborhoods as places like Los Angeles became "horizontal cities" that spread across the landscape rather than rising up to the sky in large downtown buildings.

World War II and the cold war also transformed the demographic landscape of the West in profound ways. Long a region of diverse peoples, war-related industries attracted large migrations of African Americans, Chicanos, and American Indians to urban centers throughout the West. Likewise, a shortage of agricultural laborers led to an increased migration of people from Mexico through the government's *bracero* program, which brought in hundreds of thousands of agricultural and railroad workers. These new migrations into and within the region often reflected older hopes of finding a wider set of opportunities in the West, but they also met with the types of backlash that characterized the late nineteenth century. The internment of Japanese Americans during World War II was a clear expression of one hundred years of anti-Asian bias. The so-called Zoot Suit riots in Los Angeles, when several thousand white soldiers, sailors, and civilian men attacked Mexican American youths in June 1943, reflected the degree to which racial violence continued to define relations between whites and nonwhites in the American West. This was hardly unique to the western United States, but the vast and diverse numbers of new residents pouring into the region intensified social, ethnic, and racial distinctions and fit older historical patterns that had long distinguished the West from the rest of the nation.

While the segregated mosaic of western cities only sharpened in the postwar era, the West seemed a bastion of the untroubled good life to many nonresidents when the struggle for civil rights captivated the rest of the country. It was as if the entire region were a Hollywood Western, a land of untroubled morality tales where individual men stood tall, fought hard, and triumphed over injustice. Whether in the image of a cowboy on the silver screen, or in the life of a beach bum surfing San Onofre, the West seemed to remain a place where individualism mattered. To an electorate worried about corporate conformity, yet equally fearful of racial diversity and the threat of communism, such qualities made western politicians like Richard Nixon, Barry Goldwater, and Ronald Reagan especially appealing to a national audience. Whether in politics, art, or entertainment, the imagined virtues of the frontier continued to inform a widespread conception of the West as a place to pursue happiness, prosper, and be true to oneself.

Such qualities had long attracted a wide assortment of people to the West and might explain the variety of unique religious groups that have formed in or moved to the region. From the nineteenth-century Mormons in Utah to the "Rajneeshees" in central Oregon during the 1980s, to all the arch conservative and free-spirited cults, religions, and churches in between, the West has been home to the richest spiritual mix in the history of the planet. These characteristics might also explain why the counter-cultural movements of the 1960s and 1970s took hold so firmly in a region equally noted for its social conservatism. Indeed, it is because of this cultural and ideological polarity that the cultural changes that rocked the nation at this time would affect the American West in especially profound ways.

In the 1950s the relatively widespread if unequal prosperity throughout the region partly explains why the West did not see the types of public racial violence that plagued the South. Nevertheless, the civil rights movement inspired a variety of potent attempts to redress a long history of inequity in the West. With what seemed like a sudden burst into the national consciousness, western-based groups like the Black Panthers, the American Indian Movement, and the United Farm Workers, as well as Asian-Pacific students at colleges and universities on the West Coast, laid bare the racial fault lines that had long divided the region and quickly transformed parts of the "alternative culture" movement into a powerful drive for social justice. In the process, these movements subverted older assumptions about the West, made claims to a region they had long shaped and called home, and inspired a radical transformation in how the history of the American West should be understood.

To the degree that it still emphasized the types of frontier processes that Frederick Jackson Turner had described at the end of the nineteenth century, western history became increasingly irrelevant in the decades following World War II and interest in the field as a professional discipline dropped off considerably. However, it was profoundly reshaped and invigorated in the 1980s by historians who had come of age in the midst of earlier social justice movements. Often described as "New Western historians," scholars such as Patricia Nelson Limerick and Richard White emphasized that the history of the American West did not revolve around the closing of Turner's frontier. They argued instead that the region has been continually an ongoing contest for resources and opportunities. Unlike Turner, who limited his concerns to Anglo-American farmers, the New Western historians have also focused on the ways that native peoples, Latinos, East Asians, and African Americans have played major roles in the history of the West. More than a product of simple westering tendencies, these scholars have presented the West as a place where different groups have conflicted and interacted with each other to shape the region's social, economic, and cultural history.

The term "frontier" has long carried powerful cultural biases, which has led some scholars to dismiss it with a certain expletive quality as the "F" word of western history. In an effort to retain some of its useful applications, others have chosen to redefine the concept in more value-neutral language, such as "cultural contact zone" or "arenas of conflict and cooperation." Besides avoiding the insulting implications of Turner's Victorian language, these newer conceptions of the frontier allow for a more nuanced interpretation of diverse historical interactions. No longer viewed as an outward moving line of American expansion or the meeting point of two cultural monoliths, one "civilized" and the other "savage," the new scholarly discourse on frontiers views them as dynamic places that often involve multiple groups of people who draw on various cultural backgrounds.

Whether the frontier is redefined or ignored, older notions about westward expansion still remain powerful shapers of the region, its residents, and how both are perceived in other parts of the nation and around the world. Late-twentieth-century scholarship on frontiers suggested new ideas about the West, but older patterns that find their meaning in a simpler understanding of the frontier remain imbedded in the region they created. Movements to deny public schooling to the children of immigrants from Latin America, the growth of white separatist movements in Idaho, and efforts to define Indian treaty rights as special privileges that discriminate against non-Indians all reflect various efforts to define the West and its residents according to older notions of the frontier. Such examples represent extreme positions that are not always widely shared across the region, and all are vigorously challenged in ways that were not possible in the mid-twentieth century. Nevertheless, such attitudes draw strength from outside the region as well, where the West remains a fantasy landscape—a sort of Disney Frontierland writ large.

The conflation of the West with the frontier is also becoming one of the most financially viable ideas in the region, as tourism converts the rural West into a playground for people from urban and suburban areas. In places like Vail, Colorado; Bend, Oregon; or Jackson Hole, Wyoming; visitors are enticed with the opportunity to "relive the spirit of the Old West." Though based on a comfortable, holiday version of the frontier, the powerful appeal of these places and the history they purport to represent is a strong indication of the degree to which the regional West remains tied to ideas about the frontier. These sentiments go beyond the appeal of a vacation in the Rocky Mountains, however. The rural West is increasingly becoming a place where residence is predicated on access to recreational and scenic amenities. In the process, new homes and developments are transforming old mining towns and ranches into carefully designed places for an enticing form of "western living." For those displaced by these changes, or those left behind by the affluent refugees who are fleeing the urban centers of the region for its less crowded interior, the struggle over how the West is defined, and who is a westerner, remains a central feature of the region. Likewise, the effort to connect identity and locale to a particular conception of the frontier remains firmly in place.

494

See also **Agrarianism and the Agrarian Ideal in Early America; Prophetic Native American Movements; Expansion and Empire** *(volume 1);* **Native Americans** *(in this volume); and other articles in this section.*

BIBLIOGRAPHY

Primary Works

Bowles, Samuel. *The Parks and Mountains of Colorado: A Summer Vacation in the Switzerland of America.* Edited by James H. Pickering. 1868. Reprint, Norman, Okla., 1991. Page references in the text are from the reprint edition.

Boyd, Julian, ed. *The Papers of Thomas Jefferson.* 27 vols. Princeton, N.J., 1950– .

Cole, Thomas. *Thomas Cole: The Collected Essays and Prose Sketches.* Edited by Marshall Tymn. St. Paul, Minn., 1980.

Emerson, Ralph Waldo. "The American Scholar." In *The Collected Works of Ralph Waldo Emerson: Nature, Addresses, and Lectures.* Edited by Robert E. Spiller and Alfred R. Ferguson, pp. 52–70. Cambridge, Mass., 1971.

Jefferson, Thomas. "Notes on the State of Virginia." In *The Life and Selected Writings of Thomas Jefferson.* Edited by Adrienne Koch and William Peden, pp. 187–288. New York, 1944.

Lipscomb, Andrew A., and Albert Ellery Bergh, ed. *Writings of Thomas Jefferson.* 20 vols. Washington, D.C., 1903–1904.

Roosevelt, Theodore. *The Wilderness Hunter.* 1893. Reprint, New York, 1909. Page references in the text are from the reprint edition.

———. *The Works of Theodore Roosevelt.* 26 vols. New York, 1906–1910.

Turner, Frederick Jackson. "The Significance of the Frontier in American History." In *The Frontier in American History,* pp. 1–35. New York, 1920.

Whitman, Walt. *Leaves of Grass.* Boston, 1881–1882.

Secondary Works

Adelman, Jeremy, and Stephen Aron. "From Borderlands to Borders: Empires, Nation-States, and the Peoples in Between in North American History." *American Historical Review* 104 (June 1999): 814–841.

Athearn, Robert. *The Mythic West in Twentieth-Century America.* Lawrence, Kans., 1986.

Cronon, William, George Miles, and Jay Gitlin, ed. *Under an Open Sky: Rethinking America's Western Past.* New York, 1992.

Deverell, William. "Fighting Words: The Significance of the American West in the History of the United States." *Western Historical Quarterly* 25 (summer 1994): 185–206.

Dippie, Brian W. *The Vanishing American: White Attitudes and U.S. Indian Policy.* Middletown, Conn., 1982.

Goetzman, William H., and William N. Goetzman. *The West of the Imagination.* New York, 1986.

Hyde, Anne Farrar. *An American Vision: Far Western Landscape and National Culture, 1820–1920.* New York, 1990.

Klein, Kerwin Lee. *Frontiers of Historical Imagination: Narrating the European Conquest of Native America, 1890–1990.* Berkeley, Calif., 1997.

Kolodny, Annette. *The Land Before Her: Fantasy and Experience of the American Frontiers, 1630–1860.* Chapel Hill, N.C., 1984.

Limerick, Patricia Nelson. *The Legacy of Conquest: The Unbroken Past of the American West.* New York, 1987.

Limerick, Patricia Nelson, Charles E. Rankin, and Clyde A. Milner, eds. *Trails: Toward a New Western History.* Lawrence, Kans., 1991.

Marx, Leo. *The Machine in the Garden: Technology and the Pastoral Ideal in America.* New York, 1964.

Matsumoto, Valerie, and Blake Allmendinger, eds. *Over the Edge: Remapping the American West.* Berkeley, Calif., 1999.

Mitchell, Lee Clark. *Witnesses to a Vanishing America: The Nineteenth-Century Response.* Princeton, N.J., 1981.

Pearce, Roy Harvey. *Savagism and Civilization: A Study of the Indian and the American Mind,* rev. ed. of *The Savages of America.* Berkeley, Calif., 1988.

Pomeroy, Earl. *In Search of the Golden West: The Tourist in Western America.* New York, 1957.

Prown, Jules, et al. *Discovered Lands, Invented Pasts: Transforming Visions of the American West.* New Haven, Conn., 1992.

Ronda, James P., ed. *Thomas Jefferson and the Changing West.* Albuquerque, N. Mex., 1997.

Rothman, Hal K. *Devil's Bargains: Tourism in the Twentieth-Century American West.* Lawrence, Kans., 1998.

Slotkin, Richard. *Gunfighter Nation: The Myth of the Frontier in Twentieth-Century America.* New York, 1992.

Smith, Henry Nash. *Virgin Land: The American West as Symbol and Myth.* 2d ed. Cambridge, Mass., 1970.

Truettner, William H., ed. *The West as America: Reinterpreting Images of the Frontier, 1820–1920.* Washington, D.C., 1991.

Utley, Robert. *The Indian Frontier of the American West, 1846–1890.* Albuquerque, N. Mex., 1984.

West, Elliott. *The Way to the West: Essays on the Central Plains.* Albuquerque, N. Mex., 1995.

White, Richard. *"It's Your Misfortune and None of My Own": A History of the American West.* Norman, Okla., 1991.

THE IDEA OF THE SOUTH

Paul V. Murphy

The custom of identifying a particular region of the United States as the "South" is deeply rooted in American history but often a matter of some imprecision. Does the South embody only the eleven states that seceded from the Union in 1860 and 1861 to form the Confederate States of America, or does it include border states such as Kentucky and Missouri? What of the state of Oklahoma, which only entered the Union in 1907 but is often aligned with Texas? Or, is the South a region chiefly distinguished by certain cultural characteristics, as, for example, a high membership in evangelical Christian churches, a preference for country music, or an adherence to rural values? With this in mind, should the South include the lower half of Illinois and Indiana and exclude Miami, Florida, and northeastern Virginia? Such questions emphasize the fact that the American South is, in fact, an idea, one that began to gain currency at the time the nation was formed. The boundary of the American South is a matter of convention, enclosing a geographical region marked by a variety of climatic conditions, soil characteristics, and geographical features. When Charles Mason and Jeremiah Dixon surveyed the line between Pennsylvania and Maryland in the 1760s, it should be noted, they were resolving a boundary dispute, not distinguishing North and South. By the end of the American Revolution, however, the Ohio River and the Mason-Dixon line had come to demarcate a distinct American region, one defined by social and cultural customs resulting from large-scale plantation agriculture, staple crop production, and race-based slavery.

It was out of the cultural and political, as opposed to the geographical, entity of the South that a second and more complex idea of the South emerged, one that not only demarcated boundaries but also asserted an identity and assigned value. This idea began to form before the Civil War, but its heyday was roughly an eighty-year period stretching from 1865 through 1945. It retains some meaning in contemporary America, even as it is recognized as a product of human invention that only inaccurately describes social reality. This idea of the South suggested the existence of a coherent, unified, and undifferentiated people, one whose behavior and customs were both so unique and predictably alike as to suggest the operation of a single, organizing "mind," and so exotic and flamboyant as to be distinct from the majority of Americans. It was productive of stereotypes: the people of the South were passionate and violent; their lives were governed by a medieval code of honor, their society shaped by deep commitments to family, community, and place. Americans were individualistic and hard working; southerners were patriarchal and prone to laziness. Above all, the South was, according to such stereotypes, fundamentalist in religion, paradoxically swinging between displays of moral censoriousness and hedonistic abandon. Sin and sanctity were measured in equal amounts in southern life. "There is often a plaintive note about the stories we tell in the South, often the theme is sorrow," the journalist Ben Robertson recalled in a 1942 memoir of his upcountry South Carolina home, *Red Hills & Cotton.* "The world to us is filled with sin, and for our souls there is a struggle that never stops. In the South we had rather save our souls than make a lot of money." The South, where life was leisurely and unhurried, was, in the mind of Robertson and many others, an antimaterialist exception to the American mainstream.

This idea did not merely define a region and assign a geographical boundary; it characterized a people and a culture and set bounds of membership. Whites were included, blacks were not. It became a dominant modality through which writers and intellectuals, predominantly but not exclusively southern, conceived of, discussed, and criticized southern society. Its meaning and content varied, and its connotation could be either negative or positive. Although often focused on certain assumed qualities relating to family, conservative religious beliefs, and loyalty to community and place, the emphasis could differ. A commitment to chivalry and honor could be interpreted as a predilection for unreflective violence; a premium on manners and hospitality could be seen as a weakness for sham sentiment and self-delusion; a healthy love for leisure, play, and talk could be dismissed as a tendency toward laziness, self-indulgence, and florid rhetoric. The idea of the South has tended to occur in two modes: one centered on the gentry and one on the yeoman. And it has tended to signal resistance to modernization and modernity. Persistently over time, the idea of the South has suggested atavism and intransigence, a people poised resolutely against the forces of industrialization, democratization, liberalization, and homogenization, standing against, for good or ill, the forces most other Americans accept as progress. This idea of the South has fostered both admiration and distaste for southern culture on the part of both southerners and non-southerners alike.

ORIGINS OF REGIONAL IDENTITY AND SOUTHERN NATIONALISM

Some early settlers thought that the Chesapeake colonies represented an agrarian paradise, in which healthful living would be available to the hardworking emigrant. Certainly the Virginian Thomas Jefferson's agrarian republicanism drew in part from these roots. "We have now lands enough to employ an infinite number of people in their cultivation," Jefferson wrote to the statesman John Jay in 1785. "Cultivators of the earth are the most valuable citizens. They are the most vigorous, the most independant [sic], the most virtuous, & they are tied to their country & wedded to it's [sic] liberty & interests by the most lasting bonds." Not all observers agreed. A visitor from England concluded that the climate of Virginia had made its inhabitants "indolent, easy, and good natured; extremely fond of society, and much given to convivial pleasures. In consequence of this, they seldom show any spirit of enterprise, or expose themselves willingly to fatigue." Jefferson himself, in contrasting regional personality types in a 1785 letter to the Marquis de Chastellux, found southerners to be fiery, voluptuous, indolent, and unsteady whereas northerners were cool, sober, laborious, and independent. (Southerners, however, were generous and candid; northerners were "interested" and "chicaning.")

By the end of the American Revolution, then, general distinctions between North and South, and between northerners and southerners, somewhat along the lines of later stereotypes, were in place. Moreover, southern politicians were pointing to distinct regional economic interests. Yet the revolution tended to unite northerners and southerners as Americans rather than reinforce a southern regional identity. Until the outbreak of the Civil War, many southerners espoused a strong loyalty to the Union, even as they had increasingly come to identify with the South as well. A self-conscious self-identification as southerner and the beginnings of southern nationalism emerged in the 1830s following the nullification controversy—South Carolina's resistance to the federal government's power to impose tariffs. Southern nationalism grew as the economic fortunes of the coastal southern states declined and the imperative behind the plantation economy became expansion. Slavery, the plantation system, and staple-crop agriculture exerted a unifying force in the South, but southern nationalism was a defensive reaction in the South, arising more from increasing fears of slave revolt and resentment at northern moral condemnation than from the growth of a common cultural identity. Southerners wanted respect for their society and the preservation of the slave system. A rising animosity for the North and fear for their future led many southerners to countenance disunion by 1860.

Southern intellectuals did not develop a strong romantic nationalism before the war, but southern novelists had begun to develop the plantation legend, in which men were chivalrous and women were pedestalized. The first plantation romance was George Tucker's *The Valley of Shenandoah* (1824). John Pendleton Kennedy's *Swallow Barn* (1832) and William Alexander Caruthers's *The Cavaliers of Virginia* (1834), as well as later novels by William Gilmore Simms and John Esten Cooke, created and elaborated upon the Cavalier image—a refined southern gentry that could supposedly trace its roots to the well-born royalist exiles who settled Virginia in the seventeenth century. The vision of the South these authors presented was not completely sentimentalized, nor were they averse to criticizing southern institutions. Moreover, both northern and southern writers participated in the creation of the image of the romantic Cavalier and his opposite, the grasping, uncouth, and calculating Yankee businessman, and used it as a form of social criticism. By the 1850s, according to the scholar William Taylor, both stereotypes were embedded in the American imagination and expressed the essential conflict that had developed "between a decorous, agrarian South and the rootless, shifting, money-minded North." The idea of the South was implicit in such images. It was the war itself and the experience of defeat, however, that brought the idea to fruition.

CREATION OF THE IDEA OF THE SOUTH, 1865–1915

Southern nationalism was more a product of defeat in the Civil War than the force that created it, as the historian David Potter observed. It was through the war and the shared experience of defeat—both experiences that seriously distorted southern society and left it economically impoverished—that a tighter, more cohesive sense of white southern cultural identity emerged. The war, the historian Charles Reagan Wilson argued, resulted in the creation of a civil religion of the "Lost Cause," a phrase taken from an 1866 history of the Confederacy written by Edward A. Pollard. Christian clergy became the ministants of this religion, which held the war to be a moral crusade against a godless and materialistic North. The repeated appeal to the "baptism of blood" undergone by the South suggested to southerners the creation of a new, somehow spiritualized nation, one in which the war was an act of atonement and the sacrifice a source of sanctification. Confederate veterans carefully tended the memory of the war, establishing the fledgling Southern Historical Society in New Orleans in 1869. They reorganized it four years later in Richmond and, in 1876, established the *Southern Historical Society Papers,* which published a wealth of historical documentation on the Confederate military. The religion of the Lost Cause was promulgated in churches, at meetings of Confederate veterans groups, and in the violence of the Ku Klux Klan and similar prosouthern paramilitary squads. Funerals of Confederate heroes became occasions for the ritual remembrance of the war, as did Confederate Memorial Day observances and, eventually, veterans reunions. Confederate monuments spread across the southern landscape, particularly between 1890 and 1910. The United Confederate Veterans was formed in 1890, followed later in that decade by the United Daughters of the Confederacy and the United Sons of the Confederacy.

If the idea of a united, culturally cohesive South, defined in terms of moral and spiritual propositions, was born of the crucible of war and defeat, it was fostered in the late nineteenth century by probusiness reformers who sought to attract northern capital to the South in order to spur southern in-

dustrial and commercial development. The southern propagandists of a "New South," most notably newspapermen such as Henry Grady of the *Atlanta Constitution,* Richard H. Edmonds of the *Baltimore Manufacturers' Record,* Henry Watterson of the *Louisville Courier-Journal,* and Francis W. Dawson of the *Charleston News and Courier,* stressed racial accommodation (they promised paternalistic concern and fairness for blacks but not social equality, equal opportunity, or political rights) and sectional reconciliation. They criticized the South's prewar reliance on staple-crop agriculture as well as the slave economy and preached the virtues of agricultural and economic diversification. The New South spokesmen trumpeted a transformation that they already saw underway, but they were also advocating a partial modernization of the South (the embrace of industrialization but not political or racial liberalization). In doing this, they made strong cultural appeals to white identity, engaging in lavish testimonials to the virtues of the plantation South, affirming the moral superiority of southern civilization, and doing much to promulgate the "moonlight-and-magnolias" tradition of southern remembrance. "The New South," the historian Michael O'Brien observed, "helped to make permanent the very idea of a South."

The positive historical reconstruction of the Old South plantation society was a crucial element of the southern white oligarchy's successful program to end northern-administered Reconstruction, reimpose its authority over white society, and, by the 1890s, construct a sophisticated and effective system of white supremacy, which was founded upon rigid and legal racial segregation, disfranchisement of black voters, and the persistent threat of racial violence to any blacks that threatened the new order. The period from 1890 to 1915 was the historical nadir for African Americans in the South, a period in which white anti-black violence and hatred, evident most notably in ritualized lynching spectacles that drew large popular audiences, reached arguably pathological levels. Southern whites convinced a northern audience that Reconstruction had represented the ghastly imposition of ignorant, corrupt, and incompetent black rule upon the South. It was in this late-nineteenth-century atmosphere that southern whites were able to establish their most cohesive and distinctive regional identity, one that was viewed by many northerners as very positive. The plantation romance entered its most popular phase in this period and was exemplified by the work of Thomas Nelson Page, a Virginia lawyer and diplomat who traced his ancestry to antebellum aristocrats. Page's most famous story is "Marse Chan," a fond remembrance of the plantation told in black dialect by an ex-slave, which was collected with like stories in *In Ole Virginia* (1887). The black narrator hearkens back to "de good ol' days befo' de war" and declaims, "Dem was good ol' times, Marster, de bes' Sam ever see." Edwin Anderson Alderman and Joel Chandler Harris's edited collection, the seventeen-volume *Library of Southern Literature* (1907–1913), attests to the white South's self-conscious awareness of its cultural heritage and reinforces the idea of a unified South, a single people shaped by a common mind.

THE IDEA OF THE SOUTH AND THE SOUTHERN RENAISSANCE, 1920–1945

By the 1920s, the idea of the South was in full bloom, and its effect was to drive many southerners, writers and artists, journalists and academics, to a sustained probing of themselves and their region. In the years after World War I, the intense race hatred and persecution of the previous era diminished somewhat in the South; segregation was firmly established and functioning as intended, providing some breathing space for southern intellectuals. At the same time, many young southern artists and academics were gaining exposure, whether through their experiences in war, through travel, or at the South's colleges and universities, to the currents of modernism that were reshaping the broader cultural and intellectual life of America. To many of these intellectuals, the intellectual contradictions of the idea of the South were apparent, as well as, on some level, the psychic costs of being southern: the unspoken codes of authority, the rigid expectations of orthodoxy and loyalty, the sense of common identity and membership that was alternately comforting and suffocating. Some felt a nagging rub of doubt and guilt on the question of race. The idea of the South and the mythology of the Lost Cause exerted a profound hold on this postwar generation of southerners, but many were, simultaneously, pulled in cosmopolitan directions and confronted by a full-scale assault on the religious orthodoxy so central to the South (and so painfully on display, for some cosmopolitan southerners, in the 1925 Scopes anti-evolution trial in Tennessee). The result was a tremendous intellectual outpouring—the Southern Renaissance—of distinctive art and commentary produced by a generation of history-obsessed, often God-haunted, but always eloquent southerners.

The southern literary renaissance should not be narrowly conceived. It was evidenced in the productions of southern novelists, dramatists, and poets such as William Faulkner, Erskine Caldwell, Thomas Wolfe, Dubose Heyward, Julia Peterkin, Paul Green, John Crowe Ransom, Allen Tate, Donald Davidson, Robert Penn Warren, Caroline Gordon, John Gould Fletcher, Andrew Nelson Lytle, Stark Young, and the early work of Katherine Anne Porter, Lillian Hellman, and Eudora Welty, and also in the sociology of Howard Odum and Rupert B. Vance at the University of North Carolina; the journalism of Gerald W. Johnson, Wilbur J. Cash, Jonathan Daniels, and the young James Agee; the scholarship of Broadus Mitchell, V. O. Key, and C. Vann Woodward; and the criticism of Cleanth Brooks. This generation of southern writers, the scholar Richard Gray argued, were aware of the mythologies of their region and, even as they adhered to them, "they had to reinvent them, reinterpret them according to their needs, and in the process think more critically, argue more provocatively, and write with more imaginative force and daring than most of their predecessors in the region."

The southern poet and critic Allen Tate memorably attributed the renaissance to the delayed modernization of the South and his generation's experience of the sudden transition from tradition to modernity. "With the war of 1914–1918, the South reentered the world—but gave a backward glance as it stepped over the border: that backward glance gave us the Southern renascence, a literature conscious of the past in the present," he wrote. There was, of course, no prior period of southern literary brilliance to serve as antecedent for this rebirth. As Michael O'Brien observed, Tate and others, in conceptualizing such a renaissance, were tapping into a well-established Romantic paradigm by which a "renaissance" was the way in which a people's passage from tradition and folkways to urbanity and cosmopolitanism was marked. For O'Brien, the idea of the South, which came to full fruition in the interwar period, was entirely a function of the Romanticism that had seeped into southern intellectual life in the early nineteenth century. Romanticism combines a sociology of community and psychology of alienation. While not a simple response to the industrial revolution, it brilliantly addresses the psychic needs produced by people experiencing industrialization, as communities are sundered, traditions destroyed, and individuals left to navigate life in large cities more nearly alone. Romantics posited an organic relationship between a people, its land, and its culture. The efflorescence of regionalist thought in the South in the late nineteenth and early twentieth centuries comprised versions of Romantic sociology. The idea of a unified South was a careful construction of such Romantic southerners. "By no stretch of anything but a phenomenological imagination," O'Brien observed, alluding to the German intellectual traditions important to many southerners, "can so huge and diverse an area as the South be designated a community." Tate's "backward glance" formulation was misleading; southerners were indeed casting a skeptical eye at the forces of modernization, but they were also struggling with the spiritual and emotional contradictions of their culturally constructed southern identity—and were preparing to shed it.

The 1920s and 1930s witnessed an apex in regionalist thinking in America, not only in the South but across the nation. There was an interest across the nation in learning more about the South and reading southern authors. The mass audience stood ready to consume the idea of the South; New York publishers scavenged for plantation romances. Margaret Mitchell's *Gone with the Wind* (1936), which portrays a somewhat complex and ambivalent South, is the most notable success. Moreover, the national audience stood ready to consume multiple images of the South, including those of the poor whites and the yeoman farmer as well as the genteel planter. The idea of a wholesome and spiritual South, boldly resistant to modernity and corruption, could be transmitted through tales of the folk just as readily as through those of the master class. A strong southern literature of folk humor and local color developed in the nineteenth century; Appalachian "primitives" were discovered at the end of that century. In the 1920s, a spate of novels about poor whites appeared, many of them sympathetic and almost idealized. In addition, the commercial recording industry began to issue records by rural and working-class southern musicians, such as Fiddlin' John Carson and Jimmie Rodgers. "Hillbilly" music, which evolved into country-and-western music in the 1930s and 1940s, was purchased nationally by southern migrants but available to others as well. At the same time, less flattering portraits of poor southern whites emerged. T. S. Stribling and Erskine Caldwell published tales featuring poor white southerners immured in poverty, disease, and social dysfunction. The images of southern rural identity were turned by Stribling, Caldwell, and others into effective forms of social critique. Nevertheless the creation of comically grotesque characters, such as Jeeter Lester, the hero of Caldwell's *Tobacco Road* (1932), contributed to the creation of what

the historian George Brown Tindall identified as the myth of the Benighted South in the 1920s. The fabulous caricatures of southern greed and sensuality and the perversity present in the work of such writers as Caldwell and William Faulkner led to what the novelist Ellen Glasgow dubbed the school of Southern Gothic.

In 1930 a coterie of faculty and students at Vanderbilt University in Nashville, Tennessee, which included John Crowe Ransom, Allen Tate, Donald Davidson, and the young Robert Penn Warren, organized the publication of *I'll Take My Stand: The South and the Agrarian Tradition,* a collection of essays authored, according to its title page, by "Twelve Southerners." The symposium was a conscious manipulation of the idea of the South but also a serious attempt to criticize industrial capitalism and what the authors considered the mindless cult of progress in 1920s America. The Agrarians, as the group came to be called, seriously upheld subsistence agriculture as a viable alternative to industrialism, tapping into deep-rooted cultural myths when declaring that "the culture of the soil is the best and most sensitive of vocations." Industrial progress, they argued, will endow southern towns with thousands of miles of concrete walks but with no direction in which to go. It undercut artistic production that was authentically connected to the people, the wholesome culture of the yeoman, an individual's connection to nature and to God, and the elements of a good life—leisure, conversation, and hospitality. The Agrarians' counsel to fellow southerners was resistance. "Do what we did after the war and the Reconstruction: return to our looms, our hand crafts, our reproducing stock," Andrew Nelson Lytle argued. "Throw out the radio and take down the fiddle from the wall." At the core of *I'll Take My Stand* was an effort by modern southern intellectuals to redefine but retain the idea of the South. As southerners had desired for generations, the Agrarians wanted progress but on their own terms, they sought to change but not to capitulate to the features of modernization that bred alienation. They sought, in Ransom's words, to be "reconstructed but unregenerate."

Not all southerners agreed with the Agrarians. Indeed, many accused them of being hopelessly nostalgic and unrealistic. Howard Odum and those gathered around him at the University of North Carolina cared no less about their southern identity but embraced progress and sought, through expert regional planning, to improve the social and economic prospects of the region. For many others, an embrace of southernness itself posed difficulties.

Three intellectuals from the interwar period epitomize the deep ambivalence that southern intellectuals displayed toward the idea of the South at the height of its cultural authority: Allen Tate, William Faulkner, and Wilbur J. Cash. The tensions implicit in the self-conscious and intransigent appeal to the southern past threaded throughout agrarianism were manifest in Allen Tate, who, with William Faulkner, was the most important literary figure in the twentieth-century South. Tate's Agrarian phase was marked by a deeply ambivalent relation to the southern past. Torn between a patrician maternal ancestry and a more plebeian paternal inheritance, Tate signaled his personal alienation from the myth of the Lost Cause in his poem "Ode to the Confederate Dead" (1926; revised in 1937), in which the narcissistic narrator stands puzzled before a Confederate graveyard, acutely aware of but fatally separated from the dead's past sacrifice. "What shall we say who have knowledge / Carried to the heart?" he asks. Shall we, he continues plaintively, "set up the grave / In the house?" By the time of *I'll Take My Stand,* and despite an intense immersion in southern history, which resulted in two Civil War biographies, Tate was openly fretting about the vigorous sectionalism of the symposium. Over the course of the 1930s, he found southernism to be antithetical to his artistic and critical ambitions and, in that decade and beyond, moved to articulate an independent cultural stance of the man of letters and to reinterpret agrarianism as a defense of Christian humanism broadly conceived. His sole novel, *The Fathers* (1938), is a poignant admission as a southerner that southern defeat in the Civil War was, in part, due to its own flawed culture. The novel acknowledges two "fathers": both the honor-bound southern gentleman and the unscrupulous and ambitious southern businessman.

Many scholars consider William Faulkner the master spirit of the renaissance, a southern author appropriated by the post–World War II American critical establishment to serve as the nation's modernist genius. Based in Oxford, Mississippi, Faulkner created an entire history, genealogy, and geography for his imagined Yoknapatawpha County in which he set tales that present characters haunted by the weight of their southernness. Faulkner's South is truly gothic, one in which community, pride, and noble intentions are inextricably bound up with suppressed racial guilt, neurotic male attitudes toward women, and carefully ignored perversities. He satirized the emerging business class of the New South as small-minded and mercenary through his portrayal of the Snopes clan; the tragic

William Faulkner (1897–1962). © BETTMANN/CORBIS

Compson family embodies the psychic dilemma of being southern. Faulkner's *Absalom, Absalom!* (1936) is an urtext in any discussion of the idea of the South, not least because of the famous injunction, from the Canadian Shreve McCannon to his southern roommate Quentin Compson, *"Tell about the South. What's it like there. What do they do there. Why do they live there. Why do they live at all,"* that shapes the text. The book is, in fact, a sustained exploration of the meaning of southern identity, but the frustrations of this search are duplicated in the narrative. Ostensibly, the narrative is Quentin's effort to explain his native region and the story of a crude and violent antebellum pioneer, Thomas Sutpen, who carves out a plantation for himself on the frontier, but it is also, in fact, Quentin's own quest to come to terms with the South. The narrative, however, is completely disjointed: multiple narrators are used, stories are disconnected, the reader is granted only limited omniscience. Indeed, Faulkner's thickets of complex and confusing narrative recreate for the reader the jagged difficulties facing any southerner, real or imagined, who attempts to understand the South. In Faulkner's South, humans are trapped by elaborate codes of class distinction, female virtue, and racial hypocrisy and haunted by the powerful repercussions of perceived past sins. The culture of the South distorts lives, blocks understanding, and makes honor the enemy of love and honest emotion. At the end of the novel, Shreve asks Quentin why he hates the South. "I dont hate it," Quentin replies. "I dont hate it."

Wilbur J. Cash rivals Faulkner in importance as an interpreter and analyst of the idea of the South because of the impact of his one book, *The Mind of the South* (1941), published shortly before his own suicide. Cash authored a scathing attack on prevailing southern opinions, but he accepted, as well, the false assumption of a southern "mind" and, in fact, did more than many others to prolong the life of this idea. ("If it can be said there are many Souths," Cash declared, "the fact remains that there is also one South.") For years, scholars reputed Cash's work to be the single most important book to read on the South. In it, he sought to debunk the legend of the Old South, to show the parvenu roots and grasping nature of the Old South elite. He placed the southern yeoman farmer at the center of southern history; the burden of his history was to explain why this southerner historically acted against his self-evident (to Cash) class interests. The answer lay in a debilitating blindness of southerners, their inability to escape mythic constructions, such as the "proto-Dorian convention," the racial bond that united poor whites with their elite class enemies. In the end, southerners, Cash felt, had historically subscribed to a false individualism. They were, in fact, conformists, bound by what Cash called the "savage ideal," a social, political, and cultural straitjacket that demanded absolute loyalty, in which "dissent and variety are completely suppressed and men become, in all their attitudes, professions, and actions, virtual replicas of one another." The "line between what was Southern and what was not" was etched in fire, Cash melodramatically declared. What one must think and say and do is carefully defined:

> And one thought it, said it, did it, exactly as it was ordained, or one stood in pressing peril of being cast out for a damned nigger-loving scoundrel in league with the enemy. Let a man deviate from the strait way once, and by dint of much eating of meek bread he might yet win forgiveness. Let him deviate twice, three times, and men's eyes were hard and dangerous in his, women began to gather their skirts closely about them as they passed, doors that had formerly swung hospitably open slammed in his face, marriage into a decent family became difficult or impossible, the children in the village street howled and cast stones, the dogs developed an inexplicable eagerness to bite him, his creditors were likely to call in the sheriff. (p. 138)

The South was a closed society, free thinking was squelched. Indeed, Cash's book is ultimately an analysis of the southern psyche; he approached the southern mind through what he conceived to be its dark unconscious. This was a notion that made sense to critics and observers throughout the civil rights era. It also made sense, apparently, to southerners. The book was well received in the South.

REDEFINITION, 1945 TO THE PRESENT

The idea of a unitary South collapsed after World War II. Postwar historians, notably C. Vann Woodward, challenged accepted views of southern history, particularly those that posited a seamless and continuous arc to the southern past or that suggested that the South was especially unique and distinctive. Sociologists began to emphasize the diversity of the region. Moreover, the material conditions that had fostered the idea of the South shifted. The Great Depression and World War II profoundly affected the region. New Deal agricultural policy helped spur the end of the sharecropping system and encouraged the concentration and mechanization of agriculture. World War II marked a major watershed, spurring economic growth and migration to the cities. By the 1960s, the South was modernized, with more than half of its population living in urban areas. By 1980, only 3 to 4 percent of southerners farmed. Instead, the South had become part of the Sun Belt (a term coined by the political commentator Kevin Phillips in the 1960s), a region marked by heavy industrialization, diversified agriculture, and prosperity. Perhaps most important, the civil rights movement, arising among African Americans at the grassroots level in cities and rural areas, had upended the southern system of racial segregation. By the mid-1960s, segregation was in full collapse and blacks were reclaiming their right to vote.

With the attainment of modernization in the South, southerners' will to resist it by using the idea of the South lessened. With the coming of racial integration, civil rights for blacks, and relative prosperity, the usefulness of the idea of the South as a mode of social criticism also declined. Moreover, scholars began to talk explicitly of an "idea of the South," or of the myth of the South. In an essay published in 1964, George Brown Tindall suggested that the idea of the South is a "social myth," a mental picture that represents the perceptions and self-perceptions of a people. Although Tindall in fact identified a range of myths that had been operative over the years, the prevailing one was the "plantation myth," which had two dominant versions: one featured a Sunny South with courtly gentlemen, caring masters, gracious and lovely belles, and happy and contented "darkies" in the background; the other envisioned a Benighted South, a violent, miasmal swamp of social dysfunction replete with brutal and mendacious masters, oppressed and abused slaves, and thousands of poor whites—lazy, diseased, and impoverished.

Yet, even as intellectuals analyzed the idea of the South as a cultural construction, the idea itself persisted. Southerners were less likely to assert a unified society or an all-encompassing southern mind, but many continued to treasure a sense of regional distinctiveness, a sense of historical connection to ancestors and place, and a culture that resisted the blandishments of modernity and clung to traditional ways. The revolution of southern race relations shook southern society to its core, leading to various forms of white southern defensiveness as well as an extended discourse among increasingly self-regarding southerners around the question of whether the South still existed, whether the South would survive as a distinctive region or gradually become Americanized and adopt the tastes and habits of an increasingly homogenized national culture. Many southerners began to argue that the South's significance lay, in fact, in the idea that defined it and to embrace the idea of the South as a state of mind.

Conservatives found fertile territory in the South, and several Agrarians and neo-Agrarians took the lead in defining the South in explicitly conservative terms. Whereas previously, southerners had decried Yankees as soulless and money-hungry threats to southern values, now southern conservatives argued that liberals endangered the values most dear to southerners. The Catholic Canadian critic Marshall McLuhan drew close to Allen Tate and his Agrarian associates and came to argue in the 1940s that the South exemplified a humanist culture in which ideas mattered. The most conservative and southern of Agrarians, Donald Davidson, likewise associated the South with moral and intellectual traditionalism, which he felt was under attack from liberalism. "The cause of the South was and is the cause of Western civilization itself," he wrote in 1958. The claim that the South was a synecdoche for Western civilization is evident throughout *Why the South Will Survive* (1981), a neo-Agrarian symposium commemorating the fiftieth anniversary of *I'll Take My Stand*. The point reached absurd heights—and the idea of the South attained a rather attenuated meaning—with the literary scholar Marion Montgomery's contention that the Russian dissident Aleksandr Solzhenitsyn was a southerner in spirit because of the affinity of his traditionalist views with southern conservatism.

More significantly, academics, notably the sociologists Lewis M. Killian and John Shelton Reed and George Brown Tindall, began to argue that white southerners were, in fact, a distinct ethnic group. Using a variety of measures, Reed painstakingly showed the persistence of numerous beliefs and attitudes, whether regarding community, violence, religion, or a variety of other factors, both serious and frivolous, among white southerners. Moreover, southerners continued to identify themselves as different. In the 1970s, in the wake of the integration of the South and the successful presidential bid of the Georgian Jimmy Carter, southernness became chic. The South charted by Reed was a "downhome, funky, country" South of grits and black-eyed peas, pork barbecue and NASCAR racing, blues music and honky-tonk bars. Here was a tolerant, live-and-let-live South in which individualism and eccentricity, as well as a taste for good times and a serious attention to leisure, were not scorned. The co-existence of rock-ribbed evangelical Christianity with a delight in the outlaw culture of the juke joint was not a paradox but an occasion for knowing and ironic comment. Moreover, this South was explicitly multicultural; there were southern cultures, not one unitary South. As some commentators observed, evidence suggested that African Americans were returning to the South in the 1970s and asserting their own identity as black southerners.

A new, informal, let-it-all-hang-out image of the South developed, one indebted to previous images of southern hot heads and voluptuaries as well as sturdy and independent yeoman farmers. This new colorful South had many faces. One could experience southern traditionalism by attending a bluegrass concert, as that music underwent a revival in the 1960s and 1970s; visions of a family-centered and communal South were evident in "The Waltons," a 1970s television series created by the Virginian Earl Hamner Jr. and focusing on a tight-knit southern family surviving the depression in Virginia. In this South, the "rednecks," memorably portrayed as intolerant and murderous bigots in the classic hippie film *Easy Rider* (1969), became hell-raising, rebellious, but sweet-hearted good ole boys. Pickup trucks with gun racks were cultural signifiers and vestiges of rural life, not organs of oppression. The good ole boy flaunted his conservatism and regional pride in "Sweet Home, Alabama," a southern rock anthem by the group Lynyrd Skynyrd, in the country music of Charlie Daniels and Hank Williams Jr., in the good ole boy films of Burt Reynolds, and in the television series *The Dukes of Hazzard*, in which the Duke boys jumped in and out of a car named "General Lee" emblazoned with the rebel flag. The revalorized redneck became, for many, the image of the contemporary South. In her irreverent and uninhibited memoir, *Confessions of a Failed Southern Lady* (1985), Florence King recalled one of her lovers. "I could not deny that the man on the bed personified the worst aspects of the South," she wrote. "I had heard him cuss out the nigras in his work gang and seen them cringe from the pale blue fire flashing in his eyes. It was easy to imagine the rest." But, if this man represents the worst of the South, he also represents the best. "There was no telling what he would do if he got riled, yet he had an underlying sweetness, an almost female tenderness, that had saved my life and sanity. He was that many-splendored thing called a good ole boy. He said grace, he said m'am, and he loved his countries—both of them."

This idea of the South was decidedly countercultural, even postmodern. The rebellious past of the South was not forgotten but rather flaunted with a winking insouciance. Southernness became a lifestyle choice and a commodity, to be studied in the magazine *Southern Living* and in the writing of a new generation of authors and commentators, including Harry Crews, Bobbie Ann Mason, Dorothy Allison, Roy Blount Jr., and Lewis Grizzard. A distinctive southern culture persisted, but the idea of a unitary, coherent South had collapsed. The live-and-let-live culture of the good ole boy could not exert the kind of cultural grip analyzed by Tate, Faulkner, and Cash. In fact, it explicitly disclaimed such a hold. The idea of the South had posited a unitary southern mind; the postmodern South relished variety, change, and ironic disjunction. Southerners had used the idea of the South to resist modernization; postmodern southerners used their collection of cultural signifiers to subvert it.

See also **Agrarianism and the Agrarian Ideal in Early America; Slavery and Race; Secession, War, and Union; Southern Intellectual Life** *(volume 1);* **Whites and the Construction of Whiteness** *(in this volume); and other articles in this section.*

BIBLIOGRAPHY

An excellent starting point for any study of the idea of the South is Charles Reagan Wilson and William Ferris, eds., *Encyclopedia of Southern Culture* (Chapel Hill, N. C., 1989). Useful general overviews of the cultural construction of the South include Richard Gray, *Writing the South: Ideas of an American Region* (Baton Rouge, La., 1997), and Fred Hobson, *Tell About the South: The Southern Rage to Explain* (Baton Rouge, La., 1983). An important collection of essays is Michael O'Brien, *Rethinking the South: Essays in Intellectual History* (Baltimore, 1988). Also useful is Larry J. Griffin and Don H. Doyle, *The South as an American Problem* (Athens, Ga., 1995). William R. Taylor's *Cavalier and Yankee: The Old South and American National Character* (New York, 1961) is a classic and influential study. An older study is Clement Eaton, *The Mind of the Old South* (Baton Rouge, La., 1967).

Studies of southern nationalism include John McCardell, *The Idea of a Southern Nation: Southern Nationalists and Southern Nationalism, 1830–1860* (New York, 1979); Drew Gilpin Faust, *The Creation of Confederate Nationalism: Ideology and Identity in the Civil War South* (Baton Rouge, La., 1988); and Emory M. Thomas, *The Confederate Nation, 1861–1865* (New York, 1979). Also see David M. Potter, *The Impending Crisis, 1848–1861* (New York, 1976), chapter 17. The Lost Cause myth is discussed in Charles Reagan Wilson, *Baptized in Blood: The Religion of the Lost Cause, 1865–1920* (Athens, Ga., 1980), and Gaines M. Foster, *Ghosts of the Confederacy: Defeat, the Lost Cause, and the Emergence of the New South, 1865–1913* (New York, 1987). The classic account of New South ideology is Paul M. Gaston, *The New South Creed: A Study in Southern*

Mythmaking (New York, 1970). Michael O'Brien's *The Idea of the American South, 1920–1941* (Baltimore, 1979) is indispensable in any study of this topic. Also important is Daniel Joseph Singal, *The War Within: From Victorian to Modernist Thought in the South, 1919–1945* (Chapel Hill, N.C., 1982).

On the Southern Renaissance, see Richard H. King, *A Southern Renaissance: The Cultural Awakening of the American South, 1930–1955* (New York, 1980). On southern literature more generally, see Louis D. Rubin Jr. et al., eds., *The History of Southern Literature* (Baton Rouge, La., 1985), and Michael Kreyling, *Inventing Southern Literature* (Jackson, Miss., 1998). An influential study of the Southern agrarians is Louis D. Rubin Jr., *The Wary Fugitives: Four Poets and the South* (Baton Rouge, La., 1978). Also see Paul V. Murphy, *The Rebuke of History: The Southern Agrarians and American Conservative Thought* (Chapel Hill, N.C., forthcoming). Primary sources of interest from the interwar period include Twelve Southerners, *I'll Take My Stand: The South and the Agrarian Tradition* (Baton Rouge, La., 1977); W. J. Cash, *The Mind of the South* (New York, 1960); and William Faulkner, *Absalom, Absalom!* (New York, 1990). A recent biography of Wilbur J. Cash is Bruce Clayton, *W. J. Cash: A Life* (Baton Rouge, La., 1991). Two successor symposia to *I'll Take My Stand* are Louis D. Rubin Jr. and James J. Kilpatrick, eds., *The Lasting South: Fourteen Southerners Look at Their Home* (Chicago, 1957); and Fifteen Southerners, *Why the South Will Survive* (Athens, Ga., 1981).

Much of the work of John Shelton Reed is necessary to understanding the contemporary South. Representative studies include: John Shelton Reed, *The Enduring South: Subcultural Persistence in Mass Society* (Lexington, Mass., 1972); *Southerners: The Social Psychology of Regionalism* (Chapel Hill, N.C., 1983); and *Southern Folk, Plain and Fancy: Native White Social Types* (Athens, Ga., 1986). Reed has also published collections of occasional essays, including *Whistling Dixie: Dispatches from the South* (Columbia, Mo., 1990).

George B. Tindall's essay on southern mythology is contained in Frank E. Vandiver, ed., *The Idea of the South: Pursuit of a Central Theme* (Chicago, 1964).

Useful studies of contemporary southern culture include Jack Temple Kirby, *Media-Made Dixie: The South in the American Imagination,* rev. ed. (Athens, Ga., 1986); Jack Temple Kirby, *The Countercultural South* (Athens, Ga., 1995); and James C. Cobb, *Redefining Southern Culture: Mind and Identity in the Modern South* (Athens, Ga., 1999). Ben Robertson's memoir is *Red Hills and Cotton: An Upcountry Memory* (Columbia, S.C., 1991). Florence King's memoir is *Confessions of a Failed Southern Lady* (New York, 1985).

506

APPALACHIA

Henry D. Shapiro

APPALACHIA AS A REGION, AND ITS CULTURE

Between 1870 and 1920, the mountainous portions of eight or nine southern states came to be talked about as if they comprised a distinct entity, separate from the South as a whole, and from America as a whole. The new entity was called "Appalachian America," then simply "Appalachia." But it was also a new kind of entity, for no one had yet thought to define America as pluralist or to describe the nation as divided geographically into culturally distinct areas. Appalachia thus became the first American region—not as one among many, however, but as an exception to the unity and homogeneity claimed as a characteristic of post–Civil War America.

To writers and journalists, and to their editors in New York or Boston, the land and its people seemed sufficiently unfamiliar to make Appalachia "a field for fiction." The mountain people lived in the "back yards" of their respective states, far from centers of population, culture, and political power. They were cut off from the trends and tendencies of modern life, and in their isolation apparently preserved intact the civilization of earlier times— "like a mammoth in ice," said the writer John Fox Jr.

By 1890 Appalachia had begun to attract the interest of missionaries who wished to bring the good news of modern civilization to the mountaineers, and of educators, railroad agents, and entrepreneurs of extractive industry who proposed modernizing the mountaineer as a way of improving Appalachian culture and the Appalachian economy. By the end of the century, indeed, teachers and engineers had become the protagonists of mountain fiction, replacing the wide-eyed travelers who had earlier expressed astonishment at the "otherness" of Appalachia. The "primitivism" of the region functioned in fiction as in real life, as background to the action and simultaneously as justification for the destruction of landscape by the steam shovels of industrial development.

The Idea of Culture, and the Culture of Appalachia

During the nineteenth century, culture was associated with civilization as the mechanism by which the natural man was tamed and trained, and the savage made human and humane. Culture was also a measure of achievement, a marker of how far any given population had moved along a presumed continuum from primitive to modern. The movement itself was a world historical phenomenon, true and inevitable, the surest sign of the evolution of the human race toward universalism, rationalism, and altruism. Exceptions to this rule, therefore, caused consternation—and were worthy of notice.

Appalachia appeared to be such an exception. The culture of the southern mountain region seemed more primitive than civilized, although precisely how primitive depended on the point of view of the commentator and on the date of the commentary. Everyone acknowledged, however, that even Asheville, North Carolina, the great resort center of the Old and New South, lacked the amenities of life in Boston or New York. Everyone acknowledged that the mountain people lacked the manners of modern sophisticates, although this was hardly worth noting since old-time conditions and old-time usages were normally to be found in backlands, uplands, and hinterlands. But everyone also acknowledged that Appalachia was fully American, tied to the national economy, and a participant in the national polity, sharing in the contemporary American culture of capitalism and republicanism and the expectation of progress. That is precisely why its departure from the norms of modern American culture made it seem a strange land inhabited by a peculiar people.

If Appalachian otherness could be identified as a soon-to-be-remedied condition, then the existence of Appalachia posed no challenge to contemporary notions of American unity and homogeneity. If Appalachian otherness could be explained as a result of the normal operation of normal historical processes—by which isolation preserved outmoded usages, for example—then similarly the existence of Appalachia caused no trouble. But when Appalachia obtained the status of a discrete region inhabited by a distinct people, the existence of Appalachia seemed to challenge notions of American unity and homogeneity.

During the first decades of the twentieth century, the assumption of American unity and homogeneity itself began to dissipate. What appeared was an America characterized by racial, ethnic, social, economic, and geographic diversity. In this new context, Appalachian otherness became less a set of conditions to be altered than a fact to be defined, and accepted. As "culture" became what we do and why we do it, moreover, the place of culture assumed new importance as a way of organizing patterns of visibly different behaviors and beliefs. At the same time, older notions of the usefulness of race or ethnicity as markers of culture-as-accomplishment gave way before the arguments of science and the polemics of egalitarianism. What remained, or rather what was created, was a nation of regions as well as of peoples, and the beginnings of an inquiry into the relationship of people, place, and culture. From this perspective, if Appalachia were a region, then there must be a single Appalachian culture and a single Appalachian people to carry that culture.

THE ALLEGED CHARACTERISTICS OF APPALACHIA AND THE MOUNTAINEERS' REPUTATION

Well into the twentieth century, "primitive" was used to describe the people, the place, and the culture of Appalachia. Some said that the mountaineers, as a people "behind the times," thereby preserved the virtues of simplicity and the culture of a golden age. Others said that being behind the times ipso facto meant being savage, vicious, crude, and cruel. By 1900, for example, everyone "knew" that the mountaineers were feudists and moonshiners, that mountain fathers brutalized their daughters and mountain husbands brutalized their wives. In novels and short stories, the hero brought peace to the feudists, arrested the moonshiners, and defeated the brutal fathers and husbands in fair fights or by the power of right reason. In magazine articles, the schools and churches and the agents of economic development brought enlightenment and opportunities for employment that made feuding, moonshining, and child abuse no longer necessary aspects of mountain life. But did the mountaineers

behave badly because a primitive environment made them vicious? Or were they the degenerate descendants of our pioneer ancestors, unable to transcend the primitive environment of Appalachia as our forefathers had done in other regions?

The work of late-twentieth-century scholars has explained how allegations of feuding or moonshining were used locally to obtain political or economic advantage in mountain communities, and nationally to legitimize the intervention of outsiders seeking to develop the region's natural resources. Modern scholars all agree, moreover, that feuding and moonshining as characteristics of Appalachian culture had little basis in fact. It has been demonstrated also, that moonshining—the manufacture and sale of untaxed whiskey—was more prevalent in the great cities of the nation than in any rural region, and that feud violence, more usually designated gang violence, was also an urban phenomenon, while incest, child abuse, and spousal abuse have been recognized as normal patterns of American behavior, in the nineteenth century as in the twentieth. Nonetheless, even in the late twentieth century, apologists for Appalachia and Appalachian institutions had to grapple with the problem of the mountaineer's reputation, as if it were based on reality.

Defining Appalachia as a Folk Society In the 1890s William Goodell Frost, the president of Berea College, began calling the mountain people "Our Contemporary Ancestors" to justify an educational mission among the apparently savage and degenerate. According to Frost, the mountaineers possessed the strength and self-reliance of the American frontiersman. They were independent in spirit and imagination, quick to anger, and impatient of social constraint. Like Daniel Boone, they seemed best content when most completely isolated from the potential demands of neighbors for assistance. Thus, the same characteristics that made them seem antisocial to a first generation of observers, now became a warrant of their quintessential Americanness. In addition, they made baskets and wove coverlets that were just as nice and just as traditional as the ones you inherited from your New England grandmother, except these were new, and for sale.

During the next years, this image was elaborated and the details of cultural survivals in the mountains made specific, not only by journalists and benevolent workers, but also by the first generation of scholars in cultural studies. The mountaineer was said to speak what was variously called the only pure Anglo-Saxon, Old English, Elizabethan English, or

Shakespearean English to be heard in North America. Their thoughts, moreover, like their language, were said to be unaffected by slang, chewing gum, or Tin Pan Alley. The mountain farmers, who cultivated cash- and garden-crops and kept hogs, cattle, and chickens, were said also to preserve the admirable frontier economy of the hunter-gatherer. Thus the mountain people were often said to comprise the nation's only race of sharp-shooters, whose skills were honed by hunting squirrels with the Kentucky or long rifle. This trait, sometimes said to be learned and sometimes said to be innate, was also held to account for the bravery of Alvin York at the Battle of the Argonne Forest during World War I, when, armed with a single rifle, he captured 132 German soldiers. York was initially treated as an avatar of American individualism who used his American skills to defend American interests. He dropped out of the public interest after he decided to use the money he received for public appearances as an American hero to found an industrial school in Tennessee so other mountain boys would not have to grow up in poverty. Gary Cooper received an Academy Award for his title role in the 1941 movie, *Sergeant York,* but by then York had become as fictional a character as George Washington.

The mountaineers were said to preserve the superstitions of seventeenth- and eighteenth-century America, including beliefs in witchcraft, signs, black and white magic, planting by the phases of the moon, and the use of herbs, roots, and spells in folk medicine. No one thought of the mountaineers as preserving the songs of pioneer days, however: who ever heard of Daniel Boone singing? As a result, the folk music collected in the mountains beginning in the 1890s was most often treated as the naive product of a naive culture. In 1915, however, the English folksong collector Cecil J. Sharp was in the United States, promoting the British cause in World War I by reminding Americans of their ties to Merrie Olde England—and perhaps also avoiding the dislocations of war at home. One day he had a visit from Olive A. Dame of Medford, Massachusetts, the future wife of John Campbell of the Russell Sage Foundation's Southern Highland Division. Mrs. Campbell brought with her the texts of songs she had collected from mountain children, including a version of "Lord Thomas and Fair Ellinore" that she insisted was the same song as "Lord Thomas and Fair Annet," no. 73 in Francis James Child's *English and Scottish Popular Ballads* (1882–1898). Sharp was convinced, and later claimed for himself the "discovery" of Appalachia as a repository of tradi-

tional English song. But because Child's work was widely viewed as an essential source book of American culture, the implications of Sharp's discovery were also that Appalachia, instead of being America's opposite, was in fact the genuine thing, the real America.

Sharp's "discovery" of Appalachia as a preserve of traditional English culture, announced formerly in *English Folk Songs from the Southern Appalachians* (1917), was hailed on both sides of the Atlantic. Even those American scholars who had been publishing Child ballads collected in the southern mountains for a dozen years reviewed the book as if Sharp were the first to do so. The publication of Sharp's book, in any case, instantly made Appalachia an intact and functioning folk culture. Some of its creations were survivals from the past. Others were variants on the old patterns, old songs, old beliefs, or innovations consonant with the region's folk culture: new styles in weaving and basket making; in guitar, fiddle, and banjo playing; in dance music; and in the style of dance. (At the party celebrating publication of *English Folk Songs,* Sharp demonstrated for the first time the "Running Set" of Kentucky, which he claimed as the first indigenous American folk dance ever collected.)

But if the mountaineers were our pioneer ancestors and mountain culture preserved the uses of American folk culture, why did the mountain women not know how to do double-draft weaving, or the mountain men know all the fingerings for "Soldier's Joy"? And why did the little children yearn for comic books, the movies, and jobs in the cities? The only thing to do was to teach the mountaineers their "own" culture, which the folk schools and festival managers first defined and then promoted. During the first half of the twentieth century, only John C. Campbell of the Russell Sage Foundation's Southern Highland Division had the courage to insist that mountain culture was just the culture of isolated rural regions, the same in Maine or Illinois as in Kentucky or Tennessee. But even his voice foundered on his own dilemma, that without a distinct culture there could be no distinct region or people, and if there were no Appalachia, what was the unit toward which the foundation's philanthropic beneficence should be directed?

After 1920 in any case, and whatever else it was, Appalachia became a land of folkways rather than technic ways, folk culture rather than Broadway culture, and the mountaineers ipso facto the nondegenerate American population, free of contemporary neurasthenia, unaffected by the corruption of cities and modern ways. Appalachia thereby became a "healing land" to which Americans, worn out by the stresses of modern civilization, might go to restore themselves by bathing in a simpler, purer culture, and from which—in the novels at least—mountaineers leave only at peril of losing their true selves.

The Problem of Using Appalachian Culture as a Definer of Regional or Ethnic Identity

Appalachia gained a new status after 1960 as a pocket of poverty in an affluent nation. From the pluralist perspective of late-twentieth-century America, however, regional distinctiveness was itself normal. Thus, the peculiarities of Appalachian culture that seemed earlier to point to the region's exceptionalism now became mere particularities. It is these particularities, then, that the literature on Appalachian culture of the last quarter of the twentieth century tried to describe, sometimes to assert the legitimacy of alternative, nonmainstream, or "folk" cultures, sometimes to explain the cultural inhibitors preventing mountaineers from making effective use of available social services and economic opportunities. The literature of the first sort has been especially interested in folk aesthetics, including building style and decoration and the design and utilization of burial grounds and other environments—a trendy concern deriving in part from the vogue of cultural studies and the structuralism of Claude Lévi-Strauss and Michel Foucault—or in the folk technologies underlying folk aesthetics, described most fully in the Foxfire Books of Elliot Wigginton and his students at Rabun Gap, Georgia. The literature of the second sort, by contrast, has focused on *mentalité* as a basis for social system. That is, it has tried to identify the assumptions and expectations with which the mountain people make and meet their world, especially as observed by the social workers, teachers, and medical missionaries who have sought to improve life in the mountains and among Appalachian out-migrants in Cincinnati, Columbus, Cleveland, Detroit, and Chicago since 1960.

In no case, however, have these descriptions and analyses of Appalachian culture demonstrated the existence of a pattern of culture sufficiently different from the culture of the South, the culture of rural regions, the culture of small towns, the culture of deindustrialized regions of the nation, the culture of persons in or from those kinds of places, or the culture of out-migrants or emigrants anywhere, to serve as an adequate definer of Appalachia as a region or the mountaineers as a people. For example, the observation, well demonstrated by research in

Appalachia and out, that mountain people are "familial" in their modes of social organization and interactions and patterns of interpersonal dependence (an older usage talked about "clans" when discussing feuding as an Appalachian cultural affect) does not by itself define Appalachia or Appalachians, nor by itself distinguish mountain people from the members of other groups for whom "familialism" is an observable and equally self-consciously celebrated trait. What the recognition of "familialism" as an element in Appalachian culture does in fact do, is remind social service personnel that neither mountaineer children nor mountaineer adults are the isolated and independent individuals of nineteenth-century fiction or twentieth-century psychology.

Folkways as Acceptable Markers of Appalachian Culture: Hand-Loomed Coverlets and Mountain Music

Nonetheless, there are markers of Appalachian culture, apparently indigenous in origin, that have been seized upon by outsiders as proof of Appalachia's status as a region and the mountaineers' status as a people. As markers, they have been celebrated and therefore given value by the outsiders' attention, and have been accepted by the mountaineers as aspects of their own culture.

Feuding and moonshining, and the practice of incest, have been denied standing as cultural traits and categorized instead as "stereotypes" against which both mountaineers and their advocates must contend. Hunting squirrels for food has tended to disappear with the suburbanization of the region and the availability of alternative sources of protein in the mountaineer's diet. Only the production of mountain music and mountain crafts have remained as acceptable markers of the unique culture of Appalachia, and therefore as emblems of all the beliefs and behaviors that comprise the diverse patterns of Appalachian life.

At the end of the twentieth century, for example, children in the schools of Appalachia and among Appalachian out-migrants in Cincinnati and Detroit were taught to make corn-husk dolls, and children in the schools of Indianapolis were taught that Appalachian children made (and played with) corn-husk dolls, which in fact they did—at least in the schools. In Appalachia and among Appalachian out-migrants, the making of corn-husk dolls was part of an attempt to teach the mountaineer children their "own" culture, to legitimate that culture by recognizing it within the school curriculum, and to make school "relevant" by integrating a (socially acceptable) cultural usage of the client population

Mountain Music Dance, Marshall, North Carolina, 1998. © OWEN FRANKEN/CORBIS

into the work of the classroom. In Indianapolis and elsewhere, the corn-husk doll business was part of the ethnic diversity curriculum, intended to legitimate the otherness of apparently alien groups by asserting that they were like us because they also had a culture, although it differed in its details—the kinds of toys they played with, and how they got them—from our own.

Unlike cultural traits involving food choices, preferences in style of dress, or expectations of public and private behavior, the practices of mountain music and mountain crafts have significance; that is, they point beyond themselves and say something about the mountain culture they represent. What they say is that mountain culture is "traditional" or "old-timey." This is what the outsiders said about Appalachian culture at the end of the nineteenth century; it is what mountaineers continued to say about Appalachian culture at the end of the twentieth. Unlike foodways and similar aspects of everyday life, moreover, the practice of mountain music and mountain crafts requires self-consciousness and intention, plus formal training, education, or preparation. Also, while anyone can eat either white bread or corn bread, some persons will be better than other persons at making mountain music or mountain crafts, and these will become the teachers, the performers, the practitioners of those aspects of mountain culture, the professionals even among the folk.

In addition, the practice of mountain music and mountain crafts depends on the existence of a market for such cultural products and responds to the demands of that market. In 1899 William G. Frost began advertising home-loomed coverlets and handmade splint baskets for sale to the friends of Berea College in New York and New England, and in 1902 he organized Fireside Industries to teach coverlet weaving and basket making to meet the demand he had created. In subsequent years Berea and other centers of crafts production in Appalachia began experimenting with new ways to make traditional products, and tested the market for new products displaying the marks or motifs of traditional manufacture. And while the sale of Appalachian crafts has remained most vigorous outside the region, both insiders and outsiders have come to value Appalachian handicrafts for their own sake, to identify the region as a place where handicrafts production is "traditional," and to regard handcrafted items made in the mountains as more "authentic" than the same products made anywhere else.

The appearance of folk-song collectors in the mountains similarly indicated the existence of a market for traditional, especially British-derived song. According to Jean Ritchie, when Cecil Sharp came to the Hindman (Kentucky) Settlement School, "people thronged in from up and down the branches and hollows, literally standing in line

511

awaiting their turns to sing their ballads, love songs, play songs—whatever the furriners might want" (p. 189). But when Sharp became bored at hearing yet another rendition of "Barbry Ellen," Jean's sister Una and their cousin Sabrina went home to learn a tune not in the conventional repertoire—Uncle Jason Ritchie taught them "Nottamun Town"—so they could get the outsiders' attention at school the next day.

We must then ask the question that Sharp and most other collectors of folksongs preferred to ignore: What was the "common possession" of the mountain people, and what did one make of Appalachia if this "common possession" consisted of "Barbry Ellen" and the songs of Tin Pan Alley instead of a full complement of Child ballads? As it turned out, the "common possession" of the mountain people was what the market called for, and everyone could find an Uncle Jason, or a songbook, or later a phonograph or radio program from which to learn something new and unfamiliar. By the mid-1920s, professional musicians like A. P. Carter, his wife Sara, and his sister-in-law Maybelle had transformed the traditional music of Appalachia into commercial "mountain music"—on records, in concert halls, and especially on the radio—making the performance and the consumption of this new music an essential element in Appalachian identity.

The "revival" of handicrafts in the mountains and the "discovery" of mountain music has been well documented and fits easily into conceptions of Appalachian culture as something constructed by outsiders to suit the perspective of the larger American culture. But it is also true that the real mountaineers of the early twentieth century—who were as American as anyone else, of course, and sometimes lived in Atlanta or Cincinnati—were self-conscious participants in the process by which handicrafts and folksong became identifiers of Appalachian culture, as well as in the selection of which handicrafts and which musical styles best fit their sense of who they were. Around 1910, for example, Jean Ritchie's own father, Balis, prepared and published a songbook for sale in Eastern Kentucky, *Lover's Melodies, A Choice Collection of Old Sentimental Songs Our Grandmothers Sang, and Other Popular Airs.* It included versions of "Lord Thomas and Fair Ellender" but also "The Lightning Express," and "Bill Bailey (Won't You Come Home)." By the 1920s, however, the disdain of the folksong collectors and the social service workers from outside the region for comic and music-hall song, and their delight in the idea of Appalachia as an unspoiled land, forced "Bill Bailey" out of currency, or

into the side pocket of "what we do for fun" rather than as "a part of our culture."

As a result, when the producers of phonograph records began going South to record "old-timey" or "hillbilly" music, no one offered to sing "Bill Bailey" for them. Instead, when auditions were announced, professional musicians turned up wearing wool hats and bib overalls to reinforce the authenticity of their performances and their personae, but fully prepared to innovate in the style of traditional music. Indeed, the musicians knew the market before the record producers did, and took pains to assert the Appalachian origins of their style and repertoire and their own compositions. Fiddlin' John Carson of Atlanta claimed Blue Ridge descent long before he appeared on Okeh records. The vaudevillian Jimmie Rodgers became a displaced mountaineer and then a working stiff, the "Singing Brakeman." The professional musicians, performing in country clothes and claiming to be just plain folks, the promoters of concerts, records, and radio programs, and the audiences all connived at the invention of country music as a traditional art form, and at the idea that it had its origins in Appalachia.

The existence of an audience or market for mountain music in the South and among the mountaineers is worth noting, because our conventional understanding of the folk arts is that they are "lost" rather than popular or public, that they are to be discovered and appreciated by connoisseurs, and that the audience for "folk" music is not the same as the audience for "popular" music. The experiences of Balis Ritchie and A. P. Carter, however, suggest that southern (and national) audiences liked songs about both "Lord Thomas" and "Bill Bailey." In addition, the self-conscious and public consumption of traditional Appalachian culture after 1900, by celebrating and sentimentalizing the rural past of southerners (including mountaineers), may have helped the South adjust to the presence of mills, factories, and deep-shaft mines, to the disappearance of wildwoods and wildwood flowers, and to the migration of mountaineers along with other southerners to the big cities of industrializing America.

The Appalachia of the Planners, and the Appalachia of the Mind During the 1960s, when federal monies for economic development, education, and social welfare programs in Appalachia seemed to be available, and when planners were able to persuade Congress to define regions on the basis of a geography of need rather than the accidents of politics or the assertions of folklorists, Appalachia was redefined as the mountainous portions of eleven states, not all of them southern. Appalachian America in the nineteenth and early twentieth centuries consisted of portions of Virginia, West Virginia, Kentucky, Tennessee, North Carolina, South Carolina, Georgia, Alabama, and sometimes Maryland. During the 1930s, the coal-mining regions of Kentucky, West Virginia, and Pennsylvania (which had never been called Appalachian) were routinely excluded from discussions of the region because of their industrial character and the strength of unions, especially the United Mine Workers, among their "independent" mountaineer populations. After 1960, Alabama declined to be classified as Appalachian to show its resistance to federal initiatives of any kind (especially those connected to racial integration). Pennsylvania, Ohio, and New York agreed to be Appalachian despite the implication of poverty that that designation carried.

In our imagination, Appalachia is of smaller extent. As a folk culture or traditional society, it is eastern Kentucky, eastern Tennessee, and western North Carolina. As a pocket of poverty, which it is to readers of the *New York Times,* it is deindustrialized West Virginia. For the mountaineers themselves, in or outside the region, their identification as members of a group or participants in a culture is essentially a private matter—except when political action is to be taken or political benefit is to be obtained, as is the case for everyone else in America.

THE NEW APPALACHIAN SELF-CONSCIOUSNESS: APPALACHIA AS AMERICAN

The definition of Appalachia as a region because of its apparent "otherness" in a unified and homogeneous America ended when America itself became redefined as a nation of regions and peoples, and of distinct cultures. That process began in the 1920s, as a conscious campaign against the invidious distinctions of race, class, ethnicity, and geography in American life and thought. During the 1930s and 1940s, America's diversity became a theme in American culture itself, legitimating the use of American motifs in literature, art, and music and the replacement of European-based aesthetics with the principles of the "native American mind," and in the process becoming an appropriate subject for books and symposia. During the 1950s, diversity itself became a desideratum to be pursued, sometimes through the politics of inclusion, sometimes through the politics of self-exclusion. In all this

time, while Appalachia continued to seem a folk or traditional society, the region itself became just one among the regions of the nation.

After 1960, however, Appalachia also became an emblem of some dilemmas of contemporary American life, particularly the unequal distribution of goods and services across regions and among peoples, and the inevitable dislocations consequent to modernization. Appalachia appeared as a best bad example of the environmental degradation that accompanies the careless use of natural resources, of the deindustrialization and the resulting unemployment that accompany resource depletion, changing market patterns, and production shifts in the global economy of the late twentieth century, and of the terrible consequences of poverty as a permanent characteristic of a people's life. John Kenneth Galbraith's *The Affluent Society* of 1958 had warned that pockets of poverty might coexist with prosperity. After 1960, John F. Kennedy, Michael Harrington, and the *New York Times* insisted that America view Appalachia as nothing more and nothing less than a pocket of poverty in an affluent nation.

Origins: The "Depressed Areas" Problem In the spring of 1960, during the Democratic presidential primary in West Virginia, candidate John F. Kennedy asserted that poverty and unemployment were not unique to West Virginia, but that West Virginia exemplified the "depressed areas" of the nation that had been ignored by the Eisenhower administration. He would do better.

During his campaign Kennedy spoke often about industrial unemployment and the depressed areas problem and renewed his "pledge to the people of West Virginia." In the meantime, the reporters who had followed him along the Big Sandy and Tug Rivers and into the upper Ohio valley made West Virginia into an emblem of Appalachia, and Appalachia a "pocket of poverty" in an otherwise prosperous nation.

Appalachia was not included among the 110 "depressed areas" eligible for federal assistance under the Area Redevelopment Act of 1961, however, and when the Appalachian governors urged the claims of their states for emergency aid, the president promised only such help as was already authorized by law. Nonetheless, the *New York Times* reported on 9 May 1961 that Kennedy said, "The Governors are to be complimented upon their resourcefulness in the treatment of unusual multistate regional problems. It is the first time an entire section of the nation has been organized to develop an important regional program of this magnitude." What that program was never became clear.

During the next years two processes occurred. One was the separation of Appalachia out of its component states and its public identification as a distinct region of the nation. That had happened before, principally through the conventions of literature. Now its regional status seemed to derive from the hard evidence of economic circumstance rather than from the propaganda needs of benevolent workers or the imagination of geographers and culture critics during the 1930s. Pocket of poverty or not, moreover, Appalachia became the only region with claims to a distinct identity, culture, and institutional framework, and thus a model for advocates of regional planning and "intergovernmental organization" or "cooperative federalism." Within a decade it had become the actual locus of a variety of regional institutions: the Conference of Appalachian Governors and the Appalachian Regional Commission as at the start, but also the Appalachian Consortium and the Appalachian Consortium Press; the Appalachian Studies Association; writers' workshops; arts collaboratives; crafts cooperatives; popular and scholarly journals of Appalachian culture and literature; and not a few regionwide political organizations attempting regional solutions to regional problems.

A second process of the 1960s was the identification of Appalachia with industrial development and industrial unemployment, and thus with the depressed areas problem that already absorbed so much of the nation's attention. This was almost entirely the result of Harry Caudill's extraordinary book on the spoliation of the coal counties of Kentucky, published in 1963 as *Night Comes to the Cumberlands: A Biography of a Depressed Area.*

Harry Caudill and the Normalization of Industrial Development in the Mountains
Through much of the twentieth century, Appalachian culture was conventionally assumed to be rural and agricultural rather than urban and industrial. As a result, and despite John Kennedy's observations in West Virginia, Appalachian poverty at first seemed to bear no relationship to industrial unemployment elsewhere in the nation. The "depressed areas" program, moreover, was directed at unemployment conceived as a temporary problem. Harry Caudill's genius was to explain Appalachian poverty first of all as the result of industrial unemployment rather than of a paucity of natural resources or the inefficiency of the Appalachian work force, and second as a phenomenon that was not temporary but per-

manent. Where poverty in other areas might be the result of irregularities in the operation of the economic system, in Appalachia it was the result of structural conditions such that the wealth of the region—its raw materials and the value created by the labor of its residents—was siphoned off to enrich nonlocal interests. What remained was a dead landscape and a dead land.

By discussing Appalachian poverty as the product of industrial processes, and especially as the result of deindustrialization, however, Caudill effectively located Appalachian poverty and Appalachia itself within the contemporary dialogue on national problems and the emerging recognition of regional particularities as aspects of national diversity. Ironically, his work thereby facilitated the adoption of nonradical solutions to Appalachian poverty, now seen as just another instance of the inequalities of the American economic order. Thus Congress, in the Appalachian Regional Development Act of 1965, ignored the social and environmental consequences of decades of resource exploitation as merely a normal aspect of economic development, and encouraged such alternatives to an industrial economy as road construction and tourism, and the establishment of "growth centers" that might attract packaging and light manufacturing operations from other regions to the low-wage areas created by industrial unemployment. Caudill himself remained outside, a plain-speaking lawyer from Whitesburg, Kentucky, who briefly had the nation's ear as he complained about the continuing corporate exploitation of the region's natural and human resources, and of the nation's apparent collaboration in it. But all he could do was complain, or sometimes shout, as in his 1971 book, that *My Land Is Dying,* while compromisers took the new federal money and developed programs to spend it.

Caudill spoke with a kind of moral outrage that touched the American conscience and enhanced the political feasibility of "doing something" about Appalachian poverty. Within the region itself, his books made possible reassessments of the place of Appalachia within the American economy (including the publication of studies of industrial development as the process of resource exploitation rather than as "progress"). They provided a context and national legitimation for movements already under way, advocating self-help and wealth retention within the region, along with political opposition to state and county officers who facilitated the flow of wealth out of the region. His work also made possible the Appalachian phase of a contemporary dialogue on the uses of power and the consequences of powerlessness, and on exploitation and colonialism as world-historical processes. Thus, Appalachia could be discussed as being like a third-world country.

Federal Policy: The Appalachian Regional Commissions

In the spring of 1963, President Kennedy was again asked to do something about poverty and industrial unemployment in Appalachia. He agreed that the administration might take independent action. The first steps were to review existing federal programs, to establish a joint federal-state committee on the needs of the region, and, through "close cooperation between the Area Redevelopment Administrator and state officials and university heads in the region, to establish an Appalachian Institute as a center for research and training to develop the economy" (*New York Times*, 10 April 1963).

The joint federal-state committee on the Appalachian region was called the Appalachian Regional Commission (ARC) or more frequently the President's Appalachian Regional Commission. (Congress established its own Appalachian Regional Commission in 1965.) Chaired by Undersecretary of Commerce Franklin D. Roosevelt Jr. and composed of representatives of fourteen federal departments or agencies, the Conference of Appalachian Governors, and the several Appalachian states, the ARC by the fall of 1963 had decided to recommend the establishment of an independent Appalachian Development Corporation "to overcome poverty and backwardness" in the region. Its tasks would be to plan "the development of an adequate highway system to provide access to and within the region" and thereby facilitate "the development of the region's coal, timber and land resources"; to plan "the control and exploitation of the region's abundant water supply"; and to plan "the improvement of the education and health facilities available to the region's people." At public hearings in each of the mountain states, however, reporters found that "federal money for more highways and tourist facilities seemed to be the chief objective of local officials."

Kennedy was assassinated before the ARC's proposals could be passed on to Congress. His successor, Lyndon B. Johnson, was less interested in the possibilities of regional planning than Kennedy had been, and more cautious about the political complexities of regional governance. He was also unwilling to encourage any competition with his War on Poverty. As a result, the Economic Opportunity Act of 1964 transferred all human development programs already under way in Appalachia to the new Office of Economic Opportunity. Proposed legislation to facilitate the governance of Appalachia as a multistate region and to address regionwide problems of resource management was allowed to die in committee.

When the next Congress convened in 1965, a new Appalachia bill was introduced. The Republican leadership immediately announced that they would oppose the bill. Regional governance of any kind challenged the power of Congress, but in any case, they said, the bill's provisions for the construction of new hospitals in the mountains was really just an administration trick to initiate socialized medicine. Democrats in the House and Senate had no objections to regional governance, but proposed to amend the bill in order to create additional regional authorities for the Upper Great Lakes, the Upper Great Plains, and the Southwest. After much compromise, the Appalachian Regional Redevelopment Act was passed and signed into law on 10 March 1965. It created a new and permanent Appalachian Regional Commission composed of the governors of the southern Appalachian states plus Maryland, Pennsylvania, and Ohio (New York was added in August), and a single representative of the federal government. The legislation authorized the ARC to spend $1.1 billion, 78 percent of which, as requested by local officials, was for road construction to create the infrastructure necessary to industrial development (light manufacturing, assembly, packaging and shipping) and to facilitate tourism.

INSTITUTIONAL FRAMEWORK FOR A NEW APPALACHIAN SELF-CONSCIOUSNESS

From the time of its discovery in the 1870s, Appalachia was always defined by the fact of "otherness," even when the details of that otherness were unspecified, or, as was more often the case, untrue. It was Appalachia's otherness, in any case, that made it seem a discrete region, in but not of America. During the late nineteenth century and during most of the twentieth century, Appalachia's regional identity and regional identification were thus largely imposed from without, comprising facts asserted about the region and its people. Since "otherness" in all its formulations normally defined the region and its people as inadequate—primitive, behind the times, a folk-society instead of a modern society— there was little reason for the mountaineers to think about the needs of the region or to identify themselves with the region rather than the locality in which they lived or had been born.

515

The publicity given to region-wide problems after 1960, and the political struggles over formulation and then implementation of a national Appalachian policy during the next decades, helped create recognition of the region as a locus for action and brought some advantage to regional identification. At the same time, commentators like Caudill, then later John Gaventa, David Whisnant, and Helen Lewis began associating Appalachia's situation with larger themes in American life, including the relationship of power and powerlessness and the consequences of modernization. But in addition, a convergence of tendencies in American culture more generally yielded both the spirit and the institutional framework necessary for a new Appalachian self-consciousness and for the emergence of a new Appalachian literature.

The Expansion of State Universities The growth of the state universities in Appalachia, as elsewhere in the nation, involved a proliferation of campus units and the upgrading of two-year and specialized (e.g., teacher training) schools into four-year colleges. These became the venues for the development of area studies programs, and more generally for an explosion of academic subjects outside the boundaries of the traditional disciplines. At the very least, the establishment of new colleges meant the creation of new library and research collections and an increase in the number of faculty members, departments, fields of study, and student enrollments. These, in turn, created new markets (readers, viewers, and listeners as well as buyers) for high-culture products—in this case, including Appalachian journals and journalism; Appalachian poetry, fiction, drama, and film; Appalachian music and art; and the full range of analytic and descriptive studies necessary to elucidate the region, its society, and its culture. The universities did not cause Appalachian studies; they were simply the place where it happened.

The Legitimation of Group Distinctiveness A second tendency in American culture was the legitimation of group distinctiveness within a pluralist American society. Initially associated with the strategy of self-empowerment in the context of "movement" politics (Saul Alinsky's *Reveille for Radicals,* originally published in 1946, was reissued in 1969), and with the popular psychology of "I'm OK, You're OK" (the title of a 1969 book by Thomas A. Harris), it both asserted and celebrated group identity based on alleged or real ethnic, cultural, residential, or historical characteristics. Although often held to be a

central principle of the new democracy of the 1960s, it sometimes yielded group separatism instead of integration, and self-aggrandizement (including the one-downsmanship of "we are the victims") instead of egalitarianism.

In any case, the legitimation of group distinctiveness led to the identification of Appalachian Americans as one among the many ethnic groups in the national population. This fact in turn led to the development of "culturally sensitive" programs in the schools and among social service personnel at local agencies. The logic of the situation, plus the polemical arguments of Appalachian advocates (that the acceptability of Appalachians as Americans could be measured by the recognition of their special needs and the availability of special programs to meet those needs), plus the experience of social service personnel with Appalachian populations who were apparently unwilling to utilize available resources for counseling, assistance, and medical care that had been configured for a "general" American population, all seemed to demonstrate the need for group-specific social service programs. The need for these service programs, and then the existence of them, reinforced contemporary notions that Appalachians comprised a distinct group in the American population, and carried over to the end of the twentieth century older notions of Appalachian otherness.

The dilemma of Appalachia's standing, or meaning, or significance in and to American culture, and the legitimation of Appalachians as one of the ethnic groups of the American population from which it followed, yielded the emergence of Appalachian studies as a distinct field of inquiry, most notably in colleges and universities within the Appalachian states. It also yielded a first set of attempts to address the problem of Appalachia. One strategy was to write its history, to describe the past and present of its people, without ever attempting to explain Appalachian otherness, as if Appalachia were anyplace. A second strategy was to apply analogies from world history, for example, by describing Appalachia as an "internal colony." A third strategy identified culture as a "made" thing, and sought to examine its making.

Simultaneous with the development of Appalachian studies as a field or discipline, and following from the tendency toward celebration of group identity, was the legitimation of Appalachian high-culture products as art rather than folk art, story instead of folktale, and—especially through the Foxfire books—of Appalachian cultural usages as ways of doing and thinking instead of folk ways of doing and thinking. Another result was the establishment of workshops, and other kinds of institutional centers to encourage and facilitate the work of Appalachian writers, artists, filmmakers, woodworkers, and basket makers, without pretending thereby either to "preserve" the native culture of the mountains or to use the arts or crafts to facilitate the modernization of the mountaineer. Some of these centers were within the universities, sometimes associated with an Appalachian studies center, department, or curriculum; many others were independent of the universities. Some obtained independent incorporation and the appearance of permanence. Some came into existence and later disappeared as the needs and interests of local artists changed. All, however, benefited from the new availability of financial support for public activities in the arts and humanities, available from eleemosynary foundations and especially the national and state arts and humanities councils.

Up until this time, works of Appalachian literature, like American literature more generally, had seemed to deserve consideration only as examples of subliterary genres, such as the diary, tall tale, travel account, or "local color" writing, set in a rural area rather than in Boston or New York. The revolution that legitimized the examination of America and American texts generally made itself manifest in the mountains as well. Not only could one begin to notice that Fenimore Cooper's romances of the New York frontier were really no more boring than Walter Scott's romances of the Scottish frontier, but also that Harriette Arnow wrote real prose, James Still wrote real poetry, that Appalachian literature was real literature after all. Then came the question that still fills the pages of journals and forms the subject of symposia: what makes Appalachian literature Appalachian, and what is the role of "place" in the consciousness of a writer?

The Structuralist or Deconstructionist Revolution

A third tendency of importance in American culture was the structuralist revolution in academic, but especially in popular, discourse that identified ideas as cultural constructs and thus as an appropriate subject for historical and critical analysis. If ideas were neither innate nor natural to the human mind but were "made" or "discovered," they might or might not be true; but in any case, like institutions, their origins and functions might be examined, and their usefulness assessed.

The impact of this structuralist revolution on Appalachian studies may be seen clearly in the differences among volumes published for use in Appalachian studies courses, themselves manifestations of an emerging Appalachian self-consciousness. The earliest works of this genre inevitably began by addressing the question, Who are the mountaineers? The answer was always the same, and was stated in terms of eugenics rather than occupational or demographic terms: the mountaineers are descendants of good Scotch-Irish stock. This was the necessary first fact to be established in order to disprove popular notions of mountaineer degeneracy, and to legitimize Appalachia and the mountaineers as an appropriate subject for examination or object of beneficence.

Late-twentieth-century works in this genre, by contrast, take the legitimacy of their subject for granted and try to describe the real history and real characteristics of mountain life. Even those more conventional works that begin with the matter of the ethnic background of the mountain population, however, ignore the "problem" of alleged mountaineer degeneracy. Instead, they use the occasion to deny that the mountaineers are a homogeneous population descended from Scots-Irish frontiersmen, and to acknowledge ethnic—if not always cultural—diversity as a characteristic of the region.

The Examination of Appalachia as Itself

Although modern scholarship eschews the older notions of Appalachia as a strange land inhabited by a peculiar people, of the mountaineers as a degenerate population, and of the persistence or existence in the mountains of America's only folk culture, these tropes remain both available and attractive to unwary scholars and contributors to American popular culture.

Scholarship, like journalism, is a continuing interplay between the perception of reality and the application of generalizations or models to describe it, and thus to organize the data of reality. If we start with an assumption about how the world works, we may well find evidence to prove it. If we start with what someone else says as evidence of how the world works, we may well come to conclude that the world does indeed work just that way. Where we draw our data from is thus as much of an issue as the models we use to organize that data.

Works of fiction, for example, written as literature, may be read as true descriptions of their settings, that is, the places and populations that fill the stage on which the main action occurs. Thus Mary Noailles Murfree's stories, written in the 1880s, were read by college students preparing to do settlement work in the mountains after 1910. Her assertions of Appalachian otherness made the stories interesting and publishable when they were first written. They also became a basis for action thirty or more years later, however. Her descriptions of mountain life in the 1880s (actually based on observations made in the 1860s) were taken as accurate statements of contemporary conditions after the turn of the century—reinforcing, in the process, notions of Appalachia as a timeless land, untouched by the forces of modernization.

Murfree's stories can still be read at the end of the twentieth century (they have indeed recently been reprinted), and only a careful reader will notice that their world is more than one hundred years old. But even those who notice that her stories date from the 1880s and are thus about the 1880s will face the dilemma that their very historicity must mean that her vision is accurate, since her account was written close to the time of the events described.

In the schools and colleges, students are asked to distinguish between "primary" and "secondary" sources for historical study, and even pupils in the lower grades are asked to do research in "primary" documents. "Primary" documents are those of the time, rather than later accounts of the summaries in textbooks and encyclopedias. Thus for all but the most wary Americans at the end of twentieth century, stories "written close to the time of the events described" is the essential criterion for the evaluation of historical evidence. Should not this criterion then be extended to the work of all the novelists and special pleaders of the nineteenth and earlier twentieth centuries, so that those who were there on the scene "must" have been telling the truth, and Appalachia really was a strange land inhabited by a peculiar people (although it may no longer be so)? The historians Ronald Eller and Altina Waller have demonstrated that it is possible to read the records of the past without becoming entangled in the issues of Appalachian otherness, but few others have been as rigorous in their examination of Appalachian history. As a result, the peculiarities of mountain culture are regularly reasserted, sometimes rediscovered, especially by journalists in search of a story line, by novelists, by screenwriters, and sometimes even by scholars.

REGIONAL IDENTITY AND REGIONAL CULTURE

Since its founding, the Appalachian Regional Commission has had supporters, but also many detrac-

tors, and has barely survived the greediness of the states for federal development dollars and the centralizing efforts of the Reagan administration's "new federalism." It has survived, and at the end of the twentieth century remained the only federally funded regional organization in the United States, a leftover from the enthusiasm for regional planning during the midcentury years.

Whether the ARC has ever adequately served Appalachia's interests will remain a matter for debate, and whether it even represents the existence of Appalachia as a distinct region of the nation is unclear. What is clear is that the ARC did only what was politically correct in the conservative context of the time. It attempted no alteration in the existing system of resource allocation or resource development and allowed virtually no discussion of the environmental consequences of resource utilization. It planned and supervised the construction of roads. It encouraged tourist development. It facilitated the elaboration of the educational and health care delivery systems in the mountains. It smiled benignly on urban sprawl and suburbanization, and it overlooked, or perhaps oversaw the continuing deindustrialization of Appalachia.

What happened in Appalachia during the last quarter of the twentieth century was what happened everywhere else in America. Whether Appalachian culture has thus become just like the culture of anyplace else, however, is doubtful. The particularities of Appalachian culture remain: patterns of speech, conventions of dress and behavior, taste in food and the aesthetics of space, and the social systems that enforce conformity and authorize change. And while they will not be identical with the particularities that characterized Appalachia in the nineteenth or earlier twentieth centuries, they are nonetheless real, and are the elements of culture. The institutional framework created by the intellectual and social revolutions of the 1960s and 1970s also remain, as formal proof of the existence of Appalachian culture and the locus of debate over its characteristics and future. The universities are there, as are the Appalachian studies programs, the journals and the writers and the artists and the crafts workers. Most important, there are hundreds of thousands of ordinary people who are self-consciously Appalachian and have a stake in being who they are. Whatever else, there is always the landscape, which continues to look strange to outsiders' eyes, and just right to those who live there.

518

See also **Agrarianism and the Agrarian Ideal in Early America** *(volume 1); and other articles in this section.*

BIBLIOGRAPHY

Barker, Garry C. *The Handcraft Revival in Southern Appalachia, 1930–1990.* Knoxville, Tenn., 1991.

Becker, Jane S. *Selling Tradition: Appalachia and the Construction of an American Folk, 1930–1940.* Chapel Hill, N.C., 1998.

Billings, Dwight B., Gurney Norman, and Katherine Ledford, eds. *Confronting Appalachian Stereotypes: Back Talk from an American Region.* Lexington, Ky., 1999.

Campbell, John C. *The Southern Highlander and His Homeland.* 1921. Reprint, Lexington, Ky., 1969.

Caudill, Harry M. *Night Comes to the Cumberlands: A Biography of a Depressed Area.* Boston, 1962.

———. *My Land Is Dying.* New York, 1971.

Eller, Ronald D. *Miners, Millhands, and Mountaineers: Industrialization of the Appalachian South, 1880–1930.* Knoxville, Tenn., 1982.

Gaventa, John. *Power and Powerlessness: Quiescence and Rebellion in an Appalachian Valley.* Urbana, Ill., 1980.

Hevener, John W. *Which Side Are You On?: The Harlan County Coal Miners, 1931–1939.* Urbana, Ill., 1978.

Kinney, William Howland. *Recorded Music in American Life: The Phonograph and Popular Memory, 1890–1945.* New York, 1999.

Lewis, Helen Matthews, Linda Johnson, and Donald Askins, eds. *Colonialism in Modern America: The Appalachian Case.* Boone, N.C., 1978.

McGowan, Thomas A., ed. "Assessing Appalachian Studies." *Appalachian Journal* 9, nos. 2–3 (1982).

Miller, Wilbur R. *Revenuers and Moonshiners: Enforcing Federal Liquor Law in the Mountain South, 1865–1900.* Chapel Hill, N.C., 1991.

Peterson, Richard A. *Creating Country Music: Fabricating Authenticity.* Chicago, 1997.

Pudup, Mary Beth, Dwight B. Billings, and Altina L. Waller, eds. *Appalachia in the Making: The Mountain South in the Nineteenth Century.* Chapel Hill, N.C., 1995.

Ritchie, Jean. "Living Is Collecting: Growing Up in a Southern Appalachian 'Folk' Family." In *An Appalachian Symposium: Essays Written in Honor of Cratis D. Williams,* edited by J. W. Williamson. Boone, N.C., 1977.

Shapiro, Henry D. "Introduction." *The Southern Highlander and His Homeland.* Lexington, Ky., 1969.

———. *Appalachia on Our Mind: The Southern Mountains and Mountaineers in the American Consciousness, 1870–1920.* Chapel Hill, N.C., 1978.

———. "The Place of Culture and the Problem of Appalachian Identity." In *Appalachia and America: Autonomy and Regional Dependence,* edited by Allen Batteau. Lexington, Ky., 1983.

Waller, Altina L. *Feud: Hatfields, McCoys, and Social Change in Appalachia, 1860–1900.* Chapel Hill, N.C., 1988.

Walls, David S., and John B. Stephenson, eds. *Appalachia in the Sixties: Decade of Reawakening.* Lexington, Ky., 1972.

Whisnant, David E. *Modernizing the Mountaineer: People, Power, and Planning in Appalachia.* Boone, N.C., 1980.

——. *All That is Native and Fine: The Politics of Culture in an American Region.* Chapel Hill, N.C., 1983.

Williamson, J. W. *Hillbillyland: What the Movies Did to the Mountains and What the Mountains Did to the Movies.* Chapel Hill, N.C., 1995.

Williamson, J. W., and Edwin T. Arnold, eds. *Interviewing Appalachia: The Appalachian Journal Interviews, 1978–1992.* Knoxville, Tenn., 1994.

THE MIDDLE WEST

Andrew R. L. Cayton

Many people would consider the idea of the life of a Midwestern mind an oxymoron. Throughout the twentieth century, American popular culture has represented the residents of the Middle West (a region arbitrarily defined here as the area covered by the states of Ohio, Indiana, Illinois, Michigan, Wisconsin, Iowa, Minnesota, and parts of Missouri, Kansas, Nebraska, and the Dakotas) as at best stalwart, practical folks and as at worst intolerant, greedy provincials. A place of farms and small towns, retail businesses and huge industries, the Middle West is not generally associated with great artistic achievement or memorable cultural centers. One of the most popular sketches on the television show *Saturday Night Live* in the 1980s portrayed working-class Chicagoans as mindless beer drinkers whose world began and ended with "Da Bears" and "Da Bulls." It was hilarious in no small part because it zeroed in on the popular image of the Midwesterner as utterly banal.

Reinforcing this negative cultural image is the pronounced tendency of intellectual and artistic types to flee the region at the first chance they get. Midwestern expatriates have been legion. Perhaps the first notable one was the Ohio-born novelist William Dean Howells, who became the grand old man of American letters from a perch in Boston rather than Cincinnati or Chicago. Howells established a pattern emulated, among many others, by Mark Twain, Ernest Hemingway, F. Scott Fitzgerald, Richard Wright, Toni Morrison, and Jane Smiley. The Middle West has produced some of the great American artists and intellectuals of the twentieth century but (with some notable exceptions, including Theodore Dreiser, Grant Wood, and Frank Lloyd Wright) they have done their best work elsewhere.

Southern and western writers and artists often have buried themselves in their home country. Neither William Faulkner nor Wallace Stegner was a simple-minded regional booster but both lived in the midst of what they wrote about because they saw themselves (however ambiguously and painfully) as parts of some place called the South or the West.

Midwestern intellectuals do not have the same experience. They often leave and, chameleon-like, transform themselves into something unrecognizable. Who would think that the poet T. S. Eliot was born in St. Louis? Or that Bob Dylan was from Minnesota? Or that the Broadway composer Cole Porter was a native of Peru, Indiana? Even the most influential historian of the region—Frederick Jackson Turner—abandoned the University of Wisconsin in 1910 to teach at Harvard University. Occasionally, Midwestern intellectuals decide they are out of place in the East or Europe and return to their roots. Garrison Keillor, the father of the popular live radio program *A Prairie Home Companion,* is a notable example of someone who followed the well-worn path to the big lights of the city and then trod the less familiar path back to the Midwest. But in general Midwesterners who want to lead examined lives are permanent regional exiles.

MIDWESTERN CULTURES

The Middle West has never been without culture, of course. Indeed, it has always had a multiplicity of them. Born with diverse ethnic and Christian traditions, raised in one of the most prosperous regions in the world in the nineteenth and twentieth centuries, exposed to extremes of climate and human geography, Midwesterners have been people with a strong sense of how things ought to be. Normally, they have identified themselves more in terms of religions and communities—as Poles or Norwegians, German Catholics or Yankee Protestants—than in terms of regionalism. The architecture of sacred buildings in the region demonstrates the diversity of belief. But living in a multicultural world for two centuries has encouraged Midwesterners to keep public pronouncements as vague and consensual as possible.

Pigeon Creek Evangelical Church, 1915. Located in Pigeon Falls, Wisconsin, the church was completed in 1876. COURTESY OF MURPHY LIBRARY, UNIVERSITY OF WISCONSIN–LACROSSE

This tendency toward the bland reflects the distinctive economic and social structures of the region. The most important fact about the Middle West was that it originated and developed simultaneously with the greatest expansion of international capitalism in the history of the world. Planned as an embodiment of enlightened commercial pastoralism (the proceeds from the sale of which were to support the United States government), the region became in the nineteenth century a great showpiece of commercial agriculture and industry. In fact, it was the close identification of the region with market capitalism that gave it definition. Free labor was exalted; slavery was forbidden; Indians were driven away or assimilated; premiums were put on the development of land for commercial purposes. The quintessential architecture of the Middle West was a Main Street of practical commercial facades. Towns and cities, of which Chicago is the most important example, exist to absorb the natural resources of their hinterlands (lumber, grains, pork products) and transform or transship them for sale all over the world.

Hegemonic Middle Western culture by the late nineteenth century celebrated this commercial progress. No wonder that so many thoughtful residents of the region—the kind of person the novelist Sherwood Anderson immortalized in George Willard, the hero of *Winesburg, Ohio* (1919)—ran away in horror. Here was a world whose complexities and contradictions were hidden away behind illusions of consensus and conformity. Here was a world in which blind ambition (mostly material in nature) destroyed the lives of the characters in the novels of Theodore Dreiser and Booth Tarkington. Here was a world built on the labor and sacrifice of millions of unknown farm and laboring families whose tedious work and difficult lives appear in the work of Hamlin Garland, Willa Cather, Edgar Lee Masters, and Richard Wright.

To be sure, the Middle West had—and has—an abundance of highbrow and middle brow cultural institutions. Thanks to the contributions of German immigrants in the second half of the nineteenth century, there are world-class symphony orchestras in Chicago, Cleveland, Cincinnati, and St. Louis. Rare is the Midwestern city of any size without a fine art museum or an active historical society. The state universities of the region are among the finest in the country. Theater thrives in Chicago.

Still, an omnipresent boosterism compromises the vast majority of these great cultural institutions. In part, they exist for the entertainment and edification of their patrons. But they also exist as efforts at cultural refinement. They symbolize the solidity and importance of the cities in which they exist. An orchestra or an art museum in the late nineteenth century was what a professional sports team had become at the end of the twentieth century: one of the marks without which a city cannot claim national or international significance.

The close relationship between locality and institution puts a premium on consensus; it does not encourage, let alone invite, experimentation. Art exists as an ornament in the city's crown; it does not exist for its own sake. In a nation dominated by commercial culture, Middle Western cities have proved to be remarkably adept at assimilating any organization that threatens to become avant-garde. Witness the transformation of Chicago's Second City comedic troupe from a slightly anarchic, mildly irreverent group into a cultural icon of a great city; it has become an institution, which adds to the reputation and tourist appeal of its city.

Overall, we can divide Midwestern intellectual life into three major chronological periods. The first, running roughly from the late eighteenth century to the 1870s, focused on the possibilities inherent in the development of the region. The second era, covering the decades from the 1870s through the 1940s, was a great florescence in the arts in which thoughtful women and men attempted to come to terms with the society constructed in the nineteenth century and lamented the human costs of the progress their predecessors had celebrated. The third period, ranging from the 1940s to the present, covers an explosion of interest in asserting multicultural diversity in a region that seems bent on maintaining an illusion of cultural uniformity.

THE PROMISE OF THE OLD NORTHWEST, 1780s–1870s

For the first century of its existence, many people in and out of the Old Northwest considered it a kind of promised land. Established as a federal territory in 1787 by the Northwest Ordinance, the states carved out of it by the 1880s attracted a wide range of peoples. There were upland southerners, principally from Greater Virginia and the Carolinas; Yankees from New England and New York; a few African Americans; and increasing numbers of western Europeans, principally Germans, Scandinavians, and Irish.

Many of these peoples celebrated the enormous potential of the land north and west of the Ohio River. Much of their writing, talking, and singing sounded naive and promotional well into the nineteenth century. Folk songs and folktales told of wonders and prospects. Travel accounts and autobiographies spoke of the possibilities awaiting hardworking men and women in a land of plenty. Exceptions to this generalization, such as Frances Trollope's *Domestic Manners of the Americans* (1832), a bilious satire of the denizens of Cincinnati, were rare.

Most early land speculators, including the Ohio Company of Associates, John Cleves Symmes, and Moses Cleaveland, and political figures wrote or spoke in developmental terms. They argued that once Indians and white "banditti" were removed, respectable Americans could buy land, lay out farms, build cities, and establish essential social institutions such as churches, schools, and public spaces in a matter of years. In public papers and pamphlets such as the New England minister Ma-

nasseh Cutler's *An Explanation of the Soil* (1787) they detailed their vision of a polite commercial society tied into the North Atlantic world via the Ohio and Mississippi Rivers. As these early promoters faded in importance in the early 1800s, their cause was taken up, with some modifications, by professional men, including lawyers and newspaper editors.

The frontierspeople who constituted the bulk of the early settlers of the Old Northwest were also interested in development. But their plans were not nearly as grandiose. Migrating from greater Virginia (including Kentucky), they were much more concerned with the immediate acquisition of land and the maintenance of local autonomy in political issues such as questions of taxation and support for physical and cultural improvements, such as roads and schools. Often, they celebrated their lives and communities in song and stories that were transmitted orally rather than through print.

No group of people likened the Old Northwest to a promised land as explicitly as enslaved African Americans. In spite of the pervasive legal hostility to blacks north of the Ohio River in the nineteenth century, enslaved and free blacks took hope in the Northwest Ordinance's prohibition against slavery and indentured servitude. Whites generally supported the ban, in part because they thought slavery immoral and in part because they did not want blacks living (and competing for jobs and land) among them. But African Americans continued to look to the Ohio River as an American version of the Jordan River; once across it, they might find freedom.

Although few blacks were able to take advantage of the promise of the Old Northwest (in 1900, the black population of most Midwestern states hovered at around 1 to 3 percent of the total), slavery increasingly became the symbolic difference between the Old Northwest and its southern neighbors. Part of the commercial development of the region in the nineteenth century involved a relatively straightforward embracing of capitalism, a celebration of the market and free labor, and a strong emphasis on individual moral improvement. This tendency, apparent in the earliest promotional literature, was reinforced and refined with the migration of tens of thousands of New Englanders (or Yankees) into Ohio, Indiana, Michigan, Illinois, and Wisconsin.

Yankees not only brought with them evangelical fervor, they were stalwart supporters of education. They revived and detailed plans for public school systems that had languished for decades because of their costs and cultural innovations. In the second quarter of the nineteenth century, denominational colleges began to appear in the small towns of the region. The most famous ones, including Oberlin College, were zealous in their opposition to slavery, and sparked intense controversies with their neighbors. These colleges persisted, however, and trained hundreds of teachers, ministers, and other professionals who carried Protestant and middle-class notions of respectable behavior to the far corners of the Old Northwest and points beyond.

Religion—overwhelmingly Protestant until the arrival of Irish and German Catholics in the 1840s and 1850s—was at once conservative and radical. Long seen by secular politicians and promoters as essential to the maintenance of social order, religion also encouraged remarkable social experimentations. Conventional religious writings—including the *Autobiography* (1856) of Peter Cartwright and James Finley's *Sketches of Western Methodism* (1854)—detailed the hardships and ultimate triumphs of itinerant ministers. Many were published in Cincinnati, which by 1850 was the fourth largest publishing center in the United States.

Meanwhile, all kinds of religious groups and movements looked to Ohio, Indiana, Michigan, and Illinois as potential sites for the establishment of what might be called utopian communities today. The Quakers, Shakers, and Mormons were only the most famous of these groups. The image of the Old Northwest as a liberal and prosperous region attracted thousands of people who wanted to experiment with new kinds of social relationships and ideas. Some were secular in character. But for every New Harmony, Indiana, the brainchild of the English reformer Robert Dale Owen, there were many other communities whose goals were clearly sacred, such as the Amana settlements in Iowa.

By the 1850s, then, the Old Northwest was a curious mixture of boosterism and experimentation; it was at once progressive and conservative. Thousands of small towns and dozens of growing cities dotted its largely agricultural landscape; many of these urban centers, with their new colleges and growing middle class, were interested in making their cultural institutions match their economic ones. Their "persister" populations—the successful families who stayed in one place for several generations—sought self-improvement in lyceum lectures and printed materials, including magazines and books. They wanted to cultivate music and art as personal and communal ornaments. Cincinnati at midcentury was an extreme example of this quest. Only a half-century old, built on the rough

and tumble river trade and the processing of hogs, with a bustling commercial center, rife with cultural conflict (especially between Catholics and Protestants and among different classes of people), it was a city whose leading citizens wanted to refine it in the 1850s. They wanted to add a coat of cultural veneer to its economic core.

Women had always been crucial to the importance of refinement in the development of the Old Northwest. Late-eighteenth-century promoters had seen women as progenitors of a polite society; more important, they would provide the backbone of educational and religious institutions. Middle-class white women did these things, of course, but with their own twist. They found in organizing to promote moral improvement a source of female solidarity and an opening for demanding a more public role in Midwestern society. They also brought unabashed emotionalism to public discourse in the region.

This interest in speaking from the heart accounts for the popularity of sentimental music and art at midcentury. The parlor songs of writers such as the Pittsburgh-born Stephen Collins Foster were ubiquitous. Even more popular was the rise of sentimental literature. In *Uncle Tom's Cabin* (1852), the New Englander Harriet Beecher Stowe, who lived for years in Cincinnati, produced the most famous example of the genre. She also brought together many of the themes of Midwestern history, including antislavery, the importance of pietism, the need for refinement, and the image of the region as a promised land. Stowe's description of the slave Eliza's improbable escape across an icy Ohio River solidified the river's reputation as a cultural boundary.

For many people, the Civil War was the fulfillment of the promise of the Old Northwest. It was a war of liberation—and regional definition. Midwestern men, with the support of their wives, freed slaves from bondage, tramping through the evil and degenerate South with a sense of righteousness that fulfilled their historical destiny. The Old Northwest had become what its founders hoped it would be: an exemplar of a higher form of civilization, a model to the rest of the nation.

THE MEANING OF PROGRESS, 1870s–1930s

The image of the Middle West as a promised American land was always contested, of course. African Americans found abundant racism in Ohio and Indiana. White upland southerners were horrified by the moral superiority and grandiose social schemes of Yankee settlers. Germans wanted little to do with public education and temperance movements that threatened to obliterate their cultural traditions. And for working people on canals and railroads or the docks of Cincinnati, Cleveland, and Chicago, life was just plain tough.

It was only after the Civil War, however, that these contests became integral to the public landscape of the Middle West. In the last third of the nineteenth century, cities, counties, and states became more conscious of their origins. Many produced or supported the distribution of massive, multivolumed tomes that celebrated the triumph of economic and moral progress over forces of ignorance, obstructionism, and provincialism. These books were a kind of reverse version of real estate pamphlets; they celebrated the potential of future development by pointing out the success of past development. In particular, they detailed the whitewashed lives of great men—lawyers, bankers, and businessmen whose personal achievements had allegedly secured the greatness of their communities.

This public culture seemed increasingly hollow in the late nineteenth and early twentieth centuries. The Middle West by the 1890s was a place of immense contrasts: huge, industrial cities and vast expanses of farmland; a core population of respectable, middle-class citizens who insisted on individual and community progress, and growing numbers of immigrants from all over Europe who refused to surrender their ways of raising their children or enjoying their lives. These contrasts provoked a great deal of tension and unrest between the 1870s and 1930s. The Granger movement and the Populist Party of the 1890s attracted some Midwestern farmers and laborers who resented the power of railroad companies and huge corporations. Like the Knights of Labor in the 1880s, they emphasized the importance of cooperation and respect for independent labor.

Meanwhile, working-class people throughout the Middle West actively defied middle-class notions of respectable behavior. Whether the issue was sexuality or alcohol, they demanded the right to control the time and space available to them when they were away from the work place. Leisure for many of them was a time to play, to escape the drudgery of their jobs, to find solace and pleasure in free association in clubs, saloons, parks, and the streets; it was not another period of improvement.

While religion remained central to their existence, giving structure to the world in ways that their jobs did not, both men and women increasingly found solace in the commercialization of leisure. Professional sports, nickelodeons (and then moving pictures), amusement parks, and arcades began to occupy more and more of people's time—and take more and more of their wages. Respectable citizens railed against these developments but with so little effect that by the 1920s large numbers of their children had adopted the styles and habits of their working-class counterparts. The increasing availability of the automobile made parental control all but impossible to maintain. Robert and Helen Lynd's *Middletown* (1929), a primitive but landmark sociological study of Muncie, Indiana, in the 1920s, argued that Midwesterners were people whose customs were disintegrating.

If many of the intellectuals who grew up in the Midwest fled the region in the late 1800s and early 1900s, nearly all of their writings reflected the ambiguity of responses to the maturing of the region. No doubt many people had found better lives in the Midwest; it was a prosperous place with grand cities, an elaborate transportation system, and many cultural achievements. In the last area, Germans had been active in the second half of the nineteenth century, particularly in encouraging the growth of symphony orchestras. But whatever their origins, Midwestern cities in the early 1900s could boast of large concert halls and elaborate public buildings. The Art Institute of Chicago, which opened in the 1890s, was a classic example of this trend.

Still, many intellectuals at the turn of the twentieth century rejected the cultural achievements of the Middle West as little more than a veneer, shellacked over the lives of millions of people lost in a rapidly changing world over which they had little or no control. Many worried about the ubiquity of alienation and especially about the dangers of the middle-class culture of the region. One of the most persistent themes of the literature of this period is the effort of some young person to escape the humdrum, suffocating life of a Midwestern town and find fulfillment (sometimes economically, sometimes artistically) in some more vibrant place, some place more receptive to nonconformity and diversity. If many Americans had seen the Old Northwest as a promised land in the early 1800s, many saw it as a place from which one had to escape in the early 1900s. The vision had stagnated; the region was a victim of its own success, becoming what its public "founders" envisioned, its very achievement choking the creativity of its children, lost forever in the deadening atmosphere described by the writer Hamlin Garland. "The Main-Travelled Road in the

West," wrote Garland in a brief preface to a collection of short fiction entitled *Main-Travelled Roads* (1891), "is long and wearyful, and has a dull little town at one end and a home of toil at the other. Like the main-travelled road of life, it is traversed by many classes of people, but the poor and the weary predominate."

Some intellectuals found answers to this dilemma in a return to simplicity, in a celebration of what they considered to be the purer elements in the region's makeup. The historian Frederick Jackson Turner, worried about the direction of American society, focused on the rejuvenating image of the frontier; although that era was officially over, Turner suggested that it was the possibility of starting over again (no longer possible in the Midwest) that had made the United States unique. Carl Sandburg, in both his poetry and his best-selling biography of Abraham Lincoln, celebrated the simple pleasures and achievements of Midwestern life. Washington Gladden, a minister in Columbus, Ohio, encouraged his congregation to advocate practical social reforms in order to achieve a more just and Christian society.

More creatively, the Wisconsin-born architect Frank Lloyd Wright and a group of contemporaries developed what became known as the Prairie School of architecture in the early 1900s. Rejecting the box-like construction of most homes and public buildings and building on the work of Louis Sullivan and designers of the Chicago-style of skyscrapers in the 1890s, Wright and others advocated an organic style of building. They wanted human creations to embody the spirit of the land and the people who would inhabit them. Many of their designs thus incorporated the long, flat lines of Midwestern prairies and emphasized the centrality of a large place as the literal hearth of houses that were expressions of the world in which they were placed.

Novelists from Willa Cather to Ole Edvart Rolvaag, while fully cognizant of the social costs of Midwestern progress, also found much to admire in the sheer persistence of people. They celebrated the role of ethnic and religious traditions in helping people to deal with, if not overcome, the physical hardships, enormous distances, and chronic isolation of Midwestern life.

Still, the theme of deadening alienation dominated the social realism of the most famous novels of this period. Although we tend to oversimplify these complex novels, works such as Theodore Dreiser's *Sister Carrie* (1900), Sherwood Anderson's *Winesburg, Ohio*, or Sinclair Lewis's *Main Street* (1920) immortalized the image of the Middle West as a land of banal and anti-intellectual conformists (personified by the central character in another

The Robie House, Chicago, Illinois (1910). The most famous of Frank Lloyd Wright's Prairie House designs. © G. E. KIDDER SMITH/CORBIS

Lewis novel, *Babbit* [1922], who drove sensitive and creative people to despair or exile).

THE SIGNIFICANCE AND INSIGNIFICANCE OF CONSENSUS, 1940s–2000

If much of the artistic creation of Midwesterners in the early twentieth century was a critique of the world into which artists had been born or moved, it did not amount to a coherent regionalism. Writers tended to blame universal forces—soulless capitalism, huge cities, isolation—which were not peculiar to the region. They did not talk about a Midwestern identity—a phrase that only came into widespread use in the early twentieth century—in specific terms. It was a decidedly vague concept. So thoroughly was the region transformed by capitalist development in the nineteenth century (in large part because of its geographical accessibility and monotony) that there were few places or peoples for intellectuals to hold up as alternatives to the American mainstream.

Southern and western regionalists, particularly in the 1930s when regionalism was a strong intellectual movement, celebrated countercultural currents in American society: they embraced folk art or music, oral traditions, and natural environments as embodiments of a purer American spirit that had luckily escaped or resisted the spiritually deadening experiences of capitalist (and especially industrial and urban) transformation. They asserted the value of things and peoples and places they believed had been dismissed or ignored as backward and primitive. It was precisely their unspoiled character that made them valuable.

Although the Middle West had its share of topographical peculiarities and a cornucopia of diverse religious and ethnic traditions, it could not shake its popular image as "middle America" or "the Heartland." The idea of the Midwest (to the extent that there was ever an articulation of such) was that it is a middle-of-the-road region of small towns, endless prairies, and cities more renowned for their business centers, uniform suburbs, and practical architecture than intellectual life or cultural diversity. Superficially, at least, cities—especially those that emerged at major urban areas in the second half of the twentieth century—seemed as interchangeable as their airports, movie theaters, and fast-food restaurants. Were not Columbus, Indianapolis, Des Moines, and Kansas City pretty much the same thing?

No matter how much they tried, Midwesterners could not escape the booster mentality, the emphasis on success and respectability, that had defined the region in the nineteenth century. American corporations tested new products in Des Moines; the *New York Times* and other media went to Canton, Ohio, to find out what Middle America thought; and television producers set *The Mary Tyler Moore Show* (1970s) and *ER* (1990s) and other shows whose locales had to be relatively nondescript in the Middle West. The 1990s satirical television comedy *Third Rock from the Sun* used its small-town Ohio location to lampoon American culture as a whole.

Within the region, there was little effort at exploring the idea of a regional culture. Scholars and novelists tended to focus on smaller units such as cities or states rather than the Middle West as a whole. Perhaps the most important sources of translocal identity were professional sports teams. The mania for Big 10 college football and later basketball reinforced loyalty to particular states (the major exception is Notre Dame, where the translocal identity was religious and ethnic rather than regional). Interest in professional baseball, football, and later basketball often crossed state lines, building a regional following created by radio signals and then cable television. For most of the century the quintessential Midwestern team was the Chicago Cubs, an organization that promised rather than delivered greatness. In the 1990s, the Chicago Bulls' domination of professional basketball made them and their key star Michael Jordan wildly popular. Their appeal, however, was more national than regional. The Middle West never had a single team that the region (even briefly) could rally around, as New Englanders did around the Boston Red Sox or southerners, the Atlanta Braves.

Still, if no coherent regionalism developed in the Middle West, many people continued to thrive on a critique of the idea of it as bland and typical. Part of it was boosterism but part of it was a use of regional identity as way of attacking deeper problems in American society as a whole. Centers of intellectual culture were obviously major cities, particularly Chicago, which had long nurtured a community of artists and intellectuals, and, increasingly, university towns such as Madison, Wisconsin, and Ann Arbor, Michigan. State universities had long served as cultural centers but the democratization of these institutions in the decades after World War II intensified their roles as facilitators of cultural criticism. Scholars of history and literature, architecture and music, devoted much of their time to attacking hegemonic ideas and institutions and celebrating

Bascom Hall at the University of Wisconsin–Madison. The university was founded in 1849.
© BETTMANN/CORBIS

resistance to them and the construction of alternative forms of expression. Again, however, little of this was peculiarly regional in nature; if a scholar wrote about working people in Chicago, the subject was usually in the general nature of working-class culture, not Chicago or Midwestern cultures. It is notable that the most influential student-based critique of American society written in this era—the Port Huron (Michigan) Statement (1962) that became the foundation of Students for a Democratic Society—was universal in its critique of the power structure in the United States. Ironically, much of the most important cultural criticism emanating from the Middle West reinforced the popular image of the region as nondescript.

As in American society as a whole, the most profound writings by Midwesterners in the second half of the twentieth century tended to be by African Americans, women, and other "minorities" who had long seen themselves as excluded from the American mainstream. African Americans only became an important segment of Midwestern society after World War I, when the attractions of jobs in the automobile and steel industries brought thousands of migrants from the South to Cincinnati, Chicago, Detroit, and Gary. In the Midwest, the black immigrant experience was often disillusioning and painful. Complicating their lives was racism, different from the southern variety, but no less virulent. Richard Wright's *Native Son* (1940), written and set in Chicago, was a powerful indictment of the impact of racism (even well-intentioned, paternalistic racism) on African American men. Toni Morrison, a native of Lorain, Ohio, explored similar themes from a feminist perspective in works such as *The Bluest Eye* (1970) and *Sula* (1973), both of which were set in Ohio. Throughout the twentieth century, black men and women expressed their rage and resignation about life in a racist society in a variety of music styles. Poets such as Nikki Giovanni and Rita Dove wrote about the celebration and development of black identity in an overwhelmingly white society. Clearly influenced by life in the Middle West, these writers—like the Chicago-based minister and activist Jesse Jackson—were nonetheless engaging an American rather than a regional culture.

Much the same was true of female intellectuals. The most popularly successful, Ruth Hamilton and Jane Smiley, told stories about marital discord, child abuse, loneliness, family conflicts, and sexism that seemed only tangentially Midwestern in their settings. Smiley occasionally directly addressed the idea of the Midwest; there is a chapter with that title in her satire of state universities, *Moo* (1995), which describes the region as the home of zombie-like creatures of convention. But if Smiley's themes are universal, it is her ability to create and sustain a Midwestern environment that gives her writings such depth. Her Pulitzer Prize–winning reworking of King Lear, *A Thousand Acres* (1991), succeeds in no small part because she has created a place that seems truly like the rural Midwest. And *The All-True Travels and Adventures of Lidie Newton* (1998) reminds us of the centrality of the issue of slavery and regional conflict (Yankees v. southerners) to the origins of the Middle West.

The group of people who have most directly addressed Midwestern regionalism in the 1980s and 1990s are gays and lesbians. Several collections of stories, poems, and memoirs, including a volume edited by Karen Lee Osborne and William J. Spurlin, *Reclaiming the Heartland: Lesbian and Gay Voices from the Midwest* (1996), focus on the theme of being "different" in a society that seems to insist on uniformity. There is a great deal of ambivalence in these writings, mixing, as they often do, love of place and people with horror at the suffocating insensitivity and fear of change.

AN ARTIFICIAL CONSTRUCTION

Midwestern culture has always been an artificial construction. Its history is that of an idea, a popular image. Few are the residents of the region who have ever talked or written in regional terms; fewer are the scholars who have addressed the notion that there might be a regional culture. Magazines and newspapers regularly invoke the label "Midwestern," more often than not when they are discussing travel or a very tangible product such as food. As in the United States as a whole, consumerism is now a key component of regional identity. The monthly magazine, *Midwestern Living*, admirably conveys the image of the Middle West as a region of home-cooked meals, steady habits, and beautiful scenery: you can visit all kinds of quaint places where diversity is toothless, history homogenized, and ethnic and local cultures reduced to quilts and furniture that can decorate your home.

Beneath this contemporary variation of the booster emphasis on respectability, however, the Middle West remains what it has been for almost two centuries. It is a place of remarkable heterogeneity, founded and developed by all kinds of human beings who constructed both great cities and massive farmlands. It is also a place in which many people—perhaps because of the very diversity of the region's population—put a great premium on getting along with each other, on harmony at the expense of creativity. With their interests in local and family concerns, they have never developed a coherent regional consciousness. Nor do they seem eager to do so, content to nurture their distinctiveness out of sight, under the comfortable blanket of the Heartland.

See also other articles in this section.

BIBLIOGRAPHY

Atherton, Lewis. *Main Street on the Middle Border.* Bloomington, Ind., 1954.

Billington, Ray Allen. *Frederick Jackson Turner: Historian, Scholar, Teacher.* New York, 1973.

Bodnar, John E. *Remaking America: Public Memory, Commemoration, and Patriotism in the Twentieth Century.* Princeton, N.J., 1992.

Brooks, H. Allen. *The Prairie School: Frank Lloyd Wright and His Midwest Contemporaries.* New York, 1976.

Buley, R. Carlyle. *The Old Northwest: Pioneer Period, 1815–1840.* 2 vols. Bloomington, Ind., 1950.

Burg, David F. *Chicago's White City of 1893.* Lexington, Ky., 1976.

Cayton, Andrew R. L., and Peter S. Onuf. *The Midwest and the Nation: Rethinking the History of an American Region.* Bloomington, Ind., 1990.

Cayton, Mary Kupiec. "The Making of an American Prophet: Emerson, His Audiences, and the Rise of the Culture Industry in Nineteenth-Century America." *American Historical Review* 92 (June 1987): 597–620.

Cronon, William. *Nature's Metropolis: Chicago and the Great West.* New York, 1991.

Garner, John S., ed. *The Midwest in American Architecture.* Urbana, Ill., 1991.

Gjerde, Jon. *The Minds of the West: Ethnocultural Evolution in the Rural Middle West, 1830–1917.* Chapel Hill, N.C., 1997.

Grossman, James R. *Land of Hope: Chicago, Black Southerners, and the Great Migration.* Chicago, 1989.

Jensen, Richard J. *The Winning of the Midwest: Social and Political Conflict, 1888–1896.* Chicago, 1971.

Onuf, Peter S. *Statehood and Union: A History of the Northwest Ordinance.* Bloomington, Ind., 1987.

Sawislak, Karen. *Smoldering City: Chicagoans and the Great Fire, 1871–1874.* Chicago, 1995.

Shortridge, James R. *The Middle West: Its Meaning in American Culture.* Lawrence, Kan., 1989.

Smith, Carl S. *Chicago and the American Literary Imagination, 1880–1920.* Chicago, 1984.

Teaford, Jon C. *Cities of the Heartland: The Rise and Fall of the Industrial Midwest.* Bloomington, Ind., 1994.

Vitz, Robert C. *The Queen and the Arts: Cultural Life in Nineteenth-Century Cincinnati.* Kent, Ohio, 1989.

Williams, Peter. *Houses of God: Region, Religion, and Architecture in the United States.* Urbana, Ill., 1997.

Zukowsky, John. *Chicago Architecture, 1872–1922: Birth of a Metropolis.* Munich, 1987.

THE SOUTHWEST

Daniel Belgrad

The Southwest as a cultural region is characterized by a pervasively arid climate that has compelled the development of adaptive behaviors and by its persisting overlap of Native American, Mexican American, and Anglo-American cultures. As is true of most cultural regions, it is difficult to define the Southwest's exact boundaries. El Paso, Texas, and adjacent valley of Mesilla, New Mexico, constitute one of the region's most significant nodes of transportation and migration; Los Angeles, California, is another. Between them, the Southwest's boundary arcs northward, encompassing the states of New Mexico and Arizona and the southern portions of Colorado, Utah, Nevada, and California. Despite Oklahoma's aridity and its Native American populations, that state, on the northern border of Texas, is more properly considered part of the southern Great Plains; one feature that distinguishes Native American tribes of the Southwest is that by and large they still inhabit their ancestral homelands, while most of the tribes of Oklahoma were removed from the eastern United States.

Much of the early settlement of the Southwest in both prehistoric and historic times followed the river valleys: to the east, the Rio Grande; to the west, the Colorado, Salt, and Gila Rivers. When Spanish explorers arrived in the sixteenth century, these two river systems and the adjacent canyons and mesas formed the basis for two broad zones of agricultural civilizations, most notably the Pueblo. Archaeologists corroborate Pueblo traditions that trace their ancestry to the prehistoric Anasazi (Hisatsinom) civilization and to abandoned stone cliff dwellings at sites like Chaco Canyon; these city-states are believed to have been founded by migrants from far to the south. The spaces around and between these agricultural enclaves were inhabited by Athapaskan-speaking tribes more recently arrived from the north, primarily the Apaches, whose economies centered on hunting and gathering, supplemented by trading and raiding.

THE PUEBLO

The Pueblo people have never been a unified nation but are rather the inhabitants of independent villages that function like city-states (pueblos), sharing similar but not identical lifestyles and traditions. Some of the major subdivisions of the Pueblo are the Hopi, the Zuni, the Tiwa, the Tewa, and the Keresan speakers. Among Anglos, the Pueblo are renowned for their elaborately costumed ritual dances, their painted pottery, and their kachina "dolls."

According to Benjamin Whorf and Alfonso Ortiz, Pueblo languages and the traditional Pueblo worldview give precedence not to the distinction between past, present, and future but to that between what is latent ("unripe")—the future, dreams, spirits—and what is manifest ("ripe")—the past, the present, grown men and women. This structural dichotomy associates many aspects of Pueblo life, including green plants, with the spirit world. Traditional pueblo geography situates each pueblo in relation to thirteen sacred sites. Far from the pueblo (fifteen to eighty miles) in the four cardinal directions are the sacred mountains, each with a body of water that provides access to the underworld (*shipapu* or *sipofene*) of the spirits (*kachina*); close by are the sacred mesas, which offer access to the warrior brothers who guard the pueblo and mediate between the people and their gods. On the mountains and on the mesas, and at the four edges of the pueblo and in its center, are built "earth navels," shrines made of stones through which the power of the gods circulates, as described in the common prayer: "Within and around the earth, within and around the hills, within and around the mountains, your authority returns to you."

Traditional pueblo cultural life is distinguished by the characteristics of inclusivity and secrecy. Inclusivity implies that as new beliefs are integrated into the culture, old ones are not discarded. The principle of secrecy derives from the fact that

Petroglyphs, Three Rivers, New Mexico. Sierra Blanca is in the background. The Jornada
Mogollon people created these petroglyphs between 900 and 1400 A.D. © DAVID MUENCH/CORBIS

esoteric knowledge, dances, and rituals are considered the cultural property of particular groups (the moieties and kiva societies). They are the source of these groups' power and of their relevance to the larger community; this is one reason why some Pueblo consider anthropological studies and New Age imitations invasive and exploitative.

Many, though not all, pueblos are organized both by clan and by moiety. This cross-linking structure serves to integrate various social fractions into a unified whole. The clans are many and matrilineal and control the distribution of farmland; with names like Wood, Tobacco, Bear, and Bluebird, they appear to derive from extended family groups that traveled separate migratory paths and were integrated into the pueblo at different times. Some kiva societies are associated with particular clans (as the One Horn society is linked to the Water clan), probably representing how the knowledge and rituals of particular arriving groups have been integrated into the general culture of the pueblo. All Pueblo also belong either to the Summer or to the Winter moiety, each with its own chief and its major annual festival; the moieties are patrilineal and thus integrate the Pueblo across clan lines.

Traditionally, another mechanism of social integration among the Pueblo is the dynamic of gift exchange. Gifts, as of food, services, or sex (considered a gift of women to men), must be reciprocated either with other gifts or with goodwill and deference. This dynamic organizes inequalities between youths and elders, rich and poor, men and women, Pueblo and outsiders, making these social distinctions the bases of potential bonds rather than rifts.

THE SPANISH CONQUEST OF THE PUEBLO

Misunderstandings between the Spanish and the Pueblo over the principles of gift exchange and religious inclusivity developed almost immediately after first contact. The Spanish mistook Pueblo gifts for tribute, failing to reciprocate with friendly behavior; the Pueblo agreed to accept Christianity, then persisted in their own "devilish" dances. Ultimately, armed conquest triumphed over gifting, but so did the inclusivity of hybrid forms triumph over efforts to instill a "pure" Spanish Catholic culture.

The first Spaniards to encounter the Pueblo, in 1536, were Álvar Ńuñez Cabeza de Vaca, the African slave Estevanico, and two companions: the last survivors of Pánfilo de Narváez's ill-fated expedition to the west coast of Florida, lost in 1528. For eight years, Cabeza de Vaca and the others had made their way slowly across the continent, sometimes as slaves of the natives, sometimes as traveling traders or medicine men. Estevanico returned to the region in 1539, in the vanguard of an expedition led by the Franciscan Fray Marcos de Niza, and was killed by the Zuni. When Fray Marcos returned to Mexico, his description of the pueblos was quickly associated with the Spanish myth of the fabulously rich Seven Cities of Cíbola. The next year, an expedition was led by Francisco Vásquez de Coronado to find Cíbola and to conquer or destroy the pueblos. After a brutal campaign against the Pueblo, in which Cíbola seemed always just over the next horizon, Coronado left the region in 1542, and it was not until 1598, under Juan de Oñate, that the Spanish came to establish permanent settlements.

Spanish law prescribed how these settlements were to be laid out, and they generally followed a standard plan that is still visible today. At the center of the town was a rectangular public plaza, surrounded on three sides by the governor's palace, the soldiers' garrison (presidio), and the church; streets extended from the plaza in the four cardinal directions. Spanish settlers were prohibited by the king's law from taking native slaves except in "just war"—a phrase that was loosely constructed to justify regular slave raids against the Apache—and from encroaching on Native American farmlands. In reality, the large Spanish land grants often did include such lands. In addition, the Pueblo were expected to offer tribute to their Spanish overlords (encomenderos) in the form of corn, cloth, and labor.

The Spanish settlements were hierarchical, timocratic societies in which status was intimately linked to codes of honor and ritual deference, with local hidalgos (members of lower nobility) and Franciscan or Jesuit missionaries at the top and genízaros (captured or purchased Indians) at the bottom. A mestizo (mixed race) middle class quickly developed, swelling the ranks of tradesmen and small landowners (vecinos) and soon outnumbering the "Spanish" in Hispano society.

The Hispano culture of the American Southwest developed beside the pueblos and far from the New World centers of Spanish culture, resulting in unique cultural forms marked by syncretism or hybridity. Churches that synthesize Spanish baroque and local adobe models are one manifestation of this principle. Another is the secret society of the Penitentes. These societies emerged as historical vicissitudes (such as the expulsion of the Jesuits by the Bourbon king Charles III in 1767) deprived the region of clerical leaders, leaving the folk in charge of their own religious observances. The male-only society houses (moradas) of the Penitentes are reminiscent of Pueblo kivas, and their flagellation ceremonies fuse the crucifixion drama with native bloodletting fertility rituals. Similarly, the religious hymns (alabados) of the region contain lyrics that meld Pueblo and Christian perspectives, thus enabling coexistence through a "common experience diversely interpreted" (Deutsch, p. 84). Even those Hispano arts that do not show direct Pueblo influences, such as the religious folk art of retablos (paintings), bultos (sculptures), and reredos (altar screens), in their untutored quality reinforce the principle that remoteness from the centers of Spanish culture was a defining characteristic of this region.

Despite their internalization of Spanish perspective in the matachine dance, which celebrates Christian conquest of the "Pharisees," the Pueblo strove to retain their cultural integrity in the face of Hispano power. In this struggle, they were aided by the persistent tension between the governors of the province and the missionaries, who, unlike the secular clergy, did not recognize the authority of the king of Spain. The governors let the Pueblo retain their kachina worship and customary concubinage and in general worked to undermine the friars' charismatic authority; the friars in turn had more than one governor arrested in the name of the Holy Inquisition. This schism among the Spanish authorities encouraged the Pueblo to elude the encomienda and to defy missionaries and governors alike. Beginning in 1680, led by the Tewa Indian Popé, the Pueblo revolted and pushed the Spanish out of the upper Rio Grande valley. Although the Spanish authorities returned in 1693, many of the Hispano settlers and Christianized genízaros who had fled the upper valley stayed settled in the Mesilla region of present-day New Mexico. Thus, it is as a result of the Pueblo Revolt that the pueblos of the upper valley of the Rio Grande survive today while those of the lower valley have disappeared.

THE NAVAJO

The Navajo people (who call themselves the Diné) developed in the historical crucible of Pueblo, Spanish, and Apache interaction. The Navajo were Apache who adopted Pueblo agricultural techniques and other aspects of the Pueblo culture,

NAVAJO MYTHOLOGY

This excerpt from the Female Mountain-Top-Way of the Navajo, translated by Bernard Haile, describes how two old and ugly spirits, Big Snake and Big Bear Man, used trickery to seduce two willful young women, who then ran away from them only to become entangled in the Pueblo Wars.

"Are we appearing in the shape we are?" one asked the other. And they set about to dress themselves; one dressed in white shell, he put a slim white bead necklace around his neck. The other, Big Snake, also adorned himself with a slim white shell necklace, adding a white shell pendant to it. That done, Big Bear picked up the pipe, the other also filled his pipe. The first one lighted it with the sun, the other lighted his pipe with the moon. And Big Bear just took a puff from it, then began a song and told Big Snake to blow the smoke on the earth, then on the sky, then to blow it towards the east, to the west, south and north. Then he told him to blow around four times in a circle, the Bear singing right along. "Blow it along where the two women are!" he said. This he did.

It seems the tobacco [smoke] floated there to them. "What is it that smells so sweet, my younger sister!" "Leave it alone! Can bad things smell sweet?" the younger replied. "Blow it again over there!" he [Bear Man] directed the Snake. And again it floated to them. "What a sweet smell has floated to us again, my younger sister!" she said. "Blow it there again!" he [Bear Man] told him. When it floated to them it made her feel good. "What a fine smell, it certainly is sweet, my younger sister!" she repeated. She perspired freely, she threw the sweat from her brow. Again he said, "Blow it there again." When it floated to them she again said, "What a sweet smell!" By that time she was bathed in sweat. "Open up for us, let us two out, the heat is unbearable!" she said, but with little success, it seems. "Don't say that, open up for us, we are dying with heat!" she repeated. Then it seems they opened the circle for them. "We shall sit right here," she said. The two spent some time there before he blew the tobacco [smoke], which floated to them. "Whence does the smell come," the two were saying as they encircled the spot, then stood again where they had previously been seated. Again he blew it to them and the two made a sunwise circle. Again he blew it and they made the circle again. And again he blew it so that it floated to them. "What a sweet smell this is, my younger sister!" she said. As this happened no attention was paid to them by the group of dancers.

And the two girls left in the direction from which it floated to them. "From here the smell comes, my younger sister!" And when he blew it again they went on, again he blew it and they walked along the path of the smell. Again he blew it and they saw the burning fire. "From here the smell came, my younger sister!" she said, and now finally both went towards the fire and stood at the entrance. They certainly were two fine young men unknown to them who sat there covered with beads. "I will take that one for my husband, my younger sister!" she said, referring to Big Bear, "You take that other, my younger sister!" She gave her younger sister to Big Snake. "You will be his wife," she told her.

Source: Leland C. Wyman, *The Mountainway of the Navajo*. Tucson, Ariz., 1975. Pp. 170–171.

including weaving. When the Spanish brought domestic animals to the region, the Navajo began to specialize in herding sheep and goats and in weaving woolens. Never conquered by the Spanish, they remained a refuge for many Pueblo fleeing Spanish domination, but the Spanish and the Pueblo regularly joined in raiding the Navajo for slaves and livestock, and the Navajo regularly raided Pueblo and Spanish settlements as well.

Traditional Navajo society is predominantly pastoral rather than village-based. It is organized by matrilineal clans, which create far-reaching networks of trust and kinship, and outsiders are generally viewed with suspicion. The most important social unit, however, is the extended-family household, whose members share summer and winter quarters and manage a common herd. The herd is owned by the adult women and is the focus of family life; it is the source of food, clothing, status, and emotional security.

While not "individualistic," traditional Navajo place a high premium on autonomy. Thus, parents will not compel their children into particular behaviors, preferring the more indirect means of shaming; and the Navajo are reluctant to speak for others or to make appointments for fixed times in the future. Traditionally, the tribe has no formal authority structure, but men of local importance (*natani*) exercise charismatic influence.

The Navajo ideal is of *hozho,* a condition of peace established by the equilibrium of spiritual forces (*ké*). In order to maintain *hozho,* persons must observe the many behavioral guidelines and prohibitions prescribed by tradition. Singing also helps to bring *hozho,* and many traditional Navajo have songs to accompany their activities throughout the day. If *hozho* has been disrupted, a ritual sing can be commissioned by the afflicted person to restore *hozho.* If the cause of the imbalance is not known, a "hand trembler" can be called in to diagnose the source of the problem and to determine which ritual is necessary to remedy it. The different categories and structures of the ritual sings imply that some, like the Yei Bei Chai (Nightway) ritual, are adapted from Pueblo dances, while others are of Athapaskan derivation. There were once approximately forty different singing rituals, each lasting between two and nine days; today, about half of them are forgotten. Each singing ritual includes, in addition to prayers, segments of an immense mythology and oral history, accompanied by the appropriate sand paintings. In this way the heritage of the Diné was preserved, although any one singer memorized only part of it. Many of these cultural features are skillfully portrayed in the novels of Tony Hillerman.

THE ANGLO-AMERICAN CONQUEST

In 1848 the United States took the Southwest away from the young republic of Mexico, after a short war justified by the ideology of Manifest Destiny and prompted by slavery expansionists in the South. This change of flags underscored a longer period of transition in the cultural geography of the region.

Under Spanish dominion, goods and people had moved through the region primarily along a north-south axis, from the northernmost political capital of Santa Fe through El Paso to Chihuahua and Mexico City. Mexican independence in 1821 opened trade with the United States along the Santa Fe Trail, which led, from the American side, down the Missouri River, past Bent's Fort on the international boundary (in present-day Colorado), to Taos. Trade and migration gradually shifted to an east-west axis, confirmed by the construction of two railroad routes after the American conquest: the Atchison, Topeka, and Santa Fe and the Southern Pacific. The southern route, which required the acquisition of yet more Mexican land (purchased from the corrupt Mexican president Antonio de Santa Anna in 1853), was designed to serve the slave states in case of their secession.

The railroads integrated the region into a national economy, facilitating the growth of cities (El Paso, Albuquerque, Phoenix, Tucson, Los Angeles) and the development of industrial ranching, mining, lumbering, and tourism. In many towns and cities of the Southwest, the railroad became the commercial and industrial focus of an Anglo-American "new town," marginalizing the Hispano "old town" built around the Spanish plaza.

U.S. Army forts also stimulated the region's economy, through the imposition of American law, their heavy demands for beef, corn, and services, and their almost unique ability to pay in silver or gold. In 1863 Christopher "Kit" Carson led the army in an expedition to defeat the Navajo, who were then marched to Bosque Redondo near Fort Sumner for a five-year exile from their homeland. Such army operations, complemented by similar efforts by Mexican federal police (*rurales*) south of the border, largely put an end to the culture of raiding, rustling, and banditry that had long persisted in the region. Mormon farmers in central Utah found this situation encouraging and in 1875 began to found settlements from the canyonlands south to Chihuahua and Sonora in Mexico. However, Navajo society was disrupted by the enforced exile, the importation of cheap whiskey, and the imposition of a paternalistic federal authority precluding the traditional manly arts of hunting and raiding.

It was as a result of adjustments compelled by the Anglo-American conquest that the Navajo developed the crafts for which they have become famous. The woolen blankets traditionally woven by Navajo women were supplanted by woolen rugs woven for export to Anglo showrooms, sometimes with designs devised by Anglo traders based on

Persian models. Sacred turquoise stones, brought to traders during the winter as surety for payment on goods advanced on credit, were redeemed in the spring with the wool crop; and whatever additional payment the traders made in silver would be worked by the Navajo men into elaborate settings for the turquoise.

RANCHING AND MINING

The cattle industry in the Southwest began to flourish with the start of the Civil War in 1861, and by the 1870s, coinciding with the army's pacification of the Apache, the Southwest was a cattlemen's empire. As in the Great Plains region, corporations with large herds did their best to monopolize range and water rights, and the range was quickly threatened by overgrazing. Range wars erupted between sheepherders and cattlemen, which had a cultural as well as a material dimension: sheep cropped the grass very closely, ruining the range for cattle; but the feud also generally pitted a sheepherding culture of Navajos and Hispanos, who traveled on foot accompanied by dogs, against a cattle culture of Anglos on horseback.

Paradoxically, despite the appropriation of the cowboy image as an Anglo-American icon, much of the Anglo cattle culture derived from Spanish-American roots, traceable through such tools, words, and practices as the lariat, the rodeo, and daily roping. Two differences seem culturally significant: the Mexicans neither castrated the bulls in their herds to make steers nor assigned the ownership of water sources to individuals. Both of these Anglo practices were consistent with the resource management strategies of corporate capitalism.

Despite romantic tales of prospectors and placer mines, most of the mining in the Southwest, from coal and copper to uranium, has been accomplished by large corporations using industrial technologies. At the turn of the twentieth century, mining towns were almost always company towns, with miners living in company-owned housing and being paid in scrip, as described in Agnes Smedley's autobiographical *Daughter of Earth* (1929). Miners were an ethnic mix, including Italians, Greeks, Poles, Slavs, and a large number of Hispanos attracted by wages twice those of farm labor. Because the mining companies dominated the cultural institutions of the mining camps, these Hispanos did not succeed in replicating their traditional village life. In southern Colorado the managers of the Gould-Rockefeller Colorado Fuel and Iron Company took a "progressive" approach to worker relations, founding a kindergarten to train miners' children to their labor, a morale-boosting camp magazine, and a sociological department charged with instilling what they considered "American" values among those they characterized "fatalistic, patriarchal, presentist, oriental, subservient, irresponsible" Hispanos (Deutsch, *No Separate Refuge*, p. 96). But these strategies failed to avert bitter labor strikes that culminated in the infamous Ludlow massacre of April 1914.

MISSIONARIES AND PRIMITIVISTS

At the same time that the U.S. Army and industry were "Americanizing" the Southwest, Protestant missionaries and primitivist tourists were doing the same, albeit with greater ambivalence. Protestant missionaries to the Native Americans regularly interceded with the federal authorities on behalf of their congregants, although on some issues, such as the outlawing of native religions, they were unreliable spokesmen. Presbyterian schoolteachers brought progressive domesticity, English literacy, and the woman's movement to isolated Hispano villages; but their romantic appreciation for an exotic lifestyle often worked against their objectives. They were often integrated into the village community only on its own terms.

Many Anglos who first came to the arid Southwest to cure themselves of tuberculosis or other urban ills became enamored of the Native American and Hispano cultures there, seeing in them an alternative to the industrial American rat race. Mary Hunter Austin crisscrossed the Southwest desert alone on horseback for several years, collecting material for literary sketches published as *Lost Borders* (1909) and *The Land of Little Rain* (1903). Bert Phillips came to Taos in 1898, to prospect, paint, and promote tourism, and was soon joined by other artists in quest of the picturesque, including Ernest L. Blumenschein. The New York heiress Mabel Dodge arrived by automobile in 1918, married the Pueblo Indian Tony Luhan of Taos, and put the Taos art colony on the maps of the American avant-garde. D. H. Lawrence and Robinson Jeffers sought inspiration there at her invitation. Most famously, Georgia O'Keeffe became a permanent resident of New Mexico, devoting many of her paintings to modernist interpretations of its colorful landscapes. Visits to the Native American reservations of the Southwest also inspired the "Indianist" music of Arthur Farwell, epitomized by his *Navajo War Dance* for piano.

Many of these artists, writers, and musicians shared a common set of ideas that linked a modern art aesthetic to American Indian culture. Austin, Dodge Luhan, and O'Keeffe were convinced that their works could communicate something profound about the Native American worldview. The values they propounded were alertness to the environment, a different sense of time, and a feeling of community—values that they encoded in a vocabulary of color and rhythm that they identified with the cultures of the Southwest. As O'Keeffe explained her flower paintings, "Everyone has many associations with a flower—the idea of flowers. . . . Still—in a way—nobody sees it really—it is so small—we haven't time—and to see takes time, like to have a friend takes time. . . . So I said to myself, I'll paint what I see—what the flower is to me but I'll paint it big and they will be surprised into taking time to look at it—I will make even busy New Yorkers take time to see what I see."

THE DUST BOWL AND DAMS

During the Great Depression of the 1930s, a different kind of Anglo emigrant appeared in the Southwest. Pushed off farms in the southern Great Plains by drought and foreclosure, Anglo emigrants made their way across the mountains and deserts to southern California, as dramatized in John Steinbeck's *The Grapes of Wrath* (1939). They joined the stream of migrant Hispano farmworkers already laboring in California's fields and orchards and, like them, were greeted with scorn and suspicion, although, unlike the Hispanos, they were not subject to sudden deportation to Mexico.

The 1910s and 1920s had witnessed an influx of Mexican migrants into the Southwest, escaping the upheavals of the Mexican revolution. They brought with them the musical traditions of the *corrido* (saga song), *conjunto* (accordion and guitar ensemble), and mariachi. The new wave of Anglo migrants brought their music with them as well, and "hillbilly" music (later developing into "folk" and "country") became a staple of radio broadcasting in Los Angeles. The songs and patter of Woody Guthrie exemplified a folksy style of performance; the style of "singing cowboy" movies starring Roy Rogers and Gene Autry was considerably refined, in keeping with Hollywood versions of the American Dream.

In the 1930s, Los Angeles was emerging as a modern metropolis. The great dam projects of the mid-twentieth century along the Colorado River system were designed in part to preserve California's agriculture from flood and drought, but equally important were the water and electricity they provided for the expansion of cities and industries. In the 1870s John Wesley Powell, the first director of the U.S. Geological Survey, had advocated interstate cooperation in regional water management. In 1921 California and Nevada agreed to cooperate in building Boulder (later renamed Hoover) Dam, which was completed in 1936. California would get most of the water, while Nevada would get most of the electrical power and the recreational attraction of Lake Mead. Las Vegas, Nevada, was transformed from a small Mormon town to a tourist center replete with an airport, hotel-casinos, and all-you-can-eat buffets. But conservationists were upset that spectacular canyonlands had disappeared beneath the reservoir.

Dam technology also conflicted with the lifestyle of the Navajo. Sheep had become increasingly important to the Navajo economy as woven woolen rugs became their primary stock in trade with the Anglos. But drought and large herds combined to cause severe overgrazing on the Navajo reservation, leading to soil erosion and an increased runoff of silt into Lake Mead. John Collier, the federal commissioner of Indian Affairs from 1933 to 1945, tried to remedy the situation with a drastic stock-reduction program approved by a Navajo tribal council of dubious legitimacy. The result was a badly planned and poorly implemented program that further destabilized Navajo society and fed the Navajo distrust of the Anglo authorities. The coercion and wastefulness associated with the stock-reduction program overshadowed Collier's good-intentioned efforts to restore tribal sovereignty and to preserve Navajo culture by commissioning several anthropological studies.

After more Colorado River canyonlands were destroyed by the Glen Canyon Dam (completed in 1964), environmental activist David Brower of the Sierra Club led a successful campaign to oppose proposed dams in the Grand Canyon itself. The art and literature created for this struggle represent the values of an influential southwestern subculture of environmentalists and conservationists. Exemplary works include the black-and-white photography of Ansel Adams and Philip Hyde, the color photography of Eliot Porter, and fiction and nonfiction by Wallace Stegner and Edward Abbey.

The Colorado River dams and the interstate highway system stand as monuments to the exuberance of the progressive Anglo vision. Dedicated to mastering and improving upon nature, they endeavor to transcend the geographical and climatic conditions that have historically shaped the Southwest's regional culture. Since World War II, the way of life they make possible has come to dominate the region, but the drawbacks to this lifestyle have also become more visible.

WORLD WAR II

World War II promoted the expansion of industrial and military activity in the Southwest. Los Angeles became a major center of wartime production (especially for the budding aerospace industry), as well as a base for military operations in the Pacific. Atomic testing at Los Alamos and White Sands, in New Mexico, continued through the cold war era.

The antiracist ideology associated with the war effort also had an important effect on the region, laying the foundation for improved crosscultural relations. The Navajo code talkers are a case in point: recruited by the military to communicate secret orders in the syntax of their native language, they mystified Axis cryptographers.

Yet in many respects reality did not conform to ideology. African Americans had come to the region since the nineteenth century as servants, cowboys, Exodusters (as some post-Reconstruction settlers called themselves), laborers, and professionals; they continued to experience unfair discrimination during the war, as chronicled in Chester Himes's novel *Lonely Crusade* (1947). In the Mexican American barrios of Los Angeles, during a week of rioting in 1943, Anglo enlisted men hunted down local pachuco youths sporting the flamboyant zoot suits and stripped them of their clothes. Japanese Americans on the Pacific coast were interned as "enemy aliens" and stripped of their property.

AMERICAN *MESTIZAJE*

Postwar affluence encouraged the spread of the Southwest's hybrid culture (in Spanish, *mestizaje*) across the United States. The freeways, ranch houses, swimming pools, and air conditioners of southern California defined a new suburban ideal for the whole country. In art and popular music, too, Los Angeles styles began to set the trend. In the 1960s the surfer subculture, set to music by the Beach Boys, became a symbol of the good life of youth and leisure. The music of Frank Zappa evinced a more ironic attitude toward the contemporary L.A. experience, as did the pop art of Los Angeles artists like Wayne Thiebaud. Born in Mesa,

Arizona, and raised on a Mormon ranch in southern Utah, Thiebaud had worked as a cartoonist for the Walt Disney studios during the Depression, and then for the Air Force Motion Picture Unit during World War II; his paintings of garishly colored, artificial-looking desserts comment with a mixture of satire and affection on the superficiality of the new American Dream.

Hybridity and ethnic crossover continued to be the source of exciting cultural innovations in the postwar period. Johnny Otis, a pioneer in the birth of rock and roll from swing jazz and rhythm and blues, was born Greek American but joined the African American community. Richie Valens was just one of several Mexican Americans who became Anglo recording stars. The striking sculpture of the Watts Towers was built over a thirty-four-year period by Sam Rodia, an Italian immigrant who lived and married within the Hispano community. He named his majestic complex of concrete spires, studded with glass bottles and broken ceramic, Our Town: *nuestro pueblo*.

Another important category of Southwest art since the 1960s has given ethnic identity a political dimension. The Chicano movement of the late 1960s had a strong cultural orientation: Luis Valdez's Teatro Campesino ("Peasants' Theater") supported the United Farm Workers' strike against California grape growers; the poems "Aztlán" by Alurista and "I Am Joaquin" by Rodolpho Gonzales revived Mexican myth and folklore in a call for social justice. The subculture surrounding the customized cars and bicycles known as "low riders" harks back to this Chicano heritage of *la Raza* (the "Mexican race") and its mythical homeland of Aztlán, as is clear in letters to the editors of *Lowrider Magazine*. Among American Indians as well, postwar cultural developments have often been inflected with issues of identity and tribal autonomy. Examples include the divergence of Native American painters from the Santa Fe Studio style associated with older forms of Anglo patronage, the postmodernist writing of Leslie Marmon Silko, and the fight for official recognition of the Native American Church. Finally, "guerrilla theater" is a useful term for comprehending the paramilitary activities of such groups as the Black Panthers, the Brown Berets, and Rejes Lopez Tijerina's Alianza: these groups sought to achieve social change not so much through violence as through the psychological impact of their violent image.

Among Anglos the political culture of the Southwest at the end of the twentieth century was dominated by conservatives fighting to defend their language and values against the drug trade and illegal immigration. But the region is also the long-time home of Anglo countercultural enclaves. From the late 1950s through the early 1970s, Venice West, California, was a haven for beatniks and hippies. Since then, Santa Fe, New Mexico, and Boulder, Colorado, have become the unofficial capitals of New Age spirituality, an amalgam of the psychedelic "age of Aquarius," occultism, Native Americanism, and alternative medicine. College students and runaway teenagers in serapes and tie-dyed T-shirts converge on the region every summer to create the perennial commune known as the Rainbow Gathering. The more recently created Burning Man Festival annually combines art and theatricality with the challenge of desert subsistence. In the future the culture of the Southwest will probably continue to be defined by the same forces that have defined it in the past: the struggle to sustain human life on a beautiful but arid land and the provocative encounter among diverse cultural heritages of its Anglo, Hispano, and Native American inhabitants.

See also **Latinas and Latinos in the United States** (in this volume); and other articles in this section.

BIBLIOGRAPHY

Austin, Mary. *The American Rhythm.* New York, 1923.

Brody, J. J. *Indian Painters and White Patrons.* Albuquerque, N.Mex., 1971.

Chase, Gilbert. "The 'Indianist' Movement in American Music." Program Notes to *Farewell, Orem, and Cadman.* New World Records NW 213. New York, 1977.

Davis, Mike. *City of Quartz: Excavating the Future in Los Angeles.* New York, 1990.

Deutsch, Sarah. *No Separate Refuge: Culture, Class, and Gender on an Anglo-Hispanic Frontier in the American Southwest, 1880–1940.* New York, 1987.

Downs, James F. *The Navajo.* New York, 1972.

Fergusson, Harvey. *The Conquest of Don Pedro.* New York, 1954.

Greever, William S. *The Bonanza West: The Story of the Western Mining Rushes, 1848–1900.* Norman, Okla., 1963.

Gutiérrez, Ramón A. *When Jesus Came, the Corn Mothers Went Away: Marriage, Sexuality, and Power in New Mexico, 1500–1846.* Stanford, Calif., 1991.

Hillerman, Tony. *The Ghostway.* New York, 1985.

Jones, Oakah, Jr. *Los Paisanos: Spanish Settlers on the Northern Frontier of New Spain.* Norman, Okla., 1978.

Klein, Joe. *Woody Guthrie: A Life.* New York, 1980.

Loeffler, Jack. *La Música de los Viejitos: The Hispano Folk Music of El Rio Grande del Norte.* Albuquerque, N.Mex., 1999.

Luhan, Mabel Dodge. *Edge of Taos Desert: An Escape to Reality.* Albuquerque, N.Mex., 1987.

Martin, Russell. *A Story That Stands like a Dam: Glen Canyon and the Struggle for the Soul of the West.* New York, 1989.

Meinig, D. W. *Southwest: Three Peoples in Geographical Change, 1600–1970.* New York, 1971.

Myres, Sandra L. "The Ranching Frontier: Spanish Institutional Backgrounds of the Plains Cattle Industry." In *Essays on the American West.* Edited by Sandra L. Myres et al. Austin, Tex., 1969.

Nostrand, Richard L. *The Hispano Homeland.* Norman, Okla., 1992.

O'Keeffe, Georgia. *Georgia O'Keeffe*. New York, 1976.

Ortiz, Alfonso. *Tewa World: Space, Time, Being, and Becoming in a Pueblo Society*. Chicago, 1969.

Pérez de Luxán, Diego. *Expedition into New Mexico Made by Antonio de Espejo, 1582–1583*. Edited by George P. Hammond and Agapito Rey. Los Angeles, 1929.

Rosales, Francisco Arturo. *Chicano!: The History of the Mexican-American Civil Rights Movement*. Houston, Tex., 1996.

Schimmel, Julie. *Bert Geer Phillips and the Taos Art Colony*. Albuquerque, N.Mex., 1994.

Silko, Leslie Marmon. *Storyteller*. New York, 1981.

United States National Park Service. *Prospector, Cowhand, and Sodbuster: Historic Places Associated with the Mining, Ranching, and Farming Frontiers of the Trans-Mississippi West*. Washington, D.C., 1967.

Viramontes, Helena María. *Under the Feet of Jesus*. New York, 1995.

Vogt, Evon Z., ed. *People of Rimrock: A Study of Values in Five Cultures*. Cambridge, Mass., 1966.

Weigle, Marta. *Brothers of Light, Brothers of Blood: The Penitentes of the Southwest*. Albuquerque, N.Mex., 1976.

White, Richard. *The Roots of Dependency: Subsistence, Environment, and Social Change among the Choctaws, Pawnees, and Navajos*. Lincoln, Nebr., 1983.

Whorf, Benjamin Lee. "An American Indian Model of the Universe." *International Journal of American Linguistics* 16, no. 2 (1950): 67–72.

Wyman, Leland C. *The Mountainway of the Navajo*. Tucson, Ariz., 1975.

Yava, Albert. *Big Falling Snow: A Tewa-Hopi Indian's Life and Times and the History and Traditions of His People*. Edited by Harold Courlander. New York, 1978.

BORDERLANDS

Ramón A. Gutiérrez

In contemporary historical writing produced in and about the United States, the word "borderlands" has multiple meanings, each with its own particular history and genealogy. The oldest use of "borderlands" dates to the early 1900s and specifically to the historical scholarship of Herbert Eugene Bolton. Beginning in 1902 Bolton used the term "Spanish Borderlands" to refer to those areas presently within the territorial limits of the United States that had been under Spain's colonial control. From Spain's lofty imperial perspective, its North American territory was quite extensive. Geographically, it encompassed roughly everything in North America below the forty-second parallel, from the Atlantic Ocean to the Pacific. And by rights of exploration, this expanse theoretically included large parts of the Pacific Northwest. But the area of effective Spanish settlement was much smaller, continuously shifted, and slowly contracted during the late eighteenth and early nineteenth centuries. Spain established population nodes in what are now the states of Florida, Georgia, Louisiana, Texas, New Mexico, Colorado, Arizona, Nevada, and California. These former areas of Spanish colonial settlement are what Bolton called the "Spanish Borderlands." He always modified borderlands with the adjective "Spanish" and frequently wrote about Spain's borderlands in the plural. He thus referred to Georgia as "one of the Spanish Borderlands," signaling his recognition of the development of a great array of Spanish cultural variants. The Spanish Borderlands, for Bolton, came into existence with the 1492 voyage of Christopher Columbus and ended with Mexico's independence from Spain in 1821.

Until the mid-1960s the Spanish Borderlands were the only ones that received the attention of American historians. Starting in the mid-1960s, academic writers, primarily Mexican American and Chicano scholars, began referring to the Borderlands, an area that somewhat overlapped geographically Bolton's Spanish Borderlands, but was imagined as being ordered by a very different sense of time and space. The end of the Mexican War in 1848 and the establishment of a two-thousand-mile border between Mexico and the United States defined the moment of the Borderlands' conception. The exact space that defined this area was always left vague, but it did signify a very wide swath of land on both sides of the international border. Mexican American and Chicano scholars were principally interested in issues of Mexican immigrant adaptation in the United States and the complex transnational economic flows that pushed labor out of Mexico and pulled it into the United States. These scholars cared little about the pre-1848 history of the area and always looked forward to the present.

A third definition for "borderlands" that was similarly rooted in the present and less concerned about the past emerged in the late 1980s. This Borderlands was more a metaphor for cultural change than a precise place, period, or process. Borderlands were a way of describing hybridity, cultural blending, transculturation, and the conjunction of complex social identities, such as those of race, ethnicity, gender, and sexuality.

BOLTON'S SPANISH BORDERLANDS

The word "borderlands" entered the lexicon of professional historians in the United States at the beginning of the twentieth century as part of a larger movement to chronicle regional distinctiveness. In late-nineteenth-century historical writing about the United States, there was a dominant tendency to depict national development in linear, monolithic, and unitary terms. In the 1890s most histories of the United States still largely focused on the original thirteen colonies and were almost entirely Anglocentric. To change this, a number of historians wrote narratives of regional development and distinctiveness. Frederick Jackson Turner's legendary essay "The Significance of the Frontier in American History" (1893) focused on the West and by so doing provoked a wider discussion of American history. Turner maintained that a distinctive relationship between humans and environment had developed in the American West, an area he envisioned as primarily consisting of the Trans-Allegheny region. Although Turner and his students acknowledged that the French and Spanish had explored and settled areas of the midcontinent and zones west of the Mississippi River, these experiences gained no mention as part of his narrative of the American western frontier.

Others described the distinctiveness of historical events in other regions of the United States. Francis Parkman spent much of his career documenting the French presence in North America. Walter Prescott Webb theorized about the distinctiveness of the Great Plains. Bolton invented the Spanish Borderlands and gave them their most extensive and sustained definition.

Spanish Borderlands is a term most frequently associated with Bolton and with his particular hemispheric perspective on the historical development of the Americas, as viewed from the vantage of the United States. Bolton was a professional historian who trained a large number of students, and thus his theories about the Spanish Borderlands were, until the mid-1960s, primarily of interest to U.S. historians. Bolton repeatedly tried to get Mexican and Latin American historians to embrace his ideas, but few ever found them very useful or compelling. For Latin Americans writing histories of their own republics, Turner's ideas about the frontier held more interest and promise.

Bolton began writing about the Spanish Borderlands in 1902, while still an assistant professor of medieval history at the University of Texas at Austin. With the 1921 publication of *The Spanish Borderlands,* Bolton's ideas received their fullest articulation. He described several of Spain's borderlands in what became the United States—Georgia, Florida, Louisiana, Texas, New Mexico, and California. Each of these places was a distinct cultural zone that had been profoundly influenced by the interactions of Spanish colonial institutions and personnel, indigenous populations, and colonial rivals. These were the crucial historical components of Bolton's Spanish Borderlands. These analytic categories, simple as they were, gained broad dissemination and importance through the hundreds of masters and doctoral students he taught as a professor of American history at the University of California, Berkeley, between 1911 and 1940 and from 1942 to 1945.

After Bolton died in 1953, historians who embraced the Spanish Borderlands framework did so in narrower and more restricted ways. This can be determined simply through a survey of the use of the term "borderlands." Authors, most of them former Bolton students, began to divide the Spanish Borderlands into Eastern Borderlands, by which they meant Georgia, Florida, and Louisiana, and Western Borderlands, or Texas, New Mexico, and California. This division is in part driven by the fact that the Eastern Borderlands historically had been administered from Cuba, while the Western Borderlands were governed from New Spain, or what became the Republic of Mexico in 1821. The historian David J. Weber argues in "Turner, the Boltonians, and the Borderlands" (1988) that few historians had Bolton's geographic and empirical scope, and this intellectual limitation and lack of mental discipline largely explains the separation of the Spanish Borderlands into eastern and western parts. A more persuasive and less personalistic explanation is that Spain had its largest settlements and its most temporally sustained cultural impact in what became known as the Western Borderlands. Indeed, historical writing on the Eastern Borderlands was always sparse and has all but disappeared. Writing on the western segment of the Spanish Borderlands was always more extensive (Bolton's chairmanship of the history department at Berkeley probably had much to do with this), remained vibrant, and was gradually complemented by a more expansive scholarship on the borderlands.

Bolton was born near Tomah, Wisconsin in 1870, and as a graduate student of history at the University of Wisconsin in 1896 was an assistant to Turner. He received his Ph.D. in 1899, and in 1901, Bolton joined the faculty of the University of Texas at Austin. He moved to Leland Stanford Junior University in 1909, and finally settled at the University of California, Berkeley, in 1911, where he spent the rest of his academic career.

Bolton was lured to Berkeley with a promise that he would be given the financial resources to expand the Bancroft Library's holdings on Spain's presence in North America. On arriving at Berkeley, Bolton immediately outlined his vision of this project for Benjamin Ide Wheeler, president of the University of California. In a report titled *Need for the Publication of a Comprehensive Body of Documents Relating to the History of Spanish Activities within the Present Limits of the United States* (1911), Bolton asked rhetorically why Spain's presence in North America was so poorly known and understood. French settlement in the United States had been minimal in comparison to the Spanish, yet it was widely recognized and taught in schools. Spanish exploration, missionary work, industrial development, and settlement in North America had been so extensive that this experience required its own historian. This was the goal Bolton elaborated and readily embraced. Bolton believed that the fact that Spain's historic role in the development of the United States was not better known was due to the narrowness of academic training and social pedigrees. The history of the United States had, until then, been written "almost solely from the standpoint of the East and of the English colonies," largely by New Englanders, most of them trained at Harvard University. Bolton acknowledged the importance of Turner's work on the West, but cautioned that Turner's "West is a moving area which began east of the Appalachians and has not thus far reached beyond the Mississippi Valley. He and his school have contributed very little to the history of the Southwest and the Far West."

The history department at the University of California was uniquely positioned geographically to chronicle the Spanish frontier in America, Bolton explained in his report. What would be most crucial for this project were investments in the gathering of documentary collections so that the Spanish legacy in the United States could be faithfully reconstructed. According to Bolton, the Spanish epic in North American history was simple. It was defined by "Spanish exploration and conquest; the Spanish mission, presidio, pueblo, mine, and ranch; Anglo-American trappers, explorer, contraband trader, and filibuster within the Spanish domain; revolution from Spain and development under Mexican rule; and finally, Anglo-American settlement, diplomacy, and conquest." This description, in highly abbreviated form, became the basic thematic framework that Bolton and his students eventually elaborated in more detail to explain the historical development of the Spanish Borderlands.

Throughout his long academic career at Berkeley, Bolton marshaled his considerable energy to integrate the history of the Spanish Borderlands into larger histories of the United States. Toward this end, he gathered documents and published transcriptions in accessible form. So that the Spanish language did not become an obstacle to better understanding, he prepared numerous scholarly translations. He edited guides to archival collections in Spain and Mexico and personally wrote numerous books and essays detailing how Spain had explored, conquered, and colonized its various borderlands. He trained a legion of graduate students and con-

Mission San Xavier del Bac, Tucson, Arizona. Founded in 1699 by the Jesuit missionary and explorer Eusebio Kino, the mission was rebuilt by Franciscans from 1783 to 1797. It is located on what is now the Tohono O'odham reservation. © CORBIS

stantly challenged and critiqued historians he deemed too parochial and ethnocentric, asking them to imagine a more complex America, a "Greater America" that stretched beyond the territorial boundaries of the United States, and most certainly way beyond the thirteen original colonies.

While Turner and his students imagined the process of frontier expansion as a movement from east to west, this schema simply did not work for Bolton's Spanish Borderlands. Such a spatial organization of American history was too narrow. To the east-west trajectory one had to add two others: one that went from south to north and another from north to south. Spain's frontiers in the United States developed from south to north in two distinct areas. Florida, Georgia, and Louisiana were conquered, settled, and governed from Cuba and the administrative center in Santo Domingo. Settlements in Spanish New Mexico, Texas, and California were founded by people and institutions moving northward from central Mexico. The French presence in North America complicated these directional forces of change, because the French colonial movement moved from north to south.

As one of Turner's students, Bolton was considered one of Turner's most accomplished protégés. Clearly, Turner's framing of the American frontier loomed large in Bolton's own thinking. Bolton embraced Turner's spatial model and pointed it in new directions. When it came to the relationship between humans and their natural environments, Bolton took a contrary stance, asserting instead that Spanish institutions, culture, and personnel had forged the frontier in Spain's own image. The power of the Habsburg monarchs was so overwhelming that their authority stifled local initiative, personal liberty, and self-government throughout most of the Spanish Empire, save in remote California, where a moderate climate, rich land, and docile Indian labor bred a "mellower spirit."

Bolton advanced this case primarily by documenting the lives of important leaders, both civic and religious, and the baroque intrigues of European imperial rivalries in the Americas. He wrote extensively about the various conquistadores that first explored Spain's borderlands, documenting their triumphs, trials, and defeats. The selfless and indefatigable friars who endured all sorts of hardships to plant Christianity in the Americas were particularly saintly to Bolton and received only the most heroic and roseate verbs from his pen. The role of the missionaries and soldiers in establishing the missions and the presidios (colonial forts), the two frontier institutions that brought "civilization" to the most remote areas of the empire, were the topic of Bolton's most important essays, published in 1917 and 1930. The missions and the presidios, and occasionally towns, figured large in his histories.

As a great Hispanophile, Bolton gave inordinate attention to Spanish language, architecture, religion, law, festivals, and archival records. He made only scant mention of the Native American peoples and cultures with whom the Spaniards interacted, and, by contemporary standards, this was one of his major blind spots. Despite the considerable variance and complexity that existed among native peoples at the time of Spanish exploration, conquest, and settlement, Native Americans in Bolton's writings were simple and monolithic. They were mostly passive players caught up in Spain's larger territorial designs. The brutality of the wars of blood and fire the Spaniards wreaked on the Indians was rarely mentioned, and the impact of the confinement of Indians in Spanish missions went largely unnoted. Bolton's goal as an historian was to counter the Black Legend concerning the Spanish colonial experience in America. Logically, death, disease, and destruction could not figure large in that story.

Assessing the impact of Bolton's legacy in historical writing, the Latin American historian Benjamin Keen characterized it as "romantic" and "Hispanophile." Bolton would have undoubtedly found this characterization extremely satisfying, for as he himself wrote in 1930, "These Spanish Borderlands have had a picturesque, a romantic, and an important history. They had special significance as parts of the vast Spanish Empire. They are unique as the meeting place of two streams of European civilization."

Starting in the late 1940s, Bolton's cherished missions and missionaries came under searing historiographic attack from demographers and anthropologists. From Sherburne F. Cook, an animal physiologist who also taught at Berkeley, came a series of publications between 1940 and 1943 that chronicled the devastating impact the missions had on California's Indians. In 1770 California's Indian population numbered about 133,500, noted Cook, but by 1870 this number had fallen to 20,000. Much of this population decline could be blamed on the confinement of the Indians in missions. The Spanish policy of gathering the Indians into mission communities was driven not by some larger military or political goals but by a religious zeal for Catholic converts. California's Indians suffered malnutrition and starvation at the missions, and their confinement in close quarters created a fertile breeding ground for the rapid spread of disease. Forced labor, excessive punishment for putative crimes, and imposed celibacy further dispirited California's Indians and led to their rapid numeric decline. The anthropologist Henry F. Dobyns, writing in the 1960s, told an equally brutal tale of the impact of the Jesuit missions in the Pimería Alta, what is today southern Arizona.

Since Bolton's death, and particularly since the 1960s, American historians have revisited Spain's colonial legacy in the United States. Greater scholarly attention has been given to the syncretic cultural forms created through Spanish-Indian interactions, to the flow of people, culture, and ideas in complicated and unpredictable ways, to the multiplicity of Native American cultures, and to the hybridity of cultural forms created under conditions of conquest and domination. The areas in the United States that Bolton described as the Spanish Borderlands formally became part of independent Mexico in 1821. For Bolton and most of his students, the borderlands under Mexican control were of little interest, and even less so as objects of study under the post-1848 territorial control of the United States.

NATIVES TALK BACK:
INDIANS AND CHICANOS

By the mid-1960s the mute and largely stoic Indians of the Boltonian imagination started to talk back. Bolton and his students saw the Indians of the Spanish Borderlands as the Spaniards themselves had once imagined them, as little more than "savages," possessing little civilization, ensnared in superstitions rather than religion, and participating in anarchy rather than a formal government. When Native Americans talked back, writing about their own lives, memories, and histories, they recounted stories of Indian heroism, of native struggle and resistance, and of endurance, despite scholarly and popular tracts lamenting their demise. Indians had not vanished, and in the 1960s they became outspokenly militant about their cultural rights to the preservation of their languages and their lands and access to education. As participants in the worldwide movement of egalitarian aspirations sparked by students, racial and ethnic minorities, and women in the 1960s, Native Americans began to assert their own rights to self-determination. Vine Deloria Jr., Jack Forbes, and Peter Blue Cloud were just three of the Native American scholars who wrote histories of Indian activism and resistance. As these scholars so correctly pointed out, histories of Indian passivity and extinction were themselves the toxic products of colonialism. In this climate of protest, Native Americans wrote manifestos that mobilized many to action. Beginning in November 1969, Native American activists occupied Alcatraz Island in San Francisco Bay for almost a year and a half. In 1973 the village of Wounded Knee, South Dakota, was held by Native American militants for eighty-one days. These activities brought great attention to the movement for Indian self-determination and sovereignty.

A similar movement of political mobilization occurred among Mexican Americans residing throughout the southwestern United States. Defiantly calling themselves Chicanos, young Mexican American men and women in solidarity with Native Americans laid claim to their own repressed and forgotten Indian ancestry and discovered direct genealogical links to the Aztecs, the fiercest warriors that had ever roamed the Americas. They claimed the Southwest was Aztlán, their ancestral homeland, and demanded its independence from the United States. Although these militant Chicanos may have been remote descendants of the Spanish soldiers that had once conquered the Southwest, Chicanos wanted no part of this European Spanish heritage.

Rather, Chicanos proclaimed working-class origins, celebrated Mexican national roots, and were quick to point to their *mestizo* ("mixed-blood") heritage as products of racial and cultural mixing between Spaniards and Indians. Chicanos were a hybrid people who had long resided in the Southwest. They had never crossed a border. Rather, at the end of the Texas Revolution in 1836 and the Mexican-American War in 1848, and with the Gadsden Purchase in 1853, the border separating Mexico and the United States had physically crossed them. For Chicano activists and scholars writing in the late 1960s and 1970s, Spain had indeed established the institutions of colonial rule in its North American borderlands, but that legacy was one of plunder, rape, and destruction.

The triumphant and romantic Spanish Borderlands about which Bolton and his students had written so assiduously and tried so actively to establish as part of every research university's curriculum by the 1960s was rather marginalized. The Spanish Borderlands story never replaced, or even much explicated, the narrative of U.S. national development that began with the original colonies. At some research universities in the United States the Spanish Borderlands were taught as part of Latin American history, and much less so as part of western U.S. history. Given this curricular reality, when in the mid-1960s and the 1970s Native American and Chicano activists demanded the establishment of Native American and Chicano studies programs and departments, staffed by native and Chicano scholars teaching courses from minority perspectives, little had to be institutionally displaced. Courses taught in such programs occasionally touched lightly on the pre-Columbian and Spanish Borderlands periods. The politics of the day were more concerned with the present than with some remote and imagined past.

THE BORDERLANDS

In the mid-1960s and the 1970s a "new" borderlands emerged in scholarly writing. This borderlands was not preceded by the modifier "Spanish," nor was it about the multiple and temporally shifting borders of Spain's colonial settlements in what is now the United States. Instead, for the Mexican American and Chicano scholars who first elaborated this conception, the Borderlands was a unitary, single space. It was territorially demarcated by the international boundary separating Mexico and the United States. How far north and south of the legal boundary the Borderlands extended was never really specified and was always left ambiguous. There was a fair degree of overlap between the "old" Spanish Borderlands and the "new" Borderlands, particularly in the area that Bolton's students had referred to as the Western Spanish Borderlands.

What changed and what characterized the "new" Borderlands was a unique temporal scope. For Mexican American and Chicano scholars, the signing of the Treaty of Guadalupe-Hidalgo, ending the war with Mexico in 1848, was the legal event that transformed them as Mexicans into Americans, and from citizens of Mexico to marginalized minorities in the United States. Under the provisions of the Immigration Reform Act of 1965, allowing heightened levels of migration from regions formerly barred, massive numbers of Mexicans entered the United States, both as legal and illegal immigrants. This movement undoubtedly accelerated scholarly interest in the Borderlands. A thematic focus on Mexican immigrants and their adjustment to life in the United States, rather than on Spanish colonial institutions and personnel, thus logically dominated Borderlands scholarship. It examined the legal enforcement of the international border, rather than the shifting boundaries of Spain's colonial control. The original disciplinary locus for Borderlands studies was in history but very quickly expanded into the social sciences. Since most people of Mexican origin living in the United States in 1965 had crossed this border after 1900, the major issues that motivated Borderlands scholarship were immigration politics, trade, the enforcement of the United States–Mexico border, and the logic of assimilation and acculturation. Examining Borderlands scholarship as a whole, the narrative trajectory in many ways followed Bolton's lead. People moved from a weak Mexico in the south to a powerful United States in the north; traditional Mexican peasants migrated to the modernity of the United States.

It should be noted that some historians—including Carlos E. Cortés, Ralph H. Vigil, and Donald E. Worcester—tried to draw theoretical links between the Spanish Borderlands and the Borderlands. They focused on continuities and parallels between old and new problems, while urging a more profound historical understanding of the area as a whole. Other scholars totally dismissed the Spanish Borderlands. Its demise in 1821 made it an irrelevant entity to the politics and problems of the 1960s and 1970s.

As noted, Borderlands scholarship first emerged as a critique of the elite focus of the Spanish Borderlands framework. In time, it developed in two directions. The most distinct cohort of scholars founded the field of Chicano studies. Keeping 1848 as the crucial date that marked the beginning of their neocolonial status as marginalized Americans, Chicanos chronicled how the United States had seized Mexican territory at the end of the Mexican-American War. Their mission was to show how Mexicans had been deprived of their lands and rights in the United States and how they had been politically disenfranchised, proletarianized, stigmatized as racial inferiors, and discriminated against in education, housing and employment. The folklorist Américo Paredes, one of the first to map the contours of *mexicano* resistance to the Anglo-American domination along the U.S.-Mexico border, defined the Borderlands as "an historically determined geo-political zone of military, linguistic, and cultural conflict."

A second Borderlands research trajectory developed in the social sciences in the late 1970s, driven largely by public policy concerns over immigration and trade. While Chicano scholarship was largely oppositional and contestatory, this research, largely funded by federal dollars, focused most often on putative Mexican immigrant pathologies: poverty, drug use, welfare dependence, and crime. Around 1981 scholars working in this emerging area formed their own professional guild, the Association of Borderlands Scholars, and published a massive bibliographic guide, *Borderlands Sourcebook: A Guide to the Literature on Northern Mexico and the American Southwest* (1983). In 1986 the association started its *Journal of Borderlands Studies* at New Mexico State University.

BORDERLANDS AS A METAPHOR

Since the mid-1980s geopolitical relationships of domination and subordination; population movements within territories separated by an international border; and a search for ways to describe multiple personal identities have generated a new Borderlands model. In this still emerging framework the Borderlands is imagined as a liminal zone, as a space of cultural hybridity, and as a place of transculturation, where peoples, cultures, and ideas move in complex ways, defying linearity—indeed, mirroring the very logic of the new global economy. Although clearly rooted in experiences along the boundary between Mexico and the United States, in this scholarship the Borderlands is a metaphor that can be invoked to describe similar cultural processes anywhere on the globe.

The Borderlands as metaphor is found mostly in the literature of the humanities and social sciences and particularly in interdisciplinary fields such as cultural studies, women's studies, and ethnic studies. As the anthropologist Robert R. Alvarez explains, the Borderlands metaphor emerged from an iconization of the actual border between Mexico and the United States. Scholars studied the social and cultural dynamics that occurred at this particular boundary between two nation-states and from that extrapolated a metaphor for social separation, sociopolitical marginalization, and cultural conflict.

A. I. Asiwaju's 1984 inaugural address to the Berlin West African Congress at the University of Lagos exemplifies how the metaphor is used. Describing the political border between Nigeria and West Africa, Asiwaju compared it to the U.S.-Mexico border. For Asiwaju, Africa's "Borderlands" were liminal places of marginality and cultural conflict.

Gloria Anzaldúa, in her highly influential book *Borderlands = La Frontera: The New Mestiza* (1987) elaborated the Borderlands metaphor quite extensively to describe a host of personal identities and psychological states of mind born of life along the U.S.-Mexico border. For Anzaldúa, "a consciousness of the Borderlands" stems from the realization that people inhabit several cultures simultaneously. "Cradled in one culture, sandwiched between two cultures, straddling all three cultures and their value systems, *la mestiza* (the hybrid woman) undergoes a struggle of flesh, a struggle of border, an inner war . . . a cultural collision" (p. 78). According to Anzaldúa, the *mestiza*, that is, the hybrid woman born of the conflict of the Borderlands, lives with a tolerance for ambiguity and contradictions. Indeed, she is a creature of plural selves. These plural selves allow her to challenge dualistic thinking and the vulgar dichotomies generated by life along the border. Anzaldúa explains:

> To live in the Borderlands means you
>   are neither *hispana india negra española*
>   *ni gabacha, eres mestiza, mulato,* half-breed
>   caught in the crossfire between camps
>   while carrying all five races on your back
>   not knowing which side to turn to, run from . . .

> To live in the Borderlands means to
>   put *chile* in the borscht,
>   eat whole wheat tortillas,
>   speak Tex-Mex with a Brooklyn accent;
>   be stopped by *la migra* at the border checkpoints
>   . . .

> In the Borderlands
>   you are the battleground
>   where enemies are kin to each other;
>   you are at home, a stranger,
>   the border disputes have been settled
>   the volley of shots have shattered the truce,
>   you are wounded, lost in action,
>   dead, fighting back . . .

> To survive the Borderlands you must live
>   *sin fronteras*
>   be a crossroads. (pp. 194–195)

Guillermo Gómez-Peña, in *The New World Border: Prophecies, Poems and Loqueras for the End of the Century* (1996), has also contributed extensively to the canonization of the Borderlands metaphor in the academy. As a performance artist Gómez-Peña challenges artists and writers to imagine a new cartography of possibilities in America. He urges us to think not of a single map of putatively fixed and sealed colonial and modernist territorial borders with discreet centers and margins that meet along the U.S.-Mexico border, but one that depicts "a more complex system of overlapping, interlocking, and overlaid maps . . . [one] that belongs to the homeless, and to nomads, migrants, and exiles" (p. 6). Gómez-Peña's new cartography for existence places hybridity at its analytic core. The hybridity is based on the experience of border crossers, individuals who experience dominant culture from the margins and from the outside, persons who are members of multiple communities, intercultural translators, political tricksters, and nomadic chroniclers who "trespass, bridge, interconnect, reinterpret, remap, and redefine" (p. 12).

Anzaldúa's and Gómez-Peña's writings have had broad influence in the humanities and social sciences, prompting a reexamination of modernist assumptions about the unity of nation-states, the coherence of national languages, and the consistency of communities and subjectivities. The work of the anthropologist Roger Rouse on Mexican migration to and from the United States has been particularly exemplary of the deployment of the Borderlands metaphor. While Borderlands scholars in the 1970s and 1980s once thought of the international boundary as separating two rather distinct and hermetically sealed national communities, where power and innovation flowed from a single center to the margins, such a spatial model defies the realities of contemporary capitalism, explains Rouse. Studying the transnational migration circuit from the Mexican township of Aguililla, Michoacán, to Redwood City, California, Rouse shows how Mexican laborers, though separated by thousands of miles, remain active participants in the economic, political, and cultural life of Aguililla through telephone links, remittances, and information obtained from travelers. Mexicans working in Redwood City struggle to obtain "permanent resident" status in the United States as Mexican citizens so that they can go back and forth across the border and have their children educated in Mexico, where the bilingual and bicultural skills necessary to operate successfully in both countries may be learned.

Rouse splendidly points out that just as migrant laborers defy the simplistic dichotomies of previous Borderlands studies on immigration and assimilation, the capitalist enterprises that employ Mexican labor in the United States do not belong to a single national community, do not speak a single national language, and owe no particular nation-state more allegiance than any other.

How, then, must we imagine the border between Mexico and the United States? Rouse invokes Gómez-Peña's observations about life along the line separating Tijuana, Mexico, and San Diego. "In my fractured reality, but reality nonetheless, live two histories, languages, cosmogonies, artistic traditions, and political systems dramatically opposed—the border is the continuous confrontation of two or more referential codes" (p. 255).

A number of Mexican and American ethnographers, such as Michael Kearney, following Rouse's lead, have begun to study the circulation of people, money, and ideas in sophisticated ways that defy the simple dualities created by the U.S.-Mexico border. The anthropologist Carlos G. Vélez-Ibáñez has examined the complex variety of subcultures that exist on both sides of the U.S.-Mexico border to show both the hybridity of social forms and the difficulty of accounting for them neatly through discreet national boundaries. The historian David G. Gutiérrez employs a similar analytic tack in his studies of the multiplicity of ethnic Mexican experiences in the United States, focusing closely on how generation, gender, race, class, and citizenship rights have created political subjectivities.

See also **Latinas and Latinos in the United States** *(in this volume); and other articles in this section.*

BIBLIOGRAPHY

Akwesasne Notes. *Trail of Broken Treaties: BIA, I'm Not Your Indian Any More.* Rooseveltown, N.Y., 1973.

———. *Voices from Wounded Knee, 1973, in the Words of the Participants.* Rooseveltown, N.Y., 1974.

Alvarez, Robert R. "The Mexican-U.S. Border: The Making of an Anthropology of Borderlands." *Annual Review of Anthropology* 24 (1995): 447–470.

Anzaldúa, Gloria. *Borderlands = La Frontera: The New Mestiza.* San Francisco, 1987.

Asiwaju, A. I., and P. O. Adeniyi, eds. *Borderlands in Africa.* Lagos, Nigeria, 1989.

Bannon, John Francis. *Herbert Eugene Bolton: The Historian and the Man, 1870–1953.* Tucson, Ariz., 1978.

Blue Cloud, Peter, ed. *Alcatraz Is Not an Island.* Berkeley, Calif., 1972.

Bolton, Herbert Eugene. "Spanish Records at San Antonio." *Texas State Historical Association Quarterly* 10 (April 1907): 297–307.

———. "Records of the Mission of Nuestra Señora del Refugio." *Texas State Historical Association Quarterly* 14 (October 1910): 164–166.

———. *Guide to Materials for the History of the United States in the Principal Archives of Mexico.* Washington, D.C., 1913.

———. "The Mission as a Frontier Institution in the Spanish-American Colonies." *American Historical Review* 23 (October 1917): 42–61.

———. *The Spanish Borderlands.* New Haven, Conn., 1921.

Bolton, Herbert Eugene. "Defensive Spanish Expansion and the Significance of the Borderlands." In *The Trans-Mississippi West: Papers Read at a Conference Held at the University of Colorado, June 18–June 21, 1929,* edited by James Field Willard and Colin Brummitt Goodykoontz, pp. 1–42. Boulder, Colo., 1930.

———. "The Epic of Greater America." *American Historical Review* 38 (April 1933): 448–474.

———. *The Northward Movement in New Spain.* 1946.

Bolton, Herbert Eugene, ed. *Arredondo's Historical Proof of Spain's Title to Georgia: A Contribution to the History of One of the Spanish Borderlands.* Berkeley, Calif., 1925.

Cook, Sherburne F. "Population Trends among the California Mission Indians." *Ibero-Americana* 17 (1940): 1–48.

———. "The Mechanism and Extent of Dietary Adaptation among Certain Groups of California and Nevada Indians." *Ibero-Americana* 18 (1941): 1–59.

———. *The Conflict between the California Indian and White Civilization.* Berkeley, Calif., 1943.

———. "The Indian versus the Spanish Mission." *Ibero-Americana* 21 (1943): 1–194.

———. "The Physical and Demographic Reaction of the Nonmission Indians in Colonial and Provincial California." *Ibero-Americana* 22 (1943): 1–55.

Deloria, Vine, Jr. *Custer Died for Your Sins: An Indian Manifesto.* New York, 1969.

———. *We Talk, You Listen: New Tribes, New Turf.* New York, 1970.

Dobyns, Henry F. "Indian Extinction in the Middle Santa Cruz Valley, Arizona." *New Mexico Historical Review* 38 (April 1963): 163–181.

Forbes, Jack D. *Apache, Navaho, and Spaniard.* Norman, Okla., 1960.

———. *Warriors of the Colorado: The Yumas of the Quechan Nation and Their Neighbors.* Norman, Okla., 1965.

Gutiérrez, David G. *Walls and Mirrors: Mexican Americans, Mexican Immigrants, and the Politics of Ethnicity.* Berkeley, Calif., 1995.

Kearney, Michael. "Borders and Boundaries of State and Self at the End of Empire." *Journal of Historical Sociology* 4 (1991): 52–71.

Keen, Benjamin. "Main Currents in United States Writings on Colonial Spanish America, 1884–1984." *Hispanic American Historical Review* 65 (November 1985).

Rouse, Roger. "Mexican Migration and the Social Space of Postmodernism." *Diaspora* 1, no. 1 (1991): 8–23.

Stoddard, Ellwyn R., et al., eds. *Borderlands Sourcebook: A Guide to the Literature on Northern Mexico and the American Southwest.* Norman, Okla., 1983.

Vélez-Ibáñez, Carlos G. *Border Visions: Mexican Cultures of the Southwest United States.* Tucson, Ariz., 1996.

Weber, David J. "Turner, the Boltonians, and the Borderlands." In his *Myth and the History of the Hispanic Southwest.* Albuquerque, N. Mex., 1988.

NEW YORK CITY

Graham Russell Hodges

New York City's cultural and intellectual life has always been contested ground affected by myriad and endlessly changing forces. While English has been the official tongue of the city since 1664, ethnic identity and degrees of acculturation among its polyglot population have made language a key factor in understanding urban culture. The same holds true for the effects of race, religion, and sexual orientation. Scholars debate whether New York's culture stems from the elite, from its middle classes, or from its churning lower classes. An ancillary question is the comparative importance to the city's thought and art on civic institutions on the one hand and evanescent, unofficial cultural milieus on the other. For example, did the rise of university centers beginning in the mid-eighteenth century, shift the city's cultural and intellectual focus from public figures to professional academics? Is culture and intellectual life in the city public or private? In perhaps no other city in America are such questions so apt as in New York City. Because of the city's central place in the national economy, the answers speak loudly about how Americans create cultural and intellectual activity.

COLONIAL NEW AMSTERDAM AND NEW YORK

After initial settlement in 1624, New Amsterdam was a remote outpost of the Netherlands, then enjoying its golden era. During what Simon Schama calls the "embarrassment of riches" that characterized seventeenth-century Netherlands, few citizens were willing to relocate to the rude outpost in North America. Observers commented on the number of taverns, the smelly streets, and the dilapidated fort of the obscure colony. Chiefly concerned with fending off attacks by Puritan New Englanders, Swedes, and neighboring Native American nations, the Dutch government and population of the tiny colony could barely foster an intellectual culture.

Printed materials, all issued in the Netherlands, were either advertising tracts extolling agricultural or trade potential or political remonstrances between angry colonists and governors. Among the most informative was Adrien Van Der Donck's survey of the young colony. Just before the end of the Dutch era, the poet Jacob Steendam, a recent arrival from colonial ports in Africa, penned "The Complaint of New Amsterdam to Her Mother," in which he attacked Dutch indifference to New Amsterdam. Though his goals were close to earlier propagandists, Steendam's verse was matched locally only by the businessman Nicasius de Sille, who wrote poetry about New Utrecht, the Brooklyn town he founded, and of Dominie (Reverend) Hendrik Selijns, whose poems described the loneliness of life in the young colony. While printed culture was scarce, local artisans produced domestic furniture of high quality; farmhouses and barns adapted European modes to produce a distinctive American style.

As Michael Kammen has demonstrated, after the English conquest and the renaming of the city in 1664, New York's cultural and intellectual life emerged slowly. Even by 1700, there were few newspapers, printshops, and bookstores. The first printed works in the colony were its laws, issued in a pamphlet by William Bradford in 1694. The initial newspaper, Bradford's *New-York Gazette,* hit the streets for a few months in 1725, followed by John Peter Zenger's *New-York Weekly Journal* in 1733, which survived his death in 1746 and continued until 1751. Zenger was particularly noted for his role in the famous libel case of 1734 that established freedom of speech in America. Over twenty newspapers appeared in New York between 1725 and 1776. Bradford also published the first map of the city, James Lyne's *Plan of the City of New York from an Actual Survey in 1731* (1731), the first play, Governor Robert Hunter's *Androborus: A Biographical Farce in Three Acts* (1714), and the first edition of Cadwallader Colden's *History of the Five Indian*

Nations (1727). James Parker published Samuel Richardson's novel, *Pamela* (1742), in 1744, Isaac Watts's devotional lyrics in 1750, and verses of the enslaved poet Jupiter Hammon in 1760. Newspapers and books were sold at the city's growing number of bookstores and, beginning in 1754, at the New York Society Library, the first sustained collection in the city.

Ethnicity colored the cultural and intellectual activities of the colonial city. During English rule, the Dutch elite gradually acceded to imperial language and power, while the middling and poorer ranks of society clung to ethnic identifications. The principal method for anglicizing city residents was the teachings of the Church of England. Construction of Trinity Church in 1697 gave local Anglicans a means to proselytize their beliefs. Through the Trinity Charity School and by Elias Neau's famous ministry to blacks and Native Americans, Trinity attempted with some success to advance English culture. W. E. B. Du Bois, for example, argued in his *The Souls of Black Folk* (1903) that the concept of the Talented Tenth among African Americans descended directly from Neau's school. However, Anglican missionary David Humphreys noted that Africans used home religious customs for marriage and burial ceremonies. Among other ethnic groups, Anglican ministries had mixed results. The Dutch and Huguenot elite gradually accepted English rule and by the mid-eighteenth century even held church services in English. The middling Dutch and French, whether artisan or farmer, resisted. As Joyce Goodfriend has demonstrated, Dutch wives, through marriage and language, held tightly to their home culture and faith. The Anglican Church became a vehicle for elite members of other faiths to assimilate into English society. Wealthier Huguenots, Jews, and dissident denominations such as the Society of Friends gradually accepted Anglican teachings.

Ethnicity and religion were underlying factors in the furor over the establishment of King's (later Columbia) College in 1754. Designed to educate Anglicans and prepare for an American bishopric, plans for King's College faced opposition from Presbyterians led by the Livingston family. William Livingston had the previous year proposed a public college paid for by local taxes, a method that was then considered hopelessly radical. He used the pages of the *Independent Reflector* (1752–1753), his political magazine and the colony's first, to lambaste the Anglican scheme. Livingston, considered by Thomas Bender to be the first public intellectual in New York, teamed with William Smith Jr., the au-

thor of *History of the Province* (1757), the first published history of New York, and John Morin Scott, a fellow lawyer, to produce the *Independent Reflector* and its successor, the *Occasional Reverberator* (1753). Anglican political power insured the controversial school's opening and the Reverend Samuel Johnson, a fervent advocate of the American bishopric, became the first president.

The college initially attracted only a few scholars each year. One reason is that private tutorials were the preferred method of educating. Whether studying law with an experienced barrister, as Aaron Burr did, or taking an apprenticeship, as was the case with most skilled tradespeople, lengthy private study and practice was the educational method of general choice. Literacy remained illusive except to those able to afford tutors, unless educated at charity schools, such as the Trinity school for enslaved blacks, which after 1725 only favored domestics from wealthy families. True scholars were rare. Virtually alone, Cadwallader Colden corresponded with European scientists and wrote treatises on botanical diseases, gravity, calculus, and philosophy, though he lacked the brilliance of Benjamin Franklin, who tarried momentarily in New York before moving on to Philadelphia.

During the eighteenth century, apprenticeships produced a growing number of skilled craftsmen. As New York's economy grew, especially during the Seven Years' War in the late 1750s and early 1760s, the city's bourgeoisie purchased fine plate from silversmiths and goldsmiths and furniture from specialist cabinetmakers. They commissioned portraits from itinerant limners or such visiting artists as John Singleton Copley, whose visit to the city in 1771 created much excitement. Other travelers commented on the boorish quality of New York's residents. Despite concern over their morals, New York gradually welcomed touring thespians and watched performances of Shakespeare (the first in America was in New York in 1730) along with animal acts and comedies.

During the prerevolutionary decade, New York's cultural and intellectual life became politicized. Local caricaturists ridiculed English rulers; artisans produced memorabilia commemorating the Stamp Act riots of 1765, and the nonimportation movements of the late 1760s greatly augmented local crafts. New York City was the cockpit of the American Revolution; accordingly, occupying armies and three large fires roiled and devastated the city. Still, there were signs of cultural activity. The British army regularly presented plays and orchestral musicals. Of particular note were racially integrated dances. American satirists ridiculed General William Howe for attending African American formal dances during the war, but the presence of the commanding officer amidst a makeshift band of violinists, drummers, and hurdy-gurdy players was the first time a high-ranking white official publicly attended this early form of cotillion.

CULTURE IN THE NEW NATIONAL CITY

As soon as the British army left the city on 25 November 1783, a postrevolutionary culture began to emerge. Newspapers appeared spouting conflicting political beliefs. The *American Museum,* the city's first postwar magazine, appeared in 1787 and 1788. Learned societies appeared and disappeared quickly. Thomas Bender has discussed the Friendly Club (1793–1798), a close association of men of letters, professionals, and businessmen. Guided by Elihu Hubbard Smith and William Dunlap, the club promoted learned but sympathetic criticism of members' intellectual labors through earnest discussion. They queried each other about scientific progress and worried about whether learning would be destroyed by the pursuit of wealth by the "common man." Members sought to be encyclopedic, accepting some specialization but aspiring to an understanding of the whole of knowledge, or at least a passing acquaintance with it. Having won a revolution, they were optimistic that freedom, commerce, and literature could vitalize each other. In fact, commerce would succeed, but it would also destroy the nutrients that enabled the growth of the arts and literature, creating a deep division between "elite" society and later men of letters.

For the time being, however, creative planners established learned institutions. Even after New York City was no longer the political capital of the new nation, the city successfully pursued cultural supremacy as well as economic dominance by the construction of special-purpose intellectual institutions. De Witt Clinton, whose leadership led to the construction of the Erie Canal, was as well a founding member of the New-York Historical Society, the Literary and Philosophical Society, the American Academy of Fine Arts, and the Free School Society. With Dr. David Hosack, another public intellectual, Clinton used municipal funds to establish the New York Athenaeum in 1824. Such civic commitment propelled the movement over the next decades to found new universities, including the University of the City of New York (later New York University) in 1831, the Free Academy (later

the City College of New York) in 1847, and Cooper Union in 1859. The key public institution in this period was Central Park, opened in 1859 to provide the middle classes with a bucolic setting to observe each other while riding on safe roads free of the hurly-burly of the streets.

The New Yorker intellect in the early nineteenth century combined the attitudes of colonial gentry with the rising artisan class, creating a hybrid personality of European and revolutionary American outlooks. "We think in English," famously proclaimed Alexander Hamilton after the war. If early national books seemed to substantiate that aphorism, an American literature gradually took hold. The writings of Washington Irving were, initially, republican only on the surface and aristocratic at the core. Irving created a Knickerbocker school of writing, stemming from the musings of young aristocrats. His intellectual descendants included William Cullen Bryant and Gulian Verplanck, but slowly this sensibility gave way to a more democratic impulse. A linchpin figure was Edgar Allan Poe, whose 1840 short story, "The Man of the Crowd," exhibited an immense fascination with popular life, albeit with the air of the fallen aristocrat. Poe's work, including his poems and his urban sagas and detective stories, genres that he invented, deeply influenced the French writers Charles Baudelaire and Arthur Rimbaud, and the painter Édouard Manet.

Other major figures of the American Renaissance of the antebellum decades were influenced by the rise of a mechanic sensibility. The city's artisanry, confident and purposeful in pursuit of political and social power after the Revolution, institutionalized a learned culture in 1785 with the establishment of the General Society of Tradesmen and Mechanics. Composed primarily of masters, the society created an Apprentices Library in 1820, sponsored temperance organizations, and opened the Mechanics' Institute in 1822. Members, whatever wealth or rank they possessed, considered culture, as Bender has noted, a mark of respectability attained without leaving their class. Education was an indicator of self-improvement, not social mobility, and helped artisans retain trade unity and fend off the cultural hegemony of elite New Yorkers.

New York population (as defined by its twentieth-century boundaries) soared from 60,000 people in 1790 to 696,000 by 1850. Most residents remained packed into wards below Canal Street, less than a mile from Castle Garden. The Boston Post Road, known locally as the Bowery, became famous as the center for popular melodrama. Appealing broadly to egalitarian-minded artisans and Irish immigrants, inexpensive theaters introduced the characters Mose the Bowery b'hoy and Lize, his Bowery g'hal. These stock personae represented a youthful, street-tough sensibility, their elaborate costumes displaying a touch of consumerism mixed with urban pride. A disturbing element of Bowery culture of the 1840s was the "Jim Crow" minstrel show in which whites with cork blackfaces mocked African American society. Immensely popular, minstrel shows valorized white skin and manifested modern American racism. Lesser known "Chinese rooms" appeared in the 1850s in which Chinese people were exploited as freaks; lithographs endless reproduced images of a Chinese man partnered with an Irishwoman. While innocent interracial love occurred regularly in the Five Points, racist media mocked such pairings. Soon, the entrepreneurial P. T. Barnum mixed freak shows with family entertainment in his nationally famous museums. The virulent racism of much of Bowery culture did not deter the rise of moral crusades espousing temperance, female fights, pacifism, free love, and, most importantly, the abolition of slavery.

ANTEBELLUM ACTIVISM AND CULTURAL RENAISSANCE

Even though many blacks were conspicuous consumers of newly available, inexpensive clothing, the African American community was bluntly activist. At first combining its efforts with the elite Society for the Abolition of Slavery, founded by Episcopalians and Quakers in 1785, black intellectuals and activists helped to convince the state legislature to end slavery gradually, beginning in 1799. Through the African Society, founded in 1795, and then the African Society of Mutual Relief, established in 1804, black New Yorkers commemorated favorable developments. The learned Reverend Peter Williams Jr. celebrated the end of the foreign slave trade in a published speech in 1808. Black essayists, poets, and speakers continued this tradition over the next two decades. Their achievements helped fuel the free black culture, which spawned its first newspaper, the *Freedom's Journal* in 1827 (published until 1829); a second, the *Colored American,* appeared from 1837 to 1841. The African Free School, founded in 1787, was a direct descendant of Elias Neau's eighteenth-century charity school for blacks. It educated a new generation of black intellectuals, including Alexander Crummell, James McCune Smith, Ira Aldridge, James Varick, and Thomas Syd-

ney. Their political and intellectual exertions included struggle against southern slavery and the American Colonization Society, attempts to open black schools and colleges, and attempts to create black newspapers, magazines, books, theater, painting, drawing, and intellectual centers. Though not a graduate of the Free School, David Ruggles emerged in the 1830s as a black intellectual activist. During his brief but busy career, Ruggles published five pamphlets, wrote hundreds of letters to editors, edited the first black magazine, opened the first bookstore for blacks, and publicly debated and otherwise fought his opponents. As a founder of the Underground Railroad, he made it possible for slaves, including Frederick Douglass and J. W. C. Pennington, to escape from bondage and become intellectual activists. Black women also made their intellectual mark in the 1830s by founding the Society of Dorcas for the discussion of literature and politics.

Black and white middle-class New Yorkers agreed upon a gospel of self-improvement. In the streets, a ruder sensibility ruled. Centered on the Five Points in Manhattan's slummy Sixth Ward, an interracial melting pot of music, dance, gambling, and romance "presaged a Grand National opera," as Walt Whitman said. Middle-class observers, including Charles Dickens, gaped at black and white dancers and musicians. From here came popular melodrama in the 1840s about the doings of Mose and Lize, the archetypical Bowery b'hoy and g'hal, in whom Sean Wilentz and Christine Stansell have seen the origin of modern youth culture. Though cleaned up by the Moral Society in the 1850s, the Five Points anticipated the intellectual and artistic hubbub around Times Square a century later.

By the late 1840s the city was alive with political controversy over national expansion, increasingly divided over slavery, and bursting with economic energy. Poe's work announced a New York style. Walt Whitman's poetry defined it. Later described by Allen Ginsberg, his twentieth-century avatar, as the great Yawp, Whitman's poetry strived to capture the rhythms and colors of the city's hurly-burly streets. Adoring wharfingers, cartmen, butcher boys, and a thousand other urban types, Whitman, to some, created the American language out of what he saw, heard, and smelled in the public arena. Interested in politics but obsessed by culture, Whitman sought a unity of democracy and literature. Less optimistic but equally interested in the fulfillment of the empire of the common man was the novelist Herman Melville, whose greatest influence did not come until the twentieth century. Melville's most incisive work on New York was the short story, "Bartleby the Scrivener" (1853), about a copy clerk who rejected the gospel of progress.

Equally discouraged about progress in the antebellum city was its black population. As white New Yorkers denied blacks civil and political rights and lent open support to southern positions regarding slavery, the city's African American intellectuals split over their future. Some worked with the Liberty Party; others, like James McCune Smith, who reprinted David Walker's famous *Appeal* in 1847, spoke openly of armed revolt. Many others, voting with their feet, left for Canada and the west coast of Africa. Though few had been born there, black New Yorkers created an ideological conception of Africa as succor in a hostile homeland. As the slavery crisis shattered national unity in the 1850s, what had been an almost entirely African American issue thirty years before now promised to rupture the American republic. Looking back at the tumultuous 1850s, lack of awareness of the consequences of racism within the larger society insured that New York's intellectuals were generally unprepared for the Civil War.

THE CIVIL WAR AND THE GILDED AGE

New York City emerged from the Civil War with plenty of money. Having earned war profits from finance, manufacturing, and shipping, and having paid far less human cost than the defeated South, city businessmen prepared for greater dominance of the nation. Profits made during the Gilded Age from the industrialization of the South were used to rebuild the city. Monuments recognized Civil War–era figures, including Abraham Lincoln, Robert Gould Shaw, William Lloyd Garrison, and Ulysses S. Grant. Genealogical and historical societies such as the Holland and the Huguenot Society were organized to reassure the city's ruling elite of the importance of their ancestors in the city. Historians, most notably Martha J. Lamb, who edited the *Magazine of American History* from 1883 to 1893, wrote biographies of the city in the last quarter of the century. E. B. O'Callaghan and A. J. F. Van Laer collated historic city documents into bulky, fascinating collections in the mid-nineteenth and early twentieth centuries, respectively. After the turn of the twentieth century, I. N. Phelps Stokes published his voluminous masterpiece, *The Iconography of Manhattan Island* (1915).

New Yorkers built monuments to progress. A combination of private philanthropy and municipal funds created the New York Public Library, the Museum of Natural History, and the Metropolitan Museum of Art. New York's economic hegemony over the nation attracted barons of oil, steel, and railroads to the city. After creating vast art collections taken from all over the globe, they endowed New York's cathedrals of culture. The city's greatest monument was the Brooklyn Bridge, opened in 1883; it made consolidation of the city's five boroughs possible fifteen years later. Skyscrapers, made necessary by soaring real estate prices and corporate consolidation and feasible by the development of safe and rapid elevators and metal-frame interior structures, dwarfed the city's churches and formed a new urban landscape. New wealth was evident in the work of the architectural firm of McKim, Mead, and White, which borrowed from European beaux arts neoclassicism to reconstruct the city, using incandescent illumination to bathe it in light and color. The flush of cash also produced mammoth homes for millionaires along Fifth Avenue; some of them were beautiful, others gauche.

Ordinary New Yorkers, eager for self-portrait, quickly adopted the daguerreotype after its invention in 1839. Wealthy New Yorkers could have their images made at Mathew Brady's salon on Broadway. Ordinary New Yorkers could buy theirs at the photo shops that sprouted up everywhere in the city. Innovation transformed and reduced the cost of the photographic process in the next decades. New Yorkers purchased *carte de vistes* of famous leaders, actors, scenery, and themselves. *Cartes de visite* were small, mass-produced photographs mounted on cardboard which were popular in the mid-nineteenth century and were designed to be either cards of introduction or to commemorate important people, events, and places. More permanent pictures were enclosed in attractive, plastic cases.

New York artists, benefiting from the urban realism of Whitman and Poe and from the photograph, created an artistic culture that redefined modern art and intellect after 1875. As William B. Scott and Peter M. Rutkoff have demonstrated, New Yorkers incorporated European ideas of modernity and adapted them to vernacular American commercial, folk, and popular culture. Keeping urban realism in the forefront and working through painting, drama, photography, dance, and architecture, they created a culture and intellect that at the turn of the twenty-first century still defined what city life is for Americans and the larger world. This was done, Scott and Rutkoff claim, with a distinctly antiacademic bias that reflected the city's unruly character and the inability of any one school, theory, museum, or patron to define modernity. Therefore, New Yorkers sustained a dissonant dialogue noted for its diversity and controversy. That discordance was plain in the ethnic theaters of the Lower East Side, where immigrant Jews, Italians, Germans, Poles, and Lithuanians adapted traditional cultures to the Bowery theater world, creating simultaneously family entertainment and bawdy vaudeville.

Of all the immigrant groups pouring onto New York between 1880 and 1920, eastern European Jews established intellectual customs which prepared them to assimilate into local society while sustaining their own culture. In addition to the Yiddish theater, Jews formed the Educational Alliance in the Lower East Side in 1889 to help "Americanize the green-horns," as Irving Howe put it. The Alliance threw itself into communal aid and popular education. There were morning classes for children needing assistance before entering public schools; daytime classes for adults who worked on the night shift; classes in Yiddish and Hebrew; classes in cooking and sewing as well as courses on Greek and Roman history. Among the most popular formats was the lecture, by which impoverished Jewish workers could pick up knowledge on myriad subjects for a few pennies. Abetting all this was a strong literary culture in the Lower East Side. The Yiddish press, scholar-intellectuals, poets, and novelists worked in an amalgam of Hebrew and English. By the third generation, a grand narrative of Jewish social mobility and assimilation colored by anxieties of maintaining religious traditions were the principal concerns of novelists Henry Roth, Leo Calvin Rosten, and the poet Delmore Schwartz. In the second half of the century, these ethnic myths drove the novels of Philip Roth, Saul Bellow, Bernard Malamud, and Isaac Bashevis Singer.

Italians, hampered by anti-Catholic prejudice and by association with gangsterism, sustained a vital culture based upon family, church, and community. Although Italian folk artists such as Ralph Fasanella and the abstract expressionist Robert De Niro became widely known, novelists and filmmakers have emphasized the sensational history of Italian gangs. Polish New Yorkers also fostered a culture based upon traditional institutions. Jews, Italians, and Poles introduced food styles which quickly became assimilated into a New York palate.

Early forms of motion pictures, produced first by Thomas A. Edison and then quickly borrowed by vaudeville entrepreneurs, attracted large crowds. D. W. Griffith's controversial movie, *The Birth of a Nation* (1915), debuted in New York City in 1916. Though tainted by racist caricatures, the movie demonstrated the immense financial future of the medium. Movies were successful partly because they offered dreamy substitutes for the rigors of urban life. Although gay New Yorkers were seldom observed by the general public before the 1880s, George Chauncey has shown that before then they sustained traditions of masked balls, theater, and tavern culture ancillary to the Bowery world to which the city's elite flocked. Theaters and taverns produced the seedbeds for a multicultural modernity more evident in the twentieth century.

MODERNISM AND REALISM

Artists responded to the city's changing ethos by accenting realism. Initiated by novelists Edith Wharton, Stephen Crane, and William Dean Howells in the early 1890s, realism reached an apogee in the controversial publication in 1900 of Theodore Dreiser's *Sister Carrie*. Scandalous because a young mistress of two men becomes a wealthy actress, Dreiser's sprawling work portrayed a vast, overwhelming city in which George Hurstwood, the male protagonist, realizes that in a city of whales, a common fish like himself must feed at the bottom. Realism also entered the fine arts. Jacob Riis and Lewis W. Hine used the photograph to uncover poverty under the gilded cake of wealthy New York. The Eight Exhibition in 1908 shocked New Yorkers as Robert Henri, John Sloan, and six other artists grappled with the modern complexity of New York. Five years later the Armory Show of realist painters attracted huge crowds, indicating the arrival of a new sensibility and attention to the truths found in daily life. Sloan's *Sixth Avenue and Thirtieth Street* (1927) portrayed weary pedestrians in this hurly-burly neighborhood. Portraying a "girlie" show in the background, Sloan showed the ambivalent character of the city's transformation. By focusing on females in the street, Sloan's street scenes pictured ordinary women in the streets, showing how public culture had moved away from what Kathy Peiss has called the homosocial world of Victorian (or late-nineteenth-century) New York City, in which males dominated the public stage. This male domination of public space is inadvertently revealed in the masculine realism of Reginald Marsh and George Bellows in the 1920s. Even the lonely cityscapes of Edward Hopper a decade later were redolent of this masculinity. Women, however, were challenging many conventions at the turn of the century. Ruth St. Denis and Isadora Duncan feminized and mod-

Lewis Hine, Orchard Street, Lower East Side, c. 1912. This messy, multicultural world, which horrified established New Yorkers, proved irresistible to visitors seeking bargains offered in many languages. GEORGE EASTMAN/LEWIS W. HINE/ ARCHIVE PHOTOS

ernized dance, previously divided sharply between classical and vernacular.

Unfortunately, Sloan's painting omitted the neighborhood's African American population. Thirtieth Street and Sixth Avenue was in the heart of the Tenderloin, the home of much of the city's black population before they migrated north to Harlem. During this hegira, Scott Joplin popularized ragtime and introduced syncopated beats into popular music, making possible first the cakewalk dance and later the Charleston, a 1920s craze that individualized twentieth-century public dances. By 1930 a European observer commented, "America dances to a Negro beat." The great migration of blacks from the South greatly replenished New York's black population between 1890 and 1940. Within the city, the established African American society moved north from the Tenderloin district into newly constructed houses in Harlem. In the first decade of the twentieth century W. E. B. Du Bois, among the era's intellectual giants, was a key founder of the National Association for the Advancement of Colored People, with headquarters in

New York. The NAACP sought to promote the arts by awarding an annual medal for works acknowledging the significance of Pan Africanism. Similarly, James Weldon Johnson's influential anthology, *The Book of Negro Poetry* (1922), accentuated a dignified, racially based artistic vision. Neighborhood photographer James Van Der Zee exemplified this vision with his portraits of Harlem's middle classes.

If African Americans influenced modernism from within New York, European cubism and dada affected it from without. New York's galleries abounded with European modernist painters before World War I. Photographer Alfred Stieglitz celebrated European postimpressionism at his famous 291 Gallery, where he attempted to fuse artistic camera techniques to the work of van Gogh, Picasso, and Matisse. Greenwich Village became a hotbed of modernist ideas and talent. Mabel Dodge's salon on lower Fifth Avenue was a mélange of European modernist and American political radicals. A key ingredient in the culture was the new sexuality. As Ann Douglas has shown, Freudianism in the first decades of the twentieth century vali-

Reginald Marsh, *Twenty Cent Movie.* Egg tempera on board 30 × 40 in., 1936. Marsh encapsulates the erotic realism of New York's street culture and portrays the new freedom of young females in the streets. The presence of an African American male foreshadows the postwar period, when blacks would move with greater ease in the city street for the first time since before the Civil War. © FRANCIS G. MAYER/CORBIS

dated the sexuality of women and opened discussions about a variety of family and sex-related issues. "New women" exalted extramarital sex and same-sex relationships. Greenwich Village bohemians held rallies for strikes against mines in Ludlow, Colorado, owned by John D. Rockefeller. The most important literary vehicle for radical politics was Max Eastman, Art Young, and Floyd Dell's famous magazine, *The Masses.*

Christine Stansell describes how an amalgam of radical feminists, sympathetic males, and Eastern European Jewish intellectuals sustained a bohemian atmosphere in Greenwich Village. These bohemians valorized talking, writing, friendship, politics, and sexuality mixed with abundant drinking to create a modern personality originating out of radical Jewish culture. Emma Goldman personified the dress (plain shirtwaists with ties and no head covering or cheap finery), and serious demeanor of the new

Jewish Woman who espoused socialism and anarchism and ideals of female independence. In her memoirs, Goldman traced her passage from the Lower East Side to the anarchist causes to the Village's bohemian salons.

The output of the Jazz Age in the 1920s showed that commitment and optimism concerning social change was not universal among New York writers. F. Scott Fitzgerald's novel, *The Great Gatsby* (1925), while stylistically beautiful, revealed the sordid characters of the period's wealthy financiers. Eugene O'Neill's powerful drama, *The Emperor Jones* (1920), first starring an African American, Charles Gilpin, and later another African American, Paul Robeson, showed the playwright's impatience with white racism, skepticism about democratic progress, and pessimism about the future. Others found hope in art. Paul Rosenfeld's *Port of New York* (1924), a collection of essays, declared that the city was the center and source of the modern American renaissance. Agreeing with him were poets William Carlos Williams and Marianne Moore and artist Frank Stella, whose 1920 painting, *The Bridge,* proclaimed the city's triumph over nature. Much of this activity found a public forum at the New School for Social Research, founded in 1919 by disaffected academics including historians Charles and Mary Beard and political analyst Herbert Croly. There the public could attend inexpensive classes taught by key figures of the modern movement.

New York's self-perception as the nation's arts center was propelled further by the introduction of the *New Yorker* magazine in 1925. *Time, Reader's Digest, Newsweek,* and *Life* magazines debuted in the same era, but their audience was a broad cross-section of the nation, while the *New Yorker* sought an upscale audience. Also, the *New Yorker* was ostensibly just for the city's residents, although its influence and circulation soon became national and even international. Initially, the weekly featured witty stories, cartoons, and occasional newsbreaks. Cultivating the upper middle class, the *New Yorker* added lengthy stories, profiles, and a gossipy column, "The Talk of the Town." Legendary editors Harold Ross and William Shawn created a winning formula that produced a generous advertising revenue and a soaring circulation. Though authors were paid very little, publication in the *New Yorker* had prestige value and attracted the talents of cartoonist Charles Addams and novelists John O'Hara, Irwin Shaw, John Updike, and later J. D. Salinger. The *New Yorker*'s response to the Great Depression was muted, although it did feature writers A. J. Liebling and Joseph Mitchell, whose stories of the city's lower depths brightened the muted shades of most of the periodical's writing.

The *New Yorker* was carefully planned to appeal to the city's elite. As Fitzgerald and Dreiser pointed out, a significant amount of money was required to survive in New York. Accordingly modernists had to find cash. Alfred Stieglitz's photography gallery pioneered cultivation of wealthy connoisseurs, a practice increasingly more common in the 1920s and institutionalized later with the establishment of the Museum of Modern Art in 1929 and the Whitney Museum in 1930.

Money was also a key ingredient in the famed Harlem Renaissance of the 1920s, which sustained exciting, urbane novelists, painters, graphic artists, sculptors, photographers, and poets. Hailed by Alain Locke in his anthology *The New Negro* (1925), the Renaissance actually involved very few New York artists. Rather, a shifting array of black writers and poets moved through the city, where they found white patrons, particularly Carl Van Vechten, who introduced Claude McKay, Jean Toomer, Langston Hughes, and others to white, mainstream publishers. This is not to say that the artists were creatures of Van Vechten. While white patrons expected black artists to create "primitivist" art, New York's African American intellectuals created a vibrant community in Harlem, which interacted with other black artists nationally and internationally. For whites, primitivism, which they felt stemmed from Africa and pervaded black culture, was a keystone of modernism and promised to open doors to greater sexual and cultural freedoms. However paternalist was this view, it did open financial and curatorial opportunities for blacks and, as Sharon F. Patton has noted, broadened the parameters of modern art to include an African American artistic vernacular.

Van Vechten's network did not affect all black artists. More directly commercial and thus independent was the jazz world, which married southern band music with the urban blues prevalent in New York, exemplified particularly by piano players Willie "the Lion" Smith and James P. Johnson. New York jazz soon featured a big-band sound, popularized by Fletcher Henderson's orchestra and brought to artistic heights by Duke Ellington's band, which, according to William B. Scott and Peter M. Rutkoff, forced white Americans to accept black music and prepared the way for racial integration later in the century. The southern migration of blacks into the city also popularized blues music, which joined field hollers with the tough, urban lyricism found in black and tan dives in New York.

THE DEPRESSION AND WORLD WAR II

The Wall Street collapse of 1929 energized political and artistic radicalism. The 1930s were unquestionably the high point of political art and the moment when Communism had the great attraction for New York intellectuals. A number of New York intellectuals began their careers as revolutionary communists. As Alan M. Wald has argued, they stemmed from the anti-Stalinist Left and included such intellectuals as Lionel Trilling, Irving Kristol, Norman Podhoretz, Sidney Hook, and James T. Farrell. Sustaining careers as academics, novelists, and public intellectuals, they gradually moved from left to right, from advocating socialist revolution in the 1930s to endorsing American capitalism after World War II.

At first isolated and sectarian, New York's Communist Party made headway by responding to such social outrages as the Scottsboro case of 1930. The party attempted to radicalize race in the city by its concentrating efforts on Harlem and class by its early support of the taxi drivers' strike of 1934, immortalized in Clifford Odets's play, *Waiting for Lefty* (1935). The 1932 presidential election brought more artists into the party fold, and its John Reed Club in New York became the largest in the nation. However, the alliance between artists and the party was shattered seven years later by the Hitler-Stalin Pact, which facilitated the Nazi invasion of Poland.

Radical artists and intellectuals, communist and noncommunist, found work in the government-sponsored Federal Theatre Project within the Works Progress Administration. Hallie Flanagan's Federal Theatre featured left-oriented plays by Elmer Rice and *It Can't Happen Here* (1936), derived from Sinclair Lewis's novel, along with Orson Welles's all-black production of *Macbeth* in 1936 for the theatre's Negro Unit. Similar successes occurred in painting and literature. Later in the decade, the WPA sponsored murals by Aaron Douglas, called *Aspects of Negro Life* (1934), for the Countee Cullen branch of the New York Public Library in Harlem. The WPA also provided funds for the early work of African American artists Charles Alston and Romare Bearden, and printmaker Robert Blackburn, whose Printmaking Workshop on Seventeenth Street remains today a major center for black arts. WPA patronage fostered a social realism among black artists, allowing them to focus on issues such as lynching and economic exploitation. Though critically acclaimed, most of these efforts were targets of congressional investigations in the late 1930s. More commercial and resilient were the efforts of producer and musicologist John Hammond, who introduced southern folk and blues music to New Yorkers. Artists Woody Guthrie and Leadbelly paved the way for the folk revolution of the 1960s.

Meanwhile, a cultural stew boiled around Times Square. Famous throughout the twentieth century as the spot to celebrate the New Year, Times Square functioned until the latter years of the century as the prototype for New York's City's popular culture. Theaters, nightclubs, restaurants and, further down the social scale, bars, cheap eateries, and the streets were meeting places for an amalgam of elite and lower class, heterosexual and homosexual, black, Hispanic, and white seekers of culture. The overwhelming popularity of Frank Loesser's musical, *Guys and Dolls* (1950), derived from the popular vernacular of Damon Runyon and epitomized this marriage of high and low culture and Broadway's transformation from illegitimate to national theater. Journalist Walter Winchell and Runyon created the "slanguage of Lobster Alley," making Times Square argot the tongue of generations of smart-aleck New Yorkers. Their counterpart in photography was Weegee, who, equipped with a police radio in his car, specialized in candid shots of murders, fires, and sensational arrests. Weegee and other photographers of New York City street life found a ready market in the tabloid daily *PM*, which flourished between 1940 and 1948. More accomplished photographers including Berenice Abbott, Todd Webb, André Kertész, and Walker Evans gave New York's street life a mythological character. Abbott, who studied in France with Man Ray and resuscitated the career of Eugène Atget, created a beautifully formalistic approach to everyday life in New York. Like Walker Evans, Abbott sustained her art with stints as a photographer for scientific magazines. Abbott and Evans shot images of New York's people and cityscape that became iconographic symbols of urban life.

POSTWAR ARTS

Travel writer Jan Morris has observed that after World War II, New Yorkers fell in love with themselves and consciously sought national recognition for their city's personality. One means of expressing pride was talk. Anticipating the popularity of public political talk radio decades later, New York speech had a wise-guy quality to it. As Joshua Freeman has argued, every New Yorker had opinions on anything; whether it was conveyed in Spanish, Yiddish, Italian, or some form of English, New Yorker's ideas, insults, and commentary spewed forth in argots that enriched the national language. Some of this, performed by ace comedians Phil Silver and Sid Caesar, was hilarious. The ordinary guy and girl opined in know-it-all ways. Daniel Bell, the political commentator, traced this New York attitude to the Jewish petite bourgeoisie, though parallels were present in every ethnic group and occupation. The city's cabdrivers wrote innumerable memoirs. For example, James Maresca's *My Flag Is Down* proclaimed the cabby's encyclopedic knowledge of the city and by extension, the world. Ubiquitous in movies, television programs, and advertisements, the New York City cab represented the era's average guy.

This fusion of Jewish intellectuals, working class attitudes, and the arts coalesced in the *Village Voice*, a lively weekly started in 1955 by Dan Wolf, Ed Fancher, and novelist Norman Mailer to foster an iconoclastic, avant-garde press which also reflected the new ethnic heterogeneity in the Village. During the 1960s, alternative journalism flourished in the East Village, where anarchic newspapers such as the *East Village Other* and the *Rat* pushed the boundaries of free speech. The more staid *New York Review of Books*, founded in 1963, responded to the radical ethos of the 1960s by once printing the directions for making Molotov cocktails (homemade bombs).

After World War II, realism's association with socialism cost it support. Abstract expressionists Jackson Pollock and Robert Motherwell, popularized by approving articles in *Life* magazine, declared personal and artistic independence from political and ideological causes. From familiar vantage points in bars and taverns, abstract expressionists sought a politically pure art and explored the unconscious, the archtypical, and the universal, as noted by Scott and Rutkoff. Guided by Clement Greenberg's famous essay titled "'Avant-Garde' and 'Kitsch'" (*Partisan Review*, 1939), abstract expressionists distanced themselves from the left-wing art of the 1930s. Ironically, their self-conscious intellectualism alienated them from Americans outside New York, who, although more conservative than New Yorkers, readily understood and appreciated the mural and political art of the 1930s. Attentive to surrealism, which they felt offered better contact to the unconscious, New York artists studiously absorbed all the lessons of modernism over the preceding decade. By 1950 they were known as the New York school, which synthesized European modernism, especially surrealism, with American representational traditions.

While highly individualized, abstract expressionists discovered the virtues and value of solidarity; and by the mid-1950s they had become a recognizable group and commodity. Centered around the Cedar Tavern on University Place in Greenwich Village, the abstract expressionists evoked a persona of brawny, intellectual masculinity that was often spooked by femininity. Ann Eden Gibson has argued that New York's abstract expressionist world was sifted to exclude religion and cultural specificity and had no sexuality but heterosexuality, no commercial goals, and no hard-edged geometry. Exceptions to the domination of abstract expressionism by white males were few and their experiences fraught with problems. Helen Frankenthaler was one of the few women among them and was received in a condescending fashion.

Unable to ignore social issues, black artists had to go a different route. The 306 Group and Studio became in the late 1940s the center for black arts and fostered the murals and social abstractions of Jacob Lawrence. Few blacks had agents, regular galleries, or solo shows. They retained interest in realistic imagery, though transforming it stylistically through color. In the early 1960s, Romare Bearden led the path to a novel method that married earlier political concerns with a modernist and Africanist perspective.

Alienation within abstract expressionism was even sharper for gay people. Although her work exalted New York City and its global significance, lesbian Sonia Sekula was generally excluded from review as a serious abstract expressionist. In the same category were sculptor Louise Bourgeois and artist Forrest Bess, who, according to Ann Eden Gibson, found little comfort in the heterosexual climate of New York's art world of the 1950s. Doubly worse was the situation of gay African American artist Beauford Delaney.

After the war, alienation was the core message for writers. Norman Mailer's powerful psychological war novel, *The Naked and the Dead* (1948), Saul Bellow's tragic story, *Dangling Man* (1944), and his *Seize the Day* (1956), and even the enormously popular *Catcher in the Rye* (1951), by J. D. Salinger, are suffused with alienation. The same can be said for the dramas of Arthur Miller and Tennessee Williams. Worsening their feelings of despair were the McCarthyism of the early 1950s, which demanded that artists inform on each other's political flirtations with left-wing politics in the 1930s. One response to the right-wing surge of American politics was the Beat movement, which was situated almost entirely in New York City. The Beats featured the picaresque journeys of writers Jack Kerouac, Allen Ginsberg, and William S. Burroughs and photographers Robert Frank and, later, Diane Arbus, undertaken to understand an America they largely rejected. Beat writing was initially dismissed as mere typing by stylish writers such as Truman Capote. The Beats, however, survived longer than these critics and still powerfully influenced writers at the end of the twentieth century. Ginsberg, in particular, became the greatest political New York poet since Whitman by embracing a succession of causes from the anti–Vietnam War movement to gay liberation while remaining a constant public presence. The Beats thrived around Times Square in the 1950s and early 1960s, finding inspiration in its cheap dives and cinemas. Gay artists also thrived around Times

Square, as shown in the novels and plays of Burroughs, John Rechy, and Samuel R. Delaney.

African American novelists James Baldwin, John A. Williams, and John Oliver Killens described the powerful alienation of blacks toward the dominant, discriminatory white culture. One bridge between the races was Ralph Ellison. His novel, *The Invisible Man* (1951), inscribed that alienation, but in his essays he endorsed a unity of black and white American culture. More celebratory of popular culture (though no less alienated) was the bebop revolution of the late 1940s. Expressed through powerful, concise units led by Charlie Parker, Dizzy Gillespie, Lester Young, and Miles Davis (descendants of the Five Points bands of a century earlier), and articulated by female vocalists Billie Holiday, Sarah Vaughan, and Ella Fitzgerald, bebop fused dance music with hard-edged and free-form expression. Jazz influences may be found in Harlem artist Faith Ringgold's quilts, Melvin Edwards's powerful lynch fragment sculptures, and Alvin Loving's hard-edged abstract paintings. In the late 1960s that fusion was essential to the Black Arts movement shaped by Amiri Baraka (previously known as Leroi Jones) and Larry Neal, and was critical in the turn-of-the-twenty-first-century work of New York poet Jayne Cortez, and imbued the postmodernist works of painters Jean-Michel Basquiat, Howardena Pindell, and Emma Amos.

New York's dramatic world went through innumerable phases after World War II. Intense introspection was the rule at Lee Strasberg's Actor's Studio. Basing its approach on the teachings of Konstantin Stanislavsky, the studio's effect upon American acting and drama was incalculable. Among the actors who trained there were Marlon Brando, Marilyn Monroe, and Robert De Niro. More free-form was the radical Living Theatre of the 1960s, the black nationalist theater of Amiri Baraka, and the La Mama workshop on the Lower East Side as well as the attempts by gay drama of the 1980s to cope with the AIDS epidemic. In the 1990s P.S. 122, a former schoolhouse, became a center of innovative theater. Public performances included literary readings, best known at the 92d Street YMHA, St. Mark's Poetry Project, the Conversations with Writers Series at the New School in the 1980s, and the Nuyorican Cafe "poetry slams" the following decade, all of which foreshadowed author appearances at chain bookstores.

POP, ROCK, AND APPROPRIATION

The modernism of bebop and its successor, the "cool," had to share space with their illegitimate cousin, rhythm and blues, and its child, rock and roll. New York spawned major pop music talents in the 1950s, including singers Frankie Lymon and Bull Moose Jackson, songwriters Jerry Lieber and Mike Stoller, and impresario Alan Freed. New York became the focal point of any artist's performance career, as singers from Frank Sinatra in the late 1940s, Elvis Presley in the 1950s, and the Beatles and Rolling Stones in the mid-1960s could not feel validated until feted by a New York crowd. Rock's impact was felt not only among youngsters, as its influence on Leonard Bernstein's brilliant musical, *West Side Story,* demonstrated in 1957.

Popular images offered succor for talented young artists put off by the self-conscious masculinity of the abstract expressionists. In the early 1950s, a talented young illustrator named Andy Warhola turned to a marriage of commercialism and gay bohemianism. Apprenticing as a fashion illustrator, by the 1960s Warhol (dropping the *a*), began churning out dazzling pop images of soda bottles, detergents, and celebrities. Although pop originated in England in the 1950s, it found its most vital expression in New York, where Warhol along with Roy Lichtenstein quickly discovered the connections between artistic radicalism and commercial acceptance. While Warhol and Lichtenstein conceptualized general American images, Red Grooms evoked street life with huge, papier-mâché constructions of cabdrivers, skyscrapers, city buses, and other vernacular images of the city. In the 1980s Keith Haring reinvigorated pop with abstractions used as political and public messages.

New York's preeminence in popular arts meant that it defined popular music, television, and media images. As much as the Chicago basketball player Michael Jordan is known around the world, more ubiquitous global images were the Empire State Building, the taxicab, and Lincoln and Rockefeller Centers. Filmmakers, encouraged by tax breaks from the city, regularly shot motion pictures there, sending images of New York all over the world. Beginning in the 1970s, filmmakers Woody Allen, Martin Scorsese, and Spike Lee self-consciously made New York the backdrop of their films. In literature, Richard Price adapted the nervous street slang of ethnic neighborhoods into his novels. Paul Auster's *New York Trilogy* described the randomness of New York life, while Jay McInerney and Brett Easton Ellis epotimized the blank generation of the 1980s. New York's major museums concentrated on huge exhibitions that attracted millions of visitors, more than all the professional sports teams nationally. The *New Yorker,* under the editorship of Tina

Brown in the early 1990s, opened its pages to more female and gay writers. Gay New Yorkers responded to the AIDS crisis with a literature of defiance, best realized in the work of David Wojnarowicz, Paul Monette, and Larry Kramer.

Pop art quickly adapted itself into rock music, a natural habitat, where self-conscious punk bands in the late 1970s congealed beat and teenage alienation with abstract expressionist sounds. This appropriation policy colored painting, photography, literature, and music in the 1980s, when overt utilization of past masters and their art became standard. By the early 1990s, even black rap singers were generally recapturing or sampling the sounds of earlier artists. New York art remained controversial at cen-tury's end. Angry cultural disputes with members of Congress over government-sponsored art in the early 1990s, Mayor Rudolph Giuliani's decision to withdraw city funds from the Sensation exhibition at the Brooklyn Museum in 1999, and the furor over the African Burial Ground throughout the decade indicated the constant politicization of art in the city. Despite the ferocious energy of, for example, rap music, the lack of originality stems as well from the overwhelming diversity of 1990s New York City. New York was the leading urban example of a global economy and no one style could capture its ethos. At the dawn of a new millennium, New York remained as Poe had described years before: "It does not allow itself to be read."

See also **Urban Cultural Institutions; The Harlem Renaissance** *(volume 1); and other articles in this section.*

BIBLIOGRAPHY

Bender, Thomas. *New York Intellect: A History of Intellectual Life in New York City from 1750 to the Beginnings of Our Own Time.* New York, 1987.

Brooker, Peter. *New York Fictions: Modernity, Postmodernism, The New Modern.* New York, 1996.

Conrad, Peter. *The Art of the City: Views and Versions of New York.* New York, 1984.

Freeman, Joshua B. *Working Class New York: Life and Labor since World War II.* New York, 2000.

Gibson, Ann Eden. *Abstract Expressionism: Other Politics.* New Haven, Conn., 1997.

Goodfriend, Joyce. *Before the Melting Pot: Society and Culture in Colonial New York City, 1684–1730.* Princeton, N.J., 1992.

Hodges, Graham Russell. *Root and Branch: African Americans in New York and East Jersey, 1613–1863.* Chapel Hill, N.C., 1999.

Jackson, Kenneth T., ed. *The Encyclopedia of New York City.* New Haven, Conn., 1995.

Kammen, Michael G. *Colonial New York: A History.* New York, 1975.

Madoff, Steven Henry, ed. *Pop Art: A Critical History.* Berkeley, Calif., 1997.

Patton, Sharon F. *African-American Art.* New York, 1998.

Peiss, Kathy. *Cheap Amusements: Working Women and Leisure in New York City, 1880–1920.* Philadelphia, 1986.

Scott, William B., and Peter M. Rutkoff. *New York Modern: The Arts and the City.* Baltimore, 1999.

Stansell, Christine. *American Moderns: Bohemian New York and the Creation of a New Century.* New York, 2000.

Taylor, William R. *In Pursuit of Gotham: Culture and Commerce in New York.* New York, 1992.

van der Zee, Henri, and Barbara van der Zee. *A Sweet and Alien Land: The Story of Dutch New York.* New York, 1970.

Wald, Alan M. *The New York Intellectuals: The Rise and Decline of the Anti-Stalinist Left from the 1930s to the 1980s.* Chapel Hill, N.C., 1987.

Yagoda, Ben. *About Town: The New Yorker and the World It Made.* New York, 2000.

CHICAGO

Timothy Spears

In September 1893, during a visit to Chicago and the World's Columbian Exposition, the historian Henry Brooks Adams sat on the steps of the administration building and wondered about the Beaux Arts architecture spread out before him and along the shores of Lake Michigan. Had this vision of classicism evolved out of local conditions or was it a historical aberration? Adams reported that the architects and artists who had been hired to work on the exposition questioned Chicago's commitment to art and "talked as though they worked only for themselves; as though art, to the Western people, was a stage decoration; a diamond shirt-stud; a paper-collar" (*The Education of Henry Adams,* p. 341). In at least one respect, their criticism was literally true. Most of the exposition's buildings were made of staff, a papier-mâché-like substance that was plastered over chicken-coop wire and wooden frames to give the structures the appearance of solidity and permanence.

Concerns about Chicago's intellectual and aesthetic character were closely tied to the city's extraordinary rise. Settled in the 1830s by eastern entrepreneurs, Chicago was little more than a muddy frontier town when civic boosters began laying the groundwork for the city's future greatness. This vision began to materialize during the 1840s and 1850s, when Chicago became the central terminus for the nation's emerging railroad system, supplanting rival St. Louis, Missouri, as the region's economic and commercial hub, and assumed a sharper profile in the aftermath of the Great Fire of 1871, as architects and contractors rebuilt the city. By the 1880s a powerful industrial economy and a wide-open social landscape had established Chicago as the "shock city" of the Western world. While in 1860 the population was around 100,000, in 1890 it surpassed one million, with the foreign-born outnumbering the native-born by a three-to-one margin. As visitors frequently remarked, nineteenth-century Chicago was a city of violent contrasts, a judgment that the environment itself made through a juxtaposition of poor and well-to-do neighborhoods, towering skyscrapers, and a horizon that rested on Lake Michigan and the prairie. Dramatized by a series of volatile public crises such as the Haymarket Riot in 1886 and the Pullman Strike of 1894, Chicago's national image evolved along political, class, ethnic, and racial lines. Although these divisions characterize most modern American cities, Chicago's reputation as a tough, disorderly town proved especially resilient. It gained further credence in the 1920s and 1930s, when the gangster Al Capone and Hollywood seemed to work together to promote the image of the Chicago gangster, and resurfaced in August 1968 during the Democratic National Convention, when Mayor Richard J. Daley's police and Vietnam War protesters clashed in Lincoln Park.

INSTITUTIONAL UPLIFT

For Henry Adams and other skeptics, Chicago's openly commercial, industrial character raised questions about whether the city could support a vital intellectual and aesthetic culture. During the 1830s the city's raw, frontier conditions seemed inhospitable to such a culture. Still, elite Chicagoans, most of them wealthy businessmen, had lofty ambitions for their city, and during the 1870s and 1880s established a public library (1872) and the Art Institute (organized in 1869 and given its present name in 1882). These philanthropic efforts peaked in the 1890s with the founding of several important cultural institutions, including the Newberry Library in 1887; the Chicago Orchestra (later the Chicago Symphony Orchestra) in 1890; the John Crerar Library in 1894; and the Field Museum of Natural History in 1893 (initially located in the Palace of Fine Arts, one of the few exposition buildings made of genuine stonework). In 1892, supported with an originating gift made two years earlier by John D. Rockefeller, the first buildings of the University of

"A GIANT MAGNET"

In 1889, Chicago had the peculiar qualifications of growth that made such adventuresome pilgrimages even on the part of young girls plausible. Its many and growing commercial opportunities gave it widespread fame, which made of it a giant magnet, drawing to itself, from all quarters, the hopeful and the hopeless—those who had their fortune yet to make and those whose fortunes and affairs had reached a disastrous climax elsewhere. It was a city of over 500,000, with the ambition, the daring, the activity of a metropolis of a million. Its streets and houses were already scattered over an area of seventy-five square miles. Its population was not so much thriving upon established commerce as upon the industries which prepared for the arrival of others. The sound of the hammer engaged upon the erection of new structures was everywhere heard. Great industries were moving in. The huge railroad corporations which had long before recognised the prospects of the place had seized upon vast tracts of land for transfer and shipping purposes. Street-car lines had been extended far out into the open country in anticipation of rapid growth. The city had laid miles and miles of streets and sewers through regions where, perhaps, one solitary house stood out alone—a pioneer of the populous ways to be. There were regions open to the sweeping winds and rains, which were yet lighted throughout the night with long, blinking lines of gas-lamps, fluttering in the wind. Narrow board walks extended out, passing here a house, and there a store, at far intervals, eventually ending on the open prairie.

Source: Dreiser, pp. 15–16.

Chicago appeared just south of what soon became the 1893 exposition. Although Rockefeller's intention was to create a Baptist college, the university soon developed beyond its denominational roots. Under the leadership of president William Rainey Harper and board chairman Martin Ryerson, and with the continued financial support of Rockefeller, the university became the leading intellectual force in the city, attracting faculty from elite eastern universities, drawing students—men and women—from the region, and developing such innovative curricular programs as its continuing education classes for immigrants at Hull-House. By the 1920s it was one of the nation's top research universities (moving closer to models like Johns Hopkins University) and well on its way to international eminence.

WORLD'S COLUMBIAN EXPOSITION

The World's Columbian Exposition was a crucial part of the effort of civic uplift. In triumphing over New York in its bid to host the fair, boosters hoped that Chicago would soon become the nation's premier city. Managed by the architect Daniel Burnham and a planning board that included, at various times, the prominent Chicagoans Marshall Field, George Pullman, Philip Armour, and Bertha Honoré Palmer, the White City (as the utopian landscape came to be called) developed around a vision of urban order that had clear implications for the sprawling city that lay beyond the fairgrounds. With the help of eastern consultants such as the landscape architect Frederick Law Olmsted and the sculptor Augustus Saint-Gaudens, the White City gave shape to the forces of modern civilization displayed inside the buildings—scientific discoveries, industrial machinery, and the dynamo that Henry Adams designated as the principal symbol of the age. This European approach to urban order is also evident in Burnham's 1909 "Plan of Chicago," which, though not fully implemented, guided the design of the city's lakefront parks and boulevards. However anachronistic the classical architecture may have seemed to self-declared modernists like Louis H. Sullivan (who designed the Transportation Building), the White City displayed the wonders of the modern age on a heroic scale, translating Chicago's expansive industrial strengths into the lexicon of high civilization.

The exposition's Midway Plaisance offered a different vision of order. There, amid concession stands, foreign villages, state exhibition halls, a towering ferris wheel, and an array of exotic and sensual attractions (for instance, the hootchy-kootchy dancer Little Egypt), fairgoers encountered a commercial popular culture that more closely resembled the streets of Chicago. Still, as historians have argued, the Midway's pleasures likewise reinforced important social distinctions. The quasi-anthropological display of half-clothed African tribesmen reinforced prevailing notions of imperialism and racism, while the Midway as a whole organized and regulated the process of consumption, providing a model for the city's, and the nation's, developing middle classes.

Together, the White City and the Midway offered a consolidated vision of the future.

Looking back on the Columbian Exposition, the writer Henry Blake Fuller observed in 1901 that Chicago is "not yet" a city and that "we" (Fuller was a native son) "had to strain on tiptoe" to achieve the "metropolitan moment" represented by the fair ("Chicago as a Country Town"). Like Adams's skepticism, Fuller's disappointment rests on an assumption that authentic cities and their citizens should share a commitment to, if not an understanding of, a sophisticated, cultural heritage. But while Fuller and other elite critics criticized Chicago's provincial nature and lamented that the exposition did not usher in a new age of culture, they often failed to appreciate the opportunities for intellectual and aesthetic experimentation afforded by the city's fluid social structures. Intellectually, as well as economically, Chicago was up for grabs and offered chances that ambitious men and women of arts and letters seized.

ARCHITECTURE

These opportunities had already been realized in the building construction that took place during the decades after the 1871 fire. As early as the 1840s, massive grain elevators announced Chicago's vital link to the hinterland, symbolizing its central role in regional agricultural commerce. By the 1880s the city's economic rise was marked by the skyscrapers that dominated the Loop, named for the streetcar tracks (and later elevated railroad tracks) that circled the downtown. The skyscraper was made possible by two technological developments—steel-frame construction and the passenger elevator—and it established a new working environment for businesses, especially corporations whose growth during the postbellum years generated the need to house and organize a swelling fleet of white-collar workers and office equipment. Moreover, to borrow a line from Fuller's 1893 aptly titled novel *The Cliff-Dwellers,* the "soaring walls of brick and limestone and granite" that rose "higher and higher with each succeeding year" created a new, urban landscape in the streets below (p. 1).

Beginning with the construction of the ten-story Montauk Building in 1881–1882, Chicago architects established a building style that gave the city itself an international reputation for innovative design. Designed by Daniel Burnham and John Wellborn Root, the Montauk was not a wholly iron-framed structure and so was limited in height. However, its

pioneering concrete-and-steel floating foundation proved to be key in building subsequent skyscrapers. Just as significant, the Montauk was developed out of the collaborative work of architects, engineers, and real estate speculators—a convergence of forces that made the modern skyscraper a work of art, technology, and business. William Le Baron Jenney's Home Insurance Building (1883–1884), usually considered the first skyscraper built around a metal frame, reached all of twelve stories and suggested that architects need no longer be constrained by load-bearing walls. Buildings could become sleeker and soar upward, windows and glass could float free of the building, and sheathing could be treated independently of structure, design principles that reached their logical conclusion in the shimmering, glass boxes designed by Ludwig Mies Van de Rohe in the mid-twentieth century. Although the Chicago architects who helped develop these principles were very much the product of nineteenth-century training and culture, their work paved the way to the International style and Bauhaus designs of the twentieth century.

This tension between old and new pertains especially to the two most important architects to emerge from nineteenth-century Chicago: Louis H. Sullivan and Frank Lloyd Wright. Trained in the Beaux Arts tradition and employed as a young architect in Jenney's design studio, the mature Sullivan was a self-styled spokesman for the Chicago style and a critic (as in the example of the White City) of traditional design methods. His famous maxim, that "form follows function," became a rallying point for twentieth-century architects interested—as modernists—in stripping away useless ornament and facade.

Significantly, Sullivan derived this rule of thumb from his reading of the poets Ralph Waldo Emerson and Walt Whitman, who pointed him toward the idea that modern architecture should, in democratic fashion, serve all people. Like Whitman, however, Sullivan was at ease with his apparent contradictions. In his *Autobiography of an Idea* (1924) he underscored the need for "a realistic architecture based on well defined utilitarian needs" (p. 257), but he just as vociferously maintained the importance of organic design that enabled buildings to function as a part of nature. Practical realism and naturalized plasticity came together in what is widely considered Sullivan's most significant structure, the Auditorium Building, which was completed in 1889. A magnificent public space that included, among other features, a theater for operatic and orchestral performances, the Auditorium ap-

The Auditorium Building. Located at 430 South Michigan Avenue, the Auditorium Building now houses Roosevelt University. © G. E. KIDDER SMITH/CORBIS

peared straightforwardly massed from the outside—echoing Henry Hobson Richardson's architectural work in Chicago—and sumptuously appointed on the inside and was replete with ornamentation such as mosaic floors and stenciled ceilings. With his partner, the engineer Dankmar Adler, Sullivan created a organically integrated environment that allowed patrons to walk from their hotel rooms (also part of the building) to the theater to business offices in the top stories; an annex was later added, which was accessible from a tunnel that went under Congress Street. Sullivan and Adler also designed according to current technological advances, including, for instance, a sophisticated heating and cooling system. Thus, Sullivan worked along the cutting edge of technological development while drawing on the design vocabulary of Renaissance artists, the result being a structure that reflected Chicago's robust commercial culture.

Although Wright's diverse achievements stretch well beyond Chicago, the city played a crucial role in his development as an architect. Arriving in 1887 at the age of twenty, Wright eventually went to work in the offices of Sullivan and Adler. He became Sullivan's favored draftsman and was in a perfect po-

sition to absorb the technologies that were transforming architectural practice, changes such as reinforced-concrete framing and modern plumbing appliances, which Wright incorporated in his early commercial and residential designs. The World's Columbian Exposition likewise galvanized his thinking. While he came to agree with Sullivan that the Beaux Arts landscape was out of step with the future of American architecture, he saw in the White City a utopian urban space, not unlike the Broadacre City models he undertook during the 1930s. Wright was also influenced by the Japanese Ho-o-den exhibit, a low-slung, open-spaced temple, whose features are evident in many of his residential designs. Indeed, it was in the design of domestic space, where he pioneered his trademark Prairie style, that Wright made his most significant impact in Chicago. Wright designed several important public spaces in the Chicago area, for example, the Unity Temple in Oak Park (1906) and the Midway Gardens (1913–1914). Still, the homes he designed in the decade following his departure from Sullivan's firm in 1893 reveal a vision of middle-class domestic life that was tied to Chicago and the Midwest.

For better or worse, residential building had always been a significant part of the Chicago story. Balloon-style framing (developed in the 1830s) and the ready availability of lumber simplified home construction, hastened Chicago's physical growth, and eventually fueled the 1871 fire. Wright's contribution came in the form of a single-family design that utilized horizontal breadth, low roofs, and expansive hearths to organize domestic life within open, intimate spaces that also gave individuals ample privacy and independence. Like Sullivan, Wright was influenced by transcendentalism, especially the writings of Emerson, and developed an architectural style infused with the spirit and rhythms of nature. But while Sullivan's innovations went upward to define Chicago's skyline, Wright's hugged the prairie in bedroom communities such as River Forest and his own home in Oak Park. As historians have noted, Wright's evolving philosophy of domestic architecture—shaped both by his love of the Wisconsin countryside (where he grew up) and his dislike of urban crowding—was perfectly suited to the landscape of the suburb. Judging from the invitation Wright received from *Ladies Home Journal* to outline his vision of the model suburban home, this philosophy was shared by many Americans. The resulting article, "A Small House with 'Lots of Room in It,'" published in 1901, revealed the extent to which Wright's Prairie style engaged the question of how the middle class should live in modern

America. The problem preoccupied Wright throughout his career, most notably in his Usonian homes of the early 1940s, which were designed to provide standardized, affordable housing for single families.

LITERARY CHICAGO

In singling out the skyscraper as a symbol of Chicago, Fuller illuminated the city's imposing physicality and its relentlessly economic character. During the 1890s and beyond, Fuller was joined by other writers who were drawn to Chicago's gritty urban scenery, what Carl Sandburg in his poem "Chicago" called the "Stormy, husky, brawling, City of the Big Shoulders."

The city's "first" novel, Juliette Kinzie's *Wau-Bun* (1856), underscored the conjunction of geography and urban character by presenting Chicago as a frontier outpost. Thirty years later, the novelist and lawyer Joseph Kirkland, perhaps the city's first "serious" literary figure, returned to this theme in *Zury: The Meanest Man in Spring County* (1887), a realistic portrayal of farm life in antebellum Illinois that barely mentioned Chicago. The notion that Chicago's development and character were crucially linked to its place in the region received its strongest endorsement in an address that the Wisconsin historian Frederick Jackson Turner gave at the World's Columbian Exposition in 1893. In "The Significance of the Frontier in American History"—now regarded a landmark in American historiography—Turner argued that the nation's democratic institutions were the product of frontier conditions. However, because open land was no longer available as a safety valve for restless citizens, the frontier was now "closed." What Turner did not say, but was hard to deny in 1893 Chicago, was that the city had become America's new frontier.

The writers who arrived in Chicago during the 1880s and 1890s confirmed this point. Leading the way with concrete depictions of urban life, journalists such as George Ade, Finley Peter Dunne, Brand Whitlock, and Ray Stannard Baker pioneered a realistic style of reportage that quickly found a literary counterpart in fiction. The best of this work—novels like Fuller's *The Cliff-Dwellers* (1893) and *With the Procession* (1895); Hamlin Garland's *Rose of Dutcher's Coolly* (1895); Theodore Dreiser's *Sister Carrie* (1900); Frank Norris's *The Pit* (1903)—dealt frankly, and sometimes critically, with the economic, physical, and psychological conditions of urban life. *Sister Carrie*, for example, ex-plores the emotional life of consumer culture by focusing on a young woman who is drawn by desire to the magical pleasures of city life—department stores, hotels, restaurants, and theaters—a vision of pecuniary distinction that the University of Chicago economist Thorstein Veblen analyzed in his *The Theory of the Leisure Class* (1899). Although *Sister Carrie* epitomizes a tendency in Chicago fiction to depict the city as a place dominated by economic instincts and self-making, other writers, especially women, emphasized familial and communal connections. Edith Wyatt's *True Love* (1903), for instance, describes the daily rhythms of native-born, middle-class society, a world of family gatherings, developing romances, and continuity over time, while her short-story collection, *Every One His Own Way* (1901), includes ethnic Chicagoans in its portrayals of everyday life.

HULL-HOUSE

This integrative view of culture was reflected in Jane Addams's efforts at Hull-House to provide support for Chicago's poor and foreign born. Between 1889 and 1909, as part of the urban settlement house movement, Addams introduced immigrants to American democratic institutions and values—an alternative working-out of Turner's frontier thesis. In "The Subjective Necessity for Social Settlements," an address given in 1892 and reprinted in *Twenty Years at Hull-House* (1910), Addams stressed her generation's effort to translate the humanitarian impulses of Christianity into a progressive political agenda. Arguing that settlement workers should try to see the world through the eyes of the poor, she urged reformers to adapt their methods to the circumstances. Addams's experimental approach to reform rested on an important and relatively novel idea: that the environment, rather than innate dispositions, was primarily responsible for shaping social behavior. Addams herself worked to reshape the environment by establishing innovative educational programs that brought together artists, writers, and intellectuals—including John Dewey from the University of Chicago—and made Hull-House a vital community learning center.

POETICS OF MIGRATION

Hull-House was the by-product of one of modern Chicago's ongoing dramas: the influx of newcomers into the city. Well into the twentieth century, internal migration as well as foreign immigration were a generative force in the intellectual and aesthetic life of the city. Given its large immigrant population, Chicago had supported a sizable foreign-language press since the mid-nineteenth century; literary culture, particularly theater, was highly valued within the city's ethnic communities. Although language barriers limited the impact of this cultural work, ethnic Chicagoans were prominently featured in the city's literature. For example, Upton Sinclair's famous muckraking novel *The Jungle* (1906), castigated the meat-packing industry in large measure because it exploited newly arrived (and naive) immigrant laborers. In the 1930s, 1940s, and 1950s, James T. Farrell's sociologically informed novels and Nelson Algren's mean-streets fiction followed the lives of characters who could have been the children of these immigrants. During the 1910s the so-called Chicago Renaissance came to fruition largely through the efforts of Main Street wayfarers such as Sherwood Anderson, Edgar Lee Masters, and Floyd Dell; their work—for instance, Anderson's *Winesburg, Ohio* (1919) and Dell's *Moon-Calf* (1920)—often explored notions of artistic and sexual liberation in the context of internal migration.

Nowhere was the migration theme more powerfully engaged, however, than in the creative efforts of African Americans who began arriving in Chicago during the 1910s as part of the great migration from the South. Richard Wright, who came to the city in 1927, wrote autobiographically of his journey north in *Black Boy* (1945) and addressed the great migration's meaning for African Americans in *Twelve Million Black Voices: A Folk History of the Negro in the United States* (1941), a Marxist condemnation of the racism that afflicted northern, urban black areas. Wright's political, sociological perspective formed the background for his 1940 novel (and masterpiece) *Native Son,* in which the violent acts of Bigger Thomas seem the determined outcome of his impoverished, South Side existence.

Although Wright's portrayal was particularly horrific, his "blues" were of a piece with the poignant, existential forms of musical expression that emerged from the South Side during the 1930s and 1940s. There, Muddy Waters, John Lee "Sonny Boy" Williamson, and others who came to Chicago from Memphis, Tennessee, and the Mississippi delta, often on the Illinois Central Railroad, made music and sang about the gap between urban life and the homes they left behind in the South. Also, in the 1920s black jazz musicians sparked a vibrant social scene. At "black and tan" cabarets, white nightclubbers—some drawn to the seeming exoticism of African

BLUES FELL ON CHICAGO

In the fall of 1957 a young Buddy Guy left Louisiana and traveled north to Chicago, where he hoped to make a living playing the blues. Although Guy eventually thrived in Chicago, he spent his first days in the city trying, without success, to get an audition with Chess Records, and wondering if he should just go home. Here are his recollections of those first days:

I didn't know anyone in Chicago. It was winter, I had no money, and I didn't know where to go. I was trying to get back to Louisiana, but I didn't even have a dime to call my mother back at home to ask her to help me. I went without food for three days, just wandering around with my guitar.

On the third day, I met a man who owned the 708 Club in Chicago. Just to get out of the cold, I asked him if I could play the blues for him for food. He wouldn't feed me—I remember he said something like, "A hungry blues singer is a good blues singer"—but he listened to me play and said I could do some songs at his club. So I got up on the little stage and began to play. Someone in the audience called Muddy Waters at home and told him to get up out of bed and come over—that I was worth hearing—and that I said I was hungry. So Muddy got up out of bed and came to hear me play. When I was done, he gave me bread and some salami that he had brought for me, and right there and then, Muddy told me not think about going back to Louisiana. He said that I had what it took, and to stick it out in Chicago.

On Sunday afternoons, there would be a blues contest at a local club. The winner of the contest would get a prize: a big bottle of whiskey. So I went and when it came my turn to perform, I jumped up on the bar and started to play. Then I walked to the front of the club and out the door—still playing the guitar—turned around, and came back in. I had a real long guitar cord! Well, I won the bottle of whiskey, and I went back the next Sunday and won another! But I didn't drink. I was just 21 years old, and turned 22 on July 30, 1958. So I gave away the whiskey—gave everybody a drink—and, as you can guess, I became very popular with the other players.

All the great giants of blues were living in Chicago at this time. That was why I wanted to go to Chicago. I could have gone to Los Angeles or Texas from Louisiana, but Chicago was where I wanted to be. It was the place!

(Liner notes for *The Cobra Records Story: Chicago Rock and Blues, 1956–1958,* 2 discs, Capricorn 9 42012–2, 1993)

A Chicago Nightclub, 1941. Multi-instrumentalist Boyd Atkins, shown here playing alto saxophone, leads an octet. Farm Security Administration photo by Russell Lee. © CORBIS

American culture—mixed with black Chicagoans to hear the innovative art form. White musicians as well were attracted to the artistic freedom they sensed on the South Side, and in some instances, performed with black musicians.

CHICAGO SCHOOL OF SOCIOLOGY

As Robert E. Park, a University of Chicago sociologist, noted in his seminal article "Human Migration and the Marginal Man" (1928), migration played an important role in the development of this fluid, hybrid urban culture.

> Migration as a social phenomenon must be studied not merely in its grosser effects, as manifested in changes in custom and in the mores, but it may be envisaged in its subjective aspects as manifested in the changed type of personality which it produces. When the traditional organization breaks down, as a result of contact and collision with a new invading culture, the effect is, so to speak, to emancipate the individual man. . . . The emancipated individual invariably becomes to certain degree a cosmopolitan . . . a new type of personality, namely, a cultural hybrid, a man living and sharing intimately in the cultural life and traditions of two distinct peoples; never quite willing to break, even if he were permitted to do so, with his past and his traditions, and

not quite accepted, because of racial prejudice, in the new society in which he now [seeks] to find a place. He [is] a man on the margin of two cultures and two societies, which never completely interpenetrated and fused. . . . It is in the mind of the marginal man that the moral turmoil which new cultural contacts occasion manifests itself in the most obvious forms. It is in the mind of the marginal man—where the changes and fusions of culture are going on—that we can best study the processes of civilization and of progress. (pp. 888, 892–893)

Echoing commentators such as Henry Adams, Park searched for an organic, unifying process amid the tension of urban life. Like Turner's thesis, Park's vision of the marginal man presented an argument about progress; straddling and finally fusing ethnic and racial conflict, the marginal man promised a cosmopolitan end to the migratory streams that constituted this most modern of cities.

For Park and his colleagues in the sociology department at the University of Chicago—Ernest W. Burgess, Ellsworth Faris, George Herbert Mead, William F. Ogburn, Albion Small, and William I. Thomas—the city was a "laboratory" that enabled the scientific study of competition, conflict, isolation, and other cultural phenomena that made the modern city a new social ecosystem. These phenomena (and others) also constituted the chapter headings of the landmark textbook *Introduction to the Science of Sociology* (1921), which Park wrote with Burgess. Between 1920 and 1932 the Chicago school of sociology dominated the discipline and trained countless graduate students, whose research—for instance, Nels Anderson's *The Hobo: The Sociology of the Homeless Man* (1923) and Clifford R. Shaw's *The Jack-Roller: A Delinquent Boy's Own Story* (1930)— led to eye-opening investigations of Chicago subcultures that became classics in the field. These, and books like *The Polish Peasant in Europe and America* (1918) by Thomas and Florian Znaniecki, left little doubt that Chicago was a city constituted by movement and migration. Thus, while the great achievement of the Chicago school was to develop systematic, empirical methods for examining individual and group behavior—innovations that drew on the work of the French sociologist Émile Durkheim and the German sociologist Georg Simmel and reshaped the field of sociology—these disciplinary advances were also the product of a specific place and time.

CHAMPIONSHIP CITY

While the dream that lay behind the 1893 World's Columbian Exhibition—that Chicago could be America's "first city"—gradually lost its urgency, the restless, striving ambition that inspired Chicago's earliest boosters remained part of the city's image more than one hundred years after the exposition. During the post–World War II era, with the explosive growth of the mass media, Chicago became a byword for ethnic neighborhoods, pizza, blues, machine politics, baseball's Chicago Cubs, blue-collar culture, Lake Michigan, basketball's Chicago Bulls—and the list goes on. The accomplishments of many late-twentieth-century Chicagoans boosted the city's national image: writers such as Saul Bellow, Gwendolyn Brooks, and Studs Terkel; playwright David Mamet; politicians like Richard Daley, Jesse Jackson, and Harold Washington; entertainers such as Bill Murray and Oprah Winfrey; and sports stars like Ernie Banks, Gale Sayers, Dick Butkus, Sammy Sosa, and Michael Jordan. Although all these people were celebrities, their achievements promoted an image of Chicago as a city of down-to-earth, hard-working people.

Nothing has done more to dramatize Chicago's civic ambitions than its legendary devotion to its sports teams. The Black Sox scandal of 1919, football's Chicago Bears glory days in the 1940s, and the long-standing suffering of Cubs followers are some of the episodes in Chicago sports history that have tested and revealed the city's character, bringing its teams and fans to the attention of a national audience. Indeed, the success of the Chicago Bulls (six championships in the 1990s), especially the feats of Michael Jordan, is arguably the most important development in Chicago's image to take place in the last quarter of the twentieth century. Not only are the Bulls known throughout the world, but Jordan is an international icon, the most famous sports figure since the boxer Muhammad Ali. That Michael Jordan represents the hopes and dreams of Chicago—its commercial power, racial diversity, and, most of all, its cultural legacy—is a fact that Jordan himself has embraced. At the press conference announcing his retirement from professional basketball in January 1999, Jordan thanked the city for adopting him as "one of theirs" and said that in return he had "tried to step on the basketball court and get rid of the gangster mentality that Chicago was known for for a long time." The entire Bulls organization, Jordan added, "has made an effort to change the perspective about Chicago. And we're hopefully going to be known as a championship city." This is an ambition that even Henry Adams would have understood.

See also **Urban Cultural Institutions** *(volume 1); and other articles in this section.*

BIBLIOGRAPHY

Primary Works

Adams, Henry. *The Education of Henry Adams.* Edited by Ernest Samuels and Jayne N. Samuels. 1907. Boston, 1973.

Addams, Jane. *Twenty-Years at Hull-House.* New York, 1910.

Dreiser, Theodore. *Sister Carrie.* London, 1900.

Fuller, Henry Blake. "Chicago as a Country Town." *Chicago Evening Post* (1901). Henry Blake Fuller Papers, Newberry Library, Chicago.

———. *The Cliff-Dwellers.* 1893. New York, 1968.

Park, Robert E. "Human Migration and the Marginal Man." *American Journal of Sociology* 32 (May 1928): 881–893.

Sandburg, Carl. *Chicago Poems.* Urbana, Ill., 1992.

Sullivan, Louis H. *The Autobiography of An Idea.* 1926. New York, 1956.

Wright, Richard. *Native Son.* New York, 1940.

Secondary Works

Badger, Reid. *The Great American Fair: The World's Columbian Exposition and American Culture.* Chicago, 1979.

Bremer, Sidney H. *Urban Intersections : Meetings of Life and Literature in United States Cities.* Urbana, Ill., 1992.

Condit, Carl. *The Chicago School of Architecture: A History of Commercial and Public Building in the Chicago Area, 1875–1925.* Chicago, 1964.

Cronon, William. *Nature's Metropolis: Chicago and the Great West.* New York, 1991.

Crunden, Robert M. *Ministers of Reform: The Progressives' Achievement in American Civilization, 1889–1920.* New York, 1982.

Duffey, Bernard. *The Chicago Renaissance in American Letters: A Critical History.* East Lansing, Mich., 1954.

Faris, Robert E. L. *Chicago Sociology, 1920–1932.* San Francisco, Calif., 1967.

Gilbert, James. *Perfect Cities: Chicago's Utopias of 1893.* Chicago, 1991.

Grossman, James R. *Land of Hope: Chicago, Black Southerners, and the Great Migration.* Chicago, 1989.

Horowitz, Helen Lefkowitz. *Culture and the City: Cultural Philanthropy in Chicago from the 1880s to 1917.* Lexington, Ky., 1976.

Kenney, William Howland. *Chicago Jazz: A Cultural History, 1904–1930.* New York, 1993.

Miller, Donald L. *City of the Century: The Epic of Chicago and the Making of America.* New York, 1996.

Palmer, Robert. *Deep Blues.* New York, 1981.

Pierce, Bessie Louise. *A History of Chicago.* 3 vols. New York, 1937–1957.

Riley, Terence, and Peter Reed, eds. *Frank Lloyd Wright: Architect.* New York, 1994.

Smith, Carl S. *Chicago and the American Literary Imagination, 1880–1920.* Chicago, 1984.

———. *Urban Disorder and the Shape of Belief: The Great Chicago Fire, the Haymarket Bomb, and the Model Town of Pullman.* Chicago, 1995.

PHILADELPHIA

David R. Brigham

Philadelphia is centrally located on the eastern seaboard, and by the time of the American Revolution was the second largest English-speaking city in the world and the most active port in North America. By virtue of Philadelphia's prosperity, ethnic and religious diversity, and rapid population growth, it was culturally the richest city in colonial and early national America; home to the country's first secular institution of higher education; the first hospital; the first sustained public museum of art and science; a scientific society and a subscription library; many benevolent societies; and a host of theaters, circuses, and other popular entertainments. Mixing the philosophy of the Quaker religion, Scottish and English Enlightenment beliefs in practical education and egalitarianism, and a spirit of enterprise fueled by a lively mercantile economy, colonial and early national Philadelphians helped to articulate such American principles as liberty, equality, religious tolerance, utilitarianism, and self-reliance.

ESTABLISHING THE CITY OF BROTHERLY LOVE

Pennsylvania was founded by the Quaker statesman William Penn, who received a grant for the colony in 1681 and a charter in 1682. Penn's plan for the colony was distinctive in that it declared, "Any Government is free to the People under it (what-ever be the Frame) where the Laws rule, and the People are a Party to those Laws, and more than this is Tyranny, Oligarchy or Confusion" ("The Frame of Government and Laws Agreed upon in England" [1692], in Dunn and Dunn, vol. 2, 1982, p. 213). The colony was conceived as providing a haven in particular for persecuted Quakers but also for people of other faiths. Penn also established a unique basis on which to deal with the Indians, founded on fair dealing and nonviolence. The colony, however, was also shaped by the British desire to expand the empire and establish the Anglican Church in North America.

By July 1682, Philadelphia had been named, sited, and laid out on a grid plan extending from the Delaware to the Schuylkill Rivers with a park square for the city's four quadrants and its center at the intersection of present-day Broad and Market Streets and occupied today by City Hall. The squares were initially called Northeast, Southeast, Southwest, Northwest, and Centre Squares, and in the nineteenth century renamed for five of Philadelphia's civic and intellectual leaders: Logan Square (1834 for James Logan), Franklin Square (1825 for Benjamin Franklin), Washington Square (1825 for George Washington), Rittenhouse Square (1825 for David Rittenhouse), and Penn Square (1828 for William Penn), respectively. Settlement during the eighteenth century remained densest among the half dozen blocks running parallel and closest to the Delaware, though by the end of the century there were also a handful of fabulous "country" mansions in what is now Fairmount Park.

Philadelphia grew rapidly and quickly became a city of ethnic, religious, and economic diversity. As in other early American cities, the social ranks ranged from unskilled laborers to artisans, merchants, professionals, and gentlemen. The city grew from about 2,200 in 1700 to nearly 14,000 in 1750, 32,073 in 1775, and nearly 70,000 in 1800. As a prosperous port where religious tolerance was practiced, it was home not only to English, Scots, Irish, and Welsh immigrants, but also to Germans, French, Swedes, Swiss, Dutch, and Africans (free and slave). Although the city had a Quaker majority—albeit a declining one—throughout the eighteenth century Philadelphians practiced religion in Baptist, Methodist, Presbyterian, Lutheran, Moravian, Episcopalian, Catholic, and Jewish houses of faith. Philadelphia's diversity was expanded by the influx of French-speaking white and black refugees from the slave revolt in St. Domingue (later Haiti) in 1793.

The dominant socioeconomic group in eighteenth-century Philadelphia was the merchants, although divided by religious identity, ethnicity, and even social standing. The wealthiest merchants tended to be members of either the Quaker or Anglican elite, while a number of middling merchants were Presbyterian and a small minority were Jewish. The majority of Philadelphia's merchants were of English descent and depended upon strong ties to the London economy for capital and trade, though others were French, German, or Irish. In politics, their effectiveness as a collective voice was undercut by tensions among Quakers, Anglicans, and Presbyterians. The most common stance of a Philadelphia merchant during the early part of the Revolution was ambivalent recognition of the injustice of taxation without representation coupled with hesitation to endorse revolutionary action. After the war, Philadelphia's merchants gravitated toward the Federalists.

While Philadelphia's economy was primarily commercial, the majority of Pennsylvanians were farmers. Produce from the hinterland was essential to provision exporters, so the farmers, as well as other producers (such as merchants), were deeply interdependent. As a matter of republican (and self-) interest, the Agricultural Society of Philadelphia was organized in 1785. It promoted scientific agriculture by offering premiums for improvements in farming techniques. The descriptions of the premiums demonstrate that the society sought to expand the economy, not simply to improve the well-being of individual farmers.

Philadelphia's mercantile economy also required the support of a broad base of skilled mechanics from coopers to shipwrights as well as unskilled laborers to move merchandise from the docks and maintain the infrastructure of the city. Those manual laborers lived throughout the city in heterogeneous neighborhoods among merchants, lawyers, and clergy. While enterprising skilled workers might ascend to the upper middling ranks of society, more often they struggled to pay for food, shelter, and lodging. The mechanical abilities of Philadelphia's skilled workers, coupled with the financial capital of the city's merchants, formed the basis for industrial development in the early nineteenth century.

Some eighteenth-century merchants became owners of ironworks in the hinterland. After the Revolution, however, enterprising merchants and mechanics recognized the need for vastly expanding American industrial production. Philadelphians organized societies of mechanics to promote the establishment of American industries. In 1789 they created the Pennsylvania Society for Mechanical Improvements and Philosophical Inquiries, which included such prominent men as the mathematician and scientific instrument maker David Rittenhouse, the watchmaker and inventor Robert Leslie, the university professor Robert Patterson, the ironmonger Joseph Bringhurst, and the publisher Benjamin Franklin Bache. The society gained momentum in 1802 when its statement of purpose and by-laws were republished as a matter of national importance (*Aurora. General Advertiser,* 19 June 1802). The society was established "for encouraging and patronizing manufactures," and "for exhibiting, at the risk and expence of many, the most useful examples of the method of establishing and conducting them" (*Aurora. General Advertiser,* Phila., 19 June 1802). The drive to develop a manufacturing economy was hastened by the embargo of 1808 and was promoted increasingly as a matter of patriotic duty.

Those who did not achieve prosperity in Philadelphia were buoyed by public assistance and private benevolent associations. Before the Revolution, relief was carried out by the overseers of the poor who were appointed to collect the poor tax, maintain the almshouse, and drive out indigents who were not legitimate residents of the city. In 1766 a new system was established that sheltered the disabled poor and put the able-bodied to work. In 1789 leaders of Philadelphia's poor relief separated the "worthy" poor, whose misfortune deserved relief, from the "unworthy" poor, who deserved punishment.

Private relief to the poor was usually distributed based on church, ethnic, or occupational affiliation. Quakers, Anglicans, and Baptists all worked to alleviate the suffering of the poor members of their faiths by supporting widows and victims of fire, for instance. In 1786 Quakers founded the Philadelphia Dispensary, which offered medical assistance to the poor and was funded by contributions from subscribers who could then recommend two people worthy of free treatment at a time. Philadelphians sought to uplift the poor through education, including schools aimed at providing Christian education to various segments of the poor population. Ethnically based societies supported poor immigrants and other unfortunate countrymen. Early national groups, organized by trade, provided for the relief of widows and orphans of their fellow tradesmen, including stonecutters, barbers, bricklayers, and pilots.

Philadelphia's colonial and early national system of poor relief embodied genuine desires both to assist and to control the poor. The latter element is especially evident in the division of the worthy from the unworthy and in the expulsion of the nonresident poor. The dual nature of relief was most clearly embedded in efforts to reform the poor, as in the Magdalen Society, created in 1800 to set wayward women on a moral path. The contours of the ongoing debate over whether to fund poor relief publicly or privately, what role education should play in assistance, and how to allocate limited resources among those requesting support remained among the key issues in urban public policy at the end of the twentieth century.

POLITICAL LEADERSHIP IN PHILADELPHIA

Philadelphia's leadership in the political culture of revolutionary America is well-known, especially as it relates to key events in the birth of the nation and to the first official national institutions. For example, Philadelphia was the site of the writing and first reading of the Declaration of Independence in 1776 as well as the framing of the Articles of Confederation in the same year and the United States Constitution in 1787. The city also was the nation's capital 1790 to 1800.

The press was an important political establishment during the revolutionary and early national periods. Philadelphia's newspapers—the *Pennsylvania Gazette* (1728–1815), the *Pennsylvania Chronicle* (1767–1774), and the *Pennsylvania Journal* (1742–1793)—collectively presented a range of political perspectives and promoted debate about and opposition to the Stamp Act of 1765, the Townsend Acts of 1767, and the Intolerable Acts of 1774. After the Revolution, Philadelphia's newspapers helped to define the differences between Federalists and Democratic-Republicans and forced the definition of the boundaries of the First Amendment. Benjamin Franklin Bache, grandson of Benjamin Franklin and editor of the *General Advertiser* (1790–1827), and John Fenno of the *Gazette of the United States* (1789–1818), epitomized the poles of the factional debate. Bache's strong Jeffersonian republicanism and vocal opposition to the administration of John Adams were balanced by Fenno's equally strident federalism and defense of the second president. Bache's and other editors' opposition contributed to the passage of the Alien and Sedition Acts. In early tests of the First Amendment, Bache and his successor, William Duane, among others, were arrested under the Sedition Act for their Jef-

fersonian opinions. Bache died before trial and Duane was acquitted. The Alien and Sedition Acts remained in force until Thomas Jefferson became president.

Philadelphia's political culture was also played out in significant ways in the city's taverns and streets. Taverns were places in which one could read the news printed in Philadelphia's newspapers as well as those from other cities in America and abroad. Before the Revolution, news and information were exchanged and debated in taverns by ministers, political leaders, and masters of commerce alongside mechanics and sailors. Ironically, during the revolutionary era a political and economic elite became more sharply defined in contrast to the working people of Philadelphia. Tavern life now reflected that social stratification in the construction of such fashionable public houses as the City Tavern (1773). Men of other social standings continued to discuss politics in neighborhood taverns but were increasingly segregated from the elite.

The street was an important site of symbolic political expression. Philadelphians staged parades, fireworks displays, and public festivals to establish a pantheon of American heroes and villains, to mark anniversaries of significant political events, and to identify with those sharing ethnic and occupational kinship. In 1780 Philadelphians paraded an image of the traitorious Benedict Arnold through the streets and burned him in effigy. In 1783 Philadelphians erected the Roman-inspired Triumphal Arch to honor the conclusion of war with Britain. The birthday of George Washington and the anniversary of the Declaration of Independence became cause for annual celebration, though those occasions were defined first in partisan terms as Federalist and Democratic-Republican events, respectively. Other public holidays recognized French support for the American Revolution. In the 1790s commemoration of French royalty was replaced with festivals in honor of the dawn of the French republic. Celebrations of the French Revolution were also partisan, with Federalists warning against the excesses of anarchism and Jeffersonians applauding the spread of egalitarianism throughout the world.

Parades were highly ritualized public performances that embodied not only a shared interest in an occasion but also carefully mapped out social allegiances and hierarchies. Newspapers carried detailed reports of the order of processions, listing the relative position of Philadelphia's leaders as they marched through the streets. For example, the order of the procession in 1788 marking the ratification of the U.S. Constitution was published in anticipation of the event. That parade was to include allegorical floats symbolizing the union as well as militia companies, local and national political leaders, representatives of the states that had ratified the Constitution, Philadelphia's merchants, clergy, and practitioners of forty-two trades; and the faculty and students of the University of Pennsylvania and the College of Physicians. All of these elements were carefully orchestrated to symbolize the inclusiveness of the republic, the foundations of liberty and civic order, and the economic foundations of the future success of the nation. Gatherings at taverns after parades were also described by the press, circulated among printers, and reprinted as signs of common values within the new republic. Of particular note were the conventionalized toasts that were raised in honor of the president, the principles of liberty, and the growth of an independent American economy, for instance. Public celebrations were also marked by "illuminations," the display of candles or lamps in windows. Public houses sometimes hung transparent allegorical scenes in their windows, lit from behind, that were then described in detail in the newspaper. Militia companies were called to march, display their colors, and fire their weapons.

The American Revolution also marked the emergence of a growing free black population and the establishment of the first African American cultural institutions in Philadelphia. The former slaves Absalom Jones and Richard Allen emerged as the leaders of the black community and worked in close concert with socially progressive Quakers and sympathetic, though often paternalistic, ministers of various Protestant denominations. In 1787 Jones, Allen, and other free blacks created the Free African Society, which helped African Americans move from slavery to freedom. They went beyond their original nonsectarian mission of benevolence in 1790 to form their own worship services. In 1793 they served the white community by nursing the sick and burying the dead who were afflicted during the yellow fever epidemic. Their philanthropic services, it was hoped, would win them an equal place as citizens in the new republic, but that optimistic expectation proved premature. In 1791 Jones formed the African Church of Philadelphia, a nondenominational black church, which in 1794 joined the Episcopal Church and became the African Episcopal Church of St. Thomas. The same year Allen formed a small congregation of Methodists, the evangelical faith into which he had been received during revival meetings in the late 1770s. That church was known as the Bethel Church and

in 1817 developed into the first congregation of the African Methodist Episcopal Church (Nash, p. 130). Allen and Jones thus established the first independent black churches in this country and laid the foundation for considerable social and religious organizational activity among future generations of African Americans.

ENLIGHTENMENT INSTITUTIONS AND FAITH IN SELF-IMPROVEMENT

Philadelphia offered an optimistic model of self-improvement as a means of advancement up the social ladder. Benjamin Franklin's *Autobiography*, first written in 1771, offers the archetype of the self-reliant Philadelphian, from a boy of seventeen arriving in Philadelphia in dirty clothes, with nothing but "a Dutch dollar, and about a shilling in copper" (Franklin, ed. Shaw, p. 23) to a respected printer, inventor, civic leader, statesman, and man of wealth. That self-made image of Franklin also made him an appealing model of the revolutionary ideology that one's station in life should be determined by achievements rather than by birth.

Enlightenment beliefs in the human capacity for improvement inspired a number of collective endeavors in Philadelphia aimed at promoting "useful knowledge," an eighteenth-century term for intellectual efforts undertaken for practical reasons. Knowledge obtained for its own sake was considered vain and the privilege of self-indulgent aristocrats. One of the earliest expressions of that philosophy was embodied in Franklin's "Proposal for Promoting Useful Knowledge among the British Plantations in America" (1743), which articulated the principles upon which the American Philosophical Society was founded in Philadelphia. The society would collect correspondence from the American colonies about their geography, soil, flora, and fauna as well as chart the latest methods for converting those resources in order to "increase the power of man over matter, and multiply the conveniences or pleasures of life" (Franklin, ed. Shaw, p. 199).

After limited initial success, the society was revitalized in 1769 in the interest of promoting American economic independence. The categories of knowledge or inquiry with which members identified aptly suggest the scope and purpose of the society: geography, mathematics, natural philosophy, and astronomy; medicine and anatomy; natural history and chemistry; trade and commerce; mechanics and architecture; and husbandry and American

View of Several Public Buildings in Philadelphia (1790). Attributed to James Thackara and John Vallance, probably after Charles Willson Peale. The buildings are *(from left)* the Episcopal Academy, Congress Hall, the State House (Independence Hall), Philosophical Hall, the Library Company of Philadelphia, and Carpenter's Hall. THE LIBRARY COMPANY OF PHILADELPHIA

improvements. The American Philosophical Society remained in operation at the turn of the twenty-first century as the oldest learned society in the country and as an important research library in the sciences, social sciences, and humanities. Science was further advanced in Philadelphia by the Academy of Natural Sciences, which was founded in 1812 and incorporated in 1816. While the academy's membership included merchants, apothecaries, and artisans, its concentration on mineralogy, geology, and zoology marked an important step toward professionalization and specialization in the sciences.

Franklin was also the founder of the Library Company of Philadelphia, a subscription library founded in 1731 and chartered in 1742. By the spring of 1732 twenty-five subscribers had each paid forty shillings for a share in the library. The first books were purchased with the advice of the bibliophile James Logan in Philadelphia and with the assistance of the Quaker merchant and botanical enthusiast Peter Collinson in London. In the eighteenth century the company's Library Hall adjoined the hall of the American Philosophical Society near the State House, now known as Independence Hall, making that complex of buildings the intellectual and political center of the city.

Schools The University of Pennsylvania, another institution largely defined by Franklin, originated as a school established in 1740 for the education of the poor. In 1749 Franklin articulated the need to bolster the struggling academy in his "Proposals Relating to the Education of Youth in Pennsylvania" and in 1755 obtained a charter for the college. In 1779, with a charter granted by the state legislature, the college was elevated to a university, the first in North America. Franklin's plan for the college set it on a course that was unique among America's first important educational institutions. Although still rooted in classical education, Franklin and the early leaders of the school deemphasized Latin, the scholarly language, in favor of the vernacular English. The college declared itself nonsectarian and devised a curriculum that emphasized such secular pursuits as science and applied knowledge. The first provost of the College of Philadelphia was William Smith, educated at Aberdeen, Scotland, and one who shared Franklin's view of Enlightenment reform in education. He implemented a curriculum that included the classics as well as studies in natural history, physical science (math, chemistry, and physics), and government and commerce.

The college also established the first medical school in America. Most eighteenth-century American physicians were trained through apprenticeships, though a handful had the advantage of formal medical education in London, Edinburgh, or Leiden. The medical department at the College of Pennsylvania was the first of its kind in the colonies and a logical extension of the institution's commitment to practical education. The department was founded in 1765 by John Morgan, a physician trained through an apprenticeship in Philadelphia and university education at Leiden and Edinburgh. Morgan argued the need for a systematic medical education rather than the idiosyncratic kind that might be gained from an apprenticeship. The medical curriculum at the college included materia medica, chemistry, and anatomy. The legacy of the university's foundation in practical education was further embodied in the creation of the Wharton School, the first school of business in the country when founded in 1881. The scientific legacy of Franklin and his peers may be witnessed in the university's role in developing the Electronic Numerical Integrator and Computer (ENIAC) in 1946, a pioneering experiment in computer technology.

The Pennsylvania Hospital, founded in 1751, represented the confluence of Philadelphia pragmatism, acceptance of public responsibility for the indigent, and collective talent in medicine. Dr. Thomas Bond and Franklin were among the hospital's organizers. Bond conceived the idea and Franklin promoted it in his *Pennsylvania Gazette,* appealing to Christian charity by presenting the hospital in terms of the Good Samaritan. When Bond joined the faculty of the newly formed medical school of the College of Philadelphia, he took students on rounds at the hospital as part of their training. Like other charitable institutions in Philadelphia, the Pennsylvania Hospital directed its care to the worthy poor.

Established in 1787, the College of Physicians of Philadelphia helped to professionalize medical training and the practice of medicine. Dr. Benjamin Rush, who was trained in Edinburgh and was a member of the first faculty of the medical department of the College of Philadelphia, was among its founders. Other founding members included John Morgan and John Redman, who was Rush's and Morgan's teacher. Redman served as the college's first president. Rush articulated the major tenets of the college: promotion of public health; establishment of uniform standards of care in the profession; and advancement of medical knowledge. The college would achieve those goals through regular meetings of its members, publication of scientific papers, development of a botanical garden, and creation of a library.

The Public Water Supply Philadelphia's thirst for scientific inquiry was put to the test in the 1790s when the city was plagued with a series of yellow fever epidemics that killed thousands each year in August and September. People debated whether the fever was spread by ships coming from the West Indies, by inadequate sanitation, or as divine retribution for moral decline in the city. Rational voices won the argument, and the city's engineers were challenged to develop a clean public water supply. A number of solutions were offered, including a proposal from the Delaware and Schuylkill Canal Company to build an aqueduct to supply fresh water for the city. An alternative plan was proposed by Benjamin Henry Latrobe, the English-born and -trained architect and engineer who conceived of a steam-powered pump to push water from the Schuylkill to a central reservoir. A second pump would force the water into a tank high enough to ensure gravity-fed distribution throughout the city. Although opposed by those representing the commercial interests of the canal and complicated by its technical challenges, the Philadelphia waterworks was undertaken in 1799 and began supplying water in 1801. The first pump was built on the Schuylkill River and the second pump and water tank were erected at Centre Square (later Penn Square) at the heart of William Penn's city plan. Public sanitation was improved and the spread of epidemic disease was greatly alleviated in the humid months of late summer. The waterworks also facilitated fire fighting, since substantial supplies of water could now be obtained at hydrants.

Women's Education Philadelphia's egalitarianism and interest in practical education were also expressed in the development of women's education after the Revolution. In 1787 the Young Ladies Academy opened, with Benjamin Rush among its leaders. Rush articulated the philosophy of education at the academy in his published speech "Thoughts upon Female Education, Accommodated to the Present State of Society, Manners, and Government in the United States of America" (1787). Despite the apparent elimination of a barrier, women were still expected to learn deference toward men and to manage the domestic sphere. Women's education would include bookkeeping so that they could administer their husbands' probates, for instance. They would also study reading, writing, arithmetic, grammar, composition, rhetoric,

John Lewis Krimmel, *Fourth of July in Centre Square.* Oil on canvas, 22¾ x 29 in., c. 1812. The neoclassical structure in the background is the pumphouse and water tank for Philadelphia's first public waterworks. PENNSYLVANIA ACADEMY OF THE FINE ARTS, PHILADELPHIA (PURCHASE FROM THE ESTATE OF PAUL BECK, JR.)

and geography. Unlike male students, young women would not study the classics or advanced mathematics, and their exposure to science would be limited to that which would make their management of the kitchen more efficient.

Peale's Museum Useful knowledge was also pursued as a private undertaking by Philadelphia's inventive mechanics. One of the most interesting cultural institutions was established by Charles Willson Peale, who trained as a saddler and then as a portrait painter. Peale founded an eponymous museum in 1786 as the country's first sustained, independent museum of art and science. Starting modestly with a small collection of his own portraits of Revolutionary War heroes and a few fossil bones of a mastodon recovered near the Ohio River, Peale and his sons built an impressive museum of nearly 250 paintings and thousands of natural history

specimens. He articulated a philosophy of the public utility of museums based on their capacity to educate and amuse people, targeted his exhibitions and programs to both elite and popular audiences, organized his collections according to the principles of scientific classification, augmented the museum's holdings through unceasing personal effort and by soliciting donations from the community, developed an aggressive marketing campaign, instituted subscription memberships to provide a steady patronage base, and initiated the practice of selling museum souvenirs. In each of those developments Peale provided models that were more or less followed by American museums of art, science, and history into the twenty-first century. The museum eventually failed due to increasing competition from popular entertainments, and with it died the independently owned, for-profit museum. This, too, is part of Peale's legacy to American culture, as

Charles Willson Peale, *The Artist in His Museum.* Oil on canvas, 103¾ x 79⅞ in., 1822. THE PENNSYLVANIA ACADEMY OF THE FINE ARTS, PHILADELPHIA. GIFT OF MRS. SARAH HARRISON (THE JOSEPH HARRISON JR. COLLECTION)

educational programming came to be deemed not viable as a commercial venture and was sustained by substantial underwriting from corporate, governmental, and private sources.

The museum presented collections and demonstrations to advance the country intellectually and economically. Portraits were exhibited as models of civic virtue and accomplishment to be emulated by visitors as a means of bettering the republic. Peale interpreted nature through labels, publications, and lectures as a system endowed by God to be harmonious and hierarchical. Each creature was

Mr. Shaw's Blackman. Attributed to Moses Williams. After 1802. The Library Company of Philadelphia

MOSES WILLIAMS: AFRICAN AMERICAN ARTIST

Moses Williams created thousands of silhouette portraits for which he charged eight cents per person. He first traced the face of his customers with a machine called the physiognotrace, which transferred the reduced outline of a sitter's profile onto a piece of paper. Having folded the paper into quarters, Williams would then cut four identical silhouette portraits that could be exchanged among the subject's friends and family members. A piece of black paper or cloth would be placed in the hollow space cut from the paper, and a simple frame might be added to formalize the portrait. Williams had been a slave owned by Charles Willson Peale until he was freed in 1802, shortly after Peale added the physiognotrace to the museum as a souvenir concession. The success of the device in attracting new audiences provided Williams with an income that facilitated his legal independence from his former master, though it kept Williams tied to the Peale Museum.

ideally suited to its position and interdependent upon the workings of all other parts of nature. Peale offered that interpretation not only as an explication of God's work, but also as a model for how society should be organized. Peale also presented natural history collections in terms of their potential for use in a complex American economy that balanced agriculture with commerce and manufacturing. Animals and minerals were shown along with models of inventions that would help to exploit those natural stores, and America's first manufacturers were invited to contribute specimens of their products and the natural resources from which they were made.

ART AND POPULAR ENTERTAINMENT

Popular entertainments in early national Philadelphia were expected to contribute to society, not simply serve as diversions from everyday life. Proponents of the theater, in particular, had to define the stage in terms of "rational amusement"—something that simultaneously educated and entertained—in order to defend its existence. Ever since the first recorded plays were performed in Philadelphia, Quaker leaders opposed them as promoting idleness and profligacy. In laws passed by the Pennsylvania Assembly in 1779 and renewed in 1786, the theaters were banned along with profanation of the sabbath, cursing, gambling, drunkenness, and dueling. In 1789 theaters were legalized but only if they were deemed "capable of advancing morality and virtue, and polishing the manners and habits of society" (Brigham, p. 21). Such a liberalization of public entertainment also reflected the waning power of the Quakers in Pennsylvania's government after the Revolution. Still, a minority coalition of Protestant clergymen, people living outside the city, and Quakers continued the fight against the theater throughout the 1790s. Their rhetoric about the moral impact of the theater upon Philadelphia's collective well-being extended to the claim that the outbreak of yellow fever in 1793 was a sign of divine providence.

With the revival of the theater, other popular entertainments followed. Philadelphians attended equestrian circuses, classical music performances, horse races, scientific demonstrations, menageries, and dances as well as displays of fireworks, balloon ascensions, automata, panoramas and models, waxworks, and natural wonders. Whereas Francis Ricketts built an amphitheatre in 1795 to house his circus, many of the entertainments were presented by resident and itinerant performers in hotels, taverns, and "leisure gardens." For instance, Oellers's Hotel on Chestnut Street, near the State House, was the site of many fashionable balls and concerts. Philadelphia's cultivation of music was formalized in 1820 with the establishment of the Musical Fund Society, which soon supported an orchestra of 120 members.

Philadelphia's early efforts to institutionalize the visual arts each combined an academy to train fine artists with a gallery to display their work. The first institution was the short-lived Columbianum (1794), which was initiated by a number of American and European artists working in Philadelphia. The founders included Peale, the engraver William Birch, and the Italian sculptor Giuseppe Ceracchi. The Columbianum was to be an academy of art— teaching anatomy, chemistry, architecture, sculpture, history, and landscape painting, perspective, and engraving—and a place in which artists could display their paintings for the aesthetic education of the public. That project was deeply divided by factions that played out their differences in Philadelphia's newspapers, and after one exhibition the institution quickly crumbled.

In 1805 the Pennsylvania Academy of Fine Arts, a successful joint gallery and academy, was initiated. Again, Peale was one of the organizers. This time, however, the city's professional elite was among the guiding forces. These included Joseph Hopkinson, a Philadelphia lawyer who sought subscriptions from his peers in order to commission a set of casts from classical and European sculpture as a foundation from which professors might teach the art of the human figure. Learning from casts of European masterworks was to be followed by lessons from live models. After some two centuries, the tradition of lessons in cast and life drawing was still in place at the academy. Its gallery became the foundation for what is arguably the oldest fine arts museum in the United States and includes major examples of the work of such Philadelphia painters and sculptors as Peale, Gilbert Stuart, and Benjamin Rush.

Philadelphia at the end of the twentieth century reflected its material and cultural roots in the eighteenth and early nineteenth centuries, though many of the institutions established in that era were displaced in prominence by those founded later. The University of Pennsylvania remained the preeminent institution of higher education and was joined in the greater urban area during the nineteenth and twentieth centuries by Thomas Jefferson University (1824), Haverford College (1833), Swarthmore College (1864), Temple University (1884), Bryn Mawr College (1885) for women, and Drexel University (1891). The American Philosophical Society and Library Company of Philadelphia still existed at the dawn of the twenty-first century as important scholarly institutions, and the much larger Free Library of Philadelphia continued to provide democratic access to knowledge in all fields. Peale's Museum was defunct but the Academy of Natural Science and the Franklin Institute offered educational exhibits of natural and physical science. The Pennsylvania Academy of the Fine Arts continued to educate artists and displayed one of the country's finest collections of American art, though overshadowed by the encyclopedic collections of the Philadelphia Museum of Art. By the year 2000 Philadelphia had long ceased to be a political center, as the capital of the United States moved to Washington, D.C., in 1800 and the capital of the state to Lancaster in 1799 (and subsequently to Harrisburg in 1812). With the 1998 population of 1.4 million (5.9 million in the greater metropolitan area), making Philadelphia the fifth largest city in the country, it remained important to statewide and, to a lesser degree, national elections. However, its once nationally central political role was relegated to historical commemoration at the National Park Service's Independence National Historic Park. The last decade of the twentieth century marked a notable period of economic redevelopment and expansion, especially evident in the construction of new skyscrapers downtown and a flourishing service and tourism economy.

See also **Urban Cultural Institutions** (volume 1); and other articles in this section.

BIBLIOGRAPHY

Alexander, John K. *Render Them Submissive: Responses to Poverty in Philadelphia, 1760–1800*. Amherst, Mass., 1980.

Bailyn, Bernard. *Voyagers to the West: A Passage in the Peopling of America on the Eve of the Revolution*. New York, 1986.

Bell, Whitfield J., Jr. *The College of Physicians of Philadelphia: A Bicentennial History*. Canton, Mass., 1987.

Brigham, David R. *Public Culture in the Early Republic: Peale's Museum and Its Audience*. Washington, 1995.

Carter, Edward C., II. *"One Grand Pursuit": A Brief History of the American Philosophical Society's First 250 Years, 1743–1993*. Philadelphia, 1993.

Davidson, Cathy N. *Revolution and the Word: The Rise of the Novel in America*. New York, 1986.

Davis, Susan G. *Parades and Power: Street Theatre in Nineteenth-Century Philadelphia*. Philadelphia, 1985.

Doerflinger, Thomas M. *A Vigorous Spirit of Enterprise: Merchants and Economic Development in Revolutionary Philadelphia*. Chapel Hill, N.C., 1986.

Dunn, Mary M., and Richard S. Dunn, eds. *The Papers of William Penn*. 2 vols. Philadelphia, 1981–1987.

Franklin, Benjamin. *The Autobiography and Other Writings*. Edited by Peter Shaw. New York, 1982.

Greene, John C. *American Science in the Age of Jefferson*. Ames, Iowa, 1984.

Hamlin, Talbot. *Benjamin Henry Latrobe*. New York, 1955.

Kerber, Linda K. *Women of the Republic: Intellect and Ideology in Revolutionary America*. 1980. Reprint, New York, 1986.

Klepp, Susan E., ed. "The Demographic History of the Philadelphia Region, 1600–1860." *Proceedings of the American Philosophical Society* 133, no. 2 (June 1989).

Meyerson, Martin, and Dilys Pegler Winegrad. *Gladly Learn and Gladly Teach: Franklin and His Heirs at the University of Pennsylvania, 1740–1796*. Philadelphia, 1978.

Miller, Lillian B., et al. *The Selected Papers of Charles Willson Peale and His Family*. 4 vols. New Haven, Conn., 1983–1996.

Nash, Gary B. *Forging Freedom: The Formation of Philadelphia's Black Community, 1720–1840*. Cambridge, Mass., 1988.

——. *The Urban Crucible: Social Change, Political Consciousness, and the Origins of the American Revolution*. Cambridge, Mass., 1979.

Newman, Simon P. *Parades and the Politics of the Street: Festive Culture in the Early American Republic*. Philadelphia, 1997.

Scharf, J. Thomas, and Thompson Westcott. *History of Philadelphia, 1609–1884*. 3 vols. Philadelphia, 1884.

Smith, Billy G. *"The Lower Sort": Philadelphia's Laboring People, 1750–1800*. Ithaca, N.Y., 1990.

Thompson, Peter. *Rum Punch and Revolution: Taverngoing and Public Life in Eighteenth-Century Philadelphia*. Philadelphia, 1999.

Warner, Sam Bass, Jr. *The Private City: Philadelphia in Three Periods of Its Growth*. Philadelphia, 1968.

Williams, William H. *America's First Hospital: The Pennsylvania Hospital, 1751–1841*. Wayne, Pa., 1976.

ANTEBELLUM CHARLESTON

Jane H. Pease
William H. Pease

On its surface, antebellum Charleston's culture seemed smooth and uniform, ruffled only when intense conflict disrupted political life. Beneath that apparent calm, however, lay diverse cultures that required strategies and tactics deliberately devised to blunt discord. An ideological divide separated the agricultural priorities of its low-country plantation hinterland from the commercial outlook of the merchants, traders, and mechanics who pursued their economic interests in a Charleston that in 1820 was still the South's largest city. Although its prosperity was tied to rice and cotton, the city's continuance as a major port depended on the expansion of the banks, railroads, and manufacturing establishments, in which planters rarely invested. Their additional commitment to relative stasis so stifled urban incentives to modernization that by 1860 Charleston lagged not only behind major urban centers in the Northeast and Europe but behind New Orleans and Mobile as well. And as rural Carolinians emigrated westward in great numbers, Charleston's population remained essentially stable between 1820 and 1860. But since so many planters lived for much of the year in Charleston while successful businessmen often bought plantations for themselves or their children, the potential conflict between commercial and agricultural interests was blurred in a superficial harmony cemented by the priority both gave to maintaining white dominance in a political economy dependent on black slave labor.

Consequently whites living in a city almost evenly divided between those who were free and those who were not, between those of European and those of African descent, shared the commitment to social stability cultivated by planters who lived as a small and isolated wealthy minority surrounded by a rightless and propertyless black majority. City and hinterland therefore concurred that the security of this race-based socioeconomic system outweighed all other considerations. As a result, most of Charleston's social and cultural organizations, like its political ones, strove to include all white men of legitimate occupations to ensure their allegiance to things as they were. To that end, city leaders cultivated the soft style that stifled debate except on those issues deemed either absolutely trivial or so critical that they could not safely be avoided if the status quo was to be maintained.

The most ominous antebellum threat to stability was the slave insurrection that the free black Denmark Vesey and enslaved Gullah Jack plotted in 1822. Although suppressed before violence started, the possibility it represented reinforced endemic fear of slave revolt. At the same time growing abolitionist sentiment in the North, which the South's declining congressional power could not effectively counter, seemed to enhance the likelihood that a future uprising might succeed. The anxiety thus generated shaped Charleston's responses to political crises, from South Carolina's nullification of federal tariffs, which almost led to war in 1833, to the state's secession from the union in December 1860, which did lead to war.

RELIGION

White Carolinians relied first and foremost on the conservative forces of family and religion to sustain their way of life. Despite theological differences among denominations, they agreed nearly universally that the Bible sanctioned the patriarchal rule of white men over both kin and slaves. Yet, when Vesey planned his slave revolt, he was an active member of Charleston's predominantly white Second Presbyterian Church and quoted scripture to validate his revolutionary message. Although the state legislature then passed a law prohibiting black church services unmonitored by whites, it never barred African Americans from attending black-led classes within churches governed by whites. By 1855 the black members in Charleston's Methodist churches outnumbered whites five thousand to seven hundred. The proportion of black worshipers to white was similar in Baptist churches. Although in other Protestant congregations African Americans represented only substantial minorities, they often enjoyed their own separate services as well as listened from balconies set aside for their use to the preaching directed primarily to white congregations. Thus, in both the Presbyterian and Congregational churches, where the city's leading businessmen clustered, enslaved and free blacks alike were exposed to a Calvinist theology that emphasized the work ethic and fed the capitalist mentality that many planters feared was a threat to the slave labor system underlying their economic well-being.

In that respect, religion was scarcely an unqualified force for socioeconomic stasis. Yet a latitudinarianism grounded in the need for secular stability was an unusual force for civic harmony. Exceptional for the time in their tolerance for religious variety, Charlestonians largely confined religious controversy within denominational lines. Shortly after the arrival in 1821 of the Irish-born Roman Catholic bishop John England, the French-oriented St. Mary's vestry so asserted its control of church property that he had to found a separate parish church to secure his cathedral seat. Orthodox Jews organized a competing congregation when Beth Elohim, dominated by reform spirit, voted in 1839 to install an organ in the new synagogue. After second- and third-generation parishioners in St. John's Lutheran Church voted to drop German-language sermons, more recent immigrants founded St. Matthew's, where after 1840 they heard preaching in their mother tongue. And in 1846 low church Episcopalians rejected the rituals revivified by the Oxford movement by forcing the resignation of the rector who tried to introduce them in St. Michael's Church. Thus, while religion was not free from controversy, Charleston saw nothing of the religious rioting that pitted one ethnic group against another in antebellum northern cities.

Clubs were similarly elastic in serving the conservative cause. In the years following the nullification crisis, which had split Charleston voters almost evenly into opposing armed camps, men of both views joined to build a new common loyalty. Ethnic organizations like the Scots-Irish Hibernian and Huguenot South Carolina societies and professional groups like the Mechanics, Carpenters, and Fellowship societies dropped their original requirements in order to admit white men of all national origins and occupations.

ART AND CULTURAL SOCIETIES

Guided by the interrelated need for both constraint and flexibility, Charleston developed a cultural life in which the soft style of gentlemen amateurs largely dominated its artistic, literary, religious, scientific, and educational life through the institutions they founded and controlled. Moreover, they prevailed among the creators of the city's most visible intellectual and cultural artifacts. Of its sculptors and painters, only Charles Fraser, who began his professional life as a highly successful lawyer, earned his living by his art without sacrificing his social standing in club life or his post as a trustee of the College of Charleston. But instead of painting the landscapes which constituted most of his early work, it was meeting his compatriots' desire for family portraits with some four hundred miniatures of the city's elite that freed him from his law office. The other talented amateurs who remained in the city continued their business careers. The painter Henry Bounetheau remained a banker and accountant, and the sculptor John Cogdell continued as a bank president. Conversely, when he chose art as a profession, Thomas Sully left the city, returning periodically to satisfy the demand for highly romanticized portraiture.

Perhaps because there was so little demand for original sculpture or paintings other than portraits, Charleston largely lacked institutions to promote the visual arts. In 1821 local amateurs founded the South Carolina Academy of Fine Arts only to see it collapse within a decade. It was not until 1858 that the city boasted another art organization, and it was founded by wealthy and politically powerful Carolinians without the participation of practicing artists. As a result, the Carolina Art Association's exhibitions featured the European originals and copies owned by its patrons and failed to offer either training or encouragement to local talent. Literary organizations did not fare much better. The Literary and Philosophical Society, founded in 1813, soon languished, but was revived in the 1820s, then relapsed again until the mid-1840s, when it became little more than a convivial social group, dubbed the "Conversation Club." Nonetheless, throughout the antebellum period, more than any other organization, it served as a stimulus for self-consciously intellectual discussion among the city's leading lawyers, editors, clerics, professors, physicians, and other well-educated men. But only in its halcyon days did it address a broader public, sponsoring lectures that ranged from literature and philosophy to travel and chemistry and displaying its collection of

Thomas Middleton, *Friends and Amateurs in Musik* **(c. 1827).** Middleton's portrayal of his brother's drawing room reflects the elite culture created by South Carolinians' planting and mercantile wealth. The Benjamin West portrait of a Middleton ancestor *(third on wall from left)*, the other paintings with classical and European references, the musical instruments, and the jovial collegiality of the formally dressed, wine-drinking men all catch the spirit of gentlemanly amateurism. GIBBES MUSEUM OF ART/CAA

scientific specimens. In the 1850s other groups occasionally sponsored both lecture series and individual speakers, such as the locally prominent physician Samuel Dickson or the nationally famous Edward Everett, who toured from Maine to Georgia with his famous lecture on George Washington to raise funds for the Mount Vernon Society. The city, however, never instituted a consistent lyceum program.

PUBLICATIONS

More regularly, Charlestonians were informed by the popular press. The principal daily and weekly papers throughout the antebellum period were the Whiggish and business-oriented *Charleston Courier,* founded in 1803, and its chief rival, the *Charleston Mercury,* established in 1822 and a vigorous exponent of the radical sectionalism that so appealed to planter interests and values. Editors A. S. Willington and Richard Yeadon of the *Courier* and Henry L. Pinckney and R. Barnwell Rhett Jr. of the *Mercury* were major participants in and shapers of the city's political life as their journals either swallowed up or overshadowed the old Charleston *Gazette,* which William Gilmore Simms edited from 1829 to 1837, and the *Southern Patriot* (1814–1845), edited first by Isaac Harby and then Jacob N. Cardoza, who,

after 1845, edited its successor, the *Charleston Evening News.*

Despite its spirited journalistic press, Charleston never seriously competed with periodical and book publishers in Boston, New York, and Philadelphia. It launched a number of literary journals; but few lasted longer than a year or two, whether their contributors and intended audience were regional or more narrowly focused. The *Southern Literary Journal* ran only from 1835 to 1838; two periodicals were named the *Southern Literary Gazette,* but one was published only in 1828–1829, the other in 1852. An exception was the *Southern Quarterly Review,* ably edited first by Daniel K. Whitaker and later by Simms, which drew contributors throughout the South and attracted sufficient subscribers to last from 1842 until 1855. Nonetheless, authors looked to northern publishers to print and distribute their books if they wished to reach beyond the parochial limits served by local printers.

It was scarcely surprising, therefore, that Charleston showed few signs of becoming a vigorous literary center. Its most talented literary men, such as the planter-novelist Simms, who never turned his back on Charleston, and the essayist Hugh Swinton Legaré, who did leave to serve as American consul in Belgium and then as attorney general in Washington, D.C., relied on correspondence with like-minded writers elsewhere for the intellectual stimulus they perceived was lacking in a city they saw as a cultural backwater. Others chose to pursue academic careers in institutions that promised more rewards than any employment Charleston could offer. Basil Manly, scholar-pastor of the First Baptist Church, left in 1837 to become president of the University of Alabama after turning down a similar post at South Carolina College. Twenty years later, the philologist Basil Lanneau Gildersleeve chose to teach at the University of Virginia after completing his doctorate at Göttingen.

Conversely, a number of outsiders stimulated intellectual endeavor in Charleston. Prominent not only as religious leaders but in much of the city's cultural life were the Irish-born bishop John England, the Yankee Unitarian Samuel Gilman, and the New York Lutheran John Bachman. All were members of the Literary and Philosophical Society and as individuals promoted scientific inquiry and the application of knowledge to contemporary issues. The Belfast-born Presbyterian Thomas Smyth, though not an immediate participant in their circle, was an ardent pamphleteer on moral and religious issues. And together with ordained Episcopalians who, until 1838, furnished both the faculty and the president of the College of Charleston, leading clerics either sponsored or taught in schools and academies that furthered both the classical education that led to college and the professions and the English education that prepared young men for business. Bishop England established the Classical and Philosophical Seminary, whose curriculum prepared boys for secular colleges or the Catholic priesthood. The Episcopal bishop Christopher E. Gadsden and his younger colleagues, like Daniel Cobia and Christian Hanckel, conducted similar college preparatory classes while the Lutherans, under Bachman's leadership, operated separate academies that devoted serious attention to science education for both girls and boys. More directly a function of religion's centrality to cultural life, denominational periodicals flourished where literary ones did not. Bishop Gadsden edited *The Gospel Messenger* from 1827 to 1835. Benjamin Gildersleeve conducted the Presbyterian *Charleston Observer* from 1827 until 1845. And the *United States Catholic Miscellany*, which Bishop England founded in 1822, circulated until the Civil War.

SCIENCE

Unlike the relative harmony of interests among the clerics of different religious denominations, the medical community was riven by conflicts that defied the cultural imperative to restrain sharp controversy. Because combating the epidemic and endemic illnesses that flourished in Charleston's subtropical climate was so clearly a matter of individual survival as well as public health, the South Carolina Medical Society founded a medical school in 1824. But when the faculty voted to dismiss an obviously impaired alcoholic colleague, the society, reluctant to offend one of its own, not only vetoed the dismissal but insisted on its right to appoint all faculty. The professors, putting expertise ahead of collegiality, took their case to the legislature, which chartered a second medical college whose trustees were political appointees. Thus began six years of legal battles and open conflict between the two schools. Finally, in 1839 a compromise merged the schools into the Medical College of the State of South Carolina. Never again did antebellum Charlestonians confront so open a challenge to local institutions or so openly question professional expertise—albeit in the wake of the battle and of political challenges to all professional gatekeepers, the medical society lost its power to license physicians just as the Charleston bar did its ability to control admission to legal practice.

None of that, however, dampened enthusiasm for scientific activity that had no immediate impact either on privileged institutions or individual well-being. John Bachman and his son-in-law John Audubon published their *Viviparous Quadrupeds of North America* between 1846 and 1854. The medical school professor John Edwards Holbrook classified and described North American snakes, while his colleague Edmund Ravenel cataloged the shells and fossils found along the Carolina coast. Dr. Francis Peyre Porcher, who wrote several medical treatises, studied the medical properties of botanicals. Charles Upham Shepard taught at the College of Charleston and produced commercially oriented scientific reports. But, of all Charleston's scientists, Lewis Reeves Gibbes displayed most fully the widely diverse scientific interests of his place and time, ranging from plant taxonomy to the classification of chemical elements to astronomical observations. By 1853 scientists, both professional and amateur, were sufficiently numerous to found the Elliott Society of Natural History, a society with interests far broader than those of the Horticultural Society, to which many of the city's scientific enthusiasts had previously reported their observations.

Randolph Hall, College of Charleston. Designed by Charleston architect Edward Brickell White (1806–1882), Randolph Hall was built between 1850 and 1856. The College of Charleston was the first municipally sponsored college in the United States. Faculty research and publications, as well as professional associations, made the college a nationally visible science center and a major focus for Charleston's intellectual life. PHOTO, COURTESY OF THE COLLEGE OF CHARLESTON

EDUCATION

Despite their respect for knowledge, Charlestonians showed limited dedication to public education before the city council voted to fund a free common school in 1856. Until then five state-supported free schools had educated only a small portion of the city's poor white children while others were, at various periods, educated in schools sponsored by multipurpose organizations. In the 1820s, the Fellowship Society operated a primary school for orphans and children of the poor who could not be accommodated in the free schools. In 1827 the South Carolina Society opened academies for the sons and daughters of its members as did the German Friendly Society the following year. And parents who could pay the fees chose among a wide and constantly changing variety of proprietary schools. Not until 1839 did the city establish a boys' high school to replace the classical grammar school courses the private College of Charleston had of-fered from its opening in 1785 until its reorganization in 1837.

Indeed, not until Jasper Adams became president of the college in 1824 did it offer college-level courses at all. In 1837, however, declining enrollment on the ill-administered and undisciplined campus forced it to close. But a year later it reopened with municipal support, thus making advanced education available both to city boys whose parents either could not or would not send them away from home and to eligible candidates from the city's orphan asylum. Similarly broadening, its politically appointed trustees ended the Episcopalians' near monopoly of its administration and faculty by appointing a Baptist minister, William Brantly, the college's new president. Although both trustees and faculty continued efforts to make the college more representative of its potential constituencies, enrollment averaged only 50 students a year, and only 163 were granted degrees between 1838 and 1857.

All of those students were male, in keeping with the values enshrined in the city's cultural life. Where white women's destiny was marriage, motherhood, and domesticity, where ladies were understood to adorn society but not to govern, and where all African Americans were officially denied even literacy, the educational system reflected the patriarchal assumption that an extended education was a privilege reserved to white males and a very few others. Among those others were the girls who attended demanding private schools, among the best of which was the academy Acelie Togno established in 1853. Following a Philadelphia model, her school, conducted largely in French, offered a wide range of courses in literature and language, natural science, art, and music. And the city was never completely devoid of a few good schools for black pupils, mostly the children of free people of color.

ENTERTAINMENT

Like the quality and variety of its educational institutions, the diversity of the entertainment offered by Charleston differed sharply from the rural preoccupation with hunting, fishing, and outdoor sport. Nonetheless, its distinctly urban amusements suffered from the same lack of support that hampered the expansion of its economic infrastructure. In its colonial past the theater had flourished, but in the nineteenth century interest in drama fluctuated widely. Usually no more than a single legitimate theater could operate even during the three- to four-month winter season, which not infrequently was cut short by audiences too small to sustain even that much. Increasingly, over time even its supporting players came from touring companies. And the well-known lead actors who sparked most interest seldom remained in town for more than a week or two. Yet, when famous tragedians like Edwin Booth and Edwin Forrest appeared, they attracted large audiences, as did Charlotte Cushman, famous for both her male and female roles; Jenny Lind, the "Swedish nightingale"; and the daringly costumed Austrian dancer Fanny Elssler. Every season, some Shakespeare plays were performed. But always they were interspersed with lighter fare like *The Duke's Daughter* and *The Lovers' Chase*. No local dramatist emerged other than Simms, whose plays were notably less successful than his best novels. Before the 1850s little opera was performed, though the fare was ambitious when it was. In 1860 audiences had their choice of concert performances of *Il trovatore, La sonambula,* and *Lucia di Lammermoor.*

Outside the theater, music was more likely to be the stimulus for a dance or the accompaniment of a parade rather than a serious concert. In the eighteenth century the St. Cecilia Society (founded in 1762) was an amateur choral group performing a wide range of music. But by the nineteenth it had become a social club whose exclusive balls were its major attractions. The orchestra of the Union Harmonic Society died out completely. Still, where there were parties there were always musicians— talented household slaves, free blacks who made their living as musicians, or even a guest known for her expertise as a singer or pianist. Ethnic organization members often formed bands to play for their own festivities or at public functions. Occasionally, touring professionals presented public concerts. But most music was performed at home by amateurs or in churches by ill-paid organists who often supplemented their earnings by teaching many young ladies who studied music as amateurs.

READING

In the absence of a public library, Charlestonians could borrow books from distinguished but idiosyncratic private collections assembled by book lovers such as the lawyers Mitchell King and James Louis Petigru. Hardly more accessible, except to its male members and their kin, were the volumes acquired by the Charleston Library Society since its founding in 1748. And the College of Charleston's meager library was available only to faculty and students. In 1824, therefore, a group of merchants and mechanics founded the Apprentices Library Society, which by 1840 offered seven thousand volumes filled with useful instruction and sober entertainment to the city's young men. Women, unless they had male kin entitled to borrow from these libraries, necessarily relied on circulating subscription libraries or on buying books from Charleston's well-stocked bookshops. The content of Charlestonians' reading, like their access to books, was also shaped by gender. The best-educated women read French and Italian fiction and dramas in the original but seldom knew the Latin and Greek that would open the classics to them as it did to fathers and brothers who had gone no further than a classical grammar school. The most intellectually engaged women, however, read broadly in both English and European history and literature, sampled the scientific work of the geologist Charles Lyell and the explorer

Alexander von Humboldt, and gleaned reflections on their own society written by foreign travelers such as England's Frances Trollope and Sweden's Fredrika Bremer.

GENDERED CULTURE

Women almost always feared being labeled bluestockings as much as their male kin shunned being known for an "unmanly" interest in the arts. So girls were encouraged to learn sketching and watercolor painting in school while boys of the same age were warned against cultivating such talents lest they be distracted from more practical and thus more important subjects. Religious participation was similarly gendered. Women predominated among church members and communicants; men, even those not full church members, predominated among pew owners and held exclusive sway in both pulpit and vestry. Social groups likewise were governed by gender differentiation. Men's service to the community came most commonly as charitable donations from the social clubs to which they paid dues or as individual participation in municipal affairs. Women acted more commonly through benevolent societies—often church-related. Their members made and distributed clothing to the needy, visited the sick poor, and raised funds by selling goods, often objects of their own creation, at benefit bazaars. Only rarely, as in the Methodist Benevolent Society, did women and men work together.

When women organized clubs for their own recreation, they were often study and reading groups that lacked the formal structure and consequent longevity of men's clubs. They generally remained focused on their original purpose and rarely if ever expanded into clubs of general conviviality. Not surprisingly, women's stamp on Charleston's most readily discerned culture was more individual than institutional. Caroline Howard Gilman, the Massachusetts-born wife of a Charleston Unitarian minister, not only wrote poetry and novels that sold reasonably well but from 1832 to 1835 edited the *Southern Rose-bud*, a popular children's periodical, and, from 1835 to 1839, the *Southern Rose*, a magazine for women. Charleston-born Penina Moïse added a Jewish flavor to the sentimental poetry that many women published anonymously, and Sue Petigru King's four novels were satirically laden critiques of Charleston society enlivened by direct attacks on the misery marriage imposed on women.

RACE AND CULTURE

As white women carved out their own cultural zones, so did Charleston's African Americans. Their use of Gullah, a dialect that mingled English words with African grammar in a Creole language that whites seldom understood fully, if at all, nurtured a distinctive oral tradition of storytelling and preaching that preserved African values and perceptions by adapting them to the realities of life in the low country. Nowhere was that broad creolization more evident than in the religious practices of vocal responsiveness and physical display of possession by spirits, practices that reinforced the proclivity of whites to allow black worshipers significant autonomy in classes and services led by African American exhorters within ostensibly white-controlled churches. In the 1850s both Presbyterians and Episcopalians evaded legal restrictions to establish essentially independent black congregations, although they were still monitored by a white rector. In addition, by 1860 fully half of all Charleston's African Americans sat in the balconies of churches whose white congregants occupied the main floor. But in both cases the richly ambiguous message with which black class leaders endowed biblical texts promised more freedom than the white community would willingly tolerate. As a result, the city's only significant outbreak of religion-inspired rioting occurred. After a jailbreak of black prisoners in 1849, a white mob attacked the newly constructed Calvary Church, which elite white Episcopalians had erected as a mission chapel for African Americans.

In contrast to the limited incorporation that Creole religious practices offered the slave majority, Charleston's free people of color erected structures that mimicked those of the white social hierarchy from which they were excluded. Most prestigious was the Brown Fellowship, a society established in 1790 largely by skilled artisans and restricted to those of mixed European and African ancestry. Significantly, it was not until 1843 that darker men organized the Humane Brotherhood of Free Black Men. Similarly, those whose ancestry was exclusively African were barred from clubs like the Clionian Debating Society, where, from 1847 to 1851, young men of light color virtually mirrored the college debating society in their selection of topics and activities. More inclusive were the benevolent societies that African Americans formed for mutual aid. They resembled similar organizations formed by white artisans and craftsmen who were not included in the city's most prestigious clubs but who enjoyed high visibility in the militia, where they associated with other white men of all ranks, and in the fire companies, on whom all relied for public safety. Nonetheless, they, like the more ephemeral fraternal and religious ones of recent immigrants, protested the indignity and economic hardship of competing with black artisans, whether free or slave. Especially in economic hard times, they pressed to limit the employment of black craftsmen. But because many either hoped to own slaves or did own them, that sentiment was insufficient to exclude African Americans from the skilled trades, although it did block the formation of a free black fire company.

CULTURAL FLOWERING IN THE 1850s

Many Charleston organizations and institutions remained as stable as its population and its defense of slavery and patriarchy. But its economy, which, except for a few years, was depressed from 1820 to 1850, suddenly throve in the decade before the Civil War. That revival increased both personal incomes and tax revenues that could be used for cultural enrichment. It made possible the first free common schools available to all white children, which in 1857, the first full year of operation, taught twelve hundred students and by 1861 enrolled more than four thousand. In 1858 the city broke further educational ground by opening a girls high school explicitly designed to educate the teachers required for the new schools. The College of Charleston, enriched since 1848 by nearly $50,000 from private gifts and state and municipal appropriations, erected new buildings, expanded scholarship aid for worthy but impecunious students, endowed new professorial chairs, and revamped its faculty by appointing four well-trained scientists and an equal number of humanists. For the first time the library had its own building and the books to meet the basic needs of college level courses.

Just as significant for the city's intellectual life were the other spurs to scientific work that marked the decade. The presence of Alexander Bache and his United States Coastal Survey Team after 1847, a meeting of the American Association for the Advancement of Science at the college in 1850, and a subsequent flow of distinguished visitors all stimulated interest in scientific inquiry. In 1850 the college was induced to shelter a museum of natural history directed by Francis Holmes, an amateur paleontologist whose extensive collection was a major contribution to its holdings. And in 1856, the recently formed Elliott Society of Natural History,

which held its meetings and focused its activities at the college, began to issue regular publications of its proceedings.

In addition to the sciences, the humanities also flourished in Charleston throughout the 1850s. The South Carolina Historical Society, founded in 1856, immediately became a repository of documents relating to the state's past. The college appointed Frederick Porcher its first professor of history. The intellectuals such as young Henry Timrod and William Porcher Miles and the older Simms, Dickson, and Petigru who gathered at Russell's bookstore encouraged the rising poet Paul Hamilton Hayne to edit *Russell's Magazine,* a monthly literary journal published regularly in Charleston from 1857 until 1861. Beginning in the mid-1840s, a building boom sparked by the new prosperity opened opportunities for trained local architects like Edward C. Jones, Edward Brickell White, and Francis D. Lee to design public buildings that, since Robert Mills had left the state in 1830, had been left to contractor-artisans or an architect from away. Even the formation of the Carolina Art Association in 1858 resulted in part because of the expanding economy that spurred the private acquisition and public display of art.

Charleston's decline from its eighteenth-century prosperity as Britain's wealthiest mainland colony, its uneasy reliance on the labor of a black slave majority, and its failure to modernize all limited the quantity and quality even of its dominant culture. Not until the boom times of the last antebellum decade did the city fund the expansion of literacy, essential to sustaining the wide interest in literature on which support for journals and books depended. Except for the patronage of portraiture, in which practical considerations shaped aesthetic, Charleston's citizens gave little support to the visual arts. Although it failed to encourage professionals in these fields, its well-educated amateurs used the resources at hand for a richly satisfying intellectual life. More broadly, Charleston's citizens expressed much interest in medical education and scientific endeavor. And, when times were good enough to provide the resources, social clubs funded low-fee nonprofit schools and academies. Even in times of depression, the city council allocated public monies to sustain America's first municipally supported college and a municipal high school for boys. Furthermore, expanded public revenues in the 1850s were used to establish free common schools for all the city's white children, which, in turn, led to a girls high school to train teachers. But more far reaching in their cultural implications than the schools, from which half the city's youths were barred by their color, were the city's churches. While they, too, reflected the separate cultures that divided the city, within their formal services women and men, blacks and whites did worship together.

But a shared Christianity could not bridge the separate and often conflicting cultures that left Charleston uneasy, proud of its distinctive ways yet defensive whenever their excellence was challenged. On the eve of the Civil War the city seemed undoubtedly launched toward a broadened and more vibrant cultural growth. Increased support for science, art, and the humanities combined with an expanded educational system promised to enlarge the reading public, promote the publication of books and journals, increase patronage of the theater, art exhibits, and museums, and encourage a more active intellectual life. Nonetheless, that encouragement reached white women less than white men, African Americans not at all. And four years of war stifled its impetus.

See also **Southern Intellectual Life; Urban Cultural Institutions** *(volume 1); and other articles in this section.*

BIBLIOGRAPHY

Readily accessible to the general reader is the comprehensive survey Walter J. Fraser Jr., *Charleston! Charleston! The History of a Southern City* (Columbia, S.C., 1989). Michael O'Brien and David Moltke-Hansen, eds., *Intellectual Life in Antebellum Charleston* (Knoxville, Tenn., 1986), contains essays on a broad sweep of the city's culture. For a provocative introduction to the Charleston of 1820, George C. Rogers Jr., *Charleston in the Age of the Pinckneys* (Norman, Okla., 1969), cannot be surpassed. William H. Pease and Jane H. Pease, *The Web of Progress: Private Values and Public Styles in Boston and Charleston, 1828–1843* (New York, 1985. Reprint, Athens, Ga., 1991), continues the broad sweep of the city's history. There is no comparable study for the remaining years.

While no study encompasses all denominations, relevant chapters in Erskine Clarke, *Our Southern Zion: A History of Calvinism in the South Carolina Low Country, 1640–1990* (Tuscaloosa, Ala., 1996), elaborate the central role of the city's Congregational and Presbyterian churches. E. Brooks Holifield, *The Gentlemen Theologians: American Theology in Southern Culture, 1795–1860* (Durham, N.C., 1978), assesses several prominent Charleston clerics. Describing the practices of a religious community rather than its theology, James William Hagy, *This Happy Land: The Jews of Colonial and Antebellum Charleston* (Tuscaloosa, Ala., 1992), and Gary Phillip Zola, *Isaac Harby of Charleston, 1788–1828: Jewish Reformer and Intellectual* (Tuscaloosa, Ala., 1994), give special attention to Charleston's early reform movement.

The best treatment of the medical profession, especially its institutions, is Joseph Ioor Waring, *A History of Medicine in South Carolina, 1825–1900* (Columbia, S.C., 1964). Donald J. Senese, *Legal Thought in South Carolina, 1800–1860* (diss. 1970; Ann Arbor, Mich., 1990), is supplemented by George C. Rogers Jr., *Generations of Lawyers: A History of the South Carolina Bar* (Columbia, S.C., 1992).

Joel H. Easterby, *A History of the College of Charleston, Founded 1770* (Charleston, S.C., 1935), is the standard work on this critical institution and its relation to other phases of cultural life. The interaction of science and thought is probed in Lester D. Stephens, *Science, Race, and Religion in the American South: John Bachman and the Charleston Circle of Naturalists* (Chapel Hill, N.C., 2000). Many articles in David Moltke-Hansen, ed., *Art in the Lives of South Carolinians: Nineteenth Century Chapters* (Charleston, S.C, 1979), deal with the city, and Kenneth Severens, *Charleston: Antebellum Architecture and Civic Destiny* (Knoxville, Tenn., 1988), offers a comprehensive treatment of its subject. Maurie D.

McInnis and Angela Mack, eds., *In Pursuit of Refinment: Charlestonians Abroad* (Charleston, S.C., 1999) elaborates the European content of the city's culture. Charles S. Watson, *Antebellum Charleston Dramatists* (Tuscaloosa, Ala., 1976), presents a similar elaboration for the theater.

In addition to Charles W. Joyner, "'If You Ain't Got Education': Slave Language and Slave Thought in Antebellum Charleston," in O'Brien and Moltke-Hansen, eds., *Intellectual Life,* black culture is best accessed through early chapters in Edmund L. Drago, *Initiative, Paternalism, and Race Relations: Charleston's Avery Normal Institute* (Athens, Ga., 1990), and Bernard E. Powers Jr., *Black Charlestonians: A Social History, 1822–1885* (Fayetteville, Ark., 1994). Women's special cultural world is explored in Barbara L. Bellows, *Benevolence among Slaveholders: Assisting the Poor in Charleston, 1670–1860* (Baton Rouge, La., 1993), and Jane H. Pease and William H. Pease, *Ladies, Women, and Wenches: Choice and Constraint in Antebellum Charleston and Boston* (Chapel Hill, N.C., 1990).

Drew Gilpin Faust, *A Sacred Circle: The Dilemma of the Intellectual in the Old South, 1840–1860* (Baltimore, 1977), elaborates southern intellectuals' perception of their isolation so visible in Charleston. Biographies of some of the city's leading intellectuals include Michael O'Brien, *A Character of Hugh Legaré* (Knoxville, Tenn., 1985); John Caldwell Guilds, *Simms: A Literary Life* (Fayetteville, Ark., 1992); and William H. Pease and Jane H. Pease, *James Louis Petigru: Southern Conservative, Southern Dissenter* (Athens, Ga., 1995).

Major collections of manuscripts are housed in the South Carolina Historical Society, Charleston; the South Caroliniana Library, University of South Carolina, Columbia; and the Southern Historical Collection, University of North Carolina, Chapel Hill.

THE SAN FRANCISCO BAY AREA

William Issel

The public culture of San Francisco has been marked above all by ethnic and religious diversity and by robust social movements and political reform efforts. Reformers since the gold rush era have worked to make San Francisco public life open to all residents without respect for race, color, or creed. To a greater extent than in other American cities, the public culture and the intellectual life of San Francisco have been continuously infused by energies associated with this boisterous struggle over the question of who belonged in the city's mainstream and who should be kept on the margins. For this reason, the city of San Francisco and the Bay Area have earned an international reputation for liberalism and toleration.

GOLD RUSH EMPORIUM, 1848–1890

The Spanish established the first European settlement on the peninsula where the San Francisco Bay meets the Pacific Ocean in 1776, when members of an expedition dispatched from Mexico City established a presidio and a mission. The Ohlone, or Costanoan, people living in the area at the time numbered about five hundred. The first municipal survey was done in 1835, when the settlement was called the village of Yerba Buena, and the village became part of a coastal trading network that brought Yankee Americans, English, and other Europeans—some from South America—to the Pacific coast.

The American flag was raised at the Yerba Buena Plaza in July 1846, symbolizing the transfer of the settlement from Mexico to the United States. The change of name from Yerba Buena to San Francisco occurred in January 1847. One year later, gold was discovered near Sacramento on land owned by John A. Sutter, a Swiss immigrant. Because of the virtual flood of gold seekers passing through the port of San Francisco, the city population soared from one thousand to twenty-five thousand between January

1848 and December 1849, and the city joined the front ranks of urban America.

Fortune seekers from all over the world turned San Francisco into a major city during the decades after the gold rush. By 1890 San Francisco's population had increased to 299,000, and the city became the dominant urban settlement of the western United States and the eighth largest in the United States. Mansions and hotels rivaling those in New York City marked the business district and Nob Hill. The first grand opera, Vincenzo Bellini's *La Sonnambula,* was performed at the Adelphi Theatre in 1851, launching San Francisco on its long career as the opera capital of the West. The San Francisco Art Association began its work in 1871, and the Palace Hotel, the largest grand hotel in the nation, opened in 1875.

During this period, the population was well over 90 percent European American, and it remained so until the mid-twentieth century. In addition, Chinese, Japanese, and Filipino immigrants, along with Central Americans and South Americans, made their way to San Francisco. (African Americans did not comprise more than a fraction of 1 percent of the population until the years of World War II.) Chinatown, until late in the twentieth century the nation's largest, originally provided services to Chinese employed in the gold mines and expanded after unemployed Chinese construction workers moved to the crowded streets adjacent to the old Plaza after the completion of the transcontinental railroad in 1869.

San Francisco experienced something of a literary golden age during the 1860s. Bret Harte, the first editor of the *Overland Monthly,* chronicled the lore of the mining camps and the bawdy humor of city saloons to armchair adventurers all over the country. Mark Twain lived and worked in the city for two years in the mid-1860s as a journalist for the *Morning Call, Golden Era,* and *Alta California.* Twain wrote "The Celebrated Jumping Frog of Calaveras County" while in San Francisco, and its

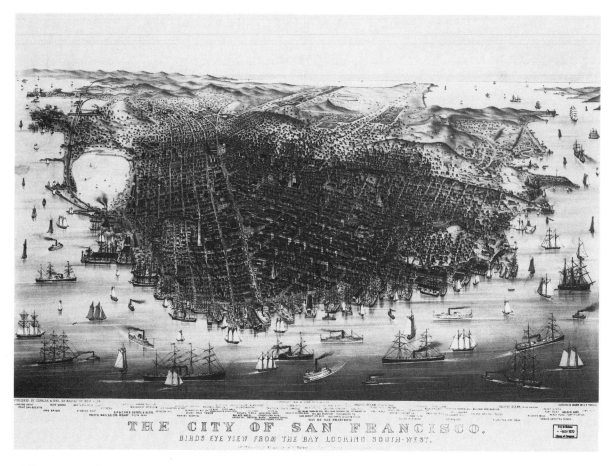

Bird's-eye view of San Francisco. Drawn by C. R. Parsons and published by Currier and Ives in 1878. LIBRARY OF CONGRESS

publication in a New York newspaper made him a national celebrity.

By the early 1870s Irish and German immigrants and migrants, from New York especially, a large proportion of whom were Roman Catholic and a sizable minority Jewish, had established themselves in the top echelons of San Francisco business, society, and culture. With the notable exception of the 1856 Committee of Vigilance, which for nearly a decade dampened Irish Catholic participation in local politics as a result of the nativist dimensions of its activities, Catholics and Jews enjoyed relative freedom from public displays of prejudice and discrimination. The Chinese population, on the other hand, experienced both routine and riotous racist attacks. This was particularly the case during the hard times of the middle to late 1870s.

From its earliest days, however, San Francisco had a notable population of European Americans inspired by a belief in democracy and equality for all, who, along with African American and Asian residents, challenged racism and white supremacy. The distance from "back east," the young male

character of the population, and the emphasis on achievement rather than group identity as the basis of status and prestige all played a part in this. So did the explicit dedication of large numbers of residents to making liberty a practical reality rather than a theory. In addition, trade unionists built the foundations for the city's labor movements; socialists and anarchists campaigned for proletarian revolution and the overthrow of the state. Women campaigned for the vote, gained a foothold in the paid workforce, and demanded equality in the union movement, the professions, and the arts. In fact, San Francisco women organized the first state organization in the United States dedicated to the furtherance of woman suffrage in the summer of 1869.

Complexities, ironies, and limitations abounded in the city's social movements and political reforms in the middle and the late nineteenth century. For example, San Francisco's most powerful politician in the mid-1850s, Senator David C. Broderick, devoted himself to building an Irish Catholic political machine as well as to fighting for the abolition of slavery. At the same time, however, during that tu-

598

multuous decade before the Civil War, thousands of San Franciscans joined the raucous vigilante movement. Ostensibly a campaign to purify the city's politics, vigilantism also targeted Irish Catholic politicians such as Broderick.

San Franciscans also debated the rights of African Americans as the nation moved inexorably toward civil war. White supremacy advocates unsuccessfully tried to exclude free African Americans from the state, and they did prohibit nonwhites from testifying in court. African American activists in the Franchise League (1852) and the Colored Convention (1855), with the support of white allies in the state legislature, succeeded in exempting blacks from the testimony law during the Civil War. African Americans won the right to vote after the ratification of the Fifteenth Amendment to the Constitution in 1870, and after 1872 Chinese and Native Americans could testify in court on their own behalf.

During the Civil War two African American women, Emma Turner and Charlotte Brown, successfully sued for damages when they were put off streetcars, but segregated service continued. African Americans and Chinese residents fought, with mixed results, against segregated schools. A San Francisco challenge led to a state "separate but equal" doctrine twenty-two years before the more famous *Plessy v. Ferguson* Supreme Court decision of 1896, but in 1875 the city allowed black and white school integration. However, when the *Tape v. Hurley* decision in 1885 affirmed the right of a Chinese girl named Mamie Tape to attend city public schools, the city established a separate "Oriental" school.

During the 1870s the Workingmen's Party of California, led by Denis Kearney, accused several Nob Hill millionaires of using their Central Pacific Railroad to impose monopoly capitalism on California. According to critics, the railroad sought to squelch all competitors in land and sea transportation. Kearney also condemned San Francisco's Chinese workers (who were barred from citizenship) for allegedly taking jobs away from white Americans. Kearney and his followers contributed to the agitation that led to passage of the Chinese Exclusion Act of 1882.

The journalist and reformer Henry George wrote *Progress and Poverty* (1879) after deciding that eradicating the economic inequality he witnessed as a Bay Area journalist required radical measures. He advocated a single tax on land that would discourage land speculation and sever the perverse correlation whereby progress and population growth led to poverty. Trade unionists organized a San Francisco branch of the Knights of Labor, and socialists influenced by Karl Marx's First International founded the International Workingmen's Association in 1882. One of the leaders of the Knights was Kate Kennedy, an advocate for woman suffrage and a leader of the successful campaign for equal pay for the city's women teachers. The Art Association (1871) and the Bohemian Club (1872) entertained the Irish poet and dramatist Oscar Wilde when he visited the city in 1882. The Sailors' Union of the Pacific, destined to be among the largest unions on the West Coast, organized in 1891, and in 1893 the San Francisco Labor Council, forerunner of today's institution of the same name, was founded.

By the end of the century, the San Francisco Bay area contained a volatile and unstable mix of conservative and radical impulses. The conservatism stemmed from the large and influential numbers of businesses and family-oriented Irish Catholic, German, Jewish, and Asian residents. The radicalism derived from the degree to which the region's gold rush experience, with its tradition-flouting and adventure-oriented individualism, continued to attract young and experimental individuals looking for alternatives and hoping to begin life anew in a place associated with exoticism and excitement.

PACIFIC METROPOLIS, 1890–1940

At the beginning of the new century, the city still stood as the metropolis of the West, with commercial dominance over Alaska, Hawaii, and much of the Pacific coast and intermountain region. The anti-Chinese racism of the late nineteenth century subsided slightly; Chinatown became a tourist attraction; and mutual tolerance usually characterized relations among the numerically dominant Irish, German, British, Italians, Scandinavians, and old-stock Americans. San Francisco reigned as the unchallenged cultural capital of the Pacific coast when the United States became an imperial power by acquiring the Philippines, Puerto Rico, and Guam after the Spanish-American War of 1898. Between that "splendid little war," as Theodore Roosevelt described it, and America's entry into the global conflagration of World War II, San Francisco lost its monopoly on regional urban power.

On 18 April 1906, an earthquake measuring roughly 7.9 on the Richter scale, and lasting forty-eight seconds, hit San Francisco and the surrounding region. Estimates later in the century put the death toll at more than three thousand, far more than the city's official 1906 figure of 674. The earthquake started fires that destroyed more than twenty-eight thousand buildings and leveled four square miles: the entire downtown and some two-thirds of the city's commercial, industrial, and residential neighborhoods.

Recovery after the 1906 disaster coincided with the forging of San Francisco's version of progressivism. In the immediate aftermath, all segments of the community experienced a brief sense of unity in facing the need to rebuild. Major disagreements over the role of planning divided the business leadership, however, and the City Beautiful plan that Mayor James D. Phelan had commissioned from the renowned Daniel Burnham was never implemented. The business community was also divided over the exposure and trial of numerous local officials who had accepted illegal payments in return for awarding franchises and contracts to favored utility corporations.

In 1911, a coalition of leading businessmen and a few conservative labor organizations elected James Rolph, self-proclaimed "mayor of all of the people," who became one of the nation's first big-city mayors who attempted to build civic unity through a program of public construction. The beaux arts city hall, civic auditorium (1915), and former public library (1916), later remodeled into the Asian Art Museum, date to this period. The San Francisco Symphony Orchestra, organized by the city's Musical Association, gave its first performance just after Rolph's election in December 1911. The symphony became one of the most successful attractions of the 1915 Panama-Pacific International Exposition, a world's fair intended to be an expression both of the city's phoenix-like recovery and of its hope that it would continue to exercise dominance over the commerce of the Pacific. Efforts at creating a Greater San Francisco, modeled on the creation of New York City in 1898, foundered when it met opposition from Oakland in the East Bay and other municipalities outside the city.

During this period San Francisco attracted large numbers of dissenters and reformers, attracted by the city's growing reputation for tolerating unconventional behavior and cultural diversity. Several causes contributed to the city's reputation. "Frisco" was the most important international port on the Pacific coast, with rough waterfront, "Barbary Coast," and "South of the Slot" districts that attracted single male adventurers, freebooters, and freethinkers from all over the world. The author Jack London, who died in 1916, made these facets of the Bay Area's culture famous throughout the world. A socialist and an adventurer, London filled his novels and stories with two-fisted masculine courage and revolutionary indignation. Some of his best-known stories, including "South of the Slot," feature San Francisco and Bay Area settings.

More "respectable" residents included large populations of white Catholics and Jews. Present since gold rush days, they lived in relative freedom from the nativism and anti-Semitism that plagued their co-religionists in other American cities. Gertrude Atherton, a product of privileged background in the city's social elite, used San Francisco high society as the material for her sentimental novels. Her high-strung and world-weary heroines looked to English gentlemen or eastern attorneys for relief from what she regarded as the cultural isolation of California.

Labor organizations emerged and developed great strength in the early twentieth century, making San Francisco unusual among American cities with respect to the power of organized labor. Influential Roman Catholic priests and Jewish rabbis supported the labor movement and added respectability to socialist, communist, and anarchist demands for universal brotherhood regardless of race and for the abolition of capitalism. A major strike in 1901, by teamsters and waterfront workers, supported by the Catholic priest Peter Yorke, led to the creation of the Union Labor Party, a union-dominated organization that captured city hall and shattered Mayor Phelan's dream of a city run by enlightened and cultured businessmen. The Union Labor Party was nearly destroyed by a graft prosecution, financed in part by Phelan, only to revive under the leadership of Mayor Patrick H. McCarthy, a building-trades leader who saw city government as appropriately run by political brokers representing wage earners. San Francisco unions also sought to extend union organization to workers in other parts of California; McCarthy, for example, also led the statewide council of building-trades unions.

San Franciscans participated in the Progressive Era women's rights campaigns. At the turn of the century Mary McHenry Keith, an attorney, and the labor leader Maud Younger, the "millionaire waitress" who called herself "the bridge that connects working women with their wealthy sisters," provided energetic leadership to the state and national campaigns. A sizable majority of San Francisco men rejected votes for California women in both 1896 and 1911, but the statewide measure passed the second time despite the San Francisco opposition.

San Francisco also became a central location for the preservation movement of the Progressive Era.

John Muir founded the Sierra Club in 1892, the best-known environmentalist group in twentieth-century America. With its first offices in the city's California Academy of Sciences, the organization helped establish the National Park Service, the California State Park Commission, Mount Tamalpais State Park, and Kings Canyon National Park. Muir's unsuccessful attempt in 1913 to stop the damming of Hetch Hetchy Valley to create a reservoir met opposition from many club members who were city residents, but in subsequent years San Franciscans often took the lead in efforts to preserve natural environments threatened by development.

Although Los Angeles passed San Francisco in total population in 1920, the city continued to grow, from 506,676 in 1920 to 634,394 in 1930, with landmarks such as the Mark Hopkins Hotel remaking the skyline during that decade. Increasing numbers of Italian Americans, already successful in agriculture, began making their mark on the public culture of the city and the state. Amadeo P. Giannini's Bank of America, a pioneer in branch banking, emerged as the leading banking institution in the state, one of the most important in the nation, and an important source of capital for the growth of the film industry in southern California. New cultural institutions appeared during the first decades of the twentieth century, including the San Francisco Ballet, the War Memorial Opera House, the de Young Museum, the Palace of the Legion of Honor, and the Palace of Fine Arts. These new institutions enjoyed enthusiastic popular support, but efforts at regional planning failed. However, the automobile contributed to growth all around the bay and strengthened the historical connections that linked San Francisco cultural life with the University of California in Berkeley, the California College of Arts and Crafts in Oakland, and Stanford University.

During the Great Depression years, San Franciscans embraced a liberal political culture in which federal government agencies with New Deal mandates for economic recovery became partners in Bay Area growth and development. The federal National Industrial Recovery Act section 7a, by encouraging collective bargaining, sparked a revival of organized labor in 1933. Militants, led by Harry Bridges, won control of a revived longshoremen's union; in 1934 shipping companies' intransigence produced a coastwide maritime strike and a brief citywide general strike. A federal mediation board settled the strike, and employers slowly made accommodations with labor militancy.

A federal Reconstruction Finance Corporation loan funded construction of the Oakland–San Francisco Bay Bridge. The New Deal Works Progress Administration (WPA) and the Public Works Administration provided funds for local parks and playgrounds. (This liberal approach to funding public outdoor culture culminated in the establishment of the Golden Gate National Recreation Area in the post–World War II years.) A state-established regional authority created the Golden Gate Bridge, but some civic projects were still paid for through local bond issues supported by city voters. The city in 1939 celebrated completion of the two great bridges, but the Golden Gate International Exposition (the cost underwritten in part by the WPA), failed to ignite enthusiasm comparable to that of the 1915 World's Fair.

By the end of the 1930s, San Francisco contained more Communist Party members proportionately than any other American city, laying part of the foundation for a radical subculture in the years following World War II but showing little immediate impact on city politics. Leftist politics made an imprint on the city's culture in the form of controversial mural projects, including those by the Mexican painter Diego Rivera at the Pacific Stock Exchange and the San Francisco Art Institute and by local artists at Coit Tower and the Rincon Annex Post Office.

A CITY SHAPED BY WAR, 1941–1975

World War II military production demands expanded San Francisco's shipbuilding facilities into one of the largest complexes in world history. Wartime expansion of bases, repair yards, and manufacturing sites in the city followed two decades of efforts by local boosters to attract military investment, and the war years contributed to the regional dispersal of such activities. Severe labor shortages stimulated large-scale migration to the city, and a dramatic expansion of the African American population from less than 1 percent to 5 percent brought the city a significant black population for the first time.

Wartime migration swelled San Francisco's total population from some 635,000 in 1940 to more than 775,000 in 1950. After the population peaked at nearly 784,000 in 1953, it gradually declined to 759,300 in 1995. The city's residential patterns began to change as large numbers of blue-collar and white-collar white families moved into racially homogeneous districts in the outer parts of the city. The Bay Area experienced considerable dispersion as new residents moved to newly constructed tracts in San Mateo County to the south or Marin, Alameda, and Contra Costa Counties to the north and east.

After World War II, San Francisco's economy changed dramatically as the city experienced the full force of the regional and metropolitan economic transformations associated with the rise of a global economy. San Francisco culture became more diverse and cosmopolitan as a result of the city's experience of World War II and the forty-five-year cold war that followed, particularly the Vietnam War. African American and Latino migrants came to the city to contribute to the World War II effort and became a substantial part of the population after the war.

By the end of the 1960s, due to federal immigration reforms in 1965, Asian and Pacific island immigrants began to flock to San Francisco and to make further alterations in the already complex social geography of the city's ethnic minority population. Refugees from the political instability of Central America during the 1970s and 1980s joined other Hispanic residents. The white population declined from 89 percent to 47 percent of the total between 1950 and 1990, while the African American share increased from 5 percent to 10 percent, the Asian from 4 percent to 36 percent, and the Hispanic from about 2 percent to 14 percent.

During World War II labor unions began the lengthy process of eliminating discrimination based on race and gender. After the war supporters of civil rights began to draw upon patriotic affirmations of America's "democratic way of life" in order to advance the cause of equality for all regardless of race, creed, or national origin. Numerous black and white reform groups in the 1940s, joined by representatives of the growing Asian, Pacific island, and Latino population, pursued racial liberalism, a program premised on belief in universal human rights. To this effect, in 1943 the San Francisco Board of Supervisors urged Congress and the president to repeal the Chinese Exclusion Act and concluded public hearings on racial discrimination by asserting that all residents of the city should be accorded "an equal opportunity to participate in the community life and to enjoy its benefits." The World War II resolutions and reports of the board of supervisors coincided with the beginning of a decades-long grassroots struggle for human rights. A variety of groups, including the Communist Party, the National Association for the Advancement of Colored People (NAACP), the Mattachine Society (a homophile organization), the Mexican American Legal Defense and Educational Fund (MALDEF), Indians United, and Chinese for Affirmative Action, mobilized on behalf of human dignity and civil rights.

An interracial civil rights campaign, more extensive and more successful than elsewhere in the nation, developed in San Francisco during the 1940s and 1950s. White Jews and Catholics cooperated with black, Asian, and Hispanic activists and succeeded in passing significant local civil rights reform legislation. Communist Party members backed the campaign for racial equality and also supported a homophile movement that attracted publicity to the city unwanted by culturally conservative residents. The city's Commission on Equal Employment Opportunity, one of the first in the nation, was established in 1957. Some conservative public officials used anticommunism as an excuse to criticize the reform programs, but the red-baiting tactic eventually backfired: in the face of such repressive tactics anticommunist liberals defended the freedom of speech of radicals with whom they often disagreed.

The 1960s witnessed a dramatic acceleration in the agitation for equality. College students demonstrated against the House Committee on Un-American Activities in 1960, led a successful strike to create the School of Ethnic Studies (one of the first in the nation) at San Francisco State College in 1968, and started the occupation of Alcatraz Island as "Indian Land" in 1969. Multiethnic and interracial civil rights organizations protested against discrimination in education, employment, and housing, and San Francisco established one of the first municipal Human Rights Commissions in 1964. Gay, lesbian, bisexual, and transgendered residents had long been a presence among the diverse population of "Baghdad by the Bay." Daughters of Bilitis, the nation's first lesbian political organization (1955) and the Society for Individual Rights (1964), which established the first gay community center in 1966, began building a gay and lesbian political movement in the late 1960s.

Even though the city's many cultural changes have often been related to its role as a staging ground for war and a leading complex of military bases and research facilities, criticism of war and militarism has marked San Francisco public culture. In 1916 the rabbi Jacob Nieto of Temple Sherith Israel joined the city's socialists and anarchists in condemning World War I as a murderous capitalist adventure. Moderates, radicals and conservatives generally agreed that World War II—against fascism, totalitarianism, and imperialism—was a "good war." After World War II the cold war against communism received considerable support in the city. At the same time the Bay Area attracted writers and artists who had been conscientious objectors during World War II. One of these pacifists, Lewis Hill, founded a listener-supported FM radio station in Berkeley, KPFA, which provided a forum for critical commentary on politics and culture during the 1950s. During the height of U.S. involvement in the Vietnam War, from the mid-1960s to the mid-1970s, during U.S. participation in Latin American civil wars during the 1980s, and during the Persian Gulf conflict of the early 1990s, Berkeley, Oakland, and San Francisco became leading centers of antiwar organizing and protest demonstrations.

CAPITAL OF THE COUNTERCULTURE, 1957–1978

From the late 1950s through the 1970s San Francisco developed an international reputation as the mecca of the Beat and hippie countercultures and as the "gay capital" of the United States. The city was not the only place where critics of "the American way of life" sought harmony with nature, sexual freedom, spiritual experimentation, poetic revelry, rock music, and psychedelics, but San Francisco did play a pioneer role in redefining American public culture. A distinctive "San Francisco rock" and several local groups, notably the Grateful Dead and the Jefferson Airplane, played an influential role in the development of the rock music scene nationally.

The civil rights movement, like the labor movement and the women's rights campaigns, had demanded equal rights to participate in the center of public life rather than being relegated to the fringes. The counterculture and gay liberation movements sought equal rights, to be sure, but also the freedom to choose to live beyond (as well as more securely within, if one desired) the mainstream. In North Beach, the Haight-Ashbury, and the Castro districts, dissenters experimented with lifestyles meant to provide models for Americans everywhere who felt themselves limited by the conventions of "Main Street, U.S.A." and who demanded liberation from tradition and authority.

The saloons, coffeehouses, restaurants, and clubs of North Beach attracted literary and political radicals during the 1920s and 1930s, such as the bohemian circle around John Barry, the "philosophical anarchist" who founded the International Radical Club in 1912. After World War II poets and writers who scorned what they saw as the materialism and militarism of America gravitated to North Beach. The neighborhood of narrow streets, low rents, and continental restaurants was reminiscent of the Left Bank in Paris but still within (yet on the edge of) the United States. A distinctive San Francisco and Bay Area style of abstract expressionism in painting developed during this period, as did a renaissance in poetry; both were centered in local art schools and colleges and attracted national attention. Several offshoots of that "scene"—including the anarchist and civil libertarian City Lights Bookstore (1953), City Lights Publishing Company (1955), and the San Francisco State University Poetry Center (1954)—continued to thrive into the twenty-first century.

Media attention provided San Francisco's Beat writers, hippie entrepreneurs, and gay and lesbian community builders with a national audience. *Life* magazine reported the "not guilty" verdict in the trial of Lawrence Ferlinghetti and Shigeyoshi Murao (from City Lights Bookstore) for selling the allegedly obscene Allen Ginsberg poem "Howl" in 1957. Several years later, *Life* dubbed the city the "gay capital" of the nation. In 1967 the television networks chronicled the thousands of hippies who listened to the Buddhist chants and Zen prayers of Beat luminaries Gary Snyder and Allen Ginsberg at the 1967 Human Be-In at the Polo Field in Golden Gate Park.

The Beat movement, the hippie counterculture, and the queer community used media and the arts in order to claim a space in the public life of San Francisco. Some drew upon classic European roots, such as the San Francisco Mime Troupe, founded in 1959 by R. G. Davis in the commedia dell'arte tradition. Others, like Gay Freedom Day, commemorating the 1969 Stonewall uprising in New York City, drew upon the model of antiwar marches and demonstrations of the 1960s.

LEFT COAST CITY, 1975–1995

By the end of the 1970s, in a pattern continued into the next century, the city became predominantly a service center for regional and Pacific basin economic development, with government, education, finance, insurance, real estate, and (during the 1990s) multimedia industries commanding a greater share of the workforce. Economic transformation expressed itself in the dramatic alteration of the city's built environment. High-rise office buildings in the central business district turned the downtown area into a mini-Manhattan. Young entrepreneurs and computer-savvy workers, especially

City Lights Bookstore at 261 Columbus Avenue. "A Literary Meetingplace since 1953" reads the store's masthead. Founded by poet Lawrence Ferlinghetti and Peter D. Martin, City Lights remains one of the great independent bookstores. COURTESY CITY LIGHTS

those associated with genetic engineering, the Internet, and e-commerce businesses made their mark on San Francisco and Bay Area social and cultural life during the middle to the late 1990s. Abandonment of the finger piers along the Embarcadero, and the demolition of the Embarcadero Freeway after damages caused by the 1989 Loma Prieta earthquake, allowed the redevelopment of the waterfront in connection with the city's most important service business: tourism. Retailing of the reminders of the city's colorful history—the cable cars and Fisherman's Wharf, for instance—allowed the hotel and restaurant business to thrive as San Francisco became a prime destination for recreational visitors and as a convention site. The city's attraction as a regional hub for Bay Area culture increased when a new home for the city's symphony orchestra, the Louise M. Davies Hall, opened in 1980 and the new downtown quarters of the California Historical Society and the Museum of Modern Art opened during the 1990s.

New immigrants from Asia, the Pacific islands, and Central America brought greater diversity to the city and greater complication to social and political reform activities after the Vietnam War. By the beginning of the 1990s the U.S. Census Bureau ranked San Francisco number one in ethnic diversity among American communities. Writers, artists, playwrights, filmmakers, and video producers found the city a stimulating place to live and work:

in the last quarter of the twentieth century, San Francisco's most famous residents included writers such as Armistead Maupin, Ishmael Reed, Maxine Hong Kingston, and Richard Rodriguez, film producers and directors George Lucas and Francis Ford Coppola, and movie actors Robin Williams and Whoopi Goldberg.

San Francisco maintained and increased its reputation as the heart of one of the nation's most liberal cultural regions even as much of the country moved in centrist and conservative cultural directions during the 1980s and 1990s. One way that Bay Area residents expressed their insistence upon the importance of direct citizen participation in decisions that affect the life of the community was their support of an extensive independent press dedicated to investigative reporting. Numerous weekly newspapers, magazines, and independent publishers operated in a deliberately irreverent spirit, including *Ramparts* magazine (1962–1975), *Rolling Stone* (1967), *Bay Guardian* (1966), and the gay-oriented publications *Gay Sunshine* (1970) and *Bay Area Reporter* (1971).

The alternative media kept Bay Area residents apprised of contests over development and redevelopment as these issues became more complicated because of the growing heterogeneity of the city's residents after the 1960s. Questions of economic advantage, neighborhood preference, racial and ethnic justice, equality for those outside the heterosexual mainstream, and the needs and rights of the disabled and the aged all received close attention. Controversies over the impact of redevelopment on the African American and Japanese American residents of the Western Addition and the displacement of elderly retired persons by the Yerba Buena Center project and by the demolition of the International Hotel were among the most contentious.

A desire to enhance the quality of human life and health and an appreciation for simplicity, craftsmanship, and the natural setting and climate have particularly marked San Francisco environmentalism. Residents from many walks of life helped to make the city a national leader in urban land-use reform policy, including tree planting in residential neighborhoods and height limitations on downtown office buildings. The first "freeway revolt" in American history occurred in San Francisco when the city board of supervisors canceled plans by state and federal highway agencies in 1959. Environmental activists have included socially prominent members of the city's historic business elite, such as Rhoda and Richard Goldman, as well as professional politicians such as Phillip Burton. Muckraking journalists such as Bruce Brugmann of the *Bay Guardian,* as well as housewives-turned-politicians such as Dianne Feinstein and Sue Bierman, worked to preserve the city's natural amenities.

Residents continued to debate redevelopment, gentrification and displacement, district election of supervisors, and access to political power by black and gay activists through the end of the twentieth century. When Dan White, a disgruntled conservative and former member of the board of supervisors, murdered liberal Democratic Mayor George Moscone and Harvey Milk, the city's first gay supervisor, in 1978, San Franciscans were shocked, but that event demonstrated an exception rather than the rule in the notoriously tolerant climate for which San Francisco is best known. The city's mayor at the beginning of the new millennium, Willie L. Brown Jr., was African American; he proudly described himself as the most liberal mayor in America, and many San Franciscans undoubtedly regarded the sobriquet "Left Coast City" as a compliment rather than an epithet.

See also **Urban Cultural Institutions** *(volume 1);* **Ethnicity: Early Theories; Ethnicity and Race** *(volume 3); and other articles in this section.*

BIBLIOGRAPHY

Albright, Thomas. *Art in the San Francisco Bay Area, 1945–1980: An Illustrated History.* Berkeley, Calif., 1985.

Bloomfield, Arthur. *The San Francisco Opera, 1922–1978.* Sausalito, Calif., 1978.

Broussard, Albert S. *Black San Francisco: The Struggle for Racial Equality in the West, 1900–1954.* Lawrence, Kans., 1993.

Chandler, Robert J. "In the Van: Spiritualists as Catalysts for the California Women's Suffrage Movement." *California History* 73, no. 3 (fall 1994): 188–201.

Cherny, Robert W. "Patterns of Toleration and Discrimination in San Francisco: The Civil War to World War I." *California History* 73, no. 2 (summer 1994): 130–141.

Daniels, Douglas Henry. *Pioneer Urbanites: A Social and Cultural History of Black San Francisco.* Philadelphia, 1980.

Davidson, Michael. *The San Francisco Renaissance: Poetics and Community at Mid-Century.* New York, 1989.

DeLeon, Richard Edward. *Left Coast City: Progressive Politics in San Francisco, 1975–1991.* Lawrence, Kans., 1992.

Ferlinghetti, Lawrence, and Nancy J. Peters. *Literary San Francisco: A Pictorial History from Its Beginnings to the Present Day.* San Francisco, 1980.

French, Warren. *The San Francisco Poetry Renaissance, 1955–1960.* Boston, 1991.

Godfrey, Brian J. *Neighborhoods in Transition: The Making of San Francisco's Ethnic and Nonconformist Communities.* Berkeley, Calif., 1988.

Issel, William, and Robert W. Cherny. *San Francisco 1865–1932: Politics, Power, and Urban Development.* Berkeley, Calif., 1986.

Lee, Anthony W. *Painting on the Left: Diego Rivera, Radical Politics, and San Francisco's Public Murals.* Berkeley, Calif., 1999.

Lotchin, Roger W. *San Francisco 1846–1856: From Hamlet to City.* New York, 1974.

McClain, Charles J. *In Search of Equality: The Chinese Struggle against Discrimination in Nineteenth-Century America.* Berkeley, Calif., 1994.

McDonough, Jack. *San Francisco Rock, 1965–1985: The Illustrated History of San Francisco Rock Music.* San Francisco, 1985.

Narrell, Irena. *Our City: The Jews of San Francisco.* San Diego, Calif., 1981.

Schneider, David. *The San Francisco Symphony: Music, Maestros, and Musicians.* Novato, Calif., 1983.

Shilts, Randy. *The Mayor of Castro Street: The Life and Times of Harvey Milk.* New York, 1982.

Smith, Richard Cándida. *Utopia and Dissent: Art, Poetry, and Politics in California.* Berkeley, Calif., 1995.

Steinberg, Cobbett. *San Francisco Ballet: The First Fifty Years.* San Francisco, 1983.

Walsh, James P., ed. *The San Francisco Irish, 1850–1976.* San Francisco, 1978.

Watson, Steven. *The Birth of the Beat Generation: Visionaries, Rebels, and Hipsters, 1944–1960.* New York, 1995.

Yung, Judy. *Unbound Feet: A Social History of Chinese Women in San Francisco.* Berkeley, Calif., 1995.

DETROIT

Peter W. Williams

On Saturday, 24 October 1998, the J. L. Hudson Company's downtown flagship store was deliberately imploded, leaving behind only a pile of dust and debris for souvenir hunters. The destruction of this Chicago-style monument to Midwestern commerce, which since 1982 had lain empty and neglected, was a brief, late, little-noted, but highly emblematic episode in the story of the Motor City. Years after massive "white flight" had depleted the city of Hudson's traditional middle-class constituency, the downtown store still symbolized for countless middle-aged suburbanites a midcentury chapter in gracious urban consumption. For the myriad African Americans who now made up the bulk of Detroit's population, though, Hudson's was remembered mainly as a bastion of white bourgeois privilege where blacks had seldom been hired as employees or welcomed as patrons. Hudson's branches still thrive in suburban malls such as Victor Gruen's Northland, in the building of which Detroit had long been in the forefront. The collapse of Hudson's downtown headquarters was something both of an afterthought and an anticlimax, reflecting a profound social transformation that had been precipitated three decades earlier in one of the most traumatic upheavals in American urban history.

The history of Detroit has always been centered on two themes represented by this incident: the pursuit of commercial gain and the meeting and clashing of disparate populations. Since its founding as a fur-trading outpost in 1701, Detroit—"the straits" in French—has undergone dramatic growth, metamorphosis, and, ultimately, shrinkage, while always retaining a reputation as a center of industry and commerce. From its colonial origins, Detroit has successively changed into a small provincial bastion of Enlightenment values; a typical emergent Great Lakes industrial city, with the requisite cultural institutions; a city uniquely dominated by a single industry on a scale that for a brief period generated a distinctive cultural flourishing; and, finally, a city torn by racial strife and deindustrialization in which an African American culture had a chance to demonstrate its viability.

THE ENLIGHTENED TRIUMVIRATE

The trading village and military post founded by Cadillac lasted some sixty years as a French settlement, and developed very little that might be called a cultural or intellectual life other than that betokened by the presence of the Catholic Church. The city accompanied the rest of French North America into the British imperial orbit in 1760, and then came under American aegis in 1796 as part of the lands falling under the Northwest ordinance. Despite the city's small population and unstable political and economic situation in the nineteenth century, three remarkable personalities came together and set the stage for the city's future cultural development. The first of these, Gabriel Richard, was an émigré French Sulpician priest who arrived in the city in 1798 and ministered not only to the city's Catholics but to Native Americans and interested Protestants in the absence of any other clergy. In primitive circumstances Richard was instrumental in founding a variety of schools that were intended for both sexes and for Indians as well as whites, a project to which Thomas Jefferson contributed financially. Richard was also responsible for establishing the city's first printing press and newspaper as well as the Michigan Historical Society. Even more remarkably, he was elected to a term as territorial delegate to the U.S. Congress in 1823, the only Catholic priest to serve in that body until late in the twentieth century. Richard died in 1832 while ministering to those stricken in a cholera epidemic.

The second figure in Detroit's initial cultural triumvirate was Augustus B. Woodward, a Columbia-educated lawyer whom Thomas Jefferson appointed chief justice of the Michigan territory's supreme court in 1805. In addition to various contributions to the development of a regional legal tradition, Woodward, like Richard, promoted a variety of civic projects, most notably in the realm of urban planning. Impressed by Pierre L'Enfant's geometric scheme for the streets of the national capital, Woodward designed a somewhat similar plan for Detroit in which wide boulevards on north-south and east-west axes intersected at regular intervals, demarcated by circular plazas surrounded by concentric rings of circular streets, with other avenues radiating out diagonally. Public buildings were to be sited in the plazas, or "grand circuses," and large lots were intended to attract substantial single-family homes. Although this scheme was later abandoned in favor of the more usual grid pattern, it still frames a portion of today's downtown, which is appropriately intersected by Woodward Avenue, one of the city's once-grand radial thoroughfares.

Another of Woodward's enduring schemes was his plan for a new sort of institute of higher learning, which he inventively dubbed the Catholepistemiad. This was the institutional expression of his 1816 work *A System of Universal Science,* a rough translation of his elaborate Hellenic coinage. Established by the territorial legislature in 1817 with the alternate name of the University of Michigania, Woodward's brainchild was staffed by Père Richard and his Presbyterian counterpart, the Reverend John Monteith, who came to be the third member of Detroit's enlightened triumvirate. Although the two clergymen valiantly attempted to teach all thirteen divisions of Woodward's curriculum between them, the school was not successful on its own terms; it provided the foundation, however, for the University of Michigan, which opened in Ann Arbor in 1841. Woodward was also instrumental in founding the Detroit Lyceum in 1818, yet another Enlightenment-style attempt to promote the commonweal through the widespread diffusion of knowledge.

Detroit grew rapidly during the nineteenth century through immigration, primarily from Ireland and Germany, as well as through the development of various industries such as the manufacture of railroad cars; the processing of metals such as brass, copper, iron and, later, steel; and a wide variety of other enterprises ranging from drugs to seeds to stoves to chewing tobacco. With the turn of the twentieth century, however, Detroit rapidly changed from a fairly typical Great Lakes industrial city into something distinctive: an American city whose name rapidly became eponymous with an entire industry. Just as Washington is synonymous with government and Hollywood with motion pictures, so

does Detroit immediately bring to mind automobiles. During the later nineteenth century, various elements fell into place that would position the city, if not inevitably, at least propitiously, to become the center for the design and manufacture of that distinctively American phenomenon, the car. By the time the possibilities of the internal-combustion engine were beginning to make themselves known, Detroit already possessed an industrial and commercial infrastructure in which marine gas-engine and malleable-iron manufacturing, wheelwrights and blacksmiths, capital from the extractive industries of northern Michigan such as timbering and mining, and a labor supply provided by the decline of those same enterprises all combined with the presence of remarkable men such as Henry Ford, William C. Durant, and the Dodge brothers. Ford's revolutionary innovations, such as the assembly line and the five-dollar day, galvanized these components into an entirely new industrial order in which a vast influx of immigrants, primarily from central and eastern Europe, vied with in-migrants from rural America to share in what seemed to them to be a hitherto undreamed-of prosperity, however exacting the price in standardized drudgery might prove. In the twenty years from 1900 to 1920, the city's population grew from 285,000 to nearly one million.

ARCHITECTURE AND ART

With the city's financial coming-of-age, Detroit began to acquire the standard cultural accoutrements of the major American cities of the era. Central here is the cluster of institutions that still impressively preside on Woodward Avenue, officially designated as the city's Cultural Center. These include Cass Gilbert's Detroit Public Library (1915–1921); Paul Cret's Detroit Institute of Arts (DIA) of 1927, which faces the library and reflects its beaux arts style; and the Wayne State University campus, which includes the school's Old Main (1898; formerly Central High School) and the Merrill-Palmer Institute (1890–1893), built as the Charles Lang Freer house and which once housed Whistler's Peacock Room. A variety of houses of worship still grace Woodward as well, especially in the area known as Piety Hill, and include Ralph Adams Cram's Cathedral Church of St. Paul (1908–1911), the aisles of which are lined with Pewabic pottery from the local Arts-and-Crafts kilns founded by Mary Chase Perry Stratton. Nearby is the Fox Theatre (1927–1928), a fortunately well-preserved "Eclectic Hindu-Siamese-

Downtown Detroit, c. 1930s. Mall Street: the Union Guardian Building (1927–1929, *far left*), the Penobscot Building (1928, *center*), and old City Hall (1871, *foreground*). © HULTON-DEUTSCH COLLECTION/CORBIS

Byzantine" extravaganza from the golden age of the movies (Eckert, *Buildings of Michigan*, p. 72).

Perhaps more representative of Detroit's commercial culture is its cluster of art-deco office buildings in the downtown area at which Woodward culminates. These include the Penobscot Building, designed by Wirt Rowland of Smith, Hynchman, and Grylls; completed in 1928, it features American Indian motifs in its exterior stone and metalwork. Rowland's nearby Guardian Building of the same period, designed to house the offices of the Union Trust Company, is an even more exuberant display of Pewabic and Rookwood tiles along with glass, metal, and terra-cotta ornament in a profusion of green, white, orange, black, and pink. The craftsmanship and materials lavished on the structure earned it the designation of "Cathedral of Finance" from a local newspaper at the time of its opening. Another local architect, Albert Kahn, was responsible for two other notable nearby skyscrapers. The General Motors Building of 1919–1921 consists of a fifteen-story central block with four projecting wings on each side, reflecting and providing an appropriate space for the vertical integration that was beginning to characterize the emergent auto indus-

try. Kahn's Fisher Building of 1927–1929 was designed not only for commercial offices but also as an elaborately decorated, self-contained mall in which urbanites might shop at tasteful stores, conduct banking necessities, have dinner, and take in a movie without having stepped outside.

Kahn, however, is most notable as the architect who was able to provide Henry Ford with the precise sort of infrastructure needed to carry out what Frederick Lewis Allen dubbed "the dynamic logic of mass production." When Ford became frustrated with the limitations of the multistoried, masonry-frame structures in which he began his operations, Kahn was at hand to design the revolutionary Highland Park Plant of 1910. Here, all auto-assembly operations took place under one roof, made possible by concrete-slab, girder-beam construction, with no open courts or dividing walls to interrupt the flow of Model T bodies. The River Rouge Plant, begun in 1917 and gradually expanded during the following decade, carried these construction principles still farther to create an uninterrupted half-mile assembly line housed under open beams and continuous glass walls that simultaneously provided improved lighting, ventilation, and fire safety.

First Moving Assembly Line, Ford Highland Park Plant, 1913. In December 1915, after less than thirteen years in business, the Ford Motor Company produced its one-millionth car. COURTESY OF THE FRANCES LOEB LIBRARY, GRADUATE SCHOOL OF DESIGN, HARVARD UNIVERSITY

Ford was drawn to Kahn as an ideal collaborator: a capable designer with a strong business sense who was willing to subordinate aesthetics to functional concerns and his ego to the outsized one of his employer. The contradiction inherent in the relationship lay in Kahn's having been the immigrant son of a German rabbi while Ford was publishing one of the major anti-Semitic screeds of the period, *The Dearborn Independent,* which featured articles such as "Jewish Jazz—Moron Music—Becomes Our National Music." The two helped to make one another rich, however, and both seemed to acquiesce in their accommodation, even though Kahn also produced designs for other major automakers and other industries at home and even in the Soviet Union (oddly enough, with Ford's blessing). Indeed, by 1938, 19 percent of the architect-designed

industrial building in the United States had come out of Kahn's enormous firm.

Kahn also designed a considerable number of other sorts of buildings, including some important contributions to the University of Michigan's campus as well as the suburban homes of Detroit's automotive executive corps. Henry Ford, interestingly, chose a different (Gentile) and probably less-talented architect for his own Dearborn home, "Fairlane," a composite of English and Scottish styles located not too far from Greenfield Village, the idealized and highly eclectic re-creation of small-town America that Ford built alongside a major museum of automotive history. Henry's son Edsel, kept perpetually under his father's thumb, was more open to cosmopolitan influences despite his father's having denied him a college education on

Charles R. Sheeler Jr., *River Rouge Plant.* Oil on canvas, 1932. After photographing Ford's River Rouge plant in 1927, Sheeler was inspired to create a series of paintings. PHOTOGRAPH COPYRIGHT © 2000: WHITNEY MUSEUM OF ART

the grounds of its impracticality, and commissioned Kahn as the architect of his own palatial Cotswolds-style home in Grosse Pointe Shores, one of the riverfront suburbs of choice for the local leaders of industry. Edsel himself achieved some distinction in the emergent field of automotive design, an area his father had scrupulously ignored until forced to pay attention to the aesthetics of his machines through competition from General Motors.

A more daring and far-reaching act of artistic patronage on Edsel's part, however, was his role in financing Diego Rivera's *Detroit Industry* murals (1932–1933) in the Garden Court of the Detroit Institute of Arts. The younger Ford and his wife had for some time been cultivated and tutored by William Valentiner, the German-born director of the

DIA who used his influence to negotiate this memorable project. Although one of the premier mural artists of the Mexican Revolution, whose open use of Marxist symbols would later lead to the destruction of his work at Rockefeller Center, Rivera was quite taken both with the Fords—he regarded Edsel as an artist in his own right—and with the material and human spectacle provided by the Rouge Plant. The resultant murals, which combine a technically realistic rendering of the means of industrial production with mythic allegorical figures, are ideologically ambiguous, readable at once as an indictment of American capitalism and as an exaltation of the combined might of the men and machines who made up the assembly line. Although public reception was originally hostile, Edsel Ford stood by

611

Rivera, and the murals remain one of the museum's treasures. Ford was also instrumental in commissioning a series of paintings and photographs of "the Rouge" by Charles Sheeler, who was fascinated by the plant's formal qualities and produced a series of images in which humans are entirely absent.

Another collaborative artistic project of enduring significance grew out of the association of George G. Booth, the Canadian-born publisher of the *Detroit News,* and Eliel Saarinen, the Finnish-born architect whose second-place-winning submission in the *Chicago Tribune* tower competition originally brought him to the United States and to a teaching position at the University of Michigan. Booth's Anglo-Canadian forebears had been craftsmen, and he had been instrumental in the founding of the Detroit Society of Arts and Crafts in 1906. He was attracted to Saarinen, who had been shaped by Finland's nationalistic recovery of its folk art tradition, as one who shared his ideals of the integration of beautiful design into the stuff of everyday life.

The institutional context for the Booth-Saarinen collaboration was the Cranbrook Educational Community, which had its roots in Booth's attempt to recover his family's Kentish past in the rolling countryside of Bloomfield Hills, a then-rural area which would eventually rival the Grosse Pointes as the preferred suburban locale for the executive set. Cranbrook began with the Booth house, designed by Albert Kahn (begun 1907) in the English manor-house style that reflected the widespread Anglophilia of the regional elite. Booth, however, was interested in more than superficial effects and used his grand house to display a number of original works he had commissioned in the Arts-and-Crafts mode, including woodwork by John Kirchmayer, an Albert Herter tapestry with a Crusader motif juxtaposing medieval knights and General Pershing, and, inevitably, Pewabic tile by his friend Mary Chase Perry Stratton.

Cranbrook House was the nucleus for a rapidly expanding set of institutions that were mostly educational but also included Christ Church Cranbrook (Episcopal) by Bertram Goodhue Associates (1925–1928). Saarinen's first design work was the Cranbrook School for boys, which would later be supplemented by elementary schools for boys and girls as well as a science institute, an art museum, and a library. Most enduring in its cultural influence, though, has been the Cranbrook Academy of Art, a complex of buildings designed by Saarinen; he became its first president in 1932. The Academy has been described in its early existence as a com-

bination of school, atelier, and art colony. For several years it resisted granting degrees or adopting a formal curriculum, attempting instead to create a community in which established artists in residence would work together with aspiring younger creative folk. The entire Saarinen family, whose campus house has been refurbished as a museum, participated in the venture; Eliel's wife, Loja, was an accomplished weaver, their daughter Pipsan designed the campus interiors, and son Eero, who also designed furniture, later emerged as a major national architect in his own right.

Under Saarinen's aegis, Cranbrook rapidly developed into a cosmopolitan island, mirroring Detroit's polyglot character in its own elite collection of artists, many of them foreign-born. A crucial early appointment was that of Carl Milles, the Swedish sculptor whose archaizing classicism was similar to that of his American contemporary Paul Manship, whose work is also represented on campus. Saarinen was eventually succeeded as president by the Hungarian-born painter Zoltan Sepeshy, whose post-cubist realism included many scenes of Michigan life; his "Woodward Avenue No. II" of 1934, for example, includes references to Father Coughlin's Shrine of the Little Flower incongruously juxtaposed with Hedge's Wigwam, an Indian-themed eatery known for its chicken pies. Commercial and industrial design were included within the Cranbrook ambit from the beginning, following the philosophy that there should be no lines drawn between pure and applied art or between arts and crafts. The furniture design of Eero Saarinen and Charles Eames, for example, helped provide a national style for the 1950s.

SOCIAL CHANGE: LABOR, RELIGION, IN-MIGRATION

The prosperity upon which the Booth and Ford fortunes were built was not shared universally, especially after the great crash of 1929. Detroit's contributions to social change have always been more in the applied than the theoretical realm, as evidenced in the labor movement, which became almost as synonymous with the city's name as that of the auto industry for which it provided the skill and muscle. Perhaps not surprisingly, Henry Ford was the most recalcitrant of the management cadre in recognizing the right of collective bargaining. The "Battle of the Overpass" of May 1937, which pitted Ford's security chief Harry Bennett and his thugs against Walter Reuther and the United Auto Workers, created such bad publicity that even Ford capitulated. In 1951, the opening of Solidarity House as the UAW's international headquarters symbolized the city's prominence in the labor movement, just as the disappearance of former Teamsters' president Jimmy Hoffa from the parking lot of the Machus Red Fox restaurant in nearby Birmingham in 1975 came to epitomize the difficulties into which the movement later descended.

Despite the predominance of the practical, Detroit did make two contributions in the realm of social debate during the overheated prosperity of the 1920s and the corresponding despondency of the following decade. Reinhold Niebuhr, whose name would become virtually synonymous with the neo-orthodox movement in American Protestant theology, took up the pastorate of Bethel [German] Evangelical Church in northwestern Detroit upon his completion of graduate study at Yale in 1915 and remained at that post until his acceptance of a teaching position at Union Theological Seminary in New York City thirteen years later. During his tenure at Bethel, the old German parish grew remarkably despite its pastor's lengthy absences for speaking engagements and began to attract many who were intrigued by Niebuhr's proclamations on social topics and the church's role as a staging ground for vigorous public debate on the issues of the day. Although Niebuhr chaired a mayoral commission on racial issues in 1926, his heart was always more in the debate over what he saw as the failure of modern industrial society not only to provide its working people with decent wages and working conditions, but even more with the spiritual poverty that mindlessly repetitive industrial work engendered. He saw organized labor as too shortsighted in its preoccupation with material advances, and identified Henry Ford as, in the words of Niebuhr's biographer Richard Fox, "the man of limitless authority whose spirit was as mechanical as his product" (*Reinhold Niebuhr*, p. 109). Many of Niebuhr's Detroit-era writings were collected in his first book, *Does Civilization Need Religion?* (1927); his second work, *Leaves from the Notebook of a Tamed Cynic* (1929), was a reflection on the conflict between his pastoral and prophetic roles during his time at Bethel.

As Reinhold Niebuhr was nearing the end of his Detroit stint, another clergyman appeared on the scene who shared both Niebuhr's concerns for social justice and his public presence, although with considerably different long-term results. Charles Coughlin was a Roman Catholic priest from Ontario who in 1926 was assigned by Bishop Michael Gallagher to Royal Oak, Michigan—then a hotbed of Ku Klux Klan activity—to build a shrine to the recently canonized St. Thérèse of Lisieux, the "Little Flower of Jesus." Coughlin openly defied the anti-Catholic Klan and took to the airwaves to raise money for his new enterprise. The material result was the octagonal Shrine of the Little Flower (Henry McGill, 1929–1931) at Woodward and Twelve Mile Road, one of the few churches designed in the art-deco style and overshadowed by a soaring limestone Charity Crucifixion Tower.

Although the Shrine has outlasted Coughlin, who died in 1979 after a forty-year career as its pastor, he is remembered today not so much for carrying out his bishop's charge but rather as the "radio priest" of the Depression years who challenged Franklin Roosevelt and lost. After the onset of hard times, Coughlin's campaign for social justice for working people, which was based on the teachings of Pope Leo XIII as well as on his own experience in a working-class parish in Kalamazoo, attracted such a vast radio audience that a new post office had to be built in Royal Oak to handle his correspondence. Coughlin's urban populism was at first directed toward helping elect Franklin Roosevelt in 1932. Before long, however, Coughlin turned against Roosevelt and helped organize the Union Party, whose 1936 nomination of William Lemke now ranks as a minor historical footnote. More alarming as the 1930s progressed were Coughlin's growing anti-Semitism and pro-Nazi sympathies; the convergent forces of episcopal disapproval and a grand-jury investigation led to his retirement from the airwaves and the end of his publication, *Social Justice*, after the outbreak of World War II.

The anti-Semitism of Ford and Coughlin provoked growing protests from Detroit's substantial Jewish community, such as that of Philip Slomovitz, the founder and editor of the *The Jewish News*. By the 1920s, Jews were only one among the manifold ethnic communities that ranked Detroit near the top of the American scale in terms of diversity. Beginning with aboriginal peoples and then the French and British, the city attracted considerable numbers of Irish and Germans in the nineteenth century. The new immigration era prior to World War I brought Belgians, Greeks, Hungarians, Italians, and Russians as well as Armenians, Lebanese, and Syrians, so that Dearborn in particular became an early major center of an American Islamic presence. Mexican immigrants created yet another kind of diversity, as did the Appalachians drawn to the city's industries during World War II, whose stories were told in Harriette Arnow's 1954 novel *The Doll-*

maker. The most conspicuous ethnic presence, however, was that of Polish immigrants and their offspring, who by 1930 numbered more than a third of a million. Hamtramck, which for many years was an independent city entirely surrounded by Detroit, and the home of the Dodge Main plant, remains a major Midwestern Polonia. Dominated by St. Florian Catholic Church—designed in 1925 by the Anglican Gothic revivalist Ralph Adams Cram—the neighborhood remains a neat enclave of working-class homes and ethnic shops, even though many of its residents have fled to Warren and other blue-collar suburbs to the north. Although a lively polka culture has existed in Polish Detroit, it has not proven as musically innovative as that of Chicago, Milwaukee, or Buffalo. Other Polish-language institutions once flourished in the area, but by the end of the twentieth century, assimilation-minded generations had substantially weakened them.

AFRICAN AMERICAN DETROIT AND THE GROWTH OF MOTOWN

In addition to the foreign-born, who in 1930 constituted nearly a third of the city's population, Detroit's population also grew with the in-migration of both Appalachian whites and blacks from the deeper South seeking employment, particularly during war-generated periods of industrial demand for labor. Tension between the races periodically erupted in lamentably memorable fashion, notably during the Civil War and World War II. By the 1930s, the Detroit ghetto had become a major center of African American life, rivaling Harlem and Chicago's South Side. During the 1930s, W. D. Fard, an itinerant seller of silks in the "Paradise Valley" black business and recreational district, made a disciple of a recent Garveyite migrant from Georgia named Elijah Poole. After Fard's never-resolved disappearance in 1934, Poole, who took on the name of Elijah Muhammad, proclaimed Fard's divinity and moved to Chicago to form the nucleus of the Nation of Islam, or Black Muslims. Malcolm X, who, despite his Lansing-area origins, had been known in the East as "Detroit Red," arrived in the Motor City after his release from a Massachusetts prison in 1952 to preside over "Mosque No. 1," the "mother church" of the Nation. More mainstream but also innovative religious leadership was provided by C. L. Franklin, who arrived in the city in 1946 from Mississippi via Buffalo. The popular sermons of this "jitterbug preacher" were not only broadcast over local radio but recorded and distributed nationally by Chicago's Chess Records, which is better remembered for its association with Chuck Berry and other early rock stars. Franklin's Gospel Caravan and the Clara Ward Singers took their show on the road nationally and provided an early platform for, among other gospel performers, Franklin's daughter Aretha.

The gulf between "saints and sinners" in black culture, historically represented by gospel music and the blues, was not an unbridgeable one in Detroit. Franklin's New Bethel Baptist Church was attended, at least periodically, by Smokey Robinson, Mary Wilson of the Supremes, Berry Gordy Jr., and, during their appearances in town, B. B. King and Lionel Hampton. Franklin, conversely, was friends with Dinah Washington and Art Tatum, and frequented nightspots such as the Flame Show Bar, where jazz, rhythm and blues, and other distinctively black urban musical genres flourished. One of the most successful bridgings of these worlds was represented by Motown Records—also known as "Hitsville USA"—and its impresario, Berry Gordy Jr. Gordy's parents were an entrepreneurial black couple from Georgia who established a successful business significantly named the Booker T. Washington Grocery Store, which employed the entire Gordy family. After various unsuccessful attempts at finding a career, the younger Gordy established Motown Records, a paradigmatic black enterprise that appealed to both the black and white taste communities. Gordy developed a musical formula with crossover appeal, recruited local talent that had honed their musical skills in gospel choirs and high-school programs as well as on street corners and in housing project stairwells, and emulated the auto industry in making record production a carefully articulated and coordinated process from beginning to end, including teaching the performers grooming and behavioral skills. He thereby succeeded in generating a sound that would epitomize a decade and make a fortune for himself in the process. The Temptations, the Supremes, Smokey Robinson and the Miracles, Martha and the Vandellas, Marvin Gaye, Stevie Wonder, and, ultimately, the Jackson Five, created a whole new genre of popular music whose appeal has outlasted its own time of creation.

As Suzanne Smith (whose *Dancing in the Streets* is a major source for this section) notes, however, the great black American success story of Motown possessed deep ambiguities. Gordy was both clever and lucky in appearing at the right time and place, when the sounds of the urban ghetto were being discovered by nonblack fans but had not yet been exploited by the major recording companies. His ability to produce a black sound that was not as threatening to whites as the earthier rhythm-and-blues genre launched him—and his carefully programmed performers—on a road to economic success that began with an emulation of C. L. Franklin's Gospel Caravan and ended with an operation more closely resembling General Motors. Ultimately, Motown became increasingly estranged from its local roots, culminating in its move to Los Angeles in 1972 and Gordy's selling his own interest to MCA in 1988 for $61 million. The road to success led ultimately not only out of the ghetto but entirely away from the Motor City itself.

UNREST AND ITS AFTERMATH

Gordy and his enterprise became involved with another contradiction: the growing difficulty of keeping together what had in fact become two separate Detroits. Beginning in the years following World War II, urban renewal—also known ironically as "Negro removal"—disrupted the old black culture that had centered on Hastings Street as the old neighborhood was condemned by the city and sold to developers or used for the welter of interstate highways that would make urban employment and suburban residence an increasingly attractive option for white folk. Motown, in short, was the exception rather than the rule in its apparent illustration of the possibility of success through entrepreneurship in the context of the inner city. The culmination of the tensions engendered by the long-term problem of finding affordable housing and a growing rate of unemployment in an era of deindustrialization took place on 23 July 1967, when police raided a "blind pig" (illegal bar) on Twelfth Street, which had replaced Hastings Avenue as the center of popular nightlife. The response was an outburst of looting and arson, much of it directed by blacks against other blacks, which was more expressive of pent-up anger than of any systematic ideology. After some delay, federal paratroops were sent in to restore order. When the dust had settled, forty-three people were dead, with more than seven hundred injured and seven thousand arrested; property damage ran to $50 million. A related incident involving the shooting deaths of three local men by police prompted widespread indignation and an investigative report by the novelist John Hersey in his *The Algiers Motel Incident.*

The city was badly polarized by what had variously been called the "Detroit Riot" or the "Great Rebellion" of 1967, with vast numbers of whites leaving the city during the next few months and the eventual election in 1973 of Coleman Young as the city's first black mayor. During his lengthy reign, Young and his rhetoric continued to exacerbate tensions with the blue-collar white suburbanites of northeastern Macomb County and their upscale counterparts in Oakland County, one of the wealthiest in the nation. A cadre of more radical black leaders came to the fore, such as Milton and Richard Henry, founders of the Republic of New Africa, and Albert B. Cleage Jr., a longtime political activist and United Church of Christ minister who commissioned an eighteen-foot mural of an African-hued Virgin Mary for his Shrine of the Black Madonna at Central Congregational Church. In his 1968 collection of sermons, *The Black Messiah,* Cleage followed the lead of the Garveyite African Orthodox Church of the 1920s in arguing that Jesus—and, for that matter, God—had been literally black. This black separatist position, however, gained few adherents either among more traditional-minded black Christians or the Marxist-oriented secular militants of the Black Power movement. Cleage was also instrumental in stimulating local cultural projects through Blacks Arts conventions and other activities at his shrine. Motown, caught in the middle, responded by allying itself cautiously with an activistic stance, releasing recordings such as the Supremes' "Love Child" (1968) and Marvin Gaye's "What's Going On?" (1971), with themes that addressed contemporary social issues. Before long, however, the entire operation had abandoned the city of its roots.

During the remainder of the twentieth century, Detroit made some economic and cultural recovery, despite ill-starred attempts such as the 1977 Renaissance Center to stimulate downtown business activity. Coleman Young was eventually succeeded by Dennis Archer, a mayor with a more irenic stance toward the white suburbs. Traditional cultural centers such as the DIA began to revive after having faced extreme stringencies, and the Charles H. Wright Museum of African American History joined the city's Cultural Center in an expanded home in 1997. Robert Graham's 1986 sculpture at Woodward and Jefferson of a giant fist as a tribute to the local boxing hero Joe Louis was a public expression of the city's gritty determination in the face of massive adversity. Despite this resurgent vitality, one cannot say that Detroit even in its heyday in the 1920s was a strong candidate to be the Paris of America, just as today it may be excessive to regard it as a collective memento mori, a horrible example of the urbanization process taken to extreme, third

615

world-like conclusions. It has never, to be sure, been home to a very impressive literary culture; only a handful of reasonably well-known local authors come to mind, such as Edgar A. Guest, a sort of urban James Whitcomb Riley and the author of now nearly forgotten verse collections such as *A Heap o' Livin'* (1916); L. E. Sissman, a poet of some distinction (*Dying, An Introduction*, 1967), who left the city for Harvard and New York; and, perhaps most representative, Elmore Leonard, the good-humoredly hard-boiled author of suspense novels such as *Glitz* (1985) and *Get Shorty* (1990). The fine arts have perhaps done better, as in the case of Cranbrook, although the observation in one local history that "Detroit has had a number of famous

artists including Alvah Bradish, John Mix Stanley, Julius Robhoven, Robert Hopkin, and Gari Melchers" (Woodford and Woodford, *All Our Yesterdays*, p. 172) may not ring entirely true today. The major examples of local cultural distinction—Kahn's factories, Booth's Cranbrook, Rivera's murals, and Gordy's Motown—are all interesting not only on their merits but also as examples of the economic bases of cultural production. In each case, the relationship between sponsors and artists was somewhat different, but in no case would the artistic products have been possible without the support of established or emerging capitalists. Whatever the Motor City may be, it is certainly a place where art and money have enjoyed an intimate relationship.

See also **Urban Cultural Institutions** *(volume 1); and other articles in this section.*

BIBLIOGRAPHY

Chafets, Ze'ev. *Devil's Night: And Other True Tales of Detroit.* New York, 1990.

Colby, Joy Hakanson. *Art and a City: A History of the Detroit Society of Arts and Crafts.* Detroit, 1956.

Eckert, Kathryn Bishop. *Buildings of Michigan.* New York, 1993.

Ferry, W. Hawkins. *The Buildings of Detroit: A History.* Detroit, 1980.

———. *The Legacy of Albert Kahn.* Detroit, 1987.

Fox, Richard Wightman. *Reinhold Niebuhr: A Biography.* New York, 1985.

Herron, Jerry. *AfterCulture: Detroit and the Humiliation of History.* Detroit, 1993.

Hersey, John. *The Algiers Motel Incident.* New York, 1968.

Hildebrand, Grant. *Designing for Industry: The Architecture of Albert Kahn.* Cambridge, Mass., 1974.

Jacob, Mary Jane, and Linda Downs. *The Rouge: The Image of Industry in the Art of Charles Sheeler and Diego Rivera.* Detroit, 1978.

Kempton, Arthur. "The Lost Tycoons." *New York Review of Books* (20 May 1999), 68–73; "The Fall of the Black Empires" (10 June 1999), 50–56.

Lacey, Robert. *Ford: The Men and the Machine.* Boston, 1986.

Nawrocki, Dennis Alan. *Art in Detroit Public Places.* Detroit, 1999.

Peck, William H. *The Detroit Institute of Arts: A Brief History.* Detroit, 1991.

Pound, Arthur. *The Only Thing Worth Finding: The Life and Legacies of George Gough Booth.* Detroit, 1964.

Schmeckebier, Laurence. *Zoltan Sepeshy.* Syracuse, N.Y., 1966.

Sinclair, Robert. *Metropolitan Detroit: An Anatomy of Social Change.* Cambridge, Mass., 1977.

Smith, Suzanne E. *Dancing in the Streets: Motown and the Cultural Politics of Detroit.* Cambridge, Mass., 1999.

Westbrook, Adele, and Anne Yarowsky, eds. *Design in America: The Cranbrook Vision, 1925–1950.* New York, 1983.

Wittkopp, Gregory, ed. *Saarinen House and Garden.* New York and Bloomfield Hills, Mich., 1995.

Woodford, Frank B., and Arthur M. Woodford. *All Our Yesterdays: A Brief History of Detroit.* Detroit, 1969.

Wrobel, Paul. *Our Way: Family, Parish, and Neighborhood in a Polish-American Community.* Notre Dame, Ind., 1979.

The author would like to thank Robert A. Benson of Miami University and Nick Salvatore of Cornell University for their invaluable contributions to this essay.

CINCINNATI

Robert C. Vitz

THE EARLY YEARS, 1815–1840

In the nineteenth century Boston and Philadelphia and then New York City dominated the nation's artistic and intellectual development. Expansion beyond the Appalachian Mountains led to the development of regional centers, and until late in the century Cincinnati served as the most important one. Its rise to prominence was in part an accident of geography and in part the result of committed citizens.

In 1812 Cincinnati, an Ohio frontier community not yet twenty-five years old, could scarcely have foreseen the astonishing growth that would soon expand its boundaries and make it the "Queen City of the West," a phrase made popular by a Henry Wadsworth Longfellow poem titled "Catawba Wine" (1854). Although the city quickly became the most important commercial center in the rapidly developing Northwest Territory, two slightly older and larger cities, Pittsburgh to the east and Lexington, Kentucky, to the south, attracted more attention in the century's first decades. However, over the next twenty years, several factors combined to push Cincinnati past its rivals: military spending during the War of 1812, the arrival of steam navigation, a rapidly increasing flow of settlers into the Ohio Valley, and the construction of the Miami and Erie Canal. By 1830 Cincinnati boasted a population of 25,000 and had surpassed both Pittsburgh and Lexington as the leading urban center in the western region. With economic supremacy in hand, the city quickly emerged as the intellectual and cultural center of the West, benefiting from its transportation links, its financial base, and the number of citizens concerned with replicating eastern urban amenities.

For most of its first forty years Cincinnati's cultural development did not markedly distinguish it from other western communities, but in the 1820s and early 1830s there were serious, if inconsistent, efforts in theater, music, and art. Appearances by professional troupes along with performances by the actors Edwin Forrest and Junius Brutus Booth led in 1837 to the opening of the National Theatre, the largest theater building west of Philadelphia and north of New Orleans. About the same time music found early public acceptance in a Haydn Society, several music academies, a short-lived amateur orchestra, and serious church choirs. The artist and ornithologist John Audubon drew four of his bird portraits while working at the city's Western Museum Society (now the Museum of Natural History and Science), itself an early effort (1818) at promoting interest in the natural sciences. More significantly, the city supported, albeit modestly, a range of literary and intellectual activities that culminated in the Semi-Colon Club (c. 1833–1845). Founded by the physician Daniel Drake, the Semi-Colon Club included sisters Catharine Beecher and Harriet Beecher Stowe, William Henry Channing, James Handasyd Perkins, Timothy Flint, Elizabeth Blackwell, Caroline Lee Hentz, and James Hall. Flint and Hall also published transitory literary journals that promoted regional writing. In the late 1830s Channing and Perkins, cousins and transplanted Bostonians, for several years turned the journal *Western Messenger* (1835–1841) into an outpost of New England transcendentalism, publishing works by Ralph Waldo Emerson, William Ellery Channing, Margaret Fuller, and John Sullivan Dwight.

THE ATHENS OF THE WEST, 1840–1860

By the 1840s Cincinnati basked in the glory of its artists. The sculptor Hiram Powers, who began his career as a maker of wax figures for the Western Museum, caught the attention of Nicholas Longworth, a wealthy landowner, vintner, and patron of art, who financially supported Powers's career first in the city and later in Italy, where he enjoyed an international reputation. Longworth also helped launch the careers of the painters William Henry

Nicholas Longworth (1782–1863). Although trained as a lawyer, the New Jersey–born Longworth came to Cincinnati in 1803, where he soon amassed a fortune in real estate. He supported artists and maintained a vineyard on the ridge behind his home; in fact, his Catawba wine inspired the Longfellow poem. His son Joseph and granddaughter Maria continued the Longworth involvement in the arts, and his great-grandson, Nicholas Longworth III, became Speaker of the House of Representatives and husband of Alice Roosevelt. CINCINNATI MUSEUM CENTER IMAGE ARCHIVES

Powell, Thomas Buchanan Read, Robert S. Duncanson, and Alexander Helwig Wyant. Including James Henry Beard, William Louis Sonntag, Thomas Worthington Whittredge, Joseph Oriel Eaton, and Godfrey N. Frankenstein, the city of Cincinnati boasted an impressive number of artists. To provide ready incomes these artists painted portraits and sculpted busts of the city's socially prominent men and women; for exhibition they frequently painted landscapes, making up an informal western branch of the Hudson River school.

While the most talented of these artists eventually headed to New York or to Europe, those who remained secured the city's reputation as a significant regional art center, complete with galleries, artist organizations, classes, and private studios. "Cincinnati! What is there in the atmosphere of Cincinnati that has so thoroughly awakened the arts of sculpture and painting?," a *New York Star* editor wondered in 1840, and five years later the *New York*

Tribune singled out "wealth, genius, and beauty" as those features which set off the "Western Metropolis" (Vitz, *The Queen and the Arts,* p. 35). In 1847 artists and patrons launched the Western Art Union, designed to encourage artists and patterned after New York's better known American Art Union. Although it lasted fewer than five years, at its peak the Western Art Union numbered almost five thousand members, stimulated interest in local artists, and had its own exhibition gallery.

As befit the nation's fastest-growing city, Cincinnati took pride in other cultural endeavors, especially music. Stephen Collins Foster, working as a bookkeeper in his brother's riverfront office, spent four years in the city (1846–1850), attending musical events, including blackface minstrel shows, and absorbing the dialect and rhythms of African American roustabouts on the levee. During his Cincinnati years he composed "O! Susanna," "Uncle Ned," "Away Down South," and possibly "Gwine to Run All Night" ("Camptown Races"). About the same time Victor Williams organized an amateur orchestra and Timothy B. Mason and Charles Aiken introduced music into the public school curriculum. A swelling influx of German immigrants soon brought even greater musical dividends. In 1846 local German singing societies organized a small outdoor musical festival, followed in 1849 by a regional Saengerfest, a three-day celebration of song and fellowship that brought choral groups from Louisville, Kentucky, and Madison, Indiana. From this activity emerged the Saengerbund of North America and ever-larger annual festivals that rotated among the principal western cities. Although Anglo-Americans were often offended by the free-flowing beer and the inclusion of Sunday afternoon festivities, for the most part German musical sophistication helped break down the nativist hostility that spawned anti-German riots in Cincinnati and other cities during the 1850s.

The decade before the Civil War brought to the city even more sophisticated musical entertainment. The recently arrived composer Frédéric Louis Ritter, German born and trained, founded the Cecelia Society, an eighty-member chorus, and an orchestra, the Cincinnati Philharmonic, more polished than the defunct amateur orchestra of the 1840s. Choral performances by the Cecilia Society and the Maennerchor, the leading all-German chorus, drew enthusiastic audiences. Thus, on the eve of the Civil War, Cincinnati had experienced solid orchestral and choral music, supported a succession of musical academies, and witnessed the emergence of the Saengerfests. As one visitor phrased it, "I have

DR. DANIEL DRAKE

In the first half of the nineteenth century Daniel Drake served as Cincinnati's most zealous advocate, as well as supplying much of the stimulus for the city's early intellectual life. Born in New Jersey in 1785 and reared in May's Lick, Kentucky, Drake studied medicine with William Goforth in Cincinnati from 1800 to 1804. After additional study in Philadelphia, he spent most of his professional life in the Queen City. He founded the Ohio Medical College, now the University of Cincinnati College of Medicine, and was affiliated with several other medical schools in the region. Although his somewhat acerbic personality resulted in occasional quarrels with colleagues, his versatile interests led many to call him the "Franklin of the West." Based on his observations and medical experience, he wrote his most important professional work, the two-volume *A Systematic Treatise . . . on the Principal Diseases of the Interior Valley of North America* (1850, 1854), but he is better known today for his many civic activities.

In *A Natural and Statistical View, or Picture of Cincinnati and the Miami Country* (1815), he provided observations on economic development, weather, the New Madrid earthquake, prehistoric mounds in the area, and medicinal plants, along with a brief history of Cincinnati that encouraged immigration into the region. In 1818 Drake helped found the Western Museum Society (now the Museum of Natural History and Science), which promoted scientific knowledge. In the 1830s, to foster intellectual activity, he organized first the Buckeye Club and then the somewhat more structured Semi-Colon Club, where members contributed their literary efforts, usually read by William Greene to preserve anonymity and protect female members from any embarrassment of public speaking. Drake served in a number of appointed positions in the city and strove tirelessly for various urban improvements. He advocated improved sanitation, canal building, and a railroad connection to the South and was instrumental in establishing libraries, educational institutions, and hospitals. He died in 1852.

found it to be the prevailing opinion, that in Cincinnati very nearly all . . . must be acquainted with the science of music" (Ritter, *Music in America*, p. 376).

During this same period Cincinnatians made several attempts to establish colleges. In 1819 the Cincinnati College opened its doors, but inadequate funding led to its demise in the 1840s. Also in 1819 Daniel Drake organized the Medical College of Ohio and in 1835 the short-lived Medical Department in the Cincinnati College, while Timothy Walker helped found the Cincinnati Law School in 1833. Twenty-five years later businessman Charles McMicken bequeathed a considerable part of his estate to the city for the establishment of a public college. Although legal obstacles and the Civil War delayed the school's opening until 1873, city leaders used the opportunity to consolidate the Medical College of Ohio, the McMicken School of Design, the Cincinnati Astronomical Society, along with several other institutions and various educational funds into the municipal University of Cincinnati. The university quickly became the center of the community's intellectual life, and among its many distinguished faculty have been President William Howard Taft, the archaeologist Carl Blegin, and the physician Albert B. Sabin.

Xavier University, initially named The Athenaeum, opened in 1831 as the first Catholic college in the old Northwest Territory. The panic of 1837 eroded its funding, however, and in 1840 the Society of Jesus took control and renamed the school St. Xavier College. For the next ninety years the school remained relatively small, maintaining a traditional classical curriculum. In 1930 it became Xavier University and it has steadily expanded its presence in the city. In 1854 Isaac Mayer Wise arrived in Cincinnati to become rabbi of the K. K. Bene Yeshurun Congregation. His efforts to modernize rabbinical training led to the founding of the Hebrew Theological Institute, now Hebrew Union College. Wise served as the college's first president. Under his leadership and later that of Nelson Glueck and Alfred Gottschalk, it became a world center for Judaic scholarship.

Rabbi Wise was part of Cincinnati's mid-nineteenth century German flowering. By 1860 German immigrants made up over 30 percent of the city's population, and they established many of their own institutions. Besides singing societies, German churches, schools, savings societies, political organizations, and newspaper offices dotted the district known as Over-the-Rhine. In 1848 recently arrived Germans established the first American Turnverein, and Turnhalle became a focal point of German-American culture, with art classes, a library, a chorus, a band, a theater, and a strong physical fitness program. Two of the most prominent Germans were Johann Bernhard Stallo, who arrived in 1839, and August Willich, an early associate of Friedrich Engels and a militant participant in the 1848 revolution, who came in 1858. Stallo went on to a distinguished career as a judge, while Willich earned recognition as a newspaper editor and Civil War general, but their lasting reputations reflect their stature as two of the leading exponents of Hegelian philosophy in the United States.

Literary and intellectual activity further swelled Cincinnati's reputation. Societies for history, horticulture, and astronomy, as well as a public library, suggest the breadth of local interests. The short-lived Cincinnati College had brought William Holmes McGuffey as its president, and he and his brother Alexander Hamilton McGuffey published their popular Readers, beginning in 1836. Although the Semi-Colon Club had expired some years earlier, and the city's most prominent writers-to-be, Harriet Beecher Stowe and poets Alice and Phoebe Cary, had departed for the East, the Literary Club appeared in October 1849. Spearheaded by Ainsworth Rand Spofford, a bookseller and later the librarian of Congress (1864–1897), the Literary Club's early members included such luminaries as Rutherford B. Hayes; Murat Halstead, editor of the *Cincinnati Commercial;* the statesman Salmon P. Chase; the astronomer Ormsby McKnight Mitchel, who single-handedly established the Cincinnati Observatory; Alphonso Taft, father of the future president William H. Taft; and the German-American

philosopher Stallo. Topical papers and lively discussions made up the weekly meetings. The club also brought Ralph Waldo Emerson to the city in 1850 for the first of his five visits. Soon after Emerson's visit, a railroad connection to the east made the city a convenient stop on a national lecture circuit that brought many of the country's finest minds to the Ohio Valley. Following the sage of Concord came the educator Amos Bronson Alcott, the theologian Theodore Parker, the clergyman Henry Ward Beecher, the educator Horace Mann, the reformer Wendell Phillips, the statesman Carl Schurz, the essayist and educator Oliver Wendell Holmes, Sr., and the naturalist Jean Louis Agassiz.

In 1856 Moncure Conway, a Unitarian minister, Emerson disciple, and transplanted Virginian, launched *The Dial,* an attempt to rekindle the literary transcendentalist flame. He published local contributions, as well as material submitted by the clergyman Octavius B. Frothingham, the young author William Dean Howells, Holmes, and Emerson. *The Dial* expired in 1861, and its passing symbolized the way the Civil War cut through artistic and intellectual matters. The war scattered people, undermined financial support, and weakened those aspects of life not directly related to the war effort. Exhibits, concerts, and literary journals decreased in direct correlation to the war's expansion, but the prewar years left Cincinnatians expecting a certain quality of life that included recognition of the arts.

However, Cincinnati's reputation as a regional cultural center ultimately rests on its accomplishments during the last quarter of the nineteenth century, a period when the city earned national recognition for its artists and distinction for its contributions to American music.

THE PARIS OF AMERICA, 1870–1900

The Civil War caused a disruption in the city's musical organizations that not even the recent opening of Pike's Opera House could offset, and some viewed the building's destruction by fire in 1866 as fatal to the city's cultural aspirations. Yet just four years later the city built the cavernous Saengerhalle to accommodate a very successful 1870 Saengerfest, and the previous year Christian Friedrich Theodore Thomas, with a highly disciplined forty-member orchestra, made the first of his annual visits to the city. Maria Longworth Nichols, the granddaughter of Nicholas Longworth, suggested that Thomas or-

Pike's Opera House. Opened in 1859, Pike's Opera House fulfilled the dream of local businessman Samuel Pike (originally Hecht). After the building burned in 1866, Pike replaced it with a more modest structure of the same name. CINCINNATI MUSEUM CENTER IMAGE ARCHIVES

ganize a major music festival that would go beyond the ethnic focus of the Saengerfests, and she used her social connections to line up financial support. Her husband, George Ward Nichols, became president of the May Festival Association. With a 108-piece orchestra led by Thomas and a chorus of almost eight hundred voices, the first May Festival in 1873 sparked a decade of extraordinary music activity. It also initiated an intense rivalry with Boston, as Cincinnati strived to become the musical center of the United States.

In 1875 the city held an even more successful second festival, and in its aftermath the retired merchant Reuben R. Springer launched a drive for a more fitting music facility. The result was the Music Hall, which opened in 1878 by hosting the third May Festival. Thomas led the orchestra and chorus in a tour de force of classical music. Local enthusiasm for the festivals, for Thomas, and for the magnificent Music Hall led to a proposal that Thomas

move permanently to the city and head a national school of music. Housed in the Music Hall, the College of Music opened in October 1879, with Thomas as its artistic and academic head and Nichols to oversee its business side. Local enthusiasts labeled Cincinnati the "Paris of America" and claimed national supremacy in musical matters. The euphoria soon evaporated.

Following a bitter disagreement between Thomas and Nichols over the school's direction, the maestro resigned and returned to New York City. A less ambitious College of Music, still under Nichols's management, eventually merged with the smaller Conservatory of Music, and the joint school continues today as part of the University of Cincinnati. Although opera supporters in the 1880s established a short-lived annual festival to parallel the May Festival, and another attempt at a permanent orchestra was made, the quarrel between Thomas and Nichols so divided the city's music community that serious music growth became impossible. Major floods in 1883 and 1884, the Court House Riot of 1884, economic problems, growing labor tension, and the decline of effective city government all contributed to the city's weakened musical state.

It was not until the mid-1890s that the city again moved forward. In 1894 socially prominent members of the Ladies Musical Club, harnessing a love of music with a new burst of civic spirit, founded the Orchestra Association, with both general membership and the board of directors restricted to women. With the support of their husbands and a more unified community, they organized the Cincinnati Symphony Orchestra (CSO). After an abbreviated 1895 season, the orchestra reached full professional status the following year under the baton of Frank Van der Stucken, who served as director until 1907. The sixth oldest symphony orchestra in the country, the CSO established a solid reputation in the twentieth century, and it has provided a podium for some of the nation's finest orchestral leaders.

THE GOLDEN AGE OF ART, 1870–1920

Frank Duveneck, born in 1848 across the Ohio River in Covington, Kentucky, also brought artistic distinction to Cincinnati. He was taught church decoration as a boy in Covington, and his natural talent and ambition led him to study at Munich's Royal Academy of Art. He returned to the United States in late 1873 for an eighteen-month stay in Cincinnati, and his presence in the city encouraged artists to break from the meticulous brushwork taught locally. Duveneck's success and influence led other Americans to follow him back to Munich, and from heavily Germanic Cincinnati came the painters John Henry Twachtman, Edward Henry Potthast, and Robert Frederick Blum, all of whom gained national distinction. Twachtman soon abandoned the muddy colors of Munich and moved under the spell of French impressionism. Before his death in 1902, he had become a leader among American artists grappling with the new emphasis on light and atmosphere, and his delicate lyricism and subdued tones ensured his place among American impressionists. Potthast, who left Cincinnati for New York in 1896, also forsook Munich's dark palette for colorful, breezy beach scenes, while Blum adopted a modest Japanese style.

During this time the city produced several other artists of merit. Elizabeth Nourse, born in Cincinnati, studied at the city's McMicken School of De-

sign before settling permanently in France where her intimate canvases of peasant mothers and children became her signature. Kenyon Cox, born in Warren, Ohio, also studied in Cincinnati before turning to Paris, where he experienced the French academic tradition. Joseph R. De Camp, who was born in Cincinnati in 1858, became a leading painter in Boston and remained closer to Duveneck's style, and perhaps for that reason enjoyed more public favor than those who turned to impressionism. Henry F. Farny, an Alsatian by birth, departed from the Munich influence as well, and devoted his life to painting the Indians of the Great Plains. Joseph Henry Sharp, a product of Bridgeport, Ohio, followed Farny in finding inspiration in the Native American. He learned sound draftsmanship at the McMicken School, but in the mid-1890s he headed for New Mexico and became a pillar of the Taos art colony.

Although other U.S. cities siphoned off the most talented of Cincinnati's artists, the city developed an expanding infrastructure of schools and art associations. At the center of this activity was the McMicken School of Design. Opened in 1869 as part of a proposed University of Cincinnati, McMicken served as the training ground for a generation of local artists. Headed for many years by the authoritarian Thomas S. Noble, the school provided a solid but conservative training in drawing and composition, with a strong emphasis on applied arts. In 1884, spurred by an unseemly public quarrel over its traditional curriculum, the school became the Art Academy of Cincinnati, attached to the recently founded Cincinnati Art Museum. Despite Noble's resistance to change, the school's ties to the museum, the influence of the museum's assistant director, Joseph Henry Gest, and the eventual return of Duveneck to the city nudged the academy toward contemporary art movements. In the 1890s the school gradually introduced a more liberal curriculum, increased the number and quality of faculty, and supported both faculty and students with an innovative scholarship program for study in Europe.

The Cincinnati Art Museum also provided strong institutional support for art and artists. In 1876 a small group of Cincinnati women sent a display of their carved furniture and decorated china and stoneware to the Centennial Exhibition in Philadelphia, and the success of this display launched both an arts and crafts movement in the city and led directly to the founding of the Cincinnati Art Museum in 1881. Intrigued by the application of art to industry, and especially by the possibilities for women, the Women's Art Museum Association, founded in 1877, sponsored lectures, classes, and exhibitions to promote a permanent museum. In 1880 local businessman Charles W. West announced a gift of $150,000, to be matched by public subscription, and in 1886 the museum, built by the Cincinnati architect James W. McLaughlin, opened its doors.

Alfred Traber Goshorn, who headed the Philadelphia Centennial Exposition in 1876, served as the museum's first president, but much of the new institution's vitality came from Joseph Gest. It was Gest who quietly pushed for exhibits by contemporary artists. He also urged the acquisition of paintings by the American painters John Singer Sargent, Edmund Tarbell, and Frederick Childe Hassam, as well as Twachtman, Potthast, Duveneck, and Farny. Shortly after the turn of the century, Mary M. Emery donated her collection of European paintings, the first of several major donations that would give the museum international stature. Although the museum never quite lived up to its appellation as "Art Palace of the West," and the Art Academy never achieved the national distinction promised by Noble, the two institutions helped support the art activity so crucial to the city's reputation.

The expanding number of artists in the city led to several organizations. In 1884 the Sketch Club, made up of students dissatisfied with the curriculum at the McMicken School of Design, included most of the city's serious painters. John Rettig, who had developed a reputation as a theater scene painter, headed the group. There is some evidence to suggest that several women also belonged to the Sketch Club, and this may have been the reason that Rettig and twelve others seceded and formed the all-male Cincinnati Art Club in 1890. For the next several decades the Art Club, which still exists, became the focal point of what passed for Bohemian art life in the city, with members holding monthly criticisms, sketching trips (often led by Frank Duveneck), and enjoying numerous parties.

Not to be outdone and resenting the male-only provision, women artists formed the Woman's Art Club in 1892. More serious than the men in their objectives, the women spurned the exuberance and levity exhibited by their male counterparts. Mary Spencer served as the first president, and virtually all of the city's significant female painters belonged to the organization. Both art organizations held highly popular annual exhibits, as did the Art Museum and the Society of Western Artists, a Chicago-based group dominated during its early years by Cincinnati artists.

Both the McMicken School and the art museum emphasized the need for sound craftsmanship and design in manufacturing. Borrowing heavily from the writings of the English art critic John Ruskin, the American arts and crafts movement sought to offset the increasing production of cheap, shoddy, machine-made goods. In Cincinnati the English-born Benn Pitman served as the local catalyst. From his woodcarving and design classes at the McMicken School, students turned out sophisticated furniture. Although hand-carved furniture never became commercially successful, Pitman also promoted china painting and encouraged a group of socially prominent women to experiment with various types of ceramic decoration. Led by Mary Louise McLaughlin and Maria Longworth Nichols, these efforts led first to the Pottery Club, an amateur organization that turned out quality individual pieces, and then to the Rookwood Pottery, the most significant of several local art potteries. Maria Nichols, supported by her father's generosity, founded the Rookwood Pottery in part to advance her own interest in glazes and design and in part to supply careers for young women artists. Although the pottery became increasingly commercial, its designers helped place Rookwood products among the world's finest hand-painted ceramic ware, and its Tiger Eye, Iris, and Sea Green glazes earned international acclaim. Rookwood Pottery captured a gold medal at the Paris World's Fair in 1889 and came away with a coveted Grand Prix at the 1900 Paris World's Fair, a remarkable achievement for a pottery style just twenty years old.

THE CITY IN DECLINE

Despite Rookwood's good fortune, the establishment of the Cincinnati Symphony Orchestra, and the number of significant artists linked to the city, the twentieth century saw a decline in Cincinnati's reputation. Population and economic growth slowed, leaving the city, once the nation's sixth largest, sliding out of the top ten. Cleveland, St. Louis, and especially Chicago surged past the "Queen of the West." By 1900 most major cities in the country had duplicated Cincinnati's cultural achievements, and New York had established itself as the nation's center for all things artistic. Indeed, as an intellectual and literary center Cincinnati had been in decline since 1861. The promise of the prewar years never materialized. Publishing houses moved to New

York, western literary journals found better opportunities in Chicago, and the specialization and professionalization of knowledge weakened amateur intellectual activities. About all that remained in the city was the Literary Club, which had gradually evolved into a genteel membership dedicated to belles lettres.

Cincinnati artists, content to follow in Duveneck's path, shunned newer art currents sweeping in from Europe. Young, aspiring painters from the region now looked to more modern and more recognizable artists in New York or Europe, and with the deaths of Farny (1916) and Duveneck (1919), the city lost its most notable artists. Music suffered as well. The symphony orchestra slowly established a solid reputation, but it never rivaled orchestras in New York, Boston, or Chicago. Thus, the brightest stars in the city's firmament remained the May Festival and the Rookwood Pottery, but even their luster dimmed. Although the May Festival ranks as one of the great monuments in the nation's musical development, a shift in interest from choral to orchestral music reduced its place in the new century, and despite Rookwood's international acclaim, the age of arts and crafts did not survive World War I and Rookwood production was suspended in 1967.

If Cincinnati lost much of its regional acclaim, its institutions continued to launch major artistic careers. Ballerina Suzanne Farrell, music director James Levine, singer Kathleen Battle, and painters James Dine and Tom Wesselman trained in the city before moving on to the national scene. The symphony orchestra benefited from the talents of music directors Ernst Kunwald, Eugene Ysaÿe, Fritz Reiner, and Thomas Schippers. Architects Michael Graves and Peter Eisenman designed signature buildings for the University of Cincinnati campus, extending the architectural heritage established by Samuel Hannaford in the previous century and continued through such striking Art Deco buildings as the Union Terminal (now the Cincinnati Museum Center) and the Carew Tower complex.

In retrospect Cincinnati played a significant role in the nation's cultural and intellectual maturation. The city served as the most important nineteenth-century western center for the arts, a result of its geographical location and unprecedented growth, and the personal fortunes acquired before the Civil

Maria Longworth Nichols Storer (1849–1932). Known for her involvement with the May Festival and Rookwood Pottery, this energetic and outspoken supporter of the arts found outlets for her own creative talent in pottery decoration, oil painting, and work in bronze. Although she spent her last thirty years in Europe, Storer remains the best-remembered member of the Longworth family. CINCINNATI MUSEUM CENTER IMAGE ARCHIVES

War secured the more permanent developments of the 1870s and 1880s. However, this momentum could not be sustained. Competition from a ring of fast-growing cities, the dominance of New York, the decline of river trade, and a decrease in the city's traditional manufacturing all suggest a gradual hardening of its economic arteries. In an era sometimes called the "age of energy," the new energy was more visible in Chicago and New York. Yet Cincinnati's contributions remain significant: early literary encouragement; support and recognition for several generations of "western" artists and musicians; Rookwood pottery's place in the nation's arts and crafts movement; and the May Festival's importance in developing appreciation for the great music of eighteenth- and nineteenth-century Europe.

See also **Women in the Public Sphere, 1838–1877; Urban Cultural Institutions; The Popular Arts** *(volume 1);* **Lyceums, Chautauquas, and Institutes for Useful Knowledge; Museums; Painting; Sculpture; Music** *(volume 3).*

BIBLIOGRAPHY

Aaron, Daniel. *Cincinnati: Queen City of the West, 1819–1838.* Columbus, Ohio, 1992.

Boyle, Richard J. *John Twachtman.* New York, 1979.

Carter, Denny. *Henry Farny.* New York, 1978.

Cincinnati Art Museum. *The Golden Age: Cincinnati Painters of the Nineteenth Century Represented in the Cincinnati Art Museum.* Cincinnati, 1979.

———. *The Ladies, God Bless 'Em: The Women's Art Movement in Cincinnati in the Nineteenth Century.* Cincinnati, 1976.

Drake, Daniel. *Physician to the West: Selected Writings of Daniel Drake on Science and Society.* Edited with introductions by Henry D. Shapiro and Zane L. Miller. Lexington, Ky., 1970.

Duveneck, Josephine W. *Frank Duveneck, Painter-Teacher.* San Francisco, 1970.

Mansfield, Edward D. *Memoirs of the Life and Services of Daniel Drake, M.D., Physician, Professor, and Author; with Notices of the Early Settlement of Cincinnati.* Cincinnati, 1855.

Ritter, Frédéric Louis. *Music in America.* 1890. Reprint, New York, 1972.

Storer, Maria Longworth. *The History of the Cincinnati Musical Festivals and of the Rookwood Pottery.* Paris, 1919.

Thomas, Theodore. *A Musical Autobiography.* 2 vols. Edited by George P. Upton. Chicago, 1905.

Trapp, Kenneth R. "Art Palace of the West: Its Beginnings." In *Art Palace of the West: A Centennial Tribute, 1881–1981.* Cincinnati, 1981.

———. "Rookwood Pottery: The Glorious Gamble." In *Rookwood Pottery: The Glorious Gamble,* edited by Anita J. Ellis. New York, 1992.

———. "Toward a Correct Taste: Women and the Rise of the Design Movement in Cincinnati, 1874–1880." In *Celebrate Cincinnati Art,* edited by Kenneth R. Trapp. Cincinnati, 1981.

Tunison, Frank E. *Presto! From the Singing School to the May Musical Festival.* Cincinnati, 1888.

Venable, William H. *Beginnings of Literary Culture in the Ohio Valley: Historical and Biographical Sketches.* New York, 1949.

Vitz, Robert C. *The Queen and the Arts: Cultural Life in Nineteenth Century Cincinnati.* Kent, Ohio, 1989.

Wade, Richard C. *The Urban Frontier: The Rise of Western Cities, 1790–1830.* 1959. Reprint, Cambridge, Mass., 1971.

NEW ORLEANS

Jeremy du Quesnay Adams

GEOGRAPHY AND CLIMATE

Few cities in the United States have been more decisively shaped by topography and climate than New Orleans. Its climate is subtropical, intensely humid. The warmer half of the year can be enervating, producing a high disease rate and a sensual cultural atmosphere. Until yellow fever was controlled in the late nineteenth century, New Orleans had the highest death rate in the Union. Morbid romanticism has tended to dominate the city's literary output; the jazz funeral and "The St. James Infirmary Blues" characterize its most creative contribution to world culture. Distinctive cemetery architecture has long been one of its visual keynotes; in the late twentieth century its most successful forms of business export were restaurants and cemetery-mausoleum management.

Were it not for sustained technological intervention, New Orleans would be virtually uninhabitable. Its highest land are the natural levees deposited by the Mississippi on its banks, but the oldest part of the city, the Vieux Carré, or French Quarter, lies about two feet below mean sea level—an anomalous situation caused by the force of that enormous river's push against the Gulf and its previous deposit of a marshy buffer zone reaching as far as twenty miles behind those elevated banks. Parts of the present city, originally marshland drainable thanks to the construction of levees under the colonial and federal American regimes (now maintained by the U.S. Corps of Engineers), lie as low as nineteen feet below sea level. Nineteen pumping stations keep New Orleans functioning. Certain themes seem inevitable in such a city's culture: the vulnerability of human life and of cultural and natural structures; the temptation—almost the imperative—of making the most of available pleasure. New Orleans would love to be "the city that care forgot," as the motto of its dominant folk institution, Mardi Gras, declares it is.

HISTORY

New Orleans was founded in 1718, the farthest thrust southward of the French North American empire. In 1763 New Orleans and the western half of the vast territory it was supposed to control for the French Crown were ceded to the Spanish king Charles III by the Treaty of Paris, which ended the worldwide conflict generally known as the Seven Years' War. With the exception of the "Isle of Orleans," the land between the Mississippi and Lakes Maurepas and Pontchartrain, France had to cede the Mississippi valley east of the river to Great Britain. In 1763 the white population of Louisiana—meaning the western half of the Mississippi valley—was officially estimated at six thousand to eight thousand, and that of the blacks and mulattos at another ten thousand. New Orleans boasted a racially diverse population of some three thousand, one third white. The Indians were a rapidly fading minority in the city. Most, though not all, of the blacks were slaves.

For forty years the Spanish Crown postponed what now appears the inevitable absorption of Louisiana by Anglo-American culture. During that time it was something of a model colony; several hundred Spaniards emigrated there, and their leading families soon directed the cultural life of the growing capital. The leading magnate of the Spanish colonial interlude was Don Andres Almonester y Rojas, scion of impoverished Andalusian nobility, who became very rich in Louisiana, eventually held most of the capital city's appointive and elective magistracies, founded numerous philanthropic institutions, and in 1794 inaugurated the church of St. Louis, "which he had built at his own expense." It would soon become the Roman Catholic cathedral. Despite the brevity of Spanish political domination, New Orleans has retained a peripheral position within the economic and cultural orbits of Spanish America.

In 1801 Napoleon forced Spain (then ruled by his brother Joseph) to cede Louisiana to France and then sold the whole Louisiana Territory to the United States in 1803 for $15 million. The colonial phase of New Orleans history lasted until 1812, when Louisiana was admitted to the Union as a state—or perhaps until 1815, when General Andrew Jackson's victory on 8 January over a superior British invading force guaranteed that the city would not be annexed by the British Empire and produced an explosion of patriotic harmony between the Franco-Spanish "Creole" population and the "Americans." The late colonial phase of the city's history overlapped with a thirty-year (1790–1820) phase of intense Anglophone and Francophone immigration. Anglo-Americans poured into Louisiana in the last years of Spanish rule, most down the Mississippi, some from the East Coast. The French émigrés, perhaps three thousand in number, were royalist exiles from the French and Haitian Revolutions. They were responsible for the survival of French culture in New Orleans: the pre-1790 Creole families were not numerous enough to resist absorption into Anglo-American culture without the élan the immigrants brought and the new Francophone institutions they created. The architect Benjamin Latrobe, shortly before his death in 1820, declared nonetheless that New Orleans would be a thoroughly English-speaking American city very soon.

In the third phase of its history, from the 1820s to the Civil War, New Orleans experienced its economic and in some ways its cultural apogee despite devastating epidemics. The 1850s witnessed a building boom, during which the city's most distinctive buildings were erected. With the occupation of the city by Union troops early in the Civil War, in April 1862, New Orleans entered a twelve-year phase of political, military, economic, and social turbulence, with long-lasting consequences. It was the first major city occupied for any length of time by the U. S. Army, which consequently lacked any traditions for this challenge. The bungled occupation turned a port city largely skeptical of secession into a hotbed of reactionary Confederate sentiment. No other Southern city was as violently instrumental in defeating Reconstruction.

This traumatic and fatally divisive interlude was followed by a forty-year period (1874–1914) of economic slippage and cultural consolidation, with the imposition of white supremacy and Anglophone culture. The city's prime entertainment became Mardi Gras, a several-week carnival period climaxing in the torchlight parades of the Krewes of Comus, Momus, and Proteus, and the midday parade of Rex, the King of Carnival, on Shrove Tuesday itself.

From 1928 to 1963 the centerpiece of Louisiana politics was a struggle between the Huey Long machine and the city's reform faction, contemptuously dismissed by Governor Long, "the Kingfish," as "silk stockings." The most successful of the anti-Long New Orleans politicians was De Lesseps Story (Chep) Morrison, mayor from 1946 to 1961. Those were years of high optimism about the city's economic prospects, based on a revitalization of its port facilities and a steady campaign of trade development with Latin America as well as with European and other North American port cities. Artistic and literary projects were encouraged as well; there was much talk of a renaissance.

New Orleans experienced increasing political and economic difficulty and coincidentally a second literary flowering, in the last third of the twentieth century. The public-school desegregation crisis of 1960 exposed the city's long-simmering racial tensions and began significant ethnic white flight upriver and across Lake Pontchartrain. During the mayorship of Maurice (Moon) Landrieu (1970 to 1978) the population of Orleans Parish became, for the first time since the early nineteenth century, over 50 percent black. Since 1978 the city's mayors have been members of the black Creole elite; their revenue-starved administrations have striven to transform this bastion of exclusive white supremacy into an authentically multicultural city. It is a different version of the New Orleanian legacy, but far from revolutionary in its appeal to old realities.

SOCIAL STRUCTURES

The social structures of this old, economically straitened, pleasure-loving and yet rancorous city are complex. New Orleans has long been one of the most ethnically diverse and multicultural cities in the United States, almost a standard exception to the national norm. It has always had the most genuinely African urban culture in the country; the historian Jerah Johnson maintained that the Native American presence lasted longer in New Orleans than in any other major U.S. city. Nevertheless, the city's discourse has been fractured by racial hatreds and intense intraracial ethnic insults.

The social and economic life of New Orleans has long been dominated by a small merchant elite collaborating with key planters, bankers, brokers, shippers, and lawyers, most of them members of the

Boston Club. It likes to think of itself as patrician and thus allows into its councils few of the self-made men who have incarnated "the American dream." As a result it has long been one of America's poorest commercial elites, and the local economy has consistently lost out in competition with other comparable cities more open to raw talent (New York in the early nineteenth century and Houston in the twentieth). For over a century that group was convinced that the best way to present its city as a beehive of dynamic capitalism was to cultivate Mardi Gras. Few of the sociocultural patterns in New Orleans make obvious sense.

For New Orleanians "Creole" is a loaded social and cultural term. Once again it does not automatically mean what most Anglo-Americans assume: a person or custom of mixed European and African (or possibly Native American) antecedents. Under the Spanish regime a *criollo* was a person of pure European blood, normally Spanish but in Louisiana also French, Italian, or British, born in the Americas, not in Europe. By the mid-nineteenth century the term was normally applied to anyone who had been in Louisiana long enough to be assimilated, and thus not (or no longer) an "immigrant." It was also widely applied to distinctive local varieties of crops or prepared foods (such as Creole mustard). By the mid-twentieth century, however, the term designated a person or cultural behavior of Franco-Spanish origins. In the twenty-first century, it applies to whites and blacks with such ancestors, to a distinctive cuisine, and to a few fading folkways.

LITERATURE

New Orleans literary output has reached two peaks. The late-nineteenth-century peak involved several literary genres in both French and English, the late-twentieth-century peak only English. Prose fiction has been the genre most widely and most successfully practiced in both languages in both periods, but poetry, literary criticism, and drama were popular as well. Consciously literary essays and longer historical and philosophical works marked the intellectual efforts of New Orleanian French culture in both centuries.

French literature got under way in the colonial period, with the publication in the 1770s of Julien Poydras de Lallande's poems eulogizing the exploits and attitudes of Bernardo de Gálvez, Louisiana's most popular Spanish governor. His *Dieu et les Nayades du fleuve Saint-Louis, à Don Bernard Galvez* (God and the Naiads of the Saint Louis [i.e., Mis-

sissippi] River) of 1777 and his short effort at epic verse, *La prise du morne du Bâton Rouge par Monseigneur de Galvez* (The capture of the bluff of Baton Rouge by My Lord de Galvez) were published in 1779 by the press of Antoine Boudousquié, one of several local printing presses. New Orleans presses produced mostly official documents and sporadic experiments in gazette-type journalism until the 1790s.

The arrival of the émigrés changed all that. They tended to be formally educated and were numerous enough to create a demand for high culture, some of which they began producing, although most of the French authors of the early and middle nineteenth century came directly from France. Native-born authors were quite productive. Bernard Marigny de Mandeville, bon vivant and indifferently educated scion of one of colonial Louisiana's first families, developer of Faubourg Marigny downriver from the Vieux Carré and the inventor of the game of craps, expressed himself ebulliently in numerous often startling essays: he supported the anti-Catholic, hyper-Anglo but anti-immigrant Know-Nothing Party that paradoxically took over the municipal government in the 1850s, but he also criticized their racist propaganda. In 1845 Armand Lanusse published *Les cenelles: Choix de poésies indigènes* (The holly-berries: A selection of native poetry), an anthology of formal lyric and elegiac poems by himself and sixteen other freemen of color. It has been hailed as the first work of African American verse literature, although, as Arlin Turner observed, their authors would have been most unlikely to identify themselves as either African or American.

The Francophone literary public was mad for theater: verse dramas in the styles of Corneille, Racine, and Molière, sung (!) as well as spoken, competed with the classic French dramatic repertory. Auguste Lussan, a French immigrant, scored a success in 1839 with *Les martyrs de la Louisiane*, celebrating the revolt of republican Creole planters against Spanish rule in 1765. Lussan wrote or adapted several other well-received plays, mostly with romantic themes set in Europe, as did the rival Creole cousins Placide Canonge and Armand Mercier.

Louisiana's premier French novelist was Alfred Mercier, brother of Armand and with him a pillar of the Athénée Louisianais and other institutions dedicated to the preservation of French in Louisiana. Born upriver in 1816, he spent over a third of his life in France. He waited out the Civil War over there (as did the architect Henry Hobson Richardson), then returned to New Orleans to practice medicine. His house at 824 Canal Street is now the Boston Club. Mercier published some of his scientific research as well as short stories and half a dozen melodramatic novels, of which the most interesting from the point of view of American culture is *L'habitation Saint-Ybars,* published in 1881 as a tardy rejoinder to *Uncle Tom's Cabin.* Generally described in that context because of its idealized (though still brutally critical) picture of antebellum slavery, it may in fact be more revealing for its romanticized, less-than-ideal image of the Creole family, at once formal and permissive, passionately fixated on its members, obsessed with death, disease, and milder forms of loss.

The Rouquette brothers, Dominique and Adrien, epitomize this transatlantic culture. Both were sent to school in Nantes and Philadelphia; Dominique became a schoolteacher and a prolific poet fascinated by local color, Adrien became a lawyer and then Louisiana's first native-born Catholic priest. In the 1860s he went as a missionary to the Choctaws north of Lake Pontchartrain. He wrote a stream of poems on such topics as Paris, the American prairielands, Daniel Boone, Christopher Columbus, Saint Paphnutius, and Thaïs. A romantic conservative, in correspondence with the clergyman Isaac Hecker and the writer Lafcadio Hearn, Rouquette composed polemical and didactic prose and verse on American politics and the contemplative life. His best known work is his complex novel *Nouvelle Atala; ou, la fille de l'esprit* (1879), as ideological as it is romantic in its defense of Native American values and its impassioned commitment to classical literature as well as to the vision of Châteaubriand (to whose *Atala* of 1801 it is a response).

The painful recognition that French had lost out as a political and commercial language in Louisiana provoked a second burst of French literature starting in the 1870s, earnestly encouraged by the short-lived Athénée Louisianais, founded in 1876. That preservation effort failed, and ultimately French literature took a backseat to the rich traditions of literature in English.

English-language journalism throve from 1803 onward, expanding steadily in output. In 1895, 119 English periodicals of different sorts were published in the city; by then there were only three French newspapers and fourteen bilingual periodicals in English and other languages (Spanish, Italian, and German as well as French). By the 1850s performances of the English dramatic repertory (preeminently Shakespeare) occurred weekly throughout the year at several theaters. The first major creative burst occurred in the late nineteenth century, with George Washington Cable as the leading figure.

Cable was born and bred in New Orleans, the son of a slaveholding, devoutly Presbyterian Southern family. He served with distinction in the Confederate cavalry, returning to New Orleans in 1865. For the next twenty years he lived and wrote there, producing short stories, sketches, and essays on his native city and the South as a whole for national organs such as *Scribner's Monthly.* In 1880, a year before Mercier's *Saint-Ybars,* Cable published the first and best of his fifteen novels, *The Grandissimes.* Long, loaded with local color, much of its dialogue in dialect (as was *Saint-Ybars*), this novel is an authentic *Kulturroman,* presenting the author's vision of collective cultural change through the narrative interaction of its stereotypical characters. Although set in 1803, Cable used this tale of tangled lineages to express his horror at post-Reconstruction white supremacy as well as antebellum slavery. *The Grandissimes,* hailed by late-twentieth-century critics as the first of the modern Southern novels, was met by violently negative reaction from white Creoles. Cable, encouraged by fellow authors Mark Twain and Joel Chandler Harris, replied to this barrage with his extended essay *The Silent South* in 1885, the year he felt it necessary to move to New England. There, in Northampton, Massachusetts, he wrote his most serious ideological statement, *The Negro Question* (1888).

New Orleans welcomed in those years its fair share of literary visitors, the most prolific of whom was Lafcadio Hearn, who lived there from 1877 to 1887 writing for the *New Orleans Item* and the *New Orleans Times-Democrat* (ancestors of the current *Times-Picayune*). His first novel, *Chita,* an exercise in local color, was published in 1889 after serial appearance in *Harper's New Monthly* magazine. The *Times-Democrat* later published some of his earliest Japanese articles, and his authorized biographer, Elizabeth Bisland, was a New Orleanian. On good terms with the conservative Rouquette, Hearn shared Cable's opposition to racial discrimination and warned against the malignity of anti-Semitism.

Kate O'Flaherty Chopin of St. Louis, a resident of New Orleans for three decades after her marriage to Oscar Chopin in 1870, abandoned local colorism for a blunt psychological realism in her more than one hundred short stories and two novels set in Louisiana, the second of which, *The Awakening* (1899), has been seen by scholars as an early example of American feminist fiction. Its heroine, Edna Pointillier, shares the author's insider-outsider relationship with the Creole establishment. Liberated from some conventional sexual and social constraints, Edna more or less abandons her family and takes a final suicidal swim in the Gulf of Mexico from Grand Isle, a hurricane-prone resort where her emancipation began. *The Awakening* met with critical outrage, and was out of print for half a century; Chopin, by then a widow, returned to St. Louis to die.

Literary creativity in both languages declined after the 1890s, but experienced a revival after the First World War. Among the visiting writers of the 1920s was William Faulkner, who wrote *Soldier's Pay* while living on Pirate's Alley in 1926. Among the long-time residents Grace King and Lyle Saxon contributed significantly to the city's published lore: King, no Creole herself, took up the cause of terminally fading Creole culture, attacking Cable with particular sharpness. Their lead was followed after World War II by John Chase (*Frenchmen, Desire, Good Children,* a meditation on the city's street names), Harnett Kane, and Frances Parkinson Keyes, the transplanted Bostonian romantic novelist. (*Came a Cavalier* is set in the 1826 Morphy-Beauregard House she lovingly restored.) The city's Caribbean linkage was reasserted by W. Adolphe Roberts, the cosmopolitan Jamaican journalist, poet, and historian who wrote *Lake Pontchartrain,* a thoughtful work of landscape history, and a trilogy of historical novels (*Royal Street* and its sequels) celebrating the Creole legacy.

This locally recognized activity culminated in a nationally recognized literary burst in the last forty years of the twentieth century. The key transitional figure was Tennessee Williams, so constant a visitor and part-time resident that the city claims him with as much validity as it has claimed Lafcadio Hearn. *A Streetcar Named Desire* (1947, Pulitzer Prize 1948), *Suddenly Last Summer* (1958), and *Vieux Carré* (1977) are his most explicitly New Orleanian plays. Shirley Ann Grau's *House on Coliseum Street* (1961) explores the struggle of reflective culture against the threat of lawless natural impulses. Walker Percy's *The Moviegoer* (1961, winner of the National Book Award in 1962) evokes the city's enveloping weather as well as its beset legacy of Anglican gentility; his *The Last Gentleman* (1966), *Love in the Ruins* (1971), and *Lancelot* (1977) gave a new, conservative Catholic twist to the long-dominant local-color tradition. Anne Rice's vampires and freemen of color have made the local scene both more exotic and nationally more familiar. Ellen Gilchrist's short stories tend to be barely fictionalized retellings of painfully true tales.

A special case is John Kennedy Toole's *Confederacy of Dunces* (1980), which won a Pulitzer Prize in 1981, more than a dozen years after Toole's suicide. His *Confederacy* reveals Toole as a lost Rabelaisian genius; the city government has honored him with a bronze statue in front of the downtown resort hotel that used to be the D. H. Holmes department store, site of his novel's opening scene.

MUSIC

New Orleans's major contribution to world culture is undoubtedly jazz. A musical genre defined primarily by rhythmic sound patterns and by individual performers' improvisation rather than by score-bound melodic and harmonic subtleties, with a non-European sense of the boundary between musical sonority and mere noise, jazz emerged and defined itself between the 1880s and the early 1920s. Its origins, like its name, are elusive. The West African rhythmic component is central, but Frederick Starr and others insist on recognition of the European harmonic element deriving from popular dance tunes, Protestant hymn-singing, Hispano-Cuban music of several types, and even formal French operatic training (the last of these specific to New Orleans). Comparably, the word "jazz" has been traced to a West African (Malenke) word for living intensely and to the Anglo-American "jack-ass," by way of a nineteenth-century Southern vulgarism for sexual relations. In any case, the term became standard in musicians' usage by 1917, the date of the oldest surviving phonographic recording of jazz, done by Nick La Rocca of the Original Dixieland Jazzband. One of the most influential of the "Alligators," or white jazz players, La Rocca demonstrates the dominant classes' acceptance of a style of music that had emerged some thirty years earlier among the predominantly black bands performing in the better bordellos of Storyville, New Orleans's licensed red-light district of thirty-eight squares alternating with the St. Louis cemeteries north of Basin Street at the northern end of the Vieux Carré. The music they played was marked by a complex, almost conversational polyphonic call and response, by breaks, riffs, and grooves, and by what the jazz trumpeter Wynton Marsalis has called a "so-what-if-it-hurts jubilation." Improvisational and unrecorded, the founders of this now worldwide genre remain dim figures: they include Alphonse Picou the clarinettist, José Ysagguire the bass player, and

Jazz Funeral Procession, c. 1984. Traditionally, players dress in black suits, white shirts, and bow ties. The bands play somber hymns or mournful spirituals on the way to the cemetery and up-tempo, joyous songs on their return. © PHILIP GOULD/CORBIS

Dee Dee Chandler the drummer. The youngest of the pioneers, Papa Celestin, played his theme-setting cornet (the "hot instrument" of the black marching bands) in the Basin Street style for three generations of New Orleans debutantes into the 1950s, when he could be heard inveighing against the immoral influence of rock-and-roll.

Storyville (named for Chep Morrison's maternal uncle, the urbane alderman Sidney Story) closed down in 1917, the year of La Rocca's recording, as a concession of the city government to the U.S. Navy's concern about venereal disease at a major naval base. Jazzmen had started to leave New Orleans even before that blow to their livelihood. Kid Ory had gone to California by then, and King Oliver—mentor of the young Louis Armstrong—to Chicago.

The trumpeter and singer Louis Armstrong and the saxophonist Sidney Bechet, ably assisted on the drums after 1928 by their fellow New Orleanian Zutty Singleton, defined and expanded the capacities and character of jazz for the next thirty years. They incorporated many of the musical techniques

of two other Afro-American genres that had evolved further upriver, blues and ragtime. Blues, dominated by the solo voice sometimes accompanied on the banjo, guitar, or piano, was sung throughout the South, with a creative center at Memphis. Ragtime, often exclusively instrumental, arose in the river ports of Missouri, especially Sedalia and Saint Louis. The laziness of the original New Orleans jazz style, breaking sporadically into spontaneous gaiety, paled before the bursts of explosive solo and orchestrated backup variations on a theme that became the hallmark of international interwar jazz. Mythic nostalgia for the cradle-land persisted, however, leading to the Dixieland revival after World War II, heralded by Louis Armstrong's Dixie Band in the 1947 film *New Orleans,* and echoed in Fats Domino's down-and-out semi-blues song "Walking to New Orleans" of 1960.

In the quarter century after the Second World War contemporary developments of international jazz were reflected in New Orleans, usually in a conservative manner, by Louis Prima and Al Hirt, whose bands maintained the Alligator legacy. Mahalia Jackson was that generation's contribution to the development of gospel singing, a parallel genre only sporadically interacting with jazz. In the 1970s, long after the creative forces of "classical jazz" had moved far from the Crescent City (to New York, Kansas City, San Francisco, Paris, and elsewhere), the Dirty Dozen Brass Band led other New Orleans musicians in maintaining the city's faded honor. Their explosive and festive music influenced Bradford Marsalis and others who adapted funk, hip-hop, and other styles of a continuing African American street culture to balance the antiquarianism of Preservation Hall, a reverent institution where musicians born well after the pioneers had died maintain the traditions of the preclassical New Orleans jazz of the 1920s.

Before jazz was conceived, opera and related classical genres ruled the musical scene in New Orleans. Frederick Starr has explored the international standing of the local operatic culture in the mid-nineteenth century as the context of New Orleans's most important classical composer, Louis Moreau Gottschalk; as Starr points out, New Orleans's opera frequently outstarred the productions of its rivals New York, Mexico City, Havana, and Rio. Its repertory included more than the expected French and Italian favorites: 1872, for instance, saw the American première of Wagner's *Tannhäuser*. However, the city's operatic primacy had faded badly by 1929, when the French Opera House on Bourbon Street in the Vieux Carré burned. After World War II opera was bravely revived in the visually and acoustically depressing Municipal Auditorium, which, like the French Opera House, also hosted Mardi Gras balls. A symphony was founded only in 1935 thanks to Edith Rosenwald Stern and was sustained largely by her philanthropy for a quarter century thereafter; it remains one of her prime gifts to the city.

ARCHITECTURE

Architecture was practiced better and longer in New Orleans than any of the other visual arts. New Orleans is, in U.S. terms, a highly abnormal city. Two neighborhoods, the Vieux Carré and the Garden District, demonstrate its distinctness. The Vieux Carré began as a market site for local Indian trade, at what is now the French Market, restored in the 1930s by the Works Progress Administration. Until the 1960s it preserved some of its former function as the metropolitan area's central wholesale food market, with retail activity on the side. Now it is

mostly an emporium for the tourist trade, the city's second source of income, so in a way it retains its symbolic centrality.

Beyond the original line of market stalls Louisiana's first colonial governor and founder of New Orleans, Jean-Baptiste Le Moyne de Bienville and the military engineers Pauger and Blondel de la Tour laid out a model eighteenth-century city of forty-four squares. The standard square measured 50 *toises* (almost exactly 300 feet) on each side; no street was to be wider than 10 *toises* (60 feet). Bienville's grid plan was loosely replicated for more than a century of subsequent urban expansion, with each new *faubourg* reoriented to the curving river front, making for fanlike intersections at the limits of these gridded developments. Bienville and his Enlightened engineers were probably unaware that they were replicating the planning norms of Alexander the Great's successors—and New Orleans does retain much of the cultural feel of Hellenistic urbanism.

Little of the surviving Vieux Carré is strictly colonial, thanks to three devastating eighteenth-century fires. The only authenticable French colonial building is the Ursuline Convent, a standard French provincial structure begun in 1745. More typical of early French influence is the standard French Quarter one-story hipped-roof cottage, a blend of Canadian and Caribbean models. The grander style of colonial townhouse is represented by "Madame John's Legacy" (632 Dumaine Street), built in French style for a Spanish officer by an American builder after the fire of 1788. Its current name derives from one of Cable's novels.

The typical French Quarter buildings—three- or four-story brick structures with wrought- or cast-iron galleries, built around courtyards—are nineteenth-century or carefully imitative twentieth-century constructions. They perpetuate an old Mediterranean residential model, however. Residential density in the Quarter is not equal to that of Rome or Naples, but close. A stylish bourgeois life active year-round was made possible in that climate by the enclosed patios, their shade enhanced by the large green leaves of fast-growing banana trees. The standard building of this type accommodates commercial activity as well, and public buildings such as banks arose among the private houses. Architecturally the most distinguished zone of the Vieux Carré is also its planned center, the Place d'Armes, which became Plaza de Armas and then Jackson Square after the victory of 8 January 1815. Three Spanish colonial buildings reworked in the nineteenth century face the riverfront across the

Gallier House, Royal Street, the French Quarter. James Gallier Jr. built this street for his use in 1857. Among his other New Orleans buildings are the French Opera House (1796) and the Luling Mansion (1865). © G.E. KIDDER SMITH/CORBIS

Square. St. Louis Cathedral, drastically redesigned in the 1850s by J. N. B. de Pouilly, perhaps New Orleans' greatest architect, is at the center; the Cabildo, seat of the Spanish state, and the Presbytère, designed to be the residence of the colonial clergy, flank the cathedral: all three buildings benefited in early stages from Don Andres Almonester's munificence. The east and west ("downtown" and "uptown") sides of the Square have been taken up entirely since 1850 by the Pontalba buildings, named after Don Andres's daughter, Baroness Pontalba. The buildings boast prime residential space on the upper floors—cafés and shops are on the ground level—with views hard to match in America across lushly gardened Jackson Square to the cast-iron balconies of the apartments facing or diagonal either to the monumental complex of cathedral-Cabildo-Presbytère or to the active riverfront crowded with ships going about their business.

The Vieux Carré was mirrored upriver in 1788 by Faubourg Ste. Marie, which was thoroughly Americanized after 1803. Partly residential, this rapidly expanding development provided the site for James Gallier's monumental Greek Revival City Hall of 1845 (now Gallier Hall), and businesses in the Anglo-American style flourished in buildings designed exclusively for commercial use. Less than twenty minutes from that central business district by one of the nation's first streetcar lines lay the city of Lafayette, annexed to New Orleans in 1855. Lafayette's core, soon called the Garden District by its promoters, is an early exercise in American suburban planning. Elegant residences in a variety of East Coast styles, separated from one another by surrounding gardens, were built for entrepreneurs from the Atlantic states and the British Isles and the occasional Creole family with an eye for the future. Among the colonnaded verandas appears the occasional cast-iron gallery, and here and there a neo-Gothic fantasy heralds the eventual arrival of Victorian syncretism. The District is not Charleston or Savannah, but the kinship is clear. What marks it as distinctively New Orleanian is the cemetery at its center and the tendency of several blocks to have one side of modest shotgun cottages to house the servants, often black. Racial and social segregation did not become complete in the Garden District until the 1970s, when property values finally expelled the poor and racial paranoia locked white residents behind their iron fences and reinforced gates. Racially fluid neighborhoods were another feature declaring the city's eccentricity in the early and mid-twentieth century.

But New Orleans's most distinctive neighborhoods are her necropoles scattered throughout the city rather than lying, in the Roman fashion, outside the walls. The oldest and most striking cemetery, St. Louis, lay originally beyond the colonial ramparts but was quickly surrounded as the Vieux Carré expanded inland. It was and remains interracial. New Orleans tombs had to be built above the ground because of the closeness of the water table to the city's surface. In the 1840s the city government and the Catholic archdiocese decided to improve the cemetery in the style of Père Lachaise in Paris. The result was standardized neoclassical tomb design, a whitewashed city of the dead with a richly variegated roofline punctuated by sculptured monuments. Some are the work of J. N. B. de Pouilly, a French immigrant who rebuilt the façade of St. Louis Cathedral and designed the splendid St. Louis Hotel and many elegant French Quarter townhouses.

CUISINE

One can say that New Orleans's most successful art forms have been music (opera and jazz, not symphony) and domestic architecture; but one should add cuisine, both haute and household. The standard touristic account of the origins of Creole cooking are fairly accurate. The colonizing French encountered a rich seafood-exploiting gastronomic tradition among the Tchoupitoulas, Choctaws, and other native peoples. The cultivation of rice by the French and then Spanish colonists largely replaced Indian corn as the basic local staple starch. To this blending process the émigrés contributed the diet of the Caribbean, itself a blend of French and West African traditions with some Mexican touches, already introduced to Louisiana kitchens by the Spanish rule. The émigrés' appetite for high culture, sharpened by the tendency of many of their wealthiest sons (and some daughters) to spend long years in Paris and elsewhere in France for their education, caused the full-scale import of haute cuisine, enjoyed and well supported by the other prosperous elements of the city's population.

Antoine's, still the city's largest and most famous formal restaurant, was founded in April 1840 by Antoine Alciatore, a recent immigrant. A richly sauced turkey dish is said to have been his earliest hit recipe. In subsequent generations Alciatore's descendants developed a wide range of dishes, adapting classic French cuisine to simpler Louisiana tastes and a larger sense of American reality. Their most famous recipe is Oysters Rockefeller, invented in 1899 by Antoine's son Jules to compensate for a shortage of imported escargots and named for America's richest man. The restaurant has never divulged the recipe and estimates that it has served that dish over 3.5 million times; any other restaurant's claim to duplicate it is firmly denounced as a fraud.

CARNIVAL

To finish this tally of cultural and intellectual achievements and disappointments, it seems fair to say that New Orleans's most creative and distinctive cultural institution has been its Carnival. New Orleans rivals Venice, Nice, and Rio de Janeiro as the home of an institutionalized carnival ritual of worldwide fame, though little imitation.

In general, Mardi Gras began in the Middle Ages as a more or less jocular worldly response to a serious Catholic liturgical time-marker, the beginning of Lent. Some anthropologists see the carnival in Catholic culture as an instance of liminality. Despite those origins, New Orleans's Carnival was organized in the late nineteenth century to boost the local economy, and in the twentieth century many New Orleanians spoke and wrote of Mardi Gras as more than the city's symbol, almost its essence, certainly its continuing raison d'être.

In the colonial era New Orleanians white and black were addicted to dancing, and the culmination of the dancing year was clearly the season leading up to Fat Tuesday, the eve of Ash Wednesday, after which such frivolities as the dance were to be suspended. There were formal balls for the Creoles, for whom dancing appears to have been much more than a social accomplishment, and ceremonial dancing for the blacks, which involved masked dancing in honor of a crown-wearing king of death. Masquing of a different inspiration, derived from Latin role-reversing *festivitas*, was popular with both racial groups. The titillation of sexual deviancy was present from the beginning: eighteenth- and nineteenth-century moralists inveighed predictably against masquing as a cover for prostitution and an occasion for female cross-dressing. In the twentieth century male impersonation of women would become a major feature of Mardi Gras and a cause for homiletic concern.

Carnival made its way through the Civil War and Reconstruction, appealing to Union troops as well as to the natives. In 1872 it began to include local and state political figures and local businessmen. A point has been made ever since to invite businessmen and civic leaders throughout the United States as well as occasional foreign dignitaries (such as the Duke and Duchess of Windsor) to join in the festivities. The goal of this organized hospitality has been to present New Orleans in a favorable light to an expanding commercial constituency.

During the late nineteenth century, parades of at least a dozen (sometimes several dozen) floats followed widely publicized routes, with flambeaux-carriers illuminating the edifyingly festive spectacle for the cheering crowds, to which masked members of the parading krewe (carnival group) flung necklaces and other trinkets. The themes of these tableaux became more instructional than polemical after Reconstruction: from a daring satire of Reconstruction government to "Plants of the Mississippi Valley," anthologized themes from Greek mythology, or celebrations of scientific progress.

Neighborhood Carnival organizations flourished among all the city's ethnic groups. White ethnic communities and middle-class groups excluded from the elite krewes and clubs founded their own balls, some far more opulent than the venerable establishment balls. Eventually, in the mid- and late twentieth century, newer elements of the business establishment—unfortunately for the city's economy, rival establishments—founded their own parading krewes. Carnival seemed on its way to becoming a nationally integrated equal-opportunity exercise in liminality.

In 1991 Carnival faced a crisis. The city Councilwoman Dorothy Mae Taylor led a successful campaign requiring Carnival organizations that received city support services such as police escorts and street cleaning to cease their racial and social exclusiveness. Krewes responded by refusing to parade. Some cognoscenti suggest that the membership of these elite clubs were finding it increasingly difficult to pay for parades worthy of their past and greeted the new city ordinances with muted outrage. Despite this boycott, in 1999 fifty-seven parades wound their way through various sections of the city between 31 January and 16 February (Mardi Gras that year.) What does Carnival mean, at least for New Orleanians? Reid Mitchell, a native son with a doctorate in American Studies from Princeton, goes so far as to "see in Mardi Gras what I hear in a really good jazz band: a model for the just society, the joyous community, the heavenly city. . . . Few people in New Orleans look for the millennium, but when the millennium comes, it will look a lot like New Orleans." Perhaps so.

See also **Southern Intellectual Life; Urban Cultural Institutions** *(volume 1); and other articles in this section.*

BIBLIOGRAPHY

American Institute of Architects, New Orleans Chapter. *A Guide to New Orleans Architecture.* New Orleans, 1974.

Benfey, Christopher E. G. *Degas in New Orleans: Encounters in the Creole World of Kate Chopin and George Washington Cable.* New York, 1997.

Cable, Mary. *Lost New Orleans.* Boston, 1980.

Cabildo, Friends of the. *New Orleans Architecture.* Vol. 3, *The Cemeteries.* Gretna, La., 1997. (This is part of a multivolume series begun by Samuel Wilson Jr., professor of architecture at Tulane, in collaboration with his students and continued by them.)

Caulfeild, Ruby Van Allen. *The French Literature of Louisiana.* New York, 1929.

Giraud, Marcel. *Histoire de la Louisiane francaise.* 4 vols. Paris, 1953–1974.

Haas, Edward F. *DeLesseps S. Morrison and the Image of Reform: New Orleans Politics, 1946–1961.* Baton Rouge, La., 1974.

Hamel, Réginald. *La Louisiane créole: Littéraire, politique et sociale, 1762–1900.* 2 vols. Montréal, Canada, 1984.

Heard, Malcolm, Jr. *French Quarter Manual: An Architectural Guide to New Orleans' Vieux Carré.* New Orleans, La., 1997

Huber, Leonard V. *Landmarks of New Orleans.* New Orleans, La., 1984

Kane, Harnett T. *Queen New Orleans, City by the River.* New York, 1949.

Lanusse, Armand. *Les cenelles: Choix de poésies indigènes.* New Orleans, La., 1845; reprint, Nendeln, Liechtenstein, 1971.

Lewis, Peirce F. *New Orleans: The Making of an Urban Landscape.* Cambridge, Mass., 1976.

Malson, Lucien, and Christian Bellest. *Le Jazz.* Paris, 1987.

Mercier, Alfred. *L'Habitation Saint-Ybars; ou, Maîtres et esclaves en Louisiane (récit social).* New Orleans, 1881; reprint with intro. and commentary by Réginald Hamel, Montréal, Canada, 1989.

Mitchell, Reid. *All on a Mardi Gras Day: Episodes in the History of New Orleans Carnival.* Cambridge, Mass., 1995.

Richardson, Thomas J., ed. *The Grandissimes: Centennial Essay.* Jackson, Miss., 1981.

Roberts, W. Adolphe. *Lake Pontchartrain.* Indianapolis, Ind., 1946.

Starr, S. Frederick. *Bamboula! The Life and Times of Louis Moreau Gottschalk.* New York, 1995.

———. *Southern Comfort: The Garden District of New Orleans,* with photographs by R. S. and J. W. Brantley. Cambridge, Mass., 1989; reprint, New York, 1998.

Tinker, Edward Larocque. *Les écrits de langue francaise en Louisiane en XIXe siécle.* Paris, 1932.

Turner, Arlin. *George W. Cable: A Biography.* Durham, N.C., 1956.

Tyler, Pamela. *Silk Stockings and Ballot Boxes: Women and Politics in New Orleans, 1920–1963.* Athens, Ga., 1996.

Vella, Christina. *Intimate Enemies: The Two Worlds of the Baroness de Pontalba.* Baton Rouge, La., 1997.

SOUTHERN CALIFORNIA

Richard Cándida Smith

The transformation of Los Angeles into one of the most exciting, vibrant cities of the world testifies to the power of the imagination to overcome natural limitations. During the last two decades of the nineteenth century, civic leaders challenged the isolation of their town by building an artificial harbor that is now the nation's second busiest port. They captured control of train routes into the region and engaged in a worldwide marketing campaign to attract tourists and settlers. The most important project for the future of the region, however, was engineer William Mulholland's proposal to transport water from the Sierra Nevadas across hundreds of miles of desert and mountains. In the 1910s he designed and constructed for the city of Los Angeles one of the world's most ambitious hydrological projects, perhaps the largest ever built by a city instead of a national government. Mulholland's team succeeded brilliantly in solving technical obstacles and eradicated the limits that relatively limited local water sources placed on growth.

Often enough as the region grew in a series of spectacular projects, failure revealed the nightmares lingering close to ambition. While Mulholland built his aqueduct system, real estate developer Abbott Kinney hoped to create a replica of Venice complete with canals and gondolas in the Ballona Lagoon south of Santa Monica. Kinney dreamed of recapturing for his hometown the glory of the once great Mediterranean city. However, he could not solve the problem of how to keep the canals from silting, and his project quickly decayed into a slum, where decomposing stucco arcades spoke to the fear of degeneracy haunting modern dreams of unlimited progress. The price of rapid growth dictated largely by the desire of local entrepreneurs to capitalize on the region's clement weather has been urban sprawl, air pollution, and racial tensions that three times in the twentieth century fueled deadly urban riots.

Home to the motion picture industry, Los Angeles is one of the most important cultural capitals of the world. Hollywood imagery had contributed to the glamorous mythos of the region, while simultaneously promoting an image of Southern California as superficial and tawdry, as a place where the shade of one's tan carries greater weight than the depth of one's thought. The image may not be entirely unfair, but it offers an incomplete representation of a complex urban center. Southern California has developed into an important center for research in many scientific fields, with particular strengths in astronomy, genetics, and organic chemistry. Continued investment over many decades in schools, museums, and other civic institutions has led to an impressive body of cultural assets that are outstanding by any standard. Los Angeles in particular has been home to scores of prominent writers, artists, musicians, architects, scientists, and educators. Distinctive and innovative approaches to literature and the arts have emerged from the region, yielding a rich artistic legacy, often exceptionally engaged with the moral and aesthetic dilemmas of a culture organized around unlimited progress. For local boosters, rapid growth demonstrated the productivity of imagination. For the many critics of Southern California life, the most insightful of whom have been local residents, regional history has demonstrated instead the destructive effects of greed. Neither booster nor critic is wrong. To understand the cultural and intellectual life in the region requires keeping the perspectives of both in mind.

CONQUEST AND A CULTURE OF GROWTH

The Tongva, Chumash, and Tataviam peoples occupied the coastal plains and valleys along the Santa Barbara channel for thousands of years. In 1769, Franciscan missionaries landed at San Diego to establish a chain of missions along the coast as far north as the San Francisco Bay region. Secular set-

Chumash Cave Painting. The Chumash used the sacred caves for religious ceremonies. © DAVID MUENCH/CORBIS

tlement from Mexico followed and, in 1781, forty-four migrants founded the pueblo of Los Angeles. The first literature from the region were accounts by Franciscans of their work, memoirs by members of the landowning aristocracy, and descriptions by French, British, American, and Russian travelers of the climate and social life during the Spanish and Mexican periods.

To these foreign commentators, the peoples of the area, be they Mexican or native, failed to grasp the value they could extract from the land upon which they lived. The historian Richard Henry Dana, in his classic account of California under Mexican sovereignty, *Two Years before the Mast* (1840), enthused, "In the hands of an enterprising people, what a country this might be!" (p. 179). Visitors affirmed the beauty and abundance of the land, which they credited to a beneficent nature that would generate untold wealth once labor tamed it. In the late twentieth century, ethnobotanists and

ecological historians have stressed that the wealth of the region before European conquest had been a product of the original inhabitants' expertise and technique. The philosophies and myths that guided their labors were largely invisible to commentators, who saw the ease with which the native peoples enjoyed their land as evidence of a corrupt moral state. The preexisting wealth of the area was both allure and temptation, for even conquerors might become sybarites. One early "explorer," Thomas Jefferson Farnham noted in *Life, Adventures, and Travels in California* (1849), a bountiful nature seduced Californians to put pleasure ahead of work, and Dana worried that Americans who settled in the far West would become lazy.

For thirty years after the American military conquest of 1846, Southern California remained a quiet pastoral region. Yankees arriving in Los Angeles, a town of sixteen hundred inhabitants in 1850, styled their new home the "Queen of the Cow Counties."

642

The city's population grew slowly to nearly six thousand by 1876, the year that the railroad arrived. By 1885, two rail companies, Southern Pacific and Santa Fé, were competing to draw tourists and settlers to the region from the eastern United States. Both railroads established literary bureaus to fund books and magazine articles extolling the potential of the land. Works by Charles Nordhoff (*California for Health, Pleasure, and Residence: A Book for Travellers and Settlers*, 1872), The California Immigration Commission (*California, the Cornucopia of the World*, 1883), and Jerome Madden (*California: Its Attractions for the Invalid, Tourist, Capitalist, and Homeseeker*, 1892) extolled the climate and the possibilities for a new culture that would blend Anglo-Saxon initiative with Mediterranean comfort.

The boosters of the region were extraordinarily effective. In the 1880s alone, the population of Los Angeles more than quadrupled and then doubled in each of the next two decades. By the 1910 census, the city had joined the ranks of the major urban centers in the United States. Between 1880 and 1930, new residents were predominantly middle-class, white Americans from the Midwest. The great waves of European immigration that transformed the major cities of the nation, including San Francisco to the north, largely bypassed Los Angeles. Carey McWilliams's *Southern California: An Island on the Land* (1946) and Robert M. Fogelson's *The Fragmented Metropolis: Los Angeles, 1850–1930* (1967), the two classic works on the development of Los Angeles prior to World War II, argue that public life in Los Angeles developed around a stark racial divide. A white, Protestant majority zealously guarding its American identity dominated a large minority of distinct nonwhite groups, fragmented and competing with each other for the lowest occupations but all equally excluded from the political process and even from many basic public services.

Although the white population of the city tended to despise the racial minorities who lived there, romantic interest in the history of the region and the cultures that the Americans had replaced found many adherents. Charles Fletcher Lummis, the first city editor of the *Los Angeles Times*, came to Los Angeles from Cincinnati in 1884 and quickly developed an enthusiasm for native culture, California's "Spanish" period, and the austere natural beauties of America's Southwest deserts. Lummis collected native crafts, and the work he saved in many cases remains the most extensive evidence of tribes destroyed by the Spanish and American conquests. Lummis launched a monthly magazine, *Land of Sunshine* (later renamed *Out West*), that encouraged exploration of the West. With considerable support from local businesses, he offered subsidies for eastern writers and artists who wanted to experience the wonders of the region. His home, El Alisal (The Sycamore), an eclectic mixture of styles that he believed synthesized the spirit of the land he had adopted, was the center of a small community of locally based intellectuals and bohemians who shared his enthusiasms, including the feminist writer Charlotte Perkins Gilman and the painter William Wendt. Lummis founded the California Landmarks Club in 1895, the beginnings of a regional historic preservation movement. In 1910, he launched the Southwest Museum, which has since built upon the personal collection he donated to the new institution. Lummis was a prolific writer, and his many books helped create a romantic geography of the region with often accurate but sometimes fanciful interpretations of the landscape and the history of the peoples who have lived there.

The cultural and intellectual life of the city developed in the context of nonstop boosterism. Regional elites wanted maximum growth in all fields, including the life of the mind. The eastern and midwestern towns they had left behind provided their models for a good cultural life. The migrants who arrived in Los Angeles after 1880 brought with them a commitment to chautauqua culture. Los Angeles was a lucrative destination for public lecturers, theater touring companies, and traveling musicians at the end of the nineteenth century. In her autobiography, Emma Goldman wrote that audiences in Los Angeles prior to 1917 were the largest she encountered anywhere in the United States and the most enthusiastic. Much of her public was hostile to her radical anarchist and feminist ideas, but she could count on drawing large numbers of informed listeners interested in debating virtually every topic she might propose.

CULTURAL INFRASTRUCTURE: LEARNING, LIBRARIES, AND MUSEUMS

Boosterism merged with a progressive culture of moral uplift to encourage the construction of schools, libraries, and museums, institutions that ensured that a rapidly expanding commercial society in a foreign land could remain attached to the best of its cultural heritage. As of 1990, there were thirty-two four-year colleges and universities in Los Angeles County and twenty-seven junior colleges. The three leading research universities in the county are the University of Southern California (USC),

The University of Southern California. The University Park Campus, south of downtown Los Angeles, with the Student Union building and Bovard Auditorium *(right)*. © ROBERT HOLMES/CORBIS

started in 1880 by the Methodist Episcopal Church as a school open to students of all faiths; the University of California, Los Angeles (UCLA), founded in 1919 as a southern branch of the older Berkeley campus; and the California Institute of Technology (Caltech), established in Pasadena in 1891 as Throop University but reorganized and renamed in 1920 when the physicist Robert A. Millikan became president.

Academic prestige has been particularly notable in science and medicine. The Nobel laureates Max Delbrück and Linus Pauling, among many others, helped establish the area as a center for research in chemistry and genetics. Los Angeles is also a focal point for astronomy and space exploration. In 1917, the astronomer George Ellery Hale opened a 100-inch telescope on Mount Wilson in the San Gabriel Mountains above Pasadena, followed within a few years by a 200-inch reflector telescope at Mount Palomar near San Diego. The Jet Propulsion Laboratory, started in 1958, has designed and managed the National Aeronautics and Space Administration's expeditions to Mars, Venus, Jupiter, Saturn, and

other planets, and has been responsible for the scientific aspects of lunar exploration.

The Los Angeles Public Library quickly developed into one of the largest and most used public systems in the United States, while universities of the area also developed excellent libraries. The University Research Library at UCLA is the third largest academic library in the United States. There are several specialized research libraries in the Los Angeles region. The Henry E. Huntington Library, Art Gallery, and Botanical Gardens in San Marino opened to the public in 1928. The library has over 3 million rare items, including Shakespeare folios, manuscripts pertaining to British and American literature, politics, and culture, and a Gutenberg Bible. The art collection focuses on eighteenth-century British painting. The William Andrews Clark Memorial Library, deeded to UCLA in 1934, has extensive holdings in seventeenth- and eighteenth-century British literature, as well as books related to the life and work of Oscar Wilde. The surgeon Elmer Belt developed a superb collection of old books and manuscripts relating to Leonardo da Vinci and his time. Belt donated his collection to UCLA, where it is now a special library. The Research Institute for the History of Art and the Humanities at the Getty Center has collected over 800,000 volumes dealing with art history, as well as extensive manuscript collections. Thanks to a several-billion-dollar endowment, this late-twentieth-century library has quickly become an essential place for the study of French postimpressionism and modernism, dada and neodada art movements, and a large variety of other art historical topics.

The Getty Center is also famous for its J. Paul Getty Museum, which has particularly strong collections in Greco-Roman antiquity, medieval manuscripts, old master painting, and photography. It is one of over two hundred museums in the greater Los Angeles region. The Norton Simon Museum of Art in Pasadena houses one of the finest private collections of old master, modern, and Asian art to be found anywhere in the world. The museum is also home to the Galka Scheyer Collection of German expressionist painting, as well as to excellent modern collections assembled by the Pasadena Art Museum between 1942 and 1974. Other particularly notable museums are the Los Angeles County Museum of Art, founded in 1910, with superb holdings in most fields; the Los Angeles Museum of Contemporary Art, founded in 1979 to showcase art produced since 1940; the Autry Museum of Western Heritage; the Southwest Museum, with strong holdings in the cultures of the indigenous peoples of the region; the Frederick R. Weisman Museum of Art at Pepperdine University, with particularly strong holdings in twentieth-century California art; the California African American Museum; the Japanese American National Museum; and the Museum of Jurassic Technology.

Los Angeles cultural institutions flourished to the degree that wealthy benefactors supported them with financial donations and personal leadership. Impressive amounts of money facilitated the acquisition of the best items available at any given time in the art or book markets. Money as well assured that the best professional talent came to Los Angeles to develop and administer collections built virtually from scratch in extraordinarily short periods. The strength of museums and libraries in the area makes them fitting cultural symbols for a region historically committed to an ethos of growth. Most collections have nothing to do with the region, California, or the American West. Materials with recognized timeless value and validated as important by the leading experts of the eastern United States and Europe received first priority.

For a city that claims to be, and very likely is, the most multicultural city in the world, Los Angeles's cultural monuments are decidedly Eurocentric. Further, though the city has been home to many lively contemporary literary and arts scenes, few cultural leaders of the region have made support of local work a personal priority. Local talent may receive excellent training in area schools, but afterward they have historically encountered a marked indifference to contemporary culture that is not part of the entertainment industry. Nonetheless, the region has developed strong autonomous traditions in literature, art, architecture, music, and dance, in large part thanks to the presence of Hollywood.

The relocation of the motion picture industry to Los Angeles in the 1910s was an important factor in spurring the development of the local arts scenes. The industry brought perennial waves of writers, artists, and musicians, as well as actors, dancers, and theater talent to the city. Their numbers far exceeded the employment capacities of Hollywood, even in its heyday, but thousands kept coming and many born in the region stayed. Despite the inadequacies in cultural support typical of American provincial cities, a lively cultural world emerged unlike that found in any American city other than New York. As pervasive and catalytic a presence as Hollywood has been for the region, however, the motion picture industry did not set the limits of the city's cultural life. Indeed, it may be that themes indigenous to Southern California writers and artists shaped the development of American motion pictures and helped create the mythic image of Los Angeles that the movies then projected around the world.

LOS ANGELES LITERATURE AND FICTION

The first locally produced work of fiction was Horace Bell's *Reminiscences of a Ranger* (1881). A humorous account of Americans living in Los Angeles between 1850 and 1870, the book is marked by a broad humor reminiscent of Mark Twain's *Roughing It* (1872) and the satires of Artemus Ward. Rather than glorify Yankee heroism, Bell poked fun at the perpetual naïveté of Americans dumb enough to leave their comfortable homes and fling themselves into a completely strange country.

The first best-selling book to emerge from the region was Helen Hunt Jackson's *Ramona* (1884). During the 1870s and early 1880s, Jackson traveled extensively in Southern California and became friends with several Californio families. She decided to write a novel that would dramatize for the American public how Yankee greed had led to the mistreatment of the Mission Indians and dispossession of the "Spanish" landowners. Jackson celebrated the culture of the Californios as one of refinement and personal integrity, as well as more caring of the Indians for whose care they were responsible. Synthesis between Yankee, Latino, and native peoples, however, was not yet on the agenda. Despite her sympathies, Jackson concluded *Ramona* with its attractive heroes, the son of a Mexican land grant owner and his Indian beloved, quitting the United States and settling in Mexico, where they could find refuge from their persecutors.

Though Jackson was highly critical of how California had developed under the Americans, her romantic enthusiasm for the region's Spanish roots fit in quite well with how real estate speculators were marketing the region. Developers responded to the novel with tour packages and the construction of a series of attractions for tourists. For at least two decades, fans of the novel poured into the region expressly to visit the "actual sites" where the fictional characters of Jackson's novel had lived and struggled.

Jackson was a tourist herself, as were most writers who initially came to the region. Mary Austin was one of the first serious writers of Southern California to speak from years of personal experience. In 1888 at the age of twenty, she moved from the East to Tejón Pass, a ranching area in the mountains north of Los Angeles. She married and moved with her husband to Owens Valley, where she raised a family for the next fifteen years. Her first novel, *Land of Little Rain* (1903), is a powerful evocation of her life as a working farm wife in the Southern California hinterlands. Austin wrote of the desert as a powerful, indifferent presence looming over the region. In her work, the desert refuses to recognize human aspirations, but provides spiritual liberation to those who learn to appreciate a beauty transformable into wealth only with great difficulty. She also wrote of the interaction of the peoples of the region and their learning from each other in the course of a common struggle.

Like the desert, Hollywood has remained a staple theme in regional literature. Here, Hollywood is not simply a setting but exteriorizes a moral state; the movie business serves as a symbol for a complex of ideas about the role of ambition and self-deception in the modern world. The first novel about modern, urban Los Angeles was Harry L. Wilson's *Merton of the Movies* (1922), a comic novel set in the newborn motion picture industry. Wilson's work—indeed, the Hollywood novel at large—inverts the boosters' myths of Southern California as a place of unlimited growth and opportunity by foregrounding the greed, failure, and moral crudeness of lives devoted to stimulating and satisfying desires. Among the most famous of the many works produced on this theme are Nathanael West's *The Day of the Locust* (1939), Aldous Huxley's *After Many a Summer Dies the Swan* (1939), John Fante's *Ask the Dust* (1939), F. Scott Fitzgerald's *The Last Tycoon* (unfinished, published 1941), Budd Schulberg's *What Makes Sammy Run?* (1941), and Evelyn Waugh's *The Loved One* (1948). William Faulkner, who also made the trek to Hollywood and worked for some time as a screenwriter, contributed to the genre with his short story, "Golden Land" (1935).

In the 1930s, the detective novel emerged as a staple of Los Angeles literature. James Cain's *The Postman Always Rings Twice* (1934) and *Double Indemnity* (1936) established the basic themes of greed and sexual desire combining to pervert all human relationships. Raymond Chandler's Philip Marlowe novels, particularly *Farewell, My Lovely* (1940), and Ross Macdonald's Lew Archer series, beginning with *The Moving Target* (1949), set high literary standards for subsequent writers, and established a vocabulary of plot twists for a style that came to be called L.A. noir. Dreams turn rotten in a tawdry, quickly built cityscape that, however young, is already decaying. In Macdonald's work, generational strife saps the victories of the founding fathers, whose hidden crimes emerge inevitably to reveal the hypocrisy of an ethos centered on growth, while Chandler foregrounded the inability of men and women to trust each other or arrive at a union that will ensure continuity.

In the late twentieth century, Joseph Wambaugh, a former Los Angeles Police Department officer, established a new standard of brutal realism for the genre with *The New Centurions* (1970) and subsequent novels that explored the culture of policemen and their spiritual confusions. The corruption of the public order marks the novels of John Gregory Dunne, such as *True Confessions* (1977). In the 1990s, Walter Mosley and Michael Nava adopted the genre to explore the dark side of the city's racial and sexual histories by creating detective heroes based in the African American and gay communities, respectively. Mosley's work follows the precedent set by Chester Himes in *If He Hollers Let Him Go* (1945), which uses noir conventions to describe the experiences of African Americans in wartime Los Angeles. Like many writers, Himes came to Los Angeles to work as a screenwriter in Hollywood. He landed a job at Warner Bros., but the racism he encountered overcame his determination to succeed. In 1944, he left Los Angeles to return to New York, but ultimately moved to Europe. Several of his novels refer to his experiences in Southern California.

Noir conventions shape many novels about life in Los Angeles that are not otherwise in the Hollywood and detective genres. Joan Didion's *Play It As It Lays* (1970) uses the freeway system as a metaphor for the aimless, wandering life of its main character, while John Rechy's classic of gay literature, *City of Night* (1963), presents a chilling portrait of male hustlers in Hollywood. Upton Sinclair's earlier *Oil!* (1927) is more realist and less symbolic, but its detailed picture of the oil boom in the Long Beach area and its corrupting effects anticipated many of the noir motifs, as did Horace McCoy's *They Shoot Horses, Don't They?* (1935), a brilliant examination of the devastating consequences of the Great Depression symbolically represented by a marathon dance held on a Southern California pier jutting out into the Pacific Ocean. Christopher Isherwood's *A Single Man* (1964) tells the story of an expatriate dying in Los Angeles in the 1940s and horrified by the doom falling simultaneously upon him and the city. Many critics consider Isherwood's book the finest novel on the émigré experience in Southern California. The poetry of Charles Bukowski, perhaps the best-known poet of the city, with themes of isolation in the midst of decay, strongly reflects noir conventions.

"Los Angeles literature" is too often limited to work that is explicitly set in the region. Authors such as Ray Bradbury, Anaïs Nin, and Octavia Butler, whose work has not privileged the region as either a setting or a theme, are not widely recognized as "Los Angeles writers," even though their creative careers were largely or entirely spent in the city. Hundreds of writers live and work in the region. They reflect the diversity of the communities and the cultures that make up an urban center of over 10 million people. In the 1980s, fully 25 percent of foreign immigrants to the United States settled in Southern California, more than double any other location in the country. These new residents have complicated the racial divisions of the region by adding a layer of ethnic diversity that is transforming the social and political life of the region. The literature of the new Los Angeles will likely intersect with the older themes that established a global symbolic understanding of the region. Nonetheless, the genres that presented Los Angeles to the world as the archetypal symbol for modern decadence will have to be transcended if experiences of taking root and making connections are also to find expression.

ART AND ARCHITECTURE

Cave paintings by the Chumash people have survived, as well as handcrafts. They provide evidence of the values of the native peoples, but the primary expression of visual art in the preconquest period was body painting, an intimate and fragile medium that requires contact with people and not simply with images. Franciscan missionaries trained native artists in European techniques, and some paintings and sculptures by these artisans have also survived, particularly in the San Gabriel Mission, where Spanish and native visual traditions are occasionally juxtaposed. Nothing survives of Tongva, Chumash, or Tataviam buildings. The Chumash had an elaborate wood construction technology, while the other native peoples built more temporary enclosed spaces from boughs and reeds.

In the American period, companies interested in promoting tourism and settlement sponsored visits by painters who would capture the natural beauties of the region. By the 1890s, permanent arts communities had taken root in the Arroyo Seco area around Charles Fletcher Lummis's home, as well as in several other semirural communities. In 1898, the then well-known French floral painter Paul DeLongpré moved to Los Angeles from France, and his gallery became a principal tourist attraction in the region. Local painting was largely derivative of the Barbizon school, but with stronger emphasis on capturing the sharp contrasts of light and shadow typical of the region on sunny days. Stanton Macdonald-Wright, a veteran of pre–World War I Paris, founded Los Angeles's first modern art society in 1916. A lively modernist scene developed through the 1920s and 1930s with a primary interest in chromatic effects that would match the colorful environment. Rex Slinkard and Mabel Alvarez were the most talented painters associated with early regional modernism. During this time, the Italian immigrant Sabato (Simon) Rodia constructed the Watts Towers, which inspired many subsequent assemblage artists in the state.

Los Angeles was an important center for the development of modern architectural styles. For several decades after the American conquest, builders shifted from the adobe used by the Mexicans to wood and brick, utilizing materials and construction techniques familiar to them from their homes in the East. In the 1890s, architects and builders began giving serious thought to how they might take better advantage of the natural environment that was the primary attraction to settlers. At the same time, the real estate booms involved widespread development of large tracts with relatively uniform style of homes. The California bungalow, popularized throughout the country by *Craftsman* magazine, became a ubiquitous feature of the Southern California landscape. Its relatively simple but elegant lines opened interior spaces to allow for greater connection to yards, while wooden porches, eaves, and porticoes presented warm façades that suggested both Japanese and European influences. The architectural firm of Charles and Henry Greene in Pasadena built versions that were more elaborate for the many wealthy easterners who wintered in that suburb.

At the same time, the quest for a distinctive regional identity encouraged a revival of Mexican building styles. Adobe construction did not reappear, but concrete and stucco superimposed a "Spanish" look upon floor plans developed for the California bungalow house. Shortly after 1900, Irving Gill developed a poured-concrete construction technique that he used to add arcaded patios and porches to homes with otherwise sleek modern lines. By 1915, the so-called Mission revival style dominated new construction, both for private housing and public buildings. Bertram G. Goodhue's pavilions for the Panama-California Exposition in San Diego established an impressive body of public buildings that combined simple planes of white wall with bands of elaborate baroque ornamentation. The 1925 Santa Barbara earthquake demolished much of the town's Victorian-era center, and the city council ruled that all reconstruction be limited to the Spanish style.

Mission revivalism was particularly popular, but it was only one expression of a broader movement to link California to a fictitious Mediterranean legacy. George Allison's design for the UCLA campus in the 1920s used a neo-Byzantine style, self-consciously imitating monuments in Ravenna and Milan. Adding to the romantic mixture increasingly defining Los Angeles buildings, there were free adaptations of Chinese and Japanese architectural styles. Frank Lloyd Wright designed several homes constructed with steel-reinforced concrete blocks that he used to evoke Aztec and Maya monumentality. There were also a number of amusing programmatic buildings, such as the now demolished Brown Derby restaurant shaped like a derby hat, or the Tail O' the Pup hot dog stand shaped like a hot dog in a bun.

Two Austrian immigrants, Richard J. Neutra and Rudolf Schindler, were the foremost exponents of the International style in Los Angeles. Schindler came to the United States before World War I to study with Frank Lloyd Wright in Wisconsin. He moved to Los Angeles in 1920 to supervise the construction of Wright's Hollyhock House. He decided to stay and over the next several years built his own home in West Hollywood. This building, now restored to its original design and open to the public as a museum, synthesized Craftsman, Japanese, and Spanish motifs into a distinctively experimental, avant-garde look that attracted commissions. Neutra settled in Los Angeles in 1926, where he found a congenial clientele in Hollywood and in the city's professional circles receptive to his theories of "biological realism." Neutra's Lovell House (1929) overlooking Griffith Park became his signature building. His design alternated horizontal bands of fenestration circling the building with brilliant white panels that served both to reflect the hot sun and to bring attention to the building in its steep hillside setting. In the interior, Neutra achieved an illusion that the floors are hovering weightlessly over the canyon the home overlooks. Schindler and Neutra designed both homes and public buildings that set a path for further developments in California architecture. While both were interested in designing large-scale housing tracts and Neutra did construct prefabricated housing for war workers in the Channel Heights Housing Project (1942–1944), neither had much influence on the tract housing that came to dominate the Southern California landscape.

West Coast painters in the 1920s and 1930s followed European modernist developments closely, but their work was seldom directly imitative and often moved in distinctive directions. Surrealism, for example, found an echo and a riposte in postsurrealism, a school led by Helen Lundeberg and Lorser Feitelson. The postsurrealists sought to examine the relation of self and environment through a focus on the normal associative processes of the mind and its ability to transform sensations into ideas. During World War II, these painters shifted their interest to exploring the space and light effects inherent to abstract geometric forms.

After World War II in Los Angeles as elsewhere, modernism became the predominant form in both architecture and painting. In vernacular architecture, the ranch house spread across the region. Cliff May developed the style in the 1930s as a modification and simplification of the Spanish revival building. The ranch house with its concrete slab flooring proved to be particularly economical for rapid construction of low- to middle-income housing. In an effort to counter the low design standards of most tract homes, John Entenza's journal *Art and Architecture* launched the Case Study House program. Entenza selected young architects to design homes that might demonstrate how scientific form improved quality and reduced costs. Entenza then found clients who would pay for having the homes constructed. Between 1945 and 1966, thirty-six model homes were designed and the majority built. Spectacular photographs by Julius Shulman did much to publicize the work of the contributors, who included Gregory Ain, Craig Ellwood, Charles and Ray Eames, Pierre Koenig, John Lautner, Raphael Soriano, and William Wurster.

Simultaneously, Richard Neutra and his partner Robert Alexander developed Baldwin Hills Village as a model for privately funded, multi-unit, low-cost housing. These efforts to change the nature of mass housing, as well as explorations with the aviation industry into the development of prefabricated homes, were frustrated by opposition from the real estate industry, private building contractors, and the building trades unions. The Case Study Homes, although designed as prototypes for low- to medium-cost housing, remained unique buildings that displayed the taste, daring, and distinction of their owners, while Baldwin Hills Village became a much-sought-after and expensive condominium complex.

While abstract expressionism dominated painting in New York and San Francisco immediately after World War II, Los Angeles artists continued working in the areas that had long been of interest to them. Oskar Fischinger and Jules Engel, both working as animators in the motion picture industry, presented forms, lines, and colors in the process of an unfolding development. In addition to painting, both worked in abstract motion pictures, a development that would find many followers in the region. Rico Lebrun and Howard Warshaw were the leaders of the so-called romantic surrealists. Lebrun's emotional imagery of the crucifixion and other religious themes received both critical and popular acclaim. John D. McLaughlin, Lorser Feitelson, and Helen Lundeberg developed an impressive body of color-field paintings. Lundeberg returned to figurative subjects after a long period of pure abstraction, and her canvases of the Los Angeles skyline under various lighting conditions were very influential. At first glance, the work of Emerson Woelffer, William Brice, and Hans Burckhardt appears close to abstract expressionism, but their gestural explorations of mark, form, and line are more in dialogue with contemporaneous French and Italian painting than with the New York school. Los Angeles painters did not have a large regional market, nor did they receive critical attention from New York. Nonetheless, the twenty years after World War II saw a remarkable explosion in the number of painters working in the region. The education provisions of the GI Bill led to dramatic increases in art school enrollments. A new arts community came into being that was completely separated from and often hostile to both the entertainment industry and to the regional tradition of boosterism. By the end of the 1950s, two new trends emerged within the local art scene that received considerable international attention: the funk and the cool.

Funk art preserved as much as possible the raw feeling of the materials artists used, whether they were paint, clay, or found objects. The California assemblage school was one of the major expressions of the funk aesthetic. Artists scoured junkyards, abandoned factories, and desert ghost towns to find abandoned objects with unusual shapes and textures, and then they re-created them into imaginative figures and scenes. Often the work addressed political and social themes, with particular emphasis on militarism, capital punishment, racial oppression, and sexual hypocrisy. A thoroughgoing critique of the cult of growth underlay the genre. By emphasizing the use of discards, assemblage artists challenged conventional public attitudes about beauty in art and preferences for sleek, modernist design that were prominent in the 1950s and 1960s. Well-known assemblagists from Los Angeles include Edward Kienholz, Wallace Berman, and George Herms. Noah Purifoy, the director of the Watts Towers Art Center in 1965 at the time of the Watts rebellion, put together an exhibition of pieces he and several other artists constructed from debris recovered from buildings burned out and looted during the conflict.

Cool art appeared to be more distant from social critical themes. The work usually had a well-polished finish and often focused on exploration of light and space, a long-standing regional interest. Robert Irwin, for example, eliminated chromaticism on his disks by using reflective paint that captured ambient light and created a variety of ephemeral coloristic illusions as viewers moved and changed their relationship to his paintings. Larry Bell and Craig Kauffman adopted new plastic materials and industrial paints developed in the aerospace industry. Other painters addressed symbols common to the region. Billy Al Bengston evoked hot rods, surfing, and military insignia in his paintings; Ed Ruscha painted and photographed gas stations, palm trees, the Hollywood sign, as well as many other mythic icons of the region. Both painters lavished technical brilliance on subjects redolent with boosterist overtones, but their work nonetheless succeeded in resisting and deflating the mythic emotional registers long associated with the images they reworked. Critics often posed cool and funk art as antagonistic trends, but many artists moved back and forth between the schools. The influence of the French artist Marcel Duchamp linked both groups. His phenomenal popularity in the local art world led to Walter Hopps curating the first retrospective that Duchamp had anywhere in the world, mounted at the Pasadena Art Museum in 1963.

Despite fluctuations in the art market, Los Angeles has continued to grow rapidly as a contemporary arts center since the mid-1960s. It has been a center for conceptual art. Judy Chicago's *Womanhouse* (1971) is a landmark in the development of feminist art. The Chicano artist collectives Los Four, Asco (Nausea), and the Self-Help Graphics and Art, Inc., emerged in the late 1960s and early 1970s to reclaim the Mexican heritage of the region from the legacy of appropriation. Mural painting had a rebirth in the region, particularly in Latino communities, but also elsewhere. One of the best known murals is *The Great Wall,* painted by Judy Baca and neighborhood youth in the San Fernando Valley in the mid-1970s. The mural presents a history of the United States as one of conquest and racial struggle, but extends the promise of an eventual triumph of hopes for justice, equality, and democracy. African American arts activists challenged the exhibition and collecting policies of local museums and forced local art critics to give more attention to exhibits by African American artists. The watercolorist William Pajaud assembled an impressive collection of African American art for Golden State Mutual Life Insurance Company, the largest black-owned business in the state of California. Alonzo Davis, Samella Lewis, John Outterbridge, Noah Purifoy, Betye Saar, and Carrie Mae Weems are among the numerous African American artists who were working in Los Angeles in 2000.

Los Angeles has become a center for pop, postmodern, and deconstructive architecture. In the 1970s and 1980s, Frank Gehry emerged as the region's best-known architect. Gehry's California Aerospace Museum (1984) is a sculpture of geometrical shapes that explode out of the ground. In his work for Loyola Law School (1984), Gehry incorporated playful quotations of older styles relevant to concepts of law and justice. In the Temporary Contemporary (1983, a branch site of the Los Angeles Museum of Contemporary Art) and in his own home in Santa Monica, he has used throwaway building materials such as sheet metal, cyclone fencing, and particleboard for decorative effect.

MUSIC AND DANCE

In the late 1930s, Los Angeles was home to a host of conductors and composers, including Otto Klemperer, who served as the conductor of the Los Angeles Philharmonic; Kurt Weill; Ernst Toch; Arnold Schoenberg, who had come in 1934 to teach at UCLA; Igor Stravinsky; Mario Castelnuovo-Tedesco; and Ernst Krenek. The weekly Monday Evenings on the Roof concert series, hosted by the Los Angeles Chamber Music Society, featured new music and premiered many of the new works by the prominent composers in the region. However, modern music remained an enclave, a specialized taste that did not interact significantly with other parts of the Los Angeles community. Efforts by Nicolas Slonimsky to introduce the work of Charles Ives and Arnold Schoenberg into the repertoire of the Los Angeles Philharmonic in the 1930s were spectacularly unsuccessful.

Nonetheless, the presence of so many important figures in modern music may have stimulated experimentation by a younger generation of Americans. Schoenberg held private classes at his home as well as at UCLA and taught the avant-garde composer John Cage twelve-tone composition techniques. A native of Los Angeles, Cage developed his musical style in his hometown before moving to New York in the 1940s. Los Angeles was a center for the California microtonalists. Cage, Conlon Nancarrow, and Harry Partch were among a number of composers who independently explored the possibilities of musical scales using more than the twelve tones developed in European music. Partch in particular became a cult figure on the West Coast. His hobo songs and his transcriptions of graffiti invoked *noir* traditions, while his mythic dance dramas synthesized European and East Asian musical forms with those of the peoples native to the American Southwest. Only the strong support of a few music patrons such as Betty Freeman and the presence of strong colleges and universities allowed experimental music to survive, if not precisely flourish.

Jazz came to Los Angeles with the motion picture industry. In 1919, Kid Ory formed the first

650

large-scale African American jazz orchestra in the city. His success in finding audiences generated many imitators and fostered the subsequent development of big band music. Benny Goodman's orchestra originated in Los Angeles before leaving to find greater success in New York. The number of African Americans living in Los Angeles jumped dramatically during World War II. A lively club scene developed in the Central Avenue area. Charles Mingus, Dexter Gordon, Eric Dolphy, Ornette Coleman, Buddy Collette, Horace Tapscott, Quincy Jones, Art Pepper, Gerry Mulligan, and Chet Baker are among the Los Angeles jazz musicians who developed international reputations. Between 1945 and 1965, a distinctively cool and intellectual jazz style developed in clubs in San Francisco and Los Angeles, often referred to simply as "West Coast jazz." After 1950, however, the club scene shrank, and musicians in the area were increasingly dependent upon recording motion picture and television scores for their incomes. While jazz remained a part of Los Angeles life, institutional support for innovative jazz music was limited. Many of the best and most innovative musicians left for New York or Europe to pursue their careers.

Los Angeles was also a center in the development of modern dance. Both Isadora Duncan and Ruth St. Denis began their careers in the region at a time when the pageant movement encouraged interest in the dramatic use of free dance form. Lester Horton, however, was the only important modern dance choreographer to maintain his base in Los Angeles between the 1920s and the 1950s. He trained a number of dancers and choreographers, including both Alvin Ailey and Bella Lewitzky. Ailey followed the usual pattern of relocating to New York where there was greater support available. Lewitzky remained in Los Angeles, successfully guiding a dance company that lasted from the 1960s to the 1990s.

LOS ANGELES AND THE CULTURE OF THE FUTURE

Given numerous strong schools, a flourishing high-technology sector, the continuing presence of the entertainment industry, and a growing core of wealthy donors and patrons, Los Angeles is likely to remain an important global center of intellectual and cultural life. The city's art and architecture scenes have achieved global visibility and in the 1990s received considerably more infrastructural support than in times past. No longer are artists and architects limited to regional imagery or themes, yet their work is often richer for its relation to a long history of concern for specific issues such as light and space. Contemporary boosters of the city refer to the international fame its artists and architects have achieved to argue that the city has finally achieved "world-class" status.

The city has long been an important center for twentieth-century world culture, but it also has had, and continues to have, many features more typical of a provincial town. Literature, theater, music, and dance could be equally strong, but they suffer from inadequacies in local infrastructure. While the cultures of Latinos, Asians, and African Americans started to receive greater visibility and some modest support toward the end of the twentieth century, multiculturality remains more a slogan rather than an actuality. A multicultural intellectual and cultural life is impossible if the city remains divided along racial and ethnic lines—a brutal fact that reflects nearly 150 years of deliberate exclusion and separation. To overcome the actual, everyday culture of the region will involve fostering a new culture that has confronted legacies of racial division and romantic appropriation. Exemplars for this culture do not yet exist elsewhere, and the provincial model for heritage preservation that has been dominant in Los Angeles—the collection of classic works from traditions important to people who have migrated into the region—will not meet the challenge. A heritage preservation particular to Southern California might entail recognizing innovations that have occurred in the course of people creating new lives for themselves in a new society. Engaging the culture that is in development needs as much if not more support than heritage continuity.

Current talk of Los Angeles as having become a global capital elevates the city's booster heritage to new levels and repeats hoary patterns. Perhaps, however, dangers can turn into assets if the provincial nature of cosmopolitan ambitions is cheerfully acknowledged. If Los Angeles has joined the ranks of world-class cities, then any place can, be it Miami, Minneapolis, or Oklahoma City. The success of Los Angeles suggests that a model of the world divided between a few cosmopolitan centers surrounded by layers of increasingly backward hinterland might someday be replaced by one in which nodes of concentrated human capital are widely dispersed in overlapping networks of shared concerns and projects across a large, diverse world. Certainly a romantic conception, but less dreary than the equally romantic image of Los Angeles as "capital of the twenty-first century."

See also **The World According to Hollywood; Asian Americans; Latinas and Latinos in the United States** *(in this volume); and other articles in this section.*

BIBLIOGRAPHY

Apostol, Jane. *El Alisal: Where History Lingers.* Los Angeles, 1994.

Banham, Reyner. *Los Angeles: The Architecture of Four Ecologies.* London, England, 1971.

Cándida Smith, Richard. *Utopia and Dissent: Art, Poetry, and Politics in California.* Berkeley, Calif., 1995.

Caughey, John, and LaRee Caughey, eds. *Los Angeles: Biography of a City.* Berkeley, Calif., 1976.

Cenzatti, Marco. *Los Angeles and the L.A. School: Postmodernism and Urban Studies.* Los Angeles, 1993.

Dana, Richard Henry. *Two Years before the Mast.* 1840. Reprint, New York, 1922. Page references in the text are from the reprint edition.

Davis, Mike. *City of Quartz: Excavating the Future in Los Angeles.* New York, 1992.

Dear, Michael J. "Postmodern Urbanism." *Annals of the Association of American Geographers* 88(1998): 50–72.

Dear, Michael J., H. Eric Schockman, and Greg Hise, eds. *Rethinking Los Angeles.* Thousand Oaks, Calif., 1996.

Farnham, Thomas Jefferson. *Life, Adventures, and Travels in California.* New York, 1849.

Fine, David ed. *Los Angeles in Fiction: A Collection of Original Essays.* Albuquerque, N.M., 1984.

Fogelson, Robert M. *The Fragmented Metropolis: Los Angeles, 1850–1930.* 1967. Reprint, Berkeley, Calif., 1993.

Gebhard, David, and Robert Winter. *Los Angeles: An Architectural Guide.* Salt Lake City, Utah, 1994.

Gordon, Robert. *Jazz West Coast: The Los Angeles Jazz Scene of the 1950s.* New York, 1986.

Gottlieb, Bob, and Irene Wolt. *Thinking Big: The Story of the Los Angeles Times, Its Publishers, and Their Influence on Southern California.* New York, 1977.

Gutiérrez, Ramón A., and Richard J. Orsi. *Contested Eden: California before the Gold Rush.* Berkeley, Calif., 1998.

Karlstrom, Paul ed. *On the Edge of America: California Modernist Art, 1900–1950.* Berkeley, Calif., 1996.

McWilliams, Carey. *Southern California Country: An Island on the Land.* 1946. Reprint, Santa Barbara, Calif., 1973.

———. *The Education of Carey McWilliams.* New York, 1978.

Ovnick, Merry. *Los Angeles: The End of the Rainbow.* Los Angeles, 1994.

Rieff, David. *Los Angeles: Capital of the Third World.* New York, 1991.

Rolfe, Lionel. *Literary L.A.* San Francisco, 1981.

Scott, Allen J., and Edward W. Soja, eds. *The City: Los Angeles and Urban Theory at the End of the Twentieth Century.* Berkeley, Calif., 1996.

Starr, Kevin. *Inventing the Dream: California through the Progressive Era.* New York, 1985.

———. *Material Dreams: Southern California through the 1920s.* New York, 1990.

Steele, James. *Los Angeles Architecture: The Contemporary Condition.* London, 1993.

Walker, Franklin. *A Literary History of Southern California.* Berkeley, Calif., 1950.

Winter, Robert. *The California Bungalow.* Los Angeles, 1980.

UTAH AND MORMONISM

Thomas G. Alexander

MORMONS AND UTAH'S PHYSICAL AND CULTURAL LANDSCAPE

Civic Development Since July 1847, when members of the Church of Jesus Christ of Latter-day Saints (LDS), also known as Mormons, began to settle in Utah, they have left an indelible imprint on Utah's land and culture. As with a number of American religions, Mormonism originated during America's Second Great Awakening (1797–1840s). In 1820 in the midst of religious revivals, Joseph Smith, then fourteen and living at Palmyra in western New York, turned to God in prayer. He experienced an extraordinarily powerful theophany in which Christ told him to join none of the churches. Later, an angelic visitor named Moroni led him to engraved plates that he translated and published as The Book of Mormon. Smith and a small body of believers organized the church in 1830. Enduring intense persecution for their communitarian religion that included theocratic politics and economics, Smith and the Mormons sought refuge in Ohio, Missouri, and Illinois. By 1844 in Nauvoo, Illinois, internal dissention and external persecution led to frequent conflicts and eventually to the murder of Smith and his brother Hyrum.

In August 1844 the majority of the Mormons voted to follow Brigham Young and the Quorum of Twelve Apostles. Renewed armed attacks led a majority in 1846 to abandon Nauvoo and to move westward. Young and the other leaders concluded that their religious beliefs and practices would induce conflict anywhere other Euroamericans had already settled, as they moved to the Great Basin. Under the leadership of Brigham Young and other general authorities the LDS Church conducted an active campaign to bring members to settle in the West. Between 1846 and 1930, the thousands of Mormons who emigrated founded some 742 towns, more than 600 of which have remained in the twenty-first century.

For nineteenth-century Latter-day Saints, Zion represented both an idea and a place. Zion meant "the pure in heart." It also meant the gathering place of Latter-day Saints who expected to build covenant communities to protect themselves from the tribulations prophesied in Matthew 24 prior to Christ's second coming. In the twentieth and twenty-first centuries, Zion has continued to mean "the pure in heart," but, like the seventeenth-century Puritans, instead of gathering to Utah, Mormons are encouraged to live in the world but not be of the world.

In the nineteenth century, as they gathered to Utah, they laid out the towns on a grid pattern similar to that of many American cities. Mormons based the plan in part on the plan of the City of Zion devised for a community in Independence, Missouri, by Joseph Smith, the church's founder. Because of federal land laws, after a U.S. land office opened in Utah in 1868, the town layouts tended to vary substantially.

Nevertheless, the ideal Mormon towns had a peculiar look to them. Young said that he wanted to be able turn a span of oxen around without backing it up, so the streets of Mormon towns were forty-four yards wide. The settlers bordered the streets with irrigation ditches and trees, especially Lombardy poplars. The Mormons laid out one-and-a-quarter-acre town lots, which they situated on ten-acre blocks. Each lot had space for vegetable, fruit, and flower gardens. In a design similar to that of New England and European towns, the Latter-day Saints placed their farms outside the settlements. In the center of town they reserved space for public and religious buildings.

Although Mormons generally established farming towns, they also promoted mining, manufacturing, commerce, and the professions. Moreover, they founded specialized settlements such as those at Parowan and Cedar City (1851) for iron manufacture; Coalville (1859) for coal; and St. George (1861) for cotton and grapes. In the 1860s and

1870s they chartered and constructed railroads, banks, and cooperative united orders. In the 1890s Mormon leaders collaborated with national business leaders to organize the Utah-Idaho Sugar Company and hydroelectric power companies. To promote the development of the territory, the Mormons organized the Deseret Agricultural and Manufacturing Society (DAMS), which the territorial legislature chartered in 1857. Among other activities, the DAMS operated a territorial fair that offered prizes for the best plants, animals, and crafts; set up experimental gardens and farms; and imported improved strains of plants and animals.

At the same time, the Mormons expected that the concentration of people in towns would facilitate educational and cultural improvement. Young believed that living close together would enable farmers to have the same cultural and intellectual advantages as other urban dwellers. To disseminate information, the church leadership began publishing the *Deseret News* in 1850.

As planned, the towns served as centers for intellectual and cultural life. In 1854, under the leadership of Wilford Woodruff, a Connecticut Yankee educated at the Farmington Academy, the Mormons organized the short-lived Universal Scientific Society, an ambitious attempt to study all knowledge. The same year, under the leadership of the former Oberlin College students Lorenzo Snow and his sister Eliza Roxey Snow, they organized the Polysophical Society, which promoted study and performances in the humanities and arts. The Polysophical Society lasted until a reformation in 1856 forced its closure. During the mid-1850s, women in various towns organized relief societies, which offered charitable help to the needy and also afforded sisterhood, education, and religious experiences to the women who joined. Relief societies were still thriving at the end of the twentieth century.

Arts, Theater, and Education   During the 1860s the Mormons promoted cultural revivals throughout the settlements. Clubs and literary organizations sprang up. Although Salt Lake City had a population of only eighty-two hundred in 1860, in 1862, the Mormons constructed the Salt Lake Theater. This extraordinarily beautiful Greek Revival structure hosted traveling theater troupes and a resident company. In dedicating the theater, Young said he expected plays to offer moral lessons while they afforded popular recreation and intellectual stimulation. The actors performed plays such as *Hamlet, Macbeth, Richard III,* and *King Lear* along with sentimental family comedies and domestic melodramas.

In the pattern established by Salt Lake City, people in many of the towns also established their own theater companies. Ordinarily these were amateur troupes, but they offered a variety of theatrical performances. In the isolated Colorado Plateau settlements in Castle Valley, for instance, amateur theater companies presented plays by 1880. Along with sentimental melodramas, companies in Huntington and Castle Dale also staged tragedies such as *Virginius* and *The Merchant of Venice.* In Mendon, a northern Utah farming community, in the early twentieth century the thespians took locally produced plays on the interurban railway to nearby Wellsville, Deweyville, and Honeyville.

Challenged at first by the vaudeville circuit and later by motion pictures, many of these theater companies failed during the 1920s. Faced with heavy expenses and the demand for renovation to meet safety codes, in 1928 the LDS Church sold the Salt Lake Theater to Mountain States Telephone, which replaced the theater with an art deco office building.

While promoting the performing arts, the theater served as seed ground for the graphic arts as well. Most of Utah's most prominent early painters were Mormon converts, many of whom had studied in Europe or the eastern United States. During the nineteenth century, Mormonism's foremost painters and musicians depended on contracts to paint scenery for the Salt Lake Theater for income and public attention. Many of the second generation of artists did not have the theater connection to support them, but beginning in 1888 a number of younger artists traveled to Paris to train under academic impressionists, and the church helped finance the Paris education of some of these artists. After returning to Utah, several painted murals in the Salt Lake Temple.

Some of the second-generation artists remained in Utah and secured university appointments. Others worked privately. Still others lived principally outside Utah. Cyrus Dallin, a Springville, Utah, native who lived in Boston, gained national fame by sculpting such renowned bronze pieces as the *Paul Revere* statue in Boston, the *Massasoit* statue at Plymouth, Massachusetts, and the *Angel Moroni* (the angel who gave Joseph Smith the Book of Mormon plates) for the Salt Lake Temple spire. Mahonri M. Young, a grandson of Brigham Young, moved to New York City, and his sculptures reside at that city's Metropolitan Museum, the Whitney Museum, and Madison Square Garden. In Utah, he designed and sculpted the *Sea Gull* monument on Temple Square (1913) and the *This Is the Place* monument (1947). Born in southeastern Idaho to Danish Mormon converts, Gutzon Borglum grew up in Ogden, Utah. He is best known for designing and carving the figures of four presidents on Mount Rushmore in South Dakota and the Stone Mountain Confederate Memorial in Georgia.

The Salt Lake Theater also served as the staging ground for musicians. Early theater orchestra directors included Charles J. Thomas and George Careless, both of whom trained in London and also directed the Mormon Tabernacle Choir. The Tabernacle Choir achieved its first national recognition under the baton of Evan Stephens, a Welsh convert to Mormonism. Named director in October 1890, Stephens took the choir to the World's Columbian Exposition in Chicago in 1893, where the Tabernacle Choir took second place in an international competition. On the heels of this triumph, the choir performed with artists such as John Philip Sousa, Ignacy Paderewski, and Dame Nellie Melba and went on to achieve worldwide acclaim. Under Stephens's successor, Anthony C. Lund (1916–1935), in 1929 it began weekly radio broadcasts. Under Lund's successor, J. Spencer Cornwall (1935–1957), choir recordings earned Peabody and Grammy awards. It has continued these successes with recordings, broadcasts, tours, and performances with renowned orchestras, under Richard P. Condie (1957–1974), Jay Welch (1974), and Jerold Ottley (1975–2000).

To promote intellectual growth, the Latter-day Saints established schools, colleges, and universities throughout the territory. The Mormon-dominated legislature chartered the University of Deseret (later renamed the University of Utah) in 1850. The church chartered Brigham Young University in 1875. LDS University in Salt Lake City persists as LDS Business College. Several colleges originally chartered by the church were transferred to state ownership during the Great Depression or had already closed during the 1920s.

THE MORMON RELIGIOUS IMPRINT

With educational, religious, cultural, and social activities, the church left its imprint on the settlements. Larger towns like Salt Lake City had up to twenty local congregations called wards. The smaller towns might have only one ward. A bishop with two counselors presided over each ward, conducted religious services, cared for welfare needs, promoted cultural activities, and organized public works. A stake president with two counselors and a twelve-man high council presided over all the wards in each county. In the twentieth century, wards generally consisted of about 350 members and stakes encompassed about nine wards, so most cities had (and still have) many wards and stakes.

Latter-day Saints considered the settlements part of God's plan for building a kingdom on earth in preparation for Christ's Second Coming. They pointed to scriptures that supported their plans to build covenant communities, to strengthen the members, to avoid calamities, and to separate themselves from worldliness.

In the wards, the members held regular religious services and cultural meetings and activities. The most important religious meetings were the weekly ward sacrament meetings, Sunday services in the stake or Salt Lake tabernacles, and monthly fast and testimony meetings. The sacrament meetings consisted ordinarily of congregational songs, prayers, choir music, sermons, and the partaking of the sacrament—the Mormon name for communion. Sunday tabernacle services included music, prayers, and sermons by general authorities and other prominent church leaders.

The monthly fast and testimony meeting resembled a Quaker meeting. Members came to the meeting after having fasted for a day. After an opening song, a prayer, and partaking the sacrament, members occupied the time as the spirit moved them. The participants ordinarily shared significant spiritual experiences and bore witness of the restoration of the Gospel, of the prophetic calling of Joseph Smith, and of the universal atonement of Jesus Christ.

In some towns the Latter-day Saints constructed temples for sacred rites. These ceremonies included the endowment, where members covenant to live moral lives and where they receive instruction about humanity's fall from divine grace, repentance, and returning to God and Jesus Christ. Mormons also attend the temples for marriages, or "sealings," that bind families together throughout eternity. The Mormons began the construction of the first of these Utah temples in Salt Lake City (constructed 1853–1893). In the 1870s and 1880s they constructed three other temples—St. George (constructed 1871–1877), Manti (constructed 1877–1888), and Logan (constructed 1877–1884). In the 1970s the church began a new round of temple construction. The first new temples in Utah were built in Ogden and Provo in 1972. Others in Utah include

Salt Lake Temple. Brigham Young broke ground for the temple in 1853, and it was finally completed in 1893. © MELVYN P. LAWED; PAPILIO/CORBIS

temples at American Fork, Bountiful, Jordan, Monticello, and Vernal.

A weekday meeting for young children, called the Primary, was organized in Farmington in 1878, and spread throughout Utah and the surrounding territories largely through the efforts of Eliza Snow. In Primary, children learned church doctrine, recited poetry, and participated in drama, crafts, and public speaking. The Sunday School sponsored Sunday morning religious instruction for adults and children. The church also undertook systems of weekday religious education for school-age children. The church sponsored religion classes for elementary school children from the 1890s through 1929, when they were discontinued in deference to the Primary.

In 1912 the church first experimented with weekday released-time religious instruction for high school students at Granite High School in Salt Lake County. Called "seminary," the program expanded until by 2000 the church had constructed buildings near high schools throughout Utah where students could take daily religious instruction under a released-time arrangement in such subjects as the Bible, the Book of Mormon, and Latter-day Saint doctrine and history. In 1926 the church set up its first Institute of Religion at the University of Idaho. This program also expanded so that institutes are located near universities and colleges throughout Utah and the United States. All of these programs sponsor social and cultural activities in addition to daily religious instruction.

No church meetings have had a greater impact on Utah's cultural, religious, and social life than the church's annual (April) and semiannual (October) conferences. Held at the Salt Lake Tabernacle, the conferences draw church members and leaders from throughout the world for instruction and discussion.

In 1965 the church launched a program called Family Home Evening, in which family members gather on Monday evenings for lessons, games, songs, and other activities. Family Home Evening has impacted the larger culture in Utah because members have achieved some success in pressuring organizations such as schools, little leagues, and cities not to sponsor competing programs on Monday evenings.

In addition, church members have an enormous impact on the social, economic, political, and spatial aspects of Utah life. The LDS Church owns buildings and property in downtown Salt Lake City and in other cities, and the city governments regularly consult with church leaders on planning matters. LDS Church members constitute the bulk of members of the legislative, executive, and judicial departments of state government as well as the mayors, city councils, county commissioners, and employees of various governmental units. Both consciously and inadvertently the Mormons influence the culture of the state and its subdivisions.

MIGRATION AND THE ETHNIC IMPRINT

Although the church has sent missionaries to nations throughout the world, most nineteenth-century converts came from North America and northwestern Europe. The northeastern and midwestern United States, Great Britain, and Scandinavia supplied by far the largest numbers. As they gathered to Zion, each ethnic group imparted a significant character to the settlements. Sanpete County in central Utah became famous for its Scandinavian settlers, and some of the Swiss peopled the town of Santa Clara in southwestern Utah.

In the twentieth century, by contrast, as the LDS Church has encouraged members to remain in their home countries, the areas of most extensive conversion have shifted. Instead of northern Europe, since World War II, the highest rates of conversion have occurred in Latin America, Asia, and Africa. Since most members no longer immigrate to Utah, the cultures of northern Europe and North America have had a much larger impact on Utah's culture than have the cultures of these other regions of the world. Nevertheless, the cultures of Mormons from Latin America and Polynesia have exercised a noticeable influence on Utah's twentieth-century culture.

In the nineteenth and early twentieth centuries, the LDS Church organization facilitated the integration of immigrants into the body of its membership while encouraging the perpetuation of their ethnic identities. In the larger cities, Scandinavians, Germans, and Dutch among other ethnic groups held services in their native languages. With church approval, they also published foreign-language newspapers such as the *Bikuben* (Danish and Norwegian), the *Beobachter* (German), and *De Utah Nederlander* (Dutch), all of which persisted into the early twentieth century.

To facilitate immigration, church leaders established the Perpetual Emigrating Fund (1849–1887) to collect donations, which they loaned to converts to help them gather to Zion. Immigrants were expected to repay the money so the fund could assist others. During the nineteenth century, many convert companies embarked on the first leg of the journey to America from Liverpool, England. Landing either in New York City or New Orleans, they made their way by wagon, rail, lake, and river to the Missouri River towns of Council Bluffs, Iowa, or Florence, Nebraska, where they left for Utah.

Until the completion of the railroad in 1869 most traveled by wagon train, but in a relatively successful experiment, between 1856 and 1860 ten companies migrated by handcart. Most of these arrived without undue hardship. Two handcart companies, however, left Florence in 1856 much too late in the season. Encountering snows on Wyoming's high plains in early October, the companies and the accompanying wagon trains suffered severe hardship from exposure and starvation. Perhaps two hundred people died out of one thousand in the companies before rescue parties from Salt Lake City saved the survivors.

RELATIONSHIP WITH THE INDIANS

When the Mormons reached Utah, the Salt Lake Valley was a no man's land between the Shoshones to the north, the Utes to the south, the Paiutes to the southwest, and the Gosiutes to the west. In general, the Mormons viewed the Indians differently from most Euroamericans. Teachings in the Book of Mormon and revelations to Joseph Smith led Mormons to consider the Indians a remnant of the House of Israel. As children of God and descendants of Israel they were fit subjects for conversion to the LDS Church, and the church leaders sent teams of missionaries to teach them the Gospel. In some cases they succeeded, and in others they failed. Violence, for instance, led the church to abandon the mission near present-day Moab. By contrast, a number of prominent chiefs such as Wakara of the Utes and Tat-se-gabbits of the Paiutes were baptized and ordained elders in the LDS church. Moreover, the Mormons assisted the Paiutes by suppressing the traffic in Indian slavery that bore heavily on their people.

At the same time, Mormon settlements stretched quickly into Indian-occupied lands. The settlement of Utah Valley encroached on the most heavily settled Ute lands. The founding in 1849 of Fort Utah, later renamed Provo, led to serious conflicts. Brigham Young tried to prevent violence by counseling members to be kind to the Indians, but the settlers often declined to observe this counsel. Serious conflicts followed the Mormon expansion. The expansion into Ute country led to the Walker War in 1853–1854, which resulted in deaths on both sides. Continued settlement also led to the Black Hawk War of 1865–1872, which occurred in part because of the effort of the federal government to remove the Utes to the Uintah Valley Reservation in eastern Utah. After these wars, although remnants of the Paiute bands remained in southwestern Utah, most of the Utes were removed to the Uintah Reservation in eastern Utah and most of the Shoshones were sent either to Idaho or Wyoming. Gosiutes were settled on two reservations in western Utah.

MORMONS AND THE GOVERNMENT OF UTAH TERRITORY

Following the end of the Mexican War and the Treaty of Guadalupe Hidalgo in 1848, the federal government began planning a government for the Mormon kingdom, which it inaugurated as part of the Compromise of 1850. The Compromise of 1850 admitted California as a free state, organized Utah and New Mexico as territories without reference to slavery, abolished the slave trade in the District of Columbia, and strengthened the Fugitive Slave Act. As citizens of a territory, the Mormons did not enjoy the degree of autonomy they might have if Utah had been admitted as a state. Since the federal government exercised plenary power in the territory, the president appointed Utah's principal executive and judicial officers. The territorial organic act allowed Utahns to elect local officials, members of the territorial legislature, and a nonvoting delegate to Congress.

The Mormons endured conflicts with many of the appointed federal officials as well as with other Euroamericans throughout the nation, especially evangelical Protestants. Although President Millard Fillmore named Young the first governor of the Territory of Utah and appointed half the first set of territorial officers from the Mormon ranks, most of the other officials who journeyed to Utah nursed a deep prejudice against the Latter-day Saints. Moreover, after these first appointees, no Mormons were appointed to territorial posts until the 1890s. The first officials established a pattern that persisted during the 1850s, by which federal appointees came to Utah, flayed the church membership with anti-Mormon rhetoric for a short time, then called upon the federal government for action against the Mormons.

In practice, however, because of the loyalty of its members the church leadership ruled no matter who was appointed to territorial positions. Locally elected officers were almost invariably Mormons, many of whom held ecclesiastical callings. In Protestant-dominated communities such a mixing of church and state would probably have gone unnoticed in nineteenth-century America. In Utah, however, such practices generated intense opposition from non-Mormons.

Shut out by the Mormons and appalled by the local culture, the outside appointees found much to deplore, including the practice of polygamy, secular rule by Mormon leaders, the support of the leaders by church members, and unsubstantiated charges of murder.

Conflicts with federal officials and especially erroneous reports by Judge William W. Drummond led President James Buchanan to believe the Mormons had mounted a rebellion against federal authority. After his inauguration in 1857, without notifying Young of his removal, Buchanan appointed Alfred Cumming of Georgia as governor and dispatched an army of twenty-four hundred men to accompany him. Fearing a replay of the anti-Mormon violence perpetrated on them by militiamen in Missouri and Illinois, Young declared martial law, and he mobilized the territorial militia to obstruct the army by burning supply trains and to prepare fortifications for a potential battle. In addition, he negotiated cooperative agreements with the Indians, ordered the Saints to abandon Salt Lake City, sent emissaries to prepare the people for potential conflict, and ordered them not to sell supplies to people passing through the territory.

Following Young's orders, Mormon settlers in southern Utah refused to sell supplies to a party of 120 Arkansan migrants. The migrants reportedly responded by verbally abusing the Mormons and stealing and trashing crops and committing acts of mayhem in southern Utah towns. The Cedar City leaders sent a rider to Salt Lake City to ask Brigham Young's advice for dealing with the Arkansans. Before the rider returned with Young's orders not to interfere with the migrants, units of the Iron County militia and a band of Paiutes had massacred the Arkansans at Mountain Meadows.

THE ISSUE OF POLYGAMY

The Mormons faced intense opposition to one aspect of their religion that had begun at the time of its founding by Smith: plural marriage. The Mormons believed their right to practice plural marriage was protected by the First Amendment, and they also espoused theological and practical arguments in defense of polygamy. They pointed out that many Old Testament prophets had practiced plural marriage. Through polygamy, they argued, righteous men and women could build family units in which they could eventually become kings and queens, priests and priestesses to God. Through polygamy, men would be freed from the temptations of fleshly indulgence outside of marriage.

In practice, both men and women found plural marriage more difficult to abide than monogamy. Although totals are difficult to calculate because of the attempt to hide the practice, perhaps 25 percent of Mormon marriages were polygamous. Divorce rates for polygamous marriages, though low by twentieth-century standards, were generally twice those of monogamous unions. Moreover, in an age when most women did not work outside the home, the large families resulted in a drain on resources and dissipation of fortunes.

Strange as it seems given the nineteenth-century rhetoric, polygamy offered some advantages to women. Most women could expect to marry intelligent, honorable, and prosperous men rather than remain single or settle for the ignorant, marginal, or ne'er-do-well. Polygamous wives tended to be somewhat more independent than their monogamous sisters, and many of the Mormon women who led in the arts, humanities, and politics in Utah territory were polygamous wives. Indeed, Mormon women made it clear in public activities and pronouncements that they supported the practice. Numerous mass meetings of women denounced the antipolygamy legislation proposed by Congress.

Polygamous wives and other Mormon women also held mass meetings and petition drives to promote woman suffrage, and they worked with national leaders like Susan B. Anthony and Elizabeth Cady Stanton to secure votes for women. Some national leaders like Representative George Julian of Indiana suggested that if Mormon women were given the vote they would throw off the shackles of the church's polygamous priesthood. But in fact there was no conflict of interest between Mormon women and the church hierarchy. Women gave sermons and participated in religious services, and Mormons had always held women in high regard. Editorials in the Mormon press showed that priesthood leaders favored woman suffrage and valued the assistance of women in various reform projects. In 1870 the territorial legislature gave women the vote. The newly enfranchised women voted just as the men did, and the citizens continued to elect Mormon leaders to prominent positions.

Outraged by the continued practice of plural marriage, the Republicans attacked polygamy as one of the twin relics of barbarism—the other was slavery. In 1862 the Republican-controlled Congress passed the Morrill Anti-Bigamy Act, which set fines and imprisonment for men convicted of marrying more than one woman. The Morrill Act remained a dead letter until 1875, when George Reynolds, Young's secretary, was convicted. In 1879 the U.S. Supreme Court sustained Reynolds's conviction in a ruling that became the basis for all future interpretation of the free-exercise clause of the First Amendment. In his opinion, Chief Justice Morrison Waite held that although the First Amendment protected belief, it did not protect citizens who cited a religious justification for acts considered criminal by the people of the United States.

In practice, however, the Morrill Act proved extremely difficult to enforce because the Supreme Court also ruled that the prosecution had to provide direct evidence of a polygamous marriage. Such evidence was difficult to secure. Wives would or could not testify against their husbands, Utah had no civil registration until after 1887, and the records of such marriages kept by officials in Mormon temples were carefully hidden from public scrutiny.

By the 1880s conditions in Utah had raised the ire of a majority of American citizens. Since prosecution under the Morrill Act proved difficult, the Vermont senator George Franklin Edmunds introduced legislation in 1882 to outlaw unlawful cohabitation. Conviction for this offense required only evidence that a man lived with more than one woman or that he held more than one woman out to the community as his wife. Subsequent prosecution led to the imprisonment of more than a thousand Latter-day Saint men. Several women also served terms in prison for contempt of court for refusing to testify in such cases.

When the Edmunds Act failed to end polygamy, in 1887 Congress passed the Edmunds-Tucker Act, which provided for the confiscation—technically called escheatment—of all of the LDS Church's secular property; the act also disfranchised Utah's women and abolished a number of local institutions or placed them under federal control.

STATEHOOD

After the passage of the Edmunds-Tucker Act, the Latter-day Saint leadership resisted the efforts of the federal government to confiscate church property, but in May 1890 the Supreme Court ruled that such escheatments were legal. Moreover, the court's decision opened the way to the confiscation of religious properties. Fearing the loss of temples, Woodruff, who then served as church president, announced in September 1890 that the church from that point forward would recommend that its members refrain from entering into contracts for plural marriages.

The church leadership had already begun cooperating with local and national business leaders and had opened discussions with national political leaders in an attempt to secure favorable treatment for the church and statehood for Utah. In 1891 Mormons and non-Mormons began to cooperate in organizing national political parties. With this new evidence of ecumenical cooperation, Utah achieved statehood in 1896.

The Mormons have continued to constitute a majority of Utah's population and play a significant role in Utah's social, cultural, and intellectual life after 1896. Over the years church members have actively supported state legislation restricting vice,

The Mormon Tabernacle Choir. Formed in 1847, the Mormon Tabernacle Choir in the 2000s comprised 320 singers. PHIL SCHERMEISTER/CORBIS

gambling, liquor consumption, and Sunday recreation. Mormons have succeeded in influencing the defeat of several federal and state measures, including the proposal in the late 1970s to base MX missiles on mobile tracks in the west; the Equal Rights Amendment, which polls showed that a majority of Latter-day Saints favored until the church leadership came out firmly in opposition; various proposals for saloon-type liquor by the drink, although the state with tacit LDS approval altered the law to permit the consumption of alcohol with meals in certain restaurants and private clubs; and parimutuel betting, which failed in a referendum in November 1992. Local ordinances have closed swimming pools on Sundays in a number of cities.

The church's cultural and educational endeavors have played a role that reaches far beyond the community of Mormon people. Brigham Young University, the nation's largest private university, influences the quality of life and the intellectual climate in the state. The Mormon Tabernacle Choir enjoys worldwide fame. In the second half of the twentieth century, a number of Utah and Mormon writers, artists, and intellectuals have achieved national recognition. These include the historians Juanita

Brooks and Leonard Arrington, the nature writer Terry Tempest Williams, the science fiction writer Orson Scott Card, the former U.S. commissioner of education Sterling McMurrin, the founder of the Utah Shakespearean Festival Fred Adams, the former NASA head James Fletcher, the entertainers Donnie and Marie Osmond, the ballet impresario Willam Christensen, and the painter James Christensen. Significantly, both of the Utahans whose statues reside in statuary hall in the nation's capitol—Brigham Young and Philo Farnsworth, the inventor of television—are Mormons.

After a century and two thirds, Mormons live in a curious dichotomy of tension and reconciliation with other Americans. In a nation with ideals of religious freedom and personal liberty, in the nineteenth century public officials subjected Mormons to nearly unremitting persecution for their religion. Although Mormons have always believed in the atonement of Christ; in faith, repentance, and baptism; and in God, Jesus Christ, and the Holy Spirit, in a misinterpretation of Mormon beliefs, some Evangelical Protestants persist in mischaracterizing the Latter-day Saints as non-Christians. Notwithstanding the Latter-day Saints abandoned plural marriage and church dictation in economics more than a century ago, misinformation about the persistence of these doctrines and practices still engenders tensions. Church dictation in political matters is more problematic. Since the 1970s, the church leadership has declined to support any political candidates and has taken stands only on issues they perceive as moral. Tensions have arisen at times because the majority of Mormons are Republicans and at times because opponents often perceive the issues on which the leadership has taken stands as political rather than moral. Nevertheless, the Church of Jesus Christ of Latter-day Saints has been arguably the most successful religion born in the United States. It continues to grow rapidly. With nearly five million members in the United States and nearly eleven million worldwide, it is the nation's seventh largest church. In Utah, Latter-day Saints constitute more than 70 percent of the population, and they have left and continue to leave their stamp on the state's and nation's cultural, intellectual, and political history and life.

See also other articles in this section.

BIBLIOGRAPHY

Alexander, Thomas G. *Mormonism in Transition: A History of the Latter-day Saints, 1890–1920.* 2d ed. Urbana, Ill., 1996.

———. *Things in Heaven and Earth: The Life and Times of Wilford Woodruff, a Mormon Prophet.* Salt Lake City, Utah, 1991.

———. *Utah, the Right Place: The Official Centennial History.* 2d ed. Layton, Utah, 1996.

Allen, James B., and Glen M. Leonard. *The Story of the Latter-day Saints.* 2d ed. Salt Lake City, Utah, 1992.

Arrington, Leonard J. *Brigham Young: American Moses.* New York, 1985.

———. *Great Basin Kingdom: An Economic History of the Latter-day Saints, 1830–1900.* Cambridge, Mass., 1958.

Beecher, Dale F. "Colonizer of the West." In *Lion of the Lord: Essays on the Life and Service of Brigham Young.* Edited by Susan Easton Black and Larry C. Porter. Salt Lake City, Utah, 1995.

Bennion, Lowell C. "A Geographer's Discovery of Great Basin Kingdom." In *Great Basin Kingdom Revisited: Contemporary Perspectives.* Edited by Thomas G. Alexander. Logan, Utah, 1991.

The Book of Mormon. Salt Lake City, Utah, 1998.

Brooks, Juanita. *The Mountain Meadows Massacre.* Stanford, Calif. 1950.

Christy, Howard A. "Weather, Disaster, and Responsibility: An Essay on the Willie and Martin Handcart Story." *BYU Studies* 37 (1997–1998): 7–74.

Doctrine and Covenants of the Church of Jesus Christ of Latter-day Saints. Salt Lake City, Utah, 1981.

Derr, Jill Mulvay, Janath Russell Cannon, and Maureen Ursenbach Beecher. *Women of Covenant: The Story of Relief Society.* Salt Lake City, Utah, 1992.

Lyman, Edward Leo. *Political Deliverance: The Mormon Quest for Utah Statehood.* Urbana, Ill., 1986.

Madsen, Carol Cornwall. *Battle for the Ballot: Essays on Woman Suffrage in Utah, 1870–1896.* Logan, Utah, 1997.

Mulder, William. *Homeward to Zion: The Mormon Migration from Scandinavia.* Minneapolis, Minn., 1957.

Olpin, Robert S. *Dictionary of Utah Art.* Salt Lake City, Utah, 1980.

Poll, Richard D., Thomas G. Alexander, Eugene E. Campbell, and David E. Miller, eds. *Utah's History*. 2d ed. Logan, Utah, 1989.

Powell, Allan Kent. *Utah History Encyclopedia*. Salt Lake City, Utah, 1994.

Swanson, Vern G., Robert S. Olpin, and William C. Seifrit. *Utah Painting and Sculpture*. Rev. ed. Salt Lake City, Utah, 1997.

Wahlquist, Wayne L., and Howard A. Christy, eds. *Atlas of Utah*. Ogden and Provo, Utah, 1981.

Part 11

NATURE, HUMAN NATURE, AND THE SUPERNATURAL

THE NATURAL WORLD

Patrick Allitt

Americans have thought about the natural world in several different ways. First, the land has been their primary means of livelihood: earth for farming and herding, forests to provide wood for building and burning, rivers for fishing, transportation, and water supply, and mines for salt, coal, oil, and gold. Second, the natural world has provided the setting for Americans' religious ideas. From the Indians, who lived in a world of wind, land, and animal gods; through the Puritans, who feared wilderness as the home of devils, and the Transcendentalists, who saw it as the abode of God; up to late-twentieth-century advocates of ecospirituality, nature has been a setting for encounters with the divine. Third, scientists throughout American history have tried to understand the workings of plants and animals and the interaction of the living and nonliving environment. Fourth, the natural world has been a source of pleasure and a place for recreation.

These four approaches have never been entirely distinct. A wandering eighteenth-century naturalist like William Bartram studied the flora and fauna of the American South according to the scientific principles of his day, but he also took pleasure in the journey and believed that his discoveries confirmed the existence of a designer-God. The typical nineteenth-century American farmer was usually a Christian, trusting in God's providence to provide for his crops, but increasingly seeking to study rational, scientific methods of improving yields. Since the early seventeenth century definitions of nature and approaches to studying and appreciating it have changed, demonstrating that "nature" is itself cultural. The world and the things in it really do exist, but there has been no permanent agreement about what is, and what is not, "natural." Some twentieth-century environmental authors, for example, treat human beings as part of nature while others regard them as alien intruders into a natural world that would be better off without them. "Nature" means, and has meant, many different things.

AMERICAN INDIANS

Despite wide variations among Indian cultures, nearly all shared the idea of an animated natural world, in which rivers, trees, hills, wind, rain, fire, plants, and animals were spiritual forces with lives of their own. Roger Williams, the founder of the first Rhode Island settlement, for example, learned from the local Narraganset Indians that to them fire was a god. One of them told him:

> This fire must be God, or Divine power, that out of a stone will arise in a Sparke and when a poore naked Indian is ready to starve with cold in the House, and especially in the Woods, often saves his life, doth dresse all our Food for us, and if it be angry will burne the House about us. (Williams, *Language of America*, p. 130)

They used fire to clear woodland underbrush, to control insect infestations, and to nurture "edge" habitats for game animals. Many Indian cultures believed that they could communicate in dreams with the spirits of the animals and that if a hunt was successful it was because the animals had consented to their own deaths, in return for the hunters' promise to treat their remains with respect. Tribes explained their origins as arising out of arrangements among the animals, during a mythic age in which they and all men spoke the same language. The Navajo, for example, believed that people and animals had collaborated to invent agriculture:

> First Man . . . brought forth the white corn which had been formed with him. First Woman brought the yellow corn. They laid the perfect ears side by side; then they asked one person from among the many to come and help them. The Turkey stepped forward. . . . He danced back and forth four times, then he shook his feather coat and there dropped from his clothing four kernels of corn, one gray, one blue, one black and one red. Another person was asked to help in the plan of the planting. The Big Snake came forward. He likewise brought forth four seeds, the pumpkin, the watermelon, the cantaloupe, and the muskmelon. His plants all crawl on the ground. (Turner, *The Portable North American Indian Reader*, pp. 181–182)

Western tribes explained the origin of common problems they faced with tales about a trickster, Coyote, and the practical jokes he played on the bear, the beaver, and other animals.

EARLY SETTLERS

The first generations of British settlers did not share the Indians' view of an animated natural world. The Book of Genesis in their Bible said that after the Creation, God had made men stewards of the earth and given them dominion over it. It is worth noting, however, that Genesis, like many of the Indians' tales, included a talking serpent who acted rather like Coyote when he beguiled the first woman into eating the forbidden fruit. It is also notable that the first settlers, like the Indians, often interpreted events in the natural world as divine signals. The Puritan divine Increase Mather, for example, saw thunderstorms or hard winters as evidence of God's displeasure and good harvests as signs of his mercy. These "special providences," and an array of European folk traditions and astrological beliefs, inhibited seventeenth-century settlers from taking an entirely pragmatic approach to the natural world. The first generation of New England settlers regarded the American landscape as, in the words of the Plymouth Colony governor William Bradford, a "howling wilderness," the home of wild beasts, wild men, and devils. They found beauty in it only when they had domesticated it according to English farming patterns.

The usual name for a farmer in colonial America was "husbandman," and settlers noted parallels between the fertility of the land and the fertility of women, both of which had to be activated or impregnated by a husband. The colonist and adventurer Thomas Morton compared New England to the biblical promised land of Canaan in a poem (1632), in which he said that the land was "Like a faire virgin, longing to be sped / And meet her lover in a Nuptiall bed." This virgin land, like the virgin of his poem, would be "most fortunate / When most enjoy'd." Otherwise its potential would go to waste (quoted in Merchant, *Ecological Revolutions*, p. 101). There was no virtue or merit in unused land—it needed a husband of its own.

New England and Virginia settlers, even those disappointed at not finding gold, described the land as incredibly plentiful. They felt justified in seizing it partly because they thought the Indians lazy not to have profited more from its many forms of potential wealth. One such form was woodland itself.

Generations of settlement had deforested England yet wood was still a vital resource for house- and shipbuilding and for firewood. The abundance of trees in America delighted them—they could build timbered houses and enjoy roaring wintertime fires of a sort only the wealthiest Englishman could afford.

THE EIGHTEENTH CENTURY

Eighteenth-century observers of the natural world occasionally took pleasure in nature quite apart from its practical uses or the clues it provided about the mind of God. Among them was the Virginia planter William Byrd II, who described a border-surveying expedition into the Appalachian ranges of western Virginia in 1728 as a jolly adventure and took pleasure even in such lands as the Dismal Swamp, which was difficult to traverse and economically worthless. He was an enthusiastic observer of wildlife, giving, for example, a close description of the marsupial opossum: "The greatest particularity of this creature . . . is the FALSE BELLY of the FEMALE into which her Young retreat in time of Danger. . . . Within the False Belly may be seen seven or eight Teats, on which the young Ones grow from their first Formation till they are big enough to fall off like ripe Fruit from a Tree (p. 248).

Byrd's blend of appreciation and close observation became more common as the eighteenth century advanced. Bartram, who toured the southern colonies in the early 1770s "for the discovery of rare and useful productions of nature, chiefly in the vegetable kingdom," published his *Travels* in 1791. It shows, on the one hand, meticulous study of the area's plants and animals, many of which had not previously been classified. On the other hand, it is full of rhapsodic evocations of the scenery. "How gently flow they peaceful floods, O Altamaha! How sublimely rise to view, on thy elevated shores, yon magnolian groves" (p. 64). Bartram's *Travels,* well received in Europe and widely translated, influenced the nature-Romanticism of the great English poets Samuel Taylor Coleridge and William Wordsworth. In his footsteps trod numerous later students of American wildlife, notably the ornithologists Alexander Wilson and John James Audubon.

Thomas Jefferson, Bartram's near contemporary, was also an acute observer of the natural world. The first half of his *Notes on the State of Virginia* (1785) describes the rivers, mountains, waterfalls, animals, plants, and climate of the state. Jefferson wrote it partly to refute the Comte de Buffon, a French naturalist who had asserted that the flora and fauna of the New World were inferior in size and variety to those of the Old World. Jefferson countered Buffon's theory by listing a huge variety of large American mammals and by observing that the skeletons of mammoths had recently been discovered near the Ohio River. He admitted that he had never seen a mammoth (some Delaware Indians had told him about it), but he was convinced that they still existed—it seemed to him inconceivable that God would create a creature only to permit it subsequently to become extinct.

Jefferson was also puzzled by the discovery of fossilized seashells several thousand feet up in the Appalachians. What could account for them being there? He examined three hypotheses: a flood of biblical proportions, a "convulsion of nature" that had suddenly raised up the seabed, or the natural formation of shells inside the rock. Then he painstakingly demolished all three, according to the best scientific methods of his day, and ended on a note of scientific agnosticism: "The three hypotheses are equally unsatisfactory; and we must be contented to acknowledge that this great phenomenon is as yet unsolved. Ignorance is preferable to error; and he is less remote from the truth who believes nothing, than he who believes what is wrong" (p. 33). Over the next eighty years rapid advances in geology and evolutionary biology would provide answers to questions about nature that Jefferson admitted his own generation could not solve. In the twentieth century the development of plate tectonics theory would indicate that a variant of the second hypothesis he had rejected was right—the Appalachian summits really were once part of the seabed.

THE EARLY REPUBLIC

Jefferson plays a central role in American political as well as intellectual history, not least for his decision to accept Napoleon's offer of Louisiana in 1803, which nearly doubled the land area of the United States and extended its frontier from the Mississippi to the Rocky Mountains. Meriwether Lewis and William Clark crossed this new territory by laboring up the Missouri River, over the Rockies, and down the Snake and Columbia Rivers to the Pacific coast (1804–1806). Sharing Jefferson's inquiring, Enlightenment temperament, they identified dozens of new plants, animals, and landforms. They, and later the explorers Zebulon Pike and Stephen Long, described a vast territory almost devoid of trees and much drier than the eastern states. It

John James Audubon and Engraver Robert Havell Jr., Pigeon Hawk (c. 1827–1830). Between 1827 and 1838, Audubon published his four-volume *The Birds of America*, containing 435 hand-colored plates of 1,065 birds. © THE ACADEMY OF NATURAL SCIENCES OF PHILADELPHIA/CORBIS

seemed to them unlikely that white settlement would be possible there. Through the first half of the nineteenth century this area was often marked on maps as the "Great American Desert."

The early nineteenth century marked the high tide of literary Romanticism, in which the novels of Sir Walter Scott enjoyed as much acclaim in America as in his native Britain. James Fenimore Cooper and Washington Irving, the two most renowned American authors of the era, used dramatic evocations of the natural world to parallel the emotional condition of their human characters in a way reminiscent of Scott. These American authors sometimes confessed to a feeling of cultural inferiority by comparison with Britain, because America lacked a feudal past, the romantic, half-ruined old abbeys and castles of Europe, and its long-cultivated rustic landscape. They compensated, however—as did a generation of American landscape painters, notably Thomas Cole, Frederic Church, and other painters of the Hudson River school—with claims that their *natural* environment was superior to anything on offer in Europe. Niagara Falls, unmatched anywhere in Europe, was their prime exhibit.

The romantic glorification of sublime nature found its religious counterpart in Transcendentalism. The essayist and poet Ralph Waldo Emerson, reacting against what he called the "corpse-cold" indoor religion of the Boston Unitarians, declared that in nature we could best communicate with God.

> In the woods a man casts off his years . . . and at what period soever of life is always a child. . . . Within these plantations of God, a decorum and sanctity reign, a perennial festival is dressed, and the guest sees not how he should tire of them in a thousand years. In the woods, we return to reason and faith. . . . Standing on the bare ground . . . all mean egotism vanishes. I become a transparent eyeball; I am nothing; I see all; the currents of the Universal Being circulate through me; I am part or parcel of God. (*Nature, Addresses, and Lectures,* p. 10)

Emerson's friend Henry David Thoreau took this idea to heart and also wrote on the spiritual elevation he gained from communing with nature. His two-year experiment in independent living beside Walden Pond (*Walden,* 1854) has become a Transcendentalist and environmental classic.

Transcendentalists were not the only religious Americans moving out of doors. In the eighteenth century the traveling English evangelist George Whitefield caused a sensation by holding outdoor revival meetings. By the time of the Second Great Awakening in the early nineteenth century, outdoor revivals were commonplace. The evangelical revival that swept through the states in those decades institutionalized camp meetings, revivals, and river baptisms, occasions for turning to God in the midst of the natural world. Revival sermons by the great evangelists Francis Asbury and Charles Grandison Finney exalted the natural world as God's spiritual theater. Slave religion also gained a new intensity in "brush arbors," outdoor and often secret religious meeting places.

Despite these religious trends, nature remained to most Americans more a source of wealth than spiritual edification. Among the Americans pushing farther west in search of new and better land in the early nineteenth century were those whose eastern farms were deteriorating. Certain crops, particularly the great southern staples of tobacco and cotton, exhaust the soil unless it is fertilized and left fallow to recuperate every third or fourth year. In their search for profits, many planters had neglected these precautions. Deteriorated tobacco lands had already made parts of Virginia and Maryland unusable by the time of the American Revolution. With the great cotton boom of the early nineteenth century, more areas of the expanding South began to suffer. One

vigorous critic of southern farming practices was Edmund Ruffin, a largely self-taught scientist and America's first soil chemist. Ruffin, a romantic, Walter Scott–loving planter, was also passionately proslavery and feared that destruction of the land would destroy the basis of the South's prosperity. Appointed South Carolina's first agricultural and geological surveyor in 1842, he urged planters to fertilize their fields with guano and clay marls, to rotate their crops, and to avoid planting techniques that led to short-term profits but then to soil erosion. He read the work of Justus von Liebig and other European agricultural chemists and passed on their insights in his *Essay on Calcareous Manures* (1832) and as editor of the *Farmer's Register* (1833–1842), but he made little headway in the face of the planters' boomer mentality. He did, however, lay the groundwork for the much more scientific approach to farming that would displace ad hoc methods in the early twentieth century. Ruffin himself, the Confederate who fired the first shot on Fort Sumter, South Carolina, committed suicide after the Civil War.

SCIENTIFIC REVOLUTION

Soil chemistry was only one of many scientific fields to take great forward strides in the mid-nineteenth century. The publication of *On the Origin of Species by Means of Natural Selection* (1859) by Charles Darwin was probably the single most momentous scientific event of the century, one that provoked biological, philosophical, and religious controversies on both sides of the Atlantic. In combination with studies of population by Thomas Malthus and the geology of Charles Lyell, Darwin, an English biologist, presented an unfamiliar and—to some readers—a threatening vision of the earth's natural history. First, he exploded the argument for the existence of God from the ingenious design of nature, which had sustained Bartram and many other naturalists over the preceding century. Plants, animals, and the inanimate world fit together so intricately, said Darwin, not because a clever and benevolent God has designed them to do so but because they are the best-adapted survivors in a perpetual struggle for existence. Second, he confirmed Lyell's view that the earth was incomparably more ancient than earlier generations had supposed. In Darwin's view, extinction (the phenomenon Jefferson had refused to believe in) was a central mechanism of natural history. Third, he implicitly refuted the idea that Genesis gave a historical account of the earth's origins. Prominent American scientists, among them the botanist Asa Gray, converted to the Darwinian view in the 1860s. Others, including the influential Harvard biologist Louis Agassiz, refused to do so. Agassiz became the standard-bearer for a dwindling band of anti-Darwinians, but the new theory prevailed among almost all serious American biologists by 1900. However, many of them, led by Edward Cope, attached a vitalist, or purposeful, element to the theory and rejected Darwin's own emphasis on natural selection through random, directionless variation.

Among religious Americans the Darwinian view of the natural world caused, and has continued to cause, controversy. Christian evolutionists like Henry Ward Beecher and Lyman Abbott argued that the theory was compatible with the central tenets of their faith, while creationists like Charles Hodge and William Jennings Bryan continued to believe in a world made by God once and for all, exactly as described in Genesis. Bryan was horrified by the brutality of Darwin's natural world and feared that accepting it would ruin Americans' morality and destroy their faith in a benign God.

The scientific study of nature intensified after the Civil War. Darwin's generation in effect created ecology, the science of the interconnection of living and nonliving things in natural settings. Among the first American ecologists was George Perkins Marsh, a Vermonter with a voracious appetite for learning (he spoke twenty languages), who published *Man and Nature* in 1864 after studying degraded landscapes in New England, Italy, and the Middle East. Now an environmental classic, *Man and Nature* emphasizes the connection between living creatures, plants, soil, and rivers and argues that man intrudes on nature at his peril: "Wherever he plants his foot, the harmonies of nature are turned to discords" (p. 32). Marsh was the first American to warn that deforestation and intensive farming have ruinous long-term consequences, including desertification, and the first to propose principles of conservation.

John Wesley Powell, like Marsh, was a self-taught scientist with a protoecological sensibility. He was the first person to make the hazardous boat trip through the Grand Canyon and to map previously unknown sections of the Green and Colorado Rivers (1869). He befriended and studied the Ute and Shivwits Indians who lived on the canyon's rim, and he lobbied in Washington, D.C., to bring an ethnographic and cartographic survey into the area. In his *Report on the Lands of the Arid Region of the United States* (1878), Powell argued that the arid desert Southwest could never support homestead farmers living on 160-acre lots, as specified in the Homestead Act of 1862. Such farms were difficult enough to manage in the humid zones of the Midwest. The farther one moved out onto the Great Plains the more difficult farming became, principally because of lack of water. The only way to organize settlement of the Southwest, said Powell, was to abandon the grid survey method and divide the land according to its watersheds, with an eye to limited irrigation farming. Most of the area, he cautioned, would never be amenable to farming or ranching. Clarence King and other leaders of the U.S. Geological Survey (founded 1878) came to similar conclusions.

The federal government, however, thought that Powell was too pessimistic. The late nineteenth century was, after all, a period of brilliant technical accomplishments, in which American inventors were brushing aside natural obstacles that had once seemed insuperable. In 1869 the first transcontinental railroad linked the two coasts and reduced ordinary citizens' travel time across country from several months (on the Oregon Trail) to less than a week. Steam trains now rumbled over the Sierra Nevada at Donner Pass, where, during the winter of 1846–1847, a stranded immigrant train was reduced to cannibalism to survive. Railroad companies ran in all seasons, connecting isolated communities and diminishing the seasonal variations in their citizens' work, diet, and communication. The presence of the railroad in turn made feasible the settlement and farming of the Great Plains. Wood for building and coal for fuel could be shipped in by train, while cargoes of grain could be shipped out to feed growing eastern cities. Wheat farming was phenomenally productive so that, by the 1930s and from then on, the chronic problem of American agriculture was overproduction.

Railroads fostered not only farming in the Midwest but also tourism in the spectacular landscapes of the desert and mountain West. The Central Pacific Railroad, for example, would halt its trains at scenic spots in the Sierra Nevada. The Santa Fe Railroad, on its more southerly route to the Pacific, arranged guided tours to Taos Pueblo and the Grand Canyon. It even paid the Pueblo Indians to don feather headdresses (a characteristic of the Plains tribes) and dance for the tourists. The Northern Pacific Railroad lobbied successfully for the creation of Glacier National Park in Montana. Being looked at, painted, hiked in, photographed, and written about—by such popular western nature writers as Mary Austin—became the principal role of large parts of Colorado, Utah, Arizona, Wyoming, Montana, and New Mexico. As Powell had foreseen, they were just too dry to farm.

CONSERVATION

The pace of technological development and western settlement raised the possibility that America might eventually run out of available land and natural resources. As the nineteenth century ended, eloquent voices began to argue for conservation. Gifford Pinchot was one. Trained in Germany, he applied scientific principles to forest management and wrote persuasively on the issue. He showed that if the development of a forest was scientifically monitored, certain trees could be harvested each year when they had reached maturity for maximum lumber yield. Seedlings would replace them and, in the following year, another selected group of mature trees would be felled. In this way, under proper management, the forest would yield lumber into the indefinite future. What was actually happening throughout the United States, he lamented, was that entire forest areas were being clear-cut all at once, making the land vulnerable to soil erosion while destroying young trees whose timber yield was negligible. Pinchot was a talented political infighter as well as a good forester. By persistent lobbying he was able to persuade his friend and patron, President Theodore Roosevelt, to create an independent U.S. Forest Service in 1905 with Pinchot as its first chief forester.

Roosevelt was already famous as a western outdoorsman, hunter, and soldier who had spent part of the 1880s living on a Dakota cattle ranch. An evocative writer, he popularized the idea that the West was a challenging natural arena where men could test their mettle against the elements. He supported the creation of national parks as well as national forests, if only to preserve, for an increasingly "soft" urban population, a place where they could flex their muscles and hunt wild beasts. His friend the author Owen Wister shared many of these ideas and embodied them in the novel that created the cowboy genre, *The Virginian* (1902).

ENVIRONMENTAL PROTECTION

Pinchot and Roosevelt had an equivocal relationship with John Muir, America's first professional environmental writer. Muir, like Powell, was raised on the hard labor of frontier farms. Living alone for long stretches in California's Yosemite wilderness, but being careful to meet publishers' deadlines in order to popularize his ideas, Muir argued that wild land should be preserved not in order to be more rationally used hereafter (Pinchot's guiding idea), but for its own sake. A nature mystic in the tradition of Emerson and Thoreau, Muir did not shrink from using explicitly religious language about the trees and valleys, and he was one of the first American writers to use the concept of "wilderness" in a wholly positive sense—something to care for and preserve rather than something to get rid of.

Most of his contemporaries regarded Muir as a crackpot; only in retrospect, especially in the wake of the modern environmentalist movement, have his ideas and values gained widespread respect. It is significant that the next great figure in the modern environmental pantheon, Aldo Leopold, should have started out in the footsteps of Pinchot rather than Muir and spent much of his career working in utilitarian conservation work. Among Leopold's jobs after graduation from the Yale Forestry School was shooting wolves and mountain lions in the desert Southwest, because they preyed on range cattle. A trigger-happy hunting enthusiast at first, Leopold's epiphany came when he approached a wolf he had shot and saw the "fierce green fire" in its eyes extinguished as it died. "I realized then," he wrote later, "and I have known ever since, that there was something new to me in those eyes—something known only to her and the mountain" (*A Sand County Almanac*, p. 130). Working as a professor of wildlife management at the University of Wisconsin beginning in 1933, he began to argue, like Muir, that living things had an intrinsic value far beyond their usefulness to men. His most famous essay, "A Land Ethic," argues that the history of ethics shows a steady widening of the moral community and that it is reasonable to assume that the circle will continue to widen, beyond the solely human, embracing animate and even inanimate things. By then he had witnessed, or seen the results of, several human-induced ecological catastrophes, including grasshopper infestations in the Midwest, the boll weevil plague among southern cotton farmers, and the Dust Bowl storms of the 1930s that destroyed thousands of acres of the western plains.

Leopold was a captivating stylist who knew how to appeal to a wide audience. Equally adept at good public relations was Rachel Carson, whose book *Silent Spring* (1962) was an early salvo in the modern environmental movement. Carson, a marine biologist, deplored the widespread use of toxic pesticides like DDT by American farmers, highway departments, and other branches of government. She argued that spraying is a short-term fix that soon backfires by creating toxin-resistant strains of the target insects. Worse, the poison kills indiscriminately and becomes concentrated at key links in the food chain, making it more, not less, deadly. Emotional passages of *Silent Spring* warned that even breast-feeding mothers might be unwittingly passing lethal chemicals along to their infants. DDT had won a Nobel Prize for its inventors in the 1940s— it was an excellent suppressant of malarial mosquitoes—but Carson's surprise best-selling book on agricultural chemicals led to congressional hearings and a ban on DDT.

The late 1960s, a period of upheaval in many areas of American life, witnessed the birth of modern environmentalism. Among its chief concerns were industrial and toxic pollution, world overpopulation, the self-indulgent and wasteful lifestyle of middle-class Americans, and urban sprawl. It appealed strongly to the puritanical side of the counterculture and coincided with a vogue for simplicity and returning to the land. Urban hippies who tried to set up organic farming communes often found the work backbreakingly difficult, especially if they eschewed modern farming equipment and chemicals. Still, the essential soundness of organic farming principles gradually "mainstreamed" them in a commercially viable way, and business farmers adapted many of them in the last three decades of the twentieth century.

ECOLOGY

Ecology, the science that underlies environmentalism, developed out of the limelight in the post-Darwinian English-speaking world and only became popular in the early 1970s. The environmental movement was often referred to as the "ecology movement," though ecology rarely provided clear lessons to environmental policy makers. It was, moreover, riven with theoretical disputes. The pioneer ecologist Frederic Clements argued early in the twentieth century that groups of plants in a region cooperate in such a way that people should think of them as a kind of organism, one that eventually achieves "adulthood" in a mature "climax community." His British critic Arthur Tansley challenged Clements's organicism and invented the term "ecosystem" to describe the combination of organic and inorganic contributors to the living things in a given time and place. "Ecosystem" became one of the principal heuristic terms in ecology. Highly technical ecologists such as Raymond Lin-

deman graphed energy transfers into and out of living things as they interacted with their nonliving environment. But by the 1980s the concept of the ecosystem in turn was under attack, from the ecologists S. T. A. Pickett and P. S. White, whose research found few long-term equilibriums, even in settings undisturbed by man. They emphasized that the "system" in "ecosystem" is in the mind of the beholder rather than out there among the actual plants and animals. In its place they offered the concept of "patch dynamics."

Whatever the ecologists' intentions, most popularizers of ecological ideas after 1960, including Paul R. Ehrlich, Garrett Hardin, Wendell Berry, and Bill McKibben, implied that the natural world, when left to itself, exhibits stable ecosystems. These writers usually characterized humans as villains who disrupt ecosystems by mowing, planting, harvesting, hunting, weeding, overpopulating, and in a hundred other ways destroying the equilibrium. Ehrlich's *The Population Bomb* (1969) and McKibben's *The End of Nature* (1989), among many other works, had a gloomy, apocalyptic tone, predicting "ecocide." By contrast their critics, including Julian Simon, Ben Wattenberg, and Aaron Wildavsky, who accepted humans as an integral part of nature rather than as an intruder into it, denied that the earth was in ecological crisis. In their view, environmental problems, while certainly serious, were manageable. Human ingenuity could overcome new difficulties, they argued, just as it had overcome them in the past.

The dispute about what is and is not natural concerned anthropologists, geographers, philosophers, and theologians as well as biologists in the 1970s, 1980s, and 1990s. Ecology and environment earned places on the academic curriculum, while environmentally attuned nature writers like Edward Abbey and Annie Dillard gained a large following. There also was a faddish side to environmentalism, fought out more in slogans and bumper stickers than in seminars. Even grade-school children began learning to save the whales, if not the whole world; to use less paper ("save the trees"); and to collect bottles, cans, and newspapers for recycling ("think globally, act locally"). The members of environmental organizations were mainly urban, white, and upper middle class, which made them vulnerable to criticism from farmers, who saw them as impractical utopians, and from working-class men who relied on extracting the resources of the natural world for their livelihoods. Irritable Oregon loggers, for example, whose jobs seemed threatened by plans to protect the forest habitat of endangered species, sported bumper stickers on their vehicles that read: "Out of Work and Feeling Hungry? Eat an Environmentalist!"

Religious denominations reconsidered their teachings in light of environmental concerns. Liberal Protestant churches, in particular, uncomfortable with the idea of "dominion," began to place greater stress on human "stewardship" of the earth. "Ecofeminists" like the Catholic theologian Rosemary Ruether argued that the exploited land was analogous to exploited women, both suffering from the blundering misconduct of "man." A defrocked Catholic priest, Matthew Fox, edited *Creation Spirituality*, a journal of nature religion, and claimed to take religious advice and instruction from his dog. The British scientist and inventor James Lovelock suggested that the earth itself could be thought of as a vast organism, an idea that also took on religious overtones when Lovelock named this superorganism after the Greek goddess "Gaia."

At the close of the twentieth century, the idea of "nature" was still contested, as it had been through much of American history. It carried positive connotations for nearly everyone, just as "unnatural" was usually pejorative, but there was no broad agreement on what it was. References to nature were usually claims about economic, religious, recreational, or scientific affairs, as before, but they nearly always carried implicit moral overtones. Homosexuality, for example, the subject of an intense debate in the last third of the century, had earlier stood condemned as unnatural. In the hands of gay rights advocates, however, it was redefined as an entirely natural phenomenon, possibly even encoded in certain strands of human DNA. The inference was clear: if it's natural, it can't be immoral.

See also **Philosophy from Puritanism to the Enlightenment; The New England Theology from Edwards to Bushnell; Agrarianism and the Agrarian Ideal in Early America; American Romanticism; Transcendentalism; Communitarianism; Pragmatism and Its Critics** *(volume 1);* **The Discovery of the Environment; Pastoralism and the Rural Ideal** *(in this volume); and other articles in this section.*

BIBLIOGRAPHY

Primary Sources

Bartram, William. *Travels through North and South Carolina, Georgia, East and West Florida, etc.* 1791. Reprint, New York, 1996.

Byrd, William, II. *Histories of the Dividing Line betwixt Virginia and North Carolina.* New York, 1967.

Carson, Rachel. *Silent Spring.* Boston, 1962.

Emerson, Ralph Waldo. *Nature, Addresses, and Lectures.* Edited by Robert E. Spiller and Alfred R. Ferguson. Cambridge, Mass., 1971.

Jefferson, Thomas. *Notes on the State of Virginia.* Edited by William Peden. 1785. Reprint, New York, 1983.

Leopold, Aldo. *A Sand County Almanac and Sketches Here and There.* Edited by Robert Finch. 1949. Reprint, New York, 1987.

Marsh, George Perkins. *Man and Nature; Or, Physical Geography as Modified by Human Action.* Edited by David Lowenthal. 1864. Reprint, Cambridge, Mass., 1965.

Thoreau, Henry David. *Walden.* 1854. Reprint, New York, 1991.

Turner, Frederick W., ed. *The Portable North American Indian Reader.* New York, 1974.

Historical Studies

Bruce, Robert V. *The Launching of Modern American Science: 1846–1876.* Ithaca, N.Y., 1987.

Craven, Avery. *Soil Exhaustion as a Factor in the Agricultural History of Virginia and Maryland, 1606–1860.* Urbana, Ill., 1926.

Cronon, William. *Changes in the Land: Indians, Colonists, and the Ecology of New England.* New York, 1983.

———. *Nature's Metropolis: Chicago and the Great West.* New York, 1991.

Easterbrook, Gregg. *A Moment on the Earth: The Coming Age of Environmental Optimism.* New York, 1995.

Foerster, Norman. *Nature in American Literature: Studies in the Modern View of Nature.* New York, 1923.

Hays, Samuel. *Conservation and the Gospel of Efficiency: The Progressive Conservation Movement, 1890–1920.* Cambridge, Mass., 1959.

Mathew, William M. *Edmund Ruffin and the Crisis of Slavery in the Old South: The Failure of Agricultural Reform.* Athens, Ga., 1988.

Merchant, Carolyn. *Ecological Revolutions: Nature, Gender, and Science in New England.* Chapel Hill, N.C., 1989.

Nash, Roderick. *Wilderness and the American Mind.* New Haven, Conn., 1967.

Opie, John. *Nature's Nation: An Environmental History of the United States.* Fort Worth, Tex., 1998.

Rothman, Hal. *Devil's Bargains: Tourism in the Twentieth-Century American West.* Lawrence, Kans., 1998.

Scheese, Don. *Nature Writing: The Pastoral Impulse in America.* New York, 1996.

Shabecoff, Philip. *A Fierce Green Fire: The American Environmental Movement.* New York, 1993.

Stegner, Wallace. *Beyond the Hundredth Meridian: John Wesley Powell and the Second Opening of the West.* 1954. Reprint, New York, 1992.

Stilgoe, John. *Common Landscape of America: 1580 to 1845.* New Haven, Conn., 1982.

———. *Metropolitan Corridor: Railroads and the American Scene.* New Haven, Conn., 1983.

Wilkins, Thurman. *John Muir: Apostle of Nature.* Norman, Okla., 1995.

Williams, Roger. *A Key into the Language of America.* 1643. Reprint, Providence, R.I., 1963.

Wilson, David Scofield. *In the Presence of Nature.* Amherst, Mass., 1978.

Worster, Donald. *Nature's Economy: A History of Ecological Ideas.* 2d ed. New York, 1994.

GOD, NATURE, AND HUMAN NATURE

E. Brooks Holifield

When John W. Draper, the president of the Medical School of the University of the City of New York, published his *History of the Conflict between Religion and Science* in 1874 and Andrew Dickson White, the president of Cornell University, published *A History of the Warfare of Science with Theology in Christendom* twenty-two years later, they canonized a martial metaphor that for decades shaped a historiographic tradition. According to this tradition, religious and scientific conceptions of nature and human nature have always been at war.

In twentieth-century scholarship, the metaphor of warfare itself came under attack. The emphasis for the last three decades of the twentieth century was on accommodation—a trend that continues into the twenty-first century. As early as 1938 the sociologist Robert Merton signaled the changing mood by arguing for a special affinity between English Puritanism and the rise of modern science. Merton's thesis generated controversy, but other accommodationist arguments proliferated. While attempting to make appropriate concessions to the older oppositional view, this essay reflects the newer perspective. It acknowledges the persistence of tension and conflict, but it contends that both conservative and liberal movements in American religious thought have, in different ways, adapted their conceptions of God, nature, and human nature to the prevailing scientific wisdom.

No synthetic account of American thought was more influential in the mid-twentieth century than the series of volumes in which the literary historian Perry Miller charted the transition from "the covenant," the religious vision of the American Puritans, to "nature's nation," a vision of American uniqueness derived from the natural grandeur of the land. For Miller, early American thought moved steadily toward various forms of naturalism, which he found implicit in the Puritan covenant theology, concealed in the religious vocabulary of the theologian Jonathan Edwards, and fully manifest in the

essays of the Transcendentalists. Critics have faulted Miller for overlooking the diversity of American thought, misreading the covenant theology, and misconstruing Edwards, but his recognition of a continuing appeal to nature and natural science in American thought, including American religious thought, has proven to be more convincing than the older metaphor of warfare.

PROVIDENCES

Long before the Europeans arrived, a religious sensibility formed by conceptions of natural harmony undergirded the rituals of North America's native peoples, but for the European explorers, missionaries, and settlers who began to inhabit the land in the sixteenth century, this native vision remained alien and distant. European promoters described the landscape as a place of beauty and plenty designed by providence to serve the ends of Europeans. They also viewed the Native Americans with assumptions of European ethnic superiority.

Competing images of nature and the supernatural marked popular colonial thought, which could embrace ancient notions of astrology, theories of alchemy, occult techniques of curing illness and predicting the future, and the practice of witchcraft, but the thinkers who strove most earnestly to harmonize traditional religious ideas with the new science were the Calvinist theologians of New England. They combined older Christian notions of divine providence and human sinfulness with theories of nature and human nature derived from Aristotelian natural history, Platonic philosophy, and post-sixteenth-century science.

The blending of worldviews is visible in the three meanings that the New England theologians assigned to the term "nature." It could refer to the created realm of "inconstant" things that are subject to generation and corruption, a realm composed of the "elementaries" of earth, air, fire, and water. It could refer also, as it had for the early Greeks, to that which is essential to anything: the growth of plants, the movement of animals, the reason and will of human beings. And it could denote, in a traditional Christian sense, humankind's corrupt estate after Adam's fall into sinfulness, a usage visible when the theologians contrasted nature and grace (Willard, *A Compleat Body of Divinity*, pp. 110–121). This doctrine of a fallen human nature prompted a few theologians—like John Cotton of Boston—to depreciate the study of the natural world because it could never heal "the sinfull defects of nature in our own spirits," but most Puritan preachers accepted the ancient principle of natural theology: even though "the book of the creature"— the natural world—remained dark without illumination from the book of Scripture, the evidence of design and order in the cosmos proved God's existence (Cotton, *Ecclesiastes*, p. 25).

By the end of the seventeenth century, the minister Samuel Willard of Boston exemplified the growing interest in natural theology when he argued that "the curious contrivances in each part" of the natural world—a world "in which the least Fly is full of wonders"—provided a clue to the divine purpose (*A Compleat Body*, pp. 37–40, 109). Some New Englanders found such clues in the new astronomy, even when it required reinterpretations of Scripture. In 1659 a New England almanac announced that the heliocentric theory of Copernicus was "the true and genuine system of the world." If the Bible appeared to differ, this was only because the biblical authors had no interest in "exactness" and wrote for "the capacity of the rudest mechanick, as of the ablest Philosophers" (Morison, *New England Quarterly*, p. 12).

It is true that Calvinist preachers saw the natural world as the continual object of providential guidance. In their theology, God governs nature through an ordinary providence that works through "second causes" and an extraordinary providence requiring immediate divine intervention. Most also distinguished between a "general" providence directing the whole creation and "special" providences governing particular events. The notion of providence sometimes functioned to legitimize assumptions about the difference in social power between the rich and the poor, men and women, and Europeans and Native Americans.

When English natural philosophers and Anglican theologians began to depict a lawlike natural order that called special providences into question, the Boston Congregational minister Increase Mather wrote his *Kometographia* (1683) and *An Es-*

This year, about the end of the fifth month, we had a very strange hand of God upon us, [in] that upon a sudden innumerable armies of caterpillars filled the country all over the English plantations, which devoured some whole meadows of grass, and greatly devoured barley (being the most green and tender corn), eating off all the blades and beards. . . . Much prayer there was made to God about it, with fasting in diverse places; and the Lord heard, and on a sudden took them all away again in all parts of the country, to the wonderment of all men. It was of the Lord, for it was done suddenly.

Source: John Eliot (17th century) in Demos, *Remarkable Providences,* (1872), pp. 375–376.

say for the Recording of Illustrious Providences (1684) to show that comets conveyed divine messages and God mysteriously intervened in the natural order. However, within a few years his son Cotton Mather, who never abandoned belief in providential events, was reading the opening chapters of Genesis as a foreshadowing of the atomistic theory of matter and summarizing the latest scientific opinion on light and gravity, planets and the sun, lightning and temperature as evidence for divine order. Cotton Mather's *Christian Philosopher* (1721) was the product of a man equally at home in the both the providential and the lawlike universe.

By the early eighteenth century, some of Mather's colleagues moved further toward the language of natural religion and natural law in their sermons and writings. In 1715, John Wise of Massachusetts found evidence in "The Light of Nature" for New England's church order and published his beliefs in *A Vindication of the Government of New England Churches;* in 1730 John Bulkley of Connecticut contended that some of the "weightiest matters" of faith came from lessons taught by "Nature, or Natural Light"—an idea that he put forth in his *Usefulness of Reveal'd Religion.* By 1759 Ebenezer Gay of Hingham, Massachusetts, was arguing in *Natural Religion* that natural law revealed a "God of Nature" whose aim was the moral virtue, not simply the salvation, of his creatures. For a few theologians, both the idea of depravity and the be-

Cotton Mather (1663–1728). Mather's writings popularized the developing sciences of Europe, including the work of Newton, in the colonies. Mather was also an early proponent of inoculation for the treatment of smallpox. LIBRARY OF CONGRESS

lief in special providences faded into the background.

This was the setting in which Jonathan Edwards made his audacious effort to encompass the new science of nature within older Calvinist sensibilities. He strove for a seamless blending of the scientific and the religious. He wrote accounts of spiders and rainbows and speculated about atoms, but he also continued the old tradition of "spiritualizing the creatures," finding religious truths in natural phenomena. Following the Anglo-Irish chemist Isaac Newton and Robert Boyle, who had formulated a mechanistic science in which matter lacks all inherent powers of attraction, Edwards saw the natural world as so dependent that it could continue to exist only because God created it anew each moment. The Newtonian sense of nature as governed by unchanging universal law found its counterpart in Edwards's view, grounded in philosophical idealism, that the uniform operation of divine law constitutes "all being in created things" (in Townsend, *Philosophy of Jonathan Edwards,* p. 72). He was more interested in nature's order than in its occasional irregularities, but he never abandoned belief in

special providences. Even in his views of human nature one finds the same blending: he drew on the new moral philosophy that postulated a "moral sense" in human nature, but he used it to reassert Calvinist views of human sinfulness.

Edwards died in 1758. The next significant outpouring of theological reflection on nature came from writers quite distant in spirit from Edwards and the Calvinist tradition. The American deists rejected Calvinist doctrines of Original Sin, all conceptions of special providence, and Christian belief in a biblical revelation. They sought, as Thomas Paine explained in his *Age of Reason* (1794), nature's God, revealed to every rational mind in the changeless laws of the natural order. For the deists, scientific understandings of nature provided norms for religious faith, and not only the wording of the Declaration of Independence but popular institutions like Masonic lodges illustrated the extent to which "nature and nature's God" could secure a place alongside the other traditions of American religious thought.

NATURAL THEOLOGY, MENTAL SCIENCE, AND THE GEOLOGICAL CRISIS

The traditionalist's answer to the deist's natural religion was a repristination of Christian natural theology. By the early nineteenth century, the common assumption among theologians was that the evidence of design in nature—the view that each natural structure serves definable predetermined purposes—bespoke the existence of a designer whom theologians identified with the God of biblical revelation. Natural order and intelligibility confirmed for them the biblical depiction of God as a personal agency who directs the world to its proper ends. The result was what Dwight Bozeman called "doxological science," the study of nature as a means of serving the God of Christian tradition (*Protestants,* p. 71).

The patron saint of science as doxology was the sixteenth-century courtier Francis Bacon, whose advocacy of a patient and humble inductive method seemed to ensure that natural science would remain within its proper bounds. Bacon's maxims reached a literate audience through the popularity of the Scottish common sense philosophy of Thomas Reid and Dugald Stewart, who emphasized the reliability of inductive scientific knowledge but also the limits of science and the congruity between scientific and religious truth. Arriving in America in the late

Some may, perhaps, doubt whether it can have been one of the objects of divine benevolence and wisdom, in arranging the surface of this world, so to construct and adorn it as to gratify a taste for fine scenery. But I cannot doubt it. I see not else why nature every where is fitted up in a loving manner, with all the elements of the sublime and beautiful, nor why there are powers in the human soul so intensely gratified in contact with those elements, unless they were expressly adapted for one another by the Creator.

Source: Edward Hitchcock, *The Religion of Geology and Its Connected Sciences*, (1854), p. 183.

eighteenth century, the Scottish philosophy found advocates in almost every religious group.

On doxological science, the theologians agreed. On human nature, they quarreled endlessly. Unitarians affirmed human freedom and the potential for moral perfection; revisionist Calvinists at the Yale Divinity School taught that sin is certain but not necessary; Methodists talked of a prevenient grace that restores free will to the sinful; Catholics likewise combined the doctrine of Original Sin with belief in a preparatory grace that restores the capacity to choose wisely; traditional Calvinists insisted that the imputation of Adam's sin to his descendants issued in a universal depravity that could be overcome only by the special grace given to the elect. What was equally striking, however, was the way in which each of these groups appealed to the new discipline of "mental science," grounded in Lockean and Scottish philosophy, to argue their case. During the 1820s, the study of mental science became virtually a prolegomenon to theology, and theological arguments often turned on such questions as whether the mind has three fundamental faculties (will, understanding, and affection) or only two (will and understanding).

A similar interweaving of theology and science could be found in other antebellum debates over human nature. Some theologians during the 1820s drew on mental science to refute the American phrenologists, who correlated human behavior with organs of the brain identifiable from the shape of the skull. Others appealed to natural history to re-

fute the American polygenists, who contended that white and black people came from separate creations and constitute separate species. Theologians generally preferred the earlier views of the College of New Jersey (later Princeton University) professor Samuel Stanhope Smith, who in 1787 had explained human difference as the result of adaptation to different climates and societies. More important in some ways than these academic debates were the conceptions of human nature implicit in widespread cultural prejudices. Most whites assumed their superiority to blacks; most males thought that certain "natural" feminine attributes consigned women to a subordinate position in the society; most Protestants viewed Irish immigrants with condescension or hostility, and most American of European descent assumed the inferiority of Native Americans. Activists like Elizabeth Cady Stanton and Lucretia Mott, who organized in Seneca, New York, in 1848 the first woman's rights convention, and black abolitionist leaders like Frederick Douglass provoked national debate when they challenged such assumptions.

Whether discussing nature or human nature, antebellum theologians could assume that science confirmed religious faith. When Samuel Miller of Princeton University published in 1803 his *Brief Retrospect of the Eighteenth Century*, he announced that science had consistently corroborated the biblical account of creation. Within the next three decades it became increasingly clear that if they wished to claim the authority of science, the theologians would have to engage in some creative reinterpretation.

During the 1820s, American naturalists began to attend to the earlier arguments of the Scottish geologist James Hutton, who had described the development of the earth as a process without a discernible beginning or end, as well as to the nebular hypothesis of the French astronomer Pierre-Simon Laplace, who had argued that the solar system originated through the gradual condensation of gaseous or fluid matter. Hutton explained the earth's surface as the result of geological processes set in motion by immense heat; other geologists explained it as the result of receding water that once covered the planet.

The disagreement assumed importance for theology after 1829, when the geologist and Yale professor Benjamin Silliman published his geological lectures with the argument that the watery explanation could easily be harmonized with Scripture if it were recognized that each of the six days in the biblical creation story was a geological period of indefinite length. Edward Hitchcock, a onetime student of Silliman and professor at Amherst College countered that a better way of harmonizing the two accounts was to interpret the first verse of Genesis as implying two creations, the first "in the beginning," the second (the six days) after an intervening "void." According to this "gap theory," the fossils originated in the first creation, human beings in the second. The fact that both theories received widespread approval among theologians reveals the depth of the desire to harmonize. The Catholic theologian Francis P. Kenrick explicitly warned theologians in his *Theologia Dogmatica* (1858) not to interpret Scripture in ways that place it in opposition to the discoveries of science. He need not have worried. Many of them implicitly made geology the norm by which the biblical account was to be interpreted. This was painfully evident to the few earnest literalists, like Moses Stuart at Andover Theological Seminary and Taylor Lewis of Union College, who insisted that philology, not geology, had to determine the meaning of the biblical narrative.

To the thinkers who gathered in 1836 around the leader of the Transcendentalist movement, Ralph Waldo Emerson, the exegesis seemed frivolous and the arguments from design mechanistic and artificial. The irony is that the Transcendentalists were far more suspicious of natural science as it was then understood than were the Christian traditionalists. Like the earlier deists, Emerson spoke for a religion of nature, which he found suffused with divinity, but unlike them he distrusted an empirical approach to the natural world because he thought that it would always fail to find the deeper spiritual truth available to the intuitive reason. And his natural religion always cloaked a certain ambivalence, for he was not quite sure whether nature was a reality to which the self had to conform or a mere appearance cloaking the omnipresence of the mind. In her *Women in the Nineteenth Century* (1844), however, Margaret Fuller used Transcendentalist ideas about natural capacities to promote individualism and self-reliance in women.

The Transcendentalists introduced to many Americans a way of seeing nature as organic rather than machine-like, and their symbolic reading of the natural world, linked with their elevated view of human nature as the vehicle of an immanent divine mind, made them enduring resources for what the historian Catherine L. Albanese called the "metaphysical" tradition in American religion—a religious vision founded in the discovery of neverending correspondences between nature and spiritual truth (*Nature Religion in America*, pp. 80–116). This romantic vision of nature has had lasting consequences. The naturalist John Muir, who met and admired Emerson, discovered in the mountains of the American West a sacred presence that elevated him into the vast mysteries of the universe, and his form of nature religion prompted a quest for preservation that eventuated in the establishing of Sequoia and Yosemite National Parks in California and heralded the rise of an environmental consciousness that grew stronger in the twentieth century.

The organic vision could also find more conventional Protestant forms. When Horace Bushnell, the pastor of the North Congregational Church, in Hartford, Connecticut, published his *Nature and the Supernatural as Together Constituting the One System of God* in 1858, he discarded the older natural theology, with its confidence that every structure exemplifies a divine design, in favor of a more chastened view of nature as often wasteful and chaotic. Bushnell was no longer convinced that natural theology could offer proofs of a personal God. But he never minimized the religious importance of nature. In fact, his theory of language depicted the natural world as a source of metaphors that illumined the religious imagination. He also helped transform liberal Protestant notions of human nature by emphasizing that children could be gradually formed by parental and social influence rather than suddenly converted by revivalist sermons. Bushnell had his suspicions of science; his universe was filled with inexplicable miracles, and his confidence in the science of the eminent Harvard University naturalist Louis Agassiz meant that he resisted after 1859 the evolutionary biology of Charles Darwin. He also promoted conventional views of "feminine" nature by opposing the drive for women's rights as unnatural. But his organic view of physical nature, his notion of theological language as symbolic, and his depiction of nature and the supernatural as intimately interrelated foreshadowed directions that his followers would pursue much further in the late nineteenth century, especially after the publication of Darwin's *Origin of Species* (1859).

EVOLUTION

The debates over Darwinian evolution have seemed to offer the prime example of warfare between religious and scientific conceptions of nature. Antievolutionary sentiment has been extensive in popular culture, with 47 percent of Americans, including one-fourth of college graduates, believing as recently as 1991 that God created men and women pretty much in their present form at one time within the last ten thousand years (Numbers, *The Creationists*, p. ix). Among American theologians, however, both liberal and conservative, the story has been far more complex.

Much of the opposition of the theologians came at a time when scientists remained unconvinced. Harvard's Agassiz, who saw each animal species as the discrete creation of a transcendent deity, represented a substantial number of biologists and geologists who contended that Darwin's theory failed to meet the criteria for a solid inductive conclusion. American scientists who adopted theories of transmutation during the 1860s gravitated toward the ideas of the French paleontologist Jean-Baptiste Lamarck, who had seen nature as filled with innate powers that enabled species to change in response to the environment and then pass the changes to their offspring. Lamarckian biology left an opening for teleology.

Darwin's chief explanatory idea—that evolution occurred through a random process of natural selection in which accidental variations enabled new species to emerge and triumph over competitors—seemed to leave no such opening. Given the religious commitments of most American naturalists, it was not surprising that only during the 1870s did they begin in substantial numbers to see natural selection as a promising hypothesis. Several were able to make this transition because the Harvard botanist Asa Gray, who had adopted Darwin's theory earlier in 1859, made a convincing case in his *Darwiniana* (1876) that natural selection is fully compatible with Christian ideas of divine order and purpose.

Darwin's religious opponents had multiple reasons for worry. When the Princeton Presbyterian theologian Charles Hodge concluded in his *What Is Darwinism?* (1874) that Darwinism is atheism, he meant that natural selection precludes teleology, a view shared, incidentally, by the Unitarian Francis Bowen. Others saw the theory as threatening the unique character of human beings as made in the image of God, or as promoting the ethical view that might makes right. Underlying some of these fears was the worrisome sense that Darwin's science was incompatible with the teachings of the Bible about creation, the fall, and redemption.

For many, however, the biblical worries were easy to overcome. Even Charles Hodge acknowledged that theologians had often appropriately re-

We have only to say that the Darwinian system, as we understand it, coincides well with the theistic view of Nature. It not only acknowledges purpose . . . but builds upon it; and if purpose in this sense does not of itself imply design, it is certainly compatible with it, and suggestive of it. Difficult as it may be to conceive and impossible to demonstrate design in a whole of which the series of parts appear to be contingent, the alternative may be not more difficult. . . . Of the alternatives, the predication of design—special, general, or universal, as the case may be—is most natural to the mind, while the exclusion of it throughout . . . leads to a conclusion which few men ever rested in.

Source: Asa Gray, *Darwiniana* (1876), pp. 311–312.

interpreted the Bible in the light of scientific learning. Ever since the seventeenth century, they had been willing to say that the biblical writers had accommodated their message to popular thought forms. Some believed that a close reading of Genesis would reveal nineteenth-century scientific truths hidden behind these ancient forms of thought. Others concluded that the Bible is a purely religious book, not a scientific account, and that its wisdom has nothing to do with the worldviews assumed by its authors.

As a result, a number of theologians, including especially conservative Calvinists, could accept even Darwin's theory of natural selection. Oberlin College professor George Frederick Wright said that Calvinists and Darwinists shared a common distaste for sentimental and romantic views of nature and that Calvinists could come to terms more easily with the suffering and apparent waste entailed by natural selection because they had always affirmed both that suffering served an inscrutable end and that the purpose of creation was the good of being itself, not the happiness of particular individuals. Asa Gray was a conservative Calvinist who recognized the harshness of natural selection but still found it compatible with a conception of design which assumes that variation has been "led along certain beneficial lines" (Moore, *The Post-Darwinian Controversies*, p. 274).

The more frequent recourse of liberal theologians was to reinterpret both Darwin and Christian tradition by accentuating God's immanence in the natural world. Overlooking the more unpleasant aspects of natural selection, some of them began to speak of God as the all-pervading efficient cause of all things, moving the cosmos along toward inevitable progress. The Congregationalist Lyman Abbott, whose *Theology of an Evolutionist* (1897) affirmed evolution while refusing to identify it with Darwinism, described it simply as God's way of doing things, while the geologist Joseph LeConte at the University of California argued in *Evolution and Its Relation to Religious Thought* (1888) that since there is no efficient force but spirit, the law of evolution is nothing other than the mode of the divine energy in originating and developing the universe. Viewed from this perspective, argued the Catholic theologian John Augustine Zahm in his *Evolution and Dogma* (1896), evolution "ennobles our conceptions of God" (p. 429). The church forced Zahm to withdraw his book from circulation, but by the late twentieth century even the popes were saying something quite similar.

The Christian liberals tried to maintain links between biblical tradition and evolutionary philosophies, but others found in the grandeur of evolution itself a sufficient grounding for a natural religion. The philosopher John Fiske spoke most eloquently for those who saw in evolution the marks of an unknowable power worthy of worship and devotion. In his *Outlines of Cosmic Philosophy* (1874), Fiske urged his readers to base their conceptions of God on science alone and assured them that the unconditioned power revealed by science is far more magnificent than the anthropomorphic God of the Bible.

Even theologians who could accept an evolutionary picture of nature sometimes found it hard to view human beings as descendants of an earlier species of animal life. It was difficult not to see mentality as a leap in the evolutionary chain that required a special creative divine act. Only gradually did religious intellectuals concede the point. When they did, the result was often a reinterpretation of several traditional doctrines. For Protestant liberals, the doctrine of Adam's fall became a symbol of human experience rather than a historical event; some reinterpreted sin as a preference for lingering "animal-like" propensities or as a failure of human beings to realize their essential nature. But the assumption still reigned that human beings are the apex of the evolutionary chain. The world had been

made for them (Roberts, *Darwinism and the Divine in America,* pp. 174–208).

By the early twentieth century such anthropocentrism came under closer scrutiny. The philosopher and educator John Dewey exemplified the kind of radical reassessment that evolutionary doctrine could produce. For Dewey, the word "God" became a way simply of pointing to all the natural forces and conditions, including human beings and human associations, that promoted the growth of ideal ends which integrated the self and directed its energies toward worthy social goals. But Dewey saw no evidence that humanity was the goal of evolution. He located the human fully in the realm of the natural and denied that human beings are the centerpiece of nature.

By the 1920s, the naturalism that Dewey represented had aroused a pressing interest in the biology of human life. The new psychology of theorists like William James and William McDougall therefore directed attention to instincts, drives, and hereditary limits of the organism. One result was a flourishing eugenics movement and a lamentable resurgence of "scientific" racism, as popular writers like Madison Grant tried to show that white "Nordics" are superior to most other European and all Asian and African people (Degler, *In Search of Human Nature,* pp. 32–55).

In the American universities, the main alternative to naturalistic philosophies came not directly from the religious traditions but from philosophical idealism. In the waning decades of the nineteenth century, philosophers like Noah Porter at Yale, Borden Parker Bowne at Boston University, and Josiah Royce at Harvard countered materialist views by arguing that the essence of the universe is the mind, or that the world is the outworking of absolute spirit, or that concepts like truth and falsity make sense only if there is an absolute consciousness to serve as a standard. The God of the idealists bore only a faint resemblance to the traditional Christian and Jewish God, but idealism influenced a few liberal theologians who saw a philosophical theology as more appropriate to a scientific age than older forms of dogmatism.

By the early twentieth century, Protestant liberals were responding to scientific conceptions of nature in two ways. The first, derived largely from nineteenth-century German theologians, was to distinguish between fact and value and to redefine theological statements as value judgments. For theologians of this persuasion, to speak of God as creator no longer meant making a quasi-scientific statement about the origin of the world; it rather

Clarence Darrow (*left*) and William Jennings Bryan during the Scopes Trial. The Scopes "Monkey Trial" was a battle over the Butler Law, which prohibited the teaching of evolution in public schools in Tennessee. AP/WIDE WORLD PHOTOS

signified simply that the world is best viewed as a gift for which gratitude is appropriate and that human beings are best seen as possessing sacred worth. The second way of responding was to make theology itself an "empirical" discipline. At its broadest, this meant that theologians would try to limit their claims to the realm of human experience. On this basis, for example, the professor Henry Nelson Wieman of the University of Chicago during the 1920s defined God as a name for the value-making process in the universe, the process that generates organic unity and wholeness and so produces the greatest possible goods for human beings who connect their lives to it.

This was the theological modernism against which Fundamentalists and evangelical Christians protested—a protest graphically symbolized in the Scopes trial by the clash between the prosecutor William Jennings Bryan and the defense attorney Clarence Darrow in a Tennessee courtroom in 1925.

The irony in their protest was that they often proved almost equally willing to import scientific norms, as they understood them, into their views of creation. The marginal notes in the *Scofield Reference Bible,* one of the favorite Fundamentalist versions, reconciles Genesis with the fossil data by employing the nineteenth-century gap theory, which had originated as an attempt to harmonize the Bible and geology. Even more telling was the Fundamentalist approbation of "creation science," which gained a wide lay audience during the 1920s, especially after the Seventh-Day Adventist George McCready Price published *The New Geology* (1923), an attempt to offer geological evidence that the earth is no more than seven thousand years old. Resurrected in the 1960s, "scientific creationism" gained momentum as a popular political force that launched aggressive campaigns to influence local school boards. It also illustrated the prestige of science in some religiously conservative circles. By defending a religious viewpoint with "scientific" accounts of nature, the creationists implicitly made science a religious norm.

CULTURE AND ECOLOGY

By the 1930s both anthropologists and psychologists were turning away from biology to embrace the idea that culture is the primary shaper of human destiny. Influenced by the research of the anthropologist Franz Boas, a host of social theorists adopted cultural interpretations, and some of them completely separated biological and social evolution. The early work of Margaret Mead, a student of Boas and of the anthropologist Ruth Benedict, especially her *Coming of Age in Samoa* (1928), introduced to a broad audience the idea that human nature is thoroughly malleable. Along with other goals, Mead and Benedict hoped that their research would shatter lingering stereotypes about gender, race, and ethnicity. Among psychologists, cultural explanation reached its apex in the behaviorist theories of John B. Watson, who argued during the late 1920s that all behavior is the consequence of environmental shaping. The vogue for Freudian psychoanalysis intensified the move toward cultural interpretations, since Freud had seen the relationship between the organism and culture as the molder of unconscious impulse. This tradition of cultural interpretation continued into the late-twentieth century and gave support to the African American civil rights movement, feminist critiques of American society, and a resurgence of ethnic pride in groups that had been disadvantaged.

Cultural approaches showed up in theology too. Biblical critics had been urging since the 1880s that the Bible reflects the mentality of ancient Semitic cultures, and theologians like Shailer Mathews at the University of Chicago began by 1900 to interpret changing conceptions of God as reflections of changes in cultural circumstances. The Protestant "realists," especially H. Richard Niebuhr at Yale and Reinhold Niebuhr at Union Theological Seminary in New York City, also emphasized the force of culture. Richard reinterpreted the concept of revelation to refer to the power of historical symbols to shape communities of faith by pointing to a transcendent reality that relativizes every human good. Reinhold described the ways in which cultural groups embody impulses of pride and self-aggrandizement that can be adequately interpreted only through the recovery of notions of human sinfulness.

The preoccupation with culture and history bespoke a diminishing interest in nature among theo-

What the ecological model offers to Christianity is a way of extending its own most basic affirmation on how others should be treated—as subjects—to nature. . . . If we are to love God with our whole heart, mind, and soul, and our neighbor as ourselves, how, in continuity with that model, should we love nature? The answer is: with the loving eye, with the eye that realizes that even a wood tick or a Douglas fir is a subject—that each has a world, goals, intentions (though not conscious), and modes of flourishing that make them good in themselves and not simply good for us.

Source: Sallie McFague, *Super, Natural Christians* (1997), pp. 164–165.

logians, but there were exceptions. Some were drawn to the categories of the British mathematician and philosopher Alfred North Whitehead, who interpreted reality as a process constantly changing in response to possibilities offered by an immanent divine creativity. Others turned their attention to the dawning awareness of ecology and environmental crisis. As early as 1954 the ethicist Joseph Sittler of the University of Chicago was writing on faith and ecology, but it took a stinging criticism in 1967 by Lynn White in *Science* magazine to elicit more widespread interest. White argued that Christian anthropocentrism and the Christian dualism between humanity and the rest of nature had contributed to the environmental disaster. As energy shortages and pollution began to make headlines in the 1970s, liberal Protestants responded by rethinking conceptions of both God and human nature in relation to the natural environment.

A number of them sought to emphasize the involvement of God in the natural world in ways that accentuated its intrinsic value. By the 1980s, "ecotheology" had become a visible form of Protestant thought. The Lutheran Paul Santmire contended that the biblical writings themselves, read with an attentive eye, convey a sense of respect for nature. Thomas Berry represented the interest in theologies of creation that found the primary revelation of the divine in the creativity manifest in nature. One group of feminist theologians, influenced by Carolyn Merchant's *Death of Nature* (1980), moved toward an "ecofeminism" that decried all dualistic separations between nature and spirit and sought to recover images of organic relatedness of God and the world, which they sometimes described as "God's Body." For these theological movements, the saving of God's creation assumed priority over the saving of isolated souls or traditional apologetic concerns.

One additional striking feature of twentieth-century American culture was the reemergence of nature religions, holistic health movements, and rituals of harmony between human beings and the rest of nature. While the novelist Annie Dillard reminded her readers that the God of nature could be brutal and unforgiving, others found in nature a source of beneficent renewal, and the 1970s saw a turn toward religious movements—often called New Age or metaphysical—that offered their adherents insights on how to tap cosmic natural energies.

Religious thinkers in America, whether traditional theologians or promoters of new religious impulses, have rarely ignored the insights of the natural sciences. The story of religion and science has had its moments of conflict, but the theme of accommodation has also woven its way through the plot, and scientific conceptions of nature and human nature have repeatedly served as either manifest or covert norms for religious thought. Nature and nature's God have left a powerful imprint on religion in America.

See also **Puritanism as a Cultural and Intellectual Force; Anglo-American Religious Traditions; Philosophy from Puritanism to the Enlightenment; The New England Theology from Edwards to Bushnell; Agrarianism and the Agrarian Ideal in Early America; Evangelical Thought; Moral Philosophy; American Romanticism; Transcendentalism; Communitarianism; The Rise of Biblical Criticism and Challenges to Religious Authority; The Struggle over Evolution; Religious Liberalism, Fundamentalism, and Neo-Orthodoxy** *(volume 1);* **Hermeneutics and American Historiography** *(volume 3); and other articles in this section.*

BIBLIOGRAPHY

General

Albanese, Catherine L. *Nature Religion in America: From the Algonkian Indians to the New Age.* Chicago, 1990.

Degler, Carl N. *In Search of Human Nature: The Decline and Revival of Darwinism in American Social Thought.* New York, 1991.

Lindberg, David C., and Numbers, Ronald L., eds. *God and Nature: Historical Essays on the Encounter Between Christianity and Science.* Berkeley, Calif., 1986.

Miller, Perry. *Nature's Nation.* Cambridge, Mass., 1967.

Mullin, Robert Bruce. *Miracles and the Modern Religious Imagination.* New Haven, Conn., 1996.

Turner, James. *Without God, Without Creed: The Origins of Unbelief in America.* Baltimore, 1985.

Providences: Seventeenth and Eighteenth Centuries

Bulkley, John. *The Usefulness of Reveal'd Religion [to Preserve and Improve that which Is Natural.]* London, 1730.

Cotton, John. *A Brief Exposition with Practical Observations upon the Whole Book of Ecclesiastes.* London, 1654.

Edwards, Jonathan. "The Mind." In *The Philosophy of Jonathan Edwards from His Private Notebooks,* edited by Harvey Townsend, Eugene, Oreg., 1955.

Eliot, John. "Records of the First Church of Roxbury, Massachusetts." In *Remarkable Providences 1600–1700*, edited by John Demos, pp. 375–376. New York, 1972.

Gay, Ebenezer. *Natural Religion, as Distinguish'd from Revealed: A Sermon Preached at the Annual Dudleian-Lecture, at Harvard College in Cambridge, May 9, 1759.* Boston, 1759.

Merton, Robert K. *Science, Technology and Society in Seventeenth Century England.* 1938. Reprint, New York, 1970.

Morison, Samuel E. "The Harvard School of Astronomy in the Seventeenth Century." *New England Quarterly* 7 (1934): 3–24.

Stoever, William K. B. *A Faire and Easie Way to Heaven: Covenant Theology and Antinomianism in Early Massachusetts.* Middletown, Conn., 1978.

Willard, Samuel. *A Compleat Body of Divinity.* Boston, 1726.

Winship, Michael P. *Seers of God: Puritan Providentialism in the Restoration and Early Enlightenment.* Baltimore, 1996.

Antebellum America: Design

Bozeman, Theodore Dwight. *Protestants in an Age of Science: The Baconian Ideal and Antebellum American Religious Thought.* Chapel Hill, N.C., 1977.

Cherry, Conrad. *Nature and Religious Imagination: From Edwards to Bushnell.* Philadelphia, 1980.

Hovenkamp, Herbert. *Science and Religion in America, 1800–1860.* Philadelphia, 1978.

Howe, Daniel Walker. *Making the American Self: Jonathan Edwards to Abraham Lincoln.* Cambridge, Mass., 1997.

Numbers, Ronald L. *Creation by Natural Law: Laplace's Nebular Hypothesis in American Thought.* Seattle, Wash., 1977.

Nineteenth-Century: Evolution

Abbott, Lyman. *The Theology of an Evolutionist.* Boston and New York, 1897.

Gray, Asa. *Darwiniana.* 1876. Reprint, Cambridge, Mass., 1963.

Hitchcock, Edward. *The Religion of Geology and Its Connected Sciences.* Boston, 1854.

Hutchison, William R. *The Modernist Impulse in American Protestantism.* Cambridge, Mass., 1976.

Marsden, George. *Fundamentalism and American Culture: The Shaping of Twentieth Century Evangelicalism, 1870–1925.* New York, 1980.

Moore, James R. *The Post-Darwinian Controversies: A Study of the Protestant Struggle to Come to Terms with Darwin in Great Britain and America, 1870–1900.* Cambridge, Mass., 1979.

Roberts, Jon H. *Darwinism and the Divine in America: Protestant Intellectuals and Organic Evolution, 1859–1900.* Madison, Wisc., 1988.

Zahm, John Augustine. *Evolution and Dogma.* 1896. Reprint, Hicksville, N.Y., 1975.

Twentieth Century: Culture and Ecology

Fowler, Robert Booth. *The Greening of Protestant Thought.* Chapel Hill, N.C., 1995.

Gustafson, James M. *Intersections: Science, Theology, and Ethics.* Cleveland, Ohio, 1997.

McFague, Sallie. *The Body of God: An Ecological Theology.* Minneapolis, Minn., 1993.

———. *Super, Natural Christians.* Minneapolis, Minn., 1997.

Numbers, Ronald L. *The Creationists: The Evolution of Scientific Creationism.* Berkeley, Calif., 1992.

Sheldon, Joseph K. *Rediscovery of Creation: A Bibliographical Study of the Church's Response to the Environmental Crisis.* Metuchen, N.J., 1992.

van Huyssteen, J. Wentzel. *Duet or Duel? Theology and Science in the Postmodern World.* Harrisburg, Penn., 1998.

Wieman, Henry Nelson. *Religious Experience and Scientific Method.* New York, 1926.

HUMANITARIANISM

Daniel Wickberg

When we speak of humanitarianism today, the images that spring readily to mind are those of international aid workers, the amelioration of third world poverty, and nonprofit organizations dedicated to improving the lives of the suffering, both locally and globally. The images are ones of social activism, and the assumption is that humanitarianism not only involves action, but essentially is a form of action. Because humanitarianism is so frequently identified with institutions, organizations, and networks of activity, it is easy to simply take for granted the impulse, the configuration of emotions, and the body of thought that lies beneath or behind it. From the point of view of intellectual and cultural history, however, it is not only the bureaucratic institutions of benevolent action at a distance that are distinctively modern; the ways of thinking, the logic, the understandings of emotion itself that are characteristic of humanitarianism today also have a relatively recent lineage. Humanitarianism is certainly a form of social activism, but it is also a sensibility—a way of seeing and experiencing the world that is a coherent configuration of ideas, emotions, and values. Before the eighteenth century, that sensibility did not exist; by the mid-nineteenth century, it had become one of the defining characteristics and outlooks of the American bourgeoisie, and in particular the New England modernizing portion of that class.

The new humanitarian sensibility helped inspire various reform movements of the late eighteenth and early nineteenth centuries: penal reform, the campaigns against capital and corporal punishment, slavery, and animal vivisection. Under the watch of late-nineteenth- and early-twentieth-century Progressivism, humanitarianism gave impetus to movements for the reform of urban living conditions, public health, and education and for the protection of women and children from labor exploitation. In the twentieth century, humanitarianism would be associated with large-scale movements such as the War on Poverty in the 1960s, international emergency relief, United Nations peacekeeping efforts, and campaigns for universal human rights. While the humanitarian sensibility or impulse should not be understood as a transhistorical or unchanging phenomenon, the development of the main body of humanitarian ideas and emotions took place in the eighteenth and early nineteenth centuries. Since then, humanitarianism has taken a number of different forms, and identified new objects of reform and concern. The sensibility itself, however, has remained largely unchanged since the nineteenth century, with one major exception—a twentieth-century secular variant of humanitarianism has completely abandoned the religious foundations that were essential to early humanitarian reform.

INTELLECTUAL ROOTS OF THE HUMANITARIAN SENSIBILITY

The roots of the Anglo-American humanitarian sensibility lay in a monumental shift of consciousness in late-seventeenth- and eighteenth-century British culture. In particular, they lay in the reaction against the view of human nature associated with the philosopher and political theorist Thomas Hobbes (1588–1679), on the one hand, and with the Calvinist tradition of reformed theology on the other. Both Hobbes and the Calvinists took a dim view of not only the human capacity for reason and self-government but also the direction of human emotions or "passions." For Hobbes, man was inevitably guided by his passions, which were at base selfish. Man's primary interests lay in self-glory and power over others, and he only agreed to submit to authority as a way to provide some security from a state of nature that Hobbes characterized as a war of all against all. Any action that appeared to be kind, altruistic, or selfless in reality hid an ulterior motive of self-aggrandizement.

The Calvinist tradition, which was instrumental in shaping both English Puritanism and Scottish

Presbyterianism, contained an image of human beings nearly as bleak and fatalistic as that of Hobbes. For John Calvin (1509–1564) and his British followers, the condition of man was to be understood only in relation to that of God. If God was omnipotent, man was feeble and weak; if God was omniscient, man's reason and capacity for knowledge was severely limited; if God was the very definition of good, man was an utter and complete sinner, deserving damnation. Man's essentially sinful nature meant that he could do good, of even the most limited sort, only by virtue of God's grace; his natural inclination was to follow his selfish passions. Calvinist theology, with its doctrines of predestination, infant damnation, and salvation through God's grace alone, justified the presence of evil, suffering, and cruelty as part of God's plan and laid them at the feet of man's sinful nature.

Neither the Hobbesian nor the Calvinist view of human nature put much faith in human reason as the engine of behavior. More important, to the extent that they saw human beings as driven by their emotions, rather than their reason, they characterized those emotions as base, selfish, and destructive. Humanity could scarcely be the source of a selfless movement to create good, nor did human beings seem to deserve any good that might come their way, seen from the perspective of the mid-seventeenth century.

The eighteenth century has often been characterized as the Age of Reason, and for good reasons. Thinkers of the European Enlightenment frequently appealed to the revolutionary power of human rationality both to discover the principles of nature, and to act as a foundation for human morality, behavior, and government. To the extent that eighteenth-century thinkers rejected the view of human nature associated with Hobbes and Calvin, they did so not only on the grounds that reason rather than emotion was the driving force of human behavior, but also on the grounds that human emotion could be good, compassionate, and sympathetic rather than selfish, sinful, and power-hungry. The eighteenth century, in intellectual and cultural circles, was as much an age of emotion as an age of reason. Humanitarianism, as it developed in the course of the eighteenth and nineteenth centuries, was based less on notions of universal reason and abstract moral principle, and more on emotional concern with suffering and concrete identification with the pain of others. The eighteenth-century revision of the meaning and purpose of emotion, then, lay at the heart of the humanitarian sensibility.

Scottish Philosophy As much as modern moral philosophy is indebted to Kantian notions of universal reason and the rational subject, modern humanitarianism flows from another source. It is indebted not to Immanuel Kant (1724–1804) but to an alternative body of eighteenth-century moral philosophy: that of the Scottish Enlightenment. Scottish thinkers such as Francis Hutcheson, David Hume, Adam Smith, and Lord Kames (Henry Home) shaped a distinctive and influential body of moral thought that laid stress on the natural emotional basis of goodwill and moral action. The benevolentist philosophy of the Scottish school had its greatest impact in America, where it came to form much of the core curriculum of the eighteenth- and early-nineteenth-century college, thus shaping the outlook of the early national elite. Influential figures such as John Witherspoon, president of Princeton; Benjamin Rush, Pennsylvania physician and prominent revolutionary; and Thomas Jefferson were deeply versed in the language and sensibility of the Scottish Enlightenment. Educated Americans read Hugh Blair and George Campbell on rhetoric, Smith, Kames, and Hutcheson on moral philosophy, Thomas Reid on epistemology, Adam Ferguson on social progress. The generally optimistic (with the exception of Hume's skepticism), emotivist and moderate outlook of Scottish philosophy had a far greater currency throughout late colonial and early national American society than is suggested by the limited portion of the society that actually read its canonical works. One need not have read Hutcheson or his students to have a general familiarity with the concept of the moral sense, anymore than one need read Freud today to be on familiar terms with the concept of repression.

Scottish philosophy, in rejecting the Hobbesian and Calvinist notions of human nature, was influenced by the Cambridge Platonists, a group of late-seventeenth-century thinkers that included Ralph Cudworth and Henry More, and more especially by the social thought of Anthony Ashley Cooper (1671–1713), third earl of Shaftesbury. Shaftesbury's popular *Characteristicks of Men, Manners, Opinions, Times* (1711) represented a celebration of human sociability and gregariousness that both affirmed the natural benevolence of man and suggested the basis for a new social order in which that benevolence and goodwill would, if left to its own devices, lead to progress and improvement. The key concepts that Scottish philosophy developed from the earlier thought of the Cambridge Platonists and Shaftesbury were the concept of the moral sense; the idea of universal benevolence; the idea of sympathy; and the idea of the sympathetic imagination. These four ideas provided the philosophical underpinnings of the humanitarian sensibility, and suggest how closely humanitarianism was tied to the development of a liberal social and political order.

Shaftesbury was the first to conceive of the notion of a moral sense as a natural human faculty, but it was Francis Hutcheson (1694–1746) who elaborated this idea and made it the key to his moral philosophy. The moral sense was understood to be a universal human faculty that allowed for immediate judgment of right and wrong. Moral judgment, from this point of view, did not involve a process of reflection and rational consideration, but an immediate perception. Hutcheson's "internal senses"—the sense of beauty, the sense of the ridiculous, and the moral sense, among others—were like the "external senses" of sight, hearing, touch, smell, and taste in that they required no logic or cognition to perceive difference. The moral sense distinguished between good and evil actions in the same way that the sense of sight distinguished between red and blue—as a matter of immediate perception rather than reflection upon perception. Hutcheson's notion that all human beings possessed a moral sense, then, implied that reasoning ability, education, and learned codes of ethics were irrelevant to moral judgment. All people, except those whose moral senses had been corrupted, knew intuitively and immediately upon perception whether a given action was right or wrong.

The idea of a universal, naturally given, presocial faculty was important in shaping the emerging humanitarianism of the eighteenth century in at least two ways. By giving man an innate capacity to make moral judgments, it freed morality from both God-given rules codified in Scripture and state-sanctioned rules codified in law; it made moral judgment a matter of essential humanity and natural being rather than a prescribed code. Humanitarianism would come to be based on a faith in human ability to immediately perceive injustice, suffering, and wrong, with no intermediaries, as a prelude to taking action against them. Second, in contrast to the Hobbesian and Calvinist images of human nature, the idea of the moral sense elevated normal human capacity to know the difference between right and wrong, and did so without relying upon reason. If the moral sense was not exactly an emotion, it was something very much more like it than anything that had existed before. Humanitarianism would make the *feeling* of wrong, rather than the abstract knowledge of it, the basis for action.

The application of Hutcheson's idea in America was significant. Thomas Jefferson's famous statement of human equality in the Declaration of Independence was based, at least in part, on the concept of the moral sense. Since the equality he referred to is clearly a moral equality and not a matter of reasoning ability or talent, Jefferson had to locate the basis of that equality in a universally held status independent of rationality. In *Notes on the State of Virginia* (1785) he makes clear that despite what he believed to be the great intellectual, physical, and temperamental differences between blacks and whites, blacks were entitled to liberty on the same ground as whites: their possession of a God-given moral sense. Hutcheson's notion of the moral sense as a universal human attribute by no means required an egalitarian social order, but a kind of moral egalitarianism would become central to the outlook of many nineteenth-century humanitarians, particularly in the United States.

Hutcheson also stressed benevolence as the motivating force for moral action. The moral sense allowed human beings to have immediate knowledge of good and evil, but their naturally benevolent nature provided the spring that compelled them to act on that knowledge, and gave a direction to their action. The late-seventeenth-century latitudinarian (persons of liberal religious beliefs) revolt against Hobbes and Calvin took benevolence as its watchword, arguing that God's own benevolence was mirrored in the natural benevolence God had implanted in the human breast. The notion that human beings are naturally good, that they are inspired by a kind of selfless goodwill, marks one of the fundamental features of modern liberalism; this generalized faith in human nature emphasized the active component of human goodness, thus orienting humankind toward moral progress, improvement, and uplift. The formation of benevolent societies by public-minded persons in the eighteenth century—such as those organizations central to Benjamin Franklin's public role in Philadelphia—found its philosophical foundations in the key concept of benevolence. As much as eighteenth- and nineteenth-century thought frequently put selfish motives or utilitarian reasoning at the center of morality, the humanitarian impulse was not itself dependent upon those motives—it was sentimentalist and benevolentist at its core.

The Sympathetic Imagination

The most powerful emotion underlying the ethics of benevolence, for eighteenth-century Scottish thinkers, was sympathy. The concept of sympathy had a far broader meaning in the eighteenth and nineteenth centuries than it has today. It included within it what the twentieth century would come to call "empathy," as well as a physiological component that emphasized sensations and the activity of the nervous system. Sympathy unified emotion, intellect, and physiology under one rubric, providing a powerful bridge between the interior worlds of persons separate in social condition and place. For many thinkers in the eighteenth and nineteenth centuries it became the most important mechanism for binding human beings to one another, for creating a sense of identity with others, especially as older forms of reciprocity and obligation prevalent in rank-ordered societies came under sustained attack. As W. E. B. Du Bois (1868–1963) said in his landmark work *The Souls of Black Folk* (1903), "The nineteenth was the first century of human sympathy,—the age when half wonderingly we began to descry in others that transfigured spark of divinity which we call Myself" (p. 235). It is no coincidence that individualism, with its exploration of the interior of the self, and sympathy, with its exploration of the interior of others, developed alongside each other in the nineteenth century. Although Du Bois ignored the eighteenth-century roots of sympathy, he clearly identified the way in which sympathy, in the nineteenth century, at once affirmed the importance of a boundless spiritual self and bridged the distance between that self and radically different others. Sympathy was a powerful and complex idea that influenced conceptions of the capitalist market, the family, sentimental literature, evangelical religion, social science, and humanitarian reform; its centrality to American culture and thought in the nineteenth century is just beginning to be recognized by historians. For Scottish moral philosophy, the first attempt to develop a system of ethics centered on the idea of sympathy was that by David Hume; the most important attempt, considering its implications for the humanitarian sensibility, was that by Adam Smith.

Smith's *The Theory of Moral Sentiments* (1759) built an entire superstructure of social relations, law, government, and morals on the foundation of humanity's natural inclination for sympathy, and the power of what he called the sympathetic imagination. The sympathetic imagination allowed a person to navigate between his own interior state and that of others by creating a fictive third party to the relation—what Smith dubbed "the impartial spectator." For Smith, the *actual* experience of others was inaccessible; the person perceiving that experience from outside could only imagine what he himself would feel if he were that person in that situation, and not the actual feelings of that person. The conclusion Smith drew from this insight was far from despairing. Instead of bemoaning the limits of imagination and man's failure to get outside of himself and truly enter into the experience of another, Smith saw the limits of imagination as a force drawing people closer to one another. Smith's member of society was aware that others could never experience the intensity or extent of his own emotions; he consequently moderated that intensity to win the approval of the person he imagined he himself would be if he were an impartial spectator to his own suffering. The result was the ubiquity of this fictional impartial spectator as a feature of consciousness, and, in fact, the basis for the voice of conscience. Smith's theory emphasized the spectatorial feature of sympathy, the idea that sympathetic engagement was always characterized by an incomplete identification with, and hence a passive viewing of, the emotions of others; one was simultaneously an engaged participant *and* an impartial spectator.

The consequences of this conception for the emerging humanitarian sensibility were profound. On the one hand, for the humanitarian, sympathy acted as a powerful motive force, bridging great social and physical distance, collapsing the mere accidents and contingencies of birth, fortune, and condition, erasing the external differences between self and other. On the other hand, the power of the sympathetic imagination involved a continuing acknowledgment that the suffering person existed at an enormous distance from the self, that the very conditions that caused that suffering were present to the senses and the imagination but could never be experienced by the self. The spectatorial element of humanitarianism thus emphasized a continuous navigation between emotional identification with those who are suffering and alienation from them. The sympathetic imagination, far more than the power of reason, laid the basis for identification with a universal "humanity," as opposed to the more narrow sympathetic bonds of family, caste, tribe, or nation. It did so, however, at the expense of making those bonds of humanity more attenuated than those that held people together in communities. "Though our effectual good offices can very seldom be extended to any wider society than that of our own country," said Smith, "our goodwill is circumscribed by no boundary, but may embrace the immensity of the universe. We cannot form the idea of any innocent and sensible being, whose happiness we should not desire, or to whose misery, when distinctly brought home to the imagination, we should not have some degree of aversion" (p. 235).

THE CULTURE OF SENSIBILITY AND EVANGELICAL CHRISTIANITY

The intellectual developments associated with the Scottish Enlightenment and its export to the British colonies in North America were part of a broader cultural revolution in the eighteenth and early nineteenth centuries. On the one hand, the changing social and material conditions of life for a sizable minority of the population supported a new philosophical and literary orientation toward cruelty, pain, and suffering. On the other, evangelical religion, with its emphasis upon the salvation of souls, the agency of man in doing God's work, and the possibility of human perfection, gave powerful impetus to putting sentimentalist ideas into action, especially in the United States of the first half of the nineteenth century. The humanitarian sensibility was not simply the product of social and material changes, such as the rise of a new middle class of merchants, industrialists, and their professional peers. Nor should evangelical religion be seen simply as animating an already existing body of thought that simply awaited a force to make it action; in fact, the very idea of necessary action as a result of consciousness of suffering is integral to the humanitarian sensibility. Evangelical religion is not an external force working on activating humanitarianism, but is part of the sensibility itself. The larger social, cultural, and religious dimensions of eighteenth- and early-nineteenth-century life are important constituents of humanitarianism, rather than causes of the new ways of thinking and acting.

A New Sensibility   One of the central features of eighteenth-century life was the increasingly widespread aversion to pain and suffering. For thousands of years, physical pain had been accepted as a normal, because unavoidable, part of life. Christianity, in fact, had developed doctrines that explained the presence of pain and suffering as necessary features of a fallen world, or as God-given means of punishing sinful behavior. One might seek to avoid pain by living righteously, adopt a passive attitude toward the inevitable presence of pain, or even embrace physical pain as a sign of the weakness of the body and the purity of the spirit. But whatever one did, it was within a framework in which the existence of pain was sanctioned by God. As

eighteenth-century commerce expanded the material wealth and comforts of a small but growing body of merchants and industrialists, it became possible for an influential set of spokesmen for that class to formulate their image of a world without pain. The idea that pain could be eliminated, that comfort could be a stable condition of life, and that suffering was unnecessary had widespread resonance, particularly as it dovetailed with the post-Calvinist image of a benevolent deity. A heightened sensitivity to pain was a cultural product of a society in which comfort and ease were rapidly becoming middle-class norms—pain was no longer an everyday experience, but was increasingly regarded as exceptional.

The development of anesthesia for use in surgical procedures in the 1840s ultimately confirmed the idea that pain was unnecessary and could be eliminated. Although an older medical and moral view of pain as essential to life and healing still prevailed in the nineteenth century, even among the humane, the possibility of eliminating suffering led many to promote the use of anesthesia. The introduction of anesthesia, from the point of view of the twentieth century, seems a logical response to pain, but there was nothing foregone about its acceptance. As the historian Martin Pernick has said, "Our twentieth-century sensibilities recoil at the thought that sane, responsible physicians could ever have opposed the use of anesthetics. . . . Yet in mid-nineteenth-century America, humane, conscientious, highly reputable practitioners and ordinary lay people held many misgivings about the new discovery" (*A Calculus of Suffering*, p. 35). In other words, having the medical means to eliminate pain was not itself enough to ensure that such means would be accepted and used. The idea that pain, under any circumstance, *should* be eliminated was a powerful and novel idea that has come to seem self-evident. Without such an understanding of both the possibility of eliminating pain and the moral imperative to do so, modern humanitarianism would not be possible.

Sensitivity to pain and suffering in the mid- to late eighteenth century, long before the introduction of anesthesia, was a matter not only of changing standards of physical comfort but also of fashion. The eighteenth-century "cult of sensibility" drew on strands of benevolentist ethics, sensationalist psychology, the new science of aesthetics, and the literary depiction of middle-class life in the novel to shape a set of widespread values and manners. The stock image of the "man of feeling" was a literary type, but also a social type. His deep sensitivity to suffering, his acute consciousness of his own emotions, his sympathetic feeling for the poor, weak victims of circumstance and cruelty, and his tendency to shed tears at the slightest provocation marked him as a recognizable figure. Just as the art connoisseur displayed a finely developed sense of taste, the man of feeling displayed his own finely developed sensitivity to suffering. Sensibility, as this exquisitely honed faculty was called, became fashionable, so much so that by the end of the eighteenth century the man of feeling had become a cultural cliché and an object of ridicule—the bleeding heart liberal of his time. To wear one's sensitive nature on one's sleeve eventually came under attack as a mannered pretension, but for a brief period it defined a model of moral manhood for an Anglo-American gentry.

The greater problem of the cult of sensibility and its fashionable excesses was that it revealed one of the central contradictions of the humanitarian sensibility. The figure of the man of feeling was valued precisely for the quality of his emotional sensitivity, but that sensitivity could easily become an end in itself. If the larger goal of sentimental ethics was to impel action through the power of sympathy, it just as often ran the risk of becoming self-indulgent; a heightened emotional awareness served as evidence of the man of feeling's own self-proclaimed superior nature, without any further need for action. The man of feeling degenerated into a self-serving dandy, swept up in a wave of emotional excess. Humanitarianism linked sympathy and compassion with ameliorative action, but the intensity of the emotional state, rather than the ameliorative action, could easily become the standard of moral judgment.

The broader concern with suffering, pain, and cruelty that underlay the cult of sensibility defined the very objects or ends of humanitarian activity. By putting cruelty first, as the philosopher Judith Shklar has phrased it, humanitarians made suffering the very criterion by which to judge whether action was demanded or not. This general abhorrence of cruelty and suffering as the worst evils possible had several interesting consequences. For one, it erased the line between humans and animals as objects of compassion. The ability to feel pain and to suffer was the criterion for inclusion in the class of beings possibly requiring aid. Nudged along after 1859 by the Darwinian erasure of some of the oldest justifications for viewing man and animals as different in kind, humanitarianism sought to apply the ethical injunction against pain and suffering to animals. Antivivisection movements and organizations

opposed to cruelty to animals were the most obvious manifestation of the introduction of sensation and capacity for pain and suffering as the baseline for creatures deserving moral consideration. Humanitarian focus on pain also led to some less-than-obvious results. As the historian Winthrop Jordan has noted, humanitarian arguments against slavery could be answered in a number of ways. Reform of slave institutions so as to meet the standards of non-cruelty could answer humanitarian objections without altering the fundamental property relations of slavery. And who was not to say, as the proslavery theorists had it, that the emerging wage labor system of antebellum America was far more cruel than the chattel slavery existing in the American South? By making freedom from pain and suffering the goal of reform, humanitarianism sometimes sidestepped issues of freedom, power, and self-determination.

The growing concern with physical pain and sensation that underwrote humanitarian ethics also had its dark side. The focus on concrete, detailed depictions of suffering of specific persons characteristic of humanitarian aesthetics was designed both to "put a human face" on suffering and to compel the observer to take action by revealing causal linkages that created suffering. But precisely because pain and suffering were increasingly removed from the everyday reality of the Anglo-American middle class, the portrayal of suffering could excite secret and forbidden pleasures in the observer. A combination of horror and titillation at the graphic description of slaves being whipped, for instance, excited the tender sensibilities of the humanitarian. The same sensationalist psychology that gave pain a new moral status in the eighteenth century also provided the foundation for the Marquis de Sade's philosophical concerns with the relationship between pain and pleasure.

Evangelical Christianity After the cult of sensibility, the other major cultural force shaping humanitarianism was evangelical Christianity. Arising initially among Protestant radicals who rejected the apparent fatalism of Calvinist doctrines, by the early nineteenth century evangelicalism inspired a proliferation of sects throughout the Republic. Influenced in part by the egalitarian political doctrines of the early nineteenth century, evangelicals rejected Enlightenment rationalism but embraced the possibility of synthesizing religious revivalism and social reform. The Second Great Awakening, or revivalism, of the first half of the nineteenth century inspired every brand of reform, from temperance, to antislavery, to the formation of utopian communities. While not all evangelicals were moved to humanitarian action, their linkage of religious doctrine and activism provided one of the powerful elements of the humanitarian sensibility.

In particular, evangelicals emphasized human agency in religious revivals, the possibility of human perfection, and the linkage between American republicanism and the coming of God's Kingdom. Rejecting what they saw as a kind of spiritual passivity associated with Calvinist doctrine, revivalists such as Charles Grandison Finney inspired wave upon wave of religious revivals in which they emphasized the human ability to achieve salvation. Human ability to achieve moral reform seemed to follow. The general evangelical elevation of humanity made man appear more godlike. The radical perfectionist wing of the evangelical movement saw the presence of God's spirit in all human beings, thus energizing a set of reforms in which the lowest and most abased of God's creatures—such as slaves—needed to be restored to the spiritual freedom that God required. The general activist orientation of evangelical religion fused with a millenarian impulse that insisted that the Second Coming would be achieved once the nation was reformed along the lines demanded by God. Instead of passively waiting for God, millenarians insisted that they were driven to take action in order to fulfill God's plan. The blending of spiritual and activist concerns in nineteenth-century evangelicalism invested humanitarianism with a sense of urgency and cosmological necessity.

CAPITALISM AND THE HUMANITARIAN SENSIBILITY

Historians have long noted the simultaneous development of humanitarian reform and capitalism but have been unable to reach a consensus about the relationship between the two. Why did the humanitarian sensibility become a powerful force in the Atlantic world at the same time that capitalism was remaking economic relationships and structures? Historians are loath to see this parallel development as a matter of coincidence. An older debate among social historians confuses the question even more by setting an interpretation of reform movements as "genuinely" humanitarian against an alternative explanation of reform as "social control." The social control thesis sees the emergence of widespread reform movements in the nineteenth century as motivated by a bourgeois de-

sire to create a tractable work force and to legitimate a new social order with merchants and industrialists at the helm. The so-called humanitarian thesis argues, to the contrary, that reform was motivated by a genuine benevolence and a desire to help those in need. This way of framing the debate proves to be unsatisfying because it creates a false opposition between a "real" humanitarianism and a mere smoke screen, and hence, an insincere humanitarianism. The real question is how the network of ideas, feelings, and beliefs that shaped the humanitarian sensibility could be at once "genuine" yet also related to the economic and social changes in the eighteenth and nineteenth centuries.

The major attempts to formulate the relationship of humanitarianism to capitalism have focused on the emergence and evolution of antislavery ideas and have tended to conflate those ideas with humanitarianism. There is, of course, a great overlap between humanitarianism and antislavery, but the two are by no means identical; arguments against slavery could be based on utility or abstract considerations of right rather than humanitarian considerations, while humanitarian arguments could be invoked to support slavery as a humane institution. That said, the emergence of a powerful antislavery opinion and movement was inspired in large part by the shift in consciousness characteristic of humanitarian thought. But the relationship of capitalism to humanitarianism remains a separate, if related, question from the relationship of capitalism to antislavery.

Historians have suggested that humanitarian reform was related to capitalism either through the medium of class interest or through the medium of the market. The first argument stresses that humanitarian reform met the ideological needs of various groups or classes interested in legitimating a newly emerging wage labor system. By stressing the formal freedom and independence of the wage worker, and focusing on the suffering of those who lacked such formal freedoms, humanitarian ideology both deflected attention from the exploitation of nominally free laborers and justified the property relations of the new capitalist order. The alternative explanation suggests that the emergence of a market economy led those active in it to formulate new conceptions of human responsibility. By becoming conscious of causal chains linking events and being able to see how to change action at a distance, the market-conscious were able to create new moral imperatives. Suffering that had once been thought of as inevitable—the suffering of strangers in distant communities, for instance—came to seem entirely preventable as capitalists engaged in ways of thinking characteristic of the market. A third argument stresses that the market was indeed important in shaping the humanitarian sensibility, but through the medium of class interest. The principle of the market was counterbalanced in nineteenth-century America by the domestic principle of the home, the "haven in a heartless world." According to this argument, it was the violation of understandings of family and moral conscience characteristic of bourgeois society that gave the impetus to humanitarianism. All three arguments have something to recommend them, but given the enormous intellectual and cultural complexity of the humanitarian sensibility, it would be unwise to insist that it arose out of either class interest or the institution of the capitalist market. Its success may be due to the needs of a capitalist social order, but its origins lie in a profound revolution in thought.

CODA: THE POST–CIVIL WAR ERA

Nineteenth-century humanitarianism reached its climax as antebellum reform and millenarian impulses were funneled into the Civil War. It is one of the central ironies of the nineteenth century that one of the greatest of humanitarian goals—the abolition of slavery—was achieved at the expense of enormous suffering on the battlefields and in the homes of Union and Confederate soldiers. The destructiveness of modern warfare, as first witnessed in the Civil War, helped undermine older ethics that had stressed the virtue of military valor and the glories of war, and gave greater weight to the modern ethics of pity and sympathy. The cultural representation of war as an arena of cruelty and unmitigated suffering, which proved to be a source of modern pacifism, is a result not so much of cruelties of modern war itself but of the humanitarian sensibility that was already so deeply ensconced in nineteenth-century bourgeois life.

More importantly, the experience of modern warfare created the model of bureaucratic action that would eventually serve twentieth-century humanitarianism so well. In wartime institutions such as the Sanitary Commission, the concerted attempt to relieve pain and suffering was wedded to the rationalist proceduralism and instrumentalism of modern institutions. In the late nineteenth century, the amelioration of suffering increasingly relied on a commitment to scientific and bureaucratic means. The problems of disease, health, urban conditions, and workplace safety, for instance, could be both construed and solved through scientific and technical means. This dispassionate commitment to rationality, efficiency, and objectivity sometimes sat uneasily with the emotional sympathetic identification characteristic of the humanitarian sensibility, but because humanitarianism valued action at a distance, in many ways it was already linked to the bureaucratic ethos. The combination of the sentimental and the scientific, the sympathetic and the dispassionate, the emotional and the efficient found in modern humanitarianism is one of the striking features of American culture in the modern era.

See also **Antislavery; Reform Institutions; Patterns of Reform and Revolt** *(volume 1);* **Social Reform; Socialism and Radical Thought; Anti-Statism** *(in this volume);* **Political Economy; Welfare; Foundations and Philanthropy; Government** *(volume 3).*

BIBLIOGRAPHY

Primary Sources

Beccaria, Cesare. *On Crimes and Punishments.* Translated by Henry Paolucci. 1764. Reprint, Indianapolis, Ind., 1963.

Du Bois, W. E. B. *The Souls of Black Folk.* 1903. Reprint, New York, 1969.

Hutcheson, Francis. *An Inquiry into the Original of Our Ideas of Beauty and Virtue.* 2 vols. London, 1725.

Jefferson, Thomas. *Notes on the State of Virginia.* 1785. Reprint, edited by William Peden, Chapel Hill, N.C., 1955.

Rush, Benjamin. *Essays, Literary, Moral, and Philosophical.* 1806. Reprint, edited by Michael Meranze, Schenectady, N.Y., 1988.

Shaftesbury, third earl of (Anthony Ashley Cooper). *Characteristicks of Men, Manners, Opinions, Times.* 3 vols. 1711. Reprint, in 2 vols., edited by Philip Ayres, New York, 1999.

Smith, Adam. *The Theory of Moral Sentiments.* 1759. Reprint, edited by D. D. Raphael and A. L. Macfie, New York, 1976.

Stowe, Harriet Beecher. *Uncle Tom's Cabin: or, Life Among the Lowly.* 1852. Reprint, New York, 1981.

Secondary Sources

Barker-Benfield, G. J. *The Culture of Sensibility: Sex and Society in Eighteenth-Century Britain.* Chicago, 1992.

Barnes, Elizabeth. *States of Sympathy: Seduction and Democracy in the American Novel.* New York, 1997.

Bender, Thomas, ed. *The Antislavery Debate: Capitalism and Abolitionism as a Problem in Historical Interpretation.* Berkeley, Calif., 1992.

Burstein, Andrew. *Sentimental Democracy: The Evolution of America's Romantic Self-Image.* New York, 1999.

Clark, Elizabeth B. " 'The Sacred Rights of the Weak': Pain, Sympathy, and the Culture of Individual Rights in Antebellum America." *Journal of American History* 82 (September 1995): 463–493.

Davis, David Brion. "The Movement to Abolish Capital Punishment in America, 1787–1861." In his *From Homicide to Slavery: Studies in American Culture,* pp. 17–40. New York, 1986.

Fiering, Norman S. "Irresistible Compassion: An Aspect of Eighteenth-Century Sympathy and Humanitarianism." *Journal of the History of Ideas* 37 (April–June 1976): 195–218.

Fredrickson, George. *The Black Image in the White Mind: The Debate on Afro-American Character and Destiny, 1817–1914.* New York, 1971.

Halttunen, Karen. "Humanitarianism and the Pornography of Pain in Anglo-American Culture." *American Historical Review* 100 (April 1995): 303–334.

Jordan, Winthrop. *White over Black: American Attitudes toward the Negro, 1550–1812.* Chapel Hill, N.C. 1968.

Laqueur, Thomas. "Bodies, Details, and the Humanitarian Narrative." In *The New Cultural History,* edited by Lynn Hunt, pp. 176–204. Berkeley, Calif., 1989.

Meranze, Michael. *Laboratories of Virtue: Punishment, Revolution, and Authority in Philadelphia, 1760–1835.* Chapel Hill, N.C. 1996.

Pernick, Martin. *A Calculus of Suffering: Pain, Professionalism, and Anesthesia in Nineteenth-Century America.* New York, 1985.

Shklar, Judith. "Putting Cruelty First." In her *Ordinary Vices,* pp. 7–41. Cambridge, Mass., 1984.

Stafford, John. "Sympathy Comes to America." In *Themes and Directions In American Literature: Essays in Honor of Leon Howard,* edited by Ray B. Browne and Donald Pizer, pp. 24–37. Lafayette, Ind., 1969.

Thomas, Keith. *Man and the Natural World: Changing Attitudes in England, 1500–1800.* London, 1983; 1996.

Todd, Janet. *Sensibility: An Introduction.* London, 1986.

Turner, James. *Reckoning with the Beast: Animals, Pain, and Humanity in the Victorian Mind.* Baltimore, 1980.

INTELLIGENCE AND HUMAN DIFFERENCE

Hamilton Cravens

When Americans overthrew British rule in 1781, they did more than merely win the ability to govern themselves. They also rejected the European notion that a society must be based on a social structure of orders, not classes—on distinct races or tribal groups within that society of orders. They created an idea new in the Western world, that a society can be based, not on the notions of the past, of history, but of the present and of the future. And they inverted the old European notion, that human nature cannot be changed, but only regulated, by the state, and insisted that the avenue to a better society involves severe restriction of the state's sovereignty over the individuals within that society. Americans believed a combination of private and public institutions would bring out the best in human nature; thus the new society's citizenry would be a new people melded out of the many different peoples of the Old World. Change the people for the better, certainly through education, the Americans argued, and society and culture would improve accordingly. And, indeed, from the 1790s to the 1870s, Americans from most, if not all, walks of life acted and spoke and thought as if the key to an individual's status is his or her character or reputation; in short, they held that skill, ability, and talent, or the lack thereof, are the product of a person's character, or morality, or sinfulness.

Education meant a new venture, schooling at public expense. But it meant other forms of persuasion as well. Hence, from the republic's beginning, intelligence was an important republican characteristic, an important asset for any good citizen. As early as 1779 Thomas Jefferson outlined a plan for public education that would give every boy in the Commonwealth of Virginia an elementary schooling in locally controlled public schools. By this means Jefferson hoped to establish an institutional process for the recruitment of an aristocracy of talent and virtue. Nothing came of Jefferson's proposal within Virginia, save for the eventual

founding of the University of Virginia, but the idea of public education at taxpayer expense grew in the revolutionary era and beyond. In 1798, for example, Dr. Benjamin Rush of Philadelphia proposed a multicultural education for the immigrant masses of his city, on the premise that the nation's independence had created a new category of duties for every American; if the republic were to succeed, youth must be trained, in these public schools, in the Christian religion, patriotism, in the understanding of citizenship, in various practical skills, and in physical culture. In short, public education at taxpayer expense was the best service that republican government could provide, for it prepared rational, civilized individuals for their responsibilities as participants in the business of government and the economy. By the early 1800s other cultural patriots and educational reformers had extended the premise of public education to girls as well as boys, at least in the states outside the South, and by the 1830s public men in the northern states were stitching together a framework of elementary public schools supported by the local taxpayer and governed by the local school board. In a very real sense, as the historian Rush Welter pointed out in the early 1960s, theories of public education and theories of representative government, not to mention their practices, became interdependent.

The Revolution's political idealism—"all men are created equal"—famously did not apply to certain categories of persons, especially to women and persons of color. The Revolution had among its consequences the eventual elimination of slavery in the Northern states and the gradual creation of a public role for white women, as well as the establishment of an individualistic republic based on universal white manhood suffrage, freedom of religion, of individual enterprise, and of common school education for white boys and girls. From the beginning there was a sense of racial differences and human intelligence in American social and scientific thought, which itself owed much to Old World discourses about the history of humanity and discussions of the differences of the various peoples of the planet. Central to that European discussion was the sense that all peoples had to pass through three stages of progress, from savagery to barbarism, and, finally, to civilization. The Americans who participated in this discourse agreed with their European colleagues that so far only white European peoples had become civilized peoples, and the nonwhite peoples remained either stagnating in savagery or perhaps making some progress toward civilization in barbarism. Hence there was in the American discussion of race the sense that darkness of skin usually signified a questionable or problematic racial heritage. The white races were ipso facto civilized, whereas the colored races were not—a highly convenient set of assumptions for a white elite in a multiracial society such as the young American republic clearly was. Far more than their European cousins, however, the new Americans had sought to construct republicanism as a political philosophy of radical laissez-faire individualism in which civilized (and white) rational individuals sought to pursue commerce and trade with a minimum of interference from government, especially a central government. Strictly speaking, the colored races were not civilized; hence they did not belong to the new republican society.

This individualistic, laissez-faire, and racist ideology was mainstream American political doctrine, shared by the Federalists and the Jeffersonians alike. Historians can find differences of opinion among Federalists and Jeffersonians on the proper laissez-faire economic policy, but few, if any, differences on the race question. And clearly there was racism and laissez-faire individualism in the ideas of the great American revolutionary Thomas Jefferson, the author of the Declaration of Independence, in his *Notes on the State of Virginia* (1785). Here Jefferson sought to defend the New World against attacks on it by European writers, such as the famous French natural historian George Louis Leclerc and the Scottish cleric William Robertson, as an environment unfit for habitation by civilized peoples. Jefferson saw African Americans as imports to the New World (which Native Americans were not) and as slaves—an inferior category of people by definition. He considered blacks as inferior to whites in all aspects of intelligence and physical powers. If they excelled whites in memory, they were inferior in foresight, imagination, and, above all, profoundly inferior in the ability to reason. If they were more ardent in sexual passions than whites, on the other hand, African Americans were less delicate. Jefferson was undecided on whether blacks constituted a separate species (polygenism) or merely a variety made different by environment and the passage of time (monogenism). What mattered most to Jefferson was defense of the New World from the attacks of those who insisted that the Old World was superior to the New. A race that had developed in the Western Hemisphere was inherently better than one only fit for slavery; thus Jefferson viewed the Native Americans more favorably than African Americans.

The Reverend Samuel Stanhope Smith was the first American to pen an anthropological work as such. As professor of moral philosophy at the College of New Jersey (later Princeton University), he published *Essay on the Causes of the Variety of Complexion and Figure in the Human Species* in 1787. He asserted that all races of man belong to the same species; indeed, it was pointless to attempt to differentiate among them. Smith was a monogenist; he believed man is a single species, despite many varieties. He believed that two kinds of factors, climate and what he dubbed the "state of society," caused whatever differences there were among the various races of mankind. The state of society constituted a catchall category of everything from diet, gait, and manners to ideas, passions, and interests. Smith stressed the ability of the human constitution to adapt to different circumstances. In his second edition, published in 1810, he answered those others, including Jefferson, who insisted that African Americans were inherently inferior to whites, by insisting that, given a chance to improve with a better climate and state of society, blacks would soon be the equals of whites. There were other Americans who discussed the relationship between intelligence and physical differences among the races of humankind in Smith's time, including Samuel L. Mitchill of New York, who did not depart from the monogenist camp but insisted that heredity is as important a cause of human differences as climate and state of society. Because of the biblical orthodoxy, most Americans who wrote about human racial differences before the 1830s dared not question the biblical injunction that humankind is a single, unitary species, but this allegiance to monogenism was no guarantee that an individual writer or thinker would not think that some races were superior to others.

In the later 1830s, however, the discourse on race changed. The radical individualism of the past several decades passed from the scene as Americans redefined their national population as constituting various groups, American in character or not. This transformation of social thought, namely the discovery or invention of the group as a category in society, in politics, in the economy, and in life more generally, took shape in the Old World no less than in the New. A famous example of the shift from the individual to the group as a fundamental category in social thought and social science came with the change from the Scottish philosopher James Mill's radical individualism to the creation of categories, or groups, in the thought of his widely read son, John Stuart Mill. All over Europe from the 1830s on there suddenly emerged a folkish nationalism, a sense of a right correlation between a language and a political and cultural identity, together with the assumption that all members of that group shared certain characteristics, including blood, physical traits, and other attributes that contributed to a national or racial or cultural "average." These ideas could be found from Iceland to the Urals, in England, Scotland, France, the German and Italian states, and among the subject peoples of the various empires of post-1830 Europe, including the Poles, the Hungarians, the Bohemians, and the peoples of Ukraine, not to mention the Greeks, the Serbs, and even the Slovenes. This fusion of nationalism and racism took shape in Europe and in America from the 1830s on.

Symptomatic of that transformation among Americans was the rise of the so-called American school of anthropology. Samuel G. Morton, a prominent Philadelphia doctor and avid student of nature, established the school with the publication of *Crania Americana* (1839). He argued for polygenism, or plurality of creation, and he did so with the methods and concepts of the new physical anthropology. He became interested in skulls around 1820, and throughout the next two decades he collected skulls of animals and people. Soon he had a large collection of Native American skulls. He became convinced that different races had different head shapes. That is, differences in cranial capacity and conformation, like color of skin, was a distinctive racial characteristic. *Crania Americana* was a comparative study of the crania of various races, including whites, Native Americans, "Mongolians," Ethopians, among other races; not surprisingly, whites came out on top of this racial hierarchy. Morton found a difference of about 11 cubic inches in the average cranial capacity of the twenty-two races he described.

Morton then shifted his focus from Native Americans to Africans and African Americans. Helped by the Egyptologist G. R. Gliddon, he studied the racial history of that ancient land. Working with the short biblical chronology of a few thousand years, in *Crania Aegyptiaca* (1844) Morton argued that the races of humans in his day were the same as those in ancient Egypt. Since that was close to the time of creation, the different races—in this instance, whites, Arabs, and blacks—must have been created as distinct and separate species or races, a conclusion that was in line with recent discoveries of hieroglyphics and artifacts in ancient Egypt. Morton won two valuable allies: Dr. Josiah Clark Nott and Professor Louis Agassiz. Nott practiced human and animal medicine in Mobile, Alabama. Rabidly he championed slavery and the South. His particular interest in race, insofar as it extended beyond politics and prejudice, was hybridization, arguing that the mixture of distinct races is a bad idea; thus when blacks and whites interbred, the offspring were less intelligent than whites but more so than blacks, were less hardy and long-lived, and less fertile, than either of the parent races. In 1845, after taking a drubbing from several scientists over a book he published the previous year in which he hooted at the monogeneticist argument, Nott wrote Morton for help on polygeneticist arguments—and got it.

In 1847, the famous Swiss naturalist Louis Agassiz, took a professorship at Harvard. When he came to America this most famous disciple of the great Georges Cuvier was a monogenist on man, for religious reasons, but a polygenist on plants and animals. In Europe he had never met anyone of African ancestry, but soon he had in America, and, as the scholar Stephen Jay Gould has shown, he confessed his revulsion at the sight of black people in a long letter to his mother at home. Soon thereafter Agassiz became a polygenist on humankind, and thus became an important member of the American school, lending it considerable prestige in American and European scientific circles. In *Types of Mankind* (1854) Nott synthesized the various writings of the members of the American school into a larger whole; and clearly this treatise in physical anthropology had implications for intelligence and human differences, for, as Nott put it, the "... intellectual man is inseparable from the physical man" (Nott and Glidden, *Types of Mankind*, p. 50).

That scientific opinion differed dramatically from popular views, at least on race, may be fairly doubted. As a whole generation of scholars following Leon Litwack's *North of Slavery* (1961) has shown, the emancipation of slaves in the North in the generation following the American Revolution produced, not a racially egalitarian society, but a fairly rigidly segregated one, a foreshadowing, as it were, of what was to happen in the South after Reconstruction. Even white abolitionists, supposedly the best friends of African Americans, used the same racial stereotypes as did the most bitter racists and segregationists, whether living above or below the Mason-Dixon line; Harriet Beecher Stowe's *Uncle Tom's Cabin* (1852) proves the point.

In the five decades following the Civil War, notions of intelligence and human difference intensified; they became far more pessimistic and deterministic than before. With regard to African Americans, there were three distinguishable threads of thought. The first, and that which was closest to the discourses of the sciences, was Darwinian in inspiration. During the 1870s and 1880s, numerous southerners predicted that black Americans would disappear as a race due to the struggle for existence with whites in the region. That struggle might be over food and work, or, perhaps, it might be a genuine tooth-and-claw racial war. Even Albion W. Tourgée, in *An Appeal to Caesar* (1884), wondered, sorrowfully enough, whether race war might not be a possibility. The census of 1890, however, made clear, as those of 1870 and 1880 had not, that fecundity among blacks was not a problem to be feared; the race was not growing faster than the white race, it would be situated, in the main, in the South, and, as some put it, because African Americans were a limited and inferior race, they would not have a large influence on southern or American life. The Georgia scientist Joseph LeConte applied the metaphors of the Darwinian struggle for existence to blacks, and found them wanting as compared with whites. Blacks were doomed, and race mixing with whites would not save them, for their progeny were damned. The German-born statistician Frederick L. Hoffman, in a series of articles expanded into a very influential book, *Race Traits and Tendencies of the American Negro* (1896), insisted that African Americans had been degenerating as a race since Emancipation and would continue to do so, further sinking into sexual license and declining health and vigor because their traits as a race determined that they were inferior to whites and could not compete with them. Joseph A. Tillinghast applied the same draconian Darwinian concepts of racial heredity to blacks in *The Negro in Africa and America* (1902). He insisted that racial heredity could only be changed slowly, through natural selection, and could not be hurried or manipulated by human agency. The racial character of blacks had been established in Africa, which showed an uninterrupted history of stagnation, inefficiency, ignorance, cannibalism, sexual license, and superstition.

A second line of argument among white southerners, and one that was far more popular in a region notorious for its anti-intellectualism, its anti-scientism, and its veneration of violence, was that African Americans were nothing but beasts, too wild to be tamed or civilized, too monstrous to live as equals among whites. Perhaps the most famous of the spokesmen of this extremist racialism was the South Carolina senator Benjamin Tillman, who argued in 1907 that blacks were losing ground to whites in the industrial competition of the races—such diseases as tuberculosis and syphilis would kill off blacks. Blacks were destined for degeneration and extinction as a race within a few generations. The southern essayist and novelist Thomas Nelson Page was not quite so virtriolic as Tillman; nevertheless he drew a line between the antebellum "darkies" who were loyal slaves, hardworking, honest, and the like, and the new postbellum "new issue" blacks who were bound by the conditions of freedom to be ground out of existence because of their immorality, laziness, and the like. Other novelists, such as Thomas Dixon, who penned such racialist novels as *The Leopard's Spots* (1902) and *The Clansman* (1905)—the latter the basis for the notorious film, *The Birth of a Nation* (1915)—insisted that the beast in the black man had to be restrained. Even lynching was not so problematic a remedy for the racial extremists. The third argument fell among the racial moderates, such as the Alabama clergyman Edgar Gardner Murphy, who, in such works as *Problems of the Present South* (1904), opposed the worst extremes of the segregationist society that was crystallizing around him, such as lynching and other forms of violence, but still believed in black inferiority and a segregated society as the only solution to the race problem. Indeed, one would have to conclude that from the days of Thomas Jefferson to those of President Theodore Roosevelt, and beyond, white racism was pervasive in American society. It was institutionalized throughout society and culture, tincturing science, religion, social mores, the world of work, indeed, all of the American experience.

Racism was extended to other groups in the nation's increasingly mixed population. In the post–Civil War decades, white Americans, especially those of Anglo-American and Protestant ancestry, increasingly criticized the new waves of immigrants coming to American shores from Asia and European immigration—and immigrants—for another quarter century. In these years immigrants from Italy, Russia, and the Austro-Hungarian Empire, in particular, seemed "darker," less competent, less ca-

702

pable of being assimilated into the American middle class, and those who saw themselves as the protectors of that class and its heritage spoke out increasingly in a growing chorus of angry and bitter voices, all with the language of blood and science. New England donated more than its fair share of these critics and commentators. Francis A. Walker, the president of the Massachusetts Institute of Technology (MIT), insisted after studying the 1890 census that the new waves of cheap laborers from these remote places were outcompeting the native-born stocks who were reducing their numbers in response to economic competition with these dark, swarthy, and less competent foreigners. According to Walker's Darwinian mind-set, survival of the fittest was not elevating the talents of the population but lowering it, for the questionable immigrants were taking the places of the sturdy old stock in society and economy—with only the most disastrous consequences in the offing. His friend, the Massachusetts senator Henry Cabot Lodge, made an intensive study of the "distribution of ability" in the American population, showing the superiority of the English heritage to all others in all things.

Soon American natural scientists joined this racist discourse. In 1899 the bright young MIT economist William Z. Ripley published *The Races of Europe,* a work of physical anthropology, in which he took recent work in the field and subdivided the peoples of Europe into three races identifiable by distinct physical characteristics. First came a northern race of tall, blond longheads, which he dubbed Teutonic. Next came a central race of stocky roundheads, the Alpines. And, finally, there was a southern race of dark, thin longheads whom he called the Mediterraneans. Ripley popularized what others had devised, and, despite his own environmentalist leanings, his work fueled notions of racial superiority and inferiority, including mentality as well as other, more physical, traits. Nor was this all. Biological scientists stitched together a new interpretation of how and why inheritance, variation, and evolution functions in all species, including humankind. The rediscovery of the Austrian monk Gregor Mendel's principles of heredity gave rise to the new science of genetics. Mendel had provided evidence that an organism's traits were sorted and recombined in predictable mathematical ratios, as if they were autonomous from one another and determined by specific chemical units in the reproductive germ plasm. Many American natural scientists erroneously read Mendel to mean that all traits of the adult organism, no matter which species, were determined by heredity at the time of conception.

This extreme hereditarianism colored American scientists' interpretations of the human mind no less than the body. Thus the American psychologists Henry H. Goddard and Lewis M. Terman introduced the Binet measuring scale of intelligence to America. In doing so they distorted the French psychologist Alfred Binet's test to be one of innate intelligence, which he specifically rejected (he saw it as a means of evaluating socially disadvantaged children for compensatory education, not unlike the Head Start programs of the twentieth century), and adopted the notion of the intelligence quotient, which the German psychologist Wilhelm Stern, with purposes very different from Binet's, had devised in 1914, several years after Binet's death. Goddard and Terman, and the other American pioneers of psychometrics, had imbibed a largely hereditarian interpretation of the human mind from such indigenous mentors as the American psychologist G. Stanley Hall, who insisted that the mind had evolved in stages from the lowliest paramecium up through the various human races to that most civilized race of all, the white northern and western Europeans, and, from abroad, the English eugenicist Sir Francis Galton and his colleague Karl Pearson, who almost double-handedly invented eugenics as a social reform and an applied science. One of the great Darwin's cousins, Galton had consistently been interested in finding a scientific way to show that heredity prevailed over environment in the making of human nature and greatness. He lacked creditable knowledge of human biology—in fact his talents in the sciences were rather circumscribed indeed, no small irony for a man who championed the superiority of the intellectually gifted throughout his life. Pearson devised a statistical tool, the coefficient of correlation, which was supposed to demonstrate how like two unlike things were by means of measuring their closeness on a scalogram; those things with a perfect correlation of a positive 1.00 were perfectly correlated, those with a negative 1.0 had none. With this Pearson applied his tool to various mental and physical measurements and declared that mental nature is as inherited as physical nature because the correlations he found for related individuals were far higher than they were for unrelated ones.

Obviously the American natural scientists who took up these arguments were looking for support for their social policy views, especially their canards and bromides on race and ethnicity. Such was the power of institutionalized racism in American society and culture. It was Lewis M. Terman's American standardization of the Binet test (the Stanford-

Binet), published in 1916, that became the fundamental American IQ, or intelligence quotient, test. The test was patterned after the Gaussian bell-shaped curve, in which one-fourth of the examinees were supposed to fail, one-half were to pass within a "normal" range (normal for their chronological age, thus the intelligence quotient being the ratio of the chronological to the mental age as measured by the test), and one-fourth were to pass at a superior (high IQ) level. Terman "standardized" the Binet test on suburban or small-town, middle-class, white children in California who were of northern European and Protestant extraction, so that it is not extreme to say that the much-ballyhooed Stanford-Binet was normed on the majority dominant subculture at the time. Terman was a liberal Republican who often voted for reformers in both major parties, and saw no conflict between those ideas and his notions that a person's IQ is fixed at birth and that northern and western Europeans of Protestant background are superior to other ethnic groups and races.

In the second decade of the twentieth century, mental testing became the largest single specialization among American psychologists and professors of education. Testing was a new field; tests appeared easy to administer, and one's results could be published as summaries of experimental investigations, thus lending their authors much professional authority and prestige. Two groups of testers quickly emerged. One studied social deviants. Following Henry Goddard's suggestion that low innate intelligence—feeble-mindedness, in contemporary parlance—caused antisocial behavior, this group attempted to demonstrate that link in studies of all manner of criminals and of people of low intelligence. In the 1910s probably the most celebrated study of this genre was Goddard's melodramatic *The Kallikak Family* (1912) in which he traced the social pathology of a particular family of innate social deviants who in turn had bred entire generations of miscreants. Insisting that intelligence—high or low—was inherited according to the Mendelian ratios, Goddard popularized the notion that the study of social problems is the same as the study of human heredity—of eugenics, or the tracing high or low intellect in related people.

The second group of testers studied comparative racial intelligence, but this time with intelligence tests, rather than measurements of physical anthropology, as had been the practice in the nineteenth century. A major event in the history of the mental testing movement was the United States Army's use of mental tests in World War I. The army suddenly needed to sort out the almost 2 million new soldiers into officers and enlisted men, and then into the many job classifications therein, and the psychologists offered their services, through the War Department. A committee of psychologists, headed by Robert M. Yerkes, a Harvard professor and president of the American Psychological Association, devised two tests, Army Alpha and Army Beta, for literates and illiterates, respectively, normed on the Stanford-Binet, with all its structural and functional characteristics, save these were group tests given in less than an hour, to recruits who were often in unfamiliar or even hostile situations. After the war, Yerkes published scientific and popular reports on the results of the army mental tests, which definitely showed a hierarchy of superior and inferior groups. Native-born recruits had the highest group averages, and of the foreign born, those from northern and western Europe had the next highest group scores, and those from southern and eastern Europe possessed the lowest group scores of any immigrants. Yerkes claimed, incorrectly, as it turned out, that African Americans had lower scores than all whites, with northern blacks scoring higher than southern blacks. Yerkes also found that those with the greatest amount of formal education and also those in professional, managerial, or even clerical occupations, stood higher in group averages than those with less schooling and less skilled jobs. Yerkes chose to interpret his results as the result of innate intelligence.

Since World War I the immigration restriction movement had been able to persuade most Americans that it no longer made sense to permit free immigration; hence the question arose, who—what groups or races, more precisely—would be permitted to enter and stay. Because the prejudices with which white, Anglo-Saxon Protestant middle-class Americans viewed immigrants and people of color were institutionalized in the larger culture, and helped shape the racial and ethnic attitudes of scientists no less than laypersons (because all were members of and participants in the larger national culture) historians cannot say that the scientific arguments of Yerkes and his associates caused the U.S. Congress to vote for immigration restriction. However, the enactment of immigration restriction legislation, initially in 1921, then permanently in 1924, owed a good deal to the scientists' formulation of the arguments and much of the evidence of racial and ethnic "superiority" and "inferiority."

There was a large debate, not merely over immigration restriction, but over the scientific notions of racial and ethnic superiority and inferiority that accompanied the restrictionist public discourse. Throughout the 1920s and into the 1930s and 1940s social scientists attacked such notions, specifically, the cultural anthropologists, who had taken over intellectual leadership of anthropology from the racist physical anthropologists after 1900 under the leadership of the German Jewish immigrant Franz Boas, a professor of anthropology at Columbia University. Boas's social policy views were those of a contemporary European social democrat and a profound antiracist, and he always sought to promote his science as a handmaiden to the good democratic society. As early as *The Mind of Primitive Man* (1911) he had questioned the racist assumptions of the polygeneticist American school, such as Morton and Knott, and their post-Darwinian successors, arguing that if the head forms of east European immigrants could change to the Nordic or "American" shape within two generations of settlement in the United States, then obviously the "softer" cultural traits could adapt to the American norm as well, thus showing that there was nothing to fear from the "new immigration" from southern and eastern Europe. Boas's argument was a historical marker, demonstrating that he had no larger conception of racial equipotentiality to offset the theory of racial superiority and inferiority which Jefferson, the American school, and their various successors in the late nineteenth and early twentieth centuries had contributed to in varying ways.

In the next decade Boas and his doctoral graduates revived and recast E. B. Tylor's conception of culture, as the habits humans acquired as the consequence of belonging to society, into something new. In their hands it became a complex theory of human cultural evolution and racial equipotentality. As such it operated on the same level as the new, post-1930 genetical theory of natural selection. Together the two theories became that era's explanation of human biological and cultural evolution. Some of Boas's later students, especially Margaret Mead in such works as *Coming of Age in Samoa* (1928) and Melville J. Herskovits in *The American Negro* (1928), outlined applications of the culture theory that were as dynamic, and thus as oriented to behavioral science (as distinct from traditional static social science) and to the dynamism of the unification of biology and the genetical theory of natural selection, as any other developments in the crystallization of the new behavioral sciences of the interwar years. These intellectual developments had the effect of undercutting the scientific authority, not to say the political and cultural utility, of notions of racial and cultural superiority and inferiority.

By the later 1920s much of the steam had gone out of the racial mental testing movement, no doubt partly the consequence of its partisans seeing the enactment of the National Immigration Act of 1924, which virtually ended immigration from southern and eastern Europe. But there were serious methodological problems with the racist interpretation of the results of mental testing as well. As the critics of the racist mental testers pointed out, the tests seemed chiefly a barometer of educational advantage and opportunity. Thus the children of immigrants from southern and eastern Europe from northern and midwestern states such as New York, Pennsylvania, Ohio, and Michigan, for instance, did better on the tests than did old-stock "Nordics" from southern states with inferior educational systems. Furthermore, northern African Americans did better than southern whites, and Asian Americans and Jews scored higher than did northern white "Nordics," in the former example by almost one standard deviation, in the latter by almost twenty points, or five points more than one standard deviation, a meaningful difference to most psychometricians. By the later 1920s and early 1930s most mental testers had retreated from the field of racial mental testing in ignominious defeat, not having surrendered their belief in innate racial differences in intelligence, but recognizing rather that they lacked a scientifically authoritative or respectable methodology to support their notions that races as races could be ranked in a racial hierarchy of superior to inferior races.

Before the 1960s, then, most Americans still acted and spoke as if there were unquestionable important relationships between intelligence and human difference. Even though many psychometricians and professors of education had shown repeatedly that women were just as intelligent as men, and persevered longer in school, most Americans had so internalized the dogma of the separate spheres of male and female abilities and social roles that females were considered by men—and even more by women—to be a group apart from men in what they could aspire to and do in the larger society. And if social and behavioral scientists, including sociologists and economists, most spectacularly the Swedish economist Gunnar Myrdal in *An American Dilemma* (1944), had argued that racial segregation of African Americans was cruel and not justified by biological or social science, this had relatively little influence outside the usual liberal and

705

social scientific circles. Indeed, Americans still believed in certain "truths": that groups, not individuals, exist; that all individuals share the traits that typify the groups to which they belong; that there exists a natural and innate hierarchy of superior and inferior groups in nature and, therefore, in society; and that no individual could vary out of the parameters of the group to which she or he belongs.

The field of animal and human development has an intellectual history that proves the point that Americans believed in these tenets. Lewis M. Terman initiated what became the longest lasting longitudinal project in American social science, the so-called genius project, or genetic studies of geniuses. With modest support from Stanford University and from the Commonwealth Fund, he selected one thousand California children who scored in the genius range on the Stanford-Binet. Originally he intended to show that geniuses, whom he believed inherit their brains, are not freaks; as the study's five volumes were published from the 1920s to the 1960s, his emphasis on innate intelligence waned and instead he and his co-workers came to emphasize how well certain traits work together, high intelligence with good body build, successful social adjustment, success in life, and so on. By the mid-1950s even Terman himself was speaking less and less about intelligence and innate human difference, and more about intelligence wherever it was found, regardless of its "causes."

But by the mid-1950s a new era had dawned in the history of American culture and society, an era of radical individualism, and of the redefinition of society as a mass of atomistic individuals, whose group membership, if any, was fleeting and transitory. Now the various European nativity groups—the so-called "white ethnics"—had become regarded by the rest of society as white. Indeed, for the first time since the Civil War, an authentic civil rights movement grew up, and, unlike that in the post-Reconstruction years, it gained considerable political power and some solid political success, as with the Civil Rights Act of 1964, the Voting Rights Act of 1965, and affirmative action programs in government and private enterprise, variously designed to allow women and people of color to compete for public goods on a par with white males, who were all now defined as "privileged." Since then there have been attempts by some scientists to restore the theory of innate racial inferiority and superiority, as in the work of the educational researcher Arthur Jensen, and with the book *The Bell Curve* (1994). However, for the most part these efforts have met with strenuous criticism, scientific as well as political. Whether they are harbingers of the future of the twenty-first century or the residual flotsam and jetsam of the past, only time will tell.

See also **European and Indigenous Encounters; Africa and America; Colonial Images of Europe and America; Manhood; Racialism and Racial Uplift; Cultural Modernism; The Behavioral and Social Sciences** *(volume 1);* **The Professional Ideal; Poststructuralism and Postmodernism; Whites and the Construction of Whiteness** *(in this volume);* **The Role of the Intellectual; Elite vs. Popular Cultures; Social Construction of Reality** *(volume 3); and other articles in this section.*

BIBLIOGRAPHY

Primary Accounts

Boas, Franz. *The Mind of Primitive Man.* New York, 1911.

Dixon, Thomas, Jr. *The Leopard's Spots: A Romance of the White Man's Burden, 1865–1900.* New York, 1902.

———. *The Clansman: An Historical Romance of the Ku Klux Klan.* New York, 1905.

Goddard, Henry Herbert. *The Kallikak Family; A Study in the Heredity of Feeble-Mindedness.* New York, 1912.

Herrnstein, Richard J., and Charles Murray. *The Bell Curve: Intelligence and Class Structure in American Life.* New York, 1994.

Herskovits, Melville J. *The American Negro: A Study in Racial Crossing.* New York, 1928.

Hoffman, Frederick L. *Race Traits and Tendencies of the American Negro.* 1896. Reprint, New York, 1973.

Jefferson, Thomas. *Notes on the State of Virginia.* 1785. Reprint, edited by William Peden, New York, 1991.

Kroeber, Alfred L. "The Superorganic." *The American Anthropologist.* New Series 19 (1917): 169ff.

Lowie, Robert H. *Culture and Ethnology.* New York, 1917.

Mead, Margaret. *Coming of Age in Samoa: A Psychological Study of Primitive Youth for Western Civilisation.* New York, 1928.

Morton, Samuel George. *Crania Americana; or, A Comparative View of the Skulls of Various Aboriginal Nations of North and South America. To Which Is Prefixed an Essay on the Varieties of the Human Species.* Philadelphia, 1839.

———. *Crania Aegyptiaca: or, Observations on Egyptian Ethnography, Derived from Anatomy, History, and the Monuments.* Philadelphia, 1844.

Murphy, Edgar Gardner. *Problems of the Present South: A Discussion of Certain of the Educational, Industrial, and Political Issues in the Southern States.* New York, 1904.

Nott, Josiah C., and G. R. Gliddon, eds. *Types of Mankind; or, Ethnological Researches, Based upon the Ancient Monuments, Paintings, Sculptures, and Crania of Races, and upon their Natural, Geographical, Philological, and Biblical History.* 1854. Reprint, Miami, Fla., 1969. Page references in the text are from the reprint edition.

Ripley, William Z. *The Races of Europe: A Sociological Study.* 1899. Reprint, New York, 1965.

Smith, Samuel Stanhope. *Essay on the Causes of the Variety of Complexion and Figure in the Human Species.* Edited by Winthrop D. Jordan. Cambridge, Mass., 1965.

Stowe, Harriet Beecher. *Uncle Tom's Cabin; or, Life among the Lowly.* Edited by Kenneth S. Lynn. Cambridge, Mass., 1962.

Terman, Lewis Madison, et al. *Genetic Studies of Genius.* 5 vols. Stanford, Calif., 1925–1957.

Tillinghast, Joseph Alexander. *The Negro in Africa and America.* New York, 1902.

Tourgée, Albion W. *An Appeal to Caesar.* New York, 1884.

Yerkes, Robert M. *Psychological Examining in the United States Army.* Vol. 15 of *Memoirs of the National Academy of Sciences.* Washington, D.C., 1921.

Secondary Accounts

Barkan, Elazar. *The Retreat of Scientific Racism: Changing Concepts of Race in Britain and the United States between the World Wars.* New York, 1992. A comparative view, emphasizing the sociology of knowledge.

Cravens, Hamilton. "The Social Sciences." In *Historical Writing on American Science. Perspectives and Prospects,* edited by Sally G. Kohlstedt and Margaret W. Rossiter. Baltimore, 1986. A study emphasizing historiography, but also a conceptual framework.

———. *The Triumph of Evolution: The Heredity-Environment Controversy 1900–1941.* Baltimore, 1988. The only full-length study of its topic.

———. *Before Head Start: The Iowa Station and America's Children.* Chapel Hill, N.C., 1993. The only full-length study of developmental science.

———. "Scientific Racism in Modern America, 1870s–1990s." *Prospects: An Annual of American Cultural Studies* 21 (1996): 471–490.

Curti, Merle. *Human Nature in American Thought.* Madison, Wisc., 1980. An able study emphasizing the inner architecture of scientific ideas as well as their social context by a major founder of intellectual history in the United States.

Fredrickson, George M. *The Black Image in the White Mind. The Debate on Afro-American Character and Destiny, 1817–1914.* Middletown, Conn., 1989. A classic study, written with passion and considerable historical insight.

Gould, Stephen Jay. *The Mismeasure of Man.* New York, 1981. A scientist's positivistic view of science gone mad, with some useful information and quotations.

Haller, John S., Jr. *Outcasts of Evolution: Scientific Attitudes of Racial Inferiority, 1859–1900.* Urbana, Ill., 1971. An able full-length scholarly work; a major contribution to its subject.

Haller, Mark. *Eugenics: Hereditarian Attitudes in American Thought.* New Brunswick, N.J., 1966. In many ways this remains the standard work on its subject.

Higham, John. *Strangers in the Land: Patterns of American Nativism, 1876–1925.* New Brunswick, N.J., 1955. One of the most insightful historical monographs written in many decades; a classic.

Kevles, Daniel J. *In the Name of Eugenics: Genetics and the Uses of Human Heredity.* New York, 1986. A comparative history of genetics and eugenics in the United States and the United Kingdom which disappoints as comparative history but which has useful information on human genetics in the last several decades.

Litwack, Leon F. *North of Slavery: The Negro in the Free States, 1790–1860.* Chicago, 1961. A classic in the field.

Stanton, William Ragan. *The Leopard's Spots: Scientific Attitudes toward Race in America, 1815–1859.* Chicago, 1960. A valuable study which unfortunately overestimates racial liberalism between the Revolution and the 1840s.

Stocking, George W., Jr. *Race, Culture, and Evolution: Essays in the History of Anthropology.* New York, 1968. A collection of essays, nuanced and sophisticated.

———. *Victorian Anthropology.* New York, 1985. A first-rate treatment of its topic.

Welter, Rush. *Popular Education and Democratic Thought in America.* New York, 1962. A classic work that makes important connections between public education and democratic culture.

PSYCHOLOGY, THE MIND, AND PERSONALITY

Robert C. Fuller

Historically, Americans have been drawn to psychological ways of thinking. The United States cultural heritage, in both its religious and secular traditions, has emphasized individuality and the importance of gaining control over one's inner life. American Protestantism, for example, places particular emphasis upon the conversion experience that is thought to signify a dramatic change in a person's inner life and bring assurance of individual salvation. And, too, the so-called Protestant Ethic encourages systematic efforts to maintain self-discipline. Prevailing beliefs about the social and economic aspects of American life have also stressed the importance of a person's inner character. Whereas European culture has traditionally assumed that social class is the principal factor determining a person's destiny in life, Americans tend to attribute the degree of their worldly success to such factors as belief, willpower, and moral character. Thus it is not surprising that by the early twentieth century psychology had fully established itself as the preeminent authority to which Americans turned in their individual quests for identity or self-fulfillment.

Psychology's contribution to modern self-understanding is, however, far from monolithic. The contemporary psychological scene is divided among a number of rival schools of thought that are so divergent and so disputatious that scholars find it very difficult to assess the cultural history of psychology as a whole. Psychology, even less than mathematics or the natural sciences, is not a cumulative science but rather an assortment of facts, presuppositions, and theories, whose relevance to human welfare depends upon the philosophical outlook of the person who puts them together. Yet a historical perspective can help explain the origin and development of the major schools of American psychological thought. This perspective also makes it possible to understand the intellectual and cultural significance of the facts, presuppositions, and

theories underlying American conceptions of mind or personality.

THE COLONIAL HERITAGE

Intellectual life during the colonial period was dominated by the interests of the Protestant clergy. Clergymen were the colonies' most learned citizens and exercised a near monopoly over the fledgling universities that had been founded for the official purpose of creating an educated ministry. These universities were steeped in the medieval tradition known as Scholasticism. Scholastic thought divided the world of intellectual thought into the three provinces of logic, physics, and metaphysics. In this system, psychology fell under the heading of physics. Yet, to distinguish it from discussions of inanimate matter, psychology was said to occupy a special branch of physics dealing with pneumatology, or the study of spiritual beings. Psychology, then, was understood to investigate the properties of the soul and the soul's relationship to the physical body that it inhabited. Since medieval Scholasticism had already developed a thorough system of definitions or propositions concerning the nature of the soul, colonial psychology consisted largely of efforts to apply these theological propositions to particular issues about the mind or personality through a series of syllogistic reasoning exercises. While colonial psychology produced a number of eloquent works, they were exercises in formal logic and had almost no connection with actual human experience.

It was traditional for the university president, almost always an ordained Protestant clergyman, to teach the courses dealing with psychology. These courses were typically concerned with cataloging the personality traits consistent with the development of moral character. Protestant theology postulated that the ultimate goal of human existence is to glorify God, both in this life and in a heavenly afterlife. It followed that the purpose of psychology was to serve this goal by preparing people for a life that pleases God and is consistent with God's plan for the salvation of individual human beings.

Debates in colonial psychology usually revolved around theological issues. In particular, the theological controversy between Calvinist and Arminian views of human nature infiltrated nearly every discussion of the human mind. Calvinists affirmed that God is the sole and sovereign ruler of the universe. This theological postulate committed them to a completely deterministic view of the universe that had several logical implications for the study of mind and personality. It led, for example, to the theological principle of predestination. Because God had already determined the fate of every individual, it followed that free will is an illusion. Many colonial Americans, however, were slowly drifting away from strict Calvinism and instead embraced the doctrine of Arminius that humans have a role in determining their own destinies and are free to choose in matters of belief and morals. Belief in free will appealed not only to industrious laypersons who were eager to make a life for themselves in the New World, but to many clergymen whose sermons were designed to convince parishioners to make conscious decisions to improve their moral and spiritual lives. It is in the context of this cultural debate that historians can appreciate the significance of the writings of the colonial clergyman Jonathan Edwards. Edwards was quite possibly the greatest American intellectual prior to the Revolutionary War. Entering Yale College at the age of thirteen, Edwards absorbed the philosophy of John Locke and its argument that the contents of the human mind are structured solely by the information supplied by the physical senses. Edwards's famous treatises, *Careful and Strict Inquiry into the Modern Prevailing Notions of that Freedom of the Will* (1754) and *A Treatise Concerning Religious Affections* (1746), built upon Locke's psychology in such a way as to support the Calvinist principle of God's utter sovereignty. Edwards argued that although humans are free to choose what they desire, their desires are determined by God. Human choice is thus not an independent power, but rather an instrument of the will of God. As Edwards's writings indicate, colonial psychology remained a handmaiden to Protestant theology's master vision of human personality as subordinate to the majesty of God.

Jonathan Edwards also wrote about the psychology of religious conversion and, in so doing, opened up a line of psychological reasoning that persists to the contemporary era. Edwards accepted Locke's reasoning that all knowledge derives from sense experience, but maintained that God's spirit awakens in people an additional "new sense" through which they receive spiritual emanations not detectable by the physical senses alone. Religious conversions, then, are caused by an individual becoming aware of "new inward perceptions or sensations of their minds." Thus Edwards was arguing all people have the psychological potential to open up to a higher order of things and thereby elevate their lives to a higher level of thought and feeling. While Edwards labored to interpret the human capacity for spiritual experience in orthodox theological terms, he nonetheless sowed the seeds for a mystical strain in American psychological thought that would postulate one's otherwise untapped potential for expanding the range of the mind and personality.

POPULAR ROOTS OF AMERICAN INTEREST IN PSYCHOLOGY

Psychology remained closely connected with Protestant theology in American university curricula until well after the Civil War. Typical in this regard were books published by Asa Mahan, president of Oberlin College and an ordained Congregationalist clergyman, such as *Abstract of a Course of Lectures on Mental and Moral Philosophy* (1841), *Doctrine of the Will* (1845), and *The Science of Moral Philosophy* (1848). Yet even while universities continued to associate psychology with moral philosophy, the general public was being introduced to new psychological ideas that heralded the progressive separation of psychology from theology. One of the first to introduce American reading audiences to new, nontheological, psychological concepts was Ralph Waldo Emerson.

The nineteenth century witnessed the gradual separation of psychology from the clergy and theology. Yet, surprisingly, Americans continued to expect psychology—even in its new, nontheological forms—to provide them with broadly spiritual understandings of the mind. Among the first to provide a new psychological vocabulary was Ralph Waldo Emerson. According to Emerson, the goal of psychological development is what he termed self-reliance. The truly self-reliant individual has grown free from social influences and has become the dynamic center of his or her own life. To be self-reliant is thus to be free, spontaneous, and capable of creatively engaging the world. In Emerson's view, however, attaining self-reliance is a spiritual art more than it is an achievement of the will. It requires that people first learn to be obedient to the dictates of their inner lives rather than the dictates of social custom. Emerson went even further and suggested that self-reliance ultimately originates in spiritual impulses that come to people from what he called the Oversoul, or God. Emerson's Transcendentalist philosophy taught the existence of a "divinity that flows through all things." The key to genuine self-reliance, according to Emerson, is learning how to cultivate a lifestyle that keeps people receptive to the "inflow" of this potent spiritual power. Emerson was providing a new, psychological vocabulary for explaining how one might adopt a spiritual outlook on life. Moreover, this psychological vocabulary made no reference to traditional biblical terminology, which appeared increasingly outdated to the era's progressive-mind thinkers.

Phrenology and mesmerism further contributed to the development of public interest in a new, nontheological science of psychology. Phrenology was an early attempt to understand the neurological basis of personality. Assuming that every personality trait has its own physiological center in the brain, phrenologists developed elaborate charts indicating the precise anatomical location of every conceivable moral and intellectual disposition. A trained phrenologist could examine the relative size of any particular area of a person's skull and, using these phrenological charts, make detailed diagnoses concerning his or her moral character. Phrenology's advocates believed that they were on the threshold of a revolutionary science that would be of invaluable service to both medicine and religion. It was thought that phrenologists would eventually be able to prescribe compensatory programs specifically designed to improve those cranial locations in which a person was deficient. For example, some phrenologists suggested that leeches could be placed on criminals' heads so as to siphon off the strength from the anatomical centers of deceit and larceny. Other phrenologists prescribed mental exercises such as memorizing moral precepts in order to stimulate growth in otherwise underdeveloped sections of the brain. Yet when all was said and done, phrenology remained a system of classification. Its efforts to spawn self-improvement programs were so wedded to a physiological materialism that they appeared discouragingly futile. Phrenology's swift exit from the American intellectual scene was in the final analysis due to the fact that its master image of human personality was incompatible with Americans' underlying assumptions about mind and personality. The evangelical and revivalistic nature of American Protestantism had convinced most of the

nation's citizens that human nature is susceptible to immediate and total renovation. Any psychology hoping to gain a widespread following would have to conform to those assumptions.

Mesmerism was far more successful at attracting popular audiences to the fledgling field of psychology. Based on the discoveries of the Viennese physician Franz Anton Mesmer, mesmerism taught that humans have unconscious mental powers that can be tapped into and utilized to promote physical healing, emotional rejuvenation, and spiritual connection with God's ever-present spiritual powers. Mesmerism thus held out psychological descriptions of the mind that meshed with American culture's roots in religious revivalism. Mesmerism, like revivalism, believed that humans are capable of being "born again" in the twinkling of an eye, provided that their inner lives are first rendered open or receptive to the inflow of a higher, spiritual power. Yet the American adherents of mesmerism thought they were championing a progressive new science of the mind that represented a significant departure from conventional religion. While most agreed that the higher power (variously called animal magnetism, etheric energy, vital force) available to people through the unconscious mind is ultimately identical to what Christians call divine spirit, they thought that they were at last bringing spiritual topics into the domain of scientific inquiry.

Mesmerism was to have a long-lasting influence upon psychology's ability to attract a popular following. By the late 1880s and 1890s the mesmerists' glowing accounts of the hidden powers available to people through their unconscious minds gave rise to a popular philosophy variously referred to as Mind Cure or New Thought. New Thought authors informed their readers that what separates people from God's infinite spiritual power is not sin or disobedience, but rather simple ignorance of the psychological laws governing human existence. Spiritual progress was said to be achieved through studying the powers of one's own mind and then systematically adjusting one's life to take advantage of these lawful powers. New Thought philosophers cautioned against paying too much attention to outer circumstances. As the New Thought author Ralph Waldo Trine expressed it, the secret of both material and spiritual abundance is to quiet the outer mind and thereby become inwardly in tune with the infinite:

> In just the degree that we come into a conscious realization of our oneness with the Infinite Life, and open ourselves to the Divine inflow, do we actualize in ourselves the qualities and powers of the Infinite

711

Life. . . . In just the degree in which you realize your oneness with the Infinite Spirit, you will exchange dis-ease for ease, inharmony for harmony, suffering and pain for abounding health and strength (*In Tune with the Infinite*, p. 16).

Other New Thought volumes are less sublime. Frank Haddock's volumes such as *Power for Success through Culture of Vibrant Magnetism* (1903), *Power of Will* (1907), and *The Personal Atmosphere: Ten Studies in Poise and Power* (1909) typify how New Thought principles gave rise to think-your-way-to-success strategies for approaching life. New Thought principles were surprisingly democratic, teaching that all people have the power to align themselves with the higher energies of the mind and exert their rightful supremacy over the surrounding world. And thus while Transcendentalism, phrenology, mesmerism, and New Thought had all stimulated public interest in nonbiblical understandings of the mind and personality, they had nonetheless perpetuated a close association between psychology and a host of philosophical and spiritual attitudes toward the meaning of life. The general public's association of psychology with spiritual concerns would later make it difficult for the first generation of academic psychologists to differentiate their discipline not only from other academic fields, but from both theology and the New Thought movement.

THE BIRTH OF THE "NEW PSYCHOLOGY"

In the mid-1870s not a single American university had a separate department of psychology. By the mid-1890s, however, nearly every university did. One reason for the rapid emergence of academic psychology is sociological in nature. The last few decades of the nineteenth century witnessed unprecedented growth in the rates of industrialization, urbanization, and immigration. Older cultural patterns—largely drawn from the religious heritage of a rural, Anglo-Saxon populace—proved increasingly incapable of helping people take their bearings on life. No longer able to construct their identity in terms of "outer" conditions, Americans now sought to define themselves in terms of "inner" realities. Put differently, as Americans found it harder to influence social and economic structures, they instead embraced ideas that promised to help them understand and control their own inner natures.

The growing prestige of natural sciences combined with these sociological factors began to deepen interest in an academic discipline of psy-chology. By the 1880s the English naturalist Charles Darwin's theory of evolution had given American universities a bold new confidence in the power of science to understand all the intricacies of biological existence. Some of the era's boldest scholars thought it was time to create a new psychology, a "psychology without a soul." Academic psychologists eschewed any connection with philosophy or theology and instead aligned their discipline with the natural sciences. Although no one dramatic event marked the emergence of psychology as an autonomous discipline, a number of events between 1878 and 1892 enabled American psychology to turn a corner. In 1878 G. Stanley Hall became the first individual to receive a Ph.D. in psychology from an American University (Harvard); in 1883 he opened a psychological laboratory at Johns Hopkins University. In 1887 G. T. Ladd published his *Elements of Physiological Psychology* and Hall inaugurated the *American Journal of Psychology*; in 1890 William James published *The Principles of Psychology*; and in 1892 the American Psychological Association was formed and would see its membership quadruple in the next decade. As research methods became increasingly sophisticated, scholars developed areas of specialization. The compilation of research data led to breakthroughs in such areas as sensation and perception, learning and motivation, physiological psychology, developmental psychology, and abnormal psychology.

Most early American psychologists considered themselves to be functionalists, meaning they were particularly interested in studying the functions that the mind performs in guiding the organism's adaptation to the environment. Because of its emphasis on how an organism functions within its environment, the functionalist orientation tended to focus on applied issues such as learning, perception, and testing. Yet historical perspective enables scholars to identify the concepts of childhood and development as the two most important contributions that the functionalist orientation made to American understandings of human nature. Prior to the new psychology, Protestant theology had tended to overlook the formative influences of childhood and focused instead upon how the conversion experience transforms unruly adolescents into morally responsible adults. In contrast, the functionalist paradigm interpreted personality growth in terms of the continuing adjustment of the individual to ever-wider spheres of social activity. G. Stanley Hall's two-volume *Adolescence* (1904) and James Mark Baldwin's *Mental Development in the Child and the Race* (1895) are representative of

WILLIAM JAMES
THE PRINCIPLES OF PSYCHOLOGY

Published in 1890, William James's *The Principles of Psychology* is to this day considered the single greatest work in the history of American psychology. One reason for this distinction is that William James was a literary genius, crafting such beautiful prose descriptions of psychological topics that the book warrants the status of a classic on its literary merits alone. More important, however, James was also the era's most celebrated philosopher and helped articulate many of the otherwise tacit assumptions about mind and personality that characterize American psychology in the twenty-first century.

Principles begins with several long, tedious chapters covering neurophysiology. While much of this material is outdated, James's attention to such important theoretical issues as mind-body interaction is so philosophically astute that even these chapters hold interest for the contemporary reader. The book then moves abruptly into lively discussions about the nature of the self, consciousness, and free will. While James conceded that it is the purpose of scientific psychology to assume that humans are fully determined by their genetic heritage and environment, his discussions of these topics nonetheless reveal his personal belief that the human mind and personality exceed all standard scientific models. In the chapter on the "stream of consciousness," James showed how consciousness is not a static entity, but consists instead of a continuous flow, ever-changing, selective in choosing what it will and will not attend to. The mind, in James's view, is thus a dynamic agent that actively goes out to, and reshapes, the surrounding environment.

Totaling over thirteen hundred pages, *Principles* became the standard textbook that shaped academic understandings of psychology for several decades. The book's influence extends even to this day in American psychology's reluctance to embrace reductionistic accounts of human nature and instead to entertain perspectives that depict the mind's active and creative potentials.

the early texts that outline the developmental principles that can account for the natural evolution of human personality. Their goal was not only to wrestle the theoretical understanding of the self away from theology, but to help parents and educators make practical application of these scientific understandings of the developmental process.

The first generation of American psychologists were hoping that their new intellectual achievement would respond to critical cultural needs. An astonishing percentage of these pioneering psychologists were sons of Protestant ministers or had themselves been enrolled in a Protestant seminary before shifting careers. These individuals were sensitive to the ways in which both the natural sciences and the new industrial economy were creating challenges that old-fashioned, Bible-based religion could not readily handle. It was their hope that psychological theories of mind and personality would provide a more culturally viable understanding of human nature and of the lawful principles that must be followed if people hope to create better lives for themselves as individuals and as a species. A perfect case in point is the career of the developmental psychologist G. Stanley Hall. Originally slated for the Protestant ministry, Hall's early encounter with the theories of Charles Darwin persuaded him that the sciences were more likely to sharpen one's understanding of the laws that govern human development that the Bible. Like so many of his college-educated contemporaries, Hall found inspiration in the writings of such Romantic luminaries as Ralph Waldo Emerson, Alfred Tennyson, Friedrich Schleiermacher, and Friedrich von Schelling. It was the German philosopher Georg Wilhelm Friedrich Hegel, however, who enabled Hall to see how scientific

713

descriptions of personality development might at the same time be understood as the process whereby nature progressively evolves toward higher stages of spiritual expression. Hegel's view of the dialectic movement of history helped Hall embrace evolution as the steady process through which a pantheistic deity moves nature toward higher stages of complexity and consciousness. In Hall's view, the evolution of human personality mirrors the broader evolutionary process through which God nourishes his creation. Hall and many other first-generation psychologists thus saw psychology as contributing to religion, not replacing it. They understood themselves to be prophets of a new, scientifically grounded vision of humanity's place in an ever-evolving universe.

By the early twentieth century the university had come to replace the church as the center of intellectual thought in America. In parallel fashion, psychology had come to replace theology as the authoritative source of information concerning the mind and personality. Yet by the time psychology had succeeded in securing full academic acceptance, it had already divided into various methodological orientations that differed radically from one another. There was no one "new psychology," but rather several new schools of psychological thought, each competing for jurisdiction over the discipline. The three most dominant of these have been the psychoanalytic, behaviorist, and humanistic schools of psychological thought. As noted in the introductory remarks of this essay, psychology consists of an assortment of facts, presuppositions, and theories whose relevance to human welfare depends upon the philosophical outlook of the person who puts them together. Each of the three major schools of modern American psychology represents a unique philosophical approach to just how humans might piece together a coherent view of mind or personality.

Psychoanalysis: Assimilation and Accommodation It was especially difficult for early psychotherapists to establish a distinct professional identity. Unlike experimental psychologists who conducted research in mechanically equipped laboratories, therapists treated patients in such uncontrolled settings as hospital bedsides and private offices. Moreover, they had to rely upon the introspection and self-reports of their patients as opposed to empirically derived statistical results. For these reasons psychotherapists sought to establish a professional identity that would align them more with the medical than the academic community.

Unfortunately, medical models did little to establish the credibility of their fledgling field. The era's medical theories tended to classify psychopathology as belonging to the general category of neurophysiological disorders. Any symptom without a neurological basis was therefore dismissed as malingering, hypochondria, or evidence of a lack of moral resolve. When early practitioners in this field did try to demonstrate the role of strictly "psychological" factors in mental illness, their theories differed little from those of the proponents of New Thought.

Thus therapeutically oriented psychologists were already drawing ideological battle lines by the time they first learned about the Austrian neurologist Sigmund Freud and his system of thought referred to as psychoanalysis. According to Freud, the unconscious is the fundamental substratum of all mental life. Freud maintained that just below the threshold of consciousness exists a myriad of thoughts or memories that may resurface at any time. More deeply imbedded in the unconscious are those thoughts and memories that remain well beneath the surface of mental life because they are repressed or have no association with language. And, most important, the unconscious also contains the id, which Freud defined as the primary carrier of instinctual biological drives. Since gratification of instinct is, biologically speaking, the true purpose of the individual organism's life, the unconscious is thus the primary source of one's motives and drives. The unconscious is, in short, an intractable agent acting solely to procure immediate, personal pleasure; it is, furthermore, oblivious and even antagonistic to the practical necessities of one's physical and social surroundings. The individual must therefore develop rational skills (called the ego) and a social conscience (called the superego) that can oppose the untamed passions arising from the unconscious. The ego and superego are saddled with the responsibility of repressing the organism's most powerful drives in order to procure a measure of personal safety and to make civilization possible.

Freud's view of human nature lacked the optimistic or utopian dimension that Americans had come to expect from psychologists. He believed that there is an irresolvable tension between the individual's instinctual drives and society's need for these drives to be repressed. In Freud's view, the very existence of civilization is predicated upon society's ability to encroach upon and impose authority over people's deepest wants and wishes. Civilization develops at the expense of the individual, who pays in terms of psychic frustration, repression, and eventually mental disorders. As a system of therapy, psychoanalysis helps people gain insight into themselves. The goal of psychoanalysis is to liberate people from an overbearing conscience and help them develop shrewd, calculating ego skills that guide them toward enlightened self-interest. According to psychoanalysis, optimal psychological health enables people to pursue whatever limited measure of personal fulfillment they can obtain while stoically accepting the inevitable compromises and renunciations that society imposes upon them in the course of everyday life.

A core of American psychologists embraced psychoanalysis as a means of establishing psychotherapy along scientific lines. A. A. Brill, Ernest Jones, and James Jackson Putnam were among those who interpreted Freud's work as having great promise for identifying the uniquely "psychological" factors in the development and treatment of mental illness. Soon others, including Morton Prince, Boris Sidis, Edwin Bissell Holt, and William White, began to champion some version of psychoanalytic theory and its cardinal postulate concerning the pivotal role of the unconscious mind. There can be little question that psychoanalysis had an immediate impact upon the burgeoning fields of psychiatry and psychotherapy, providing a vocabulary and theoretical framework that would for several decades serve as a common reference point in theoretical discussions. Nor can there be any question that psychoanalysis had an effect upon some sectors of early-twentieth-century's popular culture. That is, many disaffected intellectuals seized upon psychoanalysis as a version of existentialist philosophy. To them, psychoanalysis symbolized the inherent antagonisms existing between the individual and society and seemingly affirmed them in their search for a more "authentic" life built around the pursuit of personal pleasure and a permanent suspicion of social institutions of every kind—political, familial, and religious.

Yet, despite the valiant efforts of early converts to the psychoanalytic cause, Freud's writings failed to make much of an impression upon the accumulated stock of psychological "knowledge" in America. Even the most scientific of Freud's early American followers tended to appropriate psychoanalysis in ways that blurred Freud's tragic vision of human nature. White, Holt, and Putnam are typical examples of those who muted Freud's emphasis upon the sexual and aggressive nature of human instinct. Instead, they characterized the unconscious mind as a conduit through which people are connected with what the French philosopher Henri

Bergson termed the *élan vital,* or life force that propels nature toward progressive evolutionary growth and development. Thus, although they conceded that the unconscious contains animal-like aggressive instincts, they thought it more valuable to emphasize how the unconscious also connects humankind with a vital spiritual power capable of stimulating unlimited psychological growth. Distinguishing between the "lower" and "higher" reaches of the unconscious, many American interpreters of Freud finally blurred any distinctions between psychoanalysis and the theories of the mesmerists, James, or the New Thought philosophers. Nowhere can this be seen more clearly than in the writings of Eric Berne (*Games People Play,* 1964) and Thomas A. Harris (*I'm OK—You're OK,* 1973) who repackaged Freud's ideas for the American reading public. In best-sellers of the 1960s and 1970s, Berne and Harris acknowledged indebtedness to Freud, yet unabashedly altered psychoanalytic principles in order "to reach people where they live." In Harris's view, the unconscious has more than antisocial instincts, but includes also "a bright side . . . creativity, curiosity, the desire to explore and know, the urge to touch and feel and experience" (*I'm OK—You're OK,* p. 49). Using dozens of quotes from mystical philosophers such as Ralph Waldo Emerson and Henri Bergson, Harris's self-help philsophy assured American reading audiences that in the unconscious are the forces needed to bring humans to what religions have traditionally called redemption, reconciliation, or enlightenment. In its assimilation into American culture, then, psychoanalysis was largely accommodated to a preexisting tendency of American psychology to view the unconscious mind as a source of energies that yield creativity, self-reliance, and spiritual vitality.

Behaviorism and the Quest for Control Psychologists in the early twentieth century were constantly under attack for their lack of methodological rigor. Especially sensitive to criticism from their colleagues in the natural sciences, they became increasingly concerned with their scientific credentials. Many turned their attention toward the one field of psychology that already emulated the more established sciences, the study of animal behavior. External observation and philosophical positivism quickly replaced the introspective examination and thinly veiled vitalism that had previously dominated American psychological thought. This change in viewpoint drastically altered the relationship of psychology to Darwinian biology. Earlier American psychologists such as William James had placed a great deal of importance on the psychological implications of Darwin's theory of free variation, thereby emphasizing the mind's potential for creative change. Behaviorists, on the other hand, focused almost exclusively on Darwin's theory of environmental selection, thereby depicting humans as passive products of their surroundings. By reducing the study of behavior to factors that could be empirically measured, behaviorists hoped to produce a fully scientific school of psychological thought.

John Broadus Watson became the leading spokesperson for this exciting new direction in psychological research when, in 1913, he published his epochal article "Psychology as a Behaviorist Views It." Watson contended that the principal error of psychology in the past was its misguided use of an imprecise method, introspection, to study a nonexistent entity, consciousness. In their place he proposed the use of laboratory experiments to study outwardly observable behavior. As he put it, "Psychology as the behaviorist views it is a purely objective experimental branch of natural science. Its theoretical goal is the prediction and control of behavior" ("Psychology," p. 158). According to behaviorism, psychology could henceforth dispense with such nonempirical terms as consciousness, mind, or self. These were carryovers from the prescientific vocabularies of theology and superstition. Instead, psychology was to concentrate on detecting causal relationships between environmental influences and outwardly observable behaviors. Differences between two people could now be defined in terms of specific differences in their histories of environmental conditioning rather than referring to nebulous inner states of mind. Behaviorists contended that in time they would be able to specify the causal principles shaping human behavior with such precision that they would be capable of designing a perfect social environment.

Harvard's B. F. Skinner succeeded Watson as the movement's preeminent popularizer. His bestselling books, *Beyond Freedom and Dignity* (1971) and *Walden Two* (1948) envision a society designed according to the principles of scientific psychology. Skinner argued that a truly scientific account of human personality shifts both the credit for constructive behavior and the blame for destructive behavior to the environment that produced it. Behavioral psychology can help people design better environments that will, in turn, produce better human beings. Skinner believed that people possess almost limitless potential for scientifically directing the future evolution of human nature. He believed that it

is within humans' grasp to eliminate such undesirable behavior as pollution or crime and to equip every person with the behavioral repertoire needed to make them productive citizens of an efficient social order.

In the late twentieth century, academic psychologists muted behaviorism's radical environmentalism. New information concerning genetic influences on human behavior prompted behaviorists to qualify their views. So, too, have findings in the field of cognitive psychology caused behaviorists to pay more attention to the role that mental events have in determining behavior (through many behaviorists would still contend that these mental events are themselves under the control of the environment). Nonetheless, twenty-first-century departments of psychology in American universities continue to be dominated by the basic theoretical outlook spawned by behaviorism. Academic psychology has, for example, continued to embrace the kinds of determinism, objectivism, and philosophical positivism that Watson, Skinner, and others championed. For this reason academic psychology tends to discourage interest in topics that are difficult to quantify in favor of research on topics that can be objectively measured, quantified, and subjected to statistical analysis. To this extent behaviorism largely succeeded in excising the psyche from American psychology. Whatever the shift toward behaviorism cost psychology in terms of its ability to understand the nonempirical aspects of human personality, it succeeded in defining a program that has made steady progress toward Watson's goal of predicting and controlling behavior.

Humanistic Psychology and the Celebration of Self In the early 1960s, Abraham Maslow announced the emergence of a new orientation in American psychology. What came to be known as the third force, or humanistic school of American psychology, arose in direct opposition to both psychoanalysis and behaviorism. Its principal goal was to combat the reductionistic tendencies in modern psychology that prompted psychoanalysts to reduce human behavior to instincts or repressed memories while behaviorists reduced behavior to the contingencies of environmental reinforcement. In contrast, humanistic psychology wished to celebrate the human mind and personality by drawing attention to their "highest" potentials. As Maslow explained in the *Journal of Humanistic Psychology*'s inaugural issue (1961), this third force in American psychological thought is concerned with "human capacities and potentials that have no systematic place either in positivistic or behavioristic theory or in classical psychoanalytic theory, e. g., creativity, love, self, growth, organism, basic need-gratification, higher values, ego-transcendence" (p. vii).

Humanistic psychology has never been a fixed theoretical position, but rather a loosely knit collection of the writings of such psychologists as Gordon Allport, Rollo May, Viktor Frankl, Andras Angyal, and Eugene Gendlin. It was, however, Abraham Maslow and Carl Rogers who emerged as the movement's most distinguished theorists. Maslow argued that humans have both a lower and higher nature. While behaviorism and psychoanalysis focus exclusively on the mechanisms associated with the lower end of psychological functioning, humanistic psychology represents the attempt to derive a scientific account of humanity's capacity for "self-actualization." Maslow defined self-actualization as the individual's innate drive to transcend instinctual and environmental determinism, thereby becoming free to actualize the self's unique potentials, talents, and mission. Among these unique potentials is the capacity to have what Maslow described as "peak experiences." Likening the peak experience to the spiritual states described by the mystics of all world religions, Maslow believed that such experiences are not the property of any one theology, but rather within the province of a suitably enlarged science of psychology. Maslow's study of peak experiences shows that they are profoundly healing. They foster emotional integration and release the self's creative personal energies. Moreover, peak experiences take the individual beyond his or her accustomed way of viewing life and impart a vivid perception of the self's fundamental unity with the whole of the cosmos. To this extent Maslow and other humanistic psychologists developed a psychological theory that provided their followers with a full-blown philosophy of how people might achieve mental, emotional, and spiritual well-being.

Carl Rogers, too, championed the view that humans have an innate drive toward self-actualization. His confidence that people contain within themselves the resources for self-integration and growth provided the foundation for his "client-centered" technique of psychotherapy. Rogers believed that if a therapist provides a safe emotional environment, the client will automatically let go of acquired defenses and begin to make appropriate changes in his or her life. The warm, nonimpositional relationship established by the therapist permits clients to get in touch with a deeper level of wisdom that Rogers called the organismic valuing process. This is not, however, a simple humanistic trust in the individual's own resources for self-actualization. Paralleling Ralph Waldo Emerson's views of self-reliance and metaphysical correspondence, Rogers maintained that there is formative tendency at work in the universe, which can be observed at every level luring life toward greater wholeness, complexity, and consciousness. In his view, the client-centered technique of psychotherapy establishes the right climate that permits people to tap into this "formative tendency" and release it for the purpose of stimulating growth and self-actualization. In Rogers, much as with Emerson, Trine, James, Putnam, and Harris, Americans found a psychologically phrased theory of mind and personality with strong spiritual overtones.

MIND AND PERSONALITY IN POPULAR PSYCHOLOGY

It is somewhat difficult to draw a hard and fast line between academic and popular psychology. While publications in academic psychology are intended to address the research issues and methodological criteria currently of interest to professional psychologists, popular psychology refers to those writings specifically addressed to general reading audiences. What distinguishes a psychological theory as "popular" is thus not the credentials of its creator but its overt intention to help individuals symbolize and resolve problems that arise in the context of everyday life. Indeed, James, Freud, Skinner, and Maslow are all examples of psychologists who have successfully written works intended to be "consumed" by the general reading public. The persistence of a viable market for lectures and publications in the field of popular psychology is a good indication of Americans' interest in assimilating particular images of mind and personality into the stock of ideas with which they take their bearings on life.

While a good many psychologies have attracted popular followings by promising solutions to isolated behavioral problems such as smoking and overeating, most are concerned with regenerating the whole person. Among the most popular of these psychologies have been Thomas Harris's *I'm OK—You're OK*, Norman Vincent Peale's *The Power of Positive Thinking* (1952), and M. Scott Peck's *The Road Less Traveled* (1978). Interestingly, each of these works echoes themes that have persisted in American psychological thought since the mesmerists of the 1840s and the New Thought proponents of the 1890s. They all understand the mind as a free, willing, and creative agent. And, too, they all concur

NORMAN VINCENT PEALE
THE POWER OF POSITIVE THINKING

No person has had more of an impact upon popular understandings of the power of the mind than the Reverend Norman Vincent Peale. Preacher, author, and television personality, Peale sparked the post–World War II revival of religion with his 1952 best-seller, *The Power of Positive Thinking*. Peale's message reworked themes borrowed from Ralph Waldo Emerson and William James to reassure people that the only barrier separating them from a life of total abundance is a self-imposed, psychological one. Eschewing Christianity's traditional emphasis upon sin and the need for repentance, Peale buoyed millions with his belief that "by channeling spiritual power through your thoughts . . . you can have peace of mind, improved health, and a never-ceasing flow of energy" (p. viii–ix).

According to Peale's philosophy, there is a religious, even Christian, dimension to belief in the power of positive thinking. After all, it was Jesus Christ who proclaimed that if you have the proper faith "nothing shall be impossible unto you" (Matthew 17:20). It was Peale's task to teach readers how modern psychology provides a key to understanding what mental attitudes create a power-giving faith. Instructing people to envision God as an "electrical energy" invisibly permeating the universe, Peale labored ceaselessly to drive home his message of the power available to people through the unconscious mind:

> To me it was a revelation of the fact that in our consciousness we can tap a reservoir of boundless power . . . it is my conviction that the principles of Christianity scientifically utilized can develop an uninterrupted and continuous flow of energy into the human mind and body. (p. 37)

with Emerson that full self-reliance is both a psychological and a spiritual achievement. That is, these books not only celebrate the self's capacity to eschew social opinion and lead an individually chosen lifestyle, but they celebrate the self's capacity to find inner connection with a higher, spiritual power from which wholeness and vitality are to be derived.

Many scholars such as Donald Meyer, Russell Jacoby, Elizabeth Lunbeck, and Ellen Herman criticized psychology for diverting Americans' attention from the social and economic sources of modern discontent. In their view, psychology is the opiate of today's masses, giving the illusion of well-being when in fact its theories do nothing to solve the real causes of human suffering. Their criticisms are well founded. In many ways psychology has perpetuated rather than critically examined many of the forces that lead to the fragmentation of modern life. It has, for example, tended to reinforce the American myth of the self-made person, suggesting that both emotional wholeness and financial success are available to all who properly discipline their own minds—a cruel joke to those who by birth are fated to be victims of poverty, racism, or sexism. Yet it is perhaps too harsh to require psychology to address every human dilemma. As the intellectual and cultural history of American psychology reveals, new variations continue to rework the various facts, presuppositions, and theories that together comprise psychological knowledge. And although striking continuities persist, American psychological thought has nonetheless proven remarkably creative in generating new and more culturally relevant images of human personality.

See also **Manhood; Racialism and Racial Uplift; The Behavioral and Social Sciences** *(volume 1);* **The Ideal of Spontaneity** *(in this volume);* **Individualism and the Self; Sexuality; The Social Sciences; Memory** *(volume 3); and other articles in this section.*

BIBLIOGRAPHY

Primary Sources

Berne, Eric. *Games People Play: The Psychology of Human Relationships.* New York, 1964.

Harris, Thomas. *I'm OK—You're OK.* New York, 1973.

James, William. *The Principles of Psychology.* 3 vols. Cambridge, Mass., 1981.

Maslow, Abraham H. *Toward a Psychology of Being.* Princeton, N.J., 1962.

Peale, Norman Vincent. *The Power of Positive Thinking.* New York, 1952.

Peck, M. Scott. *The Road Less Traveled.* New York, 1978.

Rogers, Carl. *On Becoming a Person.* Boston, 1961.

Skinner, B. F. *About Behaviorism.* New York, 1974.

Trine, Ralph Waldo. *In Tune with the Infinite; or, Fullness of Peace, Power, and Plenty.* 1897. Reprint, New York, 1973.

Watson, John B. "Psychology as a Behaviorist Views It." *Psychological Review* 20 (1913): 158–177.

Secondary Sources

Boring, E. G., and G. Lindzey. *A History of Psychology in Autobiography.* New York, 1967.

Cushman, Philip. *Constructing the Self, Constructing America: A Cultural History of Psychotherapy.* Reading, Mass., 1995.

Fuller, Robert C. *Americans and the Unconscious.* New York, 1986.

Gross, Martin. *The Psychological Society.* New York, 1978.

Hale, Nathan. *Freud and the Americans: The Beginnings of Psychoanalysis in the United States, 1876–1917.* New York, 1971.

Herman, Ellen. *The Romance of American Psychology: Political Culture in an Age of Experts.* Berkeley, Calif., 1995.

Jacoby, Russell. *Social Amnesia: A Critique of Contemporary Psychology from Adler to Laing.* Boston, 1975.

Lunbeck, Elizabeth. *The Psychiatric Persuasion: Knowledge, Gender, and Power in Modern America.* Princeton, N.J., 1994.

Meyer, Donald. *The Positive Thinkers: A Study of the American Quest for Health, Wealth, and Personal Power from Mary Baker Eddy to Norman Vincent Peale.* Garden City, N.Y., 1965.

Ross, Dorothy. *G. Stanley Hall: The Psychologist as Prophet.* Chicago, 1972.

———. *The Origins of American Social Science.* New York, 1991.

ANTHROPOLOGY AND CULTURAL RELATIVISM

Julia E. Liss

The history of anthropology in the United States is also a history of cultural relativism. Cultural relativism became a mainstay of anthropology, even for its opponents, because it asserted the primacy of culture as the organizing principle of human societies and because it provided ammunition against evolutionary explanations of social development. Central to these positions of cultural primacy were a critique of biological explanations, a tendency to see cultures, in the plural, as systems or wholes, and an emphasis on the way each culture provides its own system of symbols and meanings. Critiques of cultural relativism have focused on the importance of biology over culture, the reassertion of hierarchies, and the importance of standards and truth over tolerance.

This history falls into two periods: (1) the formation of cultural relativism in anthropology from 1890 to 1950 in the work of the German-American anthropologist and founder of the culture-center school of anthropology Franz Boas and his students, Alfred Kroeber, Robert Lowie, Edward Sapir, Margaret Mead, Ruth Benedict, and Melville Herskovits; and (2) the post–World War II debates over cultural relativism in which all of its assumptions were questioned. In fact, cultural relativism is in many ways synonymous with the "Boasian revolution" in anthropology: the view that culture, defined as the shared values and beliefs of a group, should be the central concern of anthropology as a discipline, and that those values and beliefs should be understood within the context of that group, rather than as a part of an evolutionary scheme of development imposed from the outside. Ensuing generations of anthropologists both took this meaning of culture for granted and challenged its assumptions. Because Boas, Mead, Benedict, and Herskovits were exemplary in formulating cultural relativism within anthropology for the public, they have remained the focus of ongoing debates about the issue.

DEFINITIONS

Cultural relativism involves the primacy of culture in determining human societies and their relation to each other. One area of emphasis concerns the analysis of individual cultures. In its narrowest form this is methodological or descriptive relativism: elements of a culture need to be considered *in relation* to that culture, and cultures cannot be understood by external standards. Even this seemingly straightforward definition contains within it seeds of ongoing controversy about the meanings and implications of cultural relativism. If cultures must be understood on their own terms, does that necessarily imply ethical or moral relativism, the idea that judgments or values are also relative and cannot be imposed from without? Is there an inherent contradiction between descriptive relativism and cognitive or epistemological relativism, according to which it may be impossible even to understand another culture from the outside? Finally, does the relativistic idea of culture as shared values and beliefs of a group mean that aesthetic standards are also meaningless? A second area of emphasis involves the relationship of cultures to each other. Cultures may be connected, or related, historically and they may be related by comparison. The central quandaries of cultural relativism surround the questions of whether there are universals—features that transcend time, place, and cultures—or if differences are more important, and whether one can or should make moral judgments about cultures. The connection to ethical relativism raises the stakes of cultural relativism.

THE FORMATION OF CULTURAL RELATIVISM IN ANTHROPOLOGY

Franz Boas: Cultural Relativism as Method A German immigrant, Franz Boas (1858–1942) was trained as a physicist and geographer, and in new-

Margaret Mead. © Bettmann/corbis

Kantian ideas of epistemological skepticism that questioned the bases of knowledge and perception. The anthropological idea of culture that he established resembles the German one of *Kultur*, the definitive, shared characteristics of the nation's "genius." Boas's ideas about contextualism and relativism were also similar to those of American pragmatist philosophers, including John Dewey, with whom he taught at Columbia University, and his student, Randolph Bourne. As a scholar and public intellectual, and through the students he placed in anthropology departments throughout the United States, Boas lay the groundwork for cultural relativism in the discipline of anthropology. Drawing on evidence of cultural contact, linguistic borrowing, and racial intermixture, Boas based his relativism on two points: people are related and values are contingent. The role of anthropology was to illuminate this contingency and provide emancipation from the "cultural blinders" that bind humankind.

A central part of Boasian anthropology and its relativist implications came from Boas's insistence on contextualizing phenomena. Museum exhibits, he thought, should be organized by tribe and "geographical province" rather than by placing objects in chronological and developmental sequence

(Stocking, ed., *A Franz Boas Reader*, p. 62). In a study of the phenomenon of "alternating sounds"—the tendency to mishear certain linguistic elements—Boas argued that errors reflected the listener's own phonetic system: sounds are "classified according to known sensations" (p. 75). Boas popularized these conclusions in *The Mind of Primitive Man* (1911), where he argued that "race"—or physical type—was indeterminate and not fixed, related to environment and separate from culture; further, he argued that values assumed to be absolute are culturally determined, and that similarities of cultural traits "were more apparent than real" (p. 249). In *Anthropology and Modern Life* (1928), he focused on cultural bias itself—racism, nationalism, and eugenics—to reveal the dangers of judging others ("What is desirable depends upon valuations that are not universally accepted" [p. 202]). Boas laid the foundation for the emerging relativism of anthropology: by separating race from culture he helped formulate the central concept of culture and challenged the biological foundation of the hierarchical arrangement of societies. By emphasizing historical connections as distinct from social evolutionary development, Boas saw cultures as changing, contingent, and interrelated rather than fixed, absolute, and independent.

722

Boas believed that scientific, objective methods allow one to correct for bias. Conceiving of anthropology as a science of culture, he wrote,

> The scientific study of generalized social forms requires . . . that the investigator free himself from all valuations based on our culture. An objective, strictly scientific inquiry can be made only if we succeed in entering into each culture on its own basis, if we elaborate the ideals of each people and include in our general objective study cultural values as found among different branches of mankind (*Anthropology and Modern Life*, pp. 204–205).

Transcending one's own biases through science, according to Boas, enables one to see both universals and particulars and to fight against absolutes. This dual purpose was central to anthropology, which he hoped would provide self-awareness by juxtaposing the strange and the familiar, teach the values of others' ways and the arbitrariness of one's own, and allow an emancipatory cultural critique. Notably, Boas did not endorse a full-blown ethical relativism: recognizing that racism and nationalism reflected particular viewpoints did not make them acceptable alternatives. Rather, he thought they were contradicted by scientific evidence; freedom from "the shackles of dogma" through rationalism was Boas's lifelong goal. His students pushed the implications further by more closely examining individual cultures and by making cultural relativism an explicit aim of anthropology. In the 1920s and 1930s, in a period of modernist critique of cultural norms, they moved cultural relativism from a method into a doctrine.

Margaret Mead: Cultural Variety as Seen from the Inside Born into a middle-class family in Philadelphia, Margaret Mead (1901–1978) began graduate study with Franz Boas and Ruth Benedict after writing her master's thesis in psychology. A prolific author, who wrote such works as *Growing Up in New Guinea* (1930), *And Keep Your Powder Dry* (1942), and *Male and Female* (1949), Mead's work appealed to a large reading public critical of American ideas of individualism, conformity, and sexual prudery. Margaret Mead's first book was the best-seller *Coming of Age in Samoa* (1928). In it she studied adolescence in the South Pacific and pushed the Boasian agenda more firmly into the public realm. In his foreword to the book, Boas thanked Mead for "having undertaken to identify herself so completely with Samoan youth" to study adolescence and sexual maturity "in a culture so entirely different from our own." As Mead phrased the

question, "Are the disturbances which vex our adolescents due to the nature of adolescence itself or to the civilisation?" (p. 8). She presented a relativistic argument with multiple components: separating biology from culture; describing a particular culture, including a "picture of the whole social life of Samoa" in order to understand sexual maturation, presumably a universal part of the life cycle; and comparing a different system of behavior and values to one's own, in order to destabilize one's certainties and enable self-criticism. "Realising that our own ways are not humanly inevitable nor God-ordained, but are the fruit of a long and turbulent history," she concluded, "we may well examine in turn all of our institutions, thrown into strong relief against the history of other civilisations, and weighing them in the balance, be not afraid to find them wanting" (p. 174). Mead's cultural relativism meant that discreet parts of a culture, studied through participant-observation and considered in relation to the whole, enabled the anthropologist to see a culture from the inside. While one must suspend judgment about *other* cultures, comparisons also undercut a priori assumptions about the anthropologist's *own* culture, providing for social criticism and change.

For the remainder of her career, Mead wrote on sexuality, gender, and intergenerational relationships. Stressing the importance of reproduction and family life to gender roles, Mead explored the relationship of culture and biology, in various cultures, including the United States. The combination of methods and objectives—the insider's point of view, reliance on native informants, arguments for culture over biology, critique of U.S. society—made Mead the lightning rod for anti-Boasian arguments about culture and cultural relativism. In *Margaret Mead and Samoa: The Making and Unmaking of an Anthropological Myth* (1983), the anthropologist Derek Freeman advanced his argument against Boasian views on race, eugenics, and culture by attacking Mead's book, by then more than fifty years old. Charging that Mead was misled by her informants and misinterpreted Samoan society, Freeman reflected the revival in the 1980s of biological interpretations of human behavior and the extent to which Mead exemplified the opposing point of view.

Ruth Benedict: Culture and Personality Ruth Benedict (1887–1948) grew up in the Midwest and northern New York and attended Vassar College and the New School for Social Research before earning her doctorate at Columbia University. She turned her attention to the "great arc" of "potential human purposes and motivations" (*Patterns of Culture*, pp. 24, 237). Boas's student and Mead's mentor, Benedict's 1934 *Patterns of Culture* was a pathbreaking study. A best-seller when it was reissued in 1946, it was translated into over fourteen languages. Without emphasizing the historical processes that created cultures (as Boas had) or a particular problem (as Mead did), Benedict focused on cultural configurations or patterns. As Boas wrote in his introduction to the book, "It is felt more and more that hardly any trait of culture can be understood when taken out of its general setting. . . . The relativity of what is considered social or asocial, normal or abnormal, is seen in a new light" (pp. xvi, xvii). Cultural relativism posed two interrelated issues: the relation of cultural particulars to wholes, including the relation of an individual to a culture; and the relativity of morals, the varieties of normal and deviant, revealed in the context of those wholes.

In this study of the Zuñi of New Mexico, the Dobu of New Guinea, and the Kwakiutl of the Pacific Northwest, Benedict highlighted the distinctive culture and personality, the "complex interweaving of cultural traits" that comprised each one. "A culture, like an individual, is a more or less consistent pattern of thought and action," Benedict said, and the task of anthropology was to study these "cultures as articulated wholes." These cultures differed not only because of the presence or absence of certain particular characteristics but also because of their unique configuration: "They are travelling along different roads in pursuit of different ends, and these ends and these means in one society cannot be judged in terms of those of another society, because essentially they are incommensurable" (p. 223). Benedict spoke a central claim of the emerging cultural relativism: a culture is unique, outside the realm of judgment. Some, like the linguist Edward Sapir, thought that Benedict had abstracted culture from the individuals who created it. Others, including Mead, later argued that cultural integrity does not necessarily mean acceptability in an international context.

Although Benedict did not idealize the cultures she studied, her main goal was to make her readers "culture-conscious" by appreciating differences and reflecting back on their own society. Benedict thought this effort was particularly urgent in the modern world, with increased contact among peoples and rapidly changing cultural standards:

> Social thinking at the present time has no more important task before it than that of taking adequate account of cultural relativity. . . . The recognition of cultural relativity carries with it its own values, which need not be those of the absolute philosopher. . . . We shall arrive then at a more realistic social faith, accepting as grounds of hope and as new bases for tolerance the coexisting and equally valid patterns of life which mankind has created for itself from the raw materials of existence (p. 278).

Benedict extended her earlier work on cultural integration to the newer area of national character studies, exemplified by her book on the Japanese, *The Chrysanthemum and the Sword* (1946). Ironically, her liberal pleas for tolerance became the theoretical basis for cultural relativism just as it reached its most problematic historical moment during and after World War II.

Melville Herskovits: The Principles of Cultural Relativism

Melville J. Herskovits (1895–1963) was born in Ohio and originally studied to be a rabbi before abandoning his religious education in favor of history at the University of Chicago and anthropology at Columbia University under Franz Boas. He founded the first African Studies program in the United States at Northwestern University. An authority on African, Caribbean, and African American cultures, acculturation, and cross-cultural studies, Herskovits, of all Boas's students, was most responsible for articulating a theory of cultural relativism for anthropology. After the rise of Nazi Germany, which seemed to call into question the tolerance for different ways of life or at least to limit seriously the extent of relativism, Herskovits first clarified the concept of cultural relativism; a collection of essays, *Cultural Relativism: Perspectives in Cultural Pluralism* (1972), was published after his death. His initial work represents the high-water mark of early cultural relativism, presenting both its main features and the basis for the critique that has preoccupied anthropology ever since.

In *Man and His Works* (1948), an overview of "the science of cultural anthropology," Herskovits dedicated a chapter to "The Problem of Cultural Relativism." He began with a discussion of how people use their own values as criteria for understanding "ways of life that are different from [their] own." Based on "factual data" from field work that "permitted us to penetrate the underlying value-systems of societies having diverse customs," cultural relativism offered a solution to such bias: "This principle, briefly stated, is as follows: *Judgments are based on experience, and experience is interpreted by each individual in terms of his own enculturation*" (p. 63, emphasis in original). Significantly, Herskovits saw cultural relativism as a "principle," that is, not itself culture bound. He also emphasized that it existed *because of* empirical evidence assertained *through* methods, such as participant-observation, that allowed penetration of the inside of a culture. The problems of the "existence of fixed values" or "absolute moral standards," Herskovits thought, anticipating postmodernism, raised the issue of apprehending existence itself. Drawing on the work of the German linguistic philosopher Ernst Cassirer, Herskovits asked whether "reality can only be experienced through the symbolism of language. Is reality, then, not defined and re-defined by the ever-varied symbolisms of the innumerable languages of mankind?" (pp. 63–64). Although implying radical subjectivism—a system of meaning from which one could not escape—Herskovits, like Boas, retained a faith in scientific objectivity that could discover universals (such as moral systems) and particulars (their various contents) and challenge absolutism (a fixed standard). Herskovits also distinguished the "relativity of individual behavior," which would make it impossible to exert "social controls over conduct," from cultural relativism, which encouraged "respect for differences," tolerance of "many ways of life . . . [and] affirmation of the values in each culture." Herskovits's cultural relativism sought cultural universals and recognized cultural particulars. In the name of scientific objectivity, he set an agenda valuing tolerance and diversity. Against this agenda and the assumptions imbedded in it, debates about cultural relativism would forever be waged.

RESPONSES TO CULTURAL RELATIVISM

Cultural relativism developed to differentiate culture from biology and to assert its primacy in the creation of human societies, to question absolutism with universalism and particularism, and to challenge evolutionary, hierarchical schema with pluralist ones. Critiques of cultural relativism involved the challenge to culture as a central object of inquiry and a reassessment of biology, the reaffirmation of particular beliefs as superior, and the rearticulation of hierarchies. They also involved a newer critique of scientific veracity. By questioning the possibility of objectivity, which Boas and even his students had adhered to, this newer generation seemed to push the limits of cultural relativism's implications. If science itself came from a particular perspective, these postmodernists asked, on what basis could a particular argument be advanced? At the birth of the twenty-first century, the points of contention remain strikingly like those of the nineteenth and twentieth: the relative importance of culture and biology and emancipatory objectives, particularly the issue of human rights.

Clyde Kluckhohn: The Universalist Critique of Cultural Relativism Born in Iowa, Clyde Kluckhohn (1905–1960) was educated at the University of Wisconsin (where he studied classics) and Harvard University (where he earned his doctorate and taught for most of his career). His field work centered on the Navajo. Psychoanalyzed in Vienna in the 1930s, Kluckhohn was interested in both individual psychology and the psychological basis for human universals, issues that informed his stance on cultural relativism. With Margaret Mead, Ruth Benedict, John Dewey, and others, Kluckhohn participated in a conference on democracy and science just before the United States entered World War II. A Rhodes Scholar, he helped found Harvard's Department of Social Relations, where Clifford Geertz studied, and was head of its Russian Research Center. In these capacities, he was well situated to play an important role in post–World War II anthropology.

The universalist critique of moral relativism in anthropology, such as the assertion of shared values over the acceptance of particular differences, derived from the context in which Nazi Germany and the postwar Soviet Union seemed to point to the dangers of relativist thinking. The larger orientation of the period, its ideology of consensus and, in the social sciences, an emphasis on universals and social engineering, took a particularly antirelativist bent. As Clyde Kluckhohn said, "If one follows out literally and logically the implications of Benedict's words, one is compelled to accept any cultural pattern as vindicated by its cultural status; slavery, cannibalism, Nazism, or Communism may not be congenial to Christians or to contemporary Western societies, but moral criticism of the cultural patterns of other people is precluded" (*Culture and Behavior,* p. 267). The evils of the past seemed to result from the laxness of relativist thinking, while the bulwark against the evils of the present came from a return to moral certainty. "The one thing that we surely have to thank the Communists for is forcing us to take stock of our own position" (p. 297). No longer a source of cultural critique, as it had been among the Boasnians, the United States now seemed to be an ideal society, perhaps a universal model for all to emulate.

Keeping culture central, the postwar anthropologists redirected attention to the similarities among cultures that they thought had been neglected. A good example of this mid-century stock-taking was Alfred Kroeber and Clyde Kluckhohn's compendium, *Culture: A Critical Review of Concepts and Definitions* (1952). The cultural anthropologist Ralph Linton, who became chair of Columbia University's Department of Anthropology instead of Ruth Benedict, proclaimed in 1952, "Behind the seemingly endless diversity of culture patterns there is a fundamental uniformity" (in Kluckhohn, *Culture and Behavior*, p. 275). Or, as Clyde Kluckhohn said: "The human parade has many floats, but when one strips off the cultural symbolism, some of the ethical standards represented are akin . . . show[ing] their allegiance to a universal value; the prizing of the distinctive norms of one's culture" (p. 280). Tellingly, Kluckhohn turned the evidence of difference into proof of universals, criticizing the moral relativism implicit in early cultural relativism and positing a different concept of the human, a view of "human nature."

Biological Critiques of Culture

The concept of human nature involved a renewed argument about the importance of biology in human life, challenging the supremacy of culture within Boasian anthropology. If there were universals, the question went, on what were they based? "Ethical universals are the product of universal human nature, which is based, in turn, upon a common biology, psychology, and generalized situation" (Kluckhohn, *Culture and Behavior*, p. 285). Even Alfred Kroeber, who in 1917 had declared culture as "superorganic," now saw biology as an important part of human psychology. In the ensuing decades, comparative studies of human and animal behavior dominated biological and physical anthropology. The fundamental argument—that human biology defined the commonalities of human life and the limits of divergence from norms of necessity (adaptation to climate, need for food and shelter, perpetuation of the species)—remained a central thread in antirelativist critiques of the moral variant of cultural relativism and cultural determinism.

The revival of biological explanations of human similarities gave way in the late twentieth century to an interest in biological differences and, in turn, a revisiting of the whole issue of cultural diversity and hierarchies—epitomized by the publication of Edward Wilson's *Sociobiology* in 1975 and the 1994 study of intelligence testing, *The Bell Curve*, by Richard Herrnstein and Charles Murray. In the 1970s, 1980s, and 1990s, these arguments were a backlash against the social and political struggles of

the civil rights, antiwar, women's, and third world movements that destabilized the epistemological and cognitive certainty of the 1950s and early 1960s while reintroducing the importance of culture. They resulted, in turn, in a renewed cultural anthropology that reflected the lineage of cultural relativism even as it refuted most of its assumptions. The scholar David Bidney said in his 1968 essay "Cultural Relativism" that "all anthropologists are in agreement on the value of the method of cultural relativism and the relative objectivity required to report and interpret data from the perspective of the adherents of the culture," even if they disagree on their use (in Sills, *International Encyclopedia of the Social Sciences*, pp. 543–544), but within the next decade even these assumptions about consensus came under attack.

Clifford Geertz: Interpretive Anthropology and the Revival of Culture

Clifford Geertz was born in San Francisco in 1926 and has been one of the most important anthropological theorists and practitioners. His field work in Java, Bali, and Morocco combined well with his eclectic interests in interpretive anthropology. Stressing how people construct meaning through symbols, Geertz has raised important questions about how one understands others. In "Thick Description," Geertz used the British philosopher Gilbert Ryle's distinction between a wink and a twitch—one conveying meaning in a recognized symbol, one not—and the range in between that make up the "thick description" of ethnography: "A stratified hierarchy of meaningful structures in terms of which twitches, winks, fake-winks, parodies, rehearsals of parodies are produced, perceived, and interpreted, and without which they would not . . . in fact exist, no matter what anyone did or didn't do with his eyelids" (*The Interpretation of Cultures*, p. 7).

Interpretive anthropology arose as a sustained attack on both the universalism that characterized sociocultural anthropology in the 1950s and 1960s and the biologism of neo-Darwinians. Reorienting the focus to the particularities of individual cultures, Clifford Geertz returned to the priorities of the Boasians, by way of the functionalism of the American sociologist Talcott Parsons but with a different focus on culture: that is, interpreting cultures, those "webs of significance he [man] himself has spun," as one would literary texts. Geertz said in *The Interpretation of Cultures*:

> My point . . . is not that there are no generalizations that can be made about man as man, save that he is a most various animal, or that the study of culture

has nothing to contribute toward the uncovering of such generalizations. My point is that such generalizations are not to be discovered through a Baconian search for cultural universals, a kind of public-opinion polling of the world's peoples in search of a *consensus gentium* that does not in fact exist, and, further, that the attempt to do so leads to precisely the sort of relativism the whole approach was expressly designed to avoid. . . . Once one abandons uniformitarianism . . . relativism is a genuine danger; but it can be warded off only by facing directly and fully the diversities of human culture (pp. 40–41, emphasis in original).

Geertz's particularism did not admit the moral equivalence of all cultures, but it did argue for the irreducible significance of differences. The Balinese cockfight, for instance, is not functionalist evidence of status, Geertz argued: "Its function, if you want to call it that, is interpretive: it is a Balinese reading of Balinese experience, a story they tell themselves about themselves" (p. 448). In Geertz's refusal of holistic meanings, the anthropologist becomes someone who reproduces the "native's point of view" (*Local Knowledge,* p. 56) by "read[ing] over the[ir] shoulders . . . societies, like lives, contain their own interpretations. One has only to learn how to gain access to them" (*Interpretation of Cultures,* pp. 452–453). Unlike the first generation, who compared others' cultural worlds to their own society—the double-edged sword of cultural relativism—for Geertz, cultural particulars remained resolutely particular worlds. Geertz's ambivalence about the problem is reflected in the double negative of his 1984 essay, "Anti Anti-Relativism," in which he distinguished an attack on relativism's detractors from a defense of the position itself. Dismissing fears about moral nihilism and paralysis that supposedly emerged from cultural relativists' inability to claim any moral position and value above others, he asserted the fact of diversity. The anthropological data, customs, crania, living floors, and lexicons, he wrote, were the fundamental material with which anthropologists must contend.

Self-reflexive Anthropology and the Critique of Objectivity
In contrast to Geertz's optimism about gaining access to cultures' inner meanings, epistemological and political critiques of the problems of understanding others dominated cultural anthropology in the 1980s and 1990s. These stemmed from the struggles of the 1960s and 1970s and the rise of a new generation of outsiders, particularly women and people of color, claiming authority and recognition. They challenged imperialism at home and abroad, deeply implicating

anthropology because it was practiced largely by "colonial" outsiders on "native" peoples. These critics differed from earlier cultural relativists who had also been marginal to United States society and the academy: this newer generation came of age in the wake of postcolonialism and feminism. Although Herskovits discussed the situatedness or positionality of knowledge in 1948, he had countered with a belief in scientific universalism: applying his critique to anthropology itself was radical. Paul Rabinow's 1983 essay on Boas and Geertz, "Humanism as Nihilism," while it repeated earlier charges of the paralyzing effects of relativism, now located the problems in Boas's universalist science and Geertz's emphasis on aesthetics instead of politics.

The self-reflexive turn in anthropology focused on the work and world of the anthropologist. When it appeared that there were no universals and no objective position from which to observe, relativism became merely the belief system of a particular group, one possible stance among many. Relativism itself was relative, and the relativity of anthropologists became an issue. Some scholars persisted that the effort to understand others was fruitful and worthwhile, but they were more self-critical. Other anthropologists, including James Clifford, George Marcus, and Clifford Geertz, considered how ethnographers write about their ethnographic experiences, and redirected attention to the process of constructing knowledge through the texts that they produced, rather than the field work experience itself.

The history of anthropology also became a concern among anthropologists, an effort to relativize their own discipline out of the universals of scientific enterprise by historicizing it. Salvaging it for a new generation of anthropologists, George W. Stocking Jr. documented the history of Boasian anthropology, including Boas's politics of culture and the struggles over the cultural paradigm within anthropology. The problem of cultural relativism also became a subject of historical inquiry. One answer to the critiques of relativism, objectivism, and imperialism was to reemphasize the tradition of cultural criticism in anthropology. The anthropologist Elvin Hatch, for instance, separated the philosophical problems of cultural relativism from its historical manifestations as social criticism. George Marcus, Michael M. J. Fischer, Richard Handler, and James Clifford examined how anthropologists used cultural comparisons and relativism to challenge their own cultures "at home." In this sense, the history of anthropology revealed the complicated ways in which knowledge has been constructed and has, in turn, constructed the identities of others—in ethnographies, museums, art, and the law. Significantly, one source of the more recent criticisms of cultural relativism's moral bankruptcy and failure to address economics and power extends from historical studies of the discipline. Each of these examples is a response to the dilemma of cultural relativism within anthropology: that it is culture bound; that it is responsible for an inadequate politics and social criticism; but that it remains central.

"Native" or "indigenous" ethnography was another response to the problem of objectivity. If anthropology was imperialist not relativist, as scholars such as Talal Asad and Edward Said have charged, then the "natives" should anthropologize themselves. A part of the identity politics of the 1980s, and a criticism of the privileging of views of outsiders, native ethnography asserted that those on the inside could better, sometimes singularly, understand a culture. One variant of this is the claim of "third world" anthropologists on their "own" cultures' interpretations and representations. Important examples of such endeavors include the work of Lila Abu-Lughod, John Aguilar, Soraya Altorki, and Camillia Fawzi El-Solh, Hussein Fahim, and Emiko Ohnuki-Tierney. Another variant is the study of "complex" societies, including the United States. These studies, such as David Schneider's on American kinship, Michael Moffatt's on college students, Richard Handler and Eric Gable's on Colonial Williamsburg, and Sherry B. Ortner's on class in American society, give Euro-American anthropologists a supposedly legitimate area of field work—"their own"—and break down the age-old distinction of primitive and civilized underlying much of cultural relativism.

The division between native and non-native, however, is not so simple. The question of who is "native" and who is not, and whose culture is whose, is fraught with difficulty. As scholars such as Alexandra Bakalaki have shown, "third world" anthropologists often move back and forth between the institutions in which they work and study and the field ("home"). For individuals who are living between cultures, the anthropologist Lila Abu-Lughod asked in her essay "Writing against Culture," for instance, "What happens when the 'other' that the anthropologist is studying is simultaneously constructed as, at least partially, a self?" (in Fox, *Recapturing Anthropology,* p. 140). In their recent critiques of culture as "place," the idea of the integrity of cultures that underlay cultural anthropology from Arjun Appadurai, Akhil Gupta, and James

Ferguson, among others, now focus on the globalization of cultures and economies and the diasporas of peoples. The divisions between insider and outsider are collapsing, or at least changing. In some ways, these recent studies return to an earlier variant of cultural relativism—as a method to understand the workings of cultural particulars, especially their relatedness, without taking them for granted as givens—in the wake of suspicion of grand narratives and doctrines.

Present Debates and Future Concerns at the Beginning of the Twenty-First Century The ethical quandaries persist into the twenty-first century, however. Neo-Darwinian emphasis on the primacy of evolutionary biology, nature over nurture, repeats the challenge to the supremacy of sociocultural anthropology in much the same terms as debates in the nineteenth and twentieth centuries. There remains a Manichaean divide between culture and biology in which Boas and the Boasians are often resurrected as the source of the current malaise. Similarly unresolved are the problems of moral relativism attached to certain versions of cultural relativism—the connections between difference and tolerance, understanding and condoning. If objectivity and universals are called into question, on what basis can political positions be advanced? Much of the 1990s work that explicitly links anthropology with cultural relativism does so in the context of human rights. As in early challenges to relativism after World War II, when the German Chancellor Adolf Hitler and the Soviet premier Joseph Stalin were held up as the extreme examples that destroyed relativist possibilities, female genital operations were the case for the 1990s that raised the issue of the shaky relativist and antirelativist foundations from which the arguments about human rights have typically been derived. If the old goal of cultural relativism was a liberal version of freedom, on what basis, toward what ends, and by whom can emancipatory struggles be envisioned?

Many of cultural relativism's contributions to anthropology remain central to the field, particularly the evidence and importance of understanding differences. Even many for whom the methodological shortcut of studying "primitive" cultures is both impossible and objectionable still employ Ruth Benedict's technique of "understanding . . . by a détour" to study complex cultures in a global context. Even native ethnographers who promised to revolutionize the perspectives of participants and observers employ the heuristic device of strangeness.

Finally, naysayers aside, cultural relativism will not go away because it continues to speak to contemporary problems. Significantly, the more polemical arguments issued by conservatives against cultural relativism as synonymous with multiculturalism, the destruction of moral, aesthetic, and racial hierarchies, and the threat to national self-definition look to the foundational theorists and practitioners for evidence of where they have supposedly gone astray. The problems of the millennium—racial, ethnic, economic, and gender inequalities, the rise of new nationalisms and a global, mass economy of diasporic peoples—are much like those of the turn of the twentieth century that provided the context for the first generation of cultural relativists. The relations between human universals and particulars, between cultural values and economic and political power, will remain in the forefront of public life and, with them, cultural relativism will remain an issue to be fought over.

See also **The Struggle over Evolution; Racialism and Racial Uplift; The Behavioral and Social Sciences** *(volume 1);* **Whites and the Construction of Whiteness** *(in this volume);* **Ethnicity: Early Theories; Ethnicity and Race; Race; Class; The Social Sciences; Myth and Symbol; Cultural Studies** *(volume 3); and other articles in this section.*

BIBLIOGRAPHY

Overviews of Cultural Relativism

Bidney, David. "Cultural Relativism." In *International Encyclopedia of the Social Sciences,* vol. 3, edited by David L. Sills, pp. 543–547. New York, 1968.

Boas and His Students

Benedict, Ruth. *Patterns of Culture.* Boston, 1959.

Boas, Franz. *Anthropology and Modern Life.* New York, 1986.

———. *The Mind of Primitive Man.* New York, 1911.

Herskovits, Melville J. *Cultural Relativism: Perspectives in Cultural Pluralism.* Edited by Frances Herskovits. New York, 1972.

———. *Man and His Works: The Science of Cultural Anthropology.* New York, 1948.

Liss, Julia E. "Diasporic Identities: The Science and Politics of Race in the Work of Franz Boas and W. E. B. Du Bois, 1894–1919." *Cultural Anthropology* 13 (May 1998): 127–166.

Mead, Margaret. *Coming of Age in Samoa: A Psychological Study of Primitive Youth for Western Civilization.* New York, 1961.

Stocking, George W., Jr. *The Ethnographer's Magic and Other Essays in the History of Anthropology.* Madison, Wis., 1992.

———. *Race, Culture, and Evolution: Essays in the History of Anthropology.* Chicago, 1982.

Stocking, George W., Jr., ed. *A Franz Boas Reader: The Shaping of American Anthropology, 1883–1911.* Chicago, 1974.

———, ed. *Malinowski, Rivers, Benedict and Others: Essays on Culture and Personality.* Vol. 4, *History of Anthropology.* Madison, Wis., 1986.

Clyde Kluckhohn and Universalist and Biological Critiques

Degler, Carl N. *In Search of Human Nature: The Decline and Revival of Darwinism in American Social Thought.* Oxford, 1991.

Kluckhohn, Clyde. *Culture and Behavior: Collected Essays of Clyde Kluckhohn.* Edited by Richard Kluckhohn. New York, 1962. Especially relevant are the essays "Ethical Relativity: *Sic et Non*," pp. 265–285, and "Education, Values, and Anthropological Relativity," pp. 286–300.

Spiro, Melford E. *Culture and Human Nature: Theoretical Papers of Melford E. Spiro.* Edited by Benjamin Kilborne and L. L. Langness. Chicago, 1987.

Interpretive Anthropology

Geertz, Clifford. "Distinguished Lecture: Anti Anti-Relativism." *American Anthropologist* 86 (June 1984): 263–278.

——. *The Interpretation of Cultures.* New York, 1973. Especially relevant are the essays "Deep Play: Notes on the Balinese Cockfight," pp. 412–453; "The Impact of the Concept of Culture on the Concept of Man," pp. 33–54; and "Thick Description: Toward an Interpretive Theory of Culture," pp. 3–30.

——. *Local Knowledge: Further Essays in Interpretive Anthropology.* New York, 1983.

Self-Reflexive Anthropology, Including the History of Anthropology

Asad, Talal. *Anthropology and the Colonial Encounter.* London, 1973.

Clifford, James. *The Predicament of Culture: Twentieth-Century Ethnography, Literature, and Art.* Cambridge, Mass., 1988.

Clifford, James, and George E. Marcus, eds. *Writing Culture: The Poetics and Politics of Ethnography.* Berkeley, Calif., 1986.

Geertz, Clifford. *Works and Lives: The Anthropologist as Author.* Stanford, Calif., 1988.

di Leonardo, Micaela. *Exotics at Home: Anthropologies, Others, American Modernity.* Chicago, 1998.

Handler, Richard. "Boasian Anthropology and the Critique of American Culture." *American Quarterly* 42 (June 1990): 252–273.

Hatch, Elvin. *Culture and Morality: The Relativity of Values in Anthropology.* New York, 1983.

Marcus, George E., and Michael M. J. Fischer. *Anthropology as Cultural Critique: An Experimental Moment in the Human Sciences.* Chicago, 1986.

Ortner, Sherry B. "Theory in Anthropology since the Sixties." In *Culture/Power/History: A Reader in Contemporary Social Theory,* edited by Nicholas B. Dirks, Geoff Eley, and Sherry B. Ortner, pp. 372–411. Princeton, N.J., 1994.

Rabinow, Paul. "Humanism as Nihilism: The Bracketing of Truth and Seriousness in American Cultural Anthropology." In *Social Science as Moral Inquiry,* edited by Norma Haan, Robert N. Bellah, Paul Rabinow, and William Sullivan, pp. 52–75. New York, 1983.

Said, Edward. *Orientalism.* New York, 1978.

Native or Indigenous Ethnography

Abu-Lughod, Lila. "Writing Against Culture." In *Recapturing Anthropology,* edited by Richard G. Fox, pp. 137–162. Santa Fe, N.M., 1991. See also José Limón, "Representation, Ethnicity, and the Precursory Ethnography: Notes of a Native Anthropologist," pp. 115–135; Sherry B. Ortner, "Reading America: Preliminary Notes on Class and Culture," pp. 163–189; and Arjun Appadurai, "Global Ethnoscapes," pp. 191–210.

Handler, Richard, and Eric Gable. *The New History in an Old Museum: Creating the Past at Colonial Williamsburg.* Durham, N.C., 1997.

Moffatt, Michael. *Coming of Age in New Jersey: College and American Culture.* New Brunswick, N.J., 1989.

Globalization and Culture

Aguilar, John. "Insider Research: An Ethnography of a Debate." In *Anthropologists at Home in North America: Methods and Issues in the Study of One's Own Society,* edited by Donald Messerschmidt, pp. 15–26. Cambridge, U.K., 1981.

Altorki, Soraya, and Camillia Fawzi El-Solh, eds. *Arab Women in the Field: Studying Your Own Society.* Syracuse, N.Y., 1988.

Appadurai, Arjun. *Modernity at Large: Cultural Dimensions of Globalization.* Minneapolis, Minn., 1996.

Bakalaki, Alexandra. "Students, Natives, Colleagues: Encounters in Academia and in the Field." *Cultural Anthropology* 12 (November 1997): 502–526.

Fahim, Hussein, ed. *Indigenous Anthropology in Non-Western Countries.* Durham, N.C., 1982.

Gupta, Akhil, and James Ferguson, eds. *Culture, Power, Place: Explorations in Critical Anthropology.* Durham, N.C., 1997.

Ohnuki-Tierney, Emiko. "'Native' Anthropologists." *American Ethnologist* 11 (1984): 584–586.

Ortner, Sherry B. "Generation X: Anthropology in a Media-Saturated World." *Cultural Anthropology* 13 (August 1998): 414–440.

——. "Identities: The Hidden Life of Class." *Journal of Anthropological Research* 54 (Spring 1998): 1–17.

Schneider, David. *American Kinship: A Cultural Account.* 2d ed. Chicago, 1980.

Contemporary Debates on Anthropology and Human Rights

Downing, Theodore E., and Gilbert Kushner, eds. *Human Rights and Anthropology.* Cultural Survival Report 24. Cambridge, Mass., 1988.

Human Rights Quarterly is an important interdisciplinary journal that focuses on developments in the United Nations and regional human rights organizations, and is a particularly useful source for contemporary debates about rights and relativism.

Walley, Christine J. "Searching for 'Voices': Feminism, Anthropology, and the Global Debate over Female Genital Operations." *Cultural Anthropology* 12 (August 1997): 405–438.

Part 12

THE POLITICAL ORDER

NATIONALISM

Wilbur Zelinsky

The usual practice in dealing with any topic whose nature and significance are open to debate is to define relevant terms at the outset. In the case of "nationalism," whether in an American or any other context, it makes better sense to take a roundabout route, to begin by viewing this complicated, fluid concept in historical perspective.

TOWARD DEFINITIONS

Obviously there can be no nationalism without nations, a phenomenon, as concept or actuality, that appears on the scene only in modern times, that is, since the 1600s or 1700s and then only in certain portions of the world. In earlier days the only social units or spaces that really mattered to anyone but some members of the elite were local or intimate: family, neighbors, coworkers, congregation, persons and places with range of one's daily, weekly, or seasonal action-space. The fact that political states have existed for several millennia in the more advanced regions of the world in various sizes and shapes does not negate this claim. The subject populations had little knowledge of, and less affection for, the ruling monarch or prelate and actively feared the demands and exactions of his minions, while the frequent battles between competing polities could generate tragedy and devastation but never patriotic passion.

The birth of nations is a transformation that came about initially in western Europe, something we can attribute to the confluence of several factors. Prominent among them were the growing complexity and productivity of local and regional economies along with technological innovations of all sorts but most notably in the realms of transport and communication. Perhaps the most crucial development was the advent of the printing press in the mid-fifteenth century and the inception of universal literacy. With the widespread availability of printed matter, and thus awareness of distant places, events, and ideas, the "imagined community" (to use Benedict Anderson's useful term) became a practicality, and the world witnessed the emergence of the first nations.

The most succinct way to define "nation" may be that it is a real or supposed community of individuals who believe they share a common, unique set of traditions, beliefs, and cultural attributes so precious that few sacrifices are too great for the community's preservation and enhancement. Such a package of shared traits and values cherished by a given group, one that sets it apart from all other nations, is normally associated with a specific tract of the earth's surface, although there are some interesting exceptions, such as the gypsies and many dislocated Native American nations. The commonalities in question may have some basis in historical or anthropological fact, or they may have come into being belatedly, the result of some spontaneous inventiveness among community members or imposition from above by an intelligentsia or governmental entities. But differences in the origins of these social artifacts are immaterial; the actual behavior of nations has little to do with their genesis.

The relationships between the political state and the nation are varied and complex. A single state may contain within its borders two or more nations that aspire to some level of political and cultural autonomy or even independence. Conversely, a single nation may find itself straddled across the territory of two or more sovereign states. The ideal case, however, is that of the nation-state, the situation in which all of a given nation is the sole occupant of a given political state, where regime, nation, and territory are fused into a singular wholeness. Such perfected nation-states are the exceptions; a handful—for example, Japan, Iceland, Denmark, the Malagasy Republic, Portugal, Swaziland—exist among the 180 or so of the sovereign entities today of the modern world as the result of geographic and historical happenstance. Some of the more powerful centralized states have energetically pursued the policy of homogenizing their disparate ethnic and regional minorities into a unified national society—the French case is the classic example—but inevitably with mixed results at best. But the extraordinary case of the American nation-state is even more instructive. Such sociocultural engineering takes a lot of doing, either by calculated design on the part of the governmental apparatus or via the collaboration, perhaps subconscious, of countless individuals and organizations in thrall to the *Volksgeist*.

"Nationalism" is, in essence, fervent commitment to the idea of the nation on the part of its citizens (no longer subjects), indeed its apotheosis as the supreme repository of social meaning and identity, in its extreme form superseding even traditional religions and all other personal obligations. Thus we can characterize nationalism as a civic religion. The terms "jingoism" and "chauvinism" may be applied to the more manic expressions of nationalism, but nationalism is not totally synonymous with "patriotism." The latter term may be equated more realistically with devotion to the locality rather than the nation.

The collective passion we call nationalism can flourish whether or not the nation has attained political sovereignty, but obviously it is most likely to climax under the aegis of a reasonably effective nation-state. It is essential to note that, despite family resemblances, not all nationalisms are the same. The specific ways in which the nationalism scenario is played out varies markedly from one state or community to another. Furthermore, the character and intensity of nationalism can differ greatly over time in each case, as the American story amply demonstrates.

THE FIRST NEW NATION

We can divide all the nations of the contemporary world into two general classes. The first, and by far the larger, consists of those that are traditionally rooted in whole or significant part in a discrete tract of land to which they have some ancestral claim. The less numerous second category consists of a number of transplanted or "settler" societies for which this essay will use the generic term "neo-European," even though one might argue the admissibility of certain overseas groups of African or Asian origin (for example, Haiti or Trinidad). In these instances, emigrants from one or more countries in the Old World have established distinctly nontraditional nations in localities far removed from the homelands, thereby creating new types of societies that lack historical precedent despite the obvious linkage with the natal regions. The United States is the outstanding example of course, but the list also includes Canada, Brazil, Argentina, Uruguay, Chile, South Africa, Australia, and New Zealand. One might add all the remaining republics of Latin America and the Caribbean, although at a minimum Mexico, Guatemala, and Peru could qualify for a hybrid neo-European/indigenous status; and such former colonies as Fiji and Mauritius with their mixed imported populations also defy easy classification.

The transition from colonial status to autonomy and eventually into some semblance of a nation-state consummation has not been problem-free for any of the various neo-European countries. Indeed Canada and Australia have not yet completely severed the umbilical cord connecting them to Great Britain. In the case of Canada, we see a country racked by a perpetual identity crisis, exacerbated, of course, by tensions between Anglophone and Francophone communities, and unable to construct anything resembling a soul-nourishing nationalism. Lacking national heroes, suitable totems, an unambiguous flag, and virtually everything else in the toolkit of vibrant nationalism, perhaps the most potent unifying factor for the peoples of Canada is that they are not part of the United States and do not wish to be.

That there is any American story at all to be discussed here is the outcome of an improbable sequence of events. Not even the cleverest, most prescient of mid-eighteenth-century observers could have foreseen the formation of the world's "first new nation" out of thirteen disparate colonies in eastern British North America.

These colonies, usually contained with ill-defined boundaries, differed in size, physical geography, resources, economy, mode of governance, and ethnic and religious makeup. Nevertheless signs of a nascent nationhood could be detected as early as the 1750s. The first Great Awakening of the 1730s and 1740s was a pan-colonial affair, and the religious fervor it kindled transcended parochialisms to nurture an embryonic peoplehood among diversified communities. The various European conflicts waged on American soil helped to solidify larger geographic sensibilities, especially the Seven Years War (1756–1763), when troops from various colonies converged, mingled, and fought for a cause that was continental rather than local. The process intensified the Crown's subsequent gentle treatment of the mostly Catholic Québecois, probably prompted by the need to avoid a standing army among a subjugated population, but one causing collective resentment among the anti-popish future Americas. And, of course, escalating grievances generated by perceived mishandling of economic and political issues by the rulers in London led to an unlikely bid for independence waged against the strongest military and economic power of the period. The astonishing outcome was that the colonists prevailed—just barely—thanks to a series of happy accidents and the quirks of the geopolitics of those years.

Success on the battlefield did not translate into automatic nationhood. For the first time in human history, the decision makers in the now weakly united thirteen states confronted the daunting challenge of composing a nation de novo. The outlook was not promising. Few or none of the conventional building blocks for nation-building were at hand. The novel republic resided within a poorly defined, contested territory abutting unfriendly British and Spanish possessions, its terrain lacking any meaningful mythical resonance. There was no hallowed history or collection of legends to fall back on, aside from what could be borrowed from the British chronicles. The founders could hardly invoke language as a rallying cry since, despite emergent dialectical divergence, the common tongue was virtually identical with that of their former masters. A varied set of American religions, also shared with the homeland, did not offer any dominant candidate for spiritual togetherness. Another formidable obstacle was the new country's ethnic diversity, even if one ignored the virtually powerless aboriginal peoples and black slaves. Although persons of English derivation were clearly in the majority nationwide, sizeable localized contingents of Germans, Swiss, Scots-Irish, Scots, Welsh, and Dutch had to be contended with as well as other smaller clusters of non-English residents. Further compounding the problem was the fact of serious economic and political instability during the crucial decade of the 1780s.

Amazingly enough, the founders and their associates rose to the challenge despite the lack of any antecedent formula. The essential strategy—in addition, of course, to the adoption of a clever Constitution—was the deployment of an armamentarium of symbols. The richest symbolic resource of all was the American Revolution itself. This convulsion was far from being an ordinary squabble pitting one set of belligerents against another or even the standard civil war or war of liberation. Instead it was widely recognized at the time and ever after as being genuinely revolutionary in character despite its limited bourgeois objectives—the cul-

mination of the Age of Enlightenment and the intellectual and social ferment of the period. The ideological messages have reverberated throughout the world ever since.

What set the American experiment apart from all other nations past and present was an electrifying sense of providential mission. As the highly self-conscious culmination of the Enlightenment, in which the inspiring examples of republican Athens and Rome figured so prominently, the revolutionary Americans adopted many classical motifs in their cultural and social lives, including styles in architecture and the naming of places, persons, and enterprises. This newborn community, this "City upon a Hill," a light unto the world (or, alternatively, the New Israel or New Rome or Greece) was verily God's Country destined to fulfill millennia of human aspiration. This was a society offering a compact to all the peoples of the world (but preferably Caucasians) seeking the blessings of liberty, opportunity, self-expression, and brotherhood. Although the credo may have wavered at times or been perverted in unseemly ways, it remained vital to the new nation's future, with incalculable effects on both domestic and foreign policy.

GENESIS THROUGH SYMBOLS: A LIVELY NATIONALISM

During or shortly after the rupture with Great Britain, a number of novel nationalistic devices were invented or preexisting ones refashioned and infused with greater vigor. Perhaps the most striking of the new contrivances was the national hero, clearly an American first. Paramount among these larger-than-life figures was, of course, George Washington. His enshrinement began as early as 1777, and for many years thereafter the celebration of his birthday was a central event in the nationalistic calendar exceeded only by the observance of 4 July, Independence Day (another American invention), in terms of loudness and exuberance. Furthermore, his demise in 1799 prompted what may have been the greatest collective spasm of grief in national history.

But George Washington was only the first among a crowded company of hallowed luminaries that included Thomas Jefferson, Benjamin Franklin, Alexander Hamilton, Thomas Paine, Samuel Adams, John Adams, James Madison, the Marquis de Lafayette, Kazimierz Pulaski, Tadeusz Kościuszko, Patrick Henry, John Hancock, Ethan Allen, Nathan Hale, Benjamin Lincoln, Francis Marion, John Paul

Jones, Nathanael Greene, and a veritable battalion of other warriors (most of them conveniently forgotten today).

Although no national anthem was adopted during the initial burst of nationalistic exultation in emulation of the United Kingdom's "God Save the King" (evidently a British innovation), this period did experience an explosion of political ditties and triumphalistic verse. Historians followed suit with chronicles of events that were essentially panegyrics to the American cause, as did the authors of school texts and readers. It was also a golden age of political oratory as silver-tongued performers outdid one another in extolling the virtues of the young republic. Similarly, and building again upon contemporary European practice, the most accomplished of artists executed inspiring history paintings that quickened the pulse of patriotic citizens. On a less lofty aesthetic plane, many craftspeople created and marketed vast quantities of all manner of household and personal items adorned with a full panoply of nationalistic motifs.

Two of these visual props for nationalistic pride proved to be crucial in impact: the American bald eagle and the flag. Although the latter was relatively inconspicuous during its early career, the eagle quickly earned intense devotion among the nationalistic faithful. Other nation-states, then or later, may have adopted a totemistic creature as their emblem, but none, it may be safely said, achieved quite the spectacular adulation this bird of prey managed to excite. Somehow it symbolizes, at least in its initial incarnation, the very idea of liberty and whatever it is that we define as the American Dream. But not to be overlooked is another embodiment of the national ethos and identity: Miss Liberty. As a figure bearing an ideological message, rather than just an identity tag for a country, à la Britain's John Bull, she qualifies as elder sister to France's Marianne, who originated during the French Revolution and whose visage, crowned with the liberty cap, remains prominent on the French scene to this day. This was one of the many complex interconnections between two momentous revolutions: the American and French.

In contrast to the modern-day American landscape, there were few obvious manifestations of nationalism on public view during the early decades of independence. A feeble federal regime with a skeletal workforce supported by a puny army and navy was not yet especially visible. The one interesting immediate exception to this generalization took the form of a burst of enthusiasm for things classical in keeping with the self-image of America as the modern Greece and Rome; thus in the early nineteenth century there came about a widespread vogue far classical revival architecture with a specifically American flavor in the more pretentious of residential structures and such public buildings as were erected. In parallel fashion, this period witnessed a veritable epidemic of place-names referring to the ancient Mediterranean world along with a similar fad in personal names.

But there was still another landscape development dating from the infancy of the nation, indeed something mandated by the Constitution, a project that was later to play a most conspicuous role in the nationalistic agenda: the creation of a capital city for the nation. And, in a manner reminiscent of the nation itself, it was to arise de novo on a site where no urban center had previously existed. This notion may not have been completely original, given the building of St. Petersburg (which, incidentally, never totally replaced Moscow as Russia's symbolic center) several decades earlier, but its execution was innovative indeed and provided a model that was later emulated by other countries. But, however bold and grandiose was the city plan designed by Pierre Charles L'Enfant, the national capital was a sorry sight in its early years. It was not until the Civil War and thereafter that Washington, D.C., began to consummate the aspirations of its founders by turning into the symbolically potent heart of the civil religion that it emphatically is today.

The period under discussion, roughly the 1780s through the 1820s, experienced the apogee of the primal version of American nationalism. It was then that spontaneous devotion to the ideals of the Revolution permeated the masses and indeed reached fever pitch. Despite nontrivial class, sectional, and political differences, the population as a whole was as one in its worship of the heroes and principles that had brought their unique polity into being, and they gloried in it with little need for prompting from above. In terms of fundamental ideological temper, it was as homogenous a public as the country has ever seen. Those loyal to the Crown had taken their leave en masse during and just after the Revolution, and immigration from abroad was at its lowest ebb ever. If there was a climactic moment in the biography of what might be termed American Nationalism I, it occurred in the period 1824–1826: in 1824 the aged Lafayette—who, as a heroic young volunteer from France, virtually became Washington's adopted son during the Revolution—conducted his triumphant tour of all the states, and on the morning of the sanctified date of 4 July 1826 both Thomas Jefferson and John Adams met their maker just hours apart, surely evidence of the providential.

STATISM ASCENDANT

With the passage of time and the departure of the first generation of American citizens, but, more particularly, with the advent of new technologies and the expanding wealth and complexity of the economy, some significant changes in the nature of the republic's nationalism began to take shape, even if quite gradually at first. Not too coincidentally, this was also the period when large business corporations, sometimes of national scope, began to flex their muscles. This new phase, which was decisively confirmed by the Union's triumph in the Civil War, might be labeled Nationalism II or, more meaningfully, "statism." As American statism approached its peak early in the twentieth century, there was a decided convergence with other relatively advanced nation-states in terms of both spirit and operation. Many of the peculiar practices that had made early nationalistic America such a special place atrophied or were transmuted into statist forms.

Perhaps the earliest portent of things to come was the invention of Uncle Sam during the War of 1812 and his steadily increasing popularity thereafter. Eventually eclipsing Miss Liberty as the visual symbol for the United States, this genial gent must be interpreted as representing the state (but not its pesky governmental apparatus), an ever more benevolent abstraction that furnished material and spiritual security and other blessings to those within its sheltering arms, shedding grace in a downward direction to its devotees.

Another less benevolent symptom of the changing times was a crudely expansionist mood, a belief in a Manifest Destiny whereby American hegemony and the American Way would be imposed upon an ever wider swath of territory and peoples, willing or not. With rather less swagger, this was also the time when American authors and creative artists of all sorts began the long slow process of overcoming "cultural cringe," that is, feelings of inferiority with respect to their European, especially British, peers. But full parity would not be acknowledged until well into the twentieth century.

The practice of erecting monuments to national heroes and ideals, a rather uncommon occurrence even in late antebellum days, became increasingly popular after the Civil War, and rare was the town or city without such a prod to the collective memory within its symbolic center. Historical museums and piously preserved homes and other landmarks associated with a receding, ever more mythical heroic past also began to populate the scene as did impressive federal courthouses, post offices, and customhouses. With the ceremony at Gettysburg, Pennsylvania, in 1863—in which Lincoln dedicated a large burial ground for the many thousands of slain combatants, the first such hallowed space anywhere in the world—the United States had pioneered the national cemetery, and a few years later created its first national park (Yellowstone, in 1872), two ideas to be adopted widely thereafter by other countries. The late nineteenth century witnessed the rise of veterans organizations and a variety of voluntary organizations dedicated to exalting nationalist, or statist, principles. Americans also responded enthusiastically to the possibilities inherent in staging world's fairs, a phenomenon spawned in Europe in the 1850s. In terms of bolstering self-esteem and advertising the material and ideological splendor of the United States, the expositions staged in Philadelphia in 1876 and Chicago in 1893 were resounding successes.

All this while the national capital was growing in population, political muscle, opulence, and architectural grandeur. Its assemblage of monuments, tombs, museums, awesome edifices, and other tokens of the civil religion attracted increasingly large swarms of the nationalistically devout, essentially pilgrims. A not-too-subtle shift in the character of heroes also reflected the shifting temper of the times. Instead of the political, ideological, and military stalwarts of yore, the public was mesmerized by business tycoons and technological wizards. One can also detect a transformation in the national totem. As represented in stone, metal, and other media, the American eagle became more muscular in appearance, like Uncle Sam the embodiment of the state, but no longer emblematic of the liberal, even revolutionary, doctrines of 1776.

Although many expressions of American nationalism generally paralleled or anticipated developments in other advanced regions of the world, there were interesting divergences. Largely because of the peculiarities of the national ethos, the United States never seriously considered adapting a centralized, government-owned and -operated railroad or telegraph system when those new technologies became so pivotal to the economy, nor did it subsequently. Similarly, and unlike most other self-respecting would-be nation-states, never has the United States countenanced having a dominant governmentally run radio or television network.

Perhaps the most significant deviation from the standard statist program is the absence of a uniform, centralized educational system in a land where school affairs are administered by the various states and their local school boards. Yet, paradoxically enough, despite the fragmentation and democratization of school governance, American primary and secondary classrooms have been remarkably effective in inculcating a single shared vision of national identity and purpose, in molding loyal citizens as well as training them in the three Rs and other basics, perhaps even more so than in the tightly regimented systems of Great Britain, France, or Japan. More is involved here than the use of standardized texts and readers or potent images hung upon the walls. Somehow teachers and administrators have internalized the mandatory unspoken agenda. At one time, however, during the early twentieth century, the program became quite overt as a number of municipalities set Americanization projects to hasten the assimilation process among adult immigrants.

The one aspect at American statism that is truly unique has to do with the flag. As indicated previously, it was at best a minor factor in the early flush of nationalism, coming into prominence only from Civil War days onward. But when it was fully unfurled, the impact was stunning. The persistent, highly emotional controversy over flag desecration and the perennial attempts to enact a constitutional amendment to deal with the matter attest to the flag's unique position within the American value system. In no other political state has the national flag become so fetishized, indeed transformed into a literally sacred object. Old Glory ultimately came to be displayed not only on all manner of public buildings but also beside commercial shops, churches, factories, and warehouses. It hangs in classrooms, cemeteries, and parks, as well as next to countless private dwellings. It is emblazoned on currency, stamps, advertisements, tatoos, clothing, and every conceivable sort of manufactured or crafted item. It is truly ubiquitous not just as the Stars and Stripes but in abstracted form as the red-white-and-blue motif that permeates so much of the nation's built landscape. This public display of the national flag has no other remotely comparable parallel anywhere else in the world. Another indication of the pervasiveness of flag idolatry is the Pledge of Allegiance. After its introduction in the 1890s, it was adopted by virtually every elementary school in the land, so that the ritual of reciting the Pledge and saluting the flag marked the beginning at every school day.

STATISM IN CRISIS

The statist phase of American nationalism enjoyed its heyday in the first decades of the twentieth century. It was then that the United States had emerged as a legitimate claimant to great power status, but, more particularly, it was the time when faith in the omnipotence and goodness of the American nation-state had peaked and was as absolute as its champions could ever desire. But trouble was on the horizon. Perhaps the most crucial of premonitory developments was the surge of iconoclasm among historians and other scholars, such as Charles and Mary Beard, Matthew Josephson, and Thorstein Veblen, who took perverse pleasure in demystifying and debunking the mythologized American past. Similarly, relatively few serious artists, musicians, or literary figures could celebrate any longer in uncritical fashion the hallowed themes of earlier generations. Much of the blame could be assigned, of course, to the aftereffects of World War I, to its senseless carnage and the collective idiocy of the world's most highly developed nation-states.

But phases in the history of something as complicated as nationalism do not begin or end on fixed dates; instead they tend to overlap. Amid the miseries of the Great Depression of the 1930s, there emerged a lively interest and pride in American folk and regional cultures along with other populist movements associated with the New Deal and something of a revisionist, more positive evaluation of certain aspects of the American past. In the next decade, the victory of the Allies in World War II meant that the United States had become the undisputed master of the capitalist world. This turn of events led quite naturally to a new kind of American euphoria, a mood that became outright jubilation and self-congratulation as an unprecedented economic boom soon followed the military triumph.

But when the dust had settled, it was obvious enough that American nationalism, or statism, had assumed a new and unfamiliar form. Since the country is still in the midst of that transformation, it is difficult or impossible to see it in proper perspective or even give it a meaningful name, but perhaps Statism II will have to do. The one key attribute of this latest state of affairs is a loss of vitality, the perfunctory way in which the rites of state adoration are now performed. The decay of Statism I is most obvious in the manner that national holidays have come to be observed, or rather effectively ignored. Such major anniversaries as Independence Day, Memorial Day, Presidents Day, and Armistice Day (now Veterans Day) are welcomed mostly as an excuse for an extended weekend, or are occasions for irritation when post offices and other government facilities are shut.

Hard statistics on voter turnout demonstrate a continuing decline in the number of persons performing this most elemental act of citizenship, a decline that reflects, among other things, disillusionment with, or active dislike of, the executive and legislative branches of government and its multitudinous bureaucracies. Equally symptomatic of general apathy concerning matters of national moment has been the demise of the hero. During the latter half of the twentieth century, not a single contemporary figure captured widespread adulation for more than a fleeting instant. Thus, in place of the outsize characters of times past renowned for statesmanship, ideas, the amassing of fortunes, or technological feats, Americans now celebrate celebrities usually drawn from the worlds of sport and entertainment. Moreover, few of them appeal to more than special fractions of the population or display much lasting power.

But however beleaguered it may be, the nation-state always has at its disposal one powerful device for whipping up blind devotion: the waging of war. This strategy worked splendidly during World Wars I and II and, despite the opinion of some skeptics, the Spanish-American War. More recently, if ever so transiently, nationalistic passions became incandescent during the 1991 Gulf War, thanks in large part to adroit manipulation of news and propaganda. But wars, declared or otherwise, can also be more divisive than unifying in effect, as was the case with the War of 1812, the Mexican War (1846–1848), the Philippine Insurrection of 1899–1902 that followed the Spanish-American War, the Korean conflict (1950–1953), and, most notably, the war in Vietnam during the 1960s and early 1970s, which contributed so mightily to distrust of, or disgust with, higher authority. There is no question, however, that international sport, as a form of surrogate warfare, has succeeded wonderfully in invigorating statist loyalties. Winning the World Cup in soccer means the world to virtually every country except the United States, but the equally content-free quadrennial Olympic Games are guaranteed to set off a maximum explosion of flag-waving by Americans.

We have, then, a country preoccupied with consumerism, sport, entertainment, and the pursuit of pleasure in all its forms, while the demands of citizenship and national loyalty speak much less urgently to the conscience of Americans, except perhaps for survivors of earlier generations, right-wing chauvinists, and some religious fundamentalists. In any event, one can soothe any angst about national identity and one's role therein by patronizing a Disneyfied theme park, historical village, or museum or by planting a flag on the lawn. Then on to the mall or stadium.

The malaise sketched above is certainly not peculiar to the United States; indeed it was pandemic among all of the relatively mature nation-states at the end of the twentieth century. Exception must be made, of course, when we look at those stateless nations in Europe, Asia, and Africa, or even in Canada (such as the Kurds, Basques, Bretons, and Québecois), still agitating for greater autonomy or outright sovereignty, or those instances where heads of state and their henchmen have scratched the itch of ethnic resentment so as to solidify or extend their power. But for well over 90 percent of the peoples of the world the issue of political identity and state membership has been settled and is of casual interest. Less certain is the fate of the nation-state itself.

TWILIGHT OF THE NATION-STATE?

We have today a rapidly growing literature on the problems besetting the nation-state that, according to some writers, threaten its integrity and even survival. For lack of space, they need only be mentioned in passing here. Perhaps the most immediate challenge to the supremacy of the state is the growing power, wealth, and technical expertise of a small number of multinational business firms that owe loyalty to no particular state and effectively defy serious regulation by any. Another type of impotence to be noted for even the most heavily armed of countries involves their most basic responsibility: safeguarding the lives and property of their citizens. Sophisticated long-range nuclear and non-nuclear weapons and the possibility of biological or chemical attack by other powers or canny terrorists render risible any claims of absolute national security.

Perhaps equally unsettling are those environmental concerns that transcend national borders and call for international cooperation for their alleviation. Such issues, along with a variety of social, political, charitable, scientific, technological, and cultural concerns have given rise to a great host of nongovernmental organizations (NGOs) and other forms of transnational networking that tend to diminish the strength and luster of the nation-state. The globalization of culture, with its special impact upon the youth of the world, has certainly worked against the interests of sovereign states.

Not the least of the difficulties they face is the simple preservation of ethnic, or national, identity during an era when massive new flows of unfamiliar immigrants, sojourners, and refugees are crossing their borders. This has become a worldwide phenomenon, but it is perhaps nowhere more noteworthy than in the United States, where the numerical and sociocultural supremacy of the Euro-American majority is thought by some to be imperiled in the foreseeable future by rapidly swelling communities of persons of Latin American, Caribbean, Asian, and Middle Eastern origin as well as indigenous non-European stock. The predictable nativist response has been a clamor for safeguarding English (the world's least threatened language) and restrictions on immigration, altogether a rather recidivist version of nationalism.

Predictions are perilous and probably foolish, but the most likely future for the American nation-state would seem to entail some form of multiculturalism. How compatible such a condition might be with nationalism in any of its current or previous guises is, of course, beyond conjecture. What is even further beyond the power of imagination is what new shape American nationalism, or statism, might assume in the third millennium and whether a persistent belief in chosenness will persist. The only safe generalization is that whatever comes to pass in the future will not repeat, or even closely resemble, the nationalisms that have gone before.

See also **Liberalism and Republicanism; Federalists and Antifederalists; Jacksonian Ideology; Whig Ideology; Agrarianism and the Agrarian Ideal in Early America; Expansion and Empire; Secession, War, and Union; Nationalism and Imperialism** (volume 1); **World War and Cold War; Intellectuals and Ideology in Government; Resurgent Conservatism; Artistic, Intellectual, and Political Refugees** (in this volume); **Political Economy; Government; Public Murals; Memory; Myth and Symbol** (volume 3); and other articles in this section.

BIBLIOGRAPHY

Albanese, Catherine. *Sons of the Fathers: The Civil Religion of the American Revolution.* Philadelphia, 1976.

Anderson, Benedict. *Imagined Communities: Reflections on the Origin and Spread of Nationalism.* London, 1983.

Castells, Manuel. *The Power of Identity.* Oxford, U.K., 1997.

Gellner, Ernest. *Nations and Nationalism.* Ithaca, N.Y., 1983.

Hayes, Carlton J. H. *Essays on Nationalism.* New York, 1926.

———. *Nationalism: A Religion.* New York, 1960.

Hobsbawm, E. J. *Nations and Nationalism since 1780: Programme, Myth, Reality.* Cambridge, U.K., 1990.

Nye, Russel Blaine. *This Almost Chosen People: Essays in the History of American Ideas.* East Lansing, Mich., 1966.

Shafer, Boyd C. *Faces of Nationalism: New Realities and Old Myths.* New York, 1972.

Smith, Anthony D. *Nationalist Movements.* New York, 1976.

Tuveson, Ernest Lee. *Redeemer Nation: The Idea of America's Millennial Role.* Chicago, 1968.

Wecter, Dixon. *The Hero in America: A Chronicle of Hero-Worship.* New York, 1941.

Zelinsky, Wilbur. *Nation into State: The Shifting Symbolic Foundations of American Nationalism.* Chapel Hill, N.C., 1988.

DEMOCRACY

Peter S. Field
John Louis Recchiuti

PHILOSOPICAL FOUNDATIONS: DEMOCRACY THROUGH THE CIVIL WAR

"Democracy" is perhaps the most protean word in the American political lexicon. Narrowly defined, it is the form of government in which sovereignty resides with the people as a whole and is exercised directly by them (as in ancient Athens) or by officials elected by them, as in the U.S. republic itself. The term is also sometimes used to denote a society in which all have equal rights before the law, and in which there exists no hereditary privilege.

Thus, for all the word's multiple connotations, and even though Americans have never in their history assembled to vote directly on issues of moment, the ultimate sovereignty of "We, the people," as enshrined in the Constitution, has been a fundamental and cherished principle since the nation's founding.

Virtually all Americans believe themselves to be democratic, and, at least since the age of Andrew Jackson and George Bancroft, have taken immense pride in what they consider to be their democratic system of government. For many it is the institutional embodiment of Thomas Jefferson's grand assertion in 1776 that "all Men are created equal." Associated in many minds with the similarly ambiguous term "equality," democracy for almost two centuries has served to differentiate the United States from Europe and the rest of the world. As imperfectly as it is practiced, democracy to most Americans is the government best suited to a nation of free people. It also represents the unique contribution of the United States to human progress.

The Framers and Their Views of Democracy

"Democracy" did not assume its expansive, positive meaning in America until the turn of the nineteenth century, when it came to represent more than merely a form of government. In contrast to later generations, the founders used the term derisively and narrowly. John Adams and James Madison, the most precise thinkers among them, understood a democracy, in which laws are promulgated by popular majorities, to be both necessary and dangerous. Democracy was required to protect the interests of the people against those of the one and the few, so some form of democratic power was essential to any mixed and balanced form of government. It was also inherently dangerous and unstable, as popular dominion threatened to devolve into mob rule. Relying largely on the works of Aristotle and Polybius, the founders hoped in the Constitution to establish a republic that simultaneously contrasted with the monarchies of Europe and countered the forces of majoritarian democracy in the several United States. As opposition to monarchy was nearly universal, the Constitutional Convention set its sights on limiting the ability of the common people to wreak havoc. Having learned their lessons by the lamp of Whig history, Adams, Madison, Alexander Hamilton, and John Jay understood that internal dissension brought on by democratic degradation posed the greatest danger to the survival of republics. Aristotelian and Ciceronian political theory unambiguously testified to the grave dangers democratic tendencies posed for republican regimes. Democracy more closely resembled anarchy than the republicanism the founders were striving to incorporate into the new nation; as Fisher Ames put it, "our sages in the great convention intended our government should be a republick, which differs more widely from a democracy, than a democracy from despotism."

The founders and their Federalist progeny believed democracy, as unlimited rule of the majority, did not foster liberty but negated it. "Democracies," wrote Madison in *The Federalist,* "have ever been spectacles of turbulence and contention; have ever been found incompatible with personal security, or the rights of property; and have in general been as short in their lives, as they have been violent in their deaths." Unchecked direct democracy constituted nothing less than one form of absolutism, which in state after state threatened the rights of minorities. Madison especially feared for the rights of the propertied minority that could easily be outvoted by popular majorities of debtors. The preamble "We, the people" notwithstanding, the framers carefully sought to minimize the ability of the people to practice their titular sovereignty. Accordingly, the Constitution granted the people direct election only of the members of the House of Representatives. Selection of senators, presidents, and justices devolved to deliberative bodies composed of the natural aristocracy, whose distance from the will of the majority the founders sought to ensure. If the nation turned democratic, they had failed in their mission.

In the course of constructing a novel form of government, the Constitutional Convention that met in Philadelphia in 1787 sought simultaneously to base power on popular sovereignty and to safeguard the nation against the danger of overbearing majorities. The new national government inhibited the exercise of power by popular majorities by several means, including the incorporation of checks and balances, separation of powers, staggered elections, and what the political philosopher John Rawls labels "side constraints." Grounded largely in the concept of natural rights, or a higher moral law, these fetters prevented even democratically elected governments from abridging certain individual privileges, such as those famously but elusively expressed by Jefferson in the Declaration of Independence as "Life, Liberty, and the Pursuit of Happiness." The founders specifically had in mind the right to property, which could be forfeited solely by due process of law. To this day, the government cannot confiscate property without compensation, wantonly take a life, or imprison citizens without cause.

The Antifederalist opponents of the Constitution exhibited a more sanguine view of the American people and democracy. Ever fearful of the power of government and entrenched elites, Samuel Adams and Patrick Henry pilloried the conservatism of their opponents. Largely without success, they strove to make the states, with their more representative legislative bodies, the locus of political power in the new nation. It was their hope that all the states would follow the example of Pennsylvania, which for a brief period adopted a unicameral legislature and a weak, rotating executive. Antifederalists believed that because states were closer to the people, they would ensure the effective application of the principle of popular sovereignty to the emerging ruling structures and institutions. Nevertheless, even the most radically egalitarian of the Antifederalists sought nothing more than a government responsive to the will of the majority of white males of the several states. No one advocated anything approximating a multiracial polity in which a polyglot amalgam of women as well as men enjoyed full political rights.

Antifederalists notwithstanding, in no small measure the very success of the American Revolution and the subsequent adoption of the Constitution resulted from a crucial moment of consensus among most Americans, the vast majority of whom believed wholeheartedly in republican ideals. There existed fundamental agreement concerning natural rights, popular sovereignty, mixed government, and separation of powers. The consensus surrounding these republican principles helped to minimize political conflict in the decades immediately after Independence as Americans went about the business of writing state constitutions and twice creating a national government. The significance of this republican consensus is hard to overestimate, especially in the 1790s, with the advent Jeffersonian opposition to the Federalist administrations of Washington and Adams. Consensus on political terminology, though not its meanings, resulted in Federalists and Jeffersonians alike claiming to be the protectors of the true republic while elementally disagreeing on the definition of republicanism.

In order to fight their Federalist opponents and their scheme of the Hamiltonian finance, Madison and Jefferson turned to the semantics of the defeated Antifederalists. Hardly enamoured of genuine democracy, Jeffersonians increasingly deployed the term in their Democratic Clubs and in the Democratic-Republican Party in order to make utterly unmistakable the distinction between themselves and their elitist Federalist antagonists. Whereas Federalists like John Adams and Fisher Ames championed those elements in republicanism that served as the essential counterpoise to the tyranny of a democratic majority, the Jeffersonians increasingly emphasized the democratic aspects of their brand of republicanism. Jefferson and Madison and their Democratic-Republican allies appealed to a broader coalition of farmers, freemen, and artisans than did the Federalists, to be sure, but they were hardly democratic. Nevertheless, in what Jefferson styled the "Revolution of 1800," the Democratic-Republicans vanquished the Federalists by brilliantly playing up the democratic rhetoric of their republican ideals. By 1820, the founders' debates over the meaning of republicanism had reached their denouement, with the Jeffersonian definition triumphant. Jeffersonians meant by democracy—an increasingly amorphous and ideological term—something akin to a yeoman republic of independent freeholders. Increasingly, political leaders successfully employed the term not only as a counterbalance to aristocracy, as they had since the time of the revolution, but as a cudgel to attack all remnants of deferential politics. In the history of the mutating definition of democracy, Jeffersonians bridged the eighteenth century's narrow political meaning and the nineteenth century's far broader Jacksonian social construction. No sooner had democracy become part of the lexicon of party competition than its precise eighteenth-century denotation vanished.

Jacksonian Democracy The triumph of the Democratic-Republicans over the Federalists in the name of popular sovereignty—which by no means required any form of democracy—had dramatic if unintended consequences. The first third of the nineteenth century saw Federalist-era restrictions on the franchise give way and participation in national elections skyrocket, especially with the emergence of Andrew Jackson as the nation's most popular political figure. Old states followed new ones of the South and West in doing away with property qualifications and in granting universal manhood franchise. By 1854, all the states had eliminated property restrictions on suffrage; only some forms of poll taxes inhibited white males from the franchise. Similarly, an overwhelming majority of eligible voters cast ballots in the presidential elections between 1828 and 1860. As Honore-Gabriel de Riquette, comte de Mirabeau, wrote, "words are things," and Jeffersonians' almost interchangeable use of the words "democracy" and "popular sovereignty" precipitated a new era of participatory politics in the United States.

With the emergence of the Democratic Party and a full-fledged new party system in the 1830s and 1840s, national parties came to play an increasingly central role in American politics. The relationship of the Whigs and Democrats to democracy proved ambiguous at best, with the leadership of both parties claiming to be the true defenders of the people. They catered to the interests of the elites who controlled them but nonetheless unintentionally democratized the national government. As the national parties became machines intent on winning millions of votes, they fostered the liberalization of the franchise and a quantum leap in popular participation in the political process. More importantly, they undermined the founders' attempts to separate senators and presidents from popular influence, thus subverting the deliberative element

Théodore Chassériau, *Alexis de Tocqueville,* **1844.** Tocqueville sat for this portrait four years after he finished *Democracy in America.* © BETTMANN/CORBIS

that the framers had sought to incorporate into the electoral college and the senate. Even as party operatives manipulated these fledgling national institutions, popular nominations, caucuses, and grassroots organization encouraged greater popular regard for and participation in the political process. Generations of historians have attested to the significance of this opening of American politics by labeling the period "Jacksonian democracy."

In rhetoric that originated with Jefferson and reached its apotheosis in Alexis de Tocqueville, commentators increasingly invoked democracy as something of a synecdoche for the nation, with the United States and democracy becoming one and the same. With the expansion of the franchise, Americans came to understand their form of government as essentially democratic; it was a commonplace to assume that the people ruled, even if not everyone assented to the Jacksonian nostrum of vox populi vox Dei. For Tocqueville and his contemporaries among American intellectuals such as George Bancroft and Ralph Waldo Emerson, democracy served as the touchstone of American uniqueness among nations. Whatever was right and wrong with the

United States and its novel political system resulted from the popular embrace of democracy.

The Impact of Tocqueville   Alexis de Tocqueville's publication of *Democracy in America* in the 1830s, after a visit to the United States early in the decade, altered forever the definition of democracy. Henceforth the term became even more amorphous, with its meaning expanding from its previous political connotations toward a greater social significance. For Tocqueville, whose work was more sociological than political, the open political institutions of the United States were less the cause than the reflection of American society and the novel American personality. Tocqueville's two-volume classic sought to elaborate upon far more than politics; its true subject was the new democratic individual, whose distinguishing feature was an uncompromising devotion to social equality. In contrast to aristocracy and its artificial constraints, democracy for Tocqueville was the natural relation of independent individuals.

Beginning with Tocqueville, and as extended by Emerson, Henry David Thoreau, Walt Whitman, and others, democracy no longer signified a form of government merely; it implied the negation of government. Democratic dogma relentlessly reminded Americans that they were independent. Unfettered by artificial aristocratic limits and urged on by a belief system that declared each individual equal to everyone else, they were free to pursue their interests with the knowledge that they possessed the competence to govern their own lives. Under this conception, democracy defined a specific type of society (of which the United States represented the first instance) that stemmed only in part from its political institutional structure. Democracy in America denoted a social state in which individuals related to one another as entirely free agents, all artificial relations having been stripped away. Social relations devolved to political ones, which were ruthlessly democratic. "In the United States," wrote Tocqueville, "the dogma of sovereignty of the people is not an isolated doctrine which is unrelated to the habits or body of dominate ideas . . . Providence has given to each individual, whatever he is, the level of reason necessary for managing his own affairs with regard to what exclusively concerns him." A passionate faith in democratic equality permeated virtually all family, personal, and social relations, as individuals interacted "without a common bond to hold them."

Anticipating Friedrich Nietzsche, Tocqueville combined his praise of democracy with some so-bering admonitions. The pervasive "spirit of extreme equality" could be tyrannical, as Americans might be willing to sacrifice freedom in order to maintain equality. What Tocqueville called "mild democracy" inculcated a dangerous form of herd mentality. Similarly, drastic material inequities that belied "equality of condition" were always suspect and might occasion impulsive popular political action. At the same time, with no other means to display their greatness, Americans were prey to materialism, hungering to prove themselves by the sole means available in a democracy, the acquisition of vast personal wealth. Tocqueville also warned of the grave risks equality posed to autonomous thought. Freed from artificial social and political constraints, democratic individuals hardly proved intellectually self-reliant. In the realm of public opinion, Tocqueville detected the tyranny of the majority that Madison and the founders had feared would result from political democracy. Emancipated from governmental constraints and enamored by notions of perfect equality, Americans sheepishly heeded majority opinion, against which isolated individuals seemed powerless. Released from governmental oppression, Americans submitted to a new democratic form of despotism, the tyranny of public opinion.

Emerson and Whitman   Although he too worried about the dangers of materialism, atomization, and isolation, Ralph Waldo Emerson proved far more sanguine about democracy than Tocqueville. Unlike his French contemporary, who envisioned the American democrat as a new type of social being already fully developed, Emerson assumed that his compatriots were only in the natal stage of an evolutionary process that would produce a new order of man. As a result, Emerson hoped that in time and with the efforts of democratic intellectuals like himself the dangers of democracy would be overcome. As a consequence the nation would become the land of truly self-reliant individuals, whose profound realization of their own self-worth constituted the key building block for genuine respect of others. Despite the dangers of democracy, Emerson claimed it was the sole political system capable of fostering self-reliance, because it alone constituted that "society in which the most important judgment made about persons," as the political theorist George Kateb put it, "is that they are of equal worth just because they are human beings." With its democratic culture and material abundance, American society held out the great promise of promoting community by encouraging individuals to valorize humanity. Emerson's consanguinity, which Walt

Whitman and many other antebellum intellectuals shared, rested in his faith that democratic culture had only just begun to transform Americans. Where Tocqueville saw the foibles of Americans, such as they were, Emerson descried the national promise of democratic individuality. "We think our civilization near its meridian," Emerson declared in his essay "Politics," "but we are yet only at the cock-crowing and the morning star."

In 1855 a struggling journalist answered Emerson's call for a democratic poetical voice. A resident of New York, that most democratic of regions, Walt Whitman sang a paean to the United States as democracy. Despite the Civil War, or perhaps because of its faint egalitarian promise of racial justice, Walt Whitman lyrically expressed the possibilities of a nation of free individuals, who could be as exalted as their ambitions. He created a new style, a new voice commensurate to what William James would shortly call the "booming, buzzing confusion" of American society. In his deceptively deep and ambiguous *Democratic Vistas,* Whitman gave the highest literary expression to Americans' vision of themselves as unique and uniquely devoted to an elemental equality. For Whitman and the nation for whom he spoke, American exceptionalism was rooted in that utterly ambiguous term "democracy."

The Civil War The Civil War powerfully altered American society, and with it the meaning of democracy. Americans on both sides of the conflict believed they were fighting in defense of democratic ideals. Confederates invoked Jeffersonian and Jacksonian cants about fighting an overbearing and tyrannical government in the name of the people, states' rights, and liberty. So great was this devotion to local democracy that some historians have suggested it fatally hampered the Confederate war effort.

Unionists initially associated putting down the rebellion with the democratic ideals of the Constitution and the legitimate election in 1860 of Abraham Lincoln as the sixteenth president. Lincoln eloquently and irrevocably tied the Union war effort to the defense of democracy in his 1863 Gettysburg Address, when he declared that Americans "highly resolve that these dead shall not have died in vain— that this nation, under God, shall have a new birth of freedom—and that government of the people, by the people, and for the people, shall not perish from the earth."

At almost the same time, the Emancipation Proclamation fundamentally changed the meaning of the Civil War, as it turned soldiers intent on preserving the Union into freedom fighters. As blacks joined the Union armed forces and the army became a tool for liberation of millions of American slaves, the Northern war effort emphatically became the engine of democratic triumph. After Appomattox, national adoption of the Thirteenth, Fourteenth and Fifteenth Amendments to the Constitution validated the Union definition of the Civil War as one fought to preserve American democracy. As significantly, it also set the stage for extending forcefully the Declaration's promise of "all men created equal" to every American regardless of race. At the cost of 600,000 lives, the nation seemed poised to establish in law that broad, inclusive, and national definition of citizenship that characterizes modern democracy in the United States.

EXPANDING THE FRANCHISE: THE CIVIL WAR TO NEW MILLENNIUM

Constitutional Expansion of Democracy The story of American democracy as it continued after the Civil War can be traced in part through the nation's amending of its fundamental law, the U.S. Constitution. No less than nine of the fifteen constitutional amendments adopted in the 135 years from 1865 to 2000 directly address the question of democracy. Americans of African ancestry were welcomed into the democratic process by the Thirteenth (1865), Fourteenth (1868), and Fifteenth (1870) amendments to the U.S. Constitution, which ended slavery, welcomed ex-slaves to national citizenship, and universalized male suffrage, respectively. Fifty years later, passage of the Nineteenth Amendment (1920) guaranteed women the same right, which meant that now all American adult citizens, regardless of their race or sex, were legally welcomed by the U.S. Constitution to participate in the nation's democracy. Never before had the world seen such a broadly conceived democratic franchise in such a culturally, ethnically, and socially diverse polity.

Democracy at the ballot box was extended by other measures as well. In 1913 adoption of the Seventeenth Amendment made direct election of U.S. Senators law. In 1951, after Franklin D. Roosevelt had been four times elected president, the Twenty-second Amendment limited a president's terms to two, thereby avoiding potential future cult-of-personality problems. In 1961, the Twenty-third Amendment granted citizens in the District of Columbia three electoral votes for president, thus quieting, though not extinguishing, the cry "No taxation without representation." (The District of Columbia still has only a single, nonvoting member in Congress.) In 1964 the Twenty-fourth Amendment rendered the poll tax unconstitutional and heralded a new era in American civil rights and democracy. In 1971, during the Vietnam War, the Twenty-sixth Amendment lowered the voting age to include eighteen-year-olds. Although many of these amendments were relatively minor adjustments in comparison with the increases in ballot-box democracy afforded by the Fifteenth and Nineteenth amendments, they demonstrated a dedication to an ever-expanding democratic inclusiveness that characterized the post–Civil War America.

Exclusion of African Americans Constitutional expansions in the right to vote tell only part of the story of post–Civil War American democracy, however. Although African Americans were constitutionally guaranteed the right to vote in 1870, in the decades that followed they were systematically denied this right, especially in the American South. Through a complex web of state laws and extralegal tactics ranging from hectoring to lynching, whites conspired to keep Americans of African ancestry from the polls. Beginning with the Mississippi Plan of 1890, a baroque series of regulations made registering to vote increasingly difficult in many southern states. Would-be voters had to pass literacy tests, prove that their grandfather had been able to vote, or pay a poll tax for the privilege of voting.

Democracy in the Gilded Age and Progressive Era In the late nineteenth and early twentieth centuries, immigration, urbanization, and industrialization also shaped American democracy. Beginning in the 1880s "new immigrants" from southern and eastern Europe rekindled an older political movement against newcomers—especially Asians, Catholics, and Jews—judged by nativists of Protestant religious faith to be a detriment to the nation's democracy. Urbanization gave rise to the political boss and to a political corruption in the nation's cities at once expressive of, and antiethical to, the nation's democratic ethos.

Further, new concentrations of power and money attendant upon industrialization led to what many political reformers saw as the corruption of democracy by capitalism and capitalism's quislings. The wealth and power of capitalists such as Andrew Carnegie and J. P. Morgan meant that they could buy influence in government in ways not available to the average citizen. Increasingly throughout the nineteenth and early twentieth centuries, political radicals such as Eugene Victor Debs and Morris Hillquit charged that inequitable distribution of wealth made a mockery of democracy. (One estimate of the distribution of wealth in the U.S. at the end of the nineteenth century suggested that 1.4 percent of the people owned 70 percent of the nation's wealth.) When the distribution of wealth was highly skewed, democracy gave way to oligarchy, such radicals argued. For socialists and political progressives a more equitable distribution of wealth was prerequisite to commensurable democratic freedoms among citizens.

The late nineteenth century also saw the rise of the Populists, a democratically inspired movement largely among America's farmers. Populists hoped to use the power of democracy—especially the power of their members' votes—to craft legislation favorable to America's producers (farmers and workers) through such initiatives as government ownership of the railroads; a subtreasury plan through which government would subsidize the building of storage facilities for farmers' harvests as well as underwrite discounted loans, free coinage of silver, the eight-hour day, and a graduated income tax. In nineteenth- and early-twentieth-century America a majority of Americans lived in rural areas, and Populists hoped to grow a communitarian democracy among this majority. In the rising tide of industrialization, however, Populists proved to be fighting a rearguard political campaign. The agrarian-based democratic culture celebrated by Jefferson as symbol and substance of American democracy had run aground on the shoals of industrial capitalism.

During the Progressive Era (1895–1917), even as the systematic exclusion of Americans of African ancestry continued at the ballot box, the democratic nature of the American electoral process expanded in other areas. The direct primary, as well as the initiative, referendum, and recall were adopted in many states during these years, and the Seventeenth Amendment was adopted.

In the Progressive Era there arose as well the paradox of democratic elitism. Social scientists and other intellectuals, emphasizing the importance of their science-based expertise, were committed to the view that they constituted an entitled elite that ought direct the nation's political policy agenda. Yet these same intellectuals were often also committed to democracy—government of, by, and for the people, which for these men and women inherently posed the danger of rule by the uneducated and ill-informed at the expense of what was known to be best by the educated and informed few. Some resolved this paradox by concluding that experts ought to lead. As the economist E. R. A. Seligman wrote in 1916, "the university spirit is jeopardized by democracy, no less than by autocracy. For democracy levels down as well as up, and is proverbially intolerant of the expert." Others believed that the demos itself would have to become connoisseurs of science. The influential journalist and social critic Walter Lippmann wrote in *Drift and Mastery* (1914) that "[t]he scientific spirit" was "the discipline of democracy, the escape from drift." In Lippmann's view, "the discipline of science is the only one which gives any assurance that from the same set of facts men will come approximately to the same conclusions." And, at least in his turn-of-the-century writing on the subject of democracy, the American philosopher John Dewey concurred, writing in 1902 that, "Because the public is so behind the scientific times, it must be brought up." The problems confronting society, he insisted, "are essentially scientific problems, questions for expert intelligence conjoined with wide sympathy.... Yet they are at present ... almost hopelessly under the heel of party-politicians whose least knowledge is of the scientific questions involved." Modern conditions, Dewey concluded in 1902, "necessitate the selection of public servants of scientifically equipped powers." In this and in other places in his writing, Dewey, the great philosopher of twentieth-century democracy, had a tendency to idealize scientific technique. Though, to be sure, democracy for Dewey took on a meaning much larger than the expansion of the franchise, or the simple goal of economic democracy. In Dewey's eyes democracy grew to encompass a way of life, an ethical development of individuals in community. In *The Public and Its Problems* (1927) Dewey espoused confidence in the public's capacity to overcome problems of expertise:

> Inquiry, indeed, is a work which devolves upon experts. But their expertness is not shown in framing and executing policies, but in discovering and making known the facts upon which the former depend. They are technical experts in the sense that scientific investigators and artists manifest expertise. It is not necessary that the many should have the knowledge and skill to carry on the needed investigations; what is required is that they have the ability to judge of the bearing of the knowledge supplied by others upon common concerns.

Dewey was sanguine about the public's ability.

World Wars and Democracy When the United States entered World War I in 1917, President Woodrow Wilson declared that the nation was fighting "to make the world safe for democracy." In both the first and second world wars the "fight for right" was cast in the language of democracy: We are democrats, our enemies autocrats. Wartime rhetoric about democracy, however, had the ancillary effect of increasing consciousness within the United States itself that for women and minorities the nation had not made good on the promise of democracy. In the aftermath of World War I the Nineteenth Amendment guaranteed women's right to vote. Advances in civil rights for America's minorities were achieved after World War II and during the anti-communist cold war that followed.

The Civil Rights Movement and 1960s Counterculture In 1954 the Supreme Court decision in *Brown* v. *Board of Education* declared racially segregated schools unconstitutional. In the years that followed, the civil rights movement, urged forward by the leadership of Martin Luther King Jr. and by the work of the Student Non-Violent Coordinating Committee (SNCC), pressed claims for the democratic inclusiveness of the nation, culminating in the Civil Rights Act of 1964 and Voting Rights Act of 1965.

During the 1960s, in combination with the successes of the civil rights movement and the growing women's movement, an increasing emphasis on participatory, grassroots democracy led to the rise of a counterculture that questioned the allocation of power in a democracy. Tom Hayden, a leading figure in SDS (Students for a Democratic Society), wrote the Port Huron Statement (1962) to call students and "an awakening community of allies" to the cause of "participatory democracy." In explaining participatory democracy Hayden wrote in the Port Huron Statement:

> We would replace power rooted in possession, privilege, or circumstance by power and uniqueness rooted in love, reflectiveness, reason, and creativity. As a social system we seek the establishment of a democracy of individual participation, governed by two central aims: that the individual share in those social decisions determining the quality and direction of his life; that society be organized to encourage independence in men and provide the media for their common participation.

C. Wright Mills's *The Power Elite* (1956) and Herbert Marcuse's *One Dimensional Man* (1964) fueled countercultural and New Left discussions of the nature of the nation's democracy. Mills identified the existence of a power elite who subverted democracy. In his view, the power elite "are in command of the major hierarchies and organizations of modern society. They rule the big corporations. They run the machinery of the state and claim its prerogatives. They run the military establishment. They occupy the strategic command posts of the social structure, in which are now centered the effective means of the power and the wealth and the celebrity which they enjoy." The other major figure celebrated by the New Left, Marcuse, offered a comprehensive critique of modern industrial society through a synthesis of Marxian and Freudian theories. In *One Dimensional Man* Marcuse argued for a sexual basis to the social and political repression of democracy in contemporary America.

In the 1980s and 1990s, debates about free speech and political inclusion continued, often surrounding questions of multicultural democracy and issues of diversity and conformity. One critique of democratic society at the dawn of the new millennium viewed daily life as a web of domination that suppressed critical dialogue at every turn. Contrarily, others celebrated the triumph of democracy as indicated both by the more than one hundred years expansion of suffrage within the United States, as well as by the spread of democracy to many of the world's nations.

CONCLUSION

At the beginning of the twenty-first century, despite two hundred years of progress in opening the nation's democratic institutions to all of its citizens, for some Americans democracy continued to be a promise unfulfilled. Low voter turnout was but a species of the larger problems of democracy in a nation in which there were minimal chances for expression of social or economic democratic alternatives. For others, however, America's continuing adherence to democratic principles signaled what was best about the nation. From uncertain beginnings in the eighteenth century, this nation's "great experiment in democracy" proved itself a beacon for nations worldwide. In the darkest hours of European and Asian autocracies in the twentieth century, democracy in the United States remained a guiding light. American democracy, too, for all its flaws, was central to the rise of the United States from third-rate power to its much-vaunted status in the twentieth century as the richest and most powerful country in the world. In this view, it is democracy (democracy and capitalism to be more precise) that has made America the City on a Hill from which the beacon of democracy shines bright.

See also **Liberalism and Republicanism; Federalists and Antifederalists; Jacksonian Ideology; Whig Ideology; Patterns of Reform and Revolt; Nationalism and Imperialism** *(volume 1);* **World War and Cold War; Race, Rights, and Reform; Intellectuals and Ideology in Government; Second-Wave Feminism** *(in this volume);* **Race; Class; Government** *(volume 3); and other articles in this section.*

BIBLIOGRAPHY

Barber, Benjamin R. *Strong Democracy: Participatory Politics for a New Age.* Berkeley, Calif., 1984.

Chomsky, Noam. *Deterring Democracy.* New York, 1991.

Colburn, H. Trevor. *The Lamp of History: Whig History and the Intellectual Origins of the American Revolution.* Chapel Hill, N.C., 1965.

Elkins, Stanley, and Eric McKitrick. *The Age of Federalism.* New York, 1993.

Emerson, Ralph Waldo. *Collected Works.* Cambridge, Mass., 1971.

Foner, Eric. *The Story of American Freedom.* New York, 1998.

Goodwyn, Lawrence. *Democratic Promise: The Populist Movement in America.* New York, 1976.

Hamilton, Alexander, John Jay, and James Madison. *The Federalist Papers,* edited by Isaac Kramnick. New York, 1987.

Judis, John B. *The Paradox of American Democracy: Elites, Special Interests, and the Betrayal of the Public Trust.* New York, 2000.

Kateb, George. *The Inner Ocean: Individualism and Democratic Culture.* Ithaca, N.Y., 1992.

Kenyon, Cecilia M., ed. *The Antifederalists.* New York, 1966.

Keyssar, Alexander. *The Right to Vote: The Contested History of Democracy in the United States.* New York, 2000.

Kloppenberg, James T. *Uncertain Victory: Social Democracy and Progressivism in European and American Thought, 1870–1920.* New York, 1986.

Nieman, Donald G. *Promises to Keep: African-Americans and the Constitutional Order, 1776 to the Present.* New York, 1991.

Rawls, John. *A Theory of Justice.* Cambridge, Mass., 1971.

Tocqueville, Alexis de. *Democracy in America* 1838. Reprint, New York, 1945.

Warren, Mark E. *Democracy and Association.* Princeton, N.J., 2001.

Westbrook, Robert B. *John Dewey and American Democracy.* Ithaca, N.Y., 1991.

Whitman, Walt. *Democratic Vistas* 1888. Reprint, New York, 1970.

LIBERALISM

Richard J. Ellis
Robert E. Hawkinson

In 1955 Harvard political theorist Louis Hartz published a seminal account of the liberal tradition in America. Writing under the shadow of McCarthyism and in the midst of the Eisenhower era, Hartz argued provocatively that America was now and always had been a liberal society. Absent feudalism, the United States never developed the powerful, class conscious socialist movements and political parties that played so prominent a part in the politics of Europe. From the Revolution on, America had been a nation with only one political tradition worthy of the name: liberalism.

If Hartz was right, then the history of liberalism in America is nothing less than the history of American political thought. If the nation's major political parties and thinkers have always been hedged within the walls of the liberal tradition, the task of relating the story of American liberalism seems both daunting and tedious—daunting since nothing of importance is beyond the scope of the narrative; and tedious because each political epoch or movement yields the same values and beliefs.

Much, of course, depends on how one defines liberalism. To many people the word "liberalism" connotes moral permissiveness, high taxes, and big government. This is the "L" word that George Bush famously derided and Michael Dukakis artfully dodged in the 1988 presidential campaign. The percentage of Americans in the 1980s and 1990s who called themselves liberal was less than the portion who called themselves conservative or the number who counted themselves moderates. In using the term "liberal," Hartz did not have in mind, as most Americans do, the ideology of the contemporary Democratic Party. Rather he used the term in its "classic Lockean sense," unclouded by "all sorts of modern social reform connotations" (*The Liberal Tradition in America,* p. 4). For Hartz, liberalism meant limited, constitutional government, political equality, individual liberty, and the protection of private property. Using this definition, Republicans and Democrats were equally liberal, Herbert Hoo-

ver and Ronald Reagan no less than Franklin D. Roosevelt and Bill Clinton. What made America exceptional was not only the absence of a strong socialist party challenging private property but also the lack of Tory conservatives resisting political equality. In Europe the paternal Right and the socialist Left combined to create a powerful state; in America, in contrast, there was only the liberal dread of government power. Never having known feudalism, American liberals were even more antistatist than European liberals for whom the state had been a necessary instrument to batter down the walls of the old order.

By placing American political thought in comparative perspective, Hartz brought into sharp relief the distinctive character of liberalism in the United States. In Europe liberalism was housed within specifically liberal parties, flanked to the left by socialist or labor parties and to the right by paternalistic conservative parties; in America, in contrast, there was no liberal party per se because liberalism constituted the unspoken premises and unconscious attachments of virtually the entire society. Hartz did not deny the importance or the reality of political conflict within America, but he insisted that compared to Europe the most striking feature of party conflict in America was that it generally took place within the confining boundaries of a liberal consensus. Hartz was well aware that his sweeping thesis exaggerated in order to show off the contrast with Europe. When Hartz proclaimed (quoting the French political observer Alexis de Tocqueville) that America was "born equal," he was cognizant of the huge political (not to mention economic) inequalities that were present from the outset in the United States. Hartz's argument that America was a middle-class liberal society was a comparative, not an absolute, statement; compared to Europe, America was exceptional because of the absence of inherited, hierarchical status and class distinctions.

Looking outside the United States enabled Hartz to see what others, caught up in the sound and fury of American political rhetoric, had often missed. Yet if Hartz illuminated some of the unseen boundaries and limits that participants took for granted, his vision also tended to obscure the important changes and conflicts that took place within American liberalism. Moreover, the Hartzian perspective ignores or slights periodic but persistent nonliberal opposition to American liberalism. Even if Toryism and class-conscious socialism have been missing in the United States, other nonliberal ideologies have posed serious and sustained challenges to fundamental liberal tenets.

WHAT IS NOT LIBERAL IN AMERICA?

There was nothing liberal about slavery. It violated every cherished liberal principle, self-ownership and individual autonomy no less than equality before the law and equal opportunity. Those Americans who sought to justify and sustain the brutal enslavement of blacks were quick to forge illiberal ideologies and policies. Southern slaveholders used government to censor and confiscate mail from the North and in 1836 they succeeded in winning a "gag rule" that prohibited the reading of antislavery petitions in Congress. Prominent southern propagandists repudiated the Jeffersonian cant that all men are "created equal," emphasizing instead divinely ordained hierarchies of rank, order, and station. Ideologies of patriarchy and paternalism—blacks were children, the white race the fathers—flourished in the antebellum South as apologists sought to defend slavery in the face of abolitionist agitation.

Hartz recognized the illiberal character of proslavery ideology, but viewed it as a fantastic "fraud" (*The Liberal Tradition,* p. 147). Southern political thought was a "madhouse" (p. 169), in which apologists tied themselves in philosophical knots trying to defy their links to a liberal past and present. Virginia's George Fitzhugh imagined slaveholders as feudal lords and dripped contempt for northern "wage slavery," yet most slaveholders bought and sold slaves like any other commodity and produced goods for the market like any other capitalist. Patriarchal ideologies may have been good for the slaveholding conscience and self-conception, but in Congress the most reliable and effective defenses of slavery appealed to the liberal commitment to property rights. Southern defenders of slavery who assailed the abstract rationalism of Thomas Jefferson using the conservative language of eighteenth century English statesman Edmund Burke were left

without an ideological lever to transform the liberal tradition they wished to destroy. For Burke, legitimate change was never revolutionary but always emerged gradually, with a profound respect for custom and tradition. Where the tradition is liberal rights and equality, reactionary conservatives must emulate not Burke but Burke's adversaries, the French revolutionaries who pursued radical change in the name of abstract principle. This is a trap, according to Hartz, that awaits all conservatives in America. The hegemonic power of Lockean liberalism in America is confirmed, for Hartz, by the fact that after the Civil War the South's "great conservative reaction" died without leaving any significant impression on American political thought.

Fitzhugh and other "Southern Tories" may have been "forgotten . . . with a vengeance" (*The Liberal Tradition,* p. 183), but it will not do to push ascriptive, inegalitarian ideologies to the sidelines of American political thought. As Rogers Smith has emphasized, ascriptive ideologies justifying hierarchies of race, ethnicity, and gender have pervaded American political ideology and law. Liberal principles in America, according to Smith, confront not just illiberal practices or prejudices but principled, elaborated illiberal arguments. The story of race and gender in America is not solely one of hypocrisy, of liberal principles not lived by, but of rival ideological systems, of "multiple traditions" (*Civic Ideals,* p. 18). Ascriptive, hierarchical ideologies do not ineluctably wither away in the face of liberal ideals, because ascriptive ideas and institutions emphasizing innate characteristics have a distinctive political and psychological appeal that liberal ideas and institutions lack. Ascriptive visions of American citizenship reassure Americans that "regardless of their personal achievements or economic status, their inborn characteristics make them part of a special community, the United States of America, which is, thanks to some combination of nature, history, and God, distinctively and permanently worthy" (p. 38).

Yet liberalism in America did not only compete with racism, it shaped it. In the Spanish colonies of Latin America, where hierarchical distinctions and categories were widely accepted, slavery accommodated complex gradations among the races and between slaves and free persons. In the United States, in contrast, liberal principles declaring that all men were created equal ironically created ideological pressures for a more virulent form of racism in which the humanity of blacks was denied. Liberal precepts did not apply to black slaves because they were either animals, an inferior species, or mere property. In Brazil, for instance, where the humanity of slaves was conceded, the law recognized the sanctity of marriage relations among slaves, whereas there was no such recognition in Anglo-American law, which treated slaves primarily as property. Thus liberal democratic ideals have powerfully shaped illiberal doctrines of exclusion at the same time that they have often been useful weapons with which excluded groups have pricked the nation's conscience and moved the nation, however haltingly, toward inclusion.

Some of the deepest tensions within liberal political thought turn on the fact that liberalism cannot extinguish illiberal ideas and institutions without risking a fatal undermining of its own cherished principles. Freedom of speech means protecting if not promoting voices of intolerance, exclusivity, and hatred. Honoring freedom of association and freedom of religion necessarily means creating ideological and institutional space within which illiberal and antidemocratic groups and belief systems can flourish. Religious groups, like secular associations not deemed places of public accommodation, are free to discriminate and to show favoritism toward their own, just as they are free to teach servility and submission. Likewise, the liberal insistence on a boundary between public and private spheres permits patriarchal and authoritarian family relationships to persist. Liberals who defend this incongruence between public and private spheres necessarily protect illiberalism, including patriarchy and authoritarianism, religious and cultural fundamentalism, discrimination, and intolerance. However, liberals who insist on mandating congruence between private associations or relationships and liberal norms risk, in the name of equality, taking liberalism itself in illiberal directions.

The flourishing in America of multiple traditions, including nonliberal or illiberal traditions, is in part then a product of liberalism's toleration of individual speech, no matter how intolerant, of religious groups and voluntary associations, no matter how illiberal, and of private relationships, no matter how unjust or inegalitarian. Such indiscriminate tolerance has been assailed by modern-day critics of liberalism who advocate instead republicanism. Where liberalism privileges individual rights and the freedom to choose one's own values and ends, the republican tradition is said to privilege community, participation, and civic virtue. And where liberalism is neutral toward the values and ends its citizens pursue, civic republicanism avowedly "cultivates in citizens the qualities of character self-government requires" (Sandel, *Democracy's Discontent,* p. 6). While political theorists

debate the relative merits of these rival political visions, historians have debated the relative strength of these two political languages in the American past, particularly the eighteenth century. Historians touting "the republican synthesis," argued that in the eighteenth century Americans' dominant frame of reference was republican rather than Lockean liberal and that the colonists' fear of centralized executive power and trust in the civic virtue of a participatory citizenry bespoke classical republicanism rather than liberal rights. Some historians trace republican fears and faith into the nineteenth century and beyond; others believe that while America was certainly not born liberal, as Hartz believed, it quickly became so after the Revolution. Gordon Wood, in *The Creation of the American Republic* (1969), for instance, argues that the creation of the U.S. Constitution signaled the "end of classical politics" premised on virtue and the birth of a modern, liberal politics based on interest.

The efforts of political theorists and historians to distinguish between republican and liberal languages is a useful corrective to Hartz's narrative, but the distinction between liberalism and republicanism sometimes rests on a caricature of liberalism. Few real-world liberals are indifferent to character formation (hence their support for public schools and their insistence on teaching toleration and respect for principles of law and justice) or political participation (voting is seen not just as a right but as a public—though not compulsory—duty). Liberals care about both civic virtue and individual rights (see Isaac, "Republicanism v. Liberalism," p. 376, and Rorty, "A Defense of Mimimal Liberalism," p. 117–118). Fear of corrupt and centralized executive power, so prominent throughout American history, is as much liberal as republican. Only when republicanism becomes a shield for the bigotry or chauvinism of local communities intent on denying individual or minority rights—that is, only as republicanism begins to morph into illiberalism—does liberalism become clearly distinct from republicanism.

THE LIBERAL TRADITIONS IN AMERICA

Attention to such "liberal virtues" as character formation and political participation points to perhaps the most important defect of the Hartz thesis: its tendency to flatten out the liberal landscape, reducing it all to a monotonous, property-conscious Lockeanism. Liberalism is not and never has been one thing only. If there are, as Alan Ryan (pp. 291–

292) suggests, many liberalisms, we should not be surprised to find that in America, too, there has not been one single liberal tradition but rather multiple liberal traditions.

Among the most important reconstructions of the Hartz thesis was the one developed by the political scientist J. David Greenstone, who argues that within the genus liberalism are two distinct liberal species: reform liberalism and humanist liberalism. The humanist or hedonistic liberal closely parallels Hartz's Lockean liberal. This species of liberalism emphasizes negative liberty, the freedom to choose one's own goals unimpeded by external authority. The primary goal of politics is to enable individuals to define and satisfy their preferences. Preferences can be added up in either the marketplace or the voting booth, but no one can legitimately or authoritatively question the value of the other person's preference. Government may be necessary to provide public goods (roads, for instance) or to ensure that all citizens have an equal opportunity to satisfy their desires, but individual autonomy remains the primary value. Reform liberalism, in contrast, favors a more positive conception of liberty. Freedom for reform liberals means not the absence of external restraint but the cultivation of human faculties in ways that meet socially determined standards. In reform liberalism, the aim is not to do what feels good, but to do good. Politics is not about satisfying individual preferences but about articulating shared standards of what constitutes good conduct and then trying to live up to those standards, and striving to make sure that one's neighbors do as well.

For Greenstone, antebellum abolitionists (about whom Hartz had nothing to say) were quintessential reform liberals. The southern slave owners' preference for holding slaves counted for nothing because slavery was morally abhorrent. A utilitarian calculus of slavery's costs and benefits was equally irrelevant, as was the adding up of votes. A vote for slavery could not be weighed in the same scales as a vote to abolish it. Abolitionists recognized the slaves' right to be free, but they were animated by a duty to do the right thing, to follow the dictates of God and conscience, and to cleanse the sins of America from their own hands and the hands of all their countrymen, most especially slave owners themselves. Their sense of ethical obligation to others went beyond their aversion to slavery; they crusaded also against alcohol, war, competition, selfishness, hedonism, and other vices that prevented people from fully developing their human capacity. No one would accuse these liberals of being moral relativists.

But were they liberals? Is what Greenstone labels "reform liberalism" liberal at all? Or is it profoundly illiberal? Certainly the doctrine of positive liberty has its dark side—the willingness to force others to be free—but, in the case of the abolitionists at least, the vision remained identifiably liberal. To begin with, the institution abolitionists set out to destroy, slavery, was the most profoundly illiberal institution in American history. The subjugation of one human being by another violated liberalism's most cherished ideals. Moreover, prior to the Civil War at least, abolitionists committed themselves to achieving emancipation through the conversion of individual slaveholders. Their objective was to persuade slaveholders that their self-development no less than that of the slaves was dependent on abolishing the peculiar institution. The most radical of the abolitionists, the Garrisonian "nonresistants," opposed not only slavery but all institutions that coerced or constrained the individual, including government, the military, jails, political parties, even, in some cases, marriage.

The abolitionists can be viewed as paradigmatic reform liberals, but they were hardly the only exemplars of this Protestant strand of liberalism. The antebellum Whig Party, particularly in New England, was suffused with reform liberal commitments. From John Quincy Adams to Daniel Webster, Greenstone suggests, New England Whigs enacted a political culture that was liberal without being wholly Lockean. In contrast to the Jacksonian Democrats, for whom liberty meant freedom from "the moralistic meddling of the political community in private affairs" (Greenstone, *The Lincoln Persuasion*, p. 223), Whigs like Webster taught that to do exclusively as one pleased endangered the unity and harmony of the collectivity. True liberty, for Webster, meant not the liberty to act on one's every impulse but rather the liberty to cultivate one's higher self and thus avoid becoming a slave to one's baser passions.

Greenstone's bipolarity between humanist liberalism and reform liberalism, negative liberty and positive liberty, is an important step in recovering the diversity of liberalisms in America. But it is only a first step. Distinguishing between the Protestant and Lockean faces of liberalism, as Greenstone does, still leaves the Lockean mask over much, indeed most, of American political culture. Appeals to Locke and to Lockean principles have certainly been common throughout American history, but those principles have often been interpreted and invoked to advance radically different ways of life. Many Americans have certainly used Lockean principles to justify private property, economic inequalities, and competitive capitalism, but there has also been an egalitarian reading of Lockean precepts, a tradition that has attracted adherents in America since the days of Thomas Paine. From the Lockean premise that laws should secure to each man the fruits of his labor, American egalitarians have attacked large concentrations of wealth on the grounds that such holdings do not derive from productive labor. Locke's injunction that a person has a right to that property that "he hath mixed his Labour with" has been used to attack speculators, merchants, and bankers, and to uphold the rights of the workingman. A natural right to property has been employed as an ideological lever to protest an economy that left many landless. Even when Americans appealed to Locke, the radically different interpretations placed on his precepts meant that "the power of Locke in America" (Hartz, *The Liberal Tradition*, p. 8) was much less constricting than Hartz assumed.

Throughout American history one finds individuals and parties appealing to the same foundational liberal documents or ideals to advance dramatically different ideological agendas. All Americans quote the Declaration of Independence, for instance, but they frequently carry away fundamentally different understandings of those famous words, "all men are created equal." In the same way, the ideal of equality of opportunity is frequently invoked by Americans, but its meaning is rarely agreed upon. For some the accent is on the word "opportunity." No person should be denied the right to pursue the vocation or career of his or her choice. Equal opportunity for the individualistic liberal entails abolishing legal discrimination and government favoritism, and then allowing individuals to use their distinctive talents and abilities to achieve and accumulate. For other liberals the stress is on the word "equality." It is not enough that individuals be given an opportunity, they must have, as near as possible, an arithmetically equal opportunity. For the egalitarian liberal, inequalities between and within families, schools, and workplaces must be abolished so that each individual has a truly equal chance in life. Equality of condition becomes a prerequisite to equal opportunity, and unequal outcomes constitute prima facie evidence of an unfair process.

Democracy is another consensual value about which Americans have harbored distinctly different ideas. For some, democracy is primarily about competition and choice. Just as consumers express their preferences about products through the competitive marketplace, so voters express their preferences about candidates and policies through competitive elections. For other Americans, however, real democracy means direct, popular participation in the decisions that govern their lives. From the time of the Anti-Federalists through to the 1960s New Left, some Americans have derided representative government as "false democracy," an oligarchy in democratic disguise. From this perspective, periodic voting to select governing elites is less an expression of democratic participation than an abdication of democratic citizenship. Instead of being celebrated as a mechanism of democratic accountability, elections are criticized as a device for confirming and legitimating "democratic elitism."

Consensual liberal values, in short, are not incompatible with fundamental disagreements over the good life. A broad consensus on liberty, private property, equal opportunity, and democracy has not prevented Americans from contesting the meaning of these liberal values, or the relative weight that ought to be given to each of these values. Americans may all be liberal but American liberalism is not reducible to Hartz's monolithic Lockean liberalism.

THE DEVELOPMENT OF MODERN LIBERALISM

Hartz's liberalism is not only monolithic but static, roughly the same in the 1950s as it was more than two hundred years before. In Hartz's telling, American Lockean liberalism is an unchallenged and hence unconscious ideology. Unaware of their own premises and assumptions, American liberals are unable to learn or to develop. "A society which begins with Locke," Hartz explains, "stays with Locke, by virtue of an absolute and irrational attachment it develops for him" (*The Liberal Tradition*, p. 6). Later scholarship, however, emphasizes that liberalism in America has in fact been an enormously dynamic ideology that has changed markedly throughout the nation's history, particularly in the twentieth century. Although offering different appraisals as to the precise nature and timing of these changes, scholars generally presented a picture affirming what Gary Gerstle called "the protean character of American liberalism."

Nineteenth-century American liberalism was generally committed to a laissez-faire program of limited government intervention in the lives of the nation's citizens. The growth of government in nineteenth-century America was retarded not only by a Lockean commitment to liberty and property but also by a widely shared belief that government was the parent of inequality. Jacksonian Democrats, for instance, perceived no conflict between laissez-faire and economic equality, because they believed that equality of condition would be far more widespread if government stayed out of the marketplace than if it actively intervened. The natural propensity of society, as Thomas Paine taught, was toward equality. It was government, through favoritism, sweetheart deals, and the granting of special privileges, that upset "nature's own leveling process" and manufactured large and artificial inequalities (Ellis, *American Political Cultures*, pp. 43–62).

Toward the end of the nineteenth and beginning of the twentieth centuries, the received Jacksonian wisdom came under sustained scrutiny from those committed to greater equality. Inequality, it seemed increasingly clear to many Americans, had economic and not just political roots. Self-regulating markets and entrepreneurial capitalism might have many virtues, but creating equality was not among them. Or so it seemed to many turn-of-the-century reformers who began to think that the federal government might be part of the solution rather than the problem.

Hartz's caricature of early-twentieth-century progressives as backward-looking trustbusters, intent on restoring a nineteenth-century world of small property holders, does not begin to do justice to the rich ferment of Progressive Era reform. Far from being wedded to "American absolutism" (Hartz, *The Liberal Tradition*, p. 236), progressives were part of a cosmopolitan transatlantic community of reformers. Prior to the Progressive Era, Americans invariably and reflexively contrasted New World democracy with Old World tyranny. They saw nothing to be learned from European experiences, except perhaps the negative lesson of the value of avoiding standing armies, high taxes, and opulent governments. Americans looked abroad primarily to count their blessings. But under the spur of industrialization and urbanization, American reformers began to recognize in Europe common experiences and problems, and to look to England, Germany, France, Switzerland, and even Australia and New Zealand for models of industrial accident insurance, old-age pensions, and unemployment and health insurance.

Yet progressive reformers largely failed to achieve at the national level what their counterparts in other countries attained. In Britain, for instance, Liberal governments enacted workers' compensation, old-age pensions, and unemployment and health insurance in a five-year span between 1906 and 1911. In America only industrial accident in-surance was achieved at the federal level, although many state legislatures enacted other progressive labor and welfare legislation. America remained a welfare-state laggard, but not because, as Hartz claims, "Progressivism compulsively embraced the Alger ethos" (*The Liberal Tradition*, p. 235). Many progressive liberals, it is true, were wary of public social spending, but this caution was not an irrational Lockean tic but a rational, learned response based on long experience with veterans' pensions, which the Republican Party had used for many years to maintain its electoral dominance. If progressives worried about spending programs in the American context it was less because they feared a centralized state than they feared the consequences of the absence of professionalized civil service bureaucracies. For these reformers the primary task was to build up the state's administrative and regulatory capacity, not to reinforce the centrifugal pull of patronage parties. The ideology of the Liberal Party in Great Britain was not hugely different from the liberal ideology of the American progressives; what was decisively different was the political institutions that shaped what liberal reformers wanted and what they could hope to achieve.

Not that American Lockeanism is irrelevant to explaining the welfare-laggard status of the United States. Widespread public skepticism of government continued through the end of the twentieth century to act as a brake on what liberal reformers could attain. Even after the New Deal and the Great Society had radically recast the shape of American public policy and dramatically closed the gap between American and European welfare states, America continued to be distinctive in several important respects. First, and most notably, was the absence of a comprehensive system of national health insurance. Second, the welfare state in the United States tended to be far stingier and more restrictive than in other European countries. Unemployment compensation, for instance, lasted for a shorter duration and covered a lower percentage of a worker's wages in the United States than in European nations. Political institutions (checks and balances, federalism, decentralized political parties) matter here, too, but so does the power of Lockean liberalism, which enables opponents of these policies to sound warnings of "big government" and "socialized medicine" and play to the values of self-reliance and individual choice.

LIBERALISM'S WRONG TURN?

Liberalism's modern-day travails (no president since Lyndon Johnson has publicly identified himself or his policies as liberal) have induced many observers sympathetic to liberalism to try to identify modern liberalism's wrong turn and to recover its lost promise. For some libertarians, the wrong turn is traceable to the Progressive Era, in which liberals abandoned their exceptionalist faith that liberty and equality were mutually supportive, and turned their attention from power-restraining constitutionalism to power-enabling administration. Franklin D. Roosevelt's New Deal and Johnson's Great Society, in this narrative, were further steps along this mistaken state-centered path. Other scholars, however, portray a radical disjunction between the liberalism of Progressive Era reformers and the liberalism of the later twentieth century.

The historian Alan Brinkley argues that the critical transformation of modern reform liberalism occurred in the latter years of the New Deal. The 1937–1938 recession and World War II led reform liberals to retreat from their commitment to structural reform of the economy in favor of a preference for government spending. The earlier concern with problems of production and democratic control was superseded by a single-minded commitment to consumption, economic abundance, and its equitable distribution. The antimonopoly movement, for instance, which in the Progressive Era had been concerned with decentralizing power so that farmers, workers, small producers, and local merchants could control their own lives, was transformed by the head of the Justice Department's Antitrust Division, Thurman Arnold, into a crusade to lower consumer prices. Brinkley's lost liberalism is not an atomistic or reflexive Lockeanism but a democratic liberalism keenly attentive to what Michael Sandel describes as "the political economy of citizenship" (*Democracy's Discontent,* p. 250). Brinkley's account of liberalism's retreat from reform in the late 1930s and 1940s has much to recommend it, but there is reason to doubt whether American liberalism's political travails at the end of the twentieth century can be plausibly attributed to an excessive attention to economic abundance and consumption. Nor does it seem likely that greater attention to structural reform of the economy would help more liberals get elected.

The troubles liberalism faced at the end of the twentieth century are more readily understood by examining events of the 1960s and 1970s. Gareth Davies suggests that the pivotal moment came in the shift from "opportunity liberalism" to "entitlement liberalism" during the late 1960s, a shift that destroyed the Great Society and shattered the New Deal coalition of the Democratic Party. The New Deal's popular success lay in its ability to craft proposals for economic security in the individualistic language of opportunity and self-reliance. Social security, for instance, was sold and explained to the American public as a system by which individuals would save for their own retirement. The benefits an individual retiree collected would have been earned and thus deserved. Lyndon Johnson's War on Poverty was launched in the same spirit, carefully couched in the liberal language of opportunity ("a fair start in the race of life") that resonated with citizens. Other liberals, however, became increasingly attracted to a new brand of liberalism, one that would remove the stigma that attached to welfare dependency, untie the liberal knot between work and entitlement, and guarantee an income to all Americans. The guaranteed income movement failed and liberal enthusiasm for it soon subsided, but not, Davies argues, before it had wrecked the promise of the Great Society, created a public image of the Democrats as the party of welfare rather than work, and saddled the word "liberal" with the burden of welfare queens and deadbeat dads.

No account of liberalism's political problems would be complete without a discussion of race. No issue arguably did more to give liberalism a bad reputation, at least with whites. Passage of the 1964 Civil Rights Act and the 1965 Voting Rights Act was one of liberalism's finest hours, but living up to liberal ideals came at a heavy political cost of white support in the South. By defining liberalism almost entirely in terms of economic and class issues, the New Deal had enabled many southern whites to call themselves liberals, or at least to be comfortable in a party dominated by liberals. But as modern liberalism came to be redefined to include a fervent commitment to racial justice, the solid South began to crack. This much was unavoidable, but the next step was not. As long as liberalism stood for equal treatment and against racial discrimination it occupied the moral high ground, fortified by core values of American liberalism. But when liberals, frustrated at the slow pace of change, embraced affirmative action programs that classified, admitted, and hired people on the basis of race, they placed themselves dangerously at odds with liberalism itself and with the great majority of the American public who believed in "color blind" liberalism. The liberal language of "fairness" and "justice" became viewed by many Americans as code words for racial quotas and reverse discrimination.

Race is far from the only issue on which liberals have found themselves at odds with a majority of the American public. The rise of rights-based liberalism has propelled liberals to take positions on a host of social and cultural issues that are not shared by a majority of the American public. Public opinion polls in the late twentieth century consistently found that on economic and social welfare issues (for example, government spending to help the needy and the unemployed, social security, health care), Democratic Party activists had views that were just as liberal as those of rank-and-file Democrats. But on civil rights and civil liberties issues (for example, prayer in public schools, the rights of homosexuals, mandatory drug tests, police searches), Democratic Party activists had views that were far to the left of rank-and-file Democrats. Indeed the views of the Democratic rank and file on these issues were often closer to that of Republican elites than Democratic elites. Here liberals faced a genuine and intractable political dilemma: following liberal principles means taking unpopular positions in defense of often despised minorities, whether atheists, homosexuals, or criminals. Yet for liberals not to take those positions often means compromising fundamental liberal tenets.

Issues such as same-sex marriage or gays in the military reveal just how formidable is the ideological opposition liberals face, even or perhaps especially in America. Powerful nonliberal arguments that appeal to religion, morality, and tradition are successfully used by conservatives; prejudice plays its (large) part, of course, but at stake are also alternative value systems. Outside of the courts at least, conservative arguments based on morality and tradition do not wither or melt away in the face of liberal assertions of rights. The idea of liberal consensus is a liberal conceit: we have principled values, they only blind prejudices. Small and even great victories may be won by liberals, but there is no ineluctable, onward march toward ever greater liberal freedom. All of which makes liberalism's very real triumphs during the twentieth century all the more remarkable.

See also **Liberalism and Republicanism; Federalists and Antifederalists; Reform Institutions; Patterns of Reform and Revolt; Religious Liberalism, Fundamentalism, and Neo-Orthodoxy** *(volume 1);* **Race, Rights, and Reform; Multiculturalism in Theory and Practice; Anti-Statism** *(in this volume);* **Political Economy; Welfare; Individualism and the Self** *(volume 3); and other articles in this section.*

BIBLIOGRAPHY

Appleby, Joyce. *Liberalism and Republicanism in the Historical Imagination.* Cambridge, Mass., 1992.

Bercovitch, Sacvan. *The American Jeremiad.* Madison, Wis., 1978.

Brinkley, Alan. *The End of Reform: New Deal Liberalism in Recession and War.* New York, 1995.

———. *Liberalism and Its Discontents.* Cambridge, Mass., 1998.

Davies, Gareth. *From Opportunity to Entitlement: The Transformation and Decline of Great Society Liberalism.* Lawrence, Kans., 1996.

Diggins, John P. *The Lost Soul of American Politics: Virtue, Self-Interest, and the Foundations of Liberalism.* Chicago, 1984.

Ellis, Richard J. *American Political Cultures.* New York, 1993.

———. *The Dark Side of the Left: Illiberal Egalitarianism in America.* Lawrence, Kans., 1998.

Ericson, David F. *The Shaping of American Liberalism: The Debates over Ratification, Nullification, and Slavery.* Chicago, 1993.

Gerstle, Gary. "The Protean Character of American Liberalism." *American Historical Review* 99 (October 1994): 1043–1073.

Greenstone, J. David. *The Lincoln Persuasion: Remaking American Liberalism.* Princeton, N.J., 1993.

Hartz, Louis. *The Founding of New Societies: Studies in the History of the United States, Latin America, South Africa, Canada, and Australia.* New York, 1964.

——. *The Liberal Tradition in America: An Interpretation of American Political Thought since the Revolution.* New York, 1955.

Huntington, Samuel P. *American Politics: The Promise of Disharmony.* Cambridge, Mass., 1981.

Isaac, Jeffrey C. "Republicanism v. Liberalism? A Reconsideration." *History of Political Thought* 9 (summer 1988): 349–377.

Kloppenberg, James T. *The Virtues of Liberalism.* New York, 1998.

Orren, Karen. *Belated Feudalism: Labor, the Law, and Liberal Development in the United States.* New York, 1991.

Rodgers, Daniel T. *Atlantic Crossings: Social Politics in a Progressive Age.* Cambridge, Mass., 1998.

Rorty, Richard. "A Defense of Minimalist Liberalism." In *Debating Democracy's Discontent,* edited by Anita L. Allen and Milton C. Regan Jr. New York, 1998.

Rosenblum, Nancy L. *Membership and Morals: The Personal Uses of Pluralism in America.* Princeton, N.J., 1998.

Ryan, Alan. "Liberalism." In *A Companion to Contemporary Political Philosophy,* edited by Robert E. Goodin and Philip Pettit. Blackwell Companions to Philosophy series. Oxford, U.K., 1993.

Sandel, Michael J. *Democracy's Discontent: America in Search of a Public Philosophy.* Cambridge, Mass., 1996.

Shafer, Byron E., and William J. M. Claggett. *The Two Majorities: The Issue Context of Modern American Politics.* Baltimore, 1995.

Shalhope, Robert E. "Toward a Republican Synthesis: The Emergence of an Understanding of Republicanism in American Historiography." *William and Mary Quarterly* 29 (January 1972): 49–80.

Shklar, Judith N. *Redeeming American Political Thought.* Chicago, 1998.

Skocpol, Theda. *Social Policy in the United States: Future Possibilities in Historical Perspective.* Princeton, N.J., 1995.

Smith, Rogers M. *Civic Ideals: Conflicting Visions of Citizenship in U.S. History.* New Haven, Conn., 1997.

Wilson, Graham K. *Only in America? The Politics of the United States in Comparative Perspective.* Chatham, N.J., 1998.

Wood, Gordon S. *The Creation of the American Republic, 1776–1787.* Chapel Hill, N.C., 1969.

Young, James P. *Reconsidering American Liberalism: The Troubled Odyssey of the Liberal Idea.* Boulder, Colo., 1996.

CONSERVATISM

J. David Hoeveler

The term "conservatism" has embraced many different political ideals and cultural values in American history. Unlike in England and Canada, however, it has not given its name to any national political party. Conservatism can at one time express elitist prejudices and at other times populist ones. It can ascribe a significant role to government and the state or endorse a libertarian philosophy and a laissez-faire economics. Conservatism can be modernist or antimodernist, provincial or nationalist, and sometimes both. These varieties challenge the historian to understand what conditions have caused the evolution of conservatism as an American ideology. What has conservatism meant and what values and ideals has it expressed in different historical eras?

Two themes connect American conservatism as an intellectual and cultural phenomenon. One is the problem of history and tradition. European conservatism built on these entities, beginning with Edmund Burke in the late eighteenth century. The frightful disruptions and violence of the French Revolution led Burke to speak for the stabilizing influences in a nation's experience—the institutions of state, church, and class that preserve an organic community of place and memory. The United States, by contrast, has always seemed to suffer from a lack of depth, a lack of temporal longevity that connects past and present. It lacks the symbols of crown and church that preserve tradition as a contemporary reality. Instead, expansion, mobility, and the visible indices of change seem to be the norms of American life. Second, conservatives have not sat comfortably with what they see as democratic, egalitarian, and leveling forces in American life. Few conservatives have rejected democracy as such. They have looked instead for a means of incorporating aristocratic principles into democratic practices and ideals.

FEDERALISTS AND WHIGS

To conservative-minded intellectuals, the American Revolution left a legacy of problems. The new state constitutions empowered the legislative branches and placed few constraints on their authority. The result, conservatives believed, was a democratic despotism. Conservatives queried the republican ideology of the Revolution and its attribution of virtue to the common people. American nationhood seemed a weak and diminished concept under the Articles of Confederation. The United States seemed only a loose amalgam of petty states. Religion was in decline and radical, deistic ideas and agnosticism ascendant. Furthermore, in the 1790s conservatives watched with horror the progress of the French Revolution.

Early American conservatism united a nationalist political ethic with a program of religious and moral recovery. That agenda found its locus in the Federalist Party. The new Constitution of 1789 gave it opportunities. Alexander Hamilton represented the nationalist wing of the Federalists, and as secretary of the Treasury from 1789 to 1795 he advanced a program that would ally the federal government to the growing manufacturing interests and large financial class in the new nation. Hamilton sought to dissolve the power of entrenched local dynasties, quasi-feudal kingdoms thriving by inertia from the colonial era. He wanted to open the United States to enterprise, invention, and talent. The federal government would assist in making new opportunities. Hamilton thus envisioned a new American society. He would replace the old elites without embracing the leveling democracy he feared in rival Thomas Jefferson and others. The entrepreneurial elite he defined as America's best hope reflected a recurring theme in American conservatism—the quest to locate an aristocratic principle with the prevailing democratic norms of the nation.

The other wing of the Federalists balanced economics with moral and religious commitment. This wing had a New England base, effectively represented by Timothy Dwight. As president of Yale College (1795–1817), Dwight not only inspired an evangelical revival, he also articulated the Protestant churches' fears of the French Revolution. Dwight saw the revolution as the offspring of the Enlightenment, which represented to him the standards of rationalism, skepticism, and materialism. Socially disastrous effects followed, he believed, sexual immorality most visibly.

In John Adams, Federalist conservatism found a political expression. For Adams, by the time of his election to the presidency in 1796, social order had become a premium. Society, like the human individual, housed inherently unstable components, he perceived. Adams did not appeal to an aristocracy of the European kind, with its artificial titles and decorative trappings. He did look to traditional social institutions—family, church, and state—to moderate and contain the exercise of liberty, and he specified social hierarchy to assure stable democracy. Adams's Puritan heritage also instilled him with the conviction that public policy must have a public purpose.

Federalist conservatism took shape against a rival Jeffersonian libertarianism in the Republican Party. Laissez-faire economics, states' rights, and religious skepticism, the Federalists believed, constituted the main intellectual challenges posed by their opponents. The Democratic Party, in the era of Andrew Jackson, called itself "the party of liberty" and pressed a more aggressive populism into its politics. The bank war of the 1830s coincided with the Democrats' celebration of the virtues of the small businessman and farmer against the financiers, bankers, and large commercial businessmen. Such partisan views compelled the Federalists' successors, the Whigs, to make their case for modernism in the new age of industrial and financial capitalism. Whigs championed the entrepreneurial ethic, and political leaders like Horace Greeley expected the new era of machinery and the factory system to have a disciplining and sobering effect on the working classes. The Whig leader Henry Clay offered his American system, a program by which tariffs and sale of federal lands would finance a broad variety of internal improvements. Here again the federal government inherited a key role in creating a modern, efficient, integrated national economy.

Whig conservatism did not uncritically celebrate an expansive capitalism. It wanted government, as in the Bank of the United States, to have a moder-

ating effect on growth. Moreover, Whigs looked for resources that would prevent a corrosive materialism from infecting American society. They often joined their agenda to the evangelical movement in American Protestantism, an alliance intended to satisfy calls for "a Christian party in politics." This conservatism thus perpetuated a Puritan heritage that would make the state an agency of moral discipline. Popular causes among Whigs included temperance, sabbatarianism, and abolition of slavery. Whig political leaders like John Quincy Adams, Clay, and Abraham Lincoln all struggled to discipline their own personalities and to project that order and self-control onto society at large. The mob violence that killed the abolitionist Elijah Lovejoy in 1837 sickened Lincoln. He believed that if respect for the law did not prevail in America, its great democratic experiment could not succeed.

The antebellum years also saw the emergence of a southern conservatism that would supply key components of the conservative tradition in the United States. In its southern expression, conservatism set its teeth against the system of liberty. Against the growing attacks on slavery from northerners, the Virginia sociologist George Fitzhugh in the 1850s famously made his case against free society. An unbridled competitive system had turned industrial capitalism, he said, into an inhumane and oppressive economic system. It brutalized women and children and honored only the strong. It thus thrived in a social arena wholly at odds with Christian ethics. Slavery, Fitzhugh believed, supplied the humane alternative. Also in defense of slavery, John C. Calhoun, the most important political voice of the South, attacked virtually every premise of liberal ideology. He subjected the social contract theories of John Locke and Jean-Jacques Rousseau to a critique that assumed the superior perspective of society's priorities. Calhoun demolished the notion of individual rights and any other abstract derivations. He furthermore discredited the priorities of majoritarian rule, especially when the power of numbers threatened the place of the "civilized minority." As a Democrat, however, Calhoun did not share Whig nationalism, and he staunchly defended states' rights and southern sectionalism.

SOCIAL DARWINISM

Conservative ideology underwent significant shifts in the late nineteenth century. It became less associated with a particular political party as both Democrats and Republicans embraced the ideal of the minimal state in economic matters. Reform ideas found their expression more through third parties such as the Greenbacks and Populists (the People's Party). Conservatism lost its identity with the Hamiltonian and Clay tradition. The early Republican Party of the late 1850s and 1860s sponsored programs in that tradition—a homestead act, the transcontinental railroad, the Morrill Land-Grant Act for state colleges—as Lincoln and other leaders perpetuated their Whig philosophies of government. The Republicans preserved the moral tradition of the Whigs in their opposition to slavery and endorsement of civil rights for the freedmen during Reconstruction. Increasingly into the 1870s, though, the Republican Party became more dominated by business interests and reflected a protective attitude toward that constituency.

Social Darwinism, the new and dominant conservative expression, derived from the extension of Charles Darwin's theory of evolution into social attitudes and policies. Darwin published his famous hypothesis *On the Origin of Species* in 1859. The British philosopher Herbert Spencer, who would enjoy a popular vogue in the United States, had already coined the expression "survival of the fittest" in his 1851 publication *Social Statics.* The portrayal of all life as a system of intense and often brutal competition, with victory to the strong, seemed to reflect the conditions of the United States in the Gilded Age. Labor strife and class conflict prevailed throughout the era. Corporations and trusts gained ascendancy in the economic order. New immigration presented a picture of thousands of Americans in daily struggle to stay afloat. Viewed against the backdrop of a new age of steel and coal, these conditions gave a naturalistic aura to the American scene and social Darwinism reflected it.

William Graham Sumner became America's purest voice of social Darwinism. A Yale professor, he wrote the short book *What Social Classes Owe to Each Other* (1883) and fortified his arguments in dozens of scholarly articles. Influenced by the English economist Thomas Malthus, Sumner saw humanity in a statistical trap, doomed to overproduce itself and confront starvation. Sumner saw only one way out—the application of technology to production. Creation of capital, however, required individuals who would forgo immediate gratification for future higher returns. The vast majority of humans, Sumner believed, were too profligate to exercise such self-denial. To those that do, however, society owes its very life, and these individuals may justly claim full title to all their wealth, he asserted. Furthermore, these individuals can also redeem the world by passing their habits to their progeny. Society's unsuccessful should pass out of existence, Sumner believed, lest their perpetuation impair the future human race. Sumner's capitalist ethic urged against welfare programs and any socialist-like interference or redistribution of wealth. None would work and most would be emphatically dangerous. Sumner's views may have echoed the laissez-faire notions of Thomas Jefferson but they embraced none of his natural rights philosophy. Nature, Sumner believed, promised only that the race may, by sheer hard work and self-denial, just possibly survive. No public or humanitarian intervention would change the course of things. Said Sumner: a drunkard in the gutter is just where he ought to be.

From the business world itself came a ringing endorsement of social Darwinism. Andrew Carnegie, a Scottish immigrant who had accumulated immense wealth in steel, offered his celebrated work of 1886, *Triumphant Democracy.* Influenced by Spencer, Carnegie projected a much more optimistic view. A partnership of democracy and capitalism, he said, had placed the United States in world economic leadership. There were, in Carnegie's view, redemptive elements for democratic capitalism: in his famous essay "The Gospel of Wealth" (1889), Carnegie looked for an aristocracy of philanthropy, the wealthy in their public munificence, who preserved social stability and equality of opportunity.

ANTIMODERNISM AND THE CRITIQUE OF MASS SOCIETY

The first half of the twentieth century saw some of the richest expressions of American intellectual conservatism. Its exponents stood back from both triumphant capitalism and triumphant democracy. They associated both of these phenomenon with a secular society given to materialism and hedonism and they often described a resultant soulless nation of rootless and dispirited individuals. These conservatives looked for a new aristocratic principle to redeem democracy. Some were avowedly elitist. This group of conservatives had two components—one traditionalist and one libertarian.

Irving Babbitt was the major spokesman for a group known as the New Humanists. It consisted also of Paul Elmer More, Stuart Pratt Sherman, and Norman Foerster. Babbitt published *Literature and the American College* in 1908 and his most important books, *Rousseau and Romanticism* and *Democracy and Leadership,* in 1919 and 1924. In these works Babbitt presented a humanist philosophy that celebrated a principle of control in each individual, to be exercised against the dangerously expansive and lustful drives that also inhere in each personality. The principle of this dualism, the New Humanist believed, received its most powerful depiction in classical literature and in later thinkers like the English writer Samuel Johnson. Babbitt sought to locate a common humanity on this high plain and recoiled from a democratic culture in which, he said, we descend to meet. Babbitt also looked to these inner controls as the principles of an ordered society and considered these the aristocratic forms that made for an improved democracy. Without them, he said, any community will face the unwelcome alternatives of anarchy on the one hand or an oppressive, controlling state on the other. Babbitt presented a conservatism not at all enamored of the American business civilization and its capitalist order. He decried an American mentality that worshiped technology and money and cloaked its imperialistic behavior toward the rest of the world in democratic idealism.

Southerners reinforced the conservative case against modern society, focusing on industrialism and the erosion wrought by science and technology. The Agrarians began their movement at Vanderbilt University in the 1920s and in 1930 issued their manifesto *I'll Take My Stand: The South and the Agrarian Tradition.* Major contributors included John Crowe Ransom, Allen Tate, and Donald Davidson. Generally, the southern intellectuals blamed industrialism for creating modern anomie, the detachment of individuals from their community roots, and the collapse of organic society. They saw the same manifestations in modern culture. Some of the Agrarians offered the countermodel of the historic southern plantation, but none expected to see its recovery. Several of the group made their important contributions in literary criticism. Through the New Criticism they sought to isolate the poetic object from any entanglements with the exterior world. Close textual reading and the effort to experience poetry as an organic whole represented an extreme aestheticism by which the former Agrarians made their ultimate stands against the inroads of a scientific culture. Art became the point of resistance to the erosions of economic modernism.

Two world wars in the first half of the twentieth century and the experience of modern totalitarianism left many intellectuals troubled about the forces of erosion in the modern Western world. That reinforced the traditionalist conservatism be-

RUSSELL KIRK'S SIX CANONS OF CONSERVATIVE THOUGHT

1. Belief that a divine intent rules society as well as conscience, forging an eternal chain of right and duty which links great and obscure, living and dead.
2. Affection for the proliferating variety and mystery of traditional life, as distinguished from the narrowing uniformity and egalitarianism and utilitarian aims of most radical systems.
3. Conviction that civilized society requires orders and classes. The only true equality is moral equality; all other attempts at leveling lead to despair, if enforced by positive legislation.
4. Persuasion that property and freedom are inseparably connected. . . . Separate property from private possession, and liberty is erased.
5. Faith in prescription and distrust of "sophisters and calculators." Man must put a control upon his will and his appetite, for conservatives know man to be governed more by emotion than by reason. Tradition and sound prejudice provide checks upon man's anarchic impulse.
6. Recognition that change and reform are not identical, and that innovation is a devouring conflagration more often than it is a torch of progress.

Source: *The Conservative Mind,* 1953.

gun by the New Humanists. In 1949 the poet and academic Peter Viereck issued the influential work *Conservatism Revisited: The Revolt against Revolt, (1815–1949).* Viereck labeled his views "the New Conservatism." Viereck's enemy was mass society, which he saw undergirding the modern totalitarian movements. He traced the cultural roots of the problem back to the Romantic movement, with its glorification of the *Volk,* or the common people, in the early nineteenth century. Mass society had produced a leveling culture and societies of bland and manipulable citizens. He abhorred populism of any kind and alienated other conservatives in his denunciation of Senator Joseph McCarthy's zealous anticommunist campaign in the 1950s. As a traditionalist, however, Viereck endorsed the liberal political tradition of the United States. Viereck called

GEORGE WILL ON CONSERVATISM

True conservatives distrust and try to modulate social forces that work against the conservation of traditional values. But for a century the dominant conservatism has uncritically worshiped the most transforming force, the dynamism of the American economy. No coherent conservatism can be based solely on commercialism, but this conservatism has been consistently ardent only about economic growth, and hence about economies of scale, and social mobility. These take a severe toll against small towns, small enterprises, family farms, local governments, craftsmanship, environmental values, a sense of community, and other aspects of human living. . . .

Politics should be citizens expressing themselves as *a people,* a community of shared values, rather than as merely a collection of competing private interests inhabiting the same country. Instead, politics has become a facet of the disease for which it could be part of the cure. The disease is an anarchy of self-interestedness, and unwillingness, perhaps by now an inability, to think of the *public* interest, the *common* good. This disease of anti-public-spiritedness is not a candidate's disease. It is a social disease.

Source: *The Pursuit of Happiness and Other Sobering Thoughts,* 1979.

himself "a value-conserving classical humanist" and urged an ethical dimension in educational programs. He did not reject democracy, but called instead for an improved democracy and said that democracy is the best government on earth when it tries to make all its citizens aristocrats.

The postwar years also saw traditionalist conservatism flourish in the contribution of Russell Kirk. A prolific writer, Kirk first gained influence with his book *The Conservative Mind* (1953). Kirk, looking back as far as Burke, surveyed a rich accumulation of conservative writing in Europe and the United States. The book went through seven editions. Kirk, who referred to Babbitt as "my mentor," pronounced emphatically anti-modernist views and showed again that this strain of conservatism found little kinship with notions of material progress through industrial capitalism. Kirk had grown up in Michigan and recalled with disgust the "assembly-line civilization" created by Henry Ford. In his 1954 book, *A Program for Conservatives,* Kirk also gave a plenary report on what constituted a conservative life. His chapter essays explicated conservative understandings of such items as "mind," "heart," "social boredom," "community," "justice," "power," and "tradition." Kirk was a convert to Roman Catholicism, and his concern for tradition, community, religion, and order gave a medieval theme to his writings. He looked for an aristocracy of leisure, exempt from the materialist drives of the modern business order, as a counterforce to mass taste and popular culture.

Traditionalist conservatism faded in the 1960s and afterward, but it found eloquent expression in the 1970s essays of the columnist George Will. Will liked to call himself a "Tory conservative" and said that he invoked a European form of conservatism. Properly understood, Will argued, conservatism had a stake in preserving community; it could not therefore be anti-statist. Will endorsed the modern welfare state and its protective policies. Capitalism, as a relentless engine of change, he said, does not suit the conservative mentality; it ravishes small communities and rural landscapes, historic homes and buildings. Will, on the other hand, opposed liberalism's disdain for rank and hierarchy and its strident egalitarianism. Affirmative action was anathema to him.

Other conservative critics of mass society and democratic culture followed a different tack. Instead of applying the constraints of history and tradition, they embraced a libertarian ideology that would produce an elite separate from the democratic mass. Albert Jay Nock embodied both the libertarian and the elitist aspects of dissent from democracy. In his essays for the *Freeman* and in his sparkling autobiography, *Memoirs of a Superfluous Man* (1943), Nock excoriated the leveling effects of democratic society. He boasted that he never attended a public school. He decried the effects of mass literacy, as evidenced by the sensationalism and vulgarity of the popular novel and magazine fiction, and the base appeal of commercial advertising. Nock believed most people were not educable, only trainable. The only mark of an educated person, he insisted, was mastery of the classical literature of ancient Greece and Rome. All expressions of cultural modernism he found degrading. Nock's book *Our Enemy the State* (1935) conveyed classic libertarian sentiments. He objected to all measures of state intervention against citizens, from divorce laws to war: he spoke publicly in opposition to both World War I and World War II.

H. L. Mencken became the best known of the libertarian conservatives. He enjoyed cult status among many in the 1920s and symbolized the revolt of the intellectuals, of all political and cultural persuasions, from democratic culture in America. A product of the German ethnic community in Baltimore, Mencken always appreciated its distance from the American Puritan tradition, a tradition he saw as the necessary partner of American democracy. The two forces had contrived to denigrate the superior and creative individual as it honored only the conventional pieties of mass opinion. Mencken liked to say that no one ever lost money in underestimating the intelligence of the people. He looked at the United States and saw a nation of Rotarians. Mencken, a serious and important literary critic, faulted the entire literary tradition of the United States as he saw in it only the long and oppressive presence of moral idealism. In turn he championed literary modernism, especially the naturalistic writing of Theodore Dreiser. Only a true aristocracy, secure in its social status, could be entrusted to promote artistic innovation and cultural advance, Mencken asserted. He could locate no such aristocracy in America since the old days of the colonial South, but it was no surprise to him that the nation owed its liberties to the Virginia aristocracy.

H. L. Mencken (1880–1956). From 1914 to 1923 Mencken co-edited *The Smart Set,* and in 1924 he helped found the *American Mercury,* which he edited until 1933. In the latter, Mencken once wrote, "The Liberals have many tails, and chase them all." © CORBIS

COLD WAR CONSERVATISM

No issue more united and motivated conservatives than America's struggle against communism; from the time of the Russian Revolution in 1917 conservatives dreamed a "nightmare in red." The issue assumed greatest intensity in the late 1940s and 1950s, but it agitated to the end of the cold war.

Most Americans knew Whittaker Chambers as the accuser in the celebrated Alger Hiss spy case in 1948, when the former communist Chambers accused Hiss, a State Department official, of having been a Soviet spy in the 1930s. Chambers left his mark on the conservative intellectual movement. But it was through his powerful, personal account, *Witness* (1952), that the famous "Letter to My Children" that introduces the autobiography became a landmark in the conservative literature. It sounded an emotional warning about the emerging threat of world communism, a threat Chambers described as spiritual in nature. The world faced a contest of beliefs, he said: "God or Man, Soul or Mind, Freedom or Communism." Ever since, conservative writers and readers have taken the vision of those words to heart.

Cold war conservatism drew into its ranks a remarkable number of former communists, socialists, or champions of radical causes. They included Chambers himself, whose book told of his years in the Communist Party, and others like Frank Meyer, Ralph de Toledano, Max Eastman, John Dos Passos, and Will Herberg. In this group James Burnham had much influence. After education at Princeton and Oxford, Burnham joined the faculty at New York University. He worked with communist labor unions and, as a follower of Leon Trotsky, edited the *New International.* When disillusionment with the Soviet Union set in, Burnham became a powerful voice for a strong anticommunist policy. His book of 1947, *The Struggle for the World,* warned that the communist drive for world power was irrevocable; the "third world war" had already begun.

In *Containment or Liberation?* (1953) Burnham warned against any accommodation with the Soviet Union and urged that the United States take the fight directly into Eastern Europe.

The common cause of anticommunism gave a disjointed conservative movement some coalescence in the 1950s. That fact became visible with the inauguration of the new conservative magazine the *National Review*, in 1955, edited by William F. Buckley Jr. Buckley had become known to an American readership in 1951 through his book *God and Man at Yale: The Superstitions of Academic Freedom.* This recent Yale graduate wanted America to know that little of God and little of free-market economics remained at that venerable school. A wealthy Catholic, Buckley exuded aristocratic mannerisms but could pronounce in a very populist way on some issues. In 1954 Buckley and his brother-in-law Brent Bozell published the anticommunist *McCarthy and His Enemies. National Review* brought into one house conservative writers of all types—traditionalist and libertarians, religious and atheist. The diverse elements did not always coexist harmoniously. The libertarian Max Eastman and the radical individualist Ayn Rand, both atheists, found the *National Review* atmosphere too religious.

NEOCONSERVATISM

Toward the end of the 1960s a new conservative expression took shape, but it was not until the next decade that it acquired the label "neoconservativism." Unlike previous conservative expressions, it had substantial representations from Jewish intellectuals—Norman Podhoretz, Midge Decter, Irving Kristol, and Hilton Kramer, among others. Podhoretz turned the Jewish magazine *Commentary* into a major voice of neoconservatism. Catholics also made up a large proportion of neoconservatives. As in the case of cold war conservatism, neoconservatism housed many former socialists and Democratic liberals. The neoconservative movement derived from what its leaders perceived as an adverse shift in political liberalism; it had moved, they said, from the historic New Deal emphasis on equality of opportunity to a new concern with equality of results. In such programs as compulsory school busing and affirmative action, neoconservatives saw dangerous efforts to impose a statistical equality among races and sexes. Neoconservatives also voiced a strong anticommunism, directed especially at the Soviet Union. The Democratic Party's nomination of George McGovern as presidential

candidate in 1972 symbolized to neoconservatives that party's shift from the priorities of Franklin Roosevelt, Harry Truman, and Hubert Humphrey. Many, like Jeane Kirkpatrick and Irving Kristol, became Republicans.

The career of Kristol reflects the intellectual trajectory of neoconservatism. Kristol grew up in New York City, the son of orthodox East European Jews. He entered the City College of New York in 1936. His ideas were enthusiastically aligned with those of the *Partisan Review,* the leftist publication of the early New York intellectuals. By the 1950s, after the war against Nazism, a mood of accommodation with the United States had settled on the group. Kristol gradually moved to the Right and by the 1980s became known as "the godfather of neoconservatism." In 1965, with Daniel Bell, he edited the *Public Interest,* the major neoconservative publication on social policy. Kristol was influential with neoconservative think tanks such as the American Enterprise Institute, which financed the *Public Interest* and the neoconservative journal for the arts, the *New Criterion,* edited by Kramer.

However much neoconservatism seemed to be a new departure, it reflected patented conservative themes, especially in Kristol. He endorsed "bourgeois" values—the ethics of hard work, self-discipline, frugality, and delayed gratification. But he did not endorse the "capitalist" ethic, which he defined as one of unrestrained hedonism, acquisitiveness, and self-indulgence. For a long time, Kristol believed, the bourgeois ethic had kept the capitalistic ethic in check, but no longer. Kristol denounced a modern United States given over almost completely to the capitalist ethic. Parents who by hard work and savings had become affluent could not pass on to their children the self-discipline by which they had become successful. Free-market capitalism, Kristol believed, did not answer society's need for a morally disciplined citizenry. His point of view put him at odds with contemporary defenders of free-market capitalism like the economist Milton Friedman. Kristol became a *Wall Street Journal* editorialist, and he published an important collection of essays, *Two Cheers for Capitalism,* in 1978.

POPULIST CONSERVATISM

In the late twentieth century a new style of conservatism became prevalent. Many considered populist conservatism, with its deference to the common people and it anti-elitism, a bogus conservatism. In fact, however, populist conservatism had roots in different kinds of conservatism that preceded it. From Edmund Burke to Russell Kirk to George Will, traditionalist conservatism had looked to the enclaves of provincial life and folk traditions for a pluralistic resistance to mass culture in the machine age. The sociologist Robert Nisbet, from the 1950s to the 1980s, upheld the role of intermediate societies—local school boards, labor unions, fraternal groups—against the uniformity imposed by the leviathan state. Cold war conservatives believed that the broad base of American people feared the communist threat far more than did political leaders and most of the intellectual community. Buckley's 1951 book revealed an anti-elitism directed against American academe. Neoconservatism also contributed to the emerging populist conservatism. Indeed, in the Chambers-Hiss engagement, future neoconservatives sided with the rumpled Chambers against the polished easterner Hiss. The Catholic Michael Novak published his important book *The Rise of the Unmeltable Ethnics* in 1972. Novak celebrated the ethnic-immigrant culture of Eastern Europeans in the United States and found in them a healthier and more genuine humanity than he could see in the WASP elite that dominated American professional life.

Populist conservatism had a direct relationship to political change in the 1970s and 1980s. The Alabamian George Wallace, product of small-town poverty, first gained national attention with his resistance to racial integration at the state university. He found a larger cause, and a larger national appeal, when he attacked big government and the "briefcase-carrying bureaucrats" who set liberal policy such as forced busing. These people, he said, could send their children to private schools; poor whites could not. In his presidential campaigns Wallace drew surprisingly high support from northern blue-collar workers with his "country and western" conservatism. Wallace's successes helped the Republican strategists for Richard Nixon define a "southern strategy" that would see the party regain from the Democrats a political dominance in the South, at least in presidential elections.

Populist conservatism gained its most powerful formulation from the political analyst Kevin Phillips. In 1969 Phillips, an adviser to Richard Nixon, published *The Emerging Republican Majority,* in which he described a major political evolution in America. Philips found a new liberal elite, dominant in the Northeast and in the "silk-stocking districts" of major cities, and well represented in the major universities and media in the United States. Against this elite, Phillips posed a populist insurgency—among white ethnic communities, many now to be found in the newer suburbs, among lower-class Jews, and in rural areas and mill towns. The 1972 presidential election seemed to confirm these trends. Massachusetts, near the top of the states in wealth and education, was the only state to vote for the liberal Democrat George McGovern. Mississippi, lowest in wealth and education, gave Nixon his highest popular percentage.

Phillips helped influence a Republican Party strategy that prepared the way for Ronald Reagan. Reagan had surprised the experts by his 1966 gubernatorial victory in California and won attention for his battles with the University of California system. Republicans, from the time of the Vietnam War, had learned to appeal to what Nixon liked to call "the great silent majority" against the spoiled youth, the liberal elites, and the unelected officials in government and the courts, who set the liberal agenda. The emerging Reagan coalition also added many partisans of a new "religious right," in the 1970s and 1980s, especially those who identified with Rev. Jerry Fallwell's "Moral Majority" and the efforts of the conservative spokeswoman and antifeminist Phyllis Schlafly to defeat a proposed equal rights amendment to the Constitution. Reagan drew a portrait of a bloated government, hugely expensive and ineffective, and zealous in its regulations to the point of tyranny. For Reagan the populist, the problem was government itself.

CONCLUSION

Populist conservatism shows the historical habit of conversation to mix and blend. Reagan sounded populist in his antigovernment animus and his celebration of ordinary citizens against the elites that victimize them. On the other hand, this very populism allowed Reagan to open up to free-market ideology, with the promise to liberate American business from shackles imposed by liberal policy. None other than Kevin Phillips became one of the major critics of the Reagan presidency, decrying the exaggerations of wealth and poverty in America that occurred during those years. Others decried the Gilded Age atmosphere of the Reagan White House. Such a turn of events would give an opening to a more strident populist, Patrick Buchanan, to voice an anti-elitism that attacked privileged corporate power in the United States as well as government elites.

Conservatism thus suggests no permanent and inflexible standards. It embraces a variety of ideological persuasions. One may analyze and describe these in taxonomic fashion, but historical situations will always determine their precise formulations and applications.

See also **Liberalism and Republicanism; Federalists and Antifederalists; Jacksonian Ideology; Whig Ideology; Secession, War, and Union; Nationalism and Imperialism** *(volume 1);* **World War and Cold War; Resurgent Conservatism; Working Class** *(in this volume);* **Political Economy; Individualism and the Self; Race; Class; Government; Social Construction of Reality** *(volume 3); and other articles in this section.*

BIBLIOGRAPHY

Carter, Dan T. *The Politics of Rage: George Wallace, the Origins of the New Conservatism, and the Transformation of American Politics.* New York, 1995.

Curtis, Bruce. *William Graham Sumner.* Boston, 1981.

Diggins, John Patrick. *Up from Communism: Conservative Odysseys in American Intellectual History.* New York, 1975.

Dorrien, Gary. *The Neoconservative Mind: Politics, Culture, and the War of Ideology.* Philadelphia, 1993.

Dunn, Charles W., and J. David Woodward. *The Conservative Tradition in America.* Lanham, Md., 1996.

Gerson, Mark T. *The Neoconservative Vision: From the Cold War to the Culture Wars.* Lanham, Md., 1996.

Hobson, Fred. *Mencken: A Life.* New York, 1994.

Hoeveler, J. David, Jr. *The New Humanism: A Critique of Modern America, 1900–1940.* Charlottesville, Va., 1977.

———. *Watch on the Right: Conservative Intellectuals in the Reagan Era.* Madison, Wis., 1991.

Howe, Daniel Walker. *The Political Culture of the American Whigs.* Chicago, 1979.

Judis, John B. *William F. Buckley, Jr.: Patron Saint of the Conservatives.* New York, 1988.

Karanikas, Alexander. *Tillers of a Myth: Southern Agrarians as Social and Literary Critics.* Madison, Wis., 1966.

Kirk, Russell. *The Conservative Mind: From Burke to Santayana.* 1953. 7th ed., Chicago, 1986.

Lora, Ronald. *Conservative Minds in America.* Chicago, 1971.

McAllister, Ted V. *Revolt against Modernity: Leo Strauss, Eric Voegelin, and the Search for a Postliberal Order.* Lawrence, Kans., 1996.

Nash, George H. *The Conservative Intellectual Movement in America, since 1945.* New York, 1976.

Nisbet, Robert. *Conservatism: Dream and Reality.* Minneapolis, Minn., 1986.

Stewart, John L. *The Burden of Time: The Fugitives and Agrarians; the Nashville Group of the 1920s and 1930s, and the Writings of John Crowe Ransom, Allen Tate, and Robert Penn Warren.* Princeton, N.J., 1965.

Tanenhaus, Sam. *Whittaker Chambers: A Biography.* New York, 1997.

Wrezin, Michael. *The Superfluous Anarchist: Albert Jay Nock.* Providence, R.I., 1971.

CONSTITUTIONAL THOUGHT

Jack N. Rakove

In 1765, American colonists believed that the British constitution embodied the best political wisdom of the day, and they aspired to model their own governments on its example. By 1790, the theory and practice of American constitutionalism had taken a radically different form, defined largely in opposition to British precedent. That transformation was both a by-product of the revolutionary agitation that led the colonists to declare independence in 1776, and the most important consequence of the experiment in republican self-government that declaration launched. That experiment began when the states drafted new constitutions in 1776, but its culmination came with the adoption of the Constitution proposed by a federal convention of fifty-five delegates that met in Philadelphia between May and September 1787. Ever since, American constitutional theory has been concerned with understanding the meaning of that document (and its amendments) and with developing and applying the rules for its interpretation.

Three principles of American constitutionalism have made this process of interpretation a source of recurring controversy. First, and most important, the distinctive departure in American constitutionalism was to define a constitution not as a body of practices, conventions of governance, institutions, and public law, but rather as a document, adopted at a specific moment, that would operate as an expression of supreme fundamental law, specifying what government could and could not do in its name. This definition produced two underlying difficulties. It meant, first, that many provisions had to be couched in generalities that would require later interpretation, and which different parties might therefore read differently because their own interests, as well as honest disagreements, inclined them to do so. The idea that a constitution was a document of peculiarly historical authority also opened up inevitable gaps between the values and concerns of its adopters and those of later generations.

The second innate source of disputation lies in the federal structure of American constitutionalism, which allocates the sovereign powers of government between the nation and its member states, each vested with authority to enact and execute its own laws for a people who are citizens of both. Conflicts and uncertainty about the boundaries of national and state power are unavoidable for two reasons. First, those powers often overlap; both levels of government, for example, engage in economic regulation. Second, citizens rarely have abstract preferences to see a particular power exercised by one government or another; rather, they tend to favor action by whichever government seems more likely to advance their particular interests. American federalism is inherently messy, and the constitutional structure of the union thus makes efforts to map the boundaries of national and state power a recurring source of controversy.

The third basic stimulus driving the ongoing enterprise of constitutional theory lies in the role that the judiciary has played in resolving the inevitable ambiguities and controversies that the enforcement of a written constitution creates. The belief that an independent federal judiciary could act as an umpire of constitutional disputes is arguably the most striking innovation of American constitutionalism. That belief rested, in part, on the idea that the Constitution represented only another form of law, and that courts must determine whether acts of government satisfy or violate constitutional norms. But this belief also relied on a more problematic hope: that courts would be able to interpose their judgments and authority against the politically more potent institutions of representative democracy. In fact, the courts have attained that authority, but its very exercise has in turn generated continuous disputes about the scope, methodology, and even the legitimacy of judicial review.

These three principles—the concept of a written constitution, federalism, and judicial review—do not exhaust the sources of controversy, but they provide the best framework for outlining the major phases in the history of American constitutional theory. At the risk of oversimplification, that history can be divided into three long phases, punctuated by three major upheavals. The upheavals occurred with the revolutionary origins of American constitutionalism (1776 to 1791), the crisis of the Civil War and Reconstruction (1860 to 1877), and the civil rights revolution (1954 to 1965). The first of the three long phases covered the period between the Revolution and the Civil War, when issues of the nature of the federal union were at the forefront of political controversy. A second major phase began with the collapse of Reconstruction and culminated with the constitutional crisis of the mid-1930s, when the Supreme Court first overturned and then sustained key legislation associated with the New Deal of President Franklin D. Roosevelt. Finally, the third phase, which might be called the "age of rights," was an outgrowth of the civil rights revolution of the mid-twentieth century, when the Supreme Court broadly expanded the protection of individual civil liberties against the authority of the states.

REVOLUTIONARY CONSTITUTIONALISM

The invention of the American definition of a written constitution was an almost accidental consequence of the collapse of British rule over the colonies after 1774. With legal government effectively suspended, the colonists believed they had been thrust into the condition that the English philosopher John Locke called a "dissolution of government." The restoration of legal government that accompanied independence necessarily involved writing new constitutions of government. But whether these constitutions would act as supreme fundamental law, or merely serve as the equivalent of public statutes that later legislatures might revise, was unclear. The inclination to think of constitutions as supreme law became persuasive only after Americans began to evaluate the merits and defects of the original state constitutions.

The principal feature of those first constitutions was their concentration of all effective power in the legislative branch of government. While the executive and judiciary were recognized as nominally independent departments, they were too weak to check the legislature. But complaints about the misuse of legislative power grew as wartime demands forced the assemblies to legislate actively. Those

complaints not only encouraged reformers like James Madison to look for ways to enable the weaker branches to resist the "encroachments" of the legislature; they also sharpened the distinction between ordinary acts of legislation and the fundamental rules of a constitution, which, if well drafted, might impose significant restraints on legislative power.

At the national level of governance, the Articles of Confederation that the Continental Congress drafted in 1776 and 1777 were not finally ratified until 1781. This first national constitution was theoretically significant in one critical respect: it effectively recognized the division of sovereignty between national and state governments that has always characterized American federalism. The states retained sole authority to legislate and to levy taxes, while Congress controlled war and diplomacy. But Congress often depended on the states to execute its decisions, and by 1786 their inability to do so, coupled with the failure of several proposed amendments to receive the required unanimous approval of the states, led reformers to gamble on the idea of holding a special convention to consider a revision of the Articles of Confederation. The first such meeting, held at Annapolis in September 1786, did not muster enough delegates to propose anything significant, but rather than adjourn empty-handed, its members proposed a second general convention to meet at Philadelphia in May 1787.

The Constitutional Convention deliberated for nearly four months, and the document it proposed marked the culmination of the revolutionary experiment in republican constitutionalism. Merely reading its various articles and clauses will not disclose its theoretical foundations, but the notes of debate kept by its leading framer, Madison, and the extensive public commentary created during the ensuing ratification struggle, support several generalizations about its underlying theory.

First, the Constitution was explicitly framed as a statement of supreme fundamental law. Adopting a precedent first set in Massachusetts, it was framed by a special body called for that purpose alone, and then submitted to popularly elected conventions in the states, thereby securing approval through a direct expression of popular sovereignty.

Second, the deliberations of the convention rested on the proposition that any federal system requiring the voluntary compliance of the states with national measures would fail. Instead, a complete national government had to be established that could act directly upon the American people by enacting, executing, and adjudicating its own laws. This agreement in turn enabled the convention to draw appropriate lessons from the experience of the states, whose original constitutions were now regarded as hopeful but hastily drawn experiments. These lessons in turn justified significant modifications in the theory of separation of powers, by restoring the veto power to the newly designed presidency, for example, or by recognizing that courts could exercise a power of judicial review.

Third, sovereignty in America would remain a bundle of powers divided between the Union and states, rather than the concentrated ultimate authority imagined by Old World theorists like Thomas Hobbes. If sovereignty was to be united anywhere, the Constitution's supporters argued, it would reside not in any government but in the people themselves, who always retained ultimate authority to allocate powers to the various levels and institutions of government. In cases where these jurisdictions overlapped, courts would have the duty of determining whether powers were being appropriately exercised.

Fourth, Americans could no longer be regarded as a uniquely virtuous people, possessing the requisite sense of restraint and self-denial that classic theory demanded of republican citizens. Instead, in the famous formulation of Madison's tenth *Federalist* essay, the stability of the republic would depend on the fact that it embraced a multiplicity of interests whose very diversity would prevent the formation of durable national majorities capable of suppressing the just rights and interests of minorities.

In the ensuing debate, opponents argued that the Constitution would establish a consolidated national government that would deprive the states of all meaningful authority. They further protested that the omission of a bill of rights, of the kind that had been attached to the early state constitutions, would make it difficult for citizens to know when their just rights were being infringed. The supporters of the Constitution balked at making any substantive modification in the structure or powers of the national government, but they grudgingly agreed to support amendments affirming the protection of particular rights to the ratified Constitution that would take effect in March 1789. When the First Congress assembled, Madison took the lead in forcing his reluctant colleagues to adopt a limited number of amendments affirming basic rights.

PUZZLES ABOUT FEDERALISM, 1789 TO 1861

The framers of the Constitution understood that it would take time to convert its formal structure of government into working procedures. After initial precedents were set, however, they hoped that a basic understanding of the Constitution would be established. Instead, four sets of issues soon demonstrated that this hope was naive, and that disagreements over the meaning of the Constitution would operate to sharpen rather than reduce political conflict. Together, these issues implicated nearly every major structural feature of the Constitution, and thereby encouraged the emergence of a variety of theories of interpretation that have resonated in American law and politics ever since.

These controversies began in 1791 when Congressman Madison and Secretary of State Thomas Jefferson opposed the expansive interpretation of the necessary and proper clause, which Secretary of the Treasury Alexander Hamilton invoked to justify granting a national charter of incorporation to the Bank of the United States. Two years later, as the Washington administration pondered its response to the outbreak of the general European war sparked by the French Revolution, Madison and Jefferson again disputed Hamilton's broad interpretation of the prerogative powers of the presidency in controlling foreign relations. When the United States veered toward war with France in 1798 and a national government now dominated by the Federalist Party enacted two measures, the Alien and Sedition Acts, which the opposition Democratic-Republicans deemed constitutionally suspect, Madison and Jefferson respectively drafted the Virginia and Kentucky resolutions, implying that the states retained a responsibility to thwart seemingly unconstitutional national measures. Finally, after the Democratic-Republicans gained control of Congress and the presidency in 1801, the outgoing Federalists sought to entrench themselves in the federal judiciary. This in turn helped to guarantee that the practice of judicial review of legislation under the Supreme Court, now led by Chief Justice John Marshall, would prove more controversial than it otherwise might have been.

These disputes were largely political in origin, yet they quickly escalated into clashes of constitutional principle. In the bank controversy, the issue became whether the enumeration of legislative powers in Article 1, Section 8, was to be construed narrowly, or whether the necessary and proper clause allowed Congress to determine how far its authority reached. In the foreign policy disputes, the issue was framed as a choice between a British-style recognition of the prerogative powers of the presidency, or a more republican mistrust of unchecked executive power which required scrupulous congressional supervision.

The crisis of 1798 had two constitutional implications. One was whether Congress could legislate at all in the area of freedom of speech and press when the prohibitions of the First Amendment suggested otherwise. The second was whether the states could legitimately mobilize opposition to national law. In defense of their right to do so, Madison and Jefferson evoked a compact theory of the origins of the Union and its Constitution. Under this theory, the states, as the original contracting parties, retained some inviolable ultimate authority to judge the validity of national acts, or even the authority of the Union itself.

Finally, the accession of Chief Justice Marshall heralded a new departure in the history of federal jurisprudence. In the now-famous case of *Marbury v. Madison* (1803), the Court first struck down as unconstitutional an act of Congress—or rather, a single provision of the Judiciary Act of 1789—while resolving a suit filed by one of the last-minute Federalist judicial appointees of 1801, whose commission had not been delivered before the new administration took office. This was not the first time the Court had considered the validity of congressional legislation, nor did the decision seem important at the time. But Marshall's opinion robustly defended the theory that the Court can enforce constitutional norms against the mere statutory act of the legislature. After 1810, the Court increasingly applied this general theory against state laws which seemed to violate the Constitution, most notably in its decision in *McCulloch v. Maryland* (1819), which struck down a Maryland tax upon the national bank while affirming Hamilton's interpretation of the necessary and proper clause.

The coincidence of this case with the controversy over the admission of Missouri as a slave state helps to explain why the compact theory of the Union acquired a new urgency. In 1787 southern leaders believed that their region would move into parity with the more populous North, but by 1819 they knew that the South would remain a minority. By raising fears about the authority that a northern-dominated Congress might exercise over slavery, the Missouri crisis reinforced the appeal of the principle that the states, as original compacting parties, must retain some ultimate authority to determine whether their deepest interests were compatible with continued membership in the Union. Under a compact theory, it might be argued that states retained some checking authority against acts of the national government that exceeded its constitutional powers.

One expression of this theory proved too extreme to be generally acceptable even in the South. Between 1828 and 1833, opposition to the protectionist tariff of 1828 led political leaders in South Carolina to espouse the theory of nullification, which held that states could legitimately prevent the enforcement of a national act. Though that theory proved too radical to swallow, the idea that states might pursue the more drastic remedy of secession gained new credibility. Northern nationalists replied that the states had formed an indissoluble Union, and that its authority rested less on the consent of individual states than the collective voice of the "We the People" of the preamble of the U.S. Constitution, but the damage had been done.

The escalating controversy over the morality of slavery and the possibility of barring its adoption in western territories increased the stakes in this dispute. In the 1840s and 1850s, slavery became the most dangerous issue in national politics, and protagonists on all sides increasingly addressed it in constitutional terms. Because the issue was so explosive, many politicians tried to avoid dealing with it directly by arguing that its adoption in the territories should be left to the actual settlers to decide as a matter of popular sovereignty. But just as antislavery advocates argued that the Constitution clearly empowered the government to prohibit slavery in the territories, so southern leaders increasingly demanded that the government was obliged to protect slavery everywhere. In 1857, a much divided Supreme Court struggled to resolve this question in the landmark case of *Dred Scott v. Sandford*, but its decision, effectively vacating the Missouri Compromise's effort to limit the territory into which slavery could expand, only worked to strengthen the antislavery Republican Party in the upcoming presidential election. When Abraham Lincoln won the presidency in 1860 with an electoral majority completely drawn from northern free states, secessionists gained the upper hand in southern politics by arguing that slavery's survival could no longer be assured in the face of a potentially hostile national government.

CIVIL WAR AND RECONSTRUCTION

Secession was a revolutionary act, not a constitutional one, but the distinction is not especially useful. When political allegiance to a government collapses, as it did in the South in 1861, the question of whether resistance to that government is legal loses its meaning. By 1860 the dominant political forces in the South believed that the compact theory of the origins of the Union also established a mechanism for its dissolution. All the seceding states had to do was to hold popularly elected conventions that were the mirror images, in effect, of the ratification conventions of 1787 to 1788.

The challenge that secession posed to American constitutional theory, then, was less daunting than the problem of determining how the Union would be reconstituted after a Northern victory. A civil war fought to preserve the Union might also require a new view of the Constitution. By the time Lincoln issued the Emancipation Proclamation, it was evident that victory would require the abolition of slavery, an institution that the Constitution had clearly tolerated, perhaps even promoted. As Confederate territories were occupied, questions about their current and future government also arose. Both Congress and the president considered different schemes of restoring government in the South, but no permanent solution to these problems could be developed until peace came.

When it did, Lincoln's assassination soon led to a completely unexpected political situation. Republicans soon realized that his successor, Andrew Johnson, hoped to restore the South to the Union as quickly as possible, without taking the necessary steps to ensure the fruits of freedom to the millions of African Americans freed by the recent ratification of the Thirteenth Amendment, ending slavery. When former supporters of the rebellion were elected in large numbers to the Thirty-ninth Congress that convened in December 1865, the Republican majority refused to seat them. Instead, it formed the Joint Committee on Reconstruction, and simultaneously began framing civil rights legislation to protect the rights of the freedmen and a constitutional amendment to guarantee that Congress actually had the authority to enact such legislation. Ratification of the Fourteenth Amendment was made the condition for the southern states to be restored to the Union and to participate in national government.

Given that the North had fought the Civil War in the name of an indissoluble federal Union, could Congress legitimately impose conditions on the southern states for their readmission to the Union, or keep them under military occupation, or enact civil rights legislation that ignored previous notions of the boundaries of national and state power? Politicians and commentators alike offered different justifications of these actions—arguing that the South remained in the "grasp of war," or that the Republican guarantee clause of the Constitution warranted these actions. But just as secession is best described as an extra-constitutional act, so congressional Reconstruction rested on the recognition that only extraordinary measures would redeem the promise of emancipation against a still defiant South.

The Fourteenth Amendment, ratified in 1868, marked a genuine revolution in American constitutionalism, but one whose promise long went unfulfilled. Section 1 was key. It not only overturned *Dred Scott*'s holding that African Americans were not citizens; it also imposed three major restrictions on the legislative power of the states. Henceforth no state could "abridge the privileges and immunities of citizens of the United States," or "deprive any person of life, liberty, or property, without due process of law," or "deny any person within its jurisdiction the equal protection of the laws." Section 5 of the amendment authorized Congress to pursue these ends with "appropriate legislation," and so it attempted to do.

The failure of Reconstruction rested upon two conditions that Congress could not overcome. First, southern resistance and the costs of military occupation eroded the northern commitment; though Congress continued to enact civil rights acts, their enforcement proved problematic, and public opinion grew weary of the cause. Second, the Supreme Court gradually undertook the necessary interpretation of the scope and meaning of the Fourteenth Amendment and the various accompanying acts of legislation. This process began with the Slaughterhouse Cases of 1873, but its most important expression came with the Civil Rights Cases of 1883, holding that the Fourteenth Amendment covered only state action, not discriminatory acts by private individuals or enterprises. The path was open for the decision in *Plessy v. Ferguson* (1896), which affirmed that a law permitting racial segregation of railroad facilities was constitutional. In his lone dissent, Justice John Marshall Harlan insisted that the Constitution was "color-blind," but the Court, the South, and much of the white population of the entire country believed that reasonable racial distinctions were acceptable. *Plessy* has been widely understood to defend the proposition that such distinctions were legitimate so long as the separate races were treated equally.

THE ERA OF SUBSTANTIVE DUE PROCESS

Plessy stands with *Dred Scott* as a monument to the racial injustice that the Constitution and its interpretation not only tolerated but even fortified. But racial prejudice was an endemic feature of American life in this era, and the result in *Plessy* was neither surprising nor controversial. In many ways, post-Reconstruction constitutional thinking remained faithful to the respect for state autonomy that had figured so prominently before the Civil War. Rather than require federal courts to engage in wholesale review of state legislation, the Supreme Court preferred to interpret the Fourteenth Amendment as allowing the state legislatures to determine exactly which civil rights their citizens were to enjoy.

In the beginning of the twentieth century, however, the Supreme Court embarked on a new and more controversial course of judicial review. In the 1905 case, *Lochner v. New York,* the Court overturned a statute limiting the working hours of bakers as an unconstitutional infringement of an individual's right to contract one's labor. *Lochner* epitomizes the doctrine that came to be known as "substantive due process," which holds that certain rights are so fundamental as to be immune from government regulation even when a legislature claims to have a reasonable basis for action. In the coming decades, the Court would invoke this principle to overturn various acts regulating economic activity on similar grounds. The Court's vigorous application of this doctrine in 1934 to overturn key acts adopted by the New Deal Congress of 1933 to deal with the economic collapse of the Great Depression provoked a major constitutional crisis.

The Court's willingness to subject such legislation to judicial review had grown increasingly controversial since the early years of the twentieth century. In *The Supreme Court and the Constitution* (1912), Charles A. Beard, the leading Progressive era historian, had taken issue with those who argued that the Court was usurping power not granted to it by the Constitution. In fact, Beard argued, the framers had intended to vest judicial review in the Court precisely so it could check just the sort of economic legislation it was now striking down. Thus by the time the Court seemed intent on thwarting the New Deal, questions about the scope and legitimacy of judicial review had been deeply agitated in both the polity and the academy.

The crisis came in 1937. Fresh from his sweeping electoral victory in 1936, President Franklin D. Roosevelt proposed his ill-calculated "court-packing plan," whereby a new Supreme Court justice would be added to a visibly aging Court for every sitting member reaching the age of seventy, until the Court expanded to sixteen members. This radical proposal provoked a strong political reaction against Roosevelt's ostensibly dictatorial ambitions, but in the meantime, the Court shifted course. In *West Coast Hotel v. Parrish,* a decision upholding a Washington State minimum wage law, a five-member majority reversed its position in an identical case decided the previous year, and, in doing so, it effectively signaled the Court's new willingness to defer to legislative judgments in matters of economic policy. A month later, the Court upheld another key piece of New Deal economic legislation, the National Labor Relations Act. This "switch in time that saved nine," as it is called, amounted to a revolution in constitutional doctrine. When matters of economic policy and regulation were at stake, the Court implied, it would henceforth show great respect for the political choice made by Congress and the states.

THE AGE OF RIGHTS

In a footnote to another decision, *U.S. v. Carolene Products Co.* (1938), the Court issued another pregnant signal when it identified several other categories of legislation that could remain subject to careful judicial scrutiny even while conceding that economic legislation need pass only a minimal, "rational basis" test. One of these categories was legislation "directed at particular religious, or national, or racial minorities," or what the Court called "discrete and insular minorities." The most obvious group meeting this description were African Americans, still living predominantly in the ex-Confederate states which had been erecting a system of legally sanctioned racial segregation based, in part, on the Court's own decision in *Plessy.* Racially discriminatory laws limited their access to the political process (another area that the *Carolene* Court suggested could be subjected to close scrutiny) and to public facilities of all kinds, while stigmatizing them in a variety of ways. These distinctions were coming under challenge by lawyers supported by the National Association for the Advancement of Colored People (NAACP), but progress was slow, depending as it did on the facts in particular cases and the difficulty of overcoming the perception that the "separate but equal" doctrine associated with *Plessy* was still good law.

The NAACP initially made segregation of higher education its principal target, but after 1950 it shifted strategy to challenge segregation in primary education. Its great victory came in the landmark ruling in *Brown v. Board of Education of Topeka* (1954), in which the opinion written by the newly appointed chief justice, Earl Warren, held that "separate educational facilities are inherently unequal." In reaching this decision, the Court consciously avoided grounding its decision on more traditional modes of legal reasoning, including asking whether segregation was consistent with the intentions of the framers of the Fourteenth Amendment. Instead, it relied on a general principle of equality, a belief in the importance of education to democratic citizenship, and sociological evidence asserting that segregation inflicted great harm on the stigmatized race.

From the vantage point of constitutional theory more generally, *Brown* is significant for several reasons. First, though the justices foresaw the deep opposition their decision would provoke, they recognized that the Court again had a major role to play in protecting individual and minority rights against unjust laws. Second, though another decade passed before the presidency and Congress fully supported the cause of civil rights, the Court had launched a major shift in American federalism by committing the national government to act vigorously against the offensive laws of the states. Third, *Brown* gave new substance to the core principle of the legal equality of all citizens. Fourth, the rhetoric of *Brown* reflected the new importance that the cause of human rights had gained since World War II and the disclosure of the genocide against the Jews of Europe.

The Warren Court soon initiated an even more expansive interpretation of the equal protection and due process clauses of the Fourteenth Amendment and the original Bill of Rights. For a century and a half, it had been generally understood that the Bill of Rights applied only against the national government, not the states. The Court began moving gradually away from this position after World War I, but decades passed before this shift reached critical dimensions. In the 1960s, however, the movement to "incorporate" the specific protections of the first eight amendments against the states, under the authority of the Fourteenth Amendment, gained much greater force. In other decisions, the Court required state legislative and congressional districts to be apportioned on the principle of "one man, one vote," so that rural constituencies would no longer have disproportionate representation. The Court substantially broadened the protections afforded to suspects, defendants, and those convicted and imprisoned for criminal acts. Its decisions in

the area of religion tended to support the principles of strict separation of church and state. In the contraception case of *Griswold v. State of Connecticut* (1965), it recognized a general right of privacy that could not be firmly anchored in the constitutional text. Under the new leadership of Chief Justice Warren Burger, appointed in 1969 as an apparent conservative, the Court extended this principle to create a constitutional right to abortion; and it briefly struck down all laws permitting capital punishment. Finally, in *Roe v. Wade* (1973), the Court held that women had a fundamental constitutional right to secure abortions, subject only to limited restrictions by the states.

The breathtaking scope of judicial activity in this era inspired heroic praise and searching criticism. Many of these decisions—especially those relating to desegregation—required lower courts to sanction equitable remedies designed to undo the injustices, and this in turn forced these courts to take on duties that were as much executive and legislative as judicial in nature. To the liberal supporters of these decisions, the Court's willingness to act decisively in behalf of individual rights and "discrete and insular minorities" represented a long-delayed vindication of the original promise of judicial review. Leading academics, most notably the philosopher Ronald Dworkin, developed strong theories to justify a rights-oriented jurisprudence grounded more in moral principle than adherence to history or legal precedent. The willingness of the Warren and Burger Courts to accept challenges to long-standing practices also gave reformers a powerful incentive to rely on litigation rather than the more tedious and difficult project of securing legislative victories. On the other side of the political spectrum, conservatives grew increasingly critical of the reasoning and attitudes underlying the jurisprudence of the 1960s and 1970s. In their view, the Court was usurping powers that properly belonged to other institutions and the democratic process, threatening to turn itself into a platonic guardian of the public good. Conservative writers like Robert H. Bork began calling for a jurisprudence of "original intent," by which they meant that Supreme Court justices should avoid imposing their own values and preferences on the Constitution, but instead strive to recover what its language had meant to its adopters, leaving to other, elected institutions the difficult task of sorting political preferences.

This debate continued to rage through the twentieth century, making constitutional law and theory a deeply vexed subject, and every appointment of a new justice a potentially explosive event. But one work, published only a few years after *Brown*, cast the largest shadow over constitutional thinking. As a law clerk for the Court while *Brown* was being argued, Alexander M. Bickel had researched the original meaning of the Fourteenth Amendment as it related to segregation; but Warren had deliberately avoided appealing to history in his opinion. As a young law professor at Yale, Bickel published his influential work, *The Least Dangerous Branch* (1962), which discussed the problems courts faced whenever they used the power of judicial review to overturn legislation. Bickel wrote eloquently of "the counter-majoritarian dilemma" which inhered in the effort of any court to substitute its legal judgment for the political will of the community. Bickel firmly supported the desegregation decisions, yet he was aware that the Court would be better advised to use a variety of interpretative techniques and procedural rules to avoid the kind of rulings that *Brown* represents. An entire generation of constitutional law scholars took Bickel's strictures as the point of departure for their own efforts to understand what a document two centuries old should mean.

That Americans should still be debating the meaning of their venerable Constitution so passionately may seem, at first glance, a source of some alarm. But disagreements over the meaning of particular clauses matter less than the deep and seemingly permanent authority the Constitution has attained. Even as the world that its framers and amenders inhabited recedes ever further in time, the authority of the Constitution seems to wax, not wane. At some point, Americans may need to invent another new constitution—but that point still seems far distant.

See also **The Classical Vision; Liberalism and Republicanism; Federalists and Antifederalists; Jacksonian Ideology; Whig Ideology; Moral Philosophy; Secession, War, and Union; Patterns of Reform and Revolt; Nationalism and Imperialism** *(volume 1);* **Analytic Philosophy; Race, Rights, and Reform; Intellectuals and Ideology in Government** *(in this volume);* **Individualism and the Self; Law and the American Mind; Government; The History of Ideas** *(volume 3); and other articles in this section.*

BIBLIOGRAPHY

Ackerman, Bruce. *We the People.* 2 vols. Cambridge, Mass., 1998.

Amar, Akhil Reed. *The Bill of Rights: Creation and Reconstruction.* New Haven, Conn., 1998.

Bickel, Alexander M. *The Least Dangerous Branch: The Supreme Court at the Bar of Politics.* 2d ed. New Haven, Conn., 1986.

Burt, Robert A. *The Constitution in Conflict.* Cambridge, Mass., 1992.

Choper, Jesse H. *Judicial Review and the National Political Process: A Functional Reconsideration of the Role of the Supreme Court.* Chicago, 1987.

Cushman, Barry. *Rethinking the New Deal Court: The Structure of a Constitutional Revolution.* New York, 1998.

Dworkin, Ronald. *Freedom's Law: The Moral Reading of the American Constitution.* Cambridge, Mass., 1996.

Ely, John Hart. *Democracy and Distrust: A Theory of Judicial Review.* Cambridge, Mass., 1980.

Fehrenbacher, Don E. *Dred Scott Case: Its Significance in American Law and Politics.* New York, 1978.

Griffin, Stephen M. *American Constitutionalism: From Theory to Politics.* Princeton, N.J., 1996.

Hyman, Harold M., and William M. Wiecek. *Equal Justice under Law: Constitutional Development, 1835–1875.* New York, 1982.

Kalman, Laura. *The Strange Career of Legal Liberalism.* New Haven, Conn., 1996.

Kens, Paul. *Judicial Power and Reform Politics: The Anatomy of Lochner v. New York*. Lawrence, Kans., 1990.

Kluger, Richard. *Simple Justice: The History of Brown v. Board of Education and Black America's Struggle for Equality*. New York, 1976.

Levy, Leonard W. *Original Intent and the Framers' Constitution*. New York, 1988.

McDonald, Forrest. *Novus Ordo Seclorum: The Intellectual Origins of the Constitution*. Lawrence, Kans., 1985.

Neely, Mark E., Jr. *The Fate of Liberty: Abraham Lincoln and Civil Liberties*. New York, 1991.

Nelson, William E. *The Fourteenth Amendment: From Political Principle to Judicial Doctrine*. Cambridge, Mass., 1988.

Primus, Richard A. *The American Language of Rights*. Cambridge, U.K., 1999.

Rakove, Jack N. *Original Meanings: Politics and Ideas in the Making of the Constitution*. New York, 1996.

Wood, Gordon S. *The Creation of the American Republic, 1776–1787*. Chapel Hill, N.C., 1969.

INTERNATIONAL RELATIONS AND CONNECTIONS

David Sylvan

The United States is a country which has been formed by extensive and varied connections with other parts of the world. From the earliest European voyages of exploration to the massive and continuing waves of immigration from almost every continent in the world; from the intricate economic ties between the United States and elsewhere to the complex intellectual exchanges between Americans and Europeans, the United States is and always has been one of the most "international" countries in the world.

Yet—and this "yet" is a commonplace of American studies—the qualitative and quantitative extent of American ties with the rest of the world have systematically been underplayed, if not ignored, in the ways by which Americans have understood their country's international connections. Thus, the United States was seen by generations of intellectuals and politicians as isolated from other continents, notably Europe. U.S. economic and migratory connections were downplayed, while U.S. political connections (including military confrontations) were seen simply as attempts by successive American governments to distance themselves from European affairs. A classic, though by no means unique, personification of this way of thinking is Thomas Jefferson: the president who negotiated the Louisiana Purchase from France, encouraged U.S. commercial ties, sent a naval squadron to attack Tripoli, and strongly advocated a softening of naturalization laws was also the one who, in his first inaugural, praised U.S. separation "from the exterminating havoc of one quarter of the globe."

With the advent of the twentieth century, this double language came under significant political and intellectual criticism. On the one hand, politicians and policy intellectuals of various stripes began to argue in favor of long-term, institutional arrangements with other countries. On the other hand, a new academic discipline, international relations, was developed in the United States; from within its ranks, studies emerged emphasizing the extent to which the United States was indeed linked to the rest of the world and that such links were of great value to the country. Ironically, both of these trends, by virtue of their success in changing traditional U.S. policy, brought about a world in which American connections came once more under critical scrutiny.

CONNECTIONS AND THE SHAPING OF AMERICA

The United States was, from the earliest settlements, a land of immigrants. Newcomers brought with them not only their individual histories, including their language, but entire settlement patterns. These left their trace in a myriad of ideas and cultural practices, from the New England village with its centrally located church, its clustered dwellings, and its traditions of local democracy to the West Indies–influenced plantations of South Carolina, with their slave quarters and their semi-aristocratic round of social events. Of course, along with immigration came a notion of what it meant to be an American, but this concept was dependent on a presumed process which began with immigration and ended with Americanization. Up until the early twentieth century, U.S. identity thus existed symbiotically with continuing flows of immigrants from overseas.

Economically, America was highly dependent for centuries on dense and continuing connections with the rest of the world. Alexander Hamilton wrote his famous *Report on Manufactures* (1791) precisely because the new country was dependent on Europe (mostly England) for even such basic items as nails. Indeed, the United States did not run a balance of trade surplus until late in the nineteenth century. The other side of the ledger—U.S. exports to Europe—was equally important, so much so, for example, that Confederate leaders during the Civil War were able to imagine themselves as not only politically, but also economically, separate from the North.

These connections and others, such as intellectual and cultural ties, were, therefore, from earliest times a fundamental component in the shaping of American identity. In the face of these ties and the necessity of their continuation, U.S. leaders wishing to build up the United States had only one choice: to strive, where possible, to minimize their significance. This was done, to some degree, by high-tariff policies (the United States was protectionist until well into the twentieth century) and by sharp reductions in immigration when it was finally thought that immigrants were no longer needed. The major thrust, however, was to insist on political and military separation from European affairs. That such a policy was in many ways disingenuous does not mean that it was any the less heartfelt. However, this policy, designed explicitly to compensate for perceived U.S. vulnerability, would run into considerable difficulties as that vulnerability subsided.

THE POLITICIANS: THE RISE OF THE INTERNATIONALISTS

In the late nineteenth century the United States became, in a remarkably short time, an imperial power with interests and possessions ranging from the Caribbean and Latin America to the Pacific and East Asia. This led to the beginnings of joint political and military action with European states, as when Washington contributed troops to help put down the Boxer Rebellion in 1900 or when the United States participated in the Algeciras Conference in 1906. Similarly, the United States negotiated a series of arrangements with Japan during the first decade of the twentieth century, specifying the latter country's role, first in Korea and then, reluctantly, in China. In the meantime, the United States built up its navy so that when it entered World War I, it was well on the way to having the second largest navy in the world. Thus, quite apart from American intervention in the Caribbean and Latin America, the United States had begun to enter into precisely the kind of "entangling" relationships against which Washington had warned in his Farewell Address.

These actions were taken by a series of Republican administrations. When the Democrats took office in 1913, U.S. links with Europe deepened yet further. The critical event was the declaration of war on Germany in 1917, which thrust masses of U.S. soldiers into battle against the Entente powers. Woodrow Wilson went further, sending U.S. troops to Russia to fight against the Bolsheviks; there, they joined forces with the British and French. After the

Armistice, the United States was heavily involved in the negotiations in Paris over the disposition of enemy territory and the conditions of peace. And, of course, Wilson was the principal instigator of the League of Nations, arguing passionately, if unsuccessfully, for U.S. membership.

Although Wilson's proposal was rejected by the Senate, successive Republican administrations continued to advocate binding U.S. engagements with other states. The administration of Warren Harding negotiated the Washington Naval Agreements, linking American naval strength to that of Britain and Japan. Under Herbert Hoover the United States went so far as to participate in League of Nations efforts aimed at blocking Japanese annexation of Manchuria. Meanwhile, efforts continued to work out binding arrangements for repayment of American war loans. Nonetheless, internationalists felt themselves in a delicate position and U.S. military and political ties in Europe and Asia were not extended until the end of the 1930s.

American entry into World War II in 1941 marked a lasting victory for those politicians favoring extensive, long-term U.S. involvement in Europe and elsewhere. The United States sent millions of troops abroad during the war; many of them remained for decades afterwards, as part of cold war containment policy. Starting in the 1940s, the United States organized and maintained several permanent alliances. Similarly, the U.S. government set up the United Nations and insisted that it be headquartered on American soil. During the war, American officials drafted plans for multilateral economic organizations such as the International Monetary Fund and the World Bank; these, too, were located in the United States. These various policy initiatives, none of which was subsequently reversed, represent the institutionalization of both Theodore Roosevelt's military activism abroad and Woodrow Wilson's political internationalism.

This engagement with the rest of the world was important in more than simply an organizational or budgetary sense. It meant that the broad range of U.S. international connections was recognized, not as something apart from politics or as an unavoidable technical necessity, but as a voluntary, deliberately sought policy. The ideological shift was symbolized by Republican senator Arthur Vandenberg, formerly a proponent of U.S. isolation from European affairs, who became a staunch advocate of U.S. involvement in international institutions—including the United Nations, which, both in the Senate and as a member of the U.S. delegation to the UN's conference in San Francisco, he played an integral role in setting up.

When the cold war ended, some observers thought that the United States might return to a belief that it could disengage itself from permanent political and military ties outside of the Western Hemisphere. Over ten years later, at the end of the century, these predictions had not been borne out. The United States maintained troops in Germany and Japan and fought alongside its NATO allies in the Persian Gulf, Bosnia, and Kosovo in the decade after 1990. Although the United States became embroiled in budgetary disputes with the United Nations, opinion polls showed that most Americans remained in favor of U.S. membership; even opponents of the UN finally recognized that there was no chance of U.S. withdrawal. The two Bretton Woods institutions survived, and in the mid-1990s were joined by a third (itself foreseen in the 1940s), which the United States helped to push through: the World Trade Organization.

THE POLICY INTELLECTUALS

In pursuing their new policies of political and military engagement abroad, politicians were able to mirror, for a general audience, the arguments that various writers had been putting forward in narrower circles. Such writers came from various backgrounds—academia, journalism, law, and so forth—and advised politicians either directly or through their publications. Thus, when Roosevelt pushed for a naval buildup in the early 1900s, he was echoing the arguments of Alfred Mahan in his various writings about the importance of sea power in world politics as well as more general Social Darwinist arguments current on both sides of the Atlantic. Similarly, both Wilson and his principal senatorial opponent, Henry Cabot Lodge (both recipients of Ph.Ds in political science), were influenced in their advocacy (Lodge's was initially stronger than Wilson's) of a "League to Enforce Peace" by many of the historians and lawyers putting forward detailed plans for dispute adjudication among states.

During the interwar years, policy intellectuals continued to play a significant role. Walter Lippmann, who had begun his career by advising Wilson, argued strongly for continued U.S. political involvement abroad. His views were supported in certain respects by the theologian Reinhold Niebuhr, who broke definitively with pacifism in the 1930s. These two names are the tip of the iceberg:

across the nation, dozens of foreign relations leagues and institutes provided a constant stream of books and articles advocating the political and moral necessity of U.S. activism.

It was after World War II, however, that policy intellectuals had their greatest impact on and in support of internationalist policies. Officials such as George Kennan and Paul Nitze laid out the basic rationale for containment policies (the latter citing approvingly Hannah Arendt's work on totalitarianism). Scholars of military affairs such as Bernard Brodie and Herman Kahn developed fundamental notions of nuclear deterrence. Economists such as Walt Rostow put forward arguments supporting economic development as a means of combating Communism. These various ideas were then repackaged and presented both to elite audiences and, in the form of consultant advice, to politicians, by other intellectuals such as McGeorge Bundy, Henry Kissinger, and Arthur Schlesinger Jr.

An important means by which policy intellectuals made their influence felt after World War II is the enormous expansion of the U.S. foreign policy bureaucracy. To some degree, this came about via the growth of the State Department, though that involved foreign service officers more than policy intellectuals (the latter congregated mostly in specialized parts of State, such as the Policy Planning Staff and the Bureau of Intelligence and Research). The significant growth, though, was in other agencies: the Central Intelligence Agency, the National Security Council staff, and the Department of Defense. In each of these cases, numerous appointments were made and staff members hired; many of the latter had academic degrees in international relations and were, from the very start of their careers, specialists in particular aspects of foreign policy.

Although some of the policy intellectuals who entered government stayed there for many years, a more typical path—at least at the higher levels—involved a recurring cycle of government service followed by several years of extragovernmental activities. These latter sometimes were in academia: teaching jobs in political science departments or, to an increasing degree, specialized schools of international relations, such as those attached to Johns Hopkins and Tufts. However, another feature of the post–World War II era was the creation of research institutes ("think tanks") based both in Washington, D.C., and elsewhere (for example, RAND, in Santa Monica, California). Such organizations—the Brookings Institution, the American Enterprise Institute, and, somewhat later, the Heritage Foundation—provided salaries and research facilities for policy specialists, who were thus able both to carry out research and comment on various aspects of U.S. foreign relations.

With the proliferation of specialized, technical issues in international relations, the opportunities for policy intellectuals became greater than ever. Concomitantly, their work was less likely to be in the general public eye and, more and more, to be based on academic research. Of course, generalists such as Jeane Kirkpatrick and Samuel Huntington (both political scientists) still flourished even after the cold war, but increasingly their role was supplemented by that of specialists in various academic subfields.

THE ACADEMICS: THE DISCIPLINE OF INTERNATIONAL RELATIONS

For millennia, writers have studied the interactions of kingdoms, empires, states, and other forms of political organization. Commentaries on how these various political units do and should behave stretch as far back as the *Tso chuan*, the *Arthasastra*, and the histories of Herodotus and Thucydides. Subsequent writers such as Ibn Khaldun, Machiavelli, and—in a methodologically more self-conscious treatise—Vico continued this tradition. However, international relations as a scholarly field, a discipline, is far more recent, and dates back only to the 1920s.

Wright, Lasswell, and Deutsch   The key location was the University of Chicago political science department. It had been built up with the aim of studying politics in a rigorous and systematic way, and it is no exaggeration to say that the modern discipline of political science was largely shaped at Chicago in the 1920s. Among the stars of the department was a specialist in international law, Quincy Wright, and one of the department's own graduates, the polymath Harold Lasswell. Working separately, they developed the basic theoretical approaches and research methodologies that, to this day, mark the study of international relations.

Apart from his work in law, Wright published two massive works. The most significant was the huge, interdisciplinary *Study of War* (1942). In it, Wright attempted to gather and test numerous hypotheses about where, when, and how wars occurred, what their consequences might be, and how they might be avoided in the future. He deliberately borrowed from psychology, anthropology, econom-

ics, and numerous other fields; he also had his research assistants (many of whom subsequently went on to distinguished careers of their own) gather the first large-scale, systematic data set on wars over the centuries. Although Wright's work has been improved on since its initial appearance, subsequent studies of war have followed very much in its footsteps.

Lasswell was more prolific than Wright. He carried out the first genuinely international collaborative research project, gathering data in over fifty countries on the relationship of psychological phenomena such as insecurities and reasoning styles among elites to the kinds of foreign policies pursued by different states. He also pioneered the study of propaganda and political symbols, and served as an adviser to the U.S. government on radio broadcasting during World War II. In the 1950s and 1960s he centered his work at Yale, where he trained a new generation of political scientists and pioneered research into the comparative study of values in politics. Interestingly, even though Lasswell was first and foremost a scholar, he was able to foresee important emerging tendencies in world politics, one of which was the growth of what would now be called the national security state.

The basic methodological orientation of both Wright and Lasswell combined precision with extensive comparison. Hypotheses, drawn originally from various fields, were put forward and modified, then tested against data from numerous countries, of which the United States was only one. Implicit in this approach was the notion that the United States was a country just like others and that its leaders responded to the same concerns as their counterparts in other states. Moreover, the policy implications of both Wright's and Lasswell's work were, although varied, concordant in one respect: that states wishing to protect themselves and to defend their interests more effectively had, of necessity, to work with other states. In this way, the thrust of both scholars' work was that engagement with the rest of the world was not only unavoidable but highly useful.

Among Lasswell's colleagues at Yale was a younger scholar, Karl Deutsch. In the 1950s, he had done pathbreaking work on the roots of nationalism, arguing that it stemmed first and foremost from the growth of communicative networks between persons. Deutsch extended this work to the phenomenon of integration—the merging together of political institutions—and was able both to analyze and to make predictions about the course of European unification. After going to Yale, where he began to collaborate with Lasswell, Deutsch began to study how various governmental phenomena, such as decision making, could usefully be seen as involving flows of information. In his later years, Deutsch began to collaborate with scholars elsewhere on the study of war and of general trends in international relations.

Deutsch extended the methodological orientation of both Wright and Lasswell, emphasizing above all the importance of transactions in international relations. For Deutsch, transactions were what constituted the bulk of peaceful international relations (and, for that matter, of decision making within states): flows of goods, people, and information of various sorts. Thus, trade, investment, tourism, immigration, letter writing, radio broadcasts, and so forth comprised, in their totality, international relations outside of war. Deutsch found that dense networks of transactions across borders made it increasingly difficult for people in different countries to regard each other as enemies. In this sense, transactions were a cause of what Deutsch called "security communities." This not only was an implicit argument in favor of European integration (itself supported by the U.S. government) but of continued U.S. efforts at creating and strengthening international regimes that fostered extensive transaction flows.

Starting in the late 1950s other scholars, some of whom were colleagues or former students of Wright, Lasswell, or Deutsch, others of whom were influenced by their work, began dealing with a variety of research topics in international relations. Some focused on small groups in foreign policy or on decision making under crisis situations; others on the functioning of international organizations, on long-run tendencies in "balance of power" systems, and on the structure of political and economic ties between different countries. These various studies, extraordinarily disparate in their subject matter and methods of data collection, were nonetheless marked by a considerable agreement that international relations should be studied in a social scientific manner: by formulating hypotheses, testing them rigorously against data, and, eventually, cumulating results. The United States was in this regard one case among others; to separate it out from other countries made no sense. Moreover, even though international relations scholars varied considerably in their political orientations, they agreed that the United States neither could nor should disengage from the rest of the world. Hence, the emerging discipline of international relations

lent social scientific support to the pro-connection stance of both policy intellectuals and U.S. politicians.

By the 1960s the notion of international relations as a social science had spread to the top one hundred or so universities and liberal arts colleges in the United States. In turn, the explosion of graduate studies led to a new generation of doctoral students trained along these lines and thus to the ever-more-widespread diffusion of social scientific international relations across American academia. This trend had numerous consequences, intellectual and otherwise; the most important, however, was the effect on the way in which undergraduates began—then and for decades thereafter—to see the world.

Schuman and Wolfers A good case in point is the career of Frederick Schuman, who received his doctorate at the University of Chicago with Lasswell and Wright. Schuman taught for several decades at Williams College in Massachusetts; there, his courses in international relations durably marked generations of undergraduates. In that era, the State Department and other agencies concerned with foreign policy, such as the Central Intelligence Agency, recruited heavily from the Ivy League and other elite colleges and universities. Schuman's teaching thus represented a first, and for that reason, intellectually powerful, exposure to international relations. Moreover, Schuman wrote *International Politics* (1933), one of the first textbooks in international relations, and maintained it, through various revisions, for close to forty years. Though eventually superseded by Hans Morgenthau's *Politics among Nations* (1948), Schuman's text dominated college syllabi in the principal feeder schools of U.S. foreign policy makers for decades.

From the first edition of his book, Schuman's argument was the very Lasswellian one that the "only prospect for intelligently directed change" (p. 835) was for elites in the United States and elsewhere to build up a new internationalism of "international collaboration between the nation-states" (p. 842) via systematic economic cooperation, a web of day-to-day ties among democratic states, and new political arrangements to which positive symbols could be attached. This emphasis on the practical necessity of economic and political multilateralism, grounded in social scientific studies of various international connections, was first formulated by Schuman in the 1930s; it came to dominate U.S. foreign policy for over half a century and arguably still holds sway at the beginning of the twenty-first century.

Another example of a Lasswell-influenced scholar whose teaching and writing was of paramount importance in introducing undergraduates to international relations is that of Arnold Wolfers, who taught for several decades at Yale. Wolfers, although cast as a "realist" (that is, a believer that international relations revolves essentially around force and the pursuit of power), was at pains in both his teaching and his writing to emphasize the multifaceted nature of foreign policy goals, the necessity of collective action by groups of states in order to attain those goals, and the obligation of elites to shape public opinion if they were to carry out such action. As with Schuman, Wolfers's reasoning was social scientific in nature: putting forward hypotheses about state goals and interaction, testing those hypotheses against various empirical cases, and connecting his claims to those made in related disciplines. Small wonder, then, that successive generations of American foreign policy makers turned over and over, far more so than their counterparts in other countries, to social scientists when making various decisions. In this way, the discipline of international relations went hand in hand with the influence of policy intellectuals.

However, if the most apparent impact of the establishment of international relations as a social science discipline is found in the worldviews of foreign policy makers—bureaucrats and politicians—in the United States, a more broad-based effect is equally discernible. In almost every college and university in the United States, international relations was established either as an undergraduate major in its own right or as a recognized subfield of political science. Starting in the 1980s, enrollments in undergraduate international relations courses began to increase at a growing pace. As a result, large numbers of students were exposed to ongoing international relations research. One would thus expect that, with the passage of time, Americans would come to see themselves as both inescapably connected with the rest of the world and as obliged to continue, indeed to extend, those connections.

GLOBALIZATION AND CONNECTIONS

To some degree, this expectation has been borne out. Public opinion polls over the past half century have consistently shown a strong level of support for close U.S. collaboration with other countries, whether in the United Nations or in other multilateral forms of cooperation, ranging from economic links, through cultural ties, to various forms of joint action (for example, on fighting crime and disease). This sense of connectedness is that of a good in itself: American involvement with the rest of the world is considered as positive, both for its effects in solving problems and, more generally, as representing the way in which international relations should be carried out. The one exception to this pro-engagement stance is a general reluctance to back U.S. combat operations abroad. Only after troops have been committed has there been a "rally round the flag" effect, which in turn has only been sustained as long as casualties have been low.

However, both the mass public's and U.S. policy makers' generally favorable view of U.S. connections is conditioned on U.S. leadership over other countries. When other states, whether allies or adversaries, are seen as defying the United States, support for cooperation with such states drops. The problem for politicians, policy intellectuals, and academic specialists in international relations committed to the necessity and usefulness of U.S. connections with the rest of the world has thus been how to maintain public support for those connections in the face of a long-term decline in U.S. leadership. This decline is not a matter of U.S. weakness but of the simple fact that the conditions of 1945, when most European states were prostrate and accepting of American leadership in the newly created multilateral institutions, were unique and could not last.

Up until the 1990s, challenges to U.S. leadership were finessed within the United States by reference to national security considerations. Arguments were repeatedly made by specialists in international relations that even if multilateral cooperation did not benefit the U.S. immediately, such cooperation was vital over the longer run in fighting the cold war. Thus, for example, even as successive American presidents were putting pressure on Japan and Germany regarding their trade surpluses with the United States, they were also attempting to head off efforts at stronger retaliation with the argument that these states were, after all, U.S. allies and that it was in the national interest that they be kept strong.

With the end of the cold war, such arguments lost much of their power. Moreover, it was apparent that Communist-style alternatives to market mechanisms had proven unsuccessful, which meant that the original post-1945 multilateral economic institutions would now need to be extended to include dozens of new state members. International relations specialists in the United States had therefore to plan for new economic arrangements, with all that such planning implied about the inevitable need to make concessions to other states, without any longer being able to use the security argument as a means of dampening domestic dissent.

By the mid-1990s, this strategy was reaching its limits. It became increasingly difficult to negotiate new multilateral agreements, since domestic opponents of such accords were able to slow down or completely block them. Plans for an extension of the North American Free Trade Agreement beyond Canada and Mexico had to be shelved in the face of labor opposition; the draft of an accord on multilateral investment had to be dropped because of protests by various groups; the Kyoto Protocol on greenhouse gas emissions was not ratified by the Senate due to criticism from the coal and automobile industries; proposals to expand UN peacekeeping operations, even without U.S. troops, went nowhere because of U.S. budgetary restrictions; a treaty establishing an international criminal court, an idea pushed for years by the United States, went unsigned by that country because of Pentagon opposition; and, as the century ended, proposals to start a new round of trade negotiations under the auspices of the World Trade Organization were stymied, among other reasons, due to domestic U.S. protests.

Certainly, the opponents who were able to block the various multilateral initiatives of the late 1990s were heterogeneous in nature. By no means did they all see themselves as conservative; indeed, many had strong links with labor unions and other forces on the left elsewhere around the world. (This internationalization of protest is not new, dating back to the socialist movement of the nineteenth century; it is, however, far more extensive than in the past.) This made their successes, if politically more tenuous, all the more important from the standpoint of the pro-connection position. No longer was it possible to convince people that cooperation per se was good: it now depended on the kind of cooperation being proposed. Since it was likely that any given kind could well end up disadvantaging one or more groups, international relations specialists therefore had to devise additional arguments on a case-by-case basis.

At the same time as domestic opposition was growing, a second shift was occurring. Increasingly, the mass media began to speak and write of "globalization" as a new and powerful trend in international relations. Such claims were profoundly ahistorical (from the earliest European voyages to the Americas and Asia, a global economy had existed) but were nonetheless strongly argued. The world was seen as subject to massive market forces, with producers and consumers everywhere facing the same competitive alternatives. These alternatives were by no means all negative; what mattered is that they were understood as invasive and, in most respects, unavoidable.

The result of these two trends is that for many Americans, international connections came to be perceived as necessary, though often with negative repercussions. In the face of this perspective, international relations specialists found themselves very much in the position of their counterparts a century earlier. The irony was that in the interim, the connectionist agenda had triumphed and that the world they were trying to maintain was very much one of their own making.

See also **European and Indigenous Encounters; Africa and America; Expansion and Empire** *(volume 1);* **World War and Cold War; Franco-American Cultural Encounters and Exchanges; Vietnam as a Cultural Crisis; American Expatriate Artists Abroad; Artistic, Intellectual, and Political Refugees; Asian Americans; German Speakers; Irish Americans; Italian Americans; Latinas and Latinos in the United States** *(in this volume); and other articles in this section.*

BIBLIOGRAPHY

Early American thought on separation from Europe extends well beyond Jefferson and Hamilton; still useful is Henry Adams's nine-volume work, the *History of the United States during the Administrations of Jefferson and Madison* (New York, 1890–1891). A good summary and extensive bibliography of this period are in Thomas G. Paterson et al., eds., *American Foreign Relations: A History,* 4th ed. (Lexington, Mass., 1995), vol. 1, chaps. 1–2. On policy intellectuals, see Alfred T. Mahan, *The Influence of Sea Power upon History, 1660–1783* (Boston, 1890); Walter Lippmann, *Drift and Mastery: An Attempt to Diagnose* the Current Unrest (New York, 1914); Reinhold Niebuhr, *Moral Man and Immoral Society: A Study in Ethics and Politics* (New York, 1936); "Mr. X" [George Kennan], "The Sources of Soviet Conduct," *Foreign Affairs* 25, no. 4 (1947): 566–582; [Paul Nitze et al.], "National Security Council Paper Number 68," *Foreign Relations of the United States, 1950* (Washington, 1976), vol. 1, pp. 234–292; Bernard Brodie, *Strategy in the Missile Age* (Princeton, N.J., 1965); Herman Kahn, *On Thermonuclear War* (Princeton, N.J., 1960); W. W. Rostow, *The Stages of Economic Growth: A Non-Communist Manifesto* (Cambridge, U.K., 1960); and Henry A. Kissinger, *Nuclear Weapons and Foreign Policy* (New York, 1957).

The two major books by Quincy Wright are *A Study of War*, 2 vols. (Chicago, 1942) and *The Study of International Relations* (New York, 1955). With Harold Lasswell there is an embarrassment of riches; among his best works are *Psychopathology and Politics* (Chicago,1930); *World Politics and Personal Insecurity* (New York, 1935); and, with the coeditor Daniel Lerner, *The Policy Sciences* (Stanford, Calif., 1951); it is interesting to see Lasswell's reflections on his former colleague and teacher, Quincy Wright, in "The Cross-Disciplinary Manifold: The Chicago Prototype," in *The Search for World Order: Studies by Students and Colleagues of Quincy Wright*, edited by Albert Lepawsky, et al. (New York, 1971). Among the most significant works of Karl Deutsch are *Nationalism and Social Communication: An Inquiry into the Foundations of Nationality*, 2d ed. (Cambridge, Mass., 1953); *Political Community and the North Atlantic Area: International Organization in the Light of Historical Experience*, with editors Sidney A. Burrell et al. (Princeton, 1957); and *The Nerves of Government: Models of Political Communication and Control* (New York, 1963). Other examples of the types of social scientific works referred to in the text are Nazli Choucri and Robert C. North, *Nations in Conflict: National Growth and International Violence* (San Francisco, 1975); Ernst B. Haas, *Beyond the Nation-State: Functionalism and International Organization* (Stanford, Calif., 1964); Graham T. Allison, *Essence of Decision: Explaining the Cuban Missile Crisis* (Boston, 1971); Robert O. Keohane and Joseph S. Nye Jr., eds., *Transnational Relations and World Politics* (Cambridge, Mass., 1972); and Morton A. Kaplan, *System and Process in International Politics* (New York, 1957).

Frederick L. Schuman's textbook first appeared under the title *International Politics: An Introduction to the Western State System* (New York, 1933), though it went through multiple editions and changed title. An excellent introduction to the writings of Arnold Wolfers is *Discord and Collaboration: Essays on International Politics* (Baltimore, 1962). Recent debates about U.S. leadership and the future of multilateral cooperation are contained in numerous works; see, for example, Henry R. Nau, *The Myth of America's Decline: Leading the World Economy into the 1990s* (New York, 1990); *America's National Interests, A Report from the Commission on America's National Interests* (Cambridge, Mass., 1996); and Arthur M. Schlesinger Jr., "Back to the Womb? Isolationism's Renewed Threat," *Foreign Affairs* 74, no. 4 (1995): 2–8.

SOCIAL REFORM

Kevin Mattson

Social reform may best be defined in contrast to political reform. While political reform focuses on changing the institutions of government, social reform scrutinizes the realm of interpersonal behavior—the way citizens interact on a daily basis. Essentially, social reform goes deeper than political reform, for it is motivated by a belief that behavior (even the smallest personal act) can be examined and changed for the better, sometimes through voluntary action, sometimes by remaking institutions. To give a contemporary example, social reform is witnessed in the cultural struggles (some would call them wars) over abortion rights that began in the 1970s, while political reform is best epitomized by the age-old struggle for campaign finance reform in America.

Social reform must be set off from revolution—that is, the complete remaking of everyday life as witnessed in historical atrocities like the cultural revolution mobilized in Communist China by Mao Tse-tung. Social reformers believe in tinkering with existing patterns of behavior and in remaking, rather than making over. Social reform springs from a pragmatic philosophy and a faith that society can be improved when citizens change their institutions and the way they act. Thus, social reformers tend to be optimistic.

From the beginning, social reform has been a part of the American character and history. After the original revolution that founded this country, Americans avoided political revolutions—in marked contrast to countries like France. Instead, Americans committed themselves to building a republic open-minded to reform and, hence, resistant to revolution. One of America's most eloquent public poets, Walt Whitman, explained that America had (unlike the Old World) already established democratic political institutions. Its challenge, therefore, was to extend the values of democratic politics to everyday life in civil society. In his classic essay "Democratic Vistas," Whitman wrote, "I say democracy is only of use there that it may pass on and come to its flower and fruits in manners, in the highest forms of interaction between men, and their beliefs—in religion, literature, colleges, and schools—democracy in all public and private life" (*Complete Poetry and Selected Prose,* pp. 474–475). In Whitman's words can be seen the radical, democratic, and commonsense basis of social reform in America.

Nonetheless, there has been more to the story of social reform in America than optimism. Some have argued that those who decide to remake society cloak sinister motives and actually force their values on others. From this viewpoint, social reform is not about democracy or humanitarian motivations but about imposition. The critics argue that reformers might speak the language of universal humanitarianism—the language that Ralph Waldo Emerson spoke (see sidebar)—but they really foist their own particularistic views on society (be those religious or secular). Whichever interpretation one agrees with—reform as democracy or domination—the criticism makes clear that the history of social reform is nuanced and not always easy to interpret. It also makes clear that by examining the legacy of social reform, we ask difficult questions about the meaning of American democracy.

THE CLASSICAL PERIOD: RELIGION AND THE ANTEBELLUM ERA

The classical period of social reform in the United States is certainly the period after the Constitution was ratified and up through the Progressive Era. By the time the authors of the *Federalist Papers* made their case for representative government and a balanced Constitution, the primary political institutions of America were in place. Attention could now be paid to who would participate in these governmental institutions (which thus far had excluded women, free African Americans, and the poor) and to issues that fell outside politics and within "civil

"MAN THE REFORMER"

Ralph Waldo Emerson, observing the tide of the numerous social reform movements in his own era, reflected in 1841: "What is a man born for but to be a Reformer, a Remaker of what man has made; a renouncer of lies; a restorer of truth and good, imitating that great Nature which embosoms us all, and which sleeps no moment on an old past, but every hour repairs herself yielding us every morning a new day, and with every pulsation a new life?" (from "Man the Reformer," *Complete Works,* p. 248). Emerson makes clear that social reform can be passionate and fervent while remaining committed to the limits of repair and remaking.

society"—an arena, as the French political observer Alexis de Tocqueville described it in *Democracy in America* (1835–1840), dominated by voluntary associations. And while the Bill of Rights separated religion from government, the realm of civil society welcomed faith with open arms. Theocracy had little future in America—except for the great experiment of Mormonism—but citizens could try to sway others that their religious belief should dictate social behavior (or even the entire structure of social life, as attempted by some of the alternative communities that sprouted up during the nineteenth century).

Most important in this regard was evangelical Protestantism, the predominant form of religious belief among middle-class Americans. In the early years of the Republic, Protestantism had shed the more stern Calvinism of yesteryear with its central focus on original sin. The religious fervor associated with the Second Great Awakening—symbolized in lively and often raucous tent meetings—and an increase in newer sects (especially Baptists and Methodists) during the nineteenth century had a concomitant component in social reform. Evangelicalism rejected the pessimistic undertones of Calvinism and Puritanism—especially the doctrine of original sin and predestination. The newer churches saw sin as a failure of an individual's will to reach the love of God rather than as a permanent state of depravity. Humans suffered from the errors of free will, but that same free will allowed them to reform

their behavior and become more complete in the eyes of God. Evangelicalism's faith in this-worldly redemption motivated much social reform throughout the nineteenth century.

Indeed, a proliferation of voluntary moral and religious societies led by evangelicals served as the backbone of many social reform initiatives during the nineteenth century. One of America's most famous preachers, the liberal Presbyterian Lyman Beecher, called for a statewide organization in Connecticut that would stand for the "Suppression of Vice and the Promotion of Good Morals." Another famous Presbyterian evangelist, Charles Grandison Finney led numerous revivals and proselytized through tract societies, arguing for citizens to reform their behavior. "God has made man a moral free agent," Finney explained to his converts, suggesting that they should make this clear in their own lives (*A Shopkeeper's Millennium,* quoted in Johnson, p. 3). After gaining reknown for his activities in New York City and Philadelphia, Finney was invited to Rochester, New York, in 1830 to save the city from vice, in what became one of the most famous campaigns of antebellum social reform. Finney crusaded to convert new believers and to counter the sins of imbibing alcohol. Temperance, Finney believed, could be seen as direct witness to an individual's good character, and hence, his or her closeness to God. One observer claimed that Finney helped shut down the "grog shops" that were sprouting up around Rochester. In fact, many working citizens resisted Finney's revival, but in general his efforts in Rochester illustrate the connection between evangelical faith and social reform.

A crucial feature of nineteenth-century social reform was the role of women in leading these movements. Women might have been shut out of politics by a "cult of domesticity," but they held enormous responsibility in family life and civil society. As the home receded in the making of economic goods during the nineteenth century, socialization took center stage in family life. The mother was the moral custodian over her children (the father's role and his tendency toward strict discipline concomitantly dwindled), and she was expected "to give up wealth, frivolity, and 'fashion,' to conquer weakness and ailments, sloth and insensitivity, and acquire a discipline and knowledge preparing her for a great calling" (Wishy, *The Child and the Republic,* p. 28). This calling focused women's attention on the home, but it could also push women out of the home. Concerned with their own family's moral standing, women reckoned with social forces that threatened the peace and haven of the domestic sphere. They especially reacted against two key aspects of the male-dominated world of business and leisure—prostitution and drinking.

Middle-class women gravitated toward missionary and Bible societies during the 1820s, giving religion a female tinge. As women grew fervent with religious belief, they became the foot soldiers of evangelical social reform. Christopher Lasch writes, "The female reformer, taking quite seriously her role as the custodian of official morality, threw herself into public causes in the belief that the influence of women would purify" social life and "lead to a general revival of religion" (*The World of Nations*, p. 45). For instance, in 1834, the New York Female Reform Society formed to combat prostitution. Members actually descended upon brothels, praying vigilantly for the women inside. In Utica, New York, women entered taverns and berated men for drinking (presaging Carry Nation, who famously invaded saloons and smashed kegs of alcohol with a hatchet at the turn of the century). This close association between social reform and women's activism lasted for quite some time, even after evangelical faith waned.

In the end, though, mothers were expected to devote the bulk of their energy to cultivating their children's morality. Childhood—as a special and distinct category of life—essentially was invented during the nineteenth century. While in colonial times, children were seen as little adults (and from a Calvinist standpoint, as sinful adults), in the nineteenth century, childhood became viewed as a phase of life distinct from adulthood and one in which the learning of morality and faith became central. Nurture replaced discipline, and nurture relied upon an appeal to the budding conscience of the child. Popular manuals offered mothers advice about child-rearing techniques suitable for moral inculcation. By the 1840s, a major result of social reform—the public school—was buttressing the efforts of mothers even more.

That the public school grew out of the same social reform spirit that fueled temperance and other movements is quite clear. Horace Mann, the most important leader in American school reform during the antebellum period, was a classic social reformer who had been involved in temperance crusades. The public school also drew upon the teaching energies of women—creating one of the first female-dominated professions that encouraged women to turn their roles as nurturers in the home to public-minded work. Hence, Mann followed on previous social reform initiatives, but also opened up a new, distinctly modern chapter in the history of social

Horace Mann (1796–1859). Mann became known as the father of American public education. © CORBIS

reform. In advocating for the creation of the public school, Mann argued that social problems could not be reformed by the voluntary activities of civil society alone but required public support (that is, taxation) and the will of government. This, in turn, required the growth of administrative bureaucracies capable of overseeing these processes. In taking this step, Mann developed a central tenet of modern and liberal belief: that solving social problems required more than private, voluntary activities.

Mann's efforts centered in Boston, and for good reason. During the 1840s, Irish immigrants flooded the city. At the same time, factories displaced the older apprenticeship system of work. Working-class children began loitering in the city's streets, making the "urchin" a central fixture in nineteenth-century urban life. Confronting this social problem, Mann argued for placing these children in schools where they could be trained to become public-minded citizens while being saved from the vices of the city's streets (that is, prostitution and saloons). As head of the state board of education (beginning in 1837), Mann called for compulsory schooling. He also argued against those within his own movement who believed schoolteachers had the right to discipline children physically. Instead, Mann argued that teachers should nurture the *conscience* of students. Mann, therefore, connected his vision of the school to the evangelical spirit that had informed social reform up to his own time, while moving beyond voluntarism. The public school became an institution closely associated with American democracy and the solution of social problems.

Mann found himself railing against a previous form of schooling that was clearly elitist—the academy system that had housed and schooled the wealthy. There was never any doubt in Mann's mind that the public school promised an inclusive and democratic culture. As he put it, "If we do not prepare children to become good citizens, if we do not develop their capacities, if we do not enrich their minds with knowledge, imbue their hearts with the love of truth and duty, and a reverence for all things sacred and holy, then our republic must go down to destruction" (quoted in Tyler, *Freedom's Ferment,* p. 239). Nonetheless, many elements of working-class Boston resisted the public school system, believing it would only benefit the wealthy and consign their children to factory life. Mann also faced a combative writer, Orestes Brownson. During the 1840s, Brownson scrutinized Mann's board of education reports. In doing so, he became one of the first social critics to argue that what might appear democratic and humanitarian could actually be a form of imposition. Brownson lambasted the board of education as a "branch of general police." Arguing that healthy communities could educate themselves without schools, Brownson suggested that Mann and his fellow board of education members "esteem [schooling as] the most effectual means possible of checking pauperism, and crime, and making the rich secure in their possessions" ("The Second Annual Report of the Board of Education," p. 412). Thus, Brownson argued, Mann used the language of democracy and humanitarianism to keep things safe for an elite.

Not surprisingly, this critique failed to sway Mann or his fellow social reformers, who succeeded in establishing public schools and continued to pour their energies into other initiatives at social reform. For instance, Mann called for prison reform. Others following his example took part in the abolitionist movement—the most important social reform movement in nineteenth-century America.

Abolitionists believed sincerely that by ending slavery, they would remake their society. As James Stewart puts it, "Abolitionists envisioned their cause leading to a society reborn in Christian brotherhood. Emancipation, like temperance, women's rights and communitarianism, become synonymous with the redemption of mankind and the opening of a purer phase of human history" (*Holy Warriors,* p. 45). The most thoughtful of the abolitionists, including William Lloyd Garrison, editor of the *Liberator* and a vocal spokesperson, made persuasive arguments that the means of abolitionists must conform to their ends—the re-creation of a beloved community. Garrison was one of the first to marry the philosophy of nonviolence to social reform. Though political decree and the military bloodshed of the Civil War would ultimately be the decisive elements in ending slavery, abolitionists left behind a strong legacy in the belief that slavery required Americans to re-examine their moral credo and live by higher ideals. They made clear that slavery required a reform in the hearts and souls of Americans.

By the 1840s, one major social problem, besides slavery, held the attention of northern evangelical reformers more than any other. This was the problem of poverty. At first, evangelical Christians seemed to fear the "urban masses" and blamed poverty on character defects. From the perspective of the historian Carroll Smith-Rosenberg, the poor seemed "a moral cancer within the body politic" (*Religion and the Rise of the American City,* p. 157). But in trying to convert the poor, evangelical Christians started to notice the need for reform of the urban environment. The New York Association for Improving the Condition of the Poor, formed in 1843, took the lead in criticizing landlords who crammed the poor into unsafe tenements. This group, along with the Children's Aid Society, provided summer camps for poor children to escape the city, if only briefly. But even with this newfound attention to the social environment, pre–Civil War social reformers believed, as Rosenberg puts it, that the "only real solutions for pauperism were ultimately moral and religious" (p. 260). Whatever their limited view of solutions, these reformers put poverty squarely on the broader agenda of future, and more modern, reformers.

CLASSICAL SOCIAL REFORM TURNS MODERN

With the Civil War and the Gilded Age, industrial capitalism was born, and the classical period of social reform underwent a change. The slavery issue had been settled, but the issue of poverty carried over directly from the antebellum period. Indeed, industrialization and urbanization only heightened the issue of poverty. Reformers still worried about the character of the poor, but they began rejecting older forms of charity work. Facing an increasingly secular culture, reformers drew on different sources of motivation than religion. As with much else, reform was *problematized* in the modern period—the assuredness of evangelicalism started to dwindle. Within the Social Gospel movement, liberal Protestants argued that the Bible could still be a source of inspiration for doing good. Walter Rauschenbusch provided an intellectually sophisticated rendering of these arguments in his *A Theology for the Social Gospel* (1917). But even so, these liberal efforts could not shore up religious inspiration from the increasing power of "unbelief" that swept middle-class Americans and the social reformers among them at the turn of the century (see Turner). Reformers started to question their motivations, wondering aloud if they were truly noble. They even started asking questions about the relationship between reform and democracy.

The lives of two reformers from the period—Frederic C. Howe and Jane Addams—reflect the increasing complexity of reform in the modern world. Howe grew up in a Presbyterian household in a small Pennsylvania town and then attended Johns Hopkins University (a very modern school). He then worked at a settlement house—the key institution of Progressive Era social reform (the most famous being Jane Addams's Hull House). As in most settlement houses, middle- and upper-class reformers moved into poorer neighborhoods to work with local citizens in order to combat poverty and urban social problems. Afterward, leaving the settlement house movement, Howe became an aide to Mayor Tom Johnson of Cleveland, Ohio, a progressive and reform-minded mayor. When Howe recounted his life in *The Confessions of a Reformer* (1925), he wrote it around the central process of "unlearning." Unlike previous evangelical reformers, Howe put his own motivation to scrutiny, openly discussing the "evangelistic morality [that] became bone of my bone, flesh of my flesh" (*Confessions,* p. 17). Howe explained that the experiences of the modern city challenged this preconceived, evangelical morality. For instance, by exploring saloons, he saw the benefits they offered working people and thus rejected the temperance movement he would have otherwise embraced. By engaging in dialogue with new immigrants, he saw how their values and customs served them well; therefore, he rejected nativism. As Howe explained it, this process of "unlearning" his moralistic inheritance was a

prerequisite to becoming a good reformer who was capable of working with people different from him. Essentially, Howe lived the life of pragmatism outlined by William James and John Dewey—he opened his mind toward new experience and made clear that effective reform demanded acceptance of a "pluralistic universe," rather than preconceived morality.

While Howe made clear that modern social reformers could question certitude, Jane Addams showed how a calling for social reform could take into account individual psychology and motivation. Addams, like Howe, had been raised in a strict family where religious certitude was key. During her coming of age, Addams went through a period of profound doubt about religion. She confessed to a friend in 1880, "I have been trying an awful experiment. I didn't pray . . . for about three months, and was shocked to find that I feel no worse for it" (quoted in Crunden, *Ministers of Reform,* p. 23). Soon thereafter, though, Addams fell into a nervous depression or what was called back then neurasthenia (a problem that touched numerous middle-class intellectuals and reformers at the time). She felt disconnected from any real engagement in life—her previous education at the Rockford Female Seminary seemed frivolous and the ideal of womanhood seemed limiting, especially since she could not bear children (because of a congenital spinal defect). Generally, she described her life during the 1880s as one of "nervous exhaustion." She felt that most middle-class women led "unnourished, oversensitive lives." This psychological and cultural crisis drove Addams on to experiment like Howe. Religious doubt, she learned, could be transcended by actively solving society's problems. In 1889, having decided to commit herself to social reform, Addams went to live with the poor in the growing city of Chicago in order to combat an increasing number of urban problems. Here she founded one of the first settlement houses in America—Hull-House.

Not only her motivations but her activities at Hull-House symbolized a turn toward modern social reform. Addams brought with her middle-class (and Victorian) values that always threatened to be imposed upon the working-class immigrants in her neighborhood. But all the while, she tried, in her own words, "to interpret democracy in social terms," that is, to break down the wall between social classes. Addams argued that the immigrants she worked with had a great deal to teach her and the other middle-class women at Hull-House. The reformer no longer prosletyzed—as reformers did during the nineteenth century and the height of

Jane Addams in 1930. The picture shows the fortieth-anniversary celebration of the founding of Hull-House. © BETTMANN/CORBIS

evangelicalism—but rather engaged in dialogue with his or her fellow citizens. Addams exhibited her pride in her fellow neighbors by exhibiting the craft work of new immigrants in her Hull-House Labor Museum. She also made an implicit argument against evangelical temperance activists, by admitting that the saloon served a social purpose and that it could not be simply abolished. Believing that an alternative to the saloon had to be offered, she created discussion groups for working-class immigrants at Hull-House. These discussions provided a space in which local citizens and settlement house workers could decide how to improve the social conditions of the neighborhood. Addams tried to work *with* her fellow citizens to improve their neighborhood. By listening to and living with poor people, Addams made clear that modern social reform required thoughtful and pragmatic action.

Addams brought the classical period of social reform into the twentieth century. Hull-House provided Addams's life with meaning and got her beyond the crisis that marked her life during the 1880s. But gradually those who worked there and at other settlement houses saw themselves less as

passionate creatures stirring with internal conflicts and more as professional employees—as what would become known as social workers. As her biographer Allen Davis points out, Addams "refused to become professionalized, and never took a salary"; nonetheless, Hull-House became "a training ground for new professional careers as experts and administrators in government, industry, and the universities" (*American Heroine,* p. 80). Social work grew to be one profession among a myriad of others, and social workers were expected to have gone to school to learn how to manage the individual cases who walked into their offices. The settlement house dwindled, as a university degree replaced committed passion as prerequisite for doing social work.

Even as it gave rise to a new generation of social workers, the settlement house led some to question if it was the right arena in which to deliver services to neighborhoods. Addams herself admitted that local and national governments had a role to play in alleviating the suffering of the poor (by passing child labor laws, for instance). But there were others who began rejecting local institutions as social service providers. Most famous was Harry Hopkins, who got his background in the settlement house movement—having worked at the Christadora House in New York City. Not only was Hopkins no evangelical (he openly betted on the horses), his career illustrated an end to the classical period of social reform. From Christadora House, he moved up a newly forming ladder in the social services world. First he directed New York's state relief program. Then, Hopkins followed his boss—Franklin Delano Roosevelt—to the White House. As a part of the New Deal, he directed the Works Progress Administration (WPA), a branch of the federal government that provided work relief to millions of Americans during the Great Depression.

Hopkins's career symbolizes a transition that was taking place within modern liberal politics—a growing suspicion among political leaders about the capacities of local and voluntary activities to deliver human services and an increasing faith in the federal government's compulsory power. No longer were well-intentioned settlement house workers in local neighborhoods enough. Rather, the federal government was to oversee the lives of the poor— as the New Deal made clear. Instead of a good-natured social worker trying to help the poor directly, the poor began receiving such things as welfare checks, public work opportunities, and even subsidized medical care. Where there was once the arbitrary acts of settlement house workers (or the

796

lack thereof), now there was the welfare state. As one historian put it, by the 1930s, the settlement house "no longer seemed quite so relevant" (Trolander, *Professionalism and Social Change*, p. 24). Or as Raymond Moley, a New Dealer himself, explained, "I have not the slightest urge to be a reformer" (quoted in Leuchtenburg, *Franklin D. Roosevelt and the New Deal*, p. 339).

The birth of the welfare state ended the classical period of social reform—an era that had focused on the problems of poverty, especially those concentrated in America's growing cities. The increasing role of government in solving issues of poverty pushed aside the efforts of local social reformers like Addams and Howe. Government programs trumped local initiatives. But that did not mean that the spirit of social reform disappeared entirely. There were other issues waiting to be solved or at least confronted through the efforts of locally oriented reformers—racial inequity most especially—that leaders of government had not fully reckoned with. Nonetheless, with the rise of the New Deal, Americans seemed to accept that governmental legislation—not the efforts of nobly motivated citizens—could more effectively solve social problems. With that idea, the history of social reform changed.

INTERPRETING SOCIAL REFORM

Historians have interpreted this classical period of social reform differently. Perhaps the most appealing and forthright interpretation of social reform is one that takes the reformers' claims at face value. Seeing these reformers in the spirit of Whitman—as citizens trying to extend the democratic values of America's political institutions into social life—historians have put an optimistic spin on their efforts. The work of Alice Felt Tyler stands as a monumental example. In *Freedom's Ferment* (1944), Tyler details the history of nineteenth-century social reform movements and fits them into the interpretative framework of what she calls "dynamic democracy." Reflecting the optimism that many Americans felt toward the end of World War II, Tyler applauds nineteenth-century social reformers as having lived during a time when "liberal and humanitarian" views "were accorded almost universal hearing." She explains that "Americans were superbly conscious of the fact that it was their duty and their privilege to lead the way in reforms that brought better care to the unfortunate, hope to the poor and downtrodden." For Tyler, the nineteenth century was a period "of social ferment, . . . full of optimism, of growth, and of positive affirmation" (p. 548).

Faith such as Tyler's—a faith that echoed the earlier optimism of Emerson—began to wane soon after Tyler published *Freedom's Ferment*. By the 1950s, historians, such as Richard Hofstadter, began viewing social reform in a more pessimistic light. In *The Age of Reform* (1955), Hofstadter finds in reform initiatives a more sinister—if often unconscious—motive. He argues that a "status revolution" explained Progressive Era reform: As new wealth displaced old (at the height of the Gilded Age), those who found themselves falling through the cracks turned to reform as a means of self-preservation. Many reformers "were Progressives not because of economic deprivations but primarily because they were victims of an upheaval in status that took place in the United States during the closing decades of the nineteenth and the early years of the twentieth century" (p. 185). Thus, reformers often wanted to preserve the past—not go forward. Though he believed the New Deal had swept away this tendency of Progressives, Hofstadter warned that social reform was often marred by "moral crusading" and hidden agendas.

Though New Left historians are thought to have broken with Hofstadter's generation of historians, there were actually many carryovers in their interpretations of social reform. One of Hofstadter's students honed the critique of social reform. Christopher Lasch essentially followed Orestes Brownson's critique of Horace Mann in his interpretation of Progressive Era social reformers. Though reformers might appear as humanitarians, Lasch argued, they were really concerned with "adjustment"—with adapting people to an inhumane social system, rather than transforming it. Lasch dissected the "manipulative note that was rarely absent from" the writings of Progressive Era reformers. As he saw it, Progressive Era reform came down to an "insistence that men could best be controlled and directed not by the old, crude method of force but by 'education' in its broadest sense" (*The New Radicalism in America, 1889–1963*, p. 146). Though reformers like Jane Addams—on whom Lasch focuses a great deal of attention—looked as though they were progressive and liberal-minded, they actually cloaked sinister motives. Lasch's dissection of what he called "social control" reappeared in the New Left's interpretation of "corporate liberalism"—a belief that corporate capitalism coopted and used reform in order to preserve itself.

New Left historians might have interpreted social reform as wracked by limits, but it took a

French historian, with far left proclivities, to see in reform even more sinister motivations. Michel Foucault drew upon Friedrich Nietzsche's dissection of the philosophical concept of good conscience and his argument that "punishment" did not improve humans but only "tamed" them (*The Birth of Tragedy and the Genealogy of Morals*, pp. 216–218). For Foucault, this principle could easily be applied to a wide array of Enlightenment-based reform initiatives. (Foucault aimed his analyses at European history, but they are easily applied to America.) In his most famous book, *Discipline and Punish* (1977), he contrasts older forms of punishment with the modern prison. The sovereign king had punished subjects in public, through methods of torture—often creating elaborate methods of dismemberment (one case provides the gruesome and provocative opening of Foucault's book). But as Europe moved through a period of Enlightenment, newer methods of incarceration appeared, most emblematically the panopticon created by Jeremy Bentham. The panopticon was an observation tower that gazed into each prisoner's cell without allowing the prisoner to look back, and in Foucault's view it entirely symbolized modern reform: the modern prison worked on the *conscience* of the prisoner, not the body, and therefore became more invasive from Foucault's perspective. Foucault saw the modern prison's aim as "not to punish less, but to punish better; to punish with an attenuated severity perhaps, but in order to punish with more universality and necessity; to insert the power to punish more deeply into the social body" (*Discipline and Punish*, p. 82). Behind humanitarian reform, Foucault saw new forms of domination more sinister and less easy to detect. (American prison reformers adopted certain elements of the panopticon, but not its entirety.)

Foucault's historical interpretation—and a larger intellectual trend toward postmodern suspicion—is a far cry from the optimism of Alice Felt Tyler. It leaves the reader with a sense of doom about the possibilities of reform within a democratic society. Common sense, though, suggests that Foucault lost sight of something quite basic. As Thomas Haskell points out, "Foucault's position contains much truth, yet in contemplating it, we must not lose sight of another truth, namely, that to put a thief in jail is more humane than to burn him, hang him, maim him, or dismember him" (*Objectivity Is Not Neutrality*, p. 236). There is a middle position between Tyler's optimism and Foucault's pessimism. Social reformers often had good intentions—and any historian must at least listen to what these reformers claimed they were doing—but they also had limits. Sometimes they could impose new forms of domination on those they purportedly helped. Sometimes they could help prop up a status quo in the best interest of the rich or some other elite (as Orestes Brownson asserted). Nonetheless, the possibility of creating a more democratic society—one that is more just in relation to all members—has existed throughout history, and some have acted on it. To conclude otherwise would be to flatten out history, to make it too one-dimensional.

How we interpret social reform is not merely an academic question. Even though the classical period has closed, there are new movements for social reform—movements against smoking cigarettes, for example, and for such things as vegetarianism and speech codes. The question of whether reform can ever be democratic—or if it always threatens to become domination—demands our attention, because the impulse to improve social conditions will never go away. Whether or not this impulse can be something more than imposition remains to be seen. How this question is resolved will tell us a great deal about the future of democracy.

See also **Antislavery; Reform Institutions; Moral Philosophy; Transcendentalism; Communitarianism; Popular Intellectual Movements: 1833–1877; Patterns of Reform and Revolt; Gender and Political Activism; Racialism and Racial Uplift; Radical Alternatives** (*volume 1*); **Second-Wave Feminism; The Discovery of the Environment; Vietnam as a Cultural Crisis** (*in this volume*); **Race; Class; The Social Sciences; Foundations and Philanthropy; Journals of Opinion; Rhetoric; Marxist Approaches** (*volume 3*); *and other articles in this section.*

BIBLIOGRAPHY

Addams, Jane. *Twenty Years at Hull-House.* 1910. Reprint, New York, 1961.

Banner, Lois. "Religious Benevolence as Social Control: A Critique of an Interpretation." *Journal of American History* 60, no. 1 (1973): 23–41.

Boyer, Paul. *Urban Masses and Moral Order in America, 1820–1920.* Cambridge, Mass., 1978.

Brownson, Orestes. "The Second Annual Report of the Board of Education." *Boston Quarterly Review* (October 1839): 393–434.

Crunden, Robert. *Ministers of Reform: The Progressives' Achievement in American Civilization, 1889–1920.* Urbana, Ill., 1982.

Davis, Allen. *American Heroine: The Life and Legend of Jane Addams.* New York, 1973.

Emerson, Ralph Waldo. "Man the Reformer." In *The Complete Works of Ralph Waldo Emerson.* Vol. 1. Boston, 1903.

Foucault, Michel. *Discipline and Punish: The Birth of the Prison.* New York, 1977.

Haskell, Thomas. "Capitalism and the Humanitarian Sensibility, Parts I and II." In *Objectivity Is Not Neutrality: Explanatory Schemes in History.* Baltimore, 1998.

Hofstadter, Richard. *The Age of Reform: From Bryan to F.D.R.* New York, 1955.

Howe, Frederic C. *Confessions of a Reformer.* 1925. Reprint, New York, 1967.

Johnson, Paul A. *Shopkeeper's Millennium: Society and Revivals in Rochester, New York, 1815–1837.* New York, 1978.

Katz, Michael B. *The Irony of Early School Reform: Educational Innovation in Mid-Nineteenth Century Massachusetts.* Cambridge, Mass., 1968.

Lasch, Christopher. *The New Radicalism in America, 1889–1963: The Intellectual as a Social Type.* New York, 1965.

———. *The World of Nations: Reflections on American History, Politics, and Culture.* New York, 1973.

Leuchtenburg, William Edward. *Franklin D. Roosevelt and the New Deal, 1932–1940.* New York, 1963.

Nietzsche, Friedrich. "The Genealogy of Morals." In *The Birth of Tragedy and the Genealogy of Morals.* New York, 1956.

Rothman, David J. *The Discovery of the Asylum: Social Order and Disorder in the New Republic.* Boston, 1971.

Schlesinger, Arthur M. *The American as Reformer.* Cambridge, Mass., 1950.

Smith-Rosenberg, Carroll. *Religion and the Rise of the American City: The New York City Mission Movement, 1812–1870.* Ithaca, N.Y., 1971.

Stewart, James Brewer. *Holy Warriors: The Abolitionists and American Slavery.* New York, 1976.

Trolander, Judith Ann. *Professionalism and Social Change: From the Settlement House Movement to Neighborhood Centers, 1886 to the Present.* New York, 1987.

Turner, James. *Without God, Without Creed: The Origins of Unbelief in America.* Baltimore, 1985.

Tyler, Alice Felt. *Freedom's Ferment: Phases of American Social History from the Colonial Period to the Outbreak of the Civil War.* New York, 1944.

Whitman, Walt. "Democratic Vistas." In *Complete Poetry and Selected Prose.* Edited by James E. Miller. Boston, 1959.

Wishy, Bernard. *The Child and the Republic: The Dawn of Modern American Child Nurture.* Philadelphia, 1968.

SOCIALISM AND RADICAL THOUGHT

Christopher Phelps

DEFINITION AND OVERVIEW

Radicalism has been, paradoxically, at the center as well as the margin of American intellectual and cultural life. The American nation, although born of a revolutionary upheaval that Europeans took as a profound challenge to the old regime, has often displayed great suspicion of—even hostility toward—its radicals who seek deeper political and social transformations. Yet American radicals, despite the stigma and repression visited upon them, have contributed beyond their numbers to many of the nation's most celebrated intellectual and cultural achievements.

Radicalism means fundamental opposition to the prevailing social order. The ambition of radicals is to cut to the root of things, as the word "radical," which shares the same Latin ancestry as "radish," literally implies. It is not unusual for the term to be applied to extremists, but it is best reserved for those on the left, from progressives to revolutionaries. Other constructions mislead, especially when they include a far right that seeks to expand racial, class, and gender privileges. Radicalism, in other words, entails a visionary, sometimes utopian, aspiration to remake the world on the basis of the principle of human equality.

Socialism is the primary form of modern radicalism. The word sometimes functions as a vague humanistic ideal, but more exactly it suggests a society of common ownership in which public use, not private gain, is the baseline of production, and in which solidarity replaces alienation and exploitation. Thus, equality of condition, not mere opportunity, is axiomatic for radicals, and culture, politics, and economics are indissoluble for them. Radicals have tended to desire the reduction if not elimination of all invidious forms of privilege based upon privately appropriated wealth, and a culture in which creative development of personality replaces self-centered individualism.

Since the early nineteenth century, radicals have tended to oppose capitalism, the modern system of production motivated by private profit and characterized by market exchange and wage labor. The radical view has been that despite economic dynamism and technological innovations, capitalism on the whole is irrational, unreliable, and exploitative. Radicals have objected to other aspects of modern society as well, including racial oppression, imperialism, and militarism, and have tended to consider these endemic, hence requiring deep structural transformation rather than mere policy changes. Radicals have played a leading role in movements to abolish slavery and racial segregation, to obtain full social and political equality for women, to challenge empire and expansion (from the Mexican-American conflict of 1846 to 1848 through the Vietnam and Persian Gulf Wars), and to achieve an environmentally sustainable society. On the other hand, in numerous instances radicals involved in one or more of these causes failed, for a variety of reasons, to extend full or consistent support to the others.

Radicalism is distinguished from other forms of political thought, such as liberal reformism, not only by the extent of its egalitarianism but by the willingness of radicals to go beyond conventional means. Radicals have deliberately violated laws—for example, Jim Crow ordinances and constraints on free expression—that they deem unjust or illegitimate. They have also been willing to sabotage property and commit acts of violence, especially in self-defense against attacks on them. Moral and strategic controversy, however, has accompanied every unconventional tactic, and some radicals have advocated "safe and legal" approaches or declared themselves principled pacifists.

The vast literature on American radicalism has returned time and again to a central question framed at the dawn of the twentieth century by the German sociologist Werner Sombart: "Why is there no socialism in the United States?" Why is the American working class not more class-conscious? Why, despite sometimes ferocious workplace militancy, have American workers often aspired to become employers rather than challenge class rule? Why does America lack a mass party like the declared social-democratic parties of Europe?

One possible answer lies in Sombart's own oft-quoted answer: "On the reefs of roast beef and apple pie, socialistic utopias of every sort are sent to their doom" (in Daniel Bell, *Marxian Socialism in the United States*, p. 4). The very strength of American capitalism has made challenges to it difficult, even if according to the precepts of historical materialism that very maturity ought to have made it ripe for the plucking. Other commentators have attributed the weakness of American socialism and class consciousness to a host of other factors: the individualism and nationalism so prevalent in American ideology, the identification of native-born workers with conventional politics as a result of the early extension of the ballot, the extraordinary ethnic diversity and racial divides in the American working class, the unusual geographic and occupational mobility characteristic of American life, the capacity of the two parties dominant since the Civil War to absorb radical demands and fend off all would-be challengers, the ferocity of governmental and extralegal repression visited upon American radicals, or the tactical, strategic, organizational, and ideological shortcomings of American radicals themselves. As historian Eric Foner has observed, however, many of these factors have actually proved radicalizing—and there are exceptions to them, too. The entire framing of debate in terms of "why is there no socialism" may prove less and less fruitful as the demise of the nominally socialist states of the Soviet Union and Eastern Europe, combined with the adaptation of western European parties to American-style campaigns and neoliberal politics, makes the United States seem in the vanguard rather than an exception.

ORIGINS OF AMERICAN RADICALISM

Although colonial America never had the landed aristocracy, feudal system, or extent of ecclesiastical domination that galvanized European social and political radicalism, the American Revolution had radical features. Enlightenment themes of reason, progress, and liberty were pronounced in Thomas Paine's pamphlet *Common Sense* (1776), a stirring plebeian call for full independence. In popular language, Paine demanded a democratic republic, opposed monarchy, and inveighed against hereditary privilege. Because the American Revolution was led by slaveholders and property owners, however, it has been a source of ambivalence for the Left. At times radicals have viewed the Revolution as a reluctant secession by a colonial elite devoted above all else to its propertied interests. At others, as during the Popular Front of the 1930s, the left has attempted to lay claim to the American fountainhead by emphasizing the Revolution's popular elements and libertarian themes.

The earliest form of American socialism was shaped, in any case, not by Paine's secularism but by Protestantism. The German sects at Ephrata in Pennsylvania and Amana in Iowa, the Shakers, and the Oneida colony of John Humphrey Noyes all exhibited a perfectionist instinct to withdraw from the sinful world to live as a community of saints, combining paternalism with common ownership of goods. Understandings of perfection varied, from the Shakers' ascetic program of celibacy to Noyes's doctrine of "complex marriage," which held the sexual impulse symbolic of spiritual union. Besides these exclusive religious ventures, there were socialist communities that aspired to be prototypes for universal social reorganization, such as the experiment inspired between 1825 and 1828 by Robert Owen. A successful textile manufacturer in Scotland, Owen sought to persuade business and political leaders to adopt his benevolent practices and enact educational reforms. On arriving in the United States, he addressed both houses of Congress, met with John Quincy Adams, and purchased land at New Harmony, Indiana, for a model of his system, which suffered severe schisms within two years.

The evangelical Protestantism of the Second Great Awakening, with its emphasis upon the responsibility of each individual to reject sin, contributed to radical abolitionism. William Lloyd Garrison's newspaper, the *Liberator*, established in Boston in 1831, was an unprecedented vehicle for demanding the immediate end of slavery and full civic equality regardless of race. Although divisions arose between those who advocated slave insurrections, like John Brown, and those, like Garrison and Frederick Douglass, who favored legislative and moral means to abolition, the radical abolitionist movement was a serious challenge to the ruling planter class of the South and to a form of property excused by the Constitution. It helped to alter public opinion and eventually spark a national crisis in the Civil War, culminating in emancipation.

Abolitionism fed many related movements, notably the women's rights campaign launched at the Seneca Falls Convention of 1848, and to many nineteenth-century reformers, these causes were congruent. Sojourner Truth, an ex-slave and abolitionist, was fervently evangelical and spoke for women's rights. Henry David Thoreau, whose essay "Resistance to Civil Government" (1849) called for active disobedience of unjust governments and wars, defended Brown's raid on Harpers Ferry. Transcendentalism, in fact, was centered in Massachusetts in the 1840s at Brook Farm, a religious-naturalist community influenced by the ideas of French utopian Charles Fourier.

Utopian socialists and radical abolitionists, however, had little connection to the labor movement before the Civil War. That was not the case with the Germans, beginning with the "'forty-eighters" forced into exile after the failed European revolutions, who became the first important immigrant ethnic group to contribute to the emergent American Left. With strong convictions, working-class loyalties, and an array of cultural institutions that by the late nineteenth century would include German-language newspapers, singing societies, gymnasiums, and labor lyceums, German American socialists played a dominant role in American radicalism through the 1890s—even, in strongholds like Milwaukee, into the 1930s and 1940s.

Ironically, given their criticisms of the utopians, the German American socialists were often insular, failing to reach native-born workers and disdainful of native-born radicals. In the Civil War period, Friedrich Sorge and others maintained active ties to the London-based Karl Marx and Friedrich Engels, who advocated trade-union action and revolutionary engagement with the main lines of historical development as against small-scale models, reformism, or adventurism. The socialists helped to establish a Yankee section of the heterogeneous First International, or International Workingmen's Association (1864–1872). After the inspiration of the Paris Commune (1870–1871), many native-born radicals grew attracted to the International, including sisters Tennessee Claflin and Victoria Woodhull, whose newspaper called for women's rights, world government, and free love, with the slogan "Progress! Free Thought! Untrammeled Lives!" To Sorge and other 'forty-eighters, *Woodhull and Claflin's Weekly* was the embarrassing work of reckless dilettantes and, when the First International lived out its last moment in New York, it was only after a purge of the native-born American reformers and their spiritualist-feminist ideas.

Conscious of their isolation, German American socialists tried to reach beyond their enclave by participating in 1876 in the formation of the first national-scale socialist party, the Workingmen's Party of the United States. In a strategic rupture that would be characteristic of the American Left, the party dissolved the following year with the defection of many (including Sorge as well as Adolph Strasser and Samuel Gompers, later to found the American Federation of Labor, or AFL) who believed it premature to run candidates before a trade union movement was securely established. Renamed the Socialist Labor Party (SLP) in 1877, the remaining party tried to bring together a multiethnic immigrant base, though it never integrated many native-born Americans. The SLP enjoyed some electoral success and established a trade union federation premised upon socialist political action before falling under the sway of Daniel De Leon, a brilliant but highly orthodox Marxist. Despite SLP hopes that he would reach new, especially Jewish, audiences, De Leon led it into sectarian sterility, epitomizing the exaggerated suspicion of others' purity that would recur in many other radical quarters.

American labor militancy rose sharply in the Gilded Age with the massive industrial eruptions that began with the nationwide railroad-centered strike of 1877, which had wide socialist participation. The 1877 upheaval was followed by other violent eruptions, including the repression of anarchists following a bombing at Chicago's Haymarket Square in 1886, a massive steel strike at Homestead, Pennsylvania, in 1892, and a strike against the Pullman Palace Car Company in Illinois in 1894 that was supported by the nation's rail workers. While reaching such intellectual heights as Henry George's economic treatise, *Progress and Poverty* (1879), Robert Koehler's paintings, *The Socialist* (1885) and *The Strike* (1886), Edward Bellamy's visionary novel, *Looking Backward* (1888), and Henry Demarest Lloyd's exposé of Standard Oil, *Wealth against Commonwealth* (1894), Gilded Age radicalism was, nevertheless, often a frustrating mishmash to socialists and anarchists, who joined it in common cause and found it better at identifying injustices than offering remedies. The Greenback movement, Knights of Labor, and People's Party drew upon the civic egalitarianism of American republicanism to favor the independent small producer—the artisan worker and small farmer. Viewing small property as the foundation of economic and civic virtue, their leaderships were suspicious of large accumulations of wealth but tended to emphasize anti-monopoly over anti-capitalism, and their economic prescriptions tended to target tax, currency, and credit rather than the realm of production seen as paramount by Marxists. Thorstein Veblen's *Theory of the Leisure Class* (1899), which excoriated elites as wasteful and parasitical, reflected this sensibility.

As Reconstruction came to an end in 1877, radicals and their organizations, such as the all-inclusive Knights, proved among the most egalitarian and tolerant of their day. Though not free of racism—native-born and Irish American labor radicals were among the most ardent exponents of Chinese exclusion—radicals were often the most principled advocates of equality. The Workingmen's Party included the first known African American socialist, Peter H. Clark. Albert Parsons, who at the time of his hanging in 1887 for his unproven role in the Haymarket bombing was the leading anarchist of his day, was a radical Texan who advocated the rights of freed people and married Lucy Gatherings, a woman of black, Mexican, and Indian heritage. Yet race could also prove divisive. Many white radicals capitulated to rising white supremacy. The demise of the Populist movement—which had elected congressmen and carried several states in the 1892 presidential election—had much to do with its ineffectiveness in the face of race manipulation by the Democratic establishment in the South. Georgia Populist Tom Watson, who had urged unity between black sharecroppers and poor white dirt farmers to fight the middlemen, banks, and railroads, was by 1912 a Catholic-baiting anti-Semite who denounced Woodrow Wilson for being "ravenously fond of the Negro," even though Wilson soon instituted segregation in federal facilities.

DEBSIAN SOCIALISM

One of the ironies in the history of American socialism is that when Werner Sombart asked, "Why is there no socialism in the United States?" in 1906, there was, in fact, socialism. The Socialist Party, which came to be the relatively durable, sizable socialist organization that radicals had been unable to forge in earlier periods, arose from the labor-farmer radicalism of the 1880s and 1890s. It was founded in 1901 as a merger of Social Democracy of America (headed by Indiana railway union leader Eugene V. Debs, radicalized by the Pullman strike) and some SLP defectors. By its height in 1912, the Socialist Party had 1,200 local elected officials and 33 state legislators, controlled municipal governments in cities ranging from Schenectady, New York, to Berkeley, California, and boasted more than three hundred sympathetic papers, including monthlies, weeklies, and dailies. The *Appeal to Reason* (1895–1922), the most successful of the socialist weeklies,

had 750,000 subscribers and printed millions of copies of its special editions. Debs, the Socialist standard-bearer, won almost one million votes (6 percent of the total) in the presidential race of 1912.

Despite the charge that American socialism has been "in the world but not of it," as Daniel Bell wrote regarding radicals' sectarianism and dogmatism, the Debs era is notable for the creative immersion of American socialists in a variety of local conditions and milieus. Even rural states like Iowa, Arkansas, and Kansas were each home to more than a dozen socialist papers. In Wisconsin, Victor Berger was elected to the House of Representatives in 1910 and five times thereafter. Among tenant farmers in Oklahoma and Texas, socialists drew upon the tradition of religious tent meetings, holding gatherings of song, food, and education that could last for days. Slovaks, Slovenes, and Bohemians in industrial Chicago, Italians in New York, and other immigrant groups joined in large numbers. By 1910 the largest-circulation Yiddish paper in the world was New York's socialist *Jewish Daily Forward,* reaching 200,000. Its editor Abraham Cahan's novel, *The Rise of David Levinsky* (1917), spoke to the quandaries of assimilation. Chicago socialist publisher Charles H. Kerr, through his book publishing and in his periodical, the *International Socialist Review* (1900–1918), promoted works by novelists Jack London and Upton Sinclair (whose best-selling 1906 novel, *The Jungle,* was first serialized in the *Appeal*), humorist Oscar Ameringer, lawyer Clarence Darrow, and muckraker Gustavus Myer. The general bent, however, was didactic, lending some credence to middle-class progressive Walter E. Weyl's 1912 diary complaint that American socialists were "second raters, . . . merely weak repeaters of other people's thoughts."

Such was not the case in Greenwich Village, where a creative New York avant-garde—including "new dance" innovator Isadora Duncan, poet Carl Sandburg, artists John Sloan and Art Young, dadaist Man Ray, and essayist Randolph Bourne—combined solidarity with artistic experimentation. In the freewheeling *Masses* (1911–1917), writers Floyd Dell, Max Eastman, John Reed, and Louise Bryant evinced modernist interest in psychoanalysis, free love, and feminism along with political sympathy for the class-struggle left wing in the Socialist Party, though others, like anarchist Emma Goldman, believed a classless society would never come about by the ballot. This cosmopolitan left embraced the Industrial Workers of the World, or Wobblies, a revolutionary union forged in 1905 that organized a number of militant industrial campaigns, one of

---

∽Oᴐᴐᴐᴐᴐᴐᴐᴐᴐᴐᴐᴐᴐᴐᴐ

"RATHER A FREE SOUL IN JAIL": EUGENE V. DEBS

These excerpts from Eugene Debs's 1918 speech in Canton, Ohio, illustrate socialist oratory at its height. The most famous speech in the history of American socialism, it resulted in a ten-year prison sentence for Debs.

I realize that, in speaking to you this afternoon, there are certain limitations placed on the right of free speech. I must be exceedingly careful, prudent, as to what I say, and even more careful and prudent as to how I say it. I may not be able to say all I think, but I am not going to say anything that I do not think. I would rather a thousand times be a free soul in jail than a sycophant and coward on the streets.

Are we opposed to Prussian militarism? Why we have been fighting it since the day the Socialist movement was born; and we are going to fight it day and night, until it is wiped from the face of the earth. . . . I hate, I loathe, I despise junkers and junkerdom. I have no earthly use for the junkers of Germany; and not one particle more use for the junkers in the United States.

Wars throughout history have been waged for conquest and plunder. . . . The master class has always declared the wars; the subject class has always fought the battles. The master class has had all to gain and nothing to lose, while the subject class has had nothing to gain and all to lose—especially their lives.

Source: Tussey, pp. 243–279.

---

which was commemorated in the "Pageant of the Paterson Strike" organized by Reed and performed by over one thousand workers at Madison Square Garden in 1913. The IWW was open—unlike the AFL—to women, blacks, and immigrants, and it created a spirited culture of jokes, cartoons, and such songs as Joe Hill's "There Is Power in a Union" and Ralph Chaplin's "Solidarity Forever."

As the increase in female industrial labor rendered the Victorian doctrine of separate spheres less and less tenable, questions of reproduction and gender resurfaced. Charlotte Perkins Gilman's *Women and Economics* (1898), which advocated women taking productive roles outside the home, was not as influential as August Bebel's *Woman under Socialism* (1879), translated by De Leon, which treated the oppression of women and exploitation of workers as parallel, with socialism the only answer. Although some socialists considered woman suffrage a bourgeois diversion, others contributed to its passage in 1920. Many publicly visible women espoused socialism, including birth-control campaigner Margaret Sanger, deaf, mute, and blind activist Helen Keller, and mineworkers' organizer Mother Jones

(known universally by that name rather than her given name, Mary Harris Jones).

Socialist advance was limited in part by theoretical weaknesses. Regulation, for example, though seen by many radicals as an initial step toward socialization (and by conservatives as socialism itself), tended to stabilize rather than transform corporate capitalism. The really crushing blow, however, came with the onset of World War I, which the Left opposed as imperial carnage. Pro-war intellectual defectors from socialism like William English Walling and Walter Lippmann became, along with the liberal *New Republic* and pragmatist John Dewey, the target of searing essays of conscience by Bourne. The Espionage Act (1917) and Sedition Act (1918) effectively criminalized dissent. The Left was set back severely by destructive government raids, postal-regulation interference, mob violence, and the confinement of leaders like Debs, who ran for president in 1920 from his prison cell. By the time the Red Scare reached its peak in the Palmer raids of 1919 and 1920, the Debsian left had been badly shattered, and although it underwent a brief revival in the 1930s under former minister Norman

Thomas, the Socialist Party never matched its prewar zenith.

AMERICAN COMMUNISM

The emergence of the Communist Party, the dominant radical organization from its birth in 1919 through the 1950s, points to another—this time internal—source of decline of the old Socialist Party. Almost all American socialists welcomed the Soviet Revolution of 1917 in Russia, which created a workers' and peasants' government, but as the inspiration sparked revolutionary momentum in the Socialist Party's foreign-language federations, moderate and right-wing Socialist leaders maneuvered to preserve their organizational control, expelling about two-thirds of the party's membership in 1919. Joined by IWW members, the expelled created two competing Communist groups, both claiming the Marxist mantle.

The early Communist movement was made up of seasoned radicals like Reed (who died of typhus in the Soviet Union in 1920) and Wobbly firebrand Elizabeth Gurley Flynn, but the Red Scare and severe factionalism caused many to drop away. At Soviet insistence the groups united in 1923 as the Workers Party, to be renamed the Communist Party in 1929. Throughout the 1920s, the Communist ranks were small. Some artists and intellectuals, like Harlem Renaissance poet Claude McKay, were attracted early on, but the appeal only became clear in the Great Depression of the 1930s, when bleak economic conditions and the rise of fascism in Europe, along with party labor organizing and activism against unemployment, racism, and war, resulted in tens of thousands of new recruits.

Professionals, intellectuals, and artists were drawn to the party through a series of institutions. In the early 1930s, when party policy was militant, the emphasis was on a class war in culture. John Reed Clubs were created to forge agitational art: propagandistic murals, posters, and drama, as well as the "proletarian literature" typified by Michael Gold's *Jews without Money* (1930), a novel that concludes with a conversion to the Left. With the turn to a Popular Front around 1935, evocations of "the people" replaced the earlier identification of class with party in party-controlled institutions like the *New Masses* (1926–1947). An alliance with liberals was fostered, a patriotic-revolutionary tradition was imagined, and broad organizations like the American Artists' Congress and the American Writers Congress were favored. The late 1930s and 1940s

Elizabeth Gurley Flynn at a Textile Strike in Passaic, New Jersey, 1926. Flynn joined the IWW at sixteen and emerged as a talented orator in its struggles for free speech. She led many labor battles including the strikes at Lawrence, Massachusetts (1912), and Paterson, New Jersey (1913). © Underwood & Underwood/corbis

were the apex of party cultural influence. Those with close ties to the Communist left included folksinger Woody Guthrie, composers Aaron Copland and Marc Blitzstein, singer Paul Robeson, playwrights Clifford Odets and Lillian Hellman, screenwriters Dalton Trumbo and Ring Lardner Jr., actor Charlie Chaplin, painter Ben Shahn, illustrator William Gropper, poet Langston Hughes, critics Kenneth Burke, Malcolm Cowley, and Granville Hicks, and novelists Theodore Dreiser, Howard Fast, and Richard Wright.

At the same time, the party came in for sharp criticism from a small but erudite group of intellectuals on the Left, notably the *Partisan Review*, once affiliated with the John Reed Clubs but reconstituted in 1936. Committed to Marxism but ardently opposed to the brutal and nationalist turn of the Soviet Union under Joseph Stalin, as well as the perceived phoniness and vulgarity of the Popular Front, the anti-Stalinist left of the 1930s and 1940s upheld revolutionary socialism, workers' democracy, and internationalism. Many were favorably disposed toward modernism and the ideas of Leon Trotsky, the exiled Russian revolutionary Marxist. Small groups led by A. J. Muste, James P. Cannon,

Communist Party Pamphlet, 1935. The text makes an appeal to architects and other professionals whose status and income level were weakened during the Depression. COLLECTION OF CHRISTOPHER PHELPS

Jay Lovestone, and Max Shachtman, as well as forums like the *Modern Quarterly* (later *Modern Monthly*) (1923–1940) and *Marxist Quarterly* (1937), attracted old *Masses* editor Eastman, philosophers Sidney Hook and James Burnham, theorist C. L. R. James, novelists James T. Farrell, Mary McCarthy, and John Dos Passos, art critic Meyer Schapiro, literary critic Edmund Wilson, and journalist Dwight Macdonald.

While the Moscow show trials from 1936 to 1938 were a pivotal moral event for the anti-Stalinist left, the Communist Party experienced far greater defections as a consequence of the Hitler-Stalin Pact of 1939, which put an end to the Popular Front, and especially Nikita Khrushchev's 1956 speech against Stalin's legacy. The late-life membership of the distinguished African American intellectual W. E. B. Du Bois and the public notoriety of black women's studies scholar Angela Davis gave the Communist Party some visibility in the 1960s and 1970s, but after 1956 the party had a permanent reputation in radical circles for an authoritarian structure and stodginess, ensuring its triviality. Most party intellectuals, including those around the journal *Science and Society* (1936–), moved toward a more independent stance.

By the late 1950s, moreover, the party had already been severely battered by the cold war and McCarthyism. The domestic antiradicalism that reached a crescendo between 1947 and 1953 put the Left severely on the defensive. All varieties of radicals were subjected to a climate of fear and suspicion, purged from the labor movement, called before congressional investigative committees, and punished by blacklists, trials, and prison sentences. Many anti-Stalinist intellectuals dropped their anticapitalism and made peace with the West—even, in the case of Burnham and Eastman, moving very far to the right. So did many ex-Communists, including Whittaker Chambers and Louis Budenz, demonstrating how repentance of youthful excess can take on religious dimensions even as a new "realism" is counseled.

A NEW LEFT AND THE DECLINE OF RADICALISM

To a greater extent than the New Left recognized, the origins of the 1960s radicalism lay in prior decades. Such periodicals as *I. F. Stone's Weekly* (later *I. F. Stone's Bi-Weekly*) (1953–1971), the *National Guardian* (later *Guardian*) (1948–1992), and Paul Sweezy and Leo Huberman's *Monthly Review* (1949–), later joined by Harry Magdoff, reflected the emergence of an independent socialist milieu out of Popular Front circles. Opposed to the cold war, they stood at a distance from the Communist Party and strongly influenced the New Left when it emerged. Irving Howe's *Dissent* (1954–), originally the vehicle of decamping Shachtmanites, was sharply critical of what it saw as naïveté and adventurism in the new radicalism, but became a gathering point for erstwhile New Left intellectuals by the 1980s and 1990s. The politics of Berkeley's Hal Draper—whose essay, "The Two Souls of Socialism" (1966), helped define democratic radicalism— and the journal *New Politics* (1961–1977, 1986–) emerged out of the anti-Stalinist Left. A. J. Muste's peace activism, C. Wright Mills's sociology of the "power elite," and William Appleman Williams's historical assessment of American empire and corporate liberalism, all widely embraced by New Leftists, first took shape in the 1950s.

There were, however, undeniably new qualities to 1960s radicalism. Inspired by the civil rights movement and opposed to the Vietnam War, students and their community allies created a heterogeneous New Left that reached a peak from 1968 to 1970. Initially rejecting class struggle and the Stalin-Trotsky debate as passé, the New Left emphasized personal commitment, politics from the bottom up, and cultural liberation. Though the new radicals were often anti-intellectual, the New Left did contribute to social thought. The Students for a Democratic Society's "Port Huron Statement" (1962), a stirring manifesto drafted by Tom Hayden, gave eloquent expression to "participatory democracy," the idea that people should control the institutions that affect their lives. Herbert Marcuse, a lingerer from the Frankfurt school of German emigrés who resided in the United States during World War II, supplied a philosophical framework in *Eros and Civilization* (1955) and *One-Dimensional Man* (1964), arguing that consumer capitalism and technological rationality had created repressive domination, not a "free world." Folksinger Bob Dylan, Beat poet Allen Ginsberg, songwriter John Lennon, and other artists and musicians of the counterculture were influenced by the political Left. In academic disciplines such as economics and literature, radical caucuses formed. In history, the journals *Studies on the Left* (1959–1967), *Radical America* (1967–), and *Radical History Review* (1970–) helped open a new social history.

By the early 1970s much of the Left realized that to dismiss working-class politics as a "labor metaphysic," as Mills had put it, was detrimental to practice beyond the campuses. A host of militant organizations like the Student Non-Violent Coordinating Committee, Black Panther Party, League of Revolutionary Black Workers, Young Lords, and American Indian Movement put racism permanently on the defensive in American culture, and both Malcolm X and Martin Luther King Jr. drew socialist conclusions before assassination cut short their lives. But to transform society, the New Left needed more allies. Recognition of that strategic deficiency only dawned as a rash of self-defeating bombings, infighting, and revival of Stalinist dogma in Maoist form, along with a winding down of the Vietnam War and the onset of economic uncertainty in 1973, caused student radicalism to wither. Significant movements, notably feminism, gay rights, and environmentalism, grew in the 1970s and 1980s but were checked by corporate offensives and a powerful right-wing political coalition. Some intellectuals, like former Barry Goldwater speechwriter Karl

Hess and *National Review* staffer Garry Wills, shifted from the Right toward the Left, but the larger tendency was in the opposite direction. Radicals David Horowitz, Ronald Radosh, Christopher Lasch, and Eugene D. Genovese moved rightward or to eclectic "beyond left or right" positions.

In film, left-liberalism was revived, championed by the likes of director John Sayles and actors Warren Beatty, Tim Robbins, Susan Sarandon, and Ossie Davis, but constrained, as ever, by commercialism and corporate oversight. Radical writers who stayed the course and succeeded in reaching mass audiences in the 1980s and 1990s included foreign policy critic Noam Chomsky, historian Howard Zinn, novelist E. L. Doctorow, literary critic Edward Said, black studies scholar Cornel West, and feminist columnist Barbara Ehrenreich. Periodicals like *The Nation* (1865–) and *In These Times* (1976–) provided a stream of topical commentary, while *Against the Current* (1986–) preserved the wavering flame of revolutionary democratic socialism and *The Baffler* (1988–) revived sardonic avant-garde criticism of business culture. Advanced Marxist thought in the universities underwent a renaissance led by the likes of literary theorist Fredric Jameson, historical anthropologist Immanuel Wallerstein, and political theorist Ellen Meiksins Wood. The British socialist theoretical journal *New Left Review* (1960–) had several American editorial associates and established a New York arm of its Verso press, which published high-visibility books by Christopher Hitchens, Mike Davis, Alexander Cockburn, and Robert Brenner, among others.

Despite its intellectual virtuosity, the socialist left in the 1990s was at a popular low ebb. Many academic radicals adopted poststructuralism or "market socialism," departing from the left heritage of universalist egalitarianism. Though American socialists had long since stopped thinking of the East as a beacon of the future—indeed, the 1968 generation had sharply rejected the bureaucratic states' claim to represent socialism—the collapse of the Eastern European states in 1989 and Soviet Union in 1991 created a powerful presumption that "socialism is dead." Socialists objected that what had failed was not socialism but a bureaucratic class system, but short of the reemergence of sizable popular movements their view had little chance of penetrating the center-right fog. At century's end, radicals and socialists had produced no lasting movements and won no fundamental shift of power, though they had aided in human rights advances that most Americans had come to take for granted.

See also **Antislavery; Communitarianism; Patterns of Reform and Revolt; Gender and Political Activism; Industrialism and Its Critics; Anti-Modern Discontent between the Wars; Radical Alternatives** *(volume 1);* **Race, Rights, and Reform; Countercultural Visions; Vietnam as a Cultural Crisis; Artistic, Intellectual, and Political Refugees; Working Class** *(in this volume);* **Welfare; Class; Journals of Opinion; Rhetoric; Marxist Approaches; Social Construction of Reality** *(volume 3); and other articles in this section.*

BIBLIOGRAPHY

Aaron, Daniel. *Writers on the Left: Episodes in American Literary Communism.* New York, 1961.

Bell, Daniel. *Marxian Socialism in the United States.* Princeton, N.J., 1967.

Bourne, Randolph. *The Radical Will.* Edited by Olaf Hansen. Berkeley, Calif., 1977.

Breitman, George, Paul Le Blanc, and Alan Wald. *Trotskyism in the United States: Historical Essays and Reconsiderations.* Atlantic Highlands, N.J., 1996.

Brick, Howard. *Daniel Bell and the Decline of Intellectual Radicalism.* Madison, Wis., 1986.

Brown, Michael E., et al. *New Studies in the Politics and Culture of U.S. Communism.* New York, 1993.

Buhle, Mari Jo. *Women and American Socialism, 1870–1920.* Urbana, Ill., 1981.

Buhle, Mari Jo, Paul Buhle, and Dan Georgakas, eds. *Encyclopedia of the American Left.* 2d ed. New York, Oxford, 1998.

Buhle, Paul. *Marxism in the United States: Remapping the History of the American Left.* New York, 1987.

Buhle, Paul., ed. *History and the New Left: Madison, Wisconsin, 1950–1970.* Philadelphia, 1990.

Cantor, Milton. *The Divided Left: American Radicalism, 1900–1975.* New York, 1978.

Crossman, Richard, ed. *The God That Failed.* 1949. New York, 1963.

Denning, Michael. *The Cultural Front: The Laboring of American Culture in the Twentieth Century.* London, 1997.

Destler, Chester McArthur. *American Radicalism, 1865–1901.* 1946. Chicago, 1966.

Diggins, John Patrick. *The Rise and Fall of the American Left.* New York, 1992.

Draper, Theodore. *American Communism and Soviet Russia: The Formative Period.* New York, 1960.

———. *The Roots of American Communism.* New York, 1957.

Egbert, Donald Drew, and Stow Persons, eds. *Socialism and American Life.* 2 vols. Princeton, N.J., 1952.

Fellman, Michael. *The Unbounded Frame: Freedom and Community in Nineteenth-Century American Utopianism.* Westport, Conn., 1973.

Foner, Eric. "Why Is There No Socialism in the United States?" *History Workshop Journal* 17 (1984): 57–80.

Freeman, Joseph, ed. *Proletarian Literature in the United States: An Anthology.* New York, 1935.

Georgakas, Dan, and Marvin Surkin. *Detroit, I Do Mind Dying: A Study in Urban Revolution.* New York, 1975.

Gitlin, Todd. *The Sixties: Years of Hope, Days of Rage.* New York, 1987.

Goldberg, Harvey. *American Radicals: Some Problems and Personalities.* New York, 1962.

Howe, Irving, and Lewis Coser. *The American Communist Party: A Critical History.* New York, 1962.

Isserman, Maurice. *If I Had a Hammer—The Death of the Old Left and the Birth of the New Left.* New York, 1987.

Jacoby, Russell. *The End of Utopia: Politics and Culture in an Age of Apathy.* New York, 1999.

———. *The Last Intellectuals: American Culture in the Age of Academe.* New York, 1987.

Johnpoll, Bernard K., and Harvey Klehr, eds. *Biographical Dictionary of the American Left.* Westport, Conn., 1986.

Kelley, Robin D. G. *Race Rebels: Culture and Politics and the Black Working Class.* New York, 1994.

Kipnis, Ira. *The American Socialist Movement, 1897–1912.* New York, 1952.

Klehr, Harvey. *The Heyday of American Communism: The Depression Decade.* New York, 1984.

Lasch, Christopher. *The Agony of the American Left.* New York, 1984.

Laslett, John H. M., and Seymour Martin Lipset, eds. *Failure of a Dream?: Essays in the History of American Socialism.* Garden City, N.J., 1974.

Lens, Sidney. *Radicalism in America.* New York, 1969.

Lynd, Staughton. *The Intellectual Origins of American Radicalism.* 1968. Cambridge, Mass., 1982.

MARHO. *Visions of History.* New York, 1983.

Miles, Michael. *The Radical Probe: The Logic of Student Rebellion.* New York, 1971.

Miller, James. *"Democracy Is in the Streets": From Port Huron to the Siege of Chicago.* New York, 1987.

Nordhoff, Charles. *The Communistic Societies of the United States.* 1875. Reprint, New York, 1962.

Noyes, John Humphrey. *History of American Socialisms.* 1870. New York, 1961.

Pells, Richard H. *Radical Visions and American Dreams: Culture and Social Thought in the Depression Years.* New York, 1973.

Phelps, Christopher, ed. "Fifty Years, Three Interviews: Paul M. Sweezy, Harry Magdoff, Ellen Meiksins Wood." *Monthly Review* 51, no. 1 (1999).

Quint, Howard H. *The Forging of American Socialism: Origins of the Modern Movement.* Columbia, S.C., 1953.

Robinson, Cedric J. *Black Marxism: The Making of the Black Radical Tradition.* London, 1983.

Salvatore, Nick. *Eugene V. Debs: Citizen and Socialist.* Urbana, Ill., 1982.

Sayres, Sohnya, et al., eds. *The 60s without Apology.* Minneapolis, Minn., 1985.

Sombart, Werner. *Why Is There No Socialism in the United States?* 1906. White Plains, N.Y., 1976.

Teodori, Massimo, ed. *The New Left: A Documentary History.* Indianapolis, Ind., 1969.

Tussey, Jean Y., ed. *Eugene V. Debs Speaks.* New York, 1972.

Wald, Alan M. *The New York Intellectuals: The Rise and Decline of the Anti-Stalinist Left from the 1930s to the 1980s.* Chapel Hill, N.C., 1987.

Warren, Frank A. *Liberals and Communism: The "Red Decade" Revisited.* Bloomington, Ind., 1966.

Weinstein, James. *Ambiguous Legacy: The Left in American Politics.* New York, 1975.

———. *The Decline of Socialism in America, 1912–1925.* New York, 1967.

Wilentz, Sean. "Against Exceptionalism: Class Consciousness and the American Labor Movement, 1790–1920." *International Labor and Working Class History* no. 26 (1984): 1–24. Replies by Nick Salvatore and Michael Hanagan in *International Labor and Working Class History* no. 26 (1984): 25–36. Rejoinder by Sean Wilentz in *International Labor and Working Class History* no. 28 (1985): 46–55.

POPULISM

Catherine McNicol Stock

The term "populism" refers most specifically to a political movement of farmers and workers in the late nineteenth century, but over time, it has come to mean much more than that. In part because the Populists advocated for the needs of ordinary men and women, populism as a larger concept in our culture refers to any political movement, form of political speech, or general style which targets the concerns of common folk. A political figure might be said to have "populist appeal," for example, if she or he came from a working-class background, rubbed shoulders with voters in diners or on the job, or even wore blue jeans or cowboy boots while on the campaign trail. Of course, politicians like Andrew Jackson had populist appeal even before the Populist Party was born. Still, understanding the actions, ideals, and contradictions of the late-nineteenth-century Populists is the best way to learn why this particular form of political behavior remains so important in our culture today.

WHO WERE THE POPULISTS?

No man or woman moved west in the nineteenth century expecting life there to be easy. The thousands of Americans and Europeans who answered the call of the Homestead Act and set off to farm the Great Plains knew that the climate would be unpredictable, the prairie sod tough enough to break a plow, and the transportation systems primitive, to say the least. Despite the promises made by some unscrupulous land agents that they might find "mango trees and cockatoos," in places like Bismarck, North Dakota, farmers and their families were rarely fooled. They moved west for long-term prosperity, not short-term gain. They dreamed of living on the land, owning their own property, and being their own bosses, unlike the growing number of wage workers in urban areas. Because they dreamed of economic independence, they endured many hardships without complaint: prairie fires, grasshopper infestations, killing frosts, droughts, and much more. In the 1880s, the climate cooperated; rainfall seemed as though it had, as scientists predicted, "followed the plow." But even in the more arid years that followed, farmers remained hopeful that their dreams would come true "next year."

Hard times at the hand of God they had come to expect. But when farmers in the West and South came to believe that not God but men—bankers, railroad magnates, and politicians—had caused their misery, their forbearance turned to anger. In the late 1880s and early 1890s, farmers organized one of the most significant political associations in American history. In the 1890 state and national elections, the Populist Party in Nebraska, Minnesota, Kansas, Colorado, Michigan, Indiana, and the Dakotas won many state seats and sent nine representatives and two senators to Washington. In the presidential election of 1892, the Populist Party candidate James B. Weaver carried four states, with over 1 million popular and twenty-two electoral votes. With grassroots support in two critically important regions, it seemed the Populist Party was on the brink of a revolutionary victory—and perhaps even an actual revolution.

ORIGINS OF THE PEOPLE'S PARTY

Farmers had organized several other associations before they united under the common banner of Populism. These initial organizations tended to focus either on a single region or single issue and rarely established themselves as independent political parties with national agendas. Nevertheless farmers brought the lessons of earlier associations with them to the Populist Party in the 1890s. As Wisconsin's famous Progressive governor Robert La Follette wrote of the earliest of these groups, "As a boy on the farm . . . I heard and felt this movement of the Grangers swirling around me. I suppose

I have never fully lost the effect of the early impression" (Stock, *Rural Radicals*, pp. 72–73).

The Grange The National Grange of the Patrons of Husbandry, or the Grange as it was commonly called, was founded in Ohio by a former farmer, Oliver Hudson Kelley, in 1867. Kelley was actively involved in the Masons, a voluntary fraternal organization, and he imagined that the Grange would serve as a similar kind of secret society for farmers, complete with a women's auxiliary. Along with educating farmers about the problems they faced, Kelley hoped that the Grange would help to ease their isolation. At first membership growth was slow. During the depression of 1873, however, more than 1.5 million farmers joined the Grange. To Kelley's surprise, however, they were interested in far more than social activities. Primary among their concerns was the power of the railroads to set rates and control costs, a concern that would dominate discussions among Populists twenty years later as well. In most parts of the West, farmers had access to only one railroad to ship their crops to market. Moreover, railroads charged more per mile the further west the farmer lived. In 1890 it cost farmers as much to ship from Fargo, North Dakota, to Minneapolis, Minnesota, as it did for them to ship from Minneapolis all the way to New York City. Soon Grangers began to refer to these corporations, as well as to all others that handled the distribution and processing of foodstuffs, like farm implement dealers, creameries, and grain elevators, as "middlemen," because they stood between the producers and the consumers of goods. The way they saw it, farmers were getting shortchanged and some city folks were starving, while the wealthy middlemen were getting rich.

Fighting back the Granger way was done like this: First, farmers began to experiment with cooperative buying, whereby they could negotiate directly with manufacturers and purchase their necessities for lower prices. Second, they tried purchasing grain elevators, packing plants, and flour mills cooperatively, so as to cut the middlemen out of their profit base. While less successful, cooperative ownership of processing facilities encouraged some Grangers to promote state ownership and/or regulation, especially of railroads. Several of these state laws were contested in the federal courts in what became known as "Granger cases." The most famous of these cases, *Munn v. Illinois* (1877), determined that certain essential industries were operated "in the public interest" and thus could be regulated without violating the Fourteenth Amendment.

The Greenback Party In the 1870s, some Grangers joined forces with eastern workers in a political party dedicated to creating economic inflation by the continued use of the paper money (also known as "greenbacks") that had been issued after the Civil War, or by the creation of a bimetalic (gold and silver) money system. They argued that despite the increased business activity, the same amount of money had been in circulation since 1865, thus each year making each dollar worth more and each debt harder to pay off. As with railroad rates, farmers in the trans-Mississippi West had to pay higher interest rates than did those in the Northeast. In currency matters as in all economic affairs, the historian David Danbom noted that "for farmers, the stick had two short ends" (*Born in the Country*, p. 153).

Currency issues were not the only links between the Greenbackers and the Populists of the 1890s. Both the Grange and the Greenback Party saw a variety of ways to empower Americans in their struggle with wealthy bankers, middlemen, and politicians. Running for the presidency in 1880, the Greenback Party nominee James Weaver's platform called for women's suffrage and a graduated income tax. When good times returned to the Midwest in the early 1880s, the Greenback Party lost considerable influence. Nevertheless its lessons would remain for a new generation of political radicals to reconsider on a larger scale.

The Farmers' Alliance A truly broad-based, sustained political movement of agrarian radicalism was begun in Texas in the mid-1880s by Charles Macune and S. O. Daws. Southern farmers shared the economic "short stick" of their northern and western brethren, but endured unique hardships as well. In the Reconstruction South, including Texas and other states of the southern frontier, a credit system known as the crop lien system kept many white and nearly all African American farmers in a state of virtual slavery. This system tied farmers to a single local merchant who provided all consumer goods, seed, and farm implements to farmers on loan until harvest. More often than not at the end of the year farmers owed the merchant more than the harvest was worth, and were forced either to give up their lease or go even further into debt.

As the leaders of the Grange and smaller southern organizations like the Agricultural Wheel had, Macune and Daws encouraged Farmers' Alliance members to engage in cooperative purchasing,

A FARMWOMAN'S HARDSHIP

I take my Pen in hand to let you know that we are Starving to death It is Pretty hard to do without any thing to Eat hear in this God for Saken country we would of had Plenty to Eat if the hail hadent cut our rye down and ruined our corn and Potatoes I had the Prettiest Garden that you Ever seen and the Hail ruined It and I have nothing to look at My Husband went a way to find work and came home last night and told me that we would have to starve he has bin in ten countys and did not Get no work It is Pretty hard for a woman to do with out any thing to Eat when she dosent no what minute she will be confined to bed If I was In Iowa I would be all right I was born there and raised there I havent had nothing to Eat to day and It is three oclock

Source: Letter from Susan Orcutt, farmwoman, to Lorenzo D. Lewelling, Populist leader in Kansas, 29 June 1894. From the Lewelling Papers, Kansas State Historical Society, as reprinted in Marcus and Burner, *From Reconstruction to the Present*, p. 100.

manufacturing, and lending. The idea was at once simple and quite radical: to put economic power back in the hands of individuals, out of the hands of powerful corporations, and thus forge a new "cooperative commonwealth." As one farmer put it, "You just wait till we control things and we'll make you town leaders hump yourselves" (*Rural Radicals*, p. 68). To bring the largest possible number of rural folk together, the Alliance encouraged and benefited from the work of farmwomen in the organization and helped to organize alliances for African American farmers. And they didn't just talk. The Alliance leaders cajoled, persuaded, and convinced. They hosted picnics, sang songs, visited families in farm kitchens, and spoke as fervently as any country evangelist. Soon ordinary men and women, black and white, talked knowledgeably of the problems of monopoly, credit, single currencies, and the "Money Power." Twenty-five thousand farmers and their families gathered for a single meeting in Kansas. As one observer put it, this was not an ordinary organization but "a religious revival, a crusade, a pentacost of politics in which a tongue of flame sat upon every man and each spake as the spirit gave

him utterance" (Billington and Ridge, *Westward Expansion*, p. 676).

In both the Southern Alliance and its northern counterpart, leaders urged members to move beyond the local and to conceive of a reconfigured political and economic reality for the nation at large. They faced two daunting challenges, however. First, in both the North and the South, men "waved the bloody shirt" with their votes—that is, they voted with the political party they had supported during the Civil War. It was asking a great deal to suggest to such men to leave their parties even to vote for a third-party candidate. As late as 1892, an Alabama congressman who changed his party affiliation remarked, "My own father would not hear me speak and said he would rather make my coffin with his own hands and bury me than to have me desert the Democratic Party" (*Rural Radicals*, p. 58). Likewise, it would not be easy to get members of the northern and southern halves of the Farmers' Alliance to forget the suffering of the war and join together in common cause.

The first effort to unite as a unified, independent political party came at a meeting of the two alliances in St. Louis in December 1889. Because many southern members still hoped to capture control of the mainstream Democratic Party in their states, delegates still did not forge an official organization. Nevertheless, they agreed on several common principles and political goals. Members approved a platform which included a graduated income tax, state ownership of railroads, an inflationary money policy, laws against massive land ownership, and the abolition of national banks. By advancing these ideas, alliance candidates won impressive victories in the 1890 election, including four gubernatorial contests, the control of ten state legislatures, and the election of more than fifty candidates to the House and Senate in the nation's capital. As one historian saw it years later, "The embattled farmers, without even a political organization, seemed on the road to national success" (*Westward Expansion*, p. 677).

THE PEOPLE'S PARTY AND THE ELECTION OF 1896

The Populist movement enjoyed the height of its power for what the historian Lawrence Goodwyn would later call only a "moment"—from 1889 to 1896. In that short time, however, farmers saw the coming together of northern and southern alliances, the creation of a third party, the 1892 presidential campaign of James Weaver, and, finally, fusion with the Democratic Party and the 1896 presidential campaign of William Jennings Bryan. Continued economic downturns, particularly the depression of 1893, convinced many that the time was ripe for a complete overthrow of the established economic and political order. Nevertheless success as a national party remained elusive.

Omaha Platform   The People's Party emerged in 1892 in Omaha, Nebraska, when thirteen hundred representatives of the two branches of the Farmers' Alliance officially inaugurated the largest third party in American history. On 4 July 1892, they endorsed the "Omaha Platform," which took the fundamental economic principles adopted in St. Louis and added a democratic vision of political life. Farmers made clear that they did not hate the government or want the "government off their backs." Instead they wanted the state to work for them on their terms. For example, they believed that the direct election of senators, the use of the initiative and referendum, and government ownership of railroad and telegraphs would ensure a government both by and for the people. Most radical of all was the subtreasury plan, which would provide interest-free loans to farmers by allowing them to store crops at government expense until the price rose to cost-of-production levels.

Fundamental to every ideal expressed in the Omaha Platform was the principle that "wealth belongs to him who creates it," not to the middlemen or corporate giants who produce nothing themselves and merely profit through the redistribution of the the fruits of other men's labors. Disparity between rich and poor threatened not only the economic foundation of the nation, the Populists reasoned, but the essence of democracy itself. As the preamble to the Omaha Platform read, "The Conditions which surround us best justify our co-operation; we meet in the midst of a nation brought to the verge of moral, political, and material ruin. . . . The fruits of the toil of millions are boldly stolen to build up colossal fortunes for a few, unprecedented in the history of mankind; and the possessors of those, in turn, despite the Republic and endanger liberty. From the same prolific womb of governmental injustice we breed two great classes—tramps and millionaires" (Hollitz, *Thinking through the Past*, p. 55).

Not surprisingly, as the Populists gained power, their detractors became more numerous, both in the east and among the land- and business-owning elites in states like Kansas, Minnesota, and Nebraska, each of which had a traditionally strong Re-publican Party. Along with discrediting their political ideas, critics attacked the political standing and personal integrity of the Populists. The noted Kansas journalist William Allen White, for example, complained that if the Populists had their way they would "drive all the decent, self-respecting men out of the state." Hardly "decent," he described the Populists as "the ragged trousers . . . the lazy, greasy, fizzle who can't pay his debts" (Hollitz, p. 66). Criticisms of female Populist leaders were even harsher, focusing crude and misogynist remarks on their appearance and sexuality. The editor of the Salina (Kansas) *Weekly Republican* described Mary Lease as so ugly that she could "set on a stump in the shade and keep the cows out of a 100 acre corn field without a gun. . . . She's got a nose like an ant-eater, a voice like a cat fight and a face that is rank poison to the naked eye" (Hollitz, p. 63).

Election of 1896   The decision made by Populist leaders after the Democratic convention of 1896 to fuse with the mainstream Democratic Party was extremely controversial at the time and historians continue to debate its significance today. Key to the decision was the currency debate. Both the Populists and the rank-and-file working-class members of the Democratic Party believed in the importance of bimetalism, particularly after the crisis of 1893. To the surprise of Populists, the silverite Democrats carried the day at their Chicago convention, as they listened spellbound to a thirty-six-year-old orator from Nebraska, William Jennings Bryan, rail against the Republican's attachment to the gold standard. "You shall not press down upon the brow of labor this crown of thorns, you shall not crucify mankind upon a cross of gold." Bryan also spoke to the heart of many of the Populists' concerns, particularly their sense that American society was passing them by. "Burn down your cities and leave our farms," he warned the delegates, "and your cities will spring up again as if by magic; but destroy our farms and the grass will grow in the streets of every city in the country" (Garraty, *American Nation*, p. 587).

As convinced as they were of Bryan's dedication to Populist ideals, rank-and-file Populist leaders still worried about fusion. Of course, they knew that their best chance for beating the Republicans lay in teaming up with the Democrats; moreover, if they selected their own candidate, they nearly insured the election of the "gold-bug" Republicans. Nevertheless some leaders felt that fusion would mean the death of their fabled organization and the essence of its most radical principles. As Tom Watson, who eventually ran with Bryan as the vice-presidential candidate, put it, "The Democratic idea of fusion [is] that we play Jonah while they play whale" (Garraty, p. 587).

Bryan faced a formidable opponent in the Republican William McKinley. He began with more money, experience, and connections than young Bryan had and, as the campaign accelerated, McKinley picked up the endorsements of almost every major newspaper in the country, including several Democratic ones. While Bryan crossed the nation on a train, traveling 18,000 miles and giving over 600 speeches, packing auditoriums and train stations and town greens every step of the way, McKinley ran a carefully orchestrated and controlled campaign from his front porch in Canton, Ohio. He hired the first example of what would become a staple in American politics—a professional fundraiser and campaign manager named Marcus Alonzo Hanna. Hanna promoted McKinley as he might any other product for sale, even, as Theodore Roosevelt suggested, a patent medicine.

The presidential election of 1896 proved that a new day had come in American politics. McKinley carried the eastern states, as expected, while Bryan carried the South and the Rocky Mountain (silver-mining) states. But throughout the Middle West, even in Iowa, Minnesota, and North Dakota, former Alliancemen voted for McKinley, suggesting that the original fusion between the southern and northern part of the Farmers' Alliance had not held fast. In all regions, businessmen and financiers voted for McKinley and spread fearful rumors about the "social revolution" that might accompany a Bryan victory. Others suggested that, rather than promoting change, the Democrats were actually afraid of it, linking their dreams with the agrarianism of the early nineteenth century and blinding themselves to the coming realities of early-twentieth-century society.

THE POLITICAL LEGACIES OF POPULISM

While the People's Party met defeat in 1896, some aspects of its political agenda and a great deal of its political rhetoric survived. First and foremost, the reforms of the Progressive Era echoed earlier Populist calls for state activism in economic and political affairs. Robert "Fighting Bob" La Follette of Wisconsin, for example, who was raised in the Granger era, championed municipal reform and government regulation of industry. Among his many reforms as governor, La Follette adopted the direct primary system, increased corporate taxes,

limited campaign financing, passed income and inheritance taxes, and established state regulation of railroad, water, gas, electric, and telephone companies. Like many Populists, as well as the middle-class experts and professionals of the Progressive movement, La Follette believed that government could work for the people, not just for special interest groups and corporations. These connections were not lost on political observers of the time. As one put it, the Progressive governors—Albert Cummins of Iowa, John Johnson of Minnesota, and Joseph Folk of Missouri along with La Follette— "caught the Populists in swimming and stole all of their clothing except the frayed underwear of free silver" (Stock, p. 73).

Smaller organizations in the West retained the Populists' rural and agrarian outlook and appeal, as well as some of its more revolutionary goals. In North and South Dakota, for example, the Non-partisan League (NPL) organized in direct opposition to the new liberal farm organizations of the early twentieth century, like the American Farm Bureau Federation, which rather than simply serving farmers also allowed businessmen and politicians to be members. For the NPL organizer Arthur C. Townley, there was nothing more important than understanding and improving the lives of small farmers. Indeed, Townley may have been the most persuasive and effective farm organizer in American history. For twelve months he drove his Model T across the plains to visit farmers in their yards, fields, barns, and kitchens. He promoted state ownership of terminal elevators, flour mills, packing houses, and cold-storage plants, state inspection of grain and grain dockage, exemption of farm improvements from taxation, and state-funded hail insurance. In a single year, he recruited 40,000 members to the NPL. In 1918 North Dakotans elected an NPL candidate for governor and attorney general. The latter, William "Wild Bill" Langer, would serve as governor in the 1930s and as U.S. senator for more than twenty years afterward. In the depths of the Great Depression, when thousands of Dakotans were losing their farms to foreclosure, Langer was known to have said, "Treat the banker like a chicken thief. Shoot him on sight" (Stock, p. 83).

In the 1930s, several more agrarian organizations took up the cause of the small farmer against corporate interests, big farm organizations, and, sometimes, the government itself. The Farmers Union, for example, fought in Congress against the Roosevelt administration's proposed domestic allotment programs. Rather than have the government's agents dictate what and where they could plant in order to receive federal aid, the Farmers Union supported a plan based on the "cost-of-production," which, like the subtreasury plan of the 1890s, assured farmers of a minimum price for their crops. This concept was put into action by the Farmers Holiday Association, which blockaded roads to keep farmers from bringing crops to market until they had reached the cost of production. They used the slogan, "Stay at home—Buy nothing—Sell nothing." As one leader put it, "We'll eat our wheat and ham and eggs and let them eat their gold" (p. 83).

Perhaps the longest-lasting contribution of the People's Party to American politics has been the use of populist rhetoric as an effective political tool. According to the historian Michael Kazin, in contemporary politics Populism defines a way of speaking more than any specific content of political speech. As he puts it, "[Populism is] a language whose speakers conceive of ordinary people as a noble assemblage not bounded narrowly by class, view their opponents as self-serving and undemocratic, and seek to mobilize the former against the latter" (*The Populist Persuasion*, p. 1). Indeed, he suggested Populism as a political style in the twenty-first century contradicts the radical implications of the original People's Party by reinforcing the classlessness of American society and protesting "social and economic inequalities without calling the entire system into question" (p. 2). Thus candidates as different as Jimmy Carter, Pat Buchanan, Ross Perot, Steve Forbes, and Jesse Ventura have all variously been called "populist" in their appeal.

THE CULTURAL LEGACIES OF POPULISM

Three generations of historians have debated the meaning of the People's Party in American culture. They have done so with an ardor usually reserved for great historical figures, military conflicts, or political movements of long gestation. But because the election of 1896 proved to be such a turning point in the American past, and because the vision of the Republicans and the Populists for America's future were so divergent, the larger significance of the Populist movement continues to fascinate twenty-first-century historians. Indeed, historians differ considerably over whether the Populists were people to admire and emulate or were people whose worst instincts ultimately nullified their fondest desires.

In many respects the Populist vision in both its original iteration and its many political derivations was one of egalitarian relationships based on productivity, honesty, and democracy. Many Populists also imagined a world where the bonds of class superseded the divisions of gender and race. For example, the People's Party endorsed women's suffrage and empowered many women to leadership in the most public of political venues. Similarly, Populist leaders saw unity in the troubles of African American farmers in the South and encouraged them to set up Alliance divisions of their own, and in some cases to integrate Alliance divisions. Finally, in their support of progressive taxation policies, inheritance taxes, and corporate regulation, the Populists aggressively sought to redistribute wealth from the haves to the have-nots.

On the other hand, the Populists could be, as the historian Richard Hofstadter put it, at once "illiberal" and "ill-tempered." The anti-Semitism of some Populist literature was unadulterated and unabashed. Both Ignatius Donnelly of Minnesota and Mary Lease of Kansas warned of the sinister plans of "Jewish bankers" to turn Americans into peasants and serfs. Likewise, William "Coin" Harvey's popular tract, *Coin's Financial School*, told of a Jewish banker named Baron Rothe whose plan was to "bury the knife deep into the heart" of America (Bennett, *Party of Fear*, p. 178). Southern Populists were directly linked with racial oppression and the reinvigoration of the Ku Klux Klan in the 1920s. Tom Watson supported Jim Crow legislation in the 1910s, and when the governor of Georgia commuted the sentence of Jewish factory owner, Leo Frank, in the sex assault and murder of thirteen-year-old Mary Frank, he called on the men of Georgia to give Frank "exactly the same thing we give Negro rapists." Heartened by Frank's lynching, Watson wrote that "another Ku Klux Klan" should be organized "to restore HOME RULE" (MacLean, p. 920).

Thus the most important legacy of the People's Party is that it forces us to face the contradictions in American politics and culture. If the Populists were not just liberal, and if they were not just conservative, they force us to look at politics beyond Left and Right. If they represent both the best and the worst of America, then they force us to see how closely intertwined these strands of thought have been. Most of all they force us to acknowledge that concern for the people is still utmost in American political life—especially among the people themselves.

See also **Agrarianism and the Agrarian Ideal in Early America; Patterns of Reform and Revolt; Industrialism and Its Critics** *(volume 1);* **Working Class; Pastorialism and the Rural Ideal; Regionalism; The Frontier and the West** *(in this volume);* **Technology; Political Economy** *(volume 3).*

BIBLIOGRAPHY

Primary Sources

Emery, Sarah E. V. *Seven Financial Conspiracies Which Have Enslaved the American People.* 1888. 2d ed., New York, 1975.

Harvey, William H. "Coin." *Coin's Financial School.* 1894. Cambridge, Mass., 1963.

Hollitz, John. *Thinking through the Past: A Critical Thinking Approach to U.S. History.* Vol. 2, *Since 1865.* Boston, 1997.

Marcus, Robert D., and David Burner, eds. *From Reconstruction to the Present.* Vol. 2 of *America Firsthand.* New York, 1989.

Peffer, William Alfred. *The Farmer's Side: His Troubles and Their Remedy.* New York, 1891.

Pollack, Norman, ed. *The Populist Mind.* Indianapolis, Ind., 1967.

Tindall, George Brown, ed. *A Populist Reader: Selections from the Works of Populist Leaders.* New York, 1966.

Watson, Thomas E. "The Negro Question in the South." *The Arena* 6 (October 1892): 510–550.

Secondary Works

Argersinger, Peter. *The Limits of Agrarian Radicalism: Western Populism and American Politics.* Lawrence, Kans., 1995.

Bennett, David H. *The Party of Fear: From Nativist Movements to the New Right in American History.* Chapel Hill, N.C., 1988.

Danbom, David. *Born in the Country: A History of Rural America.* Baltimore, 1995.

Garraty, John A. *The American Nation: A History of the United States.* New York, 1995.

Goodwyn, Lawrence. *The Populist Moment: A Short History of the Agrarian Revolt in America.* New York, 1978.

Hicks, John D. *The Populist Revolt.* Minneapolis, Minn., 1931.

Hofstadter, Richard. *The Age of Reform: From Bryan to F.D.R.* New York, 1955.

Kazin, Michael. *The Populist Persuasion: An American History.* New York, 1995.

Maclean, Nancy. "The Lynching of Leo Frank Reconsidered." *Journal of American History* 78 (1991): 911–935.

Ostler, Jeffrey. *Prairie Populism: The Fate of Agrarian Radicalism in Kansas, Nebraska, and Iowa, 1880–1892.* Lawrence, Kans., 1993.

Ridge, Martin. *Ignatius Donnelly: The Portrait of a Politician.* Chicago, 1962.

Saloutos, Theodore, ed. *Populism: Reaction or Reform?* New York, 1968.

Stock, Catherine McNicol. *Rural Radicals: Righteous Rage in the American Grain.* Ithaca, N.Y., 1996.

Watkins, Marilyn. *Rural Democracy: Family Farmers and Politics in Western Washington, 1890–1925.* Ithaca, N.Y., 1995.

Woodward, C. Vann. *Tom Watson: Agrarian Rebel.* New York, 1938.

ANTI-STATISM

Robert Avila

In the United States, the term "anti-statism" has been used to describe varying degrees of opposition to state power. At one extreme, it is synonymous with anarchism, or "no-statism," while at another it applies to groups whose opposition goes no further than checking the expansion of federal bureaucracy. The broad application of the term reflects at once the deep roots of the mistrust of state power in the American political tradition, and the tendency of anti-statist arguments to ground themselves in that tradition. There is, however, an important distinction between individuals and groups opposed to the expansion of the federal government into certain areas of social life, and those who deny the legitimacy of any government at all. While both positions can be considered "libertarian" in the sense of defending individual rights against institutions and initiatives that threaten to undermine those rights, the latter position is more properly an anarchist one, or an extreme libertarianism that promotes a society without geographical borders, based exclusively on voluntary cooperation. It is with the latter position that this essay is chiefly concerned, a definition of anti-statism that places it at the libertarian extremes of American radicalism. Here American individualism comes into direct conflict with state authority per se, and the extension of basic cultural values leads American radicals on the right and left toward a renunciation of the state itself.

Though in the United States at the end of the twentieth century the term is more often associated with the far Right, libertarianism, which holds the freedom of the individual as the highest good, anti-statism has historically had left and right (i.e., socialist and capitalist) variants. Libertarian arguments derive from three principal ideological sources: classical liberalism, Christian fundamentalism, and nineteenth-century socialism. In each case, anti-statist conclusions result from a logical extension of basic principles in the direction of a social ideal that guarantees perfect individual freedom—usually defined as the elimination of all coercive authority. On the socialist end of the libertarian spectrum (which includes "anarchist communists" and "Christian anarchists"), this ideal weds economic equality (socialism) with political freedom (liberalism). On the other end of the spectrum, laissez-faire libertarians (including nineteenth-century "individualist anarchists" and twentieth-century "anarcho-capitalists"), look to private property and the free market to regulate social relations between individuals.

THE VARIETIES OF ANTI-STATISM

Observers of the American scene have long noted that a key characteristic of the country's political life is a pervasive distrust of government. This distrust has taken many forms. The insistence on "small government" goes back to the founding of the country and the opposition to the constitution of 1787 launched by the Antifederalists. Desiring a weak constitution that gave maximum play to state governments in a federated system, the misnamed Antifederalists argued that the strong central government desired by their opponents at the constitutional convention in Philadelphia promised a new tyranny as perfidious as that recently thrown off by the revolutionary war. But the Antifederalists and their latter-day counterparts behind "states' rights" initiatives were not anti-government per se.

Even armed opposition to the government, a tradition that reaches back to the rebellion of Massachusetts farmers led by Daniel Shays in 1786 and 1787, has rarely been in the cause of dismantling it entirely. Shays and other rebel farmers, for example, wanted relief from taxes and associated judgments and punishments in the economic depression following the war of independence, and indeed petitioned the state government for redress before resorting to insurrection. In fact, self-styled patriots from Daniel Shays (an officer in the Continental army) to Timothy McVeigh (awarded the Bronze Star in the Gulf War) have usually felt they were charged with taking the government back in the name of the people.

By contrast, the most consistent anti-statists—those verging on or embracing anarchism—have seen in the concentrated power of government both the greatest threat to individual liberty and the principal cause of social injustice. As the most coercive of institutions, the state itself is the greatest enemy. As that entity with a monopoly of force within a given territory, the state alone has the authority to insist that all individuals within its domain conform to certain social norms deemed necessary. Such authority relies on an assumption of legitimacy, backed by an implicit or explicit threat of violence against dissent. As the anarchist Alexander Berkman wrote:

> *All* Anarchists agree on this fundamental position: that government means injustice and oppression, that it is invasive, enslaving, and the greatest hindrance to man's development and growth. They all believe that freedom can exist only in a society where there is no compulsion of any kind. All Anarchists are therefore at one on the basic principle of abolishing government. (*What Is Communist Anarchism?*, p. 211)

This common antagonism toward the state, the foremost expression of an extreme individualism and anti-authoritarianism, unites an otherwise disparate group of self-professed anarchists or anti-statists.

Fundamentally, anarchists regard all coercive authority as illegitimate. Their opposition extends to its exercise in institutions from the family on up through the state. They argue that no entity, be it the state, the Church, "the people" taken as a whole, or an electoral majority, can rightfully force an individual to act against his or her own conscience or desire. The liberty of an individual is absolute, and ends only where the equal liberty of another begins. Accordingly, the proper (and natural) basis of social relations is the spontaneous and voluntary association of free individuals. Most anarchists view human beings as innately social and capable not only of moral autonomy but of cooperating among themselves to fulfill social needs in the absence of some supreme authority. Institutions built on coercive authority are not only corrupt but superfluous.

Moreover, anarchists regard the idea of government by consent as a myth, the specious foundation of which is made clear as soon as an individual tries to withhold consent.

For anti-statists the fundamental conflict in society is between liberty and authority. Class conflict and most forms of political and economic exploitation are ultimately traceable to it. This focus differs from the emphasis on economic relations in Marxist theory. Moreover, while Marxism includes a critique of the state, in practice it accepts the idea of a socialist state (the "dictatorship of the proletariat") as a necessary transition to pure communism. While between anarchism and Marxism the goal of the social revolution remains very similar—a stateless society of free individuals—the means of achieving this end are quite different. Indeed, from an anarchist perspective, Marxist praxis remains fundamentally at odds with such a goal since no state will ever "wither away" on its own. On the contrary, the state only tends to expand its power. Mikhail Bakunin, the nineteenth-century founder of revolutionary anarchism, predicted that a state won in the name of the workers would end merely by replacing one set of rulers with another. "State," wrote Bakunin, "means domination, and any domination presupposes the subjugation of the masses and, consequently, their exploitation for the benefit of some ruling minority" (*Bakunin on Anarchy*, p. 277). Bakunin assumed a socialist state would be even more oppressive because it would monopolize the economic as well as the political realm.

Anarchism, emphasizing the problem of power, has thus provided an important left critique of Marxism since the mid-nineteenth century, one that tended to gain in significance with the historical unfolding of purportedly Marxist states in the twentieth century. But, while targeting the state as the principal hindrance to individual freedom and social harmony, anarchists differ on how best to overcome it. In the United States, Christian, individualist, and socialist forms of anti-statism have prescribed very different methods of achieving an anti-authoritarian society.

CHRISTIAN ANTI-STATISM

Probably the earliest example of American anti-statism dates back to Puritan New England and the Antinomian schism of 1636 and 1637. In a period when church and state were still intimately related, the Protestant tenet of unmediated communion between the individual and the divine could undermine the claims of civil as well as ecclesiastical authority. Popularly invoked by Anne Hutchinson, John Wheelwright, and their followers, direct revelation threatened the theocratic hierarchy of the

Massachusetts Bay Colony and led to the banishment of the Antinomians (literally, those "against the law"). Hutchinson, in particular, followed the logic of Protestant theology to conclusions that bordered on anarchism, as historians of American anti-statism have been wont to point out. The logical extension of a universal capacity for divine revelation elevated the individual conscience over all temporal authority. This is the ethical basis of Christian anti-statism as it developed in the United States.

The Antinomian schism presaged a series of challenges to the future nation-state in the name of a radical Christian individualism. In the early nineteenth century William Ellery Channing, the leading voice of Unitarianism, insisted on the innate goodness of human beings and argued for the moral perfection of the individual through the dictates of conscience. In assailing the dominant Calvinist view of a depraved mankind, Channing reflected a romantic belief in the potential for earthly salvation characteristic of his time and much of American anti-statist thought. Similarly, Quaker pacifism, which aroused widespread suspicion and scorn in the revolutionary period, arose from an insistence on freedom of conscience and the "divine light" in every soul. The same current of positive individualism ran through the Anabaptists, the Shakers, and other, smaller, Protestant sects, contributing to a Christian fundamentalism that would shape the history of American nonviolence from abolitionism to the antinuclear campaigns of the cold war era. At its most radical, the philosophy of nonresistance approached a Christian anarchism, or a rejection of all temporal authority.

Thus, John Humphrey Noyes could argue that religious faith canceled out worldly authority entirely. The founder of perfectionism and the Oneida Community of New York (1848–1880), Noyes proposed self-government as the highest aim of a Christian life. Modeling his renunciation of civil government on the Declaration of Independence, Noyes suggested at once a logical extension of both liberal and Christian individualism. Like William Lloyd Garrison (who was much influenced by him), Noyes found the most compelling case for this renunciation of the state in its support of slavery, a supreme violation of Christian law and of the inherent rights of individuals guaranteed by the state's own constitution.

In the Christian nonresistance of Garrison, Adin Ballou, and others, the anti-statist tendency in Christian individualism reached its most articulate stage. In the "Declaration of Sentiments" (1838) drafted by Garrison, Christian nonviolence grounded a demand for the immediate abolition of slavery in a Christian conscience that superseded any worldly authority and explicitly denied the legitimacy of the state. Slavery was but the most egregious example of a usurpation of divine authority by impious men. Such an argument dissolved national borders entirely and shared much with the Christian anarchism developed independently by Russian novelist and philosopher Leo Tolstoy a half century later.

Anti-authoritarian Christian individualism, which regarded worldly power as a usurpation of divine prerogative, continued in the twentieth century to inform movements for social change, including the growing pacifist movement. The *Catholic Worker,* founded by Dorothy Day and Peter Maurin in 1933, exemplified the continuation of this anti-authoritarian Christian radicalism well into the twentieth century. The paper and the movement named for it were at the forefront of anti-statist movements in the postwar period, including opposition to nuclear proliferation and the Vietnam War, and played an enduring part in the continuing evolution of nonviolence in the United States.

INDIVIDUALIST ANARCHISM

American "individualist anarchism"—which dates from the social experiments of Josiah Warren in the 1820s—grew largely out of the liberal ideology of the American Revolution. As the anarchist and scholar Rudolf Rocker pointed out, individualist anarchists of the nineteenth century "were influenced in their intellectual development much more by the principles expressed in the 'Declaration of Independence' than by those of any of the representatives of libertarian socialism in Europe" (*Pioneers of American Freedom,* p. xx). Indeed, Benjamin R. Tucker, the greatest American exponent of individualist anarchism, defined anarchists as "simply unterrified Jeffersonian Democrats" (*Instead of a Book,* p. 14). Reflecting a logical elaboration of classical liberalism, these right libertarians followed John Locke in tying liberty to property, seeing the latter as a natural extension of the individual and a guarantee of his or her freedom. Far from being an imitation of European ideas "alien" to American traditions, this school of anti-statist thought arose before any anarchist movement could be found in Europe. Indeed, more than a decade would pass before the French philosopher Pierre-Joseph Proudhon appropriated the label "anarchist" to signify his desire for a stateless society based on voluntary cooperation.

Some historians have been eager to stress individualist anarchism's qualitative break with the liberal tradition. In *The Superfluous Anarchist* (1972), Michael Wreszin has argued that individualist anarchists, in their hostility to the state, had more in common with Ralph Waldo Emerson and Henry David Thoreau than with Thomas Jefferson, who ultimately remained deeply invested in the political system. While self-consciously building on the distrust of power articulated by Jefferson, Thomas Paine, and other representatives of the American liberal tradition, these American radicals differed fundamentally from their predecessors on the role and nature of government. Where Paine had praised society as "in every state . . . a blessing" and berated government as the product of "wickedness," the latter was nevertheless "a necessary evil," and he and others correspondingly put their trust in limited government and the rule of majorities (Foner, ed., *The Life and Major Writings of Thomas Paine*, p. 4).

Anarchists, by contrast, saw no role for government in the institutional sense and majority rule as merely another mode of coercion. As Tucker wrote:

> The essence of government is control, or the attempt to control. He who attempts to control another is a governor, an aggressor, an invader; and the nature of such invasion is not changed, whether it is made by one man upon another man, after the manner of the ordinary criminal, or by one man upon all other men, after the manner of an absolute monarch, or by all other men upon one man, after the manner of a modern democracy. (*Instead of a Book,* p. 23)

Majority rule was thus untenable from the point of view of equal liberty. Moreover, it was "impossible" anyway since, as Voltairine de Cleyre pointed out, "any government, no matter what its forms, will be manipulated by a very small minority" (Silverman, ed., *American Radical Thought*, p. 156).

This point of departure from classical liberalism is echoed by modern right-wing libertarians like Murray Rothbard, economist and co-founder of the Libertarian Party. Speaking for the "individualist anti-statists" of his generation, Rothbard has drawn a direct line from nineteenth-century individualist anarchism (what he also refers to as "property rights anarchism") to modern day "anarcho-capitalism."

> Originally, our historical heroes were such men as Jefferson, Paine, Cobden, Bright and Spencer; but as our views became purer and more consistent, we eagerly embraced such near-anarchists as the voluntarist, Auberon Herbert, and the American

individualist-anarchists, Lysander Spooner and Benjamin R. Tucker. One of our great intellectual heroes was Henry David Thoreau, and his essay, "Civil Disobedience," was one of our guiding stars. (Silverman, p. 292)

The reference to Thoreau underscores the significance for American libertarians (left and right) of Thoreau's example, his stand against coercive government, and the Emersonian ideal of "self-government" he embodied. At the same time, the bold embrace of a free market system suggested in the very label "anarcho-capitalist" differs appreciably from the social-minded reforms proposed by their nineteenth-century counterparts, as a brief discussion of the beginnings of American individualist anarchism makes plain.

Josiah Warren, the founder of American individualist anarchism, came, like many later adherents, from an old New England family. A successful inventor and accomplished musician and orchestra leader, he joined the Welsh socialist Robert Owen's communitarian venture at New Harmony, Indiana, in 1826. After the collapse of the enterprise the following year, Warren began to piece together his own version of a just system of social and economic relations. Blaming the failure of New Harmony on the stifling of individuality through, among other things, majority rule and the collective ownership of property, Warren devised a system whereby individual freedom might be maximized while economic relations remained entirely equitable. He applied his ideas in 1827 in his famous "time store," which operated on the principle that cost should determine price in all economic transactions. A minimal charge was allowed for overhead and the time taken up in the transaction of business (the latter measured by a clock on the wall). His system was based on a labor theory of value with "labor notes" forming the medium of exchange. The success of the experiment encouraged him to propagate his ideas, summed up in the phrase "equitable commerce," in two books that achieved wide circulation, as well as in *The Peaceful Revolutionist*, established in 1833 and most likely the first anarchist periodical. Warren also founded two communities, one in 1847 in Ohio named Utopia, the other in 1851 in New York called Modern Times. Both, to varying degrees, met with what Warren considered marked success for experimental ventures, surviving for years as prosperous communities without formal government, operating on the free and equitable exchange of labor and allowing for complete autonomy in matters of belief, dress, and sexual relations.

Warren's ideas attracted and were developed by reformers responding to the political and economic ferment of the Jacksonian period, much of which was tied to widespread dissatisfaction with the banking system (especially following the panic of 1837) and the development of business monopoly. In this environment many eagerly embraced a vision of an equitable society based on Warren's cost principle. European libertarians had some influence on the development of American individualist anarchism as well. Especially in the area of finance, Warren's system was enhanced by the French anarchist Pierre-Joseph Proudhon and the application of Proudhon's "mutualism," to which the former's concept of equitable commerce bore striking resemblance. This was done most famously in the work of William B. Greene, who took the concept of interest-free or "mutual banking" (in his 1850 book of that title) from the French anarchist. Proudhon's influence on Tucker—a student of Warren's and by the 1880s the preeminent expositor of individualist anarchism—was symbolized by Tucker's adoption of Proudhon's phrase, "Liberty the mother not the daughter of Order," for the masthead of his journal, *Liberty*, founded in 1881. Also central to Tucker's anarchism was the egoistic philosophy of the German Max Stirner and the work of the English philosopher Herbert Spencer, whose chapter in *Social Statics* (1850), "The Right to Ignore the State," was reprinted by Tucker. In the work of the American abolitionist and reformer Stephen Pearl Andrews, Warren's equitable commerce mingled with still other currents of nineteenth-century European thought, including the ideas of the French socialist Charles Fourier and the Swedish mystic Emanuel Swedenborg.

In applying these ideas a few, like Andrews, accepted that industrialization made wage employment and economies of scale inevitable. But most individualists, like the jurist Lysander Spooner, looked back to a preindustrial society of single-family farms and small proprietors, a vision that reflected a waning era in which the frontier was still open, land still relatively available, and bureaucratization not as yet highly developed. Although their attacks on monopoly and "government by corporation" went to the center of economic trends, the frontier orientation of nineteenth-century individualists like Warren was ultimately at odds with American realities, especially after the Civil War. The closing of the frontier, the rise of the corporation, the increasing regulation and industrialization of the workforce, the expansion of bureaucracy, and the cultural changes that resulted made the social and economic agenda of individualist anarchism increasingly anachronistic.

But if the solutions it offered were less relevant, its critique of power was not, and the latter made the individualist brand of American anarchism still viable into the twentieth century, if initially only to an even smaller and more elitist coterie of critics. Tucker's relentless attacks on monopoly found an echo in the social criticism of Albert Jay Nock. He assailed American big business in the 1920s for wrapping itself in "impostor-terms" like individualism and free enterprise when, in fact, "American business never followed a policy of *laissez-faire*, never wished to follow it, never wished the State to let it alone" (Wreszin, *The Superfluous Anarchist*, pp. 127–128). Later, Nock criticized the New Deal liberalism that supposed the state to have finally become the servant of the people instead of the powerful. Nock's writings would themselves enjoy a rediscovery beginning in the 1950s, and we have already noted the rediscovery (and reworking) of the individualist tradition by self-titled anarcho-capitalists like Rothbard, and by Karl Hess in the 1960s. In fact, the 1960s and the decades following it dramatically demonstrated the continuing relevance of American anti-statist thought in general and its individualist form in particular.

COMMUNIST ANARCHISM

If anarchism in its individualist form is largely an extension of liberalism, its (non-Christian) communist form is principally an extension of socialism. By the latter half of the nineteenth century, a secular form of socialist anti-statism had grown directly from European socialism; specifically, the "anti-authoritarian socialism" associated with the anarchist Bakunin, Marx's rival in the International Workingmen's Association (the First International). Bakunin and his followers identified themselves as "collectivists," corresponding to an economic arrangement that in its outline of the future society called for collective ownership of the means of production but preserved the wage system in a basic form by linking individual production to material compensation. After Bakunin's death in 1876, anarchism of the socialist stripe evolved a more strictly communist agenda, where all material needs of an individual would be met regardless of the work contributed. This was done largely through the writings of Peter Kropotkin, the foremost theorist of anarchist communism.

Karl Hess in 1969. Hess's anti-statist philosophy found a place on both sides of the political spectrum. He worked for Joseph McCarthy and Barry Goldwater, but then protested the Vietnam War and worked with the Black Panthers. Asked to define the perfect anarchist, Hess replied, "A good friend, a good lover, and a good neighbor," and then added, "What did you expect, a lot of rules?" © WALLY MCNAMEE/CORBIS

Unlike the predominantly native-born and middle-class representatives of individualist anarchism, the adherents of anarchist communism in the United States tended to be working class, and the majority—like the movement's leading American exponents, Johann Most, Emma Goldman, and Alexander Berkman—were immigrants. Many came from southern and eastern Europe or from Germany, while others were from England, France, Mexico, and Japan. One of the movement's earliest organizational expressions was the 1883 congress in Pittsburgh, convened under Most's leadership. At that time the movement was concentrated in New York City and Chicago. Most, who had arrived in the United States the previous year, first formulated the social and economic doctrine accepted by the American movement at Pittsburgh. It was, strictly speaking, still a Bakuninist "collectivism." Only by the end of the decade would anarchist communism, as it had come to be formulated in Europe, become the dominant form of socialist anarchism in the United States. The American movement, however,

produced no significant theoretical development of anarchist communism. Instead, the emphasis was on propagandizing the cause, organizing newspapers and communities, working on behalf of labor, and gathering material support for the movement. Contact with the anarchist movement in Europe (also in Mexico and, to a lesser extent, Japan) was also important, and several attempts at international congresses were made.

Significantly, the Pittsburgh Manifesto, of which Most was the principal author, put forward a revolutionary agenda of armed class struggle, calling for the violent overthrow of the state and its replacement with "a free society based upon cooperative organization of production" (Jacker, *The Black Flag of Anarchy,* p. 97). The call for class war pointed to at least two features of this anti-statist movement in the coming years. First, it tended to add to the demographic and ideological distance between individualist and communist anarchism, since their positions on violence were quite distinct. While individualist anarchists sometimes employed hostile

826

and even incendiary language with regard to the state, they increasingly rejected acts of political violence as illegitimate, insisting that social change would come peacefully through education. At the same time, individualists rejected the extreme pacifism of the Christian anarchists and nonresistants. They reserved the right of self-defense, the individual's natural right, as they saw it, to repulse invasion by force. Anarchist communists, on the other hand, while by no means consistent on the issue of violence, tended to be more militant. Coming from countries with more repressive governments, like Russia, Italy, or Spain, many communist anarchists saw political violence as a legitimate and necessary part of a revolutionary movement. Berkman's own 1892 attempt on Henry C. Frick, manager of the Carnegie steel plant at Homestead, Pennsylvania, reflected the influence of a Russian populist pattern of political assassination ("propaganda of the deed"). Such violence, however, was not more prevalent than violence in the labor movement as a whole, even at its height in Europe and the United States in the 1880s.

Second, the call to armed struggle, while it more often reflected a rhetorical posture than a political agenda, ultimately helped to strengthen the establishment case against anarchism. Labeled an attack on the American way of life, and blamed for isolated acts of violence done in its name (in particular, the assassination of President William McKinley in 1901), the communist anarchists met considerable opposition from the establishment, including the passage of federal anti-anarchist legislation in 1903. Although as a political philosophy anarchism had nothing to do with violence per se, the rhetoric of violence, the actions of isolated individuals, and the efforts of media and government to stigmatize the anarchist as a bloodthirsty assassin all worked to associate anarchism with willful destruction in the public mind. To a lesser extent, this veneer of political violence was projected onto the individualist school as well, despite pains taken by Tucker and others to distinguish their position on the matter. Ultimately, as the trial of Nicola Sacco and Bartolomeo Vanzetti in 1921 suggested, the movement was never able to detach itself from the inflammatory image of the bomb-throwing nihilist it had helped to create in the late nineteenth century.

Anarchist communism inherited an international revolutionary outlook and tradition from its European leadership and constituency, and, of the three main types of American anti-statism, it has been the one most susceptible to charges of being "alien" to American institutions. Nonetheless, in making its case to immigrant and native alike, anarchist communism came inevitably to draw on and root itself in the American radical tradition. Even the Pittsburgh Manifesto invoked Jefferson in defense of its call for revolution. Especially in the writings and speeches of Emma Goldman, by the turn of the twentieth century the most influential American propagandist of anarchist communism in the English language, the movement placed itself in a larger American context.

Anti-statism in the American labor movement was most clearly expressed in the development of syndicalism. American "anarchosyndicalism," embodied by the Industrial Workers of the World (IWW), was a radical industrial unionism championing "one big union" of all workers, skilled and unskilled, of both sexes and all races. It eschewed politics, envisioning the overthrow of capitalism at the point of production through the mechanism of the general strike and its replacement by a system of autonomous, federated labor unions as the organizational basis of a future socialist society. While the founding leadership and rank and file of the IWW in 1905 reflected a broad range of opinion and political orientation (from the Marxism of Daniel De Leon to the indigenous industrial unionism of Bill Haywood and the Western Federation of Miners), its program was thus anti-statist. Anarchosyndicalism in the United States, however, never achieved the numbers, influence, homogeneity, or theoretical sophistication it did in western Europe. The IWW, whose dues-paying membership peaked at about 100,000, was more immediately grounded in American conditions, and expressed itself in a vernacular of typically American working-class values even as it spoke of "the historic mission of the working class." After a dozen years of labor militancy that included historic strikes and free speech campaigns, the IWW met serious repression by government and business during and after World War I and was severely weakened as a result.

THE TWENTIETH CENTURY

If violence served ultimately to undermine the anarchist movement at the turn of the century, the twentieth-century legacy of "total war," with its mass destruction abroad and inevitable clampdown on civil liberties at home, tended to sharpen and disseminate anti-statist arguments. The liberal writer Randolph Bourne, for example, read America's entry into World War I in terms of a logic of state power summarized in his famous phrase, "war

827

is the health of the state." Moreover, Bourne's critique of the relationship between prowar intellectuals and the state (which Emma Goldman saw fit to reprint in her journal, *Mother Earth*), marked an enduring facet of anti-statist thinking. Later, the view of intellectuals as "opinion makers" in the service of the state would be expanded by Paul Goodman, Murray Rothbard, and Noam Chomsky, among others. Similarly, World War II and its aftermath brought Dwight Macdonald, one of the New York intellectuals around the *Partisan Review,* to his own version of anti-statism, expressed in his influential journal, *Politics.*

In the 1960s the Vietnam War contributed to the single greatest revival of anti-statism in the twentieth century. More than any single event in this turbulent period, Vietnam both augmented the larger political and social ferment and focused it in a crisis of state. Carl Oglesby, president of Students for a Democratic Society (SDS), pointed to this crisis, calling the war "unparalleled," since it was "the first to be fought under slogans so transparently hypocritical" and "the first in which the reputation of the state has been unconditionally, repeatedly, and publicly laid on the line" (Silverman, ed., *American Radical Thought,* p. 351). The crisis brought anarchism a significant revival on the extreme right and left of the political spectrum. Left and right libertarianism also drew closer together politically than perhaps at any other time, as radicals on both sides recognized the greatest threat to American ideals in the power of the state. In 1969 anarchist factions in both the SDS and the right-wing Young Americans for Freedom (YAF) tried to persuade their respective bodies to adopt an extreme anti-statist position. The YAF Anarchist Caucus, for example—which invoked Bakunin, William Lloyd Garrison, and the Declaration of Independence in professing solidarity with the student movement and third-world liberation struggles—called on the membership to oppose U.S. foreign policy, mobilize against the draft, and join in a social revolution as "the only logical and possible method through which the immediate and total abolition of the State and its inherent injustice can be brought about" (Silverman, *American Radical Thought,* p. 270). Both attempts were unsuccessful, though they marked the significant presence of anti-statist thinking across the political spectrum.

A decentralist approach to political action evident throughout the New Left (especially in alternative institutions like cooperatives, communes, community centers, and newspapers) resulted in part from the ineffectual nature of mainstream politics with respect to seemingly intractable and systemic problems: war, poverty, urban unrest, racism, the draft. The corresponding emphasis on nonauthoritarian structures, "community power," and a general challenge to authority spread to all realms of social life including education, the family, and relations between the sexes. These areas had historically been of concern to anarchists, and important contributions were made at the time by elder spokesmen of that tradition like Murray Bookchin and, especially, Paul Goodman. Disillusionment with the old institutions of reform, including the corporate liberalism of the postwar period, was fed too by a rejection of a technological society that limited human potential in the name of control. This idea of the individual as victim of mass society, expressed in Herbert Marcuse's *One-Dimensional Man* (1964), also reflected older anarchist critiques of materialism and mass culture. These sometimes translated into a disdain for "mass man." As various commentators have noted, anarchism's extreme individualism could have an elitist aspect on both sides of the libertarian spectrum.

The stress on mass culture reflected a greater emphasis on psychological systems of oppression (and a concern with the cultural realm in general, expressed in popular terms by the anti-institutional counterculture of the 1960s and the punk rock movement of the 1970s). More traditional attacks on government mingled or competed with individuals and groups looking to circumvent, rather than to directly assail, the state. Edenic and anti-technological expressions like anarcho-primitivism existed alongside more traditional anti-statist critiques of power like those of Noam Chomsky. Although theoretically these two modes of anti-statism are not incompatible, the distinction could prove a source of tension within anarchism over the proper terrain of revolutionary struggle. By the end of the twentieth century, Bookchin, for example, the leading theorizer of anarchist social ecology, attacked what he called "lifestyle anarchism" in the name of the older socialist and working-class tradition. While most of the radical leaders of the 1960s who remained in politics were gradually drawn into its conventional statist mode, by the end of the century, an anti-statist outlook remained an organizing feature in specific political movements on the left and right. From the 1980s Earth First!, for example, carried the decentralist tradition of the New Left into the environmental movement, while on the right, extreme libertarianism continued to enjoy a vogue, especially from the 1980s, when it helped to underwrite the Reagan presidency.

Armed opposition to the federal government appeared sporadically up to the end of the twentieth century. But rather than anarchists, these militants were professed patriots of a highjacked constitution. The right-wing militia movement has been inhabited by persons who believe their government has been stolen from them. Historian Garry Wills has placed them in a long tradition of American "insurrectionists" beginning with Daniel Shays and including John Brown and Timothy McVeigh. Despite important differences between them, such figures echo a populist strain in American politics that has, since the nineteenth century, championed the individualism of the small holder against the monopolistic forces of an industrial and post-industrial age. This populism perceives not only an immediate economic and political disadvantage in the face of concentrated wealth, but the destruction of the Jeffersonian ideal itself, the yeoman farmer and self-sufficient artisan considered by Jefferson and his generation as the backbone of a democratic republic.

Populism gave voice to the plight of the small farmer and, to some extent, that of the new industrial worker at the end of the nineteenth century, and it attacked a political establishment seen as venal and undemocratic. But for all its opposition, independent initiatives (such as cooperatives), and demands for fundamental reforms, populism remained invested in the political system, seeking redress through government. Like latter-day populists on the right and left, these radicals and reformers ultimately desired to reclaim the government in the name of the people. There is therefore a basic distinction between such limited anti-governmentalism and the thoroughgoing libertarianism on the right and left outlined above.

At the end of the twentieth century, the distrust of government continued to be a central and even cherished part of the American political tradition, yet the relation of anarchism, or extreme anti-statism, to that tradition remained obscure. This despite a number of historical treatments of major anarchist figures and the movement as a whole since the 1960s, as well as a growing interest in anarchism as a legitimate contribution to political philosophy. One reason for this seeming irrelevance was that the history of revolutionary anarchism since the 1880s encouraged a popular dismissal of extreme anti-statism as violent, fanatical, and foreign. Another was the nature of the anarchist position itself, which put it beyond more mainstream libertarian discussions of limits to state power and could inhibit practical political action. Still another reason was the overshadowing presence of statist forms of radicalism and reform, from New Deal liberalism to Marxism. Finally, while offering a compelling critique of authority, anarchists left relatively few texts or organizations behind and have been short on practical proposals. Anarchism's anti-authoritarianism might share some of the blame for this, since it tends to undermine the development of strong organizational structures, but it is also a question of emphasis. As historian David De Leon has noted, American anti-statists "have concentrated on emancipation, on breaking the prisons of authority, rather than on planning any reconstruction. They are abolitionists, not institution-builders. . . . They generally presume that the freed spirit will require little or no guidance" (*The American as Anarchist*, p. 4). Except for a continuing tendency toward experimentation with alternative social arrangements, anarchism's most lasting legacy has been its critique of the state and authority in general. This critique properly belongs among the most consistent expressions of a native American radicalism.

See also **Law (Colonial); Liberalism and Republicanism; Federalists and Antifederalists; Whig Ideology; Agrarianism and the Agrarian Ideal in Early America; Prophetic Native American Movements; Secession, War, and Union; Patterns of Reform and Revolt; Nationalism and Imperialism; Anti-Modern Discontent between the Wars** (volume 1); **Vietnam as a Cultural Crisis; American Expatriate Artists Abroad; Artistic, Intellectual, and Political Refugees; Utah and Mormonism; The Natural World** (in this volume); **Individualism and the Self** (volume 3); and other articles in this section.

BIBLIOGRAPHY

Avrich, Paul. *Anarchist Portraits*. Princeton, N.J., 1988.

Bakunin, Mikhail. *Bakunin on Anarchy*. Translated and edited by Sam Dolgoff. New York, 1972.

Berkman, Alexander. *What Is Communist Anarchism?* (Also published as *Now and After: The ABC of Communist Anarchism.*) 1929. Reprint, New York, 1972.

Bookchin, Murray. *Post-Scarcity Anarchism*. Berkeley, Calif., 1971.

Carter, April. *The Political Theory of Anarchism*. New York, 1971.

De Leon, David. *The American as Anarchist: Reflections on Indigenous Radicalism*. Baltimore, 1978.

Foner, Philip S., ed. *The Life and Major Writings of Thomas Paine*. New York, 1993.

Goldman, Emma. *Anarchism and Other Essays*. New York, 1911.

Jacker, Corinne. *The Black Flag of Anarchy: Antistatism in the United States*. New York, 1968.

Johnpoll, Bernard K., with Lillian Johnpoll. *The Impossible Dream: The Rise and Demise of the American Left*. Westport, Conn., 1981.

Lynd, Staughton, and Alice Lynd, eds. *Nonviolence in America: A Documentary History*. Rev. ed. Maryknoll, N.Y., 1995.

Martin, James J. *Men against the State: The Expositors of Individualist Anarchism in America, 1827–1908*. Rev. ed. Colorado Springs, Colo., 1970.

Nettlau, Max. *A Short History of Anarchism*. Translated by Ida Pilat Isca. Edited by Heiner M. Becker. London, 1996.

Perry, Lewis. *Radical Abolitionism: Anarchy and the Government of God in Antislavery Thought*. Ithaca, N.Y., 1973.

Reichert, William O. *Partisans of Freedom: A Study in American Anarchism*. Bowling Green, Ohio, 1976.

Rocker, Rudolf. *Pioneers of American Freedom: Origin of Liberal and Radical Thought in America*. Translated by Arthur E. Briggs. Los Angeles, 1949.

Rothbard, Murray. *For A New Liberty*. New York, 1973.

Silverman, Henry J., ed. *American Radical Thought: The Libertarian Tradition*. Lexington, Mass., 1970.

Tucker, Benjamin R. *Instead of a Book, by a Man Too Busy to Write One*. New York, 1893.

Wills, Garry. *A Necessary Evil: A History of American Distrust of Government*. New York, 1999.

Woodcock, George. *Anarchism: A History of Libertarian Ideas and Movements*. New York, 1962.

Wreszin, Michael. *The Superfluous Anarchist: Albert Jay Nock*. Providence, R.I., 1972.